The Conspiracy Trial

The Conspiracy Trial

Edited by Judy Clavir and John Spitzer

The Bobbs-Merrill Company/Indianapolis/New York

The Bobbs-Merrill Company, Inc.

A Subsidiary of Howard W. Sams & Co., Inc.

Publishers / Indianapolis • Kansas City • New York

Copyright © 1970 by Judy Clavir and John Spitzer
Library of Congress catalogue card number 70-126301

Manufactured in the United States of America

To Fred Hampton and Mark Clark, our brothers who were sentenced and
executed in Chicago, Illinois, on December 4, 1969, without even
the gesture of a trial.

Free Bobby Seale!

Table of Contents

Foreword—Leonard I. Weinglass

This book, the most complete report of the Chicago Conspiracy Trial to date, is of value not merely because of what it contains about the trial itself, but also because of what it reveals about the contesting forces confronting each other in the 1970s. For, to a remarkable degree, the proceedings in Chicago dealt not only with the disturbances at the time of the Democratic National Convention but focused on and exposed what the United States had actually become by the close of the Decade of Protest.

Beginning with the unprecedented claim by the Attorney General of the United States that he had the unquestioned right to wiretap the defendants if he thought national security required it, down to the seemingly endless parade of paid FBI informers (one of whom worked with full press credentials for a CBS-TV affiliate) and government agents who testified without embarrassment to their having infiltrated the demonstrators' ranks and urged the use of violent tactics, the proceedings unmasked a heretofore hidden face of government. This face led one juror to exclaim at the trial's conclusion, "For the first time in my life I was afraid of my government."

Also revealed were the current nature and makeup of the Movement. Witness after witness for the defense testified about the ongoing struggle to liberate the country from racism, an immoral and illegal war, and the residual effects of a dying culture. Yippies, Mobe spokesmen, leaders in the civil rights movement, authors, intellectuals and scores of other people swept up by these events discussed the basis from which the emerging culture and anti-war movement were formed, as well as the methods employed by each, ranging from nonviolence and guerrilla theater to the use of karate and weapons for self-defense.

It has been stated that political trials have frequently marked turning points in history. If this be true of the Chicago trial, perhaps some of the reasons lie within the following pages.

Introduction—William M. Kunstler

When I was first asked to write this introduction, I had serious doubts as to what I could possibly add to even a condensed version of the transcript of the Chicago trial. But as I read over those portions selected by the editors, I soon realized that stenographers' minutes, no matter how dramatic, cannot begin to convey to those who did not sit in Judge Hoffman's courtroom their true sense and meaning. History may well be unalterable, but it is not beyond fruitful elaboration.

As I pored over the material, I was able to supply for myself the sights and sounds, as I remembered them, that characterized the various courtroom episodes which, collectively, made up the scenario of a historic trial. I could almost hear again the high-pitched theatrical tones of Judge Hoffman, Assistant Prosecutor Schultz's explosive roars of seemingly outraged innocence, the bailiff's daily sibilant pronouncement of the name of the case and its docket number, and the sporadic chuckles, cheers and shouts that emanated from the abbreviated spectators' section. The witnesses' faces, forms and modes of expression materialized in my memory as I absorbed words and phrases that had once convulsed a courtroom with laughter or tears, or exposed, in sudden blinding clarity, the thin line that often divides truth from falsity.

It would require a full-length book if I were to attempt to flesh out the bare bones of each segment of the edited transcript. But, putting time and space considerations entirely aside, it would serve no useful purpose to do so. Just as a significant criminal trial is frequently a microcosm of life itself, so the re-creation of certain segments of the former may be tantamount to epitomizing the whole.

Even observers not overly friendly to the defendants were convinced, as the trial rolled along, that Judge Hoffman was determined to do everything in his power to guarantee convictions on every count of the indictment. One of his favorite techniques in seeking to attain this goal was that of discreditation. In this connection, no insult was too gross, no humiliation too excessive, no degradation too cruel. When this otherwise rather urbane and witty man stooped to conquer, his forehead frequently touched the ground.

On the trial's very first day, for example, he ordered the arrest of four young lawyers who had assisted in the preparation of certain early motions.* The ostensible reason for this extraordinary action was that these attorneys had sent telegrams to him indicating

---

*These lawyers were Michael J. Kennedy, Dennis J. Roberts, Prof. Michael E. Tigar and Gerald B. Lefcourt. The first three were from California while Mr. Lefcourt practiced in New York.

that they would not be present in Chicago because they had only been retained "for the purpose of preparing and arguing certain of the pretrial and discovery motions." Without batting an eye, the judge, obviously relishing the first public exhibition of his awesome power, directed his clerk to issue bench warrants "for the apprehension of those lawyers who are obligated in law to be here."

The interplay between court and prosecution that was to become so routine during the trial was never more evident than during this episode. Whether the script had been prearranged or was the result of a tacit understanding, it clearly indicated the shape of things to come. Prosecutor Foran, acutely aware that Hoffman's earlier refusal to delay the trial six weeks in order to give Charles R. Garry, Bobby Seale's lawyer and the chief trial counsel for all of the defendants, time to recover from a needed gall bladder operation had raised serious constitutional questions, attempted to use the impending arrests to settle that issue once and for all.

"By the way, your Honor," he purred, after asking for orders directing the four lawyers to appear in court, "I would like to add one further statement, that if the defendants are prepared at this time to represent to this court that they are satisfied with their counsel in this case who are present here in this court and will waive any claim that their Sixth Amendment rights are abridged, then we would ask the court not to issue an order to have Mr. Lefcourt, Mr. Kennedy, Mr. Tigar and Mr. Roberts brought in before the court immediately." When we protested that the defendants would not agree to"ransom their Sixth Amendment rights for the needless visit to this court of four attorneys," Judge Hoffman promptly issued his arrest orders. A few days later, after two of the lawyers had been jailed,* he was forced by a combination of public pressure and whatever internal influences were brought to bear upon him to vacate these outrageous and thoroughly vindictive orders.

I set forth this episode in some detail because it is an excellent prototype of so many others of parallel motivation. The judge seldom missed an opportunity to hold up the defendants and/or their attorneys to scorn and ridicule and, at the same time, to furnish the government with golden opportunities to attempt to patch up his more obvious constitutional violations. With such efficient teamwork, it is small wonder that we at the defense table were soon convinced that Lewis Carroll had remarkably accurate prophetic powers.

When he wasn't engaged in trying to discredit the defendants and their legal team, the judge utilized every Macchiavellian tactic at his disposal to undermine their case. These ranged from his refusal to permit an otherwise unoccupied defense lawyer to leave the courtroom to interview prospective witnesses to his insistence on Saturday sessions after the prosecution had rested. In addition, he saw to it that the jury never knew that former Attorney General Ramsey Clark had willingly come to Chicago to testify for the defendants, deliberately tainted the only youthful member of the jury by showing her a threatening letter supposedly signed by "The Black Panthers" which she would ordinarily have never seen, and prevented Dr. Ralph D. Abernathy from taking the stand solely and simply because he had, due to unsatisfactory plane connections from Atlanta, arrived in the courtroom eighteen minutes late.

In dramatic impact, however, his treatment of Bobby Seale completely overshadowed his other excesses. Although Seale consistently stressed the fact that, if he could not have Garry "in my service," he wanted to be his own lawyer, the judge was just as determined to prevent him from so doing. The slender reed upon which he relied was the fact that I had, just before the trial began, filed a notice of appearance for Bobby.

Shortly before the trial was scheduled to open, Seale, who was then in custody in San Francisco because of serious conspiracy charges originating from Connecticut, had

---

*Tigar, a professor of Law at UCLA, was arrested in Los Angeles and flown in handcuffs to Chicago. Lefcourt paid his own way from New York to Chicago where he voluntarily surrendered to the United States Marshal. The arrest warrants for Kennedy and Roberts were quashed by a federal judge in San Francisco.

been spirited incommunicado out of California. After a six-day cross-country trek by automobile, he arrived in Chicago where he was promptly incarcerated in the antique Cook County Jail. Upon Garry's request, we asked Stu Ball, a young lawyer awaiting admission to the District of Columbia bar, to prepare and file a motion permitting Chairman Fred Hampton of the Illinois Black Panther Party* to visit Seale.

Parenthetically, in the process of denying this motion, Judge Hoffman treated young Ball with a brutal ferocity that was as unjustified as it was sadistic. Although Ball had informed him that he was not yet a practicing attorney, Hoffman said first that he would hear him "as a human being," and then, with the open encouragement of the prosecution, proceeded to berate him unmercifully for allegedly deceiving the court as to his professional status. He later compounded this breach of all ethics and morality by spitefully refusing the application of Ball's father, a respected Chicago attorney and the former president of Montgomery Ward, to admit his son to practice in the federal courts.

I arrived in Chicago on Sunday, September 21, the day after the denial of the Hampton motion. The next morning, again at Garry's insistence, I went to the lockup on the 24th floor of the Federal Building and asked to see Seale. I was informed that I could not do so without a notice of appearance which I filed at once with the clerk of the court, adding the words "pro tem" after my signature. I was only then permitted to visit Bobby.

Two days later, just before jury selection began, Len Weinglass and I filed separate notices of appearance. In order to make sure that we were each able to cross-examine every witness, we had arbitrarily divided up the eight defendants into two groups— Weiner, Hayden, Hoffman and Davis in one, and Seale, Dellinger, Froines and Rubin in the other. I signified that I represented the latter group.

However, before the jury had been selected and sworn, Seale informed us that, if he couldn't have Garry in his corner, he wished to defend himself. Judge Hoffman was notified at once of this request, both by Seale and myself, but he refused to honor it as he was to do throughout Bobby's six-week connection with the trial. From this point on, Seale attempted to represent himself at every appropriate instance, such as standing up to cross-examine a witness who had testified against him, but ran each time into the obdurate (and untrue) refrain that "You have a lawyer to speak for you."

The transcript cannot begin to convey the steadily mounting tension in the courtroom as Seale struggled heroically to exercise what is perhaps one of a citizen's most fundamental rights—to defend himself against serious criminal charges which might have cost him ten years of his life. I will never forget how desperately this proud Black man tried to question hostile witnesses, protest against the incorrect designation by the prosecutor of a clenched black fist on a sweatshirt as "the black power symbol" instead of "the power to the people sign," and make several highly relevant motions. When he was finally chained and gagged for his persistence, I knew that morality had fled the room, and all I could splutter in my hopeless frustration was that I felt "so utterly shamed to be an American lawyer at this time."

On the afternoon of November 5, Judge Hoffman, who had learned that even the tightest of gags could not silence a man determined to insist upon his constitutional rights, ordered Seale severed from the case. In so doing, he found the Black Panther Chairman guilty of sixteen separate contempts and sentenced him to three months on each one. Yet, although the judge took almost two hours to delineate Bobby's sins, the words that I remember best are not those that came from his lips, but rather Seale's ringing denunciation "of a racist decadent America where the Government of the United States does not recognize the black man's constitutional rights, and have never recognized them. . . ."

In retrospect, I now see that what most affected the judge and his actions was his utter inability to understand the defendants and their rather complex motivations. Had he only been able to surmount his own predetermination of their life styles, their characters and their goals, he might have been able to sit fairly in judgment upon them. As it

---

*On the night of December 4, 1969, Hampton, while asleep in his bed, was shot to death by Chicago police officers under the command of the State's Attorney for Cook County.

was, he used the judicial process against them exactly as Don Quixote had flailed his spear against a windmill's rotating vanes, destroying, along the way, his own credibility and undermining the very system he thought he was saving.

Perhaps the best and most poignant illustration of the overriding insensitivity that made it impossible for him to approach the defendants as human beings occurred when he was about to sentence Tom Hayden for contempt. The latter had reached the end of his pre-sentence remarks when he hesitated for a moment and then, his eyes brimming with unexpected tears, he said, "I was trying to think about what I regretted about punishment . . . and that is I would like to have a child." A man of any sensibilities would have ignored the remark and proceeded to impose sentence, but the judge, wholly unmoved by the momentary revelation of the soul of another man, could not refrain from observing that "there is where the Federal System can do you no good."

That callous quip was perhaps the best measure of the system's chronic inability to gauge correctly the worth of those who question its essential integrity.

IN THE UNITED STATES DISTRICT COURT
NORTHERN DISTRICT OF ILLINOIS
EASTERN DIVISION

UNITED STATES OF AMERICA
Plaintiff
vs.
DAVID T. DELLINGER, et al.,
Defendants

No. 69 CR-180

TRANSCRIPT OF PROCEEDINGS had at the
hearing of the above-entitled cause before the
Hon. JULIUS J. HOFFMAN, one of the judges of said
court, sitting in his courtroom in the United
States Court House at Chicago, Illinois, on the
24th day of September, A.D. 1969, at the hour of
10:00 o'clock a.m.

PRESENT:

HON. THOMAS A. FORAN, United States Attorney,
MR. RICHARD G. SCHULTZ, Asst. United States Attorney, and
MR. ROGER CUBBAGE, Attorney, Department of Justice,
    appeared on behalf of the government;
MR. WILLIAM KUNSTLER and
MR. LEONARD I. WEINGLASS,
    appeared on behalf of the defendants.

Pretrial

THE CLERK: 69 CR 180, United States of America vs. David Dellinger, Rennard C. Davis, Thomas E. Hayden, Abbott Hoffman, Jerry C. Rubin, Lee Weiner, John R. Froines and Bobby G. Seale, for trial.

Your Honor, there are several motions here.

There is a motion of all defendants to disqualify judge under United States Code, Title 28, Section 455.

THE COURT: Who will present the motion?

MR. BIRNBAUM: If the Court please, I should like to advise the Court that as a matter of record Mr. Bass and myself were retained as local counsel in accordance with the local rules; that our function and role in this case has been to act as local counsel for the purpose of assistance in the pretrial motions. It is my understanding that Mr. Kunstler and Mr. Weinglass have at this date filed an appearance on behalf of the eight defendants and they will act as counsel, trial counsel throughout the whole trial.

THE COURT: Mr. Kunstler—not that I dispute Mr. Birnbaum's word—has he made an accurate statement?

MR. KUNSTLER: He has made an accurate statement. We will serve notice on the United States Attorney in a few minutes.

THE COURT: As counsel for all defendants?

MR. KUNSTLER: The way it is, your Honor, Mr. Weinglass will be representing four of the defendants and I will be representing four of the defendants.

THE COURT: Have you prepared and are you ready to file appearances in behalf of those four?

MR. KUNSTLER: They have already been filed, your Honor. They were filed this morning.

THE COURT: All right. Nunc pro tunc, Mr. Kunstler, as of the time you filed them, whenever it was, I give you leave to appear as additional counsel.

MR. KUNSTLER: I must inform the Court that all the defendants take the position that they are not fully represented in court because of Mr. Garry's absence.

THE COURT: Mr. Kunstler, that aspect of the case has been considered by the United States Supreme Court. I am bound by the ruling of Mr. Justice Marshall.

I will hear from the Government on the observations of Mr. Kunstler.

[3]

MR. FORAN: Your Honor, first of all there have been nine attorneys in this case, all of whom have filed general appearances for these defendants. None of those appearances has been withdrawn. As recently as two days ago three of the attorneys who have filed general appearances in this case sent telegrams addressed to me. The three attorneys were Michael Kennedy, Michael Tigar and Dennis Roberts. The telegrams read in exactly the same words, each one of them, and if I may read them to you:

"I hereby wish to formally advise the Court of the withdrawal of my representation in the matter of United States against Dellinger, et al., 69 CR 180. At no time was it my intention to serve as trial counsel, that role being delegated by all defense counsel and the defendants to Charles Garry, chief trial counsel, William Kunstler and Leonard Weinglass."

I responded, your Honor, yesterday by telegram to each of those counsel:

"We do not consider your telegram of withdrawal as attorney in this case and will request the Court to order your appearance in court for trial in this case."

Your Honor, I now move that this court order the appearance in court of Michael J. Kennedy, Michael E. Tigar and Dennis J. Roberts.

It has been the law in the Federal court for over one hundred years, your Honor, and never challenged successfully that an appearance once filed cannot be withdrawn without the consent of the Court. No consent has been given or even applied for in this case.

By the way, your Honor, I would like to add one further statement, that if the defendants are prepared at this time to represent to this court that they are satisfied with their counsel in this case who are present here in this court and will waive any claim that their Sixth Amendment rights are abridged, then we would ask the Court not to issue an order to have Mr. Lefcourt, Mr. Kennedy, Mr. Tigar and Mr. Roberts brought in before this court immediately.

MR. KUNSTLER: Your Honor, as far as the suggestion of the United States Attorney is concerned that these defendants waive their constitutional rights, in effect ransom their Sixth Amendment rights, for the needless visit to this court of four attorneys, this is as outrageous a statement as I have ever heard in a Federal court. They will not waive their Sixth Amendment rights.

I think that ransoming or bargaining with Sixth Amendment rights should not be countenanced by this court.

THE COURT: Please don't repeat. You are no more forceful the second time than you are the first, and the first time you were forceful, so I am not going to go through repetition.

MR. KUNSTLER: If your Honor says I was forceful, I will accept that observation and stop.

THE COURT: I didn't say I agreed with you. You were forceful.

MR. KUNSTLER: I interpret the remarks as your signals meaning agreement.

THE COURT: You don't know me very well, but I tell you in advance of this, and this promises to be a long one, I suspect, you don't have to repeat. My hearing is good and I think I can understand after all the years what a lawyer, especially a young lawyer like yourself, is saying to me.

MR. KUNSTLER: Your Honor is too kind.

THE COURT: There will be an order on Mr. Michael J. Kennedy, Mr. Michael E. Tigar, Mr. Dennis J. Roberts and Mr. Gerald B. Lefcourt to attend here as expeditiously as possible, and I direct, Mr. Clerk, the issuance of bench warrants for the apprehension of those lawyers who are obligated in law to be here.

MR. KUNSTLER: What about Mr. Garry, your Honor? He is also obligated in law—

THE COURT: You let me take care of my orders and you take care of yours.

Is there another motion?

MR. BIRNBAUM: If the Court please, that motion is still pending which was called.

THE COURT: Oh, I will hear you, Mr. Birnbaum. I had forgotten that. Mr. Kunstler interrupted you.

MR. BIRNBAUM: I have just been advised by Mr. Weinglass that he wishes to address the Court with reference to my proceeding on this motion.

MR. WEINGLASS: If the Court please, there is a defendant in court, Mr. Bobby Seale, who is sitting here. He is entitled to counsel. As of now he does not have counsel.

THE COURT: That is not a fact, as it appears in the record.

MR. WEINGLASS: Mr. Birnbaum and Mr. Bass have withdrawn from the case as trial counsel. Mr. Seale is not represented here in court.

THE COURT: Mr. Weinglass, I direct you to sit down.

MR. WEINGLASS: If the Court please, I would like to know—

THE COURT: I would like you to sit down or I will ask the marshal to escort you to your chair.

MR. WEINGLASS: I will sit down, but I do so under protest.

THE COURT: Then do so.

MR. BIRNBAUM: Mr. Kunstler has asked leave of the Court to argue this motion on my behalf.

THE COURT: The motion as filed here reads this way: "To disqualify judge under USC, Title 28, Section 455."

I will hear you, sir.

MR. KUNSTLER: We have made a motion for your Honor's disqualification based on a transcript of proceedings before you held in this court on the twenty-seventh day of August, 1969.

In that transcript, as your Honor can read for himself, you indicate that Mr. Foran is your attorney in the mandamus proceedings. We submit on the basis of that alone, the use of the United States Attorney as your attorney in a mandamus proceeding which is a separate and distinct proceeding from the trial of this cause, that your Honor ought to disqualify himself.

THE COURT: The defendants have moved to disqualify the judge on the ground that he has entered into an attorney-client relationship with the prosecuting attorney and therefore cannot be impartial in this case.

I hold that a judge who has been a nominal correspondent in an earlier mandamus proceeding arising out of his denial of certain motions of defendants is not disqualified from hearing this suit.* No relationship is created which would justify a disqualification under 28 USC, Section 455.

Mr. Clerk, the defendants' motion styled "To disqualify the judge" will be and is denied.

THE CLERK: Motion on behalf of all defendants for a pretrial hearing on constitutional facts.

THE COURT: When was this motion served on the Government and a copy left with the court?

MR. WEINGLASS: If the Court please, the motion was served on the United States Attorney this morning in this courtroom.

THE COURT: The motion has been handed in here in violation of the rule. As it is presented, I deny it.

MR. WEINGLASS: You deny the opportunity—

THE COURT: I deny the motion as being improperly submitted to the Court under the law.

MR. WEINGLASS: If the Court please, in light of the denial of this motion, this motion will be withdrawn and resubmitted tomorrow to the Court in proper form.

THE COURT: You can't withdraw what has been submitted, sir.

MR. WEINGLASS: Are you suggesting, sir, that a motion for a hearing on constitutional facts which has not even been read by the Court is going to be denied seriatim, out of hand, without argument?

THE COURT: I only suggest what I have said.

MR. WEINGLASS: If your Honor please, pursuant to that motion—

THE COURT: Mr.—What is your name, Weinglass?

MR. WEINGLASS: Weinglass.

THE COURT: The motion has been denied and I will hear no further argument on it.

---

*Refer to Appendix II for text marked with asterisks.

Mr. Clerk, will you please swear the veniremen, the prospective jurors?

THE CLERK: The prospective jurors will please rise and be sworn to answer questions.

(venire sworn)

THE COURT: Ladies and gentlemen, before we go ahead, I would ask the marshal, please, to call twelve prospective jurors to the jury box.

THE MARSHAL: As I call your name, bring your personal belongings with you.

THE COURT: Ladies and gentlemen, in order to move this trial along and to save the time of all of us consistent with the rights of everybody concerned, I am going to tell you briefly what this case is about, and to call your attention to some matters which I deem to be of importance.

Ladies and gentlemen, this is a so-called criminal case. I say so-called because this case appears on the criminal calendar of the court, but of course the designation "criminal case" does not mean that the defendants, or any one of them, are guilty of any crime. They have been charged in an indictment filed in court by a Federal grand jury with the commission of certain offenses, and, of course, the burden of proof is on the Government. It is the duty of the prosecution to satisfy you, if you come to be selected as jurors in this case, beyond a reasonable doubt before you arrive at a verdict of guilty with respect to any defendant.

The accused sitting at that table over there, all of them as they sit at the defense table, with their lawyers, are as innocent as anyone in this court and will so remain until you, the jurors, if you come to be selected as jurors, have convicted them or any one of them, if you do come to convict them or him by your verdict or verdicts.

Now, ladies and gentlemen, because it is the jury's solemn duty to consider this case solely upon the evidence presented in the courtroom, that is to say, oral testimony given by witnesses from the witness stand and any documentary or physical exhibits that might be received, it becomes my responsibility now as a matter of law to direct each and every one of you prospective jurors that henceforth and as long as you are connected with this case in any capacity and until you have been finally discharged from service in the case, not to read any newspaper or magazines or listen to radio and not to look at or listen to television programs.

I also direct and order you to exercise the utmost care that you do not inadvertently expose yourself to any of the reports concerning this case. On occasion, you might be riding downtown, let us say, on a bus and look over a man's shoulder and see an article in a newspaper. I would suggest that if this happens you turn your head the other way.

Likewise I must direct you and order you as not to communicate with any person or allow any person to communicate with you on the telephone or in any manner with regard to any aspect of this case. It is my duty and obligation under the law to direct and order you, ladies and gentlemen, not to discuss the case among yourselves at any time until and if you are chosen as jurors in this case, and then only when you come to deliberate on a possible verdict or verdicts. But until that time, if that time ever comes, there is to be no discussion among yourselves about the case and you are directed again not to listen to others discussing the case if you happen to be present where the case is discussed.

September 25, 1969

THE COURT: Now, ladies and gentlemen, I ask each and every one of you who have served as jurors in any court in any kind of a case to please raise your hand.

(show of hands)

THE COURT: As I anticipated, there are many who have served as jurors and my next question is addressed to those of you who have just indicated that you have had previous jury service. Did something happen in any case in which you participated as a juror which would lead you to conclude that you could not give the Government and the defendants and each one of them a fair and impartial trial in this case? Will you please so indicate by raising your hands?

No one has raised his hand, hence I conclude that all of the prospective jurors, despite their previous jury service, feel that they can be fair and impartial to all of the parties in this case.

I ask you, ladies and gentlemen of the jury, whether there is any reason you can think of now, that would lead you to feel that if you are selected by the lawyers as jurors in this case you could not be fair and impartial in this case, giving the United States of America, Mr. David T. Dellinger, Mr. Rennard C. Davis, Mr. Thomas E. Hayden, Mr. Abbott H. Hoffman, Mr. Jerry C. Rubin, Mr. Lee Weiner, Mr. John R. Froines, and Mr. Bobby G. Seale a fair and impartial trial?

If there is such a reason, will you please raise your hand?

No one has raised his hand, hence I conclude that all of you prospective jurors are of the opinion that if you are selected to serve as jurors here, there is no reason in your respective minds why you could not give each and every one of these defendants and the Government the kind of fair and impartial trial that everyone charged with the commission of an offense in this country is entitled to have under the Constitution of the United States.

• • • • •

THE COURT: You are Judith A. Sage, and you live in chicago. Is that right?
THE VENIREMAN: Yes, sir.
THE COURT: What does your family consist of?
THE VENIREMAN: I am Miss, I am not married.
THE COURT: What is your business or occupation if you have one?
THE VENIREMAN: I am a secretary for Social Security.
THE COURT: How long have you been in that office?
THE VENIREMAN: About eight years.
THE COURT: Miss Sage, would the fact that you are a government employee influence your judgment with respect to any verdict or verdicts that you might come to sign in this case?
THE VENIREMAN: No, sir.
THE COURT: Do you live with your parents?
THE VENIREMAN: Yes, my parents—my mother and my father.
THE COURT: What is your father's occupation?
THE VENIREMAN: He is a policeman.
THE COURT: Of which police force is he a member?
THE VENIREMAN: Chicago.
THE COURT: Chicago. How long has he been a member of the Chicago police force?
THE VENIREMAN: Twenty-four years.
THE COURT: Miss Sage, do you feel that the fact that your father is a member of the Chicago police force and has been for many years would affect your judgment as a juror if you were selected in this case?
THE VENIREMAN: No, Judge.
THE COURT: Thank you, Miss Sage.

• • • • •

THE COURT: You are Mr. William G. Haase?
THE VENIREMAN: Yes, your Honor.
THE COURT: May I please have your family situation, Mr. Haase?
THE VENIREMAN: I have a wife and two children.
THE COURT: What is your business or occupation?
THE VENIREMAN: I am a supervisor for the Chicago Transit Authority.
THE COURT: How long have you been with the Chicago Transit Authority?
THE VENIREMAN: Ten and a half years.
THE COURT: You are out on the street seeing that things go right, is that it?
THE VENIREMAN: I am with the elevated.
THE COURT: Is your wife employed outside the home?
THE VENIREMAN: No.

• • • • •

THE COURT: You are Thomas M. Curtin?
THE VENIREMAN: That is correct.
THE COURT: You live in Arlington Heights, Illinois, is that right?
THE VENIREMAN: That is correct, your Honor.

THE COURT: Please tell me about your family situation.
THE VENIREMAN: I am single.
THE COURT: Do you live with your parents?
THE VENIREMAN: Yes, I do.
THE COURT: Your business, sir, or occupation?
THE VENIREMAN: I was just hired by Baxter Laboratories in Morton Grove, Illinois. I have not yet been to work for them.
THE COURT: Who was your former employer?
THE VENIREMAN: I just graduated from the University of Illinois.
THE COURT: You are with a good company.
    What is your father's occupation?
THE VENIREMAN: He is retired, your Honor. He formerly worked for W. H. Barber Chemicals here in Chicago.
THE COURT: Your mother, I take it, is not employed?
THE VENIREMAN: That is correct.

· · · · ·

THE COURT: Mr. United States Attorney, I tender these twelve prospective jurors.
    Mr. Marshal, will you call one prospective juror to the box?
THE MARSHAL: Jean Fritz.
THE COURT: You are Jean Fritz. You live in Des Plaines, Illinois. Is that right?
THE VENIREMAN: Yes, sir.
THE COURT: Will you tell me about your family situation?
THE VENIREMAN: Three daughters and one son.
THE COURT: And a husband?
THE VENIREMAN: Yes, sir.
THE COURT: I won't tell him that you left him out. What is your husband's business or occupation?
THE VENIREMAN: He and I run a store.
THE COURT: Where is the business located?
THE VENIREMAN: In Des Plaines.
THE COURT: Tell me about your children. How old are they?
THE VENIREMAN: Two are married. And I have a boy still and a girl in Chicago.
THE COURT: Your boy is where?
THE VENIREMAN: Home.
THE COURT: At home and goes to public school?
THE VENIREMAN: Yes, sir.
THE COURT: His age, please?
THE VENIREMAN: Nine.

· · · · ·

THE COURT: Gentlemen of the Government?
MR. FORAN: Your Honor, the Government will tender this panel.
THE COURT: Mr. Kunstler, the Government tenders these twelve prospective jurors.

· · · · ·

MR. KUNSTLER: Your Honor, before exercising our peremptories, we would like to move to challenge three of the jurors for cause. I will start in this order: juror number eight, Miss Sage. We feel that the fact that her father is a city policeman of such long standing, and because this case so inextricably involves the police of this city, that she cannot but be subliminally affected by that relationship. I would think that under those circumstances she ought to be excused for cause.
THE COURT: I will call upon the Government to reply to that motion.
MR. FORAN: Your Honor, the Government accepted the statements of the jurors under oath that they could be fair. We tender the panel.
THE COURT: Mr. Kunstler, with the oath administered as carefully as the clerk of this court administers the oath to jurors, I expect that they told the truth. I haven't the right to deprive a policeman's daughter of her right as a citizen to serve on a jury.
    The motion of the defendants for leave to challenge the three named jurors for cause will be denied.
MR. KUNSTLER: Your Honor, we are going to exercise a peremptory challenge. We do

so under protest because we feel the jury has not been asked a single relevant question to this case by the court.

MR. SCHULTZ: We object to an editorial comment being made by Mr. Kunstler.

THE COURT: I sustain the objection.

MR. KUNSTLER: Your Honor, then, because we are forced to, the defense would peremptorily challenge Mr. Haase.

THE COURT: Mr. Haase, you may leave the box. You are excused. Call another, Mr. Marshal.

THE MARSHAL: Kristi A. King.

THE COURT: Are you Kristi A. King?

THE VENIREMAN: Yes, I am.

THE COURT: Will you tell me about your family situation, please?

THE VENIREMAN: I am single. I live with my parents, my mother and my father.

THE COURT: Do you have an occupation?

THE VENIREMAN: Yes, I am a customer representative.

THE COURT: For which firm?

THE VENIREMAN: Dennison Copier.

THE COURT: What is your father's occupation?

THE VENIREMAN: He works for Illinois Bell.

THE COURT: What is his position with them?

THE VENIREMAN: He is management.

THE COURT: Is your mother employed outside the home?

THE VENIREMAN: Yes, she is a purchasing agent.

THE COURT: For which company?

THE VENIREMAN: For Northern Illinois Electric Supply Company in Crystal Lake.

THE COURT: Do you have any sisters and brothers?

THE VENIREMAN: Yes, sir, I have a brother that is twenty-nine, and a sister that is twenty-six.

THE COURT: What are their respective occupations?

THE VENIREMAN: My brother is West Coast manager for Wurlitzer.

THE COURT: The musical instrument company?

THE VENIREMAN: That's correct.

THE COURT: And your sister?

THE VENIREMAN: My sister is also a customer representative. She works for Savin Business Machines.

THE COURT: How long has she been with the Savin Company?

THE VENIREMAN: About four months.

THE COURT: Before then?

THE VENIREMAN: Before then, she worked for VISTA.

THE COURT: VISTA. Tell me about VISTA. What is VISTA?

THE VENIREMAN: She was a recruiter for VISTA. She went to different college campuses and recruited.

THE COURT: What is it?

THE VENIREMAN: It is basically the domestic Peace Corps.

THE COURT: All right, gentlemen of the Government?

MR. FORAN: The Government will tender the panel, your Honor—

THE COURT: Mr. Kunstler?

MR. KUNSTLER: We have no further peremptories, your Honor.

THE COURT: All right.

Mr. Clerk, will you please swear the members of the jury and the alternates, please?

(whereupon the jury is sworn to try the issues)

THE COURT: I can now call you ladies and gentlemen of the jury.

Ladies and gentlemen of the jury, we are about to recess. I must order you not to read the newspapers or any other journals, not to talk with anybody about this case o let anybody speak with you about it, not to discuss the case among yourselves. If anybod attempts to talk with you about this case, please get in touch with one of the Unit States marshals who will lay the matter before me.

Opening Statement on Behalf of
the Government by Mr. Schultz

September 26, 1969

MR. SCHULTZ: Ladies and gentlemen of the jury, Mr. Foran, counsel for the defendants:

The Government, ladies and gentlemen of the jury, will prove in this case, an overall plan of the eight defendants in this case which was to encourage numerous people to come to the city of Chicago, people who planned legitimate protest during the Democratic National Convention which was held in Chicago in August of 1968, from August 26 through August 29, 1968. They planned to bring these people into Chicago to protest, legitimately protest, as I said, create a situation where these people would riot, and the defendants, in perpetrating this offense crossed state lines themselves, at least six of them, with intent to incite this riot.

We will prove, ladies and gentlemen of the jury, that the defendant David Dellinger, who sits right there, the defendant Rennard Davis, who sits next to him, and Thomas Hayden, who is standing—that these three—

THE COURT: I will excuse you, ladies and gentlemen of the jury, for a few minutes. Mr. Marshal, will you take the jurors out?

(jury excused)

COURT: Who is the last defendant you named?

CHULTZ: Mr. Hayden.

URT: The one that shook his fist in the direction of the jury?

DEN: That is my customary greeting, your Honor.

RT: It may be your customary greeting but we do not allow shaking of fists room. I made that clear.

EN: It implied no disrespect for the jury; it is my customary greeting.

T: Regardless of what it implies, sir, there will be no fist shaking and I cau- repeat it. That applies to all of the defendants.

hal, bring the jury back.

(jury enters)

: May I proceed, your Honor?

Yes, Mr. Schultz.

MR. SCHULTZ: Thank you, your Honor.

In promoting and encouraging this riot, the three men whom I just mentioned, Dellinger, Davis and Hayden, used an organization which they called the National Mobilization Committee to End the War in Vietnam. They used this organization to plan these activities. The office was located at 407 South Dearborn Street, Chicago, Illinois, just a block south of this Federal Building.

The defendants Dellinger, Davis and Hayden joined with five other defendants to create the riots in Chicago during the time the Democratic National Convention was convened here.

Two of these defendants, the defendant Abbie Hoffman who sits—who is just standing for you, ladies and gentlemen—

THE COURT: The jury is directed to disregard the kiss thrown by the defendant Hoffman and the defendant is directed not to do that sort of thing again.

MR. SCHULTZ: —and with them a man named Jerry Rubin who is standing here—these two men called themselves leaders of the Yippies.

Two more of these individuals are Lee Weener—

MR. WEINER: Weiner.

MR. SCHULTZ: —Lee Weiner, who just stood, who is a research assistant in the Department of Sociology at Northwestern University, calls himself a professor at Northwestern University, and John Froines—John Froines is standing at the far corner of the table; he is an assistant and was at the time an assistant professor of chemistry at the University of Oregon—Lee Weener and John Froines joined—

MR. WEINER: Weiner.

MR. SCHULTZ: —joined with Davis, Dellinger and Hayden.

And the eighth person, the last person who joined, is a man named Bobby Seale. Bobby Seale sits near the corner of the table and he was the fifth person who joined with the first three.

Ladies and gentlemen of the jury, the Government will prove that each of these eight men assumed specific roles in it and they united and conspired together to encourage people to riot during the Convention. We will prove that the plans to incite the riot were basically in three steps. The first step was to use the unpopularity of the war in Vietnam as a method to urge people to come to Chicago during that Convention for purposes of protest.

The second step was to incite these people who came to Chicago, to incite these people against the Police Department, the city officials, the National Guard and the military, and against the Convention itself, so that these people would physically resist and defy the orders of the police and the military.

And the third step was to create a situation where the demonstrators who had come to Chicago and who were conditioned to physically resist the police would meet and would confront the police in the streets of Chicago so that a riot would occur.

We will prove that the defendants Dellinger, Davis, Hayden, Rubin and Hoffman made what are called nonnegotiable requests and unreasonable demands upon the City of Chicago and the Chicago Park District for certain permits—nonnegotiable demands.

First they demanded when these people arrived in Chicago to sleep in Lincoln Park. At one point they were talking in terms of up to or exceeding 500,000 people who were coming to Chicago to sleep in Lincoln Park and they demanded free portable sanitation facilities, they demanded free kitchens and free medical facilities.

The second demand, nonnegotiable demand, was for a march to the International Amphitheatre where the Democratic National Convention was taking place. Although they were told that the United States Secret Service said that a permit could not be authorized because of the danger to the security of the President and the Vice-President and the candidates, the defendants demanded a permit for a march.

You will hear evidence, ladies and gentlemen, that the defendants privately discussed that they did not really want that permit to march to the Amphitheatre, they would have to go through neighborhoods which they thought were hostile neighborhoods, and the marchers might be seriously injured. And the second reason why they reallly didn't want to march was that it was a six-and-a-half-mile march and if they made it, the people, thousands of people who did make the march, would not be able to engage in what the defendants called militant actions in the Loop; there would be nobody to disrupt the Loop.

The Government will prove that in organizing this action many of the defendants met with one another and planned the actions. The Government will not prove that all eight defendants met together at one time, but the Government will prove that on some occasions two or three of the defendants would meet together; on other occasions four would meet; on some occasions five of them would meet together to discuss these actions, and on several occasions six of the defendants met together to discuss their plans.

We will prove these meetings in two ways: one, by the testimony of people who were present, and, two, by the testimony of Chicago policemen who are charged with the responsibility of surveilling, following, certain of the defendants just prior to and during the Convention.

We will prove, ladies and gentlemen, that at these meetings prior to the Convention, the defendants planned the following actions: On Wednesday, August 28, 1968, which was the day that the Democratic Party was to nominate its candidates, they planned to flood the Loop with demonstrators, create disturbances in the Chicago Loop, so, as the defendant Davis stated, "the Loop would fall."

We will prove, ladies and gentlemen, that at these meetings the defendants planned that if they ever did make it to the International Amphitheatre, they would lock the exits at the International Amphitheatre and prevent any of the delegates or anyone else from leaving the International Amphitheatre, so that, as they said, the National Guard and the military would have to be called out to permit the delegates to get out of the Convention.

At these meetings that I am discussing, they agreed to arrange for people to defend and hold Lincoln Park against the police so that if the police tried to clear Lincoln Park, the people would fight them. They also stated that they planned to create enough disturbances throughout the city of Chicago during the time that the Convention was meeting in Chicago that the Federal troops would have to be called out so that it would look as though the Democratic Party was so illegitimate that it had to be protected by Federal troops. That was part of their plan as we will prove to you.

The Government will prove that in executing these plans, all the defendants except the defendant Bobby Seale, who didn't join the conspiracy until Tuesday, August 27, when he came to Chicago, planned to set up what they called marshal training programs. They said that they planned to train thousands of marshals to control their groups.

People were taught their so-called marshals' techniques with which to fight the police starting two weeks prior to the Convention. They taught the marshals judo chops; they taught them a snake dance which was a group of people who were to develop locomotion and charge and break police lines. They planned that at their training sessions in Lincoln Park prior to the Convention.

And they also at their training sessions trained their marshals in freeing arrested persons, people who were being arrested by a policeman, by throwing themselves upon the policeman so that the person whom he was arresting could break free.

The Government will show that not only were these plans made prior to the Convention, but we will show you that the defendants during the Convention carried out these plans by speaking directly to people in the streets and in the parks, trying to incite them to commit the acts that I have just told you they planned.

The defendants Davis, Rubin, Hoffman and Hayden incited the crowds as follows:

On one occasion, the defendant Davis instructed marshals to split the demonstrators, to split the people into small groups and to infiltrate into the Loop and to thin the police lines in order to reduce the effectiveness of the Chicago police.

We will prove that during the Convention the defendant Rubin instructed people in the street to arm themselves with anything they could find, and to hold Lincoln Park even at the cost of their lives.

We will prove that during the Convention the defendant Hoffman in the streets or in the parks spoke to the people and urged them to obtain weapons and on Wednesday, the twenty-eighth, they should storm the Hilton Hotel.

We will prove, ladies and gentlemen, that the defendants, the four that I mentioned, told the people to make it to the Amphitheatre against police officers by any means necessary. We will prove also that on Thursday, the twenty-ninth of August, the defendant Hoffman encouraged a large crowd to kidnap the Deputy Superintendent of Police, James Rochford, and to hold him as a hostage so that the people could get what they wanted. We will prove that, ladies and gentlemen.

We will prove that these people, the four that I mentioned, told people to go into the Old Town area of Chicago and tear it up; that they encouraged people to build barricades in Lincoln Park to be used in fighting the police when the police moved to clear the parks.

We will prove that these defendants instructed demonstrators, people in Chicago whom the defendants brought to Chicago, to break into small groups and fight the police in guerrilla bands which, the defendants said, was the most effective way of fighting the police.

During the Convention, we will prove, that the defendant Bobby Seale flew to Chicago. He flew here, as I said before, on Tuesday, the twenty-seventh of August, and he gave a speech Tuesday night to a crowd and he gave another one on Wednesday to a crowd. He told the crowd that every black man should get a .357 Magnum revolver, should get a .45 automatic pistol and an M-1 rifle, and then stop running in large groups and take direct action in small groups of four or five people and encircle the police, whom he called pigs. He said that "if a pig comes up to us unjustly," he said, "if he comes up to us unjustly, we should bring out our pieces and start barbecuing that pork, and if they get in our way, we should kill some of those pigs and put them on a morgue slab."

He so told the people.

Next the participation of the defendants Lee Weiner and John Froines. These were two key marshals who worked closely with Davis and Hoffman and Rubin and they committed a number of acts for purposes of disruption and violence.

The defendants Froines and Weiner on Thursday, August 29, arranged to make and to explode Molotov cocktails. They planned to explode them in the underground Grant Park garage to divert hundreds of police and troops and National Guard to the fire, leaving the remaining demonstrators who were in the park unguarded and free to invade the Loop. They called their venture a diversionary action to divert the police.

We will prove also that the defendant Froines obtained an acid called butyric acid, which is a foul-smelling chemical—it smells like vomit—and he secured this chemical and had some girls pour it into a downtown hotel.

Now, as to the defendant Dellinger's participation during Convention week, Dellinger was the principal architect. He was the principal architect especially of the riots which occurred on Wednesday, the twenty-eighth of August, 1968. His plan was to organize and to assemble people, as many people as possible, on Wednesday, the twenty-eighth, at the Bandshell in Grant Park.

Prior to the assembly, the defendant Dellinger planned with some of his codefendants to present two alternatives to the people whom he massed at the Bandshell on Wednesday afternoon. The first alternative was to leave the Bandshell area and have a peaceful march —that is what they called it—to the International Amphitheatre without permits. And the second was to have the remaining people invade the Loop in small groups for the purpose of guerrilla action.

We will prove that the defendants planned with Dellinger that Dellinger would lead this so-called peaceful march. Dellinger said that the police and the Guards stopping this march would require a number of troops and police taking them away from other areas so that the people who planned the guerrilla action in the Loop, would not be prevented from invading the Loop and infiltrating the Loop.

We will prove, ladies and gentlemen, that at the Bandshell, Dellinger introduced a number of speakers who gave speeches to the crowd urging them to move out of the park in guerrilla bands and to fight the police.

The defendant Hayden gave one of the speeches. He said to the crowd:

"Make sure," he said, "that if blood is going to flow, let it flow all over the city. If gas is going to be used, let it be used all over Chicago. If we are going to be disrupted and violated, let this whole stinking city be disrupted and violated. Begin to find your way out of here. I will see you in the street."

The crowd then broke up, and it infiltrated into the city. They infiltrated primarily at Balbo and Michigan. Thousands of screaming demonstrators, ladies and gentlemen, that Wednesday evening blocked the streets and refused to clear them. They ignored the police orders to clear the streets and go into the Grant Park area, and when the police attempted to finally move them, they resisted and the riot broke out at about eight o'clock on Wednesday night.

In sum, then, ladies and gentlemen, the Government will prove that the eight defendants charged here conspired together to use interstate commerce and the facilities of interstate commerce to incite and to further a riot in Chicago; that they conspired to use incendiary devices to further that riot, and they conspired to have people interfere with law enforcement officers, policemen, military men, Secret Service men engaged in their duties; and that the defendants committed what are called overt acts in furtherance of the conspiracy, that is, they took steps to accomplish this plan, this conspiracy.

The overt acts are things that they said to incite the people, and they are set forth in the indictment, and the Government will prove the charges in Count I of the indictment. As to the other counts, the Government will prove that the defendants Dellinger, Davis, Hayden, Hoffman, Rubin and Seale traveled from out-of-state to Chicago, Illinois, with the intent to organize to incite and to promote a riot as the government has charged in Counts II, III, IV, V, VI, VIII of the indictment, and, finally, the government will prove that the defendants Froines and Weiner taught and demonstrated to other people the use and making of an incendiary device, incendiary devices to be used to further this disorder as charged in Count VII of the indictment.

Ladies and gentlemen of the jury, the government will prove each of the defendants guilty as charged in each of the counts of the indictment.

Thank you.

THE COURT: Is it the desire of any lawyer of a defendant to make an opening statement?

MR. KUNSTLER: It is, your Honor.

THE COURT: All right. You may proceed, sir.

MR. KUNSTLER: Your Honor, it is 12:30.

THE COURT: I know. I am watching the clock. You leave the time-watching to me. Mr. Kunstler, I will watch the clock for you.

MR. KUNSTLER: Your Honor, will you permit us to complete the opening statements?

THE COURT: I will determine the time when we recess, sir. I don't need your help on that.

MR. KUNSTLER: Your Honor, since we both represent different defendants, I will lead with my presentation of the opening statement. Mr. Weinglass represents four defendants separately from me and he reserves the right to make an opening statement should he desire.

Opening Statement on Behalf of Certain Defendants by Mr. Kunstler

Ladies and gentlemen of the jury:

My name is William M. Kunstler. I am an attorney from the city of New York and I am one of the attorneys in this case. You must realize that these statements, both made by defense counsel and made by Government counsel, are nothing more or less than trying to indicate what each side hopes the evidence will show. They are not evidence in this case any more than the closing statements will be.

Now the Government has presented what it considers its table of contents to the book that will unfold before you.

The problem, of course, with a table of contents once you make the table known to the prospective readers is that the book must follow the table and if the table of contents reads one way and the book the other way, then the jury, of course, will draw its own conclusions. We concede or state to you that the book that we present will be the true book and that the table of contents which the government has presented to you is for some other book that is not in this trial; that what the Government has presented to you are its fond hopes of what they consider the book to be.

MR. SCHULTZ: Objection, your Honor.

MR. FORAN: Objection. This is argument.

THE COURT: I sustain the objection.

MR. KUNSTLER: We hope to prove before you that this prosecution which you are hearing is the result of two motives on the part of the Government—

MR. SCHULTZ: Objection as to any motives of the prosecution, if the Court please.

MR. KUNSTLER: Your Honor, it is a proper defense to show motive.

THE COURT: I sustain the objection. You may speak to the guilt or innocence of your clients, not to the motive of the Government.

MR. KUNSTLER: Your Honor, I have always thought that—

THE COURT: I sustain the objection, regardless of what you have always thought, Mr. Kunstler.

MR. KUNSTLER: The evidence will show as far as the defendants are concerned that they, like many other citizens of the United States, came to Chicago in the summer of

1968 to protest in the finest American tradition the National Convention of the party in power.

They organized to do so. They were conscious of their rights as citizens to so demonstrate and protest, and it was their purpose to do exactly that, to do what the Constitution gave them the right to do.

We will show that they hoped that this protest would be a significant one; that this protest would have an effect upon the country in which they live and the world in which that country is a part.

There was, as you will recall, and the evidence will so indicate, a turmoil within the Democratic Party itself as to whether it would enact a peace plan as part of its platform. This too would be influenced by demonstrators. The possibility of influencing delegates to that National Convention to take an affirmative strong stand against a continuation of this bloody and unjustified war, was one of the prime purposes of their coming to Chicago.

At the same time as all of this was going on, the evidence will show that there were forces in this city and in the national government who were absolutely determined to prevent this type of protest, who had reached a conclusion that such a protest had to be stopped by all means necessary, including the physical violence perpetrated on demonstrators. Long before a single demonstrator had set foot in the city of Chicago in the summer of 1968, the determination had been made that these demonstrations would be diffused, dissipated, destroyed as effective demonstrations against primarily the continuation of the war in South Vietnam.

Now we hope to show by our evidence that what actually happened in the streets of Chicago was not a riot caused by demonstrators but a riot engineered by the police of this city. We are going to show that the police of this city embarked on an organized conspiracy of berserk brutal action against these demonstrators; that the nightstick became the symbol of what demonstrators could expect who were demonstrating against the sensitive, delicate issue of the continuance of the war in Vietnam.

We will demonstrate that free speech died here in the streets under those clubs and that the bodies of these demonstrators were the sacrifices to its death.

The defense will show that the real conspiracy in this case is the conspiracy to curtail and prevent the demonstrations against the war in Vietnam and related issues. The real conspiracy was against these defendants. But we are going to show that the real conspiracy is not against these defendants as individuals because they are unimportant as individuals; the real attack was on the rights of everybody, all of us American citizens, all, to protest under the First Amendment to the Constitution, to protest against a war that was brutalizing us all, and to protest in a meaningful fashion.

Mr. Schultz has referred in his opening constantly to the so-called desire of the demonstrators to infiltrate the Loop, to destroy property and the like. I think you will find as the evidence unfolds that there was one unalterable object of the demonstrators' desire. They wanted to demonstrate. That is why they came. They were not bands of thieves, coming to Chicago to enjoy the luxury of rioting in the streets. The purpose of their visit, as the evidence will show, was solely to demonstrate meaningfully against this war. That purpose will shine through this case and all of the obfuscation of the Government's case, which it must do to convince you, to show that the intent was something else other than what I have indicated, all of that will dissolve in the case which the defendants will present in this court.

I just want to say as my parting words in this opening statement that the defendants will stand before you and will present before you a classic example of the Government against the people, of the people attempting, as they have throughout the history of this country and other countries to come in and present a grievance in the right and appropriate place and to go down in the streets with their head split apart and their rights violated with billy clubs which have in one form or another from the earliest time of recorded history been the device to, as the last resort, destroy dissent. At one time it was the spear; at another time it was the noose; and today or in August of 1968 it was the billy club wielded indiscriminately against demonstrators, newsmen, women, children, young men, old men, here in the streets of Chicago.

Dissent died here for a moment during that Democratic National Convention. What happens in this case may determine whether it is moribund.

MR. SCHULTZ: Objection, your Honor.

THE COURT: I sustain the objection. I direct the jury to disregard the last statement of counsel for the defendants.

MR. KUNSTLER: Thank you, ladies and gentlemen.

THE COURT: Is there any other defense lawyer who wishes to make on opening statement to the jury?

I take it that your standing there means yes, you do, Mr. Weinglass.

MR. WEINGLASS: Yes, your Honor, that is correct.

Opening Statement on Behalf of Certain Defendants by Mr. Weinglass

If your Honor please, ladies and gentlemen of the jury:

My name is Leonard Weinglass. I have been previously introduced to you by the Court. I am an attorney of the State of New Jersey and a member of the bar of that state.

This trial, like every other trial, is an attempt on the part of the parties to the litigation to recreate here in this courtroom and before you a reality of the events that occurred sometime previous.

Now a major national political convention is an event which occurs in this country just once every four years. It is a major event. It is the only time when all of our elected officials of a given party, and a number of people whom they represent, come together as a single body.

It is also the only time when the people of this country can go before the elected representatives of their party and their delegates, and express to the people whom they have elected and the people who represent them their disinclination toward the policies or the positions which their party is taking.

It was for that reason that a number of people had to come to Chicago and did come to Chicago.

Now Mr. Kunstler in his opening indicated that the persons who came to Chicago were by and large those who felt a sense of personal moral anguish over what they considered to be the wrongful conduct of this country carried forward by the Democratic Party who was then in office and the war in Vietnam.

There was also another group of people who came here not for the purpose of protest, and not even for the purpose of demonstrating, in fact, but for the purpose of showing the public, and the leaders, and the rulers of this country that there was emerging within the country a new culture, and this group was generally called the Yippies.

Now the Yippies came here for a conclave very similar to the one which was widely publicized last month at Woodstock, New York, a conclave which was then to be known as Festival of Life.

At the culture conclave which was to be the Festival of Life, they had invited a number of rock group bands which are singing bands with instruments, and other performers who are relevant to the youth culture movement in this country.

Approximately four months before coming here, they had applied to this city for the right to use a small area—I think it was approximately 50 or 60 acres—of a 1,285-acre park in this city known as Lincoln Park.

Now there has been allusion to certain nonnegotiable demands which could not possibly be met, and some suggestion that they were made because they knew they couldn't be met. I leave the judgment of what is a nonnegotiable demand to you, but you are going to hear some interesting evidence on that issue, because the City could have met those demands if the persons responsible for that decision would not have been persons who were so fearful, and so misunderstood the young in this country, that they could not meet and talk to them in a reasonable, rational way. It is as one journalist suggested in her commentary—

MR. FORAN: Your Honor, I object to what one journalist suggested.

THE COURT: I sustain the objection. Please confine your opening statement, Mr. Weinglass, to what you think the evidence in this case will reveal.

MR. WEINGLASS: I think the evidence in this case will reveal to you that the attitudes of the men who dealt with these young people were such as to be people who were afraid, who had preinclinations and predispositions against listening and talking to them, and I think this evidence will show that these young people never had a chance to come to this city and meet peacefully when the Convention was being held here.

The evidence will indicate that the National Mobilization Committee, being war protesters, filed applications for the right to march. They did not want to march into the secured compound which was then the International Amphitheatre. They wanted to march up to the barbed wire, and they made that very clear.

They negotiated for several months with the City for the right to march to that compound, and at the end, when they were denied the right to march, they came to this building with attorneys, and they filed a suit, seeking the right to march. They did everything they could to gain that right.

When they were denied, they attempted the march just the same, but they attempted it and made it in a peaceful and nonviolent manner, and we will bring before you ample proof in the nature of photographs and films so that you may see for yourselves visually what happened when these people who held a peaceful rally, where they had two permits to hold the rally, then attempted to move to the Amphitheatre where they could hold a second rally.

Now there's been some allusion to the evidence in this case by Mr. Schultz as to words which were used by the defendants, words which he characterized, as he must, as being inciteful.

I might say to you at the outset I do not ask you to accept, or like, or understand, or agree with any of the speeches which my clients might have given.

MR. FORAN: Your Honor, once again, counsel continues to argue the case. It is improper.

THE COURT: I sustain the objection. Do I make myself clear to you?

MR. WEINGLASS: I am having a little difficulty applying your Honor's ruling to my opening statement.

THE COURT: I understand you have some difficulty. If you want me to speak more loudly, I will.

MR. WEINGLASS: It is not difficulty of hearing.

THE COURT: If you persist, I will have to deprive you of the right to proceed further because of your disregard of my instructions.

MR. WEINGLASS: We want to bring before you a full, a clear picture of what happened before and during the Convention, and we intend to use our right to cross-examination to do that during the presentation of the Government's case, and then go ahead during our case with a full development by way of a number of witnesses, films, and experts so that you will have in your hands and before you a complete version of what happened here before and during the Convention.

Now, while the Government is presenting its case, my co-counsel, Mr. Kunstler, and myself will be making certain objections. We will be making objections before you and to the Court, and the Court will rule on those. I want you to know at the outset we do not make those objections for the purpose of keeping information from you. One objection which you will be hearing frequently is an objection known as hearsay.

MR. FORAN: Your Honor, objection. If your Honor please—

THE COURT: I have repeatedly cautioned you. I caution you again, Mr. Weinglass. I think you understand me. You persist in arguing and telling the jury what you propose to do in respect to objections.

MR. WEINGLASS: Yes, I thought that was the purpose of an opening statement.

THE COURT: That is not the function of an opening statement. I have cautioned you time and time again. I caution you once more.

MR. WEINGLASS: My last comment to you, ladies and gentlemen of the jury, and it will be brief, is that we of the defense, and I do not mean this in any way by personal flattery, but we of the defense do consider you in this courtroom to be the highest authority, and we will—

THE COURT: Ladies and gentlemen of the jury—

MR. FORAN: This is argument.

THE COURT: I will sustain the objection—I will excuse you for a few minutes.

(jury excused)

THE COURT: Mr. Weinglass, I have repeatedly admonished you not to argue to the jury, not to tell the jury anything other than what in your opinion the evidence will reveal.

I think your persistency in disregarding the direction of the Court and the law in the face of repeated admonitions is contumacious conduct, and I so find it on the record.

Bring in the jury, Mr. Marshal.

MR. WEINGLASS: Your Honor has tried to stop me from speaking; however, it is the only way in which—

THE COURT: I am not stopping you at this time. I am the governor of the trial under the Supreme Court's direction, and you are going to do it according to the law.

MR. WEINGLASS: It will be done that way, your Honor. My understanding of the law is that I have a right to address the jury. If my right to speak is restricted, we have no defense in this court. We cannot defend clients unless the attorneys can talk.

THE COURT: You know exactly what you can say. You are too smart a lawyer not to know what I am saying, and I have expressed my views on the record.

Bring in the jury, Mr. Marshal.

(jury enters)

MR. WEINGLASS: I will not comment further in my opening. I will have a chance at the end of this case to speak to you, as will the Government. However, I do ask you during the course of the presentation of the Government's case to keep an open mind and to await before making your judgment the opportunity which we have to go ahead and bring evidence before you.

Thank you.

THE COURT: Does any other defense lawyer wish to make an opening statement?

Just a minute, sir, who is your lawyer?

MR. SEALE: Charles R. Garry.

MR. FORAN: Your Honor, may we have the jury excused?

THE COURT: Ladies and gentlemen, I am sorry, I will have to excuse you again.

(jury excused)

THE COURT: Mr. Kunstler, do you represent Mr. Seale?

MR. KUNSTLER: No, your Honor, as far as Mr. Seale has indicated to me, that because of the absence of Charles R. Garry—

THE COURT: Have you filed his appearance?

MR. KUNSTLER: Filed whose appearance?

THE COURT: The appearance for Mr. Seale.

MR. KUNSTLER: I have filed an appearance for Mr. Seale.

THE COURT: All right. I will permit you to make another opening statement in behalf of Mr. Seale if you like. I will not permit a party to a case—

MR. KUNSTLER: Your Honor, I cannot compromise Mr. Seale's position—

THE COURT: I don't ask you to compromise it, sir, but I will not permit him to address the jury with his very competent lawyer seated there.

MR. KUNSTLER: If I were to make an opening statement, I would compromise his position that he has not his full counsel here.

THE COURT: Bring in the jury, Mr. Marshal.

Mr. Seale, you are not to make an opening statement. I so order you. You are not permitted to in the circumstances of this case.

(jury enters)

THE COURT: Will you call your first witness?

MR. FORAN: Your Honor, the Government will call Mr. Raymond F. Simon.

Testimony of Raymond Simon

MR. FORAN: Will you state your name, please?

THE WITNESS: My name is Raymond F. Simon.

MR. FORAN: What is your occupation?

THE WITNESS: I am an attorney-at-law. I am Corporation Counsel of the City of Chicago.

My duties as corporation counsel of the City of Chicago are to be house counsel for the City, to represent the mayor, the aldermen, the department heads, and to represent the City of Chicago as a corporate entity in all litigated matters in which the City is a party.

MR. FORAN: Were you Corporation Counsel during the summer of 1968?

THE WITNESS: Yes, I was.

MR. FORAN: Calling your attention to August 8, 1968, did you attend a meeting that day?

THE WITNESS: Yes, in one of the conference rooms in the suite of offices of the mayor.

MR. FORAN: Were any of the defendants present?

THE WITNESS: Mr. Hoffman and Mr. Rubin were present at that meeting.

MR. FORAN: All right. Now who else was present at that meeting?

THE WITNESS: Mr. David Stahl, the mayor's administrative officer; Mr. Richard L. Elrod, a colleague of mine in the City Law Department—there were perhaps four other persons, Hoffman and Mr. Rubin.

MR. FORAN: Mr. Simon, would you state the conversation? Who said what?

THE WITNESS: Mr. Hoffman speaking to Mr. Stahl in particular said that he wished to obtain a permit for the use of Lincoln Park. He said that he wanted the mayor to grant the permit and he wanted the city to furnish sanitary facilities and health facilities for the use of Lincoln Park.

MR. FORAN: Did he say what they wanted to use the park for?

THE WITNESS: They wanted to use the park to sleep in. They wanted to use the park in general, to have permission to use the park under their own control for what they wanted to use it for.

MR. FORAN: And what did you say?

THE WITNESS: I said if there is a desire to get a permit for the use of the park facilities, it should be addressed to the Park District, but that the mayor of the City of Chicago had no authority over the Park District and he had no authority to grant or deny that permit.

MR. FORAN: Now, calling your attention to August 21, 1968, in the morning, where were you?

THE WITNESS: I was in this building in the courtroom of Judge William Lynch.

MR. FORAN: What brought you there?

THE WITNESS: There was a lawsuit filed by the National Mobilization Committee to End of the War in Vietnam and Mr. Rennie Davis, Tom Hayden, Mark Simons and others filed against the City of Chicago, the Park District, the Police Department, the sheriff and others.

The attorney for Mr. Davis was Mr. Stanley Bass.

MR. FORAN: What happened there in court, Mr. Simon?

THE WITNESS: We went into the chambers of Judge Lynch.

MR. FORAN: Was there a conversation at that time? What was said in that conversation, Mr. Simon?

THE WITNESS: I said to Mr. Davis that the City was predisposed to issue a permit for a march and assembly if Mr. Davis was willing to accept a reasonable proposal. The two initial permit applications, were for the day of August 28, for permission to have a march through the Loop which would begin at eleven o'clock in the morning. The second application for that same day, the twenty-eighth of August, which was the day on which the national Democratic Party was to hold nominations, they were to hold an assembly with marching at the Amphitheatre commencing at seven o'clock and proceeding until midnight.

I said, "If you are interested in what you allege in your complaint, that is, to exercise your constitutional rights of speech and assembly, then I think these rights can be afforded full protection and you can exercise them if we have a march but one that is a little more reasonable."

And I said, "I would like to suggest some alternatives and I would like to invite you to suggest alternatives to me if you have some other ideas on what might be an acceptable march."

MR. FORAN: What happened then?

THE WITNESS: Well, Mr. Davis said he wanted to meet within eyesight of the Amphitheatre and he proposed two sites right at the Amphitheatre, one just in front of the Amphitheatre on Halsted Street and the other to the west of the Amphitheatre.

I pointed out that the area from 38th on Halsted to 45th and Halsted was restricted; that this area was set off and no one was permitted in that area and this was because of the security precautions that were taken for the Convention; they were regulations that were made primarily at the direction of the United States Secret Service Department.

MR. FORAN: What did Mr. Davis say?

THE WITNESS: Well, he said he wanted to use the site at the Amphitheatre, and he said if the City wants to avoid violence, then what you should do is take all of the police and all of the Guardsmen away from the Amphitheatre on the night of the nomination, and let the National Mobilization Committee police itself. "We will use our marshals."

MR. FORAN: Did Judge Lynch say anything at that time?

THE WITNESS: Yes, Judge Lynch said to Mr. Davis, "Are you assuming to take over the role of the Police Department in protecting the city?"

MR. FORAN: What did Mr. Davis say?

THE WITNESS: He said yes, that it was his experience that the police actually cause violence.

MR. FORAN: What happened then?

THE WITNESS: Well, that really is about all that transpired during that session. We recessed then until the following day.

MR. FORAN: What happened on the following day?

THE WITNESS: Well, we came back to Judge Lynch's courtroom, and then we recessed to Judge Lynch's chambers, the way we had the preceding day.

MR. FORAN: What, if anything, did Mr. Davis say at that time, Mr. Simon?

THE WITNESS: As the conference in Judge Lynch's chambers resumed, Mr. Davis said that the offer to use the Bandshell for an assembly on Wednesday the twenty-eighth of August was acceptable, that they would like to have an assembly there between I think the time was one and four o'clock in the afternoon.

He said that in regard to the other proposals, that it was necessary for his group to meet at the Amphitheatre.

I said to him that there was no authorization to use the parks for sleeping, and I asked him if he would please commit himself to abiding by this ordinance requirement.

MR. FORAN: What did Mr. Davis say?

THE WITNESS: Well, he said no, and he said, "The park is being made available to the members of the National Guard. It could be made available to our people."

I said that there was no authorization to hold a meeting, to sleep in the parks, to use the parks. I urged him to seek hotel accommodations.

MR. FORAN: Then what did he say?

THE WITNESS: Well, he said that his members couldn't really be housed in hotel accommodations, that many of them didn't have money, and that what they really wanted was the use of the park so that they could sleep there and meet all night, and he said, "If the City doesn't give us the park, there will be tens of thousands of people without a place to stay, and they will go into the parks, and the police will drive them out, and they will run through the streets of the city, and there'll be disorder, and conflict, and problems, and the police will fight back, and there will be tear gas, and Mace, and billy clubs."

MR. FORAN: What happened then?

THE WITNESS: That was substantially all that happened at that session.

MR. FORAN: Did you then have legal argument in that case?

THE WITNESS: Yes, and then the legal argument ensued, at the conclusion of which Judge Lynch said that he would take the matter under advisement, and he would issue a written opinion before noon the following day, and we should return to his courtroom.

MR. FORAN: Did he issue that opinion the next day?

THE WITNESS: Yes. The following day he read a memorandum of opinion from the bench in which he denied the relief requested and dismissed the lawsuit.

MR. FORAN: That is all, your Honor.

(jury excused)

THE COURT: The clerk of the court has just handed me an order of the United States Court of Appeals. I will read it to you for your information.

"This matter comes before the court on the petition for issuance of a writ of mandamus ordering respondent, Hon. Julius J. Hoffman, United States District Judge for the Northern District of Illinois, Eastern Division, to:

"1. Withdraw his orders of arrest; and

"2. Grant them a continuance of this case until Charles R. Garry is well enough to rejoin the two other attorneys selected by petitioners as co-counsel on the trial of this case.

"On consideration whereof, it is ordered by the Court that the said petition for writ of mandamus be and the same is hereby denied."

MR. SCHULTZ: Your Honor, may I ask one thing before the jury comes in? We have been served with notice of motion for Monday to have a hearing on the constitutionality of questions relating to ordinances and statutes.

The reason why I am bringing it up now is that if your Honor is not going to hold a hearing in that matter, that you stay the subpoenas because I have an understanding that Ramsey Clark, the former Attorney General of the United States, had been subpoenaed for that hearing on Monday and I would ask the Court to stay the subpoena.

THE COURT: I doubt, Mr. Schultz, that I have the authority to quash the subpoena directed to a witness even though he be such a distinguished person as the former Attorney General of the United States.

I think Mr. Schultz' suggestion that subpoenas be stayed—I think you said a man named Johnson, Lyndon B. Johnson, was subpoenaed also, is that right?

MR. KUNSTLER: We don't know if he has been served yet but the subpoena is out.

THE COURT: It wouldn't be nice to take him from the comforts of his ranch in Dallas or wherever it is—Johnson City—if we couldn't reach him on Monday or for any reason we weren't going to hear the motion.

MR. KUNSTLER: Your Honor, I think we would agree to the stay of the subpoenas. I think the suggestion is a reasonable one.

THE COURT: I don't even know who the witnesses are but I know there were three important names dropped during the week and I was very much impressed. I am sorry in a way that I am not very sympathetically disposed toward the motion. I would like to participate with the former President of the United States on the witness stand as close to me as Mr. Simon is here, but—

MR. KUNSTLER: There is a way to do that, your Honor.

THE COURT: What do you say?

MR. KUNSTLER: I say there is a way to do that and that is to grant the motion.

THE COURT: Yes. It would have to be a legal way.

If anyone wants to prepare an order based on the stipulation with respect to subpoenas, I will be glad to sign it.

MR. SCHULTZ: We will prepare one with defense counsel.

THE COURT: Now, Mr. Kunstler, you referred to the other matter. I think it is only fair to these two lawyers who are here in custody that we give immediate consideration to it.

MR. SULLIVAN: It is my understanding that these defendants are willing that Messrs. Tigar, Lefcourt, Kennedy and Roberts not be present during the trial of this case and not participate in the trial as defense counsel, and they are willing to agree to their withdrawal as trial counsel. They are, as I understand it, satisfied to be represented in the trial of this case by Messrs. Garry, Kunstler and Weinglass, and that they do not waive any claim of prejudice arising from the absence of Mr. Garry.

THE COURT: I don't care to participate in negotiations. I don't want to participate in a bargaining session. As you know, I am not a bargainer.

We have two men here who have flaunted the authority of the Court and I have the court to protect, but I am inclined to give sympathetic consideration to any agreement that you might work out with the United States Attorney. It should be understood that the alternative is that these men must know that they must remain in custody if there isn't a resolution of the issues here.

MR. SULLIVAN: Your Honor, I believe that the Government and Mr. Kunstler and Mr. Weinglass and I have reached some agreement, subject of course, to your Honor's views.

I would like to read the following statement and then the defendants can affirm it in any way you desire.

"Each of the defendants state that they do not seek or require the representation of Mr. Tigar, Mr. Lefcourt, Mr. Kennedy and Mr. Roberts as counsel in this case and each expressly waives any and all claim of prejudice arising from Messrs. Tigar's, Lefcourt's, Kennedy's or Roberts' withdrawal as their attorneys in his case, and each of said defendants consents to said withdrawals."

That is the end of the statement.

The attorneys whom I represent here, Messrs. Tigar and Lefcourt, desire to move for permission to withdraw as attorneys for the clients for whom they filed appearance.

THE COURT: What is the position of those defendants in respect to who their lawyers are now?

MR. SULLIVAN: Your Honor, it is difficult for me to speak for these defendants because I don't represent them. I think Mr. Kunstler has to make those statements.

THE COURT: If he is going to say the same thing he said before, he needn't waste my time or his.

MR. SULLIVAN: I tried my best anyhow.

THE COURT: You are doing the best you can for these lawyers who are in difficulty.

Let them be remanded to the custody of the United States Marshal, without bail.

MR. SULLIVAN: If the Court please—

THE COURT: I don't bail a lawyer contempter.

MR. SULLIVAN: Your Honor, are they to remain in custody for the rest of their lives?

THE COURT: For when?

MR. SULLIVAN: For the rest of their lives? Is there no term?

THE COURT: I will determine on the disposition of this case Monday morning at 10:00 o'clock. They are now held in contempt. I didn't intend and you know you were talking foolishly when you said the rest of their lives.

When the order is entered finding them in contempt, I will impose a sentence.

I am not going to let these men play horse with the Court the way some of these lawyers have done with me. Bear that in mind, sir.

That will be all.

(the Court is adjourned)

September 29, 1969

THE CLERK: There are several motions here, your Honor. There is a motion to permit additional counsel for Michael E. Tigar and Gerald P. Lefcourt.

MR. FORAN: Your Honor, the government feels that your Honor might give some consideration to vacating the orders of contempt and permitting these men to withdraw and get on with this case that needs to be tried.

THE COURT: May I inquire, Mr. Foran, whether the other two lawyers who were not in attendance on Friday have appeared?

MR. FORAN: Yes, your Honor. They are in the courtroom.

MR. KENNEDY: Michael Kennedy. May I be heard, your Honor?

THE COURT: Certainly, Mr. Kennedy. We are glad to see you here.

MR. KENNEDY: I do not appear here in response to the Court's process which was quashed, the bench warrant that was issued for my arrest which was quashed in San Francisco after I was arrested.

I appear here of counsel with Mr. Sullivan to represent my colleagues, Mr. Tigar and Mr. Lefcourt. I do not appear in response to the Court's bench warrant.

MR. ROBERTS: If I might address the Court, I am Dennis J. Roberts.

I join my brother Kennedy in his remarks.

MR. SULLIVAN: Might I be heard on Mr. Foran's remarks?

THE COURT: Yes, certainly.

MR. SULLIVAN: Your Honor, on Friday I asked you to release the men on bond and you denied that motion and there was no opportunity for me even to open my mouth to ask you to release these men over the weekend.

Your Honor directed the United States Marshal to incarcerate these lawyers over the weekend without bond because they didn't come to a trial which is routinely done as I know of my personal knowledge although—

THE COURT: I heard the remarks of the United States Attorney. As nearly as I can judge, these are young attorneys from out of this district. It is the law to require lawyers in criminal cases not to send a telegram and say they are withdrawing, but to present a motion for leave to withdraw. I have no desire to damage the professional careers of young lawyers; but even young lawyers must comply with the law.

Agreeable with the motion and suggestion of the Government, the contempt proceedings against the two lawyers who were here and the two other lawyers who were not here will be vacated, set aside, and leave will be given to them to withdraw.

MR. SULLIVAN: I know that I have repeatedly stated to your Honor it is my understanding those defendants don't want to waive their point about Mr. Garry's absence.

THE COURT: What we are saying here today, I am willing to say that does not apply to Mr. Garry, Mr. Garry's absence.

MR. MEYERS: If the Court please—

THE CLERK: There is a motion, your Honor, on behalf of amicus curiae, one hundred lawyers, to declare a mistrial and drop contempt proceedings.

THE COURT: I deny that motion not only as moot but I deny the motion because you have no standing, sir.

MR. MEYERS: But I am here on behalf of a hundred lawyers.

THE COURT: In respect to amicus curiae, one hundred lawyers, I deny that because they do not have standing at the trial under this indictment and the pleas of not guilty entered pursuant thereto.

MR. MEYERS: May I have the privilege of stating my—

THE COURT: No, no.

MR. FORAN: Your Honor—

THE COURT: No. This is not a public forum. It is a branch of the United States District Court.

MR. MEYERS: I am an officer of the court, your Honor, and I have appeared before you before. You know that.

THE COURT: You have no standing here and by "standing," I use the word in a legal sense, you have no standing in this case. I don't allow lawyers to appear by the hundreds without even their names being mentioned. Your motion is denied in the entirety.

MR. MEYERS: May I have my name on the record? My name is Irving Meyers and I appear in behalf of one hundred lawyers from various parts of the country in an effort to file a petition amicus curiae.

THE COURT: Miss Reporter, that lawyer requested that his name appear on the record. That you may have, sir.

THE CLERK: Defendants' motion for hearing on the constitutionality of questions relating to ordinances and statutes.

MR. WEINGLASS: I refer your Honor to the relevant codes of the City of Chicago and of the Chicago Park District, respecting the granting of permits for sleeping in the park after eleven o'clock and for marching on the streets of this city.

I submit that under a 1969 holding of the United States Supreme Court in the case of Shuttlesworth vs. the City of Birmingham, that both of these statutes are on their face unconstitutional.*

These defendants and the other persons who came to this city had the right as citizens of this country to seize the initiative and use the parks and the streets in the manner in which they intended. I cite for that authority United States Supreme Court once again in the case of Shuttlesworth vs. Alabama, wherein the Court stated:

"Our decisions have made clear that a person faced with such an unconstitutional licensing law may ignore it and engage with impunity in the exercise of the right of free expression for which the law purports to require a license."

Now this evidential hearing which was called for in Shuttlesworth came up in that case in the following manner: Reverend Shuttlesworth on April 12, 1967, intended to have a march in the city of Birmingham. One week prior to April 12, 1967, he sent an aide to the city hall seeking an application for a parade permit. That city official was met in the city hall by one Mr. Bull Connor. Mr. Bull Connor advised that aide that he would not permit a parade to be held and I believe he indicated words to the effect, "The only march I am going to permit by your group is when I march you off to jail."

The application was never acted upon. Reverend Shuttlesworth encouraged the people to march and fifty-two persons did, in fact, march. Reverend Shuttlesworth was arrested for marching without a permit, as was the rest of the group. The United States Supreme Court overturned that conviction.

I submit this case cries out even more than the Shuttlesworth case for a full and open hearing on whether or not this statute, this licensing ordinance, is constitutional, and secondly, whether or not in this particular instance it was constitutionally applied by the authorities who had the power under the licensing statute to act.

THE COURT: Who will reply for the Government?

MR. SCHULTZ: Your Honor, this isn't the Shuttlesworth case where people are being prosecuted for the violation of a statute in which the constitutionality is questioned. The defendants in this proceeding are not charged with violation of those statutes, and whether they are constitutional or unconstitutional is absolutely irrelevant to this case. It has no bearing whatever on this case.

THE COURT: Mr. Weinglass, you may reply.

MR. WEINGLASS: Mr. Shuttlesworth was prosecuted for being disorderly and further-more inciting to riot, the very type of statute we are being prosecuted for.

The Supreme Court vacated both on the ground that he had a right to ask people to march, which we had a right to do, and he had a right to march himself. I think we are, in fact, in the exact same position.

THE COURT: It is the view of the Court that Shuttlesworth vs. City of Birmingham is inapposite.

Mr. Clerk, the defendants' motion for a hearing is denied.

Testimony of Raymond Simon Resumed

(jury enters)

THE COURT: Who will cross-examine this witness.

MR. WEINGLASS: If your Honor please, I shall begin the cross-examination. Mr. Simon, could you tell the jury when it was that Mr. Davis first applied to this City for a permit to march on the street?

THE WITNESS: I believe July 25, 1969.

MR. WEINGLASS: Can you tell the jury today in fact why it was that Mr. Davis' application of July 25 for a parade permit had not been acted on in the one month that the Department had his application?

THE WITNESS: Yes, I can tell them, Mr. Feinglass [*sic*]. The reason was that the duration of the march and assembly would have covered thirteen hours, and it would have involved the Loop area of Chicago, and would have involved the area just next to the Amphitheatre. It was too huge a burden. That was the reason.

MR. WEINGLASS: Mr. Simon, the Department acted within approximately ten or eleven days on Mr. Davis' application for the Bandshell. He submitted it on July 25 and they served him with notice on August 6 that they would not accept that application, is that not correct?

THE WITNESS: Yes, that is correct.

MR. WEINGLASS: Could you tell the jury why they also didn't act within the same period of time on his application for a march or procession in the streets?

THE WITNESS: Well, I think the hope was that we could accommodate a reasonable march if we could get agreement on the part of the National Mobilization Committee that they wouldn't insist on carrying it through on the Amphitheatre.

MR. WEINGLASS: If I show you two transcripts, could you identify those transcripts?

THE WITNESS: Yes, those appear to be the transcripts of the hearings before Judge Lynch on the twenty-first and twenty-second.

MR. WEINGLASS: There was also a request for an evening parade, is that correct?

THE WITNESS: Yes.

MR. WEINGLASS: Now would you tell the jury what Mr. Davis did with respect to that request?

THE WITNESS: He said he was going to march to the Amphitheatre after I told him that the time covered by that application was in violation of state law.

MR. WEINGLASS: I show you both transcripts and I ask you to look through them, Mr. Simon, and tell the jury where in those transcripts Mr. Davis says he will march even though it is illegal to march.

I refer you to page 7. Is it not a fact that Mr. Davis said to you and the Court :

"You indicated that night marches, or marches from the period of four to seven, which is what we had proposed, would cause problems and was not, in your judgment, in the interest of the City—we want to tell you that we are extremely flexible about how such an assembly might constitute itself, including that people go to such an assembly as pedestrians, rather than in a march—"

MR. FORAN: I object. That is totally the improper way to introduce this.

THE COURT: I sustain the objection to reading a document that apparently has not been received in evidence.

MR. WEINGLASS: It has been marked for identification.

THE COURT: We have thousands of exhibits that are marked but that never become exhibits in evidence, sir.

MR. WEINGLASS: Now, Mr. Simon, Mr. Davis indicated to you that his group would prefer to have an assembly near, I think you characterized it as within eyeshot of, the Amphitheatre. Is that correct?

THE WITNESS: Yes, they insisted that it was necessary to have it there.

MR. WEINGLASS: They proposed, did they not, four sites out of the security area? Isn't that a fact?

THE WITNESS: They proposed sites which were not under the jurisdiction of the City, and I told them that we couldn't give permits over there.

To tell you the truth, I am really vague on whether they proposed that as an acceptable site.

MR. WEINGLASS: If your Honor please, the defendants have retained the services of a bus company in the city which has a chartered bus available to us, and at this time I would request that the jury and the Court be permitted to drive out to the Amphitheatre area where we can see for ourselves the area that we are talking about.

THE COURT: I like this courtroom that the late Mies van der Rohe provided for us.

If you don't mind, we will try this case here. Treating your remarks as a motion to give the Court a bus ride—

MR. FORAN: To which the Government objects.

THE COURT: —with the members of the jury and others, I deny the motion.

May I interrupt you, Mr. Weinglass?

Your associate, Mr. Kunstler, has handed up a matter here in writing. I promised him that when he did it, I would hear it, and I want to keep my word.

(jury excused)

MR. KUNSTLER: Your Honor, without repeating any of the long history of the controversy with reference to the lawyers which was disposed of this morning, I am moving on behalf of all defendants for a mistrial in this case or, in the alternative, again for the disqualification of this Court.

Our first ground is that your Honor illegally, unlawfully and unconstitutionally ordered and directed the arrest of some of the pretrial lawyers in the case; that equally illegally you effectuated the imprisonment and appearance in court while in custody of these attorneys; that you refused, again we claim unconstitutionally, to set bond for these attorneys, and again, equally unconstitutionally, you attempted to coerce the defendants by these arrests and imprisonment and denial of bail to waive their Sixth Amendment rights to counsel of their choice; and that you have during the course of the trial degraded, harassed and maligned in diverse ways and fashions these and other of defendants' attorneys, and because of this you have so prejudiced this case that there can no longer be a fair and impartial trial—all we claim in violation of the Constitution and laws of the United States. This has the effect of creating in the minds of the jury the appearance that the lawyers in this case are either criminals or in some way so unorthodox that any impartial judgment by a jury would be rendered impossible.

I have already been informed by some attorneys, your Honor, that there is a chilling effect which has been sent into operation here, the same chilling effect referred to in the United States Supreme Court decision in Dombrowski against Pfister* and that many attorneys who are assisting us have expressed their feelings about their vulnerabilities to harassment if not worse in assisting the defendants in this case.

We feel that it would be, to close this argument, the better part of discretion and in the interest of justice for your Honor to grant the motion for a mistrial or, in the alternative, to reconsider whether you ought to think in terms of disqualifying yourself so this case may proceed before another judge. I make the motion strongly and emphatically, your Honor, and feel that it is meritorious and should merit your earnest consideration and should be granted in one aspect or the other.

Thank you, your Honor.

THE COURT: Mr. Foran?

MR. FORAN: Your Honor, I don't know that in my career of over twenty years before the bar that I have ever been so conscious of the need that there be a recognition in this case that under our Constitution and law a case be tried in the courtroom. Some of the conduct of counsel for the defendants in this case has been so incredibly unprofessional that it is remarkable that the Court has kept as good-natured as he has.

Your Honor, what has been going on in this courtroom in connection with the conduct of the defense is so clearly a ploy to try this case not in the classic American tradition of the trial in the courtroom within the rules of law, but in the press, I suggest that the purpose of this emergency motion is an additional attempt to put in evidence in the press as distinguished from the court.

The government objects most strenuously to this motion to disqualify.

THE COURT: Mr. Clerk, the motion styled "Emergency Motion" filed by the defendants for a mistrial or, in the alternative, for the disqualification of the Court, will be denied. The Court directs the clerk of the court to impound this document for such consideration as the Court may give to it at some future time during or after this trial.

MR. KUNSTLER: Your Honor, I object to that last statement. There is another intimidation being practiced here upon the attorneys that we now have to be sorry about what happens to us for filing the paper, and I would like the record to so indicate.

THE COURT: You always have to worry in this courtroom, Mr. Kuntsler, when you make remarks or make allegations in a document such as you made over your signature. That will be all.

MR. KUNSTLER: We made—

THE COURT: That will be all, sir.

(jury enters)

THE COURT: Now you may continue with your cross-examination, Mr. Weinglass.

MR. WEINGLASS: Now the City was not only sued by the National Mobilization Committee for failure to grant assembly areas, it was also sued by the Yippies, were they not?

THE WITNESS: Yes, Mr. Feinglass [*sic*], and the suit against the City also related to the parks.

MR. WEINGLASS: Mr. Simon, could you tell the ladies and gentlemen of the jury what the basis of the Yippies' suit was against the City?

MR. FORAN: I object to that, your Honor.

THE COURT: I sustain the objection.

MR. WEINGLASS: Mr. Simon, is it not a fact that the City was sued by still a third group the week before the Convention, the Committee for an Open Convention, for failure to grant an assembly permit to that group?

MR. FORAN: I object to that.

THE COURT: I sustain the objection.

MR. WEINGLASS: Did you ascertain from the Park District why it was that they never acted either affirmatively or negatively on the National Mobilization's application to use the park?

THE WITNESS: I think the reason was there was never any permit agreed upon for the whole day. The idea of the negotiations was to try to achieve an accord so that we would authorize parades and assemblies.

MR. WEINGLASS: Fine. Now could you explain to the jury why the negotiations which you have just described did not occur until the National Mobilization and the Yippies filed a lawsuit against the City—

THE WITNESS: Well, I—

MR. WEINGLASS: —to compel those negotiations?

THE WITNESS: I don't know that there was no negotiation. I rather suspect there were many meetings, and I think other city officials were being phoned and having discussions with the applicants during that period of time.

MR. WEINGLASS: But in any event, Mr. Simon, it is a fact, is it not, that within three hours on August 22, you were able to accomplish an agreement with Mr. Davis and the National Mobilization for an assembly site during the daytime by merely making a phone call to the Park District? Isn't that a fact?

THE WITNESS: Well, it is a fact that we talked to the park officials between the morning and afternoon sessions, or between the afternoon and the following morning session, whichever it was, when Mr. Davis said he would take the assembly and they said, "Fine, we will issue the permit." That's true. That was done.

MR. WEINGLASS: With respect to the law which does not permit staying in the park beyond eleven, was that requirement waived for the Boy Scouts?

THE WITNESS: Apparently, yes.

MR. WEINGLASS: With respect to the law that requires the park to be cleared by eleven, was that requirement waived for the National Guard?

THE WITNESS: I don't know that the Park District issued or didn't issue a permit. I don't really know.

MR. WEINGLASS: If the Court please, I have completed my cross-examination.

THE COURT: I will permit additional cross-examination by Mr. Kunstler.

MR. KUNSTLER: Thank you, your Honor.

Mr. Simon, you come out of the same ward as the mayor?

THE WITNESS: I did. I grew up back of the stockyards.

MR. KUNSTLER: And would it be a fair statement to say that you are sort of a protégé of the mayor?

THE WITNESS: I suppose my dad might take some credit for educating me, and so on. I worked under the mayor's tutelage, sure. I think I would be proud to be considered that, Mr. Counselor, if that is the point you are making, yes.

MR. KUNSTLER: That is exactly the point I am making, Mr. Simon. You are very fond of the mayor, is that correct?

THE WITNESS: Yes, that is correct.

MR. FORAN: Your Honor, I object. I don't know why I should have to keep getting up to object.

THE COURT: I think it is inappropriate since there is an objection. I am not here to determine a witness' affection for the mayor of the city. What has that got to do with the charges here?

MR. KUNSTLER: Your Honor, it goes to his credibility. The mayor is, in our opinion, a party here, and that goes to his credibility.

THE COURT: I must have misread this indictment. I hadn't seen that the mayor was indicted in this indictment.

MR. KUNSTLER: No, your Honor, his name does not appear there.

THE COURT: That's right, it doesn't. I sustain the objection to the question.

MR. KUNSTLER: Now, just one question. Have you discussed your testimony here today with the mayor at all?

THE WITNESS: No.

MR. KUNSTLER: When was the last conversation you had with the mayor?

THE WITNESS: I talked to the mayor Sunday after Mass at the Catholic Lawyers Guild where the mayor was presented a citation as a courageous leader and an outstanding Catholic lawyer in government at the Ambassador Hotel.

MR. KUNSTLER: Now on August 21, in the transcript of the hearing, reference was made to a statement by Mayor Daley the day before that an ounce of prevention was worth a pound of cure. Do you recall that statement?

THE WITNESS: Mr. Davis said that.

MR. KUNSTLER: Didn't the mayor say it, too?

THE WITNESS: I don't recall him saying it, although it wouldn't have been unlike him to say it; he believes in that.

MR. KUNSTLER: Don't you think from your experience of five years now as corporation counsel of the City of Chicago that an ounce of prevention here would have been to say yes, let the people sleep in the park?

THE WITNESS: No.

MR. KUNSTLER: And we will not have the trouble that Mr. Davis rather accurately prophesied?

THE WITNESS: I don't think so, Mr. Kunstler. I think the decision was a wise one to make and it was made on the basis of a lot of intelligence and a lot of intelligent planning and nobody was killed in our city, nobody was seriously injured, the Convention went on and the Mobilization Committee and others were here in the city and the City of Chicago was able to have its Convention and nobody was killed.

What was asked was that we suspend a lot of good, reasonable laws; that you stay the park curfew; forget, you know, orderly assembly; forget the regulation of traffic. "Let us take it over ourselves."

What I am saying is you have got to be responsible when you are in charge of the

Government. You can't afford the luxury of the liberalism of saying, "Be more and more permissive; let anything go on," and then everybody would have obeyed the law. That is a speculation.

I represent the City of Chicago, Mr. Kunstler. I know what they were doing at that time. They were striving as hard as they could and in as deep earnestness as they could to have it be orderly in the city. They didn't want another Robert Kennedy assassination here. They didn't want Senator McCarthy or McCarthy workers, or all the rumors that were bouncing in in the intelligence reports, they didn't want that to happen in an assembly in the middle of the night in Lincoln Park, and have a young girl supporter of Senator McCarthy killed. We didn't want that to happen, and it didn't happen. I think we made the right decision by not letting them take over the park.

MR. KUNSTLER: No further questions.

THE COURT: You may go, sir.

(witness excused)

Ladies and gentlemen of the jury, we are about to recess until tomorrow morning at 10:00. My usual order to you is you are not to read the newspapers or any other journals. You are not to talk with anybody about this case or let anybody speak with you about it. If anybody attempts to communicate with you about the case in any manner whatsoever, please notify the United States Marshal. I order you not to listen to radio or look at television.

Mr. Marshal, the Court will be in recess until 10:00 tomorrow morning.

September 30, 1969

THE CLERK: Renewed emergency motion to disqualify the judge.

MR. KUNSTLER: I am prepared to argue that now, your Honor, and I would just briefly summarize it.

THE COURT: I have read it carefully.

MR. KUNSTLER: I understand, sir.

THE COURT: I have read every line of it.

MR. KUNSTLER: But I think it is important at least to indicate generally what is in it.

Your Honor, on September 26, Mr. Weinglass made his opening statement in which your Honor held that his "persistency in disregarding the direction of the Court and the law in the face of repeated admonitions is contumacious conduct, and I find it on the record."

Now, according to one newspaper reporter who is under subpoena and is waiting outside to testify if your Honor would have a hearing on this matter, you were overheard to say in the elevator, "Now we are going to hear this wild man Weinglass."

If that statement is true and correct, then I think that there is absolutely a valid just cause for your Honor to disqualify himself in this matter.

We think that the statement indicates a prejudice on your part against one of the trial counsel which cannot but affect the defendants in this case, that it is no longer possible for them to have a fair and impartial trial before you.

THE COURT: Mr. Clerk, the motion of the defendants styled "Renewed emergency motion to disqualify the Honorable Julius J. Hoffman as judge in this matter" will be denied, because the papers filed in support thereof do not state grounds for the relief sought.

MR. FORAN: Your Honor, a matter has come up that I think must be discussed by your Honor and counsel for the defense and my gentlemen on the record in chambers if possible.

THE COURT: I don't ordinarily conduct chambers discussions in criminal cases, Mr. Foran.

MR. FORAN: Well, it is an extremely unusual situation. I think it should be discussed.

THE COURT: Does your suggestion mean that there will be in attendance only counsel and the reporter and myself?

MR. FORAN: I guess so.

THE COURT: I have the key.

MR. WEINGLASS: Your Honor, we have no objection to that arrangement.

Discussion in Chambers

MR. FORAN: Judge, the reason for the request for the interruption was I was informed just about the time we were to come to court by the FBI that one of the jurors had received a letter or her family had received a letter that certainly could be of a threatening nature. We have no evidence at all of who sent it, but it clearly indicates a connection with this trial. I was informed by one of my assistants then that a copy of that letter had arrived and that is when I asked for the recess. It is addressed to the King family, Crystal Lake, Illinois. It is written in script: "You are being watched. The Black Panthers."

Here it is, your Honor.

MR. SCHULTZ: I think we ought to add for the record, your Honor, we found out about this when the FBI so informed our office after the mother of the King girl found the letter. She apparently telephoned the FBI.

Then we understand that the girl's father who apparently works downtown stopped in to the FBI office to tell them the same thing. There have been no other contacts by the FBI other than responses in talking to the mother and to the father. That is all.

THE COURT: Now my own marshal, gentlemen, was handed this morning this communication addressed to the Peterson family.

MR. WEINGLASS: If your Honor please, it wasn't clear to me: was the marshal handed this by Mrs. Peterson?

THE COURT: He is here. Where did you get that?

THE MARSHAL: From Mrs. Peterson.

MR. FORAN: Your Honor, I would think that we ought to probably question those two jurors and find out whether or not they feel any threat or prejudice or whether they think it would affect their impartiality at all.

THE COURT: I will be glad to entertain any suggestions from counsel for the defendants.

MR. WEINGLASS: If the Court please, in light of the fact that these documents do appear similar, they do indicate perhaps a pattern and perhaps all of the jurors should be questioned.

MR. FORAN: As to whether they had received anything like it, you mean?

MR. WEINGLASS: Yes. I don't know why these two particular jurors were singled out.

MR. KUNSTLER: I think the record should also indicate that the newspapers in Chicago did publish the addresses of each one of the jurors. I saw it in at least two newspapers.

MR. FORAN: Yes, they did.

THE COURT: There is a suggestion by Mr. Feinglass—

[34]

MR. KUNSTLER: Mr. Weinglass is going to be Mr. Feinglass before this trial is over. I may put in a change of name application for him.

THE COURT: It is Feinglass—oh, it is Weinglass? Did I say Feinglass? It is Weinglass.

MR. SCHULTZ: Since we have no indication that any of the other twelve jurors have received this communication, I don't see any reason for bringing them out individually. We could ask these two jurors, Peterson and King, singly, about their communications, but as to the other twelve jurors, I don't see calling them out individually when we have no reason to believe any of them received communications.

THE COURT: At the moment, Mr. Weinglass—I got it right that time—I am not sympathetic to assuming the risk of either frightening the other jurors when there is no evidence here that they did receive them or a similar communication. I certainly have been very forceful, in telling them to let me know if anybody attempts to communicate with them. These may just be pranks, if you can call them that. I don't even know—I have never tried anybody who has been identified with this organization. I don't know whether such an organization really exists in Chicago. They not infrequently refer to the crime syndicate but I never have seen the articles of incorporation of the crime syndicate. I don't know. There is nothing in the record thus far that identifies this organization.

MR. SCHULTZ: There will be, your Honor, in the government's case in chief, mention of the Black Panthers. There is going to be testimony of a Black Panther rally on Tuesday night in Lincoln Park during the convention, Bobby Seale being a representative of the Black Panthers.

THE COURT: Before we proceed here, gentlemen, do I understand that the defendants consent to your being here?

MR. KUNSTLER: Yes, your Honor. They consent to us being here subject to consultation with them.

THE COURT: How about you, Mr. Weinglass? Is that your understanding?

MR. WEINGLASS: Yes, that is my understanding subject to the caution that I am advised by Mr. Seale that he had fired me as his attorney.

MR. KUNSTLER: I would say the same thing.

THE COURT: All right. Then we do not have Mr. Seale's consent to this meeting. Is that right?

How can you consent in behalf of a man who you say has discharged you?

MR. KUNSTLER: I suggest—I agree with your Honor. I think that Mr. Seale ought to be here; that he is essentially pro se at this moment, and that he ought to be here.

THE COURT: I will hear from you on that subject, Mr. Foran, please.

When I say Mr. Foran, it is only because he is older, Mr. Schultz, not necessarily wiser.

MR. SCHULTZ: I am taller, your Honor.

THE COURT: What do you say?

MR. SCHULTZ: I am taller than he is.

MR. FORAN: That is only because he has got more hair, Judge.

Mr. Kunstler's appearance is of record. Mr. Birnbaum's appearance is of record. They still remain of record for Mr. Seale. And they spoke for him this morning.

MR. FORAN: Yes, they did, your Honor.

THE COURT: You, gentlemen of the defense side, are in luck. You are going to represent your client Mr. Seale, but I think in the light of Mr. Seale's position, we must go into the courtroom.

MR. KUNSTLER: Before you go out, I would just indicate that the reason that Mr. Birnbaum and I have not withdrawn for Mr. Seale, despite being fired, is that we felt that would deny him access to any communication with the outside world. So that is why we remained with him, so we at least could see him for both morale purposes and having that access, but not to represent him in a legal way.

THE COURT: Up to this meeting this afternoon, you represented to me he was your client. You spoke for him, all of them. He authorized you to come in for him.

MR. KUNSTLER: That is correct.

THE COURT: And I regard you—I will get it right this time—Mr. Weinglass and Mr. Birnbaum as his lawyers, and you so remain as far as the Court is concerned.

MR. BIRNBAUM: I have made it abundantly clear to the Court on many different occasions that my appearance in this case has been solely for the purpose of local counsel. I have not participated in this case in any way.

THE COURT: I think we will have to recess this meeting. We will go into court and we will have the defendants attend.

(in open court; jury excused)

MR. SCHULTZ: May I address the court?

THE COURT: You certainly may.

MR. SCHULTZ: Your Honor, we went into chambers, and decided that for the protection of the defendants, we were not going to make this public.

However, I represent to the Court that after the session, the defendants, five of the defendants, or actually, six, all but Seale and Rubin, announced they were going to give a press conference and they did, at which time in this Federal building, they announced publicly to the public media that two jurors had received letters.

The announcement was made that two jurors had received letters, and that this was perhaps some kind of a trick by the Government, that is, that the Government may be responsible for having these letters sent. There was insinuation by the defendants at this press conference that perhaps the Government wasn't pleased with the jurors, and that is why they did it.

Bobby Seale's letter was read where this is, according to him, a fascist plot, I think it was called.

I am not going to waste the Court's time with the representation that we did not send it, or either of them, or anything of that nature. I just thought that for the record, the fact that the defendants, except the two in custody, held a press conference without their attorney's presence should be noted on the record at this time.

MR. KUNSTLER: I would like the record to indicate that both Mr. Weinglass, Mr. Birnbaum, and myself informed your Honor's chambers at approximately one o'clock that the defendants intended to make public the situation, and we also informed Mr. Foran at the same time from your chambers of that situation.

The defendants have seriously made a statement that they believe that the two letters in question were sent in some way by some agent of the Government in order to prejudice them further in this trial. That is their position. I think they have publicly stated it, and that is the position which they take.

THE COURT: I will let you try to prove that right now. That is a very grave charge against an officer of the Government.

MR. KUNSTLER: Well, we obviously can't prove it, your Honor.

THE COURT: Then don't say it.

MR. KUNSTLER: This is the clients' position. That is my statement.

THE COURT: I think for an officer of the Court to say or to imply that some agent of the Government, perhaps as fine a United States Attorney as we have ever had in this district within my memory—to make a statement like that is irresponsible.

MR. KUNSTLER: No, your Honor.

THE COURT: In my opinion, when you cannot support it by a single shred of evidence.

MR. KUNSTLER: Your Honor, only by implication, but we have a suggestion. We do want to join in an investigation to prove exactly what happened. We don't feel the FBI is the proper agent to make this investigation.

THE COURT: You can do all of the investigating you want, but this trial will go on.

In order to insulate the jury, Mr. Clerk, there will be an order sequestering the members of the jury sua sponte.

Mr. Marshal, I direct you at an appropriate time after this hearing to see to it that the members of the jury are sequestered, and that the newspapers and other journals and radio and television are kept from them, and any other people who might try to talk with them.

MR. KUNSTLER: Your Honor, may I just say that we object to the sequestration. The jury ought to be instructed we did object and it is not at the will of the defendants.

THE COURT: I will overrule the objection. Mr. Marshal, bring in the jury.

MR. SCHULTZ: Your Honor, the jury will not be instructed as to why they are being sequestered?

THE COURT: No. I will tell them it is on the order of the Court.

MR. KUNSTLER: And over the objection of the defendants, your Honor.

THE COURT: Oh, yes. The objection of the defendants will be overruled.

MR. KUNSTLER: No, will the jury be informed we object?

THE COURT: Do you want me to do that?

MR. KUNSTLER: That we object to their sequestration, yes.

THE COURT: I see no objection to that. I certainly will.

(jury enters)

THE COURT: You may sit down.

Good afternoon, ladies and gentlemen of the jury. I must inform you that circumstances have arisen in this case and you may not like to hear this but I perceived my obligation, my duty under the law. Circumstances, I repeat, have arisen which in the opinion of the Court require what we call in the law the sequestration of the jury. That means, unfortunately, that you will be housed at a very comfortable hotel until this trial is over.

One of the lawyers for the defendants objected to this order and I overruled the objection.

The purpose of my entering this order on my own motion, and I accept full responsibility for it, is to preserve the integrity of this trial and to see to it that people don't talk to you who aren't entitled to speak to you; that you do not see newspapers or any other journals or listen to radio or television and look at television.

Mr. Marshal, you may take the jury home.

You are excused until tomorrow morning at ten o'clock.

October 1, 1969

MR. KUNSTLER: Your Honor, may I address the court briefly?

THE COURT: Yes, you may.

MR. KUNSTLER: The defendants made allegations yesterday which I repeated to the court that there was Government involvement in the two threatening letters that were the subject of our discussion yesterday.

THE COURT: I do not believe those were your words but you may proceed.

MR. KUNSTLER: Your Honor, we want very much to have an evidentiary hearing set to lay the foundation on the part of the defense for the inference of Government involvement and I might indicate we have six witnesses whom we would propose to call.

One is Bobby Seale, one of the defendants on trial, who would testify as to the Panther discipline, how they sign their letters ordinarily and the use of the term "Black Panther Party for Self Defense" or some variation thereof rather than "The Black Panthers."

We would propose to call John Wall, the former Assistant United States Attorney, who tried U. S. vs. Spock and who is quoted by Jessica Mitford in her book as being the source of the information that there were five thousand security checks on prospective jurors.

We propose to call Mr. J. Edgar Hoover as to the involvement of the FBI in any such checks in this case.

We propose to call Mr. Stanley as to the existence of any records in his possession or that he knows about referring to these security checks.

THE COURT: Who is Mr. Stanley?

MR. KUNSTLER: Mr. Stanley is the FBI Agent who is sitting at the prosecution table.

We propose to call Attorney General John Mitchell as to this procedure, if it was applied in this case, and if any records thereof exist, and we also propose to call a mathematician who will testify as to the permutation possibilities that on a random selection of jurors for the sending of threatening letters, that these two particular jurors would be so selected, and this mathematician will give the percentagewise figure as to how that permutation might be.

We would propose to hold this evidentiary hearing in order to lay the circumstantial basis to try to support the charge which the defendants made yesterday.

THE COURT: Will the Government reply to the statements of Mr. Kunstler?

MR. FORAN: Your Honor, the Government objects to the totally frivolous, idiotic proposal that you have hearings to determine inferences of possibilities of circumstantial evidence of a totally unjustified, totally ridiculous charge. I wish really—well, your Honor, the Government objects to it. It is so—I wish the showboat tactics would stop.

MR. KUNSTLER: Your Honor, again our motion, as your Honor has styled it, has been answered solely by vituperations against counsel, so we again will not stoop to answer such vituperations.

MR. SCHULTZ: Your Honor, may I say something?

THE COURT: Yes, you may.

MR. SCHULTZ: Your Honor, we have a system in this Government where the Government has to prove a case beyond a reasonable doubt. We have got a system here, where before charges can be brought in a felony, a grand jury has to review it and find probable cause. All I can say is thank God for a system like that because if we had men like this running our government, making charges on mathematicians' allegations, we would be in a sad state.

THE COURT: I don't think, Mr. Kunstler, that what went on, if anything went on—and I do not know what went on—in the trial of Dr. Spock has anything to do with the trial of the defendants in this case.

But on your statement, sir, and, as I say, treating it as a motion, the objections of the government will be sustained and the motion denied.

Mr. Marshal, will you please go to the jury room and request Juror Kristi A. King and Juror Ruth L. Peterson to accompany you to the courtroom, one at a time.

Will you just have a seat in the jury box, please.

You are Miss, is it, Kristi A. King?

MISS KING: That's right.

THE COURT: So that you will understand why you are asked to come in here, Miss King, the court is conducting a proceeding here in connection with certain letters alleged to have been received by certain of the jurors, including yourself.

Will you please look at Government's Exhibit A for identification—

Mr. Marshal, will you show it to the juror?

—and let me know whether you have seen the original of that document at any time.

MISS KING: No, sir, I haven't.

THE COURT: You have never seen it?

MISS KING: No, sir.

THE COURT: Do you know whether any member of your family brought it to your attention or not?

MISS KING: It wasn't brought to my attention, no, sir.

THE COURT: All right.

Read it, Miss King. Read it, please.

MISS KING: It says, "You are being watched. The Black Panthers." It's addressed to the King family.

THE COURT: Having now seen it, will you please tell me whether, having seen and read that document, you can continue to be a fair and impartial juror in this case, treating the United States of America and all eight of the defendants fairly and impartially, and render a verdict or verdicts according to the evidence and the law which will be given to you in this case? Do you still think you can do that?

MISS KING: No, sir.

THE COURT: What did you say?

MISS KING: No, sir.

THE COURT: You do not think so.

MISS KING: No.

MR. KUNSTLER: Your Honor, I must make an objection for the record.

This juror had never seen this letter before your Honor showed it to her. The most minimal investigation by the Federal Bureau of Investigation would have revealed from her father and from her mother that she had not so seen it.

THE COURT: What do you object to, my question?

MR. KUNSTLER: I am objecting that your Honor has revealed this letter to this juror and that your Honor has caused this juror to make the statements that she has just made.

When Miss King said she had not seen that letter, I think it was your Honor's duty then to discontinue questioning in this case, because now the Court has revealed the letter.

THE COURT: I asked you for suggestions as to the procedure you wanted to follow, and you said you wanted me to interrogate these witnesses—these jurors. That is in accordance with the law of this circuit, sir.

MR. KUNSTLER: But your Honor went too far when your Honor learned that this juror had not seen the letter at all.

THE COURT: I overrule the objection of counsel for the defendants.

In the circumstances, gentlemen, I have no alternative, since the juror has said that, having seen this letter, she cannot function fairly and impartially as a juror.

Mr. Marshal, let me have the first alternate juror's card.

MR. KUNSTLER: Your Honor, I think the interrogation now should go further here, because what you have done, you have excused this juror and I think she should be questioned as to her knowledge of the Panthers, what they are, what her thoughts are, and so on.

THE COURT: The Panthers aren't indicted here, sir. I am not trying the Panthers. I know nothing about them.

MR. SEALE: But I am a member of the Panther Party.

MR. KUNSTLER: We think they are indicted, your Honor, in the eyes of the public.

THE COURT: Mr. Marshal, will you please instruct that defendant to remain quiet during this discussion.

MR. WEINGLASS: If the Court please, may I just be heard on a point of law with respect to this matter.

I submit your Honor has not gone as far as the Appellate Courts require the Court to go. The asking of a single question of the juror under the doctrine of the Patriarcha case* is not sufficient. The Court must proceed with an interrogation as to whether or not this juror understands the nature of the communication, who might possibly have sent it, who might be prejudiced by the receipt of the letter, what is the present state of mind, what the present state of the mind of the juror is, and whether or not this juror could accept the evidence in spite of that state of mind and change her mind to accord with the evidence as given in this trial.

THE COURT: The Court in that case, Mr. Weinglass, was dealing with prospective jurors, not members of the jury.

MR. WEINGLASS: That is correct.

THE COURT: Did you know that? That is true, isn't it?

MR. WEINGLASS: That is quite true, your Honor, but what the Court was addressing itself to was getting a fair panel and I think we have that same problem here. I will not mention fair trial again. I know that disturbs the Court.

THE COURT: It doesn't disturb me. It is ludicrous to say that a defendant in the United States District Court is entitled to a fair trial.

I know of no judge anywhere who goes as far in a voir dire in that area as I do.

MR. KUNSTLER: Your Honor has not been around very much.

THE COURT: I will be glad to hear from the Government as to the request of counsel for the defendants.

MR. SCHULTZ: All of the preliminary questions that Mr. Weinglass wants you to ask relate to the ultimate question, and the ultimate question has been categorically stated by the juror, and I think that having read the letter and having as clearly as she has stated and repeated her answer that she could not be fair, I think that it would be unfair to the juror now to subject her to a series of questions.

THE COURT: I will not interrogate this juror as to her knowledge of this—what do they call it—the Black Panthers, if, indeed, such an organization exists and I don't know whether it exists. I repeat, I am not trying any organization here; I am trying eight individuals.

I think in law if a prospective or actual juror says under oath—and this juror is under oath—that she cannot be fair to the parties, one or the other, that is sufficient.

MR. WEINGLASS: Your Honor—

THE COURT: A juror has a right to say he cannot be fair.

Miss King, you are excused from further service. I order you not to talk with anybody about this case, and not to talk especially with any of your fellow jurors. If anybody attempts to talk with you about this case, you communicate with the United States Marshal who will lay the matter before me.

Alternate Juror Kay Richards will be substituted at an appropriate time for Juror Kristi A. King.

Let the juror, Ruth L. Peterson, take the jury box.

Mrs. Peterson, so that you will understand what we are doing here, it is merely to conduct an inquiry with respect to a communication which has been brought to my attention. I show you Government's Exhibit B for identification.

Mr. Marshal, will you hand that to the juror?

You are Ruth L. Peterson?

MRS. PETERSON: Yes.

THE COURT: The Marshal is handing you Government's Exhibit B-2 for identification. Have you ever seen it before?

MRS. PETERSON: Yes.

THE COURT: Tell me the circumstances, please, under which you did receive it.

MRS. PETERSON: We received this in the mail—when was it? Tuesday—no, Monday. Pardon me, Monday.

THE COURT: When you say "we," you mean your family?

MRS. PETERSON: My family, yes. My son, he was expecting a letter from his boy friend because he was in the service and—well, my husband took in the mail that day, and it was folded in between a magazine and then he looked in the magazine, you know, and there the letter was.

THE COURT: Having seen that letter, do you still feel that you can fulfill your assurances given to the Court that you can be a fair and impartial juror, continue to be here?

MRS. PETERSON: Yes.

THE COURT: And that you can give these eight defendants who sit at that table as well as the United States of America a fair and impartial trial?

MRS. PETERSON: Yes.

THE COURT: You do?

MRS. PETERSON: Yes. I think it is my duty to.

THE COURT: All right.

THE COURT: This juror will be permitted to remain on the jury.

(juror excused)

MR. KUNSTLER: Your Honor, before the jury comes in, the defense would move for the unsequestration of the jury at this point and that they be allowed to continue the rest of the trial unsequestered. We think it is more humane.

THE COURT: I will deny the motion.

Assuming there is such a word as—what did you call it?

MR. KUNSTLER: I said "Unsequestered," your Honor. We meant that they should not be locked up during the trial.

THE COURT: I treated your motion as such.

Testimony of David Stahl

(jury enters)

MR. FORAN: Will you state your name, please.

THE WITNESS: David E. Stahl.

MR. FORAN: What is your occupation?

THE WITNESS: I am the mayor's administrative officer.

As the mayor's administrative officer I am concerned with the administrative management of the city, with its reporting systems, with its budget, with the general administrative management and operation of the city.

MR. FORAN: Calling your attention to March 26, 1968, did you have a meeting on that day?

MR. KUNSTLER: Your Honor, I object to anything before the date of even the very statute we are proceeding under here. This is March 26, 1968. The statute wasn't enacted until April 11, I believe, 1968.

THE COURT: Well, the United States Attorney has a book in his hand. It might be helpful to you and to me both, Mr. Kunstler.

MR. FORAN: Your Honor, evidence which occurred before the date of the statute has been held as admissible not only in this circuit but in four others.*

THE COURT: I will let the witness answer over objection.

THE WITNESS: On March 26 I was attending a meeting of the Chicago City Council, and when I was called to the tenth floor of City Hall to meet with Jerry Rubin and Abbie Hoffman—

MR. FORAN: Do you see Mr. Hoffman and Mr. Rubin here in the courtroom?

THE WITNESS: Yes, sir.

MR. FORAN: Will you point them out to the jury, please.

THE WITNESS: Mr. Hoffman just stood up and waved his hand.

Mr. Rubin is sitting there in the yellow striped polo shirt.

THE COURT: I was about to ask whether the defense concedes that Mr. Rubin and Mr. Hoffman have been identified. It is rather important in this case. There is somebody named Hoffman up here and one down there. I don't want the witness to be confused—

MR. KUNSTLER: We will concede, your Honor, that the witness pointed not to the bench but to our table when he pointed to the person named Hoffman.

THE COURT: All right. The record may then indicate that the witness has identified Mr. Rubin and Mr. Hoffman, the defendant, in open court.

MR. FORAN: What was said at that meeting, Mr. Stahl?

THE WITNESS: I was told by Abbie Hoffman that the Youth International Party would be holding a Festival of Life in Grant Park during the week of the Democratic National Convention; that there would be 500,000 young people attending this Festival of Life; that they would be entertained by rock bands and that they were going to sleep in Grant Park.

MR. FORAN: Now was there anything further said at that meeting or did you say anything to them?

THE WITNESS: No.

MR. FORAN: I call your attention to August 2, 1968. Did you have a meeting on that date?

THE WITNESS: Yes, with Rennie Davis, Mark Simons and three other members who I was told were part of the Mobilization Committee to End the War in Vietnam.

MR. FORAN: What was said by whom, stating who said what?

THE WITNESS: Mr. Davis said that the City of Chicago should develop a contingency plan for dealing with two to three hundred thousand people who would be coming to Chicago during the Democratic National Convention to protest the war in Vietnam. Mr. Davis indicated that this would be a peaceful protest but he advised and said that we should make a distinct effort to keep the hippies away from the Negroes and that this would be an incendiary situation. Mr. Davis also said that the intensity of feeling with

[41]

regard to the Vietnam war was very high. He said that he personally would rather die here than in Vietnam.

He said that there would be a march to the Bandshell in Grant Park, and then a march to the International Amphitheatre on August 28. He said on August 29 there would be an assembly at the Bandshell in Grant Park, and he said that the parks, a number of parks in the city would be required by the Mobilization Committee for sleeping and for speeches.

MR. FORAN: What did you say to him?

THE WITNESS: I told Mr. Davis that the Mayor's office does not issue permits for either the Chicago Park District facilities which are under the jurisdiction of a separate governmental body, or for the use of a public right-of-way which is a function of the Parade Board in the Department of Streets and Sanitation.

I advised him that it was my understanding that sleeping in the parks was not permitted by a Chicago Park District ordinance and that therefore I thought that was probably a request that he was not going to be succesful in obtaining. I also said that I thought that it was unlikely that demonstrations were going to be permitted at the Amphitheatre based on the understandings I had been given by the Secret Service.

MR. FORAN: Now, calling your attention to August 7 in the evening, did you have a meeting on that day?

THE WITNESS: Yes. In the Mayor's office conference room, with Abbie Hoffman, Jerry Rubin, Ed Sanders, Richard Goldstein and Paul Krassner.

MR. FORAN: Will you state the conversation, Mr. Stahl, saying who said what?

THE WITNESS: Mr. Rubin said that they were going to begin their week, their Festival of Life, by holding classes in defense against the police from August 20 to August 24. He said that Chicago had a national reputation of being a hostile system, that they didn't like it.

Abbie Hoffman said then that he was prepared to tear up the town and the Convention. He said that he was willing in die in Lincoln Park. Mr. Hoffman then said that if we were smart, we, the City was smart, we would give them $100,000 and they would sponsor the Festival of Life or, he said, better still, we would give them—give him a hundred thousand dollars and he would leave town.

He said that their Festival of Life would include body painting, nude-ins at the beaches, public fornication, discussion of the draft and draft evasion.

MR. FORAN: What did you say to him, if anything?

THE WITNESS: I suggested to him again that the Chicago Park District ordinances, as I understood them, prohibited sleeping in the park but that if a permit for sleeping in the park was going to be obtained, they would have to obtain it by application to the Chicago Park District and not to the Mayor's office.

MR. FORAN: Now, calling your attention to August 10, 1968, did you have a meeting on that date, Mr. Stahl?

THE WITNESS: Yes.

MR. FORAN: Who was there?

THE WITNESS: Mr. Davis, Mark Simons and three other members of the Mobilization Committee to End the War in Vietnam.

I was by myself.

MR. FORAN: Would you state the conversation, Mr. Stahl?

THE WITNESS: Yes. Mr. Davis said that the city's failure to issue the permits was an invitation to violence. He said that we should expect 100,000 members of the Mobilization Committee to be in Chicago during the week of the Democratic National Convention.

He also said that we should use little visible police in dealing with members of his group, his organization, during the Convention as they regarded the Chicago Police as the Gestapo.

MR. FORAN: Now, calling your attention to August 12, 1965, did you have a meeting on that day?

THE WITNESS: Yes.

MR. FORAN: Will you state the conversation, Mr. Stahl, saying who said what?

THE WITNESS: Mr. Dellinger told me that he had just recently returned from Paris where he had been studying street riots of the students at the Sorbonne. He said he was studying these because he was anxious to know why they failed, and was interested in the whole subject of demonstrations and street activities. He said he was, however, not interested in violence or disturbing the delegates or the Convention, the Democratic National Convention, that was going to take place in Chicago. He said that he believed in civil disobedience, that the activities of the Mobilization Committee at the Pentagon, where they invaded the building, were an example of the kind of civil disobedience that he believed in.

MR. FORAN: Mr. Stahl, do you recall anything further of his conversation in that first exchange?

THE WITNESS: No, I do not.

MR. FORAN: Have you exhausted your recollection of that first exchange?

THE WITNESS: Yes.

MR. FORAN: Did he say anything concerning the march to the Amphitheatre—

MR. KUNSTLER: Your Honor, I object to that. He exhausted his recollection and now the U. S. Attorney is giving him the script, and I object to that.

THE COURT: I will let him answer.

THE WITNESS: Mr. Dellinger said that whether there was going to be a demonstration and a march to the Amphitheatre was not an issue, that the question of the Mobilization Committee having a demonstration within eyeshot of the Amphitheatre was nonnegotiable.

MR. FORAN: Did anyone else say anything then?

THE WITNESS: Yes. Mr. Davis made a rather lengthy discussion of the program of the Mobilization Committee during the Democratic National Convention.

He said that on August 25 there would be picketing of various Loop locations, including possibly the hotels where delegates were staying, the United States Government Induction Center, Chicago Police Department, and other locations.

He said that on August 28 the Mobilization Committee would assemble in Grant Park and then picket at various locations in the Chicago Loop.

He said that on August 29 there would be a rally—the Mobilization Committee would sponsor a rally at the Grant Park Bandshell between one o'clock and five o'clock in the afternoon.

I suggested to Mr. Davis that the applications which he had filed with the Department of Streets and Sanitation for the use of the public right-of-way was probably not going to be issued because of the requirements of security at the Amphitheatre.

I suggested also to him that the permit applications for the use of the Grant Park Bandshell should be submitted, as they had been—that he had taken the proper action in submitting them to the Chicago Park District.

MR. FORAN: Now, calling your attention to August 26, 1968, did you have a meeting on that day?

THE WITNESS: Yes, with David Dellinger, Professor Sidney Peck, and four other members of the Mobilization Committee.

MR. FORAN: Your Honor, at this time I would like to offer the evidence of this conversation with respect to the defendant Dellinger only.

THE COURT: Ladies and gentlemen of the jury, the testimony which this witness is about to give is offered by the Government only with respect to the defendant Derringer and to no other defendant at this time.

MR. KUNSTLER: I think your Honor meant Dellinger.

THE COURT: Dellinger, that's right.

MR. FORAN: Will you give the conversation, Mr. Stahl?

THE WITNESS: Mr. Dillinger said that we must issue a permit—

THE COURT: I am going to get back at you, Mr. Witness. I mispronounced the defendant's name. You said Dillinger. It's Derringer. We were both wrong. You mean Mr. Derringer, do you not?

MR. FORAN: Dellinger.

THE WITNESS: Mr. Dellinger said that it was necessary that a permit be issued for sleeping in Lincoln Park in order to minimize destruction. He said that there was much anger over the arrest of Tom Hayden and that that anger was going to seek expression. He said that we should immediately designate a place where ten to forty thousand members of the Mobilization Committee could assemble within eyeshot of the International Amphitheatre. He concluded the meeting by asking for a meeting with the mayor.

MR. FORAN: What occurred then?

THE WITNESS: He left with his group, and a press conference was held out in front of the mayor's office.

MR. FORAN: That's all, your Honor.

THE COURT: Is there any cross-examination of this witness?

• • • • •

MR. WEINGLASS: You are appointed by the mayor and you serve at his pleasure?

THE WITNESS: I am appointed by the mayor with the advice and consent of the Chicago City Council.

MR. WEINGLASS: And you are subject to removal in the same manner by the mayor?

THE WITNESS: That is correct.

MR. WEINGLASS: Did you ever offer the National Mobilization Committee a street or a site for an assembly?

THE WITNESS: No.

MR. WEINGLASS: Did you ever offer the National Mobilization Committee a street to march on or a parade route?

THE WITNESS: That is not my function, to issue parade permits for the use of the public right-of-way.

MR. WEINGLASS: Mr. Stahl, what was your function in meeting with the National Mobilization people?

THE WITNESS: My function was to maintain communication. I should make it clear that at no time did I ask for any of the meetings which were held in my office or anywhere else in the city. These meetings were held at the request of the Mobilization Committee and the Youth International Party.

MR. WEINGLASS: They were. And could you tell the jury why these people found it necessary to come to you?

MR. FORAN: I object to that, your Honor.

THE COURT: I sustain the objection.

MR. WEINGLASS: By communicating do you mean to tell us that after they expressed this concern that they weren't getting the permits they sought, that you would go back to the appropriate city agencies and find out why they weren't getting any action?

MR. FORAN: Your Honor, we keep asking for states of mind that are outside the scope of the original examination.

THE COURT: Do you object to the question?

MR. FORAN: Yes, I object.

THE COURT: I sustain the objection.

MR. WEINGLASS: After these people told you that they weren't able to get action on their permits, what did you do?

THE WITNESS: I told them to go back to the sources from which, or for which they had made their applications and to pursue their discussions with them at the appropriate bodies.

MR. WEINGLASS: Did you yourself ever go to the mayor and inform the mayor of this fact, that they weren't getting action?

MR. FORAN: Objection, your Honor. Here we go again.

THE COURT: I sustain the objection.

MR. WEINGLASS: Did you do anything other than listen to their complaints, Mr. Stahl?

THE WITNESS: I discussed the applications which they had pending on one occasion with officials of the Park District and on one or two occasions with the Commissioner of the Department of Streets and Sanitation.

MR. WEINGLASS: Now, if my understanding is correct, all of the meetings with Abbie and Jerry occurred in City Hall?

MR. FORAN: Your Honor, I object to the constant reference to these two little—to Abbie and Jerry. Let's call the defendants by their proper names.

THE COURT: I agree.

MR. FORAN: It is an attempt to give a diminutive attitude to men who are over thirty.

THE COURT: They should not be referred to in the United States District Court by their
—I nearly said Christian names; I don't know whether that would be accurate or not, but
by their first names.

Call them your clients—or if you don't like that, call them by their surnames.

MR. WEINGLASS: Do you remember having an interview by the Federal Bureau of
Investigation on October 8, 1968?

THE WITNESS: Yes.

MR. WEINGLASS: Do you recall telling the agent who interviewed you that you could
not recall which individual made which statement at the meeting you had on August 7
with Abbie Hoffman, Jerry Rubin, Paul Krassner, Richard Goldstein, and Ed Sanders?

THE WITNESS: Yes, I recollect making that statement.

MR. WEINGLASS: Now can you explain to us how you didn't know who made what
statement in October of 1968, just about three months after August, and now you can
recall very explicitly one year later who made what statement?

THE WITNESS: The meeting in October was a very brief and very quick meeting. Since
that time I have had a great deal of time to reflect on my notes, to reassemble in my mind
what went on at these meetings, and now to the best of my recollection I can identify
these statements with particular individuals.

MR. WEINGLASS: Now you also testified on the August 7 meeting with Jerry Rubin
and Abbie Hoffman that there was some mention of one hundred thousand dollars, is that
not correct?

THE WITNESS: That is correct.

MR. WEINGLASS: Did you take that discussion seriously, Mr. Stahl?

THE WITNESS: Yes, I most certainly did.

MR. WEINGLASS: Did you ask him a follow-up question like "Do you mean that
seriously? Are you trying to bribe me? Are you trying to bribe the city?"

THE WITNESS: No. I simply recorded the statement that was made, which I have
testified to.

MR. WEINGLASS: But when you got this serious offer of one hundred thousand dollars,
you did nothing to pursue it; did you ask him if he was trying to bribe you?

MR. FORAN: You mean he should have given him the one hundred thousand dollars,
is that what you are suggesting?

THE COURT: I don't know what you mean by that question.

MR. WEINGLASS: Did you ask him if he was trying to bribe you or bribe the city?

THE WITNESS: No, I did not pursue that line of questioning.

MR. WEINGLASS: Did Abbie pursue it?

THE WITNESS: No, there was no further discussion of it.

THE COURT: You mean Mr. Hoffman? We have gotten away from the first names.

MR. WEINGLASS: I am sorry. Mr. Hoffman.

Now in your August 10 meeting with the National Mobilization where you testified
on direct that Rennie and Mark were present as well as three other people—

MR. FORAN: Your Honor, here we go again. Now another twenty-nine-year-old being
"Rennie baby." I object to the diminutive familiar child terms for mentally grown men.

MR. KUNSTLER: Your Honor, I did not hear "Rennie baby."

MR. WEINGLASS: "Rennie baby?"

MR. FORAN: "Rennie and Mark"—I mean, that is foolishness.

MR. KUNSTLER: I object to that, your Honor.

THE COURT: I sustain the objection to the question.

MR. KUNSTLER: Would your Honor order the jury to disregard the "Rennie baby"
remark as unfounded?

THE COURT: If the United States Attorney said that, I certainly do. Crowd the "baby"
out of your minds. We are not dealing with babies here.

MR. WEINGLASS: Now, you also testified that you had a meeting with some National
Mobilization people, I believe Mr. Dellinger in particular, on August 26, is that correct?

THE WITNESS: That's correct.

MR. WEINGLASS: I believe you testified that they were somewhat angered over the
arrest of Thomas Hayden, is that correct?

THE WITNESS: That's correct. They said that anger was going to seek expression.

MR. WEINGLASS: Did they also bring to your attention their request that the police officers who were sweeping Lincoln Park not remove their name plates before engaging in that activity?

THE WITNESS: They made the request at the meeting that police officers not remove their stars and name plates. I pointed out to them that it was my understanding that that morning Superintendent Conlisk had reissued the order to the Chicago Police Department, for the benefit of those who may have forgotten it, that under no circumstances were the officers of the Chicago Police Department to remove their stars and name plates. So that action had already been taken.

MR. WEINGLASS: Now, do you know what compelled that action on the part of the Police Department?

MR. FORAN: I object to this, your Honor.

THE COURT: I sustain the objection.

MR. WEINGLASS: At this point I will ask my co-counsel, Mr. Kunstler, to proceed with this cross-examination.

MR. KUNSTLER: Mr. Stahl, did you have any discussion with the Mobilization Committee that met with you on August 12 of alternative routes or alternative locations for a rally in the vicinity of the Amphitheatre?

THE WITNESS: No, I did not discuss it.

MR. KUNSTLER: Now I will ask you whether the following question and the following answer were put and made by you to the grand jury:

Q. "What did you discuss at that meeting?"

A. "That was the most lengthy meeting we had. We discussed in considerable detail the whole range of activities that the National Mobilization to End the War in Vietnam was planning for that week. We discussed, for instance, the rallies and marches. We discussed their plans for the Amphitheatre. We began to propose alternative locations possible for a rally in the vicinity of the Amphitheatre."

And that is not the complete end of your answer—it goes on much longer—but I am asking you whether that answer, that portion, was made by you to that question?

THE WITNESS: Yes. Assuming you are reading it correctly, yes.

MR. KUNSTLER: Mr. Stahl, if I am not reading it correctly, my brethren there will let me know, I assure you.

So, it is true, is it not, Mr. Stahl, that you were proposing alternative locations for a rally at the Amphitheatre, isn't that correct?

THE WITNESS: No, that is not correct.

MR. KUNSTLER: Who was proposing them?

THE WITNESS: The Mobilization Committee.

If you look at the whole sentence, you will see I said "we" in every case when I should have said "they."

MR. KUNSTLER: Mr. Stahl, you were under oath to this grand jury, is that correct?

THE WITNESS: That is correct.

MR. KUNSTLER: Are you indicating to me that every time you see the word "we" in this answer I should change it to "they"?

THE WITNESS: No. I would have to look at the whole sentence to see, but I think when we say "we proposed," when that testimony says "we proposed alternative locations," I did not propose any alternative locations.

MR. KUNSTLER: Well, then, who is "we"?

THE WITNESS: The "we" is the Mobilization Committee.

MR. KUNSTLER: Are you serious? Is this a serious answer?

MR. FORAN: Oh, come on, now.

Your Honor, this man was alone talking to all of these people.

THE WITNESS: I am perfectly serious.

MR. FORAN: And they were coming in giving a whole statement, and he is in this argumentative fashion trying to play Perry Mason.

MR. KUNSTLER: He does pretty well, your Honor. If I can do half as well as Perry Mason—

MR. FORAN: As a television actor, you do, Mr. Kunstler.

THE COURT: Mr. Marshal, I will ask you to maintain order out there.

MR. KUNSTLER: Mr. Stahl, you testified today as to what happened at that August 10 coffee shop meeting. Now, during that discussion apparently there was some talk of the Chicago Police being like the Gestapo, is that correct?

THE WITNESS: Mr. Davis made a statement along those lines, yes.

MR. KUNSTLER: What to you does that mean? What is the Gestapo?

THE WITNESS: The Gestapo was a German—well, it was the storm troops of the Nazis during the Second World War.

MR. KUNSTLER: Have you ever seen pictures of the Gestapo in action?

MR. FORAN: Oh, come on. Your Honor, I object.

Here we go, back on Channel Seven.

THE COURT: I sustain the objection.

MR. FORAN: Or Five.

MR. KUNSTLER: Mr. Stahl, did you think there was any merit to Mr. Davis' suggestion that police not be so visible? Do you think it made any sense?

THE WITNESS: Not in view of all of the other things which were said, which were planned—the attitudes and inclinations of those who were going to be leading the demonstrations. It seemed to me as a public official that the proper thing to do would be to have a maximum amount of police available in order to be able to handle the kinds of demonstrations that were being proposed, civil disobedience, tearing up the town, marching with or without permits, these kinds of things.

MR. KUNSTLER: Well, when they said "tearing up the town" on August 7, 1968—you continued to meet with them after August 7, despite that statement, is that correct?

THE WITNESS: That's correct.

MR. KUNSTLER: Did you refer that statement to anybody?

THE WITNESS: I discussed it with officials in the Police Department.

MR. KUNSTLER: You did. Did you discuss it with the mayor?

THE WITNESS: I may have. I don't recall. I didn't go in and give the mayor a blow-by-blow description of all things that were said at these meetings.

MR. KUNSTLER: But you think that was a rather important thing that was said to you about tearing up the town?

MR. FORAN: Oh, your Honor, here we go again.

MR. KUNSTLER: Your Honor, if the remark "here we go again" is an objection, I never heard it.

MR. FORAN: I really am going to refer you to Wigmore's tonight, Mr. Counsel. Instead of watching yourself on TV, you can study evidence.

THE COURT: I sustain the objection.

MR. KUNSTLER: But I think you ought to admonish the U. S. Attorney because of the constant threat of remarks. He has a television bug in his mind that is apparently bothering him, and I think that your Honor ought to do something about it. The proper way to object is to say "I object," not "Channel Seven" or "Channel Five."

MR. FORAN: Your Honor, that is the proper way until counsel with his claque—

And by the way your Honor, I would like to have your Honor tell counsel's group in the courtroom that they are not to respond by laughter and comments.

THE COURT: I have already admonished the marshal to see to it that order is maintained.

MR. KUNSTLER: Your Honor, a bit of laughter is not disorder, and I think sometimes—

THE COURT: It is in this courtroom. This is either a serious case or it isn't. I don't waste my time.

MR. KUNSTLER: I know, but when your Honor makes a quip and people laugh—

THE COURT: It is not intended to provoke laughter.

MR. KUNSTLER: But it does, your Honor, and we all know that it does.

THE COURT: I am not a humorist.

I think we have just about reached the time when we normally recess.

(the court is adjourned)

October 2, 1969

THE COURT: I have something. I have a message to all of the lawyers, both for the Government and the defendants here.

I recommend, if you haven't read it, Rule 1.07 of the Local Rules of the Court. The title of that rule: "Public Discussion by Attorneys Appending or Imminent Criminal Litigation." I recommend that you read the rule carefully. You have Chicago counsel, and the rule is available in the library.

It has been reported to me that one of the lawyers in this case has gone on television to discuss some aspects of the case. I didn't see the performance, but I feel that I should remind all of the lawyers in the case of this rule, and I don't want to see a repetition of what happened, if it did happen, and I do not have a tape of what did happen yet.

MR. KUNSTLER: I would just like to say, your Honor, that since you brought—

THE COURT: I interrupted what you were presenting because you were the man who was on television.

MR. KUNSTLER: I was the attorney.

THE COURT: So it is alleged. I didn't see it.

MR. KUNSTLER: The "alleged" could be dropped, your Honor. I freely admit that I was on a panel show which was taped before your Honor brought the rule to the attention of the attorneys.

THE COURT: Well, consider yourself admonished in that area.

MR. WEINGLASS: If the Court please, Mr. Seale has asked me to request the Court to permit him to have lawbooks in the jail facility to which he is presently confined. I do not represent him and he would like the assistance of some law reading for purposes of his own defense. He has been denied any material up until now and he would like to have it.

MR. SCHULTZ: Your Honor, if I might say this: Mr. Seale has written a couple of handwritten motions. One where he fired his lawyer and then there was one subsequent to that which was a press release. I have observed Mr. Kunstler leaning over Mr. Seale's shoulder during this week while Mr. Seale had his handwritten papers there. I have been advised by other people in the courtroom that it appeared that Mr. Kunstler was directing him on his writing of these papers.

This is just a ploy, your Honor. This is clearly just a ploy.

MR. SEALE: May I say something, your Honor? May I please say something?

THE COURT: I am listening to the United States Attorney, if you don't mind.

MR. KUNSTLER: I want the record to quite clearly indicate that I do not direct Mr. Seale in any way. He is a free independent black man who does his own direction.

THE COURT: Black or white, sir—and what an extraordinary statement, "an independent black man." He is a defendant in this case. He will be calling you a racist before you are through, Mr. Kunstler.

MR. KUNSTLER: Your Honor, I think to call him a free independent black man will not incite his anger.

THE COURT: Your appearance is on file in writing and I respect that appearance and it will remain there.

As far as books are concerned, Mr. Weinglass, I don't run the County Jail—if that is where he is being confined. I do not have any jurisdiction over the library.

Mr. Marshal, please bring in the jury.

(jury enters)

Testimony of David Stahl Resumed

MR. KUNSTLER: Mr. Stahl, yesterday on your direct, you indicated, as I understood it, that you took seriously Mr. Hoffman's request, as you put it, for one hundred thousand dollars to either sponsor the Festival of Life or to get out of town, is that correct?

THE WITNESS: Yes.

MR. KUNSTLER: I am going to ask you, Mr. Stahl, whether the following question was asked of you during your grand jury testimony.

"Q. Did you take them seriously?

"A. I had mixed feelings about it at the time but subsequently I became informed of what I was told was an OEO grant that had been made to the Youth International Party in New York City in the amount of one hundred thousand dollars and based on that information, I had reason to believe, you know, I then believed that this was a bona fide offer that was being made."

Did you check on whether there was an OEO grant?

THE WITNESS: No, I did not.

MR. KUNSTLER: Do you know today whether there was an OEO grant?

THE WITNESS: I do not know whether there was an OEO grant.

MR. KUNSTLER: Now, as I understand it, the City of Chicago or the Police Department has an Intelligence Bureau, is that correct?

THE WITNESS: There is an Intelligence Unit within the Chicago Police Department, yes.

MR. KUNSTLER: Known locally as the Red Squad?

MR. FORAN: Oh, your Honor. Your Honor, I object to it and ask—

MR. KUNSTLER: Well, if the answer is yes, your Honor—

THE WITNESS: I don't know of a Red Squad in the Chicago Police Department.

THE COURT: I will let the question and answer stand.

MR. KUNSTLER: Did you receive any reports from any Chicago agency, including the Intelligence Unit, as to the possibility of numbers of people coming to Chicago?

MR. FORAN: Your Honor, I object, and I move to stop this cross-examination for improper—

THE COURT: I sustain the objection. I would request counsel to do his best to ask questions which are appropriate under cross-examination.

I deny at this time the motion of the government to discontinue the cross-examination of this witness.

MR. KUNSTLER: Now, in all of your discussions with either Jerry Rubin, Abbie Hoffman, Dave Dellinger, Rennie Davis, or any of the people with them at any of the meetings to which you testified, did anyone ever say to you, "If we don't get the permits, we're going to do violent acts in this city?"

THE WITNESS: Not in precisely that language, no.

MR. KUNSTLER: Well, did they do it in any language?

THE WITNESS: Yes. Mr. Dellinger said on Monday that permits for the use of the parks should be issued in order to minimize destruction.

MR. KUNSTLER: To minimize destruction. And did he indicate to you from whence the destruction would come?

THE WITNESS: It certainly wasn't coming from the Chicago Police Department.

MR. KUNSTLER: It was your impression that Mr. Dellinger did not want violence, isn't that correct?

THE WITNESS: Mr. Dellinger would frequently disclaim any interest in having violence associated with any of their demonstrations.

MR. KUNSTLER: And you had no reason to disbelieve him, did you?

THE WITNESS: He had indicated to me in other conversations he believed in civil disobedience.

MR. KUNSTLER: Well, civil disobedience is not necessarily violence, is it?

THE WITNESS: I don't know what it is. I think you would have to ask Mr. Dellinger what civil disobedience is. I didn't use the term.

MR. KUNSTLER: Have you ever read Thoreau?

THE WITNESS: No, I have not read Thoreau.

MR. KUNSTLER: I commend it to you. Have you ever read the works of Mahatma Gandhi or Martin Luther King with reference to civil disobedience?

MR. FORAN: Your Honor, I object to that.

MR. KUNSTLER: Or William Jennings Bryan?

THE COURT: I sustain the objection.

MR. KUNSTLER: I noticed your Honor's middle name and I thought that that had a connection between Mr. Bryan.

THE COURT: I tell you that I haven't the time here to go into all of these great literary figures that you are mentioning. They are all very interesting. I am sure you have read them all or you wouldn't ask about them, but they are not germane to the issues here, Mr. Kunstler.

MR. KUNSTLER: After your meetings with the Yippies and with the Mobilization group, as you have testified to, did you recommend to anybody that the defendants and the others who were there should be followed or placed under surveillance.

MR. FORAN: Objection, your Honor.

THE COURT: I sustain the objection.

MR. KUNSTLER: No further questions.

Testimony of Robert Murray

MR. SCHULTZ: Will you please state your name?

THE WITNESS: Robert Murray.

MR. SCHULTZ: What is your occupation, please, Mr. Murray?

THE WITNESS: I am a Police Sergeant with the Chicago Police Department.

MR. SCHULTZ: Mr. Murray, during the week of the Democratic National Convention in August of 1968, where were you assigned, please?

THE WITNESS: I was assigned to Lincoln Park.

MR. SCHULTZ: While you were in Lincoln Park during the Democratic National Convention, Mr. Murray, how were you dressed?

THE WITNESS: I was dressed in casual clothes, wash pants and jacket.

MR. SCHULTZ: On Sunday evening, August 25, 1968, in Lincoln Park, between nine and ten o'clock at night, did you have occasion to observe a person named Jerry Rubin?

THE WITNESS: Yes, sir, I did.

MR. SCHULTZ: At the time that you saw Rubin what, if anything, did he have on his head?

THE WITNESS: He was wearing a football helmet.

MR. SCHULTZ: When you observed Rubin, what, if anything, was he doing?

THE WITNESS: The first time I observed him he was standing there and he was talking with a newsman from ABC.

MR. SCHULTZ: Would you relate, please, what you heard?

THE WITNESS: The conversation was on a first-name basis and the newsman said, "Well, Jerry, how do you feel your program will be accepted on the college campuses this fall?" and I heard Mr. Rubin say, "Well, I feel that it will be accepted very well by the kids because they are fed up with the power structure."

The newsman said, "Well, we are going to get some coffee. We haven't had our coffee yet." and Mr. Rubin said, "Well, wait, don't go right now. We're going out in the ball field," and he pointed in the direction of the ball field, and he says, "We want to see what these pigs are going to do about it," pointing to the police officers that were standing in front of this park house.

MR. SCHULTZ: How many police officers were standing there?

THE WITNESS: There were ten policemen and one sergeant.

MR. SCHULTZ: Were they dressed in police uniform?

THE WITNESS: Yes, they were.

MR. SCHULTZ: Would you continue?

THE WITNESS: He said, "We're going out to the ball field. We want to see what these pigs are going to do when we go out there." And the newsman said, "Well, when are you going?" And he said, "Right now." He said, "OK, we'll wait." And Mr. Rubin and the other man he was with walked out onto the ball field and I just stood there behind the newsman.

MR. SCHULTZ: What occurred then?

THE WITNESS: Then I heard this man that was with him say to Mr. Rubin, "Now's the time for the flares or the fires." I don't know which word it was.

MR. SCHULTZ: Then what did you hear, please?

THE WITNESS: I heard Mr. Rubin say, "No, not now," and the other man said, "Nothing's happening. Now's the time for the flares or fires."

Then I heard Mr. Rubin say, "OK, go get them." And at this, this man turned and went out of the park going west.

MR. SCHULTZ: Then what occurred, please?

THE WITNESS: Then Mr. Rubin turned and he began to shout in a loud voice, and he used some profanity.

MR. SCHULTZ: Your Honor, I want to ask that the witness be permitted to state what was said, even though some of those words are profane words, your Honor. They are four-letter words.

THE COURT: It occurs to me that it isn't necessary to obtain the permission of the Court. A witness may testify to what he heard. I don't mean to say that people will necessarily enjoy hearing profane words, but if profane words were spoken, part of a conversation, part of something an individual had said, I think it is appropriate in law that the witness so testify.

MR. SCHULTZ: Would you relate what Rubin said when he was waving with his arm?

THE WITNESS: He looked over his shoulder, and he says, "Look at these motherfucking pigs standing over here."

He says, "They have to be standing in the park protecting the park, and the park belongs to the people. Let's get these fuckers out of here."

MR. SCHULTZ: Then what occurred, please?

THE WITNESS: Well, the people began getting up, picking up their belongings and blankets and started walking over by him, and they also shouted the same things.

MR. SCHULTZ: As the people started to get up, did you observe Rubin at that time?

THE WITNESS: Yes, sir.

MR. SCHULTZ: Did he say anything else?

THE WITNESS: Yes, sir. He says, "The pigs are in our park. They're—" the same word I just used—"m-f-ers, they're shitheads," and he began to walk toward them.

MR. SCHULTZ: What, if anything, did the people who got up—what did they start to do, please, Mr. Murray?

THE WITNESS: The people with Mr. Rubin were yelling, "They're m-f-ers and they're s.o.b.'s."

MR. SCHULTZ: Where was Rubin in relation to the other people as he was walking to where the policemen were?

THE WITNESS: He was right in front of them.

MR. SCHULTZ: What did the police do as the crowd approached them?

THE WITNESS: They backed up against the wall.

MR. SCHULTZ: Would you relate, please, what, if anything, you observed Rubin do?

THE WITNESS: Well, as the crowd approached and stopped they were yelling things, and Mr. Rubin yelled, "Your children are pigs, you're pigs, why don't you get out of the park? Let's get them out of the park!" and the crowd was yelling "White honky m-f-ers, get out of our park!" And then I heard Mr. Rubin say, "Look at them. They look so tough with their arms folded. Take off your guns, and we'll fight you hand to hand." And the crowd began to yell the same things.

MR. SCHULTZ: Then what occurred, please?

THE WITNESS: Then I observed Mr. Rubin take a cigarette butt and flick it.

MR. SCHULTZ: And then what occurred, please?

THE WITNESS: Well, then people in the crowd started throwing cans, bottles, stones, small rocks, paper—newspapers that had been crumpled—paper bags, food wrappings.

MR. SCHULTZ: What, if anything, were the ten policemen and the sergeant doing at this time, please?

THE WITNESS: Well, some of the police officers were ducking, and some of them were just standing there in a position like this. *(demonstrating)*

MR. SCHULTZ: Did you observe where Rubin went—if he went anywhere—near the end of this ten-minute period that you have just described?

THE WITNESS: Almost everyone in this crowd of approximately 200 was screaming something, and I observed Mr. Rubin, who was to my right, start walking backwards out of the crowd.

MR. SCHULTZ: Now, calling your attention to the twenty-sixth of August, did you have occasion to see the defendant Jerry Rubin in Lincoln Park on that night?

THE WITNESS: Yes, sir, I did.

MR. SCHULTZ: Would you relate what you heard, please?

THE WITNESS: I heard Mr. Rubin saying that the pigs started the violence, and he says, "Tonight, we're not going to give up the park. We have to fight them. We have to meet violence with violence." He says, "The pigs are armed with guns and clubs and Mace, so we have to arm ourselves," with any kind of weapon they could get.

MR. SCHULTZ: Do you recall any further statements by him at this time?

THE WITNESS: I don't recall what else he said, but he ended it with saying, "And don't forget our gigantic love-in on the beaches tomorrow."

MR. SCHULTZ: Did you have occasion to see Rubin again that night?

THE WITNESS: I saw him walking through the park, walking up to small groups, having a conversation with them and leaving, going from group to group.

MR. SCHULTZ: What did you hear said, please?

THE WITNESS: I heard him say that "we have to fight the pigs in the park tonight," that "we're not going to let them take the park."

MR. SCHULTZ: Now, just before eleven o'clock that evening—this is on Monday night, August 26, 1968—what, if anything, did you observe the crowd do?

THE WITNESS: Well, I observed the crowd—people in the park running through the park, gathering up—carrying park benches and tables. All the tables in the park, they were carrying them to the northeast corner of the park. They were breaking branches off the trees, big limbs. There was lumber, carrying it like over their shoulders, and they were taking all the wastebaskets that were in the park, and some of them the regular type basket and others box-shape, and they were carrying it back to this northeast corner of the park. At this time many people were entering the park, and this crowd became larger and larger by the minute, and they kept piling different items on top, and jamming baskets in between tables and benches, and they were shouting, "Hell, no, we won't go! The park belongs to the people! Fuck Lynsky! Kill the cops!" Things like that.

MR. SCHULTZ: And while the crowd was shouting these things, what, if anything, did the police do?

THE WITNESS: Well, a car approached with microphones on the roof, and it was making an announcement that the park was closed and anybody in the park was violating the ordinance, and that anybody found in there would be placed under arrest, and of course, when this car would start the announcement, the shouts and screams were louder, and then rocks—some of the people behind the barricade ran to the left of the barricade and came closer to this police car and threw rocks at it.

MR. WEINGLASS: If your Honor please, I object to this line of questioning. There has been no foundation. There have been no preliminary questions as to what defendant, if any, was nearby relating to this incident.

THE COURT: You may justify the asking of the question.

MR. SCHULTZ: Yes, your Honor. Two hours prior to this incident, this witness testified the defendant Rubin encouraged this action. This is the product or part of the product—

MR. WEINGLASS: That is precisely what I was talking about. I think this is most unfair to permit a summation in front of the jury.

THE COURT: I overrule the objection.

MR. SCHULTZ: And then after the police car was hit by the objects, what occurred, please?

THE WITNESS: Shortly after, eight to ten policemen approached.

MR. SCHULTZ: And what occurred, please?

THE WITNESS: Objects came from the crowd, from behind the barricade again, bricks and stones, mostly, bottles and cans, and one policeman turned, started running back, fell down, and they cheered, and the policemen retreated.

Then they came up again but behind them came a skirmish line, one line of policemen shoulder-to-shoulder behind them, and the police shot gas—I should say threw gas—at the barricade.

MR. SCHULTZ: Then what occurred?

THE WITNESS: Well, everything, objects just pulled out from behind the barricade, people behind the barricade rolled these wastebaskets that were filled with paper, they lit them and they rolled them down the incline at the policemen.

Finally just as the police got close to the barricade, everybody started running out of the park.

MR. SCHULTZ: Did you run out of the park?

THE WITNESS: Yes.

MR. SCHULTZ: Your Honor, I have no further questions on direct examination.

• • • • •

MR. KUNSTLER: Now, you have testified on direct, as I understand it, that on Sunday, August 25, you had been in Lincoln Park, is that correct, at some time, about between 9:00 and 10:00 P.M.?

THE WITNESS: That's correct.

MR. KUNSTLER: Were you told to watch any particular people?

THE WITNESS: No, sir, I was not.

MR. KUNSTLER: Did you know Jerry Rubin before you entered the park?

THE WITNESS: No, sir, I did not.

MR. KUNSTLER: Had you ever seen him before?

THE WITNESS: Personally, no, sir.

MR. KUNSTLER: Had you seen pictures of him?

THE WITNESS: Yes, sir, on TV and newspapers and magazines.

MR. KUNSTLER: When you saw him in the park that day, you recognized him because you had seen him on TV and in magazines, is that correct?

THE WITNESS: Well, I thought it was him, and then there was a boy standing next to me, a teen-ager, and he said, "There's Jerry Rubin with the helmet. Now things will start happening."

MR. KUNSTLER: And there is no doubt in your mind, is there, Sergeant, that this was Sunday, August 25?

THE WITNESS: No, sir, there's no doubt.

MR. KUNSTLER: Is it not true, Sergeant Murray, that you told the FBI that this incident occurred on Monday, August 26, 1968, instead of Sunday, August 25, 1968?

THE WITNESS: That's correct.

MR. KUNSTLER: When did you come to the conclusion that what you had reported as to the incident some two weeks afterwards happened on a different day than you told the FBI?

THE WITNESS: I found out my mistake the first time that I was interviewed by a U. S. Attorney, who was U. S. Attorney Cubbage.

MR. KUNSTLER: Now, you also told the FBI, did you not, that the second incident which you have described as happening on August 26, on Monday evening, you told the FBI, did you not, that that occurred on Tuesday night, August 27?

THE WITNESS: That is correct.

MR. KUNSTLER: And is it your testimony now that that, too, was a mistake?

THE WITNESS: Yes, sir, it is.

MR. KUNSTLER: Now, when you first saw Mr. Rubin between nine o'clock and ten o'clock on the 25th, as you now testify, what was he wearing in addition to the football helmet?

THE WITNESS: Well, the football helmet was white, it had a blue stripe down the middle, it had a number "88" on the back. He had a sweater or sweatshirt, as I recall, tied around his waist with the sleeves like tied in front, and I believe he was wearing blue jeans or work clothes, as I would describe them.

MR. KUNSTLER: You said Rubin said some remarks to the police such as "you're pigs," and "get out of the park" and "take off the guns and we'll fight you," and so on.

WITNESS: Yes, sir.

MR. KUNSTLER: Now, at that moment I think you said that Jerry Rubin flicked a cigarette butt, is that correct?

WITNESS: That's right.

MR. KUNSTLER: Had you seen Jerry Rubin smoking up to this time?

WITNESS: No, sir, I didn't.

MR. KUNSTLER: Never saw him smoke, did you?

WITNESS: No, sir.

MR. KUNSTLER: When did you see him light his cigarette?

WITNESS: I didn't see him light the cigarette.

MR. KUNSTLER: How did the cigarette suddenly appear in his hand, if you know?

WITNESS: I don't know.

MR. KUNSTLER: It suddenly is there, is that what you are saying?

WITNESS: Yes. He was right to my right, and he took his arm like this, and that's when I saw him flip the cigarette like this.

MR. KUNSTLER: When he flicked the cigarette, what else happened?

WITNESS: Well, other people started throwing things.

MR. KUNSTLER: Was that the signal in your mind for other people to throw cigarettes? Is that what you regarded it as?

MR. SCHULTZ: If the Court please, I object to that.

THE COURT: I sustain the objection.

(the court is adjourned for the day)

October 3, 1969

MR. KUNSTLER: Your Honor, in the hope of possibly nipping this in the bud, I would like to ask your Honor to at least caution the prosecution to adhere to Canon 7 of the American Bar Association's annually adopted standards and I am referring to the one called "Ethical Consideration" which states:

"A lawyer should not make unfair or derogatory personal reference to opposing counsel. Harangue and offensive tactics by lawyers interfere with the ordinary adminis- tration of justice and have no proper place in our legal system."

The remarks that were made by Mr. Foran and Mr. Schultz over the course of this trial on the personal level, the references to television actors and Channel Seven and the like, as well as others which are in the record—

THE COURT: I made a reference to your appearance on television.

MR. KUNSTLER: But not in a derogatory way, your Honor.

THE COURT: I would say a lawyer should always be a gentleman in court. Ours is first of all, Mr. Kunstler, a profession of good manners. I insist on a lawyer having good man- ners before I even determine whether he is a good lawyer.

MR. KUNSTLER: Your Honor, we were called unethical. I can't think of a grosser insult to an attorney in a courtroom than to be called unethical by opposing counsel. If that is not derogatory—

THE COURT: I wish you would read a document you filed here which I have ordered impounded, and I don't know how you describe that—

MR. KUNSTLER: Your Honor, that is a legitimate attack in a disqualification motion and your Honor knows that as well as I do. That is a legitimate attack.

THE COURT: Don't tell me what I know. I know what that document is because I am a student, I hope, of English. And you should follow the same rules, Mr. Kunstler, and I will ask the Government lawyers to do as I suggest.

Mr. Schultz, if you think some very forceful criticism of counsel on the personal level is indicated, in such an event please ask me to exclude the jury.

MR. SCHULTZ: We will do that, your Honor.

THE COURT: Mr. Marshal, please bring in the jury.

(jury enters)

You may continue with the cross examination of this witness, Mr. Kunstler.

MR. KUNSTLER: Sergeant, you testified on direct that on Monday evening you saw a barricade being built, is that correct?

THE WITNESS: Yes, sir.

MR. KUNSTLER: Did you see any physical contact between the police and the people in the vicinity of the barricade.

THE WITNESS: No, sir. I saw bricks and bottles and I saw some of them hitting the policemen.

MR. KUNSTLER: Did you see any of the policemen hit by any of this material?

THE WITNESS: Well, there was one of them that went down as if he was hit, but I couldn't see him get hit. But I saw others being hit as they turned running, I saw things hitting them.

MR. KUNSTLER: Now, Sergeant, just a few more questions, and I am now going back to the preceding night.

Sergeant, I want you to detail for me exactly what Mr. Rubin was wearing on the night of Sunday, August 25, when you first saw him.

THE WITNESS: He was wearing a football helmet. It had a blue stripe down the middle, I would estimate a half-inch stripe, down the middle of this helmet, from the forehead to the neck.

MR. KUNSTLER: Now, you mentioned something about the numbers "88," as I recall. Where were they?

THE WITNESS: On the back, one "8" on the left of the stripe and one "8" on the right of the stripe.

MR. KUNSTLER: Now, Mr. Rubin had this helmet on his head, I understand, during all of the time you saw him on Sunday night.

THE WITNESS: Yes, sir.

MR. KUNSTLER: Can you just describe for us the length of Mr. Rubin's beard that night?

THE WITNESS: Well, it—it was not long.

MR. KUNSTLER: But would you say in a matter of inches?

THE WITNESS: Half inch, quarter inch, half inch, something like that.

MR. KUNSTLER: What about Mr. Rubin's height? How tall would you say he was?

THE WITNESS: Five-seven.

MR. KUNSTLER: And how much did he weigh, if you can estimate?

THE WITNESS: About 145 pounds.

MR. KUNSTLER: Now, are you absolutely certain that the man you saw that night with the football helmet with "88" on it was the same defendant, Jerry Rubin, who is sitting here in court today?

THE WITNESS: Yes, sir.

MR. KUNSTLER: There is no question in your mind whatsoever?

THE WITNESS: No, sir.

MR. KUNSTLER: All right. May I have the witness, please?

MR. SCHULTZ: Objection.

THE COURT: May you have what?

MR. KUNSTLER: I want him to look at a man, your Honor, and ask him if that was not the man he saw in the park that night.

THE COURT: I sustain the objection.

MR. KUNSTLER: Your Honor, it is like a document. It is perfectly proper to ask if this was the man he saw.

MR. SCHULTZ: Your Honor, it might be out of order, but it will save time. I won't object to that.

THE COURT: You won't object to it?

MR. SCHULTZ: No.

THE COURT: I thought you did. Your objection is valid.

If the Government doesn't object, let him walk in.

(Robert Levin enters the courtroom.)

MR. KUNSTLER: Would you put the helmet on, please?

Are you absolutely sure that this is not the man you saw that night in Lincoln Park?

THE WITNESS: Absolutely.

MR. KUNSTLER: You are absolutely certain?

THE WITNESS: Yes, I am. He's too big.

MR. KUNSTLER: Would you turn around also and show him the back of the helmet.

THE WITNESS: That's a motorcycle helmet.

MR. KUNSTLER: That is not the helmet that you saw that night?

THE WITNESS: No, it was a football helmet.

MR. KUNSTLER: Your Honor, I have no further questions.

MR. SCHULTZ: Your Honor, may we have for the record an identification of this individual who walked into the courtroom?

THE COURT: Yes. Tell us who your exhibit is.

MR. KUNSTLER: Your Honor, the exhibit is a man named Robert Levin, L-E-V-I-N.

Your Honor, I would just like to mark this helmet for identification as Defendants' D-15.

MR. WEINGLASS: This was your first assignment as an undercover agent, is that correct?

THE WITNESS: That's not correct. I at no time was told that I was an undercover agent.

MR. WEINGLASS: Do you recall in your interview with the Federal Bureau of Investigation characterizing yourself as an undercover person?

THE WITNESS: They may have said I was undercover, but I said I worked plainclothes and milled in the crowd and tried to get information.

MR. WEINGLASS: Now, when you were told to gather information, were you told to gather information about any particular person?

THE WITNESS: No, sir, I was not.

MR. WEINGLASS: You were just to wander through the park?

THE WITNESS: Yes, sir, I was.

MR. WEINGLASS: And report back to your superiors?

THE WITNESS: Yes, sir.

MR. WEINGLASS: Could you tell the jury how it is that you are able to recall approximately thirteen months later the precise words used by Jerry Rubin on Sunday night, August 25, without the benefit of a single note, a single recorded word, or any other note to refresh your recollection?

MR. SCHULTZ: Objection, if the Court please.

MR. WEINGLASS: Could you tell us how you could recall the precise words used, Sergeant?

THE WITNESS: Well, when I sat down and really thought about it, and I thought about this incident, it came back very clearly because I was shocked at what was happening, and I remembered it.

MR. WEINGLASS: So, approximately two months later you sat down and you tried to remember and you remembered verbatim what Jerry Rubin said on Monday night, August 26, in the thirty-second speech, is that correct?

THE WITNESS: Yes; I remembered what others said too there.

MR. WEINGLASS: Now you did not testify that you heard Jerry Rubin that night say anything about erecting a barricade?

THE WITNESS: No.

MR. WEINGLASS: You can't tell this jury from your own observations that Jerry Rubin had anything to do with the erecting of the barricade?

THE WITNESS: No. I didn't hear Mr. Rubin say at any time, "We are going to build a barricade," no.

MR. WEINGLASS: As a matter of fact, Jerry Rubin wasn't in the park at the time the barricade was up, isn't that true?

MR. SCHULTZ: Objection, if the Court please.

THE COURT: I will sustain the objection.

MR. WEINGLASS: Sergeant Murray, as I understand your testimony, you never saw Jerry Rubin with a weapon in his hand.

THE WITNESS: That is correct. I never saw him with a weapon.

MR. WEINGLASS: I have concluded my cross-examination.

THE COURT: All right. Mr. Marshal, the court will be in recess until two o'clock.

• • • • •

THE COURT: Mr. Kunstler, you have something you wanted to indicate.

MR. KUNSTLER: It is a very simple matter, your Honor. It has to do with the fact that some of the defendants have asked me to ask your Honor whether from time to time, if the occasion arises and they do have to go to the men's room, they might leave without interrupting the trial and come right back.

THE COURT: Well, if it be understood that they waive their constitutional right to be present here.

MR. KUNSTLER: I think under those circumstances, your Honor, they would certainly waive their constitutional rights.

THE COURT: Please call your next witness, gentlemen of the Government.

Testimony of Arthur Aznavoorian

MR. FORAN: Will you state your name, please, and spell it for the court reporter?
THE WITNESS: Officer Arthur Aznavoorian.
MR. FORAN: What is your occupation?
THE WITNESS: Police officer, City of Chicago.
MR. FORAN: Were you on duty during the Democratic National Convention in August 1968?
THE WITNESS: I was.
MR. FORAN: What were your duties during that period of time, starting about the twenty-fourth of August?
THE WITNESS: I was assigned to follow Mr. Jerry Rubin.
MR. FORAN: Now, calling your attention to Saturday, August 24, at approximately 11:15 A.M., where were you?
THE WITNESS: I was at the corner of Sedgwick and Wisconsin.
MR. FORAN: Did you see Mr. Rubin at that time?
THE WITNESS: Yes, I did.
MR. FORAN: What was he doing?
MR. WEINGLASS: If your Honor please, we have a motion with respect to this witness.

(jury excused)

This witness is one of several officers of the Police Department of this city who were assigned the task of maintaining surveillance of the defendant Jerry Rubin. It is our position that for any law enforcement officer of this country to invade privacy on a twenty-four-hour-a-day basis is a violation of the Fourth Amendment right.*

The basis of the motion is not exclusively the Fourth Amendment, but the First Amendment as well, since Mr. Rubin was here to register his protest, his dissent, to gather peacefully and assemble with his fellow citizens and petition the Government for change. His First Amendment right to assemble and petition the government was also jeopardized by the surveillance.

THE COURT: The defendants contend that when surveillance is conducted on a constant, twenty-four-hour-a-day basis, it constitutes an unconstitutional invasion of privacy in violation of the Fourth Amendment and that the fruits of such surveillance are inadmissible as evidence.

The right to speak and to assemble does not include a right to do so in public unobserved.* The defendants' motion to suppress the testimony of the witness on the stand and other police officers who took part allegedly in a twenty-four-hour surveillance of the defendant Rubin will be denied.

October 7, 1969

(jury enters)

MR. FORAN: What occurred, Mr. Aznavoorian, when you saw Mr. Rubin at the corner of Sedgwick and Wisconsin?
THE WITNESS: He walked west on Van Buren to a restaurant located at 63 West Van Buren, in the company of three or four other men.
MR. FORAN: What happened then?
THE WITNESS: He stood in there about twenty minutes. He came out again. He walked east on Van Buren to the Old Colony Building and entered.

I stood there about a half hour, and he came out again. He observed me. He pointed me out to the fellows he was with. He walked south on Plymouth Court to the Eisenhower Expressway, west on the north side of the street of the Expressway to Dearborn, north on Dearborn back to Van Buren, and then east on Van Buren back to Plymouth Court. He did this twice.
MR. FORAN: What was he doing while he was walking?

[58]

THE WITNESS: Just walking in and out of doorways of stores that are located on both sides of the street.

MR. FORAN: Now, calling your attention to Monday, August 26, about noontime, where were you?

THE WITNESS: In Lincoln Park.

MR. FORAN: What was occurring in the park?

THE WITNESS: A news conference was being held with major TV and newspapers.

MR. FORAN: Was Mr. Rubin there?

THE WITNESS: Yes, he was.

MR. FORAN: Did you recognize anyone else there with him?

THE WITNESS: Abbie Hoffman was there, Stew Albert was there, Keith Lampe was there, Mr. Ginsberg was there, and a few others I can't remember now.

MR. FORAN: Now, about fifteen minutes after the press conference was over, was Mr. Rubin still within your eyesight.

THE WITNESS: Yes, he was. He was talking to a group of people. Mr. Rubin stated that "We are going to give instructions. We are going to give instructions and lessons on how to fight the pigs in self-defense (Mr. Hoffman was)." And he pointed northeast by the ball field, and he said, "We are going to line up. We are going to go there now."

MR. FORAN: After he made this statement, what occurred?

THE WITNESS: The group and Mr. Rubin started walking toward the school by the ball field. When Mr. Rubin got approximately ten or fifteen feet away, he stopped, and the rest of the group continued on. I observed Mr. Hoffman in the middle of the group there on the side, waving his arms up [demonstrating], kicking his knee up and foot out, what the rest of the people were doing also there.

MR. FORAN: By the way, did you recognize anyone else with Rubin during that day?

THE WITNESS: Yes, I did.

MR. FORAN: Who did you see him with?

THE WITNESS: Officer Pierson.

MR. FORAN: How was Officer Pierson dressed?

THE WITNESS: He had a black jacket on, helmet, beard, dark pants.

MR. FORAN: What were they doing when you saw them?

THE WITNESS: They were talking. I tried to get close to them. They would walk away, and just walk away from me, and continue talking. There was papers nailed to the trees. They would look up to the trees. I couldn't get that close.

MR. FORAN: I have no further direct examination, your Honor.

MR. KUNSTLER: Mr. Aznavoorian, can you indicate for the jury what your instructions were with reference to Jerry Rubin, what your duties were?

THE WITNESS: To observe and follow him, and to report back orally.

MR. KUNSTLER: Orally. Did you keep any notes as to what you testified on direct?

THE WITNESS: No, I did not.

MR. KUNSTLER: The first day that you testified about here today, anyway, was Saturday, August 24, and I think you said, as I recall it, that you saw Mr. Rubin earlier, at 11:15, is that correct?

THE WITNESS: Yes.

MR. KUNSTLER: From the time you first testified you saw him on Saturday until the last time you saw him on Wednesday, I believe, or Tuesday, did you ever see him with a helmet, carrying a helmet, or wearing a helmet?

THE WITNESS: No, I did not.

MR. KUNSTLER: Did you ever see a helmet in his vicinity with the number "88" on it?

THE WITNESS: No.

MR. KUNSTLER: I am talking now about the time near the Old Colony building—Mr. Rubin went back and forth with reference to a restaurant, is that correct?

THE WITNESS: Yes.

MR. KUNSTLER: Mr. Rubin then began to walk, and as you described it, he walked from Plymouth Court to the Eisenhower Expressway. And then, as I understood it, he went east on Van Buren, or north on Dearborn, and then east on Van Buren back to Plymouth Court?

THE WITNESS: Yes.

MR. KUNSTLER: He kept going in a circle, did he not?

THE WITNESS: Just about.

MR. KUNSTLER: Was he going in and out of doorways?

THE WITNESS: Yes, he was.

MR. KUNSTLER: It was obvious to you that he was playing games with you?

THE WITNESS: Yes, he was playing games.

MR. KUNSTLER: Now during that whole day, that is Saturday, the twenty-fourth, did Mr. Rubin ever use one obscenity in your presence, one profane word?

THE WITNESS: No, he did not, to my recollection.

MR. KUNSTLER: In fact, it is your recollection at no time during any of your surveillance on any of these days did he use any obscenities, isn't that correct?

THE WITNESS: It is to my recollection. No, he did not.

MR. KUNSTLER: On Sunday, August 26, Rubin went into the park and you have testified that sometime around noon there was a press conference there, is that correct?

THE WITNESS: Yes, there was.

MR. KUNSTLER: What did Mr. Rubin do during the press conference?

THE WITNESS: He sat on the ground.

MR. KUNSTLER: Was there any discussion at that press conference of what had happened to the people on Sunday with reference to the police?

MR. FORAN: I object, your Honor, as outside the scope.

THE COURT: The form is bad. You may ask him what was said.

MR. KUNSTLER: What was said by the speakers at the press conference? Identify the ones, if you can.

THE WITNESS: Well, there was one statement that comes out in my mind. I think Mr. Lampe, Keith Lampe, introduced Stew Albert and Stew Albert had a patch on his head and they were stating that he received this yesterday, sometime yesterday.

MR. KUNSTLER: What kind of a patch was it?

THE WITNESS: It was stitches.

MR. KUNSTLER: Medical patch?

THE WITNESS: Medical patch.

MR. KUNSTLER: As I understand it, after the press conference was over, Rubin said something about self-defense and I think he used the word "pigs," is that correct, in connection with that? In connection with the word pigs, what did he say, as you recall?

THE WITNESS: He was with a group of people and he stated that Abbie Hoffman was giving lessons in self-defense and instructions on how to fight the pigs.

MR. KUNSTLER: Did there not come a time subsequent to this, Mr. Aznavoorian, when Mr. Rubin was tear-gassed by the Chicago Police? Do you know that?

THE WITNESS: He wasn't tear-gassed by the police as far as my—as far as I was concerned.

MR. KUNSTLER: As far as Mr. Rubin was concerned during the time you have testified to which I believe is from August 24 through August 27 when you were relieved at 2:00 P.M. on that day, did you ever see him smoking a cigarette?

THE WITNESS: No, I did not.

MR. KUNSTLER: Did you become conscious at all during this surveillance that Mr. Rubin does not smoke?

MR. FORAN: Your Honor, I object to that.

THE COURT: I sustain the objection.

MR. KUNSTLER: During all of this period did you ever see him throw an object at another human being?

THE WITNESS: Wednesday.

MR. KUNSTLER: Wednesday he threw an object?

THE WITNESS: Yes. He threw a sweater.

MR. KUNSTLER: At who?

THE WITNESS: At me.

MR. KUNSTLER: I take it you were uninjured by the sweater?

THE WITNESS: Yes, I wasn't injured.

MR. KUNSTLER: Right. And can you just explain the circumstances of the sweater being thrown?

THE WITNESS: Yes. We were walking into Lincoln Park and Mr. Rubin reached down, grabbed a handful of grass and put it in his mouth, one of the pieces of grass in his mouth, and he was walking in the park with this grass and his sweater fell. With this he picked up his sweater, tied it around his waist and started walking. All of a sudden he started coughing, his eyes were running, and he took the sweater from off his waist and started to rub it across his eyes. He was using it like a towel. And I started coughing and it seems that Mr. Rubin got mad and he just threw the sweater at my direction. Nancy [Kurshan] came running out from the park, he picked up the sweater and they walked out of the park.

MR. KUNSTLER: Did you ever report this sweater incident to the grand jury, for example?

THE WITNESS: No, I did not.

MR. KUNSTLER: You didn't take that as a threat to you—

THE WITNESS: No.

MR. KUNSTLER: I have no further questions, your Honor.

THE COURT: Mr. Weinglass, do you desire to cross-examine this witness?

MR. WEINGLASS: Yes, I do, your Honor.

Mr. Aznavoorian, how did you know who Jerry Rubin was when you first started your assignment?

THE WITNESS: I had a photograph of him.

MR. WEINGLASS: And Jerry Rubin knew that you were a police officer from Saturday, I believe you testified, on through Wednesday, is that correct?

THE WITNESS: To my best recollection, he knew about it Sunday morning.

MR. WEINGLASS: Did he ever engage you in a conversation about that?

THE WITNESS: Yes, Sunday. This was about twelve-thirty, twelve-fifteen, Sunday afternoon. Mr. Rubin comes running across Clark Street or Wells Street with a group of reporters, a couple of men with tape recorders, and he was pointing me out hollering, "I fooled you last night! I fooled you!"

There was a little short fellow with him, with a mustache, glasses, and a beard. He says, "This man is a famous playwright from New York. I am going to make you famous."

And they started asking me questions. With this, I just turned my back and walked away from him. He was following me. These reporters were sticking a microphone in my face, and so forth, and I was just turning my back and walking away from them.

MR. WEINGLASS: Now, that press conference that you saw on Monday morning, did you hear Mr. Albert at any time while you were standing there read to the press a statement, a telegram he had sent to the United Nations asking for an investigation of the police?

THE WITNESS: I don't recall.

MR. WEINGLASS: Is it possible that Mr. Albert did read a telegram asking for an investigation of the police?

MR. FORAN: I object to that, your Honor.

THE COURT: I sustain the objection.

MR. WEINGLASS: Officer Aznavoorian, are you familiar with what happened in the park Sunday night?

THE WITNESS: No, I am not.

MR. WEINGLASS: You are not aware of the fact that the police cleared the park?

THE WITNESS: Oh, in that matter, yes.

MR. FORAN: I object.

THE COURT: I sustain the objection to the question.

MR. WEINGLASS: Did you hear Mr. Rubin at the time he called for the course in self-defense allude in any way to what happened the night before in the park?

THE WITNESS: No, I did not.

MR. WEINGLASS: No further questions.

THE COURT: You may step down, sir.

Please call your next witness.

Testimony of Richard L. Thompson

MR. SCHULTZ: Please state your name.

THE WITNESS: Richard L. Thompson.

MR. SCHULTZ: What is your occupation, please, Mr. Thompson?

THE WITNESS: I am a policeman with the Chicago Police Department.

MR. SCHULTZ: On November 20, 1967, did you have occasion to attend a meeting?

THE WITNESS: Yes. The meeting was with CADRE.

MR. SCHULTZ: Would you tell the Court and jury what CADRE is?

THE WITNESS: CADRE is the Chicago Area Draft Resisters.

MR. SCHULTZ: How were you dressed, please?

THE WITNESS: I was dressed in a wash shirt and khaki pants and gym shoes, sneakers.

MR. SCHULTZ: Who made speeches to the group, please?

THE WITNESS: There were three guest speakers and the moderator was Paul Ruppert. The guests speakers were David Harris, Bob Ross and Rennie Davis.

MR. SCHULTZ: Would you please relate to the Court and jury what, if anything, the defendant Davis said at that meeting relating to civil disobedience or the Democratic National Convention?

MR. KUNSTLER: Your Honor, how leading can we get? He is telling him what area to concentrate on.

THE COURT: Am I here to answer questions? If you think the question is objectionable—

MR. KUNSTLER: I object, your Honor.

THE COURT: I would say, Mr. Schultz, the question is suggestive of the answer. Therefore, I sustain the objection.

MR. SCHULTZ: Would you tell the Court and jury, please, what the defendant Davis said during the approximately last half of his speech.

THE WITNESS: He talked about civil disobedience and said that persons who were not going to participate directly in civil disobedience should support those who are participating and that they should support them by financial means or support them by forming a circle around them to prevent or hinder arrest by the police.

He then talked about the coming Democratic Convention and said that there would be demonstrations and civil disobedience to disrupt the Convention and that they would do anything possible to disrupt the convention.

MR. SCHULTZ: Calling your attention to Thursday, August 29, 1968, during the Democratic National Convention, did you have occasion to participate in any march?

THE WITNESS: Yes.

MR. SCHULTZ: When the march was returning back toward Grant Park, did you have occasion to observe any ranking police officer with the marchers?

THE WITNESS: Yes, Deputy Superintendent Rochford.

MR. SCHULTZ: Where did the march return to specifically?

THE WITNESS: To the Logan Statue.

MR. SCHULTZ: What occurred at this time, please?

THE WITNESS: As we were returning to the Logan statue, someone put their hand on my shoulder and said, "Are you with me?"

As I turned around, I noticed that it was Abbie Hoffman. I said, "What do you mean, am I with you?"

He said, "Well, you see the guy in front of us, the guy with the stars on his shoulder?" He was pointing at Deputy Superintendent James Rochford. And he said, "Well, you see that cat? When we get up to the top of the hill, if the cat don't talk right, we're going to hold him there and then we can do whatever we want to and the police won't bother us."

At this time he walked away from me. I said, "Yes, I'm with you."

MR. SCHULTZ: No further questions on direct, if the Court please.

MR. WEINGLASS: Officer Thompson, you testified on direct that you attended a meeting at the University of Chicago on November 20, 1967, is that correct?

Would you tell the jury what your purpose was in attending such a meeting?

[62]

THE WITNESS: The purpose was, I was participating as a policeman in the Intelligence Division to attend the meeting to see what the results or what the organization had plans for as far as the future was concerned.

MR. WEINGLASS: Now, in attending this meeting as an Intelligence Officer, did you bring with you a notebook?

THE WITNESS: No, I didn't.

MR. WEINGLASS: Did you bring with you any recording device?

THE WITNESS: No, I didn't.

MR. WEINGLASS: You testified that Mr. Davis spoke about civil disobedience, is that correct?

THE WITNESS: Yes, he did.

MR. WEINGLASS: Was he talking about civil disobedience in the context of draft resistance?

THE WITNESS: Both draft resistance and the Democratic Convention.

MR. WEINGLASS: Did Mr. Davis at any time in his presentation to CADRE refer to violence of any sort?

THE WITNESS: Only in the words of civil disobedience.

MR. WEINGLASS: Now to your way of thinking, is civil disobedience necessarily a violent action?

THE WITNESS: Not at all times.

MR. WEINGLASS: Mr. Davis, when he spoke about civil disobedience, did not refer to it as or in a violent context, did he?

THE WITNESS: Yes, when he said they would form circles around the persons who were participating in civil disobedience to disrupt the Convention, that they would prevent the arrest or protect the people from being arrested.

MR. WEINGLASS: But when he talked about forming circles, aren't you confusing that with the fact that he mentioned that in connection with burning draft cards?

THE WITNESS: No, I am not.

MR. WEINGLASS: And there is no doubt in your mind that you might have misunderstood or misinterpreted the words of Mr. Davis?

THE WITNESS: No, I didn't.

MR. WEINGLASS: You testified that on August 29 you were in Grant Park near the Logan Statue?

THE WITNESS: That is correct.

MR. WEINGLASS: Now when Abbie said to you, "Are you with me?" was this the first time he had ever talked to you?

THE WITNESS: Personally, yes.

MR. WEINGLASS: So he didn't know who you were?

THE WITNESS: No, he didn't.

MR. WEINGLASS: And he was just approaching you as a complete and total stranger?

THE WITNESS: Approached me as a member of the march. He said, "If the cat doesn't talk right when he gets to the top of the hill, then we'll hold him, and we'll do what we want to him and the police won't bother us."

MR. WEINGLASS: Didn't Abbie Hoffman also indicate to you that, "We're going to hold him here by asking him questions until he lives up to the commitments he's made to us and we can march"?

THE WITNESS: He didn't say anything like that to me.

MR. WEINGLASS: Was it your impression, Officer, that Abbie Hoffman meant that you were to physically seize Deputy Superintendent Rochford?

THE WITNESS: That's what he said.

MR. WEINGLASS: Did he say "physically seize him"?

THE WITNESS: No, "hold him." He didn't say how.

MR. WEINGLASS: Did you see Abbie Hoffman, or any of these other people he talked to, make any gesture or movement toward Deputy Commander Rochford?

THE WITNESS: No, I didn't.

MR. WEINGLASS: I am finished.

MR. KUNSTLER: Your Honor, before the court is in recess, we do have one application for you out of the presence of the jury.
THE COURT: The jury is excused.

(jury excused)

MR. WEINGLASS: If the Court please, this officer, who is a city policeman, testified that he went as an undercover agent to a meeting of citizens which had no apparently unlawful purpose, a meeting of a group known as CADRE, and he went there on specific instructions to gather intelligence of this lawful meeting of citizens of this city.
THE COURT: Wasn't there some suggestion, sir, that the matter of burning draft cards was to be considered at that meeting?
MR. WEINGLASS: I submit to the Court that the right of persons to meet, to assemble, to discuss outstanding political and social questions on a university without fear of intimidation or surveillance by police officers is paramount, and to allow police officers to attend those meetings and make intelligence reports is a violation of the First Amendment rights of the persons present.
    For that reason I ask that Officer Thompson's testimony concerning the November 20, 1967 meeting be stricken.
MR. FORAN: Your Honor, I object to their motion.
THE COURT: The motion of the defendants to strike—I will wait until the laughter ceases. I didn't intend to be funny this time.
    Do you approve of your client laughing out loud while the Court is making a decision on a motion made by them, sir?
MR. KUNSTLER: I didn't hear it. I was talking to Mr. Davis.
THE COURT: You seemed to be enjoying their laughter because you smiled yourself.
MR. KUNSTLER: Your Honor, a smile is not forbidden in the Federal Court, I don't think.
THE COURT: When a defendant or some defendants make a motion, and then that they should laugh out loud while the Court is giving consideration to the motion—
MR. KUNSTLER: My smile, your Honor, was at Mr. Davis.
THE COURT: The motion of the defendants to strike from the testimony of the witness Thompson who has just left the stand that portion of his testimony dealing with occurrences on November 20, 1967, will be denied.
MR. KUNSTLER: Your Honor, you alluded that I was laughing or smiling. I think I ought to put it on the record that Mr. Davis complimented Mr. Foran on making a good point with that last observation and I smiled.
THE COURT: As long as you are putting things on the record, I think I will put on the record the posture of one of your clients. This is the United States District Court. Have a look at him lying down there like he is on the ground. I won't discipline him at this time but I call attention to it on the record, as you put it.
MR. KUNSTLER: It may reflect his attitude, your Honor, toward what is going on in the courtroom.
THE COURT: Oh, I think it does. I think it does reflect his attitude.
MR. KUNSTLER: Then it is free speech.
THE COURT: And that attitude will be appropriately dealt with at a—can't three marshals back there deal with those comments?
    This court will be in recess until ten o'clock tomorrow morning, Mr. Marshal.

(court adjourned)

Testimony of Robert Pierson

October 8, 1969

THE COURT: Good morning, ladies and gentlemen of the jury.

MR. SCHULTZ: Please state your name.

THE WITNESS: My name is Robert Pierson.

MR. SCHULTZ: What is your occupation, please, Mr. Pierson?

THE WITNESS: I am a Chicago police officer assigned to the Sixth District Tactical Unit.

MR. SCHULTZ: Have you had any leaves of absence since you became a Chicago police officer?

THE WITNESS: Yes, sir, I have had two. The first was in 1959 through 1960 and that is when I left to go with the United States Army Intelligence. The second leave of absence was in 1963 through 1966.

MR. SCHULTZ: Where did you go during those three years, please?

THE WITNESS: I went with the Palmer House Hotel as the director of safety and security.

MR. SCHULTZ: Now in August of 1968, specifically where were you employed, please?

THE WITNESS: I was employed as an investigator for the State's Attorney's office of Cook County.

MR. SCHULTZ: Did you have any assignment during the Democratic National Convention?

THE WITNESS: My assignment was as an undercover investigator.

MR. SCHULTZ: Did you in any way alter your physical appearance to conduct your assignment as undercover investigator?

THE WITNESS: Yes, I did. I allowed my hair to grow long. I allowed myself to go without a shave for approximately four to six weeks. I purchased the attire of a motorcycle gang member, which is motorcycle boots, a black T-shirt, black levis and a black leather vest and a motorcycle helmet.

MR. SCHULTZ: Did you obtain a motorcycle?

THE WITNESS: Yes, I rented a motorcycle.

MR. SCHULTZ: Now, calling your attention to Friday, August 23, 1968, where did you go, please?

THE WITNESS: I went to Lincoln Park.

MR. SCHULTZ: What did you do at the park?

THE WITNESS: I talked with different members of the motorcycle gang and others, Yippies and people that I saw in the park that day. I stayed around the park area and talked with them, until the early evening hours of Friday.

MR. SCHULTZ: Now, calling your attention to the following day, which is Saturday, August 24, did you have occasion to go to Lincoln Park on that day?

THE WITNESS: Yes, sir, I did.

MR. SCHULTZ: Who were you with on Saturday in Lincoln Park?

THE WITNESS: I was with a fellow known as Gorilla who headed a motorcycle gang, and another fellow by the name of Banana, and other members of the motorcycle gang.

MR. SCHULTZ: Did you go home on Friday night and Saturday night?

THE WITNESS: No, sir, I did not; I went to an apartment on the North Side.

MR. SCHULTZ: Now, calling your attention to Monday, August 26, 1968, did you have occasion on that day to go to Lincoln Park?

THE WITNESS: Yes, sir, I did.

MR. SCHULTZ: Who did you meet with, please?

THE WITNESS: Fred Jordan.

MR. SCHULTZ: After meeting with Fred Jordan, did you have occasion to have a conversation with him?

THE WITNESS: Yes, I did. Jordan brought me over and introduced me to Abbie Hoff-

[65]

man. He said, "Abbie, this is Bob. He will be one of your bodyguards. He handles himself well."

Hoffman shook my hand, said that he was glad to have me with him, and at that time Jordan also pointed out two other men that were bodyguards for Hoffman.

I said to Hoffman that last night's confrontation was a pretty good one. And Hoffman said to me last night, "They pushed us out of the park, but tonight, we're going to hold the park." He then said that, "We're going to—" and he used a foul word, "F—up the pigs and the Convention."

MR. SCHULTZ: What was the word, please, will you relate it?

THE WITNESS: He said "fuck."

MR. SCHULTZ: Then what did he say, please?

THE WITNESS: He said that, "If they push us out of the park tonight, we're going to break windows," and again he used a foul word.

MR. SCHULTZ: The same word?

THE WITNESS: Yes, and he said, "We're going to f—up the North Side." And he also said that, "We're going to create little Chicagos everywhere."

MR. SCHULTZ: What did you say when Hoffman told you this, please?

THE WITNESS: I told him that he could count on me helping him in every way in doing my best to keep him from being arrested.

MR. SCHULTZ: Now, Mr. Pierson, after leaving the defendant Hoffman, where did you go please?

THE WITNESS: I went back to the Lincoln Park area near the fieldhouse.

MR. SCHULTZ: Did you have a conversation with Fred Jordan?

THE WITNESS: Yes, sir, I did. Jordan brought me over to the same area I previously showed you, east of the fieldhouse, and introduced me to Jerry Rubin.

MR. SCHULTZ: Do you see that person whom you identified as Jerry Rubin in the courtroom here?

THE WITNESS: Yes, sir.

MR. SCHULTZ: Would you point to him, please?

THE WITNESS: He's the man behind the attorney there with the yellow and red shirt and the black arm band.

MR. SCHULTZ: When you met the defendant Rubin at that time, did he look the way he looks now?

THE WITNESS: No, sir. His hair was very long and disarrayed, and his beard was possibly slightly longer.

MR. SCHULTZ: What happened after the conversation with Jordan, please?

THE WITNESS: Jordan brought me over and introduced me to Jerry Rubin. He said, "Jerry, this is Bob Levin. He will be your personal bodyguard. He can be trusted, and he handles himself well." Rubin shook my hand and said that he was glad to have me with him.

MR. SCHULTZ: Your name wasn't Levin at that time, was it, sir?

THE WITNESS: No, sir.

MR. SCHULTZ: What occurred after this introduction, please?

THE WITNESS: There was a commotion to the south of where Rubin and I were sitting, and we saw two men being placed in a squadrol. We walked over.

MR. SCHULTZ: What occurred when you arrived, please?

THE WITNESS: Rubin asked one of the people standing there what had happened, and they told him that Tom Hayden and Wolfe Lowenthal had been arrested.

MR. SCHULTZ: Did you have a conversation with Rubin at the time?

THE WITNESS: Well, as we were walking away, Rubin kicked at the ground and said, "F—n' pigs," and he said, "We cannot stand a bust, especially from one of the Federal pigs."

MR. SCHULTZ: Let me just interrupt you and ask you if you know what the word "bust" means?

THE WITNESS: It means "arrest," and he said that "tonight, we're going to hold the park, and if we're pushed into the streets, we're going to . . ." again, f—up the Old Town area.

MR. SCHULTZ: During this conversation, did anyone have occasion to join you and Rubin?
THE WITNESS: Yes, sir, a girl by the name of Nancy joined us.
MR. SCHULTZ: After Nancy joined you and Rubin, what occurred, please?
THE WITNESS: We walked across the park over to where the large group of people had gathered which was west of the sidewalk. A person came out and met us. He was one of the marshals.
MR. SCHULTZ: What, if anything, was said, please?
THE WITNESS: He told Rubin that a march was being formed to go down to Police Headquarters to free Rubin and Lowenthal.
MR. SCHULTZ: What did you do then?
THE WITNESS: I then went and got my motorcycle, drove over to 12th and State, parked the motorcycle, and I met the march at about 9th and State.
MR. SCHULTZ: Did you have occasion to meet Rubin in the march?
THE WITNESS: Yes, sir. I did.
MR. SCHULTZ: Now when you arrived at police headquarters, did you see any policemen in the area?
THE WITNESS: Yes, there were uniformed officers in front of the building on State Street and on the side of the building on 11th Street. Rubin said, "There are too many pigs here. Let's go to the Hilton."
We went east on 11th to Michigan Avenue and then north on Michigan Avenue. When the march was midpoint past the Logan statue, the crowd broke and ran up the statue screaming, "Take the hill."
They climbed the statue and displayed the Viet Cong flag, the red flag and the black flag.
MR. SCHULTZ: Now, did Rubin say anything at this time, at the time the people were rushing up with the flags?
THE WITNESS: While looking at the people rushing up the hill to the statue and seeing the flags, Rubin said that this was better than Iwo Jima.
MR. SCHULTZ: What occurred after the people went up to the top of the statue and Rubin made this statement?
THE WITNESS: I saw Rennie Davis with the microphone and the loudspeaker system.
MR. SCHULTZ: Did you hear what Davis at this time was saying on the megaphone?
THE WITNESS: Davis said, "Hold the statue. Don't let the pigs move you out."
MR. SCHULTZ: All right, now, Mr. Pierson, calling your attention to the next day which is Tuesday, August 27, did you have occasion to go to Lincoln Park on that day?
THE WITNESS: Yes, sir, I did.
MR. SCHULTZ: Did you have occasion to meet with Jerry Rubin?
THE WITNESS: Yes, sir. Rubin and I sat and talked for a while.
MR. SCHULTZ: And while you were sitting and talking, what occurred, please?
THE WITNESS: We saw some people tacking newspaper articles on some trees that were right along here. The first article that I remember looking at had the headline, "The Battle of Chicago." When looking at this article, Rubin said to me that we have got to create little Chicagos everywhere, that we've got to have riots in every city. I told him that he could count on my being wherever he wanted me to go and to protect him from being arrested by the pigs.
MR. SCHULTZ: Do you recall any additional articles that the two of you looked at?
THE WITNESS: Yes, sir, we again walked over to another tree where there was another picture and another article. One of the pictures showed a policeman with a club, and Rubin looked at me and said, "Look at that fat pig. We should isolate one or two of the pigs and kill them."
MR. SCHULTZ: What did you say?
THE WITNESS: I agreed with him, and then we walked over to a group of marshals that were sitting on the west side of the sidewalk in the park.
MR. SCHULTZ: Would you relate the conversation that occurred at this time?
THE WITNESS: Yes, sir. Rubin, afer sitting down, said to the marshals, "We've got to

do more to keep the crowd active so that we have them to help hold the park tonight," and "We want them in the park for the Bobby Seale speech that is going to be here tonight."

MR. SEALE: I object on the ground my lawyer Charles R. Garry is not here. You know my lawyer is not here, your Honor, and I want my lawyer here to speak when he mentions my name and testifies against me.

THE COURT: Ask him to sit down, Mr. Marshal, please.

THE MARSHAL: Sit down, Mr. Seale.

MR. SCHULTZ: Your Honor, this little episode for the benefit of the jury is intended simply to misconstrue the fact that this man originally had four lawyers to start with, and I think that should be on the record in front of the jury.

MR. KUNSTLER: Your Honor, I object to calling it a little episode for the benefit of the jury. I think he should be admonished for it.

THE COURT: I will direct the jury to disregard the incident but I shall deal appropriately in due course with the incident.

MR. KUNSTLER: I make an objection to your Honor's last remark.

THE COURT: I overrule your objection, sir.

MR. SCHULTZ: Would you continue to relate the conversation, please?

THE WITNESS: Yes, sir. One of the marshals asked Rubin, "Jerry, did you see the newspaper articles on the tree and did you see the pictures of the newsmen that had been injured?" Rubin said, "Yes." And the marshal said, "Now the newsmen will be on our side." And Rubin agreed, and then Rubin also said that now we have the newsmen on our side, now we need the people on our side. One of the ways to get this would be to start fires in the Loop that would cause the armed forces and police to come out in force, and it would show the people all over the country that we are living in a police state.

MR. SCHULTZ: What occurred then?

THE WITNESS: Nancy, Rubin and I went over to a tavern to make a telephone call, but just prior to going there, Rubin said to me that he would like to have the—take the crowd in Lincoln Park down to Grant Park and Bobby Seale give his speech there, and I told him that it would be a good idea, that it would really foul up traffic at that time of day.

MR. SCHULTZ: Did you have a conversation with Rubin after he left the tavern?

THE WITNESS: Yes, sir, I did. Rubin said that he had contacted the Peace and Freedom people about having the Bobby Seale speech held at Grant Park and they had told him they did not want it there because there was too much of a chance of Seale's being arrested there. They would rather keep it in Lincoln Park where they could get him away if the pigs tried to arrest him.

MR. SCHULTZ: Now, on the way back to Lincoln Park from the tavern, was there any conversation?

THE WITNESS: Yes. Rubin said to me that Abbie Hoffman had had a meeting with the Blackstone Rangers earlier that day, Tuesday, and that the Blackstone Rangers had agreed to come to Lincoln Park and help hold the park and fight the pigs. Rubin told me that he did not believe that they would do this and asked me what I thought, and I told him that I agreed with him, I also did not believe that the Rangers would come and join in the fight.

MR. SCHULTZ: All right. Now what, if anything, occurred after this conversation when you arrived in Lincoln Park?

THE WITNESS: Two people walked up to us. One of them had an aerosol can and another a plastic bag. The man with the plastic bag said to Rubin, "We are going to fill this bag with human shit and we are going to throw it at the pigs tonight." And Rubin laughed and said, "Good. It will make good food for the pigs."

MR. SCHULTZ: Had you made any notes earlier that day?

THE WITNESS: Yes, sir.

MR. SCHULTZ: What had you done with the notes that you had made, Mr. Pierson?

THE WITNESS: When I was not with Rubin and I was standing a short distance away, I would get the attention of one of the Chicago Police Intelligence personnel; I would wad up the note, throw it on the ground, and they would come and pick it up.

On other occasions I would go down in the washroom in the field house and leave notes after again getting the attention of one of the Intelligence personnel and leave the note behind the plumbing facilities down there.

MR. SCHULTZ: At about seven o'clock in the area where the people were assembling, what, if anything, occurred?

THE WITNESS: We sat down and one man gave a speech and then Phil Ochs sang a song and as Phil Ochs was completing his song, Bobby Seale, Stew Albert, some of the Black Panthers and some of the Headhunters arrived and stood right next to where we were seated.

MR. SCHULTZ: What occurred at the time that Albert arrived with Bobby Seale?

THE WITNESS: Well, Phil Ochs completed his song and then Jerry Rubin gave a talk and after his talk Bobby Seale gave a talk.

MR. SCHULTZ: Do you recall any of what the defendant Rubin said?

THE WITNESS: Yes, sir. Rubin said that America is not free and that the elections are phony.

He also said that we have got to disrupt or stop the election on Election Day.

He said that we have got to become fighters and take this country away from the people that run it and we have got to take to the streets in small groups, and I believe he ended his speech with "See you in the streets tonight."

MR. SCHULTZ: Now afer Rubin spoke, who spoke next please, if anyone?

THE WITNESS: Bobby Seale.

MR. SCHULTZ: Do you recall any of the speech made by Bobby Seale?

THE WITNESS: Yes, sir. Again it was long but I remember part of it.

In some of the speech, he made mention of Huey Newton and some of the other people in the Black Panther Party. He also said that the time for singing "We Shall Overcome" is past, that now is the time to act, to go buy a .357 Magnum, a .45, and a carbine and kill the pigs, that we've got to break up into small groups, and create guerrilla warfare everywhere, that we can no longer be arrested in large groups or killed in large groups, that we've got to break into small groups and surround the pigs.

MR. SCHULTZ: Mr. Pierson, when the defendant Rubin was speaking, what was the crowd doing?

THE WITNESS: Well, at different points during the speech, they would applaud and cheer.

MR. SCHULTZ: And when the defendant Seale spoke, what, if anything, did the crowd do?

THE WITNESS: The exact same thing. They would applaud and cheer.

MR. SCHULTZ: At about 11:30 at night, that is, Tuesday night, August 27, 1968, were you still with Rubin, Mr. Pierson?

THE WITNESS: Yes, sir, I was.

MR. SCHULTZ: What occurred in your presence and Rubin's presence at about 11:30 that night?

THE WITNESS: The police asked the crowd to leave the park. When no one left, the police began to advance in a line across the park. When they got maybe twenty-five or thirty feet away, the crowd began to pelt the police with these rocks, and bottles, and other objects that they had gathered. The police then came and they had a truck with lighting equipment on it, and they had some tear gas guns on it, and they shot the tear gas into where we were. We would run a short distance until we got away from the tear gas, and then we would stand and continue yelling, and screaming at the police.

MR. SCHULTZ: You say, "We would stand and yell and scream." Would you describe, would you tell us first who "we" is?

THE WITNESS: Well, "we" would be Rubin, Albert, Nancy, Judy, Vince, Al, myself, and a number of unidentified people.

MR. SCHULTZ: Was Rubin yelling at the police?

THE WITNESS: Yes, sir.

MR. SCHULTZ: All right, now, where did you go, please?

THE WITNESS: We went on to Clark Street right over here by this triangle.

MR. SCHULTZ: What occurred at that point?

THE WITNESS: There was a CTA bus heading in a southerly direction, and the people began kicking at the doors and trying to break the windows, and they began rocking the bus, trying to roll it over.

MR. SCHULTZ: Did Rubin do anything to the bus?

THE WITNESS: Not that I recall, no, sir.

MR. SCHULTZ: All right, after the group attacked the bus, what occurred next please?

THE WITNESS: We then continued to run westerly away from the police because by now, they were out of the park, coming onto Clark Street. As we were running Judy handed Rubin and I each a small bottle of paint. At this time, a police car had come east on Wisconsin and had parked. As we ran by it, we both threw the bottles of paint at the police car, and I didn't hit and I don't know that Rubin's bottle hit the police car either.

MR. SCHULTZ: After throwing the paint at the police car, Mr. Pierson, where did you go?

THE WITNESS: We then continued to run west and north off of Lincoln Avenue over to Armitage.

MR. SCHULTZ: What occurred near Cleveland and Armitage, please?

THE WITNESS: We ran west on Armitage to Cleveland and Armitage. At this intersection, Judy took a match and lit a large barrel, trash barrel on the corner, and started it on fire. We then ran another half a block west of Cleveland on Armitage, and at this time, a CTA bus was going west on Armitage. Al and Stew Albert threw rocks at the bus, and I remember Al, the one he threw, went right through the bus window. We then ran further west.

MR. SCHULTZ: Actually, did you observe Rubin throw any rocks at that bus?

THE WITNESS: No, sir, I don't recall him throwing any.

MR. SCHULTZ: Then what occurred, please?

THE WITNESS: Then we got to a porch about a block-and-a-half west of Cleveland on Armitage. We walked up on the porch, sat down and laughed about what we had done, and sat and watched the Fire Department respond and put out the fire, and then we saw the different cars respond to approximately where the bus had been rocked.

MR. SCHULTZ: All right. Now, calling your attention to Wednesday, August 28, at approximately eleven o'clock in the morning, would you tell the Court and the jury, please, where you went, Mr. Pierson?

THE WITNESS: I went back to Lincoln Park.

MR. SCHULTZ: Whom did you meet in Lincoln Park, please?

THE WITNESS: I met Wolfe Lowenthal, a fellow by the name of Steve, a girl by the name of Mary, and myself, and we went in Steve's car, which was a Volkswagen, from Lincoln Park to Grant Park.

MR. SCHULTZ: Did you meet anybody in Grant Park across from the Hilton?

THE WITNESS: Yes, sir, I met Jerry Rubin, Stew Albert, Nancy, Judy, Vince, Al and this other girl that had been with us on Tuesday night.

MR. SCHULTZ: Where did you go, please?

THE WITNESS: We walked over up Balbo to Columbus and cut through the park there and went over to the Bandshell.

MR. SCHULTZ: Mr. Pierson, will you relate the conversation that you had with Rubin shortly after arriving in the park?

THE WITNESS: Rubin told me that Robin was going to bring a live pig to the Bandshell and that he wanted me to go with him and take the live pig up on the stage when he gave his speech because this would cause the police to come in to retrieve the pig and would cause a confrontation between the crowd and the police.

Rubin said that he and Abbie Hoffman, Tom Hayden, Bobby Seale and other out-of-state leaders had gone to their out-of-state people and told them to bring back to their home cities the revolution that had started in Chicago, and that two of the issues that were good to keep pushing with the people were the Vietnam issue and the civil rights issue as these kept the crowds together.

MR. SCHULTZ: Calling your attention to the middle of the afternoon, about three o'clock in the afternoon, do you recall any specific incident that occurred while you were with Rubin?

THE WITNESS: Yes, sir, there was a flag-lowering incident.

MR. SCHULTZ: Would you relate what occurred, please, while you and Rubin were standing there?

THE WITNESS: A few people had lowered the American flag and had raised a red flag or attempted to raise one. At this time the police moved in to retrieve the American flag.

MR. SCHULTZ: Then what occurred, please?

THE WITNESS: Then as this happened, the crowd began to pelt the police with various objects. The crowd then surged toward the police and Rubin and I and Stew Albert and others that were with us were surging toward the police, and at this time a marked police car came from behind us.

When it got to the midst of where Rubin, Stew Albert and others that we were with were standing, the crowd began to jump on the car and try to roll the car over. Rubin began to yell, "Kill the pigs! Kill the cops!"

The police car finally got out of the crowd and got over to in front of the flagpole. Rubin continued to scream "Kill the pigs! Kill the cops!"

When the police got out of the car, they were hit with various objects that were thrown from the crowd.

At this time there was an announcement on the stage of the Bandshell by Steve telling the crowd sit down, don't attack the police and they won't attack you. The crowd began to sit down and Rubin ran over and screamed at Steve to stay off of the microphone and let the crowd do their thing. The crowd by this time, though, had begun to settle down and sit down.

Rubin walked over to where Stew Albert and I were, and he said, "Robin is here, he has the live pig. Let's go get the pig and start it all over again."

We than walked around the crowd over to where Robin was supposed to have his car and have the live pig in the car.

We walked around the back of the crowd and we saw two people that I recognized and one of them said, "There's Pierson."

With that I told Rubin that I would meet him a little later, that I had to go over and use the washroom. So I turned around and left.

MR. SHULTZ: Where did you go, please?

THE WITNESS: I went over onto Columbus Drive by the sidewalk and listened to some of the other speeches and then later I went over and reported to Deputy Superintendent Rochford.

MR. SCHULTZ: Did you discontinue your undercover surveillance at that time?

THE WITNESS: Yes, sir, I did.

MR. SCHULTZ: No more questions on direct examination.

THE COURT: Who will cross-examine this witness?

MR. KUNSTLER: We have one request, your Honor.

(jury excused)

October 9, 1969

THE COURT: I will hear you, Mr. Weinglass.

MR. WEINGLASS: Yes. If your Honor please, this motion seeks to have the Court instruct the jury that they be permitted to take notes of the proceeding. I think we are all in agreement that this will be a long, a lengthy trial.

What we are interested in in the trial of this matter is a well-reasoned verdict by the jury based upon an intelligent evaluation of all of the evidence and in a matter as complicated as this case, as lengthy as we think it will take, we think that process will be aided appreciably if the jury would be permitted to take notes on the testimony.*

THE COURT: Will the Government reply?

MR. FORAN: Your Honor, the way to assure that the jury is not misled as to facts is for counsel for both sides to fulfill their obligation and not argue matters not in evidence at the close of the case and for the judge to properly rule upon objections in the course of the argument on the misrepresentation of fact by counsel.

Since it is within the sound discretion of the Court* and generally is strongly disapproved by trial judges on the assumption that counsel will fulfill their obligations to argue properly, the Government objects to it.

THE COURT: Mr. Weinglass, I have had similar motions made—not often in the many years I have served on this bench. And I on those occasions have declined to permit the taking of notes by jurors in the belief that the possibility that such notes will serve to aid recall during deliberations is outweighed by a number of important disadvantages.* There is a danger that if some jurors elect to take notes while others do not, those who do take notes will derive therefrom undue influence during the course of deliberations.

It would clearly be prejudicial to the Government for such note-taking to begin after part of the Government's case has already been presented.

I have never permitted it to be done. It is a matter within my discretion, and accordingly I exercise my discretion and against this motion.

Mr. Clerk, the defendants' motion for the Court to instruct the jury that they may take notes during the course of the trial will be and is denied.

Testimony of Robert Pierson Resumed

(jury enters)

THE COURT: Who will cross-examine the witness, Robert Pierson?

MR. KUNSTLER: Mr. Pierson, your father is a retired police lieutenant, is that correct?

THE WITNESS: Yes, sir, he is.

MR. KUNSTLER: Is your uncle in the Chicago Police Force today?

MR. SCHULTZ: Objection.

THE COURT: I sustain the objection.

MR. KUNSTLER: Your Honor, we can show an interest, I think, a family connection. I don't see where that is objectionable.

THE COURT: There is nothing to indicate here that this witness' relatives are involved. I will let my ruling stand, sir.

MR. KUNSTLER: Mr. Pierson, from 1963 to date, have you spent any time in a hospital for mental reasons, for treatment of any mental condition?

THE WITNESS: No, sir.

MR. KUNSTLER: You have not?

THE WITNESS: I have not.

MR. KUNSTLER: Mr. Pierson, was your discharge from the army for medical reasons?

THE WITNESS: My discharge from the United States Army was an honorable discharge after serving my full period of time.

MR. KUNSTLER: Was it for medical reasons? Was it a medical discharge?

THE WITNESS: No, it was after serving my period of time.

MR. KUNSTLER: Mr. Pierson, I am going to show you Defendants' D-20 for identification and ask you if you know what that magazine is.

THE WITNESS: Yes, sir, I do. It is *Official Detective* magazine, the December 1968 issue.

MR. KUNSTLER: Does it contain an article by you about the events in Chicago in August 1968?

THE WITNESS: It contains an article for which I signed a release on a byline by me. A Mr. Brannon mailed to me a list of, I believe it was either twenty-two or twenty-four questions to which I sent answers to those questions.

MR. KUNSTLER: Were you paid for this article?

THE WITNESS: Yes, one hundred dollars.

MR. KUNSTLER: After you read the article, did you find some things were inaccurate in it?

THE WITNESS: Many things that were inaccurate as far as what I had told Mr. Brannon.

MR. KUNSTLER: Is it your testimony that the inaccurate statements in here are not statements which you made to Mr. Brannon? That is all I am asking.

THE WITNESS: That is true .

MR. KUNSTLER: Now, at some time during your period in Lincoln Park of the times you have testified, August 23 through August 28, were you, yourself, struck by a police club?

THE WITNESS: Yes, sir, I was.

MR. KUNSTLER: How many times did that occur?

THE WITNESS: Two or three times.

MR. KUNSTLER: At that time, were you throwing rocks?

THE WITNESS: I was standing with a group that had thrown objects at the time that I was with them.

MR. KUNSTLER: I would like the witness to be directed to answer yes or no.

THE COURT: You may answer that question yes or no if you can.

THE WITNESS: No, I was not.

MR. KUNSTLER: Did you ever throw rocks at the police during any of these days in the park?

THE WITNESS: Yes, I did.

MR. KUNSTLER: When was that?

THE WITNESS: On Monday night.

MR. KUNSTLER: Did you hit any policemen?

THE WITNESS: No, I did not.

MR. KUNSTLER: Did you ever call policemen "pigs" during this period of time?

THE WITNESS: I referred to them as pigs.

MR. KUNSTLER: Did you ever scream during any of this period of time any epithet whatsoever?

THE WITNESS: Yes, I would join in some of the chants that were yelled at the police during that time I was assigned to this undercover assignment.

MR. KUNSTLER: Were you given instructions to call cops "pigs" and throw things at them? Was that part of your assignment?

THE WITNESS: No.

MR. KUNSTLER: You volunteered for this assignment, didn't you?

THE WITNESS: Yes, sir, I did.

MR. KUNSTLER: When did you first get the apartment on the North Side, after August 16, or before?

THE WITNESS: The apartment was not one which I rented. It was an apartment belonging to a member of our staff, and I merely used it during this period of time.

MR. KUNSTLER: Were you there alone or with somebody?

THE WITNESS: There were times I was there alone, and there were other times I was there with someone.

MR. KUNSTLER: Was a person named Sunny with you at any time at that apartment?

THE WITNESS: Yes.

MR. KUNSTLER: That is a girl, is it not?

THE WITNESS: Yes, it is.

MR. KUNSTLER: And how much time did she spend there?

THE WITNESS: I don't recall.

MR. KUNSTLER: Did she stay overnight?

THE WITNESS: No, sir.

MR. KUNSTLER: Do you know who Sunny is?

THE WITNESS: Yes, sir.

MR. KUNSTLER: Who is she?

THE WITNESS: One of the members, a female member of the cyclists' gang.

MR. KUNSTLER: When you testified before the grand jury, do you recall testifying about Mr. Hoffman and Mr. Rubin? I am talking about the incidents in which they said something about "We are going to create little Chicagos everywhere," or words to that effect.

THE WITNESS: I believe I was asked questions about those events, yes.

MR. KUNSTLER: I will show you your grand jury testimony, D-19, and ask you if anywhere in that testimony you related to the grand jury anything about these statements. I think you will find Mr. Hoffman's on 172.

THE WITNESS: Thank you.

MR. KUNSTLER: Does that contain any reference to creating little Chicagos anywhere?

THE WITNESS: I do not see it here.

MR. KUNSTLER: Mr. Pierson, do you have your statement in front of you, the statement you made? It is our Exhibit No. 22.

THE WITNESS: My police report, sir? Yes, sir, I do.

MR. KUNSTLER: Would you look through that and see where there is any reference to this language attributable either to Mr. Hoffman or Jerry Rubin?

THE WITNESS: No, sir, I do not find any.

MR. KUNSTLER: You do not find any?

THE WITNESS: No, sir.

MR. KUNSTLER: Thank you. I have no further questions, your Honor.

MR. WEINGLASS: You spent Friday, Saturday and Sunday establishing your cover as an agent with the Headhunters, isn't that correct?

THE WITNESS: That is, as well as talking to the various groups of people in the park.

MR. WEINGLASS: When your cover was established by Sunday, you were then intro-duced to Abbie Hoffman and Jerry Rubin on Monday, is that correct?

THE WITNESS: I was introduced to them on Monday, yes.

MR. WEINGLASS: By this same gentleman by the name of Fred Jordan?

THE WITNESS: That is correct, sir.

MR. WEINGLASS: Who did you meet at the Headhunters? Who was your first contact with the Headhunters?

THE WITNESS: A fellow by the name of Banana.

MR. WEINGLASS: When you met him, were you alone or were you with Sunny?

THE WITNESS: I believe I had been talking to Sunny when I met Banana.

MR. WEINGLASS: Wasn't it, in fact, Sunny, the female motorcyclist, who introduced you to Banana?

THE WITNESS: It is possible that she did. I don't recall just how we met.

MR. WEINGLASS: Is there any particular reason why you can't recall who introduced you to Banana but you do recall who introduced you to Rubin and Hoffman?

THE WITNESS: No particular reason.

MR. WEINGLASS: The reason you are having difficulty can't be attributed to any sensitivity over Sunny's role in all this, could it?

THE WITNESS: No sensitivity at all.

MR. WEINGLASS: That was the first time you ever met Sunny, was Friday?

THE WITNESS: I had seen her before but the first time I was with her was on Friday.

MR. WEINGLASS: Where had you seen Sunny before?

MR. SCHULTZ: Objection, if the Court please.

THE COURT: I sustain the objection.

MR. WEINGLASS: Sunny didn't know you were a police officer, did she?

MR. SCHULTZ: Objection, if the Court please.

THE COURT: I sustain the objection.

MR. WEINGLASS: You took Sunny back with you to your apartment, isn't that correct?

THE WITNESS: It was not my apartment, as I believe I stated, sir. It was an apartment belonging to one of our Assistant State's Attorneys, and she was present in that apartment on occasions where I would be making notes, yes, sir.

MR. WEINGLASS: And did Sunny observe you making notes?

THE WITNESS: I don't believe that she was watching me when I made notes at any particular time.

MR. WEINGLASS: Weren't you somewhat concerned that Sunny would find out that you were a police officer?

MR. SCHULTZ: Objection.

THE COURT: I sustain the objection.

MR. WEINGLASS: Was any attempt made by you to hide the fact that you were a police officer while you were in the apartment with Sunny?

MR. SCHULTZ: Objection.

THE COURT: I sustain the objection.

MR. WEINGLASS: Did you ever see the defendant Jerry Rubin in this period of time from Monday to Wednesday when you spent a good deal of time with him wearing a helmet?

THE WITNESS: No, sir, I did not.

MR. WEINGLASS: Now you came into the park Monday morning and you were in-troduced to Abbie Hoffman, is that correct?

THE WITNESS: Yes, sir.

MR. WEINGLASS: And it was during that period of time that you spent alone with him that he related to you that the park should be held that night, isn't that correct?

THE WITNESS: Yes, sir, among other things.

MR. WEINGLASS: Were there any witnesses to your private conversation with Abbie?

THE WITNESS: Not that I am aware of.

MR. SCHULTZ: His name, if the Court please, is Abbott Hoffman, not Abbie. I would ask that Mr. Weinglass refer to him by his proper name.

MR. WEINGLASS: Yes. I am sorry. Were you aware that there were two police officers who were following Abbie at a certain distance—Abbie Hoffman?

THE WITNESS: No, sir, I am not. I was not aware of that.

MR. WEINGLASS: Then after approximately an hour with Abbott Hoffman, you were introduced by the same gentleman to Jerry Rubin, am I correct on that?

THE WITNESS: I was subsequently introduced to Jerry Rubin.

MR. WEINGLASS: Where did you and Jerry Rubin go?

THE WITNESS: We walked east from the field house down the knoll and sat down and talked for a while.

MR. WEINGLASS: This was another private conversation you had with one of the defendants, is that correct?

MR. SCHULTZ: Objection, if the Court please, as to the form of the question.

THE COURT: I sustain the objection.

MR. WEINGLASS: Now, from the time that you met Jerry Rubin at either 12:30 or 1:00 until the time you left this park after the protest march was formed, did you ever see Jerry Rubin participating in a self-defense class which was being taught by the defendant Abbie Hoffman?

THE WITNESS: No, sir, I did not.

MR. WEINGLASS: And, I ask you if Officer Aznavoorian placed these two defendants there at that time, would he be mistaken?

MR. SCHULTZ: Mr. Weinglass is construing facts to suit himself, and then putting them in the witness' mouth and asking a question.

THE COURT: Do you object?

MR. SCHULTZ: I certainly do.

THE COURT: I sustain the objection.

MR. WEINGLASS: I can't phrase a question, I understand now, based on what a prior witness testified to?

THE COURT: I am ruling on the propriety of that question or the impropriety of it, Mr. Weinglass.

MR. WEINGLASS: Now, there was a "Free Hayden" protest march, as you describe it, being formed in the park after you were with Jerry Rubin for a period of time, correct?

THE WITNESS: Yes, sir, there was a march.

MR. WEINGLASS: Was anyone throwing anything from the line of march?

THE WITNESS: No, sir, I did not see anyone throw anything from the march.

MR. WEINGLASS: It was an orderly march, wasn't it, Officer?

THE WITNESS: To the best that I can recall, yes.

MR. WEINGLASS: The protest march proceeded to Logan statue, is that correct?

THE WITNESS: Yes, sir.

MR. WEINGLASS: Walking orderly toward the statue, is that correct?

THE WITNESS: No, they ran up the hill of the statue screaming, "Take the hill!"

MR. WEINGLASS: Aside from the young man who was up on the statue, did you see any arrests being made?

THE WITNESS: I don't recall, sir, any arrests made.

MR. WEINGLASS: You said Davis said, "Hold the statue. Don't let the pigs move you out." Is that correct?

THE WITNESS: To the best I recall, that is what he said.

MR. WEINGLASS: And after he said that, what did you see? Did anyone move to hold the statue?

THE WITNESS: Some remained, some left.

MR. WEINGLASS: Officer Pierson, you know as a law enforcement officer, is there anything illegal about a group of people in the middle of the day going up to the statue?

MR. SCHULTZ: Objection.

THE COURT: I sustain the objection.

MR. WEINGLASS: You testified that at a given point Tuesday morning, you once again found yourself alone with Jerry Rubin and had a private conversation with him?

THE WITNESS: After a period of time, yes.

MR. WEINGLASS: One of those comments, I believe you testified to, was Jerry Rubin said words to the effect that, "We should isolate one or two of the pigs and kill them." Is that correct?

THE WITNESS: That is correct, sir.

MR. WEINGLASS: Did you ask him where this was going to happen?

THE WITNESS: No, sir, I did not.

MR. WEINGLASS: Did you ask him who was going to do this?

THE WITNESS: No, sir, I did not.

MR. WEINGLASS: Did you ask him when this was going to happen?

THE WITNESS: No, sir, I did not.

MR. WEINGLASS: In other words, you didn't say anything after he said this to you?

THE WITNESS: I agreed with him that it should be done.

MR. WEINGLASS: Did you think it might be helpful for your superiors in order to protect the policemen to know these details?

THE WITNESS: I felt that any information that would be furthered toward this statement, I would learn, and I would have adequate time to notify my superiors.

MR. WEINGLASS: Now you also testified that you understood, I believe, in a conversation with Jerry Rubin that Abbie Hoffman had had a meeting with the Blackstone Rangers sometime prior to that time, and the Blackstone Rangers were coming into the park?

THE WITNESS: Yes.

MR. WEINGLASS: As a matter of fact, it was the Blackstone Rangers who discovered you on Wednesday, isn't that correct?

THE WITNESS: That is true, sir.

MR. WEINGLASS: Did you see any Blackstone Rangers in Lincoln Park on Tuesday?

THE WITNESS: Yes, sir, I did.

MR. WEINGLASS: How many did you see?

THE WITNESS: Very few. I saw none of what they refer to as the Main 21, or the principal members of the gang.

MR. WEINGLASS: Do you recall being asked the following question before the grand jury?

"In other words, you were never able to observe anything that would lead you to believe that the Blackstone Rangers or any other sizable Negro group in fact joined forces with the hippies to help hold the park?"

Do you recall that question?

THE WITNESS: I would have to say that I do recall that question.

MR. WEINGLASS: Well, what was the answer you gave to that question?

THE WITNESS: The answer is "Absolutely not. There was no gang or group that I know of, of Negro residents of our city that did in fact join with those people."

MR. SCHULTZ: Objection. That does not in any way whatever contradict his testimony. It is improper impeachment.

THE COURT: I strike the question and the answer, and direct the jury to disregard it.

MR. WEINGLASS: Officer Pierson, I think we are up to—going chronologically—Tuesday afternoon, August 27, late in the afternoon in Lincoln Park. There were a number of people assembled in the park for a rally, were there not?

THE WITNESS: There were different groups all over the park area, yes.

MR. WEINGLASS: Did Jerry Rubin indicate to you that this was to be a rally of the Peace and Freedom Party?

THE WITNESS: No, sir, he did not.

MR. WEINGLASS: Did Jerry Rubin indicate to you that he was, in fact, a Vice-Presidential candidate for the Peace and Freedom Party running on a national ticket with Eldridge Cleaver?

THE WITNESS: No, he did not.

MR. WEINGLASS: Now, who spoke?

THE WITNESS: I believe Jerry Rubin was the first to speak.

MR. WEINGLASS: Have you ever made a note of the speech?

THE WITNESS: Yes, sir, I made notes of the speech.

MR. WEINGLASS: Do you have these notes, Officer Pierson?

THE WITNESS: No, I do not. They were destroyed after my report was submitted.

MR. WEINGLASS: Do you remember Jerry Rubin talking about the oppression of black people in America?

THE WITNESS: I think he did make reference to that, yes, sir.

MR. WEINGLASS: Do you remember Jerry Rubin saying these words: "We're not interested in protecting the privileges of the white race because white people in this country have been oppressing blacks for the past hundreds of years, and we're a white generation that says finally, 'No, you're not going to continue.' If the cops are going to beat on blacks, they're going to beat on us, too."

Do you recall Jerry Rubin saying words to that effect?

THE WITNESS: In essence, sir, yes, sir.

MR. WEINGLASS: And do you recall Jerry Rubin expressing his criticism of the City of Chicago and the massive propaganda campaign that the City had engaged in to keep people away from the city and to reduce the size of the demonstration?

THE WITNESS: Some reference to that effect, yes, sir.

MR. WEINGLASS: When you say "some reference," Officer Pierson, what do you recall, if anything, he said about this?

THE WITNESS: Well, some of the things you are saying, sir, is bringing back to memory Rubin's speech of that night, and it was, as I say, a lengthy speech, and I merely reflected the main points.

THE COURT: We are at a point, Mr. Weinglass, where we usually recess.

(court is adjourned)

October 10, 1969

MR. KUNSTLER: Your Honor, we have moved to vacate the order of sequestration of the jury in this case which was made by your Honor's sua sponte motion on September 30, 1969.

We feel that the sequestration order itself, the fact that this jury will be sequestered for what appears to be a considerable period of time, can only serve to be of disadvantage to the defendants in this case.

First of all, they are incarcerated away from family and friends—

THE COURT: Not incarcerated.

MR. KUNSTLER: Well, they are in the custody of deputy marshals, they cannot go home, they cannot leave the custody of those marshals, they are dependent upon those marshals for almost all of the sustenance of life. The marshals take care of the hotel, the food and the wants and needs of those jurors.

We feel that such custody makes them or tends to make them antagonistic to the case itself and particularly to the defendants. It also places them in the custody of the United States which, as your Honor has pointed out, is the plaintiff in this action, and there will be a tendency toward them to favor the United States.

If the United States is to have them in custody, it would seem only fair that there ought to be observers, as there are in political situations, of both parties at their custody, what they see, what they read, what television they are shown, and so on, all of which can have a marked effect on these jurors. They see nothing of the defense whatsoever during their custody except in the courtroom. They see the presence of the United States Government, the plaintiff in this action, at every turn of their waking day and well into night. For all of these reasons, we respectfully ask that the sequestration order be vacated.

THE COURT: The motion, Mr. Clerk, of the defendants, styled "To vacate jury sequestration order," will be denied.

Bring in the jury, please.

(jury enters)

Testimony of Robert Pierson Resumed

MR. WEINGLASS: Mr. Pierson, when we stopped yesterday we were discussing the rally in Grant Park on Tuesday night, August 27, where you testified you heard Jerry Rubin deliver a speech to an assemblage and you also heard Bobby Seale deliver a speech to an assemblage, is that correct?

THE WITNESS: That is correct, sir.

MR. WEINGLASS: I believe you gave us some description of that assemblage; however, I would like to ask you whether or not—and you are an experienced police officer—looking out at that crowd you would describe that group of people as being a dangerous group of people?

THE WITNESS: No, sir, I would not.

MR. WEINGLASS: Would you describe that assemblage as an orderly gathering?

THE WITNESS: Yes, sir, I would.

MR. WEINGLASS: Now you heard Jerry Rubin speak for a period of time. Was there any change in the mood of that assemblage?

THE WITNESS: Not that I noticed.

MR. WEINGLASS: Did the group become violent in any way?

THE WITNESS: No, sir.

MR. WEINGLASS: Now, Officer Pierson, I am now going to direct certain questions to you concerning Mr. Seale's speech.

However, I would like to request the Court that I am not Mr. Seale's attorney, I am not questioning this witness with respect to the substantive counts against Mr. Seale. I am questioning him solely in my capacity as counsel for four of the alleged coconspirators.

THE COURT: Mr. Weinglass, you may cross-examine this witness. You may ask any questions you think are proper. You are not permitted to designate on whose behalf you are asking the questions.

MR. WEINGLASS: I just wanted the record to show clearly that I am not acting as Mr. Seale's attorney.

THE COURT: Mr. Weinglass, we have, I think, the most competent official reporter in the United States Courts of this district. Everything you say and anybody says here is for the record. Please don't remind me constantly what you are saying is for the record.

MR. WEINGLASS: Now, Officer Pierson, did you see Bobby Seale come to the park that night?

THE WITNESS: Yes, sir, I did.

MR. WEINGLASS: Did Jerry Rubin have any meeting at all while you were in his presence with Bobby Seale on the evening of August 27?

THE WITNESS: No, sir, he did not.

MR. WEINGLASS: Now Bobby Seale arrived with, I believe you said, several of—in the company of several persons, some of whom you described as Black Panthers?

THE WITNESS: Yes, sir.

MR. WEINGLASS: In the course of this employment have you had occasion to familiarize yourself with the Black Panther Party?

THE WITNESS: Limitedly, yes.

MR. WEINGLASS: Will you tell us what you know about the Black Panther Party?

MR. SCHULTZ: Objection, if the Court please. That doesn't qualify.

THE COURT: I sustain the objection. I am not trying any defendant, as far as I can see here, named the Black Panther Party. We are trying eight individuals.

MR. WEINGLASS: I believe the defendant Seale was introduced to this jury by the prosecutor as the Chairman of the Black Panther Party. I have a right to clarify—

THE COURT: He is not being tried as the Chairman.

MR. WEINGLASS: How long did Bobby Seale speak that night?

THE WITNESS: I believe his speech lasted anywhere from twenty minutes to a half hour.

MR. WEINGLASS: Did you hear Bobby Seale talk about the black and white community forming a black and white coalition around Huey Newton's defense?
THE WITNESS: Yes, I believe he did.
MR. WEINGLASS: Is there any particular reason why you didn't tell the jury when you were telling the jury what you heard Bobby Seale say, why you didn't tell the jury about the black and white coalition that he spoke of?
MR. SCHULTZ: Objection.
MR. WEINGLASS: You indicated at one point in his speech Mr. Seale said words to the effect that, "People should buy .357 Magnums—"
THE WITNESS: Yes, sir.
MR. WEINGLASS: "—and .45s."
THE WITNESS: Yes, sir.
MR. WEINGLASS: Did he also say they should keep them in their homes?
THE WITNESS: I don't recall that being said.
MR. WEINGLASS: Officer Pierson, you are a police officer, and I ask you this question. Is there anything illegal about buying a .357 Magnum?
MR. SCHULTZ: I object to the last question.
THE COURT: I sustain the objection.
MR. WEINGLASS: I ask you the same question about buying a shotgun. Is there anything illegal about that?
MR. SCHULTZ: Mr. Weinglass knows that is equally objectionable, and yet he is asking that. I object and ask the Court to order Mr. Weinglass not to intentionally ask questions that he knows are not proper in law.
THE COURT: I sustain your objection to the last question.
MR. WEINGLASS: Did Bobby Seale ever call for the assassination of Mayor Daley in his speech?
THE WITNESS: The best that I can recall of his speech is that during the speech, he made mention of killing the pigs. He made mention of various political leaders. Whether he in fact mentioned Mayor Daley as one of those political leaders, I do not recall.
MR. WEINGLASS: But the only reference to killing the pigs is when he talked about self-defense, and a pig unjustly attacking us in an unjust manner, that we have a right to barbecue some of that pork as a matter of self-defense, isn't that the context and the only context in which he referred to the pigs?
THE WITNESS: That is what you have said, Mr. Weinglass. That is not what I have said.
MR. WEINGLASS: Now did you discuss Bobby Seale's speech with the FBI?
THE WITNESS: I believe I was asked about the Bobby Seale speech, yes.
MR. WEINGLASS: Do you recall telling the agents that Bobby Seale said that—Bobby Seale called on the group to kill Mayor Richard J. Daley?
THE WITNESS: Again, Mr. Weinglass, those are not my exact words. Whether I specifically mentioned Mayor Daley or not, I do not know, but I don't recall those being my exact words.
MR. WEINGLASS: Do you recall having a second interview on September 27 wherein you were asked to comment about what Bobby Seale had said in Lincoln Park at approximately 6:30, August 27, 1968?
THE WITNESS: I was questioned by representatives of the FBI in the latter part of September.
MR. WEINGLASS: Do you recall telling Agent Garrish on September 27 that Bobby Seale told the crowd, "When the opportunity arises, kill Mayor Richard J. Daley himself"?
THE WITNESS: No, I do not recall using those exact words.
MR. WEINGLASS: Is that all you said about what he said about assassinating leaders?
THE WITNESS: Well, his speech, as I said before, had the words "barbecuing pork," which in my interpretation is killing the pigs.
MR. WEINGLASS: Did you ever attend a Black Panther Party rally?
MR. SCHULTZ: Objection.
THE COURT: I sustain the objection.
MR. WEINGLASS: Now in the front of your report, Officer Pierson, you have a list of common definitions, do you not?

THE WITNESS: Yes, sir.
MR. WEINGLASS: Yippie slang, isn't it, so that your superiors will be able to interpret the Yippie slang that is in your report, the common everyday usage, right?
THE WITNESS: Yes, sir.
MR. WEINGLASS: Do you also have a definition for Black Panther talk?
THE WITNESS: No, sir.
MR. WEINGLASS: Do you have any definition of what barbecuing the pork might mean?
MR. SCHULTZ: Objection, if the Court please.
THE COURT: I sustain the objection.
MR. WEINGLASS: Now, can you explain to the jury why you did not contain any reference to Mayor Daley in your report of September 9, or any threat of an assassination to Mayor Daley and why you insisted on telling the FBI on two separate occasions very explicitly Bobby Seale called for the killing of Mayor Daley himself?
MR. SCHULTZ: Objection. He didn't say that, if the Court please.
MR. WEINGLASS: You and Jerry Rubin and a few people had dinner and then you came back to Lincoln Park, isn't that correct?
THE WITNESS: That is correct, sir.
MR. WEINGLASS: How did things appear in the park when you got back?
THE WITNESS: Well, I got back and there was a pray-in, as they called it, being conducted. There were people walking around putting vaseline on their face, there were people gathering different objects to throw at the police.
MR. WEINGLASS: Did you see what occurred to that gathering of people later that evening when the police came into the park and gassed the people who were in the park?
THE WITNESS: Many things happened, Mr. Weinglass. Some people were throwing rocks and bottles and other objects at the police, and the police were advancing. They had a light truck, and there was gas shot into the crowd.
MR. WEINGLASS: Was there gas shot into the vicinity of the pray-in?
THE WITNESS: Yes, sir, where they were.
MR. WEINGLASS: Did you see these policemen beat these people and club the ministers?
THE WITNESS: I do not remember any police officer hitting any member of the ministry.
MR. WEINGLASS: Was this one of the nights you were throwing rocks at the police yourself?
THE WITNESS: I don't recall having thrown a rock on Tuesday night at the police.
MR. WEINGLASS: Is it possible you might have thrown a can or stick, or some other object to provoke the police?
THE WITNESS: I threw a bottle of paint later on that evening.
MR. WEINGLASS: Do you recall being asked by the grand jury the following question:
    "Mr. Pierson, did you ever observe, yourself, Jerry Rubin throw an object at the police?
MR. SCHULTZ: If the Court please, what he should do is ask him: "Did you see Jerry Rubin throw an object at the police?" If he says "yes," then he can read this question and answer.
THE COURT: It seems to me, Mr. Weinglass, those are two different situations.
MR. WEINGLASS: If your Honor please, I spent a good deal of time with this witness—
THE COURT: I have spent a good deal of time listening to you also. Do you want a gold star for the time you spent?
MR. KUNSTLER: Your Honor, I object to that, those insulting remarks to cocounsel.
THE COURT: I don't insult lawyers.
MR. KUNTSLER: Sir, you just have, your Honor.
THE COURT: Don't make a suggestion like that again, sir. If you will sit down, Mr.—
MR. KUNSTLER: Kunstler is the name, K-U-N-S-T-L-E-R.
THE COURT: I will let my ruling stand.
MR. WEINGLASS: Did you ever see Rubin throw an object at the police, Jerry Rubin?
THE WITNESS: At the police themselves, no.

MR. WEINGLASS: So when you testify that you saw Jerry Rubin throw a paint container at a police car, you were carefully drawing a distinction between throwing something at the police and throwing something at a car with police in it?

THE WITNESS: I definitely believe there is a difference, yes, sir.

MR. WEINGLASS: And when the grand jury asked you if Jerry Rubin ever threw anything at the police, you did not tell them about the police car incident, did you?

MR. SCHULTZ: Objection, if the Court please.

THE COURT: Sustained.

MR. WEINGLASS: Did you ever see Jerry Rubin bring a sleeping bag to the park for the purpose of staying all night?

THE WITNESS: No, sir, I did not.

MR. WEINGLASS: Did he ever attempt to stay and hold the park when the police came to the park?

THE WITNESS: Yes, we remained there Tuesday night and then when the police came and finally forced us about, we left.

MR. WEINGLASS: You left. People were fighting the police in the park?

THE WITNESS: Yes.

MR. WEINGLASS: People were throwing things?

THE WITNESS: Yes.

MR. WEINGLASS: People were engaged in hand-to-hand combat with the police?

THE WITNESS: Yes.

MR. WEINGLASS: But Jerry Rubin was leaving?

THE WITNESS: Yes, as I was, because of the tear gas. We were running away from it.

MR. WEINGLASS: There was no attempt on his part to fight the police?

THE WITNESS: Not to fight, no.

MR. WEINGLASS: Or to throw anything at the police?

THE WITNESS: I did not see him throw anything at the police at that time.

MR. WEINGLASS: Now on Wednesday at approximately 3:00 P.M., in the course of the rally, you testified on direct about a flagpole incident, is that correct?

THE WITNESS: Yes, sir, I did.

MR. WEINGLASS: Officers moved in to the flagpole area for the purpose of arresting the individual who took the flag down, is that correct?

THE WITNESS: The individual or individuals, and retrieved the American flag.

MR. WEINGLASS: Was the flag taken all the way down?

THE WITNESS: I believe it ultimately was, yes.

MR. WEINGLASS: Was the flag first lowered to half-mast?

THE WITNESS: I believe it was, yes.

MR. WEINGLASS: Do you know the flying of the American Flag at half-mast—do you know what signal that is intended to convey?

MR. SCHULTZ: Objection.

THE COURT: I sustain the objection.

MR. WEINGLASS: At what point did you begin to move toward the flagpole?

THE WITNESS: When the crowd began throwing the objects at the police, then we moved over to watch what was happening.

MR. WEINGLASS: So Jerry Rubin, yourself and Stew Albert moved over to watch?

THE WITNESS: Yes, we moved in toward the crowd at that time.

MR. WEINGLASS: Then a police car appeared on the scene?

THE WITNESS: Yes, that is correct.

MR. WEINGLASS: Did the crowd part to let the car go through?

THE WITNESS: No, sir, they jumped on the car and started to rock the car and tried to tip it over.

MR. WEINGLASS: Did you jump on the car and try to tip it over?

THE WITNESS: I was right next to the back of the car.

MR. WEINGLASS: You had your hands on the car, didn't you, Officer Pierson?

THE WITNESS: I had my hands on the car, yes.

MR. WEINGLASS: You were rocking that car, weren't you?

THE WITNESS: No, I was not.

MR. WEINGLASS: What were you doing with your hands on the car?

THE WITNESS: I just stood right there in the crowd so that I was not conspicuous.

MR. WEINGLASS: Jerry Rubin didn't have his hands on that car?

THE WITNESS: No, he did not. He at that time was yelling to kill the pigs, kill the cops.

MR. WEINGLASS: Were you trying to stop the rocking with your hands on the car?

THE WITNESS: Well, it happened so quick—I was not trying to rock it; I did not push on it to rock it. I was just right there. I, if anything, tried to stabilize it.

MR. WEINGLASS: Could you tell the jury what the crowd was yelling, if anything, if you heard anything as the car was going through the crowd?

THE WITNESS: Yes, sir. When the car went through the crowd, Rubin began yelling "Kill the pigs! Kill the cops!" And the crowd picked up the chant and hollered the same thing.

MR. WEINGLASS: When you left the park, you went to see a high-ranking police officer of the Police Department of the City, did you not?

THE WITNESS: Yes, sir, I did. I reported to Deputy Superintendent James Rochford.

MR. WEINGLASS: And then you went subsequently to the precinct, is that correct?

THE WITNESS: Yes, sir, I did.

MR. WEINGLASS: And your mission was over?

THE WITNESS: Yes, sir, it was.

MR. WEINGLASS: Now, isn't it a fact, Officer Pierson, that your mission failed?

MR. SCHULTZ: Objection, if the Court please.

THE COURT: I sustain the objection.

MR. WEINGLASS: No matter what you did during the course of the three days that you were with Jerry Rubin, you were unsuccessful in your attempt to encourage him to even throw a pebble, isn't that correct?

THE WITNESS: No, sir, it is not correct. I never tried to encourage him to do anything like that.

MR. WEINGLASS: Wasn't it you who threw the rocks at the police and not Jerry Rubin?

MR. SCHULTZ: Objection.

THE COURT: I sustain the objection.

MR. WEINGLASS: May I have the basis of the prosecutor's objection?

THE COURT: I have sustained the objection. I will let my ruling stand.

MR. WEINGLASS: Will the Court inform me of the basis of it since the prosecutor has not?

THE COURT: Just continue with your examination.

MR. WEINGLASS: Isn't it a fact that it was you who suggested that the park be held at night against the police to Jerry Rubin?

THE WITNESS: Absolutely not.

MR. WEINGLASS: Isn't it a fact that it was you who suggested that the Peace and Freedom rally be held in Grant Park to tie up the traffic?

THE WITNESS: No, sir, it was not.

MR. WEINGLASS: Wasn't it part of your mission to compromise the demonstrators by getting them into a position with the police whereby they would be committing criminal acts?

THE WITNESS: No, sir, it was not.

MR. WEINGLASS: Didn't you have a long discussion with the FBI about this very subject?

MR. SCHULTZ: Objection. Objection, if the Court please, as to whether or not he had a discussion with the FBI on this subject.

THE COURT: I sustain the objection.

MR. WEINGLASS: Isn't it a fact, Officer Pierson, that because you never saw Jerry Rubin do anything improper or commit any criminal act, that you had to invent these private conversations which were unwitnessed that you have testified to?

MR. SCHULTZ: Objection.

THE COURT: I sustain the objection.

MR. WEINGLASS: Now, in response to a question asked of you by Mr. Kunstler about the possibility of your confinement in Wesleyan Hospital, I believe you answered you had not been in Wesleyan Hospital, am I correct?

THE WITNESS: No, Mr. Kunstler asked me had I ever been confined to the hospital at Wesley Memorial Hospital. I repeated his question and then I answered no, I had not.

MR. WEINGLASS: Now, did you ever go to Wesley Hospital in the presence of and accompanied by a man by the name of Kloeckner for treatment during the year 1963 or 1964?

THE WITNESS: I recall your asking a question about a man by that name that I believe to be known as Mr. Gluckner. I did go over, I was taken over to the Wesley Memorial Hospital one evening for a short period of time and went home the same evening.

MR. WEINGLASS: Do you recall the reason for your going to the hospital that evening?

THE WITNESS: Sometime before that I had had an aerosol can explode and split my head open and split my nose and break the nose here. From that time I had had a few dizzy spells. On one occasion I happened to be in my father's office and I went down to my knees from one of these spells. He took me over to the Wesley Memorial Hospital to see if there was any problem.

MR. WEINGLASS: Now, from that time to the present have you received any additional treatment for the head injury?

THE WITNESS: I have had tests as a result of that, yes.

MR. WEINGLASS: Were the nature of those test neurological or orthopedic?

MR. SCHULTZ: Objection. We don't have to go into this man's medical history to determine the results of a face injury. There is no basis for this.

THE COURT: I sustain the objection.

MR. WEINGLASS: I have completed my cross-examination.

Your Honor, I would like to call the Court's attention to an oversight on my part. Mr. Seale is unrepresented and would like to conduct examination.

THE COURT: That is not true. Don't say that to me again. It is not true.

MR. SEALE: I would like to cross-examine the witness.

THE COURT: Your appearance is here on file.

MR. SEALE: What about my lawyer? He is not here, your Honor.

MR. WEINGLASS: His lawyer is Charles R. Garry of San Francisco.

THE COURT: I have heard that before.

MR. WEINGLASS: He is his attorney.

MR. SEALE: I still want to cross-examine the witness.

THE COURT: Call your next witness, please.

Testimony of Frank Riggio

October 13, 1969

MR. FORAN: Will you state your name, please?

THE WITNESS: Frank Riggio.

MR. FORAN: What is your occupation, Mr. Riggio?

THE WITNESS: I am a detective with the Police Department, City of Chicago.

MR. FORAN: Calling your attention to August of 1968 during the Convention, were you given any specific assignment?

THE WITNESS: I was to keep Rennie Davis under surveillance.

MR. WEINGLASS: At this point, this witness having identified himself now as a surveillance agent, on behalf of the defendant Rennie Davis I make the objection that a twenty-four-hour surveillance constitutes a constitutional invasion of a citizen's privacy contrary to the Fourth Amendment and I object to this witness being permitted to give any testimony in a court of law on the ground that his conduct constituted a violation of the United States Constitution.

THE COURT: I will overrule the objection.

MR. FORAN: Calling your attention to August 25, 1968, did you see either Davis or Hayden?

THE WITNESS: Yes, we were in Lincoln Park. My partner and I began to follow Mr. Davis and Mr. Hayden, who were walking together by themselves. They would come to a group of people and stop and talk and then proceed through the group, and then as my partner and I would try to follow, the group would close up and block our way and make it difficult for us to keep Mr. Davis and Mr. Hayden in sight.

MR. FORAN: How long did you follow them around the park that day?

THE WITNESS: Oh, approximately two hours.

MR. FORAN: As you were following them from group to group, at about that time, at ten o'clock, what occurred?

THE WITNESS: Mr. Davis and Mr. Hayden came to a group of people where they stopped and talked to Wolfe Lowenthal. As they stopped and talked to him, Mr. Davis began to proceed toward Stockton Drive. Mr. Hayden and Mr. Lowenthal began to walk off in a different direction. My partner and I began to return to our own vehicle.

MR. FORAN: As you approached the front of your vehicle, what happened?

THE WITNESS: As we approached the front of the vehicle, we could hear a hissing noise coming from the vehicle. We then proceeded around the side of the vehicle and we observed two figures crouched at the right rear tire. At this time, my partner and I shouted to the two figures and identified ourselves as police officers. As we approached the two figures stood up, one ran off—as I approached I noted it was Tom Hayden stood at the rear tire of the vehicle, I could see that the tire of the vehicle was, for all intents and purposes, flat.

I pursued the figure who had run off toward the group of people who were in the park at the time. He ran a short distance, stopped and turned around and faced me, at which time I grabbed him and began to bring him back to the vehicle. All this time my partner had stayed with Mr. Hayden at the rear of our vehicle.

MR. FORAN: Who was it, by the way, that you had?

THE WITNESS: It was Mr. Wolfe Lowenthal.

MR. FORAN: What happened when you got back to the vehicle?

THE WITNESS: When we got back to the vehicle we informed Mr. Hayden and Mr. Lowenthal that they were under arrest for the damage they had done to the squad car and we told them to get into the vehicle.

MR. FORAN: What happened at this time?

THE WITNESS: Mr. Hayden and Mr. Lowenthal at this time refused to get back into the vehicle, and they began to struggle with both my partner and myself. They began to pull

[85]

away from us, shove us. They braced themselves against the opening of the rear door and would not get into the vehicle.

During this time they began to shout, "Help! Get these policemen! Don't let these policemen arrest us! Help us! Don't let them get us!"

MR. FORAN: What happened then?

THE WITNESS: At this time the crowd began to run over to the vehicle and began to force my partner and myself along with Mr. Hayden and Mr. Lowenthal into the corner formed by our open door and the vehicle itself. The crowd began to scream, "We're not going to let you arrest them!" Somebody yelled, "Get their guns!" Another one yelled, "Get the police! Get these policemen and turn them over to us! We're not going to let you take them!"

MR. FORAN: What occurred then?

THE WITNESS: At this time we informed Mr. Hayden and Mr. Lowenthal that we couldn't possibly effect their arrest at this time but that on the next occasion that we saw them, we would place them under arrest, and at this time they ran off with the crowd of people.

MR. FORAN: What was the crowd doing as they ran off?

THE WITNESS: Screaming and clapping, jumping up and down.

MR. FORAN: Now, did you have occasion to see Hayden and Lowenthal again?

THE WITNESS: The next day I saw them, I believe it was the twenty-sixth of August, in Lincoln Park.

MR. FORAN: Did you see Hayden?

THE WITNESS: Yes. When we first saw them we stopped and informed a uniformed sergeant and a squad of uniformed policemen that our intention was to arrest these two men and to have them pull up a wagon as we approached the group.

MR. FORAN: What happened as you approached the group?

THE WITNESS: As we approached the group, Mr. Hayden and Mr. Lowenthal stood up and informed the group, "Here come the two coppers from last night. They are going to arrest us."

At this time, my partner and I walked into the group and informed Mr. Hayden and Mr. Lowenthal that they were under arrest, and at this time the squadrol had pulled up into the crowd.

MR. FORAN: Now, what did you do then?

THE WITNESS: As we began to walk Mr. Hayden and Mr. Lowenthal into the squadrol, the crowd began to scream, "You can't arrest them!" and "Why are you taking them?" and "We won't let you arrest them!"

MR. FORAN: Do you remember any particular persons in the crowd?

THE WITNESS: I remember one young lady and one young man in particular.

MR. FORAN: Do you know that man's name, Mr. Riggio?

THE WITNESS: Not offhand, no.

MR. FORAN: Will you look over there and see if you can find him at that table?

THE WITNESS: It is the fellow in the blue shirt sitting right over there [*Indicating*].

MR. FORAN: May the record show, your Honor, that the witness has identified Mr. John Froines?

MR. FORAN: Mr. Riggio, at that time did you have a conversation with Mr. Froines?

THE WITNESS: I did. The defendant said, "I demand to know why you are arresting these two." I informed him they were being arrested for a violation that had occurred the previous night. He then stated that, "We are not going to let you take them. If you try to take them all hell is going to break loose in this city."

MR. FORAN: What happened then?

THE WITNESS: At this time, with the help of the uniformed patrolmen, I got into the squadrol along with the defendants Hayden and Lowenthal, and proceeded to 1121 South State Street.

MR. FORAN: What did you do when you got there?

THE WITNESS: We began our normal booking procedures of the two defendants.

MR. FORAN: Calling your attention to later on that same evening, close to midnight, where were you?

THE WITNESS: We were at the intersection of Michigan and Balbo Avenue.

MR. FORAN: Who did you see there at the corner of Balbo and Michigan?

THE WITNESS: I saw the two defendants, Rennie Davis, Tom Hayden, and also Wolfe Lowenthal, crossing the intersection of Balbo.

MR. FORAN: What did you and your partner do at that time?

THE WITNESS: I fell into step behind Mr. Davis. My partner fell into step behind Mr. Hayden.

MR. FORAN: What, if anything, happened as you crossed the street?

THE WITNESS: I heard Mr. Hayden, who was a step or two in back of me, say, "Here he comes again," or "Here he is again." And then he said, "You," and he used a profanity.

MR. FORAN: What words did he call you?

THE WITNESS: He said, "Here he is again, you motherfucker." At that time I turned around and observed the defendant Hayden spit at my partner, at which time my partner grabbed Mr. Hayden and Mr. Hayden then fell to the street. The crowd was beginning to rush to the incident which was now occurring.

Mr. Davis turned and began to shout, "They've got Tom again. Let's go help Tom," and they began to rush back toward my partner and Tom Hayden. At this time, with the help of uniformed officers, we pushed the crowd back across Balbo Drive.

MR. FORAN: What did you do then?

THE WITNESS: At this time after the crowd had gotten back, I went back to my partner and Mr. Hayden, and we took Mr. Hayden to a squadrol and placed him in a squadrol.

THE COURT: I think we have reached the time when we normally recess.

October 14, 1969

THE CLERK: Your Honor, there are several motions. Motion on behalf of the defendants to suspend session of trial and for alternative relief.

THE COURT: Mr. Kunstler, I will hear you.

MR. KUNSTLER: Your Honor, we have made a motion for the suspension of the session of the trial schedule for tomorrow and your Honor has before you our motion together with an affidavit by both David Dellinger and Rennie Davis supporting the motion and the motion is based on the fact that tomorrow has been declared to be a day called Vietnam Moratorium.

THE COURT: By whom?

MR. KUNSTLER: I will get to that, your Honor.

THE COURT: That is very important at the outset.

MR. KUNSTLER: Yes. This was started some months ago by essentially a small group which was located on college campuses. It has spread rapidly throughout the United States and I call your attention to today's *Chicago Sun-Times* where the headline on page 28 is "Viet Moratorium Picks Up Support Here."

As your Honor sees in the affidavits it has been recognized by the officials of many cities.

The mayor of the city of New York announced the day before yesterday that flags would be flown at half-mast and he would participate in memorial services in respect to the Vietnam Moratorium.

The purpose of the moratorium, your Honor, is essentially to protest the continuation of the war in Vietnam and to urge withdrawal of American forces from that area. Just in passing, I think your Honor ought to know that there are at least eighteen United States senators and forty-seven congressmen who are also in direct support of the moratorium.

These defendants came to Chicago, your Honor, to bear witness against this brutal imperialist war. They feel they are prosecuted for doing so. They think it is very fitting and proper that they be permitted to join the millions of their countrymen who desire to put an immediate end to a course of national action which they and their millions of countrymen believe to be the height of utter immorality.

Now, your Honor, on the legal side of it, it is not unusual at all for courts to close in situations of this sort. Just recently when President Eisenhower died, the President of the

United States proclaimed a day of mourning and I am sure this court was closed as were others in the Chicago area and throughout the United States.

THE COURT: Yes, on order of the Executive, the President of the United States.

MR. KUNSTLER: We understand that. All I am using the illustration for is to show that it is not unusual to take what is not ordinarily a national holiday and to indicate that courts can close under such circumstances.

THE COURT: It is unusual here to shut down the courts and elsewhere, Mr. Kunstler, absent an order from a competent authority. I have received no order from the acting Chief Judge of the Court, and no order from the Executive Committee of the Court which is responsible for the administration of the court. I have had no order from the President of the United States through the Attorney General or any other authorized representative. I feel, therefore, that I am without the authority to allow this motion.

MR. FORAN: Your Honor, the Government would like to make some comment on Mr. Kunstler's motion.

Your Honor, these men have been charged by a Federal grand jury, and there has been some evidence presented in this case that these men partook in a cynical plan to use two of the tragic issues of American society, the war and the tragic flaw of American character, racism, to generate for themselves the right to tear down the legal and formal structure of the Government of the United States.

That these men should now with such cynicism ask to join what may well be a totally sincere effort by a great many people, American citizens, to protest a war—and I might add that many of us feel the tragedy of war, especially some of us who have fought in one —your Honor, it is a situation where there were photographs in the newspaper last week of some of these defendants participating in activities with the Weathermen group of the SDS who were doing their thing—

MR. KUNSTLER: Your Honor, I don't think this is any answer to a motion. A political speech is being given here by the prosecution. He hasn't answered—

THE COURT: I think yours was somewhat political—just a touch political, Mr. Kunstler.

MR. KUNSTLER: I fail to see where the Weathermen come in to the motion I have made.

MR. FORAN: The Weathermen, of course, your Honor, announced that their method of protest was to protest the war in Vietnam and the tragic flaw in the American character of racism. These men who would have offered support to that group would now intend to corrupt what may well be a sincere effort of many American citizens to protest the war and racism, and the Goverment suggests that the support of the ideals of this nation might well be better handled by all of us doing our duty including trying this case before this Court.

MR. KUNSTLER: If your Honor please, I think that the remarks of the United States Attorney are wholly uncalled for. It was just a personal attack on these defendants, who are making what is, I think, a rather fervent request before your Honor.

And I think it is as important, your Honor, to protest more than some thirty thousand American deaths and Lord knows how many Vietnamese deaths that have occurred in that country as it is to mourn one man in the United States, and if courts can close for the death of one man who lived a full life, they ought to close for the deaths of thousands and millions of innocent people whose lives have been corrupted and rotted and perverted by this utter horror that goes on in your name and my name—

THE COURT: Not in my name.

MR. KUNSTLER: It is in your name, too, in the name of the people of the United States.

THE COURT: You just include yourself. Don't join me with you. Goodness. Don't you and I—

MR. KUNSTLER: You are me, your Honor, because every citizen—you are a citizen the way I am a citizen.

THE COURT: Only because you are a member of the bar of this court am I obligated to hear you respectfully as I have done.

MR. KUNSTLER: No, your Honor, you are more than that. You are a citizen of the United States.

THE COURT: Yes, I am.

MR. KUNSTLER: And I am a citizen of the United States, and it is done in our name, in Judge Hoffman's name and William Kunstler's name.

THE COURT: That will be all, sir. I shall hear you no further. Mr. Clerk, the defendants' motion for an adjournment on October 15 or alternatively for permission to be absent from this Court on that day will be denied.

THE CLERK: There is another motion, your Honor, on behalf of the Government, for issuance of a subpoena upon Joseph Rhine.

MR. SHULTZ: Good morning, your Honor.

THE COURT: Mr. Shultz.

MR. SHULTZ: Your Honor, Mr. Rhine is a material witness on behalf of the Government, relating to the travel of the defendant Bobby Seale. Mr. Rhine has gone to Israel and we are asking the Court to issue an order permitting a subpoena to issue on the witness Joseph Rhine.

MR. WEINGLASS: If your Honor please, since this motion involves one defendant, as represented by the Government, and that is the defendant Seale, I would ask the Court's permission to have the defendant Seale argue this motion against the Government on his own behalf.

THE COURT: Mr. Seale has counsel.

MR. SEALE: I don't have counsel, Judge. I don't stand up because—

THE COURT: Mr. Kunstler filed his appearance for Mr. Seale. The record shows it orally and in writing, sir.

MR. WEINGLASS: I respectfully submit to the Court that Mr. Seale very strongly and explicitly indicated to this court that he has released all of his attorneys of record, that he appears in this courtroom with only one attorney and that is Charles R. Garry, and that that attorney is—

MR. SEALE: Hey, you don't speak for me. I would like to speak on behalf of my own self and have my counsel handle my case in behalf of myself.

How come I can't speak in behalf of myself? I am my own legal counsel. I don't want these lawyers to represent me.

THE COURT: You have a lawyer of record and he has been of record here since the twenty-fourth.

MR. SEALE: I have been arguing that before that jury heard one shred of evidence. I don't want these lawyers because I can take my own legal defense and my lawyer is Charles Garry.

THE COURT: I direct you, sir, to remain quiet.

MR. SEALE: And just be railroaded?

THE COURT: Will you remain quiet?

MR. SEALE: I want to defend myself, do you mind, please?

THE COURT: Let the record show that the defendant Seale continued to speak after the Court courteously requested him to remain quiet.

Bring in the jury, Mr. Marshal.

MR. KUNSTLER: Your Honor, he wants to defend himself. He has made a motion to that respect. The Constitution says that any man that wishes to defend himself may do so.

THE COURT: You speak of the Constitution as though it were a document printed yesterday. We know about the Constitution way out here in the Middlewest, too, Mr. Kunstler. You would be amazed at our knowledge of constitutional law.

MR. KUNSTLER: Isn't that a little unfair, your Honor? We are not here from different parts of the country—

THE COURT: I am getting a little weary of these thrusts by counsel and I don't want any more of them. I had occasion to admonish you before. Bring in the jury.

(jury enters)

THE COURT: You may cross-examine this witness, Mr. Kunstler.

MR. KUNSTLER: Thank you, your Honor.

Testimony of Frank Riggio Resumed

Mr. Riggio, my name is William Kunstler. I am one of the attorneys for the defendants. On Sunday, August 25, in Lincoln Park, you were arresting Hayden and Lowenthal —for what?

THE WITNESS: For obstructing us.

MR. KUNSTLER: As far as you know, how were they obstructing you?

THE WITNESS: If we had received an emergency call or any sort of communication from the squad operator we wouldn't be able to fulfill it with a flat tire.

MR. KUNSTLER: And then you indicated Mr. Hayden screamed for help.

THE WITNESS: Correct. Mr. Lowenthal also screamed.

MR. KUNSTLER: And then what happened?

THE WITNESS: A large group of people began to form around our vehicle.

MR. KUNSTLER: And you reached a decision that it would be the better part of discretion not to effectuate an arrest at that moment, is that correct?

THE WITNESS: Correct.

MR. KUNSTLER: Did anybody in that group strike you?

THE WITNESS: No, they did not.

MR. KUNSTLER: Did anybody in that group throw anything at you?

THE WITNESS: I don't recall them throwing. They may have.

MR. KUNSTLER: And when you last had contact with Lowenthal and Hayden, did you tell them you would arrest them the next day?

THE WITNESS: Before we released Lowenthal and Hayden to the crowd, we informed them that they would be arrested by us at the next convenient time.

MR. KUNSTLER: Now that brings us to Monday, August 26. There came a time when you saw Tom Hayden and Wolf Lowenthal?

THE WITNESS: Correct. They were in a group of people who were southeast of the field house.

MR. KUNSTLER: Did you find yourself in the center of this group again as you had the night before?

THE WITNESS: Yes.

MR. KUNSTLER: Now when you went to arrest Mr. Hayden or Mr. Lowenthal, the two of you, did Mr. Hayden or Mr. Lowenthal tell the crowd, "Help, get these coppers, keep them from arresting us," or anything similar to what you had heard the night before?

THE WITNESS: No, nothing like the night before. They just informed the crowd that they were being arrested.

MR. KUNSTLER: Did you explain when you were in the middle of this group with Mr. Hayden and Mr. Lowenthal why you were arresting them?

THE WITNESS: I believe we told them obstructing a police officer, resisting arrest, and I don't know if it was disorderly conduct in there too.

MR. KUNSTLER: But it is true, is it not, Officer, that these arrests that you were making there were for activities that occurred on another day, is that correct?

THE WITNESS. Correct.

MR. KUNSTLER: Did they offer any resistance at any time from the time you walked up to them and said, you are under arrest, and the time you took them and put them in the squadrol?

THE WITNESS: No, they did not.

MR. KUNSTLER: Detective Riggio, you had testified, as I recall, that Mr. Froines had demanded to know why you were arresting Lowenthal and Hayden. Then at that moment, as I remember, you indicated that Mr. Froines said something, demanding that you release the two men, or, as you put it, I think, "all hell would break loose in the city," is that correct?

THE WITNESS: Correct.

MR. KUNSTLER: You continued with the arrest, did you not?

THE WITNESS: Correct.

MR. KUNSTLER: Did all hell break loose in the city, to your knowledge?
THE WITNESS: My opinion, yes.
MR. KUNSTLER: Your opinion was all hell broke loose because of these arrests?
THE WITNESS: Yes.
MR. KUNSTLER: Were you somewhere where all hell broke loose after these arrests?
THE WITNESS: I was in the police building when the march occurred at the police building and I could observe what was occurring in the street.
MR. KUNSTLER: And that is what you call "all hell breaking loose?"
THE WITNESS: That is what I call "all hell breaking loose."
MR. KUNSTLER: Describe "all hell breaking loose."
THE WITNESS: The tie-up in the traffic around the police building, the fact that the police building had to be secured by police personnel at the entrance to the building, and the amount of people who were chanting and screaming and shouting outside the police building.
MR. KUNSTLER: That is what you characterize as "all hell breaking loose," is that correct?
THE WITNESS: That is what I do, yes.
MR. KUNSTLER: You are smiling when you say that. Is there any reason for that smile?
THE WITNESS: No reason for my smile.
MR. KUNSTLER: Did you see the marchers throw anything at the policemen?
THE WITNESS: I did not observe that long.
MR. KUNSTLER: How long did you observe?
THE WITNESS: A matter of a minute.
MR. KUNSTLER: It was in that minute that you made the determination that all hell had broken loose?
THE WITNESS. Correct.
MR. KUNSTLER: In your definition people marching on the sidewalk, crossing the street, shouting something which you could hear from the thirteenth floor, this was a definition of "all hell breaking loose" in Chicago?
THE WITNESS: Correct.
MR. KUNSTLER: And all of this, do you attribute to Mr. Froines' remarks in the park?
THE WITNESS: In my opinion, yes.
MR. KUNSTLER: You think he instigated all of that?
THE WITNESS: That is my opinion, yes.
MR. KUNSTLER: Detective Riggio, did you ever tell the FBI about the incident, forgetting Mr. Froines' name, did you tell them that an unknown male said these words to you in Lincoln Park?
THE WITNESS: Yes, I did.
MR. KUNSTLER: I will show you D-34, which is a report labeled FBI report on September 25, 1968. I ask you whether it in any way refreshes your recollection as to whether you told them about this incident by looking through the documents themselves?
THE WITNESS: I did tell them about this incident, yes. I don't have to look at the documents.
MR. KUNSTLER: There is no question in your mind that you told them?
THE WITNESS: I believe I did, yes.
MR. KUNSTLER: Now does any mention of that appear in any of those reports?
THE WITNESS: These are not my statements.
MR. FORAN: Object, your Honor.
THE COURT: I sustain the objection.
MR. KUNSTLER: After you had gone to the police station with Hayden and Lowenthal, did you go back to 407 South Dearborn to pick up Rennie Davis again?
THE WITNESS: I believe we went by there, yes.
MR. KUNSTLER: Did you finally find them again?
THE WITNESS: Yes, I did, shortly after midnight of the twenty-sixth.
MR. KUNSTLER: After you saw Davis, what did you do?
THE WITNESS: I fell into step behind Mr. Davis.
MR. KUNSTLER: Behind Mr. Davis. Where did Mr. Bell fall in step?

THE WITNESS: Behind Mr. Hayden.

MR. KUNSTLER: Now you have testified, I believe, there was a crowd of people in the vicinity, is that correct?

THE WITNESS: Correct.

MR. KUNSTLER: Is it your testimony that the crowd in some way interfered with the arrest of Mr. Hayden?

THE WITNESS: The crowd was not permitted to get to Officer Bell or Tom Hayden.

MR. KUNSTLER: And when you say the crowd was not permitted, what did the police officers say to the crowd?

THE WITNESS: The police officers told the crowd to go back along with me, and we held them back from going toward the incident that was occurring.

MR. KUNSTLER: When you say "held back," did you seize people? Did you grab them?

THE WITNESS: Grabbed people, pushed them, just kept people from running past.

MR. KUNSTLER: How many did you grab?

THE WITNESS: Oh, Mr. Davis and a few others.

MR. KUNSTLER: You grabbed Mr. Davis?

THE WITNESS: I didn't say I grabbed Mr. Davis. I held Mr. Davis from going back. I stopped Mr. Davis from going back.

MR. KUNSTLER: Where was Mr. Hayden?

THE WITNESS: Mr. Hayden was laying in the street toward the southwest corner of Michigan and Balbo Drive.

MR. KUNSTLER: How did Mr. Hayden get to the ground?

THE WITNESS: Mr. Hayden fell to the ground.

MR. KUNSTLER: Is it what you would call going limp?

THE WITNESS: I would call it that, yes.

MR. KUNSTLER: Mr. Hayden wasn't offering any resistance, was he?

THE WITNESS: Yes, he was, sir, by pulling away from Officer Bell.

MR. KUNSTLER: Do you recall seeing Officer Bell punch Mr. Hayden to the ground?

THE WITNESS: Officer Bell did not punch Mr. Hayden to the ground.

MR. KUNSTLER: Now, with Mr. Hayden on the ground, did the crowd throw anything at you?

THE WITNESS: Nothing struck me, sir.

MR. KUNSTLER: You weren't hit with any fists, were you?

THE WITNESS: No, I don't recall being hit.

MR. KUNSTLER: You weren't hit with any stones or sticks?

THE WITNESS: No, I was not.

MR. KUNSTLER: Brass knuckles?

THE WITNESS: I was not.

MR. KUNSTLER: I have no further questions.

THE COURT: With that I think we can recess for the day.

October, 15, 1969

MR. DELLINGER: Mr. Hoffman, we are observing the moratorium.

THE COURT: I am Judge Hoffman, sir.

MR. DELLINGER: I believe in equality, sir, so I prefer to call people Mr. or by their first name.

THE COURT: Sit down. The clerk is about to call my cases.

MR. DELLINGER: I wanted to explain to you we are reading the names of the war dead.

THE MARSHAL: Sit down.

MR. DELLINGER: We were just reading the names of the dead from both sides.

THE MARSHAL: Sit down.

THE CLERK: No. 69 CR 180. United States of America vs. David T. Dellinger, et al. Case on trial.

MR. KUNSTLER: Your Honor, just one preliminary application this morning. The defendants who were not permitted by your Honor to be absent today or to have a court recess for the Vietnam moratorium brought in an American flag and an NLF Flag which they placed on the counsel table to commemorate the dead Americans and the dead Vietnamese in this long and brutal war that has been going on.

The marshal removed those from the table. First he took the NLF Flag after directing me to order the client to have it removed which I refused to do, and then he removed it himself, and then subsequently he removed the American flag.

THE COURT: We have an American flag in the corner. Haven't you seen it during the three-and-a-half weeks you have been here?

MR. KUNSTLER: Yes, but we wanted the juxtaposition, your Honor, of the two flags together in one place.

THE COURT: Mr. Kunstler, let me interrupt you to say that whatever decoration there is in the courtroom will be furnished by the Government and I think things look all right in this courtroom.

MR. KUNSTLER: Your Honor, I am applying for permission to have both flags on this Vietnam Moratorium Day.

THE COURT: That permission will be denied. That is a table for the defendants and their lawyers and it is not to be decorated. There is no decoration on the Government's table.

MR. KUNSTLER: That is the Government's wish, your Honor. We don't tell them what to do or what not to do.

THE COURT: But I tell everybody what to do as far as the decorations of this courtroom are concerned and we are not going to have the North Vietnamese flag on the table, sir.

Your motion for flags to be placed on the table, flags of any nation, is denied, and at the same time I point out that standing in the courtroom—and it has been here since this building was opened—is an American flag.

ABBIE HOFFMAN: We don't consider this table a part of the court and we want to furnish it in our own way.

THE MARSHAL: Sit down.

THE COURT: I will ask you to sit down.

Bring in the jury, Mr. Marshal.

(jury enters)

MR. DELLINGER: We would like to propose—

MR. SCHULTZ: If the Court please—

MR. FORAN: Your Honor. If the Court please, may the marshal take that man into custody?

MR. DELLINGER: A moment of silence—

MR. SCHULTZ: Your Honor, this man—

THE COURT: Mr. Marshal, take out the jury.

(jury excused)

MR. DELLINGER: We only wanted a moment of silence.

MR. FORAN: Your Honor, this man has announced this on the elevator coming up here that he was intending to do this.

MR. DELLINGER: I did not. I would have been glad to, but I did not.

MR. FORAN: Your Honor, I object to this man speaking out in court.

THE COURT: You needn't object. I forbid him to disrupt the proceedings. I note for the record that his name is—

MR. DELLINGER: David Dellinger is my name.

THE COURT: You needn't interrupt my sentence for me.

MR. DELLINGER: You have been interrupting ours. I thought I might finish that sentence.

THE COURT: The name of this man who has attempted to disrupt the proceedings in this court is David Dellinger and the record will clearly indicate that, Miss Reporter, and I direct him and all of the others not to repeat such occurrences.

MR. KUNSTLER: Your Honor, I just want to object to Mr. Foran yelling in the presence of the jury. Your Honor has admonished counsel many times on the defense side for yelling, but particularly when the jury was halfway out the door.

MR. FORAN: Your Honor, that is outrageous. This man is a mouthpiece. Look at him, wearing an arm band like his clients, your Honor. Any lawyer comes into a courtroom and has no respect for the Court and acts in conjunction with that kind of conduct before the Court, your Honor, the Government protests his attitude and would like to move the Court to make note of his conduct before this court.

THE COURT: Note has been duly made on the record.

MR. KUNSTLER: Your Honor, I think that the temper and the tone of voice and the expression on Mr. Foran's face speaks more than any picture could tell.

THE COURT: Mr. Kunstler—

MR. FORAN: Of my contempt for Mr. Kunstler, your Honor.

MR. KUNSTLER: To call me a mouthpiece, and for your Honor not to open his mouth and say that is not to be done in your court, I think that violates the sanctity of this court. That is a word that your Honor knows is contemptuous and contumacious.

THE COURT: Don't tell me what I know.

MR. KUNSTLER: I am wearing an armband in memoriam to the dead, your Honor, which is no disgrace in this country.

I want him admonished, your Honor. I request you to do that. The word "mouthpiece" is a contemptuous term.

THE COURT: Did you say you want to admonish me?

MR. KUNSTLER: No, I want you to admonish him.

THE COURT: Let the record show I do not admonish the United States Attorney because he was properly representing his client, the United States of America.

MR. KUNSTLER: To call another attorney a mouthpiece and a disgrace for wearing a black armband—

THE COURT: To place the flag of an enemy country—

MR. KUNSTLER: No, your Honor, there is no declared war.

MR. HAYDEN: Are you at war with Vietnam?

THE COURT: Any country—

Let that appear on the record also.

Bring in the jury. I don't want—

MR. KUNSTLER: Are you turning down my request after this disgraceful episode? You are not going to say anything?

THE COURT: I not only turn it down, I ignore it.

MR. KUNSTLER: That speaks louder than words, too, your Honor.

THE COURT: And let that appear of record, the last words of Mr. Kunstler, and, Miss Reporter, be very careful to have them on the record.

(jury enter)

THE COURT: I say good morning again, ladies and gentlemen of the jury. Will the witness please resume the stand?

Testimony of Frank Riggio Resumed

MR. WEINGLASS: Now, it was your assignment to watch Mr. Davis?

THE WITNESS: Correct.

MR. WEINGLASS: Wasn't it also your assignment to threaten Mr. Davis, to tell him to get out of town?

THE WITNESS: That is incorrect, sir.

MR. WEINGLASS: You never threatened him?

THE WITNESS: I don't recall threatening Mr. Davis.

MR. WEINGLASS: You don't recall? But it is possible, isn't it?

THE WITNESS: I did not threaten Mr. Davis or tell Mr. Davis or Mr. Hayden to get out of town.

MR. WEINGLASS: You are positive of that?

THE WITNESS: I am fairly positive of that, yes.

MR. WEINGLASS: Fairly positive? Could you explain to the jury why, when I asked you that just a minute ago, you said you couldn't recall.

THE WITNESS: I already explained that, sir. I can't recall because I didn't make the statement.

MR. WEINGLASS: Isn't it a fact that you were armed and you had a weapon?

THE WITNESS: Naturally, sir.

MR. WEINGLASS: That you struck Mr. Davis on occasion?

THE WITNESS: No, I never struck Mr. Davis.

MR. WEINGLASS: You told him he had better get out of town or he would be killed?

THE WITNESS: No, sir, I never said that.

MR. WEINGLASS: Wasn't the purpose of your mission to drive these two young men out of town so they wouldn't have their peaceful demonstration?

THE WITNESS: No, sir, that was not the purpose of my mission.

MR. WEINGLASS: Didn't you discontinue on Tuesday when you found out that they couldn't be driven out of town, or Mr. Davis was doing nothing wrong?

THE WITNESS: No, sir, that is not true.

MR. WEINGLASS: Nothing further.

Testimony of Dwayne Oklepek

MR. FORAN: Will you state your name, please?

THE WITNESS: Dwayne Oklepek.

MR. FORAN: What was your occupation in the summer of 1968?

THE WITNESS: I was a reporter for the *Chicago Today*.

MR. FORAN: Was that a full-time occupation?

THE WITNESS: No, that was just a job for the summer. I was a senior at Cornell College in Mount Vernon, Iowa.

MR. FORAN: Now, during the summer of 1968 were you given any special assignment?

THE WITNESS: Yes, I was. I was to go to Mobilization headquarters and work with them as a volunteer worker.

MR. FORAN: Were you given any instructions about revealing your identity or your occupation?

THE WITNESS: I was only told to tell the Mobilization people that I was a reporter if I was asked.

MR. FORAN: How long did you work at that office?

THE WITNESS: From July 24 until August 30, 1968, almost every working day.

MR. FORAN: What were your duties while you worked there?

THE WITNESS: I made phone calls to secure housing for demonstrators who were coming into the city for the Convention, I typed form letters, did some filing and answered the telephone when it rang.

MR. FORAN: What hours did you ordinarily work?

THE WITNESS: Well, I ordinarily got there about nine or ten in the morning and stayed until three or four in the afternoon, at least. That would be an average day.

MR. FORAN: Now, calling your attention to August 9, 1968, in the morning, where were you?

THE WITNESS: I was in the Mobilization office.

MR. FORAN: Were any of the defendants present in the office on that day?

THE WITNESS: Yes, they were. Mr. Davis, Mr. Hayden and Mr. Froines.

MR. WEINGLASS: Your Honor please, I object. I feel that the Government has not laid a proper foundation. They have not demonstrated in any way through any evidence that there was an unlawful association among the defendants. They can, therefore, not proceed to introduce evidence of any particular acts or conversations.*

THE COURT: We have considered this problem, and I overrule your objection.

MR. FORAN: Now, what occurred, if anything?

THE WITNESS: Mr. Davis walked in with Mr. Hayden and said that there was going to be a meeting, what he termed the corps of marshals, on the west side of the main room, and he said that anyone who is in the office at that time who wished to participate in this first meeting of the corps of marshals should go into that room.

MR. FORAN: Was there a conversation in that room at that time?

THE WITNESS: There was.

MR. FORAN: Who said what, Mr. Oklepek?

THE WITNESS: Mr. Davis began speaking first. He pulled out a street map of the city of Chicago and set it up so we could all look at it, and began to point out the various routes which he said the Mobilization was trying to get for a march on August 28, 1968. Then Mr. Davis began to speak about what he termed the perimeter defense of Lincoln Park. Mr. Davis said that he expected that if demonstrators tried to sleep in the park past the announced curfew time of 11:00 P.M., that some time after midnight they could probably expect the park to be surrounded by police and/or National Guardsmen and that arrests would begin after that time.

Mr. Davis said in order to combat this situation, all of the separate groups of demonstrators who were sleeping in the park should have designated places to go in the event arrests occurred, and that these groups should attempt to break out of the park through the police lines, or past the police lines, to avoid the arrest situation.

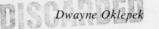

MR. FORAN: Did he say where they should go?

THE WITNESS: Mr. Davis felt that the separate groups should form up and then attempt to move their way south to the Loop area, where Mr. Davis said they should, in his own words, "tie it up and bust it up." He went on to say he thought that these groups should try to disrupt traffic, should smash windows, run through the stores and through the streets.

MR. FORAN: Was there anything else said at that time, that you recall?

THE WITNESS: Someone objected at that time to marching down 35th Street and along Halsted. He said there were a great many viaducts along these two routes, and that people conceivably could get on them and attack the demonstrators by throwing missiles at them, and things like that. Mr. Davis said, and these again are his own words, "We will put marshals on those things and they will shoot the shit out of anyone who opens up on us."

MR. FORAN: Do you recall anything else that was discussed at that meeting?

THE WITNESS: Someone asked Mr. Davis what would occur if it were impossible for the demonstrators to get out of Lincoln Park at all at night if an arrest situation commenced, and Mr. Davis said, "That's easy, we just riot."

MR. FORAN: Now, do you recall anything that occurred at that meeting, right at the end of the meeting, Mr. Oklepek?

THE WITNESS: Yes, I do recall some assignments being made.

MR. FORAN: What were those assignments, Mr. Oklepek?

THE WITNESS: Each of the people in that room was to make detailed maps of certain blocks of the downtown area and of certain places which were going to be demonstration targets during Convention week.

MR. FORAN: Were you to draw one of these maps?

THE WITNESS: Yes.

MR. FORAN: Did the meeting break up then?

THE WITNESS: Yes, it did.

MR. FORAN: Now, calling your attention to August 15, 1968, in the afternoon, where were you, Mr. Oklepek?

THE WITNESS: I was in Lincoln Park on the baseball field which is adjacent to LaSalle Drive at the southernmost end of the park.

Dave Baker took the twenty-five or thirty people who were there and lined them up side by side in rows of five or six so that they all faced in one direction and then he put one line in back of another so that there were five lines of five or six people all facing the front.

He had with him an eight-foot-long pole which was about an inch-and-a-half in diameter, round so that it fit very well into the palm of a hand, and he gave this pole to the front row of people and told them to link arms like this [*indicating*] and grasp the pole with both hands. Then each of these successive rows in back of this first row also linked arms and then every other person in between these two people on the end reached forward and grasped the belt of the person in front of them.

Then the formation moved as close together as possible so that it could run without any person stepping on the heels of the person in front of him and then Mr. Baker bega to chant something to sychronize our foot movements and the entire group began to jo place. Then after that Mr. Baker instructed us to begin moving forward and we be move in straight lines across the park, and after we had done this for a few min got a bit skilled at it, he began having us move in wavy lines and make turns faster and slower at his command.

After about fifteen minutes of this, Mr. Baker and Mr. Froines and gan to simulate attacks on this group such as might be expected from to hit people who were in strategic positions in the formation to try a or trip them to demonstrate to us how we should be alert for these sort of attacks could do to the entire formation.

MR. FORAN: At the completion of the training, did you o cerning it?

THE WITNESS: Mr. Hayden told the group that this same type that Japanese students had used to precipita vented then President Eisenhower from visiting tha together in this kind of formation, getting them moving and chanting and yelling, aroused their emotions, sustained their spirits, got them very excited.

He said that this formation was very good for breaking through police lines and that in the event of an arrest situation, this formation would be used during Convention week to break police lines and to try to escape from Lincoln Park, for instance. He also said that it was good for moving people over large distances in the event of a riot situation.

MR. FORAN: Now, calling your attention to August 15, 1968, in the evening, where were you, Mr. Oklepek?

THE WITNESS: At Mobilization headquarters at 407 South Dearborn.

MR. FORAN: How many people were there?

THE WITNESS: Approximately eight or ten.

MR. FORAN: And were any of the defendants present at that meeting?

THE WITNESS: Mr. Hayden, Mr. Davis and Mr. Froines were there.

Someone suggested that the marshals have what they termed political discussions. He specifically asked how Chicago police should be handled differently than army troops or National Guardsmen, if they should. At this point, Mr. Hayden said—this is becoming rather obscene.

MR. FORAN: Go ahead.

THE WITNESS: Mr. Hayden said, "Fuck them all. They are all pigs."

Mr. Froines then said that he believed that army troops would be more likely to be lenient with demonstrators than the Chicago policemen because the majority of army troops are draftees that would have been conscripted against their will, and, therefore, would be very sympathetic to the antiwar cause of the demonstrators. Mr. Froines felt that National Guardsmen would be even easier to handle because they would have been citizens only a few hours before their getting into uniform. They would be used to exercising their constitutional rights, and that, therefore, they would be susceptible to the logic of the demonstrators; that a genuine effort should be made among the demonstrators to get the National Guardsmen to literally join them in their demonstration.

Mr. Davis then said that there would be no way to deal logically or rationally with the Chicago police; that they were the most belligerent and uncompromising and unthinking law enforcement agency which the demonstrators would face, and that there was no hope of avoiding a confrontation with the Chicago police.

MR. FORAN: Calling your attention to August 24 in the afternoon, where were you?

WITNESS: I was in Lincoln Park.

AN: What was going on there?

ESS: There was snake dance training going on, and another group which was

te techniques.

id you see any of the defendants directing those snake dances and those

articipating in them?

bjection, leading.

believe it is leading in view of the witness' preceding answer. I

or may answer, sir.

weren was leading one of those groups.

M in Lincoln Park that afternoon, did you participate in a

MR. KU dants?

the Chicago

at that conversation?

d, and what was said?

standing about three feet apart. We were

t four feet in front of us, and the three

practicing self-defense tactics which

ple who were practicing—

on, "which would be used against

I don't think there is anything at this point that indicates this witness was told who these were to be used against.

THE COURT: Overruled. I overrule the objection.

MR. FORAN: Go ahead, Mr. Oklepek.

THE WITNESS: He turned his head from watching these people who were practicing these tactics and said to Mr. Baker, "Let's not mess around with this. Let's just go and get them."

MR. FORAN: Do you recall any further conversation at that time?

THE WITNESS: Yes. Mr. Hoffman was addressing a group of people who had been practicing snake dancing. He said that groups of people in the snake dance formations in different formations could be used to distract police in the event that police tried to arrest a large group of people.

He spoke about guerrilla theatre tactics. That is, spontaneous demonstrations which could occur at a moment's notice, and said that in the event that demonstrators had inspiration to do one of these things, they should immediately get together in a group and position themselves logistically in order to confront whatever situation they were in.

MR. FORAN: Now do you recall any further conversation on that day by any of the defendants?

THE WITNESS: I remember a statement made by Mr. Hayden. I remember a conversation that to the best of my recollection took place on that day.

MR. WEINGLASS: There is no foundation for where or when to this question and I object to it on that basis.

MR. FORAN: To the best of his recollection it was on this day in Lincoln Park. He is not certain it was that day and there is nothing I can do about changing that, your Honor.

THE COURT: You may answer, sir.

THE WITNESS: Mr. Hayden made the statement. He said we should have an army and get guns.

MR. FORAN: Will you indicate where you were on August 28 at 7:30 P.M.

THE WITNESS: I was on the west side of Michigan Avenue, in the doorway of the building directly adjacent to the Sheraton-Blackstone Hotel.

MR. FORAN: What was going on?

THE WITNESS: Well, the crowd was very agitated. There was chanting, a great deal of movement, people in the crowd pressing to get into the intersection, pressing up toward the Hilton Hotel. They were chanting. They were very agitated. One youth was atop a traffic light here in the middle of the intersection. They were waving flags, chanting, very agitated, very excited.

MR. FORAN: Do you remember any of the chants?

THE WITNESS: They were chanting, "Daley must go." They were chanting, "Dump the Hump." They chanted, "Hell, no, we won't go," and the other one, I believe it was, "NFL is going to win, Ho, Ho, Ho Chi Minh," among others, which I have forgotten.

MR. FORAN: How long did you stand there?

THE WITNESS: Well, I was moving south and north as the tear gas came and went, until about two o'clock in the morning.

MR. FORAN: Now, Mr. Oklepek, calling your attention to the next morning, August 29, where were you?

THE WITNESS: I was in Mobilization headquarters, again.

MR. FORAN: Were any of the defendants present?

THE WITNESS: Yes, Mr. Dellinger was present.

MR. FORAN: Did you have a conversation with him?

THE WITNESS: Yes. I asked Mr. Dellinger what sort of demonstration was to take place that afternoon in Grant Park, and he said, "A short one. We have won a moral victory and now we have to get everyone home in one piece to use it."

MR. FORAN: That is all, your Honor.

You may cross-examine.

MR. KUNSTLER: Mr. Oklepek, would you describe your role with reference to the Mobilization as that of a paid informer?

THE WITNESS: No.

MR. KUNSTLER: Were you paid for what you did?

THE WITNESS: Not to inform, no.

MR. KUNSTLER: Did you inform?

THE WITNESS: That was reporting; it was not informing.

MR. KUNSTLER: Mr. Oklepek, do you recall making a rather lengthy statement to agents of the Federal Bureau of Investigation on October 1, 1968?

THE WITNESS: Yes, I do.

MR. KUNSTLER: I want to show you Defendants' 35 for identification and ask you if this is the statement which you made.

THE WITNESS: Yes, this is the statement.

MR. KUNSTLER: Were the statements that appear in Defendants' Exhibit 35 for identification true and correct at the time you signed it?

THE WITNESS: Yes, they were.

MR. KUNSTLER: I am going to ask you, Mr. Oklepek, whether on the first day of October, 1968, you did not make this statement:

"On May 19, 1968, I was hired by Jack Mabley, Associate Editor of the *Chicago American,* a newspaper published in Chicago, Illinois, for the purpose of obtaining data on individuals connected with, and activities of organizations known as the Students for a Democratic Society [SDS] and the National Mobilization Committee to End the War in Vietnam [NMC]. I was to obtain this data through becoming associated with these organizations, but without disclosing my connection with the *Chicago American.* For this work I was paid the regular starting salary of a newspaper reporter, amounting to $140 per week."

Did you make this statement?

MR. FORAN: Your Honor, I object to counsel reading from a document not in evidence.

THE COURT: I sustain the objection.

MR. KUNSTLER: Your Honor, this is classic impeachment procedure.

THE COURT: I think it is neither. It is not classic and not impeachment. I sustain the objection.

MR. KUNSTLER: What did Mr. Mabley say to you?

THE WITNESS: He said, "Would you object to infiltrating SDS and National Mobilization in order to get stories which will be pertinent to the Democratic National Convention?" or something to that effect. I said yes, I would do it.

MR. KUNSTLER: Now, after Mr. Mabley offered you the assignment, and you said you had no objection, what did you do to embark on it?

THE WITNESS: The first thing I believe I started doing was just walking through Old Town to a few places there where I thought from previous experience that I might meet some people who were connected with SDS.

MR. KUNSTLER: You just walked around Old Town?

THE WITNESS: I went down to SDS headquarters a few times.

MR. KUNSTLER: Was one of your assignments to infiltrate SDS with reference to the Democratic National Convention?

THE WITNESS: Yes. Mr. Mabley said I should try SDS.

October 16, 1969

MR. KUNSTLER: Mr. Oklepek, what were your first duties when you went to Mobilization Headquarters?

THE WITNESS: I believe the first day I began doing something clerical, either typing letters or making phone calls to secure housing for demonstrators who would be coming into the city. I typed a letter which was a fund-raising letter for the Summer of Support of 1968.

MR. KUNSTLER: Now, did your duties remain much the same from July 24, 1968, until—I think your last day at Mobilization headquarters was August 30, 1968?

THE WITNESS: Well, when marshal training began in earnest around the thirteenth, once that began, that occupied much of the time, more of the time than those other duties.

MR. KUNSTLER: Did someone tell you you were to be trained as a marshal?

THE WITNESS: Yes.

MR. KUNSTLER: You didn't volunteer to be a marshal, is that correct?

THE WITNESS: Yes, I did.

MR. KUNSTLER: Oh, you did. What is it? You volunteered or someone told you?

THE WITNESS: On the first meeting on August 9, I was in the room when Rennie Davis said, "I would like this group to be trained as marshals before August 24, 1968." So I was told, but I did volunteer.

MR. KUNSTLER: He said more than that, didn't he? Didn't he also say, "Anyone who is interested in attending this meeting"?

THE WITNESS: Yes, he did say that.

MR. KUNSTLER: You were interested because you wanted to report to Jack Mabley, isn't that correct?

THE WITNESS: Yes.

MR. KUNSTLER: That was the main reason, the only reason for your interest?

THE WITNESS: No.

MR. KUNSTLER: Did you support the aims of the demonstrations?

THE WITNESS: Well, which demonstrations and which aims?

MR. KUNSTLER: Did you know what the main aims were of Mobilization—for example, with reference to the Chicago Convention?

THE WITNESS: They wished to nominate a candidate for President who would be responsive to the will of the people. They were demonstrating sentiment against the war in Vietnam, against social injustice, and I am all for that.

MR. KUNSTLER: You support that wholeheartedly, do you not?

THE WITNESS: Yes.

MR. KUNSTLER: You supported it then and you support it now?

THE WITNESS: Yes.

MR. KUNSTLER: Mr. Oklepek, were you ever told in the taking of this assignment by Mr. Mabley that he or someone else had informed Mayor Daley of your assignment?

THE WITNESS: I really don't remember.

MR. KUNSTLER: Do you know whether Mayor Daley or the FBI had been informed of your assignment?

MR. FORAN: Your Honor, I object to this.

THE COURT: I will sustain the objection.

MR. KUNSTLER: Now, at the meeting of August 9, 1968, I believe you stated on your direct examination that Mr. Davis had made some sort of remark about the viaducts in the white community on Halsted north of Garfield Boulevard.

As I recall your testimony, the remark was, "We'll put marshals on those things and they'll shoot the shit out of anyone who opens up on us."

Now at the time Mr. Davis made the remark, isn't it a fact, Mr. Oklepek, that everybody attending that meeting laughed?

THE WITNESS: Most of them did, that is true.

MR. KUNSTLER: Up to that time, August 9, 1968, had you heard any discussion from anybody in the Mobilization office about guns?

THE WITNESS: I don't recall any conversation about guns before that point, no.

MR. KUNSTLER: Did you see any guns before that time, before August 9?

THE WITNESS: No, I did not.

MR. KUNSTLER: Did you ever see any person in Mobilization wearing a gun?

THE WITNESS: Not that I could see, no.

MR. KUNSTLER: You say not that you could see. Are you saying that you saw the outlines under their coats?

THE WITNESS: I saw bulges under their coats.

MR. KUNSTLER: Oh, you saw bulges. Did you say to yourself at that time, "Those are guns?"

THE WITNESS: I said to myself at that time, "Those are bulges."

MR. KUNSTLER: "Those are bulges." Extremely accurate.

Would you just indicate for me whether at any time of your connection with Mobilization from the twenty-fourth of July until the thirtieth of August, 1968, that you ever saw a firearm on any person in the office or in any connection with Mobilization people?

THE WITNESS: Not that I could observe on their person, no.

MR. KUNSTLER: Is it not a fact that you heard the marshals instructed on, I believe, August 13, that they were under no circumstances to carry weapons at all, because that would provoke the police?

THE WITNESS: Dave Baker did say that, yes.

MR. KUNSTLER: Were you conscious or aware during your work for Mobilization that attempts were being made to get a permit from the City of Chicago or permits to conduct demonstrations?

MR. FORAN: Objection.

THE COURT: I sustain the objection.

MR. FORAN: He didn't make the attempts.

MR. KUNSTLER: Did you hear any negotiations being carried out over the telephone or in person for permits by National Mobilization leaders?

THE WITNESS: No, I did not hear any negotiations.

MR. KUNSTLER: Was there a lot of discussion about these permits or the attempt to get them, in the office?

THE WITNESS: Yes, there was.

MR. KUNSTLER: That was a pretty general subject, was it not, the attempt to obtain permits?

THE WITNESS: Yes.

MR. KUNSTLER: In fact, didn't you state to the FBI that you were very impressed with these efforts to obtain permits?

MR. FORAN: Objection.

THE COURT: The form of the question is bad. I sustain the objection.

MR. KUNSTLER: If you will turn to page 9 of D-35 for identification, I want to ask whether you told the FBI the following:

"At the same time I was impressed with the negotiations mentioned as being carried on by NMC leaders with officials or representatives of the city government of Chicago and the apparent efforts to be thorough and leave no avenue uncovered as regards obtaining legal authority for any specific activity being planned."

Did you say that?

MR. FORAN: Objection, your Honor, as reading from a document not in evidence and I ask the jury be directed to disregard the question.

THE COURT: Yes. The jury is directed to disregard that question.

MR. KUNSTLER: Mr. Oklepek, did there come any time while you were in the office working that you would look through the Mobilization files?

THE WITNESS: Yes, there were such occasions.

MR. KUNSTLER: Is it not true that in doing so you found nothing whatsoever that would indicate anybody was planning any trouble at the Democratic National Convention?

THE WITNESS: I didn't find anything that seemed to indicate anything was going to happen at the Democratic National Convention.

MR. KUNSTLER: Your Honor, is something happening—my colleagues say something is happening in the courtroom. I don't understand what is happening except that the marshals have asked people to leave.

THE COURT: I know nothing about it.

MR. KUNSTLER: Could we find out, your Honor?

THE COURT: I will excuse the jury with the same order, ladies and gentlemen, that I gave you before.

(jury excused)

THE MARSHAL: Ladies and gentlemen, spectators, I will not have talking and no finger waving or any distraction whatsoever, especially near the jury. Do I make myself clear? So it won't interrupt the proceedings.

THE COURT: Do you want to make a statement, Mr. Kunstler?
MR. KUNSTLER: I still don't know what happened. The marshal walked over and made a statement, a unilateral statement about which I know nothing.
THE COURT: I am asking you why you brought the matter to my attention.
MR. KUNSTLER: Because, your Honor, my colleagues called my attention to the marshals—and we always have three or four standing at the door all during the trial, something defense objects to anyway, giving an air of force, that it is necessary to keep order in this courtroom, and then it was called to my attention—
THE COURT: I have never tried a case where I did not have at least one marshal in the courtroom.
MR. KUNSTLER: No, your Honor, I understand that, your Honor, but four standing—
THE COURT: If you understand it, don't comment.
MR. KUNSTLER: Your Honor, I would like the record to show one, two, three, four, five, six, seven marshals—one just left, which was eight marshals in the courtroom at one time. Also three black people were asked to leave, your Honor. We don't know why.
THE COURT: I will say that the matter of having spectators leave is entirely in the hands of the marshals, a matter of security.
MR. KUNSTLER: I think we are entitled to know. This record may be read by another court and the public trial issue is involved.
THE COURT: Are you anticipating a conviction?
MR. KUNSTLER: Yes, I am.
THE COURT: Your clients have pleaded not guilty.
MR. KUNSTLER: I know, your Honor, but we have our own thoughts about what is going to happen to them and I have to be prepared for a conviction.
THE MARSHAL: I see the three that were out are back in, Mr. Kunstler. They came in about two seconds after they went outside and and they were asked to keep quiet.
MR. DELLINGER: Two seconds after we protested.
A SPECTATOR: I beg your correction. There are still two out and the third was just let out.
THE MARSHAL: By their own choosing.
THE SPECTATOR: The last two—
THE COURT: Will the marshal have that lady sit down or ask her to leave? I will direct her to leave if she makes any statement in the courtroom.
MR. KUNSTLER: There are apparently two more outside, your Honor, of the ones that went out. So maybe the marshal's comment is not entirely correct. If there are two more outside, they ought to come back in.
MR. SEALE: I think there is a bit of racism involved, myself.
MR. KUNSTLER: Your Honor, it was called to my attention and I looked around and I saw black people being taken out of the courtroom. The only thing I have—
MR. FORAN: Your Honor, may the record also show that a number of marshals are black people, that over close to half of the courtroom is black people, and your Honor this is—this is, you know, our daily routine for exciting articles in the newspapers. It is so utterly ridiculous, your Honor, that the Government would ask that we go on with the trial.
MR. KUNSTLER: I ask your Honor to please order the marshal to bring back any two that are still not in the courtroom. I understand two are still outside.
THE COURT: I will not order the marshal to do anything because I don't have any evidence of any wrongdoing on the part of the marshal.
    And all I get from your clients constantly is a laugh. Just this last second they sit there and laugh at a judge of the highest trial court in the United States. That is what I have been getting. Perhaps you think that is proper as a lawyer admitted to practice here by the courtesy of this court.
    We will recess, Mr. Marshal.
MR. KUNSTLER: Your Honor, before the jury comes in, I want to just indicate to your Honor that I have been informed by a law school graduate who has done some work with us—that she overheard one of the marshals outside the room indicate that the black people in the courtroom on the right side were not to be seated up to this afternoon on the front

row, because it was felt that that would intimidate the jury, and I think that that is a rather serious thing, if decisions are being made by the marshals on the basis of the race of the spectators and as to where they are seated in the courtroom.

I wanted to bring it to your Honor's attention, because I think an effort should be made—

THE COURT: I observe, Mr. Kunstler, that there are people of the Negro race sitting right close up front. I see one, two, three, four, five, six people from here in the first row of spectators' seats.

MR. KUNSTLER: I stated, your Honor, up to the noon break the situation was as I have indicated. Now there seems to be some black people on the—

THE COURT: Anyone who knows me—I have to repeat to you, sir, you don't know me. You don't practice law in this jurisdiction. Anyone who knows me knows there is no discrimination in any case over which I preside, and there will be none.

MR. KUNSTLER: Your Honor is taking this personally.

THE COURT: My decision in the South Holland case was the first desegregation case decided in the North, and I followed the command of the United States Supreme Court and the Constitution.

For anyone to even suggest that there is discrimination on racial grounds in this courtroom means that he isn't informed.

MR. KUNSTLER: Your Honor, all I am saying is that two witnesses who are presently seated in the courtroom heard this remark from a marshal.

THE COURT: There has been no discrimination, and there is no discrimination now; there was none this morning.

Bring in the jury please, Mr. Marshal.

(jury enters)

MR. KUNSTLER: Didn't the National Mobilization Committee leaders constantly stress that the purpose of the marshals, their very function, was to avoid violence, if possible?

THE WITNESS: They were to prevent demonstrators from being arrested.

MR. KUNSTLER: You are telling me that is all you ever heard was said to you or the other marshals by any leader of the National Mobilization Committee, that the sole purpose of the marshals was to prevent demonstrators from being arrested?

THE WITNESS: Yes, or to get arrested themselves to prevent such arrest of demonstrators.

MR. KUNSTLER: Now, will you look at Exhibit D-50 for identification at the portion I have underlined about the purposes of the marshals.

Is that what you told the readers of *Chicago Today* in your bylined article?

MR. FORAN: I object to that.

THE COURT: I sustain the objection.

MR. KUNSTLER: Have you ever said anything contrary to what you have just told us here?

THE WITNESS: I don't believe so, no.

MR. KUNSTLER: Did you ever tell or say anywhere that one of the purposes of the marshals was to protect the marchers from unwarranted assault from police and indigenous population? Didn't you say that?

THE WITNESS: Not that I remember.

MR. KUNSTLER: Then I take it your testimony is that you have never written or said that one of the purposes of the marshals was to protect the marchers from assaults by police and indigenous population?

MR. FORAN: I object to that.

MR. KUNSTLER: Now you were present, were you not, in the vicinity of Grant Park on August 28, 1968?

THE WITNESS: Yes, I was.

MR. KUNSTLER: During that time, did you see or smell the use of tear gas?

THE WITNESS: Yes.

MR. KUNSTLER: During that time, did you see policemen clubbing demonstrators?
THE WITNESS: Yes.
MR. KUNSTLER: During that time, did you see them clubbing women and children?
THE WITNESS: I did not see them clubbing children.
MR. KUNSTLER: All right. Did you see them clubbing women?
THE WITNESS: That is difficult to answer yes or no. When two people are striking each other at close quarters, who was clubbing who?
MR. KUNSTLER: Did you see women with clubs?
THE WITNESS: I saw women using implements as clubs, yes.
MR. KUNSTLER: And you never saw a policeman throw or club a woman to the street, is that correct?
THE WITNESS: No, I did not.
MR. KUNSTLER: Did you see them club men to the street?
THE WITNESS: Yes.
MR. KUNSTLER: Did you see people lying on the ground, demonstrators?
THE WITNESS: I saw people lying on the ground, yes.
MR. KUNSTLER: Did you see people bleeding in the streets?
THE WITNESS: Yes, I saw people bleeding on that street.
MR. KUNSTLER: Did you see any policemen chasing after demonstrators, running after them?
THE WITNESS: Yes, I did.
MR. KUNSTLER: And did you see them catch up with any of the demonstrators?
THE WITNESS: Yes, I did.
MR. KUNSTLER: Did you see them then club the demonstrators after they caught up with them?
THE WITNESS: In some cases.
MR. KUNSTLER: And did those clubs land on heads—
THE WITNESS: In some cases.
MR. KUNSTLER: —as you watched? And did you see blood spurt under those clubs?
THE WITNESS: When they hit their heads, yes.
MR. KUNSTLER: It has a squashy sound, doesn't it, if you heard it?
MR. FORAN: Now, come on. I object.
MR. KUNSTLER: I will withdraw the question.
    Did you hear the sound of a club hitting a bare head?
THE WITNESS: Four times, three or four times.
MR. KUNSTLER: That is not a very pleasant sound to hear, is it?
THE WITNESS: I suppose not, no.
MR. KUNSTLER: You suppose not. Did it ever pass or cross your mind that the marshal training program had been eminently justified by what happened?
MR. FORAN: Object.
THE COURT: Sustained.
MR. KUNSTLER: Before we get to the next, I want to ask you one question. Were you aware that the people in the National Mobilization office at a certain period of time, particularly somewhere between August 9 and August 20, considered you an informer? Did you come to that conclusion?
MR. FORAN: I object to that.
THE COURT: I sustain the objection.
MR. KUNSTLER: Did anyone, Mr. Froines or Mr. Davis or anyone else, ever tell you that they were suspicious of your motives in being in the office?
THE WITNESS: On August 28, in the afternoon, I saw Mr. Weiner who was walking across Columbia Drive and asked him a question about the demonstration, and he said, "What do you care, you're on their side anyway," and kept on walking.
MR. KUNSTLER: That was August 28. What about Mr. Davis, prior to that?
THE WITNESS: I do not remember.
MR. KUNSTLER: Your Honor, I have no further questions.

October 17, 1969

MR. FORAN: Mr. Oklepek, did you tell the grand jury that Mr. Hayden had suggested that an army be trained?

THE WITNESS: Yes, I did tell them that.

MR. FORAN: Did you tell the grand jury that Mr. Hayden had made many, many violent statements?

MR. KUNSTLER: Objection to that.

MR. WEINGLASS: Objection, your Honor.

MR. WEINGLASS: Leading, prejudicially leading question.

THE COURT: On redirect examination I will permit the question, over objection. He may answer that.

THE WITNESS: Yes, I did.

MR. FORAN: Did you tell the grand jury Hayden was always in favor of some violent confrontation as opposed to anything peaceful?

MR. KUNSTLER: Your Honor, I object to that. Same reasons the prosecutor objected every time we would go into the grand jury.

THE COURT: I will let him answer over objection.

MR. FORAN: Do you remember telling the grand jury that, Mr. Oklepek?

THE WITNESS: Yes, I do.

MR. FORAN: Do you remember telling the grand jury that Mr. Hayden had suggested that the demonstrators fight their way through all the cops?

THE WITNESS: Yes.

MR. KUNSTLER: I object to that, your Honor. It is certainly not proper redirect.

THE COURT: I think this subject was explored by the defense on cross-examination. I will let him answer over objection.

MR. WEINGLASS: Your Honor please—

THE COURT: Over objection I am permitting the answer to the question.

MR. WEINGLASS: I have—

THE COURT: Do you hear me?

MR. WEINGLASS: I have a second objection which wasn't stated by Mr. Kunstler.

THE COURT: I don't permit another objection after I have ruled, sir. That is my practice. You may answer the question.

MR. FORAN: Go ahead, Mr. Oklepek.

THE WITNESS: Yes, I remember telling that to the grand jury.

MR. FORAN: Did Mr. Hayden say that?

THE WITNESS: To the best of my recollection, he did, yes.

MR. FORAN: I have no further questions.

Testimony of Carl Gilman

MR. SCHULTZ: Please state your name.
THE WITNESS: Carl Gilman.
MR. SCHULTZ: Mr. Gilman, will you tell the Court and jury what your occupation is?
THE WITNESS: Newsman.
MR. SCHULTZ: From what city?
THE WITNESS: San Diego, California.
MR. SCHULTZ: Mr. Gilman, have you on any occasion ever received any money from the Federal Bureau of Investigation?
THE WITNESS: Yes, sir, around $150 a month on an average.
MR. SCHULTZ: For what have you received this $150 and reimbursement of expenses?
THE WITNESS: For reports I filed with the Bureau.
MR. SCHULTZ: Now, calling your attention to July 25, 1968, in the evening about 8:30, would you tell the Court and jury where you were, please?
THE WITNESS: At San Diego State College, Life Science Building, Room 300.
MR. SCHULTZ: What was occurring at approximately 8:30 at that time and at that place?
THE WITNESS: There was a rally. David Dellinger was the speaker at that rally.
MR. SCHULTZ: Will you relate to the Court and the jury the last part, the very last part of the speech which Mr. Dellinger gave?
MR. WEINGLASS: If your Honor please, I object to this question. I object to this witness relating any speech given by a person before an open public rally at a college campus as being in violation of the First Amendment of the United States and I would like to argue this outside of the presence of the jury.
THE COURT: I don't think that question is so complicated. We have gone into it on pretrials and I will let you argue your objection to it right here.
MR. WEINGLASS: If your Honor please, the United States Supreme Court in 1966 in the case of Elfbrandt vs. Russell,* held that it would be constitutionally impermissible to permit the Government to proceed in a prosecution by introducing into evidence speeches made, opinions held, that did not constitute a clear and present danger in the circumstances in which they were made, and to permit a jury to hear the contents of the speech, the public speech, as part of a criminal prosecution, would be to have an inhibiting effect on the First Amendment right of free speech.

Justice Douglas in his opinion examines the dangers that are inherent in permitting the Government to do what is now contemplated, to have undercover agents or paid informers appear at public rallies held in public places and to report in a later criminal prosecution the content of a speech made by one of the speakers. To permit this type of prosecution to proceed with this type of evidence would have the effect of chilling the desire of the people of this country to engage in open and public debate.*

It becomes particularly objectionable in a situation such as the one presented by this case where the Government is intending to prove as part of its case a state of mind of the defendants and then attempts to prove that state of mind by offering into evidence constitutionally protected speeches of the defendants.
MR. SCHULTZ: May I reply, your Honor?
THE COURT: Certainly.
MR. SCHULTZ: Your Honor, what Mr. Weinglass is saying is that if somebody makes a speech in public, that speech can never be used against that person in a subsequent criminal prosecution because if it were, people would be afraid to speak freely and therefore their First Amendment rights would be inhibited.

Now to follow logically with that argument, what Mr. Weinglass is saying is that nobody can be prosecuted in public for making incriminating statements. For example if an individual were to walk to the corner of State and Madison and he were to say, "I am going to murder Mr. X tomorrow," and then tomorrow Mr. X is murdered and the individual who made that statement is seen in the vicinity, then when the Government or the state would try to prosecute that case, according to Mr. Weinglass' argument they could not introduce before a jury the fact that in public the man said "I am going to do it," because it would chill his right to speak.

Well, that would destroy all prosecution. In fact, most prosecutions, including this one, are statements made in public. Fortunately, it is not the law. If Mr. Dellinger at his speech said things which he sort of wished he didn't say, but he said them anyway, they should be heard by the jury so the jury can evaluate them to determine what he was thinking, what his intentions were, what he wanted other people to do.

THE COURT: Over the objection of the defendant, I will permit the witness to answer.

MR. SCHULTZ: Mr. Gilman, to the best you can, please, would you relate to the Court and to the jury the entire speech that the defendant Dellinger gave on that July 25, 1968, meeting?

THE WITNESS: He started off his speech by talking about a trip that he had made to Hanoi. He also discussed his trip to Paris, France, where he talked to representatives of the North Vietnamese delegation at the Paris peace talks.

He also went into a speech about the war in Vietnam, and he was opposed to it, and discussed the Vietnam war and how it is a political war.

MR. SCHULTZ: Now, at the end of the speech, would you relate what he said?

THE WITNESS: "Burn your draft cards. Resist the draft. Violate the laws. Go to jail. Disrupt the United States Government in any way you can to stop this insane war."

MR. SCHULTZ: Now, when he said that, what, if anything, occurred?

THE WITNESS: The audience applauded. People stood up and whistled and yelled and screamed. They were very excited.

MR. SCHULTZ: If the Court please, if the marshals would—it is very disrupting to have the audience laughing during the court proceedings.

THE COURT: I direct the marshals to admonish the spectators that they will be asked to leave if they do not refrain from noisy laughter.

MR. SCHULTZ: All right. As soon as he finished saying, "Disrupt the United States, stop the insane war," what occurred?

THE WITNESS: As the applause died down, Mr. Dellinger said something and I missed the first word or perhaps the first two words, and after that he said, "I am going to Chicago to the Democratic National Convention where there may be problems."

Then the audience applauded, stood up and yelled and screamed and whistled.

MR. SCHULTZ: Then what occurred, please?

THE WITNESS: Then as the applause died down, he shook his fist like this [indicating] and said, "I'll see you in Chicago," like that, and the audience applauded, stood up for five minutes and applauded and Mr. Dellinger walked off the podium and that was the end of the rally.

MR. SCHULTZ: That is all on direct.

THE COURT: Cross-examination?

MR. WEINGLASS: If your Honor please, I renew my objection at this point. There is no mention of Mr. Dellinger's intention to commit any crime, either directly or indirectly in the city of Chicago from what I heard, so I don't think the speech as given by this witness even passes muster under the prosecutor's test.

THE COURT: I thought I heard the witness testify about burning draft cards.

MR. KUNSTLER: That is not what he is being prosecuted for, your Honor, for burning draft cards, for encouraging the burning of draft cards.

THE COURT: You are right about that.

MR. KUNSTLER: So it should be stricken; your Honor, you agree with me?

THE COURT: Oh, no. No. I shall not interpret his speech. That is the responsibility of the jury. But I deny Mr. Weinglass' motion.

You may cross-examine.

MR. KUNSTLER: Mr. Gilman, did there come a time—your Honor, is someone being removed from the courtroom? Again another black person, I see.

MR. SCHULTZ: Say—this repeated comment about "another black person"—

A SPECTATOR: You hate black people or something?

MR. SCHULTZ: This constant repetition is not warranted, this attempt to make it appear that there is racism in this courtroom. And that response, your Honor, is so outrageous— it is they who are engineering and who are looking for racism—

I ask your Honor to order the people in this courtroom to stop making remarks about racism.

MR. KUNSTLER: Your Honor, it's only been black people ejected that I have seen.

THE COURT: I don't know how from your position you can see what person has been ejected. I'm facing the door. I've never seen anybody ejected. And I don't think that it is proper for a lawyer to refer to a person's race. It isn't fitting that you do it as far as the member of that race is concerned.

I have to repeat to you that in this courtroom, sir, there has never been any such thing as racism, as any lawyer who practices here—and you don't, regularly—knows. And I direct you now, I order you now, not to refer to the ejection of a black person again.

MR. KUNSTLER: I will not, your Honor, if black people are not constantly ejected from this court.

THE COURT: I order you not to, sir. That is my order.

MR. KUNSTLER: I think that violates the constitutional rights, your Honor, of these clients.

THE COURT: I think I am as familiar with the Constitution as you are, sir, and you will now proceed with your cross-examination of this witness.

MR. KUNSTLER: How many times after your first meeting did you call the FBI to bring something to their attention?

THE WITNESS: Hundreds of times.

MR. KUNSTLER: How many times did the FBI call you during the same period of time?

THE WITNESS: Just call me?

MR. KUNSTLER: Called you to initiate some investigation on your part.

THE WITNESS: Maybe five times.

MR. KUNSTLER: Did the Federal Bureau of Investigation contact you with reference to Mr. Dellinger?

THE WITNESS: No, sir, not that I can recall.

MR. KUNSTLER: Did you initiate this on your own—

THE WITNESS: Yes, sir.

MR. KUNSTLER: —initiative?

THE WITNESS: Yes, sir.

MR. KUNSTLER: In San Diego, do you recall whether someone introduced Mr. Dellinger, or he just started to speak?

THE WITNESS: Someone introduced him. The person gave a brief history of Mr. Dellinger's life.

MR. KUNSTLER: Did he tell you that Mr. Dellinger was a lifelong pacifist? Did you hear that?

THE WITNESS: Yes, sir.

MR. KUNSTLER: Didn't he say that Mr. Dellinger had once or at some time in the past served three years in jail for nonregistration regarding the draft even though he was exempt as a seminary student?

THE WITNESS: Yes, sir. I vaguely remember hearing something about that.

MR. KUNSTLER: You didn't make any notes of that, did you?

THE WITNESS: No, sir.

MR. KUNSTLER: Did not Mr. Dellinger in his speech state that he was an advocate of nonviolence?

THE WITNESS: He may have.

MR. KUNSTLER: Now, during his speech you said that he mentioned his trip to Paris, is that correct?

THE WITNESS: Yes, sir.

MR. KUNSTLER: Did he say in his mention of that speech that while there he had met with Averell Harriman on two occasions at Mr. Harriman's invitation?

THE WITNESS: I cannot recall that. I do not remember.

MR. KUNSTLER: Did he discuss at all at this time or did he mention at that time that Mr. Harriman was negotiating with reference to a peace treaty with the North Vietnamese and the Viet Cong in Paris?

THE WITNESS: Yes, I think that was probably brought in. I don't remember exactly what he said in that reference.

MR. KUNSTLER: Do you remember that Mr. Dellinger indicated that his discussions with Ambassador Harriman were mainly about methods in stopping the war in Vietnam?

THE WITNESS: No, I do not remember that.

MR. KUNSTLER: Now, in his speech that night, did Mr. Dellinger discuss anything about his role in the release of American prisoners who had been held by the North Vietnamese or the Viet Cong in Vietnam?

THE WITNESS: Yes, he said that he had gone to Hanoi and he went on to say that the prisoners that were being released were being taken to Thailand and brainwashed by the United States Government to save face in Southeast Asia.

MR. KUNSTLER: Do you remember him mentioning at all that the prisoners had been taken off a civilian plane in Laos at the intervention of President Johnson and taken by military plane to Thailand? Do you recall that in the speech?

THE WITNESS: I remember that he accused the U. S. Government of taking the servicemen to Thailand.

MR. KUNSTLER: Didn't Mr. Dellinger say to this group that the purpose of these prisoner releases was to get the prisoners home to their families and that the United States Government was frustrating that purpose by this type of action?

THE WITNESS: I cannot recall that.

MR. KUNSTLER: Just one last question: Do you not remember that in discussing problems in Chicago that Mr. Dellinger made reference to a statement that went something like "Shoot to kill, shoot to maim"?

THE WITNESS: I do not remember that.

MR. KUNSTLER: No further questions.

THE COURT: You may go, sir.

THE WITNESS: Thank you.

(witness excused)

THE COURT: Please call your next witness.

Testimony of Robert A. Casper

MR. FORAN: Will you state your name, please?

THE WITNESS: Robert A. Casper, Special Agent of the FBI.

MR. FORAN: Calling your attention to July 23, 1968, at about seven o'clock in the evening, where were you?

THE WITNESS: I was on the corner of 48th Street and Park Avenue in New York City. A demonstration was in progress at that time.

MR. FORAN: Were there a number of speakers at this rally?

THE WITNESS: Yes, sir. Approximately seven individuals spoke at the rally.

MR. FORAN: Did Jerry Rubin speak at this rally?

THE WITNESS: Yes, sir, he did.

MR. WEINGLASS: If your Honor please, we objected this morning on this ground, and I object again. The prosecutor is proceeding once again to offer evidence of a constitutionally protected speech given before a public rally, and unless that speech was in and of itself criminal in nature, that speech cannot be used in this court against any of the defendants. If the prosecution continues in this way, we will see happening in this court the beginning of the end of free speech before public rallies.

THE COURT: I have had occasion to look at the cases you cited this morning, and I find they are inapposite, Mr. Weinglass. At this point I overrule your objection.

You may continue with the examination of the witness.

MR. FORAN: Would you state in substance and in words what Mr. Rubin said on that occasion, Mr. Casper?

THE WITNESS: Yes, sir. He said that people should mass and cause disruptions to the election system in the United States.

He said in Chicago during the Convention and on Election Day these disruptive tactics should be such that the candidates would not be able to campaign publicly, and he also said that thousands and thousands of people will be in Chicago so as to implement this, these disruptive tactics.

MR. FORAN: Then how did he finish his speech?

THE WITNESS: He finished his speech by facing the—north, towards the Waldorf-Astoria, raising his left hand, and using an obscenity.

MR. FORAN: That is all. You may cross-examine.

MR. WEINGLASS: Your Honor, we have another motion.

THE COURT: All right. You may make another motion.

(jury excused)

MR. WEINGLASS: If I understand the witness correctly, I feel that what the witness has said is still not permissible evidence in this case, and we have a case which was decided by the United States Supreme Court this year.*

In that case a member of the Ku Klux Klan in the state of Ohio advocated at a meeting of fellow Klan members that the Klan should march on Congress on July 4, 400,000 strong, and indicated that by marching in such large numbers on that day they should compel Congress to close and remain closed for a period of time until their demands were met.

It's the Supreme Court's opinion that even if Mr. Rubin advocated that this assemblage should in the future commit acts of violence and force, his words are still entitled to the constitutional protection of the First Amendment because the only words that are not is wherein he tells that group that they must immediately resort to force and violence, thereby creating at the time he uttered the words a clear and present danger.

MR. FORAN: Your Honor, this argument—I thought it had been articulated so clearly so many times, it just keeps coming up over and over again.

We are talking about admissibility in evidence of a statement tending to show intent to do something and these are public speeches that are not anywhere near what these

[111]

cases are cited concern, and the cases in fact are directly opposite to what the position is, and the Government objects to the motion.

THE COURT: I will deny the motion.

Now, are you ready to cross-examine?

October 20, 1969

MR. KUNSTLER: Now, is it not true, Mr. Casper, that most of Mr. Rubin's speech had to do with Election Day 1968, rather than with the Democratic National Convention?

THE WITNESS: No, sir, I don't think that is accurate.

I believe that his speech was on the election system in substance as opposed to Election Day and I say this because of some statements he made.

MR. KUNSTLER: In any event, it is true that Mr. Rubin did talk about demonstrations in connection with the coming election campaign, did he not?

THE WITNESS: Yes, sir, he did.

MR. KUNSTLER: Was it from that statement that you reached the conclusion that this would involve also the Democratic National Convention?

MR. FORAN: Objection, your Honor.

THE COURT: I sustain the objection.

MR. KUNSTLER: What did you base your conclusion that Mr. Rubin called for disruptive tactics at the Democratic National Convention if he didn't say it exactly as you have so testified?

THE WITNESS: I believe I said I didn't recall what he said exactly, sir.

MR. KUNSTLER: How did you reach that conclusion then?

THE WITNESS: Well, it was hardly a conclusion. He said anywhere, any time, the so-called candidates appeared they would mass and demonstrate, to a degree, make it impossible for them to appear publicly.

MR. KUNSTLER: All right. Then did you conclude from that, that meant that this was calling for disruptive tactics at the Democratic National Convention?

MR. FORAN: I object to that.

THE COURT: I sustain the objection.

MR. KUNSTLER: I have no further question, your Honor.

THE COURT: You may go, sir.

(witness excused)

THE COURT: Ladies and gentlemen of the jury, I will permit you to go now until two o'clock. There are matters to be considered here out of your presence.

(jury excused)

THE CLERK: There is a motion here of defendant Bobby Seale pro se to be permitted to defend himself.

THE COURT: I will hear you, Mr. Seale.

MR. SEALE: I want to present this motion in behalf of myself. I am not a lawyer, but I do know that I as one of the defendants have a right to defend myself and I feel and know that it should be looked into by the judge of this court, Judge Hoffman, and I feel that it has not been looked into.

I have made attempts at defending myself by asking to cross examine one witness who testified against me. I made attempts to object to witnesses testifying against me because my lawyer Charles R. Garry was not here.

I understood quite a while back after arraignment, in fact, the same day that I was arraigned on these charges, that Charles R. Garry would be the only one who would defend me here, that all other lawyers who would appear in court would appear in court only for pretrial motions and pretrial proceedings. There is where I stood and this has been my contention all along. But I hope that it becomes clear with respect to the developments of the situation here now, so I present this motion and I read it:

I, Bobby Seale, demand and move the Court as follows: because I am denied the lawyer of my choice, Charles R. Garry, I cannot represent myself as my attorney would be doing, but because I am forced to be my own counsel and to defend myself, I require my release from custody, so that I can interview witnesses, do the necessary investigating, do necessary factual research and all other things that being in custody makes impossible; 2) the right to cross examine witnesses and examine witnesses of my choice; 3) the right to make all necessary motions that I as a layman can think of to help my defense and prove my innocence, and to argue those motions; 4) the right to do any and all other things for myself that I am forced to do because I am denied the services of my lawyer, Charles R. Garry.

I have signed the statement and I feel that some investigation should be done on my behalf so that it can be clear in this courtroom and the record can show I have a right to defend myself here presently with respect to the past developments and there is only one who has actually testified against me by name and I think that has to be considered on my part.

THE COURT: Have you finished, sir?

MR. SEALE: Yes.

THE COURT: All right.

MR. KUNSTLER: Your Honor, the other defendants would like to join in this motion. I am doing it not to represent him but the other defendants who do have a stake because we are in a conspiracy indictment.

I would like to call your Honor's attention to Adams vs. U. S. ex rel. McCann,* where the Supreme Court said:

"The right to assistance of counsel and the correlative right to dispense with a lawyer's help are not legal formalitisms. They rest on considerations that go to the substance of an accused's position before the law.

"The Constitution does not force a lawyer upon a defendant. He may waive his Constitutional right to assistance of counsel if he knows what he is doing and his choice is made with eyes open."

I might indicate to your Honor that although I filed a pro tem notice of appearance in order to see Mr. Seale on, I think, September 21, and I filed another notice of appearance on September 24 when Mr. Weinglass filed for four and I filed for four, I was informed by Mr. Seale on, I believe, September 29 that he did not desire to have me or any of the other attorneys who had appeared for him with the exception of Mr. Garry, whose notice still is on file to represent him in any way, and I have been told this on numerous occasions since then.

Your Honor indicated to me on September 30 that even were I to file a notice to withdraw my notice of appearance, your Honor would deny it. But nevertheless, in view of Mr. Seale's strong stand throughout, I am filing such a motion before your Honor, and I just want to call your Honor's attention that Canon 44 of the Canons of Professional Ethics indicates that if a lawyer is informed by his client that the client does not wish him to proceed in the case, that it is essentially unethical for the lawyer to continue to represent him.

I would strongly recommend, on behalf of all defendants, that the motion of Mr. Seale be granted.

MR. SEALE: Your Honor, Mr. Kunstler said that on the twenty-ninth he was informed that I didn't want him for my attorney. Correct that, because it was a Friday, the twenty-seventh, if I am not mistaken, that I filed a written statement firing all of these other lawyers who represented me on pretrial motions and proceedings.

So for that, this motion today—I just got a note they were doing this in support of the rest of the defendants, but as I listened to it, it was good, and I am saying this here because I know I have gotten some attacks from the Government saying we were playing games over here.

I am not playing no game with my life being stuck on the line, and I want to put that into the record to explain my situation.

THE COURT: Mr. Schultz.

MR. SCHULTZ: May we briefly reply, your Honor?

Your Honor, this is a ploy. It's just a simple, obvious ploy. The ploy is so obvious.

When the lawyers cross-examine a witness on Mr. Seale's speech, they qualify it by saying, "Well, I'm doing this on behalf of my clients," or whatever they think of. When Mr. Kunstler stands here and argues that he is arguing Mr. Seale's motion for seven other clients when he only represents three other clients, I might add, it's silly. It's ludicrous. The defendants are trying to make a record, they are trying to create error in the record.

Now, they know perfectly well that if Mr. Seale were to cross-examine witnesses here and argue to the jury, we would have a mistrial in this case in two minutes. He would destroy the other defendants' rights to a fair trial. There is absolutely no doubt about that. They know perfectly well, him not being a lawyer, him not being versed in the law, that there would be reversible error and there would be nothing that we could do about it.

It's a game they are playing with this Court. There is no basis in law whatever in this motion, none at all, and we are asking that the motion be denied.

MR. SEALE: Your Honor, may I just reply?

THE COURT: Yes. You may reply, Mr. Seale.

MR. SEALE: A signed statement was filed here at least a month or so before the trial began by Mr. Charles R. Garry who flew out here. The statement was brought to me in jail, prior to this trial, that Mr. Charles R. Garry would be the only one representing me, so this idea of a ploy and all, this is not true.

I talked to my lawyer on the phone from the Cook County jail, and he said that he would definitely have to enter the hospital unless he risked his life. That was that Thursday night. That next morning I brought my written statement here that I wrote in jail myself.

THE COURT: The defendant, Bobby Seale, has handed up to the Court—it was handed up this morning—a longhand document, which begins as follows: "I, Bobby Seale, demand and move the Court as follows."

I, of course, shall order the document filed. It is signed not "Bobby Seale, Defendant," but in this manner: "Bobby Seale, Chairman, Black Panther Party."

I know of no such designation in the pleadings in this case. However, I shall treat the document as a motion of the defendant, Bobby Seale, and that motion as a matter of law for leave to appear pro se, and further, for relief on bail.

The defendant Seale is now represented by competent counsel, Mr. Kunstler, Mr. Kunstler having filed his appearance in Mr. Seale's behalf and having so stated in Mr. Seale's presence.

Now the defendant Bobby Seale comes in today and has moved to be allowed to act as his own counsel and release on bail in order to perform certain function as he says are necessary to his defense.

The right to discharge one's counsel and appear pro se is not unqualified if an accused seeks to exert it after trial has commenced.* I find now that to allow the defendant Seale to act as his own attorney would produce a disruptive effect. Moreover, the denial of the defendant's motion to appear pro se would not be prejudicial to his case. On the contrary, the complexity of the case makes self-representation inappropriate and the defendant would be more prejudiced were he allowed to conduct his own defense than if his motion were to be denied.

Mr. Clerk, the motion of the defendant Bobby Seale to appear pro se will be denied as will his motion for release on bail.

Will you bring in the jury, Mr. Marshal.

(jury enters)

MR. SEALE: I would like to say, Judge, that you denied my motion to defend myself and you know this jury is prejudiced against me.

THE COURT: I will ask you to sit down.

MR. SEALE: You know that; the jury can't go home to their loved ones and their homes, and you know they have been made prejudiced against me.

THE COURT: Ladies and gentlemen of the jury, you are excused.

(jury excused)

MR. SEALE: They have been made prejudiced against me, I know. I should be allowed to defend myself. I should be allowed to speak so I can defend myself.

THE MARSHALL: Be quiet.

MR. SEALE: Don't tell me to shut up. I got a right to speak. I need to speak to defend myself.

THE COURT: Mr. Seale, I must admonish you that any outburst such as you have just indulged in will be appropriately dealt with at the right time during this trial and I must order you not to do it again.

MR. SEALE: In other words, you are saying you are going to put me in contempt of court for speaking on behalf of myself?

THE COURT: Will you be quiet? That is all. You have lawyers to speak for you.

MR. SEALE: They don't speak for me. I want to represent myself. Charles R. Garry is not here in my service. I have explained to you in the past what the situation was. I was put in jail and everything else. Now you are saying you are going to put me in jail, you are going to put me in jail, that's one thing. You are going to put me in contempt of court because I am speaking in behalf of myself.

The jury is prejudiced against me all right and you know it because of those threatening letters. You know it, those so-called jive threatening letters, and you know it's a lie. Now how can that jury give me a fair trial?

THE COURT: Mr. Marshall, will you go to that man and ask him to be quiet?

MR. SEALE: I will speak for myself. They can't speak on behalf of myself. I still want to defend myself, and I know I have a right. I just want to let him know. That racist, that fascist. You know, the black man tries to get a fair trial in this country. The United States Government, huh. Nixon and the rest of them.

Go ahead and continue. I'll watch and get railroaded.

MR. SCHULTZ: If the Court please, there is one thing that has not been placed on the record, whenever the defendants have wanted to meet with Mr. Seale and the lawyers, the marshals have made arrangements to bring them to a room where all of them could get together.

MR. SEALE: I would like to put something on the record. You weren't in that room unless you got a tape recorder in there and—

THE MARSHAL: I am asking you to keep quiet.

MR. SEALE: That man is lying on me.

THE MARSHAL: All right.

MR. SEALE: I met with these defendants and argued with these so-called cats about so-called defending me. I want that for the record, too.

THE COURT: Bring in the jury, Mr. Marshal.

(jury enters)

THE COURT: Call your next witness, please.

Testimony of Kenneth Carcerano

October 21, 1969

MR. FORAN: Will you state your name, please?

THE WITNESS: Kenneth Carcerano.

MR. FORAN: What is your occupation, Mr. Carcerano?

THE WITNESS: Police officer of the City of Chicago.

MR. FORAN: Now, calling your attention particularly to Monday, August 26, 1968, did you see Rennie Davis on that night?

THE WITNESS: Yes, I did.

MR. FORAN: Where?

THE WITNESS: At Lincoln Park.

MR. FORAN: About what time did you see him in Lincoln Park?

THE WITNESS: Approximately 12:35 A.M., which would be Tuesday morning.

MR. FORAN: What did you see there?

THE WITNESS: At that time the police had formed a skirmish line running north and south through the park. West of the police had been erected a barricade, running parallel to the police line. The barricade was constructed of picnic tables, litter baskets, boards, tree branches.

MR. FORAN: How long was it?

THE WITNESS: I would say it was approximately seventy-five feet, one-hundred feet. It varied in height. Some places it was waist-high; others it was hat-high.

MR. FORAN: As you saw Mr. Davis, what were the police doing?

THE WITNESS: The police were approximately ten feet east of the barricade and were attempting to cross that barricade.

MR. FORAN: Now, did you hear Mr. Davis say anything?

THE WITNESS: Yes, I did. Davis was yelling through a bullhorn, "Fight the pigs. Don't let the pigs take the park. The park belongs to the people." He was shouting obscenities at the police.

MR. FORAN: What was the crowd doing while Davis was shouting in this bullhorn?

THE WITNESS: The crowd was screaming, men were fighting the police, they were right on the barricade fighting the police. Many objects were being thrown at the police at that time.

MR. FORAN: I would like to call your attention at this time to the next night, that would be Tuesday night, late in the evening. Where were you?

THE WITNESS: I was in front of the Conrad Hilton Hotel.

MR. FORAN: Did you see the defendant Davis at that time?

THE WITNESS: Yes, I did. He was having a conference with Deputy Superintendent James Rochford in front of the Hilton. After the conversation Davis crossed the street, and over a portable loudspeaker announced that the demonstrators would be allowed to remain in Grant Park overnight.

MR. FORAN: What happened then?

THE WITNESS: Davis was approached by a young male Negro, whose name I do not know.

MR. FORAN: Did you overhear a conversation?

THE WITNESS: Yes, I did. The male Negro said to Mr. Davis, "I represent the revolution, and I want a revolution now. The pigs are here now. My people are ready. Let's confront the pigs now."

MR. FORAN: And what did Davis say?

THE WITNESS: He said, "Not now. Later. Cool it."

MR. FORAN: And was there anything further said?

THE WITNESS: The male Negro then said to Davis, "You're a square John anyway," and he walked away from him.

MR. FORAN: Mr. Carcerano, I want to call your attention to Thursday afternoon—this is the twenty-ninth, in the afternoon, where were you?

THE WITNESS: I was in front of the Conrad Hilton Hotel.

MR. FORAN: Would you name some of the people who gave speeches in Grant Park.

THE WITNESS: Mr. Hayden, Mr. Davis, Mr. Dellinger, Mr. Sidney Peck, Senator Eugene McCarthy, and Dick Gregory.

MR. FORAN: What did you hear Mr. Hayden say over that loudspeaker, Mr. Carcerano?

THE WITNESS: Mr. Hayden began by predicting Columbia University uprisings throughout the nation.

He then stated, to the best of my recollection, what the demonstrators had gained was bringing into a fruition a vanguard of people who were experienced in fighting for their survival under military conditions and that this invaluable experience would have a consequence far beyond that week. He talked about the strategy of overheating the nation's military machinery and that this philosophy would continue throughout the campaign, wherever Humphrey and Nixon went, the threat of protest was sure—the troops would be called out to guard them.

He said that this was not only a Chicago policy but a national policy, and that the Left would be there to assure it and expose it.

At that time there was a collection taken to raise money for the bond of Jerry Rubin. I believe Mr. Davis was the next speaker.

MR. FORAN: What did Mr. Davis say?

THE WITNESS: Mr. Davis began by relating the experience of his arrest and beating by what he called the fascist pigs. He stated that he had been singled out for this beating because of his leadership position. He then went on to state that the activities of the National Mobilization Committee were terminated and that any group of persons wishing to assume leadership of the crowd was welcome to it.

MR. FORAN: I think that's all, your Honor.

MR. KUNSTLER: Mr. Carcerano, what time did you first see Mr. Davis in Lincoln Park?

THE WITNESS: Approximately 12:30 A.M.

MR. KUNSTLER: Now at the time you first saw Mr. Davis, where was he standing?

THE WITNESS: He was approximately ten feet north of myself, twenty feet west of the barricade which had been erected, toward the south end of that barricade.

MR. KUNSTLER: Did you see at any time nightsticks land on the heads of demonstrators after the police broke through the barricade?

THE WITNESS: Yes, sir.

MR. KUNSTLER: Did you see the police using nightsticks on the demonstrators?

THE WITNESS: Yes, I did, sir.

MR. KUNSTLER: Did you see at any time nightsticks land on the heads of demonstrators?

THE WITNESS: Yes, I did, sir.

MR. KUNSTLER: Were these demonstrators with bare heads?

THE WITNESS: Some of them were, sir.

MR. KUNSTLER: Did you see that they were bleeding, some of them were bleeding from the head?

THE WITNESS: Yes, I did.

MR. KUNSTLER: Did you see any other type of wound on the demonstrators outside of the head injuries?

THE WITNESS: I saw demonstrators limping, holding parts of their bodies.

MR. KUNSTLER: What parts of their bodies?

THE WITNESS: Arms, back.

MR. KUNSTLER: Did you see people holding their groins?

THE WITNESS: I don't recall.

MR. KUNSTLER: Did you see any policemen bleeding from head wounds?

THE WITNESS: Yes, I did, sir.

MR. KUNSTLER: Would you describe whom you saw?

THE WITNESS: I saw several police officers with blood on their faces. I don't know where the wound was but they had blood on their faces, on their shirts.

MR. KUNSTLER: Did you see any demonstrators with clubs clubbing policemen?

THE WITNESS: Yes, I did, sir.

MR. KUNSTLER: Would you describe that? Whom did you see and where?

THE WITNESS: Demonstrators had manned the barricade. They were either on the barricade or behind the barricade and as the police line approached the barricade, the demonstrators were swinging at the police with clubs and sticks and boards, besides throwing missiles at the police.

MR. KUNSTLER: From your own observation there, if the police had not attempted to go over the barricade and get the demonstrators, from your experience would it not have been a peaceful scene?

MR. FORAN: I object to that.

THE COURT: I sustain the objection.

MR. KUNSTLER: Now, on Thursday, August 29, you say you were in front of the Hilton. I think you said that three of our defendants here, Rennie Davis, Dave Dellinger and Tom Hayden, were some of a number of speakers who addressed these 2,000 people, is that correct?

THE WITNESS: Yes, sir.

MR. KUNSTLER: Senator McCarthy spoke, isn't that correct?

THE WITNESS: Yes, sir.

MR. KUNSTLER: Didn't Senator McCarthy tell the group that he had met his commitments and that he would expect them to fulfill theirs, or words to that effect?

THE WITNESS: Words to that effect.

MR. KUNSTLER: Did Senator McCarthy discuss what had happened to the people in the streets of Chicago because of the actions of the Chicago police?

THE WITNESS: I don't recall, sir.

MR. KUNSTLER: Now, Mr. Davis spoke about the fact that he had been beaten, is that correct?

THE WITNESS: Yes, sir.

MR. KUNSTLER: Would you describe his physical condition as you observed it?

THE WITNESS: At that time I believe Mr. Davis had a bandage wrapped around his head, his forehead area, the back of the head.

MR. KUNSTLER: Didn't you see blood on him?

THE WITNESS: I didn't see blood on him, sir.

MR. KUNSTLER: Was it a large bandage?

THE WITNESS: Yes, sir, a fairly large bandage.

MR. KUNSTLER: Your Honor, I have no further questions.

THE COURT: Mr. Marshal, the court will be in recess until ten o'clock.

October 22, 1969

THE CLERK: Motion on behalf of William Kunstler for leave to withdraw as counsel for defendant Bobby G. Seale.

THE COURT: I will hear you, Mr. Kunstler.

MR. KUNSTLER: Thank you, your Honor. On September 22 when I arrived at the Federal building I was informed by John Adams, the Deputy Marshal, that I could not see Mr. Seale unless I filed a notice of appearance. I then filed one writing in the words "pro tem" opposite my name at the bottom of the notice of appearance.

On September 24 I filed a notice of appearance which was a full notice for defendants Jerry Rubin, David T. Dellinger, John Froines and Mr. Seale. Following that I was informed by Mr. Seale several days later that he did not desire me or any other lawyer to represent him in the absence of Charles R. Garry.

I think at that time, as I recall, he filed in this court a handwritten statement in which he said exactly what I am telling your Honor, that he had discharged all other attorneys since he could not have Mr. Garry.

Subsequently to that I have informed your Honor both in your chambers on September 30, on innumerable times in this court that Mr. Seale has taken this action and that I represent him only in a very, very token way by the mere fact that that notice of appearance was filed and I do not represent him for any other purpose other than that token one of the filing of the notice of appearance.

THE COURT: You forget that as an officer of this court here at the sufferance of the Court you assured me that you had filed his appearance and that you would represent him.

MR. KUNSTLER: I might say, your Honor, I think the Canon of Ethics does indicate that a lawyer who is discharged should not proceed further in the case.

THE COURT: That is not the law. Nor is it in the Canon of Ethics. Does the Government desire to be heard?

MR. FORAN: Yes, your Honor. A full appearance by Mr. Kunstler was of record on September 24, when this case began. There were substantial proceedings taken in this court before this court prior to the time that Mr. Seale first made mention of a desire to discharge Mr. Kunstler.

The status of the law, your Honor, is clear.* Once the obligation, the professional obligation of representation is assumed by a lawyer, he has no right to withdraw whether his client tells him to or asks him to or not; that it is then subject to the sound discretion of the Court as to whether or not this right prior to the beginning of the trial of a client to defend himself is overcome in the Court's discretion by the strong likelihood that the discharge of a lawyer in the midst of a trial would result in total destruction of court proceedings—total disruption of court proceedings to the prejudice of a fair trial.

On that basis, your Honor, the Government asks the Court to deny the motion.

MR. KUNSTLER: Your Honor—

MR. SEALE: Can I speak on that and answer his argument?

THE COURT: No. This is not your motion, sir. Your motion has been decided.

MR. SEALE: In other words, I can't speak in behalf of myself?

THE COURT: Not at this time, sir.

MR. SEALE: Why not?

THE COURT: Because this is your lawyer's motion.

MR. SEALE: That ain't my lawyer.

THE COURT: This is not your motion. This is the motion of Mr. William Kunstler for leave to withdraw as your lawyer.

MR. SEALE: Well, this man has misconstrued a whole lot of things concerning my right to defend myself and he knows he did.

They can jack you up and get you to sit up there and say rotten, crazy stuff concerning my right to defend myself.

THE COURT: I would request the marshal to ask the young man to sit down.

MR. SEALE: Well, I want my right to defend myself and this man knew, I indicated to him he was not my counsel at the very beginning when I first got here and arrived here and was in jail.

THE COURT: That motion—since you will not listen to the Court, you may sit down.

Have him sit down, Mr. Marshal.

MR. SEALE: I still want my right to defend myself. A railroad operation, and you know it, from Nixon on down. They got you running around here violating my constitutional rights.

MR. KUNSTLER: Mr. Seale has taken a very strong stand, and he just reiterated it again this morning a few seconds ago, that he does not desire—

THE COURT: That motion has been decided.

MR. KUNSTLER: I realize that.

THE COURT: I don't want to hear either from you or him on that subject. Permitting a withdrawal in this case by Mr. Kunstler is clearly inappropriate. We are now four and one-half weeks into trial and Mr. Kunstler has actively engaged in the defense of Bobby Seale, a defendant, along with other defendants. A withdrawal by an attorney so intimately acquainted with the facts of the case at this juncture would require either a pro se appearance which is inappropriate here for the reasons which the Court stated, or would require a mistrial.*

Mr. Clerk, the motion of Mr. William Kunstler to withdraw as attorney for the defendant Bobby Seale will be denied.

Call your next witness.

MR. SCHULTZ: Your Honor, before the next witness testifies, would it be possible if the Court would permit the Government—we have the picture of the boy with the black power symbol fist on his sweat shirt that was identified by Officer Carcerano as the boy who spoke with Rennie Davis. We would like to offer it at this time—

MR. SEALE: That's not a black power sign. Somebody correct the Court on that. It's not the black power sign. It's the power to the people sign.

THE COURT: Mr. Marshall, will you stop the talking, please.

MR. SEALE: Yes, but that is still wrong, Judge Hoffman. It's not a black power sign. It's a power to the people sign, and he is deliberately distorting that, and that's a racist technique.

MR. SCHULTZ: If the Court please, this man has repeatedly called me a racist—

MR. SEALE: Yes, you are. You are, Dick Schultz.

MR. SCHULTZ: And called Mr. Foran a racist—

THE COURT: Ladies and gentlemen of the jury, I will ask you to leave the court. Mr. Marshal, remove the ladies and gentlemen of the jury.

(jury excused)

Mr. Seale and Mr. Kunstler, your lawyer, I must admonish you that such outbursts are considered by the Court to be contemptuous, contumacious, and will be dealt with appropriately in the future.

MR. KUNSTLER: Your Honor, the defendant was trying to defend himself, and I have already indicated my—

THE COURT: The defendant was not defending himself.

MR. SEALE: I was, too, defending myself. Any time anybody gives me the wrong symbol in this courtroom is deliberately—

THE COURT: He is not addressing me with authority—

MR. SEALE: —distorting, and put it on the record.

THE COURT: Instruct that man to keep quiet.

MR. SEALE: I want to defend myself and ask him if he isn't lying, and he is going to put that lying crap on the record? No siree—I am not going to sit here and get that on the record. I am going to at least get it be known—request that you understand that this man is erroneously representing symbols directly related to the Party of which I am Chairman.

MR. SCHULTZ: If the Court please, if nothing else, this has pointed up the reasons why Mr. Seale should not represent himself and Mr. Kunstler should represent him.

THE COURT: I think I pointed up the reason in deciding that motion. Among the reasons was just precisely what is going on now, what has gone on. Return the jury.

I admonish you, Mr. Seale, that outbursts such as you have just been guilty of will be appropriately dealt with at a proper time in the future.

(jury enters)

THE COURT: Is there any objection to Government's Exhibit 14 for identification?

MR. KUNSTLER: Your Honor, I object on the grounds that it is probative of absolutely nothing in this case. It's a picture of an unidentified black youth. He has on his shirt the power to the people symbol of the clinched fish which has been characterized here as black power, but which is not the correct characterization. It is not probative of anything in this case.

THE COURT: You may reply, Mr. Schultz.

MR. SCHULTZ: Our purpose of putting this exhibit into evidence was simply because witnesses have identified this picture as being a photograph of the young boy whom there has been considerable testimony about. He is the one who wanted the people to go now and Davis said, "not now." I think that the jury should have the opportunity to at least look at the photograph that witnesses have identified, this individual being the center of some discussion on the examination.

THE COURT: Over the objection of the defendant, Government's Exhibit 14 for identification will be admitted into evidence.

Please call your next witness.

Testimony of Andrew Rodriguez

MR. SCHULTZ: Please state your name.

THE WITNESS: My name is Andrew Rodriguez.

MR. SCHULTZ: And your occupation, please.

THE WITNESS: I am a detective with the Chicago Police Department.

MR. SCHULTZ: Now, calling your attention to Monday night, August 26, 1968, did you have occasion to go to Lincoln Park?

THE WITNESS: Yes, I did. I arrived at Lincoln Park at 11:00 P.M.

MR. SCHULTZ: And were you at the park when the park was cleared that night?

THE WITNESS: Yes, I was.

MR. SCHULTZ: Where were you when the police were clearing the park that night, that Monday night, or actually early Tuesday morning, wasn't it?

THE WITNESS: I was stationed or standing in the west parking lot of Lincoln Park.

MR. SCHULTZ: While you were standing, did you see the police and the demonstrators move further?

THE WITNESS: The demonstrators moved first, followed shortly by the police.

MR. SCHULTZ: How were you dressed that night?

THE WITNESS: In sport jacket, sport shirt and slacks.

MR. SCHULTZ: After the demonstrators moved by you, what occurred next please?

THE WITNESS: Well, the police line came through, and I stood there for a while, and then I joined the police line and assisted them in clearing the demonstrators.

MR. SCHULTZ: Then where did you go, please?

THE WITNESS: I crossed over to this small island. It's part of the intersection, I believe, which separates Clark Street from LaSalle Street.

MR. SCHULTZ: Now, while you were standing at the island did you have occasion to observe anybody whom you recognized?

THE WITNESS: Yes. At the corner of Eugenie and LaSalle, right in front of the car agency, I recognized Rennie Davis.

MR. SCHULTZ: What was Rennie Davis doing?

THE WITNESS: At that time he was walking from group to group of people and more or less conversing with them.

MR. SCHULTZ: After you observed that for two to three minutes, what, if anything did you do, please?

THE WITNESS: I crossed over and I walked over to the middle of LaSalle Street.

MR. SCHULTZ: What occurred just when you arrived in the middle of LaSalle Street?

THE WITNESS: Well, I observed Mr. Davis shouting, facing the crowd and shouting, "Let's fight the pigs. Let's fight. Let's get them. Let's go. Let's go."

MR. SCHULTZ: What occurred when or about the time that Davis started to yell, "Let's get the pigs. Let's fight the pigs. Let's go. Let's go"?

THE WITNESS: Well, the people picked up the shouting of obscenities at the police line and some of them began throwing objects at the police.

MR. SCHULTZ: Did you see what objects were being thrown, please?

THE WITNESS: I saw something that resembled either bricks or stones and I heard the sound of glass breaking.

MR. SCHULTZ: Did you see Davis throw anything?

THE WITNESS: No, I did not.

MR. SCHULTZ: What did the police do when the objects were thrown from the crowd toward the police?

THE WITNESS: They began to march or run toward the demonstrators. The majority of the demonstrators began to run south on LaSalle Street.

MR. SCHULTZ: And the ones who didn't run, what did you observe them do?

THE WITNESS: There was several that I saw who remained and were fighting or struggling with the police, the uniformed policemen.

MR. SCHULTZ: Did you see where Davis went?

THE WITNESS: No. The last I saw him was when he, too, was walking rather fast south on LaSalle Street.

MR. SCHULTZ: Was Davis—would you tell the jury whether or not Davis was still shouting and yelling while the police were moving through?

THE WITNESS: Well, when the police began to sweep over, Davis was still shouting, "Let's fight the pigs, let's get the pigs. Let's stop them. Let's go. Let's go."

MR. SCHULTZ: That is all, your Honor, for direct.

THE COURT: Then, Mr. Marshal, that having been done, we will recess until two o'clock.

(recess taken to 2:00 P.M. the same day)

MR. SEALE: You are a pig for kicking him out.

SPECTATORS: Right on. Right on.

THE MARSHAL: This honorable court will now resume its session.

THE SPECTATORS: Oink oink.

MR. KUNSTLER: Your Honor, if I can just make a—

Oh, are you going to call the case?

THE CLERK: 68 CR 180, United States of America vs. David T. Dellinger, et al., case on trial.

MR. KUNSTLER: Your Honor, if I could make one application—the other seven defendants have purchased a birthday cake for Chairman Bobby Seale whose thirty-third birthday is today and they have requested me to ask your Honor's permission since the marshals would not let them bring the cake to Mr. Seale, the only way they can get it to him is in the courthouse, but they would request permission to at least bring it to him and present him with the cake before the jury comes in.

THE COURT: Mr. Kunstler, I won't even let anybody bring me a birthday cake. I don't have food in my chambers. I don't have any beverages. This is a courthouse and we conduct trials here. I am sorry.

MR. KUNSTLER: The cake is not to eat here, your Honor.

THE COURT: Your application will be denied.

Will you bring in the jury, please, Mr. Marshal.

MR. SCHULTZ: If the Court please, can we wait until the defendants appear?

THE COURT: Oh, the defendants are not here? Will you please get the defendants, Mr. Marshal?

MR. DAVIS: They arrested your cake, Bobby. They arrested it.

THE COURT: One more outburst like that, ladies and gentlemen on the spectator seats, and the courtroom will be cleared of spectators. Just one more. That is the second time that has occurred.

MR. SEALE: Don't say nothing no more, brothers. Just sit in the court and observe the proceedings. OK? All right.

THE COURT: And, Mr. Seale, I will issue the orders around here.

MR. SEALE: They don't take orders from racist judges, but I can convey the orders for them and they will follow them.

THE COURT: If you continue with that sort of thing, you may expect to be punished for it. I warned you right through this trial and I warn you again, sir.

Bring in the jury.

MR. SEALE: We protested our rights for four hundred years and we have been shot and killed and murdered and brutalized and oppressed for four hundred years because of—

THE COURT: There is another instance, that outburst may appear of record and it does.

Did you get it, Miss Reporter?

THE REPORTER: Yes, sir.

MR. SEALE: I hope you got my part for the record, too, concerning that. Did you get that, ma'am?

THE REPORTER: Yes, sir.

MR. SEALE: Thank you.

THE COURT: And that outburst also.

MR. DELLINGER: I think you should understand we support Bobby Seale in this—at least I do.

THE COURT: I haven't asked you for any advice here, sir.

MR. SEALE: All I have to do is clear the record. I want to defend myself in behalf of my constitutional rights.

THE COURT: Let the record show that the defendant Seale has refused to be quiet in the face of the admonition and direction of the Court.

MR. SEALE: Let the record show that Bobby Seale speaks out in behalf of his constitutional rights, his right to defend himself, his right to speak in behalf of himself in this courtroom.

THE COURT: Again let the record show that he has disobeyed the order of the Court.

Bring in the jury, Mr. Marshal.

MR. SEALE: Please do.

THE COURT: Will the witness resume the stand?

(jury enters)

You may cross-examine this witness.

MR. KUNSTLER: Thank you, your Honor. Detective Rodriguez, I call your attention to August 26, that evening, in fact, when you were, as I understand it, at Lincoln Park at approximately 11:00 P.M., is that correct?

THE WITNESS: Yes.

MR. KUNSTLER: What were the demonstrators doing?

THE WITNESS: The majority of them were running.

MR. KUNSTLER: Did you notice whether some were crying? Did you see their faces?

THE WITNESS: No, I didn't see their faces.

MR. KUNSTLER: Did you hear any of them coughing?

THE WITNESS: No.

MR. KUNSTLER: Did you hear any obscenities from the police that night?

THE WITNESS: No.

MR. KUNSTLER: You never heard a single "damn"?

THE WITNESS: I heard mutters but I didn't hear any shouts.

MR. KUNSTLER: What did you hear muttered by the police?

THE WITNESS: Son of a bitch.

MR. KUNSTLER: What else?

THE WITNESS: That's about all. Son of a gun, words to that effect.

MR. KUNSTLER: The police said "son of a gun"?

THE WITNESS: Some of us do.

MR. KUNSTLER: Now, how many people did you see police clubs land on?

THE WITNESS: Five to ten.

MR. KUNSTLER: Were they men and women?

THE WITNESS: They appeared—there was a combination of both men and women being struck.

MR. KUNSTLER: Now of the people you saw, let's take one of the women, for example, if you can keep in mind one of the women you saw. What was she doing when she was struck by the policeman's club?

THE WITNESS: She was striking the policeman. She also had a club, a stick.

MR. KUNSTLER: She had a stick. Where was she hit, by the way?

THE WITNESS: I can't be exact about it. Somewhere on the upper part of her body.

MR. KUNSTLER: How many of the people, the five to ten that you saw hit by sticks, were running when they were hit?

THE WITNESS: The five or ten that I did see were standing toe-to-toe with the police.

MR. KUNSTLER: Toe-to-toe slugging it out?

THE WITNESS: Yes.

MR. KUNSTLER: And then the policeman would use his stick on the person with whom he was struggling, is that correct?

THE WITNESS: To defend himself, yes.

MR. KUNSTLER: And in no instance is it your testimony you saw any policemen strike any person who was running?
THE WITNESS: I saw sticks being swung at people who were running, yes.
MR. KUNSTLER: Did you see people bleeding?
THE WITNESS: I saw people bleeding, yes.
MR. KUNSTLER: Did you hear any obscenities from the police at that time?
THE WITNESS: "Those damn son of a guns," or, you know, "son of a b—'s."
MR. KUNSTLER: Use the actual words, Officer.
THE WITNESS: "Those damn son of a bitches are really tough," words to that effect.
MR. KUNSTLER: You were in casual clothes, is that correct?
THE WITNESS: Yes.
MR. KUNSTLER: And you sought cover because you were afraid, isn't that correct?
THE WITNESS: I was afraid of being hit with an object, yes.
MR. KUNSTLER: Were you also afraid of being hit by the police?
THE WITNESS: No.
MR. KUNSTLER: Did it cross your mind that you were in casual clothes, the police might not be able to distinguish between you and a demonstrator?
THE WITNESS: Just at that moment I placed my police badge on the lapel of my coat.
MR. KUNSTLER: You thought it was time to let the police know you weren't a demonstrator, isn't that correct?
THE WITNESS: Right.
MR. KUNSTLER: No further questions.

Testimony of Louis Salzberg

October 23, 1969

MR. SCHULTZ: Please state your name.

THE WITNESS: Louis Salzberg.

MR. SCHULTZ: Where do you live, please? In what city?

THE WITNESS: New York City, New York State.

MR. SCHULTZ: Mr. Salzberg, what is your occupation, please?

THE WITNESS: I'm a press photographer.

MR. SCHULTZ: Mr. Salzberg, have you received any money from the Federal Bureau of Investigation?

THE WITNESS: Yes, for services which I performed, such as photographs and information.

MR. SCHULTZ: And approximately how much money have you received from the FBI for the services that you have rendered?

THE WITNESS: I would have to say somewheres around seven, eight thousand dollars.

MR. SCHULTZ: Mr. Salzberg, calling your attention to March 14, 1968, did you have occasion to attend a meeting?

THE WITNESS: Yes, sir. Washington Square Methodist Church, Greenwich Village, New York.

MR. KUNSTLER: Your Honor, I would like to object to any testimony with reference to any period prior to the first period mentioned in the indictment, which is considerably after March 14, 1968.

MR. SCHULTZ: The statements made prior to the first date charged in the indictment are admissible to show the intent. The intent doesn't have to be proved from the period of the indictment. If things occurred before which show what is in a man's mind, that is admissible so that the jury can impute the intent relating to the crime that is charged during the period that is charged in the indictment.

THE COURT: I overrule the objection.

MR. SCHULTZ: Mr. Salzberg, what organization, if any, sponsored this meeting which you attended?

THE WITNESS: The Resistance.

MR. SCHULTZ: Was there a featured speaker at that meeting, please?

THE WITNESS: Yes. Tom Hayden.

MR. SCHULTZ: If the Court please, may the witness get off the stand and identify—

THE COURT: Yes, you may step down, sir, and identify the person you are talking about, if you can.

MR. DELLINGER: [*rising to address witness*] Quite a letdown. I am really disappointed in you.

MR. SCHULTZ: May the record show that the witness had identified Thomas Hayden.

THE COURT: The record may so indicate.

MR. SCHULTZ: Did Hayden in his speech say anything at all about Chicago?

THE WITNESS: Tom Hayden said that he and Dave Dellinger were planning demonstrations in Chicago for the National Convention. He asked everyone at this meeting to please come to Chicago for these demonstrations. He also said that they were hoping to get at least 20,000 people to Chicago for these conventions. He also said that it was the purpose of the National Mobilization Committee to—he used profanity at that point.

MR. SCHULTZ: Would you relate exactly what he said, using the profane word, please.

THE WITNESS: He said it was the purpose of the National Mobilization Committee to fuck up the Convention in Chicago.

MR. SCHULTZ: Then what did he say, please?

MR. SALZBERG: He related some plans that were being made in California by hippie and Yippie groups. He also mentioned that he was hoping there would not be any racial

[125]

riots among the blacks in Chicago before the Convention because this would turn off a lot of people, and a lot of people would not come out in August.

MR. SCHULTZ: That's all, your Honor. That's all we have on direct.

• • • • •

MR. KUNSTLER: Mr. Salzberg, can you indicate to us what your regular non-FBI occupation is.

THE WITNESS: Press photographer.

MR. KUNSTLER: Are you employed by anybody now?

THE WITNESS: I am self-employed.

MR. KUNSTLER: Is that with something called the New York Press Service?

THE WITNESS: Yes.

MR. KUNSTLER: Prior to New York Press Service, by whom were you employed?

THE WITNESS: *El Tiempo,* a Spanish language newspaper in New York City.

MR. KUNSTLER: Now, when you formed New York Press Service, did you ask Mr. Dellinger for a letter of recommendation?

THE WITNESS: Yes.

MR. SCHULTZ: Objection.

THE COURT: I sustain the objection.

MR. KUNSTLER: Now, when you began to work with the Federal Bureau of Investigation, did you apply for such work or did the FBI contact you?

THE WITNESS: The FBI contacted me and asked me if I would cooperate with the FBI in supplying photographs and I said yes I would.

MR. KUNSTLER: Were those photographs of certain activities in New York City?

THE WITNESS: Yes.

MR. KUNSTLER: What type of events were these?

THE WITNESS: Demonstrations, picket lines, rallies of some sorts.

MR. KUNSTLER: Did you notify the people in charge of any of the events you were photographing that you were in addition to being a photographer at *El Tiempo,* you also were a photographer for the FBI?

THE WITNESS: No one knew I was a photographer for the FBI, including my own wife.

MR. KUNSTLER: Where was the FBI located?

THE WITNESS: The FBI office is at 69th Street and Third Avenue, I believe. It's 201 East 69th Street.

MR. KUNSTLER: What is the telephone number?

THE WITNESS: LE 5-7700.

MR. KUNSTLER: Can you indicate for the jury where you would normally deliver these photographs?

THE WITNESS: The agent would mention a street corner where he would be. I would drive by with my car, pick him up; we would drive to another area, park, conduct whatever business we had. I would probably drive him back to a bus stop or to a train station, drop him, and I would continue on my way. There were other places where we would meet in the Bronx, up by the Bronx Zoo. That's when we had extensive things to discuss, and we spent lengthy time in the car.

MR. KUNSTLER: From January of 1969 on, your income from the FBI jumped appreciably, did it not?

THE WITNESS: Yes, it did.

MR. KUNSTLER: You got $290 in January, $500 in February of '69, $600 in March of '69, $600 in April, $600 in May, $600 in June, $600 in July, $600 in August, and then you had a sudden drop to $300 in September, is that correct?

THE WITNESS: Yes.

MR. KUNSTLER: Did that drop reflect any reluctance on your part to come to Chicago and testify in this case?

THE WITNESS: I don't know. I really don't know how to answer that as to why the drop in September except for the fact that possibly that list was made up in September and they paid me until that date.

MR. KUNSTLER: Didn't you have a discussion with the Federal Bureau of Investigation about testifying in this case?

THE WITNESS: Yes.

MR. KUNSTLER: And didn't you tell the agent that if you testified in this case it would cut off your income from the FBI because now you would be known as an FBI informer? Didn't you tell someone that?

THE WITNESS: Well, it was discussed, yes.

MR. KUNTSLER: Now have you received your second monthly installment or bi-monthly installment for October?

THE WITNESS: No, I have not.

MR. KUNSTLER: They owe you that right now, is that right?

THE WITNESS: The FBI owes me nothing.

MR. KUNSTLER: Now you like this kind of work, don't you, with the FBI?

THE WITNESS: I wouldn't say I like it. I feel it is a necessity.

MR. KUNSTLER: And it pays pretty well, doesn't it?

THE WITNESS: No.

MR. KUNTSLER: What was your income last month from other sources than the FBI?

THE WITNESS: Not very much.

MR. KUNSTLER: How much?

THE WITNESS: Other than the two photographs from Abbie Hoffman, which is $100, possibly two pictures for United Press International, which is about $30.

MR. KUNTSLER: Now, to call your attention to the meeting of March 14, 1968, it was a meeting sponsored by the Resistance, isn't that correct?

THE WITNESS: That is correct.

MR. KUNTSLER: Can you indicate whether the Resistance is an organization that to your knowledge is an advocate of violence?

THE WITNESS: They have performed some violent acts——

A DEFENDANT: That is a lie.

THE WITNESS: —against the draft or in their resistance to the draft they have performed some violent acts.

MR. KUNSTLER: What were those violent acts?

THE WITNESS: Handcuffing themselves to fences, when the police tried to come near them they would kick and fight and resist. I would like to bring one example where some 115, I believe, was arrested at CCNY in New York for harboring a deserter, and as the police asked them to leave, they resisted. They had to be bodily carried out, and some even fought and were arrested on resisting arrest, and so forth. This I consider violence.

MR. KUNSTLER: Weren't ministers involved in that second incident you have referred to?

MR. SCHULTZ: Objection, if the Court please.

THE COURT: I sustain the objection.

MR. KUNSTLER: Now, at this meeting on March 14, 1968, this was held in the Methodist Church, is that correct?

THE WITNESS: That is correct.

MR. KUNSTLER: Did you report what Mr. Hayden's speech was to the FBI after the speech?

THE WITNESS: Yes, I did, by telephone.

MR. KUNSTLER: You had the notes in front of you when you spoke so you wouldn't forget anything, is that correct?

THE WITNESS: Right.

MR. KUNSTLER: You related everything Tom Hayden said, is that correct?

THE WITNESS: Not everything that Tom Hayden said as to what he said about Vietnam and as to what he said about racism in America, but I did tell everything he said about Chicago.

MR. KUNSTLER: He indicated, as far as I understood your direct testimony, what the purpose of MOBE was in going to Chicago, did he not?

THE WITNESS: Right.

MR. KUNSTLER: Then you used an obscenity and said that's what he said about fucking up the convention, or words to that effect, is that it?

THE WITNESS: That was his quote.

MR. KUNSTLER: That was about the key thing that you told the FBI, wasn't it?

THE WITNESS: In my mind, yes.

MR. KUNSTLER: Now, do you remember being interviewed by the Federal Bureau of Investigations with reference to this matter on March 15, 1968?

THE WITNESS: It was the following day which was the fifteenth. I related my information by telephone.

MR. KUNSTLER: All right. I show you D-67 for identification and ask you when did you read the report?

THE WITNESS: Approximately two weeks after I got the—

MR. KUNSTLER: You read through it, made corrections, signed each page with your code name, lined out some things, put in different things. Did you include the words that Mr. Hayden said?

THE WITNESS: No, I did not. I didn't include it because—Could I answer?

MR. KUNSTLER: I didn't ask you why, but if you want to tell me, go ahead.

THE WITNESS: I would like to.

MR. KUNSTLER: I am sure you would like to. Go ahead.

MR. SCHULTZ: Objection to Mr. Kunstler's aside.

THE COURT: Yes. "I'm sure you'd like to," those words may go out, and the jury is directed to disregard them.

MR. KUNSTLER: All right. Then you may explain.

THE WITNESS: Could I explain that? All right.

I did mention to him that a very important statement about the MOBE is omitted from this report, and the agent related to me that any reports that I was to phone in could not have any obscenities in it. They will not print them, and I asked him why, and he told me that they have young girls as stenographers, and they will not print them that way.

MR. KUNSTLER: That isn't wholly true, is it, Mr. Salzberg?

THE WITNESS: Yes, it is.

MR. KUNSTLER: Was not a question asked of Mr. Hayden about violence in Chicago?

THE WITNESS: Yes.

MR. KUNSTLER: And did not Mr. Hayden say in words or substance that that was not the intent of the Mobilization?

THE WITNESS: No, I don't recall that.

MR. KUNSTLER: Did he answer the question, huh?

THE WITNESS: He answered—the question was whether or not there would be violence of the—what do you call it—of the blacks in Chicago, speaking of summer—

MR. KUNSTLER: The blacks are the "what do you call its?"

MR. SCHULTZ: If the Court please—

THE WITNESS: Don't twist my words.

THE COURT: Just a minute, sir.

Mr. Kunstler, if you interrupt the witness again, I will have to discontinue your cross-examination.

MR. KUNSTLER: I was affronted by the statement.

THE COURT: Please don't do it again.

I accept your apology for this, but don't do it again. You are not running this courtroom yet, Mr. Kunstler. Please bear that in mind.

THE WITNESS: The question was whether or not there would be summer violence in Chicago, rioting, and Hayden answered to that that he hoped it would not be. It was not their purpose to excite any of the black ghettos to violence in Chicago.

MR. KUNSTLER: I have no further questions.

THE COURT: Mr. Weinglass, do you want to cross-examine this witness?

THE MARSHAL: If your Honor please, Mr. Kunstler, I request that newspapers be removed from the table, sir, completely.

MR. KUNSTLER: The newspapers are part of our work here.

THE MARSHAL: Prior to the last recess, one of the defendants was holding one of these newspapers up, sir.

(jury excused)

THE COURT: Now, I ask you out of the presence of the jury to advise your clients not to do that. If you don't want to do that, I will act in a manner that I think is appropriate. It doesn't look dignified for newspapers to be read in the United States District Court. I like to read newspapers myself, especially when perchance something complimentary is said about me, but I don't read one up here. You wouldn't respect me if I did.

MR. SCHULTZ: I would like to make one observation for the record. At 12:30 this morning or 12:30 early this afternoon, when the jury was adjourned, after the jury stood up, defendant Hoffman—in fact, he had the same article that he has in front of him there—

ABBIE HOFFMAN: Yes, I was going to show it to—

MR. SCHULTZ: He held up the newspaper for them to see and—

ABBIE HOFFMAN: It ain't a newspaper. It is the *Berkeley Tribe* and doesn't tell lies, so it isn't a newspaper.

THE COURT: You know, when I was out there trying cases, if my client started to talk when another lawyer was speaking, Mr. Kunstler, I told him to remain quiet. Now, I can direct him to remain quiet. We are not running a circus. This happens to be a court—even though there are those who don't share my views.

ABBIE HOFFMAN: I was just trying to be helpful, your Honor.

THE COURT: I will not hear from your client.

MR. SCHULTZ: He held up the paper that's before him now, held it out so the jury could see it, motioned to the jury, and pointed repeatedly to a headline. That's what he did.

MR. RUBIN: What does the headline say?

MR. KUNSTLER: Does your Honor want me to put this into the record? It's headed, "Peace Creeps Run Amuck."

THE COURT: You may do anything you like, sir, as far as putting it into the record. I haven't asked you to put anything into the record, you know that.

Testimony of Louis Salzburg Resumed

MR. WEINGLASS: Mr. Salzberg, have you recently been arrested in the city of New York?

MR. SCHULTZ: Objection.

MR. WEINGLASS: I shouldn't say "recently." In the month of April 1969.

MR. SCHULTZ: Objection, if the Court please.

THE COURT: I sustain the objection.

MR. WEINGLASS: May I ask the basis of that objection?

THE COURT: Certainly. It is not proper as a matter of the law of evidence. It is not proper impeachment.

MR. WEINGLASS: Correct, and I am not using it, your Honor, for impeachment.

THE COURT: If you say it is correct, then why do you ask it?

MR. WEINGLASS: My purpose in asking about this is to indicate that this man is being employed by the FBI, not only as an informer but as an agent provocateur, and in fact he did cause a violent provocation in the city of New York as a paid person for the FBI, and I thought that should be on the record.

MR. SCHULTZ: Objection, if the Court please.

THE COURT: I will let my ruling stand.

MR. SCHULTZ: And I move to have those statements made by Mr. Weinglass that he just made stricken from the record, if the Court please.

THE COURT: I will strike it and direct the jury to disregard it.

MR. WEINGLASS: Mr. Salzberg, are you a member of an antiwar group yourself?

THE WITNESS: Several.

MR. WEINGLASS: And can you tell the jury the names of those organizations?

THE WITNESS: I am on the steering committee of the Vietnam—Vets for Peace. I am on the steering committee of the Fifth Avenue Vietnam Peace Parade Committee. I am a member of the Vets and Reservists to End the War in Vietnam. I am a member of an organization called the Crazies.

MR. WEINGLASS: Are you informing on all of those organizations for the FBI?

MR. SCHULTZ: Objection, if the Court please.

THE COURT: I sustain the objection.

MR. SCHULTZ: If the Court please, Mr. Rubin is sitting here making very noticeable comments. Just one—he called one of your rulings pathetic. If the Court would please—and it's very difficult for me—

MR. RUBIN: It is difficult for me—you keep hopping up and down.

MR. KUNSTLER: I heard the remark, and he did make an observation on the ruling which I think he has a right to make under his free speech rights.

MR. SCHULTZ: There is no free speech rule, if the Court please, in the middle of a proceedings in the District Court to say what you want to say whenever you want to say it and just sit and speak aloud—that is not free speech.

THE COURT: I will not permit out loud talking at your table. I heard the noise, but I didn't know who it was.

ABBIE HOFFMAN: It wasn't me.

THE COURT: I direct everybody at that table not to speak out loud during this trial until they are called to speak in some manner that entitles them to be heard that way.

Continue, please, with your cross-examination.

MR. WEINGLASS: Mr. Salzberg, were you being paid by the FBI in April of 1969 when you disrupted a speech by Hubert Humphrey in the City of New York?

MR. SCHULTZ: If the Court please, I object to the question.

THE COURT: I sustain the objection.

MR. WEINGLASS: Were you being paid by the FBI in July of 1969 when you convinced the Fifth Avenue Parade Committee not to support the Black Panther Party in the United Front Against Fascism conference?

THE WITNESS: I never did that. I never said it.

MR. SCHULTZ: If the Court please—your Honor, I object to the question. I ask that question be stricken.

THE COURT: It may go out. I sustain the objection. I strike it and direct the jury to disregard it.

MR. WEINGLASS: Mr. Salzberg, were you charged with the crime of forgery in April of 1969?

THE WITNESS: The actual charge is possession of a forged implement. It doesn't mean that I forged anything personally.

MR. WEINGLASS: Has the FBI made any promises to you about the disposition of the charges now pending against you, if you would appear in court here today and testify as you have done?

THE WITNESS: No, it never has. Never.

MR. WEINGLASS: No talk of that at all?

THE WITNESS: None whatsoever.

MR. WEINGLASS: I have nothing further.

THE COURT: Is there any redirect examination?

MR. SCHULTZ: Just a couple of questions.

What is the forged document that you are charged with?

THE WITNESS: It was a ticket to eat a meal at the LID, which is, if I remember correctly, Industrial—L—I—D—Liberal Industrial something, which is LID.

MR. SCHULTZ: That is all, your Honor.

THE COURT: You may step down, sir.

Testimony of Frank D. Sweeney

MR. FORAN: Will you state your full name and spell it, please.

THE WITNESS: My name is Frank D. Sweeney.

MR. FORAN: Where are you employed?

THE WITNESS: I am employed by the Dreyer Advertising Agency, New York City.

MR. FORAN: Now, Mr. Sweeney, have you ever obtained any money from the Federal Bureau of Investigation?

THE WITNESS: Over a period of time, approximately, I would say, around $300.

MR. FORAN: What was that money paid to you for?

THE WITNESS: It was paid to me for expenses and service to attend meetings.

MR. FORAN: These meetings that you would attend, would you report to the FBI about them then?

THE WITNESS: That is right. I would report to the FBI.

MR. FORAN: Now, directing your attention to July 25, 1968, about 8:00 o'clock in the evening, where were you?

THE WITNESS: I was at the Hotel Diplomat, which is on West 43rd Street in New York City. I attended a meeting of the Fifth Avenue Peace Parade Committee.

MR. FORAN: Were there any speakers at this meeting?

THE WITNESS: Cora Weiss, Tom Hayden were two of them.

MR. FORAN: Will you state, Mr. Sweeney, what Mr. Hayden said at that time?

THE WITNESS: He said that the war in Vietnam was immoral, it was a war of genocide and that the United States was an outlaw nation. He said that because the United States was an outlaw nation, it had broken all of the rules, and therefore the peace demonstrators could break all the rules, too.

He talked about demonstrations in Berkeley and Paris and Berlin and he specifically referred to the upcoming Democratic Convention in Chicago. He spoke about the fact that the North Vietnamese were shedding blood and the peace demonstrators when they went to Chicago should be prepared to shed blood, too. He said there would be more arrests in Chicago and right through the election than the jails could hold.

MR. FORAN: That is all.

October 24, 1969

THE COURT: Is there any cross-examination?

MR. WEINGLASS: Mr. Sweeney, this was a meeting of the Fifth Avenue Peace Parade Committee, was it not?

THE WITNESS: That is right.

MR. WEINGLASS: Will you tell the jury what this committee is?

THE WITNESS: Well, as far as I can tell, it was a group that was against the war in Vietnam and by the speakers there, it probably had pretty much the inclination of a radical group, possibly.

MR. WEINGLASS: The inclinations of a radical group? Is that because they were against the war in Vietnam?

THE WITNESS: No, no, because I think the way they talked, they wanted to destroy the government.

MR. WEINGLASS: It that right? Do you tell the jury—could you tell the jury what they said that indicated they wanted to destroy the government?

THE WITNESS: From Tom Hayden's speech, in terms of the way he talked, it wasn't just planning that these things were all going to happen in Chicago, and there was going to be bloodshed, and that to me is destroying the government.

MR. WEINGLASS: You deduced that conclusion from the words you heard Tom Hayden use which you related to this jury?

THE WITNESS: The whole tone of the speech was inflammatory and provocative.

MR. WEINGLASS: Now, when Mr. Hayden said that the demonstrators were going to shed blood in Chicago, you felt that was inflammatory, did you not?

THE WITNESS: Those are part of the things that he said.

MR. WEINGLASS: And when Mr. Hayden said that the United States is an outlaw nation and because the United States is breaking the rules the peace demonstrators could break the rules, you thought that was inflammatory, did you not?

THE WITNESS: Yes.

MR. WEINGLASS: He did not call at that point for any specific acts of violence, did he?

THE WITNESS: Not that I remember.

MR. WEINGLASS: As a matter of fact, all he gave was the one statement that you can remember?

THE WITNESS: I remember that very well, yes.

MR. WEINGLASS: Did you hear Mr. Hayden on this evening start his speech by saying the following words:

"We have to understand that the United States Government is attempting to end the antiwar movement rather than ending the war itself."

MR. FORAN: I object to counsel reading from a document not in evidence.

THE COURT: I sustain the objection.

MR. WEINGLASS: Nothing further.

THE COURT: You may go, sir.

Testimony of Michael Kilian

MR. FORAN: Will you state your name, please.

THE WITNESS: Michael Kilian.

MR. FORAN: What is your occupation, Mr. Kilian?

THE WITNESS: I am a reporter for the *Chicago Tribune*.

MR. FORAN: Do you know Thomas Hayden?

THE WITNESS: Yes, I do.

MR. FORAN: Did you have occasion to see Mr. Hayden during the month of May 1968?

THE WITNESS: Yes, I did. In an office building on South Dearborn Street.

MR. FORAN: Now, what occurred when you first arrived at this building, Mr. Kilian?

THE WITNESS: I went into an office—I believe it was on the fourth floor—and asked for Mr. Hayden.

MR. FORAN: What occurred then?

THE WITNESS: I was taken into a side office just off that room and introduced to Mr. Hayden.

MR. FORAN: Did you have a conversation with Mr. Hayden at that time?

THE WITNESS: Yes, I did.

MR. FORAN: Toward the end of your conversation with Mr. Hayden, what occurred, Mr. Kilian?

THE WITNESS: Someone came in the room and said there was a long-distance call for him from New Jersey. He went outside of the room and took the call in the next room.

MR. FORAN: Was the door between the office you were in and the next room open or closed?

THE WITNESS: It was open.

MR. FORAN: Could you hear Mr. Hayden's voice?

THE WITNESS: Yes, I could.

MR. FORAN: What did you hear him say?

THE WITNESS: He said, "Fine. Send them on out. We'll start the revolution now. Do they want to fight?"

MR. FORAN: Now, after you heard Hayden make these statements, what occurred?

THE WITNESS: I wrote them down in my notebook.

MR. FORAN: What did you do then?

THE WITNESS: I waited another five to ten minutes, and then walked out of that office into the main office.

MR. FORAN: When you walked out into the main office, did you see Mr. Hayden?

THE WITNESS: No.

MR. FORAN: That's all.

THE COURT: Cross-examination.

MR. KUNSTLER: Mr. Kilian, you say you worked for the *Tribune* for some three years?

THE WITNESS: Yes.

MR. KUNSTLER: And you are fully familiar with most of its policies as to whom it supports politically and so on.

THE WITNESS: I read the edi—

MR. FORAN: I object to that. That's immaterial.

THE COURT: Sustain the objection.

MR. KUNSTLER: Can you indicate to the jury whether the paper has been a supporter of Mayor Daley?

MR. FORAN: I object to that.

THE COURT: I sustain the objection.

MR. KUNSTLER: Did you take notes on what Hayden said?

THE WITNESS: Yes.

MR. KUNSTLER: Do you have those notes?

THE WITNESS: No, I do not.

MR. KUNSTLER: Can you remember a single phrase, sentence, paragraph that Mr. Hayden said between the "hello" and your first remark that you have attributed to him today, "Fine. Send them out."

THE WITNESS: I have a general recollection of his asking about mutual acquaintances.

MR. KUNSTLER: Did it sound like a social conversation?

THE WITNESS: Primarily, I would imagine.

MR. KUNSTLER: Is it your normal custom as a reporter to eavesdrop on conversations and use them without notifying the person you are interviewing?

MR. FORAN: Objection, your Honor.

THE COURT: I sustain the objection.

MR. KUNSTLER: I have no further questions, your Honor.

THE COURT: All right. Then we will have to recess.

• • • • •

MR. KUNSTLER: Your Honor, we have one application before the jury comes in.

Your Honor, I have been informed by Dave Dellinger, one of the defendants herein, that he has just received a direct personal communication from Xuan Oanh of the North Vietnamese delegation to the Paris peace conference. Mr. Oanh has asked Mr. Dellinger and Mr. Davis to come to Paris this weekend to receive certain information regarding American prisoners of war and this is similar to the communication received by Mr. Dellinger some months ago when this Court granted relief or extension of bail limits for Mr. Dellinger to go to Paris and which eventually resulted, as your Honor recalls, in the voyage of Mr. Davis to North Vietnam and the release of three prisoners of war.

The letter received by Mr. Dellinger indicates that the North Vietnamese may be prepared to release some important information regarding American prisoners of war to Mr. Dellinger and Mr. Davis which I am sure would be of interest to everyone concerned. They have made reservations and, anticipating a successful application to your Honor—

THE COURT: Who gave them the idea that their application would be successful?

MR. KUNSTLER: Well, your Honor, it is important to make the reservations on a week-end because of the fact that it is very crowded.

THE COURT: I appreciate that, but—

MR. KUNSTLER: They have no information, your Honor, except your Honor's previous actions in connection with exactly the same request some time ago.

I might indicate, your Honor, that this will in no way disrupt this trial and is nothing more than essentially extending their bail limits to include Paris, France from Friday, tonight, through Sunday of this weekend, and that the results of their trip might very well have the potential of releasing certain information about American prisoners of war and hopefully of releasing, as it did the last time, under exactly the same situation, of releasing three prisoners of war back to the United States.

THE COURT: Treating your observations as a motion, I deny the motion.

Bring in the jury, Mr. Marshal.

(jury enters)

Testimony of Michael Kilian Resumed

MR. WEINGLASS: Did you think Mr. Hayden meant literally what you thought you heard, that "We'll start the revolution now"?

MR. FORAN: Objection, your Honor.

THE COURT: I sustain the objection.

MR. WEINGLASS: Were you frightened, Mr. Kilian, when you heard these words?

MR. FORAN: Objection, your Honor, as to what the witness thought.

THE COURT: I sustain the objection.

MR. WEINGLASS: Were you fearful that you might be caught up in the revolution that was about to begin?

MR. FORAN: Objection.

THE COURT: I sustain the objection.

MR. WEINGLASS: Did you run back to your paper and—

MR. FORAN: Objection.

MR. WEINGLASS: —tell your paper the revolution is about to begin, you just heard it?

MR. FORAN: Objection, your Honor.

THE COURT: Sustain the objection.

MR. WEINGLASS: No further questions.

THE COURT: We have reached the time when we normally recess.

Ladies and gentlemen of the jury, my usual instructions.

October 27, 1969

THE COURT: Ladies and gentlemen of the jury, good morning.

MR. SEALE: Good morning, ladies and gentlemen of the jury. I hope you don't blame me for anything.

THE COURT: Mr. Marshal, will you tell that man to sit down.

THE MARSHAL: Take a seat, Mr. Seale.

MR. SEALE: I know—

THE COURT: Mr. Marshal, I think Mr. Seale is saying something there.

MR. SEALE: I know I am saying something. You know I am speaking out for the right to defend myself again, don't you, because I have that right as a defendant, don't I?

THE COURT: I don't know what you are going to say and you have a very competent lawyer of record here.

MR. SEALE: He is not my lawyer and you know I fired him before that jury was even picked and put together.

THE COURT: Will you ask him to sit down, Mr. Marshal?

THE MARSHAL: Sit down, Mr. Seale.

MR. SEALE: What about my constitutional right to defend myself and have my lawyer?

THE COURT: Your constitutional rights—

MR. SEALE: You are denying them. You have been denying them. Every other word you say is denied, denied, denied, denied, and you begin to oink in the faces of the masses of the people of this country. That is what you begin to represent, the corruptness of this rotten Government for four hundred years.

THE MARSHAL: Mr. Seale, will you sit down.

MR. SEALE: Why don't you knock me in the mouth? Try that.

THE MARSHAL: Sit down.

THE COURT: Ladies and gentlemen of the jury, I regret that I will have to excuse you.

MR. SEALE: I hope you don't blame me for anything and those false lying notes and letters that were sent that said the Black Panther Party threatened that jury, it's a lie, and you know it's a lie, and the Government did it to taint the jury against me.

(jury excused)

You got that? This racist administrative Government with its superman notions and comicbook politics. We're hip to the fact that Superman never saved no black people. You got that?

[136]

MR. KUNSTLER: I might say, your Honor, you know that I have tried to withdraw from this and you know that Mr. Seale—

THE COURT: I don't know what you tried to do. I know your appearance is of record, and I know I have your assurance orally of record that you represent this man.

MR. KUNSTLER: Your Honor, you can't go on those semantics. This man wants to defend himself.

THE COURT: This isn't semantics. I am not fooled by all of this business.

MR. SEALE: I still demand the right to defend myself. You are not fooled? After you have walked over people's constitutional rights?

THE MARSHAL: Sit down, Mr. Seale.

MR. SEALE: After you done walked over people's constitutional rights, after you done walked over people's constitutional rights, the Sixth Amendment, the Fifth Amendment, and the phoniness and the corruptness of this very trial, for people to have a right to speak out, freedom of speech, freedom of assembly, and et cetera. You have did everything you could with those jive lying witnesses up there presented by these pig agents of the Government to lie and say and condone some rotten racists, fascist crap by racist cops and pigs that beat people's heads—and I demand my constitutional rights—demand—demand—

THE COURT: Will the Marshal bring in the jury, please.

Please call your next witness.

Testimony of William Frapolly

MR. FORAN: Will you state your name, please?

THE WITNESS: William Frapolly.

MR. FORAN: What has been your occupation for the last two years?

THE WITNESS: I have been a student at Northeastern Illinois State College.

MR. FORAN: Have you been a member of any organizations during that time?

THE WITNESS: Yes. Northeastern Illinois State College Peace Council, SDS, the Chicago Peace Council, Student Mobilization, and National Mobilization.

MR. FORAN: When did you join the Students for a Democratic Society?

THE WITNESS: Late in June of 1968.

MR. FORAN: Now, during this period of time has your appearance altered any?

THE WITNESS: Yes, I have grown sideburns approximately to here. My hair is exceedingly long, I have grown a goatee, and I have grown a mustache.

MR. FORAN: Now, during this period of time have you been otherwise employed?

THE WITNESS: Yes, as a member of the Chicago Police Department.

MR. FORAN: When did you first join the Chicago Police Department?

THE WITNESS: I first joined the Chicago Police Department in June of 1966.

MR. FORAN: What is your rank now, sir?

THE WITNESS: I am a patrolman.

MR. FORAN: Now, calling your attention to July 16, 1968, in the afternoon, where were you?

THE WITNESS: On July 16 I attended a meeting at Northeastern Illinois State College.

MR. FORAN: What, if anything, occurred?

THE WITNESS: I filled out a form from the National Mobilization Committee stating I would like to be a marshal for the Democratic National Convention.

MR. FORAN: Now, calling your attention to Friday, August 9, 1968, in the morning, where were you?

THE WITNESS: I went to National Mobilization Committee headquarters. I walked in, I asked someone where the marshals' meeting was. They directed me to the room on the west end of the building.

MR. FORAN: Do you remember any of the people who were in that room?

THE WITNESS: Yes. Rennie Davis was there, David Dellinger, Lee Weiner, Richard Bosciano, Ben Radford, Robert Karlock, Ken Friedman, Dwayne Oklepek, Irv Bock, and there were many other people there.

MR. FORAN: Now you named Rennie Davis. Do you see Mr. Davis here in the courtroom?

THE WITNESS: Yes.

THE COURT: Please step down, Mr. Witness, and point to the man you think is—

MR. FORAN: Walk over toward him, Mr. Witness.

A DEFENDANT: Oink oink.

(Witness identifies defendants and returns to stand.)

MR. FORAN: Now as you entered the meeting, what was being said, if anything, and by whom?

THE WITNESS: Mr. Davis was talking about the march routes on the twenty-eighth. He was saying that they had two plans to march on that night to the Amphitheatre. The first plan was to assemble in Washington Park and then to move west from Washington Park to Halsted and then north on Halsted to the Amphitheatre.

He said he had an alternative, to mass somewhere else in that general area and use the same approximate route to the Amphitheatre. After that he asked for other suggestions.

I suggested the IIT parking lot at 35th and State and I said there would be enough room to mass the large number of people they said would come.

Someone pointed out there was an overpass we would have to walk through and it might be dangerous. Mr. Davis made a comment at that and then I modified that plan and said, "Well, we could mass at Comiskey Park that night."

MR. FORAN: Did anyone make any response to that suggestion?

THE WITNESS: Yes. There was somebody in the room—I think it was Irv Bock, he said the Sox were playing a night game so we couldn't use that area.

After that Mr. Davis began to talk about other things that would happen during the convention.

MR. FORAN: Go ahead. What did he say?

THE WITNESS: He said on the twenty-seventh there would be many small demonstrations throughout the city. He said the purpose of these was to stretch the police force out. He suggested that in one area we could have a nonviolent demonstration and in another area we could have a very militant demonstration, and this would keep the police busy all day. And he also mentioned having a mill-in on Tuesday and Wednesday.

MR. FORAN: Did he describe what a mill-in was?

THE WITNESS: He said a mill-in would be to get anywhere from fifty to a hundred thousand people into the Loop, and then these people would go through the Loop and they would try and disrupt it. He said, "We would block cars driving down the street, we would block people coming and going out of buildings, we would stop people from walking down the street. We would run through stores. We would smash windows and generally try and shut the Loop down."

MR. FORAN: All right. Go ahead. What else was said?

THE WITNESS: He talked about a rock festival that was planned on the twenty-fifth. He said, "We are going to invite the McCarthy kids, the young delegates and children of prominent people that would be here for the Convention." He said "We would lure them here with music and sex." Then he said, "We will keep the people there after eleven o'clock because we will keep the bands going."

MR. FORAN: Now, calling your attention to August 15 in the afternoon, where were you?

THE WITNESS: I was in Lincoln Park.

MR. FORAN: Were any of the defendants present?

THE WITNESS: Rennie Davis was present and Tom Hayden was present.

MR. FORAN: Do you remember any other persons that were present other than Mr. Davis and Mr. Hayden?

THE WITNESS: Yes. Ben Radford was there, Dwayne Oklepek, I was, of course, there, Dave Baker was there. I think there were five of us there. Irv Bock was there.

MR. FORAN: What occurred?

THE WITNESS: Ben Radford said to Davis, "I saw one of those jeeps and it looked like they are going to string out barbed wire in front of us." Davis said, "Is there any way we can stop it?" And I said, "Yes, we could set up a grappling hook and a rope and throw it into the wire and that would snap it." Mr. Davis said, "That's a good idea. We'll use it if they use the jeeps." Then we formed up in a snake dance practice and began to snake dance.

MR. FORAN: What occurred after that?

THE WITNESS: Well, a man from CBS asked if he could photograph the snake dance. Davis said, "Well, there aren't too many of us here today and we just started practicing and we aren't in that good shape, so if you come back next week when we have more people, it will be more impressive when we have practiced it and you can have the exclusive rights to film it."

MR. FORAN: What did you do then?

THE WITNESS: I drove a few people down to Mobilization.

MR. FORAN: What occurred when you arrived?

THE WITNESS: We sat around for a minute or two and then Davis said, "Well, we are going to start the meeting now."

MR. FORAN: Were any of the defendants present at that meeting?

THE WITNESS: Yes. Davis and Hayden. Dave Baker was there, and Richard Bosciano.

MR. FORAN: Was there a conversation at that meeting?

THE WITNESS: Yes, there was. Mr. Davis made a comment that we should have a different attitude toward police than troops. Mr. Davis said the Federal troops from Fort

Bragg will be brought in and that we should be very nice to these people, we shouldn't harass them or provoke them, we should just try and organize them, show them that they are doing the wrong thing.

Then he said the second group would be the National Guard. He said the National Guard is only—well, he said, "They are only a bunch of fucking draft-dodgers anyway," and that we shouldn't provoke them that much, we should talk to them and try to get them to join our side.

He said the last groups would be the Chicago police. He said, "We all know what bastards they are anyway, and that we can't avoid a confrontation with them, so we are going to harass them, provoke them, and we are going to keep this up through the whole Convention, and that should be our attitude toward the police, we should do it whenever we get a chance."

MR. FORAN: Calling your attention to Saturday, August 17, in the afternoon, where were you?

THE WITNESS: I was in Grant Park that afternoon.

MR. FORAN: Would you name some of the persons who were present?

THE WITNESS: John Froines was there, Tom Hayden, Ben Radford, a person by the name of Shaughnessy from the Chicago area draft resisters.

MR. FORAN: Was there a conversation at that time?

THE WITNESS: Yes, there was. Radford said it was going to be rough going on the march on the twenty-eighth. He said, "We'll be going through many hostile areas, and even if we had a permit, we'd have a problem marching through there."

Hayden said, "That's true, and we might not even have a march that day, but no matter what happens, we're going to have a vigil at the Amphitheatre that night."

He said that the vigil people should bring enough food and water to last for five or six hours, and that we'd wait there until the candidate was nominated and then we'd use a snake dance to leave that area.

MR. FORAN: Do you recall anything else being said?

THE WITNESS: Yes. Someone suggested to Mr. Hayden that if we don't have the march, we could have a mill-in.

Hayden said, "We're going to think about that. It's a good suggestion. We'll get all the people we could, upwards to a hundred thousand people, and go through the Loop, run into stores, keep people from coming out of their office buildings to go home, stop cars on the street, stop people from walking down the street, and even break windows."

MR. FORAN: Do you recall anything further being said at that meeting?

THE WITNESS: To the best of my recollection, I don't.

MR. FORAN: Now, calling your attention to the twentieth of August, 1968, in the afternoon, where were you?

THE WITNESS: Well, I walked into Lincoln Park, and there were people standing around, and a small marshals' meeting happened that day. John Froines and Lee Weiner were there.

MR. FORAN: Now, what was said, Mr. Witness?

THE WITNESS: Well, at this meeting Lee Weiner said that we were going to have the march on the twenty-eighth, and we are going to work on the march route. He said that we'd have communications set up between marshals and that we'd have scouts out ahead of the marshals that would relay information back. He said that the marshals would probably wear helmets. Everyone in the group agreed that they should. Then Terry Gross said, "Also, we're going to have flares, and we're going to have those lighted." He said these could be used as a weapon to keep anyone away from the marchers. Someone said—I think it was John Froines—he said they'd burn at about 4,000 degrees Fahrenheit and would be very effective in keeping anyone away from the marchers. Everyone liked the idea.

MR. FORAN: Now, what occurred then?

THE WITNESS: Well, this meeting broke up, and about ten minutes later we went into another meeting.

MR. FORAN: Were any of the defendants present?

THE WITNESS: Yes. Weiner and Froines were at this meeting. So was Abbie Hoffman.

MR. FORAN: Do you see Mr. Hoffman here in the courtroom?

THE WITNESS: Yes, I do.
MR. FORAN: Would you step down and point him out, please.
THE WITNESS: Mr. Hoffman is sitting with the leather vest on, the shirt—he just shot me with his finger. His hair is very unkempt.

Lee Weiner talked about the march on the twenty-eighth. He said that people should get in shape for it and they should practice the snake dance.

After that, Abbie Hoffman was telling everyone that he had gotten a book from one of the news companies that was here that listed all the delegates' hotel numbers, the hotels they were staying in and their room numbers, and he said he was going to pass this out, he was going to mimeograph it so that everybody could have a copy of it and that if people wanted to harass a delegate, they could go there at night or three or four in the morning and harass that person. He said that it was a good thing that everybody should have it so they could go around and find the delegates.
THE COURT: Mr. Foran, I think we have reached a point where we will recess for the morning session.

(jury excused)
(court in recess)

MR. SEALE: I want to make a request, Judge Hoffman, that my wife be let in with my son and that the marshal, Deputy Marshal Richard Jones, has attempted to harass her and tell her he was going to lock her up because she had my son here. He just come here over the weekend, and that he be allowed—
THE COURT: Mr. Marshal, you take care of the requests of anybody here as far as admission to the courtroom is concerned.
MR. SEALE: In other words, my son can't come in, right?
THE COURT: Mr. Marshal, I have not addressed this man. Will you undertake to see what he wants and do what is fair under the law.
MR. KUNSTLER: Your Honor, while you are on the subject, a lot of people have been forced to stand outside by the marshals waiting to come up, and it was twenty-nine degrees this morning, and I would think that they should be allowed to stand in the building rather than out in the cold, and perhaps your Honor could give some directions—
THE COURT: I am not the custodian of the courthouse. The marshal is in charge of seating in the courtroom, sir.

I walked to lunch today, and I wasn't so cold.
MR. KUNSTLER: But your Honor didn't stand in twenty-nine degree temperature waiting to get into this building from 7:30 on.
THE COURT: We do the best that we can, and it is entirely up to the marshals. Mr. Marshal, bring in the jury.

(jury enters)

THE COURT: You may continue, sir, with the witness.
ABBIE HOFFMAN: There are around fourteen marshals.
MR. RUBIN: Military state.
MR. KUNSTLER: We have an army of marshals here in the back of the room, and I think that is not necessary and gives an aura to this trial which it shouldn't have.

Look at them, your Honor. You can see one, two, three, four, five, six, seven, eight men there.
THE COURT: I think, if you don't mind, the marshals will look after security in this courtroom.
MR. KUNSTLER: I know, but the jury sees this, your Honor. It gives a false impression to the jury.
THE COURT: Yes. Yes, they do. The jury heard what went on this morning also. I can't help that.
MR. FORAN: Your Honor, I object to all the statements made by Mr. Kunstler as improper.
THE COURT: I sustain the objection, and I wish you would proceed with the direct examination of this witness which I directed earlier.

MR. FORAN: Now, calling your attention to Monday, the twenty-sixth of August, in the afternoon, where were you?

THE WITNESS: I was in Lincoln Park, just south of the fieldhouse.

MR. FORAN: Were you alone, or were you with someone?

THE WITNESS: No, I was with John Froines and Lee Weiner, and there were other people I don't recall.

MR. FORAN: Now, was there a conversation at that time?

THE WITNESS: Yes, there was. John Froines said, "The marshals acted as better street fighters than they did controlling the crowd. Last night showed that we can fight in the street." Froines said people should break into small groups and that these groups should be violent and that people should tonight leave the park and run into Old Town, disable cars and smash windows. Everyone in the group agreed with this, and they called these groups affinity groups.

MR. FORAN: Now, what happened then?

THE WITNESS: Well, during the conversation Hayden and Wolfe Lowenthal approached the group. Hayden said, "I'm going to be arrested," and then two officers in plainclothes came up and arrested him. They also arrested Wolfe Lowenthal.

MR. FORAN: Then what happened?

THE WITNESS: I saw John Froines yelling at a police officer. Someone in the group said that the Legal Defense Committee should be called, and myself and Rowan Berman placed a call to the Legal Defense Committee.

MR. FORAN: All right. Now, calling your attention to late that night, near midnight, where were you?

THE WITNESS: Myself and two other people were walking out of the Conrad Hilton, and as we were walking out, the doorman was talking to Rennie Davis, Tom Hayden, and two other people.

MR. FORAN: What was the conversation?

THE WITNESS: The doorman said they couldn't enter the hotel, and either Davis or Hayden said, "Well, we are going to go visit some friends in a room."

The doorman said, "I'm sorry, I can't let you in."

At this point a Chicago police officer in uniform came over and asked what the problem was.

The doorman said he couldn't let these people in. The police officer asked Davis and Hayden to move away from the door.

MR. FORAN: Where did you go?

THE WITNESS: We walked out to Balbo and then walked east on Balbo to the corner which is Michigan Avenue. Then we crossed Balbo walking north.

MR. FORAN: What occurred when you were crossing the street, if anything?

THE WITNESS: When we were crossing the street, Davis and Hayden were behind me. I heard a shout and I turned around and Hayden was facing a police officer in plainclothes.

MR. FORAN: And what occurred?

THE WITNESS: After that Hayden was walking away, the police officer grabbed him and Hayden went limp and fell to the ground.

MR. FORAN: And what happened then?

THE WITNESS: He tried to roll away and the officer restrained him. Davis said, "Look what they're doing to Tom. Let's do something about it."

MR. FORAN: And what, if anything, occurred?

THE WITNESS: I remember the person next to me taking about two steps forward and there were some Chicago police officers there and they pushed him back along with the rest of the group and moved us north on Michigan.

MR. FORAN: Now, calling your attention to the evening of the next day, Tuesday, August 27, where were you on that day?

THE WITNESS: I was in Lincoln Park also that day. There was a Free Huey rally going on.

MR. FORAN: How many people were attending that particular rally?

THE WITNESS: I would say a thousand or two thousand people.

MR. FORAN: Did you recognize any of the speakers?

THE WITNESS: I heard Jerry Rubin give a speech, Phil Ochs sang and then a person who identified himself as Bobby Seale spoke.

MR. SEALE: I object to that because my lawyer is not here. I have been denied my right to defend myself in this courtroom. I object to this man's testimony against me because I have not been allowed my constitutional rights.

THE COURT: I repeat to you, sir, you have a lawyer. Your lawyer is Mr. Kunstler, who represented to the Court that he represents you.

MR. SEALE: He does not represent me.

THE COURT: Ladies and gentlemen, I will excuse you.

(jury excused)

THE COURT: Now you just keep on this way and—

MR. SEALE: Keep on what? Keep on what?

THE COURT: Just sit down.

MR. SEALE: Keep on what? Keep on getting denied my constitutional rights?

THE COURT: Will you be quiet?

MR. SEALE: Now I still object. I object because you know it is wrong. You denied me my right to defend myself. You think black people don't have a mind. Well, we got big minds, good minds, and we know how to come forth with constitutional rights, the so-called constitutional rights. I am not going to be quiet. I am talking in behalf of my constitutional rights, man, in behalf of myself, that's my constitutional right to talk in behalf of my constitutional rights.

THE COURT: Bring in the jury, Mr. Marshal.

MR. SEALE: I still object to that man testifying against me without my lawyer being here, without me having a right to defend myself.

Black people ain't supposed to have a mind? That's what you think. We got a body and a mind. I wonder, did you lose yours in the Superman syndrome comic book stories? You must have to deny us our constitutional rights.

THE COURT: Are you getting all of this, Miss Reporter?

MR. SEALE: I hope she gets it all.

(jury enters)

THE COURT: I note that your counsel has remained quiet during your dissertation.

MR. SEALE: You know what? I have no counsel here. I fired that lawyer before that jury heard anything and you know it. That jury hasn't heard all of the motions you denied behind the scenes. How you tricked that juror out of that stand there by threatening her with that jive letter that you know darned well I didn't send, which is a lie. And they blame me every time they are being kept from their loved ones and their homes. They blame me every time they come in the room. And I never sent those letters, you know it.

THE COURT: Please continue with the direct examination.

MR. FORAN: Now, later on that evening, about ten o'clock, where were you?

THE WITNESS: I was in Lincoln Park.

MR. FORAN: Now what were you doing there?

THE WITNESS: When I first arrived in Lincoln Park, I was walking through the crowd. I came upon John Froines, Marilyn Katz, Terry Gross and another person. Marilyn Katz showed us a group of guerrilla nails she had.

MR. FORAN: Would you describe them?

MR. WEINGLASS: If your Honor please, I am going to have to object at this point. The prosecution is attempting to bring into this case what the prosecution attempted to bring into the case in United States vs. Benjamin Spock.*

What I am referring to is they are trying to bring into this case conduct and statements of third persons who are not here in court and cannot defend themselves and are not here for purposes of cross-examination.

What the government is attempting to do now is to show Mr. Froines' intent to be part of an illicit conspiracy by introducing evidence of what a third person has done or said and that the Government cannot do. I object to it.

THE COURT: Mr. Foran.

MR. FORAN: Your Honor, of course Mr. Weinglass misstates the Spock case. The Spock case didn't have anything at all to do with statements made by persons in the presence of the defendant. In one instance the defendant is present—that is in this instance; in the Spock case the defendant was not present. It is a clear distinction in the law. The case is clearly not applicable to this evidence.

MR. WEINGLASS: May I repeat what I read from the Spock case?

THE COURT: Don't repeat. Don't repeat. I listened to you very carefully.

Mr. Weinglass, your objection is not well taken, sir. The objection will be overruled.

MR. FORAN: Would you describe what guerrilla nails are?

THE WITNESS: She had two types. One was a cluster of nails that were sharpened at both ends, and they were fastened in the center. It looked like they were welded or soldered. She said these were good for throwing or putting underneath tires.

She showed another set that was the same type of nails sharpened at both ends, but they were put through styrofoam cylinder. There was a weight put through the middle of it which was another nail, and they were all put together through the styrofoam with something that looked like liquid solder.

MR. FORAN: To whom was she showing these objects?

THE WITNESS: Showing them to everyone in the group, including John Froines.

MR. FORAN: Was anything further said at that time?

THE WITNESS: Yes. John Froines said he liked both of them and that he wondered if we could get some more.

MR. FORAN: Now, I will call your attention to the next morning, Wednesday morning, the twenty-eighth of August. Where were you?

THE WITNESS: I was at 407 South Dearborn, National MOBE headquarters.

MR. FORAN: Would you name some of the people that were there?

THE WITNESS: Well, there was John Froines and Lee Weiner, Marilyn Katz, myself. Let's see. David Dellinger was there. Tom Hayden, Rennie Davis. There were other people I don't remember their names.

MR. FORAN: All right. What was said and by whom?

THE WITNESS: Well, the meeting started off with Davis saying, "We're going to have a rally today, and we need some speakers for it." He said, "I've been thinking about having some of the people that were injured speak, and we could get them up and have them talk about how their injuries happened."

Hayden didn't like this idea. He said, "In a revolution you expect injuries, and those injuries aren't supposed to be displayed. The injured people shouldn't be displayed. They should be accepted, and the struggle should go on."

Davis after that said, "Well OK, Tom. We won't do it. But how about you speaking?"

Hayden said, "Yeah, I'll speak."

People were throwing out names. I remember somebody saying to let Jerry Rubin speak because he gave a good speech on Tuesday night. They also said Tom Neumann from New York was a very violent speaker.

Then Dellinger made a comment. He said, "It looks like we're not going to have the march to the Amphitheatre today," and he said, "We should have a march anyway, and we know it's not going to make it, but we should try it anyway." He said they could use the march as a diversion to get people out of Lincoln Park.

MR. FORAN: Out of which park?

THE WITNESS: Out of Grant Park, I'm sorry.

MR. FORAN: Go ahead.

THE WITNESS: Davis said, "That's a good idea. We can have your march start, and we'll use that as a diversion. We'll only get about a hundred people to go to that. Then we can pull people out of Grant Park and we can either have a rally across from the Hilton or we can just go into the Loop and have the mill-in."

MR. FORAN: Then did you talk to anyone further at the meeting?

THE WITNESS: Yes, I did. I had a conversation with John Froines.

MR. DELLINGER: Mr. Foran, do you believe one word of that?

MR. FORAN: Your Honor, may the record show the comment from the defendant Dellinger, your Honor?

THE COURT: Yes. Mr. Dellinger has made several comments from time to time. The record may indeed show—

MR. DELLINGER: I asked Mr. Foran if he could possibly believe one word of that. I don't believe the witness believes it. I don't believe Mr. Foran believes it.

THE COURT: And continue to take his words. I admonish you, sir, not to interrupt this trial by your conversation or your remarks. You have a very competent lawyer representing you. You are not permitted to speak while he represents you.

MR. FORAN: Would you state the conversation that you had with Mr. Froines.

THE WITNESS: Yes. I said, "John, I saw you out in the street last night near Wells and Eugenie."

He said, "Yeah, I was out there."

And I said, "You were doing pretty good."

And he said, "Yeah, we hit a couple of cops' cars."

Then he said, "You know, the marshals are better street fighters than they are at controlling the crowd. It really worked out nice."

MR. FORAN: Now, calling your attention to the next day, Thursday, August 29, in the afternoon, where were you?

THE WITNESS: I was at Grant Park, sitting on the grass, across the street from the Conrad Hilton.

MR. FORAN: Did you see anyone that you knew?

THE WITNESS: Well, in that area I saw Hayden and Davis, John Froines, Lee Weiner, Craig Shimabukuro, and many other people there.

MR. FORAN: Did you have a conversation with any of them?

THE WITNESS: I had a conversation with Lee Weiner and John Froines.

MR. FORAN: What was said, Mr. Frapolly?

THE WITNESS: Well, John Froines was talking about how he had purchased butyric acid and that he used the butyric acid in hotels and restaurants the night before. He said it really cleared out some of the restaurants. He said butyric acid smells like vomit.

Then Shimabukuro asked Weiner if I was all right, and Weiner said yes. Then Shimabukuro proceeded to tell me about some plans that were being set up for that night. He said I was to meet in the middle level of the Grant Park garage and that I wasn't supposed to bring anybody with me or tell anybody about what we were going to do. We were supposed to meet there about 7:30 and that we were going to fire bomb it. He said that the materials needed would be bought by someone and that I should be there at 7:30.

MR. FORAN: Now, do you recall anything else being said at that time?

THE WITNESS: Yes. John Froines said he had four cans of gasoline and that he didn't know exactly how he was going to use them. He said he would either use the gasoline tonight or use the butyric acid.

MR. FORAN: Now, calling your attention to the next day, Friday, August 30, where were you?

THE WITNESS: Friday, August 30, I was in Downers Grove, Illinois. There was a farm that National Mobilization was having a picnic at that day.

MR. FORAN: Who were some of the people that were there? Would you name them?

THE WITNESS: Well, Davis and Hayden, Froines, Weiner, Vernon Grizzard, I think Richard Bosciano was there, Irv Bock.

MR. FORAN: Was there a conversation at that time?

THE WITNESS: Yes, there was. John Froines said, "Did anybody see the article in the *Tribune* this morning?" And he said, "There's got to be a spy in here." He said, "They know too much about what's going on," and he said he had given some butyric acid to some girls the night before and that they got caught, and he said, "That spy's got to be real high up in National Mobilization, and if I get my hands on him, I'll fix him." Lee Weiner said when he had gotten to the underground garage that night, he was walking down there, and he said he saw some men—he said they were police—questioning Craig Shimabukuro, and when he saw this, he left. He said he didn't know if Shimabukuro was arrested or on his way back to California or where, because no one had seen him that day.

Then Froines started talking about how he purchased the butyric acid. He said he went to Walgreen's, and as he was in Walgreen's he was smelling hair remover. He said there was a brand his mother used when he was a kid, and it was very foul smelling, and after about 15 minutes in Walgreen's smelling all different brands of hair remover, the saleslady became rather suspicious, and Froines left. Then he said he got the idea to use butyric acid.

He said he went to Central Scientific, and when he bought the acid he had to show three different types of identification, and he had to sign a receipt for it. Then he went and got containers for it, and then he said he gave the acid to the girls to use on the night before, and he said they got a kick out of using it.

After that, Froines talked about setting up an underground chemist network. He says there has to be a need for a biochemist in the movement, and then he started talking about how tear gas was made. He said they could get together and they could have the formulas for making tear gas, Molotov cocktails, Mace, and other devices. He thought it was a very good idea.

MR. FORAN: Do you recall anything else being said at that meeting?

THE WITNESS: No, I think my recollection is exhausted.

MR. FORAN: That's all, your Honor.

October 28, 1969

THE CLERK: There is a motion on behalf of the defendant Seale.

MR. SEALE: I have another written motion respect to—

THE COURT: I can't hear you, sir. When I say I can't hear you, I hear you but I am not permitted under the law to hear you make a motion. You have a lawyer of record here. But I tell you that I have read your motion carefully, considered it, and I deny it.

MR. SEALE: You don't want to hear me read the motion?

THE COURT: I read it. I am the one that has to read it.

MR. SEALE: I want it for the court record. I will present it myself in behalf of myself in my own defense.

THE COURT: It will be of record.

I direct the clerk to file it.

MR. KUNSTLER: Your Honor, I have three applications which I would like to make. One is on behalf of all defendants except Mr. Seale. I move for a mistrial on the basis of your Honor's persistent refusal to allow Mr. Seale to defend himself. The defendants take the position that this being a conspiracy trial, that this adversely affects all defendants in this trial and therefore for all of the reasons that have been stated to your Honor before we feel that there should be a mistrial in this case because of your Honor's refusal to permit Mr. Seale to have the constitutional right to defend himself as his attorney as he has expressed to your Honor on numerous occasions.

That is my first application.

THE COURT: I will deny the motion.

What is your next motion?

MR. KUNSTLER: Your Honor, I am moving for a one-day adjournment of this trial so that Mr. Weinglass and I can consult with Mr. Garry in San Francisco. There is other legal action contemplated in an effort to obtain for Mr. Seale his right to be able to represent himself in this action, and Mr. Garry has indicated that he would very much like to consult with Mr. Weinglass and myself because of our intimate knowledge of what has gone on in this courtroom.

Mr. Garry is confined to his home. I spoke to him last night and he has not been to his office since the operation and cannot travel to Chicago. Therefore we would have to travel to him. I would request your Honor's permission to grant such a motion for tomorrow morning.

THE COURT: I deny the motion.

MR. KUNSTLER: Now that it has been denied, I would ask your Honor to grant permission for one of co-counsel here, Mr. Weinglass or myself, to be absent tomorrow to consult with Mr. Garry.

THE COURT: Only on these conditions, Mr. Kunstler; that first each and every defendant in this case stand up at his place at the defense table and agree that either you or Mr. Fineglass look after his interests.

MR. KUNSTLER: Weinglass, your Honor.

THE COURT: Mr. Weinglass. I will begin over again.

Only under these conditions: That each and every defendant consent to the absence of either yourself or Mr. Weinglass, and on this further condition, that you live up to your oral and written representation to me that you represent Mr. Seale.

MR. SEALE: Since you say each and every defendant, I ain't going for it no way. He ain't my lawyer so—

MR. KUNSTLER: Your Honor, I don't think I could even ask the defendants to make any comment on that. I know what their reaction would be.

THE COURT: If you know, the motion will be denied.

(jury enters)

Testimony of William Frapolly Resumed

MR. KUNSTLER: Mr. Frapolly, I understand yesterday you testified that you had been or were a student at Northeastern Illinois State College?

THE WITNESS: That is right, sir.

MR. KUNSTLER: Are you still a member of the student body in good standing?

THE WITNESS: No, I am not.

MR. KUNSTLER: You were expelled, were you not, for throwing the president off the stage physically?

THE WITNESS: No, I wasn't, sir.

MR. KUNSTLER: What were you expelled for?

THE WITNESS: I was expelled for being with a group of people that threw the president off the stage.

MR. KUNSTLER: Did you help to organize and plan this physical attack on the president of this university?

THE WITNESS: No, I did not, sir.

MR. KUNSTLER: Were you participating in discussions about it?

THE WITNESS: That is correct.

MR. KUNSTLER: Now when you were participating in those discussions, is it not true that you were receiving pay from the Police Department of the City of Chicago?

THE WITNESS: That is correct, sir.

MR. KUNSTLER: Is it not true that you were instructed by the Police Department to participate in this physical attack on the president of the University?

THE WITNESS: That is not correct, sir.

MR. KUNSTLER: Now you testified yesterday that in doing this work you grew sideburns, a mustache, a goatee, and let your hair grow long, is that correct?

THE WITNESS: That is correct.

MR. KUNSTLER: Can you give some indication to the jury how life was for you with long hair and a goatee?

MR. FORAN: Objection, your Honor.

THE COURT: I sustain the objection.

MR. KUNSTLER: Didn't you tell the grand jury how awful life was for you with long hair and a goatee in this city?

MR. FORAN: Objection.

THE COURT: I sustain the objection.

MR. KUNSTLER: Now you started, you say, on February 13, 1968, to do this work and you kept it up until September of 1969, is that correct?

THE WITNESS: No, sir.

MR. KUNSTLER: When did you stop?

THE WITNESS: I stopped—my cover was officially blown yesterday.

MR. KUNSTLER: Oh, officially blown yesterday by your testimony, is that correct?

THE WITNESS: That is correct, sir.

MR. KUNSTLER: Now yesterday you revealed yourself to the world for what you were, is that correct?

MR. FORAN: I object to that, your Honor.

THE COURT: I sustain the objection.

MR. KUNSTLER: When you testified before the grand jury you were known as Richard Rowe, weren't you?

THE WITNESS: That's correct, sir.

MR. KUNSTLER: Even the grand jury didn't know your true name, is that correct?

THE WITNESS: That's—that's correct.

MR. KUNSTLER: Now, when you came into the meeting at National Mobilization, do you remember a discussion about the twenty-seventh of August?

THE WITNESS: As I recall, I said there would be many demonstrations, some large, some small, on the twenty-seventh.

MR. KUNSTLER: But did you say that the small demonstrations had a purpose to, quote, stretch the police force out, end quote?
THE WITNESS: Yes, I remember that.
MR. KUNSTLER: Now, do you remember testifying before the grand jury in this case?
THE WITNESS: Yes, I did.
MR. KUNSTLER: Are you certain that you told the grand jury that the purpose of the demonstrations, the small demonstrations which you described for us yesterday, was to stretch the police force out or words to that effect?
THE WITNESS: I think I did.
MR. KUNSTLER: Are you certain?
THE WITNESS: No, I'm not.
MR. KUNSTLER: Then I ask you to look at your testimony on pages 22 to 26 and refresh your recollection as to whether you did or did not tell them that.
MR. FORAN: Your Honor, I object to this form.
THE COURT: I sustain the objection.
MR. FORAN: We will be reading grand jury forever. I call the Court's attention that the words "decentralize the demonstrations" are right in the grand jury testimony. I just found that, luckily.
MR. KUNSTLER: Why doesn't Mr. Foran replace the witness and testify? He is doing what you are forbidding me to do. He is reading—
MR. FORAN: I am trying to point up the reason that these are improper questions.
MR. KUNSTLER: Your Honor, the words "decentralize the demonstrations" hasn't got a bloody thing to do with stretching out the police force.
THE COURT: Oh, they don't have a bloody thing to do with it.
I sustain the objection.
MR. KUNSTLER: Why can't he look at the testimony and refresh his recollection? I don't understand that.
THE COURT: Well, maybe I have to repeat what I said to you some time ago.
When you get to be as old as I am, you might be able to understand it.
MR. KUNSTLER: You are not certain that you told the grand jury that, are you?
THE WITNESS: That's correct.
MR. KUNSTLER: By the way, Mr. Frapolly, prior to coming into this courtroom yesterday, how many meetings had you had with the United States Attorney in this case about your testimony?
THE WITNESS: There were about three.
MR. KUNSTLER: Now did not Mr. Foran at any of these meetings say to you that your previous reports and testimony didn't implicate the defendants enough and you ought to elaborate a little more?
THE WITNESS: No, he didn't.
MR. KUNSTLER: Nothing like that at all?
THE WITNESS: No.
MR. KUNSTLER: When you testified before the grand jury, did you have any notes with you at that time?
THE WITNESS: Yes, I did. I had the reports from the FBI. When I walked in the room Mr. Abel, my control officer, said to me, "I am going to ask you questions." He said, "It might be better to read the reports from the FBI that you have in front of you, because they are written in the third person and as you are speaking, you might reveal your identity if you spoke from the first person."
MR. KUNSTLER: Is it your testimony that a great deal of the testimony before the grand jury that you have in front of you was reading from FBI reports prepared by the FBI?
THE WITNESS: Yes, sir.
MR. KUNSTLER: Now there came a time that you have testified to on this meeting of August 9, this first meeting of the marshals, when Mr. Davis started to mention something about a mill-in in the Loop, is that correct?
THE WITNESS: Yes, sir.

MR. KUNSTLER: And you gave us a graphic description yesterday, did you not, of what a mill-in in the Loop was, didn't you?

THE WITNESS: Yes, I did.

MR. KUNSTLER: Was that a particularly significant thing that Mr. Davis said?

THE WITNESS: I think it was.

MR. KUNSTLER: Did you remember whether you told the grand jury about this significant thing?

THE WITNESS: I think I did.

MR. KUNSTLER: Would you look at pages 22 to 26 of the grand jury minutes which are the only pages with reference to the August 9 meeting and let me know whether it refreshes your recollection as to whether you did or you didn't?

THE WITNESS: I didn't find anything in there that—

MR. KUNSTLER: You did not. Does that refresh your recollection as to what you told the grand jury about this significant thing?

THE WITNESS: It does.

MR. KUNSTLER: You did not tell them, did you?

THE WITNESS: That's correct.

MR. KUNSTLER: Now, I show you D-78 for identification and ask you if you can identify that document.

THE WITNESS: Yes. That's my control officer's report, sir.

MR. KUNSTLER: And do you know whether your control officer's report contained any reference to this significant thing that Rennie Davis said?

MR. FORAN: I object to that, your Honor.

THE COURT: Sustained.

MR. KUNSTLER: Now, you have also stated on your direct that Rennie Davis said something about luring the McCarthy kids, the young delegates, and children by music and sex, do you remember that?

THE WITNESS: Yes, I do.

MR. KUNSTLER: Did you tell the grand jury anything about sex?

THE WITNESS: I don't think I did, sir.

MR. KUNSTLER: Did you tell the FBI anything about sex?

THE WITNESS: I think so, sir.

MR. KUNSTLER: Would you look at D-79, which is the FBI report, which you have testified you had before you when you testified for the grand jury, and let us know whether that appears in that FBI report.

MR. FORAN: I object to that.

THE COURT: Sustain the objection.

MR. KUNSTLER: Is it not true that you told the grand jury that one of the reasons for inviting McCarthy delegates and so on, young people, to the park was so the police would not invade the park?

MR. FORAN: I object to that, your Honor; no foundation. It is improper form.

THE COURT: That is not the way to do it. I sustain the objection.

MR. KUNSTLER: Your Honor, I guess the Appellate Court will have to tell me how to do it then.

THE COURT: Oh, I don't threaten very easily, sir.

MR. KUNSTLER: I am not threatening, your Honor. I just think it is classic impeachment.

THE COURT: I don't try to second-guess an Appellate Court, and I don't want a cheap remark like that made again by you, sir.

MR. KUNSTLER: Your Honor, it is not a cheap remark. It is a heartfelt remark, and we are following the book on this.

THE COURT: Yes, it is. I will not permit a lawyer to threaten me.

MR. KUNSTLER: I am not threatening. I am saying we will take it somewhere else.

THE COURT: Your client has a right to appeal, sir. He has a right to appeal to the United States Supreme Court. I do the best I can here.

MR. KUNSTLER: Is it not true that Mr. Davis said absolutely nothing that you have attributed to him with reference to the Federal troops, the National Guard and the Chicago police?

THE WITNESS: Mr. Davis made all those comments.

MR. KUNSTLER: And did you tell the grand jury that he so did?

MR. FORAN: Objection.

THE COURT: I sustain the objection as I did a moment ago.

MR. KUNSTLER: Did you not tell the grand jury that these remarks might have been said by David Baker alone?

MR. FORAN: Your Honor, I object to that.

THE COURT: In any event I sustain the objection.

MR. KUNSTLER: Did Mr. Baker also discuss the Federal troops and the National Guard and the Chicago police?

THE WITNESS: Yes, Mr. Baker said that it would be good to try and organize Federal troops.

MR. KUNSTLER: That is all he said?

THE WITNESS: He made other comments which I don't remember.

MR. KUNSTLER: Is that what Mr. Foran told you to say on the witness stand?

THE WITNESS: Mr. Foran has told me nothing to say.

MR. KUNSTLER: Nothing. You knew, did you not, that Mr. Dave Baker was not a defendant in this case before you started to testify, didn't you?

THE WITNESS: Yes.

MR. KUNSTLER: And you knew Mr. Davis was, didn't you?

MR. FORAN: I object to that.

THE COURT: I sustain the objection.

MR. KUNSTLER: Now on that day that we are discussing, which is the seventeenth of August, you testified about a later meeting which was, I understand, at Grant Park, is that correct?

THE WITNESS: That is correct, sir.

MR. KUNSTLER: Was John Froines present at that meeting?

THE WITNESS: Yes, he was.

MR. KUNSTLER: When you gave the list of names to the grand jury as to who was present at that meeting, did you not omit the name of John Froines?

THE WITNESS: It's possible, sir, but he was there.

MR. KUNSTLER: It's possible that you did omit his name, is that correct?

THE WITNESS: Yes, it is possible.

MR. KUNSTLER: Now at that meeting there was some statement by one of the participants that the march might have rough going.

Do you recall that?

THE WITESS: Yes, I do, sir.

MR. KUNSTLER: And Tom Hayden said that if there was rough going, that instead of the march there should be a vigil at the Amphitheatre?

THE WITNESS: He said that fifty to a hundred thousand people would mass at the Amphitheatre. He said people would break into small groups. They'd have discussions about what was going on, about the candidate, and then they'd reform into a snake dance and leave the area.

MR. KUNSTLER: They'd leave the area by a snake dance?

THE WITNESS: Yes, sir.

MR. KUNSTLER: Fifty to a hundred thousand people would snake dance through the streets of Chicago, is that what Mr. Hayden said?

MR. FORAN: Objection, your Honor. And I also would like the record to note the character of the noises and giggling and laughing from the defense table.

THE COURT: Yes. I've repeatedly asked that there be no loud laughing, and there was after that question.

MR. FORAN: Your Honor, may the record show that the defendant Froines just made a comment saying, "We laughed—we laughed because it was a stupid answer."

I'd like to put that in the record also.

MR. KUNSTLER: We have no objection to that going into the record, your Honor.

THE COURT: It stands on the record then, and I will sustain the objection to the last question.

MR. KUNSTLER: Didn't you state on direct that a suggestion was made by Mr. Hayden that if they couldn't have a march, that they should have a mill-in at the Loop?

THE WITNESS: Yes, I did, sir.

MR. KUNSTLER: So the first thing would be to run through the streets of the Loop, knocking over automobiles, I think you said, and breaking windows and running through the department stores, and then reforming and going for the vigil.

MR. FORAN: Objection, your Honor. I object to counsel's testifying.

THE COURT: I sustain the objection.

MR. KUNSTLER: Did anyone suggest, when that suggestion was made, that it might be a little bit difficult to go down into the Loop, run through like wild men, and then come back and have a vigil?

THE WITNESS: I don't recall that being said, sir.

MR. KUNSTLER: Are you putting these forward as serious suggestions from the witness stand as to what happened?

MR. FORAN: Your Honor, I object to that.

THE COURT: I sustain the objection.

MR. KUNSTLER: Now you testified that at midnight on August 26 Rennie Davis and Tom Hayden had a discussion with the doorman of the Conrad Hilton Hotel, is that correct?

THE WITNESS: That is correct, sir.

MR. KUNSTLER: And I think you said that you heard them say something about they had a friend in a room and they wanted to visit him, is that correct?

THE WITNESS: Yes, sir.

MR. KUNSTLER: Did you ever mention that to the grand jury?

THE WITNESS: I don't recall, sir.

MR. KUNSTLER: Would you look at page 2 on there and see if that refreshes your recollection as to that episode?

MR. FORAN: I object to that.

THE COURT: I sustain the objection.

   The fact that a witness at this trial in this court omits to say something to a grand jury is not relevant. I know of no law that compels a witness before a grand jury to volunteer testimony.

MR. KUNSTLER: Yet, your Honor, in this peculiar nature of this grand jury testimony, I am asking your Honor to look at it.

THE COURT: I don't agree with you that it is peculiar.

MR. KUNSTLER: But this is unique, your Honor, because this witness has said he read to the grand jury somebody else's reports, the FBI reports, which he read verbatim to the grand jury.

THE COURT: What he did there is of no importance here. I will let my ruling stand. I sustain the objection.

   I tried to make that clear to you but without success.

MR. KUNSTLER: I have no further questions.

THE COURT: Mr. Weinglass, do you want to cross-examine this witness?

MR. SEALE: I would like to request to cross-examine the witness.

THE COURT: You have a lawyer here.

MR. SEALE: That man is not my lawyer. The man made statements against me. Furthermore you are violating Title 42, United States Criminal Code. You are violating it because it states that a black man cannot be discriminated against in his legal defense. It is an old Reconstruction law and you won't recognize it, so I would like to cross-examine the witness.

THE MARSHAL: Sit down, Mr. Seale.

MR. SEALE: Hey did you see me make a speech in Lincoln Park, William—Mr. William Frapolly? Did you see me make a speech in Lincoln Park?

THE COURT: Mr. Marshal, will you ask that man to be quiet.

   And, Mr. Seale—

MR. SEALE: Did you see me make a speech in Lincoln Park supposedly on August 27, Tuesday—supposedly on August 27, Tuesday?

THE COURT: Let the record show that the defendant Seale keeps on talking without the approval of the Court and in spite of the admonition of the Court and in contempt of the Court.

MR. SEALE: Do you know a Robert Pierson? A lying agent?

THE COURT: You needn't answer any of those questions. Let the record show that the defendant—

MR. SEALE: Let the record show you violated that and a black man cannot be discriminated against in relation to his legal defense and that is exactly what you have done. You know you have. Let the record show that.

THE COURT: The record shows exactly to the contrary.

MR. SEALE: The record shows that you are violating, that you violated my constitutional rights. I want to cross-examine the witness. I want to cross-examine the witness.

THE COURT: I admonish you, sir, that you have a lot of contemptuous conduct against you.

MR. SEALE: I admonish you. You are in contempt of people's constitutional rights. You are in contempt of the constitutional rights of the mass of the people of the United States. You are the one in contempt of people's constitutional rights. I am not in contempt of nothing. You are the one who is in contempt. The people of America need to admonish you and the whole Nixon administration.

MR. HAYDEN: Let the record show the judge was laughing.

MR. SEALE: Yes, he is laughing.

THE COURT: Who made that remark?

MR. FORAN: The defendant Hayden, your Honor, made the remark.

MR. SEALE: And me.

THE COURT: Ladies and gentlemen of the jury, we are going to recess a little earlier tonight. I would ask the lawyers and the parties to remain.

The jury may go. The witness may go.

THE COURT: You may sit down.

I must admonish the defendant and his counsel—

MR. SEALE: Counsel ain't got nothing to do with it. I'm my own counsel.

THE COURT: You are not doing very well for yourself.

MR. SEALE: Yes, that's because you violated my constitutional rights, Judge Hoffman. That's because you violated them overtly, deliberately, in a very racist manner. Somebody ought to point out the law to you. You don't want to investigate it to see whether the people get their constitutional rights. Sixty-eight-thousand black men died in the Civil War for that right. That right was made during the Reconstruction period. They fought in that war and 68,000 of them died. That law was made for me to have my constitutional rights.

THE COURT: Do you want to listen to me for a moment?

MR. SEALE: Why should I continue listening to you unless you are going to give me my constitutional rights? Let me defend myself.

THE COURT: I am warning you, sir, that the law—

MR. SEALE: Instead of warning, why don't you warn me I have got a right to defend myself, huh?

THE COURT: I am warning you that the Court has the right to gag you. I don't want to do that. Under the law you may be gagged and chained to your chair.

MR. SEALE: Gagged? I am being railroaded already. I am being railroaded already.

THE COURT: The Court has that right and I—

MR. SEALE: The Court has no right whatsoever. The Court has no right to stop me from speaking out in behalf of my constitutional rights.

THE COURT: The Court will be in recess until tomorrow morning at ten o'clock.

THE MARSHAL: Everyone will please rise.

MR. SEALE: I am not rising. I am not rising until he recognizes my constitutional rights. Why should I rise for him? He is not recognizing—

THE COURT: Mr. Marshal—

MR. SEALE: I am not rising.

THE COURT: Mr. Marshal, see that he rises.

THE MARSHAL: Mr. Seale—

THE COURT: And the other one, too. Get all of the defendants to rise.

THE MARSHAL: Mr. Hayden, will you please rise.

THE COURT: Let the record show that the defendant Mr. Hayden has not risen.

THE MARSHAL: I would request counsel to tell their clients—Mr. Kunstler, will you advise your clients to rise?

MR. WEINGLASS: If the Court please, it is my understanding that there is no constitutional or legal obligation on the part of the defendants to rise so long as his failure to rise is not disruptive.

THE COURT: You advise your clients not to rise, do you?

MR. WEINGLASS: I have no obligation to advise my clients to rise. He is doing nothing disruptive in this courtroom.

THE COURT: We will determine that later.

MR. KUNSTLER: I might add the clients are in protest of what you have done in their opinion to Bobby Seale's right to defend himself.

MR. WEINGLASS: They are sitting silently.

THE COURT: Will you advise your clients to rise, Mr. Kunstler?

MR. KUNSTLER: Your Honor, if you direct me to, I will advise them.

THE COURT: I direct you to.

MR. KUNSTLER: Then I will pass on the direction. You directed me to. I now pass on the direction to them. They have heard you direct me but I cannot in good conscience do more than that. They are free and independent and they have to do what they please.

I have now passed on the direction.

THE COURT: Let the record show that none of the defendants has risen.

The court will be in recess, Mr. Marshal.

October 29, 1969

THE COURT: Mr. Marshal, bring in the jury.

ABBIE HOFFMAN: There are twenty-five marshals in here now, and they all got guns. There's two practically sitting in the jury box.

MR. WEINGLASS: If the Court please, within observation of your Honor is a phalanx of marshals literally. I believe there are ten standing in the narrow aisles leading to the doorway of this courtroom. There are three more standing at another door, one more standing at another door.

Now, the jury is about to be brought in. They will enter from that door. The first thing that they will see as they walk into this room is a group of twenty marshals standing in a very ominous posture, and I cannot begin my cross-examination of a witness. The jury cannot sit here unmoved by that.

THE COURT: If you don't want to cross-examine, that is up to you, sir.

Bring in the jury.

MR. KUNSTLER: Your Honor, we are objecting to this armed camp aspect that is going on since the beginning of this trial.

THE COURT: It is not an armed camp.

MR. SCHULTZ: If the Court please, before you came into this courtroom, if the Court please, Bobby Seale stood up and addressed this group.

MR. SEALE: That's right, brother. I spoke on behalf of my constitutional rights. I have a right to speak on behalf of my constitutional rights. That's right.

MR. SCHULTZ: And he told those people in the audience, if the Court please—and I want this on the record. It happened this morning—that if he's attacked, they know what to do. He was talking to these people about an attack by them.

MR. SEALE: You're lying. Dirty liar. I told them to defend themselves. You are a rotten racist pig, fascist liar, that's what you are. You're a rotten liar. You are a fascist pig liar.

I said they had a right to defend themselves if they are attacked, and I hope that the record carries that, and I hope the record shows that tricky Dick Schultz, working for Richard Nixon and administration all understand that tricky Dick Schultz is a liar, and we have a right to defend ourselves, and if you attack me I will defend myself.

SPECTATORS: Right on.

MR. SCHULTZ: If the Court please, that is what he said, just as he related it. In terms of a physical attack by the people in this—

MR. SEALE: A physical attack by those damned marshals, that's what I said.

THE COURT: Let—

MR. SEALE: And if they attack any people, they have a right to defend themselves, you lying pig.

THE COURT: Let the record show the tone of Mr. Seale's voice was one shrieking and pounding on the table and shouting. That will be dealt with appropriately at some time in the future.

MR. KUNSTLER: Your Honor, the record should indicate that Mr. Schultz shouted— went up here in a very loud shouting voice and stood at this lectern and shouted quite loudly in the courtroom.

THE COURT: Yes, he raised his voice and I think he raised his voice—if what he said was the truth, I can't blame him for raising his voice.

MR. SCHULTZ: If the Court please, just for the purposes of the record, the people who are on the right, most of them, responded to Mr. Seale's remarks before the Court came in with "Right on" and the rest of whatever it is they say.

MR. SEALE: Will you please tell the Court I told them to keep their cool because I didn't want a spontaneous response to any kind of activity that might go on. Would you please tell the Court I said to keep cool.

MR. HAYDEN: They did nothing when Bobby Seale was physically attacked. They did nothing.

THE COURT. Will you remain silent, you defendants, please. You have a lawyer.

MR. HAYDEN: Just as he ordered them to.

THE COURT: Mr. Marshal, bring in the jury.

MR. KUNSTLER: I want to indicate Mr. Seale was attacked in the courtroom by the marshals, thrown out of his chair on the ground, and I think the record must indicate that.

MR. FORAN: Your Honor, in response to Mr. Kunstler's usual misrepresentation, Mr. Seale was not thrown on the ground. He was placed in his chair while he was standing screaming at—

MR. SEALE: I wasn't placed in my chair. I was shoved in my chair.

MR. FORAN: —and pounding on the desk, and he was put forcibly in his chair in an attempt by the marshals to keep order in this courtroom.

MR. KUNSTLER: Your Honor, I observed what I observed, and Mr. Seale was thrown into the chair and the chair was tipped over backwards.

THE COURT: I saw it. I will make my findings in due course.

   Ladies and gentlemen of the jury, good morning.

MR. SEALE: Good morning, ladies and gentlemen of the jury.

MR. DELLINGER: Good morning.

THE COURT: The witness will please resume the stand.

MR. SEALE: I would like to request the right again to cross-examine this witness because my lawyer, Charles R. Garry, is not here and because I have also been denied my rights to defend myself in this courtroom. I am requesting and demanding, in fact, that I have a right to cross-examine this witness, sir, at this trial.

THE COURT: Mr. Marshal, take the jury out.

MR. DELLINGER: And all the defendants support Bobby Seale's right to have a counsel of his choice here and affirm that he has been denied that right.

MR. SEALE: Why don't you recognize my constitutional rights—

THE COURT: I have recognized every constitutional right you have.

MR. SEALE: I want to cross-examine. You have not. You have not recognized any constitutional rights of mine.

THE COURT: All I want to tell you is this: if you speak once again while the jury is in the box and I have to send them out, we will take such steps as are indicated in the circumstances.

   Bring in the jury, Mr. Marshal.

MR. SEALE: If a witness is on the stand and testifies against me and I stand up and speak out in behalf of my right to have my lawyer and to defend myself and you deny me that, I have a right to make those requests. I have a constitutional right to speak, and if you try to suppress my constitutional right to speak out in behalf of my constitutional rights, then I can only see you as a bigot, a racist, and a fascist, as I have said before and clearly indicated on the record.

Good morning, ladies and gentlemen of the jury.

THE COURT: Mr. Weinglass, will you please continue with the cross-examination of this witness if you desire to?

Testimony of William Frapolly Resumed

MR. WEINGLASS: Now on Wednesday morning, August 28, you were at a meeting at the National Mobilization office, were you not?

THE WITNESS: That is correct.

MR. WEINGLASS: You testified that you heard the participants in that conversation discussing what would happen if the march to the Amphitheatre could not occur, isn't that true?

THE WITNESS: As I remember, they said the police would probably stop them.

MR. WEINGLASS: They said that, and then what did they say they would do if the police would stop them?

THE WITNESS: Well, Mr. Dellinger said he would lead the march.

MR. WEINGLASS: What did Mr. Dellinger say that his march and the demonstrators would do if they were stopped?

THE WITNESS: They would stop.

MR. WEINGLASS: They would stop?

THE WITNESS: Yes, because the march was to be used as a diversion so the main amount of people could get out of Grant Park.

MR. WEINGLASS: And you are testifying that Mr. Dellinger said that his march would be used as a diversion, is that correct?

THE WITNESS: I don't recall if those were his words, sir, but he did say it would be used as a diversion.

MR. WEINGLASS: Now during the period of time that you functioned as an under-cover agent from August 9 to August 30, did you ever have an opportunity to talk to Mr. Dellinger privately?

THE WITNESS: I think I was in the same room with he and Rennie Davis once watching something on television.

MR. WEINGLASS: Did you ever have a chance to discuss with Mr. Dellinger his personal philosophy of nonviolence and pacificism?

MR. FORAN: I object, your Honor.

THE COURT: I sustain the objection.

MR. WEINGLASS: Isn't it a fact, Mr. Frapolly, that when these men discussed what would happen if they were stopped by the police on the way to the Amphitheatre, they only discussed one alternative and that was to have a peaceful rally in Grant Park across from the Hilton Hotel?

THE WITNESS: That is not correct, sir.

MR. WEINGLASS: Do you remember testifying before the grand jury in this district on February 1, 1969?

THE WITNESS: Yes, I do.

MR. WEINGLASS: Did you testify honestly before the grand jury?

MR. FORAN: I object to that.

THE COURT: I sustain the objection.

MR. WEINGLASS: Isn't it a fact that in your answer before the grand jury you told the grand jury that the only alternative that was discussed was an assembly in the park across the street from the Hilton for another rally?

THE WITNESS: I said another alternative. There were others besides this one.

MR. WEINGLASS: But you didn't bother relating that to the grand jury, did you?

MR. FORAN: I object to that statement.

THE COURT: I sustain the objection.

MR. WEINGLASS: Do you recall being asked questions by the special agents of the FBI as to what the demonstration leaders intended to do if the police stopped their march to the Amphitheatre?

THE WITNESS: They asked me something like that. I don't recall if that was the exact question, sir.

MR. WEINGLASS: Do you recall telling them that the alternative which was discussed was that people should assemble in the park across from the Conrad Hilton Hotel for another rally?

THE WITNESS: That was part of what I told them, sir.

I told them there would be a rally in Grant Park or people would go to the Loop.

MR. WEINGLASS: Did the FBI appear interested when you said that people would go to the Loop?

MR. FORAN: Objection.

THE COURT: I sustain the objection.

MR. WEINGLASS: Could you read that report which is an FBI report and tell the jury whether anywhere in that report there is any indication that you told them people would go to the Loop?

MR. FORAN: Objection, your Honor. That is not his statement.

THE COURT: I sustain the objection.

MR. WEINGLASS: Now, you testified that you spent a good deal of time, I believe, with John Froines, one of the defendants in this case?

THE WITNESS: Some time, yes, sir.

MR. WEINGLASS: Did you get to know Mr. Froines personally?

THE WITNESS: How do you mean, personally, sir?

MR. WEINGLASS: Well, do you know that he has a Ph.D. in chemistry from Yale University?

THE WITNESS: Yes, I learned that.

MR. WEINGLASS: You heard some discussion about fire bombings, isn't that true?

THE WITNESS: Yes, I heard John Froines, Lee Weiner, and Craig Shimabukuro.

MR. WEINGLASS: Isn't it a fact that you know from what John Froines told you that he doesn't even know how to make a fire bomb or a Molotov cocktail?

THE WITNESS: He said he didn't know how to make a Molotov cocktail, though he wasn't the only person in the group.

MR. KUNSTLER: Your Honor, if I could interrupt for just a moment and ask for a five-minute recess.

Dr. Benjamin Spock is in the courtroom, and the defendants would like to consult with him. He has to leave at 11:50.

THE COURT: Does it relate to this case?

MR. KUNSTLER: Yes, your Honor.

MR. FORAN: I have no objection to it, your Honor.

THE COURT: All right. We will take a brief recess so that the defendants can consult with Dr. Benjamin Spock.

MR. KUNSTLER: We would like to introduce him to your Honor. He is sitting in the courtroom.

MR. FORAN: Your Honor, I object to that.

THE COURT: My children are grown, Mr. Kunstler.

Mr. Marshal, the court will be in recess.

(brief recess)

THE COURT: Continue, please, with the cross-examination of this witness.

Testimony of William Frapolly Resumed

MR. WEINGLASS: Now, during the period of time that you were acting as an under-cover agent in the month of August 1968, did you see karate training sessions being held in Lincoln Park?

THE WITNESS: I saw karate demonstrated, sir.

MR. WEINGLASS: In watching it, was your impression that the instructor was actually attempting to give instruction in karate or was it all just a staged affair for camera?

MR. FORAN: Objection.

THE COURT: Sustained.

MR. WEINGLASS: When the karate instruction was being given, did you hear people laugh?

THE WITNESS: I think there might have been some people laughing, sir.

MR. WEINGLASS: Was the atmosphere in the area of the exercise one of frivolity, play-fulness?

MR. FORAN: Objection.

THE COURT: Sustain the objection.

MR. WEINGLASS: I have nothing further.

THE COURT: Is there any redirect examination?

MR. SEALE: Before the redirect, I would like to request again—demand—that I be able to cross-examine the witness. My lawyer is not here. I think I have a right to defend myself in this courtroom.

THE COURT: Take the jury out.

MR. SEALE: You have George Washington and Benjamin Franklin sitting in a picture behind you, and they was slave owners. That's what they were. They owned slaves. You are acting in the same manner, denying me my constitutional rights being able to cross-examine this witness.

THE COURT: Mr. Seale, I have admonished you previously—

MR. SEALE: I have a right to cross-examine the witness.

THE COURT: —what might happen to you if you keep on talking.

We are going to recess now, young man. If you keep this up—

MR. SEALE: Look, old man, if you keep up denying me my constitutional rights, you are being exposed to the public and the world that you do not care about people's constitutional rights to defend themselves.

THE COURT: I will tell you that what I indicated yesterday might happen to you—

MR. SEALE: Happen to me? What can happen to me more than what Benjamin Franklin and George Washington did to black people in slavery? What can happen to me more than that?

THE COURT: And I might add since it has been said here that all of the defendants support you in your position that I might conclude that they are bad risks for bail, and I say that to you, Mr. Kunstler, that if you can't control your client—

MR. SEALE: I still demand my constitutional rights as a defendant in this case to defend myself. I demand he right to be able to cross-examine this witness. He has made statements against me and I want my right to—

THE COURT: Have him sit down, Mr. Marshal.

MR. SEALE: I want my constitutional rights. I want to have my constitutional rights. How come you won't recognize it? How come you won't recognize my constitutional rights? I want to have the right to cross-examine that witness.

MR. SCHULTZ: May the record show, if the Court please, that while the marshals were seating Bobby Seale, pushing him in the chair, the defendant Dellinger physically at-tempted to interfere with the marshals by pushing them out of the way.

THE COURT: I tell you that Mr. Dellinger—if that is his name—has said here that they support the performances of this man, the statements of this man.

MR. KUNSTLER: They support his right to have a lawyer or to defend himself.

THE COURT: You told me you were his lawyer.

[159]

MR. KUNSTLER: Your Honor—

MR. SEALE: He is not my lawyer.

THE COURT: I have the transcript right here.

MR. KUNSTLER: Your Honor, we have gone over that.

MR. SEALE: I told you I fired him before the trial began.

THE COURT: You haven't explained—

MR. KUNSTLER: I have explained it fully. I have been discharged—

THE COURT: No, you haven't, and you will.

MR. KUNSTLER: I told you on the twenty-seventh and I told you on the thirtieth.

THE COURT: I tell you some day you will have to explain it.

MR. KUNSTLER: That is another threat to the lawyers, your Honor. We have had so many that—

THE COURT: Now, Mr. Kunstler, I will tell you this, that since it has been said here that all of the defendants support this man in what he is doing, I over the noon hour will reflect on whether they are good risks for bail and I shall give serious consideration to the termination of their bail if you can't control your clients, and you couldn't yesterday afternoon.

MR. SEALE: I am not—I am not a defendant—he is not my lawyer. I want my right to defend myself. I want my right to defend myself.

MR. KUNSTLER: Your Honor, they said they supported fully his right to defend himself or have his lawyer of choice, and if that is the price of their bail, then I guess that will have to be the price of their bail.

MR. SEALE: I have a right to defend myself. That's what you—

THE COURT: Will you, Mr. Marshal, have that man sit down?

MR. SEALE: You trying to make jive bargaining operations and that's different from the right I have.

   I have a right to defend myself. I still have a right to defend myself whether you sit me down or not. I got a right to speak on behalf of my defense, and you know it. You know it. Why don't you recognize my right to defend myself?

MR. SCHULTZ: May the record show that the defendant Dellinger did the same thing just now?

THE COURT: I saw it myself.

MR. KUNSTLER: Your Honor, he is trying to see what is happening.

THE COURT: Mr. Marshal, we will recess.

   Mr. Kunstler, will you ask your clients to rise?

MR. KUNSTLER: If you will direct me, your Honor, I will ask them to rise.

THE COURT: I direct you to ask your clients to rise and I tell you that I will not retain on bail in this court men who defy the United States District Court and I will give them the noon hour, the noon recess, to think about it.

MR. KUNSTLER: They are protesting, your Honor, and I think that is protective of the First Amendment.

THE COURT: They will have to obey the law in the process of protesting, sir. Now if they prefer to sleep in the county jail, let them reflect on it.

MR. KUNSTLER: I have passed your direction on.

THE MARSHAL: This honorable court will take a brief recess.

(recess)

MR. KUNSTLER: Your Honor, at the close of the session this morning you asked the defendants, as I recall, to reflect upon their support of the right of Bobby Seale to assert his constitutional right to defend himself or to have a lawyer of his choice in this courtroom, and I want to report back to you that they have reflected as follows:

   They want to point out to the Court that from the very beginning of this trial they feel that their constitutional rights have been infringed upon by the Court in the following circumstances:

   First of all, your Honor ordered the arrest of four of their pretrial attorneys which ultimately resulted in two of them being incarcerated at the very beginning of this trial.

Following that your Honor told me in open court that the keys to the jailhouse were in the defendants' hands; that if they waived their right to counsel argument with reference to Mr. Garry, then the jailhouse would open for these attorneys.

Since that time there has been a constant rain from the bench of threats of contempt over both attorneys and clients in this case. I recall myself that when I used the word "prejudicial" in an argument, and it was contained, I believe, in an affidavit of one of the defendants in a disqualification motion, your Honor ordered the document impounded with all the implication and threat therein that there was something horrendous performed by both lawyers and clients that would result in future punishment to one or the other.

When Mr. Weinglass attempted his opening statement, again a threat was expressed that he would be in essence dealt with later. During one of his cross-examinations this was also done, again another threat on the record to intimidate and deter this attorney.

In essence, almost any remark that the Court has not liked has in some way found itself embodied in language which a reasonable person could interpret as a threat of future action.

When laughter has occurred in the courtroom spontaneously, the same type of approach has been met from the bench.

Just this morning when I indicated again my status in this case with reference to Mr. Seale, I was informed by your Honor that this was something that I would meet again at some future time.

This what we consider to be a blanket and overall umbrella of intimidation has surrounded this trial from its very beginning and we think has not only infringed upon the right of counsel in this case but has been attempted to intimidate and deter defendants and their counsel from a vigorous defense to these charges.

Furthermore, there has been an attempt to make the defendant Seale waive his right to counsel argument as the price of the visit of an attorney from this trial to Mr. Garry in San Francisco.

We finally come to today, to a threat to revoke bail of the defendants who dare to support Mr. Seale's position that he wants to assert his constitutional right to defend himself in this court if he cannot have his counsel of choice.

Now I might indicate in passing on the bail question that the defendants have always been present in court, that none of them have ever had a default in bail, and that their action in this court of protesting the treatment of Bobby Seale, has never been disruptive of this courtroom, and has not been done during any ongoing business of the Court that has been going on and been disrupted.

Then lastly, your Honor, the armed camp atmosphere which we have objected to here. We have counted nineteen marshals in the courtroom this afternoon alone. There is no space in the aisle for anyone to stand because of the profusion of marshals presently standing there.

We hold, your Honor, with the Supreme Court language in Morre vs. Dempsey* that the armed camp atmosphere which is easily seen by every juror as he comes in is denying these defendants any chance of a fair trial.

The defendants want me to say that under no circumstances will they let their liberty stand in the way of the assertion of the constitutional rights of Bobby Seale to defend himself, and if the price of those rights is that they must remain in jail, then that will have to be the price that is paid. Many have paid much greater prices in the past for the defense and assertion of constitutional rights.

MR. FORAN: Your Honor, after listening to Mr. Kunstler's statement, I must say that sometimes I feel like one of the characters in Alice in Wonderland that just went through the looking glass.

I have never, your Honor, in twenty years of practice, heard attorneys like Mr. Kunstler and Mr. Weinglass refuse to direct their clients to conduct themselves with decency and courtesy in a courtroom. Mr. Kunstler has represented in open court time and time again that the only appearance he filed for Mr. Seale was what he calls, in his own self-style, a pro tem appearance, a temporary appearance so that he would be able to talk to him in the marshal's lockup. This is not so. Mr. Kunstler has also filed a general appearance for Mr. Seale, and only after three and a half or four weeks of trial did he ever make a motion to withdraw in this court in proper form, knowing full well that a motion to withdraw need not be sustained by the Court.

I think, your Honor, that someone should say what is obvious, that if there is a valid Sixth Amendment point in this case—and I do not for a moment concede that there is—but if there is, this record is replete with the preservation of that point for appellate review, and the constant reiteration of it can be for no valid legal purpose. Its conceivable constant reiteration is for the purpose of the disruption of this trial. In each instance that Mr. Seale has had outbursts in this courtroom, starting on last Wednesday, just prior to that outburst Mr. Seale had a conversation with Mr. Davis, with Mr. Hayden and Mr. Dellinger. Within two minutes Mr. Seale spoke up, out of order, in the courtroom.

Your Honor, I felt it necessary to reply to Mr. Kunstler because I considered that the grossest type of misrepresentation by an officer of the court that I have ever heard. It is my belief that a lawyer who is a professional need not say whatever his client asks him to say, that in fact on many occasions a lawyer in his honor to the law and in his honor to his own profession would say, "Forget it. I wouldn't make any such comment."

It seems to me that many of the people who do attend this court, these courtroom sessions, with an interest in the law itself, should know that we, as lawyers, that our major obligation above all others is our oath to uphold the law, and that if the law is to be changed, that this Government, the only one in the world, provides for an opportunity to change law by law and not by disruptive tactics and not by the grossest kind of attack on the very values of the law itself.

MR. SEALE: Since he made all of these statements, can I say something to the Court?

THE COURT: No, thank you.

MR. SEALE: Why not?

THE COURT: Because you have a lawyer and I am not going to go through that again.

MR. SEALE: He is not my lawyer. How come I can't say nothing? He had distorted everything, and it relates to the fact I have a right to defend myself.

THE COURT: Well, I have been called a racist, a fascist—he has pointed to the picture of George Washington behind me and called him a slave owner and—

MR. SEALE: They were slave owners. Look at history.

THE COURT: As though I had anything to do with that.

MR. SEALE: They were slave owners. You got them up there.

THE COURT: He has been known as the father of this country, and I would think that it is a pretty good picture to have in the United States District Court.

MR. KUNSTLER: We all share a common guilt, your Honor.

THE COURT: I didn't think I would ever live to sit on a bench or be in a courtroom where George Washington was assailed by a defendant in a criminal case and a judge was criticized for having his portrait on the wall.

MR. KUNSTLER: Your Honor, I am just saying the defendants are not for disruption. They are for peace. The judge of the court sits there and won't let a codefendant have his attorney of record or defend himself.

Then I have nothing further to say, your Honor.

THE COURT: Bring in the jury, please.

MR. SEALE: What about Section 1982, Title 42 of the Code where it says the black man cannot be discriminated against in my legal defense in any court in America?

THE COURT: Mr. Seale, you do know what is going to happen to you—

MR. SEALE: You just got through saying you observed the laws. That law protects my right not to be discriminated against in my legal defense. Why don't you recognize that? It's a form of racism, racism is what stopped my argument.

THE COURT: Hold the jury, Mr. Marshal.

Mr. Seale, do you want to stop or do you want me to direct the marshal—

MR. SEALE: I want to argue the point about this so you can get an understanding of the fact I have a right to defend myself.

THE COURT: We will take a recess.

Take that defendant into the room in there and deal with him as he should be dealt with in this circumstance.

MR. SEALE: I still want to be represented. I want to represent myself.

THE MARSHAL: Mr. Kunstler, will you instruct the defendants, sir, that it is the order of the Court that they will arise upon the recess?

MR. KUNSTLER: If that is a direction of the Court, I certainly will pass it on.

THE COURT: Let the record show none of the defendants have stood at this recess in response to the Marshal's request.

The court will be in recess for a few minutes.

MR. SEALE: Let the record show that—

THE MARSHAL: This court will take a brief recess.

MR. SEALE: Let the record show—

(brief recess)

MR. FORAN: Your Honor, if Mr. Seale would express to the Court his willingness to be quiet, would the Court entertain the possibility under those circumstances of Mr. Seale being unbound and ungagged?

THE COURT: I have tried so hard, with all my heart, to get him to sit in this court and be tried fairly and impartially, and I have been greeted on every occasion with all sort of vicious invective.

Mr. Seale, not only Sixth Amendment rights, but all of your constitutional and statutory rights have been and will be preserved in this trial. I want you to conduct yourself in a manner that is gentlemanly and hear the evidence of the witnesses as it is given from the witness stand. I assure you that if you have any evidence when the time comes, we will listen attentively, and all we want is you to be respectful to the Court. If you will assure the Court that you will be respectful and not cause the disorder and commotion that you have up to now, I am willing that you resume your former place at the table, and in the same physical condition that you were in prior to now.

I ask you, therefore, and you may indicate, by raising your head up and down or shaking your head, meaning no, whether or not I have your assurance that you will not do anything that will disrupt this trial if you are permitted to resume your former place at the table along with the other defendants and the layers. Will you, sir?

MR. SEALE [*gagged*]: I can't speak. I have a right to speak. I have a right to speak and be heard for myself and my constitutional rights.

THE COURT: Will you give me your assurance, sir? If you will give me your assurance, will you please indicate by raising your head up and down.

MR. SEALE [*gagged*]: Give me your assurance that you will let me defend myself.

THE COURT: I can't understand you, sir.

MR. SEALE [*gagged*]: I want to defend myself. I have a right to speak in behalf of my constitutional rights, and you just violated my constitutional rights to speak on behalf of my constitutional rights.

THE COURT: Mr. Marshal.

Well, Mr. Foran, I tried to do what you suggested. Is there anything you want to say in the light of my questioning of Mr. Seale?

MR. FORAN: No, your Honor. I would also like the record to show, your Honor, that just prior to Mr. Seale speaking through his gag, the defendant Davis was whispering to him.

THE COURT: Did you want to say something, sir?

MR. KUNSTLER: I wanted to say the record should indicate that Mr. Seale is seated on a metal chair, each hand handcuffed to the leg of the chair on both the right and left sides so he cannot raise his hands, and a gag is tightly pressed into his mouth and tied at the rear, and that when he attempts to speak, a muffled sound comes out.

MR. SEALE [*gagged*]: You don't represent me. Sit down, Kunstler.

THE COURT: Mr. Marshal, I don't think you have accomplished your purpose by that kind of a contrivance. We will have to take another recess.

Let the record show again the defendants have not risen.

(short recess)

MR. KUNSTLER: Your Honor, for the record, I would like to indicate that their co-defendant is handcuffed and legcuffed to a metal chair with a gag deep in his mouth consisting of a cloth and covered with layers of adhesive tape. I also want the record to indicate that he has passed a note across the table in which he indicates that the handcuffs and the leg irons are stopping his blood circulation and he wants this brought to the Court's attention.

I might also indicate, your Honor, that the remarks of Mr. Foran that Mr. Seale was being spoken to prior by one of the other defendants, the implication being that he was being told what to do, and so on, is a thoroughly racist remark. Mr. Seale is a black man who is not told what to do by white people. He makes his own decisions. I think the record ought to clearly indicate that.

(jury enters)

THE COURT: Ladies and gentlemen of the jury, I must tell you that in a trial by jury in a Federal court in the United States, the judge is not a mere moderator under the law but is the governor of the trial for the purpose of assuring its proper conduct, and fairness, and for the purpose of determining questions of law. The law requires that the judge maintain order and to take such steps as in the discretion of the judge are warranted, and, accordingly, the marshals have endeavored to maintain order in the manner that you see here in the courtroom.

Mr. Weinglass, do you wish to cross-examine this witness?

MR. KUNSTLER: Your Honor, before Mr. Foran proceeds, I just want to move for the other seven defendants other than Mr. Seale for the removal of the irons and the gag on the ground that he was attempting only to assert his right to self-defense under the Constitution and I move on behalf of the other seven defendants for the immediate removal of the gag and the arm and leg cuffs.

THE COURT: Mr. Kunstler has made a motion in behalf of the seven other defendants.

I direct you, ladies and gentlemen of the jury, to not hold it against any of the seven other defendants when these measures are taken with respect to the defendant Mr. Seale. These measures indicate no evidence of his guilt or lack of guilt of the charges contained in the indictment. These measures have been taken only, as I say, to ensure the proper conduct of this trial which I am obligated to do under the law.

The motion of Mr. Kunstler will be denied.

MR. SCHULTZ: If the Court please, I just want to make this statement for the record. The Government had joined in Mr. Kunstler's motion. I just want the record to show that. Your Honor requested Mr. Seale if he would remain silent that these measures would not have to be taken.

MR. KUNSTLER: I think the jury ought to know the price of Mr. Seale not having the handcuffs and the gag was to give up his right to defend himself. That is the price he had to pay.

MR. FORAN: Your Honor, I object to Mr. Kunstler's statement and I ask that it be stricken from the record and that the jury be directed to disregard it.

THE COURT: I am going to let that one on the record. I am going to deny your motion, Mr. Foran. I sustain the objection but I let the remark remain on the record.

Now, Mr. Foran, do you have any redirect examination?

MR. FORAN: Yes, your Honor.

Testimony of William Frapolly Resumed

MR. FORAN: Mr. Witness, do you recall Mr. Kunstler asking you whether you had been expelled from school for being with a group of people that had prevented the president of the school from speaking?
THE WITNESS: Yes, I do.
MR. FORAN: What was the group of people that you were with, Mr. Witness?
THE WITNESS: I was with SDS at that time.
MR. FORAN: Were all of them members of the Students for a Democratic Society chapter at Northwestern Illinois?
THE WITNESS: No, they weren't. I was the only one.
MR. FORAN: And who were the others in the group?
THE WITNESS: They were members of the national staff of SDS and other people that were working in Chicago.
MR. FORAN: Now, had you advised your superiors that this event was going to occur?
THE WITNESS: Yes, I did.
MR. FORAN: What did they tell you?
THE WITNESS: They told me that I should not break the law and that I should not become engaged in any violence.
MR. FORAN: Did you become engaged in any violence in the course of that incident?
THE WITNESS: No, I did not.
MR. FORAN: That is all, your Honor.
THE COURT: Is there any recross-examination?

October 30, 1969

MR. WEINGLASS: Mr. Frapolly, you indicated to the prosecutor that you had received instructions from your superior to the effect that you were not to participate in any violent actions, is that correct?
THE WITNESS: That is correct, sir.
MR. WEINGLASS: Now do you consider the forcible removal of the president of a university from the speaker's lectern a violent action?
THE WITNESS: Yes, I consider people removing him a violent action. But I was not to take part in the violence, sir, but I was to be there to observe what happens.
MR. WEINGLASS: Isn't it a fact that you were the only student of the entire group at Northeastern University and the others were all outsiders and it was you who showed them how to get to the stage?
THE WITNESS: That is correct, sir.
MR. WEINGLASS: You indicated that you also were arrested for a sit-in, is that true?
THE WITNESS: That is correct, sir.
MR. WEINGLASS: Do you consider a sit-in to be a violent act?
THE WITNESS: In some ways it was violent, sir.
MR. WEINGLASS: So then you yourself ignored the instructions you received from your superiors, is that correct?
THE WITNESS: No, sir.
MR. WEINGLASS: Did you think that sitting in and refusing to move when you were told and being arrested was a violation of your instructions from your superiors not to be violent?
THE WITNESS: No, I did not, sir.
MR. WEINGLASS: If your Honor please, the buckles on the leather strap holding Mr. Seale's hand is digging into his hand and he appears to be trying to free his hand from that pressure.
   Could he be assisted?
THE COURT: If the marshal has concluded that he needs assistance, of course.
   I will excuse you, ladies and gentlemen of the jury, with my usual orders.

[165]

MR. KUNSTLER: Your Honor, are we going to stop this medieval torture that is going on in this courtroom? I think this is a disgrace.

MR. RUBIN: This guy is putting his elbow in Bobby's mouth and it wasn't necessary at all.

MR. KUNSTLER: This is no longer a court of order, your Honor; this is a medieval torture chamber. It is a disgrace. They are assaulting the other defendants also.

MR. RUBIN: Don't hit me in my balls, motherfucker.

MR. SEALE: This motherfucker is tight and it is stopping my blood.

MR. KUNSTLER: Your Honor, this is an unholy disgrace to the law that is going on in this courtroom and I as an American lawyer feel a disgrace.

MR. FORAN: Created by Mr. Kunstler.

MR. KUNSTLER: Created by nothing other than what you have done to this man.

MR. ABBIE HOFFMAN: You come down here and watch it, Judge.

MR. SEALE: You fascist dogs, you rotten, low-life son-of-a-bitch. I am glad I said it about Washington used to have slaves, the first President—

MR. DELLINGER: Somebody go to protect him.

MR. FORAN: Your Honor, may the record show that that is Mr. Dellinger saying someone go to protect him—and the other comment is by Mr. Rubin.

THE COURT: Everything you say will be taken down.

MR. KUNSTLER: Your Honor, we would like the names of the marshals. We are going to ask for a judicial investigation of the entire condition and the entire treatment of Bobby Seale.

THE COURT: Don't point at me in that manner.

MR. KUNSTLER: I just feel so utterly ashamed to be an American lawyer at this time.

THE COURT: You should be ashamed of your conduct in this case, sir.

MR. KUNSTLER: What conduct when a client is treated in this manner?

THE COURT: We will take a brief recess.

MR. KUNSTLER: Can we have somebody with Mr. Seale? We don't trust—

THE COURT: He is not your client, you said.

MR. KUNSTLER: We are speaking for the other seven.

THE COURT: The marshals will take care of him.

MR. RUBIN: Take care of him?

THE COURT: Take that down.

The court will be in recess.

(brief recess taken)

THE COURT: Let the record show that none of the defendants have risen other than Mr. Froines and—

MR. SCHULTZ: Hayden.

THE COURT: —and Mr. Hayden.

THE MARSHAL: The court will now resume its session.

THE COURT: Will you continue with your cross-examination?

MR. WEINGLASS: If your Honor please, just before that I would like to inform the Court that the reason why the other defendants are not rising is because Mr. Seale is not able to rise due to the fact that he is shackled to his chair and they are sitting in silent protest of that fact.

I further would like to inform the Court that standing here at this lectern as I am just five feet from a man who is shackled and gagged and bound and who, when the jury is not in this courtroom—

THE COURT: Will you continue with your cross-examination?

MR. WEINGLASS: —is physically assaulted by the marshals—

THE COURT: If you have any observation about any other thing, I will permit you to make it at the end of your cross-examination.

MR. WEINGLASS: I am attempting to explain to the Court why it is impossible for me at this point to proceed with my cross-examination of this witness.

THE COURT: If it isn't possible, then you may sit down.

THE COURT: Do you want to continue with your examination?

MR. WEINGLASS: I do not.

THE COURT: Then you may sit down.

MR. WEINGLASS: At this point I would like to ask the Court as a motion of the defendants to poll the jury to see whether or not the jurors feel that they can continue in this case with orderly deliberations while one man is sitting here receiving the treatment that Mr. Seale is being given in this courtroom.

THE COURT: Deliberations—

MR. WEINGLASS: May we have a voir dire examination for this purpose?

MR. FORAN: Your Honor, may the jury be excused?

THE COURT: Yes.

Ladies and gentlemen of the jury, you may be excused with the usual orders.

(jury excused)

MR. FORAN: That statement of counsel was the grossest attempt to corrupt the jury that I have ever seen attempted by any lawyer, and the Government protests and asks that counsel be admonished.

MR. WEINGLASS: Mr. Foran is speaking of gross attempts, your Honor. I have tried a number of Federal cases, but I have never heard a prosecutor make such personal attacks on an adversary as Mr. Foran has. He has never answered me in this case with a citation of law to the cases that I have cited. Instead he prefers the tactic of attacking the attorneys personally and your Honor knows it is a canon of ethics that an attorney cannot do that, no less an attorney who represents the United States in this courtroom.

Now I insist that your Honor admonish Mr. Foran. I have just made a motion, it is a legal motion, it is proper. Mr. Foran knows there is nothing improper about it. However, he insists in answering that motion by a personal attack on me saying that it is the grossest misconduct.

Well, we have had gross misconduct in this courtroom. We have had Mr. Foran sitting at counsel table acting as an attorney but seconding as some kind of an agent, watching who we talk to at this table, holding private conferences and then advising this Court, as Mr. Schultz did, of a private comment that Mr. Kunstler gave to him out of the presence of the Court. And we haven't, by the way, advised the Court of Mr. Schultz' answer to Mr. Kunstler. Mr. Kunstler in that private conversation asked him about the quality of the witnesses who he is bringing here. Mr. Schultz said, "We are scraping the bottom of the barrel."

MR. SCHULTZ: That is not true. That is not true. Mr. Weinglass was not there. Mr. Weinglass, if the Court please—

MR. WEINGLASS: Mr. Kunstler advised me of that and that is true.

MR. SCHULTZ: If the Court please, Mr. Weinglass' conduct in this case is a shameful thing, a shameful thing.

THE COURT: Mr. Weinglass, you made a vile—

MR. WEINGLASS: You are going to have to hear me because I am at the lectern and not Mr. Schultz.

Are you going to permit him to interrupt me?

THE COURT: Yes.

Now you have—

MR. WEINGLASS: I am at the lectern—

THE COURT: You made a vile accusation about the—

MR. WEINGLASS: I have asked the Court for the personal privilege to answer the comments of the prosecutor, and I have been denied it. I am being denied it after waiting for the prosecutor to finish his argument. Now Mr. Schultz interrupts me in the middle of mine and your Honor recognizes him, and that is the kind of treatment, duplicitous treatment that has been going on here for five weeks, and I object to it. I object to it.

Now—

THE COURT: You may continue, sir.

MR. WEINGLASS: I would be remiss in my duty to my client if I stood in this courtroom with fifteen marshals standing at the door, one man gagged and bound, the marshals striking at him and not ask the Court simply to ask the jury if they could continue to deliberate in this trial. I see nothing improper with that.

The only thing improper is Mr. Foran's answer. And I plead with this court to cite to Mr. Foran the canon of ethics which admonishes attorneys in an adversary proceeding to refrain from making a personal attack on the opposing attorney.

Not only have you permitted it, you have added to it your own intimidation of me personally that I will be dealt with later.

THE COURT: That wasn't intimidation, sir; that was—

MR. WEINGLASS: I accepted that as intimidation.

THE COURT: You are mistaken. This court doesn't intimidate lawyers. It cautions you not to repeat your conduct.

MR. WEINGLASS: Well, I would like to know what I did this morning that intimates contumacious conduct.

THE COURT: I told you, I will not answer your question.

MR. SCHULTZ: I think that is proper—the Government is entitled to a fair trial here, too, and Mr. Weinglass is doing everything he can to deprive us of that. It is incredible that Mr. Weinglass could come back here to the rostrum and ask the Court to permit Mr. Seale to continue to disrupt the trial. The ruling will be reviewed by the Seventh Circuit and if necessary by the United States Supreme Court if there is a conviction in this case and if Mr. Seale is right it will come back here for a new trial. But no, they don't want that. They want to disrupt the trial by misconduct.

Mr. Weinglass and Mr. Kunstler together are assisting these defendants in all their efforts to disrupt, to destroy these proceedings, to corrupt the judicial process.

MR. KUNSTLER: Your Honor, the point here is not some appellate point. Mr. Seale wants to defend himself now, he wants to have his trial now and defend himself now and not some day in the future on some future trial.

What Mr. Schultz is saying is that Mr. Seale must sit back, take your assurance that he has a good appellate point and some day after he is convicted and reversed in the Supreme Court come back here and retry this case. We want to try the case now.

THE COURT: I would tell you, sir, that the United States District Judge who practiced law in the courts of the United States and sat on state and Federal benches for fifty years has to sit here, sir, and have a defendant call him a pig?

Listen to him now.

MR. KUNSTLER: Your Honor, we cannot hear him because of the binding and gag on him.

MR. SCHULTZ: If the Court please, Mr. Kunstler said Mr. Seale wants his trial now, he doesn't want to wait for a judical review. He wants it now.

If the Court please, that is representative of the whole philosophy of the defense that we see. If they don't get what they want now, they demand it by disruption in this case, disruption of the judicial proceeding.

Now Mr. Seale has made his record in this court, his record is clear. Your Honor has ruled. His attorneys, Mr. Kunstler and Mr. Weinglass, now are both—

MR. WEINGLASS: How did I become his attorney all of a sudden?

MR. SCHULTZ: Sit down, Mr. Weinglass.

MR. WEINGLASS: You know better than that. He knows better than that, your Honor. You should have instructed him that I am not Mr. Seale's attorney.

MR. KUNSTLER: The right of a black man to defend himself—

THE COURT: I will not hear you any longer.

MR. KUNSTLER: —after three hundred years of slavery—

THE COURT: I will hear you no longer.

MR. KUNSTLER: But, your Honor, this is a sovereign right which is a right black men fought and died for.

THE COURT: Will you ask that man to sit down, Mr. Marshal?

MR. HAYDEN: Your Honor, could I address you?

THE COURT: No, you may not, sir. You have a lawyer. That is what lawyers are for.

MR. HAYDEN: All I want to say is that—
THE COURT: Sit down, please.
MR. HAYDEN: Bobby Seale should not be put in a position of slavery.
THE COURT: Mr. Marshal—
MR. HAYDEN: He wants to defend himself.
THE COURT: Tell that man to sit down. What is his name?
MR. HAYDEN: My name is Tom Hayden, your Honor.
THE COURT: All right. Mr. Hayden.
MR. HAYDEN: I would just like to—
THE COURT: Let the record show that Mr. Tom Hayden rose and addressed the Court, persisted in speaking despite the Court's direction that he sit down.
Bring in the jury, Mr. Marshal.
MR. DELLINGER: What about the motion? There was a motion for voir dire of the jury? He hasn't ruled.
MR. WEINGLASS: Your Honor, will you rule on my motion? I made a motion to voir dire this jury.
THE COURT: The form of the motion is bad; therefore I deny it.
MR. WEINGLASS: May I have an opportunity to rephrase the form of the motion?
THE COURT: No.

(jury enters)

THE COURT: Ladies and gentlemen of the jury, I must repeat in substance some of the observations I made to you yesterday about the unusual and extraordinary things that occurred in this court.
These incidents are not to be considered by you in determining the guilt or innocence of any of the defendants and I order you to disregard the incidents as you saw them and as you heard them.
Mr. Seale, I will ask you to refrain from making those noises. I order you to refrain from making those noises.
MR. DAVIS: Ladies and gentlemen of the jury, he was being tortured while you were out of this room by these marshals. They come and torture him while you are out of the room. It is terrible what is happening. It is terrible what is happening.
MR. FORAN: That is Mr. Davis, your Honor.
THE COURT: Ladies and gentlemen of the jury, my usual order—

(jury excused)

Who is that man who was talking?
A DEFENDANT: Your Honor, he is being choked to death—tortured—
MR. SEALE: The Judge is not—he is not trying to give you no fair trial. That's what you are. You are lying. You know exactly what you are.
MR. HAYDEN: Now they are going to beat him, they are going to beat him.
ABBIE HOFFMAN: You may as well kill him if you are going to gag him. It seems that way, doesn't it?
THE COURT: You are not permitted to address the Court, Mr. Hoffman. You have a lawyer.
ABBIE HOFFMAN: This isn't a court. This is a neon oven.
MR. FORAN: That was the defendant Hoffman who spoke.
MR. SCHULTZ: Prior to that it was Mr. Hayden who was addressing the jury while they were walking out of here.
MR. HAYDEN: I was not addressing the jury. I was trying to protect Mr. Seale. A man is supposed to be silent when he sees another man's nose being smashed?
ABBIE HOFFMAN: The disruption started when these guys got into overkill. It is the same thing as last year in Chicago, the same exact thing.
THE COURT: Mr. Hoffman,you are directed to refrain from speaking. You are ordered to refrain from speaking.
It is clear after this morning that I think we cannot go ahead. I would be glad to

entertain first suggestions from the Government and then from the defense as to whether or not this trial shouldn't be recessed until two o'clock.

MR. FORAN: Your Honor, I would like to see if we couldn't continue.

THE COURT: All right. Then we will take a brief recess.

MR. HAYDEN: I thought you were going to ask the defendants.

MR. WEINGLASS: Are we part—weren't we being invited to participate in the dialogue between the—

MR. SCHULTZ: It is they who are disrupting this trial and now they want to make the decision as to whether or not we should proceed. It is incredible. It is they who are fostering this and they want to advise the Court—

THE COURT: I have ordered a recess.

THE MARSHAL: Everyone please rise.

MR. HAYDEN: Stand up. Stand up. Don't let them have any pretext.

THE COURT: Let the record show that Mr. Hayden asked the people—

MR. HAYDEN: I ask the people there to do what they were told and they did it.

THE COURT: Mr. Hayden, do not try to fill my sentences out for me, and you are not permitted to speak except as you may come to be a witness in this case. You are not permitted to speak out loud. You may, of course, consult with your lawyer.

MR. SCHULTZ: There are three defendants who have not risen, Mr. Dellinger, Mr. Rubin and Mr. Hoffman.

THE COURT: Mr. Seale, do you mind looking over here? Can you look over here? All right. I will talk to you even though you don't.

Mr. Seale, I would like to get your assurance that there will be no repetition of the conduct engaged in by you this morning and on occasions prior to this morning.

You have—you are on trial here under an indictment to which you have pleaded not guilty. The burden is on the Government to prove you guilty; you do not have any burden whatsoever. All you have to do here is to sit in your chair and listen.

I would like to get from you, sir, your assurance as an American citizen that you will not be guilty of any disruptive act during the continuance of this trial.

May I have that assurance? You know that if you continue to be disruptive the Court will have to deal appropriately with such conduct.

May I have that assurance? And if you can't speak I would like to have you raise your head up and down, or if you refuse to give me that assurance, please shake your head from the left to the right and the right to the left.

Mr. Marshal, bring in the jury and let the record show that the defendant did not reply in the manner—

MR. WEINGLASS: If your Honor please—

THE COURT: —in which I asked.

MR. WEINGLASS: If your Honor please, Mr. Seale, while the Court was addressing him, was endeavoring to answer the court by writing in spite of his hands being manacled to the chair.

Of course, he can't answer the Court verbally since he is also gagged and so I would like to read and then offer into the record as an exhibit the following note which Mr. Seale has written.

"I want and demand my right to defend myself, to be able to object acting as my own defense counsel, to be able to continue to argue my motions and requests as any defendant or citizen of America."

And the note is not complete since the Court has indicated the jury would be brought in. I would like to have it marked as an exhibit.

THE COURT: It may be marked as an exhibit.

MR. SCHULTZ: If the Court please, before the jury is brought in here, we have one brief motion.

Yesterday when Mr. Seale was manacled and the jury was in the courtroom the young lady sitting next to him was holding his hand as tenderly as she possibly could.

I would ask that this display not be permitted in front of the jury.

THE COURT: I do not know the lady.

MR. WEINGLASS: She has been introduced in the court the first day of the trial. She is one of the four legal people of our staff, Mickey Leaner.

THE COURT: In view of the statement of the United States Attorney, I do not wish her to be close to the defendant Seale.

MISS LEANER: I would like to say, your Honor, this statement is not true.

THE COURT: I have indicated, young lady, that I will not hear from you.

I will instruct the marshal now sitting there not to permit this lady—what is her name?

MISS LEANER: Marie—Jean Marie Leaner.

THE COURT: —not to have any physical contact with the defendant.

Bring in the jury.

Please call your next witness, Mr. Foran or Mr. Schultz.

Testimony of Joseph John Healy

MR. SCHULTZ: Please state your name.

THE WITNESS: Joseph John Healy.

MR. SCHULTZ: Your occupation?

THE WITNESS: I am a police lieutenant with the Chicago Police Department.

MR. SCHULTZ: Lieutenant Healy, would you tell the Court and jury what your present duties are?

THE WITNESS: I am the commanding officer of the organized crime section of the Intelligence Division.

MR. SCHULTZ: Prior to being the commanding officer of the organized crime section of the Intelligence Division, what was your title, please?

THE WITNESS: I was commanding officer of the subversive section of the Intelligence Division.

MR. SCHULTZ: Calling your attention to approximately six o'clock in the evening on August 29, 1968, were you on duty?

THE WITNESS: I was in the area of, I believe, the Conrad Hilton Hotel.

MR. SCHULTZ: At approximately six o'clock in the evening, Mr. Healy, what, if anything, occurred?

THE WITNESS: I went with eight or ten of my men to the eighth floor of Police Headquarters.

MR. SCHULTZ: What, if anything, did you do on the eighth floor of Police Headquarters?

THE WITNESS: I obtained the services of another eight or ten or twelve police officers from the internal investigations section, and the twenty of us drove immediately to the Grant Park garage, the second level underground.

MR. SCHULTZ: At approximately what time did you and the twenty or so men arrive at the underground Grant Park garage?

THE WITNESS: Approximately 7:15 P.M.

MR. SCHULTZ: At approximately 7:30 on that evening, August 29, 1968, would you tell the Court and the jury, please, what if anything you observed?

THE WITNESS: I observed Craig Shimabukuro enter. He walked in, he started walking back and forth through the rows of cars up and down looking through the windows of these cars.

After about four or five minutes of walking he approached my car, looked in my window. I got out of the car and I identified myself as a police officer to Mr. Shimabukuro.

MR. SCHULTZ: Did you have a conversation with Mr. Shimabukuro after you got out of the car?

THE WITNESS: Yes, sir, I did.

MR. SCHULTZ: And then where did you go, if you went anywhere, please?

THE WITNESS: I reentered my automobile, where we had further conversations with Mr. Shimabukuro.

MR. SCHULTZ: And after that conversation, what did you and Mr. Shimabukuro do?

THE WITNESS: Myself and Mr. Shimabukuro and the other three police officers got out of my automobile, and walked into a fire stairwell.

MR. SCHULTZ: What were you doing, please?

THE WITNESS: I was standing at the doorway to the fire stairwell looking out, looking in a southerly direction.

MR. SCHULTZ: And at approximately 7:45 what, if anything, did you observe, will you tell?

THE WITNESS: I observed Lee Weiner and four or five other persons enter into the same doorway that Mr. Shimabukuro entered.

MR. SHULTZ: And would you describe to the Court and the jury what, if anything, you observed the defendant Weiner do?

THE WITNESS: He and the people who were with him walked in, looked around, looked in the cars standing on the west wall. They continued walking in a northerly direction, stopping two or three times, apparently in conversation, and they walked out of my sight, which would be about probably half or two-thirds of the way down that walk.

Approximately four or five, six minutes later, they again came back walking in the same direction that they had just left, walking in a southerly direction against the west wall.

MR. SCHULTZ: And what if anything did you see the defendant Weiner or the individuals he was with do when they walked in the southerly direction?

THE WITNESS: They continued looking all directions, they looked down the aisles, appeared to be looking in the cars that were parked in the parking area.

MR. SCHULTZ: Is everything that you testified here today, did it all take place in the City of Chicago and the State of Illinois?

THE WITNESS: Yes, sir.

THE COURT: Cross-examination?

Mr. Seale, remember my admonition to you, please.

MR. KUNSTLER: Now, Lieutenant Healy, you testified that you had been a member or the commanding officer of the subversive section of the Intelligence Division of the Chicago Police Department. What were the duties of the Subversive Section during your tenure there?

THE WITNESS: To gather information on any type of subversive organizations operating in the City of Chicago.

MR. KUNSTLER: How did you determine what was a subversive organization?

THE WITNESS: It is a very vague question, sir. Any organization that we thought could create a problem for this country or for our city.

MR. KUNSTLER: Lieutenant Healy, when you say create a problem for the city or the country, what do you mean?

MR. SCHULTZ: Objection, if the Court please.

THE COURT: I sustain the objection.

MR. KUNSTLER: Was one of the organizations which you investigated as subversive the National Mobilization Committee to End the War in Vietnam?

MR. SCHULTZ: Objection.

THE COURT: I sustain the objection.

MR. KUNSTLER: Was one of the organizations you investigated as subversive the Yippies?

MR. SCHULTZ: Objection, if the Court please.

THE COURT: I sustain the objection.

MR. KUNSTLER: Did you ever have occasion to investigate the activities of Dr. Martin Luther King?

MR. SCHULTZ: Same objection, if the Court please, out of the scope.

THE COURT: I sustain the objection.

MR. KUNSTLER: Did you consider it subversive for an organization to advocate peace in Vietnam?

MR. SCHULTZ: Objection, if the Court please.

THE COURT: I sustain the objection.

MR. KUNSTLER: Is the name of the subversive division the "Red Squad"?

MR. SCHULTZ: Object.

THE COURT: I sustain the objection.

MR. KUNSTLER: While you were with the subversive section did you ever supply any reports to the mayor of this city?

MR. SCHULTZ: Object.

THE COURT: Sustain the objection.

MR. KUNSTLER: Your Honor, I have no further questions.

• • • • •

MR. WEINGLASS: Now, you testified that you and a number of other officers went to the underground parking garage on Thursday night, August 29, is that correct?

THE WITNESS: That's correct.

MR. WEINGLASS: And that at a given point in time you saw a gentleman who you have identified as Mr. Shimabukuro enter the garage? And after observing him for a period of time you had occasion to converse with him?

THE WITNESS: That's correct.

MR. WEINGLASS: Was Mr. Shimabukuro then placed under arrest?

THE WITNESS: No, sir, he was not.

MR. WEINGLASS: Now, some time thereafter you testified that you saw an individual who you identified as the defendant Weiner come into the garage?

THE WITNESS: That's correct.

MR. WEINGLASS: Now, you did not stop this individual who you testified was Mr. Weiner, did you?

THE WITNESS: No, sir, I did not.

MR. WEINGLASS: You had an opportunity to walk up to him and have a conversation with him?

THE WITNESS: If I had so desired, I could have walked up to him, yes.

MR. WEINGLASS: If you so desired you could have arrested him?

MR. SCHULTZ: Object, if the Court please, to the form of the question.

THE COURT: Sustain the objection.

MR. WEINGLASS: When you saw this person who you described as Mr. Weiner, did he have the keys to the car in his hand?

THE WITNESS: Not that I observed, no.

MR. WEINGLASS: Have you ever been in the underground garage when people came in and looked for their automobiles?

MR. SCHULTZ: Objection, if the Court please.

THE COURT: I sustain the objection.

MR. WEINGLASS: Lieutenant Healy, if you would have observed an infraction of the law by any of these people you described, would you have then arrested them?

THE WITNESS: If they had violated the law that I had understood they were in to violate, absolutely.

MR. WEINGLASS: But you never saw them violate that law that you understood that they were to violate?

THE WITNESS: No, sir.

MR. WEINGLASS: Nothing further.

MR. SEALE [*gagged*]: I would like to cross-examine the witness. I want to cross-examine the witness.

THE COURT: Ladies and gentlemen of the jury, I will have to excuse you.

MR. SEALE [*gagged*]: My constitutional rights have been violated. The direct examination is over, cross-examination is over, I want to cross-examine the witness.

THE COURT: Ladies and gentlemen of the jury, you are excused until tomorrow morning at ten o'clock.

(jury excused)

THE COURT: Now I want to tell you, Mr. Seale, again—I thought you were going to adhere to my directions. You sat there and did not during this afternoon intrude into the proceedings in an improper way.

MR. SEALE [*gagged*]: I never intruded until it was the proper time for me to ask and request and demand that I have a right to defend myself and I have a right to cross-examine the witness. I sit throughout other cross-examinations, I never said anything, and I am not attempting to disrupt this trial. I am attempting to get my rights to defend myself recognized by you.

THE COURT: You have employed one of the most competent criminal lawyers I have ever seen.

MR. SEALE [*gagged*]: He is not employed by me. He is not, and you know Charles R. Garry is my only lawyer. He is not here.

THE COURT: I must tell you, sir, that time is running out. If you are going to persist in this sort of thing, the Court will have to deal appropriately with your conduct.

MR. SEALE [*gagged*]: I have a right to object. I have a right—

THE COURT: Mr. Marshal, the court will be in recess.

MR. SEALE [*gagged*]: I have a right to my constitutional rights.

October 31, 1969

MR. WEINGLASS: If your Honor please, Mr. Seale is having difficulty. He is in extreme discomfort. He has written me a note that the circulation of blood in his head is stopped by the pressure of the bandage on the top of the skull and would it be possible to have those bandages loosened?

MR. SCHULTZ: Your Honor, I think that we are, of course, concerned. Perhaps we should take a couple of minutes before the jury comes in and they can loosen it. He looks very uncomfortable.

MR. KUNSTLER: I would like to reiterate I am calling for an end of this. I think this is absolutely medieval. I don't think you have seen it in your experience nor have I seen it in mine.

I am moving now in behalf of the other seven defendants that this be stopped. Let this man defend himself. You could stop this instantly, stop any disturbance in the courtroom if you let him defend himself.

THE COURT: The record does not indicate that I could stop Mr. Seale.

MR. KUNSTLER: You can, your Honor. He asks one thing of you and that is the right to defend himself.

THE COURT: He is being treated in accordance with the law.

MR. KUNSTLER: Not the Constitution of the United States, your Honor, which is the supreme law. He has a right to defend himself.

THE COURT: I don't need someone to come here from New York or wherever you come from to tell me that there is a constitution in the United States. Why should I have to go through a trial and be assailed in an obscene manner?

MR. KUNSTLER: But, your Honor, that is a reaction of a black man to not being permitted to defend himself. If you had said to him, "Defend yourself," none of this would have happened.

THE COURT: I have had black lawyers in this courtroom who tried cases with dignity and with ability. His color has nothing to do with his conduct.

MR. KUNSTLER: He feels he is being denied a right which the Constitution gives him and one particularly applicable to black people, 1982 of Title 42.

THE COURT: If that is a motion, I deny the motion.

We will recess for a short time.

(brief recess)

MR. KUNSTLER: Your Honor, before the jury comes in, the defendants would like to move to adjourn until Monday so that we can have an opportunity to send the lawyers to California to consult with Mr. Garry. We feel that it is impossible to continue as human beings with the trial of this case under the present circumstances; that it is impossible for essentially white men to sit in this room while a black man is in chains and continue—

THE COURT: I wish you wouldn't talk about the distinction between white and black men in this courtroom. I lived a long time and you are the first person who has ever suggested that I have discriminated against a black man. Come in to my chambers and I will show you on the wall what one of the great newspapers of the city said editorially about me in connection with the school segregation case.

MR. KUNSTLER: Your Honor, this is not a time for self-praise on either side of the lectern.

THE COURT: It isn't self-praise, sir. It is defense. I won't let a lawyer stand before the bar and charge me with being a bigot.

MR. KUNSTLER: For God's sakes, your Honor, we are seeking a solution of a human problem here, not whether you feel good or bad or I feel good or bad.

THE COURT: Please don't raise your voice to me. I don't like that. You tell me first precisely who is going to San Francisco and what is that person going to say to Mr. Garry?

MR. KUNSTLER: Your Honor, I can't tell you that. Mr. Garry is just leaving his home for the first time after his operation to return to some limited type of practice.

THE COURT: Your motion, your application, will be denied. There is no showing here. You haven't said what you propose to do.

MR. KUNSTLER: Your Honor, I can't say anything more than we will meet. If we knew what we were going to do, no meeting would be required.

THE COURT: You have two very competent lawyers. You have a long-distance telephone call to Mr. Garry—

MR. WEINGLASS: If your Honor please, so far as the court record is concerned, Mr. Garry is still a trial attorney in this case, although he hasn't been able to attend due to his physical condition.

Now we are going out to confer with the third attorney of record in this matter. Your Honor is asking us to reveal the course of our deliberations.

THE COURT: No. I want to know what result, in your opinion, might be accomplished by this visit, whoever goes to San Francisco.

MR. FORAN: Your Honor, I find it interesting that these motions are made of course with no notice to us at all so that we can look into these matters. I point out also, your Honor, that if in fact the purpose of discussion with the people in San Francisco is simply to see a man's physical condition, that it could easily be handled on the telephone.

Nevertheless, your Honor, there is no one more reluctant to see Mr. Seale in the condition in which he sits than I, except possibly your Honor, in this entire courtroom.

Because of the fact that there is a possibility that this is simply a valid attempt to make some kind of contribution to the proper proceeding of this trial, because of this and for no other reason, the Government would have no objection to a recess until ten o'clock on Monday morning.

THE COURT: Since you, as United States Attorney for the Northern District of Illinois, representing the Government in this case, along with Mr. Schultz, have no objection, I'll go along, but with great reluctance. I believe, however, that we should have assurances from the defendants here that there will be no speeches made vilifying the Court or you or anybody connected with this case.

I don't want to be lying in bed peacefully looking at television and suddenly see one of the defendants and hear him characterize me as a blackmailer. I don't want that to happen. It isn't a pleasant thing for a man who has devoted all of his adult life to the law to hear. It isn't a pleasant thing to hear.

MR. FORAN: I know it, your Honor.

THE COURT: And I would ask Mr. Kunstler to give us that kind of an assurance.

MR. FORAN: I would certainly expect that he would, your Honor.

THE COURT: Quite apart from any constitutional right of free speech, I don't want a speech to be made on some campus in California telling how wicked the judge in Chicago is, and the prosecution, how wicked the President of the United States is. One would think that this present President of the United States had appointed me from some remarks of a defendant.

MR. KUNSTLER: Your Honor, the defendants have decided that the only person that will go representing the defendants as a defendant will be Thomas Hayden. So I would propose that Mr. Hayden indicate in answer to your Honor's query as to assurances. He is right here, so—

THE COURT: If he is willing to, he may.

MR. HAYDEN: The purpose of my going to see Mr. Garry is to try to explore with him the crisis that has developed in this courtroom. I am sorry if anyone thinks that I am going to California to be on television. However, one gag is enough, and I will not preclude the possibility of my speaking in California, although I have no plans whatsoever to speak there right now. The primary plan is to speak to Mr. Garry but on principle I think that one gag is enough.

MR. FORAN: Your Honor, I still do not object to the motion. I think sometimes an event and a time come together, Judge. I think maybe this is the trial. Let's see about goodwill. Let's see about fair trial. Let's see who wants to see what is right and wrong.

I have no objection, your Honor, I accept the responsibility for what these men do.

THE COURT: I shall place the responsibility squarely on your shoulders, Mr. Foran, for anything that occurs later as a result of granting leave to Mr. Hayden to depart the jurisdiction to confer with Mr. Garry.

Bring in the jury, Mr. Marshal.

Ladies and gentlemen of the jury, while you were out a request was made by counsel that this trial be recessed until Monday morning, and after hearing statement of counsel, the Court agreed that the trial be recessed until Monday morning at ten o'clock.

November 3, 1969

MR. WEINGLASS: If the Court please, following this Court's decision to grant the application made on Friday, myself and two of the defendants, Tom Hayden and Jerry Rubin, flew to California to confer with Mr. Garry.

It is clear, based on my conversation with Mr. Garry and with his physician, that it is both physically and medically impossible for Mr. Garry to attend this case at this time.

Now I have received from Mr. Garry a statement which is in his own hand and he has asked me to read his position to the Court so that it will be clear and on the record.

"Statement of Charles R. Garry, November 2, 1969.

"The crisis in this trial has been precipitated by the gross violation by the Government and the trial judge of the fundamental constitutional rights of Mr. Bobby Seale, a black American citizen and national Chairman of the Black Panther Party.

"Mr. Seale's fundamental American constitutional right to counsel of his own choice was violated by the refusal of the Government and the trial judge to agree to adjourn the commencement of this trial until the seriously ill counsel of his own choice, the undersigned, Charles R. Garry, could attend.

"Once the trial had started, Mr. Seale's fundamental American constitutional right to defend himself which he demanded be afforded to him was unlawfully and without any cause in law denied to him by the Government and the trial judge and in flagrant violation of the Constitution the Government and the trial judge proceeded with the trial.

"Furthermore, Mr. Seale was then and still is inhumanely and cruelly punished, insulted and degraded by the Government and the Court solely for attempting to assert a right which every American citizen has and that is the right to defend himself against accusations of crime.

"Accordingly, there is now only one way out of the present crisis in the Chicago trial consistent with the mandate of the Constitution that every American, black or white, is entitled to equal justice under the law. The Government must forthwith confess error in open court that Mr. Seale's constitutional right to counsel of his own choice was violated and must voluntarily dismiss the present case as having been irretrievably prejudiced against Mr. Seale and all of his codefendants.

"Meanwhile, Mr. Seale must be immediately accorded by the Government and the trial judge his constitutional and statutory right to defend himself. He must be released forthwith from all physical bonds, gags and shackles. He must be released from all restraints upon his liberty so that he may defend himself and receive full and adequate apologies and compensation by the Government for the brutal, cruel, unusual and unconstitutional punishment inflicted upon him during the past two weeks of this trial.

"Even if I were physically and medically able to take part in a major trial, which I am not according to my physicians, my participation could in no way cure the fundamental constitutional infirmity with which it is already plagued. Accordingly, participation by me in this trial long after it is started would violate my basic professional responsibilities and might well be deemed malpractice.

"If this proposed course of action is not immediately implemented, all avenues under the Constitution and laws of the United States will at once be pursued to enforce and protect not only Mr. Seale's fundamental constitutional rights but the integrity of the mandate and promise of our Constitution that all Americans, black and white, are entitled to equal justice and freedom under the law.

"Signed, Charles R. Garry."

I make my closing arguments on behalf of the remaining defendants, not Mr. Seale: that the inhuman treatment of Mr. Seale be stopped, and that Mr. Seale from this point on be permitted the right which every American citizen has in this court, and that is the right to stand at this lectern and plead his own case.

I ask the Court to consider this motion again. It has been made and denied, but in light of what has occurred in this courtroom in the last several days, and in the interest of having this case proceed in an orderly fashion, I ask the Court to reconsider its position and permit Mr. Seale to defend himself.

THE COURT: Will the Government reply?

MR. SCHULTZ: If the Court please, the judiciary is a very delicate thing. It is not constructed in such a way that it can defend itself against violence in the courtroom. It simply is too delicate to be able to handle it. When somebody becomes violent in the courtroom as has happened in this case, then the courts have permitted binding and shackling, and the Court has done what it has to do under the law. Inhuman—none of us like to see, and I am certain the Court too, the defendant Seale gagged. None of us do. It was an abhorrent sight which occurred here, but it was something that he deliberately brought on himself.

The defendant Seale is not gagged now. We don't want the defendant Seale to be gagged. We don't think it helps the Government in the eyes of the jury, to be very candid about it. It is a situation where the sympathy is for the defendant, there is no question about that. However, if that is the only way we can proceed with the trial, then that is the only way we can proceed.

I would ask that the Court inquire of the defendant Seale now that he knows Garry will not be here, if he will permit the trial to proceed without violent, obscene outbursts as we have had in the past, and he will permit the Court to proceed with the trial without a gag.

THE COURT: I will permit you to reply if you care to, Mr. Weinglass.

MR. WEINGLASS: Can't Mr. Schultz understand that a man is sitting here on trial facing the possibility of a ten-year jail sentence without his attorney being in this courtroom? And that his right is a simple question to defend himself, and there have been twenty-five witnesses called, there has been no cross-examination for him, his question has been denied by this Court, and he has requested repeatedly that he be given the right to cross-examine them; it has been denied.

THE COURT: I did the very best I could and endured it as long as I could. I have never in all the years—we are all saying things here that we said before. Your report here as a result of your visit to California doesn't do anything other than repeat things that have been said before by all of us.

I would close this discussion, sir, by pointing out that I have before me a document called an appearance. It reads this way:

"I hereby enter the appearance of Bobby G. Seale as defendant in the above-entitled case and that of William M. Kunstler as attorney for said defendant."

It is signed in Mr. Kunstler's own hand, "Attorney for the Defendant."

I am reading from the record.

MR. WEINGLASS: But the record is being distorted. You are reading from September 24, 1969.

THE COURT: After that date it is discretionary with the judge, with the trial judge, as to whether or not a lawyer may withdraw.

I will end this discussion now, sir. I will finish this discussion.

MR. SEALE: Can I add something on behalf of myself?

MR. WEINGLASS: May Mr. Seale be heard before your Honor rules?

THE COURT: No.

MR. WEINGLASS: He is still being denied his right to be heard, your Honor. He sat quietly throughout this entire argument.

THE COURT: I am not hearing anything further in connection with this motion.

I treat your remarks, your original remarks, as a motion of the defendants to permit Mr. Seale from here in to try his own case and I deny that motion because Mr. Seale has a record attorney here and that appearance is right here.

Now, Mr. Seale, while I want to say this to you—

MR. SEALE: And I can't say anything back after you say this?

THE COURT: I don't hear defendants—

MR. SEALE: I want to say I was shackled and one day here my blood circulation stopped in my hand so I moved my hand. Another day they had this type of guard that tightens up so when you move your head, my blood circulation stopped in my head, and I was accused of disrupting the court. I don't know why I was gagged inside of that lockup there. They tried to force something inside of my mouth. I had a temperature running for tonsillitis, I knew I would get exhausted, and I told them before they tried to force that—they grabbed my nose, I almost lost my breath. Another day here one of my blood circulation was going out, and so many marshals come on me, one of them, they accidentally struck me in the testes, my testicles. I struggled and I struggled and I got that gag off. I accused you—I accused you of cruel and unusual punishment right here, and I want to say that the way that I have been treated is inhumane.

Even the words "fascist" and "racist" and "pig"—I am getting ready to sit down—have come in the form of my argument, I am trying to persuade you to see the right for me to have the right to defend myself. I want my right to defend myself. You got that?

THE COURT: I urge you to conduct yourself in an orderly manner so that this trial will not be disrupted.

Mr. Marshal, will you bring in the jury?

MR. KUNSTLER: Your Honor, we have a motion which I would like to make at this point for all of the defendants except Mr. Seale.

In the light of your decision on Mr. Weinglass' motion, we move here now for a mistrial in this case for all of the defendants and we do so because we believe these seven defendants have standing in a conspiracy case when a codefendant is prevented from exercising the defense which he desires to exercise in this case, the right of self-defense.

Your Honor has stated that race is not an issue here. I submit that one of the grounds of our mistrial is that race is very much an issue. It happens that the fact of the matter is that Mr. Seale is a black man, and Mr. Seale feels that that is one of the reasons why he was indicted, that the Government wanted a cross-section of the dissident movement in the United States, and as one symbol of that, Mr. Seale was selected as Chairman of the Black Panther Party for Self Defense.

THE COURT: I go only by the face of an indictment, sir. I have here the indictment. That is all I can tell you.

MR. KUNSTLER: I might say to you in the Freedom Rider case, where I first heard a judge say, "This is not an issue of race," I have learned that race is very much an issue in every case involving a black man, and that—

THE COURT: It never has been as far as I am concerned. Whether or not a white juror has a prejudice, a feeling of prejudice against a black man, I can never tell. Whether there is some member of a jury that has a peculiar affection for a black man, I can never tell. But I know how I have treated cases in this case involving members of the black race, and I am satisfied in my own mind and heart that I have no prejudice and don't deserve to be called what I was called by this defendant. There is nothing I can do about it, but I don't deserve it.

MR. KUNSTLER: Your Honor, the first civil rights act this country ever passed was the Act of 1866—which was to be the most comprehensive civil rights act ever passed. In that act the Congress said that "all persons within the jurisdiction of the United States shall have the same right in every state and territory to sue, be parties, give evidence, and to the full and equal benefit of all laws and proceedings for the security of persons and property as is enjoyed by white citizens." They were talking about black citizens.

That is Section 1981 of Title 42. One of those rights, your Honor, that they are talking about which white citizens had under the Federal Code is now contained in Section 1654 of Title 28 which states:

"In all courts of the United States, the parties may plead and conduct their own cases personally or by counsel."

That is one of the specific rights which was picked up by the Civil Rights Act of 1866.*

Mr. Seale is urging, as Dred Scott did one hundred twelve years ago, the right that every white man has, and that is to plead and conduct their own cases personally. That is what he wants, and that is what he is talking about.

THE COURT: You are making an argument that does not go to your motion.

MR. KUNSTLER: I am submitting on behalf of the seven other defendants, all white men, that there should be a mistrial in this case because of what has happened to co-defendant in this case, a black man, and that this has affected them as well as him, and, therefore, they ask your Honor to grant a mistrial.

I think under all the circumstances, justice calls for your Honor to grant this motion.

THE COURT: Does the Government want to reply?

MR. FORAN: Only with this comment, your Honor. No man, black, white, green, or polka-dotted has any right to disrupt the judicial proceedings in the court of the United States.

MR. SEALE: He keeps getting up and saying that I'm disrupting, deliberately disrupting. He says I'm disrupting. I'm not disrupting. I have sat and listened to the testimony and have not said one thing in this courtroom, and when a person sits up there and makes testimony against me, I have a right to cross-examine that man. The next thing you know, you have got twenty marshals coming on me, or ten marshals, "sit that man down."

There are cases in history of disgruntled people attacking people. I am not attacking the members of the jury or attacking nobody else. I get up to argue, and he gets up to argue, too, and that is where the disrupting was. You know you're trying to put slick words in the record, but I'm wise to you and the people are going to get wise to you, too.

THE COURT: Mr. Clerk, the motion of the defendants Dellinger, Davis, Hayden, Hoffman, Rubin, Weiner, and Froines, respectively, made by Mr. Kunstler for a mistrial, will be denied.

Will you bring in the jury, Mr. Marshal.

(jury enters)

THE COURT: Ladies and gentlemen of the jury, good morning. Will you please bring your next witness to the witness stand?

Testimony of Robert Schwartz

MR. SCHULTZ: Please state your name.

THE WITNESS: Robert Schwartz.

MR. SCHULTZ: What is your occupation, please?

THE WITNESS: I am in the sales department of Central Scientific Company.

MR. SCHULTZ: What are your general duties as sales representative of Central Scientific?

THE WITNESS: I take orders over the phone plus other clerical work.

MR. SCHULTZ: Mr. Schwartz, I hand you now what is in evidence as Government's Exhibit No. 18 and ask you to look at the document and tell the jury according to the documents what was ordered from Central Scientific.

MR. SCHWARTZ: This document requests two one-kilogram size bottles of butyric acid at $2.30 per one-kilo bottle.

MR. SCHULTZ: Mr. Schwartz, according to the document, who telephoned Central Scientific and placed the order?

MR. SCHWARTZ: The name given here is Dr. J. Froines.

MR. SCHULTZ: No further questions.

MR. KUNSTLER: Mr. Schwartz, my name is William Kunstler, one of the defense attorneys.

Mr. Schwartz, with reference to Government's Exhibit No. 18 which you have identified as the invoice, I am going to show it to you and ask you a few questions about it.

Do you know of your own knowledge who telephoned in that order to you?

THE WITNESS: The name says Dr. J. Froines. I assume that is the name.

MR. KUNSTLER: But do you know of your own knowledge who telephoned it in to you?

THE WITNESS: I wouldn't know except the customer's voice over the phone.

MR. KUNSTLER: Did you recognize the customer's voice on the phone?

THE WITNESS: No, I didn't.

MR. KUNSTLER: In fact, weren't you shown a picture of Dr. Froines by the FBI before you testified here?

THE WITNESS: I believe I was.

MR. KUNSTLER: And you weren't able to identify that person, were you?

THE WITNESS: No.

MR. KUNSTLER: Do you remember who picked up the order?

THE WITNESS: No, I don't.

MR. KUNSTLER: I have no further questions of this witness.

THE COURT: You may go, sir.

Testimony of Donald L. Townsend

MR. SCHULTZ: Please state your name.

THE WITNESS: Donald L. Townsend.

MR. SCHULTZ: What is your occupation, please?

THE WITNESS: Detective for the Chicago Police Department.

MR. SCHULTZ: Detective Townsend, calling your attention to August 30, 1968, early in the morning, would you tell the Court and jury where you were stationed, please?

THE WITNESS: I was at the Palmer House Hotel.

MR. SCHULTZ: Calling your attention specifically to approximately 2:15 in the morning, 2:15 A.M., where did you go?

THE WITNESS: I went down to the basement of the Palmer House, just outside of a lounge known as the Charade A-Go-Go.

MR. SCHULTZ: What, if anything, did you observe in front of the lounge of the Charade A-Go-Go, please?

THE WITNESS: I observed two females that were in custody of security officers for the Palmer House.

MR. SCHULTZ: At the time you arrived there, did you smell anything?

THE WITNESS: Yes, sir, a very strong noxious odor like vomit.

MR. SCHULTZ: What, if anything, did you do regarding the two girls?

THE WITNESS: I placed them in custody and took them up to our security room.

MR. SCHULTZ: Did you determine the names of the two girls, please?

THE WITNESS: Yes, sir. Constance Brown and Kathy Boudin.

MR. SCHULTZ: Did you have occasion to conduct any searches?

THE WITNESS: I searched the purses of both young ladies that were in custody.

MR. WEINGLASS: If your Honor please, at this point I am going to object to the prosecution's introduction of this evidence. A proper foundation has not been laid.

Your Honor will recall from the reading of the Spock case that it imposes a requirement on the Government that before it can introduce an act or a statement of an alleged co-conspirator, it must first show that that co-conspirator unequivocally joined in to an alleged conspiracy.

Now the Government has not offered any proof that these young ladies unequivocally joined into any alleged unlawful agreement. There must be very strong showing tying these people into the alleged network of the conspiracy, and there hasn't been, and I object to it on that ground.

THE COURT: I overrule the objection.

MR. SCHULTZ: Would you tell the Court and jury, please, Mr. Townsend, what, if anything, you found in Brown's purse?

THE WITNESS: I found two closed vials containing clear white liquid emitting a noxious odor.

MR. SCHULTZ: Did you find anything else in Brown's purse?

THE WITNESS: Yes, sir, we found some papers.

MR. SCHULTZ: Now, I will show you what has been marked for identification Government's Exhibit No. 22. Do you recognize that exhibit, please.

THE WITNESS: Yes, sir. It is an expired passport belonging to one Thomas Hayden bearing his name and his photograph.

MR. SCHULTZ: That is the original or a copy?

THE WITNESS: That is a copy.

MR. SCHULTZ: While at the Palmer House, what did you find in Kathy Boudin's purse?

MR. KUNSTLER: Your Honor, that name is Boudin. She happens to be the daughter of one of America's great lawyers, Leonard Boudin, and I think the name ought to be correctly pronounced.

THE COURT: Be sure to pronounce her name correctly and if necessary tell the witness that she is the daughter of one of America's great lawyers if you know that to be a fact.

MR. SCHULTZ: What, if anything, did you find in Miss Boudin's purse, please?

THE WITNESS: I found three glass vials containing a clear white liquid espousing noxious odor as vomit.

MR. SCHULTZ: After you searched these two purses while you were at the Palmer House, did anyone else conduct a further search?

THE WITNESS: Yes, Policewoman Ryan.

MR. SCHULTZ: After Policewoman Ryan conducted a search while you were at the Palmer House, what, if anything, did she give you?

THE WITNESS: She gave me a Greyhound Terminal bus locker key.

MR. SCHULTZ: And what did you do with that key, please.

THE WITNESS: I gave it to Detective McMillan.

MR. SCHULTZ: What, if anything, occurred then?

THE WITNESS: Detective McMillan came into police headquarters and handed me a package. It was a one-and-a-half-gallon bottle containing a clear liquid and twenty-five vials containing clear liquid.

MR. SCHULTZ: Where are the vials and the bottle, if you know?

THE WITNESS: They have been destroyed.

MR. SCHULTZ: No more questions on direct, if the Court please.

MR. KUNSTLER: Detective Townsend, you have testified that while you were down at Police Headquarters, as I understand it, Detective McMillan handed you a package, is that correct?

THE WITNESS: That is right, sir.

MR. KUNSTLER: Would you indicate just what that package was, what it looked like?

THE WITNESS: It was a brown box, a cardboard box I would say approximately a foot and a half by a foot wide containing, as I stated before, a one-and-a-half-gallon bottle with clear liquid and twenty-five glass vials containing a clear white liquid.

MR. KUNSTLER: And there is no doubt in your mind now that that was a one-and-a-half-gallon bottle?

THE WITNESS: To the best of my knowledge, sir, it was, yes.

MR. KUNSTLER: Do you recall being interviewed by the Federal Bureau of Investigation on October 16, 1968, with reference to this incident?

THE WITNESS: I remember being questioned, yes, sir.

MR. KUNSTLER: I show you D-87 for identification and ask you to look at page 40. Did you not tell the FBI that this was a half-gallon bottle and not a gallon and a half?

THE WITNESS: I don't recall that, sir.

MR. KUNSTLER: Would you look then at the second full paragraph and indicate whether that refreshes your recollection as to what you told the FBI?

THE WITNESS: They have half-gallon but I don't recall telling them that.

MR. KUNSTLER: Do you know at this moment whether you told them gallon or half-gallon or gallon and a half?

THE WITNESS: I am almost positive I told them gallon and a half, and they omitted the word "one."

MR. KUNSTLER: You think you might have omitted the word "one?"

THE WITNESS: I can always be mistaken, yes, sir.

MR. KUNSTLER: Now where is this bottle right now?

THE WITNESS: It has been destroyed. I gave an order to destroy after the court hearing.

November 4, 1969

MR. KUNSTLER: I am going to show you D-88 for identification and I ask you if you can tell us what that document is.

THE WITNESS: This is an inventory receipt.

MR. KUNSTLER: Who made that inventory receipt?

THE WITNESS: I did, sir.

MR. KUNSTLER: Does that indicate whether it was a one-and-a-half gallon bottle or a half-gallon bottle?

THE WITNESS: A half-gallon bottle.

MR. KUNSTLER: I have no further questions, your Honor.

MR. WEINGLASS: I have no further cross-examination.

THE COURT: You may go, sir.

(witness excused)

MR. SEALE: Mr. Townsend—

Will you hold the witness up for a moment, please?

THE COURT: Your lawyer has examined the witness.

MR. SEALE: In other words, you are going to run all the witnesses off the stand so I can't cross-examine them.

THE COURT: Mr. Marshal, will you ask Mr. Seale to take his seat at the table, please.

THE MARSHAL: Mr. Seale, will you take a seat, please?

MR. SEALE: Can I please get an answer from you? Is that what you are going to do?

THE COURT: I am not here to be questioned, sir, by you. Just sit down.

MR. SEALE: You can't call this witness back so I can't try to have a right to cross-examine him?

THE COURT: I will have to excuse you, ladies and gentlemen of the jury, with the usual orders.

(jury excused)

THE COURT: Mr. Seale, I do not permit defendants to examine witnesses in those circumstances. So I urge you to cease interrupting the trial.

MR. SEALE: I am making a request, a motion, or statement to the effect that every witness that comes on that stand is virtually testifying against me whether he mentions my name or not, and especially those witnesses who in fact testified against me and mentioned my name on that stand. I want a right to cross-examine the testimony of witness against me.

THE COURT: I urge you, Mr. Seale—

MR. SEALE: You call it interrupting. I'm not interrupting.

THE COURT: Your motion was denied, sir.

MR. SEALE: That is a denial of my constitutional rights right there. I have to make motions in behalf of myself. I don't know all of these formalities that the lawyers know in the courtroom. I could easily learn it if you would coach me and allow me to defend myself and cross-examine the witness and ask pertinent questions.

THE COURT: Now, are you going to discontinue?

MR. SEALE: I am making a motion, another request on behalf of myself as a defendant in this case.

THE COURT: The motion, as you characterize it, will be denied, sir, and I ask you to take your chair. Bring in the jury.

MR. SEALE: I take my chair on the basis of what I have said.

Testimony of Bill H. Ray

MR. SCHULTZ: Please state your name.

THE WITNESS: Bill H. Ray.

MR. SCHULTZ: Your occupation, please, Mr. Ray?

THE WITNESS: Deputy Sheriff.

MR. SCHULTZ: Where are you a Deputy Sheriff, please?

THE WITNESS: San Mateo County, California.

MR. SCHULTZ: In what city in San Mateo County, please?

THE WITNESS: Just south of San Francisco.

MR. SCHULTZ: Were you on duty on August 27, 1968?

THE WITNESS: Yes, I was.

MR. SCHULTZ: Calling your attention to that date, August 27, a Tuesday, 1968, where were you on duty, please?

THE WITNESS: San Francisco International Airport.

MR. SCHULTZ: About 11:20 in the morning, what if anything did you observe at the airport, please?

THE WITNESS: I observed three male Negro adults walking just about parallel to us heading in the same direction. I noticed them—

MR. SCHULTZ: Could you identify any of them at that time?

THE WITNESS: Yes, I could.

MR. SCHULTZ: Who, please?

THE WITNESS: Bobby Seale.

MR. SCHULTZ: Do you see him in the courtroom?

THE WITNESS: Yes, I do.

MR. SEALE: I object to the testimony on the basis of the grounds that you have denied me my right to have my attorney, Charles R. Garry.

MR. SCHULTZ: I think in front of the jury, it should be stated that Mr. Kunstler filed an appearance on behalf of the defendant Seale.

MR. SEALE: I would like to argue the point, that Mr. Kunstler has not had a pretrial conference with me.

THE COURT: Mr. Seale—

MR. SEALE: I have never sat down and talked with this man before this trial at all, never, never, and I want to argue that point. The only man I talked to was Charles R. Garry, and you know it. I sent a motion in here one month before this trial, signed by my name, that Charles R. Garry was the only man that I consulted with in this trial.

THE COURT: Will you please sit down?

MR. SCHULTZ: May I continue?

THE COURT: You may continue, Mr. Schultz.

MR. SCHULTZ: Would you identify the person whom you say you saw was Bobby Seale on that August 27, 1968?

THE WITNESS: He is the gentleman sitting at the corner in the light blue and dark blue pullover, the man who just spoke.

MR. SCHULTZ: May the record show that the defendant Seale has been identified by the witness?

THE COURT: The record may so indicate.

MR. SEALE: And may the record show that I am a black man, too, being railroaded?

MR. SCHULTZ: After you saw the defendant Bobby Seale at the airport, what if anything did you do, please?

THE WITNESS: We followed behind the three of them to Gate 46, American Air Lines.

MR. SCHULTZ: And what if anything did you observe at Gate 46 of American Air Lines, please?

THE WITNESS: We saw the three of them approach the ticket counter and purchase a ticket.

MR. SCHULTZ: Did you see what was used to purchase the ticket, please?

THE WITNESS: Yes. Rolls of coins and cash currency, bills.

MR. SCHULTZ: And after the purchasing of the ticket, did you see where the defendant and the two other men went, please?

THE WITNESS: They were escorted to the waiting flight.

MR. SCHULTZ: Where was that flight bound, if you know?

THE WITNESS: To Chicago and Detroit.

MR. SCHULTZ: Were you at the gate when that flight departed?

THE WITNESS: I was.

MR. SCHULTZ: At what time was that to the best of your knowledge?

THE WITNESS: Approximately 11:40.

MR. SCHULTZ: In the morning?

MR. RAY: Yes, sir.

MR. SCHULTZ: No further questions on direct examination.

We have some material under 18 U.S.C. 3500.

MR. SEALE: I would like to get a copy of that 3500 material so I could go over it because it is necessary for me to prove my innocence in this trial that is being held against me. I do not have an attorney, but I can defend myself. I want to be able to cross-examine this witness here.

THE COURT: I have, Mr. Seale—

MR. SEALE: You are railroading me.

THE COURT: —the appearance, what we call in court a written appearance, a general appearance signed in person by Mr. William Kunstler for you.

MR. SEALE: You never asked me: did I ask him to put in an appearance for me? This man made an appearance on his own accord. He signed something to come into jail before this trial started.

I did not ask this man, I did not consult this man. I do not want this man for my lawyer at all, and you are forcing me to keep him.

THE COURT: Ladies and gentlemen of the jury, I will excuse you for this evening.

Mr. Marshal, court will be in recess until ten o'clock tomorrow morning.

November 5, 1969

THE COURT: Are you ready to proceed with the cross-examination, gentlemen of the defense side?

MR. SEALE: Yeah.

THE COURT: Bring in the jury, Mr. Marshal.

(jury enters)

THE COURT: Mr. Kunstler, do you have any cross-examination of this witness?

MR. KUNSTLER: Your Honor, since this witness only related facts relevant to Mr. Seale who has, as your Honor knows, discharged me, I have no questions.

THE COURT: I don't know that, and please—

MR. KUNSTLER: I have no questions.

THE COURT: Please don't tell me what you think I know.

If you don't want to cross-examine this witness, you needn't.

MR. KUNSTLER: The canon of ethics indicates that if a lawyer is dicharged he is to take no further steps in a case.

MR. SCHULTZ: If the Court please, the Court has not discharged Mr. Kunstler who didn't ask for discharge until the trial had proceeded about a month. Mr. Kunstler has a responsibility under the Constitution to defend Mr. Seale. He has a responsibility to this Court.

Mr. Kunstler cannot turn his back on the Court to which he is legally bound to defend this man and let this man not have counsel, because that means that the defendant then without counsel will have been deprived of his Sixth Amendment rights merely because Mr. Kunstler wants to play fast and loose with the defendant's constitutional rights. Mr. Kunstler has a legal obligation by order of this Court, and he cannot deny that.

MR. KUNSTLER: Your Honor, I strenuously object to these words "fast and loose." Mr. Seale has made his position quite clear. He has done it in front of the jury, and he has done it out of the presence of the jury. He has been bound and shackled because he wants to defend himself, and, therefore, I think the remarks are uncalled for and should not be countenanced by this court.

THE COURT: The last statement you made is not a fact.

MR. KUNSTLER: It is a fact, your Honor.

THE COURT: He was bound and shackled because he insulted the United States District Court on a number of occasions.

MR. KUNSTLER: Your Honor, every one of what you term insults came in connection with a demand that you give him one simple thing, let him handle his own defense, a right accorded to defendants throughout the country. Your Honor could merely say, "Defend yourself," and that is the end of the matter, no shackling, no gagging, and the trial proceeds. That is all we want to do, and we think he has a constitutional right as an American citizen to do it.

THE COURT: You don't want to cross-examine this witness?

MR. KUNSTLER: I have given you my reasons why.

THE COURT: You may sit down. Do you want to cross-examine this witness, Mr. Weinglass?

MR. WEINGLASS: If your Honor please, I certainly do not represent Mr. Seale, and I have no questions of this witness.

MR. SEALE: I would like to approach the lectern.

THE COURT: You may not cross-examine, sir.

MR. SEALE: Well, I think I have a right to cross-examine.

THE COURT: No, you have no right in the circumstances of this case.

MR. SEALE: Why did you follow me, could you please tell me, Mr. Witness—

THE COURT: Mr. Seale—

MR. SEALE: —at the airport?

THE COURT: Mr. Seale, I ask you to sit down.

MR. SEALE: Have you ever killed a Black Panther Party member?

THE COURT: Mr. Seale, I will have to ask you to sit down, please.

MR. SEALE: Have you ever been on any raids in the Black Panther Party's offices or Black Panther Party members' homes?

THE COURT: Mr. Seale, this is the third time I am asking you to sit down as courteously as possible.

MR. SEALE: Why don't you let me cross-examine the witness and defend myself?

THE COURT: Because you are not entitled to.

MR. SEALE: I am trying to defend myself. I'm being railroaded.

THE COURT: Will you sit down, sir.

MR. SEALE: This here man is testifying against me. Somebody has to cross-examine him.

THE COURT: But not you.

MR. SEALE: Me, myself, my own person have no right to defend myself? This is erroneous. It is a complete, complete overt, fascist attempt, fascist operation—

THE COURT: Ladies and gentlemen of the jury—

MR. SEALE: —of denying me my constitutional right.

THE COURT: Ladies and gentlemen of the jury, I ask you to leave the courtroom.

(jury excused)

MR. SEALE: How about that? You are talking about insulting you. You are the one that is insulting me, insulting the people of the world, insulting the people of America, and you know it.

THE COURT: Gentlemen, we will recess until two o'clock.

• • • • •

THE COURT: There is a matter that I wish to take up, gentlemen, before we proceed further with this trial. As I think everyone who has attended this trial must, if he is fair, understand the Court has done its best to prevent the repeated efforts to delay and obstruct this trial which I think have been made for the purpose of causing such disorder and confusion as would prevent a verdict by a jury on the issues presented by the indictment and the pleas of not guilty thereto.

I must now, as I perceive my duty and obligation to, take proper steps to ensure that the trial as it continues be conducted in an atmosphere of dignity, an atmosphere that the defendants and each of them are entitled to have prevail in the trial of this case. As we all know, the defendant Bobby G. Seale has been guilty of conduct in the presence of the court during this trial which is not only contumacious in character but of so grave a character as to continually disrupt the orderly administration of justice.

MR. SEALE: That is a lie. I stood up and spoke in behalf of myself. I stood up and spoke in behalf of myself and made motions and requests.

THE COURT: I don't permit anybody to speak while I am talking.

MR. SEALE: I stood up and walked to the lectern and demonstrated the fact I wanted to cross-examine the witness. You are talking about disrupting the proceedings of this trial? That's a lie. That's a lie.

THE COURT: You are making it very difficult for me, Mr. Seale.

MR. SEALE: You are making it difficult for me, Judge Hoffman.

THE COURT: I tried not to—I have done my best. I have done my best.

MR. SEALE: When you say I disrupt, I have never tried to strike anybody, I have never tried to hit anybody. You know that. And in my arguments and motions I called you a racist and a fascist and a pig, and that's what I consider you as, and my arguments and my motions will always carry that as long as my constitutional rights are being denied. So it is a lie, and you know it.

THE COURT: I find, I repeat, that the acts, statements and conduct of the defendant Seale each constitute a separate contempt of this Court; that each constituted a deliberate and willful attack upon the administration of justice in an attempt to sabotage the functioning of the Federal judicial system; that this misconduct was of so grave a character as to continually disrupt the orderly administration of justice.

I find that it is necessary that I deal with his conduct at this time. I have tried—I have endeavored on many occasions to make it clear to the defendant that his conduct was contumacious but I was not successful even right down to a few moments ago in persuading him to so conduct himself as we expect individuals to conduct themselves in the courts of the Federal system.

The Court also notes that a reading of the record cannot and does not reflect the true intensity and extent of the disruption which in some instances were accompanied by a physical violence—

MR. SEALE: That is a lie.

THE COURT: —which occurred in the presence of the Court.

MR. SEALE: That is a lie. I never attack anyone, and you know it. I never struck anyone and you know it.

THE COURT: Accordingly I adjudge—

MR. SEALE: I will stand up in any court in America and say that.

THE COURT: Accordingly I adjudge the defendant Bobby Seale guilty of the several criminal contempts. In citing specific acts and statements of the defendant Seale as contemptuous, the Court has selected only the most flagrant acts.*

I find that the acts, statements, and conduct of the defendant Bobby Seale constituted a deliberate and willful attack upon the administration of justice, an attempt to sabotage the functioning of the federal judiciary system, and misconduct of so grave a character as to make the mere imposition of a fine a futile gesture and a wholly insignificant punishment. Accordingly, I adjudge Bobby G. Seale guilty of each and every specification and the defendant Seale will be committed to the custody of the Attorney General of the United States or his authorized representative for imprisonment for a term of three months on each and every specification,* the sentences to run consecutively.

There will be an order declaring a mistrial as to the defendant Bobby G. Seale and not as to any other defendants.

---

*See Appendix III.

MR. SEALE: Wait a minute, I got a right—what's the cat trying to pull now? I'm leaving the—I can't stay?

THE COURT: The court will be continued until tomorrow morning at ten o'clock for signing the certificate of contempt and to continue with the trial in respect to the other seven defendants.

THE MARSHAL: Everyone please rise.

MR. SCHULTZ: If the Court please, we have the jury to inform.

THE COURT: Oh, yes, I'm glad you reminded me.

MR. SCHULTZ: Will your Honor set a trial date for the defendant Seale?

THE COURT: Yes. Yes.

MR. SEALE: I demand an immediate trial right now.

THE MARSHAL: Sit down, please. Come to order.

MR. SEALE: I demand an immediate trial right now.

THE COURT: Yes, we will give you a trial date.

MR. SEALE: I am talking about now. I don't want to be taken out. I have a right to go through this trial.

THE COURT: A mistrial has been declared with respect to you, sir. Your trial will be conducted on April 23, 1970, at ten o'clock in the morning.

MR. SEALE: I want it immediate, right now, though.

THE COURT: I am sorry, I can't try two cases at one time, sir.

Mr. Marshal, the court will be in recess until ten o'clock tomorrow morning.

THE MARSHAL: Everyone will please rise.

MR. SEALE: I still want an immediate trial. You can't call it a mistrial. I'm put in jail for four years for nothing? I want my coat.

THE AUDIENCE: Free Bobby. Free Bobby.

November 6, 1969

MR. WEINGLASS: If the Court please, we have an oral motion for a mistrial.

THE COURT: A what?

MR. WEINGLASS: Mr. Kunstler will now address himself to our motion as well as other related matters.

MR. KUNSTLER: May it please the Court, we have here, a very fundamental issue.* The severance out and the mistrial, as to Bobby Seale, come much too late in the game. There has been evidence in this record about Mr. Seale to convince the jury of the existence of a conspiracy. The evidence about Mr. Seale, about his speech in Lincoln Park, was gone into by at least two witnesses in great length and is well impressed in the jury's mind. They will remember such things as .357 Magnums, and the word that one of the witnesses tried to put into this record, that when Mr. Seale said "barbecue pork," he was referring to killing policemen. This is forever engraved on their memory, and the fact that your Honor might say in a direction to the jury, "Put this out of your mind," cannot reasonably be expected to be of any avail.

Not only does the jury have this very inflammatory evidence to consider, they will not relate it to Mr Seale alone; they are going to relate it to every one of the defendants since the Government has chosen to group them together in an unlawful conspiracy. Now we are in the position where these defendants don't even have their codefendant here to rebut any of this. He is out of the case. The severance of his case from theirs has irreparably prejudiced them.

Secondly, your Honor, there is a violation of basic American constitutional rights which is so fundamental that we feel it makes this entire proceeding null and void. There is a public interest in the Thirteenth, Fourteenth, and Fifteenth Amendments. The public interest in these war amendments is so powerful and so compelling that the defendants feel that eliminating from this case a black man has irreparably damaged them as well as him. The courts have held that where fundamental rights of black people are violated, white people who are involved in the same litigation have perfect standing to demand that the proceeding against them be vitiated.*

So for these reasons we urge your Honor to grant the mistrial for all defendants remaining in this case, but we further say that there is one step your Honor should take even in the denial of a mistrial if your Honor should so decide. We feel we are entitled to at least have your Honor query the jury. Your Honor did that with the letters. I think your Honor owes it to the law and to the defendants to at least query them.

Your Honor has frequently said when requests are made, "That is not an unreasonable request." I don't think this is an unreasonable request to have this query made and I think it is the very least that the law and the defendants deserve.

THE COURT: Mr. Clerk—

MR. FORAN: Your Honor—

THE COURT: Based on the record in this case and the applicable authorities which the Court has examined prior to coming in here this morning, the motion of the seven other defendants for a mistrial will be denied, as will the application of those defendants to have the Court interrogate the jurors.

Mr. Marshal, please bring in the jury.

(jury enters)

THE COURT: Good morning, ladies and gentlemen of the jury. I have this announcement to make to you: Yesterday the Court for what it regarded as valid legal reasons entered an order of mistrial as to Bobby G. Seale, and he will be tried at some time in the future. The trial will proceed now only in respect to the remaining seven defendants.

Testimony of Richard Perez

[Richard Perez, a news cameraman for CBS, New York, identifies two films he took during the Democratic National Convention in Chicago. The first shows Dave Dellinger forming the march to the Amphitheatre in Grant Park on Wednesday, August 28. The second is an interview with Tom Hayden, by CBS reporter Jack Lawrence, filmed on the night of August 28. Both films are shown to the jury over the objections of the defense. The sound track of the Hayden interview runs, in part, as follows:]

Mr. Lawrence: *Tom, after the events of the last few days, how would you summarize the effectiveness and success of the Mobilization in Chicago?*

Mr. Hayden: *Well, I think it's been a tremendous success. We accomplished everything that we expected to accomplish. I think we exposed the way in which the politicians turn to military force whenever they're confronted by people who have questions that they can't answer. I think that we strengthened a movement which will make its presence felt by creating a lot of little Chicagos everywhere Nixon and Humphrey go to campaign this fall.*

Mr. Lawrence: *Mayor Daley issued a strong statement and the Police Department today labeled you an enemy of the state, a Communist. How do you reply to that?*

Mr. Hayden: *Well, this is the usual scapegoat technique that assumes that crowds like this are led by a handful of terrorists who have superior skill and information, and really, it does a discredit to the people here in the demonstrations, because they really have been leading themselves.*

It would be a great mistake to think that by exterminating or repressing a few leaders, this would have some kind of a negative effect on the movement that's growing against the war, against the whole government.

Mr. Lawrence: *Mayor Daley believes that you are a violent and dangerous man.*

Mr. Hayden: *Well, I think that if you want to understand the establishment . . . they project their own problems to other people so if he says I am violent and dangerous, that would be truer of himself, and I think he proved that this week. His policies have created a situation of clear and present danger for all of the citizens of Chicago. His policy is very similar to the entire national policy from Vietnam to the ghettoes to the campuses, which I think is suicidal, because it will be resisted and force will lead to counterforce. America will simply be destroyed as a country rather than submit to a Daley or a Johnson or a Humphrey dictatorship.*

Testimony of John Braddock

[Mr. Braddock, a newsreel cameraman for ABC, filmed a speech by Tom Hayden in the early morning hours of Wednesday, August 28, in Grant Park across from the Hilton Hotel. The film is identified by Mr. Braddock and shown to the jury with no objection by the defense. The text runs, in part, as follows.]

Mr. Hayden: *We have found that our primary struggle has not been to expose the bankruptcy of the Democratic Party, they have done that for themselves. Our primary struggle is our struggle for our own survival, for our own survival as a movement, for our own survival as an emerging culture facing military suppression at every step of its emergence.*

Now tonight when we were here people in Lincoln Park were pushed out under a blanket of gas. So I would suggest that we simply get our sleep here.

And a final point addressed to the people inside the hotel and the people who have come from the hotel to be with us here. What would be very good, I believe, what would be very good for you to do in the morning is welcome us into the hotel, into your rooms, more particularly into your bathrooms so that we can clean up because we have a lot of work to do tomorrow.

Tomorrow is the day that this operation has been pointing toward for some time. We see before us at this hour the realities of American society exposed before us, daring us to take a step. But we are going to take the step. We are going to gather here. We are going to make our way to the Amphitheatre by any means necessary.

November 7, 1969

THE CLERK: Your Honor, there is a motion here on behalf of—motion by Francis J. McTernan for bail pending appeal on behalf of Bobby G. Seale.

THE COURT: I hear you as additional counsel for the defendant Bobby Seale.

MR. McTERNAN: Thank you, your Honor. I consider myself Mr. Seale's only attorney here. However, I think we have made our position clear on the record.

Your Honor, the sole question I present to you this morning in this motion is an application for bail pending appeal.

The first point which I think is substantial—is the question of the right to a jury trial. Your Honor is undoubtedly familiar with the Chef case and Broom vs. Illinois,* where the Supreme Court of the United States has held so far as Federal summary contempt are concerned that if the sentence imposed exceeds six months, then it is considered a serious offense and not a petty offense, and the mandate of the United States Constitution, the Sixth Amendment, is that the defendant has a right to trial by jury.

In this case, your Honor, although there were sixteen three-month sentences, in totality the sentence was four years. The Court very clearly stated that where sentence exceeds six months, then the mandate of the Sixth Amendment comes into play and the case must be tried before a jury.

Whether or not the Supreme Court will agree with my argument that I have just made that it is the totality of the sentence rather than the individual sentences which determines whether it is a petty offense or a serious offense, I submit to your Honor that the question is arguable. Nor is it an unsubstantial question of law to assert that one has a right to defend himself.

THE COURT: The conduct of this defendant is contemptuous quite apart from that.

MR. McTERNAN: Your Honor has made that clear, that that is your position.

THE COURT: You can disagree with the judge, but you don't call him a pig and fascist in the process of disagreeing with him. You disagree and you sit down when you are told to sit down. We are not running a corner store here.

MR. McTERNAN: Your Honor, I would like to develop the argument that we are dealing first with a layman and not a lawyer. Secondly, we were dealing with a black man who comes out of a black—

THE COURT: Oh, I don't want to hear another thing about a black man. The only

[192]

person who mentioned black men in this court for the first time was your client. You don't know me sir, but I am as good a friend of the black people in this community as they have, and if you don't believe it, read the books. You are the one that brings up this black man thing again. I am weary of hearing about it because he has not been discriminated against.

I have known literally thousands of what we used to call Negro people, and who are now referred to as black people, and I never heard that kind of language emanate from the lips of any one of them. I have had fine Negro lawyers stand at that lectern and at the lectern across in the old courthouse, and I never heard a lawyer, a Negro lawyer use that kind of language, or any Negro witness, or any Negro defendant in a criminal case. I never did.

MR. McTERNAN: Your Honor, that is precisely the point I am getting to, that a different culture exists in the ghetto than exists in this courtroom, than exists in the rest of the city.

And you and I as white professionals do not see that culture, we never get an opportunity to see that culture or to know what is going on in that culture. We could bring expert witnesses in here who would explain the culture and explain Mr. Seale's conduct in a noncriminal manner, and I say, your Honor, that that presents a substantial question for the appellate court to consider. I submit Mr. Seale should be granted bail on appeal pending an appeal on the contempt citation and thereafter be returned or thereupon forthwith be returned to the custody of the Sheriff of the City and County of San Francisco, State of California.

THE COURT: Does the Government desire to be heard?

MR. FORAN: Yes, your Honor. First of all, the defendant Seale was clearly guilty of contempt. The only question really that might be considered a valid question, if your Honor please, concerns the length of the sentence. There is no question at all that the conduct was contemptuous, that it was so contemptuous that it deserves the maximum penalty. So that the real question of the issuance of bail now at this time is moot.

I would call something else to the Court's attention and that is that Mr. Seale is not only under a charge but that he is under a charge on a nonbailable offense. He is under a charge in New Haven, Connecticut, for conspiracy to commit murder. He is not entitled to be on the street even under the Constitution. I feel, your Honor, that the motion is untimely, that it is moot, and at this time the motion itself is frivolous.

THE COURT: Gentlemen, we have here the motion of the defendant Seale for bail. My view is that anyone who has sat through this trial and heard the words of the defendant and watched his conduct can't but reach the conclusion that the defendant was guilty of dangerous acts of violence in open court, that he by his words intends to seek to destroy and overturn the American judicial system.

He has severely disrupted the normal trial processes of our judicial system and I think such conduct is a major threat to the continued existence of our democratic system. His shouting in open court, his insulting characterization of the trial judge, of the United States Attorney, the Assistant United States Attorney, the marshals, to me mean that he is a dangerous man. If he is a dangerous man, as I conclude and find, it would be gross error to permit him to be free on bail. I deny the motion for bail pending appeal.

Ladies and gentlemen of the jury, good morning.

THE JURORS: Good morning.

Testimony of Dick Elliott

[Mr. Elliott, a newsman for radio station WIND, identifies a tape recording he made of a statement by Abbie Hoffman at a press conference on August 27, 1968. The tape is played to the jury over the objections of the defense. Its text runs, in part, as follows:]

Abbott Hoffman: *We don't consider our action of leaving Lincoln Park as a retreat. We're never going to retreat. We're consistently going to fight for our right to be in that park, but the police just push us out in the street, and what do they expect thousands and thousands of people to do? It seems they care more about a city ordinance about not sleeping in the park than they do about the destruction of Chicago.*

Testimony of Barbara Callender

MR. SCHULTZ: Please state your name.

THE WITNESS: Barbara Callender.

MR. SCHULTZ: Mrs. Callender, will you tell the Court and jury what your occupation is?

THE WITNESS: I am a policewoman with the Chicago Police Department.

MR. SCHULTZ: On Sunday and Monday, that is, August 25 and August 26, 1968, where were you assigned, please?

THE WITNESS: I was assigned to Lincoln Park.

MR. SCHULTZ: How were you dressed, please?

THE WITNESS: I was dressed in what you might call hippie clothes, plain jeans, a shirt, a man's sweater, my hair worn down and loosely, and either sandals or gym shoes.

MR. SCHULTZ: Now, calling your attention to Sunday, August 25, 1968, at about 5:30 in the evening, where in Lincoln Park were you?

THE WITNESS: At about 5:30 I was in an area which was referred to as the Command Post area. It was several picnic tables that were set up Saturday and Sunday and other days from which they dispensed mimeographed information from this place.

MR. SCHULTZ: What, if anything, did you observe?

THE WITNESS: I saw Jerry Rubin in that area. He got up on top of the table that was there as part of that command post area and he started to shout, to give a speech, and to talk to the people that were in the park.

MR. SCHULTZ: Mrs. Callender, will you relate, please, what you heard Rubin say from the command post?

THE WITNESS: He said many things but I remember these few. He said "The park belongs to the people. Don't let the pigs push us from the park." And after each one of these statements that he would make, the crowd would cheer. Then he said, "Wednesday is the big thing. Arm yourselves and fight the pigs."

He said "We are not getting anywhere this way. We've got to break into smaller groups and wait for instructions from my marshal."

And he said, "Above all, the Convention must be stopped."

MR. SCHULTZ: Were there any obscenities in the speech?

THE WITNESS: Every other word was an obscenity, especially the four-letter word.

MR. WEINGLASS: Your Honor, is that relevant? Are my clients being tried for that?

THE COURT: You asked me that question. I don't ordinarily answer lawyer's questions but since you asked so politely, I say yes.

MR. WEINGLASS: It is relevant?

THE COURT: That is right.

MR. SCHULTZ: Calling your attention to shortly before 10:00 P.M. on that Sunday, August 25, 1968, did you have occasion to see the defendant Rubin again?

THE WITNESS: Yes, I did see him. He was standing on one of those tables and he was talking to another gentleman, Tom Hayden. Then Rennie Davis walked over to where Jerry Rubin was standing and they talked together for a few minutes.

MR. SCHULTZ: Then what?

THE WITNESS: Then Jerry Rubin got back up on the seat and he started to give another speech.

MR. SCHULTZ: Will you please relate the speech?

THE WITNESS: Once again he said many things but I remember him saying, "The park belongs to the people."

Then he said, "Pigasus for President." And everybody shouted and cheered.

He said, "Wednesday is the big thing. We disrupt the Convention."

Then he said, "Down with the blankety-blank pigs, fascist pigs." And the crowd cheered.

MR. SCHULTZ: In this speech were there any obscenities?

THE WITNESS: Yes, it was, you know, interspersed generously with obscenities again, mostly that four-letter word. It seemed like every other word was that.

MR. SCHULTZ: When you heard his voice, what, if anything, was occurring in the area?

THE WITNESS: Well, shortly after his last speech there was a lot of pictures being taken, there was bright lights being turned on. The park was full of emotional people. There was all kinds of flags.

MR. KUNSTLER: Your Honor, I object to this—how she could possibly tell about emotional people?

THE COURT: That is right. I sustain the objection.

MR. SCHULTZ: Would you please describe what you heard the defendant Rubin say over the megaphone about an hour later?

THE WITNESS: Some people with a flag and other people started out through the south-west corner of the park and the majority of the people in the park started to follow them and Jerry Rubin said, "Don't leave. Don't leave the park. We have got to make a stand tonight. We have got to fight the pigs."

MR. SCHULTZ: Now did you have occasion to see the defendant Rubin on Monday, August 26, 1968?

THE WITNESS: Yes, he was again up on the table with a megaphone and making another speech.

MR. SCHULTZ: Would you relate please what you can recall of his speech?

THE WITNESS: He screamed into the megaphone, "The pigs slaughtered us in the park last night. Let's get those blood-thirsty blankety-blank pigs."

Then he said, "Arm yourselves with anything that you can find and fight the pigs. Follow my marshals. They must be stopped." And he said, "Hold the park at all costs. Wednesday is the big thing—we march on the Convention."

MR. SCHULTZ: And again, as to obscenities, were there any obscenities in his speech?

THE WITNESS: Yes, sir.

MR. SCHULTZ: Later Monday night, did you have occasion to see the defendant Rubin again?

THE WITNESS: Yes, right before the building of the barricade, he got back up on that table at the command post and made a speech.

MR. SCHULTZ: First, will you relate the tone of voice, if you can relate it, that Rubin used in giving this speech.

THE WITNESS: He was very emotional, very upset.

MR. KUNSTLER: Your Honor, again, I raise my objection.

THE COURT: Yes, I sustain the objection.

MR. SCHULTZ: Would you relate, please, what you heard him say.

THE WITNESS: "Now is the time to make our stand. Arm youselves with anything you can find and follow the marshals. If we don't band together now, all is lost."

Then he said, "Hold the park at all costs even if it means giving up your own life."

MR. SCHULTZ: What did the crowd do while the defendant Rubin was making the statement you just related?

THE WITNESS: The crowd moved up over the hill and started to drag picnic tables and big wastepaper baskets and piled them up on top of one another. There was a lot of mimeographed papers on the ground, and some film. It was all thrown on top of this, and it was lit. Everyone was shouting, and the one phrase they kept repeating was, "Hell no, we won't go. Hell no, you can't make us go," and this was just like a chant. They started to throw things at the police that were lined up down there. They had sticks, and bottles, and stones, pieces of tile, and other debris that they were throwing in the area toward the policemen.

MR. SCHULTZ: We have no further questions on direct examination.

· · · · ·

MR. KUNSTLER: Mrs. Callender, when you arrived in the park on Sunday were you armed?

THE WITNESS: Yes, sir, I was.

MR. KUNSTLER: What kind of a weapon were you carrying?

THE WITNESS: I only have one. It is a .38 Colt Cobra.

MR. KUNSTLER: Where were you carrying this gun?

THE WITNESS: In my bag.

MR. KUNSTLER: When you entered the park at four o'clock what were people in that area doing with reference to the Presidential nomination, if anything?

THE WITNESS: They were shouting and they were yelling and they were referring to "Pigasus for President, Pig for President."

MR. KUNSTLER: As their candidate, right? Is that what you understood it?

THE WITNESS: I didn't quite understand "Pig for President." I understood what they were saying.

MR. KUNSTLER: Right. Did you take this as a satire on the nomination process?

MR. SCHULTZ: Objection.

THE COURT: I sustain the objection.

MR. KUNSTLER: Did you find anything legally wrong in what they were doing with that type of an approach to the Presidential nominations?

MR. SCHULTZ: Objection.

THE COURT: I sustain the objection.

MR. KUNSTLER: Now had you ever seen Jerry Rubin before Sunday night?

THE WITNESS: No, sir, I had not.

MR. KUNSTLER: What drew your attention first to the man you say is Jerry Rubin?

THE WITNESS: To be quite frank, I found him to be a very obnoxious man and this drew my attention to him and I just started to follow him.

MR. KUNSTLER: Is your attention often drawn to obnoxious men?

MR. SCHULTZ: Objection, if the Court please.

I ask that the defendant Rubin not speak aloud for everybody to hear, if the Court please.

MR. KUNSTLER: Your Honor, he is speaking to me.

THE COURT: The defendant Rubin and others. I do direct them and the defendant Rubin not to speak aloud.

MR. KUNSTLER: Would you indicate what was obnoxious about him?

THE WITNESS: This is one of the things—and just the obnoxious manner. I can't quite put it into words, it is too difficult.

MR. KUNSTLER: He was personally obnoxious to you, is that what you are saying?

THE WITNESS: Yes, sir.

MR. KUNSTLER: And so that was your reason for following him?

THE WITNESS: No. My reason for following him was I felt that he might possibly be one of the leaders and that is what I was there to find out.

MR. KUNSTLER: You didn't even know who he was, did you?

THE WITNESS: No, sir, I did not.

MR. KUNSTLER: Now you have indicated that he gave a certain speech in which I think you said he said something about "The park belongs to the people. Don't let the pigs push you from the park," and so on, and "Wednesday is the big day."

THE WITNESS: Right.

MR. KUNSTLER: You said, I think, every other word was an obscenity?

THE WITNESS: Every other word was the F word.

MR. KUNSTLER: What obscenity is that?

THE WITNESS: Pardon me. It is a four-letter word. Would you like me—I am not in the habit of saying it.

MR. KUNSTLER: You have heard it, have you not?

THE WITNESS: Oh, yes.

MR. KUNSTLER: You have heard it down at the stationhouse, haven't you?

MR. SCHULTZ: Objection, if the Court please. That is not a fair question.

MR. KUNSTLER: You say literally that word beginning with F—was every other word uttered by Jerry Rubin during that speech? You don't mean that, do you?

THE WITNESS: Well, let's just take one—he would say the f—n' park and the f—n' police and every time you would have a verb, that was the adjective—I mean, every time you would have a noun, excuse me, that would be the adjective for every noun that he used.

November 10, 1969

MR. KUNSTLER: Isn't it true, Mrs. Callender, that you told the grand jury Jerry Rubin's speech and never uttered one word of anything about "arming yourselves," or "driving the pigs out of the park?" Isn't that true?

THE WITNESS: Well, I wasn't telling you everything that he said in his speech, and, no, at the time of the grand jury I did not say that.

MR. KUNSTLER: You did not say that. Is there any reason why you didn't tell them these things you remembered so vividly when you testified before the grand jury?

THE WITNESS: When I testified before the grand jury, I wasn't asked a lot of things I knew and they asked me what he was saying. That is all.

MR. KUNSTLER: Now you saw Jerry Rubin talking to Thomas Hayden, as I think you said on direct, at approximately ten o'clock. Had you seen Tom Hayden before?

THE WITNESS: No, I had not.

MR. KUNSTLER: Can you describe what Mr. Hayden looked like then?

THE WITNESS: Yes. His hair was fairly close to regular length. He has kind of a pocked face. I don't remember any mustache or anything. Kind of beady eyes.

MR. KUNSTLER: Beady eyes?

THE WITNESS: Yes.

MR. KUNSTLER: You don't like these defendants, do you, at all?

MR. SCHULTZ: Objection, if the Court please.

MR. KUNSTLER: I can show motivation, your Honor. This goes to motivation.

THE COURT: I don't know what the word means so I don't know whether you have laid a proper foundation.

MR. KUNSTLER: All right. I will ask. How do you feel about Tom Hayden?

THE WITNESS: How do I feel about him personally?

MR. KUNSTLER: Yes.

THE WITNESS: I have nothing against him.

MR. KUNSTLER: You have nothing against any of them, have you?

THE WITNESS: No.

MR. KUNSTLER: Even when they have beady eyes and are obnoxious?

THE WITNESS: Beady eyes, sir, is a very small eye.

THE COURT: I don't know what the word beady means.

MR. KUNSTLER: Neither do I, your Honor. I am trying to find out.

THE COURT: You interpreted the word to mean something that was uncomplimentary.

MR. KUNSTLER: Well, I took the witness' tone of voice—

THE COURT: It may mean great big dark brown eyes, as far as I am concerned. I don't know what it means.

MR. KUNSTLER: All right. And then you say, I believe, that after Tom Hayden talked to Rennie Davis, then Rennie Davis spoke to Jerry Rubin, is that correct?

THE WITNESS: Yes, sir.

MR. KUNSTLER: Then did Rennie Davis speak to Dave Dellinger?

THE WITNESS: I don't remember.

MR. KUNSTLER: Then did you see Dave Dellinger then speak to Bobby Seale?

MR. SCHULTZ: Objection, if the Court please. Objection.

THE COURT: I sustain the objection.

MR. KUNSTLER: Now after the speech at 10:30 or so, you indicated that you heard Jerry Rubin over a megaphone, is that correct, at some future time?

THE WITNESS: Yes, sir.

MR. KUNSTLER: When did you first recognize it as Jerry Rubin's voice?

THE WITNESS: It seemed to be the first voice that I had heard earlier when he was speaking at 10:00 or 10:30.

MR. KUNSTLER: Is it your testimony that you both saw and heard Jerry Rubin at the command post at approximately eleven o'clock on the night of Sunday, August 25?

THE WITNESS: My testimony is that I heard him and I saw a man with a megaphone that I believed to be him.

MR. KUNSTLER: All right, if the man wasn't speaking and you hadn't heard a voice to identify him by, was it Jerry Rubin that you saw on the microphone?

THE WITNESS: If I hadn't heard the voice, no, I could not positively identify it as Jerry Rubin.

MR. KUNSTLER: Now this speech which you heard given on Monday night in Lincoln Park, this was much longer than just saying "Arm yourselves and fight the pigs" or words to that effect, wasn't it?

THE WITNESS: At 7:30 on Monday night, it was a lengthy speech, yes.

MR. KUNSTLER: Out of that lengthy speech, is all you can remember what you have told this jury, as to the verbatim quote?

THE WITNESS: Yes, sir.

MR. KUNSTLER: You can't remember a single other thing he said in actual quotations other than what you have told the jury?

THE WITNESS: No, sir, I tried to recall everything I could to the best of my knowledge.

MR. KUNSTLER: Now when the barricades started to be built, where were you?

THE WITNESS: Up on the barricades, sir.

MR. KUNSTLER: In fact, there came a time, did there not, when you were right on top of the barricades, isn't that correct?

THE WITNESS: Yes, sir.

MR. KUNSTLER: And there came a time when you were up there screaming, isn't that so?

THE WITNESS: Yes, sir.

MR. KUNSTLER: What were you screaming?

THE WITNESS: I was screaming with the rest of the crowd, which was screaming, "Hell, no, we won't go."

MR. KUNSTLER: Who were you screaming that at?

THE WITNESS: Just screaming it.

MR. KUNSTLER: When the crowd said something about killing pigs, what did you say? Did you join in that?

THE WITNESS: No.

MR. KUNSTLER: You only said, "Hell, no, we won't go"?

THE WITNESS: Yes, sir.

MR. KUNSTLER: And you have testified, I believe, that there was a fire built on top of the barricades, is that correct?

THE WITNESS: Yes, sir.

MR. KUNSTLER: Now isn't it true that that fire was built behind the barricades?

THE WITNESS: No, it was built—part of it was on top of the barricade, sir.

MR. KUNSTLER: How near to you or to where you were standing on top of the barricades was the fire?

THE WITNESS: It was right in front of me, right here [*indicating*].

MR. KUNSTLER: In fact, you lit it, didn't you?

THE WITNESS: I beg your pardon?

MR. KUNSTLER: I said you lit it, didn't you?

THE WITNESS: No, sir, I didn't.

MR. KUNSTLER: You are positive you didn't light pieces of paper on top of the barricade?

THE WITNESS: I am positive I didn't light any paper.

MR. KUNSTLER: I think you testified that after people were shouting, "Hell, no, we won't go," in which you joined, that somebody started to throw something, is that correct?

THE WITNESS: Yes, sir. The people from the barricade were all throwing stones.

MR. KUNSTLER: How many?

THE WITNESS: Two-thirds of them.

MR. KUNSTLER: You actually saw them do it?

THE WITNESS: I saw them being thrown. I saw them coming over my head, yes, sir.

MR. KUNSTLER: Now at any time during this forty-five minutes did you say to yourself, "My God, people are throwing rocks, and I am up on the barricade. I had better get out of here"?

THE WITNESS: Yes. It occurred to me a couple of times.

MR. KUNSTLER: Now, from your own observations at the Democratic National Convention on these two nights, did you see any policemen beat any demonstrators?

THE WITNESS: No, sir.

MR. KUNSTLER: Did you see any policemen gas demonstrators?

THE WITNESS: No, sir.

MR. KUNSTLER: Did you see any policemen do anything wrong?

MR. SCHULTZ: Well, objection as to the form of the question.

THE COURT: I sustain the objection.

MR. KUNSTLER: You would want to do anything you could, would you not, to make sure the police looked good in this trial, isn't that correct?

MR. SCHULTZ: Objection, if the Court please.

THE COURT: I sustain the objection.

MR. KUNSTLER: Mrs. Callender, if you thought that a lie would make the Chicago Police Department look good here, would you lie?

THE WITNESS: No, sir.

MR. KUNSTLER: You never would?

THE WITNESS: No.

MR. KUNSTLER: No further questions, your Honor.

THE COURT: Ladies and gentlemen of the jury, you may have heard more years ago than I care to remember there was a so-called Armistice Day on November 11. The name has since been changed to Veterans Day. Is that what they call it?

THE MARSHAL: Yes.

THE COURT: And that falls on Tuesday, November 11. Hence, all Federal courts throughout the country at the direction of the President of the United States will be closed. The session of court will be recessed therefore until Wednesday, November 12, at ten o'clock.

November 12, 1969

MR. KUNSTLER: Your Honor, I have one oral motion to make.

On November 5, 1969, a subpoena was served on the personnel officer or custodian of records of the Mid-Continent Import and Export Company, Navy Pier, Chicago, Illinois. This, according to our information, is the secret headquarters of the Red Squad, an office which is used to cloak the secret activities of this covert branch of the Intelligence Division of the Chicago Police Force. Now the subpoena was served on one Miss Hamilton who was identified as the personnel officer or custodian of records of the Mid-Continent Import and Export Company on the Navy Pier.

We asked among other things for the personnel officer to bring all the employment records of persons employed by the Mid-Continent during the years 1964 through 1968, including but not limited to names and addresses, present addresses, phone numbers, duties and assignment.

The subpoena was served, the necessary payments were made, and Miss Hamilton did not appear on November 10, 1968, and we ask that a bench warrant be issued by this court to produce Miss Hamilton together with the necessary records before this court so that they may be made available to the defense.

THE COURT: Issuing a warrant for the arrest of somebody is rather a serious thing.

MR. KUNSTLER: Of course. We are making it as a rather serious request.

THE COURT: You stood up, Mr. Schultz. Is there anything you would like to say?

MR. SCHULTZ: Yes, your Honor. If what Mr. Kunstler says is true, then the Corporation Counsel's office of the City of Chicago would represent the Chicago Police Department and could respond to the subpoena tomorrow when we can determine whether or not, first, it has been properly served and, secondly, whether or not Mr. Kunstler's investigation is accurate.

THE COURT: Let the subpoena be filed and we will have the clerk call it tomorrow. In the meantime, certainly you are not anxious to have me send a young girl to jail if you can get the assurance of the Corporation Counsel that she will attend. Will you bring in the jury, please?

Ladies and gentlemen of the jury, good morning.

Is there anything somebody at that table wants to say?

MR. RUBIN: I was speaking to my attorney.

THE COURT: I will wait. Your client wants to talk to you, Mr. Weinglass, while I am talking. I will be glad to wait.

ABBIE HOFFMAN: We think you ought to come to Washington this Saturday and protest the trial.

MR. SCHULTZ: We are getting our next witness, your Honor.

Testimony of Irwin Bock

MR. SCHULTZ: Please state your name.

THE WITNESS: Irwin Bock.

MR. SCHULTZ: Your occupation, please.

THE WITNESS: Chicago police officer.

MR. SCHULTZ: Prior to being a Chicago police officer, Mr. Bock, what was your occupation?

THE WITNESS: I was in the United States Navy.

MR. SCHULTZ: Between the time you left the United States Navy and the time you were employed by the Chicago Police Department, what was your occupation, please?

THE WITNESS: I worked for American Air Lines as a sales representative.

MR. SCHULTZ: Where are you presently assigned?

THE WITNESS: I am assigned to the subversive unit.

MR. SCULTZ: Have you ever worn a Chicago police uniform?

THE WITNESS: No sir, I have not.

MR. SCHULTZ: Since becoming a Chicago policeman, have you joined any organizations?

THE WITNESS: Yes, I have. I joined the Veterans for Peace here in Chicago. I am at present a member of the executive committee of that organization. I am on the executive board of the Chicago Peace Council.

MR. SCHULTZ: Mr. Bock, are you or have you been since you became a member of the Chicago Police Department a member of any other organization?

THE WITNESS: Yes, sir, I am at present on the steering committee of the New Mobilization.

MR. SCHULTZ: While a member of these organizations that you have just related to the Court and to the jury, were you in your undercover capacity as a Chicago police officer?

THE WITNESS: Yes, sir, I was.

MR. SCHULTZ: Do you recall when you first saw the defendant Davis?

THE WITNESS: It was on July 27, 1968, at the University Church of Disciples on the South Side of Chicago. A meeting had been called by the National Mobilization. Rennie Davis acted as the chairman.

MR. SCHULTZ: Would you relate please, to the Court and to the jury what Davis said at that meeting?

THE WITNESS: He said it was felt by the National Mobilization steering committee that demonstrations should be held at the time of the Democratic Convention. Davis said that the City is planning to hold a celebration for President Johnson's birthday, and he said that the National Mobilization is going to counter that celebration with a celebration of their own, and intermingled in the march would be hundreds of Viet Cong and American flags to show solidarity between the Viet Cong and the American Peace Movement.

MR. SCHULTZ: Mr. Bock, would you relate what else, if anything, was said by the defendant Davis on July 27, 1968, at the University Church of Disciples?

THE WITNESS: Rennie Davis said 2500 marshals were being trained by the National Mobilization. He said these marshals would be used in the event of a direct action with the police. He said that other groups such as the Southern Christian Leadership Conference, the Black Panthers, the Yippies would all be coming into the city. Rennie Davis said that on August 28, 1968, there would be a vigil and rally held at the site of the Amphitheatre. He said that this was not to disrupt the Democratic Convention but it would show the world that there would be war in the streets until there is peace in Vietnam. He said that it would also show the world that it takes police and National Guards to protect the Democratic National Convention.

MR. SCHULTZ: Now, calling your attention to August 1, 1968, at about 7:30 in the evening, do you recall where you were, please?

THE WITNESS: I attended a meeting of the Chicago Peace Council at the Lawson YMCA in Chicago, Illinois.

MR. SCHULTZ: Were any defendants in this case present at that meeting?

THE WITNESS: Rennie Davis was present.

MR. SCHULTZ: Would you relate what Davis said, please?

THE WITNESS: Rennie Davis said that on August 28, that there would be a march to the Amphitheatre. He said that if the permits were not granted or that the demonstrators were not allowed to get to the Amphitheatre, that, joined by the dissident McCarthy students over the fact that Hubert Humphrey had gotten the nomination, they would return to the Loop, flood the Loop with demonstrators, cause disturbances in the Loop, and he said the Loop would fall.

MR. SCHULTZ: Do you recall, Mr. Bock, the next time you saw the defendant Rennie Davis?

THE WITNESS: Yes, sir, three days later, on August 4, at a meeting at the Moraine Hotel in Highland Park.

MR. SCHULTZ: Were any other defendants present?

THE WITNESS: Dave Dellinger and Tom Hayden. Dave Dellinger spoke first at the meeting. He welcomed the people. He said that "a lot of you have come from the far ends of the country. We haven't come here to disrupt the Democratic Convention, nor have we come here to support any candidate to that convention." He then introduced Rennie Davis as the coordinator of the actions for Chicago.

Davis said to the people that on August 24 movement centers would open up throughout the Chicago area. He said on the following day, August 25, that there would be a huge picket held in the Loop area. He said that we would test the police on this day to see what reaction they would have toward the demonstrators, to see whether or not they took a hard stand or a soft stand. Davis said that on August 29 a rally would be held in the Grant Park area at the Bandshell and from this rally a mill-in would take place in the Loop. The mill-in would be set up so that it would close down such places as banks, draft boards, Federal buildings, police headquarters. Davis said the Loop would be closed on that day.

MR. SCHULTZ: After Davis finished speaking, what, if anything occurred, please?

THE WITNESS: Dave Dellinger adjourned the meeting or the morning session and said we should have lunch. The majority of the people left the meeting hall in the hotel and went toward the beach area.

MR. SCHULTZ: Specifically where on the beach area did you go with your lunch?

THE WITNESS: I joined a group of people close to where Rennie Davis and Tom Hayden were standing.

MR. SCHULTZ: Did you have occasion to overhear anything that the defendants Davis and Hayden were saying?

THE WITNESS: Yes, sir. Rennie Davis said that the demonstrators could use the snake dance as they do in Japan to break police lines. Tom Hayden replied to Davis and said, "Yes, we can do that," or "That's great, but the demonstrators need something else to use against the police." He said, "We have the formula for Mace and if we place this in the squirt-type bottle such as a Windex bottle or an atomizer-type bottle, the demonstrators then could use that against the police."

MR. SCHULTZ: Did you hear any more of the conversation?

THE WITNESS: No, sir, I did not.

MR. SCHULTZ: Now, Mr. Bock, when is the next time you saw either Davis, Dellinger, or Hayden?

THE WITNESS: That was August 9. Rennie Davis was at the National Mobilization office, Abbie Hoffman, Tom Hayden, and Lee Weiner, a David Baker—I believe Steve Buff and Richard Bosciano were also present, and there were about ten other people.

MR. SCHULTZ: Do you recall anybody else being present at that meeting, any other defendants?

THE WITNESS: A John Froines was present also.

MR. FROINES: Why didn't he say Dellinger?

MR. SCHULTZ: Do you recall if any other defendant was present?

THE WITNESS: Dave Dellinger was also at that meeting.

MR. SCHULTZ: Was Froines present at that meeting, do you recall?

MR. KUNSTLER: Your, Honor, I think that that is a leading question.

THE COURT: I heard the witness say Froines was there. I wrote down the name of Froines in my notes.

MR. KUNSTLER: Then I object to the question. It has been asked and answered.

THE COURT: I think that is a valid objection. The witness has testified Froines was there. I sustain it.

MR. SCHULTZ: Please relate what occurred at that meeting.

THE WITNESS: A Benjamin Radford spoke up and said that there are several danger areas that the National Mobilization should take into consideration in determining the route of the march to the amphitheatre. Radford said that one specific area was that of the Bridgeport area. This was predominantly white and predominantly against the antiwar movement. He said that they would hold demonstrations and cause the demonstrators not to go to the Amphitheatre.

He said that taking a large body of marchers into the black community would make that community hostile to that march, and that they probably would hold demonstrations and stop the march from going any further. Rennie Davis said that he had talked to the Blackstone Rangers for a safe pass or an escort to get through the black community.

The conversation then turned toward the alternatives for that route. An individual within the meeting suggested that we move the staging area from State and Wacker to the Amphitheatre and he suggested the use of the parking lot around White Sox Ball Park. I suggested that there would be a ball game on that day and that I would check into it and see whether or not there was.

MR. SCHULTZ: Do you recall any further conversation at that meeting?

THE WITNESS: Hayden said that he, Rennie Davis, and Abbie Hoffman had been making plans for diversionary tactics to take place while the main march was going to the Amphitheatre. These diversionary tactics were the breaking of windows, pulling of fire alarm boxes, the setting of small fires, and that they had two purposes.

Davis said the first purpose was to divide the police in such a way that it would take the entire police force to either watch the demonstrators or put down the disturbances. He said that this would necessitate the calling of the police away from the Amphitheatre and would allow the demonstrators to go to the Amphitheatre and confront the war makers.

Tom Hayden said that if the South and West Sides would rise up as they did in the April riots in Chicago here, the city would have a lot of trouble on their hands. Abbie Hoffman turned to Hayden and said, "It would be like another Chicago Fire." Davis then introduced a David Baker, who he said had been active during the Detroit riots in a militant capacity. He said that Baker's group would be coming to Chicago to aid in the training of the National Mobilization marshals.

Abbie Hoffman said that the Yippies would aid in the diversionary tactics on August 28 and that he wanted the National Mobilization marshals to aid the Yippies on August 25 in defense of Lincoln Park.

MR. SCHULTZ: Mr. Bock, calling your attention to August 13, 1968, in the early afternoon, do you recall where you were?

THE WITNESS: Yes, sir, I do. I was at the south end of Lincoln Park near the field house.

MR. SCHULTZ: Did you see any of the defendants there at that time?

THE WITNESS: Yes, sir, I did. Rennie Davis, Tom Hayden, and Lee Weiner.

MR. SCHULTZ: Did you observe anything occur in the presence of the defendants Hayden, Davis and Weiner and in the presence of yourself?

THE WITNESS: Yes, sir. David Baker instructed the people present in the snake dance.

MR. SCHULTZ: What, if anything, occurred, please?

THE WITNESS: The people practiced the snake dance as Baker had instructed it and Tom Hayden, Rennie Davis and Lee Weiner took part in that practice both as a demonstrator and in a leadership role in the snake dance.

MR. SCHULTZ: Did you take part in the snake dance?

THE WITNESS: Yes, sir, I did.

MR. SCHULTZ: Mr. Bock, you said that the defendant Froines was there. Do you see the defendant Froines in the courtroom?
THE WITNESS: Yes, sir, I do.
MR. SCHULTZ: Do you see the person on his left?
THE WITNESS: Yes.
MR. SCHULTZ: Do you know who that person is?
THE WITNESS: Jerry Rubin.
MR. SCHULTZ: If the Court please, may the record show that the witness has identified the defendant Froines and the defendant Rubin.
THE COURT: The record may so show.
MR. KUNSTLER: Your Honor, I don't understand what the defendant Jerry Rubin has to do with this. There has been no identification that he was present.
MR. SCHULTZ: No, he wasn't present but he will shortly make an identification of Rubin and while he was making identifications, he might at least point out who he is.
THE COURT: That is simplification, Mr. Schultz, but I don't think you are entitled to have an individual identified until there has been some testimony as to whether or not he was there.
MR. SCHULTZ: All right, your Honor.
    Please relate what was said by the defendant Davis.
THE WITNESS: Davis suggested that we split into three groups. He would take one group and handle the orientation.
    Tom Hayden would take another group and handle targets.
    John Froines would handle, would take another group and handle the training of the marshals.
MR. SCHULTZ: Then what occurred, please?
THE WITNESS: We split up into the three groups, and I stayed with the group which Rennie Davis was with.
MR. SCHULTZ: Now, calling your attention to three days later, that is August 18, did you have occasion to attend any meeting?
THE WITNESS: Yes, sir, I did, at the Welsh Hall on Noble Street.
MR. SCHULTZ: Were any defendants present at that meeting?
THE WITNESS: Yes, sir. Rennie Davis and John Froines. Davis welcomed the people, thanked them for coming, and he was glad to see there were so many new faces in the crowd. He said that we would now receive a series of staff reports from people working in specific fields. He introduced John Froines as the first speaker. Froines stood and told the people that marshal training was going on in the park. They were receiving training in first aid, guerrilla tactics and defensive tactics.
    He said there was a group of marshals making maps and diagrams of the hotels at which delegates would be staying for use as demonstration sites during the Democratic Convention.
    After Froines spoke, Mr. Davis introduced a Fred Gardner.
MR. SCHULTZ: What if anything occurred while Mr. Gardner was speaking, please?
MR. KUNSTLER: Your Honor, that is absolutely a leading question. "What if anything occurred while Mr. Gardner was speaking?" is to tell this witness that something did occur, and he should testify to it. I object to it.
THE COURT: He said "if anything." Perhaps he will say "nothing."
MR. KUNSTLER: Your Honor, I will make my observation, that he will not say "nothing."
THE COURT: You are quite a prognosticator. You seem to know in advance what the answers of the witness are going to be.
MR. KUNSTLER: In this case I think I do, your Honor.
THE COURT: I overrule the objection. I strike the observation of Mr. Kunstler, "in this case," and so forth. I direct the jury to disregard it.
MR. SCHULTZ: What if anything occured?
THE WITNESS: Some people had gone up to ask Froines a question. This individual asked John Froines what he meant by guerrilla tactics. Froines answered and said that

guerrilla tactics were the same as mobile tactics, and they were the breaking of windows, pulling of fire alarm boxes, setting fires, and he left it at that.

THE COURT: We have reached the point of recess.

• • • • •

MR. SCHULTZ: In the hall after the recess this morning at about 12:30 or earlier this afternoon I overheard the tail end of a conversation between the defendant Davis and the witness Mr. Bock who was standing in the corridor. I didn't hear very much of it and what I heard seemed to relate to him as a witness and I think that it would be appropriate for the Court to inquire of the witness as to what conversation he had with the defendant Davis in light of the Court's instruction that nobody is to talk with the witness regarding his testimony here.

THE COURT: I will permit you to.

MR. SCHULTZ: Mr. Bock, did you have a conversation with the defendant Davis shortly after the 12:30 recess?

THE WITNESS: Yes, sir.

MR. SCHULTZ: Would you relate what occurred, please.

THE WITNESS: Davis walked up to me, your Honor, and said, "Aren't you ashamed of yourself?" and he said he was surprised at me.

MR. SCHULTZ: Did you say anything to him?

THE WITNESS: No, sir, I did not.

MR. SCHULTZ: Well, I don't think that that is a serious violation of the Court's order. Certainly, though, it is improper conduct.

THE COURT: I am not sure that I share your view about that, Mr. Schultz. However, I will reflect on it at an appropriate time during this trial.

Bring in the jury, Mr. Marshal.

And the Court notes that after the last remark the defendants in unison laughed aloud at the Court.

MR. WEINGLASS: Your Honor—

MR. DELLINGER: We are not ashamed to laugh.

THE COURT: You may continue, sir, with the direct examination of this witness.

MR. SCHULTZ: Thank you, your Honor.

Now what occurred after Mr. Gardner spoke to the group?

THE WITNESS: Rennie Davis then introduced Barbara Britts. She told the people that the Medical Committee on Human Rights would aid demonstrators when they got hurt and there would be first aid stations set up. She said that the marshals were receiving first aid training.

Mr. Davis then introduced Irving Birnbaum. He said that one hundred lawyers and law students had formed a Legal Defense Committee for their aid when they got arrested during that time and that the Chicago Peace Council had set up a fund to help bail individuals out of jail.

MR. SCHULTZ: All right. Now the next day, Monday, August 19, in the morning, do you recall where you went?

THE WITNESS: Yes, sir, I do. I went to the offices of the National Mobilization at 407 South Dearborn in Chicago.

MR. SCHULTZ: Who was there, please?

THE WITNESS: On arriving I saw Rennie Davis and several staff people in the office. I went over to where Rennie Davis was standing and asked him where everybody was.

Just after I had talked to Rennie Davis, Abbie Hoffman came in.

MR. SCHULTZ: What occurred when the defendant Hoffman came in, please?

THE WITNESS: Abbie Hoffman walked in with five or six other people and he stated that he had just stolen a booklet from the studios of the NBC television network. He said the booklet contained four diagrams of the hotels at which the delegates were staying. He said there were only fifty of these books in existence, and now we have one of them. He said it also contains what floors the delegates were on, and, in fact, showed some of the rooms in which delegates would be sleeping. Rennie Davis said that this was good, because he had just set up a committee of marshals to make the very same thing. He said the National Mobilization would pay for the reprinting of that booklet.

MR. SCHULTZ: Now, calling your attention to that afternoon of the same day, August 19, which was a Monday, 1968, do you recall where you went in the afternoon?

THE WITNESS: Yes, sir, I do. I went to Lincoln Park around the fieldhouse.

MR. SCHULTZ: Were there any defendants present when you arrived?

THE WITNESS: Abbie Hoffman was there, Rennie Davis, and John Froines, a Wolfe Lowenthal, a David Baker, and about fifteen other marshals, plus sixty to seventy other people.

MR. SCHULTZ: Would you relate, please, what occurred that afternoon in Lincoln Park?

THE WITNESS: Wolfe Lowenthal instructed the crowd that gathered in a tactic to be used against the police and the National Guard. He said that by rolling up a *Ramparts* magazine very tightly into a cylinder and holding it between both hands and raising it above your head, you could protect yourself from any blow that was struck at you.

He said a second part of that tactic or movement was that the person would raise his leg to waist level and then kick straight out. He said that you could place the kick to the police or the National Guard's groin. He then demonstrated how both movements could be done simultaneously to add effect to the kick.

MR. SCHULTZ: Was there any other training that you recall?

THE WITNESS: Yes, sir. They trained in the snake dance, and there was some training in mobile team tactics.

MR. SCHULTZ: Now, calling your attention to Wednesday, August 21, in the early afternoon, with what defendant or defendants did you have a conversation?

THE WITNESS: I talked with Lee Weiner. Weiner told me of a marshals' meeting that was to take place at the offices of the National Mobilization at four o'clock that afternoon.

MR. SCHULTZ: Did you go to that meeting?

THE WITNESS: Yes, sir, I did.

MR. SCHULTZ: Who was present at the meeting?

THE WITNESS: Rennie Davis, John Froines, Lee Weiner, and about fifteen marshals that were to participate during the Democratic Convention.

MR. SCHULTZ: Was there a conversation at that meeting?

THE WITNESS: Rennie Davis said, "We have several alternatives that we can do on August 28 in relation to the march that had been announced."

He said, "First of all we could have the march as we had announced."

He said, "Secondly, we could have a rally take place in the Grant Park area, with a confrontation.

"The last alternative is to hold a rally and then take over some buildings in the Loop area."

He said, "This could be accomplished by giving speeches during the time of that rally to incite the crowd for such a takeover." He illustrated a takeover such as the one that took place at Columbia, physically blocking the entrances and exits so no one could enter or leave. He said, "The people would be arrested in such a situation rather than just merely dispersed."

He then suggested three buildings for possible discussion. One was the Federal Building, one was the Pick-Congress and the other was the Conrad Hilton.

Lee Weiner said at this point that this was too important to discuss here and that we ought to discuss this at his apartment later that evening.

MR. SCHULTZ: You say Weiner said this?

THE WITNESS: I beg your pardon, it was John Froines.

MR. SCHULTZ: If the Court please, I would ask the Court again if he would direct the marshals to direct the defendants and their lawyers to stop laughing out loud as they just did. Mr. Kunstler was probably more guilty of it than any of the defendants.

THE COURT: I direct the marshal to go over there to the defendants' table and request them as we have done repeatedly in the past not to laugh loudly during this trial. This is a trial in the United States District Court. It is not a vaudeville theatre.

MR. KUNSTLER: But, your Honor, we are human beings, too. You can't make automatons out of us, or robots; we are human beings and we laugh occasionally, and if it comes irrepressibly, I don't really see how that really becomes a court matter.

MR. SCHULTZ: Mr. Kunstler is laughing so he can influence the jury with the impression that this is absurd. That is why he is laughing aloud because he—

If Mr. Dellinger would stop talking when we are addressing the Court—

MR. DELLINGER: I am trying to tell something to my lawyer. It is absurd. It is—he is a vaudeville actor.

THE COURT: You have made your observation, sir.

MR. SCHULTZ: May I proceed, your Honor?

After that meeting at the offices of the National Mobilization Committee, where did you go, please?

THE WITNESS: We adjourned the meeting and I went to eat dinner.

MR. SCHULTZ: After you ate dinner, where did you go?

THE WITNESS: I met John Froines, Richard Bosciano, and Steve Buff and drove them out to the meeting.

MR. SCHULTZ: Mr. Bock, please relate the conversation that occurred that evening.

THE WITNESS: Lee Weiner said that we should have a march anyway without a permit since this would provoke an arrest situation. He said he could see the headlines the next day saying "100,000 Demonstrators Arrested Confronting the Democratic Convention."

He said, however, he favored Rennie Davis' last point personally. He said there could be a rally held in Grant Park at the Bandshell, speeches could be given to incite the crowd on the takeover of a building in the Loop area.

He said that the Conrad Hilton would be the best building—for various reasons.

He said that because of the size of the Conrad Hilton, it would be better only if we took over one floor of the Hilton, and he said the fifteenth floor would be best.

Lee Weiner said we probably would get help from within.

John Froines said that such a takeover would be like Columbia, the physical stopping of anybody coming or going in that building. He said it would receive the necessary publicity since the cameras and the press and TV were already situated there.

He said that he and Lee Weiner would report to Rennie Davis the following day the decision of the marshals that evening.

MR. SCHULTZ: All right. Now calling your attention to the next day, which is Monday, August 26, 1968, specifically the early afternoon of that day, where did you go, please, on Monday?

THE WITNESS: I went to Lincoln Park near the fieldhouse at the south end of Lincoln Park. I saw Lee Weiner sitting with a group of people about fifty feet east of the fieldhouse.

MR. SCHULTZ: Now, Mr. Bock, would you please relate the conversation that occurred when you arrived at that group?

THE WITNESS: Lee Weiner said that we could have used flares last night in the park. We could have thrown the flares into the police cars.

MR. SCHULTZ: And at this point in the conversation, what, if anything, did you do?

THE WITNESS: I left the meeting and made a phone call.

MR. SCHULTZ: Whom did you call, please?

THE WITNESS: My control officer.

MR. SCHULTZ: Please relate what you observed and what occurred as you returned to the group?

THE WITNESS: On returning to the group, Tom Hayden came running up to the group and said "They are going to arrest me. They are going to bust me." He moved into the center of the group that was standing by now.

Right after he approached the group or came into the group, three police officers arrived. They told Mr. Hayden and Mr. Lowenthal that they were under arrest, and at this point a police wagon arrived and they proceeded to put Mr. Hayden and Lowenthal inside the police wagon.

There was a considerable amount of shouting by various people in the crowd. John Froines said "We should have stopped the arrest."

MR. SCHULTZ: Now, calling your attention to that night, that Monday night at about seven o'clock in the evening, this is Monday, the twenty-sixth of August, 1968, at seven that evening, do you remember where you were?

THE WITNESS: I was in Lincoln Park, roughly just northwest of the fieldhouse.

MR. SCHULTZ: Did you see any of the defendants at that time?

THE WITNESS: Yes, sir, Rennie Davis, Jerry Rubin, Lee Weiner and John Froines.

MR. SCHULTZ: Now you have mentioned Jerry Rubin. Do you see him in the court-room here?

THE WITNESS: Yes, sir. He is not in the courtroom.

MR. KUNSTLER: Your Honor, Mr. Rubin has left for a commitment which he had to keep. He has left with us a waiver of any rights. I will read it to your Honor.

THE COURT: I shall not accept a written waiver. Here we had to wait until this witness started to testify about him for you to even inform me about the written waiver. You are lawyer enough to know that a defendant in a criminal case may not walk out of his trial without leave of Court whether he waives or not.

THE MARSHAL: Mr. Rubin, I can't locate him in the rest room or on the floor, sir.

THE COURT: Mr. Schultz, I do not think that we can continue with this witness if he is to testify as to some alleged incident or conversation involving the defendant Rubin.

MR. SCHULTZ: Yes, your Honor.

THE COURT: I think we shall have to recess until tomorrow morning. Ladies and gentlemen of the jury, we shall recess until tomorrow morning with my usual orders.

Mr. Clerk, let a bench warrant issue for the arrest of the defendant Rubin. Let his bail bond be terminated.

MR. KUNSTLER: Your Honor, I want to put into the record, then, the written waiver by Mr. Rubin so it is part of the record of this case.

THE COURT: You might put it in the record. File whatever he has, sir, Mr. Clerk.

Mr. Marshal, the court will be in recess until ten o'clock tomorrow morning.

Nov. 13, 1969

THE CLERK: Motion of James B. Conlisk and James J. McDonough to quash subpoena for production of documents.

MR. ASPEN: If the Court please, my name is Marvin Aspen. I am an Assistant Corporation Counsel. I represent James B. Conlisk, Superintendant of Police of the City of Chicago and Mayor Richard J. Daley.

I am here in response to a subpoena duces tecum served on Mid-Continent Import and Export Company.

This subpoena, your Honor, was purportedly served on a Miss Rose Hamilton who is the secretary of the Assistant Director of the Port Authority for the City of Chicago, a Mr. William Barry. She has no connection with or knowledge of the Mid-Continent Import and Export Company.

For several years, up until December 1967, the Subversive Unit of the Chicago Police Department had quarters at Navy Pier and on the door of their quarters they put the name Mid-Continent Import and Export Company. The fact was there was no such company, it never was incorporated, it never existed. It never did any business. This was just a name on the door so people in the area would not be suspicious of people coming in and out of an unmarked door.

THE COURT: May I interrupt, Mr. Aspen, to say here is a subpoena purportedly served on some company identified as the Mid-Continent Import and Export Company. Now either there is such a legal person and the service is valid or there is no such person.

MR. ASPEN: There is no legal person, your Honor. I only want to give you the background.

There is no such company, there are no such records, and there never has been, so the issuance of a further subpoena would be of no avail in regard to this name. I want to make it perfectly clear that we do not represent this fictitious company.

MR. KUNSTLER: Then, your Honor, I wonder why he is here.

MR. ASPEN: I am here representing Miss Rose Hamilton, as I have told the Court before.

THE COURT: You will file your affidavit, Mr. Aspen?

MR. ASPEN: Yes, your Honor. We will file our affidavit today.

MR. KUNSTLER: Your Honor, at the close of yesterday's session you ordered the issuance of a bench warrant for the arrest of Jerry Rubin and the termination of his bail bond and I am moving your Honor to rescind that order, to reinstate his bail bond, and to release him on that bond.

I might indicate, your Honor, that Mr. Rubin had accepted a few days ago an engagement at Rutgers University to speak to the entire student body of that university. The plane connections were such that to leave after 4:30, which would be the ordinary adjournment time of this court, would have made it extremely difficult to make that airplane. Mr. Rubin signed the waiver and left the courtroom. Mr. Rubin did notify Mr. Foran in writing that he was going to make this trip. He took a cab to O'Hare and en route heard the radio indicate that your Honor had ordered his arrest and when he had confirmed what had happened in court, he returned immediately to our office.

I called your Honor's office and spoke to a young lady in the office and asked her to contact your Honor with reference to the possibility of a hearing. She indicated she would, and if she reached you, she would call me back. She did not call me back and so about a half hour later, I called your Honor's apartment hotel.

THE COURT: I do not live at a hotel.

MR. KUNSTLER: Whatever it is, they rang your apartment and I was informed that you were not at home; in fact there was no answer at the apartment. I therefore took Mr. Rubin to the Federal building and turned him in sometime around 8:20 to the U.S. Marshal who then took him to the Cook County jail where he spent the night.

I might also indicate that the witness who was on the stand had already identified Mr. Rubin in open court.

If we misunderstand, then we are sorry, but I think we are dealing here with a situation which is so minimal in consequence in this case it certainly—

THE COURT: You may regard it as minimal. I do not regard it as minimal when a defendant on trial in the United States District Court deliberately absents himself during the trial without leave of Court, just gets up and leaves and doesn't tell or doesn't get leave of the Court. You can characterize that as minimal, but I do not go along with you on that, sir.

MR. KUNSTLER: All right, your Honor, I would just like to state in concluding, your Honor, that I think that the punishment imposed upon Jerry Rubin does not fit the crime. He was forced last night to spend the night in the county jail. If there is punishment merited, then I think that that is sufficient punishment for him.

In closing, your Honor, I would indicate to you that Mr. Rubin is present here, and I would like to have permission for him to make a brief statement to your Honor—

THE COURT: He may make it.

MR. RUBIN: As to yesterday, your Honor, I felt that it was sufficient to sign a statement stipulating that I would withdraw my constitutional rights to be here. I did not intend to defy you or the court, and I was very shocked when my bail was revoked because I did not know I was doing anything wrong.

I did not walk out on the trial. That is absolutely wrong. I like being here. It is interesting. I have been here every day at 10:00 and 2:00 and stayed here to the end.

THE COURT: That is the best statement I have heard here during the trial. You said you enjoyed being here.

MR. RUBIN: It is good theater, your Honor. So walking out of the trial, I didn't do. The most thing I am guilty of is misunderstanding; I thought that signing the statement would be enough.

THE COURT: I am going to grant your motion to vacate my order of yesterday and, Mr. Clerk, I direct you to reinstate the bail bond which was ordered terminated—but I must caution not only Mr. Rubin but every other defendant that I expect that they attend every trial session here and all of each session.

Bring in the jury, Mr. Marshal.

MR. SCHULTZ: Mr. Bock, when we finished yesterday we were at Monday night, August 26, 1968, at Lincoln Park. You were at the fieldhouse area and you saw Davis, Weiner, Froines and Rubin standing together with some other people. Would you relate what conversation occurred when you approached this group, please, at about seven o'clock on the evening of Monday, August 26?

THE WITNESS: Rennie Davis said that the people reacted well to Tom Hayden's arrest and that they stood up well to the police at the statue.

He said, "We should have a wall-to-wall sit-in in front of the Conrad Hilton. When the police come to break these people up, that they would break into small bands and go directly into the Loop causing disturbances. They could break windows, pull fire alarm boxes, stone police cars, break street lights."

Mr. Rubin then said that they ought to do these things and they ought to do one more. He said they could start fires in the Loop.

Mr. Froines then said that the demonstrators would need things to use against the police. He said that they could purchase ammonia from many stores in the city and if they placed this ammonia into small bottles or something that would break, they could throw this at the police. He said by adding soap or soap chips to the ammonia, it would prolong the effects of the ammonia on the police officers or National Guard.

Lee Weiner said that they could let the air out of tires at the stop lights or stop signs in the Loop, jam up the traffic.

A Walter Gross said that it would be faster if we just slashed the tires and then Lee Weiner agreed and said it would.

MR. SCHULTZ: Did you see any of the defendants later on that night, that Monday night?

THE WITNESS: No, sir, I did not.

MR. SCHULTZ: Now, calling your attention to the following morning, that is the morning of August 28, 1968, where did you go that following morning, please?

THE WITNESS: I went to the offices of the National Mobilization at 407 South Dearborn.

MR. SCHULTZ: What occurred, please?

THE WITNESS: A meeting that was scheduled for that morning.

MR. SCHULTZ: Would you relate, please, Mr. Bock, what was stated at that meeting?

THE WITNESS: Mr. Dellinger spoke first and said that the City would not allow the permits for the National Mobilization to march to the Amphitheatre. He said, "They just won't let us go there."

Tom Hayden said that if the City doesn't give in to our demands, there would be war in the streets and there should be.

Mr. Dellinger said that we should have the march anyway and attempt to go to the Amphitheatre, and that when stopped by the police we sit down and practice the old form of nonresistance and nonviolence.

He said the majority of the police would be watching the marchers and this would give an opportunity to others to do a more militant action.

Someone suggested that Jerry Rubin give those speeches since usually he gives a good speech and excites a crowd. Someone else suggested that Tom Hayden give those speeches since he had previously been arrested and the people know Tom Hayden.

Rennie Davis said that no, he would give the speeches that afternoon.

MR. SCHULTZ: If the Court please, would the Marshal again be instructed to order the defendants and the people sitting in the vicinity to stop laughing. Would you continue?

THE WITNESS: Rennie Davis said it would be better if the march that started out would be stopped immediately since the people would not get too tired to do any actions later that evening. He said those people that went with the militant action should go immediately into the Loop without any march at all. He said there would probably be injuries in that group of people.

MR. SCHULTZ: All right, now, calling your attention to the next day, which is Thursday, the twenty-ninth of August, in the morning, do you recall where you went, please?

THE WITNESS: I went across the street from the Conrad Hilton into Grant Park.

MR. SCHULTZ: And did you see any of the defendants in Grant Park when you arrived there, please?

THE WITNESS: Yes, sir. John Froines and Lee Weiner.

MR. SCHULTZ: Would you relate what occurred, please, on arriving with the group?

THE WITNESS: On arriving, I noticed that Wolfe Lowenthal's arm was bandaged and in a sling, and a companion of his had bandages on also. He told me that he had injured his arm last night in the street.

Weiner said we should have had some cocktails last night. Craig Shimabukuro asked Weiner whether he meant Molotov cocktails or not. He said he did. "They're easy to make. All it takes is gasoline, sand, rags, and bottles."

Weiner said a good mobile tactic would be to pick a target in the Loop area and bomb that target. He said a better diversionary tactic would be the bombing of the underground garage. "Because of the size of the underground garage, it would take an enormous amount of police to protect that area and to search it."

He said or when it was bombed, that it would also take an enormous amount of fire equipment to put any fires out down there. Weiner then asked me if I could obtain the bottles necessary to make the Molotov cocktails. I told him I would. Weiner said that he and Craig Shimabukuro would then obtain the other materials necessary to make the Molotov cocktails, and that we were to meet back in Grant Park one hour from the time we left after the meeting.

At this point, a gentleman came by with a camera, and Lee Weiner said, "That guy just took our pictures. Let's split."

MR. SCHULTZ: After this conversation was over, where did you go, please?

THE WITNESS: I went to phone my control officer.

MR. SCHULTZ: After you telephoned your control officer, where did you go?

THE WITNESS: I returned to the Grant Park area across from the Conrad Hilton and saw John Froines. I walked up to John Froines and asked him if he had seen Craig Shimabukuro or Lee Weiner, whether or not they had returned.

He said that they hadn't, or he hadn't seen them, and he was looking for them also.

I suggested that we split up and each go a different way and see if we can locate them because of the meeting that was scheduled.

We then split up at this time.

MR. SCHULTZ: After this meeting with the defendant Froines did you see either Froines, Weiner or Lowenthal, or Shimabukuro later that day?

THE WITNESS: No, sir, I did not.

MR. SCHULTZ: Calling your attention to the next day, which is Friday, August 30, 1968, do you recall what if anything you did?

THE WITNESS: I went out to a picnic that was held in Downers Grove at the Nettle-hopper Farm.

MR. SCHULTZ: What did you do after you arrived?

THE WITNESS: We played baseball.

MR. SCHULTZ: And after you finished playing baseball, what occurred, please?

THE WITNESS: By now a large group of people had come to the picnic and I saw Tom Hayden, Rennie Davis, Lee Weiner and John Froines with other people seated close to the house.

MR. SCHULTZ: Relate, please, the convention that occured when you arrived at this group.

THE WITNESS: Just as I arrived, a man in a business suit and holding a pad asked Rennie Davis and Tom Hayden a question, "What has the National Mobilization gained from the demonstrations during the Democratic Convention?"

Rennie Davis answered first and he said that we had won America and that the American people now are on the side of the peace movement.

Tom Hayden said that this was the first step toward the revolution and that the second step would be coming soon.

MR. SCHULTZ: Then what occurred, please?

THE WITNESS: Lee Weiner said that the police had arrested Craig Shimabukuro in the underground garage last night. He said that had the police awaited five more minutes, they would have caught him with the necessary materials in his car to make the Molotov cocktails. Weiner said that there must be a police agent high in the staff of the National Mobilization.

John Froines agreed with Weiner, saying there is someone high in the staff of the National Mobilization who is a police agent. Tom Hayden said that he would like to get his hands on that s.o.b. Froines said that "I would like to get my licks in on him, too."

John Froines said the next time the National Mobilization plans anything they will have enough things to use against the police and National Guard so that he wouldn't have to use his own identification to buy the butyric acid which was used earlier that week.

MR. SCHULTZ: At that point, what, if anything, did you do?

THE WITNESS: I made an excuse that I had to work and left the area.

MR. SCHULTZ: No further questions on direct, your Honor.

• • • • •

MR. KUNSTLER: Mr. Bock, you testified on direct that you joined the United States Navy at one time. When was that?

THE WITNESS: I joined the United States Navy in December of 1957.

MR. KUNSTLER: Do you remember having an interview with Mr. Irving Birnbaum at all about your Navy service?

THE WITNESS: Yes, sir, I do.

MR. KUNSTLER: And do you recall telling Irving Birnbaum that you left the Navy because you couldn't stand what was happening to young men that you were instructing in Vietnam?

THE WITNESS: Yes, sir.

MR. KUNSTLER: Were you telling Mr. Birnbaum the truth?

THE WITNESS: No, sir.

MR. KUNSTLER: So you were lying to Mr. Birnbaum, is that correct?

MR. SCHULTZ: Objection, if the Court please.

THE COURT: Sustain the objection.

MR. KUNSTLER: Now, when you took the stand here originally yesterday, you took an oath, did you not?

THE WITNESS: I did.

MR. KUNSTLER: Have you not testified on direct examination that some of the defendants here were talking in terms of setting off bombs, or Molotov cocktails, in the Grant Park garage?

THE WITNESS: Yes, sir.

MR. KUNSTLER: And you have also mentioned that some of the defendants talked in terms of setting fires in the Loop?

THE WITNESS: Yes, sir.

MR. KUNSTLER: Did you also testify that some of the defendants were advocating violence toward the policemen and members of the National Guard?

THE WITNESS: Yes, sir.

MR. KUNSTLER: Now, do you recall executing an affidavit in the presence of Irving Birnbaum on June 30, 1969?

THE WITNESS: No, sir, I do not.

MR. KUNSTLER: I will ask you, does your signature appear on the third page of this document?

THE WITNESS: Yes, it does.

MR. KUNSTLER: And was it signed? Did you sign that document before a notary public?

THE WITNESS: That I do not know.

MR. KUNSTLER: Was Mr. Birnbaum present when you signed it?

THE WITNESS: He was seated, yes, sir.

MR. KUNSTLER: Now, when you signed this document, had you read it?

THE WITNESS: Yes, I did.

MR. KUNSTLER: And did you notice that it indicated that you had been duly sworn upon your oath before signing it?

MR. SCHULTZ: Objection, if the Court please, as to the form of that question.

THE COURT: I sustain the objection.

MR. KUNSTLER: Did you discuss with Mr. Birnbaum what was in the document?

THE WITNESS: Yes.

MR. KUNSTLER: After you had your discussion with Mr. Birnbaum, did you sign the document?

THE WITNESS: After he made some comments on the document itself, yes, sir.

MR. KUNSTLER: During your conversation with Mr. Birnbaum, did you not tell him that you had never heard any of the eight persons, including Bobby Seale, who had been indicted in this court, suggest any criminal activity to be performed by demonstrators coming to Chicago?

THE WITNESS: I told Mr. Birnbaum that.

MR. KUNSTLER: And did you not tell Mr. Birnbaum also that you had never seen any of these defendants perform an act of a criminal nature?

THE WITNESS: I did.

MR. KUNSTLER: In fact, you signed this paper which recites that, isn't that correct?

THE WITNESS: Yes, sir, it does.

MR. KUNSTLER: Did you not also tell Mr. Birnbaum that all of the instructions which you heard given to marshals and prospective marshals for the Democratic National Convention were defense in nature?

THE WITNESS: Yes, sir, I did.

MR. KUNSTLER: Did you not tell Mr. Birnbaum that after a general discussion and review of the events of that week, there was no discussion whatsoever of incendiary devices, fire bombing or the destruction of any public facility of the City of Chicago?

THE WITNESS: The statement in that text, yes, sir.

MR. KUNSTLER: Did not the statement contain the following phrase:

"I, Irv Bock, having been duly sworn, upon my oath, do hereby depose and say by way of voluntary statement:—"

Did it not contain that statement?

THE WITNESS: That sentence is in that document.

MR. KUNSTLER: Did you ever, after signing it, contact Mr. Birnbaum and say, "Mr. Birnbaum, I would like the statement back; it is untrue?"

THE WITNESS: No, sir.

MR. SCHULTZ: Objection, if the Court please.

THE COURT: I sustain the objection.

MR. KUNSTLER: Did you ever tell Mr. Birnbaum that you had told him a series of lies?

MR. SCHULTZ: Objection.

THE COURT: I sustain the objection.

MR. KUNSTLER: If you lied to Mr. Birnbaum as you have admitted, are you also lying here in this courtroom?

MR. SCHULTZ: Objection.

THE COURT: I sustain the objection.

MR. KUNSTLER: Before signing this document, had you ever had an interview with Mr. Weinglass?

THE WITNESS: Yes, sir, I did.

MR. KUNSTLER: Did you tell Mr. Weinglass the truth in answer to his questions?

THE WITNESS: No, sir, I did not.

MR. KUNSTLER: Did you lie to him as you were to lie later to Mr. Birnbaum?

MR. SCHULTZ: Objection.

THE COURT: I sustain the objection.

MR. KUNSTLER: How did you eventually get to Mr. Weinglass?

THE WITNESS: Lee Weiner called me on the phone.

MR. KUNSTLER: And asked you to see Mr. Weinglass?

THE WITNESS: Yes, sir.

MR. KUNSTLER: Were you then supposedly working at American Airlines?

THE WITNESS: Yes, sir.

MR. KUNSTLER: But in fact, you were not, is that correct?

THE WITNESS: That is correct.

MR. KUNSTLER: Did you give the people at the Mobilization the information that you worked for American Airlines?

THE WITNESS: Yes, I did.

MR. KUNSTLER: And that was untrue, was it not?

THE WITNESS: Yes, sir.

MR. KUNSTLER: Were there arrangements made with American Airlines if anybody called to tell them that you would return the call?

MR. SCHULTZ: Objection.

THE COURT: Sustain the objection.

MR. KUNSTLER: Is it not a fact, Mr. Bock, that you were telling all of these untruths in order to accomplish a purpose that you had? Isn't that correct?

THE WITNESS: Yes.

MR. KUNSTLER: And is it not true also that you are also telling untruths today and yesterday to accomplish another purpose?

MR. SCHULTZ: Objection.

THE COURT: I sustain the objection.

MR. KUNSTLER: Is it your expectation that after your admission of all of these untruths, that you expect this jury now to believe—

MR. SCHULTZ: Objection from the very inception of that question. Mr. Kunstler knows that that is improper.

THE COURT: You ought to know better, Mr. Kunstler, and at this point, we will recess, ladies and gentlemen of the jury.

• • • • •

THE MARSHAL: We will have quiet in the courtroom, please.

MR. DAVIS: Why don't you arrest this lying police spy. He has filed an affidavit.

MR. FORAN: I would like to have those remarks on the record, Miss Reporter.

MR. KUNSTLER: I suggest to you, Miss Reporter, that no one has authority to ask you to put those comments in the record.

MR. FORAN: The remark was "Why don't you arrest that lying police spy?" Miss Reporter.

MR. DELLINGER: And that District Attorney who is teaching him to lie.

MR. FORAN: Take that also, Miss Reporter.

MR. DELLINGER: That is a fine way to get to be Senator.

MR. KUNSTLER: Now, Mr. Bock, did your control officer tell you to give Mr. Weinglass a misleading statement about the facts of any questions which Mr. Weinglass might ask you?

THE WITNESS: I was told by my control officer that I probably would be the best one to know the answers to the questions that Mr. Weinglass would ask and to give him a statement so that my identity as a police officer was not known to Mr. Weinglass. I gave a statement to Mr. Weinglass of what I think he wanted to hear.

MR. KUNSTLER: Knowing all the time that what you told him was an untruth, isn't that correct?

THE WITNESS: That is correct.

MR. KUNSTLER: Did you have discussions about your testimony here with any member of the U.S. Attorney's office prior to testifying?

THE WITNESS: Twice—three times at the most.

MR. KUNSTLER: Were there any other meetings with the U.S. Attorneys outside of their office?

THE WITNESS: No more than four times.

MR. KUNSTLER: That makes approximately seven meetings. Did not Mr. Schultz ask you whether any of the comments which you had made in this three-page statement were true?

THE WITNESS: I believe he asked something similar to that, yes.

MR. KUNSTLER: What did you tell him?

THE WITNESS: I said that in overall nature of the entire statement, taken as it is, it represented a falsehood to Mr. Weinglass because of keeping my identity as an undercover police officer.

MR. KUNSTLER: It was important to you, was it not, that you maintain your undercover role?

THE WITNESS: If I was to work, yes.

MR. KUNSTLER: That was important enough to tell untruths for, is that correct?

THE WITNESS: To individuals, yes.

MR. KUNSTLER: So you are not above telling an untruth when it is important to you, is that correct?

MR. SCHULTZ: Objection.

THE COURT: Sustain the objection.

MR. KUNSTLER: Your Honor, I think it is a proper question as to credibility.

THE COURT: It may go out, and the jury is directed to disregard it.

MR. KUNSTLER: Mr. Bock, when did you join the Veterans for Peace?

THE WITNESS: I would say it would be probably the second week in December of 1967.

MR. KUNSTLER: Can you indicate to the Court and to the jury whether as a member of either Veterans for Peace or the Chicago Peace Council you were active in plans for the demonstration in Washington tomorrow?

MR. SCHULTZ: Objection, if the Court please.

THE COURT: I sustain the objection.

MR. KUNSTLER: Did you participate in any discussion or activities in connection with the October 15 Moratorium against the war in Vietnam?

MR. SCHULTZ: Objection.

THE COURT: I sustain the objection.

MR. KUNSTLER: Is it not a fact that you told people both in the Chicago Peace Council and Veterans for Peace that you intended to go to Washington tomorrow to protest the war in Vietnam?

MR. SCHULTZ: Objection.

THE COURT: I sustain the objection.

MR. KUNSTLER: Mr. Bock, did you have an invitation from somebody to attend a meeting on the ninth of August at the Mobilization offices?

THE WITNESS: Well, if you call it an invitation, saying "come down if you want to," yes.

MR. KUNSTLER: Was that from Rennie Davis?

THE WITNESS: Yes, sir.

MR. KUNSTLER: Who initiated the telephone call?

THE WITNESS: I did.

MR. KUNSTLER: What did you say to Rennie Davis on the telephone when you started the conversation?

THE WITNESS: I acquainted him—I said "Hey, this is Irv," and I guess he said, "Who?" and I said, "Irv Bock. I represent, you know, the Vets, and I am interested in becoming a marshal."

MR. KUNSTLER: What did Rennie Davis say to you?

THE WITNESS: "Fine," he said, "we're setting up a meeting to take place," and if I want to, I should come down.

MR. KUNSTLER: And you wanted to, didn't you?

THE WITNESS: Yes.

MR. SCHULTZ: Objection to that question.

THE COURT: He has answered the question. I will let the question and answer stand.

MR. KUNSTLER: Now when you walked into that office, some of the defendants were present, is that correct?

THE WITNESS: Yes.

MR. KUNSTLER: Was there a William Frapolly present?

THE WITNESS: I don't recall whether he was there or not.

MR. KUNSTLER: Do you know him?

THE WITNESS: I knew him.

MR. KUNSTLER: Do you know that he had a connection with the Police Department?

THE WITNESS: No, sir, I did not.

MR. KUNSTLER: Now, someone suggested, did they not, during this meeting that the staging area for the march to the Amphitheatre be moved from State and Wacker to the parking lot around the White Sox Ball Park, isn't that correct, Comiskey Field?

THE WITNESS: Yes.

MR. KUNSTLER: Who was that person?

THE WITNESS: I don't recall who said that.

MR. KUNSTLER: Could it have been William Frapolly making that statement?

THE WITNESS: I don't recall.

MR. KUNSTLER: You thought there might be a night game between the White Sox and some other American League Club that night which would fill the parking lot with cars, is that correct?

THE WITNESS: Yes.

MR. KUNSTLER: Was there a night game that night?

THE WITNESS: I don't know if there was or not.

MR. KUNSTLER: Did you know when you were having this discussion about Comiskey Park that you were having a dialogue with another police officer?

THE WITNESS: No, sir, I did not.

MR. KUNSTLER: When you went over to listen to what Davis, Hayden, and Froines were discussing on the fifteenth, is it your testimony that you just stood there and listened to the conversation?

THE WITNESS: Well, I walked up and said—we greeted each other, that is, "What do you say?" or something to that effect, and they started talking.

MR. KUNSTLER: Did anyone turn to you and say, "Listen, this is a private conversation. Go back to the training," or words to that effect?

THE WITNESS: Not to my knowledge.

MR. KUNSTLER: Did you have anything to tell anyone when you went over there to this group that was having a conversation?

THE WITNESS: No.

MR. KUNSTLER: You just went there to listen and report to your control officer, isn't that correct?

THE WITNESS: Yes, sir.

MR. KUNSTLER: And no one raised an eyebrow when you just horned into the conversation?

MR. SCHULTZ: Objection.

THE COURT: I sustain the objection.

MR. KUNSTLER: Isn't it a fact that you never heard any such conversation at any such fieldhouse on that day?

THE WITNESS: No.

MR. KUNSTLER: It is not a fact?

THE WITNESS: No.

MR. KUNSTLER: When is the next time that you saw any of the defendants in this case?

THE WITNESS: On the eighteenth, at a meeting held at the Welsh Hall, on Noble Street.

MR. KUNSTLER: Now, I think you related on your direct that Rennie Davis introduced a series of people to give reports, is that correct?

THE WITNESS: Yes, sir.

MR. KUNSTLER: And I think you gave us Froines' remarks on that occasion, and then someone replaced Mr. Froines as a speaker, is that correct?

THE WITNESS: Mr. Davis called on Fred Gardner.

MR. KUNSTLER: Now, where were you standing or sitting while Fred Gardner spoke?

THE WITNESS: Close to the front, within two rows of the front and to the left of center.

MR. KUNSTLER: How many people were seated in front of you in the two rows?

THE WITNESS: Not every seat was filled, so I would say that there were about ten people at the most.

MR. KUNSTLER: So between you and Mr. Froines were two rows of seats and then a table at which Froines was seated, is that correct?

THE WITNESS: Yes.

MR. KUNSTLER: Now, while Mr. Gardner was speaking, you heard a conversation between Mr. Froines and three or four people?

THE WITNESS: Yes, sir.

MR. KUNSTLER: And you could hear that clearly?

THE WITNESS: Yes, sir.

MR. KUNSTLER: Over Mr. Gardner's voice, is that correct?

THE WITNESS: Yes, sir.

MR. KUNSTLER: Did somebody ask Mr. Froines a question?

THE WITNESS: Yes, sir.

MR. KUNSTLER: What was that question?

THE WITNESS: The question that was asked of Mr. Froines was what he meant by guerrilla tactics.

MR. KUNTSLER: You could hear that question while Mr. Gardner was giving a report from a person whose face was turned away from you?

THE WITNESS: Yes, sir.

MR. KUNSTLER: Now, did you report this incident to your control officer?

THE WITNESS: I did.

MR. KUNSTLER: I show you D-95 for identification and ask you if you can identify this.

THE WITNESS: Yes, sir. It is a control officer's report.

MR. KUNSTLER: Are you certain, Mr. Bock, that you told your control officer about this conversation about guerrilla tactics that Mr. Froines is supposed to have had with these three people that walked up that day?

THE WITNESS: Yes.

MR. KUNSTLER: Does it appear in that report?

MR. SCHULTZ: Objection. That is not his report.

THE COURT: I sustain the objection.

MR. KUNSTLER: Tell us how you remember this particular conversation of Mr. Froines'.

THE WITNESS: Because it happened and I remember it happening.

MR. KUNSTLER: And did you write it down somewhere?

THE WITNESS: Yes.

MR. KUNSTLER: Where are the notes on this conversation?

THE WITNESS: They were destroyed.

MR. KUNSTLER: Were they destroyed before you made your report to your control officer?

THE WITNESS: I used the notes that I was able to jot down at various times to aid me in making my report to my control officer.

MR. KUNSTLER: Mr. Bock, are you going to Washington tomorrow?

MR. SCHULTZ: Is that a question?

MR. KUNSTLER: That is a question.

MR. SCHULTZ: Objection.

THE COURT: I sustain the objection. You may go on.

MR. KUNSTLER: I would like a recess, your Honor. I am going to Washington. I would like to join that protest.

THE COURT: You continue with your cross-examination. You just continue. Are you going with him, is that the reason you were asking?

MR. KUNSTLER: No. If he would like to accompany me, he is free to do so, but I would like the opportunity, your Honor—

THE COURT: You just continue with your cross-examination, sir. I will let you know when we recess. You have a habit of trying to determine when the court recesses here.

MR. KUNSTLER: No. I have a right, your Honor, to protest in Washington and to make my plane to get there. Your Honor is going beyond the normal recess time and I would not like that to interfere with my First Amendment rights to go to Washington, and I am asking your Honor who has recessed at the Government's request on frequent occasions—

THE COURT: You will finish when I tell you you may finish, sir. There is only one person that determines the hours of court here. That is one of the few prerogatives I have. Counsel for the defense does not determine the hours of court.

MR. KUNSTLER: Your Honor, at this time I would like to indicate that all of the defendants would like to waive their constitutional rights to be present here. They would like to join the protest.

THE COURT: The defendants will remain here and you may continue with your cross-examination.

MR. FORAN: Your Honor, may we have the jury directed to disregard the improper remarks of counsel?

THE COURT: Yes. The jury may disregard the requests about Washington and constitutional rights. This is a trial here; it is not in Washington.

And the Court notes the loud laughter at the Court of several defendants, including Rubin.

MR. KUNSTLER: Now, you testified as to this conversation which you heard over Fred Gardner's report. How much of Fred Gardner's report did you hear?

THE WITNESS: Just a small portion.

MR. KUNSTLER: Because you were busily listening to Mr. Froines, is that correct?

THE WITNESS: I would say yes.

MR. KUNSTLER: Now, you stated that in the afternoon session Mr. Davis discussed whether it would be a hard line or a soft line as far as the police were concerned. Did he not state that they wanted to see whether the police were going to act as they did on April 27 when they clubbed and beat demonstrators or as they acted on May 4 when they did not? Do you recall that?

THE WITNESS: I believe he did use those dates as an example.

MR. KUNSTLER: Do you know of your own knowledge what happened to the peace demonstrators in Chicago on April 27?

MR. SCHULTZ: Objection.

THE COURT: I sustain the objection.

MR. KUNSTLER: Were you involved in any way on April 27 with any undercover activities in connection with the peace march on April 27 to the Civic Center?

MR. SCHULTZ: Objection.

THE COURT: I sustain the objection.

MR. KUNSTLER: Did you participate in that march?

MR. SCHULTZ: Objection.

THE COURT: I sustain the objection.

November 18, 1969

MR. KUNSTLER: Mr. Bock, on Tuesday, August 27, what did you do in the evening?

THE WITNESS: I followed a march to the streetcar barns at Shubert Street and Clark.

MR. KUNSTLER: Was that in connection with a Chicago Transit Authority strike?

THE WITNESS: I believe it was, yes.

MR. KUNSTLER: Now, is your testimony here that this occurred on Tuesday night, the march to the barns, is that correct?

THE WITNESS: On the twenty-seventh, yes, sir.

MR. KUNSTLER: Have you ever told anybody else that it occurred on a different night?

THE WITNESS: I believe so, yes, sir.

MR. KUNSTLER: Was that the grand jury?

THE WITNESS: I don't recall what I told the grand jury.

MR. KUNSTLER: Well, I will show you D-97 for identification—and ask you if this refreshes your recollection as to what you told the grand jury as to what happened the night of this march.

THE WITNESS: Well, in testifying before the grand jury I used—I told the grand jury at that time, yes sir.

MR. KUNSTLER: In your testimony to the grand jury you gave them the wrong date, isn't that correct?

THE WITNESS: I did.

MR. KUNSTLER: Isn't it a fact, Mr. Bock, that what makes your memory so accurate today is the fourteen hours you spent in discussing your testimony with the prosecution?

MR. SCHULTZ: Objection.

THE COURT: I sustain the objection.

MR. KUNSTLER: Can you give us any reason why you told the grand jury a different date than you told this jury?

THE WITNESS: I believe I can. In testifying before the grand jury I used the FBI reports and in the FBI reports the date is wrong as to the time of the march or as to the date of the march. They placed it on another day.

MR. KUNSTLER: Are you telling this jury that your testimony before the grand jury was not your own independent recollection but what the FBI said?

MR. SCHULTZ: Objection.

THE COURT: I sustain the objection.

MR. SCHULTZ: If the Court please, would the Court instruct Mr. Dellinger to stop laughing aloud and whispering to me during this examination?

MR. DELLINGER: It is so funny.

THE COURT: I have done that often during this trial, and I have been told by counsel that they want to laugh. I do direct him again not to laugh in a manner that is so loud.

MR. KUNSTLER: Who told you to use the FBI report in testifying?

THE WITNESS: I believe I was handed the report by Mr. Schultz a short period before walking into the grand jury room.

MR. KUNSTLER: Did Mr. Schultz tell you that this was the script that you were to follow?

THE WITNESS: He did not.

THE COURT: Mr. Kunstler, there is a great architect, Mies van der Rohe, who lately left us. He designed that lectern as well as this building and it was a lectern, not a leaning post. I don't permit lawyers to lean on that thing. I don't want you to do it.

MR. KUNSTLER: Your Honor, the U.S. Attorney questions from the back of this table and leans on his material.

THE COURT: I don't care about that.

MR. KUNSTLER: Why am I different?

THE COURT: I haven't seen the United States Attorney put his elbow on that thing and lean on it as though it was a leaning post and I wouldn't permit them to do it or you.

MR. KUNSTLER: Perhaps I am tired, your Honor. What is wrong about leaning on it?

THE COURT: If you are tired then let Mr.—

MR. KUNSTLER: Mr. Weinglass.

THE COURT: —Weinglass take over.

MR. KUNSTLER: May I place my hands like this, your Honor?

THE COURT: Yes. Yes. That is not leaning.

MR. KUNSTLER: Now, you testified that you had told both Mr. Birnbaum and Mr. Weinglass what they wanted to hear when they interrogated you as to the conduct of the marshals and the defendants, isn't that correct?

MR. SCHULTZ: Objection.

THE COURT: I suggest you put a question and if it is one that is proper, I will let him answer if there is no objection.

MR. KUNSTLER: When you testified before this jury on direct, were you not telling them what you thought the U.S. Attorney and the Chicago Police Department wanted to hear?

THE WITNESS: If you are saying that I lied, no, sir, you are wrong.

MR. KUNSTLER: You lied before, did you not?

MR. SCHULTZ: Objection, if the Court please.

THE COURT: I sustain the objection.

MR. KUNSTLER: Is it not true, Mr. Bock, that what you told Mr. Weinglass and Mr. Birnbaum was, indeed, the truth and what you told this jury was a lie as to any violence which you have put in the mouths of any of the defendants in this case?

THE WITNESS: That is not true.

MR. KUNSTLER: I have no further questions.

THE COURT: Mr. Weinglass, do you have any cross-examination of this witness?

•   •   •   •   •

MR. WEINGLASS: Officer Bock, the time period that you spent with the defendants covers approximately August 9 through August 30, am I correct in that?

THE WITNESS: With some meetings prior to August 9, yes.

MR. WEINGLASS: And during this period of time you have told us that you have over-heard conversations between them and other people, conversations about flares by some of the defendants, is that true?

THE WITNESS: Yes.

MR. WEINGLASS: And you testified that you overheard conversations about fire bombs by some of the defendants, is that true?

THE WITNESS: Yes, sir.

MR. WEINGLASS: And you testified you overheard conversations by some of the defendants about occupying a building in this city, is that true?

THE WITNESS: Yes, sir.

MR. WEINGLASS: And you testified that at times you heard conversations from some of these defendants about setting small fires in the Loop area?

THE WITNESS: Yes, sir.

MR. WEINGLASS: And you testified that you heard some of these defendants talk about breaking windows?

THE WITNESS: Yes, sir.

MR. WEINGLASS: And these were all conversations you overheard that you testified about?

THE WITNESS: I would say yes, sir.

MR. WEINGLASS: Now, I ask you, Officer Bock, to look at these seven men who are sitting at this table and I ask you whether or not it is a fact that throughout this entire period of time that you were with them, in their company, in their presence with them at the meetings, with them on the streets of this city, with them in the parks of this city, you never once saw any one of them ever commit a single act of violence?

MR. SCHULTZ: Objection to the form of the question.

THE COURT: I sustain the objection.

MR. WEINGLASS: Did you see any of them strike a policeman?

THE WITNESS: No, sir.

MR. WEINGLASS: Did you see any of them throw a rock?

THE WITNESS: I don't believe I did.

MR. WEINGLASS: Did you see any of them break a window?

THE WITNESS: No, sir.

MR. WEINGLASS: Did you see any of them hit a police car?

THE WITNESS: Not physically see them, no sir.

MR. WEINGLASS: Did you see any of them holding or using a flare?

THE WITNESS: No, sir.

MR. WEINGLASS: Did you see any of them making a fire bomb?

THE WITNESS: No, sir.

MR. WEINGLASS: Now, you testified that you attended, I believe it is, six sessions of marshal training in Lincoln Park. Were there any more?

THE WITNESS: None that I can recall at this point?

MR. WEINGLASS: Now, as I understand your testimony, at all of these training sessions you testified that the training involved an exercise known as "washoi," an exercise known as "skirmish line," and an exercise which you have described as rolling a magazine over the head and extending the leg out in a kicking direction.

THE WITNESS: If you are speaking about the snake dance training, yes.

November 19, 1969

MR. WEINGLASS: Now you and I have discussed marshal training once before, haven't we?

THE WITNESS: I believe we did, yes.

MR. WEINGLASS: We did at lunch and we did later in my office, didn't we?

THE WITNESS: I believe so, yes, sir.

MR. WEINGLASS: Do you remember telling me—and I wrote this in the statement which you signed—that "it appeared to me to be just a bunch of kids were getting together in the park and having a good time?" Do you recall telling me that?

THE WITNESS: I don't recall that I used those words to you or not, sir.

MR. WEINGLASS: Do you remember telling me they did not appear to have their heart and soul into anything of a serious nature?

THE WITNESS: I believe I may have said something to that effect, yes, sir.

MR. WEINGLASS: Did you also—do you also remember telling me the only instruction they received was strictly defensive?
THE WITNESS: I may have. I believe I did say that to you, yes, sir.
MR. WEINGLASS: Now, you told the jury that you had to lie to me in order to protect your identity as a police officer, isn't that true?
THE WITNESS: Yes, sir.
MR. WEINGLASS: But didn't it occur to you, Officer Bock, that if what you told me was untrue, that my factual investigation from all the other people who were present would clearly indicate that you had lied to me?
MR. SCHULTZ: Objection.
THE COURT: I sustain the objection.
MR. WEINGLASS: Wasn't just the reverse the truth, that you had to tell me the truth so that I wouldn't suspect you of being a police agent because you knew I had talked to all of the other people who had been there?
THE WITNESS: I don't believe it would indicate that to me, no, sir.
MR. WEINGLASS: Didn't you feel that you had to tell me the truth at that point to protect your identity?
THE WITNESS: I didn't tell you the truth at that point.
MR. WEINGLASS: Weren't you concerned at all that in my discussion with other people who were present I would find out that only you gave me a different story than everyone else?
MR. SCHULTZ: Objection.
THE COURT: I sustain the objection.
MR. WEINGLASS: Now, Officer Bock, the office on Dearborn Street which you testified you went to for meetings was the National Mobilization office, was it not?
THE WITNESS: Yes, sir, at 407.
MR. WEINGLASS: Were you not told by Mr. Davis that the people in the National Mobilization were aware of the fact that the rooms had been bugged by the police?
MR. SCHULTZ: Objection.
THE COURT: I sustain the objection.
MR. SCHULTZ: That is not so. Those rooms were not bugged by the police. Objection if the Court please.
MR. WEINGLASS: I think we can dispense with the witness if Mr. Schultz will be sworn to tell us what rooms the police are bugging in this city and what rooms they are not. I think that might be helpful.
THE COURT: I will let him answer the question over the objection of the Government.
THE WITNESS: As to being bugged by the police, I would say it came up several times in the offices and I don't recall whether Mr. Davis said that.
MR. WEINGLASS: Do you recall telling the grand jury that Davis said it?
THE WITNESS: I don't recall that, no, sir.
MR. WEINGLASS: Now, on August 21, at approximately four o'clock you attended a National Mobilization meeting for marshals, did you not?
THE WITNESS: Yes, sir, I did.
MR. WEINGLASS: It was at that meeting that you testified you heard Mr. Davis referring to occupying a building in the Loop, did you not?
THE WITNESS: Yes, sir.
MR. WEINGLASS: You called your control officer and you told him about what happened at that meeting, did you not?
THE WITNESS: Yes, sir; I did.
MR. WEINGLASS: Is there any particular reason, Officer Bock, that your control officer in his report doesn't even mention anything about the seizure or the occupation of the Hilton Hotel?
MR. SCHULTZ: Objection.
THE COURT: I sustain the objection.
MR. WEINGLASS: Now, I believe you testified that there was some discussion about the occupation of the Hilton Hotel at the meeting that night as well, was there not?
THE WITNESS: Yes, sir, there was.

MR. WEINGLASS: I believe your further testimony is that it was to be approved later at a subsequent meeting of the steering committee?

THE WITNESS: Well, people would report the decisions of the marshals to Mr. Davis, and I imagine he would in turn report at the steering committee.

MR. WEINGLASS: At either one of those meetings, the one the next night or the following night, was one word mentioned about the Hilton Hotel?

THE WITNESS: Not that I recall.

MR. WEINGLASS: Wasn't it the fifteenth floor which the police raided when they raided the McCarthy headquarters?

MR. SCHULTZ: Objection.

THE COURT: I sustain the objection.

MR. WEINGLASS: Aren't you confusing that with this alleged conversation which you are testifying you heard?

MR. SCHULTZ: Objection.

THE COURT: Sustain the objection.

MR. WEINGLASS: Did you ask when they were going to occupy the Hilton?

THE WITNESS: No, sir.

MR. WEINGLASS: Do you think that might be important for the police to know?

MR. SCHULTZ: Objection.

THE COURT: I sustain the objection.

MR. WEINGLASS: Officer Bock, directing your attention to Thursday morning, August 29, at approximately 11:00 A.M., you testified you were present at a conversation between the defendants Weiner, Froines, I believe Wolfe Lowenthal was there, Craig Shimabukuro, and one or two others, is that correct?

THE WITNESS: Yes.

MR. WEINGLASS: During the course of this conversation I believe you testified that you heard some mention of fire bombs.

THE WITNESS: Yes, sir. Mr. Weiner asked me if I could obtain the bottles necessary to make the Molotov cocktails.

MR. WEINGLASS: Did you ever see any of the ingredients of the so-called Molotov cocktails?

THE WITNESS: No, sir, I did not.

MR. WEINGLASS: Did you report this conversation?

THE WITNESS: I reported that, yes, sir.

MR. WEINGLASS: As a result of your conversation do you know if a number of men were dispatched to the underground garage in Grant Park?

MR. SCHULTZ: Objection.

THE COURT: I sustain the objection.

MR. WEINGLASS: Mr. Bock, in my interview of you did you not tell me that there was no discussion in that conversation of incendiary devices, fire bombing or the destruction of any public facility in the City of Chicago?

THE WITNESS: In order to maintain my cover, I told you that, yes, sir.

MR. WEINGLASS: Now, I told you that, did I not, I represented two of the people who were supposedly present at that conversation, Lee Weiner and John Froines? Did I not?

MR. SCHULTZ: Objection. That has no bearing, no probative—if Mr. Dellinger will stop talking to me when I am trying to address the Court—

MR. DELLINGER: I don't talk to you.

MR. SCHULTZ: And mumble to me every time I am trying to make an objection—

MR. DELLINGER: Don't go making up things, Richard Schultz. I didn't talk to you. I don't mind your making all of these phony objections, but when you start lying about me, too, I think that is disgusting.

THE COURT: Mr. Dellinger—

MR. DELLINGER: I didn't say a word to him, Judge.

THE COURT: You just said enough to me to admonish you not to make any more remarks like that.

MR. FORAN: Your Honor, I was sitting here, too. I overheard the remarks.

MR. DELLINGER: You are adding a lie to his lie, and I say that on my word.

THE COURT: I see that you are not accepting my admonition, sir, and I ask the reporter to make note of that.

MR. WEINGLASS: Mr. Bock, in the course of your meetings with these defendants did you ever hear the phrase "mobile tactic"?

THE WITNESS: I believe that phrase was mentioned, yes. I think Mr. Froines mentioned that at a meeting that was held at the Welsh Hall.

MR. WEINGLASS: Did you ever receive instruction in your marshal training in mobile tactics?

THE WITNESS: Yes, sir. We were verbally instructed by Mr. Davis when he said that if the demonstrators came into an arrest situation, that the marshals should break them up into smaller groups and use the mobile tactic he called a scatter tactic, where a marshal would lead demonstrators away and they would harass their pursuers, whether they were police or counter-demonstrators.

MR. WEINGLASS: And the marshals were to lead the mobile tactics, according to your testimony?

THE WITNESS: That is what Mr. Davis said, yes.

MR. WEINGLASS: There was no explanation as to what the harassment would be from your testimony?

THE WITNESS: He did not spell it out to us.

November 20, 1969

MR. WEINGLASS: Now, Officer Bock, thinking back over your entire testimony for this past week, are you able to explain to the jury why it was that you heard so much about violence supposedly from these seven men and yet saw so little of what they did?

MR. SCHULTZ: Objection.

THE COURT: I sustain the objection.

MR. WEINGLASS: As you reflect on it all, have you reached any conclusion in substance as to what all these conversations were about and how it was that none of these conversations ever manifested themselves in action?

MR. SCHULTZ: Objection.

THE COURT: I sustain the objection.

MR. WEINGLASS: Officer Bock, is there any part of your testimony now you would like to change?

MR. SCHULTZ: Objection.

THE COURT: I sustain the objection.

MR. WEINGLASS: I have no further questions.

THE COURT: Is there any redirect examination?

MR. SCHULTZ: Just a few questions, your Honor. Do you recall Mr. Kunstler asking you if you testified to what you thought the United States Attorney wanted to hear? Do you remember him asking you that?

THE WITNESS: He asked me a question similar to that, yes, sir.

MR. SCHULTZ: Did Mr. Foran, the United States Attorney, ever suggest to you in any way what it was that he wanted to hear?

THE WITNESS: He told me he wanted as much as I could recall and that it should be the truth.

MR. SCHULTZ: Did Mr. Foran in any way ever suggest to you that you should in any way falsify any testimony at all in this courtroom?

THE WITNESS: No, sir.

MR. SCHULTZ: Did I suggest to you in any way what I wanted you to say?

THE WITNESS: No, sir, you did not.

MR. SCHULTZ: Did I ever suggest that you should falsify anything in this courtroom?

THE WITNESS: No, sir.

MR. SCHULTZ: Did any agent of the FBI ever make any of these suggestions to you that I have just made?

THE WITNESS: No, sir, they did not.

MR. SCHULTZ: Did anybody in the world ever make such a suggestion to you?

THE WITNESS: No, sir.

MR. SCHULTZ: That is all, your Honor.

THE COURT: Within the limits of the redirect examination, I will permit recross-examination.

MR. KUNSTLER: When you went to see the U.S. Attorneys, Mr. Schultz and Mr. Foran, they told you to just tell the facts here in court, is that correct?

THE WITNESS: They told me to tell as much as I could recall, yes, sir.

MR. KUNSTLER: Now, if you had lied to this jury under oath here, would you admit it from the witness stand?

MR. SCHULTZ: Objection.

THE COURT: I sustain the objection.

MR. KUNSTLER: Is it your statement or is it your testimony today that you have told this jury the absolute truth in response to every question asked of you by the U.S. Attorney?

THE WITNESS: As best as I could recall, yes, sir.

MR. KUNSTLER: As best as you could recall and as best as the reports you read could assist you, is that correct?

MR. SCHULTZ: Objection.

THE COURT: Sustain the objection.

MR. KUNSTLER: I have no further questions, your Honor.

Testimony of Joseph Hale

MR. FORAN: Will you state your name, please?

THE WITNESS: Joseph Hale.

MR. FORAN: What is your occupation, Mr. Hale?

THE WITNESS: I am an investigator assigned to the State's Attorney office of Cook County.

MR. FORAN: What was your occupation in August of 1968?

THE WITNESS: I was assigned to the subversive unit of the Chicago Police Intelligence Division.

MR. FORAN: Now, calling your attention particularly to the afternoon of August 29, 1968, at approximately 3:15 that afternoon, where did you go?

THE WITNESS: I was at the Bandshell in Grant Park at this time.

MR. FORAN: Now, where were you with respect to the flagpole?

THE WITNESS: I was west of the flagpole and south of the pole and the Bandshell. I was moving through the crowd.

MR. FORAN: What were your duties at that exact moment?

THE WITNESS: I was assigned as a photographer with one of the six Police Department photo teams.

MR. FORAN: Now, at this time what did you observe, Mr. Hale?

THE WITNESS: Well, at approximately 3:15 I heard some noise. I looked up at the flag-pole, and I noticed the American flag being lowered from the top, and feeling that this was an unexpected action, I took a shot of the flag as it was descending down the flagpole. In fact, the flag was at half-staff when I got a photo of it.

MR. FORAN: What occurred then?

THE WITNESS: I then moved over to the other side of the flagpole where I saw two or three uniformed police officers apparently placing someone under arrest.

MR. FORAN: What occurred then?

THE WITNESS: Well, at this particular time a plastic bag of a brownish solution came sailing out of the crowd toward the police officers at the base of the flagpole, and the plastic bag literally exploded at this time, covering some of the officers and other by-standers with this brown solution. Then immediately after that another plastic bag came sailing out of the crowd at the police officers, and then this literally just exploded and a bluish solution was discharged.

MR. FORAN: Did you see any other missiles thrown?

THE WITNESS: Chunks of concrete came hurtling out of the crowd, three-by-three squares of plastic tile were being thrown. I remember sticks, tin cans, and at one point I saw a jar of mustard thrown at the officers.

MR. FORAN: How many police officers were there?

THE WITNESS: I'd say at the most at this time, sir, my rough guess would be maybe fifteen to twenty uniformed officers. There couldn't have been many more than that.

MR. FORAN: Did you attempt to arrest any of these people?

THE WITNESS: Yes, sir. I did. I came up behind one individual. I, of course, was in civilian clothes, and this gentleman was swinging a club. He had just struck a uniformed officer across the back, and I grabbed him from behind, and I said, "I'm a police officer. You're under arrest," and there was a struggle. I went down to my knees, and people were all around me. I reached out, I grabbed two, two individuals, and as it turned out, they were two females.

MR. FORAN: At that time did you see any of the defendants in this case?

THE WITNESS: No, sir. At this time I didn't.

MR. FORAN: All right. Now, what happened after this struggle that you were involved in?

THE WITNESS: Well, at this particular time, with the two females in custody, I was assisted by a uniformed police officer, and we handcuffed the two females and placed them in a squad car.

MR. FORAN: What was the crowd doing when you returned?
THE WITNESS: They were still throwing missiles. The concrete and the sticks and just about anything else that could be picked up and thrown.
MR. FORAN: Now at that time did you see any of the defendants?
THE WITNESS: Yes, sir.
MR. FORAN: Whom did you see?
THE WITNESS: I saw Mr. Rubin. Mr. Rubin was running through the crowd up in the front rank of demonstrators waving his arms. He appeared to be visibly agitated and was shouting, "Kill the pigs."
MR. FORAN: All right. And what was the crowd doing while Mr. Rubin was—
THE WITNESS: They were still throwing the missiles.
MR. FORAN: That is all.
THE COURT: Cross-examination?

· · · · ·

MR. KUNSLER: Officer Hale, hadn't you been informed prior to coming to Grant Park that there had been a permit issued for a rally at the Bandshell?
THE WITNESS: To be truthful, sir, I had not. As I walked over the Grant Park area, I got a leaflet from a uniformed police officer stating that certain individuals had the right to conduct a rally at the Bandshell but they would not be able to march on the Amphitheatre.
MR. KUNSTLER: The incident at the flagpole was approximately 3:15, is that correct?
THE WITNESS: I believe it is.
MR. KUNSTLER: What did you see happening with the flag?
THE WITNESS: I saw the American flag being lowered from the top of the flagpole down toward the ground.
MR. KUNSTLER: Did you see it stop at a certain point on the flagpole?
THE WITNESS: I—my first recollection, as I said earlier, I snapped a photo of the flag at half-staff. I don't remember seeing the flag being taken from the rope or whatever it was affixed to.
MR. KUNSTLER: Do you know what that symbol means, a flag at half mast?
MR. FORAN: Objection, your Honor.
THE COURT: Sustain the objection.
MR. KUNSTLER: When you saw the flag being lowered, is it not true that at that moment you thought in your mind that this was a confrontation you had been expecting, or the police had been expecting?
THE WITNESS: Yes, sir. I did feel that this perhaps might have been the start of a confrontation.
MR. KUNSTLER: You expected a confrontation, did you not?
THE WITNESS: Yes, sir. I was in the Intelligence Division.
MR. KUNSTLER: Was this the general consensus of the Intelligence Division, that there would be a confrontation between police and demonstrators?
MR. FORAN: Objection, your Honor.
THE COURT: Sustain the objection.
MR. KUNSTLER: Isn't it true, Officer Hale, that the Intelligence Division had been telling the police throughout the city that there was going to be a confrontation?
MR. FORAN: Objection.
THE COURT: Sustain the objection.
MR. KUNSTLER: Now at this particular time what was the crowd doing?
THE WITNESS: At which time, sir, when the flag was—
MR. KUNSTLER: Flag is at half-mast; you have just snapped it.
THE WITNESS: Up until the time I remember snapping the photo of the officers placing this individual under arrest, the crowd was nonviolent, but as they took this individual and started to move him away, the plastic bags first came sailing.
MR. KUNSTLER: Isn't it correct that the policemen who had arrested him were at that moment beating him with nightsticks?
THE WITNESS: To answer truthfully, sir, I remember focusing in on the individuals. I

didn't see any nightsticks raised or anything. They had their hands full, I remember, trying to restrain this individual who was kicking and tugging and tussling.

MR. KUNSTLER: Didn't you hear people in the crowd saying in words or substance, "Stop beating him!" with reference to the young man?

THE WITNESS: Yes, sir.

MR. KUNSTLER: Would you describe the missiles you said people were throwing to us?

THE WITNESS: A chunk of concrete would be a piece of a sidewalk, a retaining wall. What came to my mind was, "Where did they get the concrete?" I have been stoned, I had bottles thrown at me by whites and blacks on civil rights marches, but never concrete, and this was a first.

MR. KUNSTLER: It was a new experience?

THE WITNESS: Yes, sir.

MR. KUNSTLER: I believe you even saw a jar of mustard, is that correct?

THE WITNESS: That is correct, sir.

MR. KUNTSLER: Did you pick up the jar of mustard?

THE WITNESS: I either picked up the jar of mustard or the mayonnaise jar that was thrown. I was just glad that the mayonnaise was in a plastic jar.

MR. KUNSTLER: And you photographed the mayonnaise and the mustard?

THE WITNESS: Yes, and the can of beans that was left from the lunch.

MR. KUNSTLER: A thorough job.

Now, after you had photographed the mustard, the mayonnaise, the can of beans, the concrete—

THE WITNESS: The concrete and the tiles.

MR. KUNSTLER: Anything else?

THE WITNESS: Yes, sir. Sticks.

MR. KUNSTLER: Sticks. Did you see any of the people who were throwing this collection of culinary articles and the concrete?

THE WITNESS: Yes, sir, I did. I remember taking photos of some of the people and also at this time I cautioned some of the uniformed officers who wanted to charge into the crowd to get these people. For their own safety I remember speaking up and telling the men to stay in one group. It looked like a bad situation.

November 21, 1969

MR. KUNSTLER: Now, did you see officers using their nightsticks on any person?

THE WITNESS: No, I didn't.

MR. KUNSTLER: What did the officers do?

THE WITNESS: Well, they were ducking the missiles that were being thrown, and they couldn't do much of anything besides look out for their own welfare.

MR. KUNSTLER: Well, prior to ducking the missiles, is it not true that those officers advanced and attacked the crowd?

THE WITNESS: No, sir. They couldn't have possibly advanced and attacked the crowd, not a handful of uniformed police officers.

MR. KUNSTLER: I'm not asking what they could possibly have done. Didn't you see them go into the crowd swinging nightsticks?

THE WITNESS: I did not.

MR. KUNSTLER: Did you consider the lowering of the American flag a desecration of the American flag?

MR. FORAN: Objection, your Honor.

THE COURT: I sustain the objection.

MR. KUNSTLER: Is it not true that within your sight that when the police officers saw the flag being lowered, that they lost all self-control and attacked the crowd?

THE WITNESS: No, sir, that's not true.

MR. KUNSTLER: Now, Officer Hale, when you attempted to arrest the young man, you testified that two females, I believe was the way you put it, interfered with that arrest, is that correct?

THE WITNESS: That's correct.

MR. KUNSTLER: Now, one of these females was a black woman, was she not?

THE WITNESS: That's correct, sir.

MR. KUNSTLER: And the other was a white woman.

THE WITNESS: Yes.

MR. KUNSTLER: Were you on your feet when you seized them?

THE WITNESS: I believe when I was on my knees I reached out and grasped the two.

MR. KUNSTLER: Where were the girls when you were on your knees?

THE WITNESS: They were on me.

MR. KUNSTLER: Sitting on you?

THE WITNESS: Not quite sitting on me, but they were kicking and fighting me, striking me with their fists.

MR. KUNSTLER: Did you have a blackjack in your possession at that time?

THE WITNESS: No, sir.

MR. KUNSTLER: Is it not true that the other officers and you began to beat these two young women on the stomach and back?

THE WITNESS: That's completely false, sir.

MR. KUNSTLER: You've seen that charged against you, have you not?

THE WITNESS: Not against me, sir.

MR. FORAN: I object to that, your Honor.

THE COURT: Sustain the objection.

MR. KUNSTLER: And is it not a fact that the two girls were dragged to the squadrol?

THE WITNESS: I don't remember dragging, sir. We handled them as gently as possible, but as I say, they were kicking, resisting arrest, and we had to get them from the scene and place them in a police vehicle out of the way.

MR. KUNSTLER: Did you see Rennie Davis at any time after the incident at the flag-pole?

THE WITNESS: I thought I had seen Mr. Davis but I wasn't sure.

MR. KUNSTLER: Did you see Mr. Davis at any time after this episode with blood on his head?

MR. FORAN: I object to that, your Honor.

THE COURT: I sustain the objection.

MR. KUNSTLER: Now, when the fifty or so additional policemen arrived at the Band-shell, that made a force of about sixty-five there, is that correct?

THE WITNESS: That is correct.

MR. KUNSTLER: Now, this is around four o'clock, is that correct?

THE WITNESS: It could be. I can't give specific times.

MR. KUNSTLER: Now, after the fifty additional policemen arrived, what did the police do?

THE WITNESS: I remember them forming a skirmish line and then a wedge formation. I don't remember which came first.

MR. KUNSTLER: Did the skirmish line when formed advance on the nearest element of the crowd?

THE WITNESS: Yes, the line advanced.

MR. KUNSTLER: Now, was the nearest element of the crowd moving toward the police or stationary?

THE WITNESS: As I remember, they moved forward; the crowd at this time was not giving way for the police officers.

MR. KUNSTLER: Officer Hale, my question is was the crowd moving toward the police-man before the police began their skirmish line toward the crowd?

THE WITNESS: I don't know.

MR. KUNSTLER: And as the police approached the crowd, did you see any people lock their arms in the crowd to push the crowd back away from the advancing police?

THE WITNESS: I saw some of the people lock arms but they weren't apparently—they were not pushing anybody back from the police. The demonstrators appeared to be standing fast.

MR. KUNSTLER: Did you see the line, the police line, the wedge eventually reach the front row of the demonstrators?

THE WITNESS: Yes.

MR. KUNSTLER: Then did you see the police line or wedge break into individuals?

THE WITNESS: If I remember correctly now, I believe the command was given for the officers to engage in this thrusting motion with the baton, and this in the crowd control training is a necessary part. As the officer advances, the command would be, "on guard." The left foot is advanced forward at the same time the baton is thrust forward, the baton is withdrawn, the right foot is brought up, and the baton is brought back. It is a step in this manner [*indicating*].

MR. KUNSTLER: Did that take place here on that day?

THE WITNESS: Yes, sir, it did.

MR. KUNSTLER: And did there come a time when the officers began to engage in individual actions by using the batons other than to thrust?

THE WITNESS: I couldn't say. I didn't advance with them; I couldn't give you any further testimony in that respect.

MR. KUNSTLER: Did you learn after this episode that a great many demonstrators and people who were there had been injured by the police?

MR. FORAN: Objection.

THE COURT: I sustain the objection.

MR. KUNSTLER: Mr. Hale, at the time of the flagpole episode that you have described, what would you say was the attitude of the crowd as you observed it?

THE WITNESS: My attitude, my personal opinion, is it was in an ugly mood.

MR. KUNSTLER: Now, in the forty-five minutes that elapsed before the fifty additional police came, did you notice any change in the crowd?

THE WITNESS: No, I didn't.

MR. KUNSTLER: It was exactly the same as it had been at the flagpole?

THE WITNESS: I would say it was, yes.

MR. KUNSTLER: By the time the fifty officers arrived on the scene, there were almost no missiles being thrown, isn't that correct?

THE WITNESS: There were still missiles being thrown sporadically at the police.

MR. KUNSTLER: Well, would you say it had died down considerably by the time the fifty policemen came?

THE WITNESS: It had died down, yes.

MR. KUNSTLER: Now, despite the fact that the rock throwing or whatever was being thrown had died down, the policemen lined up and advanced on the crowd, isn't that correct?

MR. FORAN: Object to that.

THE COURT: Sustain the objection.

MR. KUNSTLER: You said on direct that you saw Jerry Rubin, is that correct?

THE WITNESS: Yes, sir.

MR. KUNSTLER: And where did you see him first that day?

THE WITNESS: I saw Mr. Rubin the first time that day up with the front rank of demonstrators.

MR. KUNSTLER: And would you describe him when you first saw him?

THE WITNESS: Well, basically Mr. Rubin looked the same as he looks today.

MR. KUNSTLER: What about the hair, is that the same?

THE WITNESS: Approximately. It could have been a bit—

MR. KUNSTLER: What about now?

THE WITNESS: Now it's a bit shorter.

MR. FORAN: Your Honor, may the record show that Mr. Rubin just took off the wig he's been wearing for the last—

THE COURT: Is that what he took off? I didn't know. I don't know about wigs. But will you concede that your client took off his wig?

MR. KUNSTLER: Now, what was he doing when you first saw him?

THE WITNESS: He was waving his arms. He was shouting.

MR. KUNSTLER: Was he doing anything else?

THE WITNESS: No.

MR. KUNSTLER: Didn't you tell us on direct examination that he was running through the crowd?

THE WITNESS: Well, he was moving, moving through the crowd. "Running" possibly would have been the wrong word to use, but he was moving through the crowd.

MR. KUNSTLER: And I think you said you heard Jerry Rubin say something about "killing the pigs," I think is the way you put it, is that correct?

THE WITNESS: That's correct.

MR. KUNSTLER: And you heard that very distinctly, did you?

THE WITNESS: Yes, sir.

MR. KUNSTLER: Now, do you recall being interviewed by the Federal Bureau of Investigation on September 27, 1968, regarding this incident?

THE WITNESS: I remember being interviewed. I don't remember the exact date.

MR. KUNSTLER: Do you remember whether or not you told them about Jerry Rubin?

THE WITNESS: No, I don't believe I did at the time.

MR. KUNSTLER: Now, when was the first time that you told anybody about Jerry Rubin?

THE WITNESS: When I was at the State's Attorney's office, I told one of the assistant State's Attorneys about what I had seen.

MR. KUNSTLER: Now you remember testifying before the grand jury in this case, do you not?

THE WITNESS: Yes, sir.

MR. KUNSTLER: Do you recall telling the grand jury that what he said was either "Get the pigs" or "Kill the pigs"?

"I couldn't make it out with all the shouting and screaming"—do you recall saying that?

THE WITNESS: I may have.

MR. KUNSTLER: Now, what is your testimony now, was it "Get the pigs" or "Kill the pigs" or both?

THE WITNESS: It was both.

MR. KUNSTLER: Did you not tell the grand jury that you couldn't really make out what Mr. Rubin was saying because of all the noise?

MR. FORAN: I object to that, your Honor.

THE COURT: I sustain the objection.

MR. KUNSTLER: Did you keep your eye on Jerry Rubin from that point?

THE WITNESS: No, I didn't.

MR. KUNSTLER: Did you tell anyone, "Maybe we had better watch that man, he is dangerous"?

THE WITNESS: There was no supervisory official on the scene at the time and I did not tell anyone to keep an eye on him, no.

MR. KUNSTLER: You did, however, tell the police with you some time or another after this episode to form a skirmish line, did you not?

THE WITNESS: Yes, I did.

MR. KUNSTLER: In fact, was it not true that you thought of yourself at this moment something like General Custer?

MR. FORAN: I object to that, your Honor.

THE COURT: Yes. That is taking us back a little beyond the direct examination.
    I sustain the objection.

MR. KUNSTLER: But you told the grand jury, did you not, that you felt like General Custer?

THE WITNESS: Yes, sir.

MR. FORAN: I object to that, your Honor.

THE COURT: I sustain the objection.

MR. KUNSTLER: I have no further questions, your Honor.

THE COURT: Is there any redirect examination?
MR. FORAN: Yes, your Honor.

. . . . .

When the flag was coming down, Mr. Hale, did you see who was taking it down?
THE WITNESS: Yes, sir. He was a young white male I would say between seventeen and twenty.
MR. FORAN: Did the flag eventually come totally off the flagpole?
THE WITNESS: The flag was removed from the flagpole, from the rope, yes, sir.
MR. FORAN: Was anything else put on the flagpole in its place?
THE WITNESS: There was a red—a red cloth, red flag sent up to the top of the flagpole.
MR. FORAN: That is all.
THE COURT: At this point, I think we will recess until ten o'clock Monday morning.

Testimony of Richard Schaller

MR. SCHULTZ: Please state your name.

THE WITNESS: My name is Richard Schaller.

MR. SCHULTZ: Mr. Schaller, what is your occupation, please?

THE WITNESS: I am an intelligence analyst with the United States Naval Investigative Service.

MR. SCHULTZ: Now, calling your attention to Wednesday, the twenty-eighth of August, 1968, at about two in the afternoon, where were you, please, Mr. Schaller?

THE WITNESS: I was in Grant Park in Chicago.

MR. SCHULTZ: At the time that you were present, did you have any recording equipment with you, Mr. Schaller?

THE WITNESS: Yes, I did. It was a Panasonic RQ 3100 Model cassette recorder.

MR. SCHULTZ: What, if anything, was occurring in Grant Park?

THE WITNESS: There was scheduled to be a rally sponsored by the National Mobilization Committee.

MR. SCHULTZ: Did the rally begin there?

THE WITNESS: Yes, it did.

MR. SCHULTZ: Approximately how many people would you estimate were at that rally?

THE WITNESS: In my estimation, 15,000.

MR. SCHULTZ: Did you record any of the proceedings at the Bandshell on August 28?

THE WITNESS: Yes, I did.

MR. SCHULTZ: Now, after recording on both of these cassette cartridges, did you transfer the recordings from those cassettes to any other recording?

THE WITNESS: Yes. I transferred it to a reel recorder.

MR. SCHULTZ: I will show you Exhibit No. 42 for identification, Government's Exhibit No. 42, which is another reel, and I ask you if you recognize that reel.

THE WITNESS: This represents excerpted speeches in sequential order.

MR. SCHULTZ: I'll show you a transcript which is Government's Exhibit 43 for identification and ask you to look at that, please. Do you recognize that transcript?

THE WITNESS: This transcript is a verbatim transcript of the excerpted speeches as recorded on this reel.

MR. SCHULTZ: The Government offers into evidence Government's Exhibit 42 for identification which is the tape recording, and Exhibit 43 for identification which is a transcript of that tape recording.

MR. WEINGLASS: Your Honor, we have one continuing objection and that objection we stated repeatedly. We feel that it's improper, constitutionally improper—

THE COURT: Don't tell me, it's chilling.

MR. WEINGLASS: Your Honor—

THE COURT: Were you about to use that word?

MR. WEINGLASS: I was about to get into the chilling effect.

THE COURT: Through this trial you have almost frozen the Court up here by repeating the word "chilling" so often.

MR. WEINGLASS: Well, I am frankly chilled by some of the testimony I've heard and the evidence I have seen.

THE COURT: Well, I use a different word in giving you my reaction to some of the things I have seen during this trial.

MR. WEINGLASS: If your Honor please, this witness circulated through a crowd at a peaceful rally. That rally had a permit. There was nothing unlawful about it. For people to know that Naval intelligence officers are taping the words of the speakers, as well as members of the audience, does create a chilling effect.

THE COURT: Who first used that word in a legal opinion? Where did you first get it? What opinion?

MR. WEINGLASS: I think the Supreme Court in Dombrowski—

THE COURT: I knew it was in some Supreme Court opinion.

MR. WEINGLASS: It was the United States Supreme Court in the Dombrowski case.

THE COURT: You like it, don't you?

MR. WEINGLASS: I think it's valid. I think the Supreme Court accurately characterized what happens to a citizenry attempting to protest against their Government in power when the Government sends agents in with recorders to record what they say.

The Supreme Court said the right of dissent must be very carefully protected so that the less strong amongst us will still feel safe to come out and express their opinions.

When the President of the United States speaks of a silent majority, I would like to speak of a silenced majority, and what's happening in this court is silencing the majority, and that is precisely why this court cannot permit it to go ahead. It is not—

THE COURT: We are speaking to exhibits here now. I wish you wouldn't make a stump speech every time I ask you to indicate your position with respect to admissibility.

Over the objections of the defendants, the Court will admit into evidence Government's Exhibits 42 and 43, respectively, for identification, as Government's Exhibits 42 and 43.

MR. SCHULTZ: May we play the exhibit now?

THE COURT: You may. [*the tape is played*]

Before the next controversial speaker could we have the people that have buckets that are trying to collect some bread to pay for all these things, the air fares, and all that stuff, could they come back up here? The next speaker is the Youth International Party's Jerry Rubin.

Jerry is an old friend. A bit insane you know, but this is the time for madmen. Because you have to have more madmen to deal with the madmen we've got. Jerry? Is Jerry around? Jerry?

Jerry Rubin: *Welcome to the most important convention that is going on in this city. What we've seen these last two days is something that has been happening all last year in the country, Columbia, Berkeley, San Francisco, New York. The birth of a new white street revolutionary. We're ready to go to jail, ready to get clubbed on the head and ready to die to change the country. We're not suggesting to the old men who are Democrats what they should do. We are saying to the Democrats get the fuck out of town. Resign. We can run the country better than you can.*

First of all, we don't believe in America first, we believe in the world first and we're not interested in what's good for America. We're interested in what's good for the world. That's different than what those people over across town are interested in. They're just interested in what's good for America. Well, fuck 'em.

Second of all, we're not interested in protecting the privileges of the white race. White people have been oppressing blacks for the past hundreds of years. We're a white generation that says "no, we're joining the blacks." There is only one way to join the blacks. It is putting ourselves in the same risks that blacks are in. If cops are going to beat on blacks they are going to beat on us too. We're going to take the risks. And if anything happens to Huey Newton they're going to have to do something to us. We're not going to let them do it.

We don't believe in the value of money, or property that comes under the individual profit system. We don't want the world run like that; we want the world to run along the principle of cooperation. We're not interested in protecting our property. The hell with property.

There is going to be an election coming up and people are asking themselves what that election should be. It's a phony election. First of all, everybody in the world should have the right to vote in an American election because America controls the world, and there ought to be on Election Day demonstrations in every town and city throughout the world against the phoniness of the American election and, if possible, we ought to try and stop the election from taking place.

Most people think this is a free country because they never try to change the country. If they try to change it they see how free it is. So we came here to express our point of view about the Convention and what do we have? For twenty-four hours a day, seven days a week I've got six cops tailing me. That is because the only way that they can nominate a pig for President is by bringing out all the pigs to protect the pig they nominated.

I want to end now because we've got a lot of work to do tonight. We've got to break up into small groups and go throughout the city and convince as many people as possible to try to get out of the Old Town area and try to get into the downtown area then to do whatever they think is necessary to make our point. See you on the streets tonight.

Dave Dellinger: *We know that anybody who comes in here in this concentration camp which is Chicago has come in here under different circumstances than any of the other mobilizations or large meetings that we have had. We're coming alive and we're fighting back. But even the Chicago police have estimated that there are 15,000 people in this park right now. And I think under these circumstances that's pretty good.*

All right, another fighter, Greg Sandow, from the Resistance.

Greg Sandow: *David! Would you light this for me? This is my delinquency notice that my draft board sent me. . . . That was my delinquency notice that my draft board sent me.*

Sometimes what we have been doing here in Chicago is like we all going back to our cities a couple months ago and said, "Hey man, let's come to Chicago and fight the pigs." And I don't think people would have done that, you know, if that was the plan. They wouldn't have come here and waged war on an enemy which was armed and stronger than we are. It's good and I'm with it and my heart's in the barricade, but I share exactly what Bobby Seale said when he was here yesterday. He was talking about people running around and fighting the pigs and he was talking mostly about his black brothers. "Power is the ability to define a phenomenon and make it act in the desired manner." That's kind of abstract formulation. Right?

But Bobby brings it right down where it is. He says out there pigs, pigs are a phenomenon. When those pigs hassle you, how do you want those pigs to act? You want them to go away, you want them to die.

So what you need is an organization which can compel those pigs to behave in the desired manner. And what we don't have in our park and what we haven't had yet is the organization that can make those pigs behave in the desired manner. We're gonna start it. Right! Yeah! Everybody knows what to do—we're gonna start now and it's gonna take a long time but we're gonna do it. . . .

Dave Dellinger: *All right everybody stay where you are. The marshals are at the bench site and are awaiting instructions. Everybody please sit down. Everybody please sit down and leave it to the marshals. Stay where you are and leave it to the marshals. . . . This is being done for the whole world to see. Let them see who is committing the violence here.*

All right. I have a report from the marshals. They say word-for-word there are only about fifty police. They are side-by-side, double-armed, and they are moving people out of that area, but not advancing on this area.

Unidentified speaker: *Don't rub your eyes. Breathe through your mouth.*

Dave Dellinger: *Don't listen to rumors. Wait until you hear from the marshals. Stay in your seat, it must not be a panic situation. What the police want to do is to create a disturbance here. Our marshals are handling it. We will not allow the police to provoke a riot here. Hold your places.*

Hear what Carl Oglesby has to say. Brother Carl Oglesby, rap to us and rap to the police.

All right we have already cooled it but we have an official word from Deputy Chief Nygren that as long as it is cool as it already is he is now withdrawing his men. Now withdrawing his men. Everybody—keep to your places, keep to your places. . . . Keep your eye on the badge number or if they have removed them, get their description. Carl Oglesby will end up being the most introduced speaker at this rally.

Carl Oglesby: *The Chief of the Police announces that so long as there is cool, there shall be no attack, and at one and the same moment we see the attack unfolding, we feel the attack on our heads. Is there any reason we should be surprised as to why this paradox takes place? Is there even one reason why we should be puzzled over this breakdown in ordinary processes of reasoning: that the attacker even as he delivers the blow should explain that he means not to attack us? By this time that process should have become absolutely and hopelessly familiar to us.*

The United States policy, just like a paradox, is no paradox at all. For we understand it as being the policy of a privileged elite that stands above us, that assaults our lives, that makes us—for the most part white middle-class people with the American dream in the palm of our hand—

We'll be detained for the moment. We need a doctor, medical people—medical people to the front. We need a doctor fast. Is there a doctor any place? To the platform.

Dave Dellinger: *We need one more medic to the left of the platform. Continue to sit down, keep it cool, and we'll handle it the best that way.*

Our marshals are working out our strategy and we will announce it shortly. It's very important that we keep cool and keep going while they're working this out so it will be the most effective possible logistics tactics.

We envision at this point three different alternatives amongst which people can choose. In a moment I'm going to call on someone to talk about one of them.

But one of the ways is that some of us, including myself, are going to gather at the statue back there. We will assemble peacefully, approximately eight abreast. We will be prepared to march to the Amphitheatre. We've got to go! We've got to go! This is intended to be led by myself—a nonviolent march—march to the Amphitheatre.

Secondly there will be some people who believe that it is important to get away from here and to regroup and take other action.

Thirdly there will be people who want to just sit quietly here while the one group is forming for the nonviolent march and the other group is forming for their regroupment and action.

Tom Neumann: *Some of us here, we know that this rally is extraordinary. It began for us when one of our brothers went right to the pole to set the flag at half-mast. No one since then has mentioned the rightness of his act. Then followed the unprovoked charge of the pigs into our space to get that man and a resistance, a correct resistance by us to that charge. No one from here has mentioned the correctness of that resistance.*

Pigs smashed into our space this afternoon. Pigs smashed in and people resisted, and yet from this speaker's rostrum only called "sit! be quiet! be still!" Many of us feel that we are going to have to liberate our space, we are going to have to fight for it. If they take over our space, we will take over their space. We have been told to sit down. When the pig sits down, we'll sit down. When the pig runs, we'll run. When the pig crawls, we've won.

Rennie Davis had his head smashed and there was not a mass move by these people in this crowd to defend this park and to show our anger at them. You know what we have to do. When they push us out of our space as they have now done in this park, we will move into their space. If they gas us, they will have to gas their streets. If they beat us, they will have to beat their Sunday shoppers, their walkers in their streets, their delegates, their wives, their sons.

We are no longer waiting for them to make moves. We have decided, some of us, to move out of this park in any way that we can, to move into their space in any way that we can, and to defend ourselves in any way that we can.

Unidentified male: *The medical people have water; dampen either a handkerchief, your undershirt or a piece of your blouse or shirt. Hold it over your mouth and take short breaths. Do not breathe through your nose. If you get the gas in your eyes it will burn. Do not rub your eyes. Take off—all you women with pierced earrings or loose jewelry, take it off at this time. The marshals will direct you if our march to the Amphitheatre does not work.*

Dave Dellinger: *In line with what I have been saying, the nonviolent march can be gathering over there quietly—those who want to be leaving in connection with the recommendations of Tom Neumann can begin to be splitting. Now I introduce a Presidential candidate, Pigasus.*

Jerry Rubin: *I want to introduce to you the only candidate that can defeat Richard Nixon, the only candidate, the only candidate—get back—the only—hey! Bring him back!*

Dave Dellinger: *All right, be sure the marshals are gathering at the monument for the nonviolent march and the other marshals are conferring for the other action.*

Jerry Rubin: *The Republican Party has nominated a pig for President and a pig for Vice-President. The Democratic Party is going to nominate a pig for President and a pig for Vice-President. And our campaign slogan is "Why take half a hog, when you can have the whole hog?" And so we're nominating a pig for President. We're requesting Secret Service protection because those Democratic and Republican pig politicians have tried to kill our candidate and have already arrested one of our candidates and placed him in jail.*

Our pig promises to run on the following principle, the same principle this country has always been governed on—garbage.

Today's pig demands debate with Hubert Humphrey Hog and Richard Milhous Pig and George Piggy Wallace in a four-pig debate on national television.

Dave Dellinger: *All right, I want to inform the people who are going on the nonviolent march to the Amphitheatre that it will be led by Veterans of the Vietnam War, by people from the poor people's campaign, by Allen Ginsberg, Jean Genet, William Burroughs and myself, and others.*

All the marshals please get over by the beginning of the march. And now I introduce Mr. Underground, Tom Hayden.

Tom Hayden: *May I briefly remember Rennie Davis. Rennie Davis is in the hospital with a split head. He's going to be all right, but he would want you to do for him what he is unable to do because he is in the hospital—and that is make sure that if blood is going to flow, let it flow all over the city. If gas is going to be used—let this gas come down all over Chicago and not just all over us in this park. That if the police are going to run wild let them run wild all over the city of Chicago and not over us in this park. That if we are going to be disrupted, and violated, let this whole stinking city be disrupted and violated, let this whole military machine which is aimed at us—around the city, don't get trapped in some kind of large organized march which can be surrounded. Begin to find your way out of here. I'll see you in the streets.*

Dave Dellinger: *And I'll see you with Allen Ginsberg and the others at the monument for this nonviolent march. Each to his choice.*

Unidentified person: *This is the end. You're walking out into your fucking death and it's worth it. This is the end. Today has been the end here and the end is coming. Death.*

Testimony of Richard Schaller Resumed

THE COURT: Has the direct examination of the witness been concluded?

MR. SCHULTZ: I have just about three or four more questions.

THE COURT: Let him resume the stand.

MR. SCHULTZ: At about 3:20 in the afternoon what, if anything, occurred that you observed, please?

THE WITNESS: At 3:20 Greg Sandow was speaking, and I glanced to my left over my shoulder and noticed someone on the flagpole. He had the American flag that was flying from the pole under his arm, proceeding down the pole.

I removed myself from there, and by the time I had gotten around the corner of the Bandshell, there were plainclothes police officers emerging from around the western side of the shell. There was a hail of missiles coming in, of various types, and landing in the immediate area. By this time some of the uniformed officers were on the scene and moved in, attempting to apprehend the young man at the pole.

When I turned to look again, he was down, and they were—was a scuffle going on, and by this time there was many different scuffles going on. I could not isolate one from another. It was total chaos.

There was some form of smoke grenade or—I'm not just certain what it was. A cannister was fired.

MR. SCHULTZ: Fired by whom?

THE WITNESS: By the police.

MR. SCHULTZ: And then what happened after that object landed?

THE WITNESS: I recall a young man rushed in and picked up the cannister and threw it back among the police officers, which forced them to disperse to the north. This evoked a big cheer from his supporters.

MR. SCHULTZ: After the cannister was thrown back at the police, what occurred, please?

THE WITNESS: At this point I could observe in the distance, in the south, coming over the bridge, what we presumed to be reinforcements, a platoon of officers. Simultaneously, there was a platoon, I believe, coming in from the north end of the park. I moved from the west side of the Bandshell around to the rear of it, over to the east side of the shell.

MR. SCHULTZ: Would you describe the objects that you had seen when you were on the west side of the Bandshell, the objects which you saw thrown?

THE WITNESS: Well, there were chunks of what I'd call concrete, rock aggregate mixed with mortar. There was tin cans containing garbage.

There were other objects that appeared when they hit to sort of explode and spew out a colored liquid. After the rally was over, walking up the walk, I was curious to know what the objects were that contained the colored articles, and I picked one up on a stick. It appeared to be a plastic Baggie-type container and contained the colored fluid, and in holding it up I detected the aroma of what I determined to be urine.

THE COURT: I didn't hear that last.

THE WITNESS: I determined it to be urine by odor.

MR. SCHULTZ: Now, Mr. Schaller, do you know who Rennie Davis is?

THE WITNESS: Yes, I do.

MR. SCHULTZ: Did you have occasion to see him with any blood on him?

THE WITNESS: Yes. It was during, I believe, Carl Oglesby's speech. I went over to the tree which was just to the right of the Bandshell and I observed in a prone position on his back Rennie Davis. He appeared to have his eyes closed and he had a cut on the right side of his head, blood had come down, flowed down the side of his head onto his shirt, and I got down within about several feet to observe and I can't say whether he was conscious or not. I verified to my satisfaction that it was he, and then I resumed my position again near the loudspeaker.

MR. SCHULTZ: That is all for direct examination, your Honor.

[238]

THE COURT: Ladies and gentlemen, we are about to recess until ten o'clock tomorrow morning.

(court is adjourned)

November 26, 1969

(jury out)

THE CLERK: Your Honor, there is a petition for writ of habeas corpus.

THE COURT: I will hear you, Mr. Weinglass.

MR. WEINGLASS: This is an application to the Court to request the Court to issue a writ of habeas corpus ad testificandum to bring to this court an individual by the name of John Sinclair who presently is in the custody of Warden Raymond J. Buckhoe of the Marquette Prison, Marquette, Michigan, in order to avail Mr. Sinclair the opportunity of testifying in this case on behalf of the defendants.

Mr. Sinclair is in a very peculiar position. He is one witness who we could not duplicate. He is the only person available to us in the country who could testify exclusively about the plans of the Youth International Party to have a Festival of Life which included the bringing to this city of a number of rock bands.

John Sinclair will testify that he spent several months working exclusively on bringing to this city as part of the peaceful intention of the Youth International Party a group of musicians who were to perform in Lincoln Park as part of the Youth International Party's week of festivities.

If he is not permitted to come to this court, we cannot make out an essential and credible part of our defense and that is that we had a peaceful intent. We have no one else that could offer that testimony, and if Mr. Sinclair is not brought here, then I think the defendants are being deprived of their right, their Sixth Amendment constitutional right to present a full and adequate defense to the jury.

THE COURT: I don't recall reading—I don't know whether or not you stated the alleged crime for which the proposed witness stands convicted and for which he is in prison in Marquette prison.

MR. WEINGLASS: He is in prison as a result of a narcotics offense. He was allegedly found in possession of two marijuana cigarettes and for that he was sentenced by the court in Michigan to a term of nine-and-a-half to ten years.

THE COURT: I don't think any judge in this building would sentence a man nine-and-a-half to ten years for the possession of two marijuana cigarettes. I just don't think that would happen here. Maybe they are more severe in Michigan.

MR. WEINGLASS: Your surprise and shock at the length of the sentence is one shared by all of the defendants in this case and I think by a large part of the population in the country.

THE COURT: It is a sentence that goes beyond the minimum Federal sentence for first offenders in narcotics cases, almost twice as much.

MR. WEINGLASS: That is correct.

THE COURT: I will decide this petition. In view of the large number of others who were similarly situated, it seems doubtful that Mr. Sinclair could add appreciably to what other witnesses could testify to. Taking into account the inconvenience of securing an out-of-state prisoner, I do not believe that the interest of justice requires the issuance of the writ requested by the defendants based on the papers filed here.

Mr. Clerk, the petition of the defendants for a writ of habeas corpus ad testificandum will be denied.

MR. KUNSTLER: Your Honor, the defendants have asked me to ask your Honor for a recess. We made a decision this man is a key witness for our defense. Your Honor has made a decision in your discretion not to allow us to have this key witness.

THE COURT: Which the law permits me to do.

MR. KUNSTLER: The law permits, but the defendants have a right to decide what they are going to do now when they have been denied a key witness to the defense. We would like a recess to discuss that.

THE COURT: I deny the motion for a recess. I don't take recesses—
MR. DELLINGER: Aw Jesus—fascist—
THE COURT: Who is that man talking, Mr. Marshal?
MR. DELLINGER: That is Mr. David Dellinger and he is saying that that is an arbitrary denial. We know who is key to our defense and we want to put on our key defense witnesses.
THE COURT: Mr. Marshal, ask that man to sit down.
THE MARSHAL: Sit down, Mr. Dellinger.
MR. DELLINGER: I think that is acting like a fascist court like Mr. Seale said when you make decisions of that kind and deprive us of our witnesses. Because he has already been persecuted in one court, now you are persecuting him and us in another one.
MR. DAVIS: Why don't you gag all of us, Judge?
THE COURT: Who said that?
MR. DAVIS: Bobby Seale said that.
MR. SCHULTZ: The defendant Davis said that, your Honor.
THE COURT: The defendant Davis. Did you get that, Miss Reporter?
    Bring in the jury.

(jury enters)

Testimony of Richard Schaller Resumed

MR. KUNSTLER: Mr. Schaller, can you indicate what the Navy's interest was in Lincoln Park?

THE WITNESS: I can.

MR. KUNSTLER: Would you do so?

THE WITNESS: None.

MR. KUNSTLER: Then you were not operating under Navy instructions, is that correct?

THE WITNESS: That's correct.

MR. KUNSTLER: Now, if you were not operating under Navy instructions, whose instructions were you operating under?

THE WITNESS: Would you permit me to explain? In June of 1968, as a consequence of the assassination of Robert—Senator Kennedy, the responsibilities of the United States Secret Service were expanded to include protective functions for other candidates.

As a consequence, on the eve of two major Conventions for which they were concerned with security, they felt a necessity to request assistance from various other Federal agencies.

They requested that we collect and disseminate any information that has a bearing on the planning of activities concerning the Democratic Convention, arrival of demonstrators, protest organizations, dissident groups that was going on at that particular time.

MR. KUNSTLER: Mr. Schaller, prior to the arrest of the young man at the flagpole, you had been recording speeches from the Bandstand, isn't that correct?

THE WITNESS: That's correct.

MR. KUNSTLER: And after the apprehension of the young man, there came a time, did there not, when Mr. Dellinger began to speak over the microphones and tell the crowd to stay where they are and to remain calm, isn't that correct?

THE WITNESS: Yes.

MR. KUNSTLER: Now, did you watch any of the police using their nightsticks on the persons of demonstrators?

THE WITNESS: I didn't see any during that period other than in this chaotic confusion, there was these nightsticks, batons, being used. They came up through the crowd, you could see them, as well as the demonstrators' signs.

MR. KUNSTLER: Did there not come a time when Mr. Oglesby was speaking and interrupted his speech and asked for a doctor to come to the front of the platform?

THE WITNESS: There was, sir.

MR. KUNSTLER: Did you see whether anybody responded to that?

THE WITNESS: I didn't observe the response to it. I mainly followed from what was being said over the speaker.

MR. KUNSTLER: Now, it is at that precise moment, is it not, in the tape that you said "Goddamn, that gas stinks, doesn't it?"

THE WITNESS: That is true, sir.

MR. KUNSTLER: That is your language, isn't it?

THE WITNESS: That is right.

MR. KUNSTLER: Then Mr. Dellinger comes on again, does he not, after Mr. Oglesby interrupts his speech to ask for medical aid, and again says, "Keep cool," does he not?

THE WITNESS: He does, sir.

MR. KUNSTLER: Now, Mr. Schaller, is it not true that Dick Gregory spoke that day?

THE WITNESS: It is true he spoke.

MR. KUNSTLER: Does—do Dick Gregory's remarks appear in the transcript or the tape?

THE WITNESS: No, they do not, sir.

MR. KUNSTLER: Now, who else spoke that day who does not appear in the transcript or the tape?

THE WITNESS: On the tape and transcript presented to the jury, I believe Norman Mailer, Jean Genet, and—

MR. KUNSTLER: Jean Genet spoke in French, did he not?

THE WITNESS: He did. And someone translated it.

MR. KUNSTLER: Who else?

THE WITNESS: William Burroughs.

MR. KUNSTLER: You were doing some of your own editing, were you not, as to what to record and not to record?

THE WITNESS: If I found a speech particularly boring, I would turn the mike off to conserve tape.

MR. KUNSTLER: Whose speeches did you find so boring you didn't record?

THE WITNESS: I found Gregory rather rambling. I also found Burchard and Brock lesser lights without much substance in their talk for my purpose there, as I understood my purposes.

MR. KUNSTLER: Well, when you say your purposes, wasn't it one of your purposes to try to record what you would consider flamboyant speeches?

THE WITNESS: No, that is not.

MR. KUNSTLER: Or speeches that you could interpret as violent speeches?

THE WITNESS: No, it was not.

MR. KUNSTLER: When was the first time that you saw Rennie Davis that day?

THE WITNESS: When he was lying prone on his back, just east of the Bandshell under a tree on a grassy area.

MR. KUNSTLER: Now, at that point his face was covered with blood, was it not?

THE WITNESS: Blood had trickled down the side, back of the ear, along the neck, spattered on his neck.

MR. KUNSTLER: I will show you D-104 for identification and ask you if you know who this is.

THE WITNESS: That's the defendant, Rennie Davis.

MR. KUNSTLER: I have no further questions.

THE COURT: You may go Mr. Witness.

(witness excused)

THE COURT: Do you have another witness?

MR. FORAN: Yes, sir.

Testimony of James M. Rochford

MR. FORAN: Will you state your name, please?

THE WITNESS: James M. Rochford.

MR. FORAN: What's your occupation, Mr. Rochford?

THE WITNESS: I'm a Deputy Superintendent. I serve with the Chicago Police Department.

MR. FORAN: How long have you been with the Chicago Police Department?

THE WITNESS: I'm serving my twenty-third year.

MR. FORAN: Now, calling your attention specifically to 5:00 P.M., August 28, 1968, where were you?

THE WITNESS: About 5:00 P.M. on the twenty-eighth of August, I was in the Ninth Street Chicago Park District Service Yards. This was the field command post for the Chicago Police Department and the National Guard from which all field decisions emanated.

MR. FORAN: Now at about 5:00 P. M. did anything particular occur?

THE WITNESS: Yes. About 5:00 P.M., the rally in Grant Park began to break up and a long column of people had assembled on the east side of Columbus Drive. This march was stopped by the Chicago Police Department, and about 5:15 or somewhere near that time, the marchers sat down.

MR. FORAN: Now, at that time did you have a conversation with anyone?

THE WITNESS: Yes. At approximately 6:30 P.M. Mr. Sidney Peck and some others came for a conversation.

MR. FORAN: How long did that conversation last?

THE WITNESS: About ten or fifteen minutes.

MR. FORAN: What occurred then?

THE WITNESS: Mr. Peck wished to return and have a further consultation with his superiors, and I went along with him to meet his superiors in the interests of saving time.

Mr. Peck and I and others crossed Columbus. We reached the point approximately 150 feet from the intersection of Balbo Drive and Columbus Drive, and there we met Mr. Dellinger.

MR. FORAN: Now, when you met with Mr. Dellinger, Deputy, who was present?

THE WITNESS: Mr. Dellinger, Mr. Peck, Mr. Richard Elrod, Assistant Corporation Counsel, a member of my staff, and others that I couldn't identify at this time.

MR. FORAN: Now, at this location where you met Mr. Dellinger, where was this group of people that you mentioned previously were lined up for the parade?

THE WITNESS: Well, the majority was still on the sidewalk.

MR. FORAN: Did you have a conversation at that time with Mr. Dellinger.

THE WITNESS: Yes, I did. I was introduced by Mr. Peck to Mr. Dellinger. I identified myself. I stated the Police Department was interested in peace. The Police Department was ready to permit the group to stay at the Bandshell. We were willing to permit the group to reassemble east of the hotel in Grant Park.

MR. FORAN: Did you have any conversation with him concerning the march to the Amphitheatre?

THE WITNESS: I said that the march would not be permitted to the Amphitheatre but I was willing—

MR. FORAN: How did Mr. Dellinger respond, if at all?

THE WITNESS: Mr. Dellinger said to me, "We are going to march. We are going to the Amphitheatre." He said, "I do not have to listen to you."

MR. FORAN: And what did he do then?

THE WITNESS: He wasn't paying too much attention to me. Suddenly a mass of people just left the sidewalk and flooded into the streets. And then he turned and walked from me, walked away.

MR. FORAN: What happened then?

THE WITNESS: At that time I decided that I had to find the head of the column and

[243]

stop the march so I walked through the people to Michigan Avenue near 11th Street. This I believed was the head of the intended march.

I called for tactical teams of police officers and commanded them to clear Michigan Avenue starting at 11th Street. As the tactical teams moved north on Michigan Avenue, the crowd then moved onto the sidewalk.

MR. FORAN: How far did the police move north?

THE WITNESS: We moved north slowly and continuously until we reached Balbo.

MR. FORAN: And what occurred when you reached there?

THE WITNESS: The crowd at that point would not leave the street. They stayed in the center of the street. The center of Michigan Avenue and Balbo was totally blocked with people.

MR. FORAN: About what time was this?

THE WITNESS: The best of my recollection, this was about 7:30.

MR. FORAN: And how many people would you estimate were in the street there at Michigan and Balbo?

THE WITNESS: At that intersection, totally, as far as I could see in all directions, my best estimate, there was approximately 7,000 people in that general intersection. The thrust of the crowd was in a south direction, and building up rapidly. The noise level was indescribably loud. A person could not really think with the amount of noise from the crowd.

MR. FORAN: Were you giving any orders at that time, Mr. Rochford?

THE WITNESS: Yes, for the people to leave the roadway. "Please go up on the sidewalk, go into the parkway," and the crowd would chant, "Hell no, don't go. Hell no, don't go."

MR. FORAN: Were there other chants that—

THE WITNESS: Yes, there were. They ranged from "Peace now, peace now. Dump the Hump, Dump the Hump. Fuck LBJ, fuck the pigs. Let's go. Let's go. Go now," and this went on and on and on and on and on, and the mood of the crowd changed continuously before your eyes.

MR. FORAN: Did you see any missiles being thrown?

THE WITNESS: At first, 7:30, the missiles were occasional. As the time went on, it became contagious, the missile-throwing. One would come and then another and then another, and they ranged from bottles and rocks and boards and ash trays and shoes— every describable and conceivable missile was in the air.

MR. FORAN: Now, calling your attention to about 7:45, did anything unusual happen at that time?

THE WITNESS: I got several tactical teams and deployed a wedge in the crowd. We opened the crowd and through it came a mule train. The mule train passed through the police line, went south on Michigan Avenue, away from the mob.

MR. KUNSTLER: Your Honor, I object to that characterization of the group as a mob.

THE COURT: Mule train?

MR. KUNSTLER: No, he said, "went away from the mob."

MR. FORAN: He said the mule train went away from the mob, Judge. He just described 7,000 screaming people standing in the middle of the intersection of Balbo and Michigan, throwing missiles, and Mr. Kunstler wants to get into semantics.

THE COURT: I will let his answer stand.

MR. FORAN: What happened then, Mr. Rochford?

THE WITNESS: Little incidents were breaking out, quickly, between police officers and members of the crowd. There was spitting and shoving and pushing and fighting, and the officers responded, and they charged the crowd, and the crowd charged back, and a serious disorder broke out.

MR. FORAN: What time was that that it broke out?

THE WITNESS: To the best of my recollection, it was near eight o'clock.

MR. FORAN: How long did this general melee continue?

THE WITNESS: Well, the fighting went on for twelve to fifteen minutes, and at that time I was able to regain control of the group—the police officers—and we went about opening the street up and making arrests of everyone that remained in the roadway.

MR. FORAN: And where did your police line go?

THE WITNESS: Moved forward. It advanced north on Michigan Avenue.

MR. FORAN: How many arrests were made there at Balbo and Michigan that night?

THE WITNESS: I couldn't say exactly but on that date I believe approximately 150.

MR. FORAN: How many police officers were injured on that date?

THE WITNESS: One hundred ninety-eight police officers were injured through the Democratic Convention which would include the—

MR. KUNSTLER: Your Honor, that is not responsive to the question. I move that both answers be stricken.

THE COURT: I will strike the reference to what happened through the Democratic Convention but the remainder of the answer may stand.

MR. WEINGLASS: Your Honor, I object to the witness testifying about any numbers of arrested or injured.

MR. FORAN: I will ask another question.

MR. WEINGLASS: Well, it is not clear. Could the jury be directed to disregard this witness' testimony on arrested and injured people?

THE COURT: All right. I will without any equivocation, then, strike the answer of the witness and direct the jury to disregard it.

You may withdraw that question.

MR. FORAN: Yes, your Honor. I have no intention of asking it again. I don't do that when the Court rules against me. I don't ask the same question over again.

How many arrests did you actually order at Balbo and Michigan, Mr. Rochford?

THE WITNESS: I believe twenty-seven.

MR. FORAN: That is all, your Honor.

December 1, 1969

MR. KUNSTLER: Deputy Superintendent Rochford, who is your immediate superior?

THE WITNESS: Superintendent James B. Conlisk, Jr.

MR. KUNSTLER: And he is the highest officer in the police force, is he not, in Chicago?

THE WITNESS: That is correct.

MR. KUNSTLER: And who appoints the Superintendent of Police in the city of Chicago?

THE WITNESS: There is in the city of Chicago a group of men known as the Police Board. They screen candidates and submit three names to the mayor of the city of Chicago.

MR. KUNSTLER: And the mayor makes the final decision, is that correct?

THE WITNESS: That is correct.

MR. KUNSTLER: Now who made the decision that there would be no march to the Amphitheatre? What person relayed that decision to you unless you made it yourself?

THE WITNESS: There was a request for a march by some people. In the interest of the community, the police officer assigned to the parade board was instructed to oppose the request for a march. They went to the United States Court. The request to have a permit was denied.

I considered it in the best interest of the City not to permit a march.

MR. KUNSTLER: Had anyone in the City government told you that the march was not to proceed at any costs or words to that effect?

THE WITNESS: No, sir, they did not.

MR. KUNSTLER: You didn't hear from the mayor about it?

THE WITNESS: I did not. No, I did not.

MR. KUNSTLER: Mr. Stahl?

THE WITNESS: No, I did not.

MR. KUNSTLER: Did the name Daley come up in your discussion at all?

THE WITNESS: The name Daley comes up almost every day. I have no recollection that it did, no.

MR. KUNSTLER: But it comes up very frequently in reaching important decisions, does it not, this name Daley?

THE WITNESS: Well, it has nothing to do with any decision that I make, if that is what you are implying.

MR. KUNSTLER: I am asking you this: Do you ever receive from Superintendent Conlisk any instructions which he says, "These are the Mayor's desires," or words to that effect?
THE WITNESS: No.
MR. FORAN: I object to that.
THE COURT: I sustain the objection.
MR. KUNSTLER: Now, with reference to the area of the Amphitheatre itself, you had some 1,200 officers there, did you not, during the Democratic National Convention?
THE WITNESS: I would say that's a fair estimate.
MR. KUNSTLER: Were there also National Guardsmen available to you during Convention week?
THE WITNESS: That's correct.
MR. KUNSTLER: How many were there of those?
THE WITNESS: About 5,500.
MR. KUNSTLER: Now, do you know of a man by the name of Major General Turner?
THE WITNESS: Major General Carl Turner, yes.
MR. KUNSTLER: Who is he? Would you tell the jury who he is?
THE WITNESS: He was the United States Provost Marshal, which is the highest officer in the United States Army whose role relates to military police.
MR. KUNSTLER: Were there any Federal troops present in Chicago at that time, the time of the Convention week?
THE WITNESS: There were Federal troops here, I believe, as observers. There were none activated anywhere within the boundaries of the city.
MR. KUNSTLER: Were you not informed that if Federal troops were needed, they could be requisitioned through General Turner?
THE WITNESS: Oh, absolutely no. That's not true.
MR. KUNSTLER: That wasn't told to you?
THE WITNESS: No. Federal troops, in order to bring them, there has to be an order by the President, and he would get a request from the governor.
MR. KUNSTLER: But was it not your understanding that General Turner was going to serve the purpose of the liaison man between the Federal authorities with reference to Federal troops and the Chicago Police Department?
THE WITNESS: Absolutely not.
MR. KUNSTLER: He is the same man, is he not, that is being investigated now for selling guns privately for private profit?
THE WITNESS: I wouldn't—
MR. FORAN: Objection, your Honor. Clearly improper.
THE COURT: I sustain the objection.
MR. KUNSTLER: Now, at five o'clock, you have indicated in your direct testimony, the rally at Grant Park began to break up, is that correct?
THE WITNESS: That's correct.
MR. KUNSTLER: And I think, as you said, a march had begun to form after the rally broke up, is that correct?
THE WITNESS: Yes.
MR. KUNSTLER: Now at this time or shortly thereafter did you not hear from somewhere that the National Guard had released some CS gas in Grant Park—at least in one of the roads running through Grant Park?
THE WITNESS: That was later, yes.
MR. KUNSTLER: And what time was that?
THE WITNESS: It was, I would say, ten or—five to ten minutes after I had talked with Mr. Dellinger.
MR. KUNSTLER: As you stood there, the crowd was all over the streets?
THE WITNESS: That's correct. There was a massive movement going on.
MR. KUNSTLER: Is it possible, Superintendent Rochford, that the sudden movement of the people off the sidewalk into the street could have taken place some time after the gas was set off?
MR. FORAN: Objection, your Honor.

THE COURT: I sustain the objection.
MR. KUNSTLER: You heard that it was CS gas, did you not?
THE WITNESS: Probably.
MR. KUNSTLER: What is CS gas?
THE WITNESS: Well, there are two major gases used in riot situations, CS and CN. I do not know the chemical makeup of the two gases. Neither one is injurious to people. It's irritating more than—sickening gas.
MR. KUNSTLER: Do you know whether this particular gas, CS gas, has been outlawed by the Geneva convention on arms?
MR. FORAN: I object.
THE COURT: I sustain the objection.
MR. KUNSTLER: Did you make any inquiries through your own sources as to what happened at that area prior to the release of gas?
THE WITNESS: I didn't make a complete and factual investigation of the circumstances under which gas was used when a mob of people were attacking Guardsmen. They certainly had the right to use gas to protect themselves, and they used it, which is their right.
MR. KUNSTLER: Isn't it true that you heard that the Guard—somebody in the Guard has been trigger-happy and released gas there as the crowd was proceeding orderly out of Grant Park?
THE WITNESS: I have no recollection of hearing that.
MR. KUNSTLER: Then you walked through the crowd alone, is that correct?
THE WITNESS: That's correct. I went down to Michigan Avenue and south on Michigan Avenue to a point about 11th Street, near 11th Street.
MR. KUNSTLER: What did you do then?
THE WITNESS: I called for police officers and started to remobilize them from Columbus. "Get them up on the sidewalk. Get them moving. Let them open the street."
A dangerous situation existed. If there was a fire to appear there, the Fire Department couldn't get through. If an emergency, an explosion occurred, equipment couldn't get through. The street had to be opened.
MR. KUNSTLER: Well, at this time did it ever occur to you that it might be a far safer thing to let the line march south on Michigan Avenue so it could be diverted further south of the hotel area? Did that ever cross your mind?
THE WITNESS: No.
The thing that continually crossed my mind is opening the street, this unlawful assembly in the street, the street had to be opened in order to make it safe for the movement of all citizens. That was foremost in my mind. I had no intention of permitting a mob to take over the street. That was in my mind, not to let the mob have their head and march to the Amphitheatre.
You see, there was no demonstration here. There was a mob of people unlawfully assembled in the roadway that we were moving off the street. People on the sidewalk were citizens minding their own business, watching, moving about freely. It's the street that was the major concern of the Police Department.
MR. KUNSTLER: Do you know how many police officers there were in the skirmish line coming northward by the time it approached Balbo and Michigan?
THE WITNESS: Fifty or one hundred.
MR. KUNSTLER: Another police skirmish line had been formed on Balbo itself, is that correct?
THE WITNESS: Yes. There was a batallion of police officers redeploying from the 9th Street yard area coming out to assist me. As they came down Wabash, they saw the crowd in the street at Balbo and they formed a skirmish line in Balbo.
MR. KUNSTLER: And that skirmish line began to push toward Michigan Avenue, is that correct?
THE WITNESS: Not push. To—
MR. KUNSTLER: Well, you describe it.
THE WITNESS: To open up the street.
MR. WEINER: Bill, the executioner is mumbling and I can't hear him.

MR. KUNSTLER: Your Honor, is it possible to tell the witness to keep his voice up?

THE COURT: I think it is possible.

MR. FORAN: May the record show the comment? Did you get that comment?

MR. DELLINGER: He was speaking to his lawyer.

THE COURT: Yes, I heard that. It is in the record.

MR. KUNSTLER: It was a remark to me, your Honor, and—every time like a little tattletale—

THE COURT: Perhaps it was a remark to you, I don't challenge that; I don't know to whom it was directed, but the jury heard it.

MR. KUNSTLER: Your Honor, Mr. Foran I don't think even heard it but Mr. Schultz whispered in his ear and then we have this little schoolhouse episode going on of reporting to your Honor what the bad boys are doing.

THE COURT: You may think these are schoolhouse episodes—

MR. KUNSTLER: Your Honor, they are what we used to call tattletales.

THE COURT: If they are, you are going to be disillusioned. Characterizing a witness in the United States District Court out loud by one of the defendants is not a schoolhouse play.

MR. KUNSTLER: So now we have two skirmish lines, do we not, one coming north on Michigan and one going east on Balbo?

THE WITNESS: That is correct.

MR. KUNSTLER: Is it not true that the skirmish line going east would be forcing people in the street into the people who were going north on Michigan?

THE WITNESS: No, that is not true.

MR. KUNSTLER: Can you explain to me how it is not true?

THE WITNESS: Well, in tactical movement of people you never move people against people. You permit escape routes. In a movement east and a movement north, the release of the crowd could go east or it could go north.

MR. KUNSTLER: If the police are forcing people east on Balbo into Michigan, isn't it possible that the people being forced east will run into the people being forced north?

THE WITNESS: It wasn't a constant quick pressure. It was a movement. There was much room to go east and much room to go north. The only pressure was to move people out of the street.

MR. KUNSTLER: But isn't it true, Superintendent Rochford, that if the people that were north of skirmish line 1 on Michigan Avenue had wanted to leave the area by going west on Balbo, it would have been impossible to have done so with the police line, skirmish line 2 on Balbo approaching Michigan?

THE WITNESS: No, that's not correct, Mr. Kunstler. Anyone could have left that area at any time. Any person in that crowd that wanted to go on the sidewalk was free to do so. If a person in the road came up to a police officer and said, "I want to get out of here," the police officer would pass him through the line and say, "Get out, up on the sidewalk," or they would motion them to the sidewalk.

MR. KUNSTLER: Did you see that happen?

THE WITNESS: Over and over and over.

MR. KUNSTLER: Now, did there not come a time shortly after skirmish line 2 has passed through the intersection that the people in skirmish line 1 began to use their night-clubs on the people in Michigan Avenue?

THE WITNESS: There were some—some use of night batons, yes.

MR. KUNSTLER: There was quite a lot, wasn't there? Didn't you see a lot of sticks going up in the air?

THE WITNESS: I don't know, quite a bit. There was some.

MR. KUNSTLER: Well, you tell me how many you saw.

THE WITNESS: I saw several. That's not quite a bit.

MR. KUNSTLER: Is that two?

THE WITNESS: That's more than two.

MR. KUNSLER: Well, is it more than ten?

THE WITNESS: It could be ten. But it was not in proportion to the number of officers.

MR. KUNSTLER: When did the police in skirmish line 1, from this point, begin to use their nightsticks that you saw?

THE WITNESS: Well, skirmish line 1 used their batons as they are trained to do it. One or two officers, when he would go to make an arrest and the person would resist and run, it's a natural thing for that baton to go into the air, so there was an occasional use of the baton in skirmish line 1.

MR. KUNSTLER: Was there any in skirmish line 2?

THE WITNESS: There was an occasional one, yes. There was some aggressive use of the baton. The baton is a police weapon given a police officer to defend himself and he is the best judge of when to use it.

MR. KUNSTLER: Did you see yourself any batons land on any heads?

THE WITNESS: Oh, yes.

MR. KUNSTLER: When they landed, did you see the blood squirt from the impact?

THE WITNESS: I am not aware of any squirting blood from anyone's head. I saw little trinkles of blood.

MR. KUNSTLER: Little what?

THE WITNESS: Trinkles of blood. I saw it on police officers; I saw it on demonstrators, yes.

MR. KUNSTLER: But you saw it on quite a few demonstrators, did you not?

THE WITNESS: I think I saw it on more police officers than I did on demonstrators.

MR. KUNSTLER: Did you see people with nightsticks assaulting police officers?

THE WITNESS: I don't think they had nightsticks. I think there were a few clubs, a few baseball bats.

MR. KUNSTLER: You saw the baseball bats hit the policemen there?

THE WITNESS: I saw them there. I saw them in the air. I saw—

MR. KUNSTLER: Did you see them hit any police officers?

THE WITNESS: I saw a wild scene, I saw police officers hit. There was a line standing in front of me of police officers, and a rock came right through the crowd and hit a police officer and broke his—

MR. KUNSTLER: Did you see any baseball bats hit any policemen?

THE WITNESS: I did not see any, but I saw them there. I saw a wild melee, a fight.

MR. KUNSTLER: Is it not true that during that twelve to fifteen minutes you completely lost control of the police officers in skirmish line 1?

THE WITNESS: That is not true.

MR. KUNSTLER: That is not true?

THE WITNESS: That is not true. There were several minutes where I did not have full responsiveness to my direction by all police officers.

MR. KUNSTLER: And is it not true that during these several minutes that you, yourself, were shocked at what the Chicago police officers were doing to civilians in the streets of Chicago?

THE WITNESS: I was hurt.

MR. KUNSTLER: You were hurt?

THE WITNESS: Oh, absolutely.

MR. KUNSTLER: And is it not also true, Superintendent Rochford, that you did see Chicago police officers going beyond the bounds of what was required to handle this particular crowd?

THE WITNESS: Not per se. You must understand the policy of the Chicago Police Department is to overcome force against it with superior force, and we will use sufficient force to overcome resistance.

MR. KUNSTLER: Well, isn't it true that you saw Chicago police officers beating people who were already on the ground?

THE WITNESS: In some instances, yes, but the person on the ground was kicking and fighting back. There was not a submitting to the authority of the police officer, and that needs to be delineated. When a police officer places a person under arrest and they resist, the officer may use superior force or strength to overcome the resistance.

MR. KUNSTLER: But didn't you see, Superintendent Rochford, Chicago police officers beating people on the ground and then leaving them there and going after other people, leaving behind an unarrested person lying on the ground?

THE WITNESS: If I did and I had the opportunity to get that officer, to go back to that person and make his arrest or give me his name, I would make an investigation.

MR. KUNSTLER: Now, it is also true, is it not, Superintendent Rochford, that the night prior to this you had given specific instructions that people could remain in the park all night, isn't that correct?

THE WITNESS: I did not give such instructions.

MR. KUNSTLER: But is it true that people did remain in the park all night without being arrested or forced out?

THE WITNESS: We did not make arrests that evening for violating the park curfew, that's correct.

MR. KUNSTLER: And it is true, is it not, that there are circumstances when you would recommend a relaxation of an ordinance such as a curfew ordinance when you thought it was better all around, isn't that correct?

THE WITNESS: Circumstances always change police decisions. Knowing all these things that I knew at the time, I feel that was the best decision under the circumstances.

MR. KUNSTLER: Is it not true that one of the reasons why you did not attempt to drive the people out of Grant Park on Tuesday night was that you had made a decision that this would not look right in front of the delegates in the Conrad Hilton Hotel?

THE WITNESS: That had no bearing on my decision, that fact.

MR. KUNSTLER: And you were suspending the law, were you not?

THE WITNESS: I didn't suspend it. I just—

MR. KUNSTLER: You didn't enforce it.

THE WITNESS: I didn't enforce it, that's right.

MR. KUNSTLER: Was that tactically different there because you were afraid of what the delegates might see?

THE COURT: You asked and he answered it.

MR. KUNSTLER: I think I did.

THE COURT: You are taking long enough here with your examination. I don't mind your asking new questions, but he did answer that very question. I wish you'd get along and ask some new questions.

MR. KUNSTLER: Your Honor, I do take exception to your remarks, "You're taking long enough here." This is the first time in this long interrogation that I have apparently repeated a question. I think it is the first objection that has been taken.

THE COURT: I don't share your view about that, and I ask you now, sir, to continue with this cross-examination.

MR. KUNSTLER: Your Honor, with that I am going to end my cross-examination.

THE COURT: Very well. Mr. Weinglass, do you have some questions?

December 2, 1969

MR. WEINGLASS: Deputy Rochford, on the night of August 28, you stayed in the intersection of Michigan and Balbo for a full half-hour?

THE WITNESS: That's correct.

MR. WEINGLASS: At any time in the half-hour did you see a large number of police officers charge into the intersection who were not a part of the skirmish line and charge into the crowd with their clubs swinging?

THE WITNESS: No.

MR. WEINGLASS: During the half-hour 7:45 to 8:15, did you see persons dressed in white uniforms with red crosses on their arms tending to persons on the pavement?

THE WITNESS: No.

MR. WEINGLASS: Did you see any persons with white uniforms and red crosses on their arm?

THE WITNESS: Oh, yes.

MR. WEINGLASS: And what, if anything, did you see them doing during that half-hour?

THE WITNESS: They were scurrying as part of the crowd, running, actively participating in the demonstration.

MR. WEINGLASS: Did you during that half-hour see anyone lying on the pavement who appeared to be injured?

THE WITNESS: No.

MR. WEINGLASS: Did you see any people being carried away on stretchers?

THE WITNESS: No.

MR. WEINGLASS: Is there not some training information on the proper use of the baton?

THE WITNESS: Yes, there is.

MR. WEINGLASS: I show you D-109 for identification. Is that a police training bulletin?

THE WITNESS: That is a police training bulletin.

MR. WEINGLASS: Now what does that particular bulletin deal with as part of the police philosophy?

THE WITNESS: Use of the police baton.

MR. WEINGLASS: Does that particular bulletin indicate that the baton is never to be swung as a club?

THE WITNESS: It indicates, "Never swing the baton as a club. It may be taken away from you and used as a weapon against you," which is the implication and the reasoning and the philosophy behind it.

MR. WEINGLASS: So there is a training document that says, "Never swing the baton as a club," is that true?

THE WITNESS: Yes, but it is not an absolute prohibition.

MR. WEINGLASS: Now I ask you again in light of that did you see police officers at that intersection violating the provisions of that training bulletin before your very eyes?

MR. FORAN: Objection, your Honor.

THE COURT: That document isn't in evidence. You have asked a lot of questions about it. I won't even look at the document at this time. At an appropriate time you may offer it and then we will deal with its admissibility.

MR. WEINGLASS: If the Court please, my last question to the witness did not deal with the substance of the document.

THE COURT: I sustained the objection and I will let my ruling stand.

MR. WEINGLASS: Following the performance of your Police Department during the Convention week, both you and the Department were studied and analyzed in a report by the chief police officer of the Police Department of the City of Los Angeles, is that true?

MR. FORAN: I object to that.

THE COURT: I sustain the objection.

MR. WEINGLASS: Following the performance of your Police Department during the Convention week, were your police officers examined by a psychiatrist known as Dr. Abrams, and a report submitted to you on his finding?

MR. FORAN: I object to that.

THE COURT: Sustain the objection.

MR. WEINGLASS: Is it your testimony, finally, before this jury that you were entirely satisfied with the performance of your policemen at the intersection of Michigan and Balbo between 7:45 and 8:15 on the evening of August 28?

THE WITNESS: I'm never satisfied.

MR. WEINGLASS: And could you indicate to the jury what your particular complaint about your police performance at that time was?

THE WITNESS: Well, it's not a complaint. Each and every time we have a police operation, we examine it, we go to the very basic operating level. I feel badly and was hurt that people were injured, that in this great city of Chicago this incident occurred in the manner that it did. I have concern for anyone injured. My basic responsibility is to protect life and property.

But after reconsidering all the circumstances and all the information that I had at my fingertips, I could not be too critical of this operation.

MR. WEINGLASS: So your answer to me is you found nothing wrong with what your police did, is that correct?

THE WITNESS: I didn't say that.

MR. FORAN: Objection, your Honor.

THE COURT: Sustain the objection.

MR. WEINGLASS: Being very specific, what did you find wrong with what your police did, if anything, at that intersection?

THE WITNESS: Well, as I said, I really feel badly that the police were unable to control this vicious, mean, willful, unlawful crowd without injury. That I deeply regret. As far as the police tactics, some officers went a little beyond what I would expect them to do as professional police officers. That's a matter of fact. I am dissatisfied with that.

And as a result of that incident, we have revised and restrengthened our whole training program, reemphasizing more hours of training. Each and every day in this great country, tactics—dissent changes, so police procedures must be revised in order to keep pace with what's happening in the country. Revolution is very possible. Terror is very close to us.

MR. WEINGLASS: Your Honor, a very interesting speech. I really don't mind, except I do think it's not responsive.

MR. FORAN: Your Honor, he asked the questions, and then he objects to the answer.

THE COURT: I think it is responsive.

MR. WEINGLASS: You may continue with your thesis on revolution in America, and maybe we will all learn something.

MR. FORAN: May I object to that, your Honor, and ask that counsel's observation be stricken?

THE COURT: The observation of counsel for the defendants will be stricken.

MR. WEINGLASS: You may go on.

THE WITNESS: There were 198 police officers injured. I regret that. There were sixty civilians injured. I regret that. I feel that because this happened perhaps I failed somewhere.

MR. WEINGLASS: Where do you think you might have failed?

THE WITNESS: I don't know. I am continually looking for that.

MR. WEINGLASS: Well, in the fifteen months since August 28, have you found one area that you might have failed in?

THE WITNESS: It doesn't jump out at me.

MR. WEINGLASS: It doesn't. Did it jump out at you when you read the Walker report?

MR. FORAN: I object to that, your Honor.

THE COURT: Oh, we have had so many questions like that. I'll sustain the objection.

MR. WEINGLASS: Well, could you indicate finally what conclusion you came to in this process of self-appraisal? You indicated some things that you might have done wrong.

THE WITNESS: As I say, they don't jump out at me, but I am willing to listen to anything that anyone says I did wrong, hopefully become a better person for it.

MR. WEINGLASS: Now you indicated some of the men might not have performed as they should have. Could you describe to the jury any particular incidents where one of your officers did not perform as he should have at that intersection between 7:45 and 8:15?

THE WITNESS: I cannot.

MR. WEINGLASS: Did any of them act improperly?

THE WITNESS: I am told that they did, but I never saw an officer that I can identify where I could take some disciplinary action against him.

MR. WEINGLASS: So then is it your conclusion that you didn't see any of your policemen at that intersection who did anything improper?

THE WITNESS: It is my testimony that I never saw anything clearly or had a complaint against a police officer that I saw or observed or could sustain. That is my testimony.

MR. WEINGLASS: I have no further questions.

THE COURT: Is there any redirect?

MR. FORAN: Yes, your Honor.

• • • • •

You were asked whether or not you were asked to clear the mule train through the police line at Balbo and Michigan. Who participated in that conversation where that was asked?

MR. KUNSTLER: Your Honor, is this a statement of somebody out of the presence of these defendants? Then I object to it.

MR. FORAN: Your Honor, he opened the door.

MR. KUNSTLER: I object to it as a hearsay statement.

THE COURT: I don't think the rule in the first instance is a defendant need be present in a conversation. I overrule your objection.

MR. FORAN: Will you state the conversation, Mr. Rochford, saying who said what?

THE WITNESS: The black gentleman who was identified as the head of the mule train said he was gravely concerned about the safety of the old people, the women and the children in that mule train. He said, "This mob is dangerous," and he wanted to get free from the crowd.

MR. FORAN: Pursuant to that conversation, what did you say to him?

THE WITNESS: I said, "We will see if we can get you out of there." Then I ordered two wedges, two squads of police officers to come and we made an opening in the crowd and the mule train passed through the opening away from the mob.

MR. FORAN: That's all.

THE COURT: Is there any recross within the limits, please, of the redirect examination?

MR. KUNSTLER: Yes, your Honor.

• • • • •

Now, there were several mule carts, were there not?

THE WITNESS: Three wagons.

MR. KUNSTLER: As I understand your answers on redirect, somebody came up to you and said something about the danger of the crowd, is that correct?

THE WITNESS: That's correct.

MR. KUNSTLER: And I think you testified, as I recall, that that was a black person?

THE WITNESS: That's correct.

MR. KUNSTLER: Do you know who that black person was?

THE WITNESS: I do not know him by name.

MR. KUNSTLER: Isn't it true that you told the grand jury that that was Ralph Abernathy?

THE WITNESS: Not to my recollection.

MR. KUNSTLER: I will show you page 131 of your testimony before the grand jury and ask you if it does not refresh your recollection as to whether you told the grand jury it was Ralph Abernathy who came to see you.

THE WITNESS: No. This says Reverend Abernathy went to Chief Lynskey. He wasn't the man that came to see me.

MR. KUNSTLER: How did you find out Reverend Abernathy went to see Chief Lynskey?

THE WITNESS: Chief Lynskey told me. You see, I know Reverend Abernathy. I did not know this gentleman.

MR. KUNSTLER: No further questions.

THE COURT: You may go, sir.

At this point I think we will recess until tomorrow.

December 4, 1969

MR. KUNSTLER: Your Honor, the defendants respectfully ask the Court for an adjournment of trial today because of the murder of Fred Hampton early this morning by police officers here in Chicago. We ask this for two reasons: first, out of respect for Mr. Hampton who was the Chairman of the Illinois Chapter of the Black Panther Party and his associate, Mr. Clark; but, secondly, because of the emotional reaction of the defendants to what all of us at the defense table consider to be a wanton murder of an associate of many of us and for myself very personally a friend for several years. He was shot and killed this morning at close to 5:00 A.M. after fifteen State's Attorney's police announced a raid, ostensibly for searching for weapons.

It is our considered judgment that this raid, searching for guns, was staged in order to provoke a shoot-out and the murder of Mr. Hampton in particular and any other Black Panther that could be found in gun sight.

THE COURT: Why should a thing like that be presented to me?

MR. KUNSTLER: We are asking for—

THE COURT: I am not a state court judge. I don't deal with murder, if, indeed, a murder was committed.

The so-called Black Panthers, whoever they are, an organization that I have no familiarity with except as the name has been mentioned here on occasions during this trial, is not a party to this indictment. At this moment, I don't know what it is, if it does exist. I don't know what the objectives of the society are.

MR. KUNSTLER: But your Honor knows the national chairman of the Black Panther Party was included in this indictment.

THE COURT: I heard you say he was. I don't know whether that is an exalted office or not.

MR. KUNSTLER: It is an exalted office.

THE COURT: I might even concede that for the sake of this discussion he might be vice-chairman of the Elks. I don't know. I don't know anything about the so-called Black Panthers. I have no knowledge of them.

MR. KUNSTLER: Your Honor, we are never going to resolve that issue between us at this moment.

THE COURT: I have resolved it.

MR. KUNSTLER: You may say nay, but I think most of the country knows that it is an issue in this case. But that is not the point of what my motion is.

THE COURT: I don't deal with the country. I deal with the courtroom, sir. I hear a case and the evidence that comes from the witness stand and in documentary form as documents are admitted.

MR. KUNSTLER: Mr. Hampton not only cooperated with the defendants in the preparation of our defense, but, as your Honor knows, we moved in this court before your Honor, which was denied, to have him interview for us Bobby Seale in prison just before the start of this case. It has to do with our motion. He worked with us.

THE COURT: I deny your motion, sir. I have nothing to do with that organization in this case.

MR. KUNSTLER: But you have to do with our sensibilities just as we have to do with yours.

THE COURT: I deny your motion.

Bring in the jury, Mr. Marshall.

Please call your next witness, gentlemen of the Government.

(jury enters)

Testimony of Joseph F. Meany

MR. SCHULTZ: Please state your name.

THE WITNESS: Joseph F. Meany.

THE COURT: Would you state your occupation, please?

THE WITNESS: Lieutenant of Police, Chicago Police Department.

MR. SCHULTZ: Where were you stationed during the Democratic National Convention?

THE WITNESS: I was stationed at the Conrad Hilton Hotel. I was in charge of a group of one hundred men who were charged with the security of the hotel.

MR. SCHULTZ: Do you know a person named Lee Weiner, Mr. Meany?

THE WITNESS: Yes, I do.

MR. SCHULTZ: Now, Lieutenant Meany, when did you first meet the defendant Weiner?

THE WITNESS: I met Weiner in the lower lobby of the Conrad Hilton Hotel, about noontime on Sunday, the twenty-fifth of August.

Weiner said he was the liaison between the Police Department and the National Mobilization group, and he came to get permission or make arrangements for a picketing demonstration in front of the Conrad Hilton Hotel. I suggested at this time that Weiner use the east side of Michigan Avenue with a wide sidewalk and the parkway for his over-flow crowd for his picketing. Weiner told me that it was agreeable that the east side of Michigan Avenue be used for the picketing.

MR. SCHULTZ: Did you have occasion to see the defendant Weiner again after that Sunday?

THE WITNESS: I saw Weiner again on Wednesday, the twenty-eighth of August, about 12:30, or possibly 1:00 in front of the Conrad Hilton Hotel.

MR. SCHULTZ: Please relate the conversation you had with the defendant Weiner about 12:30 or 1:00 in front of the Conrad Hilton Hotel, on Wednesday, the twenty-eighth of August.

THE WITNESS: Weiner told me that there was going to be a rally at the Bandshell in Grant Park about two o'clock. He said "We have a number of good speakers who can excite the crowd. There will be agitators in the crowd to stir them up and after the crowd is stirred up and excited and red-hot, an announcement will be made of a march. Those not wanting to participate in the march will remain behind while those participating in the march would walk north on Columbus Drive to Balbo and west on Balbo to Michigan Avenue."

MR. SCHULTZ: Was there any further conversation?

THE WITNESS: Yes. I mentioned to Weiner, "You do not have permits."

MR. SCHULTZ: What did he say?

THE WITNESS: He didn't answer this, just smiled and sort of shrugged his shoulders.

MR. SCHULTZ: Was there any further conversation?

THE WITNESS: I asked Weiner why he was associating with people who would incite a crowd and he said, "I like this. This is my thing."

MR. SCHULTZ: Was that the end?

THE WITNESS: Yes. Mr. Weiner left me at this time.

MR. SCHULTZ: Your Honor, we have no further direct examination.

THE COURT: You may cross-examine, Mr. Kunstler.

· · · · ·

MR. KUNSTLER: Lieutenant Meany, are you serious about Mr. Weiner's comments to you on August 28, 1968?

MR. SCHULTZ: Objection.

THE COURT: I sustain the objection.

MR. KUNSTLER: Have you been drinking before you entered this courtroom today?

THE WITNESS: No, sir.

MR. KUNSTLER: Your Honor, we have no further questions. We just would like the air conditioning turned on.

MR. SCHULTZ: I don't quite understand that, your Honor. I don't think Mr. Kunstler throwing papers on his table is proper demeanor in—

MR. KUNSTLER: You don't understand why I want the air conditioning turned on after that testimony?

THE COURT: The remark relating to the air conditioning made by Mr. Kunstler will be stricken from the record. Is there any redirect examination?

MR. SCHULTZ: I don't know if Mr. Weinglass has any questions, if the Court please.

THE COURT: Perhaps he does.

MR. WEINGLASS: No, if the Court please. This witness is beyond the scope of cross-examination. I have no questions.

MR. SCHULTZ: I think that those statements by counsel are improper. I think they should be stricken.

THE COURT: I think they are improper, and I have dealt with Mr. Kunstler. I now deal with the statement made by Mr. Weinglass. I direct the jury to disregard it and strike it from the record.

You are excused, sir.

Please call your next witness.

Testimony of Victor Weaver

MR. FORAN: Would you state your name, please?

THE WITNESS: Victor Weaver.

MR. FORAN: What is your present occupation?

THE WITNESS: I am employed by the Social Security Administration.

MR. FORAN: Now, during the Democratic National Convention were there any special duties assigned to you?

THE WITNESS: Yes. During the Convention period our regular duties were suspended and we were told that we were to observe and report on the activities of the young people expected in Chicago for the Convention.

MR. FORAN: Now, calling your attention to August 26, Monday, in the course of your duties where were you in the afternoon?

THE WITNESS: That afternoon I was in Lincoln Park. There's a grassy knoll. I had walked around to that side and came upon a group of about forty to fifty individuals.

MR. FORAN: What was occurring when you walked up?

THE WITNESS: When I walked up, there appeared to be a meeting in progress of some sort, and as I approached, I heard a tall, heavy-set individual addressing the crowd over a portable megaphone, battery-powered type.

MR. FORAN: What did you hear being said?

THE WITNESS: Well, as I approached the group, this individual was talking, and then Abbie Hoffman came up and took the microphone.

MR. FORAN: And what did he say, if anything?

THE WITNESS: He said that we're trying to take care of some business, and that spectators should move out. He then proceeded to say that the purpose of the meeting was to form self-defense groups of five or six people and that these groups were to be assigned specific areas in Lincoln Park to hold when the police attempted to drive them out after eleven o'clock. He asked for people to step forth from the crowd to form these groups so that they would get to know each other before dark.

MR. FORAN: That's all. You may cross-examine.

· · · · ·

MR. KUNSTLER: Mr. Weaver, you were a part of an intelligence team, were you not, during the week of the Convention?

THE WITNESS: Yes, sir. Our special agents were divided into teams of two individuals, assigned to a car and then each car was assigned to an area.

MR. KUNSTLER: And you were assigned to a black team, were you not?

THE WITNESS: Yes, sir, I was.

MR. KUNSTLER: And your principal assignment was to go into the black community here in Chicago and see what you could find out?

THE WITNESS: No, sir, it wasn't. My team was assigned to the West Side of Chicago. We were to cruise around and monitor any unusual gatherings or activities that were seemingly connected with the Convention.

MR. KUNSTLER: Right. Well, that was in the Negro community, was it not?

THE WITNESS: That is the West Side, yes, sir.

MR. KUNSTLER: Now, when you went to Lincoln Park on the twenty-sixth of August, did you know that Abbie Hoffman was going to be there?

THE WITNESS: No, sir, I didn't.

MR. KUNSTLER: Did you ever see him before that time?

THE WITNESS: No, I hadn't.

MR. KUNSTLER: Can you describe what he looked like when you first saw him?

THE WITNESS: Not really, other than the wild hair and the nose which impressed me.

MR. KUNSTLER: In what way did the nose impress you?

THE WITNESS: Its size.

THE COURT: You asked for that, Mr. Kunstler.

MR. KUNSTLER: I am not objecting, your Honor. A nose is a nose is a nose.

[257]

And did you know it was Abbie Hoffman?

THE WITNESS: I didn't at the time. There were two young men in front of me, two boys talking to each other, and when I sat down one of them turned to the other and said, "That's Abbie Hoffman."

MR. KUNSTLER: And did Abbie Hoffman discuss the fact that he wanted to form self-defense teams?

THE WITNESS: This was the purpose of the meeting that he stated.

MR. KUNSTLER: Did he say self-defense teams?

THE WITNESS: Self-defense groups, as I recall.

MR. KUNSTLER: I have nothing further.

THE COURT: Do you have another witness?

MR. FORAN: Your Honor, this next gentleman is our last witness.

Testimony of Albert H. Baugher

MR. FORAN: Will you state your name, please?

THE WITNESS: Albert H. Baugher.

MR. FORAN: What is your occupation, Mr. Baugher?

THE WITNESS: I'm an assistant director for the Division of Community Service, Department of Human Resources, City of Chicago.

MR. FORAN: During the summer of 1968, did those duties include any unusual assignment?

THE WITNESS: I was assigned to work with Deputy Mayor Stahl out of his office, to assist him in arranging meetings with groups who were requesting the use of facilities during the Democratic National Convention.

MR. FORAN: Now, calling your attention specifically to July 16, 1968, in the morning, where were you?

THE WITNESS: I was at 407 South Dearborn, the headquarters for National Mobilization.

MR. FORAN: At that time, did you meet with any of the defendants in this case?

THE WITNESS: Yes, Rennie Davis.

MR. FORAN: Did you have a conversation with him at that time?

THE WITNESS: We had a conversation in the office and then immediately went down to the Old Colony Restaurant located on the first floor. I introduced myself and told Mr. Davis that I would take any information that he gave me to Mr. Stahl and that in the future if he needed any help in locating the proper departments, that I'd be glad to assist him in any way.

Mr. Davis laid out several things that he would request of the City for the National Mobilization office. First of all, he said he thought there should be high-level coordination between department heads of the city and various staffs within the National Mobilization Committee so they could be fully coordinated.

He also asked for a parade permit to the Amphitheatre and specified that they had no particular route chosen but that the parade permit would allow them to stay at the Amphitheatre until the President had been nominated at the Democratic Convention, and if it overlapped to the next day, they would want similar permission to be at the Amphitheatre.

Finally, he asked for the use of local parks where large numbers of people that were coming to the city could sleep. I warned him that there was an ordinance against sleeping in the park at that time, and he said he was aware of that.

MR. FORAN: Do you recall saying anything further to him at that time?

THE WITNESS: I then stated that I would take all the information that I had concerning what he had given to me and get it to Mr. Stahl immediately.

MR. FORAN: Now, calling your attention to August 7, 1968, in the evening, do you recall where you were?

THE WITNESS: There was a meeting with a group of people coming in from New York, and I was asked to attend. Present at the meeting were David Stahl, myself, Mr. Hoffman, Mr. Rubin, Mr. Paul Krassner, Mr. Ed Sanders.

MR. FORAN: What was said at the meeting?

THE WITNESS: Well, Mr. Hoffman started off very angrily asking what was happening in the city and why we were not cooperating with the people that were requesting the permit to use the park. He stated that kids were prepared to come to this city regardless. They knew it was going to be an armed city, and they were going to come prepared for that, prepared, perhaps, even to die if necessary to open this city up. He said he himself was ready to die in the streets to open this city up.

Mr. Rubin then asked what was happening to the permit and why hadn't the mayor granted it. He said the mayor was crazy if he thought he could turn this thing off by not giving them a permit.

Mr. Stahl asked the group how they planned to take care of the vast number of people they expected to come here with food and other matters, and Mr. Hoffman replied that they had some resources, but he suggested that if the City were smart they would pay for the whole thing themselves, or they could give them the money and they could run the whole thing and take the problem off the City's back, or better yet, he said, "You can just give us the money and we can forget the whole damned thing, and we'll leave town."

I pointed out to them that they no longer had a permit. I knew that the Free City Survival Committee, the Chicago group of hippies, had actually withdrawn their permit. They withdrew it, according to them, because they weren't getting enough cooperation from the City and because they now knew that a group of New York hippies were coming to this Festival of Life for no other reason than political confrontation and they weren't going to let a lot of people come with the expectation of a Festival of Life when they felt it was going to be a festival of blood.

Rubin said I was a damned liar and told the rest of the group that we weren't getting any place. "Let's get out of here," and they left.

MR. FORAN: Now, calling your attention to Sunday morning, the twenty-fifth of August, where were you?

THE WITNESS: I was at a Toffenetti restaurant in the Loop. I then drove Mr. Dellinger and his son and Eric Weinberg to the Conrad Hilton Hotel, where we had breakfast.

MR. FORAN: Did you have a conversation there at breakfast?

THE WITNESS: Yes, we did. Mr. Dellinger asked me about the parade permit to the Amphitheatre on the twenty-eighth. I said I didn't know anything about the parade permit at that time but I would check with Mr. Stahl later.

I pointed out to Mr. Dellinger that the routes which they had suggested for going to the Amphitheatre could be extremely dangerous. I told him that the first community he would be going through was a black community with the highest youth density in the city.

I pointed out that this community also had a great number of gangs and there was a great deal of gang violence in the area and that bringing large numbers of people into that area and bringing large numbers of police might cause an incident which would precipitate a larger disturbance and riot. I then pointed out that the next section of the route took him through an ethnic community with people whose background and families had come from Poland, Hungary and various Eastern European countries, and it could be that many of these people were not exactly in sympathy with the peace march, and the police would be very hard-pressed to protect all of the participants.

I brought up the point that after this Convention, after these protests, a lot of kids would be going back to school. They could go back with the memory of a tense but at least a peaceful summer or they could go back with the memories of a very hard summer with a riot, perhaps, in their own community.

MR. FORAN: Did Mr. Dellinger say anything to that?

THE WITNESS: He said he didn't care about the riots, that they were going to march to that parade with or without a permit and the riots were Chicago's problem.

MR. FORAN: Now, later on that same day, where were you?

THE WITNESS: I proceeded to Lincoln Park.

MR. FORAN: What was happening when you got there?

THE WITNESS: A group of about 500 people had assembled near a wooden horse ring where a band was set up with amplifiers. As I approached the band, they were not playing any music.

Mr. Hoffman approached me when he saw I was there and asked me, "Where was the fucking electricity?" I told him I had told his guys they would have to provide their own electricity. He said that didn't make any goddamned difference to him, and if they didn't have the electricity, the kids would tear the park apart.

I said I would see what I could do. I went back to the park headquarters. I talked with the police officers in charge and the park supervisor got permission to get the electricity hooked up. The band started playing.

MR. FORAN: Then what occurred?

THE WITNESS: As I was standing there, I saw Mr. Weiner and Mr. Rubin.

MR. FORAN: Do you see Mr. Weiner here in the courtroom?
THE WITNESS: Yes. He just waved at me.
MR. FORAN: How long have you known Mr. Weiner?
THE WITNESS: Three years.
MR. FORAN: Did you say anything?
THE WITNESS: Yes. I said, "Hello, Lee."

He said, "Hi, Al."

Rubin called me a fascist pig. I told him to shove it and walked back over to the truck.

At that time the police had arrested a forty-year-old man that had been drunk in the park and they were leading him away from the platform past the truck. The man was shouting at that time, "They got me now. They'll get you next. Don't let them take me."

Behind me on my right Mr. Hoffman was yelling, "Stop the pigs. Don't let them take him away."

About that time the crowd broke and started chasing the police toward this police van that was parked on a road and I could hear Mr. Hoffman say, "This is beautiful. This is beautiful."
MR. FORAN: Did you see anybody hit a policeman?
THE WITNESS: Yes, I did. I saw an older man hit a policeman with a sign that said, "Peace Now."
MR. FORAN: That is all, your Honor.
THE COURT: Ladies and gentlemen of the jury, we are about to recess until tomorrow morning at ten o'clock.

December 5, 1969

THE CLERK: Your Honor, there is a motion on behalf of the government to quash a subpoena.
MR. SCHULTZ: A subpoena was served on the Federal Bureau of Investigation in Washington.
THE COURT: When you say it was served on the Federal Bureau of Investigation, is the subpoena addressed to Hon. J. Edgar Hoover?
MR. SCHULTZ: J. Edgar Hoover was not personally served with the subpoena. Appended to the letter is a check made payable to J. Edgar Hoover in the sum of $155.

Your Honor, the subpoena very briefly is one calling for all the names of all persons under the control of the Federal Bureau of Investigation which placed under surveillance the defendants or unindicted coconspirators in this case or any organization with which they were associated. They want the names and addresses of the persons, the assignments of the persons who performed and participated in the surveillance, they want the dates of the surveillance, the places, they want the surveilling individuals' instructions, assignments, they want all of their reports.

Both of these requests are for the period April 12, 1968, to August 30, 1968. Now, your Honor, this blanket subpoena in effect calls for every single bit of information that the FBI has accumulated during the period of this indictment.*

So for those reasons, your Honor, we move that this subpoena be quashed.
THE COURT: Who will reply for the defendants?
MR. KUNSTLER: I will, your Honor.

There are persons—we have information—in the Federal Bureau of Investigation or under the control of the Director, who have been active in surveillance of many if not all of the defendants in this proceeding, of many if not all of the coconspirators who are listed as unindicted coconspirators, and of the organizations which are in one way or another involved with this prosecution.

The defense feels that we should have the right to find out who was doing the surveillance, what kind of surveillance it was, and that we can call those persons to the stand in our defense in this case.

Therefore, your Honor, we think that the subpoena ought to be honored, and that it should not be quashed, that the Federal Bureau of Investigation should not be afraid to open its records to the defense in this case where it is relevant to the defense.

THE COURT: It is clear that the defendants' subpoena is wholly for the purpose of discovery, not for the production of documents that would constitute evidence admissible at the trial.*

Mr. Clerk, the motion of the Director to quash the defendants' subpoenas duces tecum will be granted and the subpoena will be quashed. There is no delivery now. They can cancel the check.

Bring in the jury.

(jury enters)

Testimony of Albert H. Baugher Resumed

MR. KUNSTLER: Mr. Baugher, in your testimony yesterday you indicated that you had a meeting at 407 South Dearborn on July 16, 1968, with Rennie Davis, is that correct?

THE WITNESS: Yes, sir.

MR. KUNSTLER: And you indicated to Mr. Stahl, did you not, later, that Mr. Davis seemed to you to be a very reasonable person, is that correct?

THE WITNESS: At that time, I thought he was, sir.

MR. KUNSTLER: Did Mr. Davis state to you, Mr. Baugher, that the working plans and the coordination of the demonstrators coming to Chicago could be worked out with your office if the mayor was agreeable?

THE WITNESS: He might have said that, yes.

MR. KUNSTLER: Now in connection with the march to the Amphitheatre on August 28, did not Mr. Davis state to you that they were going to specifically train marshals to cooperate with the Police Department and other law enforcement officials with reference to this march?

He stated to you, did he not, that the National Mobilization Committee sought co-operation with local law enforcement officials with reference to that march—

THE WITNESS: Yes, sir.

MR. KUNSTLER: —so that there would be no trouble, if possible, did he state that?

THE WITNESS: Yes, sir, he did.

MR. KUNSTLER: He went on to state, did he not, that he was perfectly willing to work out routes with you which would not cause disturbances, if possible, in the city of Chicago, did he not?

THE WITNESS: That's correct, sir.

MR. KUNSTLER: Now, you have testified about another meeting which took place on August 7, 1968, in Deputy Mayor Stahl's office, did you not?

THE WITNESS: Yes, sir.

MR. KUNSTLER: Now, the Yippies had asked, had they not, for permission to use the parks as early as March of '68? Had they not?

THE WITNESS: The Free City Survival Committee had applied for the use of Lincoln Park, but not the New York Yippies.

MR. KUNSTLER: Jerry Rubin in fact asked "What's happening about our application for permit?" Did he not?

THE WITNESS: I think he specifically said the mayor was crazy if he didn't give them one.

MR. KUNSTLER: Did you ever check after this meeting into the status of the permit application?

THE WITNESS: The permit was withdrawn a day later.

MR. KUNSTLER: Did you find out whether a new permit was submitted subsequent to the withdrawal?

THE WITNESS: I believe a new permit was submitted, sir. I had no direct information on that.

MR. KUNSTLER: And it was submitted almost at the same time that the Free City Survival permit was withdrawn, isn't that correct?

MR. FORAN: I object to that, your Honor.

THE COURT: I sustain the objection.

MR. KUNSTLER: Abbie Hoffman suggested that the City of Chicago pay the expenses which would be incurred by the Yippies when they came to Chicago. Did he mention any figure?

THE WITNESS: I can't recall the exact figure. It could have been a hundred thousand dollars.

MR. KUNSTLER: Did you or Deputy Mayor Stahl respond to that and say, "Well, we will finance it," or, "We won't finance it," or did you ignore it?

THE WITNESS: We ignored it.

MR. KUNSTLER: And after you ignored it, then I think you testified that Abbie Hoffman said, "Listen, you can settle the whole matter. Give us the money and we will go away." Is that what he said, or words to that effect?

THE WITNESS: Words to that effect, sir.

MR. KUNSTLER: Did you take that seriously?

THE WITNESS: Yes, sir.

MR. KUNSTLER: Do you think Deputy Mayor Stahl took it seriously, too?

THE WITNESS: I don't know what Deputy Mayor Stahl took it as, sir.

MR. KUNSTLER: Did Abbie Hoffman state to you at that meeting that Spiro Agnew had offered him $200,000 to come to Chicago? Did that come up?

THE WITNESS: I don't recall that, sir. He might have.

MR. KUNSTLER: At any time did you or Deputy Mayor Stahl contact Spiro Agnew and ask him whether he had made a serious offer of $200,000?

MR. FORAN: I object to that, your Honor, and I ask Mr. Kunstler to refrain from playing to his gallery.

THE COURT: I would ask that you don't waste our time.

MR. KUNSTLER: Does your Honor want to suspend now? I am going to start a new subject.

THE COURT: I will excuse the jury. I would like the parties and the lawyers to remain a minute.

(jury excused)

THE COURT: I have a request to make of counsel and the defendants. The marshals have on occasions had to wake up the defendants who were sleeping or apparently sleeping at the defense table.

I would most respectfully request counsel for the defendants to advise their clients that the United States District Court is not a place in which to sleep. Mr. Marshal, court will be in recess until two o'clock.   • • • • •

(jury enters)

MR. KUNSTLER: Now, Mr. Baugher, did you ever learn that the Yippies and the Mobe people had gone into Federal Court seeking to get a permit?

THE WITNESS: Yes, sir.

MR. KUNSTLER: Who did you learn it from?

THE WITNESS: The newspapers.

MR. KUNSTLER: Didn't you get a feeling at this time that you had been used to stall these negotiations along so that there would be very little time left to go into court?

THE WITNESS: No, sir.

MR. KUNSTLER: You thought everybody was dealing in good faith, is that correct?

THE WITNESS: I felt we were dealing in good faith, sir.

MR. KUNSTLER: Now to your knowledge do you know whether the City ever had any intention of issuing permits?

THE WITNESS: I would have no knowledge one way or the other, sir.

MR. KUNSTLER: Mr. Baugher, didn't you say to someone when you heard that litigation had started, "Are these people going to be issued permits?"

MR. FORAN: Objection.

THE COURT: I sustain the objection.

MR. KUNSTLER: Did you ever have a discussion yourself with Mr. Stahl or anybody in the mayor's office—where someone stated to you that "If we can stall these people along enough, there just won't be time to litigate this issue up to an appeal to the various courts?"

THE WITNESS: No, sir.

MR. KUNSTLER: Mr. Baugher, what did you think the purpose of all of your meetings and your contacts were with the Yippies and the Mobe people with reference to permits?

THE WITNESS: What was my function at these meetings?

MR. KUNSTLER: What was your function?

THE WITNESS: My function was to assist the Deputy Mayor in making arrangements at the meetings, to assist him in any way I could with groups that were requesting use of various city facilities.
MR. KUNSTLER: Well, didn't people from both Mobe and from the Yippies ask you about permits?
THE WITNESS: Yes.
MR. KUNSTLER: What did you tell them?
THE WITNESS: I said I thought there was a good chance.
MR. KUNSTLER: You kept telling them that almost to the end, isn't that correct?
THE WITNESS: Yes.
MR. KUNSTLER: Why did you think there was a good chance?
THE WITNESS: I didn't know of any reason why they shouldn't be granted a permit or why a permit would not be considered. I have no understanding of how permits are granted or not granted. That is entirely out of the scope of my job and my experience.
MR. KUNSTLER: I have no further questions.

December 8, 1969

MR. KUNSTLER: Your Honor, the defendants are prepared to argue the motion for acquittal. It is the contention of the defendants that the Government has failed to prove a prima facie case as to a conspiracy to violate any one of three statutes.

The defendants are accused of a conspiracy to travel in interstate commerce, to use the facilities of interstate with an intent to incite a riot and commit acts of violence in connection with or furtherance of such a riot, and to aid and abet persons in committing acts of violence in furtherance of a riot, and to perform certain overt acts in furtherance thereof.

The Government has failed to establish any acts of the so-called conspiracy which antedate the coming to or being in Chicago in the month of August 1968. It has presented testimony alluding to six acts of some of the defendants prior to August of 1968, prior to acts committed allegedly in Chicago.

It has presented Rennie Davis speaking in Cleveland, Ohio. It has presented evidence through two witnesses, Mr. Salzberg and Mr. Sweeney, of Tom Hayden in New York when he spoke at the Washington Square Church, and at the Diplomat Hotel.

Jerry Rubin was testified to by the witness Casper as being at 48th and Park Avenue in New York City on July 23, 1968. He did say that thousands of people were expected to protest in Chicago.

You have Dave Dellinger in San Diego on July 25, 1968, where the witness Gilman said that most of the speech had to do with a trip to Hanoi, and he ended his speech, according to Gilman, with the words, "See you in Chicago."

There has been no proof offered that Abbie Hoffman traveled during this time period, nor has there been any proof offered that he used any interstate facilities. He wasn't on television or radio. They don't even have him making any speech before any group.

The statute very clearly indicates that there must be a travel in interstate or foreign commerce or the use and facilities of interstate or foreign commerce. The only use of interstate facilities that is in this record, according to my reading of it, is a statement by witness Kilian, the *Chicago Tribune* reporter, that on May 20, 1968, Tom Hayden was supposed to have received a long-distance call from New Jersey.

The Government did not offer into evidence a single airplane bill, a single telephone record or any other aspect of the use of interstate facilities. When Bobby Seale was a portion of this case, as your Honor will recall, a witness was put on the stand, Deputy Sheriff Roy, who testified that he had seen him pay in cash for a ticket, seen him on the airplane and seen the airplane boarded up and leave the airport down one of the runways.

But there is no evidence of this for any other defendant in this case. With the exception of the four out-of-state incidents which I have mentioned, what you have in this record is all in-state acts in Chicago by the defendants.

You have mere meetings, all open. These defendants according to the proof submitted

were meeting in Lincoln Park, in Grant Park, speaking to thousands of people from plat-
forms in both places. They had open meetings in the Mobilization office, in Noble Hall
and elsewhere. These were meetings at which anyone could walk in and anyone did, as
the evidence indicates, everyone from informers to people who were training as marshals,
to the press.

You have in this case the Yippies and the Mobe. You have Mobe seeking to have a
march lumped as one with the Yippies in this indictment, to show that they and other
groups were engaged in some sort of a conspiracy simply because this was the place where
the political activity of the United States was taking place. This was the single most important place in the United States at the end of August 1968 for people to come and demonstrate.

The Government has proved one thing in the presentation of its evidence. What they
have proved is that the Government of the United States is out by any means necessary to
destroy the First Amendment to the Constitution, and I think in that, they have succeeded
in so proving. And your Honor's judgment of acquittal granting our motion will be, I think,
a refreshing breath of air in what is a case which has such onerous possibilities and dangers
for the right of free speech in the United States.

MR. WEINGLASS: I would like to move, if the Court please, to Count VII of the indictment which alleges that on or about August 29, 1968, the two defendants, John Froines
and Lee Weiner, did teach and demonstrate to other persons the use, application and making of an incendiary device.

The Government called just three witnesses in order to prove the evidence required
under this count, witness Bock, witness Healy, and witness Frapolly.

Now the witness Bock, your Honor will recall, came to Grant Park on August 29 at
approximately 11:00 A.M. and he testified that he met Weiner and Froines in the company
of several other persons. And he testified, that while he was there he heard a conversation
about Molotov cocktails. That conversation was initiated by the defendant Weiner, who
suggested that perhaps Molotov cocktails should be employed, I believe, as a diversionary
tactic. And then the party known as Craig Shimabukuro asked a question about them and
in response to that question the defendant Weiner allegedly stated that they are easy to
make—it takes gasoline, rags, bottles and sand, mentioning four ingredients.

Now the witness Bock very specifically stated in my cross-examination of him that
there was no intent to convey or to instruct or to tell anyone about how to make this device. The only thing that was conveyed was the fact that there were four ingredients that
go into it. He said that "Myself and Craig will get these ingredients. Bock, you get the
bottles."

So that was the only possible intent of suggesting ingredients, a division of labor. It
can be taken to convey no other meaning. And, incidentally, the defendant Froines said
absolutely nothing about the Molotov cocktail device. The only thing that Bock places in
the mouth of the defendant Froines is a conversation relating to the place where these
devices allegedly were to be used. He said the defendant Froines said, "It is better to use
them in the underground parking garage than at any other location in the Loop."

Now the witness Frapolly came on the scene not at the time of that conversation but
some three hours and fifteen minutes later, at 2:15, and he said that he met again the defendant Froines and the defendant Weiner and Craig Shimabukuro mentioned to Frapolly
that they were going to meet in the underground parking lot at about 7:30 and perhaps
undertake this activity.

Now what does all this add up to in terms of this statute? I think the most that can be
said of the Government proofs is that they might contain enough evidence to go to the
jury on the question of an attempt to fire bomb the underground garage.* The only testimony in this case about where these alleged devices were to be used was the underground
parking garage at Grant Park. The government failed to offer any evidence to prove that
that in any way may obstruct, delay, or adversely affect commerce, specific interstate
commerce. So I don't think they have met the requirement of the statute. The count dealing with incendiary devices certainly has not been proven to a point where a jury should
even consider the evidence.

THE COURT: Mr. Schultz, I will hear you.

MR. SCHULTZ: Thank you, your Honor.

Mr. Kunstler said that the Government had failed to prove an agreement. The meetings in the evidence do establish an agreement.

The first one would be August 9, which is the first marshals' meeting where we had a meeting with Davis, Hoffman, Hayden, Weiner, Dellinger, and Froines present at the meeting in planning the marshal activities, and their programs for the demonstrations during the convention. They talked about having a mill-in.

The point is the defendants prior to the Convention and during the Convention were meeting together, discussing together their plans, what they were going to do. It was very difficult to have absolute, concrete plans because you don't know what obstacles you are going to have. You don't know what the police are going to do. They had alternative plans, many of them, which the evidence has shown were carried out, and many were not. They were the organizers of the demonstrators. They were bringing the demonstrators here, and had discussions relating to plans of violence and acts that would result in riots during the convention.

Mr. Kunstler argues that there was no travel or use of interstate facilities. We have proven that each of the defendants did travel. We have proven that Hayden, that Rubin, and that Dellinger gave speeches in cities other than Chicago and then came to Chicago. They had to travel in interstate commerce to get here. Davis did use interstate facilities to go to Cleveland, Ohio, where he gave his speech on the seventeenth.

The defendant Hoffman did use interstate facilities. He said when he arrived with Rubin on August 7, when he met Deputy Mayor Stahl and Al Baugher, that they had just flown in from New York City.

As to the telephone, we have the reference to the use of the telephone by Hayden on the New Jersey call.

We have the defendants using interstate travel to bring other people here. They specifically refer to some people from out of town. They referred to David Baker who was very active during the Detroit riots and still had his group together and was coming here from Detroit.

So we have proven the conspiracy count and I have also just now covered the substantive counts that these defendants did travel. We have them out of the state, then we have them here. They did travel in interstate commerce and when they got here they did specific acts in the street or in the park of inciting a crowd to violence, to riot.

Now, with regard to teaching and demonstrating, the count under which the defendants Froines and Weiner are charged: we did prove that they taught the use and the application. Now how did they do that? Well, at the meeting, the first meeting that Mr. Bock attended, they were discussing how they were going to use these Molotov cocktails. This is after Weiner said "They are easy to make. It takes sand, gasoline, rags and bottles. They are easy to make."

But then they discussed the application and that is what we have proven. They discussed "Well, what targets are they going to bomb in order to divert the people?" They said, "A good mobile tactic would be to pick a target in the Loop area and bomb that target."

Froines' participation in this is that he stated that the underground garage is the best choice. I think a proper instruction with regard to this count would be an aider and abettor instruction. There is Froines at a meeting when they are discussing where is the best place to use Molotov cocktails.

With regard to interstate commerce, we didn't submit any proof that it would affect interstate commerce but they were talking about bombing the underground garage to divert the police so the demonstrators would be able to go into the Loop and do their action. These actions in the Loop would be a riot, which would affect interstate commerce, and that was the purpose of bombing the Grant Park underground garage.

The last point that I want to comment on is Mr. Kunstler's statement that the Government by this prosecution, by any means necessary, is trying to destroy the First Amendment. We have the obligation to prove the statements of incitement to riot like "Get them.

Kill them," right in the middle of a riot or just before a riot, which certainly are not statements protected by the First Amendment. I don't think there is anyone who says that the First Amendment protects those kinds of speeches.

THE COURT: The Court must at this time for the purposes of the motion made for a judgment of acquittal consider the evidence most favorably to the Government. That is not to say that there might later be offered and admitted into evidence proof that might conclusively dissipate the effect of some of the evidence of the Government.

But at this time, Mr. Clerk, the oral motions made by the respective defendants through their attorneys, Mr. Kunstler and Mr. Weinglass, for a judgment of acquittal at the close of the Government's case in chief will be denied. We will expect the defense to go forward with its evidence.

Is there a witness for the defendants?

MR. KUNSTLER: Yes, your Honor. Call the first witness, please.

Testimony of Edward James Sparling

MR. KUNSTLER: Would you state your full name for the record, please?

THE WITNESS: Edward James Sparling.

MR. KUNSTLER: Dr. Sparling, can you indicate what positions you have held since, say, 1929?

THE WITNESS: I was Assistant Director of Personnel at Long Island University, 1934, a Dean of Men at Hirman College, 1934 to 1936, and Professor of Psychology. From 1936 to 1945 I was President of Central YMCA College in Chicago. In 1945 I was the founder of Roosevelt University.

MR. KUNSTLER: Now, Doctor, can you indicate what boards or commissions you have served with, say, for the last fifteen years?

THE WITNESS: I founded or I was a member of the Citizens Commission to study the disorders of the April 27 peace parade, and also on the expanded commission and studied the disorders attendant on the Democratic Convention in Chicago.

MR. KUNSTLER: Dr. Sparling, did your commission issue a report with reference to the April 27, 1968 parade?

THE WITNESS: Yes, it did.

MR. KUNSTLER: Dr. Sparling, I show you D-121 for identification and ask you if you can identify it.

THE WITNESS: Yes. This is "Dissent and Disorder," a report to the citizens of Chicago on the April 27 peace parade, August 1, 1968.

MR. KUNSTLER: Now do you know when this report was issued?

MR. FORAN: Objection.

THE COURT: I sustain the objection.

MR. KUNSTLER: Your Honor, we have to argue this out of the presence of the jury.

THE COURT: Oh, no. Argue it right here if you want.

MR. KUNSTLER: All right. I will argue it right here.

Your Honor, Dr. Sparling is going to testify that he was on the commission that put out this report.

THE COURT: You mean you would like to have him testify. He will only be permitted to testify in answer to questions that are valid as a matter of law.

MR. KUNSTLER: We are going to offer into evidence that document. We think that Dr. Sparling ought to be able to testify as to the conclusions of the report, the distribution of the report, the press which it received, so as to show how these defendants, who were preparing to demonstrate in Chicago, could reasonably prepare themselves for what might be expected from the police of this city.*

THE COURT: Does the Government care to reply?

MR. FORAN: Your Honor, there has been no foundation laid at all for the conclusions. Besides, the evidence shows in this case that there was discussion by some of these defendants concerning what they planned to do in Chicago prior to the time that the report was issued.

THE COURT: I will let my ruling stand in respect to the objections made to the question put to this witness.

MR. KUNSTLER: Your Honor, we are not going to be permitted to have this witness introduce the report?

THE COURT: That is my ruling.

MR. KUNSTLER: I just don't understand it. The hearsay rule is—

THE COURT: You will have to see a lawyer, Mr. Kunstler, if you don't understand it. Ask your next question.

MR. KUNSTLER: You won't let me question this man. I have no questions. What can I do?

[269]

THE COURT: You have no further questions?
MR. KUNSTLER: What can I do? I can't have him testify.
THE COURT: Is there any cross-examination?
MR. FORAN: No, your Honor.
THE COURT: You may go.
MR. HOFFMAN: What about the August report?
THE COURT: Mr. Marshal, keep it quiet in the courtroom.

Testimony of James Marion Hunt

MR. WEINGLASS: Will you please state your name?

THE WITNESS: James Marion Hunt.

MR. WEINGLASS: What is your present occupation?

THE WITNESS: I am assistant safety director of Curtiss Candy Company.

MR. WEINGLASS: Directing your attention to August 28, 1968, in the afternoon of that day, where were you?

THE WITNESS: I was in Grant Park.

MR. WEINGLASS: Now at approximately 3:15 what, if anything, occurred?

THE WITNESS: The American flag on the flagpole west of the Bandshell was lowered to half-mast and then lowered all the way.

MR. WEINGLASS: And did you do anything to photograph that particular event?

THE WITNESS: I moved due west of the flagpole about sixty, seventy-five yards, and photographed it just as the flap was coming down.

MR. WEINGLASS: Incidentally, how were you dressed on that day?

THE WITNESS: I was wearing a dark suit, white shirt, tie, and I was wearing a white silk handkerchief which I had seen quite a few people have which I assumed were Secret Service agents, so I assumed it would be safer that way.

THE COURT: Did you want someone to think you were a Secret Service man?

THE WITNESS: I figured it might save me getting beat up.

MR. WEINGLASS: While you were in this position what, if anything, did you see occurring?

THE WITNESS: The crowd wasn't advancing on the police. Someone was on the loudspeaker asking the crowd to move back. A few people in the crowd were throwing some things.

MR. WEINGLASS: Could you see what was being thrown?

THE WITNESS: Like, most people were throwing their lunches, fruit, tomatoes, bananas. I saw some shoes thrown, at least one helmet, pieces of sticks that were obviously parts of signs.

MR. WEINGLASS: After the marshals formed the line in front of the crowd, what, if anything, did you see the marshals do?

THE WITNESS: They locked arms in a solid line in front of the crowd and started backing up, walking backwards.

MR. WEINGLASS: What did the crowd do when the marshals did that?

THE WITNESS: Calmed down, started walking backwards with them.

MR. WEINGLASS: At that time did you hear anything on the speaker system?

THE WITNESS: The speaker was telling the crowd to back up, sit down, and was asking the police to please clear out of the area.

MR. WEINGLASS: Could you identify the speaker whose voice you heard?

THE WITNESS: I believe it was David Dellinger.

MR. WEINGLASS: Now, after you saw the crowd move into the position which you have just described, what if anything, did you see?

THE WITNESS: A platoon of helmeted police marched up and stopped, marched in front to the west and stopped about twenty yards from the crowd. Another platoon came marching in maybe thirty yards behind them. They were counting cadence and slapping their sticks in their hands. They were marching at an angle toward the crowd.

MR. WEINGLASS: Then what, if anything, did you see this platoon do?

THE WITNESS: They marched directly into the crowd in step, broke ranks when they hit the line of marshals in the front of the crowd and chopped their way a hundred yards into a tightly packed crowd, beating people all the way.

MR. WEINGLASS: And the people who you described were getting beaten, where were they?

THE WITNESS: They were the marshals in front and then they were falling over the chain railings they have there and over the benches trying to get out of the way. The people in the front of the crowd were trying to get out of the way and the people in the back of the crowd couldn't get back fast enough because they were getting tangled up in all of the benches.

MR. WEINGLASS: Then what happened?

THE WITNESS: After the police had gone about one hundred yards into the crowd, some of them started turning around and walking back. They hit a few people on the way back, and walked out back out of the crowd and formed up. The attack was simply a punitive assault upon the crowd. There was no provocation.

MR. FORAN: I object to that.

THE COURT: The last statement of the witness may go out.

MR. WEINGLASS: How long did you stay in the area?

THE WITNESS: I left the area shortly after six in the evening.

•   •   •   •   •

THE COURT: Cross-examination.

MR. FORAN: Mr. Hunt, near the flagpole there, did you see an unmarked police car?

THE WITNESS: Yes, sir.

MR. FORAN: Did you see it get hit with any rocks?

THE WITNESS: Yes, sir.

MR. FORAN: Did you see anybody hit it with a stick?

THE WITNESS: No, sir.

MR. FORAN: Did you see anybody try to rock it, try to turn it over?

THE WITNESS: No, sir.

MR. FORAN: Did you see the crowd throwing anything at the car?

THE WITNESS: I saw them throwing tomatoes at the car after the smoke was thrown at them.

MR. FORAN: You didn't see any rocks?

THE WITNESS: No, sir.

MR. FORAN: Did you see any Baggies full of liquid, anything full of liquid?

THE WITNESS: No, sir, I didn't.

MR. FORAN: Did you take any photographs of anybody throwing rocks?

THE WITNESS: No, sir.

MR. FORAN: Or throwing anything?

THE WITNESS: No, sir.

MR. FORAN: Now you say you were there and you could hear what was going on from the platform. Did you hear Mr. Dellinger speak?

THE WITNESS: I heard him talking to the crowd. I didn't hear him making a speech as such.

December 9, 1969

MR. FORAN: Did you hear Mr. Dellinger say from the stage over that loudspeaker, "We're coming alive and we're fighting back"? Did you hear Mr. Dellinger say that?

THE WITNESS: You are pulling out phrases here and there. It was a sustained appeal to the crowd not to provoke any violence and asking the police to withdraw.

MR. FORAN: Your Honor, I move to strike his answer as nonresponsive.

THE COURT: Yes. The witness' characterization may go.

MR. FORAN: Did you hear Mr. Dellinger from the bandstand say, "There will be some people who believe it is important to get away from here and to regroup and to take other action"?

    Did you hear Mr. Dellinger say that?

THE WITNESS: You haven't placed it in context, sir. We were completely surrounded by armed troops, and they said no march would be permitted to leave.

MR. FORAN: I object to that. I ask that the jury be directed to disregard it.

THE COURT: The objection is sustained and the jury is directed to disregard the observation of the witness. And no more of that sort of thing. You are a very smart man.

THE WITNESS: Your Honor, may I make a request of you, sir? I feel I need the protection of the Court, sir.

THE COURT: You are getting the protection of this Court. You are getting the protection—

THE WITNESS: This man is making testimony for me.

THE COURT: You don't need any protection because you are just being asked questions on cross-examination. If you cannot answer the question, sir, you may say, "I am unable to answer the question."

THE WITNESS: I am unable to answer the question.

MR. FORAN: Mr. Witness, did you hear that afternoon, from the Bandshell over the loudspeaker, did you hear anyone say, "Before you turn that off, I want to say something. This is the end. You're walking out into your fucking deaths, and it's worth it." Did you hear anybody say that?

THE WITNESS: I heard many things, statements to that effect, sir.

MR. FORAN: Can you answer yes or no, Mr. Witness? Did you hear it?

MR. WITNESS: I am answering.

MR. FORAN: Did you hear it or didn't you?

MR. KUNSTLER: Your Honor, this amounts to badgering of the witness. I think you have admonished us several times—

THE COURT: I do not think the witness is being badgered in view of what has occurred. You may continue with your examination, Mr. Foran.

MR. WEINGLASS: If your Honor please, there is a marshal standing over our table, and I would ask the Court respectfully to have him move back.

THE COURT: I have great confidence in that marshal. If he is standing there, he has a good reason for it.

MR. WEINGLASS: It is our understanding that we have a right to privacy at least in this room at this table. Everything we are writing can be seen.

THE COURT: I overrule your objection, sir.

MR. FORAN: Now, you were taking photographs when the flag came down on the flagpole, weren't you?

THE WITNESS: Yes.

MR. FORAN: Did you photograph anyone at the base of the flagpole hitting a policeman with a sign?

THE WITNESS: No, sir.

MR. FORAN: You photographed the red flag on the flagpole?

THE WITNESS: There was no red flag.

MR. WEINGLASS: Objection, if your Honor please. There was no testimony about a red flag.

THE COURT: I overrule your objection.

MR. FORAN: I have no further question.

THE COURT: Please call your next witness.

Testimony of Jane Meyerding

THE CLERK: Will you kindly raise your right hand to be sworn as a witness?

MISS MEYERDING: I don't take an oath because I am a member of the Society of Friends.

MR. KUNSTLER: There is another form, your Honor, I think.

THE CLERK: Do you hereby affirm that the testimony you are about to give in the case now on trial before this Court and jury shall be the truth, the whole truth, and nothing but the truth? This you do under pains and penalty of perjury?

MISS MEYERDING: I do so affirm.

MR. KUNSTLER: What is your name?

THE WITNESS: Jane Meyerding.

MR. KUNSTLER: Miss Meyerding, when the clerk asked you to take the oath, you said you cannot swear because you were a member of the Society of Friends. I would ask you what is the Society of Friends?

THE WITNESS: It is commonly called Quakers—it is a religious society. The part against swearing is a part about simplicity testimony. The Quakers have always believed that you tell the truth all the time, and therefore, you don't take an oath at one particular time, as though before you took the oath you wouldn't have told the truth.

MR. KUNSTLER: Does the Society of Friends have certain religious tenets with reference to nonviolence?

THE WITNESS: Yes.

MR. SCHULTZ: Objection.

THE COURT: Sustain the objection.

MR. KUNSTLER: Now, Miss Meyerding, you came to Chicago, did you not, around Convention week of 1968?

THE WITNESS: I came to this city on Sunday, that would be the twenty-fifth.

MR. KUNSTLER: Now, prior to coming to Chicago, did you know any of the defendants at the defense table?

THE WITNESS: No.

MR. KUNSTLER: Did there come a time after coming to Chicago that you became a marshal, a Mobilization marshal?

THE WITNESS: Yes.

MR. KUNSTLER: Now, did you attend after that any marshal meeting or training period?

THE WITNESS: I went to a marshal meeting on Wednesday in Grant Park, right before the rally began.

MR. KUNSTLER: Can you tell what was discussed among the people that were there?

THE WITNESS: They were talking about what would happen after the rally. One, that the people who didn't want to do anything after the rally would stay in the Bandshell area until the other people had left and then go home. The march would have two alternatives: One, the people who just wanted to prove that the march wouldn't be allowed would march until they were stopped and then leave. Other people might want to make more of a case of it. They would keep going when the marshals told them to stop and be arrested and take it to court.

And we did realize that there might be some people who would want to try and get to the site of the Convention on their own account and the marshals wouldn't be involved with that.

MR. KUNSTLER: Now after you had left the marshals' session, did there come a time when an incident occurred at the west flagpole in Grant Park?

THE WITNESS: Yes. The first thing I saw was the flag coming down. I saw it go to half-mast, then I saw people beginning to draw toward that area. I went forward myself to see if there was anything I could do as a marshal to calm things down.

MR. KUNSTLER: All right. Then what happened?

THE WITNESS: Then there apparently had been some trouble up front that I couldn't see because people started becoming angry in the crowd. They were beginning to form a line. Marshals, the ones who weren't forming the lines across the front of the crowd, were asking people please to sit down.

MR. KUNSTLER: Now, after the few minutes that you mentioned, did the police do anything?

THE WITNESS: Yes. I was standing behind the line of marshals and when I looked up I saw that there was a line of policemen coming toward us, starting out slowly and then gaining in speed as they came forward.

When they got to the line of marshals they kept going. They broke through. The line of marshals fell on people in back of them, and the police kept going through. They pushed everyone down and people who were trying to get up again, they would hit with their sticks. The people on the benches were packed in, there wasn't enough room between the benches, so when the policemen got to the main part of the crowd, they kind of fell on this whole heap of them. And then instead of just knocking them down, they started beating them, and it looked like they were trying to just, you know, hack their way through the crowd.

MR. KUNSTLER: Now, can you indicate what transpired just before you were arrested with reference to the incident which resulted in your arrest?

THE WITNESS: Well, I was helping a boy up off the ground, I was facing away out from the benches. At that point, I turned around toward the benches and I saw a man with his back to me bending over a girl on the ground. This was a man in a business suit. Facing me, also bending over the girl on the ground, was a policeman.

MR. KUNSTLER: Can you describe the girl on the ground?

THE WITNESS: She was black, about my height. The policemen were holding her down on the ground and hitting her.

MR. KUNSTLER: Can you describe who was hitting her—the man with the business suit, the man in the uniform, or both?

THE WITNESS: Well, the man in the business suit was holding her down by her hair with one hand and was hitting out at her with the other. The policeman, I couldn't see so well what his hands were doing.

MR. KUNSTLER: Now when you saw that, what did you do?

THE WITNESS: I ran toward them crying—I was shouting to them, "stop." I got up to them and I put out my hands toward the man with his back toward me, the plainclothes-man.

MR. KUNSTLER: Do you know who that man is now?

THE WITNESS: His name is Officer Hale.

MR. KUNSTLER: Would you indicate then what happened after you said "stop" and put out your hands?

THE WITNESS: Officer Hale turned around toward me and knocked me down on my back. Then he took me by the hair and spun me around and he was saying, "Take this one, too. Arrest them both." Officer Hale was pulling us southerly and we couldn't even stand. He was pulling us by our hands and by the handcuffs.

MR. KUNSTLER: Have you learned since that time the name of the other girl?

THE WITNESS: Desiree Oliver.

MR. KUNSTLER: Was Hale saying anything to you as he was pulling you along?

THE WITNESS: He called Desiree a black bitch. He said, "We know how to treat you animals." Those are the things I remember distinctly.

MR. KUNSTLER: How far, if you recall, did Hale pull you and Desiree Oliver?

THE WITNESS: I don't think it was more than about ten feet.

MR. KUNSTLER: And you were on your feet all of this time?

THE WITNESS: We were stretched out as he pulled us along the ground. He just had hold of our hands and was dragging us like bags or something.

MR. KUNSTLER: Were you eventually put into a police car?

THE WITNESS: Yes.

MR. KUNSTLER: Were you put in the front seat or the back seat?

THE WITNESS: Back.

MR. KUNSTLER: Did anything occur in the car while you were being taken away?

THE WITNESS: Well, the policeman got into the front seat. He asked Desiree for identification, and she reached for her bag, her purse that was lying on the seat beside her, and he, Officer Hale, also reached back toward the purse. He pushed his hand toward her and knocked her back, and then he raised his right hand. He had his stick in it, and I thought he was really going to hit her. But she brought her feet up on the top of the front seat and pushed him back, so he went backwards into the front seat. And he pulled her up with him, and as she came forward she bit him on the neck.

MR. KUNSTLER: Then what happened?

THE WITNESS: His partner got in the car with some other policemen that I hadn't seen before and took us to the police station.

MR. KUNSTLER: Were you eventually charged with a crime yourself?

THE WITNESS: Yes, I was charged with battery, aggravated battery, and mob action.

MR. KUNSTLER: Will you indicate to the jury how this charge was disposed of?

THE WITNESS: The battery and aggravated battery charges were dropped on the condition that we both plead guilty to a misdemeanor of mob action. I agreed to that. They fined me $25 and suspended the fine.

MR. KUNSTLER: I am through with my examination.

THE COURT: Cross-examination?

• • • • •

MR. SCHULTZ: Miss Meyerding, did anybody at the marshals' meeting say that the leaders of the National Mobilization Committee had earlier that day planned on there being two actions, one being a march to the Amphitheatre if they could make it, and the other being actions in the Loop?

THE WITNESS: I heard no one say that.

MR. SCHULTZ: Do you know that they had planned at the meeting to use the march, the formation of the march, as a diversion to divert the police so the other people could go to the Loop for other action?

THE WITNESS: I never heard anybody say that in my life, no.

MR. SCHULTZ: At the flagpole, you couldn't see whether there was fighting or not?

THE WITNESS: I didn't see anything at all.

MR. SCHULTZ: Now you say that you ultimately did see objects being thrown, is that correct.

THE WITNESS: Yes.

MR. SCHULTZ: And you said the heaviest thing you saw was what?

THE WITNESS: The sticks from the posters.

MR. SCHULTZ: You didn't see any rocks did you?

THE WITNESS: No.

MR. SCHULTZ: You didn't see any cans full of an object, cans that when they hit, the contents would splatter out?

THE WITNESS: No.

MR. SCHULTZ: Did you hear anybody in the crowd screaming, "Get the pigs. Get the pigs. Let's go. Let's go."

THE WITNESS: No.

MR. SCHULTZ: All right. Now you saw a man in a regular suit or sports jacket bending over a girl and you saw another police officer there also, is that right?

THE WITNESS: Yes.

MR. SCHULTZ: And you went over and jumped on Mr. Hale's back and tried to stop him, is that right?

THE WITNESS: No, that is not true.

MR. SCHULTZ: That is not true. You went over and touched his back?

THE WITNESS: I put out my hand to put it on his arm to attract his attention.

MR. SCHULTZ: At most you just touched his arm with your hand?

THE WITNESS: Yes. I didn't have a chance to do more than that even if I had intended to, which I didn't.

MR. SCHULTZ: Then when you touched his arm, he threw you to the ground, is that right?

THE WITNESS: Yes. And he turned around, he knocked me down.

MR. SCHULTZ: Then he put handcuffs on your wrists, is that right?

THE WITNESS: I am not sure whether he did or the other policeman.

MR. SCHULTZ: You were fighting and trying to get free, were you not?

THE WITNESS: I was trying to stand up.

MR. SCHULTZ: You were pushing him away and flailing your arms around, were you not?

THE WITNESS: When I am off balance, I tend to flail around, yes.

MR. SCHULTZ: And the police officers were struggling to hold onto you, isn't that right?

THE WITNESS: That could be right from their point of view, yes. It seemed to us they were trying to hold us down.

MR. SCHULTZ: Then when you got in the car, the officer turned around to reach to get Desiree's purse, is that right?

THE WITNESS: Yes.

MR. SCHULTZ: Did you ever see what he took out of her purse? Did you see him take a scissors and a knife out of the pocketbook?

THE WITNESS: I never saw him take anything out of the pocketbook.

MR. SCHULTZ: Now, Miss Meyerding, did Desiree Oliver ever tell you that she had in her pocketbook a scissors and knife and Mace in that pocketbook?

MR. KUNSTLER: Your Honor, there is no foundation for the question. It is pure hearsay.

THE COURT: I overrule the objection.

MR. KUNSTLER: It is a statement made by someone not here. How can you possibly let that in under the hearsay rule?

THE COURT: I am not obligated to explain to you, sir.

MR. KUNSTLER: I object on the ground of hearsay. As long as the record contains that, I am happy.

MR. SCHULTZ: Then at one point she lunged foward, did she not, and with her fingers scratched the front of the officer's face, didn't she?

THE WITNESS: No, I don't remember that happening at all. She was tipped the other way. She had her feet up to protect herself.

MR. SCHULTZ: She leaned forward and so far as you know she bit him on the neck, is that right?

THE WITNESS: Yes.

MR. SCHULTZ: Did you see her at that time take her fingernails of her free hand and claw at his face?

THE WITNESS: I did not see that.

MR. SCHULTZ: As I understand your testimony, in December of 1968, you pleaded guilty to the misdemeanor of mob action, is that correct?

THE WITNESS: Yes.

MR. SCHULTZ: That is all, your Honor.

THE COURT: Please call your next witness.

Testimony of Anne Patricia Kerr

THE WITNESS: Can I have the Bible, please?
THE COURT: We don't have one, I am sorry. Are you an American citizen?
THE WITNESS: No, I am British.
THE COURT: In American Courts—
THE WITNESS: I am a Methodist.
THE COURT: Yes, I can hear that. In American courts you may take an oath without putting your hand on the Bible.
THE WITNESS: But I would like to.
THE COURT: I would like it too, but I don't have a Bible in the courtroom. I am sorry.
THE CLERK: You do solemnly swear the testimony you are about to give in the cause now on trial before this court and jury shall be the whole truth, and nothing but the truth, so help you God?
THE WITNESS: Yes.
THE CLERK: You may be seated.
MR. KUNSTLER: Would you state your full name?
THE WITNESS: Mrs. Anne Patricia Kerr.
MR. KUNSTLER: And, Mrs. Kerr, where do you reside?
THE WITNESS: I live in Twickenham, London, Britain.
MR. KUNSTLER: And can you tell the Court and the jury what your occupation is?
THE WITNESS: I am a Member of the British Parliament. I was first elected in 1964.
MR. KUNSTLER: Was that on Labor or Conservative?
THE WITNESS: Labor.
MR. KUNSTLER: Mrs. Kerr, were you in Chicago during the period of the Democratic National Convention in 1968 in August?
THE WITNESS: Yes.
MR. KUNSTLER: I call your attention in particular to the afternoon of Wednesday, August 28, 1968, at approximately 3:00 P.M. Do you know where you were then?
THE WITNESS: Yes. The first floor of the Conrad Hilton Hotel.
MR. KUNSTLER: Mrs. Kerr, did there come a time when you left that afternoon?
THE WITNESS: Yes. I went out onto Michigan Avenue to see what was happening because I saw people rush to the windows. They seemed very agitated. I didn't know what was happening, so I went out.
MR. FORAN: I object to that.
THE WITNESS: To see what was happening for myself.
THE COURT: Just a minute please. What do they call a Member of Parliament in England? I want to address you properly.
THE WITNESS: Just call me Anne.
THE COURT: Well, now, we call our senators here, Senator. We call our congressmen, Congressman.
THE WITNESS: You can call me the Honorable Member for Rochester and Chatham.
THE COURT: That is a little long. I will just have to call you Madame Witness. Read her last answer.
THE WITNESS: I was trying to make it easy for you.
THE COURT: Don't make it easy for me. That is not your responsibility.
THE WITNESS: Mine is to tell the truth.
THE COURT: I would suggest you refrain from any further comment.

(record read)

THE COURT: The words "they seemed very agitated" and the words that followed may go out, and the jury is directed to disregard them.
MR. KUNSTLER: In any event, Mrs. Kerr, you did go out on the street at approximately seven o'clock, onto Michigan Avenue, is that correct?
THE WITNESS: Yes, that was about the time.

MR. KUNSTLER: Would you indicate what you saw on the street when you went out?

THE WITNESS: Yes. People were choking and coughing and sneezing. They seemed to be experiencing some sort of gas. I had never seen anything like it before in my life. So I walked—

MR. FORAN: Your Honor, I object to that and ask that the witness' volunteered comments be stricken.

THE COURT: Yes, I sustain the objection. "I never had seen anything like it before in my life," those words may go out and the jury is directed to disregard them.

MR. KUNSTLER: Now when you were on Michigan Avenue, did you have occasion to meet any person?

THE WITNESS: Yes I did. I met a young girl.

MR. KUNSTLER: Can you describe to the jury how the young girl looked?

THE WITNESS: She was tall and blonde and coughing and choking.

MR. KUNSTLER: Did you do anything with her?

THE WITNESS: I took her back to the Conrad Hilton Hotel. I then took her to the lounge where I was due to meet my husband and bought her a drink.

MR. KUNSTLER: While you were in there with this young girl, can you indicate what, if anything, happened?

THE WITNESS: Yes. The police came in and said everyone had to leave. I couldn't understand why this was so, so I asked—

MR. FORAN: I object.

THE COURT: I sustain the objection. I suggest to you, Madame Witness, that you don't volunteer any observations.

THE WITNESS: I was trying to tell the truth.

THE COURT: Yes. Oh, I don't question that, but you are going beyond the question.

MR. KUNSTLER: Did you then leave the lounge?

THE WITNESS: Yes.

MR. KUNSTLER: When you left the hotel, where did you go?

THE WITNESS: I went out across—what is it, Balbo Street? I crossed the street, went onto the pavement off Michigan Avenue and I saw a whole crowd of people across the street and I saw a line of police. I went up and asked one of the young persons what was happening, having had CS gas already—

MR. FORAN: I object to that.

THE COURT: I sustain the objection.

MR. KUNSTLER: When you went up to the young people in the street, what were they doing?

THE WITNESS: Standing still.

MR. KUNSTLER: Did you see anybody acting in a violent way?

THE WITNESS: No.

MR. KUNSTLER: Did anything happen to you as you were talking to the young people?

THE WITNESS: It all happened in seconds, minutes, I suppose. I just said to them, "What's going on?" I couldn't understand it. First of all, you know, I had been turned out of the hotel, the previous day I had had this CS gas, and I had been coughing and choking with other people, and then—

MR. FORAN: Your Honor, I object to this.

THE COURT: I sustain the objection. Now I must say to you that you are a very intelligent woman and I am sure you understand about answering the questions and not making any observations of your own that go beyond the question. If you don't do that, I am going to have to deal appropriately with it.

THE WITNESS: Milord, I don't quite understand what you mean.

MR. FORAN: Your Honor, perhaps if it was explained to the witness that opinions and ideas and thoughts on subjects are the jury's ultimate job and not the witness'—

MR. KUNSTLER: Your Honor, I will try to guide the witness with questions. Mrs. Kerr, in answering my questions, just answer the facts of what you saw without anyone else's statements to you or your own opinion.

After you were out on the street talking to the people did anything happen to you personally?

THE WITNESS: Yes, I was trying to explain. I was grabbed from behind. First of all, a voice said, "Move along there," or something like that, and I said, "I am just talking to these young people."

And I was just picked up and grabbed and thrown into a police wagon. Those are the facts, Milord. I was thrown onto my right side and I still have the bruises.

MR. KUNSTLER: Now when you were in the police wagon, were you standing when you first arrived or were you in a prone position?

THE WITNESS: I was thrown in on my right side and I picked myself up and I went to the rear of the wagon where there was a little tiny aperture. Then I was sprayed with Mace by a man outside the wagon.

MR. KUNSTLER: What part of your body was sprayed by the Mace?

THE WITNESS: My face.

MR. KUNSTLER: Can you describe to the jury the sensation of being sprayed with Mace as you felt it at that moment?

THE WITNESS: I felt as though my face was on fire.

MR. KUNSTLER: Mrs. Kerr, did there come a time when you consulted a physician with reference either to the results of the Mace or the result of being thrown into the police car and the cell?

THE WITNESS: Yes, the next day. That was in Canada. I was very damaged by this time and the British consul got the money back that I had paid over. I think this ought to come out.

MR. KUNSTLER: I will get into that.

MR. FORAN: Your Honor, I now object. This is clearly a matter—whether it was a matter for civil litigation, apparently it was settled and disposed of.

THE COURT: I sustain the objection. I direct the jury to disregard the last observation of the witness.

MR. KUNSTLER: Mrs. Kerr, can you describe to the jury and to the Court what you can recall of what happened to any portion of your face because of the spraying of the Mace?

MR. FORAN: Your Honor, I object.

THE WITNESS: Yes, to this, yes I can.

THE COURT: I sustain the objection.

MR. FORAN: Your Honor, this is not a case that involves Mrs. Kerr. Mrs. Kerr is not a plaintiff in this cause making any claim for damages for injuries.

THE COURT: I sustain your objection.

MR. KUNSTLER: Your Honor, she has been sprayed in the face by a police officer of the city of Chicago. She has testified to that. Why is it that she cannot testify as to what that did to her face?

THE COURT: That doesn't require any argument, Mr. Kunstler. I am sorry.

THE WITNESS: Humph!

MR. KUNSTLER: Now, Mrs. Kerr, since the incident with the Mace, are you still having trouble with your eyes?

THE WITNESS: Yes.

MR. FORAN: I object to that.

THE COURT: I sustain the objection.

MR. KUNSTLER: I have no further questions, your Honor.

THE COURT: Is there any cross-examination of the witness?

• • • • •

MR. FORAN: Mrs. Kerr, is that all right, to address you as Mrs. Kerr?

THE WITNESS: Whatever you like.

MR. FORAN: All right, Mrs. Kerr, did you know that the FBI was investigating any improper conduct by any police officers after the Convention?

THE WITNESS: I am not sure about that.

MR. FORAN: Did you ever talk to the FBI about your injuries?

THE WITNESS: No.

MR. FORAN: Did you ever give the names of those police officers—or, by the way, did you know the names of any of the police officers who have done any of this?

THE WITNESS: How could I?

MR. FORAN: By the way, while you were in that lounge, was there a breaking of glass that preceded the policeman coming in?

THE WITNESS: Apparently there was, but I didn't hear it. I was told by the British newspapermen afterwards that in fact the police had slung people through a glass panel and had gone in and beaten them up with battens.

MR. FORAN: Your Honor, I ask that the answer to that question be stricken.

THE COURT: It may go out.

MR. FORAN: When you went outside, do you know what time it was that you went out on the Balbo Street door?

THE WITNESS: When I was driven out by the police, you mean?

MR. FORAN: When the policeman told you to leave.

THE WITNESS: They drove everyone out of the lounge. It was about seven o'clock, I would think. It was daylight.

MR. FORAN: I have no further questions.

THE COURT: You may go. Thank you.

THE WITNESS: Thank you, Milord.

THE COURT: You may call your next witness.

Testimony of Sarah Diamant

December 10, 1969

MR. WEINGLASS: Will you please state your name?

THE WITNESS: Sarah Diamant.

MR. WEINGLASS: Mrs. Diamant, what is your present occupation?

THE WITNESS: I am a Teaching Fellow at Cornell University in American History, writing my doctoral dissertation.

MR. WEINGLASS: Now, directing your attention to August of 1968, did you during that month come to the city of Chicago?

THE WITNESS: I did.

MR. WEINGLASS: During that period of time, what if anything, did you do while you were here?

THE WITNESS: We spent almost all of our time taping and filming on the streets of Chicago any place in which we heard or saw people who were involved in some way with the Convention week in Chicago.

MR. WEINGLASS: What was your purpose in filming these events?

THE WITNESS: To use them as research material for my doctoral dissertation.

MR. WEINGLASS: Directing your attention to Wednesday afternoon, August 28, 1968, the early afternoon, where were you?

THE WITNESS: In the early afternoon we were in the Conrad Hilton Hotel at the Hubert Humphrey hospitality headquarters.

MR. WEINGLASS: When you say "we," who was with you?

THE WITNESS: My husband Ralph Diamant and James Sheldon.

MR. WEINGLASS: Now did there come a time when you left the Conrad Hilton Hotel and the McCarthy headquarters?

THE WITNESS: Yes, we did, later in the afternoon, probably just before five o'clock. We walked north on Michigan Avenue, walked up to Congress Street to where the fountains are right near the bridge and saw quite a few people coming toward us over the bridge.

MR. WEINGLASS: And did you proceed to cross over the bridge?

THE WITNESS: No, we never crossed over it. We were onto it about the center of the bridge.

MR. WEINGLASS: Now as you got to the center of the bridge, what, if anything, occurred?

THE WITNESS: A man with his head all bandaged and bloody came toward us, and he was being helped by several other people, and there was a policeman and he was shaking his finger at the policeman. I turned on my microphone and the tape recorder and signaled my husband to start shooting.

MR. WEINGLASS: Now, after you filmed this particular incident, could you see what was developing with the crowd there?

THE WITNESS: Yes, I could see over the heads of the civilians who were coming across the bridge towards me that there were Guardsmen. A line of Guardsmen with their backs toward us facing a lot of people on the bridge.

MR. WEINGLASS: What, if anything, were the Guardsmen doing with their rifles at that point?

THE WITNESS: They had them pointed towards the people on the other side.

MR. WEINGLASS: What occurred?

THE WITNESS: There was a tall noncommissioned officer in the center of the Guardsmen with a spray can in his hand and he was motioning the other men in the line to direct their rifles one way or another. They gassed the demonstrators who were facing them, and then we filmed it. He turned around and saw us standing behind him and motioned

[282]

to the man next to him, who had a rifle with some kind of a wide nozzle on it that shot gas out, and turned and gassed us.

MR. WEINGLASS: Then what did you do after you were gassed?

THE WITNESS: We turned around and went west, off the bridge. As we came off the end of the bridge, a man in a white jacket and a red cross on his arm and a big bottle of water met us. We were all coughing and sneezing and I had thrown up. He gave us water and wiped off our faces. We went back onto the bridge to see if we could—

MR. WEINGLASS: What, if anything, happened at this time?

THE WITNESS: There was a young man with dark hair who couldn't have been more than about twenty, twenty-one—he was talking to the line of Guardsmen with masks on their faces, and he finally got down on his knees in front of them and covered his face up with his hands, and he was gassed.

MR. WEINGLASS: Did you film that?

THE WITNESS: Yes.

MR. WEINGLASS: Then what else did you see occur while you were standing there?

THE WITNESS: There were two other men. One of them walked up to one of the bare bayonets and pulled up his shirt, put his stomach against the bayonet, pointed at it. The third man stood confronting the bayonets with his hands on his hips. These three people were gassed. Then the tall man with the can in his hand motioned to the man at his side again, and we were gassed again, and moved back down again west on the bridge to the water fountain and splashed our faces.

MR. WEINGLASS: Now, after you left the bridge where did you go?

THE WITNESS: Down toward the park opposite the Conrad Hilton Hotel. It was very early evening, dusk.

MR. WEINGLASS: When you got down to the park across from the hotel what did you and your group do?

THE WITNESS: We saw a large number of people congregating in the street and two covered wagons coming down Michigan Avenue. We followed them to the southern end of the Conrad Hilton Hotel on Michigan Avenue. When we got to the intersection there was a line of police in the street, and we just couldn't go any further, so we went back again to the park, to the grass opposite the Conrad Hilton Hotel.

MR. WEINGLASS: What, if anything, happened with respect to the police and the demonstrators?

THE WITNESS: There was a kind of disorganized movement on the part of the police to push the demonstrators even farther back, and they did retreat, and the next thing I saw was a small group of people kneeling in the center of the street about twenty feet from the first line of police. There was a priest, and a short woman with light brown hair, and a young man in a corduroy jacket.

MR. WEINGLASS: Now did you film that?

THE WITNESS: Yes. At that point I went toward them with the microphone, and the camera, and the tape recorder, and we recorded and filmed the people kneeling in the street and asked them what they were doing there.

MR. WEINGLASS: Could you see if there was anything being thrown from the demonstrators toward the policemen?

THE WITNESS: No, there was nothing being thrown that I could see at that point.

MR. WEINGLASS: Did the demonstrators sing anything to the police?

THE WITNESS: They were singing "America the Beautiful" at one point.

MR. WEINGLASS: Now, did you film the priest getting up and walking toward the policeman?

THE WITNESS: Yes. The young boy that was kneeling next to him got up and walked toward the police and just as they were arresting the woman who had been kneeling in the street, I heard a boy behind me shout, "Mace, Mace, Mace," and I got Maced, and Ralph grabbed me and the microphone and sort of half-carried, half-dragged me onto the sidewalk, and two young men in white jackets came over and poured a bucket of water over my head and then dried me off.

MR. WEINGLASS: Can you describe to the jury how your face and eyes felt after the Macing?

THE WITNESS: My eyes and the skin all around the top of my face were burning. I put my hand up because it hurt, and sort of clawed at it, and a boy took my hand away and said, "Don't touch it." I realized what he meant because the moment I put my hand on the skin and pulled it down, the burning followed my hand right down my face, and I wanted to throw up, and I couldn't. I just kept gagging.

MR. WEINGLASS: Did you go back into the street?

THE WITNESS: Yes.

MR. WEINGLASS: Where was the group and the crowd in the street?

THE WITNESS: They had moved back; they were moving into the intersection on Michigan and Balbo and moved back almost that far, and there was a line, a straight line of people. I got into the line facing the police.

MR. WEINGLASS: When the line moved backwards from the police, what if anything did the police do?

THE WITNESS: Then there was a sound of a siren, and some sort of truck came up from behind us, and some marshals, some Mobilization marshals with bands around their arms, motioned people to move to either side of the street and to let the truck through.

As soon as everybody broke the line and parted, police motorcycles began to come to the sides of the street and force people off the sidewalk and onto the ground, knocked people into doorways. Policemen with clubs just began coming at the people in the center of the street, and we moved, and turned around and ran up Michigan, and then we turned left.

MR. WEINGLASS: As you were running, what if anything were the police doing?

THE WITNESS: They were beating people, pushing people up against the doorways of buildings. And, I mean, we couldn't get any further onto the sidewalk we were on. And there were masses of people on the sidewalk, and some people were trying to get into building and others were being beaten into doorways. And I saw a policeman coming towards me, and I motioned to him with the microphone, that I had turned it off, and the camera was behind me. I thought he would understand I wasn't a demonstrator, and he hit me.

MR. WEINGLASS: What happened?

THE WITNESS: He hit me across the neck and shoulders.

MR. WEINGLASS: What happened to you as you were hit?

THE WITNESS: I went down, and a man, there was a man standing in the doorway where I fell, he reached down to help me up, and the policeman hit him across the bridge of his nose and knocked his glasses off.

MR. WEINGLASS: And this man who attempted to assist you and was struck himself, was he filmed?

THE WITNESS: Yes, my husband filmed him sitting there with his head in his hands and a bloody wound on his head.

MR. WEINGLASS: Now, after that occurred, after you were beaten, what happened to you?

THE WITNESS: Well, we went further west and there was a restaurant or cafeteria of some sort on the corner. We headed toward that.

By this time I was with a girl who had been helping us with the taping—she grabbed my hand as we got to the restaurant and pulled me into a newspaper kiosk. I turned around and what had happened was that a police car had stopped at the intersection and the two policemen had jumped out. One of them had grabbed a boy who was standing in front of the restaurant, and was beating him. Finally, the other policeman came and grabbed his mate and pulled him off the boy. At this point, we just ran, we just left the newspaper kiosk and ran.

MR. WEINGLASS: Now, Mrs. Diamant, during the entire course of these incidents which you have described, what, if anything, did you have in your hands?

THE WITNESS: I had a microphone, and I had a 16-millimeter Air Flex camera on my shoulder.

MR. WEINGLASS: Did you ever have a stick in your hands?

THE WITNESS: No.

MR. WEINGLASS: Did you ever have a rock in your hand?

THE WITNESS: No.

MR. WEINGLASS: Did you ever assault a police officer?

THE WITNESS: No.

MR. WEINGLASS: Did you ever shout an insult to a police officer?

THE WITNESS: No.

MR. WEINGLASS: Now I show you a film marked D-145 for identification, and I ask if you can identify that film.

THE WITNESS: Yes. Yes, it is a film we shot in Chicago.

MR. WEINGLASS: Is that film a true and accurate depiction of those events which occurred to you that day and evening and which you have testified here that you observed?

THE WITNESS: Yes, they are.

MR. WEINGLASS: And that happened to you?

THE WITNESS: Yes.

MR. WEINGLASS: At this point, your Honor, the direct examination is completed. I offer into evidence the film marked D-145 for identification. [the film is shown to the jury with no objection. The sound track follows:]

Keep moving. Justice you call it. You have no feeling. I mean, you can call me a long-haired freak, but that isn't what it's all about.

Look at the police, call me soldier boy, I want to win. I want to win. I want to win if I can.

There's nothing worse on earth than to be hit on the top of your head real hard.

Hey, you guys. Those guns. I ask you, my friends, for your future, don't leave. Don't leave; go into the street. Everybody, this is your country, and you stay in it and work with it to make sure the ideals you believe in are the ideals of the majority. We need you. America's fight is coming because you're working carefully, steadily, and forever for the best interests of our country. We can't—

Walk on the sidewalk. That's all we're asking you to do. Quiet. Walk on the sidewalk.

America, America, God shed his grace on thee. This is a free country. Call Mayor Daley. I think it is a police night. America, America. Mace, Mace, Mace. Walk, walk, walk. Leave the area, get out of here. Let's stay and see what happens here.

Hey, you, fucking, blow up the whole—

Come on, man. Peace, peace, peace. America, America. Get out of here. No, no. No, no we won't go. Hell, no, we won't go. Hell, no, we won't go. Go to hell Hubert. Go to hell Hubert. Go to hell Hubert. Walk, walk, walk, walk, walk, walk, walk. Hey, we want to stay. Hey, hey, we want to stay.

The next time anyone talks to you about law and order, I think you might suggest that the Democratic Party was the first party that ever managed to lose an election by law and order. That is what they show tonight (applause). *What they show tonight is such contempt inside and outside for the rights of American citizens that they have shone they are not fit to govern this country.*

This is the Army down here. Isn't it wonderful to be in a free country where we can speak in front of bayonets (cheers). *But these people don't care, no.*

We walk down here to let you know, to let other delegates know, and to let the world know that the streets belong to the people (applause).

December 11, 1969

THE COURT: Do you have cross-examination?

MR. FORAN: Yes, your Honor, I do. Mrs. Diamant, did you see any rocks, or bottles, or sticks being thrown from the crowd over there in Grant Park at the police line?

THE WITNESS: No, no.

MR. FORAN: Did you see anything being thrown from the crowd back here at the police line?

THE WITNESS: No.

MR. FORAN: Did you see anything come out of the windows of the Hilton Hotel?

THE WITNESS: Toilet paper.

MR. FORAN: Did you see any ash trays or light bulbs?

THE WITNESS: No.

MR. FORAN: Did you hear any glass breaking in the streets?

THE WITNESS: Yes, I heard glass breaking in the streets, yes. I saw the policemen put their plastic things down, you know, over their faces.

MR. FORAN: Did you see any policemen fall to the ground?

THE WITNESS: No, but I saw them sort of shifting away, the line was shifting, and they were pulling their visors down as though they were expecting trouble.

MR. FORAN: Now you remember in that film, Mrs. Diamant, and in your testimony, there were policemen who were squirting Mace?

THE WITNESS: I remember.

MR. FORAN: Did you know that that man was under indictment and was awaiting trial from the United States having—

MR. WEINGLASS: Your Honor, I object to that.

THE COURT: You mean the man he was squirting at?

MR. FORAN: No, your Honor, the man who was doing the squirting, the police officer.

THE WITNESS: That is encouraging.

MR. WEINGLASS: If this is Mr. Foran's way of confessing policemen's misconduct, he can do that in summation.

THE COURT: I will sustain the objection.

MR. FORAN: No further questions.

Testimony of Philip David Ochs

MR. KUNSTLER: Will you state your full name, please?

THE WITNESS: Philip David Ochs.

MR. KUNSTLER: What is your occupation?

THE WITNESS: I am a singer, a folksinger.

MR. KUNSTLER: Now, Mr. Ochs, can you indicate what kind of songs you sing?

THE WITNESS: I write all my own songs and they are just simple melodies with a lot of lyrics. They usually have to do with current events and what is going on in the news. You can call them topical songs, songs about the news, and then developing into more philosophical songs later.

MR. KUNSTLER: Now, Mr. Ochs, did there ever come a time when you met any of the defendants at this table?

THE WITNESS: Yes. I met Jerry Rubin in 1964 when he was organizing one of the first teach-ins against the war in Vietnam in Berkeley. He called me up. He asked me to come and sing.

MR. KUNSTLER: Now did you have any occasion after that to receive another such call from Mr. Rubin?

THE WITNESS: I met him a few times later in regard to other political actions. I met him in Washington at the march they had at the Pentagon incident, at the big rally before the Pentagon.

MR. KUNSTLER: Now, Mr. Ochs, have you ever been associated with what is called the Youth International Party, or, as we will say, the Yippies?

THE WITNESS: Yes. I helped design the party, formulate the idea of what Yippie was going to be, in the early part of 1968.

MR. KUNSTLER: Can you indicate to the Court and jury what Yippie was going to be, what its purpose was for its formation?

THE WITNESS: The idea of Yippie was to be a form of theater politics, theatrically dealing with what seemed to be an increasingly absurd world and trying to deal with it in other than just on a straight moral level. They wanted to be able to act out fantasies in the street to communicate their feelings to the public.

MR. KUNSTLER: Now, were any of the defendants at the table involved in the formation of the Yippies?

THE WITNESS: Yes, Jerry Rubin and Abbie Hoffman.

MR. KUNSTLER: Can you just point to and identify which one is Jerry Rubin and which one is Abbie Hoffman?

THE WITNESS: Yes, Jerry Rubin with the headband and Abbie Hoffman with the smile.

MR. KUNSTLER: Can you indicate in general to the Court and jury what the plans were for the Yippies in Chicago during the Democratic National Convention?

THE WITNESS: The plans were essentially—

MR. FORAN: I object.

THE COURT: I sustain the objection.

MR. KUNSTLER: Your Honor, one of the central roles in this case is the Yippie participation around the Democratic National Convention.

THE COURT: I don't see that allegation in the indictment.

MR. KUNSTLER: Well, the indictment charges these two men with certain acts in connection with the Democratic National Convention.

THE COURT: These two men and others, but not as Yippies, so-called, but as individuals.

MR. KUNSTLER: All right, your Honor, I will rephrase the question. Did there come a time when Jerry and Abbie discussed their plans?

THE WITNESS: Yes, they did, around the middle of January at Jerry's. Present there, besides Abbie and Jerry, I believe, was Paul Krassner and Ed Sanders. Tim Leary was there at one point.

MR. KUNSTLER: Can you tell the conversation from Jerry and Abbie, as to their plans in coming to Chicago around the Democratic National Convention?

THE WITNESS: OK. Jerry Rubin planned to have a Festival of Life during the National Convention, basically representing an alternate culture. They would theoretically sort of spoof the Convention and show the public, the media, that the Convention was not to be taken seriously because it wasn't fair, and wasn't going to be honest, and wasn't going to be a democratic convention. They discussed getting permits. They discussed flying to Chicago to talk with Mayor Daley. They several times mentioned they wanted to avoid violence. They went out of their way on many different occasions to talk with the Mayor or anybody who could help them avoid violence—

MR. KUNSTLER: Now, Mr. Ochs, do you know what guerrilla theater is?

THE WITNESS: Guerrilla theater creates theatrical metaphors for what is going on in the world outside.

For example, a guerrilla theater might do, let us say, a skit on the Viet Cong, it might act out a scene on a public street or in a public park where some actually play the Viet Cong, some actually play American soldiers, and they will dramatize an event, basically create a metaphor, an image, usually involving humor, usually involving a dramatic scene, and usually very short. This isn't a play with the theme built up. It's just short skits, essentially.

MR. KUNSTLER: Did Jerry Rubin or Abbie Hoffman ask you to do anything at any time?

MR. FORAN: I object to that.

THE COURT: I sustain the objection.

MR. FORAN: I object to it as leading and suggestive.

MR. KUNSTLER: Did you have any discussion with Abbie and Jerry about your role?

THE WITNESS: Yes. In early February at Abbie's apartment.

MR. KUNSTLER: Can you state what Abbie Hoffman and Jerry Rubin said to you and what you said to them?

THE WITNESS: They discussed my singing at the Festival of Life. They asked me to contact other performers to come and sing at the Festival. I talked to Paul Simon of Simon and Garfunkel. I believe I talked with Judy Collins.

MR. KUNSTLER: Did there come a time, Mr. Ochs, when you came to Chicago in 1968?

THE WITNESS: I came campaigning for Eugene McCarthy on M-Day, which I believe was August 15, at the Lindy Opera House, I believe.

MR. KUNSTLER: After you arrived in Chicago did you have any discussion with Jerry?

THE WITNESS: Yes, I did. We discussed the nomination of a pig for President.

MR. KUNSTLER: Would you state what you said and what Jerry said.

THE WITNESS: We discussed the details. We discussed going out to the countryside around Chicago and buying a pig from a farmer and bringing him into the city for the purposes of his nominating speech.

MR. KUNSTLER: Did you have any role yourself in that?

THE WITNESS: Yes, I helped select the pig, and I paid for him.

MR. KUNSTLER: Now, did you find a pig at once when you went out?

THE WITNESS: No, it was very difficult. We stopped at several farms and asked where the pigs were.

MR. KUNSTLER: None of the farmers referred you to the police station, did they?

THE WITNESS: No.

MR. FORAN: Objection.

THE COURT: I sustain the objection.

MR. KUNSTLER: Mr. Ochs, can you describe the pig which was finally bought?

MR. FORAN: Objection.

THE COURT: I sustain the objection.

MR. KUNSTLER: Would you state what, if anything, happened to the pig?

THE WITNESS: The pig was arrested with seven people.

MR. KUNSTLER: When did that take place?

THE WITNESS: This took place on the morning of August 23, at the Civic Center underneath the Picasso sculpture.

MR. KUNSTLER: Who were those seven people?

THE WITNESS: Jerry Rubin, Stew Albert, Wolfe Lowenthal, myself is four; I am not sure of the names of the other three.

MR. KUNSTLER: What were you doing when you were arrested?

THE WITNESS: We were arrested announcing the pig's candidacy for President.

MR. KUNSTLER: Did Jerry Rubin speak?

THE WITNESS: Yes, Jerry Rubin was reading a prepared speech for the pig—the opening sentence was something like, "I, Pigasus, hereby announce my candidacy for the Presidency of the United States." He was interrupted in his talk by the police who arrested us.

MR. KUNSTLER: What was the pig doing during this announcement?

MR. FORAN: Objection.

MR. KUNSTLER: Do you remember what you were charged with?

THE WITNESS: I believe the original charge mentioned was something about an old Chicago law about bringing livestock into the city, or disturbing the peace, or disorderly conduct, and when it came time for the trial, I believe the charge was disorderly conduct.

MR. KUNSTLER: Were you informed by an officer that the pig had squealed on you?

MR. FORAN: Objection. I ask it be stricken.

THE WITNESS: Yes.

THE COURT: I sustain the objection. When an objection is made do not answer until the Court has ruled.

MR. KUNSTLER: Mr. Ochs, I show you Defendants' Exhibit 149 for identification, and ask if you have ever seen that document before.

THE WITNESS: Yes, I have. At the Mobilization office. I was talking with Tom Hayden and Rennie Davis.

MR. KUNSTLER: Did you hear from either Rennie Davis or Tom Hayden what that document was?

THE WITNESS: Both told me that it was an appeal to John Bailey, who was head of the Democratic Platform Committee, or in some position of authority.

MR. KUNSTLER: Now can you state what, to the jury, if anything happened to that letter?

THE WITNESS: It was carried by Rennie Davis and Tom Hayden and myself to the Hilton Hotel. Rennie Davis walked up to John Bailey with the paper in his hand and introduced himself, said "Hello, I'm Rennie Davis from the Mobilization Committee. I would like to present this written request to you. I would like you to read it and I would like you to act on it if possible."

MR. KUNSTLER: What did Mr. Bailey do?

THE WITNESS: He said, "Thank you very much," that he would look into it, and he also said that he was afraid he could do nothing anyway because it wasn't his responsibility. The responsibility of Chicago was Richard Daley's and he was only on the Platform Committee which had nothing to do with policing the city.

MR. KUNSTLER: Then did you part?

THE WITNESS: Not quite. We parted company temporarily. As Mr. Bailey led his party to a press conference room, we followed closely behind and we sat there listening to a few questions and Rennie Davis again stood up and repeated essentially the same idea, that we are not getting any cooperation from Richard Daley. "Can you help us out? You have the paper"—reminding him, and once again Mr. Bailey said, "Thank you very much. I will say again I will look into the matter."

And that was it as far as this paper goes.

MR. KUNSTLER: Now, I call your attention to Sunday, August 25, 1968. Did you have any occasion to see Jerry Rubin?

THE WITNESS: Well, ultimately I saw him at his apartment in Old Town that night.

MR. KUNSTLER: Do you remember approximately what time that was?

THE WITNESS: I guess it was around, maybe, 9:30 approximately 9:30, 10:00. He was laying in bed. He said he was very ill. He was very pale. We had agreed to go to Lincoln Park that night, and so I said, "I hope you are still going to Lincoln Park." He said, "I don't know if I can make it, I seem to be very ill." I cajoled him, and I said, I said, "Come on, you're one of the Yippies. You can't not go to Lincoln Park." He said, "OK," and he got up, and he went to Lincoln Park with me, and I believe Nancy, his girlfriend, and my girlfriend Karen, the four of us walked from his apartment to Lincoln Park.

MR. KUNSTLER: And did you enter the park?

THE WITNESS: Just the outskirts, I mean we basically stood in front of the Lincoln Hotel, and walked across the street from the Lincoln Hotel and stood in the outskirts of the park.

MR. KUNSTLER: Now, did there come a time when people began to leave Lincoln Park?

THE WITNESS: Yes, I guess it was around eleven o'clock at night.

MR. KUNSTLER: What did you do at that time?

THE WITNESS: Continued standing there. We stood there and watched them run right at us, as a matter of fact.

MR. KUNSTLER: Who was with you at this time?

THE WITNESS: The same people I mentioned before.

MR. KUNSTLER: Had you been together continuously since you first left the apartment?

THE WITNESS: Continuously.

MR. KUNSTLER: And from the time you left the apartment to this time, did you see Jerry Rubin wearing a helmet at any time?

THE WITNESS: No.

MR. KUNSTLER: By the way, how long have you known Jerry Rubin?

THE WITNESS: I have known Jerry Rubin approximately four years.

MR. KUNSTLER: Have you ever seen him smoke a cigarette?

THE WITNESS: No.

MR. KUNSTLER: Mr. Ochs, you said there came a time when you left the area. Where did you go?

THE WITNESS: We walked through the streets following the crowd.

MR. KUNSTLER: And can you describe what you saw as you followed the crowd?

THE WITNESS: They were just chaotic and sort of unformed, and people just continued away from the park and just seemed to move, I think toward the commercial area of Old Town where the nightclubs are and then police clubs were there too, and it was just a flurry of movement of people all kinds of ways.

MR. SCHULTZ: If the Court please, the witness was asked what he observed and that was not responsive to the question. If you would simply tell the witness to listen carefully to the question so he can answer the questions.

THE COURT: I did that this morning. You are a singer but you are a smart fellow, I am sure.

THE WITNESS: Thank you very much. You are a judge and you are a smart fellow.

THE COURT: I must ask you to listen carefully to the questions of the lawyer and answer the question. Answer the questions; do not go beyond them.

MR. KUNSTLER: At any time, did you see Jerry Rubin enter Lincoln Park?

THE WITNESS: No.

MR. KUNSTLER: Now, Mr. Ochs, I call your attention to sometime in the vicinity of 6:00 P.M. Tuesday, August 27. Did you see Jerry Rubin?

THE WITNESS: Yes, in Lincoln Park. He asked me to come and sing at a meeting.

MR. KUNSTLER: Do you know what time approximately you sang after arriving there, how long after arriving there?

THE WITNESS: Approximately a half-hour.

MR. KUNSTLER: Was anything happening in that half-hour while you were there?

THE WITNESS: Bobby Seale was speaking.

MR. KUNSTLER: Did Jerry Rubin speak at all?

THE WITNESS: Yes, after I sang.

MR. KUNSTLER: Did you sing a song that day?

THE WITNESS: Yes, "I Ain't Marching Anymore."

MR. KUNSTLER: Did you sing at anybody's request?

THE WITNESS: At Jerry Rubin's request.

MR. KUNSTLER: I am showing you what has been marked at D-147 for identification and I ask you if you can identify that exhibit.

THE WITNESS: This is the guitar I played "I Ain't Marching Anymore" on.

THE COURT: How can you tell? You haven't even looked at it.

THE WITNESS: It is my case.

THE COURT: Are you sure the guitar is in there?

THE WITNESS: I am checking.

MR. KUNSTLER: Open it up, Mr. Ochs, and see whether that is your guitar.

THE WITNESS: That is it, that is it.

MR. KUNSTLER: Now, would you stand and sing that song so the jury can hear the song that the audience heard that day?

MR. SCHULTZ: If the Court please, this is a trial in the Federal District Court. It is not a theater. We don't have to sit and listen to the witness sing a song. Let's get on with the trial. I object.

MR. KUNSTLER: Your Honor, this is definitely an issue in the case. Jerry Rubin has asked for a particular song to be sung. What the witness sang to the audience reflects both on Jerry Rubin's intent and on the mood of the crowd.

THE COURT: I sustain the objection.

MR. KUNSTLER: Your Honor, he is prepared to sing it exactly as he sang it on that day.

THE COURT: I am not prepared to listen, Mr. Kunstler.

MR. KUNSTLER: Do you recall how long after you sang in Lincoln Park that you were somewhere else?

THE WITNESS: I arrived at the next place around seven-thirty, quarter to eight at the Coliseum.

MR. KUNSTLER: Were any of the defendants present at that time?

THE WITNESS: Abbie Hoffman was there, and I do not remember if Jerry Rubin was there.

MR. KUNSTLER: Where did you see Abbie Hoffman first that night at the Coliseum?

THE WITNESS: When he raced in front of me on the stage when I was introduced to Ed Sanders. He said, "Here's Phil Ochs," and as I walked forward, Abbie Hoffman raced in front of me and took the microphone and proceeded to give a speech. I was upstaged by Abbie Hoffman.

MR. KUNSTLER: At the time when you first saw Abbie Hoffman there that night, can you approximate as best you can the time it was when you first saw him take the microphone?

THE WITNESS: Approximately 8:30.

MR. KUNSTLER: Your Honor, I have no further questions.

• • • • •

MR. SCHULTZ: You were at the Bandshell, were you not?

THE WITNESS: Yes.

MR. SCHULTZ: What time did you arrive at the Bandshell?

THE WITNESS: I don't remember. I'd guess it was around three or after in the afternoon.

MR. FORAN: You seem to have a little trouble with time. Do you carry a watch with you?

THE WITNESS: Just lately.

MR. FORAN: As a matter of fact, when it comes to time during that week, it is pretty much of a guess, isn't it?

THE WITNESS: I guess so.

MR. FORAN: And the time you arrived at the Coliseum it was 9:00 or 9:30, isn't that right? Or at 6:00 or 6:30?

THE WITNESS: No, because the normal opening time of the shows was around 8:00 and I think the show was starting when I got there. That is a safer guess than the other time.

MR. FORAN: It is still a guess though, isn't it?

THE WITNESS: Yes, it is a guess.

MR. SCHULTZ: And now you say at the Coliseum, Abbie Hoffman upstaged you, is that right?

THE WITNESS: Yes. I was walking toward the microphone and he raced in front of me.

MR. SCHULTZ: And he led the crowd in a chant of "Fuck LBJ" didn't he?

THE WITNESS: Yes, yes, I think he did.

MR. SCHULTZ: You didn't remember that on direct examination very well, didn't you?

THE WITNESS: I guess not.

MR. SCHULTZ: Abbie Hoffman is a friend of yours, isn't he?

THE WITNESS: Yes and no.

MR. SCHULTZ: Now in your plans for Chicago, did you plan for public fornication in the park?

THE WITNESS: I didn't.

MR. SCHULTZ: In your discussions with either Rubin or Hoffman did you plan for public fornication in the park?

THE WITNESS: No, we did not seriously sit down and plan public fornication in the park.

MR. SCHULTZ: Did Rubin say at any of these meetings that you must cause disruptions during the Convention and on through Election Day, mass disruptions?

THE WITNESS: No.

MR. SCHULTZ: Was there any discussion when you were planning your Yippie programs by either Rubin or Hoffman of going into the downtown area and taking over hotels for sleeping space?

THE WITNESS: No.

MR. SCHULTZ: Did the defendant Rubin during your planning discussion tell you if he ever had the opportunity and at one of his earliest opportunities he would, when he found some policemen who were isolated in the park, draw a crowd around him and bring the crowd to the policemen and attack the policemen with rocks and stones and bottles, and shout profanities at the policemen, tell them to take off their guns and fight? Did he ever say he was going to do that?

THE WITNESS: No, he didn't, Mr. Schultz.

MR. SCHULTZ: Now, Mr. Ochs, you say that on Sunday night you were with Mr. Rubin all night, is that right?

THE WITNESS: From 9:30 maybe, until after 12:00.

MR. SCHULTZ: And of course you have been told by somebody that there is evidence that Mr. Rubin was in Lincoln Park that night, isn't that right? Well, were you told, or not?

THE WITNESS: Yes.

MR. SCHULTZ: Were you told that somebody saw him with a cigarette in his hand?

THE WITNESS: No, I was not told that.

MR. SCHULTZ: Well, what were you told, please?

THE WITNESS: I was told very little. I was told that Jerry was accused of something Sunday night.

MR. SCHULTZ: Who told you all these things?

THE WITNESS: Mr. Kunstler told me the one thing, not all these things, something that Jerry was accused of something in the park on Sunday night, and that's all I was told, nothing else.

MR. SCHULTZ: You don't want to get Mr. Kunstler into trouble, do you?

MR. KUNSTLER: Your Honor, first of all—

MR. SCHULTZ: Suddenly he backs off—suddenly he backs off. It is all too patent, your Honor.

THE COURT: Will the record show that Mr. Kunstler—

MR. KUNSTLER: Yes, I did, your Honor, I think it is a disgraceful statement in front of a jury.

THE COURT: —threw a block of papers noisily to the floor.

MR. KUNSTLER: All right. I dropped papers noisily to the floor.

THE COURT: I shall not hear from you in that tone, sir.

MR. KUNSTLER: I am sorry for putting the paper on the table, and it fell off onto the floor, but to say in front of a jury, "That is too patent" and "What are you backing off for?"—I think, your Honor, any Court in the land would hold that is unconscionable conduct, and if I am angry, I think I am righteously so in this instance.

THE COURT: That will be all.

Continue with your cross-examination.

MR. SCHULTZ: In any event, Mr. Ochs, you are absolutely sure you never really went beyond the fringes of the park with Jerry Rubin that night, isn't that right?
THE WITNESS: Yes.
MR. SCHULTZ: You just stood right along the fringes all that night, you never went in to see what was happening at the command post, did you?
THE WITNESS: No.
MR. SCHULTZ: You never walked in to see what was happening at the fieldhouse, did you?
THE WITNESS: No.
MR. SCHULTZ: That is all, your Honor.
THE COURT: You may step down.

(witness excused)

THE COURT: Don't forget your guitar.
THE WITNESS: I won't.
THE COURT: Call your next witness.

Testimony of Allen Ginsberg

MR. WEINGLASS: Will you please state your full name?

THE WITNESS: Allen Ginsberg.

MR. WEINGLASS: What is your occupation?

THE WITNESS: Poet.

MR. WEINGLASS: Have you authored any books in the field of poetry?

THE WITNESS: In 1956, *Howl and Other Poems;* in 1960, *Kaddish and Other Poems;* in 1963, *Empty Mirror;* in 1963, *Reality Sandwiches,* and in 1968, *Planet News.*

MR. WEINGLASS: Now, in addition to your writing, Mr. Ginsberg, are you presently engaged in any other activity?

THE WITNESS: I teach, lecture, and recite poetry at universities.

MR. WEINGLASS: Now, did you ever study abroad?

THE WITNESS: Yes. In India and Japan.

MR. WEINGLASS: Could you indicate for the Court and jury what the area of your studies consisted of?

THE WITNESS: Mantra Yoga, meditation exercises and sitting quietly, breathing exercises to calm the body and calm the mind, but mainly a branch called Mantra Yoga, which is yoga which involved prayer and chanting.

MR. WEINGLASS: How long did you study?

THE WITNESS: I was in India for a year and a third, and then in Japan studying with Gary Snyder, a zen poet, at Dai Tokuji Monastery, D-A-I T-O-K-U-J-I. I sat there for the zazen exercises for centering the body and quieting the mind.

MR. WEINGLASS: Are you still studying under any of your former teachers?

THE WITNESS: Yes, Swami Bahkti Vedanta, faith, philosophy; Bahkti Vedanta, B-A-H-K-T-I V-E-D-A-N-T-A. I have seen him and chanted with him the last few years in different cities, and he has asked me to continue chanting, especially on public occasions. This involves chanting and praying, praying out loud and in community.

MR. WEINGLASS: In the course of a Mantra chant, is there any particular position that the person doing that assumes?

THE WITNESS: Any position which will let the stomach relax and be easy, fall out, so that aspiration can be deep into the body, to relax the body completely and calm the mind, based as cross-legged.

MR. WEINGLASS: And is it—chanting—to be done privately, or is it in public?

MR. FORAN: Oh, your Honor, I object. I think we have gone far enough now—

THE COURT: I think I have a vague idea now of the witness' profession. It is vague.

MR. FORAN: I think I might also indicate that he is an excellent speller.

THE WITNESS: Sir—

THE COURT: Yes, sir.

THE WITNESS: In India, the profession of poetry and the profession of chanting are linked together as one practice.

THE COURT: That's right. I give you credit for that.

MR. WEINGLASS: Mr. Ginsberg, do you know the defendant Jerry Rubin?

THE WITNESS: Yes, I do.

MR. WEINGLASS: Do you recall where it was that you first met him?

THE WITNESS: In Berkeley and San Francisco in 1965 during the time of the anti-Vietnam war marches in Berkeley. I saw him again at the human be-in in San Francisco. We shared the stage with many other people.

MR. WEINGLASS: Would you describe for the Court and jury what the be-in in San Francisco was?

THE WITNESS: A large assembly of younger people who came together to—

MR. FORAN: Objection, your Honor.

THE COURT: Just a minute. I am not sure how you spell the be-in.

MR. WEINGLASS: B-E I-N, I believe, be-in.

THE WITNESS: Human be-in.

THE COURT: I really can't pass on the validity of the objection because I don't understand the question.

MR. WEINGLASS: I asked him to explain what a be-in was.

MR. FORAN: I would love to know also but I don't think it has anything to do with this lawsuit.

THE COURT: I will let him, over the objection of the Government, tell what a be-in is.

THE WITNESS: A gathering-together of younger people aware of the planetary fate that we are all sitting in the middle of, imbued with a new consciousness, a new kind of society involving prayer, music, and spiritual life together rather than competition, acquisition and war.

MR. WEINGLASS: And was that the activity that was engaged in in San Francisco at this be-in?

THE WITNESS: There was what was called a "Gathering of the Tribes" of all the different affinity groups, spiritual groups, political groups, yoga groups, music groups and poetry groups that all felt the same crisis of identity and crisis of the planet and political crisis in America, who all came together in the largest assemblage of such younger people that had taken place since the war in the presence of the Zen master Sazuki and in the presence of the rock bands and the presence of Timothy Leary and Mr. Rubin.

MR. WEINGLASS: Now, later on in the year of 1967 did you have occasion to meet again with the defendant Jerry Rubin?

THE WITNESS: Yes. We met in a cafe in Berkeley and discussed his mayoral race for the city of Berkeley. He had run for mayor.

MR. WEINGLASS: Did you have any participation in that campaign?

THE WITNESS: I encouraged it, blessed it.

MR. WEINGLASS: Now, do you know the defendant Abbie Hoffman?

THE WITNESS: Yes.

MR. WEINGLASS: Now, calling your attention to the month of February 1968, did you have any occasion in that month to meet with Abbie Hoffman?

THE WITNESS: Yeah.

MR. WEINGLASS: Do you recall what Mr. Hoffman said in the course of the conversation.

THE WITNESS: Yippee—among other things. He said that politics had become theater and magic; that it was the manipulation of imagery through mass media that was confusing and hypnotizing the people in the United States and making them accept a war which they did not really believe in; that people were involved in a life style that was intolerable to young folks, which involved brutality and police violence as well as a larger violence in Vietnam; and that ourselves might be able to get together in Chicago and invite teachers to present different ideas of what is wrong with the planet, what we can do to solve the pollution crisis, what we can do to solve the Vietnam war, to present different ideas for making the society more sacred and less commercial, less materialistic; what we could do to uplevel or improve the whole tone of the trap that we all felt ourselves in as the population grew and as politics became more and more violent and chaotic.

MR. WEINGLASS: Now, did he ascribe any particular name to that project?

THE WITNESS: Festival of Life.

MR. WEINGLASS: After he spoke to you, what, if anything, was your response to his suggestion?

THE WITNESS: I was worried whether or not the whole scene would get violent. I was worried whether we would be allowed to put on such a situation. I was worried, you know, whether the government would let us do something that was funnier or prettier or more charming than what was going to be going on in the Convention hall.

MR. FORAN: I object and ask that it be stricken. It was not responsive.

THE COURT: Yes. I sustain the objection.

THE WITNESS: Sir, that was our conversation.

MR. WEINGLASS: Now, during that same month, February of 1968, did you have occasion to meet with Jerry Rubin?

THE WITNESS: I spoke with Jerry Rubin on the phone, I believe.

MR. WEINGLASS: Will you relate to the Court and jury what Jerry Rubin said to you?

THE WITNESS: Jerry told me that he and others were going to Chicago to apply for permission from the city government for a permit to hold a Festival of Life and that he was talking with John Sinclair about getting rock and roll bands together and other musicians and that he would report back to me.

MR. WEINGLASS: Mr. Ginsberg, do you recall anything else that Mr. Rubin said to you in the course of that telephone conversation?

THE WITNESS: Yes, he said that he thought it would be interesting if we could get up little schools like ecology schools, music schools, political schools, schools about the Vietnam war, schools with yogis.

He asked if I could contact Burroughs and ask Burroughs to come to teach nonverbal, nonconceptual feeling states.

MR. WEINGLASS: Now you indicated a school of ecology. Could you explain to the Court and jury what that is?

THE WITNESS: Ecology is the interrelation of all the living forms on the surface of the planet involving the food chain—that is to say, whales eat plankton; larger fishes eat smaller fish, octopus or squid eat shellfish which eat plankton; human beings eat the shellfish or squid or smaller fish which eat the smaller tiny microorganisms—

MR. FORAN: That is enough, your Honor.

THE COURT: Yes. We all have a clear idea of what ecology is.

THE WITNESS: Well, the destruction of ecology is what would have been taught. That is, how it is being destroyed by human intervention and messing it up with pollution.

MR. WEINGLASS: Now you also indicated that Mr. Rubin mentioned nonverbal education. Will you explain what that is to the Court and jury?

THE WITNESS: Most of our consciousness, since we are continually looking at images on television and listening to words, reading newspapers, talking in courts such as this, most of our consciousness is filled with language, with a kind of matter babble behind the ear, a continuous yakety-yak that actually prevents us from breathing deeply in our bodies and sensing more subtly and sweetly the feelings that we actually do have as persons to each other rather than as talking machines.

MR. WEINGLASS: Now, Mr. Ginsberg, on March 17, where were you?

THE WITNESS: I took part in a press conference at the Hotel Americana in New York City.

MR. WEINGLASS: Who else was present at this press conference?

THE WITNESS: Abbie Hoffman and Jerry Rubin were there as well as Phil Ochs, the folk singer, Arlo Guthrie, some members of the USA band, some members of the Diggers groups.

MR. WEINGLASS: Could you indicate to the Court and jury what Jerry Rubin said?

THE WITNESS: He said that a lot of younger people in America would come to Chicago during the Convention and hold a Festival of Life in the parks, and he announced that they were negotiating with the City Hall to get a permit to have a life festival in the parks.

MR. WEINGLASS: Do you recall what Abbie Hoffman said?

THE WITNESS: He said that they were going to go to Chicago in groups to negotiate with representatives of Mayor Daley to get a permit for a large-scale Gathering of the Tribes and he mentioned the human be-in in San Francisco.

MR. WEINGLASS: Did you yourself participate in that press conference?

THE WITNESS: Yes. I stepped to the microphone also. My statement was that the planet Earth at the present moment was endangered by violence, overpopulation, pollution, ecological destruction brought about by our own greed; that our younger children in America and other countries of the world might not survive the next thirty years; that it was a planetary crisis that had not been recognized by any government of the world and had not been recognized by our own government, nor the politicians who were preparing for the elections; that the younger people of America were aware of that and that precisely was what was called psychedelic consciousness; that we were going to gather together as we had before in the San Francisco human be-in to manifest our presence over and above the presence of the more selfish elder politicians who were not thinking in terms of what their children would need in future generations, or even in the generation immediately coming, or even for themselves in their own lifetime and were continuing to threaten the planet with violence, with war, with mass murder, with germ warfare. And since the younger people knew that in the United States, we are going to invite them there, and that the central motive would be a presentation of a desire for the preservation of the planet. The desire for preservation of the planet and the planet's form was manifested to my mind by the great Mantra from India to the preserver god Vishnu whose Mantra is the Hare Krishna. And then I chanted the Hare Krishna for ten minutes to the television cameras, and it goes:

Hare krishna/hare krishna/krishna krishna/hare hare/hare rama/hare rama/rama rama/hare hare.

MR. WEINGLASS: Now in chanting that did you have an accompaniment of any particular instrument? Your Honor, I object to the laughter of the Court on this. I think this is a serious presentation of a religious concept.

THE COURT: I don't understand. I don't understand it because it was—the language of the United States District Court is English.

MR. KUNSTLER: I know, but you don't laugh at all languages.

THE COURT: I didn't laugh. I didn't laugh.

THE WITNESS: I would be happy to explain it.

THE COURT: I didn't laugh at all. I wish I could tell you how I feel.

Laugh—I didn't even smile.

MR. KUNSTLER: Well, I thought—

THE COURT: All I could tell you is that I didn't understand it because whatever language the witness is using—

THE WITNESS: Sanskrit, sir.

THE COURT: Well, that is one I don't know. That is the reason I didn't understand it.

THE WITNESS: Might we go on to an explanation?

THE COURT: Will you keep quiet, Mr. Witness, while I am talking to the lawyers?

THE WITNESS: I will be glad to give an explanation.

THE COURT: I never laugh at a witness, sir. I protect witnesses who come to this court. But I do tell you that the language of the American court is English unless you have an interpreter. You may use an interpreter for the remainder of the witness' testimony.

MR. KUNSTLER: No. I have heard, your Honor, priests explain the mass in Latin in American courts and I think Mr. Ginsberg is doing exactly the same thing in Sanskrit for another type of religious experience.

THE COURT: I don't understand Sanskrit. I venture to say the jury members don't. Perhaps we have some people on the jury who do understand Sanskrit, I don't know, but I wouldn't even have known it was Sanskrit until he told me. I can't see that that is material to the issues here, that is all.

MR. WEINGLASS: Let me ask this: Mr. Ginsberg, I show you an object marked 150 for identification, and I ask you to examine that object.

THE WITNESS: Yes.

MR. FORAN: All right. Your Honor, that is enough. I object to it, your Honor. I think it is outrageous for counsel to—

THE COURT: You asked him to examine it and instead of that he played a tune on it. I sustain the objection.

THE WITNESS: It adds spirituality to the case, sir.

THE COURT: Will you remain quiet, sir.

THE WITNESS: I am sorry.

MR. WEINGLASS: Having examined that, could you identify it for the Court and jury?

THE WITNESS: It is an instrument known as the harmonium, which I used at the press conference at the Americana Hotel. It is commonly used in India.

MR. FORAN: I object to that.

THE COURT: I sustain the objection.

MR. WEINGLASS: Will you explain to the Court and to the jury what chant you were chanting at the press conference?

THE WITNESS: I was chanting a mantra called the "Maha Mantra," the great mantra of preservation of that aspect of the Indian religion called Vishnu the Preserver. Every time human evil rises so high that the planet itself is threatened, and all of its inhabitants and their children are threatened, Vishnu will preserve a return.

December 12, 1969

MR. WEINGLASS: Directing your attention to the month of April 1965, did you have occasion during that month to meet with the defendant Jerry Rubin?
THE WITNESS: Yes.
MR. WEINGLASS: What, if anything, did Jerry Rubin say?
THE WITNESS: He said that to insure a peaceful gathering in Chicago, so that a lot of people would come, encouraged by the peaceful nature of it, that they were applying as a group to the Chicago mayor's office to get a permit, but that apparently they were having trouble getting the permit. They would continue negotiating with the City, with City Hall for that permit. He said he felt that the only way a lot of people would come is if there were really good vibrations coming out of us and that he wanted it to be a peaceful gathering.
      I told him I was scared of getting into a scene where I would get beaten up or a mob scene because I was not used to that and I didn't want to. I was just simply frightened of too large a gathering which would involve conflict and fighting and getting my head busted in, and so I asked him how he felt about it, whether he was going to work for an actually peaceful gathering or not, because I didn't want to participate unless it was going to be organized peacefully, and he said he wanted it to be peaceful because he wanted a lot of people there.
MR. WEINGLASS: Now, directing your attention to August 13 at approximately 5:30 in the afternoon, where were you in the city of Chicago?
THE WITNESS: I went up to City Hall to the mayor's office. I told Mr. Stahl that I was afraid of getting into a violent scene. I chanted the Hare Krishna mantra to Mr. Stahl and Mr. Bush as an example of what was intended by the Festival of Life and I asked them to please give a permit to avoid violence.
MR. WEINGLASS: Could you chant for the Court and the jury the mantra Hare Krishna as you did that day?
MR. FORAN: Objection.
THE COURT: I sustain the objection.
MR. WEINGLASS: Could you speak without chanting for the Court and jury the Mantra Hare Krishna?
THE WITNESS: Hare krishna/hare krishna—
MR. FORAN: I object.
THE COURT: I sustain the objection.
MR. WEINGLASS: Directing your attention to the morning of August 24, 1968, where were you?
THE WITNESS: I was on a plane coming from New York to Chicago.
MR. WEINGLASS: Now, en route to Chicago while you were on the plane, what if anything, did you do?
THE WITNESS: I wrote poetry, wrote out a statement of what I thought was going on in Chicago at the time.
MR. WEINGLASS: Could you read to the jury that poem?
THE WITNESS: Gladly. I believe you have the text.
      August 24, 1968/Going to Chicago 22,000 feet over hazed square vegetable plant floor/Approaching Chicago to die or flying over earth another 40 years to die/Indifferent and afraid, that the bone shattering bullet be the same/As the vast evaporation of phenomena cancer come true in an old man's bed/Or the historic fire heaven descending 22,000 years end the Aeon./The lake's blue again, sky's the same baby, though papers and noses rumor star/Spread the natural universe'll make angels' feet sticky./I heard

the Angel King's voice a bodiless tuneful teenager/Eternal in my own heart, saying Trust the purest joy,/Democratic anger is an illusion, democratic Joy is God,/Our father is baby blue, the original face you see, sees you./How through conventional police and revolutionary fury remember/The helpless order the police armed to protect the helpless freedom to protect, the helpless freedom the revolutionary/Conspired to honor? I am the Angel King saying the Angel King/As the mobs in the Amphitheatre, streets, Coliseums, parks and offices/Scream in despair over meat and metal Microphone.

MR. WEINGLASS: At approximately 10:30, August 24, where were you?

THE WITNESS: I was in Lincoln Park.

MR. WEINGLASS: And what occurred in Lincoln Park approximately 10:30, if you can recall?

THE WITNESS: There were several thousand young people gathered, waiting, late at night. It was dark. There were some bonfires burning in trashcans. Everybody was standing around not knowing what to do.

Suddenly there was a great deal of consternation and movement and shouting among the crowd in the park, and I turned, surprised, because it was early. The police were or had given 11:00 as the date or as the time—

MR. FORAN: Objection, your Honor.

MR. WEINGLASS: What did you do at the time you saw the police do this?

THE WITNESS: I started the chant, O–o–m–m–m–m–m–, O–o–m–m–m–m–m–m.

MR. FORAN: All right, we have had a demonstration.

THE COURT: All right.

MR. WEINGLASS: Did you finish your answer?

THE WITNESS: We walked out of the park. We continued chanting for at least twenty minutes, slowly gathering other people, chanting, Ed Sanders and I in the center, until there were a group of maybe fifteen or twenty making a very solid heavy vibrational change of aim that penetrated the immediate area around us, and attracted other people, and so we walked out slowly toward the street, toward Lincoln Park.

MR. WEINGLASS: I now show you what is marked D-153 for identification. Could you read that to the jury?

THE WITNESS: Magic Password Bulletin. Physic Jujitsu. In case of hysteria, the magic password is o–m, same as o–h–m–, which cuts through all emergency illusions. Pronounce o–m from the middle of the body, diaphragm or solar plexus. Ten people humming o–m can calm down one hundred. One hundred people humming o–m can regulate the metabolism of a thousand. A thousand bodies vibrating o–m can immobilize an entire downtown Chicago street full of scared humans, uniformed or naked. Signed, Allen Ginsberg, Ed Sanders. O–m will be practiced on the beach at sunrise ceremonies with Allen and Ed.

MR. WEINGLASS: Could you explain to the Court and jury what you meant in that last statement of your message?

THE WITNESS: By "immobilize" I meant shut down the mental machinery which repeats over and over again the images of fear which are scaring people in uniform, that is to say, the police officers or the demonstrators, who I refer to as naked meaning naked emotionally, and perhaps hopefully naked physically.

MR. WEINGLASS: And what did you intend to create by having that mechanism shut down?

THE WITNESS: A completely peaceful realization of the fact that we were all stuck in the same street, place, terrified of each other, and reacting in panic and hysteria rather than reacting with awareness of each other as human beings, as people with bodies that actually feel, can chant and pray and have a certain sense of vibration to each other or tenderness to each other which is basically what everybody wants, rather than fear.

MR. WEINGLASS: Now directing your attention to the next day which is Sunday, August 25, what, if anything, did you do in the park?

THE WITNESS: First I walked around to the center of the park, where suddenly a group of policemen appeared in the middle of the younger people. There was an appearance of a great mass of policemen going through the center of the park. I was afraid then, thinking they were going to make trouble—

MR. FORAN: Objection to his state of mind.

THE COURT: I sustain the objection.

MR. WEINGLASS: What did you do when you saw the policemen in the center of the crowd?

THE WITNESS: Adrenalin ran through my body. I sat down on a green hillside with a group of younger people that were walking with me about 3:30 in the afternoon, 4:00 o'clock. Sat, crossed my legs, and began chanting O–o–m—O–o–m–m–m–m, O–o–m–m–m–m, O–o–m–m–m–m–m.

MR. FORAN: I gave him four that time.

THE WITNESS: I continued chanting for several hours.

THE COURT: Did you say you continued chanting seven hours?

THE WITNESS: Seven hours, yes. About six hours I chanted "Om" and for the seventh hour concluded with the chant Hare krishna/hare krishna/krishna krishna/hare hare/hare rama/hare rama/rama rama/hare hare.

MR. WEINGLASS: Now, directing your attention to Monday night, that is August 26, in the evening, where were you?

THE WITNESS: I was by a barricade that was set up, a pile of trash cans and police barricades, wooden horses, I believe. There were a lot of young kids, some black, some white, shouting and beating on the tin barrels, making a fearsome noise.

MR. WEINGLASS: What did you do after you got there?

THE WITNESS: Started chanting "Om." For a while I was joined in the chant by a lot of young people who were there until the chant encompassed most of the people by the barricade, and we raised a huge loud sustained series of "Oms" into the air loud enough to include everybody. Just as it reached, like, a great unison crecendo, all of a sudden a police car came rolling down into the group, right into the center of the group where I was standing, and with a lot of crashing and tinkling sound of glass, and broke up the chanting, broke up the unison and the physical—everybody was holding onto each other physically—broke up that physical community that had been built and broke up the sound chant that had been built. I moved back. There was a crash of glass.

MR. WEINGLASS: What occurred at that time?

THE WITNESS: I started moving away from the scene. I started moving away from the scene because there was violence there.

MR. WEINGLASS: Mr. Ginsberg, very early in the morning, about 6:00 A.M. on Tuesday, where were you?

THE WITNESS: I was on the bench at the lakefront at Lincoln Park, conducting a mantra chant ceremony that had been arranged to be performed by Abbie Hoffman and Jerry Rubin, and the other people who were planning the weekly schedule of Yippie activities.

MR. WEINGLASS: What occurred at this ritual?

THE WITNESS: We got together to greet the morning with Tibetan Buddhist magic prayer formulas, mantras, beginning with Om raksa/raksa hum/hum/phat/svaha, the mantra to purify a site for the ceremony.

MR. WEINGLASS: Now, at approximately 8:00 P.M. where were you?

THE WITNESS: I came with a party of writers to the unbirthday party of President Johnson at the Coliseum.

MR. WEINGLASS: Who was with you?

THE WITNESS: The French writer, Jean Genet, poet novelist. The American novelist, William Seward. W. S. Burroughs, the novelist. The novelist, Terry Southern, who had written *Doctor Strangelove*. Myself. We all write together.

MR. WEINGLASS: Now, when you arrived at the Coliseum, did you see any of the defendants present?

THE WITNESS: Abbie Hoffman. I went down and sat next to him and kissed him, and then pointed back up at Jean Genet and told Abbie that Genet was there.

MR. WEINGLASS: Where, if anywhere, did you go?

THE WITNESS: The group I was with, Mr. Genet, Mr. Burroughs, and Mr. Seaver, and Terry Southern, all went back to Lincoln Park.

MR. WEINGLASS: What was occurring at the park as you got there?

THE WITNESS: There was a great crowd lining the outskirts of the park and a little way into the park on the inner roads, and there was a larger crowd moving in toward the center. We all moved in toward the center, and at the center of the park, there was a group of ministers and rabbis who had elevated a great cross about ten-foot high in the middle of a circle of people who were sitting around, quietly, listening to the ministers conduct a ceremony.

MR. WEINGLASS: And would you relate to the Court and jury what was being said and done at the time?

THE WITNESS: Everybody was seated around the cross, which was at the center of hundreds of people, people right around the very center adjoining the cross. Everybody was singing, "We Shall Overcome," and "Onward Christian Soldiers," I believe. They were old hymn tunes.

I was seated with my friends on a little hillock looking down on the crowd, which had the cross in the center. And on the other side, there were a lot of glary lights hundreds of feet away down the field. The ministers lifted up the cross and took it to the edge of the crowd and set it down facing the lights where the police were. In other words, they confronted the police lines with the cross of Christ.

MR. WEINGLASS: And after the ministers moved the cross, what happened?

THE WITNESS: After, I don't know, a short period of time, there was a burst of smoke and tear gas around the cross, and the cross was enveloped with tear gas, and the people who were carrying the cross were enveloped with tear gas which began slowly drifting over the crowd.

MR. WEINGLASS: And when you saw the persons with the cross and the cross being gassed, what, if anything, did you do?

THE WITNESS: I turned to Burroughs and said, "They have gassed the cross of Christ."

MR. FORAN: Objection, if the Court please.

MR. WEINGLASS: What did you do at that time?

THE WITNESS: I took Bill Burroughs' hand, and took Terry Southern's hand, and we turned from the cross which was covered with gas in the glary lights, the police lights that were shining through the tear gas on the cross, and walked slowly out of the park.

MR. WEINGLASS: On Wednesday, the next day, at approximately 3:45 in the afternoon, do you recall where you were?

THE WITNESS: Yes. Entering the Grant Park Bandshell area, where there was a Mobilization meeting or rally going on. I was still with the same group of literary fellows, poets and writers. I walked up to the apron or front of the stage, and saw David Dellinger and told him that I was there, and that Burroughs was there and Jean Genet was there and that they were all willing to be present and testify to the righteousness of the occasion, and that we would like to be on the stage.

MR. WEINGLASS: Were you then introduced?

THE WITNESS: Yes. Jean Genet was also introduced.

MR. WEINGLASS: Did you speak?

THE WITNESS: I croaked, yes.

THE COURT: What was that last? You say you what?

THE WITNESS: I croaked. My voice was gone. I chanted or tried to chant.

MR. WEINGLASS: Did you remain for the rest of the rally?

THE WITNESS: Yes. I didn't pay much attention to most of the speakers that followed. There was one that I heard, Louis Abolafia, whom I knew from New York.

MR. WEINGLASS: And who is he?

THE WITNESS: Kind of a Bohemian trickster, street theater candidate for President. He had announced his candidacy for President a number of times, and his campaign slogan was, "I have nothing to hide," and he showed himself in a photograph with his hand over his lap, but otherwise naked.

MR. WEINGLASS: Was he introduced?

THE WITNESS: No, he just appeared from nowhere and got up to the microphone and started yelling into it.

MR. WEINGLASS: Do you recall hearing what he was yelling?

THE WITNESS: "The police out there are armed and violent. You are walking into a death trap."

MR. WEINGLASS: When you heard him yelling that over the microphone, what, if anything, did you do?

THE WITNESS: I went over and sat next to him, and grabbed his leg, and started tickling him, and said, "Hare krishna, Louis."

MR. WEINGLASS: Now, when the rally was over, did you have occasion to talk with Mr. Dellinger?

THE WITNESS: Yes. He looked me in the eyes, took my arm and said, "Allen, will you please march in the front line with me?

MR. WEINGLASS: And what did you say to him?

THE WITNESS: I said, "Well, I am here with Burroughs and Genet and Terry Southern." And he said, "Well, all of you together, can you form a front line and be sure to stay behind me in the front line, be the first of the group of marchers?"

MR. WEINGLASS: And did you form such a line?

THE WITNESS: Yes.

MR. WEINGLASS: How were you walking?

THE WITNESS: Our arms were all linked together and we were carrying flowers. Someone had brought flowers up to the back of the stage, and so we distributed them around to the front rows of marchers so all the marchers had flowers.

MR. WEINGLASS: Mr. Ginsberg, I show you a photograph marked D-158 for identification, and I ask you if you can identify that photograph.

THE WITNESS: Yes. It is a picture of the front line of marchers as I described it before, consisting of William Burroughs on the extreme right, Jean Genet, Richard Seaver, his editor at Grove, myself.

MR. WEINGLASS: Now, Mr. Ginsberg, you have indicated you have known Jerry Rubin since 1965?

THE WITNESS: Yes.

MR. WEINGLASS: Would you indicate to the Court and jury whether or not you have ever seen him smoke a cigarette?

THE WITNESS: I don't remember.

MR. WEINGLASS: I mean a tobacco cigarette.

THE WITNESS: Offhand, no.

MR. WEINGLASS: Now, Mr. Ginsberg, you have had extensive training in Zen and in other religions of the East. Have you acquired an expertise in the area of peaceful assembly and peaceful intent?

MR. FORAN: I object to that, Your Honor.

THE COURT: I sustain the objection.

MR. WEINGLASS: Did you see during Convention week either the defendant Jerry Rubin or the defendant Abbie Hoffman or any of the other defendants who are seated at this table commit an act or make a speech or do anything, do any other thing to violate the precepts of your own philosophy?

MR. FORAN: Objection.

THE COURT: I sustain the objection.

MR. WEINGLASS: I have no further questions.

MR. FORAN: Your Honor, I have to get some materials to properly carry on my cross-examination of this witness. It will take some time to go downstairs to get them.

THE COURT: Are you suggesting we recess?

MR. FORAN: I would think yes, your Honor.

THE COURT: All right. We will go until two o'clock.

MR. KUNSTLER: Your Honor, we asked for five minutes two days ago in front of this jury and you refused to give it to us.

THE COURT: You will have to cease that disrespectful tone.

MR. KUNSTLER: That is not disrespect, that is an angry tone, your Honor.

THE COURT: Yes, it is. Yes, it is. I will grant the motion of the Government.

MR. KUNSTLER: You refused us five minutes the other day.

THE COURT: You are shouting at the Court.

MR. KUNSTLER: Oh, your Honor—
THE COURT: I never shouted at you during this trial.
MR. KUNSTLER: Your Honor, your voice has been raised.
THE COURT: You have been disrespectful.
MR. KUNSTLER: It is not disrespectful, your Honor.
THE COURT: And sometimes worse than that.
THE WITNESS: O–o–m–m–m–m–m–m–m.
THE COURT: Will you step off the witness stand?
MR. KUNSTLER: He was trying to calm us both down, your Honor.
THE COURT: Oh, no. I needed no calming down. That will be all.

Testimony of Allen Ginsberg Resumed

THE COURT: You have finished your direct? You may cross-examine.

MR. FORAN: Mr. Ginsberg, you were named as kind of the Yippie religious leader. Do you think that is a fair designation of your connection with the Yippie organization?

THE WITNESS: No, because the word "leader" was one we really tried to get away from, to get away from that authoritarian thing. It was more like—

MR. FORAN: Religious teacher?

THE WITNESS: —religious experimenter, or someone who was interested in experimenting with that, and with moving things in that direction.

MR. FORAN: In the context of the Yippie organization?

THE WITNESS: Yes, and also in the context of our whole political life too.

MR. FORAN: And among the others named are Timothy Leary.

THE WITNESS: Yes.

MR. FORAN: And Timothy Leary has a kind of religious concept that he attempts to articulate, doesn't he?

THE WITNESS: Yes, it is a religious concept that has a very ancient tradition in Shivite worship and in American Indian worship services or ceremonies.

MR. FORAN: And one of the parts of that religious concept is the religious experience in the use of hallucinogenic drugs, isn't it, Mr. Ginsberg?

THE WITNESS: In India, in the Shivite sect, they refer to it as *gunga* or *bhang*, which in Latin is *cannabis* and which in the American language is marijuana, or pot, or grass.

MR. FORAN: In the course of his teaching, he makes use of those drugs himself?

THE WITNESS: I think he says that they are part of the legitimate religious meditation and worship exercises.

MR. FORAN: Now when you went out to the Coliseum and you met Abbie Hoffman, you said when you met him you kissed him?

THE WITNESS: Yes.

MR. FORAN: Is he an intimate friend of yours?

THE WITNESS: I felt very intimate with him. I saw he was struggling to manifest a beautiful thing, and I felt very good towards him.

MR. FORAN: And do you consider him an intimate friend of yours?

THE WITNESS: I don't see him that often, but I do see him often enough and have worked with him often enough to feel intimate with him, yes.

MR. FORAN: You feel pretty much an intimate friend of Jerry Rubin's too?

THE WITNESS: Over the years, I have learned from them both.

MR. FORAN: By the way, you were asked on direct examination whether you had seen Jerry Rubin smoke any tobacco.

THE WITNESS: Yes, I said I didn't remember seeing him smoke.

MR. FORAN: Have you seen him smoke anything?

THE WITNESS: No, I don't remember seeing him smoke anything. I don't remember ever seeing him smoke.

MR. FORAN: Anything?

THE WITNESS: Yes.

MR. FORAN: Now, you testified concerning a number of books of poetry that you have written?

THE WITNESS: Yes.

MR. FORAN: In *The Empty Mirror*, there is a poem called "The Night Apple"?

THE WITNESS: Yes.

MR. FORAN: Would you recite that for the jury?

THE WITNESS:

> The Night Apple.
> Last night I dreamed/of one I loved/for seven long years,/but I saw no face,/only the familiar/presence of the body;/sweat skin eyes/feces urine sperm/saliva all one/odor and mortal taste.

[304]

MR. FORAN: Could you explain to the jury what the religious significance of that poem is?

THE WITNESS: If you would take a wet dream as a religious experience, I could. It is a description of a wet dream, sir.

MR. FORAN: Now, I call your attention in that same Government's Exhibit No. 59, to page 14. That has on it the poem, "In Society." Can you recite that poem to the jury?

THE WITNESS: Yes, I will read it.

In Society.

I walked into the cocktail party/room and found three or four queers/talking together in queertalk./I tried to be friendly but heard/myself talking to one in hiptalk./"I'm glad to see you," he said, and/looked away. "Hmn," I mused. The room/was small and had a double-decker/bed in it, and cooking apparatus:/icebox, cabinet, toasters, stove;/the hosts seemed to live with room/enough only for cooking and sleeping./My remark on this score was under-/stood but not appreciated. I was/offered refreshments, which I accepted./ I ate a sandwich of pure meat; an/enormous sandwich of human flesh,/I noticed, while I was chewing on it,/it also included a dirty asshole.

More company came, including a/fluffy female who looked like/a princess. She glared at me and/said immediately: "I don't like you,"/turned her head away, and refused/to be introduced. I said "What!"/in outrage. "Why you shit-faced fool!"/This got everybody's attention./"Why you narcissistic bitch! How/can you decide when you don't even/know me," I continued in a violent/and messianic voice, inspired at/last, dominating the whole room.

Dream 1947.

It is a record, a literal record of a dream, as the other was a literal record of a dream.

MR. FORAN: Can you explain the religious significance of that poetry?

THE WITNESS: Actually, yes.

MR. FORAN: Would you explain it to the jury?

THE WITNESS: Yes. One of the major yogas, or "yoking"—yoga means yoke—is bringing together the conscious mind with the unconscious mind, and is an examination of dream-states in an attempt to recollect dream-states, no matter how difficult they are, no matter how repulsive they are, even if they include hysteria, sandwiches of human flesh, which include dirty assholes, because those are universal images that come in everybody's dreams.

The attempt in yoga is to enlarge consciousness, to be conscious that one's own consciousness will include everything which occurs within the body and the mind.

As part of the practice of poetry, I have always kept records of dreams whenever I have remembered them, and have tried not to censor them so that I would have all the evidence to examine in light of day, so that I would find out who I was unconsciously.

Part of the Zen meditation and part of yoga meditation consists in the objective impersonal examination of the rise and fall and disappearance of thoughts in the mind, all thoughts, whether they be thoughts of sleeping with one's mother, which is universal, or sleeping with one's father, which is also universal thought, or becoming an angel, or flying, or attending a cocktail party and being afraid of being put down, and then getting hysterical.

In other words, the attempt is to reclaim the unconscious, to write down in the light of day what is going on in the deepest meditation of night and dream-state. So it is part of yoga which involves bridging the difference between public, as in this courtroom, and private—subjective public, which is conscious, which we can say to each other in family situations, and private, which is what we know and tell only our deepest friends.

MR. FORAN: Thank you.

You also wrote a book of poems called *Reality Sandwiches*, didn't you?

THE WITNESS: Yes.

MR. FORAN: In there, there is a poem called, "Love Poem on Theme by Whitman." Would you recite that to the jury?

THE WITNESS: "Love Poem on Theme by Whitman," Walt Whitman being one celebrated bard, national prophet. The poem begins with a quotation of a line by Walt Whitman. It begins with Walt Whitman's line:

I'll go into the bedroom silently and lie down between the bridegroom and the bride,/ those bodies fallen from heaven stretched out waiting naked and restless,/arms resting over their eyes in the darkness,/bury my face in their shoulders and breasts, breathing their skin,/ and stroke and kiss neck and mouth and make back be open and known,/legs raised up, crook'd to receive, cock in the darkness driven tormented and attacking/roused up from hole to itching head,/bodies locked shuddering naked, hot lips and buttocks screwed into each other/and eyes, eyes glinting and charming, widening into looks and abandon,/and moans of movement, voices, hands in air, hands between thighs,/ hands in moisture on softened lips, throbbing contraction of bellies/till the white come flow in the swirling sheets/and the bride cry for forgiveness, and the groom be covered with tears of passion and compassion,/and I rise up from the bed replenished with last intimate gestures and kisses of farewell—/all before the mind wakes, behind shades and closed doors in a dark-ened house/where the inhabitants roam unsatisfied in the night,/nude ghosts seeking each other out in the silence.

MR. FORAN: Would you explain the religious significance of that poem?

THE WITNESS: As part of our nature, as part of our human nature we have many loves, many of which are denied, many of which we deny to ourselves. He said that the reclaiming of those loves and the becoming aware of those loves was the only way that this nation could save itself and become a democratic and spiritual republic.

He said that unless there were an infusion of feeling, of tenderness, of fearlessness, of spirituality, of natural sexuality, of natural delight in each other's bodies into the hardened, materialistic, cynical, life denying, clearly competitive, afraid, scared, armored bodies, there would be no chance for spiritual democracy to take place in America. And he de-fined that tenderness between the citizens as, in his words, an adhesiveness, a natural tenderness flowing between all citizens, not only men and women but also a tenderness between men and men as part of our democratic heritage, part of the adhesiveness which would make the democracy function; that men could work together not as competitive beasts but as tender lovers and fellows.

So he projected from his own desire and from his own unconsciousness a sexual urge he felt was normal to the unconscious of most people, though forbidden, for the most part, to take part.

Walt Whitman is one of my spiritual teachers and I am following him in this poem, taking off from a line of his own and projecting my own actual unconscious feeling of which I don't have shame, sir, which I feel are basically charming, actually.

THE COURT: I didn't hear that last word.

THE WITNESS: Charming.

MR. FORAN: I have no further questions.

THE COURT: Redirect examination.

Nothing? You may go, sir.

THE WITNESS: Thank you.

THE COURT: Call your next witness.

Testimony of William S. Styron

MR. KUNSTLER: Would you state your name for the record?

THE WITNESS: My name is William Styron.

MR. KUNSTLER: Mr. Styron, what is your occupation?

THE WITNESS: I am a writer.—I am the author of four novels; the first one, *Lie Down in Darkness*, the second one called *The Long March*, the third, *Set This House on Fire*, and the last called *Confessions of Nat Turner*.

MR. KUNSTLER: Mr. Styron, have you received any awards for your books?

THE WITNESS: I was made a member of the National Institute of Arts and Letters, and I won the Pulitzer Prize last year for the *Confessions of Nat Turner*.

MR. KUNSTLER: Can you indicate to the jury whether you have had any military service?

THE WITNESS: I had mainly general infantry training. Toward the end of World War II, I became a security detachment officer at the United States Naval Disciplinary Barracks at Harts Island, New York, where I was the commanding officer of a battalion of naval prisoners, and where I obtained some training in the control of prisoners and of crowds in general.

MR. KUNSTLER: Now, did any of that training continue during your Korean war service?

MR. SCHULTZ: Objection, if the Court please.

MR. KUNSTLER: Your Honor, I am trying to qualify him as an expert in crowd control. The Government is free to object as to his qualifications, but I have to lay the foundation.

MR. SCHULTZ: Qualifying the witness as an expert in crowd control is wholly immaterial in this case. The case charges these defendants with inciting or conspiring to incite a riot, and an opinion by the witness of what he thinks the police did or didn't do is not material.

MR. KUNSTLER: Your Honor, one of the defenses in this case is that if there were any riots in Chicago during the Convention week, they were caused solely and exclusively by the police. The defense maintains that the police brutalized the crowd, and that, in effect, this trial that is going on here is an attempt by the Government to justify what the police did in the streets of Chicago during Convention week. And I don't think we could present the defense unless we can question a witness who has had considerable experience in crowd control.

THE COURT: I sustain the objection.

MR. KUNSTLER: Now, Mr. Styron, I call your attention to Wednesday, August 28. Can you indicate where you were at approximately five o'clock that day?

THE WITNESS: I went into—I believe it is called the Haymarket Bar of the Conrad Hilton.

MR. KUNSTLER: Now when you went into the Haymarket Bar, what was going on in the vicinity of Michigan and Balbo?

THE WITNESS: There was a thick layer of tear gas overhanging the intersection, which was causing people to scurry for shelter and to take precautions and to wipe their eyes and in general fly from the scene.

MR. KUNSTLER: You also fled from the scene, is that right?

THE WITNESS: I did.

MR. KUNSTLER: When you went into the Haymarket Bar, where did you sit?

THE WITNESS: I sat very near the window which faces on Michigan Avenue. It is a large plateglass window, unobstructed, giving a wide panorama of Michigan Avenue and Grant Park.

MR. KUNSTER: Can you state to the Court and jury what you saw as you watched while you were sitting there?

THE WITNESS: I saw only suddenly a melee, a joining together of these two forces, a battle. I saw policemen battling demonstrators and knocking them off their feet. They were knocked down and were clubbed with great abandon.

MR. KUNSTLER: What else did you see?

THE WITNESS: From where I was sitting I was only able to see a circumscribed part of the action. I saw a young girl of sixteen being clubbed and brought to her feet and eventually knocked down by two very large policemen. And they opened a gash in her head which was bleeding at the moment that they threw her into a wagon.

I saw a similar action on the part of, again, two policemen on a young man who was clubbed to the ground and, like the girl, thrown into a wagon.

MR. KUNSTLER: Did you see, Mr. Styron, what the girl or the young man were doing just prior to being beaten to the ground?

THE WITNESS: From what I could see they were doing nothing. They were merely plucked at random out of the group and beaten to the ground.

MR. SCHULTZ: Objection to the last description of "plucked at random."

MR. KUNSTLER: Your Honor it is a perfectly good English expression.

THE COURT: Well, we ought to expect good English from a writer of a Pulitzer Prize, but I think that—

MR. KUNSTLER: We have got it.

THE COURT: But I think that is an unfortunate use, with apologies to the witness. That is an unfortunate use of the word "plucked." I sustain the objection.

MR. KUNSTLER: Did you see any rocks thrown by demonstrators at the police?

THE WITNESS: I did not.

MR. KUNSTLER: Did you see anything thrown?

THE WITNESS: No, I did not.

MR. KUNSTLER: After you had watched this scene, did anything else occur that you saw?

THE WITNESS: After hearing an enormous crash at the back of the bar of breaking glass, I saw people who had been hurled through the open window being pursued through the bar and into the lobby of the hotel by the police.

MR. KUNSTLER: And did the police you saw enter the bar come through the broken window?

THE WITNESS: They did, so far as I could tell.

MR. KUNSTLER: Did you see any of the people who had been hurled through the plate glass window?

THE WITNESS: I did. I did see several people bleeding, clearly in this case from broken shards of glass. And I saw a young man who had been either stunned or had been thrown through the window with such force that he was limping so badly that he could barely get to a table to sit down.

MR. KUNSTLER: When you saw the line of police on Michigan Avenue, and the crowd come together, can you indicate or state for us whether the police were moving just prior to coming together?

THE WITNESS: Yes, they were.

MR. KUNSTLER: What were the people in the street doing just prior to the police moving?

THE WITNESS: They were arranged in a motionless line on the northern side of Balbo, where Balbo meets Michigan, and across Michigan, and simply maintaining a line.

MR. KUNSTLER: And did you see the police move into the motionless line of demonstrators?

MR. SCHULTZ: Objection.

THE COURT: Yes.

MR. KUNSTLER: Then I have no further questions.

THE COURT: I will sustain the objection.

Cross-examination.

• • • • •

MR. SCHULTZ: When did you write *Confessions of Nat Turner*, by the way?

THE WITNESS: It took me about four, four-and-a-half years, and it was published in 1967.

MR. SCHULTZ: And you got your Pulitzer Prize in 1968?

THE WITNESS: That's right.

MR. SCHULTZ: All right. Now on Wednesday in the Haymarket Lounge, could you smell tear gas?

MR. STYRON: I could smell it very clearly.

MR. SCHULTZ: While you were in the Haymarket Lounge, could you smell something that smelled like vomit?

THE WITNESS: I did not, no.

MR. SCHULTZ: When you were in the Hilton that evening, did you smell what you would describe as a stink bomb?

THE WITNESS: Not that evening. I did smell what I would describe as another bomb, but I do not believe, to the best of my recollection, that it was that evening.

MR. SCHULTZ: Now as to the stink bombs that you did smell, isn't it a fact that to your knowledge there was an attempt to neutralize that smell with an aerosol deodorant, and that was not effective?

MR. STYRON: That is what I been told.

MR. SCHULTZ: It was your understanding that there was an aerosol deodorant used to get rid of the smell?

THE WITNESS: I believe so.

MR. SCHULTZ: Then the smell became worse. It smelled like methane mingled with hairspray, did you say that?

THE WITNESS: Yes, I believe I did say that in one of my flights.

MR. SCHULTZ: Like a beauty parlor over an open sewer. Did it smell like that to you?

THE WITNESS: I am sure I said that. I am not denying it. It had a rather distinct combined odor of the ingredients of a stink bomb with a perfume of some sort which is a strange mingle, I'll tell you. By the time that I smelled the tear gas in the Haymarket Bar, that odor had vanished from the hotel, as it had from other places, but I cannot be one hundred percent sure.

MR. SCHULTZ: All right. Did you hear in the street police officers stating, "Please leave the street. Please leave the street." Did you hear that?

THE WITNESS: I heard nothing from inside the bar, largely because the glass practically makes it a hermetically sealed sort of enclosure. In fact, it made it very surrealistic. I was hearing almost nothing from outside, but seeing a lot.

MR. SCHULTZ: Did you see any bottles thrown?

THE WITNESS: No, I did not.

MR. SCHULTZ: Boards?

THE WITNESS: No, sir. I saw nothing thrown.

MR. SCHULTZ: What about a sewer cap? Did you see a sewer cap?

THE WITNESS: No, sir.

MR. KUNSTLER: I might indicate I don't recollect any evidence about a sewer cap.

MR. SCHULTZ: We haven't put it in yet, but there will be. How many people did you see running through the Haymarket into the lobby? I don't mean policemen; I mean demonstrators or people who were not policemen.

THE WITNESS: My memory is somewhat dim on that, but I would say half a dozen. I am not really sure—certainly half a dozen.

MR. SCHULTZ: That is all, your Honor.

THE COURT: You may go back to wherever you live, Mr. Styron.

Does the Defense have another witness?

Testimony of Richard Clarkston Gregory

December 15, 1969

MR. KUNSTLER: Would you state your full name for the record?
THE WITNESS: Richard Clarkston Gregory.
MR. KUNSTLER: What is your occupation, Mr. Gregory?
THE WITNESS: Comedian, entertainer, author, and lecturer.
MR. KUNSTLER: Now, Mr. Gregory, prior to 1968 had you been involved in any civil rights demonstrations throughout the United States?
MR. FORAN: I object to that, your Honor.
THE COURT: I sustain the objection.
MR. KUNSTLER: Mr. Gregory, were you in Birmingham, Alabama, in June of 1963?
THE WITNESS: Right.
MR. FORAN: Objection.
THE COURT: I sustain the objection.
MR. KUNSTLER: Mr. Gregory, did you participate in the Selma to Montgomery march with Dr. King in 1965?
MR. FORAN: Objection to that.
THE COURT: I sustain the objection.
THE WITNESS: Yes.
MR. KUNSTLER: Mr. Gregory, I am going to show you a letter which has been labelled D-159 for identification and ask you if you can identify this letter.
THE WITNESS: It is a letter I sent to Mayor Daley. It was pertaining to the Democratic Convention being held in Chicago and my feelings that they appointed Chicago for the Democratic Convention—
MR. FORAN: Objection.
THE COURT: I sustain the objection.
MR. KUNSTLER: Your Honor, on January 1, 1968, Mr. Gregory, after learning that Chicago had been selected as a site for the Democratic National Convention, categorized this as "a cruel insult to the millions of deprived citizens."
THE COURT: I have read the letter.
MR. KUNSTLER: And he wrote to the mayor of the city and he made five demands: they have to do with the fair housing laws being enacted, Negroes being appointed to top echelons of the Police Department, lifting the injunction against Dr. King on marching demonstrations in Cicero and other parts of Chicago suburbs, to guarantee the health and safety of Reverend Jesse Jackson, the originator of the Operation Breadbasket, and to ask for higher pay for policemen and firemen in Chicago.

These demands which he made are very crucial to his role later on in the Democratic National Convention. In fact, as he is prepared to testify, he indicated that his participation would be nil if the demands were not met by the mayor of the city of Chicago.
MR. FORAN: Your Honor, Mr. Gregory is not charged by the Government with any violations of the statute set forth in the indictment in this case. His motivation and what he did or did not do is totally irrelevant to the charges against these men.
THE COURT: I will let my ruling sustaining the objection stand.
MR. KUNSTLER: Now, Mr. Gregory, did you have occasion to meet Abbie Hoffman and Jerry Rubin in late January or early February of 1968?
THE WITNESS: Yes, I did.
MR. KUNSTLER: What did you say to Jerry Rubin and Abbie Hoffman, and what did they say to you?
THE WITNESS: They was asking me about participating in an entertainment phase of the Democratic Convention and to contact other entertainers and coordinate a schedule with them, and to participate myself.
MR. KUNSTLER: Did you agree to do this?
THE WITNESS: No, I didn't.

MR. KUNSTLER: What did you state to them with reference to agreeing or not agreeing to participate?

THE WITNESS: I can't tell you what I stated to them if I can't tell you about the letter—

MR. KUNSTLER: State what you stated to them referring to the letter, other than that you had made some demands.

THE WITNESS: I explained to them that some demands had been made. If those demands were not met, I would not participate in nothing here in Chicago at all because it would be like going back on my word pertaining to the issue that we can't talk about.

MR. KUNSTLER: And now, I call your attention to the week of the Democratic National Convention, and specifically to August 27, 1968, in the late evening at approximately 10:00 P.M. of that day. Do you recall where you were then?

THE WITNESS: I had been home all that day until I received a phone call from Abbie Hoffman. He asked me, you know, how come I hadn't been around at none of the demonstrations and none of the rallies, and was I planning on coming to the demonstrations or rallies, and I told him that I was not. Again we are getting into what we can't talk about.

MR. KUNSTLER: Did you consent to appear at that rally?

THE WITNESS: I told him I would be there.

MR. KUNSTLER: Did you entertain at the rally?

THE WITNESS: Yes, I did.

MR. KUNSTLER: Mr. Gregory, I now call your attention to August 28, 1968. Can you state where you were on that date at what place?

THE WITNESS: I was at home. I think at that time I received a phone call from Mr. Dellinger. He was asking me would I participate in some of the nonviolent demonstrations. He said that some members from SCLC was in town; that Reverend Abernathy was in town, and would I object to any of the protest demonstrations. Again I reiterated to Mr. Dellinger that I didn't want to get involved where I could be hit or killed and stir up black folks around the country. Then at that point he asked me, you know, would I come and participate in the rally at Grant Park.

MR. KUNSTLER: Did you agree or refuse?

THE WITNESS: I agreed I would do that, yes.

MR. KUNSTLER: Now did you appear at Grant Park that afternoon?

THE WITNESS: Yes, I did.

MR. KUNSTLER: And did you speak?

THE WITNESS: Yes, I praised the young kids that was participating in the demonstrations and I told them that I had watched all the demonstrations on television and that I would hope that they would not blame the police because the police were only following orders as handed down from Mayor Daley. And that when the Shriners come to town, they can get drunk, do anything they want to do, nobody arrests them. This is the gist of what my speech went on the brief minutes that I talked.

MR. KUNSTLER: Is your recollection exhausted as to what else you might have said at that speech?

THE WITNESS: Right, yes.

MR. KUNSTLER: I wanted to ask you whether you asked or said anything about higher pay for policemen at that speech?

THE WITNESS: Yes, but that's the same thing that's in the letter that we're not supposed to talk about.

MR. KUNSTLER: Mr. Gregory, calling your attention to approximately nine A.M. August 29, 1968, do you know where you were at that time?

THE WITNESS: I was at the Hilton Hotel. Julian Bond and Pierre Salinger came across the street to ask me would I come over, because there was a rally going on.

MR. KUNSTLER: Mr. Gregory, I show you D-164 for identification and ask you if you can indicate what that picture represents.

THE WITNESS: Yes. This is the same rally across the street from the Hilton Hotel in the park. This is after I had introduced Ralph—Dr. Abernathy.

MR. KUNSTLER: Now, Mr. Gregory, did there come a time on August 29, when the rally in Grant Park came to an end?

THE WITNESS: Yes.

MR. KUNSTLER: Approximately what time was that?

THE WITNESS: About four o'clock.

MR. KUNSTLER: Can you describe to the Court and jury what happened at approximately 4:00 P.M.?

THE WITNESS: Well, right going into 4:00 P.M., I was asking Abbie Hoffman had they had any plans for the people in the park, and if not, I would just end the rally, and if so, then let someone from one of their organizations come up and direct the various people in what they wanted them to do.

At that point, the delegation from Wisconsin was marching to the International Amphitheatre, and they sent me a message over and asked me would I announce that they were going to march to the Amphitheatre as a protest to what had happened in the streets the night before.

MR. KUNSTLER: And did you see what Abbie Hoffman did?

THE WITNESS: Well, about that time, the delegation from Wisconsin was very much in evidence. They were marching, and the crowd just left the park and headed to fall in behind the Wisconsin delegation.

MR. KUNSTLER: Now after this moment in time that you have just described, what did you and Abbie Hoffman do, if anything?

THE WITNESS: Well, everybody was following out of the park. I decided that I would go home, and I marched out of the park and was up on the sidewalk going down south on Michigan.

MR. KUNSTLER: Where is your home, by the way?

THE WITNESS: It is 1451 East 55th street.

MR. KUNSTLER: Did you see Abbie Hoffman?

THE WITNESS: Yes. At that point, a tank came around the corner, what I believe to have been a tank, with a machine gun on top, and then Abbie Hoffman just went in and laid in front of the tank, and there were several other young folks that laid down, and at that point I told my wife Lil, "I guess I have to get involved."

MR. KUNSTLER: And what did you do then?

THE WITNESS: I told Abbie, "Look at that machine gun on top of that tank. We have a very dangerous situation, and no one is leading that march at that point. And with a machine gun looking down on people, we could not afford to turn around and walk away, neither he nor I, nor could we afford to lay down in front of the tank." He was laying down in front of the tank with his finger sticking up in the air.

MR. KUNSTLER: I take it the tank stopped?

THE WITNESS: The tank stopped, yes.

MR. KUNSTLER: And what did Abbie say to you?

THE WITNESS: He said, "OK, but understand, I have nothing to do with this once we get to the park. I don't want a leadership position. I don't want them asking me, you know, 'Where are we going from here?'"

MR. KUNSTLER: Would you describe what happened after you got back in Grant Park?

THE WITNESS: Well, I explained to Abbie that "I don't want to come and get involved with your demonstration." As far as I was concerned, that was white folks' business, it was white kids getting chopped by white cops, and it was the first time America was able to see that. But somebody had to stay there because the crowd was upset, the crowd wanted to march. And so I said "Well, I will lead a demonstration to my house."

MR. FORAN: Your Honor, I object to all of this as totally irrelevant.

THE COURT: Yes. I will sustain the objection.

MR. KUNSTLER: Did Abbie Hoffman say to you, "Let's not do that; let's let them run through the Loop. It's a good idea, if they are stood up, that they go and destroy property and run amuck?"

MR. FORAN: I object to that.

THE COURT: I sustain the objection.

MR. KUNSTLER: Mr. Gregory, at any time later that evening did you have occasion to see Mr. Foran, the gentleman who is seated at the counsel table that I am pointing to?

THE WITNESS: Yes, I did.
MR. KUNSTLER: Can you state to the Court and jury where you saw him?
THE WITNESS: At 18th and Michigan.
MR. KUNSTLER: Did you have a conversation with Mr. Foran?
MR. FORAN: I object to that.
THE WITNESS: Yes, I did.

(jury excused)

MR. KUNSTLER: The reason we feel this conversation is important, your Honor, is that Mr. Gregory in his conversation with Mr. Foran, after Mr. Foran asked him "Why don't you have the demonstrators march north instead of south?" Mr. Gregory then said to Mr. Foran, "Do you really want them to go to Lake Shore Drive where you got a great many rich white folks living?"

And then Mr. Foran stated, "OK," in words or substance, "maybe you shouldn't go there."

And then Mr. Gregory said that he was just joking, he really wanted to go to his house.

And we think that is relevant to one of the basic issues in this case, which is the issue of racism.
THE COURT: I know you have spoken of racism throughout this trial. I heard no evidence here that anybody is guilty of racism except one of the defendants who charged me with being a racist with absolutely no basis of fact.
MR. KUNSTLER: He said if your Honor didn't permit him to act as his own attorney you were—
THE COURT: I want this very nice witness to know that I am not, that he has made me laugh often and heartily.
MR. KUNSTLER: Your Honor, white people have always laughed at black people for a long time as entertainers.
THE COURT: I will sustain the objections of the United States Attorney.
MR. KUNSTLER: I have no further questions.
THE COURT: Cross-examination, if any.

• • • • •

MR. FORAN: Mr. Gregory, you mentioned that Abbie Hoffman was lying down in the street out near 18th and Michigan on that afternoon?
THE WITNESS: Right.
MR. FORAN: You said that he had his finger up in the air. What was he doing?
THE WITNESS: Like this (indicating).
MR. FORAN: His middle finger stuck up in the air?
THE WITNESS: Yes.
MR. FORAN: I have no further questions.
THE COURT: Call your next witness, please.

Testimony of Ruth Migdal

MR. WEINGLASS: Will you state your name?

THE WITNESS: My name is Ruth Migdal.

MR. WEINGLASS: Can you tell the Court and jury what is your occupation?

THE WITNESS: I am an artist, and I am Assistant Professor of Art at Malcolm X College.

MR. WEINGLASS: Now, directing your attention to Sunday evening, August 25, 1968, at approximately 10:30 in the evening, where were you?

THE WITNESS: I was in Lincoln Park.

MR. WEINGLASS: Can you indicate to the Court and jury how you were dressed?

THE WITNESS: I was wearing a white coat with an armband and a red cross on it.

MR. WEINGLASS: Did you have with you any medical supplies?

THE WITNESS: Yes, I did. I had bandages and tape.

MR. WEINGLASS: Were you there alone?

THE WITNESS: There were about a dozen medical people standing around. There were more all over the area. The park was full of people, walking around, slowly. It was very peaceful and quiet.

MR. WEINGLASS: Now approximately at 11:30, were you still at the hospital site in the park?

THE WITNESS: Yes.

MR. WEINGLASS: What, if anything, occurred at that point?

THE WITNESS: There was a voice on the loudspeaker telling people that the park was closed, and everyone should leave.

MR. WEINGLASS: What, if anything, did people in the area of the hospital do at that time?

THE WITNESS: We went over to a policeman wearing a suit and told him that we had permission to remain behind.

MR. WEINGLASS: And as that police line advanced, did you advance with it?

THE WITNESS: I followed behind it.

MR. WEINGLASS: Now, as you were following the police line, what occurred?

THE WITNESS: Well, first I saw a line of police being led by an officer, and he was saying, "Hold it. Hold it," and he was losing control. They were pushing past him, and they started beating people on the heads.

MR. WEINGLASS: And what occurred to the crowd when you saw this police line going into the crowd, beating?

THE WITNESS: They started screaming, blood started pouring, and they started falling back.

MR. WEINGLASS: Now just prior to seeing this police line go into the crowd, did you see the crowd throw anything at the police?

THE WITNESS: No, sir.

MR. WEINGLASS: Now did you leave the park subsequently?

THE WITNESS: I was eventually forced out.

MR. WEINGLASS: Was there any medical vehicle in that area at that time?

THE WITNESS: There was one directly across the street from the station wagon. I saw a policeman advance on it with his club raised just as Dr. Braverman ducked into a door and he was missed by a fraction of a second from being hit on the head.

MR. WEINGLASS: When you left that area, where did you go?

THE WITNESS: I went to St. Chrysostom's. It was medical headquarters for the Medical Committee for Human Rights.

MR. WEINGLASS: Directing your attention to Wednesday, August 28, in the early evening, at approximately 7:30 at night, where were you?

THE WITNESS: I was on the northwest corner of Balbo and Michigan. I was wearing a white coat and an armband with a red cross on it.

MR. WEINGLASS: Were you alone?

THE WITNESS: No, I was with a group. I was with a medical team of about nine. We were there as medical presence to give aid to whoever would need it or might need it.

MR. WEINGLASS: Now from where you were standing at approximately 7:30 at that intersection, could you observe what was occurring in the intersection where the two streets met?

THE WITNESS: I saw lots of people, and then I saw the mule train go by. I saw a double line of police come east on Balbo to Michigan.

MR. WEINGLASS: What, if anything, did you see occur with respect to the police line?

THE WITNESS: The police waded into the people and started hitting the ones in front. I saw the people being grabbed and hit on the head with clubs, and I saw them grab the people and throw them into paddy wagons.

MR. WEINGLASS: Now after you saw this police line pass you and go into the crowd, did you leave your location?

THE WITNESS: No, I didn't.

MR. WEINGLASS: Did any of the doctors who were with you leave that location?

THE WITNESS: Yes, they ran across the street. I saw them bandaging heads and pulling people away that had fallen.

MR. WEINGLASS: Now after seeing that, and while you were still standing at the first aid station, what, if anything, occurred in your vicinity?

THE WITNESS: A bus drew up to where I was and stopped. I saw the door open and I saw red-faced, angry, very angry police coming out with their clubs up.

MR. SCHULTZ: Objection to the description.

THE COURT: Yes. "Their faces were red," that, I think, is proper. But "very angry," those words I think are improper to use.

MR. WEINGLASS: Could you describe what you saw?

THE WITNESS: Yes. I saw red-faced, blue-helmeted, blue-shirted or short-sleeve-shirted men, their arms up, a club in one arm, coming out of the bus at full speed chanting, "Kill, kill, kill," and then go across the street, and charge into the crowd and start beating heads. I ran across the street, and I held some heads while Dr. Harper put butterfly bandages on them. They were bleeding badly. And then other doctors or helpers took them away and I ran back to the corner.

MR. WEINGLASS: Now, approximately how many people did you assist in treatment that evening at that corner?

THE WITNESS: At least a dozen.

MR. WEINGLASS: Approximately how long did you stay at this intersection?

THE WITNESS: A few hours until the police started attacking us. They formed a line and they started sweeping west. The line extended across Balbo. They had been doing this from time to time, and we had been talking them out of it by telling them that we were medical presence and had to be there and this was our hospital.

At this point, though, I heard one policeman say, "Get that lady," and as I turned around to run, I felt the tip of a stick hit me. But we just took off and ran.

MR. WEINGLASS: What happened then?

THE WITNESS: I was on Wabash, and we crossed the street and walked on the east side of Wabash heading north. I was with a large group of medical personnel and a minister. I was with Dr. A. Braverman, for one.

MR. WEINGLASS: Then what did you do?

THE WITNESS: We turned south, at which point we were stopped by another policeman. The policeman asked the minister, "What denomination are you?" and he said, "I am a Lutheran." And he said, "That is as bad as being a black Jew," and we all sort of told each other to be quiet, and we kept on going.

MR. WEINGLASS: Where did you go?

THE WITNESS: I went home.

MR. WEINGLASS: Now, Mrs. Migdal, are you a member of the National Committee to End the War in Vietnam?

THE WITNESS: No.

MR. WEINGLASS: On August 25 or August 28, did you know any of the defendants seated at this table?

THE WITNESS: No.
MR. WEINGLASS: No further questions.
THE COURT: Cross-examination?

• • • • •

MR. SCHULTZ: Now, isn't it a fact that prior to your participation during the week of the Democratic National Convention, you had attended meetings of the National Mobilization Committee in the Chicago area?
THE WITNESS: Yes.
MR. SCHULTZ: When you were standing at the intersection of Balbo and Michigan or near the intersection of Balbo and Michigan, did you see demonstrators hitting at policemen?
THE WITNESS: No, I did not.
MR. SCHULTZ: Did you see demonstrators throwing anything at policemen?
THE WITNESS: No.
MR. SCHULTZ: You didn't hear any obscenities by demonstrators either, did you?
THE WITNESS: You know, I don't know what you mean by obscenities anymore.
MR. SCHULTZ: No further questions.
THE COURT: You may go.

Testimony of Angus MacKenzie

MR. WEINGLASS: Would you please state your full name?

THE WITNESS: Angus MacKenzie.

MR. WEINGLASS: What is your occupation?

THE WITNESS: I am working on a newspaper, *The People's Dreadnaught,* in Birmingham, Alabama.

MR. WEINGLASS: Mr. MacKenzie, directing your attention to August of 1968, will you indicate to the Court and jury what your age was at that time?

THE WITNESS: I was seventeen.

MR. WEINGLASS: How old are you now?

THE WITNESS: Eighteen.

MR. WEINGLASS: Now, directing your attention to Wednesday, which would be August 28, do you recall where you were on that day in the early afternoon?

THE WITNESS: Yes, I was in Grant Park. I was near the edge of the crowd close to the flagpole.

MR. WEINGLASS: After you got into the park, just as you arrived, what did you do?

THE WITNESS: I went over toward the flagpole.

MR. WEINGLASS: When you got to the flagpole, what did you do?

THE WITNESS: I climbed up on the support columns on the flagpole. I reached up to the cleat that is on the flagpole where I untied it, at half-mast.

MR. WEINGLASS: After lowering the flag to half-mast what did you do?

THE WITNESS: I retied the line around the cleat and climbed off the support columns.

MR. WEINGLASS: Now, can you explain to the Court and jury why at that particular time, you lowered the American flag to half-mast?

THE WITNESS: They killed democracy.

MR. WEINGLASS: When, Mr. MacKenzie, did it occur to you to lower the flag to half-mast?

THE WITNESS: About two minutes before.

MR. FORAN: Objection.

THE COURT: Sustained.

MR. WEINGLASS: Prior to that day, during that day up to this point in time, had you met any of these seven defendants who are seated around the table?

THE WITNESS: No.

MR. WEINGLASS: Had you talked to them?

THE WITNESS: No.

MR. WEINGLASS: Did you hear any sound as you were lowering the flag to half mast?

THE WITNESS: Yes. There was quite a bit of commotion. There were many people yelling different things, yelling, "Take it down," "Half-mast." There was a great deal of confusion.

MR. WEINGLASS: Now after you jumped off the supporting poles, what happened to you?

THE WITNESS: I was grabbed from behind by a man in a white shirt, and I was hit and beaten.

MR. WEINGLASS: Did that man ever identify himself?

THE WITNESS: No.

MR. WEINGLASS: And did other persons then come into the area where you and this man were?

THE WITNESS: Yes. Police officers.

MR. WEINGLASS: What happened after the police came into the area where you were struggling with this other man?

THE WITNESS: They grabbed me, they beat me, they lifted me off the ground and dumped me on the ground, they hit me on the head with their clubs and on the body. Yes, I was bleeding quite profusely.

MR. WEINGLASS: Did that injury require medical treatment?

THE WITNESS: My whole body was X-rayed as well as my head was sewn up, I believe, with five or seven stitches, and I still have a scar, a lump.

MR. WEINGLASS: Now after you were hit on the head as you have described and beaten, what occurred to you that you can remember?

THE WITNESS: I was led away by a detective who was screaming at me in a rage, telling me that he wanted to kill me, using profanity, he wanted to kill me. "Motherfucker," he said, and then the policemen threw me in a car there.

MR. WEINGLASS: Did you remain in that car?

THE WITNESS: No, they moved me.

MR. WEINGLASS: And what if anything occurred to you in the process of being moved?

THE WITNESS: I was choked by the neck. An officer hit me several times in the mouth with his helmet like that (indicating), causing my mouth and lip to be bloody and swell up. They drove me to Central Detention.

MR. WEINGLASS: While you were in Central Detention, what if anything happened?

THE WITNESS: I asked to make a phone call.

MR. FORAN: I object to that your honor.

THE COURT: Sustain the objection.

THE WITNESS: And they hit me for that.

MR. WEINGLASS: Mr. MacKenzie, I show you D-172 for identification, and I ask you if you can identify that photograph for the jury.

THE WITNESS: It is a picture of the flag at half-mast as I left it.

MR. WEINGLASS: Now, Mr. MacKenzie, at the time you were struck in the face with a helmet, were your hands free or were they manacled?

THE WITNESS: They were manacled.

MR. WEINGLASS: In moving the American flag to half-mast, which is a position of mourning, did you intend any disrespect?

THE WITNESS: None at all; the highest respect.

MR. FORAN: I object.

THE COURT: I sustain the objection.

MR. WEINGLASS: Was it your personal opinion and your personal view that this was a time for national mourning?

THE WITNESS: Yes.

MR. FORAN: Objection, your Honor.

THE COURT: I sustain the objection.

MR. WEINGLASS: No further question.

THE COURT: Cross-examination.

• • • • •

MR. FORAN: While you were there at the base of the flagpole and the police came in to take you into custody, Mr. MacKenzie, did any plastic bag full of liquid come in there and hit anybody? Did you see anybody with spots on their shirts?

THE WITNESS: Myself; blood.

MR. FORAN: Did you see anybody with spots of blue or yellow or red liquid on their shirts from plastic bags full of liquid?

THE WITNESS: When you are being beaten up, you are not watching for spots on people's shirts.

MR. FORAN: Now did you see anyone strike the police officers with a sign at the base of the flagpole?

THE WITNESS: No.

MR. FORAN: Did you hear anyone shouting, "Get the pigs. Get the pigs. Kill the pigs." Did you hear anyone shouting that?

THE WITNESS: No, not that I could remember. Not that I heard.

MR. FORAN: Did you see anybody spitting on the policemen?

THE WITNESS: No.

MR. FORAN: Did you see anybody jump on the policemen who were trying to get you out of there and wrestle with them?

THE WITNESS: Nobody did.

MR. FORAN: Did you hear a lot of people shouting obscenities at the police as they were leading you away?

THE WITNESS: Well, like I told you, the detective did. I don't know about the crowd.

MR. FORAN: You didn't answer the question. Did you hear it?

THE WITNESS: I heard the detective say to me that he wanted to kill me.

MR. FORAN: Did you hear anybody in the crowd shouting obscenities at the police?

THE WITNESS: No. They might have, but I didn't hear it. I was being hit, and I didn't hear it.

MR. FORAN: I have no further questions.

Testimony of Linda Hager Morse

December 16, 1969

THE COURT: Call your next witness, please.

MR. KUNSTLER: Would you state your full name?

THE WITNESS: Linda Hager Morse.

MR. KUNSTLER: Can you indicate something of your background and education?

THE WITNESS: I was born in Philadelphia, Pennsylvania. I went to high school there. While in high school I was a Merit Scholarship semifinalist. I won the Juvenile Decency Award from the Kiwanis Club, one of thirteen high school students in Philadelphia that year. I went to the University of New Hampshire after graduating from high school. Then I left college and went back to Philadelphia and worked for several years in a community organizing project for a nonviolent pacifist group. Then I went to New York City and started working for the Fifth Avenue Vietnam Peace Parade Committee in 1965.

MR. KUNSTLER: Now, Miss Morse, I call your attention to July 25, 1968, and particularly in the area of 8:00 P.M. of that day, and ask you to tell the Court and jury if you can recall where you were.

THE WITNESS: I was at the Hotel Diplomat in New York City.

MR. KUNSTLER: And at that time, what was going on?

THE WITNESS: The Parade Committee, for which I worked at that point, had organized a public meeting. The speakers included Mrs. Cora Weiss, Mrs. Beulah Sanders and Mr. Tom Hayden.

MR. KUNSTLER: What did Mr. Hayden say as you recall it?

THE WITNESS: He went through a whole analysis of United States policy in Vietnam starting out with the reasons for President Johnson's March 31 speech. He said that CBS had sent a reporter to North Vietnam to interview the North Vietnamese and the reporter learned that the North Vietnamese were about to make a major concession to the United States with regard to peace talks.

So the reporter sent back word to President Johnson that this was to occur and because of the crisis at home, because of the growing antiwar movement, because of the crisis with the dollar, and because of the crisis internationally with countries being opposed to United States policy against the war, President Johnson felt that he had to make some move to undercut the upcoming North Vietnamese move. So he made his March 31 speech where he withdrew from the race and where he called for a partial deescalation of bombing.

Tom said that this would be a seeming concession to peace to the United States people and to the Vietnamese and to the world, but that in reality it would enable the United States which was short on bomber pilots, short on planes and short on bombs at that point to concentrate its energies on the bombing of one section.

Then Mr. Hayden went into a whole long discussion of what the Vietnamese were feeling at this point to the effect, in essence, that the Vietnamese felt that they had won the war militarily and politically and that it was a matter that there was nothing to negotiate except for the easiest way for the United States to withdraw from Vietnam, and that these phony "concessions" would not do any good, and that the Vietnamese just felt that they had to continue, you know, keeping up the pressure, continue fighting and— until the Americans got out.

At that point he said that the United States had only two alternatives, you know, since it couldn't win militarily by conventional means: it had either the alternative of withdrawing or of genocide. He stated that this was a different form of colonialism nowadays, and that Vietnam would be as useful to the United States with no people in it as it would be populated by the Vietnamese, and that the United States could afford to kill off the Vietnamese.

Tom said that he thought that the United States was seriously considering nuclear weapons in Vietnam and that one nuclear bomb placed in the right place would destroy

[320]

three million Vietnamese people, and that he didn't think they could stand up under that; that they had done fantastically in standing up under the bombing and the troops so far, but that they couldn't stand up under that, and that was a real alternative to the United States at this point: it could bomb Vietnam into a dust heap. Therefore, it was the duty of every American to protest, you know, what was happening by any means possible, because it was going to be genocide in Vietnam in a short period of time otherwise.

MR. KUNSTLER: Did he explain how he had gotten some of the information about the Vietnamese?

THE WITNESS: He had just returned from Paris a week or two before that where he had been negotiating the release of three American prisoners of war, and he had successfully negotiated that release. He had spoken to both Harriman and to the North Vietnamese in Paris.

MR. KUNSTLER: In the speech was there any mention made of the forthcoming Democratic National Convention?

THE WITNESS: Yes. It was mentioned in two sentences. It was something like, you know, "we must protest the war whenever possible, you know, on our campuses, in the streets of Chicago," you know, so forth and so on.

MR. KUNSTLER: Calling your attention to Friday, August 23, do you know what you did on that particular day?

THE WITNESS: I went down to the Mobilization office and met Dave Dellinger down there.

MR. KUNSTLER: Will you state to the Court and jury what you said to Dave Dellinger, and what he said to you?

THE WITNESS: He asked me to come with him for a permit negotiation meeting, and the reason for that was they had just learned that the courts had overturned an injunction that the Mobilization had put into the court asking for permits, and therefore there were no permits for the upcoming march the next week. And so, David asked me to come along, because I had had a lot of experience in negotiating for permits, for this emergency meeting down at City Hall where they were going to ask to see Mayor Daley.

MR. KUNSTLER: As a result of this conversation, did you and Mr. Dellinger do anything?

THE WITNESS: Yes. We went down to City Hall. We went into an anteroom or waiting room outside of the mayor's offices and sat around for quite a long time asking to see Mayor Daley. There were press people down there with us from various TV stations and newspapers who had followed us down there. Finally, a man came out, a city official, and spoke to us and said that Mayor Daley would not see us and that the matter was closed at this point.

So that was the end of that.

MR. KUNSTLER: Now, I call your attention to Sunday, August 25, approximately 10:30, in Lincoln Park. Can you describe the scene when you arrived?

THE WITNESS: Some people were sitting around, singing or talking, other people were walking around. It was just kind of an ordinary park scene with a little bit of excitement.

MR. KUNSTLER: Did there come a time when you saw some policemen in the park?

THE WITNESS: Oh, yes. There was a little house in the middle of the park, and at one point a group of policemen moved in front of the house, and stood with their backs up against the house, just standing there in formation.

I went over with a group of people to see what they were doing, and there was some chanting and stuff at them. I thought it was funny—we were teasing—

MR. KUNSTLER: Did you see anything thrown?

THE WITNESS: No.

MR. KUNSTLER: Did you see Jerry Rubin at all at this time?

THE WITNESS: No.

MR. KUNSTLER: Do you know Jerry Rubin?

THE WITNESS: Yes, I have known him since 1967.

MR. KUNSTLER: Now, Miss Morse, I call your attention to Wednesday, August 28, and particularly to the time between 12:30 and 1:00 P.M. Do you know where you were then?

THE WITNESS: That is the time that I arrived at Grant Park, the Bandshell.

MR. KUNSTLER: What happened after that?

THE WITNESS: I went with the people who were going to march.

MR. KUNSTLER: Can you tell the Court and jury where, if any place, the line moved to?

THE WITNESS: It moved about a block and a half or two blocks, and then we were stopped by policemen, a large group of them.

MR. KUNSTLER: After the march had been stopped by the police what happened to the demonstrators?

THE WITNESS: People got up slowly at first in small groups, couples, you know, twos and threes, and walked away from the march and across the first park toward the bridges to get across to the second park to the Hilton.

MR. KUNSTLER: Now, did you do this yourself?

THE WITNESS: I went through the first park and came up to the first bridge. It was blocked off by National Guardsmen, and I got very frightened because we were trapped.

MR. SCHULTZ: Objection, if the Court please.

THE COURT: "I got very frightened"—those words may go out and the jury is directed to disregard them.

MR. KUNSTLER: Did you have a conversation with Dave Dellinger?

THE WITNESS: Yes, I did. I told him that I was afraid that we were encircled by the National Guardsmen and the police, and that if we attempted to march that we would be beaten and arrested, and that I thought that it was too great a risk, and we had to call off the march and go back in front of the Conrad Hilton where I thought we would be safe.

MR. KUNSTLER: Did Dave Dellinger respond to the suggestion?

THE WITNESS: He told me that he felt we had to try to march; that Vietnamese and GI's were dying and this was least we could do, was to attempt to protest the war, and we had to follow through with it.

MR. KUNSTLER: Did you cross over the first bridge?

THE WITNESS: There was a row of Guardsmen in front and some trucks behind them and they were standing there with guns and tear gas masks, and one of the trucks had some weird kind of gun mounted on it. I don't know whether it was a machine gun or to shoot tear gas or what.

MR. KUNSTLER: When you couldn't get across the first bridge, what did you do?

THE WITNESS: Went up to the second bridge which was further north, I guess. We started to trot at this point and we came up to the bridge and the Guardsmen saw us coming and they shot tear gas at us. After that tear gassing we had to go and wash our eyes out in a fountain because it was really bad. Then we ran up to the last bridge, you know, and just made it across the last bridge as a group of Guardsmen were coming up.

MR. KUNSTLER: Where did you go?

THE WITNESS: We ran across the park and then back down that big street towards the Conrad Hilton. It was dark or late dusk by this time and there were really brilliant lights shining on the crowd and people were chanting. I remember hearing, "The whole world is watching. The whole world is watching. Flash your lights. Flash your lights."

They were referring to the buildings and asking people in the buildings who were watching if they were sympathetic to us to flash their lights and there were lots of lights flashing. And people were standing around in that area and sitting on the side resting.

MR. KUNSTLER: Then what did you do yourself?

THE WITNESS: I sat there for a little while and I was exhausted and frightened and I just went home after that.

MR. KUNSTLER: I show you D-112 for identification and ask you if you can identify what is in that picture.

THE WITNESS: Yes, this is one of the bridges with Guardsmen blocking it off. And they have guns.

MR. KUNSTLER: Did you see any of that equipment before?

THE WITNESS: Yes, that gun.

MR. KUNSTLER: What type of gun is that?

THE WITNESS: Machine gun is what it looks like to me.

MR. KUNSTLER: I have no further questions, your Honor.

· · · · ·

MR. SCHULTZ: You saw one of the machine guns in the picture; you don't know what caliber it is, do you?

THE WITNESS: No.

MR. SCHULTZ: You practice shooting an M-1 yourself, don't you?

THE WITNESS: Yes, I do.

MR. SCHULTZ: You also practice karate, don't you?

THE WITNESS: Yes, I do.

MR. SCHULTZ: That is for the revolution, isn't it?

THE WITNESS: After Chicago I changed from being a pacifist to the realization we had to defend ourselves. A nonviolent revolution was impossible. I desperately wish it was possible.

MR. SCHULTZ: And the only way you can change this country, is it not, is by a violent revolution, isn't that your thought?

THE WITNESS: I believe we have to have a revolution that changes the society into a good society, and to a society that meets the ideals that the country was founded on years ago which it hasn't met since then, and I think that we have the right to defend ourselves. The Minutemen in New York City were arrested with bazookas. Housewives in suburban areas have guns.

MR. SCHULTZ: And the way you are going to change this country is by violent revolution, isn't that right, Miss Morse?

THE WITNESS: The way we are going to change the country is by political revolution, sir.

MR. SCHULTZ: Miss Morse, isn't it a fact that in your opinion, there is no alternative but revolution?

THE WITNESS: Yes.

MR. SCHULTZ: And is it a fact that you believe that the revolution will be gradual, and you and your people will gain control of the cities of the United States just like the guerrillas of the National Liberation Front are gaining control of the cities in Vietnam?

THE WITNESS: I believe that the people of the United States will regain control of their own cities just like the Vietnamese people are regaining control of their country.

MR. SCHULTZ: Isn't it a fact that you believe that the United States Government will control sections of its cities while the fighting rages in other sections of the cities not controlled by the Government of the United States?

THE WITNESS: The Government of the United States has lost its credibility today; there is fighting going on in cities in this country today. People's Park in Berkeley, the policemen shot at us when people were unarmed, were fighting with rocks, the policemen used double-buckshot and rifles and pistols against unarmed demonstrators.

That is fighting. OK. People are fighting to regain their liberty, fighting to regain their freedom, fighting for a totally different society, people in the black community, people in the Puerto Rican community, people in the Mexican-American community and people in the white communities. They are fighting by political means as well as defending themselves.

MR. SCHULTZ: Your Honor, I move to strike that as nonresponsive.

MR. KUNSTLER: Your Honor, they are intensely political questions and she is trying to give a political answer to a political question.

THE COURT: This is not a political case as far as I am concerned. This is a criminal case. I can't go into politics here in this court.

MR. KUNSTLER: Your Honor, Jesus was accused criminally, too, and we understand really that was not truly a criminal case in the sense that it is just an ordinary—

THE COURT: I didn't live at that time. I don't know. Some people think I go back that far, but I really didn't.

MR. KUNSTLER: Well, I was assuming your Honor had read of the incident.

THE COURT: We are dealing with a cross-examination of a witness, and I direct you to answer the question.

MR. SCHULTZ: Gradually the Government of the United States will be taken over by this revolution?

THE WITNESS: Yes.

MR. SCHULTZ: And that your ultimate goal is to create a nation with this revolutionary party?

THE WITNESS: Revolutionary party? My ultimate goal is to create a society that is a free society; that is a joyous society where everyone is fed, where everyone is educated, where everyone has a job, where everyone has a chance to express himself artistically or politically, or spiritually, or religiously.

MR. SCHULTZ: With regard to the revolution that we are talking about, you are prepared, aren't you, both to die and to kill for it, isn't that right?

THE WITNESS: Yes, in self-defense.

MR. SCHULTZ: And further, because the educational system is so rotten, that if you cannot change it you will attempt to totally destroy it in the United States, isn't that right?

THE WITNESS: The educational system in the United States right now is destroying millions of people in Vietnam and around the world. The aerosol bombs that are used in Vietnam, or are being prepared to be used in Vietnam for CBW warfare were prepared right in Berkeley, California, where I live, and the educational system in the country is used currently to destroy people, not to create life. I believe we have to stop the murder of people around the world and in the United States and when the educational system of this country participates in it technologically, yes, we have to put our bodies in the way and stop that process.

MR. SCHULTZ: That is part of the reason why you are learning how to shoot your M-1 rifle?

THE WITNESS: I am learning how to shoot my M-1 rifle for two reasons, sir. One of them is to protect myself from situations that I was in in Berkeley some time back where I was grabbed by two young men and taken off to the hills and molested, and housewives all over the country have guns in their houses for that very purpose. The other thing is the fact that every time I walk on the street in Berkeley and pass a police car, the policemen look out their windows and make snide comments and say, "Hi, Linda, how are you doing? You better watch out. Hi, Linda, you better be careful," and it seems like every single policeman in Berkeley knows who I am, and when policemen start doing things like what they have been doing lately, killing Fred Hampton, attacking the Black Panther office in Los Angeles, shooting people in People's Park and in Chicago, then I believe we have the right to defend ourselves.

MR. SCHULTZ: One of the reasons further for your revolution is your opposition to capitalism and imperialism, isn't that right?

THE WITNESS: That's right.

MR. SCHULTZ: And the more you realize our system is sick, the more you want to tear it limb to limb, isn't that right?

THE WITNESS: The more that I see the horrors that are perpetrated by this Government, the more that I read about things like troop trains full of nerve gas traveling across the country where one accident could wipe out thousands and thousands of people, the more that I see things like companies just pouring waste into lakes and into rivers and just destroying them, the more I see things like the oil fields in the ocean off Santa Barbara coast where the Secretary of the Interior and the oil companies got together and agreed to continue producing oil from those offshore oil fields and ruined a whole section of the coast; the more I see things like an educational system which teaches black people and Puerto Rican people and Mexican-Americans that they are only fit to be domestics and dishwashers, if that; the more that I see a system that teaches middle class whites like me that we are supposed to be technological brains to continue producing CBW warfare, to continue working on computers and things like that to learn how to kill people better, to learn how to control people better, yes, the more I want to see that system torn down and replaced by a totally different one, one that cares about people learning; that cares about children being fed breakfast before they go to school; one that cares about people learning real things, one that cares about people going to college for free; one that cares about people living adult lives that are responsible, fulfilled adult lives, not just drudgery, day after day after day of going to a job; one that gives people a chance to express themselves artistically and politically, and religiously and philosophically. That is the kind of system I want to see in its stead.

MR. SCHULTZ: Now, isn't it a fact, Miss Morse, that your learning your karate and your other skill is to use these skills in revolutionary guerrilla warfare on the streets of the American cities?

THE WITNESS: I still don't know whether I could ever kill anyone, Mr. Schultz. I haven't reached that point yet.

MR. SCHULTZ: I have no further questions on the examination.

THE COURT: All right. Does the defense want to conduct a redirect examination?

MR. KUNSTLER: Can you state to the jury what your views were about the United States and the world prior to the Democratic National Convention in 1968?

THE WITNESS: Prior to the Democratic Convention I had believed that the United States system had to be changed, but the way to bring about that change was through non-violent means, through nonviolent action, and through political organizing. I felt that we could reach policemen, that we could reach the Government of the United States by holding nonviolent sit-ins and nonviolent demonstrations, by putting our bodies on the line and allowing ourselves to be beaten if they chose to do that.

MR. KUNSTLER: Can you explain to the jury why your attitude toward your country and the world changed because of the Democratic Convention week?

THE WITNESS: The specific things that made me change my attitude were the actions on Mayor Daley's part in refusing to give us permits, in violating completely as far as I was concerned, the Constitution which allows you the right to march and demonstrate, the actions on the part of the policemen and some of the National Guardsmen in beating demonstrators horribly, and what I saw on television of what was going on inside the Convention which convinced me that the democratic process, political process, had fallen apart; that the police state that existed outside the Convention also existed inside the Convention and that nonviolent methods would not work to change that; that we had to defend ourselves or we would be wiped out.

MR. KUNSTLER: By the way, how old are you?

THE WITNESS: Twenty-six years old. Just twenty-six.

MR. KUNSTLER: That is all.

THE COURT: Please call your next witness.

Testimony of Thomas W. Pew, Jr.

December 17, 1969

MR. KUNSTLER: Would you state your full name, please?

THE WITNESS: Thomas W. Pew, Jr.

MR. KUNSTLER: What is your occupation?

THE WITNESS: I am editor and publisher of the *Troy Daily News* in Troy, Ohio.

MR. KUNSTLER: Mr. Pew, were you in Chicago during Convention week of 1968?

THE WITNESS: Yes. I came here to cover the Convention, both photographically and also to write stories. I was an accredited news reporter, accredited to attend all the Convention events.

MR. KUNSTLER: I call your attention to August 28, 1968, at approximately three o'clock in the afternoon of that day. Do you know where you were?

THE WITNESS: Yes, I was in Grant Park.

MR. KUNSTLER: Did you have your press credentials with you?

THE WITNESS: Yes, I had them around my neck. They were those electronic cards. It was the most highly regarded credentials that you could have.

MR. KUNSTLER: Did there come a time when you left that area?

THE WITNESS: I walked up Columbus Avenue in the direction of the Museum, through the park. I went to the first bridge out of the park which was blocked by the National Guardsmen, and then I went to the second bridge and I stayed there for quite some time taking photographs and interviewing people.

MR. KUNSTLER: What was going on at the bridge when you arrived?

THE WITNESS: The National Guard troops were lined up and they were preventing anybody from leaving the park.

MR. KUNSTLER: Did you watch any of the automobiles being stopped?

THE WITNESS: Yes, I did.

MR. KUNSTLER: Can you describe what went on when the automobiles were stopped?

THE WITNESS: Yes, I can. When the crowd would move close to this line of National Guardsmen, they would frequently use tear gas to move them back, and some people had been pretty severely gassed, and some of the people coming through the park in their cars had agreed to take the people that had been gassed out of the park in their cars and across the bridge. The National Guard, when a car would come up that would have anybody in it who didn't appear to be an ordinary passenger in the car, they would stop that car and force the person to get rid of their passengers. Sometimes they would let the car through, and sometimes they wouldn't let the car through. Sometimes they would make the car turn around and go back out in the other direction.

MR. KUNSTLER: Did there come a time, Mr. Pew, when you were gassed?

THE WITNESS: Yes, there did. I was kneeling down and I had my camera up to my face and I heard something land between my legs, but I didn't pay any attention to it, and I took a picture. At that point I saw some sort of explosion against my legs, and when I took the camera down from my face, I was enveloped in a cloud of tear gas. My leg was actually wet with whatever material was in this cannister or grenade, and I was completely blinded at that point.

I started staggering away trying to open my eyes to see which direction I was going, and at that point a couple of people, whom I couldn't see, came up and grabbed me and they took my camera off my neck and my camera bag off my neck. They took me by the arms and started leading me. They took me to the fountain that is just off the lake from that bridge and they washed my face off in the fountain.

When I finally got my eyes open, there was a young man standing there with my camera and my camera bag with my spare lenses and he handed them over to me and I sat down on the grass. I was having some difficulty breathing. The gas seemed to stir up a

[326]

lot of liquid in my head and nose and mouth, so I stayed there for maybe twenty minutes or twenty-five minutes, catching my breath.

MR. KUNSTLER: After you were at the fountain and after you were able to move again, where did you go?

THE WITNESS: I headed down the street to try to get in the entrance of the Hilton to buy film and I walked down the street towards that entrance on the south side of Balbo.

MR. KUNSTLER: Is that the entrance with the revolving door?

THE WITNESS: Yes. There is a small foyer and then a revolving door.

MR. KUNSTLER: Did you enter that revolving door that night?

THE WITNESS: No. When I got to the foyer I looked through the door and I saw that inside the hotel there were a lot of people, that something appeared to have happened to them, their clothes were torn and they were sort of disheveled looking, and there were also police in there on the other side of the door. There were maybe three or four uniformed policemen there and they had hold of these people inside the hotel.

MR. KUNSTLER: What else did you see?

THE WITNESS: As I approached the door they were rushing this one young man toward the door and they were going to eject him but when they got him—

MR. KUNSTLER: Can you describe him?

THE WITNESS: Yes. He was a tall sort of gangly fellow with long hair and dressed casually.

MR. KUNSTLER: How old would you say he was?

THE WITNESS: I would say he was under twenty-five. This policeman in a uniform who was inside the hotel, pushed him into the door, and he was pushing the door around toward me, but before he could get the door all the way around, the policeman inside the hotel stopped the door with his foot and then another policeman who was in the foyer stopped it with his foot on the other side, leaving the man in the little space there with a small crack facing out.

MR. KUNSTLER: Then what happened?

THE WITNESS: Then the policeman in the foyer began clubbing this man in this little area where he was trapped behind the glass. The fellow sort of struggled, but in the space there was really no place to go. He tried to back up, and then the policeman would hit him in the chest, and then he would cover his head and then he would beat him on the back of the neck, and he just kept beating him. I would say he hit him twenty-five, thirty times. He just kept beating him through this crack.

Next to me in the foyer there was a young girl. I would say that she was about thirteen, very welldressed, and she began screaming in a sort of pulsating, inhaling and exhaling scream. It was just like a solid sound. I just stood there watching, watching the policeman and I wanted to do something to try and stop the beating, but I just stood there. He kept beating him and the fellow fell down in a heap inside the doorway, and the policeman still continued to beat him. After the policeman stopped beating him, the two policemen on the other side of the door took their feet away and then they revolved the door the rest of the way around, sort of ejecting the man. Then they laid him on his back in the foyer. He showed no signs of life at all at that point. He was completely limp, and policeman who had done the beating stretched him out there. This girl continued to scream, and at that point, at that point I just wanted to do something about what was happening.

MR. SCHULTZ: Objection.

THE COURT: "At that point I just wanted to do something," those words may go out and the jury is directed to disregard them.

MR. KUNSTLER: Now, Mr. Pew, did there come a time when you reported what you had seen to anyone?

THE WITNESS: I wrote a letter to the mayor of Chicago. I sent copies of the letter to the commission that was investigating crime and violence in the United States, and I sent copies of the letter to my senator, Senator Steven Young of Ohio, and I also contacted my congressman, William McCullough, who was also on the crime commission.

MR. KUNSTLER: Of all these people to whom you sent letters and copies of your articles, did you ever hear from any of them?

MR. SCHULTZ: Objection.
THE COURT: I sustain the objection.
MR. KUNSTLER: No further questions.

 • • • • •

MR. SCHULTZ: You did not contact the Federal Bureau of Investigation, did you?
THE WITNESS: No, sir.
MR. SCHULTZ: Did you know that the Federal Bureau of Investigation was conducting an investigation into any alleged police brutality during the Democratic National Convention?
THE WITNESS: I knew the crime commission was.
MR. SCHULTZ: No, no, the Federal Bureau of Investigation of the United States Department of Justice.
THE WITNESS: No, I don't believe I did know that.
MR. SCHULTZ: Do you know whether or not as a result of that investigation any policemen were indicted for acts of violence and brutality during the Democratic National Convention?
THE WITNESS: I believe some were.
MR. SCHULTZ: Do you know whether or not any of the individual policemen whom you saw commit acts of brutality, were or were not indicted by the Federal grand jury?
THE WITNESS: I do not.
MR. SCHULTZ: That is all, your Honor.
THE COURT: Redirect examination?
MR. KUNSTLER: Mr. Pew, after you sent your letter to Mayor Daley on September 25, 1968, do you know whether he sent it to the FBI?
MR. SCHULTZ: Objection.
THE COURT: I sustain the objection.
MR. KUNSTLER: Now, did any FBI officer ever contact you?
THE WITNESS: No.
MR. KUNSTLER: Just one last question. Mr. Pew, do you know whether any Chicago officials, officials of the City of Chicago, or any officials of the Democratic party have been indicted for conspiracy to promote a police riot?
MR. SCHULTZ: Objection.
THE COURT: I sustain the objection.
MR. KUNSTLER: I have no further questions.
THE COURT: You may step down, sir.

Grant Park, Wednesday. A bloody shirt is raised in place of the American flag. (See page 232.)

(Top) Police charge the rally at the Grant Park Bandshell on Wednesday afternoon. "The left foot is advanced forward at the same time the baton is thrust forward, the baton is withdrawn, the right foot is brought up, the baton is brought back." (See page 230.) Photo: Magnum Photos, Inc.

(Bottom left) Defense Exhibit 164. Reverend Ralph Abernathy speaks in Grant Park on Thursday. To the left is Dick Gregory. (See page 311.) (Fred De Van) LIFE Magazine © Time, Inc.

(Bottom right) Defense exhibit 112. Guardsmen block off exits from Grant Park after rally on Wednesday. Mr. Schultz cross-examines Linda Morse: "You saw one of the machine guns in the picture. You don't know what caliber it is, do you?" "No." "You practice shooting an M-1 yourself, don't you?" (See page 323.)

(Top) Two of the notes scrawled by Bobby Seale while gagged and shackled to his chair. The first was submitted into evidence as Defense Exhibit 84. (See page 170.)

(Bottom left) The barricade in Lincoln Park on Monday night. "The crowd moved up over the hill and started to drag picnic tables and big wastepaper baskets and piled them on top of one another. There was a lot of mimeograph paper on the ground and some film. It was all thrown on top of this and it was lit." (See page 196.) (Fred De Van) LIFE Magazine © Time, Inc.

(Bottom right) Lee Weiner and Abbie Hoffman. "Right at that point a school bus drove by . . . and Lee said to Lt. Meany, 'See, they used to want to grow up to be policemen. Now they want to grow up to be like us.'" (See page 395.) Photo by Bill Etra.

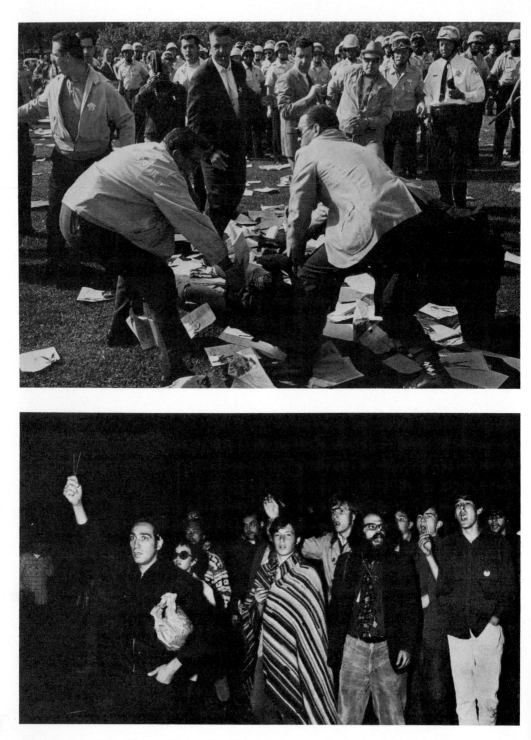

(Top) Grant Park Bandshell on Wednesday. Plainclothesmen apprehend a demonstrator. Photo by William Mares.

(Bottom) Allan Ginsberg leads the crowd out of Lincoln Park om-ing. "We walked out of the Park. We continued chanting for at least 20 minutes . . . making a very solid vibrational change of aim that penetrated the immediate area around us and attracted other people. (See page 299.) (Fred De Van)

LIFE Magazine © Time, Inc.

(Top) Specially equipped National Guard jeeps described by police undercover agent Frapolly. "I said, 'We could set up a grappling hook and a rope and throw it into the wire. . . .' Mr. Davis said, 'That's a good idea. We'll use it if they use the jeeps.'" (See page 139.)
(Bottom left) Rennie Davis lies unconscious after being beaten by police on Wednesday. "I remember hearing the voice of Carl Oglesby, 'In order to survive in this country, we have to fight.' And then I lost consciousness." (See page 481.) (Fred De Van) LIFE Magazine © Time, Inc.
(Bottom right) Motorcyclists in Lincoln Park. "I allowed my hair to grow long. I allowed myself to go without a shave for approximately 4 to 6 weeks. I purchased the attire of a motorcycle gang member, which is motorcycle boots, a black T-shirt, black levis and a black leather vest." (See page 65.) Photo by Charles Phillips.

(Top left) John Froines addresses a crowd in Lincoln Park. Next to him is Tom Hayden. "He urged the demonstrators to leave the park. He said that it was a dangerous situation to stay in the park. The park could not be safe after eleven o'clock and people should leave." (See page 455.) Photo by Charles Phillips.

(Top right) Bobby Seale speaks to the people in Lincoln Park on Tuesday. "Black people, we're saying we're lost. We seem to be lost in a world of white racist decadent America. I'm saying we have a right to defend ourselves as human beings. And if some pig comes up to us unjustly, treating us unjustly, then we have to bring our pieces out and start barbecuing some of that pork." (See page 504.)

(Bottom left) Dave Dellinger speaks to demonstrators seated on Columbus Drive on Wednesday afternoon. "Mr. Dellinger said to me 'We are going to march. We are going to the Amphitheatre.' " (See page 243.) Photo by Glenn Thoreson.

(Bottom right) Jerry Rubin with Pigasus at the Bandshell on Wednesday. "I want to introduce to you the only candidate that can defeat Richard Nixon, the only candidate . . . the only . . . hey! Bring him back." (See page 236.) Photo by Fred Mason.

Defense Exhibit 289. Police remove David Edmundson from the Logan statue Monday afternoon. "They kept pulling and kept pulling and kept pulling, and then I heard my arm break." (See page 422.)

(Top) Abbie Hoffman in Lincoln Park. "I spent most of my time right here talking to groups, forming affinity groups . . . introducing them to each other, saying that it would be safer if they stuck together." (See page 455.) Photo by Charles Phillips.
(Bottom) The National Guard blockades the exits from Grant Park on Wednesday. "When a car would come up that would have anybody in it who did not appear to be an ordinary passenger in the car, they would stop that car and force the person to get rid of their passengers." (See page 236.) (Fred De Van)
LIFE Magazine © Time, Inc.

Testimony of Jacques Levy

December 18, 1969

MR. KUNSTLER: Will you state your full name for the record?

THE WITNESS: Jacques Levy.

MR. KUNSTLER: Would you state your educational background?

THE WITNESS: I have a Ph.D. in psychology. I then took a postdoctoral fellowship at the Menninger Clinic in Topeka, Kansas, and then was asked to join the staff there.

MR. KUNSTLER: Now, did there come a time, Mr. Levy, when you left that employment?

THE WITNESS: Yes. I left the Menninger Foundation and went into the theater as a director. I went to New York City.

MR. KUNSTLER: Can you state for the Court and jury what productions you have been involved with?

MR. FORAN: I object to this.

THE WITNESS: He shouldn't object.They were all hits.

THE COURT: The last remark of the witness may go out. You are not in a theater now, sir.

MR. KUNSTLER: Mr. Levy, curb your professional enthusiasm. Can you state the plays, the years they played, and the name of the plays?

THE WITNESS: OK. In 1964, "America Hurrah." In 1967, "Scuba Duba." And then this past year, "Oh! Calcutta!"

MR. KUNSTLER: Now, Mr. Levy, did there come a time when you met Abbie Hoffman and Jerry Rubin?

THE WITNESS: Yes. I met with both Abbie Hoffman and Jerry Rubin at Abbie's home sometime in January. I can't remember the exact date.

MR. KUNSTLER: And can you indicate to the Court and jury what Abbie and Jerry said to you and what you said to them?

THE WITNESS: Yes. Abbie asked me if I had any ideas about how to go about creating an event that would be a joyous happy festival for a large group of people in Chicago. I remember Jerry Rubin saying that he thought the people would have a better time at our party than at the Democratic Party.

I said that my ideas about the theater were that the theater inside the frame of the usual theatrical house was something that the young people in this country and perhaps all over the world were no longer really interested in, and that the kind of thing that they were proposing which would be a large-scale event that would involve participation on the part of all the people involved, and not merely passively sitting and listening or watching something but becoming one with it, that that was something that I had wanted very much to do, and thought that there were ways that it could be done.

It sounded just great to me.

MR. KUNSTLER: Mr. Levy, as the result of the conversation with Abbie and Jerry, what did you do?

THE WITNESS: I went out and met with a variety of theatrical groups, leaders of theatrical groups and producers in New York, in order to try to get their support and money and cooperation to put on this Festival Life in Chicago.

MR. KUNSTLER: Mr. Levy, did there come a time when you met Jerry and Abbie again, when you were all together?

THE WITNESS: The next time that we actually met was at the Americana Hotel at a press conference.

MR. KUNSTLER: Can you state what was said by Abbie or Jerry or anybody in their presence at that press conference?

THE WITNESS: Abbie asked me if I had heard the Yippies were planning what was being called a Yip-in which was to celebrate the coming of spring, a party, essentially, at Grand Central station on midnight of March 22, I think. I said I thought it was a good

[329]

idea and that we could probably get a couple of hundred people in there and probably have a good time and not have any problems whatsoever. I was told at the time by Abbie that they had, and I subsequently found out this was true, that they had a New Year's Eve party at Grand Central Station every year so ours was just another party of that kind. Everyone who spoke at the press conference was mentioning that the Yippies were going to Chicago in August to the Democratic Convention, and that our entire basis of activities from now until the summer time would be directed toward creating a Festival of Life in Chicago.

MR. KUNSTLER: Now, was there any Yip-in at Grand Central Station?

THE WITNESS: Yes, there was.

MR. KUNSTLER: Can you describe what happened at Grand Central Station?

THE WITNESS: Yes. When I arrived at Grand Central Station at about eleven o'clock that night, there was already a growing crowd of people. I saw Abbie there and I said to him that I couldn't believe how many people were here and he said it was just extraordinary because they had done very little publicity on it and word just seemed to have gotten around everywhere, and by the time midnight came there must have been three thousand people in there, maybe more, five thousand.

The place was just jammed with people—it was like a New Year's Eve party, everybody was just having a good time and there was a lot of singing. There were people coming out of the trains that were coming into the station and when they would try to walk through the crowd, the crowd would just part and let them go through.

I saw Jerry and we exchanged congratulations to one another because we thought this was better than we expected.

MR. KUNSTLER: Did anything happen to change that atmosphere?

THE WITNESS: Yes. Then there was an incident that occurred where one or two people climbed up onto the clock in the center of Grand Central Station.

A whole group of policemen formed a wedge and began to move in toward the center of the crowd and I was at the front of that with some friends of mine, and the police began to push us with their billy clubs and to tell us to move on and I heard the police say, "Get the fuck out of here," and "Back up," and "Get out." And then the police started to charge from the other side and it was as if they were going to meet in the middle.

I saw one young man get thrown by policemen through a glass window, and I found later that he had both his arms, wrists, his hands cut, I don't know—

THE COURT: Set me right about this, Mr. Witness, please. Where did all of this that you are talking about take place?

THE WITNESS: This took place in Grand Central Station.

THE COURT: Grand Central Station in New York City?

MR. FORAN: This was their practice for Chicago, Judge, the witness testified.

THE COURT: I didn't hear that.

MR. KUNSTLER: Mr. Foran said, your Honor, this is their practice for Chicago. That is what Mr. Foran says.

Now after the Grand Central Station incident, did you have another discussion with Abbie and Jerry?

THE WITNESS: I told them that I was scared and upset. Abbie said he felt the same way. And we decided that we had to meet to find out what our next plan would be, so we met at Abbie's house.

MR. KUNSTLER: Would you state what was said at that meeting by Abbie, or Jerry, or you?

THE WITNESS: Yes, everybody, Abbie, Jerry, and myself, and everybody else at that meeting all expressed terrible concern, upset, fear, saying things that we were in an enclosed situation, so as soon as there was any kind of pushing or shoving that the crowd became very panicky and upset.

Jerry said if we weren't scared off completely, that we should try to have another event. Abbie said that he would then try to get a permit for Central Park and get the cooperation of the city to keep the police outside of the crowd so that they would be on the periphery only, and to see whether or not it would be possible for us to have a peaceful happy event with structured activity that could work without any violence or any upset or any panic going through the crowd.

MR. KUNSTLER: Now, did you see Jerry and Abbie on Easter, Easter Sunday?
THE WITNESS: Yes, I did.
MR. KUNSTLER: Where did you see them?
THE WITNESS: I saw them in Central Park.
MR. KUNSTLER: What was going on in Central Park?
THE WITNESS: It was called the Yip-out.
MR. FORAN: Objection, your Honor.
THE COURT: I sustain the objection.
MR. KUNSTLER: Will you relate to the Court and jury what Jerry and Abbie said to you and what you said to them?
THE WITNESS: Yes. They were overjoyed at the fact that this had gone so well because the police had not come in. They said that Chicago was bound to be successful because we had a wonderful experience in that park and no violence.
MR. FORAN: Objection, your Honor.
THE COURT: I sustain the objection.
MR. KUNSTLER: Your Honor, the whole point is that this witness is testifying what Abbie said comparing this event to what they expected in Chicago because this went so well, because the police were on the perimeter and they had a permit and it went all day long with rock bands—
THE COURT: Oh, yes, you have said that, but I still think that is irrelevant here.
MR. KUNSTLER: Do you recall any announcement being made over the loudspeaker system at the Central Park event relative to Chicago?
MR. FORAN: Objection.
THE COURT: I sustain the objection.

(witness laughs aloud)

THE WITNESS: Keep trying, Bill.
THE COURT: I will direct the witness to remain silent until a question is asked you and you are permitted to answer. Will you please follow that direction?
MR. KUNSTLER: At Central Park that day, after the Yip-out in Central Park, did you have any further discussions with Jerry and Abbie relative to Chicago?
THE WITNESS: Yes, the first discussion we had took place in Central Park at around seven or eight o'clock in the evening of Easter Sunday. Abbie said that he was overjoyed and very happy because this was an event that seemed to really work.

I agreed. It seemed to me that we had no problem in being able to make this kind of event work, a really great happy party in Chicago on an even bigger scale.

The important thing now, I said, was they have got to secure permits for us to be able to use a wide open space like we used in Central Park. And he said they were absolutely going to try to get those permits.
MR. KUNSTLER: Now, did you have occasion to come to Chicago around the time of the Democratic National Convention?
THE WITNESS: Yes, I did.
MR. KUNSTLER: Now, at the time you came, had you made any arrangements, definite arrangements with any theater group to come to Chicago?
THE WITNESS: No, they wouldn't come becuse we couldn't get a permit.
MR. FORAN: I object.
THE COURT: I sustain the objection.
MR. KUNSTLER: Your witness.

• • • • •

MR. FORAN: Mr. Levy, at Grand Central Station, those people that climbed up on that information booth, they broke the hands off all four faces of that clock, didn't they?
THE WITNESS: I don't know. That's what I read. I didn't see it.
MR. FORAN: Do you know how many people were at that little event?
THE WITNESS: No.
MR. FORAN: Did you know that fifty-eight people were arrested?
THE WITNESS: I didn't know that.
MR. FORAN: Did you hear any explosions there that night in the concourse?
THE WITNESS: Not that I can remember.

MR. FORAN: Did you see any bottles thrown? Did you hear any breaking glass?

THE WITNESS: Yes, when the cops threw a young guy through the glass door.

MR. FORAN: Did you know that a policeman had his skull fractured at that occurrence?

THE WITNESS: No. I read the reports the next day in the newspaper which said that there were policemen hurt.

MR. FORAN: Have you ever read Abbie Hoffman's book, *Revolution for the Hell of It*?

THE WITNESS: Parts of it. Not all of it. I skipped here and there. I never read—I didn't read about—

MR. FORAN: Did Abbie Hoffman ever tell you that he thought that the Grand Central Massacre put Yippie on the map?

THE WITNESS: Abbie Hoffman—

MR. FORAN: Did he ever tell you that?

THE WITNESS: Abbie Hoffman writes different from the way he talks.

MR. FORAN: So did he tell you that or didn't he?

THE WITNESS: And he will sometimes write things like that he would never say. He would never say something like "put anything on the map" in conversation. It is a cliché.

MR. FORAN: Did he ever tell you that?

THE WITNESS: No. I mean, he doesn't use that kind of, you know, silly cliché except when he writes.

MR. FORAN: Now, this "Oh! Calcutta!" that you directed is rather famous, isn't it?

THE WITNESS: "My learns are goided."

MR. FORAN: It was shut down in a number of cities?

THE WITNESS: No. Wrong. Wrong. Wrong. It never was shut down.

MR. FORAN: It was shut down last night in Los Angeles, wasn't it?

THE WITNESS: Not that I know of. Was it shut down last night? I don't know about that.

MR. FORAN: It is a kind of a tribal celebration of nudity?

THE WITNESS: No, absolutely not. I wouldn't have anything to do with a tribal celebration of anything.

MR. FORAN: There is a lot of nudity in it, isn't there?

THE WITNESS: It depends on what you mean by a lot.

MR. FORAN: How many at various times?

THE WITNESS: How many what?

MR. FORAN: Characters on the stage are in the nude?

THE WITNESS: Ten people on the stage in the nude.

MR. FORAN: In the nude. And what are they doing on the stage?

THE WITNESS: Dancing, singing.

MR. FORAN: In the nude?

THE WITNESS: Gliding, improvising, having what they describe as a terrifically good time and what the audience feels is a good time.

MR. FORAN: In the nude?

THE WITNESS: The audience isn't in the nude.

MR. FORAN: I have no further questions.

THE COURT: Redirect examination?

MR. KUNSTLER: Mr. Levy, after the Grand Central Terminal demonstration, did you learn that more than 200 demonstrators had been injured by the police?

THE WITNESS: I learned that a lot of demonstrators had been injured. I don't know the exact number.

MR. KUNSTLER: Did you also learn that Mayor Lindsay had publicly condemned the police action in Grand Central Station?

THE WITNESS: Yes.

MR. KUNSTLER: Thank you. I have no further questions.

THE COURT: You may go.

Testimony of Timothy F. Leary

December 19, 1969

THE COURT: Will you call the witness, please?

MR. KUNSTLER: Would you state your full name for the record?

THE WITNESS: Timothy F. Leary.

MR. KUNSTLER: Dr. Leary, what is your present occupation?

THE WITNESS: I am the Democratic candidate for Governor in California.

MR. KUNSTLER: Is that in the primary?

THE WITNESS: Yes, sir, Democratic primary.

THE COURT: Just so that the jury will be clear, do you call being a candidate an occupation, sir?

THE WITNESS: Well, it is taking most of my time at present, your Honor.

THE COURT: What is your regular occupation?

THE WITNESS: I am a religious ordained minister, and I am a college lecturer.

MR. KUNSTLER: Can you state what your educational background is?

THE WITNESS: Yes, sir, I received a Ph.D. in clinical psychology from the University of California, Berkeley, in 1950. I was two years at Holy Cross College, and a year and a half at West Point, the United States Military Academy.

MR. KUNSTLER: Now, Dr. Leary, can you state briefly your professional experience since receiving your Ph.D. in 1950?

THE WITNESS: Yes, from 1950 to 1956, I was on the faculty of the University of California and the University of California Medical School in San Francisco. I was also the director of the Kaiser Foundation Psychological Research from 1952 to 1957.

MR. KUNSTLER: And after that?

THE WITNESS: I taught at the University of Copenhagen in the Philosophy and Psychology Department in Denmark in 1958, and then in 1959 I joined the faculty at Harvard University and taught at Harvard from 1959 to 1963 in clinical psychology and personality psychology.

MR. KUNSTLER: Dr. Leary, have you been the author of any publications?

THE WITNESS: Yes, I have written two books on experimental clinical psychology and about twenty scientific articles in this field. I have written six books and over fifty scientific articles on the effects of psychedelic drugs on human psychology and human consciousness.

MR. KUNSTLER: Doctor, can you explain what a psychedelic drug is?

THE WITNESS: I will try. Psychedelic drugs are drugs which speed up thinking, which broaden the consciousness, which produce religious experiences or creative experiences, or philosophic experiences in the person who takes them

These psychedelic drugs, of course, are the opposite of the nonpsychedelic drugs like heroin, or alcohol, and barbiturates which slow down thinking, as opposed to psychedelic drugs which expand and accelerate the consciousness.

MR. KUNSTLER: Now, there came a time, did there not, Dr. Leary, when you left Harvard University?

THE WITNESS: Yes, I was dismissed from Harvard University in 1963. There were two reasons for my dismissal. One was a dispute over schedule of classes, and the other was because I was continuing to do research on the effects of psychedelic drugs which was politically risky for Harvard University to sponsor.

MR. KUNSTLER: What was the nature of that research?

MR. FORAN: I object to that, your Honor.

THE COURT: I sustain the objection.

MR. KUNSTLER: Your Honor, we want to show the background of Dr. Leary and the type of work he was doing. There has been a great misconception about the type of work he was doing. We want to explain it to the jury.

THE COURT: Dr. Leary's work isn't in issue here. He is not a defendant here.

MR. KUNSTLER: Now, Dr. Leary, do you recall when your first met Jerry Rubin?

THE WITNESS: Yes, I do. I met Jerry Rubin at the love-in at San Francisco, which was January 1967.

MR. KUNSTLER: And do you know where that love-in was held?

THE WITNESS: Yes, that was held in Golden Gate Park, and I think either seventy or eighty thousand people came to the park to participate in this love-in.

MR. FORAN: Objection.

THE COURT: I sustain the objection. Seven or eight thousand?

MR. KUNSTLER: Seventy or eighty thousand.

THE COURT: Oh, even worse.

MR. KUNSTLER: Even better.

All right, Dr. Leary, when did you first meet Abbie Hoffman?

THE WITNESS: The first time I met Mr. Hoffman was at the LSD Shrine and Rescue Center in New York City. That would be November or December of 1966.

MR. KUNSTLER: Now, lest there be any confusion, what does LSD stand for?

THE WITNESS: It was the League of Spiritual Discovery. That was a religion incorporated in the State of New York and we had a rescue center in New York where hundreds of people taking drugs could be rehabilitated.

MR. KUNSTLER: Dr. Leary, I call your attention to late January of 1968 and ask you whether you met with Jerry and Abbie during that month at that time?

THE WITNESS: Yes, I did. I met with Mr. Hoffman and Mr. Rubin and with other people and we formed and founded the Youth International Party.

MR. KUNSTLER: Now, with reference to the founding of the Youth International Party, which we will refer to as Yippie, can you state what was said by the people attending there with reference to the founding of this party?

THE WITNESS: Well, Julius Lester said that the current parties are not responsive to the needs of black people, particularly young black people. Allen Ginsberg said that the Democrat and Republican Parties are not responsive to the creative youth and to college students and high school students who expect more from society.

Abbie Hoffman, as I remember, was particularly eloquent in describing the need for new political tactics and techniques.

MR. FORAN: Objection.

THE COURT: You are not privileged to characterize the participants in that way.

MR. KUNSTLER: Even if you were impressed by what people said, don't indicate whether they were eloquent or what-have-you.

MR. FORAN: Your Honor, I object to Mr. Kunstler's comments which he knows are improper.

MR. KUNSTLER: I was trying to assist Mr. Foran.

THE COURT: I will do the directing. You ask the questions.

MR. KUNSTLER: Would you go ahead, Dr. Leary?

THE WITNESS: Abbie Hoffman said that new political methods were needed because the conventions of the Democrat and Republican Parties were controlled by machine politics which had nothing to do with the needs of the people.

Mr. Hoffman continued to say that we should set up a series of political meetings throughout the country, not just for the coming summer but for the coming years. Mr. Hoffman suggested that we have love-ins or be-ins in which thousands of young people and freedom-loving people throughout the country could get together on Sunday afternoons, listen to music which represented the new point of view, the music of love and peace and harmony, and try to bring about a political change in this country that would be nonviolent in people's minds and in their hearts, and this is the concept of the love-in which Mr. Hoffman was urging upon us.

MR. KUNSTLER: Now, at any time during this discussion did anyone make any reference to the Democratic National Convention?

THE WITNESS: Mr. Hoffman said it was important to have a large group of young people and black people and freedom-loving people come to Chicago during the Democratic Convention the following August. That it was important that people that were concerned about peace and brotherhood come to Chicago and in a very dignified, beautiful way meet in the parks and represent what Mr. Hoffman called the politics of life and politics of love and peace and brotherhood.

Mr. Rubin, I remember, pointed out that since the Democratic Party was meeting here, there was great concern about having police and having National Guard and they were bringing in tear gas. Mr. Rubin pointed out that it could possibly be violent here, and both Mr. Rubin and Allen Ginsberg said that they didn't think that we should come to Chicago if there was a possibility of violence from the soldiers or the police.

MR. KUNSTLER: I call your attention to March of 1968, somewhere in the middle of March, and I ask you if you can recall being present at a press conference?

THE WITNESS: Yes.

MR. KUNSTLER: Prior to this press conference had you had any other meetings with Jerry and Abbie?

THE WITNESS: Yes, we had met two or three times during the spring.

MR. FORAN: Your Honor, I object to the constant use of the diminutives in the reference to the defendants.

MR. KUNSTLER: Your Honor, sometimes it is hard because we work together in this case, we use first names constantly.

THE COURT: I know, but if I knew you that well, and I don't, how would it seem for me to say, "Now, Billy—"

MR. KUNSTLER: Your Honor, it is perfectly acceptable to me—if I could have the reverse privilege.

THE COURT: I don't like it. I have disapproved of it before and I ask you now to refer to the defendants by their surnames.

MR. KUNSTLER: I was just thinking I hadn't been called "Billy" since my mother used that word the first time.

THE COURT: I haven't called you that.

MR. KUNSTLER: It evokes some memories.

THE COURT: I was trying to point out to you how absurd it sounds in a courtroom.

MR. KUNSTLER: Dr. Leary, did you speak at that press conference?

THE WITNESS: Yes. I described in great detail the harassment that we had suffered in our religious center at Millbrook, New York, by the police. I describe how for the preceeding two or three months there had been a police blockade around this young people's center in upstate New York and that our houses had been ransacked at night by sheriffs and policemen and how our young children were being arrested on their bicycles on the roads outside of our houses because they didn't have identification.

And I described how helicopters had been coming over to observe our behavior and I raised the possibility that we did not want this to happen in Chicago and we hoped that Chicago would be free from this sort of unpleasant encounter, because at Millbrook we were living very peaceably, bothering nobody until we were harassed and surrounded by the police.

MR. KUNSTLER: Now, during the month of March did you have occasion to speak with Jerry Rubin?

THE WITNESS: Yes, I called Jerry to tell him about the results of the Yippie meeting in Chicago.

MR. KUNSTLER: All right. Will you tell the jury and the Court what you told Jerry and what he told you, if anything, in that phone conversation?

THE WITNESS: I told Mr. Rubin that I had never experienced such fear on the part of the young people as I did in the young people of Chicago, that they were, literally trembling about the possibility of violence in August. And I raised the issue to Jerry as to whether we should reconsider coming to Chicago.

MR. KUNSTLER: Now, up to this time in this telephone conversation had you had any conversation with Jerry Rubin or Abbie Hoffman about LSD in the Chicago water supply?

MR. FORAN: I object to that, your Honor.

THE COURT: I sustain the objection.

MR. KUNSTLER: Now, Dr. Leary, I call your attention to April of 1968, and ask you if you recall a meeting with Jerry Rubin and Abbie Hoffman?

THE WITNESS: Yes, I met with Jerry Rubin and Abbie Hoffman.

MR. KUNSTLER: What did you say?

THE WITNESS: Mr. Hoffman pointed out that since our last meeting, President Johnson had retired from office. Therefore, President Johnson would not be coming to Chicago. Therefore, the meaning of a celebration of life on our part as opposed to Mr. Johnson was lost since the man we were attempting to oppose was not going to come to Chicago.

Both Mr. Hoffman and Mr. Rubin at that time said to me before I left that they were not sure whether we should come to Chicago, and that we would watch what happened politically. At that time, Jerry Rubin pointed out that Robert Kennedy was still alive, and many of us felt that he represented the aspirations of young people, so we thought we would wait. I remember Mr. Rubin saying, "Let's wait and see what Robert Kennedy comes out with as far as peace is concerned. Let's wait to see if Robert Kennedy does speak to young people, and if Robert Kennedy does seek to represent the peaceful, joyous, erotic feelings of young people—"

THE COURT: "Erotic," did you say?

THE WITNESS: Erotic.

THE COURT: E-R-O-T-I-C?

THE WITNESS: Eros. That means love, your Honor.

THE COURT: I know, I know. I wanted to be sure I didn't mishear you.

THE WITNESS: So Mr. Rubin suggested that we hold off the decision as to whether we come to Chicago until we saw how Mr. Kennedy's campaign developed, and at that point, I think most of us would have gladly, joyously called off the Chicago meeting.

MR. KUNSTLER: You did not yourself come to Chicago, did you, during the Democratic National Convention?

THE WITNESS: No, I did not come to Chicago myself.

MR. KUNSTLER: Right. Now prior to the Convention week, did you have any conversation with Jerry Rubin?

THE WITNESS: Yes, at the end of July. I told Mr. Rubin that I had decided not to come to Chicago. Mr. Rubin asked me why.

MR. FORAN: Objection as to his reasons for not coming.

THE COURT: I should say that is irrelevant. I sustain the objection.

MR. KUNSTLER: Your witness.

THE COURT: Cross-examination

• • • • •

MR. FORAN: Dr. Leary, will you name the drugs that you said speeded up thinking?

THE WITNESS: Yes, psychedelic or mind-expanding drugs include LSD, mescaline, peyote, marijuana, and I could go on. There is a list of perhaps thirty or forty chemical compounds and natural vines and herbs. Do you want more?

MR. FORAN: No, that is enough.

Now, when you talked to Jerry Rubin in late March over the telephone from Chicago, you had a long discussion with him at that time about your fears of violence that would occur in Chicago at the Democratic Convention, did you not?

THE WITNESS: Yes, I had been told this by the young people in Chicago.

MR. FORAN: And you expressed your concern?

THE WITNESS: Well, I am always concerned about the possibility of violence anywhere at any time. I am against violence.

MR. FORAN: You asked him at that time whether or not you should reconsider coming to Chicago, is that correct?

THE WITNESS: Yes, sir.

MR. FORAN: I have no further questions.

• • • • •

MR. KUNSTLER: I have just one further question.

Dr. Leary, in answer to Mr. Foran's question about the young people, did you tell Jerry Rubin from where the young people in Chicago expected violence to come, from what source?

THE WITNESS: Well, from the militia, the National Guard. The sheriff was fighting with the police chief of Chicago at the time, and the sheriff, I believe, was enlisting vigilantes and just people off the street to be deputy sheriffs.

MR. KUNSTLER: But it was violence from the police?

THE WITNESS: And the National Guard, police, and sheriff.

MR. KUNSTLER: And not from the young people themselves?

THE WITNESS: There was no possibility of that.

MR. KUNSTLER: Thank you.

THE COURT: No further questions? You may go.

Testimony of Elizabeth Jean Snodgrass

MR. WEINGLASS: Will you please state your name?

THE WITNESS: Elizabeth Jean Snodgrass.

MR. WEINGLASS: Will you tell the Court and jury what your occupation is presently?

THE WITNESS: Registered nurse.

MR. WEINGLASS: Directing your attention to approximately 8:00 P.M. on Wednesday night, August 28, 1968, where were you?

THE WITNESS: I was at the intersection of Michigan and Balbo directly across from the Conrad Hilton.

MR. WEINGLASS: How were you attired that night?

THE WITNESS: I was attired in full nurse's uniform, white stockings, shoes, white lab coat and a red cross medical armband.

MR. WEINGLASS: Were you doing anything with respect to the Medical Committee for Human Rights on that evening?

THE WITNESS: Yes, I was.

MR. SCHULTZ: Objection.

THE COURT: I sustain the objection.

MR. WEINGLASS: Now, as you were standing at the southeast corner of Michigan and Balbo at approximately 8:00 P.M., what was occurring in the intersection?

THE WITNESS: There was a large crowd of people milling in the intersection. A large group of policeman had begun to form a direct line and without too much warning, they charged the crowd.

MR. WEINGLASS: Miss Snodgrass, when you saw the police come into the crowd, what if anything did you do?

THE WITNESS: I began to administer to people that had injuries sustained at that time, and had to move back into the park with the crowd as they were being pushed back.

MR. WEINGLASS: What occurred after you went into the park?

THE WITNESS: The policemen came after them, beating people and Macing them in the park.

MR. WEINGLASS: What did you do?

THE WITNESS: I was administering to people who had been beaten, and also taking care of people who had been Maced. We were treating people for some severe Mace burns, skin burns, and also some gas burns of the eyes. The people who had Mace injuries had severe reddened faces with blistering. Those who had not been treated immediately at the very beginning had already begun to show blisters on the face and severe eye damage.

MR. WEINGLASS: Is that injury accompanied by pain?

THE WITNESS: Severe pain.

MR. SCHULTZ: I don't know how she would know unless she was Maced.

THE WITNESS: I was.

THE COURT: I sustain the objection.

MR. WEINGLASS: Did you encounter any difficulty in treating the people?

THE WITNESS: Yes, as we were treating people in the park, many of whom had to be dealt with on the ground, we were not able to stay in any one position because we kept being pushed by the crowd and by the police and were having to pick up and move the supplies and the injured people from space to space.

MR. WEINGLASS: Now, at approximately 10:00 P.M. that night, where were you?

THE WITNESS: I was at the intersection of Jackson and Michigan as the crowd had been pushed north, and I was standing at the underground, south underground, parking lot, the ramp going down, treating people at the ramp. Around the side, there is a cement abutment with a metal railing, and I was administering to the wounds there, particularly head wounds.

   I had my back to the street at that time.

MR. WEINGLASS: What occurred?

[338]

THE WITNESS: As I was treating the people, the doctor that I was with who was facing the street grabbed me and pulled me around the edge, and I turned back to see just in time a policeman on a three-wheeler run into the wall exactly where I had been standing.
MR. WEINGLASS: What if anything did you do at that point?
THE WITNESS: At this point, I started to cry. I couldn't believe it.
MR. WEINGLASS: Now did you some time later leave the downtown section of Chicago?
THE WITNESS: I went with five other medical people to the Free Theater in the Lincoln Park area where there had been a call for medical help. I stayed outside of the car, waiting for further orders.
MR. WEINGLASS: As you were standing outside the car, did you see anything occur down the alley and on the street?
THE WITNESS: Yes, I noticed approximately four people run by the mouth of the alley, and after them, about seven or eight policemen were chasing them.
MR. WEINGLASS: What occurred?
THE WITNESS: The police had stopped at the mouth of the alley, and had turned to the medical people standing there, and had picked up some cement pieces (the sidewalk had been chipped up, and there was construction), and turned toward the medical group, and began throwing the rocks, while saying some obscenities to the group.
MR. WEINGLASS: Were you struck by a rock?
THE WITNESS: Yes, I was.
MR. WEINGLASS: And do you recall what the police said to the group?
THE WITNESS: The police picked up the rock, and he said, "Medical aides, my ass. If it weren't for you fucking bastards, the rest of the group wouldn't be here."
MR. WEINGLASS: No further direct.

• • • • •

MR. SCHULTZ: At about ten o'clock or so at Michigan and Jackson, did you see a police squadrol pull up and some youths start to push it over? Did you see that?
THE WITNESS: No, I did not.
MR. SCHULTZ: Well, did you see at about that time at Michigan and Jackson some youths attacking two or three policemen who had just gotten out of a vehicle?
THE WITNESS: No, I did not.
MR. SCHULTZ: Did you see any policeman lying on the pavement screaming that he had a broken leg?
THE WITNESS: No, I did not.
MR. SCHULTZ: Did you treat any policemen?
THE WITNESS: No.
MR. SCHULTZ: Did you see any policemen lying on the ground any time that night?
THE WITNESS: No, I didn't.
MR. SCHULTZ: Did you see any policemen hit by any objects?
THE WITNESS: No, I didn't.
MR. SCHULTZ: Miss Snodgrass, with regard to the policeman who threw rocks at you, did you report that to the Federal Bureau of Investigation?
THE WITNESS: I did make a statement to the ACLU.
MR. SCHULTZ: To the American Civil Liberties Union? You did not tell the Federal Bureau of Investigation, did you?
THE WITNESS: I think the ACLU had informed me that their files were being investigated by the FBI.
MR. SCHULTZ: Did you do anything to ascertain whether or not either the FBI or the Chicago Police Department received the affidavit?
THE WITNESS: No, but I am quite aware of their being aware of my statements, so I did nothing further.
MR. SCHULTZ: That is all, your Honor.
THE COURT: Is there any redirect examination?

• • • • •

MR. WEINGLASS: Miss Snodgrass, if any of the police would have been injured, would you have treated them?
THE WITNESS: Very definitely.

MR. SCHULTZ: I object to that.

THE COURT: I sustain the objection.

MR. WEINGLASS: Did you receive instructions from the MCHR to treat police as well as demonstrators?

MR. SCHULTZ: Objection.

THE WITNESS: Yes.

THE COURT: I sustain the objection to the question, whatever it was.

MR. WEINGLASS: Miss Snodgrass, are you aware of the fact that every policeman who was charged with an incident was acquitted of any wrongdoing?

MR. SCHULTZ: Objection.

THE COURT: I sustain the objection.

MR. WEINGLASS: I have no further questions.

THE COURT: You may go.

Please call your next witness.

Testimony of Paul Sequeira

December 22, 1969

MR. KUNSTLER: Would you give your full name, please?
THE WITNESS: Paul Sequeira.
MR. KUNSTLER: Where are you employed?
THE WITNESS: I am employed by the *Chicago Daily News* as a staff photographer.
MR. KUNSTLER: Were you so employed in and about the week of the Democratic National Convention in 1968?
THE WITNESS: Yes, I was.
MR. KUNSTLER: And I call your attention, Mr. Sequeira, to the night of August 25. Do you know where you were? That is a Sunday night.
THE WITNESS: Yes, sir, I was in Lincoln Park.
MR. KUNSTLER: Did there come a time when you were in the vicinity of the park after the park had been cleared that evening?
THE WITNESS: Yes, there was. I was in the vicinity of the intersection of LaSalle, Eugenie and Clark Streets.
MR. KUNSTLER: At that time, did you have occasion to see an automobile?
THE WITNESS: Yes, I did.
MR. KUNSTLER: Can you describe where that automobile was?
THE WITNESS: The automobile was a Corvette with three people in it. It came south on LaSalle Street from the area of the intersection at LaSalle and Eugenie and it pulled into a parking place.
MR. KUNSTLER: Can you describe who was in the car?
THE WITNESS: There was a male driving and there were two females in the front seat.
MR. KUNSTLER: Can you state to the Court and jury what, if anything, happened with relation to these two females?
MR. SCHULTZ: If the Court please, the incident that the witness is about to describe has been the subject matter of indictment, criminal indictment, prosecution and litigation in the Federal District Court. It just doesn't seem appropriate here to retry the prosecution of the policemen. I just don't see the relevancy of that at all.
THE COURT: I am not sure I understand you, Mr. Schultz. You are saying that the incident was the subject of an indictment and a result reached in the case?
MR. SCHULTZ: Yes. Three policemen were indicted as a result of this incident by a Federal grand jury.
THE COURT: Have they been tried?
MR. SCHULTZ: Yes.
MR. KUNSTLER: Tried and all acquitted, your Honor. You cannot convict a police officer in the City of Chicago, apparently.
THE COURT: Oh, that last statement may go out and the jury is directed to disregard it.
MR. KUNSTLER: Well, seven have been acquitted, your Honor.
THE COURT: You tell me I can't convict a policeman. I have convicted policemen.
MR. KUNSTLER: Let us prove here, your Honor, that these policemen were guilty of assaulting these two young people. The defendants have contended that the prosecution of the police was a sham prosecution.
MR. SCHULTZ: We prosecuted those cases as vigorously as we could, and certainly Mr. Kunstler is not going to try to establish before this jury that the Government fell down on a case by retrying a case here.
MR. KUNSTLER: I would like the record to indicate that Mr. Schultz was shouting.
THE COURT: Ladies and gentlemen, I direct you to disregard the statement of Mr. Kunstler that the prosecution to which he referred was a sham prosecution.
MR. FORAN: Your Honor, any lawyer in the world would have, before this witness took the stand, advised the Court that he was presenting evidence in this kind of a context, and

[341]

asked for a hearing outside of the presence of the jury. If he was even a decent man he would do that.

MR. KUNSTLER: Oh, your Honor.

(at this point the court is in disorder)

Your Honor, that is a disgrace.

THE COURT: Mr. Marshal.

MR. KUNSTLER: Your Honor, can we beg you to admonish once—we have never had a single admonition—

THE COURT: I will admonish the marshal to direct all of those people at that table who shouted not to do that again.

MR. KUNSTLER: The question is, are you going to admonish the United States Attorney for using the word "indecent?"

THE COURT: I will not admonish the United States Attorney because I believe it is a question that should have been brought up out of the presence of the jury.

Mr. Marshal, the court will be in recess until Monday morning at ten o'clock.

December 22, 1969

MR. SCHULTZ: Your Honor, I wanted to address myself to the question that was before you on Friday afternoon when we recessed, and that was when the witness started to testify to a transaction which involved an indictment and a trial.

The point is that whether the three policemen involved were guilty or not has no relevancy whatsoever to the issues before this jury. Furthermore, whether the Government lost the prosecution is not probative of anything in this case. It is simply irrelevant.

Now we have not objected to one incident that they have put in relating to police brutality. However, we do object at this point to an isolated act, an isolated instance in which no defendant was involved and which was not a subject of any testimony in the Government's case in chief, and therefore they are not rebutting the Government's case in chief. It is simply an isolated act of brutality which we do contend was brutality but which the jury apparently for one reason or another did not find them guilty of the crime charged.

THE COURT: Mr. Kunstler, will you reply?

MR. KUNSTLER: Yes, your Honor. First of all, when I started to interrogate this witness it was about the assaulting of two young girls by police officers. And the photograph which I was going to offer through Mr. Sequeira is the photograph of a Corvette, a photograph taken by the witness of the two girls in a car. The girl is covering her head and there are policemen with night sticks all around the car.

It is the defendants' contention that the prosecutions of the policemen were deliberately designed to pick eight scapegoats among the police and then match them up against the defendants by the Government so as to give the illusion that there was fairness on both sides. Eight defendants here, eight policemen there, and you match them up. We think the whole prosecution from its inception of all the policemen was a device, and a device simply to give the impression to the public at large that fairness was reigning in the U.S. Attorney's office in Chicago and the Attorney General's office at Washington.

Our purpose is to show that there might have been a calculated plan on the part of the Chicago police to physically assault demonstrators, and that it was the police, not the demonstrators, who caused whatever problems there were in Chicago during the Democratic National Convention.

THE COURT: In the present posture of the record there is no question hanging in air and for me to rule on, with an objection on the record to the question.

Bring in the jury.

MR. KUNSTLER: Your Honor, before you bring in the jury I have another matter. On December 24 at twelve noon a great many citizens of Chicago are going to attempt to conduct a citizen's arrest of Edward Hanrahan for the murder of Fred Hampton and Mark Clark. We all believe, after studying the reports of the last ten days or so, that the facts establish at least enough evidence to arrest Mr. Hanrahan for murder, and they want to join in that process. So we request an adjournment from twelve noon until three P.M. Do you want to rule on that?

THE COURT: I deny the motion. Bring in the jury.

Ladies and gentlemen of the jury, good morning.

MR. KUNSTLER: Mr. Sequeira, I show you D-191 for identification and ask you to identify this photograph.

THE WITNESS: It is a photograph of a Corvette car with three young people in the front seat and several police officers standing around the car.

MR. KUNSTLER: Did you see what happened to those two young people on that evening?

THE WITNESS: Yes, I did.

MR. SCHULTZ: Objection on the same basis that we have argued all morning.

THE COURT: Yes. I sustain the objection.

MR. KUNSTLER: Your Honor, I would like to offer into evidence at this time D-191, for identification.

MR. SCHULTZ: For the reasons that we have stated, we object to the introduction into evidence of the photograph.

THE COURT: The objections of the Government to Defendants Exhibits 191 for identification will be sustained.

MR. KUNSTLER: No further questions.

• • • • •

MR. SCHULTZ: Now, when you left the park Tuesday night, you went by a Dodge dealership, did you not?

THE WITNESS: Yes, that's right.

MR. SCHULTZ: And at the Dodge dealership you saw people picking up rocks and hurling them at the windows, the plate glass windows, isn't that right?

THE WITNESS: I saw a couple of bottles being thrown in the intersection, that's correct.

MR. SCHULTZ: Did you see the breaking of those windows at the Dodge dealership?

THE WITNESS: I saw them when they were broken. I didn't see the breaking of them.

MR. SCHULTZ: The bottles that you saw, were they being thrown in the direction of the Dodge dealership?

THE WITNESS: No, sir, they were not. They were being thrown from the vicinity of the Dodge dealership in the direction of the intersection.

MR. SCHULTZ: This crowd was headed south on La Salle, isn't that—

THE WITNESS: There was a large crowd that did head south on La Salle.

MR. SCHULTZ: You stayed with it or near it?

THE WITNESS: That's correct.

MR. SCHULTZ: While you were walking with this crowd, didn't you hear the window of a liquor store being broken?

THE WITNESS: Yes, I did, and I photographed it.

MR. SCHULTZ: You saw a couple of men looting the store window front, did you not?

THE WITNESS: There were two men who reached through the broken glass and picked up a bottle from the window display.

MR. SCHULTZ: And you photographed that?

THE WITNESS: Yes, I did.

MR. SCHULTZ: I will show you what has been marked for identification as Government's Exhibit No. 70 purporting to show two men. Is that a copy of the photograph which you took, Mr. Sequeira?

THE WITNESS: Yes, it is.

MR. SCHULTZ: Does that truly and accurately reflect what you observed those two men doing that Tuesday night?

THE WITNESS: Yes, it does.

MR. SCHULTZ: No further questions.

THE COURT: Please call your next witness.

Testimony of Abbie Hoffman

December 23, 1969

MR. WEINGLASS: Will you please identify yourself for the record?

THE WITNESS: My name is Abbie. I am an orphan of America.

MR. SCHULTZ: Your Honor, may the record show it is the defendant Hoffman who has taken the stand?

THE COURT: Oh, yes. It may so indicate.

THE WITNESS: Well, it is not really my last name.

MR. WEINGLASS: Abbie, what is your last name?

THE WITNESS: Well, there is some confusion about it because, well, my grandfather, he was a Russian Jew, and he decided to protest the anti-Semitism in the Russian Army and he slew—

MR. SCHULTZ: Objection. If the defendant has a last name, let him state it, but not—

THE COURT: All we want to know, sir, is your last name.

THE WITNESS: My slave name is Hoffman. My real name is Shaboysnakoff. I can't spell it.

THE COURT: There is a lawyer who has filed his appearance in the name of Abbie Hoffman for you. You gave him your name as Abbie Hoffman, did you not?

THE WITNESS: Well, no. It was the Government's idea and the name was Abbott Howard.

MR. WEINGLASS: Where do you reside?

THE WITNESS: I live in Woodstock Nation.

MR. WEINGLASS: Will you tell the Court and jury where it is?

THE WITNESS: Yes. It is a nation of alienated young people. We carry it around with us as a state of mind in the same way as the Sioux Indians carried the Sioux nation around with them. It is a nation dedicated to cooperation versus competition, to the idea that people should have better means of exchange than property or money, that there should be some other basis for human interaction. It is a nation dedicated to—

THE COURT: Just where it is, that is all.

THE WITNESS: It is in my mind and in the minds of my brothers and sisters. It does not consist of property or material but, rather, of ideas and certain values. We believe in a society—

THE COURT: No, we want the place of residence, if he has one, place of doing business, if you have a business. Nothing about philosophy or India, sir. Just where you live, if you have a place to live. Now you said Woodstock. In what state is Woodstock?

THE WITNESS: It is in the state of mind, in the mind of myself and my brothers and sisters. It is a conspiracy. Presently, the nation is held captive, in the penitentiaries of the institutions of a decaying system.

MR. WEINGLASS: Can you tell the Court and jury your present age?

THE WITNESS: My age is 33. I am a child of the 60s.

MR. WEINGLASS: When were you born?

THE WITNESS: Psychologically, 1960.

MR. SCHULTZ: Objection, if the Court please. I move to strike the answer.

MR. WEINGLASS: What is the actual date of your birth?

THE WITNESS: November 30, 1936.

MR. WEINGLASS: Between the date of your birth, November 30, 1936, and May 1, 1960, what if anything occurred in your life?

THE WITNESS: Nothing. I believe it is called an American education.

MR. SCHULTZ: Objection.

THE COURT: I sustain the objection.

THE WITNESS: Huh.

MR. WEINGLASS: Abbie, could you tell the Court and jury—

MR. SCHULTZ: His name isn't Abbie. I object to this informality.

MR. WEINGLASS: Can you tell the Court and jury what is your present occupation?

THE WITNESS: I am a cultural revolutionary. Well, I am really a defendant—full-time.

MR. WEINGLASS: What do you mean by the phrase "cultural revolutionary?"

THE WITNESS: Well, I suppose it is a person who tries to shape and participate in the values, and the mores, the customs and the style of living of new people who eventually become inhabitants of a new nation and a new society through art and poetry, theater, and music.

MR. WEINGLASS: What have you done yourself to participate in that revolution?

THE WITNESS: Well, I have been a rock and roll singer. I am a reporter with the Liberation News Service. I am a poet. I am a film maker. I made a movie called "Yippies Tour Chicago or How I Spent My Summer Vacation." Currently, I am negotiating with United Artists and MGM to do a movie in Hollywood.

I have written an extensive pamphlet on how to live free in the city of New York.

I have written two books, one called *Revolution for The Hell of It* under the pseudonym Free, and one called, *Woodstock Nation.*

MR. WEINGLASS: Taking you back to the spring of 1960, approximately May 1, 1960, will you tell the Court and jury where you were?

MR. SCHULTZ: 1960?

THE WITNESS: That's right.

MR. SCHULTZ: Objection.

THE COURT: I sustain the objection.

MR. WEINGLASS: Your Honor, that date has great relevance to the trial. May 1, 1960, was this witness' first public demonstration. I am going to bring him down through Chicago.

THE COURT: Not in my presence, you are not going to bring him down. I sustain the objection to the question.

THE WITNESS: My background has nothing to do with my state of mind?

THE COURT: Will you remain quiet while I am making a ruling? I know you have no respect for me.

MR. KUNSTLER: Your Honor, that is totally unwarranted. I think your remarks call for a motion for a mistrial.

THE COURT: And your motion calls for a denial of the motion. Mr. Weinglass, continue with your examination.

MR. KUNSTLER: You denied my motion? I hadn't even started to argue it.

THE COURT: I don't need any argument on that one. The witness turned his back on me while he was on the witness stand.

THE WITNESS: I was just looking at the pictures of the longhairs up on the wall.

THE COURT: Ask your next question, please.

MR. WEINGLASS: Would you relate to the Court and jury what employment you were engaged in in 1960?

THE WITNESS: Yes. I was offered a position as a psychologist in the State mental hospital of Massachusetts.

MR. WEINGLASS: And when you left the hospital, what employment did you engage in?

THE WITNESS: I did a number of things. I was engaged in political work. I became one of the campaign managers for a professor from Harvard named H. Stuart Hughes, who was then campaigning for senator from Massachusetts on an antiwar platform. And I also, in 1966, worked on a similar political campaign for Thomas Adams. His campaign was based on withdrawal of American troops from Vietnam.

MR. WEINGLASS: Could you indicate what other forms of work you were doing?

THE WITNESS: I worked for quite a while in the civil rights movement. I was publicity director for the NAACP in Worcester, Massachusetts. This was the place where I was born, too—I forgot to mention. And I was vice chairman of the Congress of Racial Equality, and I was field secretary for the Student NonViolent Coordinating Committee in charge of organizing Friends of SNCC groups.

MR. WEINGLASS: Now,—

THE WITNESS: I forgot something, too. I was involved with an organization called the Poor People's Corporation of Mississippi which was an attempt to set up a black-owned and operated craft cooperative in the State of Mississippi and sell those goods in the North in retail outlets and I helped to organize that.

MR. WEINGLASS: Directing your attention to the Democratic National Convention held in Atlantic City, New Jersey, during the month of August 1964, could you indicate to the Court and jury what activities, if any, you participated in around that Convention?

MR. SCHULTZ: The defendant's activities, if any, during the Convention in August of 1964 are not relevant to activities in the 1968 Convention.

THE COURT: I sustain the objection.

MR. WEINGLASS: Your Honor, this is the Democratic Convention that preceded the one in Chicago.

THE COURT: Yes, I know. I am listening very attentively. 1964 is the one before 1968. They occur every four years. I know. I know.

MR. WEINGLASS: Therefore I assume the Court agrees there is a relationship.

THE COURT: You may not ask about it.

THE WITNESS: Could I have some more water, Judge?

THE COURT: Give him some water, please.

THE WITNESS: The trial is bad for my health.

MR. WEINGLASS: Did you eventually leave the state of Massachusetts and come to the city of New York?

THE WITNESS: Yes. I left the state of Massachusetts, an $18,000 home and a lawn-mower, and moved to the Lower East Side in New York City, which is where I reside today.

MR. WEINGLASS: When you got to New York, what, if anything, did you do?

MR. SCHULTZ: Are we talking about his employment or what he did on a daily basis?

MR. WEINGLASS: Your Honor, technically this defendant has not been employed for monetary salary for years, and I cannot in fairness to him and in fairness to the work he has done characterize it in the nature of employment. He has worked for the causes he believes in. He is not employed by them.

THE COURT: I sustain the objection.

MR. WEINGLASS: What did you do in the way of work in New York after you got there in the summer of 1966?

THE WITNESS: Can I ask for a definition of "work"? Work is something you do for money, isn't it, or for some other reason? I never worked, ever. If that is what work is, it is a dirty four-letter word.

MR. WEINGLASS: How did you occupy your daytime hours—I assume even your night hours?

THE WITNESS: I opened a store called Liberty House which was the first outlet for these goods that were being made in the cooperatives of Mississippi. The handcraft was to be sold and distributed in the northern area. There were also goods that would come from other poor communities like Boone, Kentucky, and other places around the South in partic-ular that would be distributed and sold in the store, in this Liberty House store.

The profits reverted back to the Poor People's Corporation of Mississippi to open more cooperatives.

MR. WEINGLASS: Now drawing your attention to the late spring and the early summer of 1967, where were you living then?

THE WITNESS: Let's see. Late spring. I was living on 11th Street and Avenue C in a twenty-three-dollar-a-month apartment. It is a slum. The Lower East Side is a traditional place for immigrant groups trying—

MR. SCHULTZ: I don't think we need a sociological study.

THE COURT: Yes, "the Lower East Side" and the words that follow those words may go out and the jury is directed to disregard them.

MR. WEINGLASS: Your Honor, then I represent to the Court that this living experience had a great effect on the defendant, and it is something which does go to his state of mind, to his beliefs, to his philosophy, to his outlook.

MR. SCHULTZ: The issue here is when he came to Chicago, did he come here with an intent to incite, and when he arrived here, did he commit the acts that are charged. That is what is relevant here.

MR. WEINGLASS: Now, directing your attention to April 29, 1967, do you recall where you were on that day?

MR. SCHULTZ: Same objection. April 29, 1967, is long before anything relating to the Democratic National Convention.

THE COURT: I sustain the objection.

THE WITNESS: Was that the be-in that Allen Ginsberg referred to and was allowed to talk about?

THE COURT: The volunteered observation of the witness may go out.

MR. WEINGLASS: Did you do anything of a public nature in the community in which you lived, which is the Lower East Side, during the year 1967?

THE WITNESS: Yes.

MR. SCHULTZ: Oh, I will let him answer. I won't object to that.

THE WITNESS: Growing within the Lower East Side was a movement described as the hippie movement. We established various bail funds to help get people out of prison places. We helped set up crash pads and communes because a tremendous number of young children, some as low as twelve and thirteen years old, were running away from society and family life and coming to the Lower East Side. We fed and clothed and sheltered these people.

We had free food programs almost every day in Tompkins Square Park, which is like Central Park on the Lower East Side. We painted a number of large murals on the sides of buildings, and we arranged large festivals, participation festivals. For example, a sweep-in, in which three or four thousand people came and swept a huge city block and cleaned it and painted it in a very artistic way, painted fire hydrants and buildings, and things like that.

We also had tremendous festivals, like be-ins that you heard described before by Mr. Ginsberg, mass gatherings of communities of people who had a similar feeling that the values in the country were falling apart and they wanted to come together and experience a sense of joy, a new-found creativeness, and artistry. There are also guerrilla theater activities.

At this time, I was employed by the City of New York in the Youth Board Program that gave me money to carry out these things, but they gave me aside from the money, things like 200 softballs and eight bicycles for 20,000 hippies. With the softballs, we just painted them all, and hippies had a softball fight in the park. And the bicycles, we painted them white, and when the city officials came down we had maybe 200 white bicycles by then, and we would say, "There is one of the City officials floating around on a white bike."

The attitude was to take property and destroy it and turn it into art. And art would be the thing in which people would have some hope. It would be something that maybe they would be willing to die for, a work of art. Little kids would say, "Ours is the block with the big five-foot mural on it," and they would be tough about that and say to other kids, "We live on that block. We like it."

MR. WEINGLASS: How long did your employment with the City of New York last?

THE WITNESS: Two weeks. It was terminated when we threw the money in the New York Stock Exchange. They said it was bad for the city image for people to do things free.

MR. WEINGLASS: Directing your attention to the month of September 1967, will you indicate to the Court and to the jury what if anything you were doing during that month?

THE WITNESS: September 1967? Yes, I remember a number of things. Among them, a meeting with the defendant, Jerry Rubin.

MR. WEINGLASS: What did that meeting concern?

THE WITNESS: Jerry Rubin and I had a conversation. He had been observing some of these guerrilla theater-type activities.

MR. SCHULTZ: Objection. He was not asked to relate any conversation. Unless the conversation relates directly to the Democratic National Convention, I object.

MR. WEINGLASS: I represent to the Court that this conversation is relevant.

MR. SCHULTZ: Well, no, that is not sufficient. Everything to Mr. Weinglass is relevant that he puts on and everything we put on is irrelevant. That doesn't answer the question.

MR. WEINGLASS: I would characterize the Government's case as something different than irrelevant, but—

THE COURT: I assume that the lawyers will ask a witness questions that are appropriate, material and relevant. So I will let the witness tell about this asserted conversation with Mr. Rubin on the occasion described.

MR. WEINGLASS: What was the conversation at that time?

THE WITNESS: Jerry Rubin told me that he had come to New York to be project director of a peace march in Washington that was going to march to the Pentagon in October, October 21. He said that the peace movement suffered from a certain kind of attitude, mainly that it was based solely on the issue of the Vietnam war. He said that the war in Vietnam was not just an accident but a direct by-product of the kind of system, a capitalist system in the country, and that we had to begin to put forth new kinds of values, especially to young people in the country, to make a kind of society in which a Vietnam war would not be possible.

And he felt that these attitudes and values were present in the hippie movement and many of the techniques, the guerrilla theater techniques that had been used and many of these methods of communication would allow for people to participate and become involved in a new kind of democracy.

I said that the Pentagon was a five-sided evil symbol in most religions and that it might be possible to approach this from a religious point of view. If we got large numbers of people to surround the Pentagon, we could exorcize it of its evil spirits.

So I had agreed at that point to begin working on the exorcism of the Pentagon demonstration.

MR. WEINGLASS: Prior to the date of the demonstration which is October, did you go to the Pentagon?

THE WITNESS: Yes. I went about a week or two before with one of my close brothers, Martin Carey, a poster maker, and we measured the Pentagon, the two of us, to see how many people would fit around it. We only had to do one side because it is just multiplied by five.

We got arrested. It's illegal to measure the Pentagon. I didn't know it up to that point.

When we were arrested they asked us what we were doing. We said it was to measure the Pentagon and we wanted a permit to raise it 300 feet in the air, and they said "How about 10?" So we said "OK".

And they threw us out of the Pentagon and we went back to New York and had a press conference, told them what it was about.

We also introduced a drug called *lace*, which, when you squirted it at the policemen made them take their clothes off and make love, a very potent drug.

MR. WEINGLASS: Did you mean literally that the building was to rise up 300 feet off the ground?

MR. SCHULTZ: I can't cross-examine about his meaning literally.

THE COURT: I sustain the objection.

MR. SCHULTZ: I would ask Mr. Weinglass please get on with the trial of this case and stop playing around with raising the Pentagon 10 feet or 300 feet off the ground.

MR. WEINGLASS: Your Honor, I am glad to see Mr. Schultz finally concedes that things like levitating the Pentagon building, putting LSD in the water, 10,000 people walking nude on Lake Michigan, and a $200,000 bribe attempt are all playing around. I am willing to concede that fact, that it was all playing around, it was a play idea of this witness, and if he is willing to concede it, we can all go home.

THE COURT: I sustain the objection.

MR. WEINGLASS: Did you intend that the people who surrounded the Pentagon should do anything of a violent nature whatever to cause the building to rise 300 feet in the air and be exorcised of evil spirits?

MR. SCHULTZ: Objection.

THE COURT: I sustain the objection.

MR. WEINGLASS: Could you indicate to the Court and jury whether or not the Pentagon was, in fact, exorcised of its evil spirits?

THE WITNESS: Yes, I believe it was.

MR. WEINGLASS: Could you tell the Court and jury what, if anything, you did at the Pentagon at the time of the exorcism?

THE WITNESS: Yes. I passed out a number of noisemakers and brightly colored flags, various kinds of costumes and hats and things, and we attempted to surround the Pentagon. Actually I was not involved in any kind of leadership role, just me and my wife trying to do it at that time, and at that point I climbed over a fence and got arrested a few times.

MR. SCHULTZ: I am not sure I heard the last few words after "me and my wife."

THE WITNESS: My wife and me.

THE COURT: Those are your words, not mine.

THE WITNESS: None of these are my words. I am trying to use your words. I don't speak this language. I am a poet and a writer and I don't talk this kind of language so I am trying the best I can to speak your language, not my language.

THE COURT: The remarks of the witness may go out and the jury is directed to disregard them.

THE WITNESS: Where do they go when they go out?

MR. WEINGLASS: Now, drawing your attention to the first week of December 1967, did you have occasion to meet with Jerry Rubin and the others?

THE WITNESS: Yes.

MR. WEINGLASS: Will you relate to the Court and jury what the conversation was?

THE WITNESS: Yes.

We talked about the possibility of having demonstrations at the Democratic Convention in Chicago, Illinois, that was going to be occurring that August. I am not sure that we knew at that point that it was in Chicago. Wherever it was, we were planning on going.

Jerry Rubin, I believe, said that it would be a good idea to call it the Festival of Life in contrast to the Convention of Death, and to have it in some kind of public area, like a park or something, in Chicago.

One thing that I was very particular about was that we didn't have any concept of leadership involved. There was a feeling of young people that they didn't want to listen to leaders. We had to create a kind of situation in which people would be allowed to participate and become in a real sense their own leaders.

I think it was then after this that Paul Krassner said the word "YIPPIE," and we felt that that expressed in a kind of slogan and advertising sense the spirit that we wanted to put forth in Chicago, and we adopted that as our password, really.

December 29, 1969

Anita [Hoffman] said that "Yippie" would be understood by our generation, that straight newspapers like the *New York Times* and the U.S. Government and the courts and everything wouldn't take it seriously unless it had a formal name, so she came up with the name: "Youth International Party." She said we could play a lot of jokes on the concept of "party" because everybody would think that we were this huge international conspiracy, but that in actuality we were a party that you had fun at.

Nancy [Kursham] said that fun was an integral ingredient, that people in America, because they were being programmed like IBM cards, weren't having enough fun in life and that if you watched television, the only people that you saw having any fun were people who were buying lousy junk on television commercials, and that this would be a whole new attitude because you would see people, young people, having fun while they were protesting the system, and that young people all around this country and around the world would be turned on for that kind of an attitude.

I said that fun was very important, too, that it was a direct rebuttal of the kind of ethics and morals that were being put forth in the country to keep people working in a rat race which didn't make any sense because in a few years that machines would do all the work anyway, that there was a whole system of values that people were taught to postpone their pleasure, to put all their money in the bank, to buy life insurance, a whole bunch of things that didn't make any sense to our generation at all, and that fun actually was becoming quite subversive.

Jerry said that because of our action at the Stock Exchange in throwing out the money, that within a few weeks the Wall Street brokers there had totally enclosed the whole stock exchange in bulletproof, shatterproof glass, that cost something like $20,000 because they were afraid we'd come back and throw money out again.

He said that for hundreds of years political cartoonists had always pictured corrupt politicians in the guise of a pig, and he said that it would be great theater if we ran a pig for President, and we all took that on as like a great idea and that's more or less—that was the founding.

MR. WEINGLASS: The document that is before you, D-222 for identification, what is that document?

THE WITNESS: It was our initial call to people to describe what Yippie was about and why we were coming to Chicago.

MR. WEINGLASS: Now, Abbie, could you read the entire document to the jury.

THE WITNESS: It says:

"A STATEMENT FROM YIP!

"Join us in Chicago in August for an international festival of youth, music, and theater. Rise up and abandon the creeping meatball! Come all you rebels, youth spirits, rock minstrels, truth-seekers, peacock-freaks, poets, barricade-jumpers, dancers, lovers and artists!

"It is summer. It is the last week in August, and the NATIONAL DEATH PARTY meets to bless Lyndon Johnson. We are there! There are 50,000 of us dancing in the streets, throbbing with amplifiers and harmony. We are making love in the parks. We are reading, singing, laughing, printing newspapers, groping, and making a mock convention, and celebrating the birth of FREE AMERICA in our own time.

"Everything will be free. Bring blankets, tents, draft-cards, body-paint, Mr. Leary's Cow, food to share, music, eager skin, and happiness. The threats of LBJ, Mayor Daley, and J. Edgar Freako will not stop us. We are coming! We are coming from all over the world!

"The life of the American spirit is being torn asunder by the forces of violence, decay, and the napalm-cancer fiend. We demand the Politics of Ecstasy! We are the delicate spores of the new fierceness that will change America. We will create our own reality, we are Free America! And we will not accept the false theater of the Death Convention.

"We will be in Chicago. Begin preparations now! Chicago is yours! Do it!"

"Do it!" was a slogan like "Yippie." We use that a lot and it meant that each person that came should take on the responsibility for being his own leader—that we should, in fact, have a leaderless society.

We shortly thereafter opened an office and people worked in the office on what we call movement salaries, subsistence, thirty dollars a week. We had what the straight world would call a staff and an office although we called it an energy center and regarded ourselves as a tribe or a family.

MR. WEINGLASS: Could you explain to the Court and jury, if you know, how this staff functioned in your office?

THE WITNESS: Well, I would describe it as anarchistic. People would pick up the phone and give information and people from all over the country were now becoming interested and they would ask for more information, whether we were going to get a permit, how the people in Chicago were relating, and we would bring flyers and banners and posters. We would have large general meetings that were open to anybody who wanted to come.

MR. WEINGLASS: How many people would attend these weekly meetings?

THE WITNESS: There were about two to three hundred people there that were attending the meetings. Eventually we had to move into Union Square and hold meetings out in the public. There would be maybe three to five hundred people attending meetings.

MR. WEINGLASS: Were these meetings open or closed?

THE WITNESS: Oh, totally open. They totally lacked any kind of formal structure, you know, with a chairman or something like that.

MR. WEINGLASS: What activities, if any, were planned at these meetings?

THE WITNESS: There was a trip to Appleton, Wisconsin, to the grave of late Senator Joseph McCarthy to summon his spirit to join the Democratic Party in Chicago. I think the main one that most of us worked on was a raid, a mock raid on the campus of Stony Brook College outside of New York City.

MR. WEINGLASS: Would you describe that for the Court and jury?

MR. SCHULTZ: Your Honor, unless this mock raid on the campus of Stony Brook has some relationship to the Democratic National Convention—

THE WITNESS: Sure it does.

THE COURT: I can't see it. I sustain the objection.

MR. WEINGLASS: Directing your attention to March 17, 1968, and New York City, will you tell the Court and jury what, if anything, you did that day?

THE WITNESS: March 17 we had a press conference to announce to the overground press, the mass media, the fact that we were going to come to Chicago for the Festival of Life.

MR. WEINGLASS: Did you make a statement?

THE WITNESS: No, I didn't make a formal statement, although both Jerry and myself talked to newsmen individually later. There were other people. Keith Lampe spoke and gave a report on the raid on Stony Brook that we had just had previously to that, mock raid. Everybody dressed as Keystone cops and we went to Stony Brook to arrest all the whiskey drinkers.

MR. SCHULTZ: Objection.

THE COURT: I sustain the objection.

THE WITNESS: You missed a good story.

MR. WEINGLASS: I show you D-223 for identification and ask you if you can identify that document?

THE WITNESS: This document was a flyer announcing the Yip-in in Grand Central Station.

MR. WEINGLASS: What night of the week was the Yip-in?

THE WITNESS: Friday, March 22, at midnight, the first night of spring, called the spring equinox.

MR. WEINGLASS: Where did you go the following day, if you can recall?

THE WITNESS: I flew to Chicago to observe a meeting being sponsored, I believe, by the National Mobilization Committee. It was held at a place called Lake Villa, I believe, about twenty miles outside of Chicago here.

MR. WEINGLASS: Do you recall how you were dressed for that meeting?

THE WITNESS: I was dressed as an Indian. I had gone to Grand Central Station as an Indian and so I just got on a plane and flew as an Indian.

MR. WEINGLASS: Now, when you flew to Chicago, were you alone?

THE WITNESS: No. Present were Jerry, myself, Paul Krassner, and Marshall Bloom, the head of this Liberation News Service.

MR. WEINGLASS: When you arrived at Lake Villa, did you have occasion to meet any of the defendants who are seated here at this table?

THE WITNESS: Yes, I met for the first time Rennie, Tom Hayden—who I had met before, and that's it, you know.

MR. WEINGLASS: Did Jerry Rubin speak in your presence at Lake Villa at this meeting that you can recall?

THE WITNESS: Yes, I believe that he did. He made a speech that we ought to support the Polish students, the Russians were trying to impose a kind of imperialism on the Polish students, on the young people in Poland, and he put forth—

MR. SCHULTZ: Objection. That has nothing to do with what we are trying here, the Polish students and the Russians in Poland. I object.

THE WITNESS: Should I continue? I hadn't finished. It was related. What should I do now, Judge?

THE COURT: Just keep quiet until your lawyer asks you a question.

MR. WEINGLASS: There was a demonstration in Chicago against the Russian invasion of Czechoslovakia.

THE COURT: I will let my ruling stand. You may ask another question.

MR. WEINGLASS: Do you recall if you spoke at the Lake Villa meeting?

THE WITNESS: I gave a general speech on what I thought politics was, that it was the way that you led your life, not who you supported; that it didn't matter really if people supported Lyndon Johnson or McCarthy or Hitler or Attila the Hun or George Wallace, it is what they did with their lives, and how they related to each other as human beings, and that we didn't have any particular kind of program that we were bringing to Chicago, but that we were bringing a kind of life style.

I spoke at a workshop, too. There was a workshop on anticapitalism and I offered a plank that we ought to abolish pay toilets, that they were an insult to a system that was so affluent as this, and they didn't like that. They were very straight, that workshop.

MR. WEINGLASS: Was any decision reached at that meeting about coming to Chicago?

THE WITNESS: I believe that they debated for two days about whether they should come or not to Chicago. They decided to have more meetings. We said we had already made up our minds to come to Chicago and we passed out buttons and posters and said that if they were there, good, it would be a good time.

MR. WEINGLASS: Following the Lake Villa conference, do you recall where you went?

THE WITNESS: Yes. The next day, March 25, I went to the Aragon Ballroom. It was a benefit to raise money again for the Yippies but we had a meeting backstage in one of the dressing rooms with the Chicago Yippies.

MR. WEINGLASS: Do you recall what was discussed?

THE WITNESS: Yes. We drafted a permit application for the Festival to take place in Chicago. We agreed that Grant Park would be best.

MR. WEINGLASS: Directing your attention to the following morning, which was Monday morning, March 26, do you recall where you were at that morning?

THE WITNESS: We went to the Parks Department. Jerry was there, Paul, Helen Runningwater, Abe Peck, Reverend John Tuttle—there were a group of about twenty to thirty people, Yippies.

MR. WEINGLASS: Did you meet with anyone at the Park District at that time?

THE WITNESS: Yes. There were officials from the Parks Department to greet us, they took us into this office, and we presented a permit application.

MR. WEINGLASS: Did you ever receive a reply to this application?

THE WITNESS: Not to my knowledge.

MR. WEINGLASS: After your meeting with the Park District, where, if anywhere, did you go?

THE WITNESS: We held a brief press conference on the lawn in front of the Parks Department, and then we went to see Mayor Daley at City Hall. When we arrived, we were told that the mayor was indisposed and that Deputy Mayor David Stahl would see us.

MR. WEINGLASS: When you met with Deputy Mayor Stahl, what, if anything, occurred?

THE WITNESS: Helen Runningwater presented him with a copy of the permit application that we had submitted to the Parks Department. It was rolled up in the Playmate of the Month that said "To Dick with Love, the Yippies," on it. And we presented it to him and gave him a kiss and put a Yippie button on him, and when he opened it up, the Playmate was just there.

And he was very embarrassed by the whole thing, and he said that we had followed the right procedure, the city would give it proper attention, and things like that.

MR. WEINGLASS: Directing your attention to Sunday, May 13, which is Mother's Day 1968, where were you on that day?

THE WITNESS: There was what we might call a mini-festival of life, a rock concert, I believe. There were marriages taking place and there was a preparation—everybody had pies, apple pies and cherry pies and there was the beginning of a march to the police station to present the police who were on duty that Sunday, Mother's Day, with pies, apple pies.

MR. SCHULTZ: Objection. Marching to the police station on Mother's Day with pies is irrelevant.

THE COURT: You object to what is coming?

MR. SCHULTZ: I object to his continuing with the Mother's Day pies, yes, sir.

THE WITNESS: I was through with that story.

MR. WEINGLASS: It is irrelevant by Government standards. If they went to the police station carrying bombs, they would say that was relevant.

THE COURT: You may ask another question.

MR. WEINGLASS: Did a subsequent meeting occur the first week of June in New York City?

THE WITNESS: Yes. Abe Peck and Paul Simon and one or two other people from Chicago came to New York to report at what were now weekly meetings of the Yippies, to report on their luck with the City.

MR. WEINGLASS: Could you identify Abe Peck for the jury, as to who he is?

THE WITNESS: He is sitting right there. A Chicago boy. He was editor of the underground newspaper called the *Seed*.

MR. WEINGLASS: What did Abe Peck report at that meeting?

THE WITNESS: He reported that there were a number of problems arising with the Chicago Police Department; that they had had a benefit to raise money at the Electric Theater, I believe it was; that the police raided the benefit and—

MR. SCHULTZ: Your Honor—

THE WITNESS: —and arrested the owner.

MR. SCHULTZ: Your Honor, there was plenty of reason for that raid because there were violations of the law, serious violations. Obviously the defendants want to interject raids by the police because the defendants and their people were doing nothing wrong and the police just barged in for no good reason, but—

THE COURT: Do you move to strike those remarks?

MR. SCHULTZ: That is right. I ask they be stricken.

THE COURT: I strike all of the last remarks of the witness and direct the jury to disregard them.

MR. WEINGLASS: Those serious violations were building code violations by the owner of the building.

THE COURT: I have ruled.

MR. WEINGLASS: In regard to the police raid, could you indicate what else Abe Peck reported at that meeting?

THE WITNESS: He reported that in Chicago there was a curfew that began at 10:30 and literally all young people seventeen and under were criminals after 10:30 and could be arrested and yanked off the streets.

He said the attitude of the Chicago police in relating to longhaired people was going to make it particularly difficult for us to have a peaceful Festival of Life. He said it was indicative of the kind of oppression that the longhaired community around the country was receiving at the hands of police at that time.

December 29, 1969

MR. WEINGLASS: I direct your attention now to August 5, 1968, and I ask you where you were on that day.

THE WITNESS: I was in my apartment, St. Marks Place, on the Lower East Side in New York City.

MR. WEINGLASS: Who was with you?

THE WITNESS: Jerry Rubin was there, Paul Krassner was there, and Nancy. Anita was there; five of us, I believe.

MR. WEINGLASS: Can you describe the conversation which occurred between you and Abe Peck on the telephone?

THE WITNESS: Mr. Peck and other people from Chicago, Yippies—had just returned from a meeting on Monday afternoon with David Stahl and other people from the City administration. He said that he was quite shocked because—they said that they didn't know that we wanted to sleep in the park.

Abe Peck said that it had been known all along that one of the key elements of this Festival was to let us sleep in the park, that it was impossible for people to sleep in hotels since the delegates were staying there and it would only be natural to sleep in the park.

He furthermore told me in his opinion the City was laying down certain threats to them in order to try and get them to withdraw their permit application, and that we should come immediately back to Chicago.

MR. WEINGLASS: After that phone conversation what occurred?

THE WITNESS: We subsequently went to Chicago on August 7 at night.

MR. WEINGLASS: Did a meeting occur on that evening?

THE WITNESS: Yes, in Mayor Daley's press conference room, where he holds his press conferences.

MR. WEINGLASS: Can you relate what occurred at this meeting?

THE WITNESS: It was more or less an informal kind of meeting. Mr. Stahl made clear that these were just exploratory talks, that the mayor didn't have it in his power to grant the permits. We said that that was absurd, that we had been negotiating now for a period of four or five months, that the City was acting like an ostrich, sticking its head in the sand, hoping that we would all go away like it was some bad dream.

I pointed out that it was in the best interests of the City to have us in Lincoln Park ten miles away from the Convention hall. I said we had no intention of marching on the Convention hall, that I didn't particularly think that politics in America could be changed by marches and rallies, that what we were presenting was an alternative life style, and we hoped that people of Chicago would come up, and mingle in Lincoln Park and see what we were about.

I said that the City ought to give us a hundred grand, a hundred thousand dollars to run the Festival. It would be so much in their best interests.

And then I said, "Why don't you just give two hundred grand, and I'll split town?"

It was a very informal meeting. We were just sitting around on metal chairs that they had.

All the time David Stahl had been insisting that they did not make decisions in the city, that he and the mayor did not make the decisions. We greeted this with a lot of laughter and said that it was generally understood all around the country that Daley was the boss of Chicago and made all the decisions.

I also said that I considered that our right to assemble in Lincoln Park and to present our society was a right that I was willing to die for, that this was a fundamental human right.

MR. WEINGLASS: When you left that meeting, where did you go?

THE WITNESS: We went to the *Seed* office.

MR. WEINGLASS: What occurred there?

THE WITNESS: We suggested that perhaps we had been a bit naive and we should warn people that the permit negotiations were going very poorly, that the city of Chicago was a very uptight place and was making a lot of threats to the Yippie community in Chicago, and that we should resubmit a permit application the next day.

The following morning, August 8, we went to the Parks Department, and, as a group, submitted the document.

MR. WEINGLASS: Now after you submitted the document, what occurred at the Parks Department, if anything?

THE WITNESS: They just accepted the document and it was all, you know, just straight, formal stuff. "Thank you. Yep. This is right. You are doing it right."

We didn't have that attitude at all.

MR. WEINGLASS: Directing your attention to August 9 in the morning, do you recall where you were?

THE WITNESS: August 9. Yes. I believe I was at the office of the National Mobilization Committee.

There were about twenty to thirty people in the room and the only person that I can really say that I knew and recognized was Rennie Davis.

MR. WEINGLASS: Do you recall what Rennie Davis said at that meeting?

THE WITNESS: He described the difficulties the National Mobilization Committee was having in their deliberations with City officials. I said that we were having similar difficulties. I said that we had not made a decision yet about the marching on the Amphitheatre. We were concerned about what was going to happen in Lincoln Park and putting forth our alternative culture.

I will take my shirt off. OK? I'm a little warm. Could you wait a second?

I'm getting fatter. It's the neon lights: they're bad for me, for my health.

MR. WEINGLASS: What else was said other than what you have already stated at the meeting of August 9?

THE WITNESS: Rennie Davis said that the Mobilization was having orientation in a number of parks in Chicago. I said that we could do it together and our efforts should be combined in Lincoln Park.

MR. WEINGLASS: On August 14, approximately three days later, in the morning of that day, do you recall where you were?

THE WITNESS: I went to speak to Jay Miller, head of the American Civil Liberties Union. I asked if it was possible for them to work with us on an injunction in the Federal court to sue Mayor Daley and other city officials about the fact that they would not grant us a permit and were denying us our right to freedom of speech and assembly.

MR. WEINGLASS: Now, can you relate to the Court and jury what happened in court when you appeared at 10:00 A.M.?

THE WITNESS: It was heard before Judge Lynch.

There was a fantastic amount of guards all over the place.

We were searched, made to take off our shirts, empty our pockets—

MR. SCHULTZ: That is totally irrelevant. There happened to be threats at that time, your Honor—

THE WITNESS: He is right. There were threats. I had twenty that week.

THE COURT: The language, "There were a fantastic amount of guards," may go out and the jury is directed to disregard them.

MR. WEINGLASS: After the—

THE WITNESS: We came before the judge. It was a room similar to this, similar, kind of wall-to wall bourgeois, rugs and neon lights. Federal courts are all the same, I think.

The judge made a couple of references to us in the room, said that our dress was an affront to the Court.

It was pointed out by a lawyer that came by that Judge Lynch was Mayor Daley's ex-law partner. As as result of this conversation we went back into court about twenty, thirty minutes later.

MR. WEINGLASS: Did you speak to the Court?

THE WITNESS: I spoke to Judge Lynch. I said that we were withdrawing our suit, that we had as little faith in the judicial system in this country as we had in the political system.

He said, "Be careful, young man. I will find a place for you to sleep."

And I thanked him for that, said I had one, and left.

We withdrew our suit. Then we had a press conference downstairs to explain the reasons for that. We explained to the press that we were leaving in our permit application but withdrawing our Federal injunction to sue the city. We said it was a bit futile to end up before a judge, Judge Lynch, who was the ex-law partner of Mayor Daley, that the Federal judges were closely tied in with the Daley and Democratic political machine in Chicago and that we could have little recourse of grievance.

Furthermore, that we suspected that the judge would order us not to go into Lincoln Park at all and that if we did, that we would be in violation of contempt of court, and that it was a setup, and Judge Lynch planned to lynch us in the same way that Stahl was stalling us.

I pointed out that the names in this thing were getting really absurd, similarities. I also read a list of Yippie demands that I had written that morning—sort of Yippie philosophy.

MR. WEINGLASS: Now, will you read for the Court and jury the eighteen demands first, then the postscript.

THE WITNESS: I will read it in the order that I wrote it. "Revolution toward a free society, Yippie, by A. Yippie.

"This is a personal statement. There are no spokesmen for the Yippies. We are all our own leaders. We realize this list of demands is inconsistent. They are not really demands. For people to make demands of the Democratic Party is an exercise in wasted wish fulfillment. If we have a demand, it is simply and emphatically that they, along with their fellow inmates in the Republican Party, cease to exist. We demand a society built along the alternative community in Lincoln Park, a society based on humanitarian cooperation and equality, a society which allows and promotes the creativity present in all people and especially our youth.

"Number one. An immediate end to the war in Vietnam and a restructuring of our foreign policy which totally eliminates aspects of military, economic and cultural imperialism; the withdrawal of all foreign based troops and the abolition of military draft.

"Two. An immediate freedom for Huey Newton of the Black Panthers and all other black people; adoption of the community control concept in our ghetto areas; an end to the cultural and economic domination of minority groups.

"Three. The legalization of marijuana and all other psychedelic drugs; the freeing of all prisoners currently imprisoned on narcotics charges.

"Number four. A prison system based on the concept of rehabilitation rather than punishment.

"Five. A judicial system which works towards the abolition of all laws related to crimes without victims; that is, retention only of laws relating to crimes in which there is an unwilling injured party; i.e. murder, rape, or assault.

"Six. The total disarmament of all the people beginning with the police. This includes not only guns but such brutal vices as tear gas, Mace, electric prods, blackjacks, billy clubs, and the like.

"Seven. The abolition of money, the abolition of pay housing, pay media, pay transportation, pay food, pay education, pay clothing, pay medical health, and pay toilets.

"Eight. A society which works towards and actively promotes the concept of full unemployment, a society in which people are free from the drudgery of work, adoption of the concept 'Let the machines do it.'

"Number ten. A program of ecological development that would provide incentives for the decentralization of crowded cities and encourage rural living.

"Eleven. A program which provides not only free birth control information and devices, but also abortions when desired.

"Twelve. A restructured educational system which provides a student power to determine his course of study, student participation in over-all policy planning; an educational system which breaks down its barriers between school and community; a system which uses the surrounding community as a classroom so that students may learn directly the problems of the people.

"Number thirteen. The open and free use of the media; a program which actively supports and promotes cable television as a method of increasing the selection of channels available to the viewer.

"Fourteen. An end to all censorship. We are sick of a society that has no hesitation about showing people committing violence and refuses to show a couple fucking.

"Fifteen. We believe that people should fuck all the time, any time, wherever they wish. This is not a programmed demand but a simple recognition of the reality around us.

"Sixteen. A political system which is more streamlined and responsive to the needs of all the people regardless of age, sex, or race; perhaps a national referendum system conducted via television or a telephone voting system; perhaps a decentralization of power and authority with many varied tribal groups, groups in which people exist in a state of basic trust and are free to choose their tribe.

"Seventeen. A program that encourages and promotes the arts. However, we feel that if the free society we envision were to be sought for and achieved, all of us would actualize the creativity within us; in a very real sense we would have a society in which every man would be an artist."

And eighteen was left blank for anybody to fill in what they wanted. "It was for these reasons that we had come to Chicago, it was for these reasons that many of us may fight and die here. We recognize this as the vision of the founders of this nation. We recognize that we are America; we recognize that we are free men. The present-day politicians and their armies of automatons have selfishly robbed us of our birthright. The evilness they stand for will go unchallenged no longer. Political pigs, your days are numbered. We are the second American Revolution. We shall win.

"YIPPIE."

MR. WEINGLASS: When you used the words "fight and die here," in what context were you using those words?

THE WITNESS: It is a metaphor. That means that we felt strongly about our right to assemble in the park and that people should be willing to take risks for it. It doesn't spell it out because people were capable of fighting in their own way and making their own decisions and we never would tell anyone specifically that they should fight, fistfight.

MR. WEINGLASS: Did you during the week of the Convention and the period of time immediately before the Convention tell any person singly or in groups that they should fight in the park?

MR. SCHULTZ: Objection.

THE COURT: I sustain the objection.

MR. WEINGLASS: Directing your attention to the morning of August 19, 1968, did you attend a meeting on that day?

THE WITNESS: Yes. I went to the office of the Mobilization Committee.

MR. WEINGLASS: Was there a discussion?

THE WITNESS: I never stayed long at these meetings. I just went and made an announcement and maybe stayed ten or fifteen minutes.

MR. WEINGLASS: Now, do you recall what, if anything, you said at that meeting?

THE WITNESS: I told them that ABC cameramen had given me a booklet telling background material on the various delegates that were coming to the Democratic Convention. It had maps and everything of where they were staying, and I suggested that since they were going to visit the delegates, that maybe we could print up this information.

Rennie Davis said that it would be valuable information, but most of it was superfluous since it was already public knowledge printed in all the daily newspapers in Chicago.

MR. WEINGLASS: Now, do you recall where you were during the day on Friday at the end of that week, August 23, 1968?

THE WITNESS: I was in Lincoln Park, I guess. I was in Lincoln Park almost all those days.

MR. WEINGLASS: Do you recall what was happening on Friday when you were in the park?

THE WITNESS: There were classes going on in what appeared to be karate and snake dancing and self-defense, and people were talking about Mace and first aid, classes like that.

There were in these classes probably maybe fifty to sixty people on that Friday with probably two hundred people around taking pictures, two hundred to two hundred fifty people—Chicago police in uniform, undercover police, army intelligence, Secret Service, you know, Naval Intelligence, CIA—I don't know. Everybody was laughing at everybody else's clumsy efforts.

MR. WEINGLASS: Was karate being taught?

THE WITNESS: After a manner of speaking it was being taught. Some of the people that seemed to have experience were rolling newspapers and showing how to protect yourself if a billy club was brought down. It was more for people to gain discipline over their bodies and that sort of thing.

MR. WEINGLASS: Was there a course given in snake dancing on that day also?

THE WITNESS: Yes. Yes. People would have a pole and there would be about six people, and then about six people behind them, holding them around the waist, four or five lines of these people with men, women, and kids maybe eight years old in on this whole thing, and people would bounce from one foot to the other and yell "Wash oi, Wash oi," which is kind of Japanese for "Yippie," I guess.

And they would just march up and down the park like this, mostly laughing and giggling, because the newsmen were taking this quite seriously, and then at a certain point everybody would turn in and sort of just collapse and fall on the ground and laugh. I believe we lost about four or five Yippies during that great training.

The exciting part was when the police arrested two army intelligence officers in the trees.

MR. WEINGLASS: During the course of that day when you were in the park, did you notice that the police were hanging any signs in the park?

THE WITNESS: Late in the day, maybe four or five, I became aware that there were police nailing signs on the trees that said "11:00 P.M. curfew," maybe a few other words, but that was the gist of the signs.

MR. WEINGLASS: From Friday, August 23, on to the end of Convention week, did you ever discuss with any people the question of staying in the park after the curfew hours?

THE WITNESS: At a meeting on August 24, that subject came up, and there was lengthy discussion.

MR. WEINGLASS: Now, did you hear Jerry Rubin speak at that meeting?

THE WITNESS: Jerry said that the park wasn't worth fighting for; that we should leave at the eleven P.M. curfew. He said that we should put out a statement to that effect.

MR. WEINGLASS: And did you speak at that meeting?

THE WITNESS: I reported on a meeting that morning with Chief Lynskey. I had asked the Chicago cops who were tailing me to take me to Chief Lynskey who was in charge of the area of Lincoln Park. I went up to the chief and said, "Well, are you going to let us have the Festival?"

He said "No festival under any circumstances. If anybody breaks one city ordinance in that park, we clear the whole park."

He said, "You do any one thing wrong and I will arrest you on sight."

He said, "Why don't you try to kick me in the shins right now?"

And I said NBC wasn't there.

And he said, "Well, at least the kid's honest," and stuff like that.

Then I gave a speech to the police that were all assembled and I said, "Have a good time." I said, "The National Guard's coming in, they're probably going to whip you guys up, and I hope your walkie-talkies work better than ours," and stuff like that. And I just walked out.

Then we discussed what we were going to do. I said it was my feeling that Chicago was in a total state of anarchy as far as the police mentality worked. I said that we were going to have to fight for every single thing, we were going to have to fight for the electricity, we were going to have to fight to have the stage come in, we were going to have to fight for every rock musician to play, that the whole week was going to be like that.

I said that we should proceed with the festival as planned, we should try to do everything that we had come to Chicago to do, even though the police and the city officials were standing in our way.

MR. WEINGLASS: During the course of this Saturday and prior to this meeting, did you have occasion to meet Irv Bock in the park?

THE WITNESS: Oh, I met Irv Bock Saturday afternoon during some of the marshal training. Marshal training is a difficult phrase to use for Yippies. We always have a reluctance to marshals because they are telling people what to do and we were more anarchistic than that, more leaderless.

I sort of bumped into Irv Bock. I showed him a—it wasn't a gas mask but it was a thing with two plastic eyes and a little piece of leather that I got, I purchased in an army-navy store for about nineteen cents, and I said that these would be good protection against Mace.

He started running down to me all this complicated military jargon and I looked at him and said, "Irv, you're a cop, ain't you?"

He sort of smiled and said, "No, I'm not."

"Come on," I said, "We don't grow peaceniks that big. We are all quarterbacks. You've got to be a cop."

I said, "Show me your wallet."

So he said, "No, no. Don't you trust me?"

So I said, "Irv," I said, "last night there was a guy running around my house with a pistol trying to kill me," that I had twenty threats that week, and at that point I didn't trust Jerry Rubin.

MR. WEINGLASS: Now, directing your attention to Sunday, August 25, about three o'clock in the afternoon on Sunday, where were you in the park?

THE WITNESS: I was having a conversation with Chief Lynskey, I believe it was.

Chief Lynskey began the conversation and said, "According to our meeting this morning, you had agreed to provide your own generators."

I was a bit stunned because we hadn't met that morning. So I sort of played along with it and said, "No, according to our meeting this morning we were going to use the electricity in the refreshment stand." I was prepared for him to arrest me and everybody in the park right there on the spot.

I said, "Well, I guess it's time to start the rock festival." I took the cord and it was a regular electrical cord on a long black cord, maybe a hundred, two hundred feet long, and I just walked over to the refreshment stand with the police and Lynskey and kids and Yippies and everybody yelling and screaming and just stuck it in.

Right after that he slapped me on the back and said, "It looks like we're going to have a Festival."

So I said, "Yes, I guess it looks that way."

Then I asked him if we could bring the truck in.

MR. WEINGLASS: And what happened?

THE WITNESS: He said, "There's no agreement about a truck."

I mean, I was shocked. He was sort of fumbling the whole thing because there was no agreement for anything, and I said that we had this flatbed truck parked in front of the theater.

He said, "No truck. You can have the electricity but no truck."

So we decided to start the rock festival without a stage and band set up on the ground. All this time crowds kept building up. There were four, maybe five, six, seven thousand people there in the park, and people kept pushing to get to the front.

I kept talking to Lynskey saying that this was a very dangerous social situation. All they had to do was let us bring the truck in and nobody would get hurt, it would be peaceful, that's what I said.

I went over with Stew Albert to the staging area to see how we could go about getting the truck into the park.

Lynskey hadn't come back in the time that he said he would, and we went over there to talk to the next top cop in charge.

MR. WEINGLASS: What did he say?

THE WITNESS: He said that the truck would not be allowed in—he wanted to wait for a few minutes for Lynskey to come back. So we waited a few minutes, and he didn't come back, and finally he suggested that we drive the truck along the back of the snow fence and then the truck wouldn't technically be inside the park. We agreed, and we started to move the truck.

I could see a number of people moving from the back of the crowd and Stew Albert came up to me and said that the police had come through the zoo and down into the park, about 200 police, and had started clubbing people and pushing them, and there had been some arrests. He was bleeding all over his head and face. There was blood pouring profusely—

MR. WEINGLASS: About what time of day was that?

THE WITNESS: This was about 6:30 at night, Sunday night.

MR. WEINGLASS: Now, did you see the police in that area?

THE WITNESS: There were maybe 2,000 people seated, singing songs and things, and the police were lined up in rows, standing like this—cops do that, standing like that, typical cop stance.

MR. WEINGLASS: What did you do when you got there?

THE WITNESS: Well, I went up between the people and the police, and I said that the police had busted up the music festival, that it was over, that they had entered the park, and that we had a legal right to even be in the park, and they couldn't wait until 11:00 P.M., to kick the shit out of us, and they were just pouring in, and I introduced Stew and said, "Here is one of my brothers from Berkeley, you know; his blood is all our blood," and I was crying.

MR. WEINGLASS: Did you return to the park that night?

THE WITNESS: Yes, it was getting very dark, and it was getting cold. There were fires in the trashbuckets and people were sitting around singing folk songs. I spent most of my time right here talking to groups, forming affinity groups, small groups that were six or seven people, introducing them to each other, saying that it would be safer if they stuck together.

MR. WEINGLASS: Later that night, did you have occasion to talk to Commander Braasch?

THE WITNESS: Yes. I said, "Can't your police wait? It ain't even the curfew yet. I mean, already they're clubbing the crap out of people. You know, there's bloody heads all over the place."

I said "I got belted just trying to go to the men's room in the fieldhouse," and, I said, "It would be helpful if you gave us some indication of what your plans were, you know."

He said that they were going to pull up a car in this vicinity at 11:00 P.M. and announce that the curfew was in effect, that they had no intention of letting us stay in the park.

I said at that point there probably would be a symbolic test so that we could fight it out in the courts about our constitutional rights.

THE COURT: Mr. Marshal, I think at this point we will recess until tomorrow morning.

December 30, 1969

THE COURT: Bring in the jury, Mr. Marshal.

ABBIE HOFFMAN: Wait a second. We have a matter—

THE COURT: Who was that, waving and talking at me, one of the lawyers?

MR. SCHULTZ: He is acting as his own lawyer, I think. He is doing a good job of it. He shows Mr. Weinglass up.

ABBIE HOFFMAN: Wait until you get your chance.

THE COURT: Mr. Kunstler, do you have anything?

MR. KUNSTLER: Your Honor, I understand that there was a line of young people downstairs from early morning attempting to get into this courtroom. They arrive here early because if you don't get in line early you just don't get into the room. I understand that a great number of them were arrested this morning at 4:00 or 5:00 A.M. while doing nothing more than waiting in line. They were arrested for violation of the curfew law here in Chicago. We think this is particularly within the province of your Honor because this is a Federal building and the ground on which it is built is owned by the people of the United States and we do have people of the United States who are here to see a trial.

THE COURT: If they have been arrested, have they been arrested by Federal officers?

MR. KUNSTLER: I understand by city police.

THE COURT: I don't have any jurisdiction over city police.

MR. KUNSTLER: I am asking your Honor to issue an order that there be no arrests for violation of the curfew law.

THE COURT: Frankly, I didn't know there was a curfew law. I have never dealt with a curfew law. But I don't have the jurisdiction. If there is a curfew law I will certainly deny your motion because I can't say in effect that it is permissible to violate the curfew law, if indeed there is one.

MR. KUNSTLER: Your Honor, we feel that one of the points of the arrests today was because the defendant Abbie Hoffman was testifying and relates to young people, and a great many young people showed up and there are probably a great many in this courtroom right now who want to hear what Mr. Hoffman has to say.

THE COURT: I don't propose to get into a discussion of who gets admitted to this trial. I am a trial judge and not a janitor or somebody who looks after the property of the government. This trial is a public trial. Bring in the jury, Mr. Marshal.

Good morning.

· · · · ·

MR. WEINGLASS: Directing your attention to approximately two o'clock in the morning, which would now be Monday morning, do you recall what you were doing?

THE WITNESS: I made a telephone call to David Stahl, Deputy Mayor of Chicago at his home. I had his home number.

I said, "Hi, Dave. How's it going? Your police got to be the dumbest and the most brutal in the country," I said.

"The decision to drive people out of the park in order to protect the City was about the dumbest military tactic since the Trojans let the Trojan horse inside the gate and there was nothing to be compared with that stupidity."

I again pleaded with him to let people stay in the park the following night. "There will be more people coming Monday, Tuesday, and subsequently Wednesday night," I said, "and they should be allowed to sleep." I said that he ought to intercede with the Police Department. I said to him that the City officials, in particular his boss, Daley, were totally out of their minds.

I said, "I read in the paper the day before that they had 2,000 troops surrounding the reservoirs in order to protect against the Yippie plot to dump LSD in the drinking water. There isn't a kid in the country," I said, "never mind a Yippie, who thinks that such a thing could be done."

I told him to check with all the scientists at the University of Chicago—he owned them all.

He said that he knew it couldn't be done, but they weren't taking any chances anyway.

MR. WEINGLASS: Now, approximately six o'clock on Monday morning, August 26, do you recall where you were?

THE WITNESS: I went to a church with Tim Kelly. He was Catholic, and he said, "Why don't we go and pray?"

And I said, "Try anything, pray, yeah," so we prayed.

MR. WEINGLASS: Now, at anytime during the rest of that day, which is Monday, August 26, did you have occasion to meet or be introduced to a person who later became identified to you as Robert Pierson?

Yes, I believe I did. Somebody had said, "This guy is going to be your bodyguard. He is going to go with you."

I said, "Oh? So—"

That was about it.

I was with a man named Al who had a dog with him on a leash. We were leaving the park going to a car, a Volkswagen.

Pierson came as far as the car with us. Then this guy Al got in the back with his dog, and Pierson said that he was afraid of dogs and wasn't going to come and would go back to the park. He asked where we were going and stuff like that.

MR. WEINGLASS: After you left Pierson, where did you go?

THE WITNESS: I went to the police station. I believe it is at 11th and State—the central police station in Chicago. I was with Ron Kaufman and this guy Al with the dog.

MR. WEINGLASS: What happened when you got there?

THE WITNESS: When we got out of the car the police pulled their guns out of the holsters and surrounded me, just like that, and I said, "Flower power."

I said, "Oh, the dog's cool, you know, he ain't got no teeth."

And they put their guns away and I asked them where Wolfe and Hayden, who had been arrested, were, and they said they were going to be released on the other side of the building.

I went over there and waited for about a half hour until they came out.

MR. WEINGLASS: Did you meet with Tom Hayden and Wolfe Lowenthal?

THE WITNESS: Tom Hayden pointed out the two members of the Red Squad that were following him, and he said that they had made a number of threats on his life and he was afraid that they were going to kill him one of these nights. He asked me if I had had similar feelings about the Chicago police that were following me.

I pointed out to him who they were and what car they were sitting in. I said, "I have managed to con a couple of meals out of them and I got them to drive me around and give me reports about what was going on at night.

"But," I said, "they definitely informed me that I was going to be arrested on Wednesday."

I told Tom that I asked them why I was going to be arrested, and they would just smile and say, "It's going to happen."

MR. WEINGLASS: Can you tell the Court and jury where you were in Lincoln Park at approximately 11:30 Monday night?

THE WITNESS: I was walking through the barricade, my wife Anita and I.

MR. WEINGLASS: Did you see Allen Ginsberg at the barricade?

THE WITNESS: Yes. He was kneeling.

There was a crowd of people around. He was playing that instrument that he plays and people were chanting.

There was a police car that would come by and I believe it was making announcements and people would yell at the police car, you know, "Beat it. Get out. The parks belong to the people. Oink Oink. Pig Pig. Pigs are coming. Peace Now."

People were waving flags. People were running around being scared and people were running around sort of joyous. I mean, it was strange, different emotions. It was very dark in that place.

MR. SCHULTZ: The witness is not answering the question any more. He is giving another essay. I object.

MR. WEINGLASS: When the police finally came to the barricade, from what direction did they come?

THE WITNESS: They came in through the zoo.

They proceeded to climb and immediately started to club people.

They were throwing parts of the barricade, trashcans, at people.

MR. WEINGLASS: Now, at the time the police came to the barricade what did you do?

THE WITNESS: Well, I was coughing and spitting because there was tear gas totally flooding the air, cannisters were exploding all around me—I moved with the people out this way, out of the park trying to duck, picking up people that were being clubbed, getting off the ground myself a few times.

The police were just coming through in this wedge, solid wedge, clubbing people right and left, and I tried to get out of the park.

MR. WEINGLASS: Directing your attention to approximately six o'clock the following morning, do you recall where you were?

THE WITNESS: I got in the car of the police that were following me and asked them to take me to the beach—the beach part of Lincoln Park.

MR. WEINGLASS: What was occurring when you got there?

THE WITNESS: Allen Ginsberg and about—oh 150-200 people were kneeling, most of the people in lotus position which is a position with their legs crossed like this—chanting and praying and meditating.

There were five or six police cars on the boardwalk right in back, and there were police surrounding the group. Dawn was breaking. It was very cold, very chilly. People had a number of blankets wrapped around them, sitting in a circle.

I went and sat next to Allen and chanted and prayed for about an hour. Then I talked to the group. People would give talks about their feelings of what was going on in Chicago. I said, "I am very sad about what has happened in Chicago.

"What is going on here is very beautiful, but it won't be in the evening news that night.

"The American mass media is a glutton for violence, and it would be only shots of what was happening in the streets of Chicago."

I said, "America can't be changed by people sitting and praying, and this is an unfortunate reality that we have to face."

I said that we were a community that had to learn how to survive, that we had seen what had happened the last few nights in Lincoln Park. We had seen the destruction of the Festival.

I said, "I will never again tell people to sit quietly and pray for change."

MR. WEINGLASS: After this sunrise service was over, did you leave the park?

THE WITNESS: I walked through the park to the Free Theater. The Free Theater is a building with a huge courtyard. There were perhaps two or three hundred young people in small groups in the courtyard huddled around campfires with blankets over them. Many people had bandages wrapped around their feet. Many people had bandages on their heads with blood showing through.

People were roasting hot dogs and things over the fire. Some people had guitars and were singing folksongs, and there were people in white coats and white jackets going around trying to mend up some of the people. Many people were just stretched out totally unconscious, it appeared to me.

There was also a group of about ten police that were going through the area, kicking the fires and pushing the people and telling them to get out of the city, things like that.

I asked them if they had a search warrant. I said that it was private property, that we had a right to be here. They said that it didn't matter, that it was their job to drive us out of the city.

I said, "Did you check this out with Commander Braasch?"

I said, "I have just had a conversation with him, and you were supposed to leave this place alone." That was bluff, but they left.

Then I talked to the people—those that were listening. I said that this place looked like Valley Forge, with people huddled around in blankets, and that this was probably the second American Revolution, that Lincoln Park was comparable to the battle at Lexington and Concord.

I said, "The police are going to turn the whole city of Chicago into Yippies within the next two days."

MR. WEINGLASS: When you left the Free Theater, where did you go?

THE WITNESS: I hitchhiked from there to Lincoln Park. That is my general form of travel around Chicago. When I came into the park I met with a group of ministers.

MR. WEINGLASS: Do you recall what you said to them and what they said to you?

MR. SCHULTZ: I object as to what the minister said to Mr. Hoffman.

THE COURT: I sustain the objection.

MR. WEINGLASS: Your Honor, there has been no objection to other conversations but when we get into the area of ministers coming into the Park and being with the Yippies and supporting them, the Government objects on the grounds of hearsay.

MR. SCHULTZ: I don't think it is relevant in this trial as to whether or not the ministers knew what the Mobilization and the Yippies were doing, whether or not they were bilked by the Mobilization or the Yippies or whether they had a much higher or more elevated motive for these young people.

That is not relevant and that is what Mr. Weinglass is trying to get into. He wants to use the minister's good intentions and inject that into the trial and attribute it to the defendants.

THE COURT: I sustain the objection.

MR. WEINGLASS: Aside from meeting and talking to the ministers did you meet and talk to any other person while you were in the park on Tuesday in the early afternoon?

THE WITNESS: Right after that I talked to a man who said he was an official in a group called the Blackstone Rangers.

MR. WEINGLASS: If the Court please, Mr. Schultz' objection was withdrawn as soon as the words "Blackstone Rangers" were mentioned by the witness. Apparently we can have conversations with Blackstone Rangers but not with ministers under the Government's rule.

Could you relate your conversation with this man?

THE WITNESS: He said, "The police in Chicago have always treated black people this way," and that they empathized with what was happening to the Yippies in Lincoln Park. He told me they planned to bring a number of people to the park that night, that they were particularly interested in having a rally to hear Bobby Seale speak.

MR. WEINGLASS: Now, taking you back when you met with the ministers, can you relate what was said between you and them?

MR. SCHULTZ: Same objection, your Honor.

THE COURT: I sustain the objection.

MR. WEINGLASS: I would like to ask the Court what the difference is, according to the rules of evidence, as to conversation between Blackstone Rangers and the ministers—

THE COURT: I am not here to be examined, sir.

MR. SCHULTZ: I am prepared to tell Mr. Weinglass if he doesn't know. Because the defendant arranged with the Blackstone Rangers for them to come and fight for the park with weapons that night. That's the difference. That's the difference. And I will establish that on the cross examination of this witness.

THE WITNESS: It's going to be an exciting cross-examination.

MR. WEINGLASS: Both conversations took place, one after the other, but they will not permit testimony about the ministers coming in to hold a religious service. The Government is only interested in—

THE MARSHAL: Mr. Dellinger—

MR. DELLINGER: I am a little upset by the dishonesty of the Court's process—yes, my name is Dave Dellinger.

THE COURT: That man's name is Dellinger, Miss Reporter.

MR. DELLINGER: They are not interested in the truth. They just want one side of things to go in, even made-up things, but they won't allow the real things, the real truth.

THE COURT: Mr. Dellinger is continuing to speak, Miss Reporter.

MR. DELLINGER: Darned right. I hope the jury understands that too.

MR. SCHULTZ: This is unfair to the Government.

MR. KUNSTLER: Oh, your Honor—unfair to the Government—

MR. DELLINGER: The Government will go to jail for ten years, I suppose.

THE COURT: Just a minute, sir. Now Mr. Schultz, don't underestimate anybody's intelligence. Anyone who has been in a courtroom before knows that a defendant represented by able counsel doesn't speak out. Mr. Dellinger has spoken out.

MR. DELLINGER: Even when he's being railroaded he doesn't speak out.

THE COURT: I hope, Miss Reporter, you get those remarks.

MR. KUNSTLER: Your Honor, there comes a time when every human being feels a necessity to speak out, and Mr. Dellinger—

THE COURT: I didn't ask you to philosophize.

MR. KUNSTLER: I am not philosophizing, I am defending a client.

THE COURT: I have never sat in a trial, over the many years, where a defendant has spoken up on his own when—

MR. FROINES: Perhaps you can give him four years like you gave Bobby Seale.

MR. DELLINGER: We just walk politely into jail.

MR. SCHULTZ: Mr. Froines is the one who just made that comment about Bobby Seale. I am sure the Court saw that, and what's worse is the attorneys sanction it—they encourage it. Here is Mr. Kunstler standing at the podium encouraging this action.

MR. KUNSTLER: Your Honor, you are agreeing with the U.S. Attorney, I can see that.

THE COURT: And I ask you to sit down.

Mr. Marsal, please ask this lawyer to sit down.

MR. KUNSTLER: I have a right to stand and talk in defense of a client.

MR. DELLINGER: That's why we have to speak up, because you won't let our lawyers have a fair chance.

THE COURT: You may continue with the direct examination of this witness, sir.

MR. WEINGLASS: Did you ever see anyone you could identify as a member of the Blackstone Rangers in the park with any kind of weapon?

MR. SCHULTZ: Objection to the form of the question.

MR. WEINGLASS: Now, approximately 2:00 to 2:30 on Tuesday afternoon do you recall what you were doing?

THE WITNESS: I was going to have a workshop—I think I said it was going to be on insanity as a means of defense.

There were a number of workshops taking place throughout the park, underground editors were leading discussions on who to start underground newspapers. People were discussing how to make movies, political discussions.

Then a group of about fifty or a hundred people gathered around, and we sat on this hill, and I gave a speech.

MR. WEINGLASS: Could you relate to the Court and jury, Abbie, what you said?

MR. SCHULTZ: It isn't Abbie, he is a 33-year-old man. His name is Mr. Hoffman.

THE COURT: Oh, yes, but that has been gone into. If a lawyer persists in that, there is nothing very much I can do about it at this time.

MR. WEINGLASS: Could you relate to the Court as much as you can of your speech?

THE WITNESS: I think I can, Len.

THE COURT: What did he call you?

THE WITNESS: Len.

MR. WEINGLASS: Len. It is the appropriate name.

THE WITNESS: I said, "If people could carry a bag of blood, when the police went to lift up his club over his head, that they could take the bag of blood and squash it on their head and when the blood poured out, the cop would be totally freaked out by that and just walk away."

I said, "You would have to have a lot of guts to do that at that specific moment, running might be easier."

I said, "The Chicago police are teaching us the reality of America, that if we were going to continue to listen to rock music and to develop the kind of music and culture and the kind of values and attitudes toward sex and property, that we were going to have to learn to defend ourselves because the society was bent on genocide."

I said, "America is in the last stages of the empire, it was bent on devouring its children."

MR. WEINGLASS: Was there anything else you can recall?

THE WITNESS: I told them again that the Chicago police that had been following me said that I was going to be arrested, that I felt I was going to be arrested that night, and I fell asleep right there. I just went to sleep.

MR. WEINGLASS: Do you remember how long you slept for?

THE WITNESS: I just slept there for a few minutes because people were talking—then I went to the ballfield and slept there for about an hour, in the middle of the ballfield.

MR. WEINGLASS: What did you do after you slept?

THE WITNESS: I left the park with Anita and Ron Kaufman. I went to the Coliseum.

MR. WEINGLASS: Did you speak at the Coliseum?

THE WITNESS: I said, "We have won a tremendous victory, despite the fact that we have been gassed and Maced and beaten in Lincoln Park. We have proved that there were young people in the country willing to run the risks of barbed wire fences and tanks and threats of Mayor Daley and the total establishment, not only of the City of Chicago but the Democratic Party, and were willing to run those risks and come to Chicago, and it was because of that that we had won a victory, that we were a new generation that was growing in a free society in America."

"We are the vision of the founding fathers of this country," I said. "When you march to the Amphitheatre tomorrow, you should keep in mind a quote from a two-thousand-year-old Yippie with long hair named Jesus who said that when you march into the dens of the wolves you should be as harmless as doves and as cunning as snakes."

Then I got off.

MR. WEINGLASS: Now, directing your attention to approximately 6:00 A.M. the following morning, Wednesday, August 28, do you recall what you were doing?

THE WITNESS: I went to eat. I went with Paul Krassner, Beverly Baskinger, and Anita and four police officers—Paul also had two Chicago police officers following him, as well as the two that were following me. We walked and the four of them would drive along behind us.

MR. WEINGLASS: Could you describe for the jury and the Court what you were wearing at that time?

THE WITNESS: Well, I had cowboy boots, and brown pants and a shirt, and I had a grey felt ranger cowboy type hat down over my eyes, like this.

MR. WEINGLASS: What, if anything occurred while you were sitting there having breakfast?

THE WITNESS: Well, two policemen came in and said, "We have orders to arrest you. You have something under your hat."

So I asked them if they had a search warrant and I said "Did you check it out with Commander Braasch? Me and him got an agreement"—and they went to check it out with him, while we were eating breakfast.

MR. WEINGLASS: After a period of time, did they come back?

THE WITNESS: They came back with more police officers—there were about four or five patrol cars surrounding the restaurant. The Red Squad cops who had been following us came in the restaurant, four or five police, and they said, "We checked. Now will you take off your hat?" They were stern, more serious about it.

MR. WEINGLASS: What did you do?

THE WITNESS: Well, I lifted up the hat and I went "Bang! Bang!"

They grabbed me by the jacket and pulled me across the bacon and eggs and Anita over the table, threw me on the floor and out the door and threw me against the car, and they handcuffed me.

I was just eating the bacon and going "Oink Oink!"

MR. WEINGLASS: Did they tell you why you were being arrested?

THE WITNESS: They said they arrested me because I had the word "Fuck" on my forehead. I had put it on with this magic marker before we left the house. They called it an "obscenary."

I put it on for a couple of reasons. One was that I was tired of seeing my picture in the paper and having newsmen come around, and I know if you got that word on your forehead they ain't going to print your picture in the paper. Secondly, it sort of summed up my attitude about the whole thing—what was going on in Chicago.

I like that four letter word—I thought it was kind of holy, actually.

MR. WEINGLASS: Abbie Hoffman, prior to coming to Chicago, from April 1968 on to the week of the Convention, did you enter into an agreement with David Dellinger, John Froines, Tom Hayden, Jerry Rubin, Lee Weiner or Rennie Davis, to come to the city of Chicago for the purpose of encouraging and promoting violence during the Convention week?

THE WITNESS: An agreement?

MR. WEINGLASS: Yes.

THE WITNESS: We couldn't agree on lunch.

MR. WEINGLASS: I have no further questions.

THE COURT: Cross-examine.

MR. SCHULTZ: Thank you, your Honor.

• • • • •

MR. SCHULTZ: It was in December of 1967 that you and Rubin and Krassner created the Yippie myth, is that right?

THE WITNESS: And Nancy Kurshan and Anita Hoffman—that's the woman I live with. It's not just men that participate in myths.

MR. SCHULTZ: And the myth was created in order to get people to come to Chicago, isn't that right, Mr. Hoffman?

THE WITNESS: That's right, Mr. Schultz—that was one reason, to create—the other was to put forth a certain concept, a certain life style.

MR. SCHULTZ: And one of the reasons for coming to Chicago was to create a liberated area as part of your revolutionary movement, is it not?

THE WITNESS: It's a concept, yes. Free space and liberated zones are concepts in this revolutionary movement, as you call it—

MR. SCHULTZ: No, you call it a revolutionary movement.

THE WITNESS: We use the word differently, Mr. Schultz.

MR. WEINGLASS: Your Honor, if I could interrupt Mr. Schultz a minute. The Government is now going to cross-examine the witness on a book they wouldn't allow me to ask direct questions on.

MR. SCHULTZ: Your Honor, Mr. Weinglass is desperately trying to explain away this man's writings. I use the book because it obviously shows what this man's intent is.

MR. WEINGLASS: We are not ashamed of a word in this book. In fact I will have fourteen copies of the book for the jury in the morning and then they can all read the entire book.

THE COURT: No. You will not. You may have fourteen copies, but they will not go to the jury.

MR. WEINGLASS: Then you should admonish the U.S. attorney not to say that we are afraid of this book.

THE COURT: I will admonish the jury—the United States Attorney, if it is required that he be admonished.

THE WITNESS: Wait until you see the movie.

THE COURT: And you be quiet.

THE WITNESS: Well—the movie's going to be better.

Could I have a copy of the book? I've never read it. Could I have a copy—

THE COURT: The remarks of the witness may go out, and the jury is directed to disregard them.

MR. SCHULTZ: This is a copy of what is called *Revolution for the Hell of It*, and I'm showing the witness page 69, the bottom.
THE WITNESS: Yes. I think you have taken the term "liberated area" out of context, though.
MR. SCHULTZ: Put it in context, please.
THE WITNESS: It says:
"When we put on a large celebration the aim is to create a liberated area. People can do whatever they want. They can begin to live the revolution, even if only within a confined area. We will learn how to govern ourselves."
MR. SCHULTZ: Your idea of your revolution is first start with limited, confined areas, subject to your own laws and disregard the laws of the community, that's the beginning, is it not sir?
THE WITNESS: The beginning of what?
MR. SCHULTZ: Of your revolution.
THE WITNESS: I would say that it's not done in the sinister tone you imply, no, there's an element of joy. That's what "revolution for the hell of it" means. That's what "celebration" means. That's what liberation means.
MR. SCHULTZ: May I have that answer stricken, your Honor, and have the witness respond?
THE COURT: Yes, that answer may go out. Miss Reporter, please read the question to the witness.

(question read)

THE WITNESS: It's the beginning of world conquest, yes, that's right.
MR. SCHULTZ: And in these liberated areas—
THE WITNESS: One has to begin somewhere.
MR. SCHULTZ: Are you done, Mr. Hoffman, so I can—
THE WITNESS: Yes.
MR. SCHULTZ: —ask another question? Or do you want to entertain your friends?
Now, you were at demonstrations at the Pentagon which you have testified to, isn't that right?
THE WITNESS: I don't call them demonstrations, but if you want to call it that, no, I was at the exorcism of the Pentagon.
MR. SCHULTZ: And there were entertainers there, were there not?
THE WITNESS: Yes. Mr. Jerry Rubin was one. Phil Ochs was there, and, I assume, Peter, Paul and Mary.
MR. SCHULTZ: You use entertainers—
THE WITNESS: Dr. Spock.
MR. SCHULTZ: You use entertainers to attract young people to come to your—
THE WITNESS: The CIA.
MR. SCHULTZ: Are you done, Mr. Hoffman?
THE WITNESS: People in the Pentagon are entertainers, generals.
MR. SCHULTZ: You use entertainers to bring young people from all around the United States to various demonstrations, isn't that right?
THE WITNESS: Entertainers, as you would call the rock personalities, are in a sense the real leaders of the cultural revolution, yes. The idea that we have control over them is quite the reverse.
MR. SCHULTZ: Did you see numerous instances of people attacking the Guardsmen at the Pentagon, Mr. Hoffman?
THE WITNESS: I do not believe that I saw any instances of people attacking National Guardsmen. In fact, the attitude was one of comradeship. They would talk to the National Guardsmen continuously and tell them they were not the people that they had come to confront, that they were their brothers and you don't get people to oppose [their ways] by attacking them.
MR. SCHULTZ: Mr. Hoffman, the Guards and the troops were trying to keep the people from entering into the Pentagon for two days, isn't that right?
THE WITNESS: I assume that they were there to guard the Pentagon from rising in the air possibly. I mean, who knows what they are there for? Were you there?

You probably watched it on television and got a different impression of what was happening. That is one aspect of myth-making—you can envisualize hoardes and hoardes of people when in reality that was not what happened.

MR. SCHULTZ: Did you see some people urinate on the Pentagon?

THE WITNESS: On the Pentagon itself?

MR. SCHULTZ: Or at the Pentagon?

THE WITNESS: There were over 100,000 people. People have that biological habit, you know.

MR. SCHULTZ: Did you symbolically urinate on the Pentagon, Mr. Hoffman?

THE WITNESS: I symbolically urinate on the Pentagon?

MR. SCHULTZ: Yes.

THE WITNESS: I didn't get that close. Pee on the walls of the Pentagon?

You are getting to be out of sight, actually. You think there is a law against it?

MR. SCHULTZ: Are you done, Mr. Hoffman?

THE WITNESS: I am done when you are.

MR. SCHULTZ: Did you ever state that a sense of integration possesses you and comes from pissing on the Pentagon?

THE WITNESS: I said from combining political attitudes with biological necessity, there is a sense of integration, yes.

MR. SCHULTZ: You had a good time at the Pentagon, didn't you, Mr. Hoffman?

THE WITNESS: Yes I did. I'm having a good time now too. I feel that biological necessity now. Could I be excused for a slight recess?

THE COURT: Ladies and gentlemen of the jury, we will take a brief recess.

(brief recess)

MR. SCHULTZ: On the seventh of August, you told David Stahl that at your liberated area you—

THE WITNESS: What meeting was this, August 7?

MR. SCHULTZ: That's when you just flew in from New York.

THE WITNESS: Crossing state lines—

MR. SCHULTZ: At this meeting on the evening of August 7, you told Mr. Stahl that you were going to have nude-ins in your liberated zone, didn't you?

THE WITNESS: A nude-in? I don't believe I would use that phrase, no. I don't think it's very poetic, frankly.

I might have told him that ten thousand people were going to walk naked on the waters of Lake Michigan, something like that.

MR. SCHULTZ: You told him, did you not, Mr. Hoffman, that in your liberated zone, you would have—

THE WITNESS: I'm not even sure what it is, a nude-in.

MR. SCHULTZ: —public fornication.

THE WITNESS: If it means ten thousand people, naked people, walking on Lake Michigan, yes.

MR. KUNSTLER: I object to this because Mr. Schultz is acting like a dirty old man.

MR. SCHULTZ: We are not going into dirty old men. If they are going to have nude-ins and public fornication, the City officials react to that, and I am establishing through this witness that that's what he did.

THE COURT: Do you object?

MR. KUNSTLER: I am just remarking, your Honor, that a young man can be a dirty old man.

THE WITNESS: I don't mind talking about it.

THE COURT: I could make an observation. I have seen some exhibits here that are not exactly exemplary documents.

MR. KUNSTLER: But they are, your Honor, only from your point of view—making a dirty word of something that can be beautiful and lovely, and—

MR. SCHULTZ: We are not litigating here, your Honor, whether sexual intercourse is beautiful or not. We are litigating whether or not the City could permit tens of thousands of people to come in and do in their parks what this man said they were going to do.

In getting people to Chicago you created your Yippie myth, isn't that right? And part of your myth was "We'll burn Chicago to the ground," isn't that right?

THE WITNESS: It was part of the myth that there were trainloads of dynamite headed for Chicago, it was part of the myth that they were going to form white vigilante groups and round up demonstrators. All these things were part of the myth. A myth is a process of telling stories, most of which ain't true.

MR. SCHULTZ: Mr. Hoffman—

Your Honor, Mr. Davis is having a very fine time here whispering at me. He has been doing it for the last twenty minutes. He moved up here when I started the examination so he could whisper in my ear. I would ask Mr. Davis, if he cannot be quiet, to move to another part of the table so that he will stop distracting me.

THE COURT: Try not to speak too loudly, Mr. Davis.

MR. DAVIS: Yes, sir.

THE COURT: Go ahead.

THE WITNESS: Go ahead, Dick.

MR. SCHULTZ: Didn't you state, Mr. Hoffman, that part of the myth that was being created to get people to come to Chicago was that "We will fuck on the beaches"?

THE WITNESS: Yes, me and Marshall McLuhan. Half of that quote was from Marshall McLuhan.

MR. SCHULTZ: "And there will be acid for all"—that was another one of your Yippie myths, isn't that right?

THE WITNESS: That was well known.

MR. SCHULTZ: By the way, was there any acid in Lincoln Park in Chicago?

THE WITNESS: In the reservoir, in the lake?

MR. SCHULTZ: No, among the people.

THE WITNESS: Well, there might have been, I don't know. It is colorless, odorless, tasteless. One can never tell.

MR. SCHULTZ: I show you this flyer, Mr. Hoffman, and ask you if you recognize it?

THE WITNESS: No, I don't. Well, Yippie ain't even spelled that way. it's I-E, it ain't got two E's. So—

MR. SCHULTZ: Have you ever seen the flyer before?

THE WITNESS: No, I seen facsimiles to this, but I haven't seen this exact one.

This appeared in February. By then there were people publishing what you call advertisements all over the country.

We were getting notices telling us what the Yippies were planning to do in Chicago, and we would say, "Oh, that's pretty interesting."

I remember reading an interview of myself describing me with long blond curly hair, that I was six foot two, and wore bells and feathers, and telling what I and the Yippies were coming to Chicago to do.

MR. SCHULTZ: What are you answering, Mr. Hoffman? What question are you answering, Mr. Hoffman? What question are you answering, do you know?

THE WITNESS: I am saying that this was printed and published by people that I don't know.

MR. SCHULTZ: You say you saw, did you not, facsimiles of this flyer?

THE WITNESS: Actually, I didn't even look at the words in there.

MR. SCHULTZ: Well, that's what I would like you to do, if your would.

THE WITNESS: I frankly believe that the words in the English language are kind of obsolete.

MR. SCHULTZ: Look at some of the obsolete words, please and see—

THE WITNESS: Which ones would you call obsolete?

MR. SCHULTZ: Did you read that the Democrats will probably have to travel from the hotels to the Convention Amphitheatre by helicopter?

THE WITNESS: By helicopter? Good—that's future. That's great. Everybody will have a helicopter in five years.

MR. SCHULTZ: The fact is, Mr. Hoffman, that what you were trying to do was to create a situation where the State and the United States Government would have to bring in the Army and bring in the National Guard during the Convention in order to protect the delegates so that it would appear that the Convention had to be held under military conditions, isn't that a fact, Mr. Hoffman?

THE WITNESS: You can do that with a yo-yo in this country. It's quite easy. You can see just from this courtroom. Look at all the troops around—

MR. SCHULTZ: Your Honor, may the answer be stricken?

THE COURT: Yes, it may go out.

MR. SCHULTZ: I asked you whether or not you wanted to have the troops protect the delegates and make it appear that the Convention had to be held under military conditions, isn't that right?

THE WITNESS: I think that I felt that it was more of a prediction, that it was going to happen, and it is a prediction in 1972, even if all of us are in prison, that it will happen at the Republican Convention.

MR. SCHULTZ: Now, prior to the beginning of the Convention, Mr. Hoffman, that is on August 22 at about five in the morning, do you recall having coffee with some police officers?

THE WITNESS: With the policemen that were tailing me from the Chicago Red Squad? Yes. They bought me breakfast every morning and drove me around.

MR. SCHULTZ: Do you recall while having coffee with—

THE WITNESS: I don't drink coffee. I haven't drank coffee for three years. It is one of the drugs I refrain from using.

MR. SCHULTZ: Mr. Hoffman, didn't you say to a police officer named Dineen that the police had nothing to worry about until Wednesday, August 28, when you were going to march to the Amphitheatre whether you had a permit or not?

THE WITNESS: I would not have said that because it was not in my mind at that point to even march to the Amphitheatre. Maybe I was trying to sic them onto the others by saying that because we had no plans from Wednesday on.

MR. SCHULTZ: Do you know an officer named Dineen?

THE WITNESS: That was tailing me? I didn't know them by name, no. I think he was the one that asked me to get a Beatles poster for him for his kids. One of them did.

MR. SCHULTZ: Mr. Hoffman, while you were in Chicago, you deliberately told your police tails that you had had a fight with Rubin—

THE WITNESS: Yes. Deliberately.

MR. SCHULTZ: —in order to destroy any charge of conspiracy, isn't that right? Isn't that right, Mr. Hoffman?

THE WITNESS: Yes. God, I was sneaky. Yes, I told that to the policemen.
    It didn't work obviously.

MR. SCHULTZ: But the fact was that you and Rubin were really together, isn't that right, Mr. Hoffman?

THE WITNESS: You mean together in a brotherhood? In a grand conspiracy? Yes.

MR. SCHULTZ: Now, before Judge Lynch, you moved to dismiss your lawsuit, didn't you?

THE WITNESS: Yes.

MR. SCHULTZ: And you went out and held a press conference, and you told the press that because Judge Lynch was an ex-law partner to Mayor Daley it showed the judiciary and the Federal court was corrupt, and you wanted no part of it?

THE WITNESS: I said that it was tied into the political machinery, yes. I'm not the only one who said that.

MR. SCHULTZ: In fact, you thought it was a great boon to you that your case had been assigned to Judge Lynch because you could make a lot of hay out of that, isn't that right, Mr. Hoffman?

THE WITNESS: No. No, I had learned at that time that they had turned down the McCarthy people's request for a permit, and I thought if they weren't going to get it, we sure as hell weren't either.

THE COURT: Mr. Witness, we don't allow profanity from the witness stand.

THE WITNESS: Well, I wouldn't want—

THE COURT: And I don't like being laughed at by a witness in this court, sir.

THE WITNESS: I know that laughing is a crime. I already—

THE COURT: I direct you not to laugh at an observation by the Court. I don't laugh at you.

THE WITNESS: Are you sure?

THE COURT: I haven't laughed at you during all of the many weeks and months of this trial.

MR. KUNSTLER: I am not sure, your Honor, that "hell" is classified as profanity, and I think, from what has been circulated in this courtroom it is hardly profane language.

THE COURT: Well, probably not among your clients, but I—

MR. KUNSTLER: You say my clients are habituated to using "hell," which is a categorization of my clients. My clients use lots of words and your friends use lots of words—

THE COURT: I don't think you know any of my friends.

MR. KUNSTLER: You'd be surprised, your Honor.

THE WITNESS: I know your chauffeur.

MR. SCHULTZ: Mr. Hoffman, when did—I'll wait until you're finished laughing, Mr. Hoffman.

THE WITNESS: I was just laughing at your profanity.

MR. SCHULTZ: Mr. Hoffman, while you were publicly negotiating and talking with City officials and other—

THE WITNESS: Publicly? On the phone?

MR. SCHULTZ: Mr. Hoffman, while you were negotiating with City officials, you were secretly attending meetings and planning for spontaneous acts of violence during the Democratic National Convention, isn't that right?

THE WITNESS: How do you plan for spontaneous acts of violence? I would have no idea how to do that.

MR. SCHULTZ: Do you remember saying at the meeting that if the South and West Sides went up, it would be just like another Chicago fire?

THE WITNESS: No, I don't remember saying that.

MR. SCHULTZ: Did you say at that meeting that the Yippies would assist in diversionary tactics while the main march was going on?

THE WITNESS: Yippies would assist in diversionary tactics while the main march— never. No. Do you think that was a kind of agreement with the Mobilization? We had a closer agreement with the Mayor than with the Mobilization.

MR. SCHULTZ: Are you finished, Mr. Hoffman?

THE WITNESS: Yes, I'm finished.

MR. SCHULTZ: Do you want to do any headstands for us?

THE WITNESS: No, but I think I might like to go to the bathroom, if I could.

MR. SCHULTZ: Your Honor, can we go on for ten more minutes? I'd like to get this finished.

THE WITNESS: OK, I'll wait.

MR. SCHULTZ: Did you hear Mr. Davis say that on the last day of the—

THE WITNESS: Did you just ask me to do a headstand? I was going to oblige.

MR. WEINGLASS: Your Honor, Mr. Schultz has expressed a request that he do a headstand, and I think he should have an opportunity to comply with that request.

THE COURT: I don't think that was put in the form of a question.

MR. SCHULTZ: I didn't intend it to be. The witness is clowning for us, and I thought maybe in his clowning he would want to do a headstand or a cartwheel or something.

THE WITNESS: I want to comply with Mr. Schultz' request, if he wants to see me do it. I think it might start a riot.

THE COURT: No antics, Mr. Witness. No toasting the prosecutor or whomever you are raising that water glass to. We don't permit that here. You ought to know that after three months.

THE WITNESS: No. I was never told that toasting was illegal.

MR. SCHULTZ: Well, maybe we ought to take a break now. Mr. Hoffman is uncomfortable.

THE COURT: I don't know whether "uncomfortable" is the proper characterization.

The court, Mr. Marshal, will be in recess until two o'clock.

• • • • •

MR. SCHULTZ: On Saturday, the twenty-fourth, isn't it a fact, Mr. Hoffman, that you told Davis, Hayden and Weiner that if you were pushed out of the park on one of the nights, you should take over some downtown hotel? Didn't you say that, Mr. Hoffman?

THE WITNESS: No. There was no hotel that could even accommodate that many people.

MR. SCHULTZ: You were planning, were you not, Mr. Hoffman, to take over a building across from the makeshift police station in Lincoln Park during the Democratic National Convention?

THE WITNESS: What do you mean by planned?

MR. SCHULTZ: You thought about doing it, did you not, Mr. Hoffman?

THE WITNESS: I thought about doing a lot of things but that doesn't mean I planned. I did not plan that, no.

MR. WEINGLASS: Are we now prosecuting people for what they think? I think Justice Douglas wrote about this recently and the dangers of it, and I ask that the Government refrain from this type of—

MR. SCHULTZ: He is not charged with what he thought but what he thought goes to his intent in determining the issues in this case.

THE COURT: I will let him answer the question. What Mr. Justice Douglas said has nothing to do with this question.

MR. SCHULTZ: You thought about it, didn't you, Mr. Hoffman, about taking over that building across from the makeshift police station, isn't that right?

THE WITNESS: I thought that if it rained that people could stay in that building, yes.

MR. SCHULTZ: And you thought you could get about 50,000 people in that building didn't you?

THE WITNESS: It was a pretty big building. It has been empty for about five years, tied up in some court suit. It has to do with millionaires and profits. Yes, we could have got 50,000 people—50,000 people could be living free today right now in Chicago. It is still empty.

MR. SCHULTZ: And you went into that building prior to the Convention didn't you?

THE WITNESS: Did I go into that building? This might be incriminating.

THE COURT: Do you refuse to answer on that ground?

THE WITNESS: Well, if I say yes, am I guilty under some law or something?

THE COURT: You have got a good lawyer.

THE WITNESS: Well, maybe I should confer with him.

THE COURT: If your lawyer advises you not to answer, I will respect his advice.

THE WITNESS: Why don't I take the Fifth Amendment? I always wanted to.

THE COURT: Is that what you take?

THE WITNESS: Yes.

THE COURT: We will take a brief recess and let him confer with his lawyer.

THE MARSHAL: We will have quiet in the courtroom. Mr. Davis—

THE COURT: Is somebody sleeping over there? Provide a pillow, Mr. Marshal.

THE MARSHAL: Why don't you sit up?

THE COURT: Ladies and gentlemen of the jury, we are about to recess.

(brief recess)

MR. WEINGLASS: The witness is prepared to proceed.

MR. SCHULTZ: Mr. Hoffman, about a week before the Convention started, you entered the building and went into the cellar, did you not?

THE WITNESS: No.

MR. SCHULTZ: And your thought was that—that is, people could occupy this building if it rained, or in the alternative on the last day of the Convention, grab it? People would take it over, and then when everybody had left the city, you could turn it over to the poor people of Chicago? Those were your thoughts, isn't that right?

THE WITNESS: I'm not sure whether those were my thoughts or not. If you ask if I wrote such a thing in a book, yes.

MR. SCHULTZ: Now at that time, then, you wrote, did you not, that you dismissed the thought of attempting to take over a building right across the street from police headquarters? Isn't that right, Mr. Hoffman?

THE WITNESS: Did you ask me if I had the thoughts or if I wrote I had the thoughts? There is a difference.

MR. SCHULTZ: It is a convenient difference, isn't it, Mr. Hoffman?

THE WITNESS: I don't know what you mean by that, Mr. Schultz. I have never been on trial for my thoughts before.

MR. SCHULTZ: Calling your attention to Thursday, the twenty-ninth of August, you were still in the city of Chicago, were you not?

MR. WEINGLASS: Your Honor, that is outside the scope of the direct examination. My questioning concluded with Wednesday night, August twenty-eighth. I object.

MR. SCHULTZ: Your Honor, one of the charges in the indictment was what Mr. Hoffman did Thursday, which Mr. Weinglass attempted to avoid, but he did brink it in his last series of questions. Therefore I am entitled to go into it on cross-examination.

THE COURT: I overrule the objection. I will permit the witness to answer.

MR. WEINGLASS: There has been no testimony offered by the witness on direct examination on the day in question.

THE COURT: Mr. Weingrass [sic], I must caution you again when there is a ruling, the argument ceases. That is good courtroom procedure. I have ruled, and I overrule the objection.

THE WITNESS: Weingrass?

MR. WEINGLASS: I did not ask him a question about Thursday, August 29.

THE COURT: I will ask you to sit down.

MR. WEINGLASS: I concluded on Wednesday.

THE COURT: Mr. Marshal, will you ask that lawyer to sit down?

MR. DELLINGER: Boy, oh boy!

MR. KUNSTLER: Your Honor, this is legitimate argument.

THE COURT: Mr. Marshal, will you have that lawyer sit down? This one also.

MR. KUNSTLER: Your Honor, I don't think we have to stand here in fear of being made to sit down every time there is a legal argument.

THE COURT: I know you have no fear. I don't say these things because I think you have fear. I make these rulings under the law.

I will ask you to sit down.

MR. SCHULTZ: Mr. Hoffman, you were in Chicago, Illinois, on Thursday, August 29, 1968, were you not?

MR. WEINGLASS: Your Honor, that question is proof of the fact that there was no testimony offered on direct examination on that. I think that another objection is appropriate.

THE COURT: I overrule your objection.

THE WITNESS: I consider that an unfair ruling and I am not going to answer. I can't answer.

THE COURT: I direct you to answer.

THE WITNESS: Well, I take the Fifth Amendment then.

MR. SCHULTZ: Your Honor, the witness has taken the stand to defend the charges here. He has testified on direct examination and he has waived his Fifth Amendment right.

THE COURT: I order you to answer, sir.

THE WITNESS: What does that mean?

THE COURT: I order you to answer the question, sir. You are required to under law.

THE WITNESS: I just get yes or no, huh?

Yes, I was there.

All my years on the witness stand, I never heard anything like that ruling.

MR. SCHULTZ: Mr. Hoffman, in the afternoon on that Thursday you participated in a march, and then you laid down in front of an armored personnel carrier at the end of that march, at 16th or 19th on Michigan, laid down on the street?

THE WITNESS: Was that what it was? I thought it was a tank.

It looked like a tank.

Do you want me to show you how I did it? Laid down in front of the tank?

MR. SCHULTZ: All right, Mr. Hoffman. Did you make any gestures of any sort?

THE WITNESS: When I was laying down? See. I went like that, lying down in front of the tank.

I had seen Czechoslovakian students do it to Russian tanks.

MR. SCHULTZ: And then you saw a Chicago police officer who appeared to be in high command because of all the things he had on his shoulders come over to the group and start leading them back toward Grant Park, didn't you?

THE WITNESS: He came and then people left and went back to the park, yes.

MR. SCHULTZ: Did you say to anybody, "Well, you see that cat?", pointing to Deputy Superintendent Rochford. "When we get to the top of the hill, if the cat doesn't talk right, we're going to hold him there, and then we can do whatever we want and the police won't bother us." Did you say that to anybody out there, Mr. Hoffman?

MR. WEINGLASS: That's the testimony of the intelligence officer, the intelligence police officer of the Chicago Police Department.

THE WITNESS: I asked the Chicago police officers to help me kidnap Deputy Superintendent Rochford? That's pretty weird.

MR. SCHULTZ: Isn't it a fact that you announced publicly a plan to kidnap the head pig—

THE WITNESS: Cheese, wasn't it?

MR. SCHULTZ: —and then snuff him—

THE WITNESS: I thought it was "cheese."

MR. SCHULTZ: —and then snuff him if other policemen touched you? Isn't that a fact, sir?

THE WITNESS: I do not believe that I used the reference of "pig" to any policemen in Chicago including some of the top cheeses. I did not use it during that week.

January 2, 1970

MR. SCHULTZ: Mr. Hoffman, have you written that while you were at that intersection, you stated to another person, the following:

"I told him the rap to the cops was a bluff, and my strategy was to get the head cop down there, grab him, and get us through."

I'm asking you if you ever made that written statement.

THE WITNESS: That was not the statement that I made to Dick Gregory. It was wilder than that.

Do you want me to tell you what it was? I said, "The top cop is going to come down here in about five or ten minutes."

Gregory said, "What are we going to do if he comes down?"

I said, "I don't know. Why don't we cook him and eat him?"

He said, "I'm a vegetarian."

I said, "Well, maybe I'll do it. I got nothing to do this afternoon."

That was the nature of the general kinds of discussions in which me and Dick Gregory engaged.

MR. SCHULTZ: Now, the first person you saw bleeding in Chicago during the Convention was Stew Albert, isn't that right?

THE WITNESS: That's right.

MR. SCHULTZ: By the way, Albert is one of Jerry Rubin's closest friends, is he not, to your knowledge?

THE WITNESS: Yes. He's right in the courtroom here, too. Still has the scars.

MR. SCHULTZ: You and Albert, Mr. Hoffman, were united in Chicago in your determination to smash the system by using any means at your disposal, isn't that right?

THE WITNESS: Did I write that?

MR. SCHULTZ: No, did you have that thought?

THE WITNESS: That thought? Is a thought like a dream? If I dreamed to smash the system, that's a thought. Yes, I had that thought.

THE COURT: Mr. Witness, you may not interrogate the lawyer who is examining you.

THE WITNESS: Judge, you have always told people to describe what they see or what they hear. I'm the only one that has to describe what I think.

MR. WEINGLASS: I object to any reference to what a person thought or his being tried for what he thought. He may be tried for his intent.

THE COURT: Overrule the objection.

THE WITNESS: Well, I had a lot of dreams at night. One of the dreams might have been that me and Stew were united.

MR. SCHULTZ: Mr. Hoffman, isn't it a fact that one of the reasons why you came to Chicago was simply to wreck American society?

THE WITNESS: My feeling at the time, and still is, that society is going to wreck itself. I said that on a number of occasions, that our role is to survive while the society comes tumbling down around us; our role is to survive.

We have to learn how to defend ourselves, given this type of society, because of the war in Vietnam, because of racism, because of the attack on the cultural revolution—in fact because of this trial.

MR. SCHULTZ: Mr. Hoffman, by Thursday, the twenty-ninth, the last day of the Convention, you knew you had smashed the Democrats' chances for victory, isn't that a fact?

THE WITNESS: No. My attitude was it was a type of psychic jujitsu where the people smash themselves—or the party wrecks themselves. The same way this trial is.

MR. SCHULTZ: By Thursday there was no doubt in your mind when you saw the acceptance speech that you had won, and there would be a pig in the White House in '69?

THE WITNESS: Well, that was our role in coming here, to nominate a pig. That pig did win. He didn't actually—which one did?

MR. SCHULTZ: And you went out for champagne, and you brought it back to Mobilization headquarters and toasted the revolution, you did just that, right?

THE WITNESS: We drank some champagne. It was warm, warm champagne.

MR. SCHULTZ: And toasted to your success, to your victory, isn't that right?

THE WITNESS: We toasted to the fact that we were still alive.

That was the miracle as far as I saw it, is still being alive by that last Thursday.

MR. SCHULTZ: That's all, your Honor.

THE WITNESSS: Right on!

THE COURT: Have you finished your cross-examination?

MR. SCHULTZ: Yes, I have.

THE WITNESS: Right on!

THE COURT: Redirect examination.

MR. WEINGLASS: Could you explain to the jury and to the Court what you understand by the term "Yippie myth?"

THE WITNESS: This would be difficult but I will attempt it.

The term "myth" refers to an attitude, a subjective historical view of what is going on in society or in history past or history future. It is a subjective reality; the alliance between what actually happened and between thoughts and wonders and dreams and projections for the future is blurred together. For example, people's prejudices about what they see, since it is subjective, play a great role.

There is a famous experiment in psychology in which a man, a white man in a business suit, stabs a young black man in a film and it is flashed very rapidly. White people, because they have a tendency to be racists, will switch it around, invariably switch it around so that the young black man has the knife and the one with the business suit on is getting stabbed; that is, the victim in a sense now becomes the criminal.

The events that happened in Chicago would be a type of that kind of myth, a kind of subjective analysis.

If there was a conspiracy on the part of the Government and the city officials, you see, to form violence, they would have to project that on someone else. They would have to call the victims the conspiracy that fostered the violence.

Everybody participated in the Yippie myth and those people that participated most would be those people, newsmen and people in power who instantaneously can get on the news and hold press conferences and say whatever they want and have it absolutely reported.

MR. WEINGLASS: No further questions.

MR. SCHULTZ: I have no questions.

THE COURT: You may step down.

Call your next witness please.

Testimony of Stuart Meacham

MR. KUNSTLER: Will you give your name, please?

THE WITNESS: Stuart Meacham.

MR. KUNSTLER: What is your present occupation?

THE WITNESS: I am the peace education secretary for the American Friends Service Committee.

MR. KUNSTLER: Dr. Meacham, can you describe briefly your educational background?

THE WITNESS: I went to grade and high school in Birmingham, Alabama. I went to college at Davidson College in North Carolina, and following that I went to theological seminary and received a Bachelor of Divinity degree at Union Theological Seminary in 1934. I was first a pastor of two Presbyterian churches in Birmingham, Alabama, between 1934 and 1937. After that I was employed by the National Labor Relations Board until 1946. I transferred from the NLRB in 1946 to the Department of Labor as a special assistant to the Secretary of Labor and was assigned to the commanding general of U.S. Forces in Korea as a labor adviser there.

MR. KUNSTLER: Did there come a time when you left the Department of Labor?

THE WITNESS: In the spring of 1948 I became an assistant to the president of the Amalgamated Clothing Workers of America. Then I accepted an appointment in India for the Methodist Church. I was employed in 1957 by the American Friends Service Committee and became the peace education secretary about two years following.

MR. KUNSTLER: Now, Dr. Meacham, do you hold any position with the National Mobilization Committee?

THE WITNESS: Yes, I do. I'm one of the cochairmen.

MR. KUNSTLER: Who is the other cochairman?

THE WITNESS: Well, there are about six of us: Cora Weiss, Dave Dellinger, Don Kalish, Douglas Dowd, Sidney Lenz, Sidney Peck, Terry Hallinan.

MR. KUNSTLER: Now, Dr. Meacham, prior to Chicago did you have any conversations with any of the defendants with reference to the Democratic National Convention?

THE WITNESS: Yes, I did. At a place called Lake Villa, YMCA camp near Chicago, March 22 to 24.

MR. KUNSTLER: At the meeting at Camp Villa, who was present?

THE WITNESS: There were about 200 people there, and among the people that are on trial here, Dave Dellinger, Rennie Davis and Tom Hayden; also Abbie Hoffman and Jerry Rubin were present.

MR. KUNSTLER: Now, Dr. Meacham, I show you Defendants' 235 for identification and ask you if you can identify this document.

THE WITNESS: This document is one which was given out to the people who came into the March 22-24 conference, and I got one of the copies at that time.

MR. KUNSTLER: Do you know who the authors of this document were?

THE WITNESS: Rennie Davis and Tom Hayden.

MR. KUNSTLER: Can you just indicate briefly what the document is about without reading it?

MR. FORAN: I object, your Honor.

THE COURT: You may not go beyond identification.

MR. KUNSTLER: What was done with this document at Camp Villa?

THE WITNESS: It was distributed, and it was referred to from time to time by people speaking of different issues.

MR. KUNSTLER: Did the document refer in any way to the Democratic National Convention?

MR. FORAN: Your Honor, I object to this.

THE COURT: Sustain the objection.

MR. KUNSTLER: Was the document used in the discussions at Camp Villa?

THE WITNESS: Yes, it was.

MR. FORAN: Object to that, your Honor.

[376]

THE COURT: I sustain the objection.

MR. KUNSTLER: I would like to offer into evidence, your Honor, as Defendants' 235 for identification, a document written by Rennie Davis and Tom Hayden with reference to the Democratic National Convention.

MR. FORAN: Your Honor, I object to it since this witness did not write it himself. There is no foundation laid.

THE COURT: I will look at it.

(document handed to the Court)

MR. KUNSTLER: Your Honor, I might say before your Honor rules that the paper contains recommendations against violence by Mr. Hayden and Mr. Davis.

MR. FORAN: Your Honor, I object to this. He is trying to testify.

THE MARSHAL: Mr. Davis—and you too, Mr. Rubin, please keep quiet.

THE COURT: It is not possible, Mr. Kunstler, for the Government to cross-examine this witness on this document with intelligence. It is a twenty-one page document not authored by this witness.

MR. KUNSTLER: If the defendants take the stand, the authors of this document, one or both, and it is offered into evidence through them, the Government will raise the objection it is a self-serving statement and we will have to—

THE COURT: I will make such rulings as I think are indicated if, when and as the document is reoffered. Will you continue with the direct examination of this witness?

MR. KUNSTLER: Just so I understand, your Honor's ruling is based on the fact it can't be cross-examined on because this isn't the author? That is the ruling?

THE COURT: I sustained the objection of the Government to it. That is the ruling.

MR. KUNSTLER: All right. Now, can you state what Dave Dellinger said at the conference?

THE WITNESS: There was a statement by Dave toward the beginning of the conference on the morning of the twenty-third. He said that he hoped that at the Democratic Convention it would be possible for the coalition of peace and antiwar organizations to mount activities which would give expression to the aspirations of the American people for a new direction in our lives, where we are not depending on violence and suppression and crushing the Vietnamese or crushing the black people in our own country, but where we would begin to use the resource that we have here in our country for the good of all people.

That was the main thrust of what he had to say.

MR. KUNSTLER: Did Tom Hayden say anything after that?

THE WITNESS: Tom said, "I have been travelling around over the country and I find that there are many people in the United States who are prepared to support more strongly than ever protest and dissent against our policies in Vietnam, and against the neglect and the repression of people in the ghettoes of our major cities." He said that he believed that there would be a very lively opportunity during the months preceding the Convention to do two kinds of things out across the country.

One would be to organize a caravan that would be composed of actors who would move from place to place, putting on dramatic skits that would raise the social and the moral and the political issues that the people are confronted with today.

He said, secondly, he believed that there was an opportunity for there to be state and area assemblies at this grassroots feeling of the people across the country against the war and against poverty and discrimination against the black people of our country.

MR. KUNSTLER: Was Jerry Rubin present at the conference?

THE WITNESS: Yes, Jerry was present. Jerry announced that the Youth International Party intended to carry on in Chicago a Celebration of Life and that he hoped that all of those who were there would come and join.

MR. KUNSTLER: Now, did there come a time during this Saturday night session when Rennie Davis spoke in particular about D-235 for identification?

MR. FORAN: I object.

THE COURT: Sustain the objection. Please don't refer to that document. Objection to it has been sustained.

MR. KUNSTLER: Did there ever come a time when Rennie Davis spoke about an organization?

THE WITNESS: Yes, he said that he felt that it was important that we begin now, that is, in March to anticipate the Chicago Convention in August. He spoke in favor of a proposal that there be a continuing group that would stay in touch with rapidly moving developments.

MR. KUNSTLER: Now, Dr. Meacham, did the conference come to any decisions with reference to Chicago?

MR. FORAN: Objection.

THE COURT: I sustain the objection.

MR. KUNSTLER: Would you state what was decided at the conference?

MR. FORAN: Objection.

THE COURT: I sustain the objection.

MR. KUNSTLER: Now, I call your attention to July 4, 1968, and ask if you recall whether you had a conversation with any of the defendants on that day.

THE WITNESS: Yes, I did, with Rennie Davis. He was calling from Chicago.

MR. KUNSTLER: Will you state what he said to you and what you said to him?

THE WITNESS: He said to me, "Stuart, we have been asked by the Democratic Republic of Vietnam representatives in Paris to get three people from the peace and anitwar movement in the United States to come to Paris and then to go on to Hanoi for the purpose of facilitating the release of three American flyers who are now held in detention camps there, whom the Democratic Republic of Vietnam has decided to release."

He said, "If you were asked to participate in such a mission, would you be willing to accept the invitation."

I said to him that I was very much interested in doing this and would like very much to do it.

MR. KUNSTLER: I call your attention to July 6, 1968. Do you know where you were then?

THE WITNESS: On July 6. I believe that was the day that I left for Paris, and I went from New York to Paris on July 6.

MR. KUNSTLER: Now, on that date do you recall having a conversation with Tom Hayden?

THE WITNESS: Well, actually the conversation I had with him was two days later.

MR. KUNSTLER: And where did that take place?

THE WITNESS: That took place in Ambassador Harriman's office.

MR. KUNSTLER: Was the ambassador present?

THE WITNESS: Yes, he was.

MR. KUNSTLER: And will you state what was said by anybody at that conference on that day?

THE WITNESS: Well, Ambassador Harriman said to us that he was delighted that we were going to Vietnam on this mission, and he said that he would want to facilitate our successful accomplishment of the mission in every way that he could.

I said to Ambassador Harriman that I hoped very much that there would be no pressure put on the pilots to come back by American military aircraft. And Ambassador Harriman said, "Well, when you have been talking with the men at Hanoi, you will have worked them over, so they'll have to have a chance to have explained to them what their rights are when they get to Vientiane."

Tom spoke up and said, "You're insulting us," and Ambassador Harriman turned to him and said, "What did you say?"

And Tom said, "You're being insulting," and Ambassador Harriman said, "I wish to apologize. I withdraw the statement about working them over."

We continued the discussion about military aircraft or civilian aircraft. This was the main substance of the discussion.

January 5, 1970

MR. KUNSTLER: Now did you eventually go to Hanoi?

THE WITNESS: Yes, I did.

MR. KUNSTLER: Did you eventually succeed in releasing three American airmen and bringing them out of Vietnam?
MR. FORAN: Objection.
THE COURT: I sustain the objection.
MR. KUNSTLER: Your Honor, part of the reason why people came to Chicago was to protest against the war in Vietnam and since Mr. Hayden was important in setting up a release mission that released three American flyers, it would seem to me that this witness could testify as to the fruition of that effort.
THE COURT: It may seem that way to you; it doesn't seem to me, Mr. Kunstler.
MR. KUNSTLER: The witness is with you.

• • • • •

MR. FORAN: The National Liberation Front is what is commonly called here in the United States the Viet Cong, isn't it?
THE WITNESS: Well, I commonly call it the National Liberation Front.
MR. FORAN: It is also known as the Viet Cong, isn't it?
THE WITNESS: It calls itself the National Liberation Front.
MR. FORAN: Do you know whether or not it is called the Viet Cong here in the United States?
THE WITNESS: I know some people call it the Viet Cong, yes.
MR. FORAN: You also referred to some negotiations with the Democratic Republic of Vietnam. That in the United States is commonly referred to as the North Vietnamese government or the Hanoi government, isn't that correct?
THE WITNESS: Well, I have called it the Hanoi government. I have called it the North Vietnam government, and I have called it the Democratic Republic of Vietnam. As I understand it, the Judge wants us to be correct.
MR. FORAN: These representatives, Mr. Meacham, of the Democratic Republic of Vietnam or the Hanoi government informed you that they wouldn't deal with the United States government but that they would deal with the peace movement in the United States, isn't that correct, about the release of the prisoners?
THE WITNESS: No, they didn't inform me that they wouldn't deal with the United States government. They said that they were dealing with the peace forces directly and they did not want to deal with the government on the release of prisoners until the issue of prisoners was dealt with in the full context of the negotiations in Paris.
MR. FORAN: I have no further questions of this witness.
THE COURT: Please call your next witness.

Testimony of Larry Dutenhaver

MR. KUNSTLER: Will you state your full name?

THE WITNESS: Larry Dutenhaver.

MR. KUNSTLER: What is your profession or occupation, Mr. Dutenhaver?

THE WITNESS: I am an ordained minister of the United Methodist Church.

MR. KUNSTLER: I call your attention, Reverend Dutenhaver, to the night of Monday, August 26, at approximately 8:30. Do you know where you were that evening?

THE WITNESS: Church of Three Crosses.

MR. KUNSTLER: Who else was present?

THE WITNESS: Well, there were about seventy people that were representatives of the churches in the Lincoln Park area, both Roman Catholic and Protestant.

MR. KUNSTLER: Now at the end of that meeting what, if anything, did you do?

THE WITNESS: We moved from the church to the park, to distribute a mimeographed sheet that would tell people where there was help available, medical help.

MR. KUNSTLER: Reverend Dutenhaver, how were the ministers dressed?

THE WITNESS: Most of them wore clerical collars, and all people wore a white armband with a cross on it.

MR: KUNSTLER: Reverend Dutenhaver, after you entered the park, what did you do?

THE WITNESS: We walked among the people. We talked with some people.

MR. KUNSTLER: When you say you talked to some people, what did you say to them?

MR. FORAN: Object to that, your Honor. It's hearsay.

THE COURT: I sustain the objection.

MR. KUNSTLER: Your Honor, it is not hearsay from what he said. It is hearsay what other people said. He is here to be cross-examined on what he said. That is not a hearsay statement.

THE COURT: There is no way to adequately cross-examine the witness on that kind of a question and answer.

MR. KUNSTLER: It is my understanding that the words of a witness are never hearsay.

MR. FORAN: Your Honor, outside of the presence of the defendant they are hearsay.

THE COURT: I will let my ruling stand, Mr. Kunstler.

MR. KUNSTLER: Reverend Dutenhaver, did there come a time when you saw policemen in the park?

THE WITNESS: Yes, I saw the policemen lining up. Then the police proceeded across the park, coming towards the park, and the next thing was the shooting of some tear gas into the crowd.

MR. KUNSTLER: And after the tear gas what happened?

THE WITNESS: People were crowded together quite a bit and the tear gas kept hitting very close to the people and on top of people, and people started moving out quickly. Some were sitting on the ground, some were staggering to their feet and trying to walk out of the park.

MR. KUNSTLER: Now, did you see the police do anything else that night in that area?

THE WITNESS: They finally stationed themselves about halfway up the street between Eugenie and Wisconsin and stopped. At that point there was an injured boy laying right at the feet of them and I tried to get through the line to bring a medic to give him assistance. His head was bleeding.

MR. KUNSTLER: Go on. What did you do?

THE WITNESS: First they would not let me through. I asked if there was a sergeant or someone in charge.

I finally talked to someone else, a sergeant, I believe, and he said, "All right, you can go through." I brought a medic back and the boy was treated.

Then as we left they opened the line to let us go through again and I was labeled a fake, a son of a bitch—a fucking fake was one of the terms, a son of a bitch.

MR. KUNSTLER: By who?

THE WITNESS: By the policemen.

[380]

MR. KUNSTLER: Reverend Dutenhaver, I call your attention to Tuesday evening, August 27, approximately 10:15 P.M. that evening. Do you know where you were?
THE WITNESS: We were in the park.
MR. KUNSTLER: Were you alone or were you with other people?
THE WITNESS: I was with about two hundred clergy, laymen of the churches and people from the community. We conducted a service in the middle of the park.
MR. KUNSTLER: After you entered the park with the two hundred people you have mentioned, the clergy, what did you do after you arrived at the place where you held this service?
THE WITNESS: We proceeded together with our armbands to identify ourselves as part of the church and carried a large cross, a wooden cross.
MR. KUNSTLER: Then what did you do, you and the group?
THE WITNESS: The group sang, people from the park who were there originally spoke, clergymen who were in the group spoke. It was a community happening.
MR. KUNSTLER: Then what happened?
THE WITNESS: A small delegation was chosen by the group to go to see Commander Braasch.
MR. KUNSTLER: Were you in that group?
THE WITNESS: Yes.
MR. KUNSTLER: Will you relate what you or any member of the group said to Commander Braasch and what he said to the group?
MR. FORAN: Objection. Hearsay.
THE COURT: I sustain the objection.
MR. KUNSTLER: Then what did you do?
THE WITNESS: We walked outside. We saw at that time a large number of police getting out of vans and they were marching in file, whistling "Hi ho, hi ho, it's off to work we go." And also we received a number of the same kinds of abuses that we had heard earlier.
MR. KUNSTLER: How long did you remain in the park?
THE WITNESS: I remained in the park until the tear gas drove us out about a quarter of twelve.
MR. KUNSTLER: When you came out of the park where did you go?
THE WITNESS: I went west on Eugenie onto Wells Street, to the corner of North and Wells.
MR. KUNSTLER: What happened?
THE WITNESS: At that point a patrol car pulled up on North Avenue and as the car pulled up a brick came from the other side of the street where there were people and smashed into the police car.
    The two officers that were in the car jumped out of the car. The one officer had a pistol on top of the car at an angle. Then there was another, a shotgun or a rifle in the hands of the other policeman.
    Both fired across the street above the head of the crowd, three or four times.
MR. KUNSTLER: Now, after these shots rang out, what happened?
THE WITNESS: Very quickly a man with a brown suit came running up and put the officers into the police car, and I think with the youth that they had just beaten also put in the car, they took off going west on North Avenue.
MR. KUNSTLER: Was that the last you saw of them?
THE WITNESS: Yes.
MR. KUNSTLER: Did you have any occasion to see any more guns in the hands of policemen and in patrol cars?
THE WITNESS: All the police cars came by the church a number of times at very high speed with guns even sticking out the windows.
MR. KUNSTLER: Was that on both Tuesday and Wednesday nights?
THE WITNESS: Yes.
MR. KUNSTLER: I have no further questions.
THE COURT: Is there any cross-examination of this witness?

• • • • •

MR. FORAN: Reverend Dutenhaver, that police car which you saw get hit with a brick, where was that exactly?

THE WITNESS: It was on North Avenue facing west on the wrong side of the street.

MR. FORAN: You saw a number of squad cars get hit with rocks and bricks during that week, didn't you?

THE WITNESS: The next night, Wednesday night, which was really a different scene.

MR. FORAN: At Clark and LaSalle Street you saw groups of young people just stoning every police car that had come by, didn't you?

THE WITNESS: On Wednesday.

MR. FORAN: You saw as many as four or five police cars in forty-five minutes get stoned by people as they went by, didn't you?

THE WITNESS: On Wednesday. But there was some real confusion in talking about Wednesday over and against Tuesday. There are two entirely different kinds of people and groups.

Wednesday there wasn't really much of the gathering of the cross section of the people. It was what we called the greasers. We knew who some of them were from the neighborhood.

MR. FORAN: You said these kids were pretty tough, didn't you?

THE WITNESS: Yes.

MR. FORAN: When the police pulled up in the squad car and the brick came through the side window and those police got out and fired the guns across the street, they fired them tilted upwards, didn't they?

THE WITNESS: Yes.

MR. FORAN: Over the heads of the crowd.

Wednesday night you saw a couple of policemen do the same thing, didn't you?

THE WITNESS: Yes. My concern at both points was that there were apartment buildings.

MR. FORAN: On Wednesday night they were barraging them with rocks.

THE WITNESS: Right.

MR. FORAN: And as they'd come by in the police cars, they'd shout at them, too, wouldn't they, yelling, "Pig, pig!" as they threw the rocks at the police car?

THE WITNESS: Wednesday night, yes.

MR. FORAN: I have no further questions.

THE COURT: Any redirect examination?

MR. KUNSTLER: Just a few, your Honor.

In response to one of Mr. Foran's questions, you said that you thought that the group that you saw in the Lincoln Park area on Wednesday night was different than the groups you had seen in that area on Monday and Tuesday.

THE WITNESS: Very definitely.

MR. KUNSTLER: Would you state how they were different?

THE WITNESS: By dress, generally black leather jackets, and gray baggy pants, combat boots, longer hair—termed in the neighborhood as greasers.

MR. KUNSTLER: Did you recognize some of them as local youths?

THE WITNESS: Some were, and conversation found out that some were from Cicero.

MR. KUNSTLER: I have no further questions.

January 6, 1970

THE COURT: Call your next witness, please.

MR. KUNSTLER: Your Honor, is it possible to conduct this direct examination without having twenty marshals standing right behind me? We haven't had that for other witnesses.

THE COURT: I leave the matter of security, Mr. Kunstler, to the United States Marshal. I find him to be a very competent man.

MR. KUNSTLER: I see eleven at the back door, your Honor, and at least six, seven in the rest of the room. I would just like the record to note that.

Testimony of Richard Joseph Daley

MR. KUNSTLER: What is your name?

THE WITNESS: Richard Joseph Daley.

MR. KUNSTLER: What is your occupation?

THE WITNESS: I am the mayor of the City of Chicago.

MR. KUNSTLER: Is that the chief executive officer of the City of Chicago?

THE WITNESS: It is referred to occasionally as that.

MR. KUNSTLER: Now, Mayor Daley, how many executive departments do you have in the City of Chicago?

THE WITNESS: Approximately thirty-five.

MR. KUNSTLER: By whom are they headed?

THE WITNESS: Cabinet officers appointed by the mayor and confirmed by the City Council.

MR. KUNSTLER: How are they removed?

THE WITNESS: They are only removed by cause and also by trial before the Police Board.

MR. KUNSTLER: Have you ever had occasion to remove the head of any executive department yourself?

MR. FORAN: Objection, your Honor.

THE COURT: I sustain the objection.

MR. KUNSTLER: Have you ever had occasion to remove a superintendent of police?

MR. FORAN: Objection, your Honor.

THE COURT: I sustain the objection.

MR. KUNSTLER: Mayor Daley, who appoints the Police Board?

THE WITNESS: The mayor of the City of Chicago.

MR. KUNSTLER: Now with specific reference to the superintendent of police, what is his name?

THE WITNESS: James Conlisk.

MR. KUNSTLER: Was Superintendent Conlisk recommended by the Police Board?

MR. FORAN: I object to this. Now it is immaterial.

THE COURT: I sustain the objection.

MR. FORAN: Let's get on to the Democratic Convention if we are going to get there.

MR. KUNSTLER: Now, who was the chairman of the Park Commission in 1968, specifically during the period from the first of the year going through August?

THE WITNESS: The proper designation is president, not chairman. The president was William McFetridge.

MR. KUNSTLER: Is this the same William McFetridge who announced your first candidacy for mayor in 1954?

MR. FORAN: Objection, your Honor.

THE COURT: I sustain the objection.

MR. KUNSTLER: He was for many years a very close personal friend of yours, is that correct?

MR. FORAN: I object to that. It is clearly immaterial. It is a leading form of question.

THE COURT: I sustain the objection.

MR. KUNSTLER: Your Honor, this is a key portion of our interrogation, the relationship of the witness to—

THE COURT: It may be a key portion but—

MR. FORAN: Then let him ask the proper questions, your Honor.

THE COURT: I am ruling on it only as a matter of the law of evidence, sir. Whether it is key or not isn't important to me.

MR. KUNSTLER: Is it not true, Mayor Daley, that Mr. McFetridge once said the parks were not for dissenters?

MR. FORAN: Objection.

THE COURT: I sustain the objection.

MR. KUNSTLER: Mayor Daley, do you know a Federal judge by the name of Judge Lynch?
THE WITNESS: Yes.
MR. KUNSTLER: William Lynch.
    At one time did you practice law with him?
MR. FORAN: Your Honor, I object to the form of the question.
THE COURT: I sustain the objection.
MR. KUNSTLER: Mayor Daley, what is your relationship with Thomas Foran, the U.S. Attorney who is in this courtroom today?
THE WITNESS: I think he is one of the greatest attorneys in this country and the finest man I have met in private and public life.
MR. KUNSTLER: Your Honor, I would ask that that answer be stricken as not responsive as to what is his relationship.
THE COURT: I would like to have that said about me, but I agree with you that it is not responsive.
MR. KUNSTLER: Your Honor, something is happening in the rear row. I don't know what it is.
THE COURT: Will you let the marshals take care of the rear row?

(jury excused)

A SPECTATOR: The marshals are interrupting the trial.
MR. KUNSTLER: Your Honor, something is happening in the back row. A marshal is going down—a woman marshal is going down—
VOICE: Ouch!
    Ow, don't step on me, please!
VOICES: He isn't doing anything.
    She didn't do anything.
MR. KUNSTLER: Your Honor, that is one of our staff people. I don't understand—I would like the Court to inquire—
THE COURT: Regardless of who the person is, if the person has been disorderly, the marshal must ask the person to leave.
VOICES: What's going on?
    Leave him alone.
    Hey, leave him alone.
    Leave him alone.
    Ouch!
    Leave her alone.

(shouts and screams)

VOICES: Stop it.
    Hey, stop that.
    Leave them alone.

(shouts and screams)

VOICES: You're hitting Frank in the face.
    Leave him alone. Leave him alone.

(shouts and screams)

VOICES: Just leave him alone.
    You're still hitting him.
    Leave him alone.
MR. KUNSTLER: The defendants request to know what happened.
THE COURT: The marshals will explain at an appropriate time.
MR. KUNSTLER: We have information, your Honor, that some of the people doing the removing are not marshals, but employees of the City of Chicago, and we have a man standing there with his coat on who obviously is not a marshal. We would like to know who he is.

MR. WEINGLASS: He is the one who was hitting Frank.

THE COURT: If everybody will be quiet and listen to the testimony of the witness, the questions of the lawyers, there will be no disorder.

MR. KUNSTLER: We have asked your Honor to conduct an inquiry. Nothing could be fairer than that. I am not asking you to believe—

VOICES: Hey! Hey!

For crying out loud!

Come on, will you!

For Christ's sake!

MR. FORAN: Your Honor, that is the defendant Davis going back there, running to the spectator section of the courtroom.

(shouts and screams)

VOICES: Leave him alone!

THE COURT: The place for Mr. Davis is at the defendants' table and in his chair.

Bring in the jury, Mr. Marshal.

The Court directs the spectators to be orderly. If any spectator is not orderly, he will be appropriately dealt with by the Court.

MR. KUNSTLER: Your Honor, I just want to request if the person in the brown suit is a marshal. Since some of our people have been beaten up, I would like to know who that man is.

MR. FORAN: Oh, your Honor.

MR. DELLINGER: It's true.

MR. FORAN: —I object to the comment of Mr. Kunstler, your Honor. That's outrageous. I ask the jury be directed to disregard his comments.

THE COURT: Yes, I do direct the jury—

MR. KUNSTLER: Your Honor, if he will show his badge, we will be happy.

THE COURT: He doesn't have to be a marshal—

MR. KUNSTLER: To stand there in the position of authority?

THE COURT: I don't know who he is. I don't know most of the marshals.

MR. KUNSTLER: Your Honor is not going to ask him for the production of the badge?

THE COURT: No, no. No, no.

MR. KUNSTLER: Your Honor, it's our information this is a personal bodyguard of the witness.

THE COURT: Will you please proceed, sir, with the direct examination of this witness? Otherwise I will direct the witness to leave the witness stand.

Testimony of Richard Joseph Daley Resumed

MR. KUNSTLER: Mayor Daley, do you hold a position in the Cook County Democratic Committee?

THE WITNESS: I surely do, and I am very proud of it.

I am the leader of my party. I am the leader of the Democratic Party in Cook County.

MR. KUNSTLER: Mayor Daley, do you hold any position with the National Democratic Committee?

MR. FORAN: I object to that.

THE COURT: I sustain the objection.

MR. FORAN: If we are going to the Convention, let's get on to the case that is involved here.

MR. KUNSTLER: Now, Mayor Daley, on April 15 did you not order your Police Department to shoot to kill and to shoot to maim black people in the City of Chicago?

MR. FORAN: Your Honor, I object to the question, on the ground that it is leading, suggestive, immaterial, irrelevant and clearly improper.

MR. KUNSTLER: Your Honor, I have to ask a leading question in order then to move—

THE COURT: No, you don't have to. I won't permit you to.

Go ahead and ask your next question.

MR. KUNSTLER: Where were you on April 15, Mayor Daley?

THE WITNESS: I am home at 3536 Lowe Avenue where I live.

MR. KUNSTLER: Did you leave your home at any time on April 15 to go to a press conference?

MR. FORAN: I object to that. If this witness—this witness has been subpoenaed by the defense concerning the charges in this indictment.

There is nothing whatever in evidence concerning anything involving April 15.

THE COURT: I sustain the objection.

MR. KUNSTLER: Then at this moment, your Honor, I would move to have the Mayor declared a hostile witness.

THE COURT: Why, the mayor has been a most friendly witness.

I deny the motion.

MR. KUNSTLER: Your Honor, I have made no argument. I have asked now to have the jury excused—

THE COURT: Go ahead. Your motion is denied.

MR. KUNSTLER: I call your attention, Mayor Daley, to the week of August 28, 1968. Did you attend any sessions of the Democratic National Convention?

THE WITNESS: I did.

MR. KUNSTLER: And were you there during the nominating speeches for the various candidates?

THE WITNESS: I was.

MR. KUNSTLER: Mayor Daley, on the twenty-eighth of August, 1968, did you say to Senator Ribicoff—

MR. FORAN: Oh, your Honor, I object.

MR. KUNSTLER [continuing]: —"Fuck you, you Jew son of a bitch, you lousy motherfucker, go home"?

MR. FORAN: Listen to that. I object to that kind of conduct in a courtroom. Of all the improper, foolish questions, typical, your Honor, of making up questions that have nothing to do with the lawsuit.

THE COURT: May I suggest to you, sir, that this witness is your witness and you may not ask him any leading questions even of the sort that you proposed—especially, rather, of the sort that I heard a part of a moment ago.

MR. KUNSTLER: I have the source, your Honor. I will be glad to read it into the record.

THE COURT: I order you now, Mr. Kunstler, not to ask leading questions. Under the law you may not ask him such questions.

MR. KUNSTLER: Well, your Honor, then I would renew my motion out of the presence of the jury to have a hearing on the question of whether he is or is not a hostile witness.
THE COURT: I will be glad to do that. I'll excuse you, ladies and gentlemen of the jury, for a few moments.

(jury excused)

MR. KUNSTLER: Your Honor, Rule 43(b), Federal Rule of Civil Procedure, states that a party may interrogate any unwilling hostile witness by leading questions and contradict and impeach him in all respects as if he had been called by the adverse party.*
   Witnesses procured by the U.S. Attorney, particularly Mr. Simon, indicated that the City of Chicago had in every way cooperated with these defendants in the procuring of permits and that the City of Chicago had refused permits.
   In fact, if your Honor recalls, Mr. Baugher testified that he couldn't understand why the permits were not issued.
   Your Honor, the only way we are ever going to get to the truth of this matter is by being able to ask cross-examination questions of the Mayor. He is the chief executive officer, as he testified, of the City of Chicago.*
THE COURT: The motion of the defense will be denied. The Court finds that there is nothing in the testimony of the witness that has indicated hostility. His manner has been that of a gentleman. He's answered questions straightforwardly, pursuant to the oath administered by the clerk of the court.
   Bring in the jury.

(jury enters)

MR. KUNSTLER: Mayor Daley, who is David Stahl? Do you know him?
THE WITNESS: He is a very fine young man, the Deputy Mayor, who is interested in public life. He is a former vice-president of one of the outstanding corporations in Chicago and he is doing an outstanding job for the people of our city.
MR. KUNSTLER: I will assume with all of the people I ask you about they are very fine young men and so on.
   It will save time.
THE WITNESS: I would say that anyone that served in government today is a fine young man because of what they are trying to do.
MR. KUNSTLER: I direct your attention, Mayor Daley, to March 28, 1968; do you recall any conversation or meeting with Mr. Stahl with reference to the Youth International Party?
THE WITNESS: I gave Mr. Stahl the same instructions I gave any other department, certainly, to meet with them, to try to cooperate with them, and do everything they could to make sure that they would be given every courtesy and hospitality while they were in the city of Chicago.
MR. KUNSTLER: Did you consider that the use of nightsticks on the heads of demonstrators was hospitable?
MR. FORAN: Objection, your Honor.
THE COURT: I sustain the objection.
MR. FORAN: It's a leading question.
MR. KUNSTLER: Prior to the Democratic National Committee choosing Chicago for its 1968 convention, did you have any discussions with Mr. Bailey or any other official of the Democratic National Committee?
THE WITNESS: Yes.
MR. KUNSTLER: Did those instructions relate to the coming of the Convention to Chicago?
MR. FORAN: Your Honor, I object to that as a leading question.
THE COURT: I sustain the objection.
MR. KUNSTLER: Did you discuss in any of these discussions the war in Vietnam?
MR. FORAN: Your Honor, I object to the question.
THE COURT: I sustain the objection.

MR. KUNSTLER: In any of those discussions with Mr. Bailey, did you have any conversation about the black community in Chicago?
MR. FORAN: Same objection exactly, your Honor. Object to it.
THE COURT: I sustain the objection.
MR. KUNSTLER: Mayor Daley, in your experience as the mayor of this city which goes back, I understand, to 1955, have you ever had knowledge of people sleeping in Lincoln Park overnight?
MR. FORAN: Your Honor, I object to the form of the question. It is leading.
THE COURT: That is right. I sustain the objection.
MR. KUNSTLER: Your Honor, we have tried to get a declaration of a hostile witness here without success. You have the discretion, your Honor, to declare a hostile witness which would make things—
THE COURT: If that is true I do not choose to exercise my discretion to suspend the law.
MR. KUNSTLER: Did any of these defendants to your knowledge attempt to meet with you with reference to the Democratic National Convention prior to August 25?
MR. FORAN: Object to the leading character of the question, your Honor, and I ask that counsel be admonished.
THE COURT: I sustain the objection, and I remind you of my order, Mr. Kunstler.
MR. KUNSTLER: Mayor Daley, do you believe that people have the right to demonstrate against the war in Vietnam?
MR. FORAN: Your Honor, I object to the form of the question. It's an improper question.
THE COURT: I sustain the objection to the question.
MR. KUNSTLER: Now, Mayor Daley, you've testified that you were at the Democratic National Convention on Wednesday, August 28, and I questioned you about a statement with reference to Senator Ribicoff.
Can you indicate what you did say to Senator Ribicoff on that day?
MR. FORAN: Your Honor, I object to the form of the question, and again I ask that counsel be admonished.
THE COURT: I sustain the objection, and I remind you again and admonish you, Mr. Kunstler, of my order.
MR. KUNSTLER: Your Honor, I have tried to reiterate ten times that in view of the nature of this witness, it is impossible to examine him and get to the truth of anything with these restrictions—
THE COURT: This witness is no different from any other witness.
MR. KUNSTLER: But, your Honor, that isn't so. He is different from any other witness. He is the Mayor of the city—
THE COURT: The fact that he happens to occupy a high public place—other than that, he is a witness. In this court he is just a witness.
MR. KUNSTLER: We are trying, your Honor, to get to the truth of what happened during Convention week.
THE COURT: You must get at the truth through proper questions, sir.
MR. FORAN: Through the law of evidence, your Honor, that it has taken five hundred years to achieve.
MR. KUNSTLER: Your Honor, it is obvious to me that in view of the Court's rulings and in view of the restrictions under which I am working, that it is impossible to question this witness adequately as we have desired to do.
I would now, in view of the responses to my last twenty questions here, like to read into the record an offer of proof of what we had hoped to prove through this witness if we had been able to ask him either impeaching or questions as a hostile witness.
I have prepared that offer of proof and would be prepared to read it into the record at this point.
THE COURT: I will excuse you for a few minutes, ladies and gentlemen of the jury.

(jury excused)

MR. KUNSTLER: Your Honor, the defendants make the following offer of proof. Had the Mayor been designated a hostile witness, the defendants would have offered proof through his testimony to show the following:

1. That there was a conspiracy, overt or tacit, between Mayor Daley and the Democratic administration of Lyndon B. Johnson to prevent or crush any significant demonstrations against war, poverty, imperialism, and racism, and in support of alternative cultures at the 1968 Democratic National Convention.

2. That the members of this conspiracy planned and executed the use of every means at their disposal, including the open and blatant encouragement of violence toward demonstrators by police and other military forces, in order to prevent or crush such public exhibition of dissatisfaction with American domestic and foreign policies.

3. That in so doing the conspirators were determined to continue the fraudulent myth that the people of the United States had a real voice in their government and that they would have a significant choice in the national election of 1968 between candidates supporting virtually identical policies of war, imperialism, racism, and the continued degradation and exploitation and oppression of youth, ethnic, socio-economic, racial and other minorities.

4. That Mayor Daley obtained and maintains in power in Chicago by the creation and maintenance of a corrupt political machine which is supported by those individuals and corporations standing to gain the most by a continuation of present American domestic and foreign policies.

5. That this political machine is determined, whatever the cost, to prevent meaningful solutions to the problems presently facing the people of the United States and those of the rest of the world.

6. That the conspirators have embarked on a program of intense and brutal repression against all those who are seeking such solution, including but not limited to individuals and organizations committed to the end of the war in South Vietnam and the immediate and unconditional withdrawal of American troops therefrom, the right of black people and other racial, ethnic, or socio-economic minorities to control their own communities, the right of rebellion against oppression, and the bedrock right of all people to adopt a new way or style of life.

7. That in furtherance of this conspiracy, Mayor Daley, among other things:

(a) On April 15, 1968, ordered his police to respond to the assassination of Dr. Martin Luther King, Jr., with orders to shoot to kill arsonists and shoot to maim or cripple looters in the black community.

(b) Attempted first to obstruct the peace parade of the Chicago Peace Council on April 27, 1968, and then brutalized the marchers therein as a warning to peace demonstrators to stay away from the Democratic National Convention.

(c) Attempted first to obstruct the demonstrations at the Democratic National Convention in August of 1968 and then harassed, victimized, and brutalized the participants therein.

(d) Attempted to mislead the people of Chicago and the United States as to the nature and cause of such obstructive and brutal tactics.

8. That in furtherance of this conspiracy, Mayor Daley utilized the services of members of his political machine, including those of Thomas Foran, the United States Attorney for the Eastern District of Illinois and a former assistant Corporation Counsel of the City of Chicago.

9. That the indictment in this case was procured as a result of the said conspiracy in order to:

(a) shift the deserved blame for the disorders surrounding the Democratic Convention from the real conspirators to deliberately selected individuals symbolizing various categories and degrees of dissent from American foreign and domestic policies.

(b) punish those individuals for their role in leading and articulating such dissent and

(c) deter others from supporting or expressing such dissent in the future.

10. That the indictments of eight Chicago policemen, simultaneously with the instant one, were deliberately planned and procured to match the charges against the defendants and thus give the fraudulent illusion that an even-handed standard of Justice was being applied.

11. That Mayor Daley and his administrators have for years victimized the black

community in the City of Chicago by means which include chronic police violence, economic oppression, and the abuse of Federal and state programs.

12. That Mayor Daley and his administration have for years harassed, intimidated, and terrorized young people in the City of Chicago who have adopted and maintained life styles of which he disapproves including the wearing of long hair and unconventional clothing.

13. That Mayor Daley maintains power in Chicago by a combination of:
    (a) political patronage;
    (b) furthering the interests of the city's financial and mercantile communities;
    (c) oppression of racial, ethnic, socio-economic and other minorities.

14. That behind the mayor are powerful corporate interests who determine broad public policy in Chicago but are responsible to no one elected or public body. These interests govern Chicago for self-serving private gains instead of social needs: urban renewal works to enrich these private interests and against poor and working people who are robbed of their homes; no public programs effectively halt the polluting of our air and water by these powerful interests. The city practices genocide against the black community and in particular the Black Panther Party, which no group of citizens can effectively check or reverse without dislodging these private interests from their control over public officials and institutions.

VOICE: Right on.

MR. KUNSTLER: This is our offer of proof. This is what we would have hoped to have proved had we been able to have the mayor declared, as we think he ought to be, a hostile witness.

THE COURT: Your offer is made a part of the record, sir.

MR. KUNSTLER: With that, your Honor, we have no further questions because of the reasons I have indicated.

THE COURT: Is there any cross-examination? Oh, just a minute. We must have the jury in.

(jury enters)

Testimony of Richard Joseph Daley Resumed

MR. FORAN: Mr. Daley, in your conversations with anyone did you ever suggest that a permit be denied to any applicant or applicants for a march permit relating to the Democratic Convention?
THE WITNESS: No, I never did.
MR. FORAN: In your conversations with anyone did you ever suggest that a permit be denied to any applicant or applicants for a permit to use any of the parks in this city?
THE WITNESS: No.
MR. FORAN: That is all.

Testimony of Carl Oglesby

MR. WEINGLASS: Will you please state your full name for the record?

THE WITNESS: Carl Oglesby.

MR. WEINGLASS: What is your present occupation?

THE WITNESS: I am a writer, a playwright, songwriter, a singer, a lecturer.

MR. WEINGLASS: Now, prior to your becoming a full-time writer, lecturer, songwriter, would you indicate to the jury what your occupation was?

THE WITNESS: For about eight years, up until 1965, I worked first at what is now Goodyear Aerospace Corporation, and then for five years with what is now Bendix Aerospace Corporation, as finally the supervisor of a technical publications department.

MR. WEINGLASS: At the termination of that employment, what did you do?

THE WITNESS: I joined Students for a Democratic Society.

MR. WEINGLASS: Did you have any particular capacity with the Students for a Democratic Society?

MR. FORAN: Objection, your Honor.

THE COURT: I sustain the objection.

MR. WEINGLASS: Now, directing your attention to the middle of the afternoon of January 24, 1968, do you recall where you were on that day at that time?

THE WITNESS: I was in New York City. There was a meeting going on made up of about forty New Left people.

MR. WEINGLASS: Now, can you explain to the Court and jury what you mean by the phrase "New Left"?

THE WITNESS: Yes. That is a general way to refer to the movements for social change that developed in this country toward the end of the fifties and took shape in SNCC and SDS around 1960, '62, '63, in that period.

MR. WEINGLASS: Could you indicate who was present at this meeting of the new left?

THE WITNESS: I wouldn't try to remember. Tom Hayden, Dave Dellinger and Rennie Davis were there.

MR. WEINGLASS: Do you recall, Mr. Oglesby, who was the first to speak at that meeting?

THE WITNESS: Rennie Davis.

MR. WEINGLASS: What did he say?

THE WITNESS: Rennie Davis started out that meeting by arguing that it would be very important for the Movement to respond somehow to the Democratic National Convention that would be held in August so that we could make our case to the country. Davis argued that neither the Republican nor the Democratic party will successfully join the question of the Vietnam war or racism in the American society.

It is important for the Movement, if it is going to maintain its presence and grow, that it have some positive way of relating to the events that were going to unfold that year—that is to say, the campaigns and the Conventions, and so on.

MR. WEINGLASS: Now, in giving that answer, you indicated that Rennie Davis referred several times to the Movement. Would you explain to the jury what you mean by the Movement?

THE WITNESS: I would be glad to.

MR. FORAN: Objection.

THE COURT: I sustain the objection.

MR. WEINGLASS: After Rennie Davis spoke, what occurred?

THE WITNESS: I made a few comments on his ideas.

MR. WEINGLASS: After you spoke, who spoke, if you can recall?

THE WITNESS: Tom Hayden. Tom Hayden said that I was wrong to think that violence was likely in Chicago. It was his opinion that it would be quite likely, quite easy, for us if we were careful to organize an entirely peaceable demonstration to express our political views.

MR. WEINGLASS: Now, did you hear David Dellinger speak at that meeting?

[392]

THE WITNESS: Yes, but I don't recall in particular anything that he said.

MR. WEINGLASS: Now, directing your attention to July 1 and 2 of that year, which is 1968, do you recall where you were on those days?

THE WITNESS: Yellow Springs, Ohio. Tom Hayden visited us on the first and second.

MR. WEINGLASS: Now, during that two-day period that he visited you, what were you doing?

THE WITNESS: We had rather lengthy discussions of the plans for the demonstration at the Convention.

MR. WEINGLASS: Do you recall what Tom Hayden said to you at that time?

THE WITNESS: He was prepared, he said, at that time to accept the idea that I had been right when I had suggested a high possibility of violence in any demonstration at the Convention time for the Democrats. He argued that in Chicago one could see the beginning of a politics of intimidation where it was virtually the explicit purpose of those in authority to convince people that they could come to Chicago only at grave personal peril.

That was why the very peaceful demonstration in Chicago in April had been attacked by the police, he said.

There was, he argued, a gathering storm of repression. It was the function of this repression to shut up the dissent, to make people understand that they couldn't, even if they wanted to, have the most peaceful, the most docile kinds of demonstrations of their political views.

Because this situation was developing, it was all the more important that we insist on our rights of peaceable assembly and protest. If we conceded the issue at that point, struck with fear over the obvious physical and military advantages that the police forces have over unarmed, untrained protesters who have no intention of doing violence to anybody— if we tucked tail and ran, then we would be giving up not only on the particular points that we wanted to make about the war in Vietnam and racism in American cities, we'd also be giving up on our requirement to fight for that right that belongs to every American, the right of peaceable assembly, the right to express our views.

MR. WEINGLASS: Now, directing your attention to the middle of that month, did you have occasion at that time to talk to any of the other defendants who are seated here at the counsel table?

THE WITNESS: Yes, Rennie Davis called me sometime around the middle of July. I was in Yellow Springs still.

MR. WEINGLASS: Would you relate to the Court and jury what was said by Rennie Davis to you?

THE WITNESS: As I recall, there were essentially two points that he made. One had to do with the kids who were working for Senator McCarthy. These people didn't properly see themselves as being in the Movement but they saw themselves as being against the war, he said, and it was necessary for us not to take a harsh and holier-than-thou attitude towards the people who were working for McCarthy even though it was our view that the campaign of McCarthy was doomed from the beginning.

Rennie pointed out that the only way serious and real change could be made in the country was by developing a base of people who were willing to involve themselves in organizing another kind of political power, by means of which the rule of the two political parties could be challenged or at least shaken.

The other point that Davis brought out was, again, the question of violence in Chicago.

Responding to statements by Mayor Daley, behavior of the Chicago police, and so on, Davis said that he understood and it was important for us to prepare to be attacked. We would have to start seriously thinking about a medical capability, for example. We would have to start thinking seriously about having a team of marshals to do some peace-keeping duty around the demonstrations.

January 7, 1970

MR. WEINGLASS: I have no further questions.

THE COURT: Is there any cross-examination of this witness?

MR. FORAN: Yes, your Honor, there is.

• • • • •

MR. FORAN: You had a conversation with Tom Hayden in Ohio in the first part of July?
THE WITNESS: Yes.
MR. FORAN: In the course of that conversation Hayden told you that he expected violence in Chicago in August during the Convention, didn't he?
THE WITNESS: You've got it a bit wrong. I can refresh your memory.
MR. FORAN: Well, the way he put it is that he felt that you were right when you had predicted violence was going to happen in Chicago in August.
THE WITNESS: Yes. He had come around to the view that there was more to be said for my earlier view than he had earlier thought.
MR. FORAN: Now, isn't it a fact, Mr. Oglesby, that Mr. Hayden told you that the type of demonstration that they were planning would make it necessary for Federal troops to be called out to protect the Convention? Didn't he tell you that?
THE WITNESS: No. No.
MR. FORAN: Isn't it a fact that he told you that the objective of the demonstration that he and these other people were planning in Chicago was that they wanted to show the whole world that the Democrats couldn't hold a Convention unless it was protected by the troops?
THE WITNESS: No, I don't recall hearing anything like that.
MR. FORAN: Now, you had a conversation by phone with Davis in the middle of July?
THE WITNESS: Yes.
MR. FORAN: He told you that the objective of the plans that he and Hayden and the others were making for the demonstration in Chicago was to either destroy or at least shake up the political system, wasn't that correct?
THE WITNESS: Well, no.

You see, the point is that the political system is already shaken up. Otherwise the political system wouldn't have responded to our demonstration in Chicago with the obstinacy, with the repression, that it responded to that with, you see. The whole thing, the subject of all these conversations, is very simple. These guys are saying—
MR. FORAN: Just answer the question. Is it correct, that's all?
THE WITNESS: It is neither correct nor incorrect. It is neither right nor wrong. It is neither yes nor no.

I can explain all those riddles if you give me two seconds—or make that two minutes.
MR. FORAN: Davis also told you that he also expected violence in Chicago during the Convention, didn't he?
THE WITNESS: Expected, yes—it's the same as in the case with Tom.
MR. FORAN: Now, isn't it a fact that Davis told you, concerning the McCarthy people, that he and the people with him who were planning the Convention were going to get the McCarthy kids to join up with the movement by using the Yippie festival of life in Lincoln Park to draw them in? Didn't he tell you that?
THE WITNESS: No.
MR. FORAN: Didn't Davis tell you in your long conversation with him that if some of the McCarthy supporters got hurt in the violence that it would generate sympathy for the Movement? Didn't he tell you that?
THE WITNESS: I don't recall that in particular but it is very likely that he did say that. I mean, it could easily have been said.
MR. FORAN: I have no further questions.
THE COURT: You may step down, sir.

(witness excused)

THE COURT: Please call your next witness.

Testimony of David Evans

MR. WEINGLASS: Will you state your full name?

THE WITNESS: My name is David Evans.

MR. WEINGLASS: What is your present occupation?

THE WITNESS: I am a graduate student in sociology at Northwestern University.

MR. WEINGLASS: Now, directing your attention to the early part of August 1968, did you have occasion at that time to meet with Lee Weiner?

THE WITNESS: Yes, I did.

That meeting took place at Northwestern University. Steve Buff was also present.

MR. WEINGLASS: And at that meeting did a conversation take place?

THE WITNESS: Lee asked Steve and myself if we would come down and join with him in working up this corps of marshals.

MR. WEINGLASS: Now, directing your attention to Wednesday, August 28, at approximately noon, do you recall where you were?

THE WITNESS: Yes. I was in the Mobilization office.

MR. WEINGLASS: Who was there?

THE WITNESS: Lee Weiner was there. He came up to me and spoke to me.

MR. WEINGLASS: Do you recall what he said?

THE WITNESS: Yes. He said, "Dave, I'm going over to the Hilton to talk with Lieutenant Meany, who is in command of the Hilton police detail, about the march. Why don't you come along with me?"

We left the building and walked to the Hilton and walked up to the front of the Hilton and asked for Lieutenant Meany. After a few minutes, he came out and asked what we wanted.

MR. WEINGLASS: Will you relate what that conversation was?

THE WITNESS: Yes. Lee told Lieutenant Meany that we were having a rally in Grant Park that afternoon at the Bandshell.

He said that after the rally we would be also having a march that was going to be going for the Amphitheatre.

He asked Lieutenant Meany not to have any police at the site of the rally, because he was afraid that that would upset the crowd of people that would be there.

He said that he hoped we would be allowed to march but that if we were stopped, what he wanted was that Lieutenant Meany or whoever was in command of the police should announce clearly the order to halt.

The reason for this was that many of the people were planning to engage in nonviolent civil disobedience. If stopped by the police, they planned to submit to a mass arrest.

Lee said to Lieutenant Meany that he wanted it to be so that these people could be arrested in an orderly fashion without there being any confusion and possibly, as a result of that, any violence.

Lieutenant Meany replied, saying that if we obeyed the law or followed the law, we wouldn't have anything to fear from the police.

He also said to Lee, "I want you to remember that this is our city. These streets are our streets, and we don't intend to be driven off them, you know, by a bunch of outsiders."

Lee then asked Lieutenant Meany if he would give this information to his superiors. He said that he would.

MR. WEINGLASS: Is that the full conversation?

THE WITNESS: No. Right at that point, a schoolbus drove by which was filled with boys about ten years old, and they were all jumping up and down and making the "V" sign like that [*demonstrating*], and Lee said to Lieutenant Meany, "See, they used to want to grow up to be policemen. Now they want to grow up to be like us."

And Lieuenant Meany said, "I hope not," and then that was the end of the conversation.

MR. WEINGLASS: No further direct.

• • • • •

January 8, 1970

MR. FORAN: When you were going over to the Hilton with Weiner, it was just the two of you that were going together?

THE WITNESS: Yes, that is right.

MR. FORAN: Weiner told you, didn't he, that the purpose of going over there to see Lieutenant Meany was to actually let the police know about the march, let them know the specific routes so they would be ready to stop it right away? Wasn't that the purpose of him going over there?

THE WITNESS: No.

MR. FORAN: He did tell Lieutenant Meany exactly where the march was coming, didn't he, from the Bandshell?

THE WITNESS: Yes, right.

MR. FORAN: And didn't he, on the way over there, say that the purpose of using that route was so that the police could stop the marchers immediately and the crowd would be near the Hilton Hotel so that they could take other action and not have to march to the Amphitheatre?

THE WITNESS: No.

MR. FORAN: Didn't he say to you that he could just see the headlines, "Thousands Arrested Confronting the Convention?" Didn't he tell you that?

THE WITNESS: No.

MR. FORAN: Is the answer that you don't recall if you heard him say that, or that you never heard it?

THE WITNESS: Strictly speaking, I don't recall.

THE COURT: I don't understand the expression "strictly speaking." You haven't used that before.

THE WITNESS: I don't recall.

MR. FORAN: I have no further questions.

THE COURT: Call your next witness, please.

MR. WEINGLASS: Your Honor, without excusing the jury, our next witness is waiting for his shoes and if I may have a few minutes—

THE COURT: Well, I have seen people come in here almost without shoes so he may come in without his shoes. I will excuse him. Bring your next witness to the stand.

• • • • •

MR. SANDERS: I don't swear.

THE COURT: Why not?

MR. SANDERS: I affirm.

THE COURT: Why do you affirm?

MR. SANDERS: Because I believe in telling the truth.

THE COURT: Are you a member of any church or religious sect which requires you not to swear?

MR. SANDERS: I am a theosophist.

THE COURT: You will have to take an oath if you want to be a witness.

MR. SANDERS: Well, I won't affirm in the name of a deity. I will affirm in the name of galactic substances or something.

THE COURT: I am sorry, sir. I won't take—

MR. SCHULTZ: Your Honor is absolutely right but, nevertheless, so we can hear what the man has to say, we won't object to the affirmation.

THE COURT: Administer the affirmation.

THE CLERK: You do hereby affirm that the testimony you are about to give in the cause now on trial before this Court and jury shall be the truth, the whole truth and nothing but the truth, and this you do under pains of penalty of perjury?

MR. SANDERS: I do.

Testimony of Ed Sanders

MR.WEINGLASS: Will you please state your name?
THE WITNESS: Ed Sanders.
MR. WEINGLASS: Where do you reside?
THE WITNESS: In the Lower East Side of New York City.
MR. WEINGLASS: Prior to residing in the Lower East Side where did you live?
THE WITNESS: In Jackson County, Missouri.
MR. WEINGLASS: Do you recall what it was that brought you from Jackson County, Missouri to New York?
THE WITNESS: Reading Allen Ginsberg's "Howl" in shop class in high school in 1957.
MR. WEINGLASS: Mr. Sanders, could you indicate to the Court and to the jury what your present occupation is?
THE WITNESS: I am a poet, songwriter, leader of a rock and roll band, publisher, editor, recording artist, peace-creep—
MR. SCHULTZ: What was the last one, please?
THE COURT: Peace-creep?
THE WITNESS: Yes, sir.
THE COURT: Will you please spell it for the reporter?
THE WITNESS: P-E-A-C-E, hyphen, C-R-E-E-P.
THE COURT: Peace-creep, Mr. Schultz.
THE WITNESS [continuing] —and yodeler.
MR. WEINGLASS: Now in connection with your yodeling activities—
MR. SCHULTZ: Your Honor, this is all very entertaining but it is a waste of time. We don't have to do anything in connection with his yodeling to get to the issues in this case.
THE COURT: You may finish your question.
MR. WEINGLASS: Mr. Sanders, can you identify these two items?
THE WITNESS: They are two phonograph records. The records were produced by me, by the group, The Fugs, of which I am the leader and head fug, so to speak.
MR. WEINGLASS: Now, Mr. Sanders, have you also written a book about the Yippies?
MR. SCHULTZ: Leading, objection.
THE WITNESS: Yes.
THE COURT: I sustain the objection.
     Mr. Witness, will you wait when there is an objection so that I can indicate my view of the objection? Will you do that?
THE WITNESS: I'll try.
MR. WEINGLASS: Now, directing your attention to the latter part of November in the year of 1967, did you have occasion to meet with any of the defendants seated here at the counsel table?
THE WITNESS: I met with Jerry Rubin. There was a conference at the Church Center for the UN in New York City.
MR. WEINGLASS: And at the time of that meeting did you have a conversation?
THE WITNESS: Yes. I mentioned the Monterey Festival, which was a free festival featuring all the rock bands in America. Mr. Rubin said it was inspirational that some of the major rock bands in America were willing to play for free at a large tribal-type gathering of people, and I said it was really great and that we should consider convening something for the following summer or in the following year of a similar nature, that is, a free rock festival composed of all the major rock bands in America.
     Then Keith Lampe said, "Why don't we hold it next summer, you know, sometime in August?" And it was agreed—at that point everybody decided it would be a wonderful idea to have a free rock festival denoting the new life styles emerging, and that we would get in touch with Abbie Hoffman and other people and have a meeting right away.
MR. WEINGLASS: Now, directing your attention to the evening of January 4, 1968, do you recall where you were on that evening?

THE WITNESS: Yes. I went to Jerry Rubin's house in New York City to get briefed on a meeting that had taken place.

MR. WEINGLASS: What took place at that meeting you had with Jerry Rubin?

THE WITNESS: Well, first we had a period of meditation in front of his picture of Ché on the wall for a half hour.

THE COURT: Picture of whom?

THE WITNESS: Ché, Ché Guevara. Ché, the great revolutionary leader.

THE COURT: Oh. Would you spell it for the reporter.

THE WITNESS: C-H-É.

Then we practiced for about a half hour toughening up our feet walking around in Baggies full of ice, and then Jerry informed me about the circumstances of the meeting that had taken place, forming the Youth International Party, and that it was decided to hold a free rock festival in Chicago during the time of the Democratic National Convention, and that the convening would be a convening of all people interested in the new politics, guerilla theater, rock and roll, the convening of the hemp horde from all over the various tribes in the United States. I was asked by Jerry if I would help coordinate, since I knew the major rock groups in the United States, if I would contact them and ask them if they would play.

I said I would be happy to and that I would proceed forthwith in contacting these major rock groups, and that I did.

MR. WEINGLASS: Now, had you ever discussed with either Jerry Rubin or Abbie Hoffman in person your contacts with these major rock groups?

THE WITNESS: Yes.

MR. SCHULTZ: Your Honor, would you please ask Mr. Weinglass not to ask leading questions, not to lead the witness?

We keep on getting up and getting up. It becomes embarrassing. For people who don't know the legal rules, it looks very bad for the Government to constantly be getting up.

THE COURT: I appreciate that, Mr. Schultz.

MR. SCHULTZ: I am begging—I am begging defense counsel to ask questions properly.

THE COURT: Don't beg.

MR. SCHULTZ: That is what it is.

THE COURT: Don't beg. You needn't beg. I will order them not to ask leading questions.

MR. WEINGLASS: Now, directing your attention to March 27, do you recall where you were in the evening of that day?

THE WITNESS: I was at my home in the Lower East Side.

MR. WEINGLASS: What, if anything, occurred while you were at home that evening?

THE WITNESS: I received a phone call from Jerry Rubin.

MR. WEINGLASS: Could you indicate to the Court and to the jury what the conversation was that you had with Jerry Rubin on the telephone that night?

THE WITNESS: Well, he said that he was very—he had gone to Chicago and that they had placed a petition for a permit, filled out the necessary forms with the necessary officials in Chicago.

Then I said to him, "I hear that you're thinking about nominating a pig for President, an actual pig, oinky-oink, you know, Pigasus, the Immortal."

Then I said—well, I let it be known, as a pacifist and a vegetarian, I had heard there was a faction within the hippie hemp horde that was advocating a big pig roast after the election at which point the pig would be made into bacon, lettuce and tomato sandwiches, and that I was a spokesman for the vegetarians and I was opposed, philosophically opposed to this.

And so it was agreed tentatively at that point that there would be no bacon, lettuce and tomato sandwiches made of our presidential candidate.

MR. WEINGLASS: Now, directing your attention to the date of August 7, at approximately nine o'clock that evening, do you recall where you were on that date and at that time?

THE WITNESS: Yes, I was in an interior office somewhere near Mayor Daley's office for a meeting with Al Baugher, David Stahl, Richard Goldstein, myself, Jerry, Abbie, Krassner, I guess.

MR. WEINGLASS: Do you recall what was said at that meeting?

THE WITNESS: I addressed Mr. Stahl and Mr. Baugher, saying that for many months we had planned a Festival of Life with the basis of free music and that I had negotiated with rock groups and singing groups to come to Chicago on that basis and that we needed permits, and we needed the use of the park for our various festival activities.

MR. WEINGLASS: Now, what, if anything, were you doing during the course of that meeting?

THE WITNESS: I was making notes for a document that had been requested by various editors and people about the Yippie program for the Festival of Life. You know, poetic rendering of it.

MR. WEINGLASS: Now, I show you D-252 for identification, and I ask you if you can identify that document.

THE WITNESS: Yes. I wrote it. I mailed it out to various editors and publishers who had requested me for a statement.

MR. WEINGLASS: Your Honor, the defense offers Defendants' Exhibit D-252, identified by the witness.

Now, how many paragraphs appear on that document?

THE WITNESS: Eighteen.

MR. WEINGLASS: And could you read to the jury those paragraphs which are marked.

THE WITNESS: "Predictions for Yippie activities in Chicago:

"A. Poetry readings, mass meditation, fly casting exhibitions, demagogic Yippie political arousal speeches, rock music and song concerts will be held on a precise timetable throughout the week, August 25 to 30.

"A dawn ass-washing ceremony with tens of—

THE COURT: I didn't hear that last.

THE WITNESS: Excuse me.

"A dawn ass-washing ceremony with tens of thousands participating will occur each morning at 5:00 A.M., as Yippie revelers and protesters prepare for the 7:00 A.M. volley ball tournaments.

Three —oh, no, five, excuse me.

"The Chicago offices of the National Biscuit Company will be hi-jacked on principle to provide bread and cookies for 50,000 as a gesture of goodwill to the youth of America.

"The Yippie ecological conference will spew out an angry report denouncing Chi's poison in the lakes and streams, industrial honkey fumes from white killer industrialists and exhaust murder from a sick hamburger society of automobile freaks with precise total assault solutions to these problems.

"Poets will rewrite the Bill of Rights in precise language detailing 10,000 areas of freedom in our own language to replace the confusing and vague rhetoric of 200 years ago."

"B. Share your food, your money, your bodies, your energy, your ideas, your blood, your defenses. Attempt peace.

"C. Plan ahead of time how you will probably respond to various degrees of provocation, hate and creep vectors from the opposition."

MR. SCHULTZ: I didn't get that. Creep what?

THE WITNESS: It is a neologism. Creep vectors.

"D. Learn the Internationale.

"E. Bring sleeping bags, extra food, blankets, bottles of fireflies, cold cream, lots of handkerchiefs and canteens to deal with pig spray, love beads, electric toothbrushes, see-through blouses, manifestos, magazines, tenacity.

"Remember we are the life forms evolving in our own brain."

MR. WEINGLASS: Now, August 27, at two o'clock in the afternoon, do you recall where you were?

THE WITNESS: Yes, I was at the Coliseum.

MR. WEINGLASS: How long did you stay at the Coliseum?

THE WITNESS: From approximately 2:00 P.M. to approximately midnight. I was the master of ceremonies at the Johnson birthday festivities, and I was in the process of coordinating the program and introducing people.

MR. WEINGLASS: Do you recall what time you introduced Abbie Hoffman?

THE WITNESS: Approximately. It must—about 8:30, quarter to nine.

MR. WEINGLASS: Were you present when he spoke?

THE WITNESS: I was.

MR. WEINGLASS: I have no further questions.

THE COURT: All right. Is there any cross-examination of this witness?

MR. SCHULTZ: Yes, your Honor.

• • • • •

MR. SCHULTZ: Now, you said, I think, that on January 4, 1968, you went to Rubin's house, is that right?

THE WITNESS: Yes.

MR. SCHULTZ: And that you meditated before a picture of Ché Guevara, is that right?

THE WITNESS: Yes.

MR. SCHULTZ: Is this the same Ché Guevara who was one of the generals of Fidel Castro in the Cuban revolution?

THE WITNESS: Yes.

MR. SCHULTZ: How long did you meditate before his picture?

THE WITNESS: About a half hour.

MR. SCHULTZ: In Mr. Stahl's office on August 7, did you hear Hoffman say that the Festival of Life that you were discussing with Deputy Mayor Stahl and Al Baugher would include nude-ins at the beaches, public fornications, body painting, and discussions of draft and draft evasion? Did you hear that?

THE WITNESS: Nudism, draft counseling, the beach thing, but he didn't use the word "public fornication."

MR. SCHULTZ: He didn't use that word. What word did he use in its place?

THE WITNESS: Probably fuck-in.

MR. SCHULTZ: This was a very important meeting for you, was it not, because if you didn't get the permit, there was a possibility that your music festival would be off, isn't that right?

THE WITNESS: The concept of the meeting was important; the substance turned out to be bilious and vague.

MR. SCHULTZ: And you wanted those permits badly, did you not?

THE WITNESS: We sorely wanted them.

MR. SCHULTZ: While you were writing this document, you were also listening to what was going on at the meeting, weren't you?

THE WITNESS: I was keeping an ear into it.

MR. SCHULTZ: Will you read number four of that document, please.

THE WITNESS: Four.

OK.

Psychedelic long-haired mutant-jissomed peace leftists will consort with known dope fiends, spilling out onto the sidewalks in pornape disarray each afternoon."

MR. SCHULTZ: Would you read eight, please?

THE WITNESS: "Universal syrup day will be held on Wednesday when a movie will be shown at Soldiers Field in which Hubert Humphrey confesses to Allen Ginsberg of his secret approval of anal intercourse."

MR. SCHULTZ: Will you read nine, please.

THE WITNESS: "There will be public fornication whenever and wherever there is an aroused appendage and willing aperture."

MR. SCHULTZ: Did you read thirteen?

THE WITNESS: You want thirteen read? "Two-hundred thirty rebel cocksmen under secret vows are on 24-hour alert to get the pants of the daughters and wives and kept women of the convention delegates."

MR. SCHULTZ: Did you ever see these principles, or whatever they are, published in any periodical?

THE WITNESS: Yes, a couple.

MR. SCHULTZ: They were published before the Convention began, weren't they?

THE WITNESS: Right. Before.

MR. SCHULTZ: I have no more questions, your Honor.

THE COURT: Ladies and gentlemen of the jury, we are about to recess until ten o'clock tomorrow morning.

Ladies and gentlemen, good night. You may go.

(jury excused)

I want to announce that we have conveniently arranged a private gentlemen's rest room right through that door. From here in, the defendants, when they have occasion to use such facilities, will have a private one. There is the door, and they will not be permitted to go out in the hall.

Ten o'clock tomorrow morning.

Testimony of Mark Lane

January 9, 1970

MR. KUNSTLER: Mr. Lane, will you state your full name?

THE WITNESS: Mark Lane.

MR. KUNSTLER: What is your occupation?

THE WITNESS: I'm an attorney and I'm also an author.

MR. KUNSTLER: Now, Mr. Lane—

THE MARSHAL: Excuse me, Mr. Kunstler. Will you sit down, sir?

MR. KUNSTLER: Your Honor, Mr. Rubin is, I think, seeking to go to the men's room.

THE COURT: We made an order on that yesterday.

MR. KUNSTLER: But that's a jail cell, your Honor, with an open, uncovered toilet.

THE COURT: That is not a jail cell. It's a men's room, and he may use that.

MR. KUNSTLER: It's the first men's room I ever saw with bars, your Honor.

THE COURT: There are locks on the doors.

MR. KUNSTLER: But—

THE COURT: He may use that because they violated the privilege I have given them before. The marshals report that they have gone out and held conferences in the hall, they've gone places other than the regular public men's room. That is a place they will use when they have to go.

MR. KUNSTLER: Your Honor—

THE COURT: There will be no argument about it.

MR. KUNSTLER: Your Honor, we did not expect that. You said facilities had been made available.

MR. SCHULTZ: Your Honor, this is not a professional way of questioning your Honor's ruling. The proper way, instead of violating it first is to explain to your Honor, "We don't want that room."

MR. KUNSTLER: Well, your Honor, I had no idea—

THE COURT: I will hear no further argument, Mr. Kunstler.

THE MARSHAL: Sit down, Mr. Rubin.

MR. RUBIN: I want to go to the bathroom. That's a jail.

THE COURT: Then you may sit down if you don't want to use the facilities there.

MR. DELLINGER: Convicted us already.

MR. DAVIS: Guilty until proven innocent.

MR. KUNSTLER: There is no argument on that, your Honor?

THE COURT: Go ahead and examine this witness.

MR. KUNSTLER: Mr. Lane, just briefly, can you give us your educational background, after leaving high school?

THE WITNESS: After high school, I entered the Army during World War II at the age of eighteen.

MR. SCHULTZ: This is not educational background, if the Court please. Mr. Lane is an attorney and should know—

THE WITNESS: I learned a great deal in the Army.

MR. KUNSTLER: Your Honor, the Army is an educational factor, and he did go into the Army right after high school.

THE COURT: I will let him answer. Were you in the Army?

THE WITNESS: Yes, I have already so testified, Judge.

THE COURT: Oh, now, you won't get anywhere being that way with me.

THE WITNESS: I beg your pardon?

THE COURT: That kind of a reply to me just won't get you anywhere, sir.

THE WITNESS: I am not trying to get anywhere.

THE COURT: You are going to be respectful or we are going to do something about it.
   You may continue with the direct.

MR. KUNSTLER: You were in the Army for what years?

THE WITNESS: During 1945 and 1946.

MR. KUNSTLER: Can you indicate whether there came a time when you entered politics?

THE WITNESS: Yes. In 1956 I was an executive assistant to a United States congressman, Alfred E. Santangelo. In 1960 I was one of the two campaign managers chosen by Robert Kennedy to serve as the campaign manager for the New York City area for John F. Kennedy in his campaign for the Presidency of the United States.

That same year I was a candidate for the state legislature, asembly in New York State, and I was elected at that time.

MR. KUNSTLER: Now, how long did you serve in the New York State Legislature?

THE WITNESS: Just one term. I did not run for reelection. That was an education as well.

MR. SCHULTZ: If the Court please, would the witness be instructed not to ad lib about what was and what was not an education but simply to answer the questions.

THE COURT: I direct the witness to answer the questions and do not go beyond the questions.

MR. KUNSTLER: Now, after not choosing to run for the New York State Legislature—

THE COURT: And take your pipe out of your mouth when you are on the witness stand.

THE WITNESS: Even when I'm listening to the question?

THE COURT: Yes. We don't allow smoking.

THE WITNESS: I have no tobacco in here.

THE COURT: Just put it in your pocket, please.

MR. KUNSTLER: Now, Mr. Lane, can you state when you first met Tom Hayden?

THE WITNESS: Yes. It was during my campaign for Congress in 1961. Mr. Hayden worked in the campaign for the Democratic Party.

MR. KUNSTLER: Now, I call your attention to some time in the middle of June of 1968.
Did you have an occasion to meet Mr. Hayden again?

THE WITNESS: Yes, I did, in the city of Chicago, in the bar at the Hilton Hotel.

MR. KUNSTLER: Would you relate the conversation between you and Mr. Hayden, identifying who said what?

THE WITNESS: Yes. Mr. Hayden said that he was deeply concerned about the political situation in the United States. He asked me if my investigation into the assassination of President Kennedy had led me to a conclusion.

I informed him that both my investigation and the investigation conducted by the District Attorney of New Orleans with whom I had worked led me and led him to conclude that the Central Intelligence Agency was responsible for the assassination of President Kennedy.

Mr. Hayden told me that he had just come from Los Angeles where he had met with Robert Kennedy. He told me that Robert Kennedy had said to him that he was anxious to talk with him, Mr. Hayden, about the plans for the demonstration in Chicago during August.

Mr. Hayden told me that he was deeply shocked and traumatized by the assassination of Robert Kennedy, and he asked me if I thought that it was possible that that assassination and the assassination of Malcolm X and the assassination of Martin Luther King could have been the result of actions by the same group.

I told him that I believe that certainly it was possible, perhaps likely.

He told me that he was concerned about the use by the establishment of the death of Martin Luther King. He said that an open housing bill had been passed a week after the death, supposedly as a memorial to Martin Luther King, but that Senator Thurmond and some other Southern Democrats—

MR. SCHULTZ: If the Court please, if I may interrupt at this point to make an objection as to the relevancy of this conversation, and the argument that I make, be made out of the presence of the jury.

THE COURT: Very well.

I will excuse you, ladies and gentlemen of the jury, with my usual orders.

(jury excused)

MR. SCHULTZ: The witness is about to explain a discussion which he and the defendant Hayden had regarding the statute on which these defendants are indicted. The mere discussion of this statute is not relevant to this proceeding.

THE COURT: I can't tell in advance.

MR. SCHULTZ: May we inquire so that your Honor can make that determination and if so we can have a ruling?

THE COURT: I don't know that I agree with you, Mr. Schultz, that the responsibility is on the Court to interrogate—

MR. SCHULTZ: May I do it, then, your Honor?

THE COURT: Let Mr. Kunstler examine the witness out of the presence of the jury.

MR. KUNSTLER: I will do that, certainly.

Mr. Lane, would you explain what Mr. Hayden said to you relevant to this statute which you have testified to?

THE WITNESS: He told me that the bill had been passed as a memorial to Martin Luther King but that it carried with it the so-called antiriot rider, and that he was concerned that provisions of this rider would permit the Federal government to move into local situations as they had not done down in the South.

He said to me since he had been active in Mississippi, he told me, he found that the Federal presence was not often felt there, but that he was afraid that this statute would permit the Federal Government to move where they might want to move such as into the situation which he and others were working for, and that is an answer to the Democratic Convention in the streets of the city of Chicago.

MR. KUNSTLER: That is the extent of it, your Honor.

THE COURT: Suppose that question and answer were to be presented in the presence of the jury; what would your position be, Mr. Schultz?

MR. SCHULTZ: I do think that the self-serving aspects of the statement about the Federal government not moving into the South and selecting where it wants to go, I think those are not relevant and are grossly prejudicial. The rest I think, since it relates to his fears relating to the Convention, might be proper.

MR. KUNSTLER: There is nothing self-serving in making a parallel observation that the Federal government did not have its presence in the deep South when there were the attacks on black people and their supporters from '61 on.

THE COURT: That's your favorite word, isn't it, "attack"? I have sat here three months plus, and I just haven't seen—heard anything about attacks on black people, any evidence—

MR. KUNSTLER: You have heard of Medgar Evers, your Honor?

THE COURT: Not in this case.

MR. KUNSTLER: But I said attacks on black people in the South—

THE COURT: I know I have done more for the black people in this area than anyone I know, and I am continuing to try to do it.

"Racist fascist," is that what I was called so many times?

MR. KUNSTLER: Your Honor, I don't think you are on trial here.

THE COURT: What did you say?

MR. KUNSTLER: You are not on trial here. Tom Hayden is on trial.

THE COURT: That's right, I agree with you unqualifiedly.

If you insist on having the witness relate what he has just related, I will let him do it, but I will not let the witness go beyond that.

(jury enters)

MR. RUBIN: Your Honor, could Mr. Schultz be directed not to make remarks? He sarcastically pointed to the bathroom in there and said "Go to the bathroom" to me.

MR. SCHULTZ: As I walked back to the counsel table, your Honor, Mr. Rubin was laughing at me and snickering at me, and I pointed to the bathroom. I did that, your Honor—

MR. RUBIN: He said, "Go to the bathroom"—

MR. SCHULTZ: Your Honor—

MR. RUBIN: —like it was a victory for you to force us to go to the bathroom in jail.

MR. SCHULTZ: I said that. It was not very professional of me, your Honor. Apparently I succumbed a little bit to Mr. Rubin's harassment that started four months ago and of the defendants that started four months ago, a procedure and technique they have been using on authorities and policemen all of their lives. They have been trying it on your Honor and on Mr. Foran and myself, and I did, I succumbed, and I pointed to the bathroom, and that was improper, and I'm sorry, very sorry, that I did that.

MR. KUNSTLER: Do you want to be a witness? You can sit up there.

Your Honor, can I call Mr. Schultz for a few moments? If he'd like to testify, I have no objection.

THE COURT: No, you may not. You may not, and we won't have—

MR. KUNSTLER: Then I would like to have the record contain a motion for a mistrial at this time. Mr. Schultz—

THE COURT: And the record may contain the Court's order denying it, Mr. Kunstler.

Now, you will please proceed to the examination of this witness.

MR. KUNSTLER: Mr. Lane, you were about to relate a conversation in which Mr. Hayden was discussing a statute with you. Would you continue from the point where you stopped?

THE WITNESS: Yes. He made reference to a so-called antiriot statute and that this antiriot amendment was offered by Senator Thurmond and other Southern Democrats. He told me that he was fearful that this bill which gave the Federal government the right to move into local situations would be used by the Federal government in order to suppress dissent.

I asked him what his plans were in the Chicago area, and he said that although he was not active in the Democratic Party any longer, he and others were planning an alternate convention in the streets of Chicago, so that the voice of the Democrats which had been recorded in primaries all throughout the country could be heard somewhere, if not in the official Amphitheatre of the Democratic Party.

He told me, however, that although this was to be a nonviolent alternative, he was fearful that the persons who were responsible for the assassinations and responsible for suppressing dissent would either use violence against those who offered an alternative or would use this statute against them. He said that the statute could get anyone who spoke out for civil rights or anyone who engaged in any kind of lawful protest.

MR. KUNSTLER: Now, Mr. Lane, after this conversation, did you have occasion to come to the city of Chicago again?

THE WITNESS: Yes, I did. I think it was August 27, 1968.

MR. KUNSTLER: And I call your attention to the evening of August 27. Do you know where you were, say, around nine o'clock?

THE WITNESS: I was at an unbirthday party for Lyndon Johnson. I went there with Dick Gregory.

MR. KUNSTLER: At that time what was your relationship to Dick Gregory?

THE WITNESS: He had been a friend of mine for years. He was a candidate for the President of the United States. I was running with him as the candidate for Vice-President.

MR. KUNSTLER: I take it you were not a successful candidate.

THE WITNESS: We peaked a little too early, I'd say.

THE COURT: You don't want me to strike that, do you, as being—it's not responsive to the question.

MR. KUNSTLER: I accepted that as an answer.

Will you state for the judge and jury what Dick Gregory said at the unbirthday party.

THE WITNESS: He said that it was a rather insane society which permitted the mayor of the City of Chicago to talk continually about law and order when the Mafia ran the town. He also said that everything we are involved in in the coming difficult days must be nonviolent, no matter how much tear gas there may be in the street against us, we cannot let anyone turn us around.

MR. KUNSTLER: Now, Mr. Lane, I call your attention to August 28, 1968, and ask you if you know where you were at approximately 4:30 in the afternoon?

THE WITNESS: In Grant Park near the Bandshell.

MR. KUNSTLER: What was going on at that time?

THE WITNESS: A meeting had evidently just disbanded and persons were beginning to line up in ranks of four or five across. I joined the line. The line of march marched for a short distance because there were a row of Chicago police officers and several hundred National Guardsmen standing around the front of the line of march and so everyone stopped.

MR. KUNSTLER: After the march was stopped by the line of police, what did you do?

THE WITNESS: I stayed there for a while and listened to the statements that were being made over a bullhorn.

MR. KUNSTLER: Do you know what those statements were?

THE WITNESS: Yes. I believe Mr. Dellinger was speaking and he was urging persons to remain in the line of march only if they were thoroughly and definitely committed to the doctrine of nonviolence.

January 12, 1970

THE COURT: I think at this time we will recess until Monday morning, January 12.

MR. WEINGLASS: If the Court please, this is a motion for a mistrial which is being made on behalf of all of the defendants. The basis of the motion involves a statement made by Mr. Schultz.

The Court will recall that in the course of yesterday morning's proceedings there was occasion for a colloquy between the Court and defense counsel and some of the defendants with respect to the use of the bathroom facilities on this floor. In the midst of that Mr. Schultz stated to the Court:

"Apparently I succumbed a little bit to Mr. Rubin's harassment, a technique they have been using on authorities and policemen all of their lives."

Now, your Honor, that statement is the basis for the motion for mistrial. With these seven men on trial allegedly for inciting to riot, the prosecutor saying in front of the jury that these men had all their lives been harassing authorities and policemen has the same effect as the prosecutor in a bank robbery case offering to a jury his own testimony that these men have engaged in prior criminal activity in the nature of robbing banks.

I think the statement is highly prejudicial, it was made with premeditation by the United States Attorney—in this case, Mr. Schultz—and is a clear ground for a mistrial.

MR. SCHULTZ: May I reply, your Honor?

THE COURT: Yes.

MR. SCHULTZ: Your Honor, since this trial began in September there have been colloquies, one-way colloquies from the defense table to Mr. Foran and myself.

They have been going on on a daily basis. They have been profane, they have related to our religious—that is, my religious convictions—they have related to our morals and they have gone on on a regular basis every single day.

Yesterday morning, as I walked back, Rubin was making additional comments to me and I simply pointed to the bathroom. Then he told me that he was going to do it on me. That is what he said. Instead of going to the bathroom.

That was the colloquy. I said nothing.

THE COURT: Mr. Marshal, will you maintain order, please at that table.

THE MARSHAL: Sit up, Mr. Davis. Sit up.

A DEFENDANT: Don't touch him.

THE MARSHAL: Nobody is touching him. You shut up, too, Mr. Dellinger.

MR. DELLINGER: You don't have to say to shut up.

MR. SCHULTZ: That little colloquy is typical of what has been happening here. That is the device that they use against authorities and they have been trying it on your Honor for the last three and a half months and have found it very unsuccessful. They succeeded with me momentarily this morning.

Now, the comment that I made I think should be stricken. I want to point out, though, for the record, that comment was belated, it should have been said perhaps three months ago out of the presence of the jury.

THE COURT: The motion of the defendants for a mistrial will be denied and in denying that motion let me say that I entered an order here forbidding the defendants from going out at their pleasure ostensibly to what has been referred to not infrequently by counsel as the bathroom. I have never sat in a case where lawyers mention that word as often. I wonder if you, Mr. Marshal, can keep that man quiet while I am speaking.

THE MARSHAL: Mr. Dellinger—

THE COURT: Let the record show that after I requested the marshal to keep Mr. Dellinger quiet he laughed right out again out loud.

MR. DELLINGER: And he is laughing now, too.

THE MARSHAL: And the defendant Hayden, your Honor.

MR. KUNSTLER: Oh, your Honor, people can't help it sometimes, your Honor. You have laughed yourself.

THE COURT: I really have come to believe you can't help yourself. I have come to believe it. I have never been in a case where I have seen such bad manners.

MR. KUNSTLER: I know, but your Honor, when you make a joke and the courtroom laughs, nobody is thrown out.

THE COURT: Just sit down. I have not made any jokes.

Yesterday, because it was brought to my attention that the defendants, and several of them have, when it was thought that they were going to what has been referred to as the bathroom in this case, went out into conferences in the hall, to other rooms in the courthouse, even to another courtroom, yesterday I entered an order directing that if the defendants had to make use of toilet facilities, they use the one to my left, over there, where the door is.

This morning Mr. Rubin, flagrantly violating the order, got up and started to walk out, and it became necessary for the marshal to bring him back, and it is more than passing strange that he didn't use the facilities that were offered him by the Court.

MR. RUBIN: I have to go to the bathroom.

THE COURT: Let the record show that Mr. Rubin immediately got up and walked into the facilities that were offered him by the Court.

Oh, I've been through something like this before, but not often, not in the many years on the bench have I seen such circus behavior.

I repeat, I deny the motion for a mistrial, and when the jury comes in, I shall direct the jury to disregard the remarks of Mr. Schultz.

Bring in the jury, Mr. Marshal.

Will the witness please resume the stand?

(jury enters)

Testimony of Mark Lane Resumed

MR. KUNSTLER: Mr. Lane, after you left the park on Wednesday afternoon, as you indicated, and arrived on Michigan, where did you go?

THE WITNESS: We walked toward the Hilton Hotel.

MR. KUNSTLER: About what time did you arrive in the vicinity of Balbo and Michigan?

THE WITNESS: Probably about seven o'clock or perhaps a half hour earlier.

MR. KUNSTLER: Now, I show you D-262 in evidence and ask you if you can state what that picture depicts.

THE WITNESS: Yes. This shows a group of black people who were driving a mule train onto Michigan Avenue. This picture was taken moments after the police fired tear gas in the vicinity of the mule train. At least two of the persons have handkerchiefs to their mouths and one—in one case, one person is putting a handkerchief to an elderly black man's face to guard against the tear gas.

MR. KUNSTLER: Now, after the mule train exited, what did you do?

THE WITNESS: Remained there.

MR. KUNSTLER: Now, I show you Defendants' Exhibits 263 and 264 in evidence and ask you if you recognize those pictures, what they portray.

THE WITNESS: Yes. I recognize both pictures. They were taken by Caroline Mugar.

A large number of police officers came running, charging, up Balbo with their clubs in front of them. This took place at exactly 7:56 as can be seen by the clock in the background of the photograph.

The police without warning charged into the young people who were seated in the street and started clubbing them about the head and face and body. The police also had Mace and sprayed a number of the people they were able to catch. Both Miss Mugar and I were able to run quickly enough into the park at that time to escape being clubbed.

MR. KUNSTLER: Now, just prior to the police charge, did you see any of these people who were in the intersection, the non-police people, doing anything?

THE WITNESS: They were sitting there and they were chanting. One would ask the question, "What do we want?" And those who were seated in the roadway would answer, "Peace." And the question was asked, "When do we want it?" And the chant came back, "Now."

MR. KUNSTLER: I have completed the direct examination of this witness.

THE COURT: Cross-examination.

· · · · ·

MR. SCHULTZ: Mr. Lane, there were approximately one thousand people who began the march on Wednesday afternoon in Grant Park, is that correct?

THE WITNESS: I don't know how many there were. There were several hundred certainly.

MR. SCHULTZ: Most of the demonstrators at the Grant Park area seemed to drift away and there seemed to be about a thousand who remained for the march of which you were one of the thousand, isn't that right?

THE WITNESS: Is that your testimony? I didn't say that.

MR. SCHULTZ: Did you hear my question? Is my question accurate?

THE WITNESS: Your question is a statement which is completely false. Now would you like to hear the facts?

THE COURT: Oh, now, don't—that will be enough of that. You will be respectful to the lawyers, all of them in this case.

MR. SCHULTZ: Sir, isn't it a fact that you on a previous occasion have stated most of the demonstrators drifted away, about one thousand remained? Have you made that statement regarding the march in Grant Park?

THE WITNESS: Not based upon anything which I saw. I testified in the courtroom about what I saw.

[408]

MR. SCHULTZ: Have you on a prior occasion stated regarding that march, that n
the demonstrators drifted away, but about a thousand remained for the march?

MR. KUNSTLER: If Mr. Schultz is reading from something, I think he ought to sho
to the witness.

MR. SCHULTZ: I first want to know if he said it.

THE WITNESS: I may have written that based upon what I read in the newspaper, but I
never said that, that I knew that to be a fact.

MR. SCHULTZ: I will show you your book, *Chicago Eyewitness,* which you have identified as Defendants' Exhibit 256 for identification, and refer you to page 46.

THE WITNESS: Yes, I said I read that in the newspaper.

MR. SCHULTZ: Isn't it a fact that in the introduction to your book, introducing the book
itself, you stated, "I report what I saw"?

THE WITNESS: Yes, I just said that, and I explained it.

MR. SCHULTZ: Well, would you show me where in the book you state that the writing
that "most of the demonstrators drifted away and a thousand remained for the march"—
where you state you obtained that from a newspaper account?

THE WITNESS: State what?

MR. SCHULTZ: May the question be read, your Honor?

THE COURT: Yes. Please, Miss Reporter, read the question.

(question read)

THE WITNESS: No place in the book because I didn't state that in the book.

MR. SCHULTZ: Now, when 7:56 arrived and the intersection was being cleared, did you
see the demonstrators throwing sticks or ashtrays or shoes or little balls with nails in them
or rocks or rocks with spikes? Did you see any of those objects?

THE WITNESS: I just saw the demonstrators turn and run to get out of there as quickly
as they could.

MR. SCHULTZ: The mule train had not arrived at the intersection, had it, at 7:56?

THE WITNESS: I think it was there before, if I recollect.

MR. SCHULTZ: Was it in the intersection at 7:56 or had it left the intersection?

THE WITNESS: It was not in the intersection at that time, I don't believe.

MR. SCHULTZ: Isn't it a fact, Mr. Lane, that on a prior occasion you stated that the
mule train was in the intersection after the first police charge?

THE WITNESS: I don't recall. There were a number of police charges. I don't believe
that it was there at that time.

MR. SCHULTZ: Did you see the police officers fire tear gas at that mule train, Mr. Lane?

THE WITNESS: I did not see the officer fire the tear gas, no. I saw a mass of tear gas
erupt near the mule train.

MR. SCHULTZ: And this was after the first police clearing of the intersection at 7:56,
wasn't it, sir?

THE WITNESS: I think it was before the 7:56 clearing, I believe.

MR. SCHULTZ: Isn't it a fact, sir, that you have stated on a previous occasion that the
police cleared the intersection the first time, then the mule train was in the intersection,
that the police tear-gassed the mule train, and then charged a second time? Haven't you
stated that on a prior occasion?

THE WITNESS: I may have quoted newspapers about that, but I don't believe I said that
I saw it in that fashion. I may have been referring to statements in the press.

MR. SCHULTZ: In the book which you stated "I report what I saw"?

THE WITNESS: Yes, I did report—

MR. SCHULTZ: Is that where you were referring to—

THE WITNESS: Yes, I did report what I saw. Also I quoted from newspapers.

MR. SCHULTZ: Mr. Lane, when was it that you told the defendant Hayden that the
Central Intelligence Agency was responsible for the assassination of President Kennedy?

THE WITNESS: Sometime during June, I believe, of 1968.

MR. SCHULTZ: And when did you tell Mr. Hayden that it was likely that the Counter
Intelligence Agency [*sic*] of the United States was responsible for the assassination of
Malcolm X, Robert Kennedy, and Martin Luther King?

THE WITNESS: I think I talked with him in June, primarily about Robert Kennedy and Malcolm X.

MR. SCHULTZ: And Martin Luther King at the same time?

THE WITNESS: No, that was later.

MR. SCHULTZ: Mr. Lane, isn't it a fact that you testified last Friday that in your conversation with Mr. Hayden in June of 1968 you said that it was possible that the assassination of Malcolm X and the assassination of Martin Luther King could have been the results of actions by the same group, referring to the CIA?

THE WITNESS: If I mentioned Dr. King at the same time, then I misspoke, obviously.

MR. SCHULTZ: You misspoke just now?

THE WITNESS: No, I didn't—

MR. SCHULTZ: You misspoke on Friday?

THE WITNESS: That is what I said.

MR. SCHULTZ: No further questions.

THE COURT: Do you have any redirect examination, sir?

• • • • •

MR. KUNSTLER: Yes, I do.

Mr. Lane, in your book which is identified as D-256 for identification, you refer, do you not, throughout the book to quotations from various newspapers?

THE WITNESS: Yes, that is correct. In fact, the opening portion—

THE COURT: Is your answer yes?

THE WITNESS: Yes. That is right. There is more to the answer.

THE COURT: There isn't any more.

THE WITNESS: No?

THE COURT: Because that answers the question, sir.

THE WITNESS: Oh.

MR. KUNSTLER: Mr. Lane, you wanted to elaborate your answer with reference to my last question. Will you do so?

MR. SCHULTZ: No. That is an improper question. I object.

THE COURT: I sustain the objection.

MR. KUNSTLER: Now, would you explain to the jury how you wrote your book? First of all, how many days did it take?

THE WITNESS: Five days.

MR. KUNSTLER: When you wrote the book, what did you have available to you?

THE WITNESS: Just my notes, not even the photographs.

MR. KUNSTLER: Mr. Lane, I think I have no further questions.

• • • • •

MR. SCHULTZ: I have just a couple, your Honor.

Isn't it a fact that you represented your book as being a personal account of "What I Saw"?

THE WITNESS: A good portion of it is, yes.

MR. SCHULTZ: Are you saying now that some of the events that are in your book were not accurately recorded in your book?

THE WITNESS: I am saying that portions of what appear in the book clearly came from news statements.

MR. SCHULTZ: Mr. Lane, isn't it a fact that you represented your book as follows in your introduction:

"Yet at the outset I do affirm as well that I honestly and carefully recorded the events as they transpired and with the same degree of caution I have tried to present them accurately to you."

THE WITNESS: That is correct. Yes. I certainly did say that. It is accurate.

MR. SCHULTZ: That is all, your Honor.

THE COURT: Please call your next witness.

Testimony of Mark Simons

MR. WEINGLASS: Will you state your name?

THE WITNESS: Mark Simons.

MR. WEINGLASS: What is your present occupation, Mr. Simons?

THE WITNESS: I am completing my third year of law school at the University of Chicago.

MR. WEINGLASS: Calling your attention to the first week in July of 1968, during this week did you have occasion to meet with Rennie Davis?

THE WITNESS: Yes, I believe on July 3 I had a conversation with him. He asked me if I would make some phone calls for him attempting to set up meetings with city officials to negotiate for park permits, parade permits and rally sites. He said that he had information that Deputy Mayor Stahl would probably be a good man to get into contact with in terms of his closeness to the mayor and apparently not unsympathetic view toward peace demonstrators.

MR. WEINGLASS: As a result of that conversation what, if anything, did you do over the following two week period?

THE WITNESS: I attempted to call Deputy Mayor Stahl about twelve or thirteen times, approximately, during that time.

MR. WEINGLASS: Were you able to contact him by telephone?

THE WITNESS: No. I was unsuccessful.

MR. WEINGLASS: Did you ever eventually have a conversation with Mr. Stahl?

THE WITNESS: Yes, I did, on July 26.

MR. WEINGLASS: Did you at that time have a conversation with Rennie Davis?

THE WITNESS: Yes, I did. I told him that I had finally been able to get in touch with Mr. Stahl and that I thought that perhaps our outlook might be a little worse than he had originally assumed on Mr. Stahl; that he, Mr. Stahl, had seemed very agitated on the phone when I had identified myself as being from the Mobilization. Stahl had complained about a statement that Rennie had made the day before to the Justice Department, apparently asking them to investigate the Chicago police prior to the Convention.

I didn't know what Rennie had said, so all I could tell Mr. Stahl was that I thought the two of them should get together to work out this problem along with the more important problems dealing with the Convention.

MR. WEINGLASS: And was a meeting subsequently arranged between Rennie Davis and David Stahl?

THE WITNESS: Yes. On the next Tuesday we set up a meeting to take place on August 2.

MR. WEINGLASS: Mr. Simons, I show you D-278 for identification and ask you if you can identify that document.

THE WITNESS: Yes. This is the permit application that was filed with the City on the twenty-ninth of July.

MR. WEINGLASS: Does that application indicate the type of activity which is requested for a permit?

THE WITNESS: Yes, it does. "Parade and assembly."

MR. WEINGLASS: And for what date is the application made?

THE WITNESS: The twenty-eighth of August, seven o'clock at night until midnight.

MR. WEINGLASS: Could you read to the jury the activities applied for in that permit application?

THE WITNESS: It says, "Would begin with picket line moving counter-clockwise. Picketing would terminate at nine o'clock. Rally at nine o'clock would continue until delegates had left convention hall. Assembly would then disband."

MR. WEINGLASS: I show you a five-page document marked D-279 for identification, and I ask you to look at that document, and tell the Court and jury what that document is.

THE WITNESS: This is the memorandum that we prepared to be sent to the Park District.

MR. WEINGLASS: When you say "we," who prepared the document?
THE WITNESS: Rennie and I.
MR. WEINGLASS: Does the name of the author appear on the document?
THE WITNESS: It says "From Mark Simons."
MR. WEINGLASS: At this time the defense offers the memorandum identified by this witness as D-279 in evidence.
MR. FORAN: Your Honor, the Government will object to this.
THE COURT: You would rather do it out of the presence of the jury?
MR. FORAN: Yes, your Honor.
THE COURT: I will excuse you for a short time, ladies and gentlemen of the jury.

(jury excused)

MR. FORAN: Your Honor, the document is replete with statements that if it was signed by the defendants would be clearly self-serving in nature. Such statements as, "In every conceivable way the National Mobilization Committee is organizing to insure a peaceful and orderly demonstration at the Democratic Convention." It doesn't have even the pur-ported signature of the National Mobilization Committee.*
MR. WEINGLASS: If your Honor please, this document was prepared by this witness. He testified so under oath, together with Rennie Davis, one of the defendants. Now, Mr. Foran characterizes it as self-serving. I think by that he means this document tends to prove innocence, not guilt, but this document was prepared by this witness with one of the defendants and submitted to the Park District approximately one month prior to the time of the Convention. It is written ample proof of their intention, and it was not written with any self-serving intent in mind at that time. It's the first statement the National Mo-bilization made to an official of the Park District relating to their intent. So I submit it's a very relevant, very important document.
THE COURT: The objection of the Government to Defendants' Exhibit 279 for identi-fication will be sustained.
MR. DELLINGER: Oh, ridiculous.
THE COURT: Who said "ridiculous"?
MR. DELLINGER: I did. It was ridiculous. I stand on that fact. You don't want us to have a defense. You are a hypocrite.
THE COURT: Did you get all of those remarks, Miss Reporter?
MR. DELLINGER: I stand by them, too. You earned them. It really brings the whole system of justice under discredit when you act that way. What Mayor Daley and the police did for the electoral process you are now doing for the judicial process.
THE COURT: Mr. Marshal—
MR. DAVIS: We want a fair trial.
MR. DELLINGER: You don't think it is a fair trial, do you?
THE MARSHAL: Just be quiet, Mr. Dellinger.
MR. DELLINGER: You are being paid by the same company but you ought to be able to think for yourself a little bit.
THE COURT: Bring in the jury.

(jury enters)

Ladies and gentlemen, the Court sustained the objection to Defense Exhibit 279 for identification.
MR. WEINGLASS: On the afternoon of August 5, Mr. Simons, do you recall where you were?
THE WITNESS: Yes. I was in the coffee shop in the building that the Mobilization head-quarters was located in. I was at a meeting that Rennie Davis and a couple of other Mo-bilization leaders, I believe Mr. Dellinger, were having, with two members of the Justice Department community relations unit, Richard Salem and Clark Roberts, for about half an hour.
MR. WEINGLASS: Were you present during the entire meeting?
THE WITNESS: Yes. Yes.
MR. WEINGLASS: Was Rennie Davis present during the entire meeting?

THE WITNESS: Yes.

MR. WEINGLASS: Do you recall the conversation at that meeting?

THE WITNESS: Well, Rennie explained to both Mr. Roberts and Mr. Salem how the negotiations with the City had been going. He said that so far we hadn't been getting positive responses, but we hadn't been getting negative responses, either, but that we were beginning to think that time towards the Convention was getting close and that it was necessary that real negotiations begin to take place.

Then Mr. Roberts said that they had gone to see Mayor Daley, earlier that week. And that the Mayor had told them that communications were fine but that there would be no park permits given for sleeping. Rennie and myself both were kind of surprised, and I said, "Well, that's the first real negative response we've gotten," and that none of the people we had talked to had indicated that was true.

Then Rennie said that we were planning to set up a meeting on the twelfth of August between the national leaders of the Mobilization and representatives of the mayor's office and representatives from each of the City departments that we had negotiated with.

Roberts said, "Well, we'll, you know, try to help you get that set up." And that was pretty much the substance of the meeting.

MR. WEINGLASS: Now, I show you a document marked D-281. Do you recognize that document?

THE WITNESS: Yes, I do. It was a letter that I sent to representatives of several agencies inviting them to a meeting that I had set up with the deputy mayor at his office on the twelfth of August.

MR. WEINGLASS: Did you prepare that letter?

THE WITNESS: Yes, I did.

MR. WEINGLASS: Did that meeting of August 12 take place?

THE WITNESS: Yes, it did.

MR. WEINGLASS: Were you present?

THE WITNESS: Yes, I was.

MR. WEINGLASS: Who was there from the mayor's office?

THE WITNESS: Mr. Stahl.

MR. WEINGLASS: Who responded to your letter of August 8 to the Department of Sanitation at that meeting?

MR. FORAN: I object.

THE COURT: I sustain the objection.

MR. WEINGLASS: Who responded from the Park District to your letter of August 8?

MR. FORAN: Objection.

THE COURT: I sustain the objection.

MR. WEINGLASS: Who responded for Mr. Foran's office, the United States Attorney's office, to your letter of August 8?

MR. FORAN: Objection, your Honor.

THE COURT: I sustain the objection.

MR. WEINGLASS: Besides Mr. Stahl, who else was there in an official capacity?

THE WITNESS: From the City?

MR. WEINGLASS: Yes, or any other agency.

THE WITNESS: Mr. Elrod was there from the Corporation Counsel's office. I believe Mr. Baugher was there from the mayor's youth department.

MR. WEINGLASS: Who else was there?

THE WITNESS: Rennie Davis, David Dellinger, Robert Greenblatt, Gene Cerutti, myself, I believe Dennis Cunningham was there.

MR. WEINGLASS: Do you recall the conversation that occurred during this meeting?

THE WITNESS: As we were sitting down, Rennie asked Mr. Stahl where were the other people from the City departments. Mr. Stahl said he didn't know but he didn't believe that they would be there.

Then I believe that Dave Dellinger, though it could have been Rennie, outlined the activity that the people would be undertaking during the week of the Convention, and he went day by day.

Toward the end of the description, Mr. Elrod cut in and said, "If you don't get permits, what do you plan to do? Will you march anyway?" And there was no immediate response.

Then Mr. Dellinger continued with his description of what the plans were during the Convention, and then as the meeting was breaking up, someone asked, and I believe that it was Rennie, asked Mr. Stahl to attempt to set up a meeting with the representatives of the City departments that afternoon, and that we would be back at the Mobilization office waiting for his call.

And then the meeting broke up.

MR. WEINGLASS: How long did you stay at the Mobilization office?

THE WITNESS: I stayed until about 3:30.

MR. WEINGLASS: What happened at 3:30?

THE WITNESS: Right before then Mr. Stahl called.

MR. WEINGLASS: Following that conversation, where did you go?

THE WITNESS: I went to Hyde Park to report the substance of the conversation to Rennie Davis, David Dellinger, and three or four other people there.

I told them that Mr. Stahl had called, that he said that a policeman was going to come to the Mobilization office to meet with the Mobilization people.

I think David Dellinger told me to contact Stahl to tell him that we wanted to meet with the police officer, that we didn't want to pass up any chance to meet with a representative of any City department, but that I was to inform Mr. Sahl prior to any meeting that we would not accept that meeting in lieu of the larger meeting.

MR. WEINGLASS: No further questions.

THE COURT: I think at this point we will adjourn until tomorrow at ten o'clock.

January 13, 1970

THE COURT: Mr. Kunstler, I am ready to hear you.

MR. KUNSTLER: We are asking that the State's Attorney of Cook County, Edward V. Hanrahan, be enjoined from prosecuting the defendant Jerry C. Rubin under a 1968 indictment of the grand jury of the circuit court of Cook County. In essence it states that Jerry Rubin is accused of the offense of mob action in that he allegedly commanded, encouraged and requested the use of force and violence to disturb the public peace by two or more persons.

The statute under which Jerry Rubin stands indicted here along with the other defendants contains a built-in double jeopardy aspect. It states in essence that if there is a conviction in the state court, it would eliminate the Federal prosecution, and the place of the charge under the state indictment is the Bandshell area in Grant Park between 2:30 and 4:00 P.M.

Robert Pierson and Joseph Hale were the two most prominent witnesses here who testified as to that incident. Now their testimony here will be duplicated in the state prosecution. The facts which they alleged here will be the same facts in the state prosecution.

I might just indicate briefly that under the Fifth Amendment and the Fourteenth Amendment incorporating the Fifth Amendment:

"No person is permitted to be subject to the same offense to be twice put in jeopardy of life or limb."

Now, if Mr. Rubin is tried again in another forum under a different statute but covering the same facts and covering the same type of testimony as has been presented in the first trial, then he is in danger of multiple prosecution for the same offense.

We ask your Honor in the alternative, assuming you feel no jurisdiction, to strike all testimony which is previously in this record by Pierson and Hale which relates to the incident at the Bandshell between 2:30 and 4:00 on August 28.

MR. JALOVEC: It is our position, your Honor, that we would not consent to your Honor granting the request by defendant for the simple reason that we do not feel that this Honorable Court has jurisdiction to hear this.

Your Honor, we do not know what is going to happen in the state court until that witness or a witness actually takes the stand. But if jeopardy attachs, it would only be when a witness did take the stand.

Your Honor, this motion is premature in this case, because for jeopardy to attach, there must be an acquittal or conviction.

THE COURT: It is well recognized that the constitutional prohibition of double jeopardy and the guarantee of due process of law do not bar successive Federal and state prosecution based on the same acts of the defendant.*

Mr. Clerk, the motion of the defendant Jerry C. Rubin for an order enjoining the State's Attorney of Cook County from prosecuting him under Indictment No. 68-3812 in the Illinois Courts or for alternative relief will be denied.

MR. JALOVEC: Thank you very much, your Honor.

THE COURT: Bring in the jury.

(jury enters)

THE COURT: Cross-examination of this witness.

Testimony of Mark Simons Resumed

MR. FORAN: Now, the permit application that you filed, did you file it yourself?

THE WITNESS: Yes, I did.

MR. FORAN: Now that application asks for—the time of this activity out at 39th to 47th Street is from 7:00 P.M. to midnight, isn't it?

THE WITNESS: Yes. I seem to recall that.

MR. FORAN: And you know that nighttime demonstrations and marches are barred by statute and were then, don't you?

THE WITNESS: I neither know that now, nor knew that then.

MR. FORAN: You knew that the Secret Service had said that this area on Halsted Street was out of bounds for demonstrators, didn't you know that?

THE WITNESS: At the trial, the injunction suit for the parade permit, I believe that that was brought up by the City.

MR. FORAN: Well, you had been told that by Mr. Stahl hadn't you?

THE WITNESS: That is not true.

MR. FORAN: You knew when you went over to the Park District, didn't you, that there was a park ordinance that specifically forbade sleeping overnight in the parks?

THE WITNESS: I believe that I knew of the eleven o'clock ordinance, yes.

MR. FORAN: Now, once you heard about the Yippies' plans for Lincoln Park, you never for a moment believed the public authorities would suspend a law to accommodate them, did you?

THE WITNESS: I wasn't working with the Yippies to negotiate their permits and I assumed that they had contacted people who they thought were good enough to do that.

MR. FORAN: Now, you heard Davis tell Stahl at the Palmer House coffee shop on August 2 that since there might be as many as 200,000 people coming to Chicago, that this was going to be a very incendiary situation.

THE WITNESS: I recall no such statement.

MR. FORAN: Did you hear Davis say to Stahl on August 2 at the Palmer House coffee house that he, Davis, would personally rather die here in Chicago than in Vietnam?

THE WITNESS: Absolutely not. I never heard him say that.

MR. FORAN: Now, the Amphitheatre as the terminal point of the march was nonnegotiable, wasn't it?

THE WITNESS: In my understanding it was highly desired. I can't say what "nonnegotiable" means.

MR. FORAN: Well, you heard Dellinger tell Stahl that at the August 12 meeting, didn't you, that it was nonnegotiable?

THE WITNESS: I don't recall that.

MR. FORAN: Did you hear Mr. Davis say at that meeting that the question of the Mobilization Committee having a demonstration within eyeshot of the Amphitheatre was nonnegotiable?

THE WITNESS: I'm not sure. I don't think the term "nonnegotiable" was ever used.

MR. FORAN: Did you hear Mr. Dellinger say that this city, Chicago, had better pay attention to what was happening around the world? Did you hear him say that?

THE WITNESS: Yes, but he was referring to Vietnam and—

MR. FORAN: Didn't he mention it in context with what had happened at Berkeley, at Columbia, at the Pentagon, at Paris?

THE WITNESS: I recall him mentioning none of those, none of those places. Vietnam I recall. I don't recall Berkeley or Columbia, or the other places, or Paris.

MR. FORAN: I have no further questions.

THE COURT: You may go.

(witness excused)

THE COURT: Please call your next witness.

[416]

Testimony of Julian Bond

MR. KUNSTLER: Would you state your full name, please?

THE WITNESS: My name is Julian Bond.

MR. KUNSTLER: What is your present occupation?

THE WITNESS: I am a member of the Georgia House of Representatives.

MR. KUNSTLER: Now, Representative Bond, did you take your seat at the opening of the Georgia House of Representatives immediately after your election?

THE WITNESS: No, I didn't. I was still then working for the Student Nonviolent Coordinating Committee and we issued a statement in opposition to the war in Vietnam, said that we thought it was aggression, expressed sympathy with young men who could not because of their conscience enter the military.

Because I agreed with that statement, members of the legislature objected to my being seated and voted to exclude me from membership.

I ran in a second election which was to fill the vacancy which was created when I was unseated and I won that election. A special committee of the House met again and voted again to bar me from membership.

In December of 1966 the Supreme Court ruled unanimously that the Georgia House of Representatives was wrong and that I should have been seated, and subsequently in November of 1966 I had run a third time and won again, and so in January of 1967 I took my seat.

MR. KUNSTLER: Do you recall what the Supreme Court said about free speech and opposition to the war in Vietnam?

MR. FORAN: I object to that.

THE COURT: I sustain the objection.

MR. KUNSTLER: Now, Representative Bond, I call your attention to April 5, 1968, at approximately 11 P.M. on that day, do you recall where you were?

THE WITNESS: I was in the city of Nashville, Tennessee, in a motel room.

MR. KUNSTLER: Did you have a conversation with Thomas Hayden on that day?

THE WITNESS: Yes, I did.

MR. KUNSTLER: Would you describe that conversation, what Mr. Hayden said and what you said?

THE WITNESS: He mentioned he was interested in demonstrations at the Democratic National Convention which was then some months away. This was the day after the murder of Martin Luther King. As we were speaking there was gunfire and sirens, police sirens in the streets of the city of Nashville. Looking out the window you could see flashes from what we assumed to be guns.

The city was cordoned off into sections; the black neighborhoods had been segregated by the police in the city. Tom said that he was afraid that the same sort of thing might happen in the city of Chicago. He was afraid that police violence in this city might occur in the city of Chicago during the Democratic National Convention and expressed time and time again his fear that such violence might result. He asked me whether or not I thought delegates at the Convention would participate in any demonstrations and I told him I didn't know.

MR. KUNSTLER: Do you recall anything else about the conversation?

THE WITNESS: That was the gist of it.

MR. KUNSTLER: Now, Representative Bond, you attended the Democratic National Convention, did you not?

THE WITNESS: Yes, I did.

MR. KUNSTLER: In what capacity?

THE WITNESS: I was a cochairman of the group called the Georgia Loyal National Democrats. We were an insurgent group that challenged the handpicked delegation selected by Governor Lester G. Maddox from Georgia.

MR. KUNSTLER: Do you recall what the racial composition of your delegation was?

MR. FORAN: Objection, your Honor.

THE COURT: Sustain the objection.

MR. KUNSTLER: Now, I call your attention to Tuesday, August 27, 1968. Did you have a conversation with Mayor Richard J. Daley?

THE WITNESS: Yes, I did.

MR. KUNSTLER: Where did that take place?

THE WITNESS: It took place in the Amphitheatre at the site of the Convention.

MR. KUNSTLER: Now, would you relate what you said to Mayor Daley and what Mayor Daley said to you?

MR. FORAN: Your Honor, I object to that.

THE COURT: I sustain the objection.

MR. FORAN: No matter who the conversants are, if there are no defendants present, that is hearsay evidence, and I object to it.

·THE COURT: I have sustained the objection.

MR. KUNSTLER: Was your conversation with Mayor Daley anything about demonstrations?

THE WITNESS: Yes, it was.

MR. FORAN: I object to that, your Honor.

THE COURT: I sustain the objection.

MR. KUNSTLER: Now, Representative Bond, I call your attention to August 28, around midnight and ask you if you know where you were at that time.

THE WITNESS: Yes. I spent some time in Grant Park across the street from the Conrad Hilton Hotel.

MR. KUNSTLER: Were any of the defendants present there at that time?

THE WITNESS: Thomas Hayden was there.

MR. KUNSTLER: Did you speak at that time?

THE WITNESS: Yes, I did.

MR. KUNSTLER: Would you state what you said to the crowd in Grant Park?

THE WITNESS: I said that I had an impulse to—

MR. FORAN: Objection, your Honor.

THE COURT: I will sustain the objection to the question.

MR. KUNSTLER: Your Honor—

THE COURT: You may ask another question, sir.

MR. KUNSTLER: I call your attention to Thursday night or early Friday morning that is, either the twenty-ninth or the thirtieth. Can you describe where you were at that time?

MR. FORAN: Object to that, your Honor. The evidence shows that both Mr. Davis and Mr. Dellinger that afternoon in Grant Park had announced to the crowd that the Mobilization Committee had no further interest in the demonstrations in Chicago.

MR. KUNSTLER: Your Honor, they have some of the defendants at the Downers Grove picnic on Friday, and I think if the Government has extended it to Friday, the thirtieth of August, I am entitled to inquire about the twenty-ninth of August.

THE COURT: I will sustain the objection.

THE MARSHAL: Mr. Hoffman, will you be quiet? Quit laughing.

MR. DAVIS: This is a joke.

THE COURT: Did you hear me, sir? I said I would let my ruling stand.

MR. KUNSTLER: Now, Representative Bond, calling your attention to the Amphitheatre itself, can you describe for us what security measures were taken there and who were the law enforcement officials, private or public, involved?

MR. FORAN: Objection, your Honor.

THE COURT: I sustain the objection.

MR. KUNSTLER: When you were at the Amphitheatre, did you see any City of Chicago policemen in the vicinity?

MR. FORAN: I object to that. I object to what occurred at the Amphitheatre. There is nothing in—

THE COURT: I sustain the objection.

MR. KUNSTLER: I have no further questions.

THE COURT: Is there any cross-examination of this witness?

MR. FORAN: No, your Honor.

THE COURT: You may go, sir.

Testimony of Clark Kissinger, Jr.

MR. KUNSTLER: Would you please state your full name?

THE WITNESS: Charles Clark Kissinger, Jr.

MR. KUNSTLER: What is your occupation?

THE WITNESS: I am unskilled factory worker now.

MR. KUNSTLER: Where are you working?

THE WITNESS: I would rather not answer that question, since I understand a previous witness has been fired from his job.

MR. FORAN: What is he talking about? Your Honor, I object to the comment.

MR. KUNSTLER: Your Honor, Mr. Hunt was discharged by the Curtiss Candy Company after he testified for the defendants and I am not going to make this witness answer a question if he doesn't want to on where he works.

MR. FORAN: Your Honor, I object to the answer and I ask that it be stricken.

THE COURT: I strike it and direct the jury to disregard it.

MR. FORAN: Maybe he was fired because he was a bum or didn't work. I don't know, your Honor. The implication that—

MR. KUNSTLER: Oh, Mr. Hunt was fired, your Honor, directly after testifying here.

MR. FORAN: The Government knows nothing about that matter, and this is typical of the comic book way that that man runs a case.

MR. KUNSTLER: Now, your Honor, that is an outrageous statement. We can prove what happened to Mr. Hunt.

THE COURT: This is the way it will be done. I do not insist that the witness give his address. I strike the observation of Mr. Kunstler dealing with somebody named Hunt and direct the jury to disregard it.

MR. KUNSTLER: Do you strike the observation of Mr. Foran dealing with comic book defense and words to that effect?

THE COURT: I would describe it differently but I will let that stand. You may continue, sir, to examine this witness.

MR. KUNSTLER: Mr. Kissinger, do you know the background of Thomas Foran, the U.S. Attorney?

THE WITNESS: Yes, I do.

MR. KUNSTLER: Would you indicate—

MR. FORAN: I object.

THE WITNESS: He served for thirteen years as a Special Assistant Corporation Counsel—

THE COURT: I sustain the objection.

THE WITNESS: —in charge of land acquisition for the Department of Urban Renewal.

MR. FORAN: Your Honor, I object to that, and I ask that this witness be instructed—

THE COURT: Yes, the volunteered remarks of the witness may go out.

MR. KUNSTLER: Now, Mr. Kissinger, I call your attention to the night of Sunday, August 25, 1968, at approximately ten o'clock to ten-thirty o'clock on that evening. Do you know where you were?

THE WITNESS: Yes. I was in Lincoln Park near the fieldhouse.

MR. KUNSTLER: In what capacity were you there?

THE WITNESS: I was an accredited press representative to the Democratic Party Convention, and I was there covering the events in the Lincoln Park prior to the official opening of the Convention.

MR. KUNSTLER: What did you see?

THE WITNESS: I was walking toward the field house, and I saw a plain unmarked car parked sort of alongside the field house at an angle, and there was a young man on the opposite side of the car from myself letting air out of the rear right tire on the car.

MR. KUNSTLER: Can you describe that man?

THE WITNESS: No, I could just see the top of his head and his back, and he was on the other side of the car hunched over by the tire.

[419]

MR. KUNSTLER: Then what happened?

THE WITNESS: Then I heard some commotion. I turned around and I saw two men grabbing hold of Tom Hayden. They had him one on each side, by each arm, and they were coming sort of from the south. They were moving him rapidly toward the car, like he doesn't want to go, and he starts to yell, "Help, help," and—first they sort of threw him up against the car, and then they tried to put him into the back seat, and a whole bunch of people came running up and stood around and started asking what's going on and so on.

MR. KUNSTLER: Was Tom Hayden the young man you saw behind the car letting the air out?

MR. FORAN: Objection, your Honor. He said he couldn't recognize him.

THE COURT: I sustain the objection.

MR. KUNSTLER: Where was Tom Hayden when you first saw him?

THE WITNESS: He was being moved towards the car by the two men.

MR. KUNSTLER: How far from the car was he?

THE WITNESS: Oh, thirty, forty feet.

MR. KUNSTLER: What, if anything, happened to the young man who was letting the air out of the tire?

MR. FORAN: Objection to the form of the question, your Honor.

THE COURT: I sustain the objection.

THE WITNESS: I did see more than that.

THE COURT: Is there anything in addition to that that you want to tell the jury, sir?

THE WITNESS: Yes. I saw the person who I believed to be the person that let the air out of the tire moving away toward the northwest.

MR. KUNSTLER: Did you ever get a chance to look at him?

THE WITNESS: No, I never saw his face. He had long dark hair. Hayden at that time had short hair.

MR. KUNSTLER: Your Honor, I have no further questions.

THE COURT: Cross-examination?

• • • • •

MR. FORAN: When you first saw this incident at the field house, Mr. Kissinger, how far were you from the car?

THE WITNESS: I don't recall exactly. I suppose anywhere from twenty to forty feet.

MR. FORAN: What was the lighting in the park there?

THE WITNESS: It was pretty dim.

MR. FORAN: It was a little hard to see at that time at that location?

THE WITNESS: Yes, it was.

MR. FORAN: Was the man kneeling at the wheel when you first saw him Wolfe Lowenthal?

THE WITNESS: I didn't see—I subsequently met an individual named Wolfe Lowenthal at the time of the trial. I never knew him until that time.

MR. FORAN: Do you know whether the man kneeling at the right rear wheel was Wolfe Lowenthal?

THE WITNESS: No, I don't.

MR. FORAN: Could it have been?

THE WITNESS: It could have been just anybody with long hair.

MR. FORAN: That is all.

Testimony of David Edmundson

January 14, 1970

THE COURT: Call your next witness.

MR. WEINGLASS: Would you state your full name for the record?

THE WITNESS: David Lee Edmundson.

MR. WEINGLASS: What is your present occupation?

THE WITNESS: I'm a student at Jefferson State Junior College in Birmingham.

MR. WEINGLASS: Now, Mr. Edmundson, directing your attention to the early part of the month of August 1968, how were you employed, if at all, at that time?

THE WITNESS: I was a volunteer worker for McCarthy in Birmingham, Alabama.

MR. WEINGLASS: In the month of August 1968, did you have an occasion to come to the city of Chicago?

THE WITNESS: Yes, sir, I did.

MR. WEINGLASS: Directing your attention to Monday, August 26, at approximately two o'clock in the afternoon, do you recall where you were?

THE WITNESS: I was in Lincoln Park. A march was in the process of being formed to protest the arrest of Tom Hayden.

MR. WEINGLASS: Did you do anything with respect to this march that was being formed?

THE WITNESS: Yes, sir. I carried a speaker on the top of my head like this throughout about eighty-five percent of the march. The rest of the time I was working as a marshal.

MR. WEINGLASS: During the period of time that you were carrying the speaker with the attached microphone, did you observe persons speaking through the microphone?

THE WITNESS: Yes, sir, I did.

MR. WEINGLASS: Could you identify any of those persons here in court today?

THE WITNESS: John Froines, Rennie Davis, and a third person I have never seen since.

MR. WEINGLASS: During that period of time when you were carrying the speaker and Rennie Davis was speaking through the microphone could you hear what he was saying?

THE WITNESS: Yes, sir. He kept instructing the demonstrators to stay on the sidewalk. He also at various times told the marchers where we were going and why we were going there.

MR. WEINGLASS: When the line of march got down to the Police Headquarters at 11th and State, do you recall what, if anything, occurred?

THE WITNESS: Rennie Davis got on the P.A. microphone and said and I quote—"We are going to take this protest on to the people that are really responsible for the arrests. We are going to the Hilton to protest it to the Democratic Party."

MR. WEINGLASS: And after Rennie Davis made that announcement, what happened?

THE WITNESS: We began to march again, toward the Hilton.

MR. WEINGLASS: Now, as the march approached the southern end of Grant Park, where the statue of General Logan is situated, what did you observe?

THE WITNESS: I observed a lot of people coming from behind me running toward a grassy knoll on which was an equestrian statue and they were surrounding the statue and some of them began to climb up on it.

MR. WEINGLASS: What did you do when you saw the people do that?

THE WITNESS: I handed the speaker to a person that was marching beside me and I started to run for the statue. I reached the statue and I climbed up it.

MR. WEINGLASS: What portion of the top of the statue did you reach?

THE WITNESS: Directly behind the erect figure of General Logan and on the back side of the horse. I was handed a flag when I reached the top.

MR. WEINGLASS: Do you know what flag that was?

THE WITNESS: No, sir, I did not at that time. I waved it for a few minutes, and then someone on the ground yelled up and said to tie it on the head of General Logan, and he threw up a necktie, and I began to tie it onto General Logan's head. I was very, very engrossed in trying to keep the flag up there.

MR. WEINGLASS: What was the next thing you recall occurring that you were able to observe?

THE WITNESS: This person on the statue next to me nudged me and asked me if I was going, to which I replied no, I was tying the flag up there. The next time I looked over there, he was gone, so I imagine he jumped down.

MR. WEINGLASS: When you looked over, was there anyone else on the statue with you?

THE WITNESS: No, sir. There were policemen around the base of the statue, one of the policemen told me to come down. I handed the necktie down and I handed the flag down to a police officer.

MR. WEINGLASS: Then what did you do?

THE WITNESS: I began to search for the fastest and quickest way down. The policeman I handed the flag to called up to me, "Are you scared? Do you need some help?" He then told me to come to the rear of the horse and to slide down the tail, and if I were to fall, he would catch me.

He was standing there until I got about a third of the way down, in full vision, and then he put his hand on his nightstick and began to draw it out of its sheath, and he ducked under the statue out of my field of vision.

MR. WEINGLASS: After seeing that, what did you do?

THE WITNESS: I went back up the statue. The next thing I remember after seeing the policeman duck out of my sight, I remember a police officer grabbing my left leg and trying to pull me off. My back was against General Logan's back. I was turned, facing the saber side of the statue, and then I went off the side, and I tightened my grip on the saber to avoid falling, and my arm got wedged in the hilt of the saber.

MR. WEINGLASS: Now, approximately how far down is it from the side that you were on to the ground or the base where you could jump?

THE WITNESS: Approximately thirty feet.

MR. WEINGLASS: What happened then?

THE WITNESS: Two policemen on the ground grabbed my legs and started pulling on them, and the police officer that initially grabbed my leg had climbed all the way up and was hitting me with very short choppy punches in the back of the head. I was trying to tell the policemen on the ground that my arm was caught in the hilt of the saber and that their pulling on it was breaking it.

MR. WEINGLASS: What, if anything, did they reply?

THE WITNESS: Nothing. They just kept pulling, and they kept pulling, and then—

MR. WEINGLASS: Then what happened?

THE WITNESS: I heard a voice say, "Let me up there. I'll get the s.o.b." and the next thing I knew, there was this police officer facing me, hitting me in the groin and in the lower midsection.

MR. WEINGLASS: Do you know how many times you were struck by that officer?

THE WITNESS: Three that I know, three that I remember.

MR. WEINGLASS: After that happened, what occurred?

THE WITNESS: A third policeman joined in the pulling on the legs. All during this time, I was telling the officer who was looking me in the face that they were breaking my arm. They kept pulling and pulling and pulling, and then I heard my arm break.

MR. WEINGLASS: After you heard that, what happened to you?

THE WITNESS: Well, the next thing I was conscious of, I was in handcuffs, there was a police officer on either side of me, and I was being dragged away to the police car.

MR. WEINGLASS: Approximately what time was it that the police took you into custody?

THE WITNESS: About 4:30 in the afternoon.

MR. WEINGLASS: Did you receive medical treatment for your arm?

THE WITNESS: The first medication I got for pain was at twelve o'clock that night.

MR. WEINGLASS: Can you describe for the court and jury how your arm felt from 4:30 until midnight?

MR. FORAN: Objection, your Honor.

THE COURT: I sustain the objection.

MR. WEINGLASS: Now, Mr. Edmundson, were you subsequently operated on for this injury?

MR. FORAN: Objection, your Honor.

THE COURT: I sustain the objection.

MR. WEINGLASS: Mr. Edmundson, are you now wearing a metal plate in your arm?

THE WITNESS: Yes, sir.

MR. FORAN: Objection, your Honor.

THE COURT: Sustain the objection.

MR. WEINGLASS: Would you roll up your sleeve, your right sleeve, and show your arm to the jury.

MR. FORAN: Objection, your Honor.

THE COURT: You needn't do that. I sustain the objection.

MR. WEINGLASS: Mr. Edmundson, I show you a photograph marked 289 for identification. Can you identify that photograph?

THE WITNESS: Yes, sir.

MR. WEINGLASS: Do you appear in that photograph?

THE WITNESS: Yes, sir.

MR. WEINGLASS: Where were you at the time it was taken?

THE WITNESS: I was on the equestrian statue of General Jonathan A. Logan in Grant Park.

MR. WEINGLASS: There is no further direct testimony.

THE COURT: Cross-examination?

• • • • •

MR. FORAN: While you were marching along in that march, Mr. Edmundson, there were a number of chants going on, weren't there?

THE WITNESS: Yes, sir.

MR. FORAN: Do you remember hearing the chant "What do we want?" and the crowd answering "Revolution?" "When do we want it?" and the crowd would answer "Now?" Do you remember that chant going on?

THE WITNESS: Yes, sir.

MR. FORAN: Mr. Edmundson, you now know what kind of a flag it was someone handed you, don't you?

THE WITNESS: Yes, sir.

MR. FORAN: What kind of a flag was it?

THE WITNESS: It was the flag of the National Liberation Front.

MR. FORAN: Better known as the V.C. Flag, the Viet Cong Flag?

THE WITNESS: Yes, sir.

A DEFENDANT: That isn't the correct name.

MR. FORAN: Now, after you climbed back up onto the statue, after you started to slide down the tail, you climbed right up onto General Logan's head, didn't you?

THE WITNESS: I have no recollection of doing that. I have been shown photographs of doing that.

MR. FORAN: And you would throw your hands up and give the "V" sign time after time, wouldn't you?

THE WITNESS: I have seen photographs of me doing that, yes, sir.

MR. FORAN: Did you hear the crowd roar every time you would do that?

THE WITNESS: No, sir.

MR. FORAN: Now, when you were—when these police officers were trying to get a hold of you up there on the statue, you were kicking them, weren't you?

THE WITNESS: No, sir, I was not.

MR. FORAN: I have no further questions.

THE COURT: Redirect examination?

MR. WEINGLASS: Mr. Edmundson, Mr. Foran on cross-examination asked you about some of the chants you heard during the line of march. I think he specifically asked you about a chant "Hell, no, we won't go." Were you chanting that yourself?
THE WITNESS: No, sir, I was not.
MR. WEINGLASS: Do you know what that chant is?
THE WITNESS: Yes, sir.
MR. FORAN: Objection to what it is.
THE COURT: I sustain the objection.
MR. WEINGLASS: Your Honor, the difficulty with that one particular chant—and I hope the Court will hear me out,—
THE COURT: I will not hear any argument on that.
MR. WEINGLASS: No argument at all?
THE COURT: No, not on that one. It is too simple. Mr. Marshal, I am not here to be laughed at by these defendants, particularly Mr. Rubin.
THE MARSHAL: Mr. Dellinger, also, will you refrain from laughing?
MR. DELLINGER: That is a lie. And it wasn't Mr. Rubin. We laugh enough and you can catch us when we do but you just happened to get that one wrong.
MR. HOFFMAN: It wasn't Jerry. It was me.
THE COURT: That was Mr. Dellinger.
MR. KUNSTLER: That was not Mr. Dellinger.
THE COURT: I saw Mr. Dellinger talking. If anybody else did—
MR. DELLINGER: You did not see me talking. My lips were not moving. That is not the first time you have lied in this courtroom. My lips were not moving.
THE COURT: Did you get those last remarks?
MR. SCHULTZ: It was the defendant Hoffman.
MR. DELLINGER: If you can make an honest mistake, that's all right, but to lie about it afterwards and say you saw me talking when you didn't, that is different.
THE COURT: Will you ask that man to sit down?
MR. DELLINGER: You will go down in infamy in history for your obvious lies in this courtroom of which that is only the most recent one.
THE MARSHAL: Sit down, sir.
MR. DELLINGER: It is absolutely true, what I am saying.
THE COURT: Mr. Marshal, will you ask him to be quiet.
MR. DELLINGER: You will be ashamed of that for the rest of your life, if anything can shame you.
MR. SCHULTZ: Your Honor, it was the defendant Hoffman sitting immediately behind Dellinger who made those remarks.
THE COURT: I have never sat in fifty years through a trial where a party to a lawsuit called the judge a liar.
MR. DELLINGER: Maybe they were afraid to go to jail rather than tell the truth, but I would rather go to jail for however long you send me than to let you get away with that kind of thing.
THE COURT: Mr. Marshal, do I have to tell you again, sir?

(clapping)

THE COURT: Will you let the record show—I don't know, I get twisted between the defendants—the one in the middle.
MR. WEINER: Weiner.
A DEFENDANT: Davis.
MR. WEINER: Weiner.
THE COURT: Mr. Weiner applauded after that speech.
MR. KUNSTLER: So did half the courtroom, your Honor. I think that ought to be in the record.
THE COURT: I order those who applauded and who were seen by the marshals to be taken out of the courtroom.
　　Now, Mr. Weinruss—
MR. WEINGLASS: Weinglass, your Honor.

THE COURT: Whatever your name is. Continue with the examination of this witness.

MR. WEINGLASS: Is that not a chant that you often heard in the Movement meaning, "Hell, no, we won't go to Vietnam"?

THE WITNESS: Yes, sir.

MR. FORAN: Objection, your Honor, and I ask that it be stricken.

THE COURT: I sustain the objection. I strike the witness' answer and direct the jury to disregard it.

MR. WEINGLASS: I have no further redirect.

THE COURT: Please call your next witness.

Testimony of Arlo Guthrie

January 15, 1970

MR. KUNSTLER: What is your name?

THE WITNESS: Arlo Guthrie.

MR. KUNSTLER: Mr. Guthrie, what is your occupation?

THE WITNESS: I am a musician. I am an actor and a writer.

MR. KUNSTLER: By the way, Mr. Guthrie, was your father Woody Guthrie, the writer of "This Land is My Land"?

THE WITNESS: Yes.

MR. FORAN: Objection, your Honor.

THE COURT: Sustain the objection.

MR. KUNSTLER: Now, Mr. Guthrie, you stated that you were an actor. Could you elaborate on that?

THE WITNESS: Well, I've done one film, "Alice's Restaurant."

MR. KUNSTLER: Is that playing in Chicago now?

THE WITNESS: I believe so.

MR. FORAN: Your Honor, this is a long trial and this silly stuff—

THE COURT: I sustain the objection.

MR. KUNSTLER: Now, Mr. Guthrie, I call your attention to mid-January of 1968. Do you recall meeting with Jerry Rubin and Abbie Hoffman?

THE WITNESS: Yes. I met them in New York at an underground radio station. Abbie and Jerry were talking to me about having a Festival of Life here in Chicago.

MR. FORAN: Could we have who said what, please, your Honor?

THE COURT: Yes. We don't expect you to have all that other talent and still know how to be a good witness.

THE WITNESS: Abbie wanted me to come down and sing at a Festival of Life here in Chicago. What I said to Abbie was that it would be rather difficult, you know, for me to get involved in that kind of thing because we had a lot of trouble before with festivals and gatherings because of police violence.

Abbie asked me if I had any song or any kind of theme song for the festival, and I said yes. "Alice's Restaurant," and Jerry said, "What's that?" He had never heard it, and I proceeded to tell him about "Alice's Restaurant."

MR. KUNSTLER: What did you tell him?

THE WITNESS: Well, I told him that it was about Alice and Ray Brock, who live in a church in Stockbridge, Massachusetts, and that she ran a restaurant. They lived in a church and they had a lot of room in the church, and having all the room in the church, they decided that they didn't have to take out their garbage. We had a big Thanksgiving dinner, and after we took out the garbage and we went to the garbage dump, but it was closed. There was a sign across the entrance saying, "Closed on Thanksgiving," and we drove around looking for another place to put the garbage. We found one and dumped it. We went back to the church and ate some more.

The next morning I got up. We got a phone call from a police officer who wanted to know who had dumped the garbage. He had found my name on a piece of paper in the middle of the pile, and said it was illegal to dump there, to come down to the police station and pick up the garbage. So I went down, and he arrested me, and I went with my friend, and we all went over to the garbage, looked around. We went to court, got fined twenty-five bucks, and eventually picked up the garbage.

And it was after that that I went down for my induction physical examination thing in New York City at Whitehall Street, and I went through a lot of tests and examinations, I had examinations and all kinds of things. I eventually went to see a psychiatrist.

THE COURT: Did you pass?

THE WITNESS: Excuse me?

[426]

THE COURT: Did you pass the examination?

THE WITNESS: Not yet. Anyway—

MR. KUNSTLER: Your Honor, this is a story of "Alice's Restaurant."

THE COURT: Oh, this didn't happen to him?

THE WITNESS: Yes, it did.

THE COURT: Oh. You're mistaken. You're mistaken, Mr. Kunstler.

Did you pay the $25 fine?

THE WITNESS: Yes, I did.

Anyway, I finally came to see the very last person in the induction center who had asked me if I had ever been arrested. I told him yes, I was. He said, "What for?" I said, "Littering," and he said, "Did you ever go to court?" and I said, "Yes," and I was unacceptable to the draft because I had been a litterbug in Stockbridge, Massachusetts.

The end of the song is the chorus which goes: [*sings*] "You can get anything you want—"

THE COURT: Oh, no, no. No. I am sorry.

MR. KUNSTLER: Your Honor, that's what he sang for the defendants.

THE COURT: I don't want the theater owner where this picture is shown to sue me.

MR. KUNSTLER: We'll represent you, your Honor.

THE COURT: No singing. No singing. No singing, sir.

MR. KUNSTLER: Mr. Weinglass and I, free of charge, will represent you.

THE COURT: I will reserve my comment on that one.

You, please don't sing.

MR. KUNSTLER: Can you say the words of the chorus?

THE WITNESS: "You can get anything you want at Alice's Restaurant/You can get anything you want at Alice's Restaurant./Walk right in—it's around the back/About half a mile from the railroad track, and/You can get anything you want at Alice's Restaurant."

MR. KUNSTLER: Now, I call your attention, Mr. Guthrie, to the opening week, approximately, of July 1968. Do you know where you were?

THE WITNESS: I was on the front porch of the Viking Hotel in Newport, Rhode Island. Abbie and Jerry approached me, and asked me if I would come to Chicago to sing the song.

I said to both of them that I was still concerned about the fact that the permits had not been granted yet, and that I would not attend and that I would do my best to have other people not attend if the permits weren't granted because of the fear of police violence.

MR. KUNSTLER: Now, did you go to Chicago?

THE WITNESS: No, I didn't.

MR. KUNSTLER: And would you state to the Court and jury why you did not go to Chicago?

MR. FORAN: Objection, your Honor.

THE COURT: Sustain the objection.

MR. KUNSTLER: No further questions.

THE COURT: Is there any cross-examination?

MR. FORAN: I have no cross-examination.

THE COURT: You may go.

(witness excused)

THE COURT: Call your next witness, please.

THE MARSHAL: Let's have quiet in the courtroom, ladies and gentlemen.

Testimony of Cora Weiss

MR. KUNSTLER: Would you state your full name for the record?
THE WITNESS: Cora Weiss.
MR. KUNSTLER: Mrs. Weiss, what is your occupation?
THE WITNESS: I am a housewife.
MR. KUNSTLER: Do you have any relationship with the Mobilization Committee?
THE WITNESS: I am a national cochairman of the New Mobilization Committee.
MR. KUNSTLER: I call your attention, Mrs. Weiss, to the evening of July 25, 1968, and I ask you if you know where you were.
THE WITNESS: I spoke at the Hotel Diplomat in New York City under the auspices of the Fifth Avenue Peace Parade.
MR. KUNSTLER: Did anybody else speak?
THE WITNESS: Tom Hayden spoke.
MR. KUNSTLER: Would you state what Tom Hayden said?
THE WITNESS: I remember distinctly that he talked about the only alternative to genocide was the total withdrawal of troops from Vietnam, and I remember he quoted General Westmoreland and the man who said that we have to destroy a town in order to save it, to demonstrate what he meant by genocide.

And because these were the only alternatives, he said that we had to raise the issue of the total withdrawal of troops from Vietnam as the only viable solution to the war.
MR. KUNSTLER: Did he say anything else that you can now recall in that speech?
THE WITNESS: I believe that he said that we should go beyond the perimeter of dissent which is limited by waiting for elections, that we should continue our protest, and I believe he used a phrase, "the rules of the game," meaning the electoral process, the elections.
MR. KUNSTLER: Now, Mrs. Weiss, I show you D-302 for identification and ask you if you can identify that.
THE WITNESS: These are the children who survived the massacre of Pinkville whom I saw in North Vietnam two weeks ago.
MR. SCHULTZ: Object. Objection. That has no relevancy. If Mr. Kunstler is going to pursue this, we have to argue this, we should excuse the jury.
THE COURT: I will excuse you for a few minutes, ladies and gentlemen of the jury, with my usual orders.

(jury excused)

MR. SCHULTZ: There is no question but what Mr. Kunstler is trying to do is get before the jury the recent development of what is called the massacre of My Lai in Vietnam.

Now, that has no probative value in this case. It's only being injected here in an attempt to turn the jury, to get to the jury's sympathies, wholly unrelated to the merits of the charges and the evidence in this case.
MR. KUNSTLER: Your Honor, this massacre at Song My occurred in March 1968 before the Democratic Convention. There is an example of genocide which was testified to by the witness as being a portion of Mr. Hayden's speech in July of 1968. It seems to me it's perfectly proper to indicate that this was one of the motivations why people went to the Democratic National Convention. I was going to next show her a letter written by a survivor of the Song My massacre to the women of the United States and the women of the world.
THE COURT: If you want to have some other exhibits identified, I will let you protect your record by having them identified.
MR. KUNSTLER: I will show the witness Defendants' 304 for identification and ask her to state for the record what that document is.
THE WITNESS: This is a letter written in the hand of Vo Thi Lien, who is a twelve-year-old child, who is orphaned, and came from the village of Song My, in Quang Ngai Province, South Vietnam, whom I met and spent a day with several weeks ago.

MR. KUNSTLER: Now, your Honor, while the jury is out, I would like to ask the witness to read into the record the English translation of the letter from—

THE COURT: I will let you—even though I already conclude from the identification that the exhibit has no place in the trial of this case.

MR. DAVIS: Before she reads that, we have been admonished many times at this table for laughing in the courtroom. I wonder now if you would admonish Mr. Foran for laughing during this entire episode when we have been talking about the massacre of women and children in Vietnam.

MR. FORAN: Your Honor, I wonder how loud the screams from the defense table would be if the Government put in evidence of what the Weathermen, led by that young man, Hayden,—if we had put in evidence that they came charging out of Lincoln Park two-and-a-half months ago and rampaged all over the North Side of Chicago. That's why I'm laughing, because it's absolutely idiotic that they should be offering this kind of evidence in this case, and they know it, your Honor.

MR. WEINGLASS: In light of what the U.S. Attorney has said I would like this Court in light of the fact that there are persons here from the press and the public, to admonish, openly and in public, the United States Attorney for this reckless, premeditated charge against men who sit here as innocent persons, who are part of the citizenry of this country which Mr. Foran supposedly serves, and to make that charge of a crime without convincing a grand jury or having any testimony—

MR. FORAN: What about the soldiers, your Honor, who have not been found guilty of the charge at Pinkville?

THE COURT: We will strike the remarks of Mr. Foran from the record.

MR. FORAN: Your Honor, Mr. Foran will concede that he lost his temper in the face of the offer made by these gentlemen and is sorry he made the remark.

MR. WEINGLASS: Would your Honor invite Mr. Foran to the lectern where he could make a public confession of a misstatement of the truth of a fact?

THE COURT: He has done everything that is necessary, in my judgment.

MR. WEINGLASS: He's done virtually nothing except say he lost his temper.

THE COURT: That will be all, Mr. Weinglass.

MR. KUNSTLER: I might add, your Honor, that many of the American soldiers involved have confessed publicly that they participated in the murders at Song My.

THE COURT: Will you read the Defendants' Exhibit 304 for identification into the record, Mrs. Weiss?

THE WITNESS: "I am Vo Thi Lien, twelve years old, a native of My Hoi Block, Song My Village, Quang Ngai province. I have survived the murder by GI's of 502 inhabitants of my village early last year. My Hoi alone lost 87 people, including eighteen of my dearest relatives. Now I wish to tell you in detail how the massacre was committed.

"Aunties,

"The weather was fine at dawn on March 16, 1968. As usual, people were going about their work, heading for their fields with spades on their shoulders, or sailing off on their boats, or pounding coconut bark to make coir. Suddenly, from Mount Ram and other places, enemy artillery heavily pounded my village. Everybody hurried into safety.

"When the shelling ended, people got out of their shelters. But at that very moment eleven choppers rushed in from the Chu Lai airfield and landed troops. Realizing that the enemy had come for a sweep, they scurried back to cover.

"The enemy now made for My Hoi. My paternal grandfather and grandmother and myself were in an underground. Grandmother set out to see whether, as usual, they had withdrawn after plundering houses and setting fire to them. Unexpectedly, a volley hit her right at the entrance. Without even a moan, she collapsed by my side. Then there was a flash and an explosion and I lost consciousness.

"When I came to, I was frightened and trembling so much that I could hardly stand on my feet. I felt slimy bits of flesh of grandmother thrown by grenades on my body. In tears, I crawled out of the trench to see who had died and who had survived.

"Aunties, you can never imagine what a horrible scene of carnage I then saw. All the fifteen members of Le's family were a heap of bodies maimed beyond recognition, eight piled on the brink of the underground and seven with severed heads or limbs. Small pieces of flesh were all over the place. Other families were exterminated to the last man. Mrs. Mot with her child, Mrs. Trinh with her five daughters and sons. Mrs. Hoa and Mrs. Mui each with their four little ones. Corpses were sprawling in clusters on the ground, chests pierced by bayonets, broken skulls with brains spilling, and bodies with pieces of flesh carved off by grenade splinters.

"Survivors told me what had happened while I were lying senseless in the shelter. American soldiers after raping Mrs. Ngo, who was near her time, killed her with rifle shots. The fetus was ejected from her womb. And as her three panic-stricken children burst out crying, they shot them dead immediately.

"My own beloved ones died not less horribly. Soldiers dragged auntie Vo Thi Phu out of her shelter and tried to assault her, but as she desperately resisted, they gunned her down as her one-year-old baby was crawling toward her body for a suck. They threw straw on mother and child and set fire to them both. My uncle's wife Le Thi Hong was also killed by gunshots.

"It was terrible. In one day my populous village had become a deserted, devastated place with just a few survivors.

"Aunties, American troops have massacred not only my fellow villagers. I have met many friends of mine from different parts of South Vietnam, not a few of them orphaned by American bombs and bullets. I hope that you will do your best so that not one more GI will be sent to South Vietnam, that you will call for the immediate repatriation of all American troops so that my country suffers no more destruction and no more mass killing like the one in my native village, and so that other friends of mine will not experience horrors and suffering like mine.

"I wish you good health, respectfully yours,

Vo Thi Lien."

MR. SCHULTZ: Objection.

THE COURT: I sustain the objection. Not only do I sustain the objection, I order counsel for the defendants to make no reference to the exhibits before the jury.

MR. SCHULTZ: And would you also instruct the witness, your Honor, who apparently is losing her composure, not to make any reference to her recent trip and to these materials that we have been discussing, because they are not relevant to our prosecution?

THE COURT: Yes, I will instruct the jury.

MR. SCHULTZ: May we inquire of the witness who apparently was crying a moment ago whether or not a brief recess would be—

THE WITNESS: No, it won't be necessary but I am a mother and I have three children and I am sorry that I lost my composure.

THE COURT: Ladies and gentlemen of the jury, while you were out the defendants through their counsel offered Defendants' Exhibits 302, 303 and 304, respectively, for identification. The Court sustained the objection of the Government to those exhibits and I order counsel to make no further reference to them.

MR. KUNSTLER: In view of your Honor's ruling on that, we have no further questions of this witness.

THE COURT: All right. Is there any cross-examination of this witness?

• • • • •

MR. SCHULTZ: The defendant Hayden, when he gave that speech, made reference to the Democratic National Convention coming up in August, didn't he?

THE WITNESS: Yes, he spoke of Chicago.

MR. SCHULTZ: And he said that there were going to be the largest mass arrests in America's history during the upcoming elections and nominations, didn't he?

THE WITNESS: Not that I recall.

MR. SCHULTZ: He said, didn't he, that the peace demonstrators should have contempt for the rules because the United States has broken the rules and the peace demonstrators now have a right to break the rules?

THE WITNESS: The rules of the game for the electoral process. We shouldn't just wait to vote to change the man in office or the policy in office, that we have to keep on raising dissents and to keep on demonstrating.

MR. SCHULTZ: He said that the United States had violated the law and that the peace demonstrators should have contempt for the rules, didn't he?

THE WITNESS: He said the United States had violated the laws of mankind.

MR. SCHULTZ: As a matter of fact, he said that the demonstrators should be prepared to shed their blood?

THE WITNESS: I don't recall if that is the exact phrase, but he spoke of it would not be the first time that blood might have to be shed, our blood as demonstrators, for a cause.

MR. SCHULTZ: That is all.

THE COURT: Call your next witness.

Testimony of Thomas Paterson Alder

MR. WEINGLASS: Will you please state your full name for the record?

THE WITNESS: My name is Thomas Paterson Alder.

MR. WEINGLASS: Where do you reside?

THE WITNESS: Washington, D. C.

MR. WEINGLASS: What is your present occupation?

THE WITNESS: I am a lawyer and president of Public Law Education Institute, which is a research and educational organization in Washington.

MR. WEINGLASS: Directing your attention to the month of August 1968, by whom were you employed?

THE WITNESS: During the latter part of July and the month of August I was director of the Commission of the Democratic Selection of Presidential Nominees.

MR. WEINGLASS: Did your commission have any official sanction within the Democratic Party?

MR. FORAN: Your Honor, I object to the leading and suggestive form of the question.

THE COURT: I sustain the objection.

MR. WEINGLASS: Now, directing your attention to Monday night, August 26, 1968, at approximately 10:30 in the evening of that night, do you recall where you were?

THE WITNESS: I was on the third floor of the Conrad Hilton Hotel. I had two members of my staff in my company at that time: Mr. Jeffrey Cowan, associate director of the commission, and Mr. Simon Lazarus, who was an editor on the commission staff.

MR. WEINGLASS: Now, at 10:30, what, if anything, did the group of gentlemen whom you were with do that you could observe?

THE WITNESS: Mr. Cowan and Mr. Lazarus separated from myself through the lobby to the Balbo Street entrance to the Hilton Hotel.

MR. WEINGLASS: Now, when you got to the entrance, Balbo Street entrance, of the Conrad Hilton Hotel, what, if anything, did you observe?

THE WITNESS: As I reached that entrance, I noticed that Mr. Cowan and Mr. Lazarus were outside the glass doors talking with Mr. Tom Hayden. The suggestion was made by Mr. Cowan that we go back up to the office of the commission and turn on the television, and see if there was a news wrap-up on the convention. Everybody turned and started to go to the door.

We were met by, I take it, an employee of the Conrad Hilton Hotel who pointed to Mr. Hayden and said, "He can't come in."

I asked—I asked why we could not have a guest in our room. The response from the man was that Mr. Hayden couldn't go into the building, that he was under orders, or those were his orders.

I asked then to see the person who had given those orders or his superior. He turned and then walked through the hotel lobby toward the Michigan Avenue entrance. I followed him, thinking that we were going to his immediate superior. Instead, he went onto the sidewalk in front of the hotel on Michigan Avenue, went directly to an officer of the Chicago Police Department.

The group, including Mr. Hayden and Mr. Cowan and Mr. Lazarus then proceeded off the curb of Michigan and Balbo. I noticed in the corner of my left eye, the figure of a man, well over six feet tall, well over, I would say, 200 pounds, in a red and orange shirt, short-sleeved sport shirt, running across Michigan Avenue.

He ran into this crowd of people with his hand raised, pointing down this way, saying, "Get him, that's him. Get him." When I looked I saw this man and a police officer struggling over Mr. Hayden who was on the ground, being held down but at the same time pulled, seemingly dazed, saying over and over as he was dragged past the intersection, "What did I do? What did I do?"

He was then taken, Mr. Hayden, by these two officers to a police van which was not far south on Michigan Avenue, and I did not see him thereafter.

MR. WEINGLASS: How far were you in distance from Tom Hayden at the point in your testimony you indicated you saw this man run toward Tom Hayden?

THE WITNESS: It must have been a matter of some thirty or forty feet at the most.

MR. WEINGLASS: No further questions.

THE COURT: Is there any cross-examination of this witness?

• • • • •

MR. FORAN: Did you see anyone walking behind Mr. Hayden as he crossed the street?

THE WITNESS: Between Mr. Hayden and the curb on the south side of Balbo, in that pedestrian walkway, there were people crossing.

MR. FORAN: But there were some men between Mr. Hayden and the south curb, between you and Mr. Hayden, as you saw him walking north across Balbo?

THE WITNESS: There were people behind Mr. Hayden. Those people there weren't in the way of my visibility.

MR. FORAN: Did you see Mr. Hayden turn around as he was walking across the intersection and apparently either speaking or doing something to anyone behind him?

THE WITNESS: No, I did not.

MR. FORAN: No further questions.

THE COURT: You may go, sir.

Testimony of Wesley Pomeroy

January 19, 1970

THE COURT: Ladies and gentlemen of the jury, good morning.

MR. WEINGLASS: Would you state your full name?

THE WITNESS: Wesley A. Pomeroy. I am the owner and president of Pomeroy Associates, Incorporated. I am a law enforcement consultant.

MR. WEINGLASS: Prior to that what was your employment?

THE WITNESS: I was associate administrator of the Law Enforcement Assistance Administration, United States Department of Justice.

MR. WEINGLASS: Prior to March 1, 1968, do you recall what employment you were engaged in?

THE WITNESS: I had been a California law enforcement officer and administrator for twenty-six years in both state and local police departments in California.

MR. WEINGLASS: With respect to the Republican National Convention in 1964, do you recall what official position you held with respect to that convention?

MR. SCHULTZ: Objection. That is not material.

THE COURT: I sustain the objection.

MR. WEINGLASS: Your Honor, this witness was the chief law enforcement official at that Convention and we are calling him here as an expert as well as a fact witness.

THE COURT: I will let my ruling stand, Mr. Weinglass.

MR. WEINGLASS: Directing your attention to the months of July and August in 1968, do you recall where you were employed?

THE WITNESS: I was Special Assistant to the Attorney General in Washington.

MR. WEINGLASS: What particular assignment did you have in your office for the months of July and August 1968?

THE WITNESS: To function as liaison of both political conventions, in Miami Beach and in Chicago, as liaison between Federal, state, and local law enforcement officials for the Attorney General.

MR. WEINGLASS: Mr. Pomeroy, I direct your attention to July 25, 1968, at approximately 11:20 A.M.—Do you recall where you were?

THE WITNESS: Yes. We met with Mayor Daley.

MR. WEINGLASS: When you say "we," who are you referring to?

THE WITNESS: Roger Wilkins and me.

MR. WEINGLASS: Could you relate to the Court and jury what was discussed, if anything, relative to the demonstrators who were coming to the city of Chicago at the time of the Democratic National Convention?

MR. SCHULTZ: Objection. It's hearsay, your Honor, unless a defendant was present.

THE COURT: I sustain the objection.

MR. WEINGLASS: If the Court please, you have a meeting attended by a subcabinet official of the United States Department of Justice, the Mayor of this city, and one of the chief law enforcement officers in the country. The usual rule allowing hearsay does not apply here because the Government can bring in Mayor Daley or Roger Wilkins and they can refute this testimony if it is not accurate, so I submit in this case hearsay does not apply.

MR. SCHULTZ: No defendant was present. It is totally a hearsay conversation to the defendants, and therefore since the things that are said are hearsay, they are not admissible as evidence.

THE COURT: I will let my ruling, sustaining the objection to the question, stand.

MR. WEINGLASS: I direct your attention to approximately 2:30 of that day which is still on July 25. Do you recall where you were at that time on that day?

THE WITNESS: Yes. That is when I met Tom Foran. We went to his office.

MR. WEINGLASS: And who is Tom Foran?

THE WITNESS: The U.S. Attorney for this area.

MR. WEINGLASS: Were you alone?

THE WITNESS: No. Roger Wilkins and a man who was in the Community Relations Service Office here in Chicago was there.

MR. WEINGLASS: Following that conversation, what, if anything, did you do?

THE WITNESS: We went to the headquarters of the National Mobilization Committee on Dearborn Street. I don't recall the exact address.

MR. WEINGLASS: When you got to the headquarters of the National Mobilization Committee, did you meet with anyone?

THE WITNESS: Yes. A man introduced me to Rennie Davis.

MR. WEINGLASS: Following the meeting in the office, where, if anywhere, did you go?

THE WITNESS: Almost immediately we went downstairs to a small pub on the ground floor.

MR. WEINGLASS: Could you relate to the Court and jury what Rennie Davis said at that meeting, if you can recall?

THE WITNESS: Rennie Davis said that he had been attempting to negotiate with the City government in Chicago for demonstration routes and for places to hold meetings. He said that he had had difficulty in establishing a negotiating base with the City and he was afraid that if he could not do that, there might be violence during the Convention.

He asked if we would try to intercede with the City government in Chicago so that they would become more willing to negotiate with him.

MR. WEINGLASS: When you say he asked if "we would intercede," who do you mean by the reference "we"?

THE WITNESS: He was talking to Roger Wilkins, particularly, and to me, but the appeal was to the Department of Justice in Washington.

Roger Wilkins told Rennie Davis that we had met with the Mayor earlier in the day and that we were trying to get the City of Chicago to open up avenues, lines of communication with the National Mobilization Committee. He told him that the conversation with the Mayor appeared not to be too successful.

We told Mr. Davis that Mr. Foran said he had an appointment with the Mayor later that afternoon and during that meeting he would ask the Mayor to negotiate with the National Mobilization Committee.

MR. WEINGLASS: Drawing your attention to several weeks later, August 12, 1968, do you recall where you were on that day?

THE WITNESS: I was in Chicago again.

MR. WEINGLASS: Did you come alone this time?

THE WITNESS: No. Deputy Attorney General Warren Christopher and I came together.

MR. WEINGLASS: When you came here, where did you go?

THE WITNESS: I went first to the International Amphitheatre, then went to the U.S. Attorney's office, Mr. Foran's office. We went from there to the Mayor's office, Mayor Daley.

MR. WEINGLASS: What happened when you got to Mayor Daley's office?

THE WITNESS: We met with Mayor Daley, Mr. Christopher, Mr. Foran and I.

MR. WEINGLASS: Did this meeting deal with the question of permit negotiations with the National Mobilization?

MR. SCHULTZ: Objection to the form of the question.

THE COURT: I sustain the objection.

MR. WEINGLASS: What was the subject matter discussed at that meeting?

MR. SCHULTZ: Same objection. It is hearsay, your Honor.

THE COURT: I sustain the objection.

MR. WEINGLASS: Your Honor, I am not asking for the conversation. I am asking for the topic that was being discussed.

MR. SCHULTZ: The topic is hearsay.

MR. WEINGLASS: Following that meeting with the Mayor, where did you go?

THE WITNESS: We went back to Mr. Foran's office. We made a number of phone calls and we met with various people during the course of the rest of the afternoon in the U.S. Attorney's office.

MR. WEINGLASS: Was one of the phone calls you made a phone call to Rennie Davis at that time?

MR. SCHULTZ: Objection to the form of the question.

THE COURT: I sustain the objection.

MR. WEINGLASS: Directing your attention to Sunday evening, August 25, at approximately eight o'clock in the evening, do you recall where you were at that time on that day?

THE WITNESS: I was in Lincoln Park in Chicago.

MR. WEINGLASS: Was any activity occurring that you could observe?

THE WITNESS: There were several groups that were singing, there was one rather large group that was sitting down and all engaging in what I can best describe as a humming chant.

MR. WEINGLASS: Now, based on your experience as a special consultant in law enforcement and your experience covering twenty-five years as a law enforcement officer, and further based on your experience with the Republican National Convention in 1964, would you, in your professional opinion, consider the persons you observed in the park on Sunday night to be a threat to the city of Chicago, the peace and safety and welfare of the citizens who reside here?

MR. SCHULTZ: Objection.

THE COURT: I sustain the objection.

MR. WEINGLASS: How long did you remain in the city of Chicago that week?

THE WITNESS: Until the following Thursday morning.

MR. WEINGLASS: And based on what you saw in the city during that period of time and based on your experience as a law enforcement officer, would you relate to the Court and jury whether or not in your considered professional opinion the Police Department of the city of Chicago behaved in a manner consistent with reasonable standards of police enforcement?

MR. SCHULTZ: Objection, your Honor.

THE COURT: I sustain the objection.

MR. WEINGLASS: Now, I direct your attention to the defense table, and I ask you whether or not you know any other individuals seated at this table to my right.

THE WITNESS: I've met Abbie Hoffman.

MR. WEINGLASS: And could you relate to the Court and jury when you met Abbie Hoffman?

MR. SCHULTZ: Your Honor, if it's after the Democratic Convention the fact that he knows him is absolutely immaterial.

THE COURT: I sustain the objection.

MR. WEINGLASS: Did you meet the defendant Abbie Hoffman at the time of the Woodstock Music Festival in the summer of 1969?

MR. SCHULTZ: Objection, irrelevant.

THE COURT: I sustain the objection.

MR. WEINGLASS: Well, he went from a special consultant to the Attorney General to being the chief security officer at Woodstock, at the time of the music festival, and the two are related.

THE COURT: I see nothing in the indictment in this case relating to Woodstock.

MR. WEINGLASS: But Woodstock was the music festival that was intended for Chicago but was not permitted by them to be held here.

THE COURT: I will ask you to refrain from further argument on Woodstock.

MR. WEINGLASS: Well, I have no further direct examination.

· · · · ·

MR. SCHULTZ: Now, you met Davis on July 25, is that right?

THE WITNESS: Yes.

MR. SCHULTZ: Mr. Pomeroy, at that meeting did Davis tell you that regardless of what public assembly was given by the City to the demonstrators, they would reject it unless it was at the area of the Amphitheatre?

THE WITNESS: I don't recall that he did.

MR. SCHULTZ: Did he say that they were going to march whether they got permits or not?

THE WITNESS: I don't recall that he did.

MR. SCHULTZ: Did he say that they were going to stay in the parks past the curfew whether they got a permit or not to do so?

THE WITNESS: No. He said that it was inevitable that if a number of people came to Chicago, as many as he anticipated, and there were no permits or no place for them to stay, that they'd have to stay in the park.

MR. SCHULTZ: Did he say that they considered the Chicago police gestapo?

THE WITNESS: Yes.

MR. SCHULTZ: That's all, your Honor.

THE COURT: Is there any redirect examination?

　　　　　• • • • •

MR. WEINGLASS: Wasn't the purpose of your trip here several weeks later on August 12 to convince Mayor Daley to give permits to the demonstrators?

MR. SCHULTZ: Objection. Mr. Weinglass is already beyond the scope of the cross-examination.

THE COURT: I sustain the objection.

MR. WEINGLASS: I have no further questions.

THE COURT: You may go.

Testimony of Robert Garry Levin

MR. KUNSTLER: Would you state your full name?

THE WITNESS: Robert Garry Levin.

MR. KUNSTLER: What is your occupation?

THE WITNESS: I am assistant professor of psychology at Merrimac College in North Andover, Massachusetts.

MR. KUNSTLER: Mr. Levin, I call your attention to August of 1968, particularly the week of the Democratic National Convention. Do you know where you were during that week?

THE WITNESS: Yes. I was in Chicago.

MR. KUNSTLER: By the way, are you a member of the Youth International Party?

THE WITNESS: No, I am not.

MR. KUNSTLER: I call your attention particularly to Sunday at approximately four o'clock on the twenty-fifth of August. Do you know where you were?

THE WITNESS: We were at the park.

MR. KUNSTLER: How were you dressed at that time?

THE WITNESS: The same way I'm dressed now.

MR. KUNSTLER: You have something in your arms there. What is that?

THE WITNESS: It is a motorcycle helmet, my motorcycle helmet.

MR. KUNSTLER: Did you have that helmet with you when you came to Chicago?

THE WITNESS: Yes, I did.

THE COURT: If you are going to have any testimony about an exhibit, please have it marked.

MR. KUNSTLER: It is already marked, your Honor. We had this marked on, I think, the second or third day of the case. It is marked as 15.

THE COURT: In evidence?

MR. KUNSTLER: That is the famous helmet 88, your Honor, that was referred to, I think, by Sergeant Murray.

Can you describe that helmet as it was on the day that you came to Chicago?

THE WITNESS: Yes. It was in a little better condition. It had a blue stripe down the center and blue tape, 88, on the back. One of the eights is still in place but that's about all that's left.

MR. KUNSTLER: Now you entered the park, you said, at approximately four o'clock. Did you have this helmet with you?

THE WITNESS: Yes, I did.

MR. KUNSTLER: Was this helmet with you all during the evening?

THE WITNESS: Yes, it was.

MR. KUNSTLER: What time did you leave the park?

THE WITNESS: About eleven o'clock.

MR. KUNSTLER: While you were in the park did you wear that helmet?

THE WITNESS: Yes, I did.

MR. KUNSTLER: When you weren't wearing it, where was it?

THE WITNESS: It was strapped to my belt.

MR. KUNSTLER: When you took it off, did it ever leave your possession?

THE WITNESS: No.

MR. KUNSTLER: Nobody else wore it to your knowledge, did they?

THE WITNESS: Not to my knowledge.

MR. KUNSTLER: Now, I call your attention to approximately 7:00 P.M. that night or thereafter, shortly thereafter. What, if anything, happened to you at approximately that time?

THE WITNESS: When I was in the vicinity of the fieldhouse, I spoke to an ABC news reporter.

I told him that I came to Chicago because I felt that there was no clear alternative between Nixon and the almost certain nomination of Humphrey, that we were engaged in

[438]

a war, seemingly endless war, which was exploiting Southeast Asia, and that I felt this was wrong, this was both an illegal and immoral war, and I was there to protest the war and the election.

MR. KUNSTLER: Now, one question, Mr. Levin. Was your facial appearance—I am talking about the amount of hair thereon—the same then or different than it is today?

THE WITNESS: No, it was quite different. I had maybe a week's, week-and-a-half's, growth. I was just—started growing the beard then.

MR. KUNSTLER: Now, I call your attention to approximately nine o'clock on that evening. Do you know where you were at that time?

THE WITNESS: Yes. In the vicinity of the fieldhouse.

MR. KUNSTLER: Were you dressed the way you are now?

THE WITNESS: Yes.

MR. KUNSTLER: Where was the helmet that you have described?

THE WITNESS: On my head.

MR. KUNSTLER: At this time did you know that a policeman by the name of Sergeant Murray had mistaken you as Jerry Rubin?

MR. FORAN: Oh, objection.

MR. KUNSTLER: Now, at this time that you were standing there with the helmet, what happened?

THE WITNESS: After a short time, the police charged the crowd. They surged into the crowd swinging.

MR. KUNSTLER: Did anything happen sometime before the police charged the crowd?

THE WITNESS: I saw an individual flick a cigarette in the direction of the police.

MR. KUNSTLER: Where was that individual in connection to you?

THE WITNESS: Standing next to me.

MR. KUNSTLER: Can you describe him?

THE WITNESS: He was clean shaven, he had fairly long hair, and he was dressed in denims. That's about all I could say.

MR. KUNSTLER: Did the cigarette hit the police?

THE WITNESS: No, it fell short.

MR. KUNSTLER: Then what did the police do?

THE WITNESS: They charged out. Then they pulled back. They charged out again, and then they pushed the people out.

MR. KUNSTLER: At the time that you came to Lincoln Park that day or up to that time, did you know any of the defendants in this case?

THE WITNESS: No.

MR. KUNSTLER: Just one more question. Did you have your helmet with you during the entire rest of the week?

THE WITNESS: Yes, I did.

MR. KUNSTLER: And would you state to the jury why you brought a helmet with you to Chicago?

MR. SCHULTZ: Objection.

THE COURT: I sustain the objection.

MR. KUNSTLER: No further questions.

THE COURT: Is there any cross-examination?

· · · · ·

MR. SCHULTZ: Mr. Levin, at the fieldhouse, you say at seven o'clock you talked to ABC newsman, is that right?

THE WITNESS: About that.

MR. SCHULTZ: Did you say to them at seven o'clock, "You're going to go out to the ballfield to see what the pigs do when you get out there"?

THE WITNESS: No.

MR. SCHULTZ: Were you ever in front of the Conrad Hilton Hotel?

THE WITNESS: Yes, I was.

MR. SCHULTZ: Were you ripping up some signs?

THE WITNESS: Yes, I was.

MR. SCHULTZ: Did you see Rubin there?

THE WITNESS: No, I did not.

MR. SCHULTZ: Going back to Sunday night when you got to the fieldhouse, did you hear the people say "Look at the motherfucker standing there," say that to the policeman?

THE WITNESS: No.

MR. SCHULTZ: Did you see objects thrown at the policemen?

THE WITNESS: No, I didn't.

MR. SCHULTZ: Did you ever shave your beard, your growth?

THE WITNESS: Not during the Convention.

MR. SCHULTZ: Will you look at Government's Exhibit 4 in evidence showing a beard on Rubin. You say yours was about that long, is that right, during Convention week?

THE WITNESS: Yes.

MR. SCHULTZ: And you notice on the photograph that Rubin's mustache is considerably longer than the beard part. Isn't that right?

THE WITNESS: Yes.

MR. SCHULTZ: Was your mustache longer than the beard part?

THE WITNESS: No, it wasn't.

MR. SCHULTZ: Isn't it a fact, sir, that you had no beard at all during that Convention, and you have fabricated a beard in this courtroom in order to be an alibi witness for the defendant Jerry Rubin?

THE WITNESS: No. There's no fabrication at all.

MR. SCHULTZ: I will show you some pictures of yourself without a beard in front of the Conrad Hilton Hotel and ask you if that refreshed your recollection that you did not have a beard during the Convention.

THE WITNESS: The beard was considerably shorter than I recall. I had just started growing it at that point, as I said.

MR. SCHULTZ: I show you a closer one of your face, and ask you if that refreshes your recollection that you had no growth whatever during the convention.

MR. KUNSTLER: Your Honor, he has answered twice.

THE WITNESS: I was not clean-shaven. I hadn't shaved since the Convention started.

MR. SCHULTZ: Now, isn't it a fact, sir, now that you have seen the photographs of yourself during Convention week, that you had no beard at all during the Convention and that you testified here before this jury stating you had a beard because you were going to be a substitute witness, an alibi witness, for the defendant, Jerry Rubin? Isn't that a fact, sir?

THE WITNESS: It is not true.

MR. SCHULTZ: I have no further questions of the witness.

THE COURT: Call your next witness.

Testimony of Country Joe McDonald

January 20, 1970

THE CLERK: You will remove your gum, sir.

THE WITNESS: What gum?

THE CLERK: That you are chewing on.

THE WITNESS: I am afraid that I don't have any gum.

THE CLERK: You may be seated, sir.

MR. KUNSTLER: Would you state your full name, please?

THE WITNESS: Country Joe.

MR. KUNSTLER: What is your occupation?

THE WITNESS: I am a minister in the New Universal Life Church. I am a rock and roll star. I am a producer of phonograph records. Father, husband, singer, composer, poet, owner of a publishing company, and a few other things.

MR. KUNSTLER: Do you have currently a rock and roll band?

THE WITNESS: Country Joe and the Fish.

MR. SCHULTZ: For the record may we have the witness' full name?

THE COURT: I assume that his Christian name is Country. He is under oath. Is Country your first name?

THE WITNESS: Yes.

THE COURT: That is your first name or Christian name, is that right?

THE WITNESS: Some people call me Country, yes.

THE COURT: What is your real name?

THE WITNESS: Country.

THE COURT: What is your real name, sir? Were you baptized?

THE WITNESS: No, I wasn't.

THE COURT: What were you called when you went to school as a child?

THE WITNESS: Joe.

THE COURT: What was your family name?

THE WITNESS: McDonald.

THE COURT: And you are familiarly known as Country Joe, is that right?

THE WITNESS: Country Joe McDonald, yes. Joseph sometimes.

THE COURT: You still call him Country Joe even though his name is McDonald?

MR. KUNSTLER: I know, your Honor, but he is known throughout the world as Country Joe.

THE COURT: That is what you say. I have never heard of him.

MR. KUNSTLER: Are you known throughout the world as Country Joe?

MR. SCHULTZ: I object.

THE COURT: I sustain the objection.

MR. KUNSTLER: When did you first meet Mr. Rubin?

THE WITNESS: I met Jerry Rubin in 1964, October 15–16, the march to end the war in Vietnam, the march held in Berkeley, California.

MR. KUNSTLER: I call your attention to Abbie Hoffman. Do you know him?

THE WITNESS: Yes, I know Abbie Hoffman. He is that handsome fellow with the handsome jacket on.

THE COURT: Mr. Witness, when you are asked to identify anybody here, you may describe him by his apparel, but do not characterize him as being handsome or in any other such manner.

THE WITNESS: I am sorry. I have never been in a trial before.

THE COURT: I accept your apology.

MR. KUNSTLER: Do you recall when you first met Abbie Hoffman?

THE WITNESS: Yes. I first met Abbie Hoffman at the meeting at the Chelsea Hotel in New York.

MR. KUNSTLER: Now, would you state for the jury what was said by those people who participated as you can remember.

THE WITNESS: I said to Jerry Rubin, "The Yippie thing in Chicago, what do you want us to do?"

Jerry Rubin said to me, "We feel that the Democratic Convention being held in Chicago is a very important political event in the country," and that it was the responsibility of those people, young people, who are concerned with freedom in America to try to do something in Chicago that would counterbalance the evil and negative vibrations from the Democratic Convention. And since I had written the Vietnam Rag, which has become the most well-known song against the war in Vietnam, and that my group was very influential with young people in America, it was very important that we try to say something in Chicago which would be positive, natural, human, and loving, in order to let the people of America know that there are people in America who are not tripped out on ways of thinking which result only in oppression and fear, paranoia, and death.

At that point Abbie Hoffman wanted to know what the song was, then I sang the song.

It goes: [*sings*] "And it's one, two, three what are we fighting for? Don't ask me, I don't give a damn. Next stop is Vietnam. And it's—"
THE COURT: No, no, no, Mr. Witness. No singing.
THE WITNESS: "—five, six, seven—"
THE COURT: Mr. Marshal—
DEPUTY MARSHAL JOHN J. GRACIOUS: The judge would like to speak to you.
THE COURT: No singing is permitted in the courtroom.
MR. KUNSTLER: Was there any further conversation that you can recall?
THE WITNESS: My manager, Ed Denson, asked if permits had been secured and explained that it was very necessary for the bands involved that they have permits, because without a permit it would probably be impossible to get a good P.A. system, a good stage, and organization established so that a concert could actually happen.

Jerry Rubin and Abbie Hoffman said that they were working towards getting permits that we could do what we wanted to do in a legal way.

Jerry Rubin asked if it was possible for me to contact other bands and talk to them and possibly get some support for a Yippie festival in Chicago.
MR. KUNSTLER: Do you remember what the next time that you saw Abbie Hoffman or Jerry Rubin was?
THE WITNESS: I met with Abbie Hoffman, Jerry Rubin, Ed Sanders, and a few other people I can't remember towards the end of April.
MR. KUNSTLER: Will you describe who was present, and would you state what was said by whom.
THE WITNESS: Jerry Rubin asked me how I was doing in getting response for the Yippie festival.

I informed him that since our original meeting at the Chelsea Hotel, I had talked to other bands, and I found that they were constantly relating to me stories that at least two thousand civilian vigilantes were being authorized as deputies to arrest all troublemakers around the Convention, that the National Guard was being assembled to prevent people from getting close to the Convention hall, that the sewers of Chicago were being prepared as dungeons to put demonstrators in, that generally the vibrations around Chicago were very, very uptight and getting worse, that there was a possibility of incredible brutality, maliciousness, and fascistic-type tactics on the part of the police force, and that I was having a very hard time getting people to be responsive to the possibilities of anything positive happening in Chicago during the Democratic Convention.
MR. KUNSTLER: Now, Country Joe, I ask you whether you came to Chicago during Convention week?
THE WITNESS: Yes, I did. We played at the Electric Theater.
MR. KUNSTLER: Did you have occasion to meet with Jerry Rubin or Abbie Hoffman?
THE WITNESS: Yes. I met with both of them at the Electric Theater on Saturday.
MR. KUNSTLER: Would you state what was said and who said it?
THE WITNESS: Abbie Hoffman said to me "Are you going to be in the Festival?"

I said to Abbie Hoffman, no, I was not going to be in the Festival because the vibrations in the town were so incredibly vicious that I felt it was impossible to avoid violence on the part of the police and the authorities in Chicago.

I felt that my group's symbolic support of the Festival had to be withdrawn because there would be a possibility that people would follow us to the Festival and be clubbed and Maced and tear gassed by the police and that the possibility of anything positive or loving or good coming out of that city at that time was impossible, and that I had no choice but to withdraw my support.

MR. KUNSTLER: After Abbie Hoffman and Jerry Rubin left, what happened?

THE WITNESS: I performed two sets for the audience at the Electric Theater. I left the Electric Theater and on the way out was insulted by some of the people standing outside.

We tried to be polite and avoided a violent conflict and went to our car, got in our car, drove to the Lake Shore Hotel where we were staying. We were followed by three men about my age, with crewcuts, what I would say straight-looking with slacks and shirts who were drunk. One of them began yelling about having served in Vietnam and wanted to know how I could walk around the streets looking like—

MR. SCHULTZ: I object to him continuing.

THE COURT: He may continue.

MR. KUNSTLER: Then what happened?

THE WITNESS: Then I attempted to get into the elevator with my organist, David Cohen, and I was struck in the face by this person, my nose was fractured. My organist attempted to get out of the elevator to get to a phone to call the police. He was then struck in the face.

They scuffled about in the lobby. Then all three of them ran out the back door. The police were called, newspapers were called and I was taken to the hospital by the police, and they fixed my fractured nose the best they could.

MR. KUNSTLER: The witness is with you.

MR. SCHULTZ: Thank you, Mr. Kunstler.

MR. KUNSTLER: My pleasure.

• • • • •

MR. SCHULTZ: When you had your conversation with Rubin and Hoffman on Saturday night at the Electric Theater, did they tell you that during the time they were negotiating with the authorities to get permits, some of the things that Hoffman said in his writings and orally were that during the Convention the people would fight the police? Did they say that?

THE WITNESS: They couldn't say that because that would be a lie, you know.

MR. SCHULTZ: No, I am asking you whether or not one of them said that he had said that or written that?

THE WITNESS: Of course not.

MR. SCHULTZ: Or that they had said that there would be public fornication during the Convention week out in the parks?

THE WITNESS: Your Honor, I deal in words, that is my job. I write songs. I have been doing that for about ten years. Certain words have certain connotations and multimeanings to them, and in the world that I live in, in what is probably called the hippie underground, when we refer to fornication, we are not really referring to the actual sexual act of fornication at all times; we are referring to a spiritual togetherness that can be done without physical contact at all.

MR. SCHULTZ: Let me ask you this way. Did they tell you when they were negotiating with public officials that people during the Convention would fuck in the parks? Did they tell you that?

THE WITNESS: I got arrested for saying that.

MR. SCHULTZ: Did Abbie Hoffman offer to pay you, by the way, for your playing in the park?

THE WITNESS: We made it known to him that we would do everything for free.

MR. SCHULTZ: Did you tell him you were arranging with other musicians for them to do it for nothing?

THE WITNESS: No, I never said that.

MR. SCHULTZ: Did you discuss payment of the other musicians with either Hoffman or Rubin?

THE WITNESS: I don't discuss money with my friends.

MR. SCHULTZ: Oh, I have no more questions, your Honor.

THE COURT: You may go.

Testimony of Irving Birnbaum

MR. WEINGLASS: Would you please state your full name for the record?

THE WITNESS: Irving Birnbaum.

MR. WEINGLASS: And your present occupation?

THE WITNESS: I am an attorney, licensed to practice in the State of Illinois.

MR. WEINGLASS: Mr. Birnbaum, I direct your attention to the weekend of March 22 to 24, 1969, and I ask you if you recall where you were on that weekend.

THE WITNESS: I was in the company of the defendant, Mr. Lee Weiner. We were flying to New York for a conference with defendants and some lawyers.

MR. WEINGLASS: Could you relate to the Court and to the jury what Mr. Weiner said to you and what you said to him?

THE WITNESS: Mr. Weiner said to me, "I suspect that a Mr. Irving Bock, who has been active for many years in the peace movement, is an undercover policeman," and he said to me "What should we do about it?"

I said, "It's obvious what we should do about it. We should get him in and ask for a statement, and we should prepare a defense."

He said, "Why should we do that?"

I said, "There are three reasons why we should do it. One: if he's an undercover agent, he won't give us a statement because he doesn't want to blow his cover."

I says, "If he isn't an undercover agent, he will give us a statement. And if in fact he is an undercover agent and gives us a statement, we can use the statement to impeach him."

MR. WEINGLASS: Now, directing your attention to the thirtieth day of June 1969, do you recall where you were on that day?

THE WITNESS: In my office.

MR. WEINGLASS: Did you have occasion on that day while in your office to meet with Irving Bock?

THE WITNESS: Yes, I did.

MR. WEINGLASS: And could you relate to the Court and the jury what occurred in your office when you met with Irving Bock on that day?

THE WITNESS: Well, some time that evening or early late afternoon, Mr. Bock came into my office and sat down, and I said to Mr. Bock, "You know why you're here, don't you?"

He says, "Yes."

I said, "You're here because I want you to sign a statement that you gave to Mr. Weinglass, is that correct?" I said "Now you know, Mr. Weinglass has asked you all these questions, and you know you're sent here because I'm a notary public, and I want to take your statement in front of me."

He says, "Yes."

I said, "Have you seen the statement?"

He said, "No."

So I said, "Here's the statement. Will you please read the statement?"

MR. WEINGLASS: Did Mr. Bock in your presence read the statement?

THE WITNESS: Yes, sir.

MR. WEINGLASS: After he read the statement, what, if anything, did Mr. Bock do in your presence?

THE WITNESS: I asked Mr. Bock, "Is everything that you've said in this statement true and correct?"

He says, "It is correct."

I said, "Will you sign it, please?"

He says, "I will." And he signed it.

He returned it to me. I immediately notarized it, sealed it, and after I had done that I handed a copy to Mr. Bock and I says, "Here's a copy for your records." I says, "Now, Mr. Bock, since I didn't prepare this statement, I feel there are additional questions I should like to ask you, and I asked him a series of additional questions that were not included in this document.

MR. WEINGLASS: Do you recall what questions you asked him?

MR. FORAN: I object to that, your Honor.

THE COURT: I will sustain the objection.

MR. WEINGLASS: I have no further questions of the witness.

THE COURT: Is there any cross-examination of this witness?

MR. FORAN: No, your Honor.

THE COURT: You may go.

Testimony of Samuel Winfred Brown

January 21, 1970

MR. KUNSTLER: Would you state your full name, please?

THE WITNESS: Samuel Winfred Brown, Jr.

MR. KUNSTLER: What is your present occupation?

THE WITNESS: I am a coordinator of the Vietnam Moratorium Committee. I am currently on leave from Harvard University.

MR. KUNSTLER: Would you explain what the Vietnam Moratorium Committee is?

MR. SCHULTZ: Objection. That is not relevant.

THE COURT: I sustain the objection.

MR. KUNSTLER: Now, Mr. Brown, I call your attention to the summer of 1968. Do you know where you were employed then?

THE WITNESS: I was employed on the national campaign staff for the McCarthy for President campaign.

MR. KUNSTLER: Now, Mr. Brown, calling your attention to the afternoon of August 27, 1968, in the middle of the afternoon, do you know where you were?

THE WITNESS: I went to meet with Rennie Davis at the Mobilization office here in Chicago.

MR. KUNSTLER: Would you state for the jury what you said to Rennie and what he said to you?

THE WITNESS: I told him that after the events of the preceding night, Senator McCarthy was deeply disturbed by the events. And I told Rennie that I would be going to the events that evening because of Senator McCarthy's concern, and relayed to him Senator McCarthy's desire, really, to try and participate in ways which might decrease the level of violence in the city.

I told him that I had contacted the other campaigns, and that Senator McGovern had designated an individual to serve in a similar capacity that I was, and told him that I had contacted the Humphrey campaign, but they had at that point not designated anyone, and it was unclear whether they would, but that at least on behalf of Senator McCarthy and Senator McGovern, there would be people there.

MR. KUNSTLER: I have no further questions.

THE COURT: Cross-examination?

• • • • •

MR. SCHULTZ: Davis was telling you this at this meeting, that he wanted everything to be peaceful?

THE WITNESS: Yes.

MR. SCHULTZ: And of course, you wanted things to be peaceful as well?

THE WITNESS: Yes.

MR. SCHULTZ: Davis told you that because of what had happened on Monday night in the park, that there had been violence in the park, that he was concerned, isn't that right?

THE WITNESS: Actually, I expressed that concern from Senator McCarthy.

MR. SCHULTZ: Did Mr. Davis say to you that even if they didn't get a permit from the police, they were going to try to march those thousands of people to the Amphitheatre?

THE WITNESS: That was a decision that, as I recall, was not finalized at that point. We did discuss the importance of continuing a demonstration in the city, not allowing it to be stopped, and that peaceful events should not be stopped in any circumstances, and I said that I agreed with that.

MR. SCHULTZ: Did Davis tell you that they were going to give the people at the Bandshell two alternatives, one a peaceful march and the other one a nonpeaceful activity?

THE WITNESS: I don't recall that at all, no. Certainly he didn't say that.

MR. SCHULTZ: Did Davis tell you that he expected that if on Wednesday McCarthy lost the nomination, the McCarthy people would react militantly?

THE WITNESS: Well, he assumed they would be more sympathetic to efforts in the street, but he didn't use the words "angrily" or "militantly," as I recall.

MR. SCHULTZ: That's all, your Honor.

THE COURT: You may call your next witness.

THE CLERK: Will you rise and raise your right hand, sir.

• • • • •

You do solemnly swear that the testimony you are about to give in the cause now on trial before this Court and jury shall be the truth, the whole truth, and nothing but the truth, so help you God?

THE WITNESS: No.

THE COURT: All right,—

THE WITNESS: I believe in the constitutional provision for the separation of church and state, so I will choose to affirm to tell the truth.

THE COURT: Let him affirm. Administer the affirmation, Mr. Clerk.

THE CLERK: Do you hereby affirm that the testimony you are about to give in the cause now on trial before this Court and jury shall be the truth, the whole truth, and nothing but the truth?

THE WITNESS: Yes.

THE CLERK: This, you do under pains and penalty—

THE COURT: Listen to the last part of this before you say yes.

(laughter in the courtroom)

THE WITNESS: If I am going to tell the truth, I am going to tell the truth no matter what the penalties are.

THE COURT: All right, don't interrupt the clerk when he is giving you what you wanted, and that is an affirmation.

Testimony of Paul Krassner

MR. KUNSTLER: Would you state your full name?

THE WITNESS: Paul Krassner.

MR. KUNSTLER: And what is your occupation, Mr. Krassner?

THE WITNESS: I am a writer and editor.

MR. KUNSTLER: And what are you an editor of?

MR. KRASSNER: A magazine called *The Realist*.

MR. KUNSTLER: Now I call your attention to the first part of December 1967. Do you recall whether you met Abbie Hoffman and Jerry Rubin during that period?

THE WITNESS: Yes, I did. It was at Anita's and Abbie Hoffman's house and she had made this shirt for me to wear to "The Johnny Carson Show."

MR. FORAN: Objection, your Honor.

THE COURT: Yes, the witness' reference to his new shirt—at least it was new then—may go out, and the jury is directed to disregard it.

MR. KUNSTLER: I ask you if you can identify the shirt-maker in the courtroom?

MR. FORAN: Oh, your Honor, I object to this.

THE COURT: I sustain the objection.

MR. KUNSTLER: Can you identify Anita Hoffman?

THE WITNESS: Yes, the young lady who is standing.

MR. KUNSTLER: What about Nancy Kurshan?

THE WITNESS: The young lady who is now standing.

MR. FORAN: I object to this, your Honor.

THE COURT: Yes, I think it is inappropriate that the spectators here be identified by witnesses.

MR. KUNSTLER: Your Honor, I am going to object to his not being able to identify these two women. If they had been men, they would probably be indicted here as defendants because they have been in every one of the meetings. They have been stated by witness after witness as being present.

THE COURT: No volunteered statements, sir. Just ask questions, and we will get along faster.

MR. KUNSTLER: Can you state what was said at that meeting, and, Mr. Krassner, indicate who said what?

THE WITNESS: Jerry Rubin said, "Well, the Democrats are going to have their convention in Chicago in August. I guess we should have our convention, too."

Abbie Hoffman said, "Let's have a kind of alternate life style because, from the kind of military force that they have demonstrated at the Pentagon and the previous demonstrations, we know it would be masochistic to try and confront anybody like that. The only alternative is to try and show them that there is an alternative life style that is possible. This is the only sane thing to do."

And then Anita Hoffman—shall I include those witnesses too, your Honor?

THE COURT: What did you say?

THE WITNESS: Weren't you paying attention?

THE COURT: I am listening very carefully. I can't tell you how to testify. I wasn't there.

MR. KUNSTLER: I don't think the judge was present.

THE WITNESS: All right. Well then, Nancy Kurshan said, "We will have to organize this."

It was Jerry Rubin who specifically said we would call it an International Youth Festival.

I said we should have a better name for it, something that would be more catchy, and the words Youth International Party came out as a switch on "International Youth Festival," and then suddenly I shouted, "Yippie." Because the initials "Y–I–P" from Youth International Party spelled out "Yippie."

MR. KUNSTLER: Now, I call your attention to March 25 of 1968, approximately one week later, and ask if you know where you were then?

THE WITNESS: May I explain that previous answer?

MR. KUNSTLER: Go ahead.

THE COURT: No. Answer the last question.

THE WITNESS: He interrupted before I was finished.

THE COURT: Who did?

THE WITNESS: My attorney.

THE COURT: Oh, is he your lawyer?

THE WITNESS: Didn't you know that?

THE COURT: No, I didn't know that.

THE WITNESS: I thought you knew that.

MR. KUNSTLER: I call your attention to Monday, March 25, 1968, and ask you if if you know where you were at approximately 8:00 P.M. on that day?

THE WITNESS: I was at the Aragon Ballroom. There was a benefit, that night, for the Yippies and for *The Seed*, the underground paper of Chicago. I was one of the speakers at the benefit.

MR. KUNSTLER: Did you have any occasion to have a conversation with the defendants Abbie Hoffman or Jerry Rubin?

THE WITNESS: Oh, yes. This was backstage. Abbie Hoffman was there. Jerry Rubin was there. Nicholas Von Hoffman from the *Washington Post* was there.

MR. KUNSTLER: A reporter?

THE WITNESS: Yes. Jerry said that we ought to make the formal application to the City of Chicago for the permits, that we ought to do that the very next day. We proceeded to—

MR. FORAN: Who said what?

MR. KUNSTLER: Mr. Foran has suggested that you state who said what to whom as you can recall it.

THE COURT: I approve of the suggestion.

MR. KUNSTLER: I approve of it myself, your Honor.

THE WITNESS: Is everybody through approving?

MR. KUNSTLER: Everybody has approved.

THE WITNESS: Mr. Hoffman suggested—

THE COURT: Is it Mr. Hoffman or Von Hoffman? Which was it? There were two there, weren't there?

THE WITNESS: Oh, that's correct.

THE COURT: Now you are talking about Mr. Abbott Hoffman.

THE WITNESS: Abbie. Abbie.

THE COURT: All right. I want to place the various Hoffmans or Von Hoffmans—I don't want anybody to be confused about the Hoffmans.

THE WITNESS: I never call him Mr. Hoffman anyway. Abbie. Abbie said, "Let's get it done as quickly as possible."

MR. KUNSTLER: Was that as far as you can recall the extent of the conversation?

THE WITNESS: Oh, no. I just didn't want to bore the judge.

THE COURT: Oh, I'm very much interested. You're not boring me. Besides, you're obligated to answer even if you bore the Court.

MR. KUNSTLER: Just finish the conversation as you can recall it.

THE WITNESS: As I recall it, the conversation finished with Abbie saying, "We've got to do it. We got to get the permit."

MR. KUNSTLER: I call your attention to August 24, the evening of that day. Do you recall where you were then?

THE WITNESS: I was at a meeting at the Free Theater in Chicago.

MR. KUNSTLER: Would you state what you said on that occasion?

THE WITNESS: Yes. I said that even though we had a right to free speech, that we should not go beyond the curfew.

I also wrote a call to people to tell them not to go beyond the curfew.

MR. KUNSTLER: No further questions, your Honor.

THE COURT: Cross-examination. Is there any?

MR. FORAN: We just have a couple of questions.

• • • • •

MR. FORAN: How old are you?
THE WITNESS: I am thirty-seven.
MR. FORAN: Thirty-seven. You will be thirty-eight in April?
THE WITNESS: That is the way it goes chronologically.
MR. FORAN: No more questions.
THE COURT: You may go.

Testimony of Allen Katzman

MR. KUNSTLER: Your Honor, just as a preface, this is a witness that we are calling in protest because of the double jeopardy claim of Mr. Rubin. His testimony does affect Mr. Rubin, and since we have protested that he is being tried in two courts for the same offenses, I want that protest to be of record.

Would you state your full name, please?

THE WITNESS: Allen Katzman.

MR. KUNSTLER: What is your occupation, Mr. Katzman?

THE WITNESS: I am a journalist, a poet, and editor and founder of *The East Village Other*.

MR. KUNSTLER: What kind of a newspaper is it?

THE WITNESS: It's an underground newspaper.

MR. KUNSTLER: What do you mean by "an underground newspaper?"

THE WITNESS: An underground newspaper reports and participates in the cultural revolution that is happening in this country today.

It's connected with the Yippies and many other New Left organizations in the country, and it stands against the establishment press, which is bought off by big business and other concerns that deal with the economic class war in this country, and we are for peace and we are for spreading the ideals of brotherhood and love, and to make people recognize the fact that we no longer live in a system that can support human life, and therefore we must change that system.

MR. KUNSTLER: I call your attention to approximately 10:00 P.M. on August 26, 1968. Do you know where you were?

THE WITNESS: I was in Lincoln Park.

People were gathered there, and were just waiting around, and I went away from the large group of people looking for the police to see where they were hiding. I spotted the police in a ravine, about 200 policemen, waiting with walkie-talkies to be called up, and while I was waiting, I got caught while the police were moving out.

They were coming out, and I got frightened. I thought I'd be caught between the demonstrators and the police and I decided to outflank them and come around, and I got lost.

I finally saw a lighted sign and went up to it and it said "Wrong Way," and I just turned around and came back, which happened to be lucky, and I came running in the park and ran into Ginsberg, and then the tear gas started flying and there was a lot of action, and they pushed all the people out of the park, and my car was parked on LaSalle Avenue. I had come—

MR. KUNSTLER: What did you do then?

THE WITNESS: I jumped in the car, and I met a friend of mine, Jay Levin from *The New York Post*, and we put our press cards in the window, and we decided to follow the crowd down to Old Town, but that moment my gas line slipped, and we couldn't get any acceleration, and we were moving into the park at about five miles an hour. A man came out of the darkness, no identification—that is, he had no uniform or police badge—and my window on the right side where I was sitting was open, and he leaned in and started beating me with a blackjack and chains for about three minutes practically, and I—

MR. KUNSTLER: Go ahead.

THE WITNESS: I kept looking at him. I couldn't believe it, and I finally said to him, very calmly—I didn't realize how calm I was until later—I said, "What do you think you're doing?" And he stopped. I don't think anybody had ever talked—asked that question of him before, and I managed to roll up the window.

We moved along, and about fifteen more people came out of the darkness, and they broke the windows, and I got out, and I was bleeding, and they wrecked the hood of the car and front. We showed them our identification, and I said to the person—I didn't know if he was a policeman or not. They had guns and everything, but they refused to identify themselves, and they had no badges or uniforms, and I said, "Can I reach into my right-hand pocket, with my left hand? My right hand is injured." And he said, "What are you going to do? Shoot me? Have you got a gun there?"

And I said, "No, that's not my business," and I showed him my identification, and then they let us go, and then Jay Levin took me to the movement hospital in one of the churches.

MR. KUNSTLER: What had happened to your right arm?

THE WITNESS: Very badly bruised, and it now has an arthritic condition.

MR. KUNSTLER: Can you describe the condition of the car afterward?

THE WITNESS: All of the windows were broken. The hood was broken, and there were dents all over the car.

MR. KUNSTLER: Were you arrested for anything?

THE WITNESS: No, they didn't arrest me. I wasn't doing anything wrong.

MR. KUNSTLER: Now, Mr. Katzman, I call your attention to approximately 3:00 P.M. that afternoon, that is in the afternoon of Wednesday, August 28. Do you know where you were?

THE WITNESS: I was right near the flagpole, about, I don't know, twenty-five, thirty feet behind the flagpole.

MR. KUNSTLER: And what happened at that time, if anything?

THE WITNESS: Someone was pulling down the American flag, as I remember it, and I saw the police move in toward it. There was a confrontation between the person who tried to pull down the flag and the police. The police were dragging the man off, and then a lot of commotion broke out.

There was a police car, I think it was unmarked, but there was a policeman standing next to it with the door open, and things were being thrown at him.

MR. KUNSTLER: Can you state what things were being thrown?

THE WITNESS: Oh, people's lunch, a shoe, a rock, papers, you know, wadded up papers. Then the police gathered in a phalanx, about fifteen policemen, and started moving toward the crowd.

I started moving away. I was running toward the south. I saw Jerry Rubin coming from that direction.

MR. KUNSTLER: Would you state what the conversation was that you had with Jerry Rubin?

THE WITNESS: We greeted each other, and then he asked me what had happened, and I told him about the flag incident, and about the flying debris, and the police moving in, the brief skirmish.

MR. KUNSTLER: Then what did you do?

THE WITNESS: The crowd started moving back very fast again, and Jerry and I took off toward where Jerry had come from, towards the south. He ran back, and I ran behind him, and I suddenly lost him in the crowd of people. I made my way to about the other side of the Bandstand.

MR. KUNSTLER: What if anything was going on when you arrived there?

THE WITNESS: Rennie Davis was lying on the floor with his head split open and blood just pouring out.

MR. KUNSTLER: And can you estimate for us how many minutes after you last saw Jerry Rubin that you saw Rennie Davis lying on the ground?

THE WITNESS: Fifteen minutes.

MR. KUNSTLER: I have no further questions.

THE COURT: Cross-examination?

• • • • •

MR. SCHULTZ: Mr. Katzman, now Monday night, your car was in the park driving about five miles per hour when you were beaten?

THE WITNESS: Yes, sir.

MR. SCHULTZ: Did you report this assault to the Federal Bureau of Investigation?

THE WITNESS: I reported it to the Chicago Police and to the Walker Commission, and then the FBI got in touch with me. They came to my office after the Convention was over.

MR. SCHULTZ: Now this first person who hit you had a dog leash chain, right?

THE WITNESS: Yes. Well, he had two things. He had a blackjack attached to a chain.

MR. SCHULTZ: Did you not see any kind of insignia?

THE WITNESS: No badge or anything. He didn't identify himself.

MR. SCHULTZ: Now, none of these men had any weapons visible except blackjacks, isn't that right?

THE WITNESS: No, we saw shotguns. I reported it to the FBI.

MR. SCHULTZ: That's all, your Honor.

Testimony of Stephen Alan Buff

January 22, 1970

MR. WEINGLASS: Would you state your full name for the record?

THE WITNESS: Stephen Alan Buff.

MR. WEINGLASS: And what is your present occupation?

THE WITNESS: I am a graduate student in sociology at Northwestern University.

MR. WEINGLASS: How long have you known Lee Weiner?

THE WITNESS: I've known Lee Weiner since fall of 1967. I met him at Northwestern University. We're fellow students in the Sociology Department.

MR. WEINGLASS: Directing your attention to the first week in August 1968, did you have occasion during that week to meet with Lee Weiner?

THE WITNESS: Yes, I did. I met with him at the Northwestern University cafeteria in Scott Hall.

MR. WEINGLASS: At that time and place did you have a conversation with Lee Weiner?

THE WITNESS: Yes. Lee asked me if I wanted to be marshal to help train other marshals for the demonstrations surrounding the Democratic Convention which would be later that month.

MR. WEINGLASS: Did you agree at that time to act as a marshal?

THE WITNESS: Yes, I did.

MR. WEINGLASS: Now, approximately one week later, August 15, 1968, at about 3:30 in the afternoon, do you recall where you were at that time?

THE WITNESS: At 3:30 I was at marshal training in Lincoln Park.

Rennie introduced Dave Baker to the other marshals who were present. He said that Dave Baker was a student in Japan and that he knew a tactic that is used in Japan for Japanese students when they are in the street, and that we would use this as a defensive tactic.

It would be used to move people out of an area, to keep all demonstrators together, and to get them out of any particular area if a dangerous situation arose.

MR. WEINGLASS: Following Mr. Baker's remarks, what, if anything, occurred?

THE WITNESS: Then we practiced the snake dance.

MR. WEINGLASS: Moving on to two days later, which would be approximately August 17, in the morning of that day, do you recall where you were?

THE WITNESS: I was at a meeting of marshals near Buckingham Fountain. John Froines was present, Terry and Allen Gross were present, Irv Bock was present. Frapolly was present.

MR. WEINGLASS: What did Mr. Frapolly say?

THE WITNESS: Frapolly was more or less in charge of the meeting. He said that marshals should make maps of various locations of where demonstrations were to take place. He also said, after some other marshals mentioned the fact that some jeeps had driven by with barbed wire on the front of the jeeps, he said, "Maybe we can put grappling hooks on that barbed wire."

MR. WEINGLASS: When Mr. Frapolly said that, what happened in the group?

THE WITNESS: There was just laughter. It was regarded as, you know, a bad joke—or just a joke.

MR. FORAN: Objection, your Honor.

THE COURT: A joke? Those words may go out.

MR. WEINGLASS: Now, on August 20 at approximately 2:30 in the afternoon do you recall where you were?

THE WITNESS: I was at the marshal training sessions.

MR. WEINGLASS: Were any of the defendants present?

THE WITNESS: Yes. Lee Weiner was present, Irv Bock was present—

MR. WEINGLASS: No, Mr. Bock is not a defendant.

THE WITNESS: Oh, I am sorry. Lee Weiner was present, John Froines was present.

[454]

MR. WEINGLASS: Do you recall what Weiner said at that meeting?

THE WITNESS: Yes. He said that we have to make plans to both protect the parks from counterdemonstrators and to protect the parks, if people are allowed to sleep there, from incursions of plainclothes policemen who may try to do something at night when participants were sleeping in the park. So he said that we had to make plans to have sentinels around the park.

He also said that we should make plans to evacuate the park very quickly in case there was a dangerous situation, or if we were under police orders to evacuate the park, we should evacuate it quickly.

MR. WEINGLASS: Did he suggest how that was to be done?

THE WITNESS: Yes. He suggested that we use flares to light the best possible exits from the park, that we should have two sets of flares at each exit, and that over our megaphone systems we could announce to the people in the park that they leave in between the two flares.

MR. WEINGLASS: Now at approximately 9:30 Sunday night, August 25, do you recall where you were?

THE WITNESS: Yes, I was in Lincoln Park.

MR. WEINGLASS: Were any of the defendants present with you?

THE WITNESS: Yes, John Froines.

MR. WEINGLASS: Now while you were there, did John Froines do anything?

THE WITNESS: John Froines was also speaking through the microphone over the speaker system to a group that varied between 300 to 400 participants. It was a very large group. He gave the phone number of the legal committee in case of arrest. He also gave the phone number in case of injuries of the medical committee. He also urged everyone there to leave the park before eleven o'clock or when the police ordered us to leave the park.

MR. WEINGLASS: Now while John Froines was present, did anyone else use the microphone?

THE WITNESS: Yes, there was disagreement among the participants, so we had people line up behind the microphone, and as many people who wanted to speak could speak.

MR. WEINGLASS: Do you recall what some of those other persons said on the microphone?

THE WITNESS: Yes, some people said, "Listen, let's stay in the park. Forget the directions. We're staying in the park. We have every right to stay here in the park. The parks are for the people. Let's stay in the park."

MR. WEINGLASS: Now, at the conclusion of the meeting, did John Froines speak again?

THE WITNESS: Yes. He urged the demonstrators to leave the park. He said that it was a dangerous situation to stay in the park. The park could not be safe after eleven o'clock, and that people should leave.

MR. WEINGLASS: Now I direct your attention to the following Tuesday, which was August 27, at approximately one o'clock in the afternoon of that day. Do you recall where you were?

THE WITNESS: I was in front of the Polish Embassy.

MR. WEINGLASS: And what did you observe at that time at that place?

THE WITNESS: An orderly, peaceful picket line protesting imperialism and supporting self-determination for the Vietnamese.

MR. FORAN: I object to that, your Honor, the "orderly, peaceful picket line" and the rest.

THE COURT: Yes, the last sentence of the witness' testimony may go out.

MR. WEINGLASS: Mr. Buff, I call your attention to the following day, which was Wednesday, August 28, late in the morning, at approximately two o'clock. Do you recall where you were at that time?

THE WITNESS: I went to a marshals' meeting at the extreme south end of the Bandshell area in Grant Park.

MR. WEINGLASS: How many people were at the meeting?

THE WITNESS: About forty.

Rennie Davis was present, John Froines was present, and there were other marshals, many of whom I did not know.

MR. WEINGLASS: During the course of the meeting, did you hear Rennie Davis speak?

THE WITNESS: Yes. Rennie Davis said that there were three alternatives for people who were present at the rally.

The first alternative was the people could participate in a nonviolent peaceful march to the Amphitheatre. However, since the city had not issued permits, there was a danger of arrest. If they were arrested, people should sit down and allow themselves to be arrested to protest the suspension of their constitutional rights for free speech and free assembly.

The second alternative was for people to remain mobile, and he explained what mobile meant.

He said, "You know, a lot of people think that it is insane to to sit down in front of the Chicago police and to subject yourself to danger or just to sit in front of them and allow yourselves to be arrested or perhaps clubbed.

"So what other people should do is to go to the three sites of hotels in the Loop—the Conrad Hilton, the Palmer House, and the Sherman House—where most of the delegates were staying, and engage in peaceful demonstrations, just leave in small groups of friends and go to these demonstrations."

The third alternative he posed for people who had children with them, who shouldn't even go near the police, because the police had shown themselves to be irrational on the three previous nights, beating demonstrators in the parks, and these people should stay right at the rally area near the Bandshell, wait an appropriate time, and then go home or leave the area.

He said that this would be announced by Dave Dellinger over the microphone, and that the people there should be very clear as to the three alternatives, and we should separate those people so that they would know just what alternative they were deciding upon.

MR. WEINGLASS: Now, following that meeting of marshals, do you recall where you went?

THE WITNESS: Yes. In response to an announcement from the Bandshell by Dave Dellinger that there was some trouble up front, would the marshals please come up front, I started to go further to the front toward the flagpole area and toward the stage area. I had the speaker system and the mike in my hand.

MR. WEINGLASS: Now, approximately how far in distance were you from the flag pole at that point?

THE WITNESS: About 175 feet.

MR. WEINGLASS: What did you observe happening?

THE WITNESS: I saw about ten policemen. There was a slight commotion around the flagpole but there wasn't a great deal of commotion at that time.

MR. WEINGLASS: Then what happened?

THE WITNESS: Policemen left that area, and some demonstrators moved toward them. Some things were thrown in the direction of the policemen, and then a few minutes later one cannister of what I now have heard was a smoke bomb.

Demonstrators said, "It's tear gas, it's tear gas," and some of them ran from that cannister. This cannister just kind of fizzled around on the ground. It didn't discharge anything. Then another cannister was thrown by the police I didn't see where it came from, but I saw the smoky arc that it made through the air. One demonstrator grabbed it and threw it back at the police, to the cheers of the demonstrators there, and it smoked around in the area of the police.

Now, at that time more policemen came out. A first about fifty, and then I think there were more, perhaps between fifty and one hundred.

MR. WEINGLASS: Now, what did you do when you saw the police come?

THE WITNESS: When they came out, many people moved back. I walked back shouting over the megaphone, "Sit down, move back, don't throw things."

At one point I said, "You're hitting our own people."

MR. WEINGLASS: Now at the time that you were making those statements, at that point in the Bandshell, what did you observe occurring in the area in front of you in the Bandshell?

THE WITNESS: Well, I saw the police had moved up right through the crowd. Many of the participants were on their feet, looking to see what was happening in this area. I believe at that time things quieted down, but I continued the cautionary statements.

MR. WEINGLASS: What occurred at that time while you were standing in the area which you have indicated?

THE WITNESS: Someone approached me from the south, from this area.

MR. WEINGLASS: Who was that person?

THE WITNESS: Jerry Rubin.

MR. WEINGLASS: Do you recall the conversation?

THE WITNESS: Yes. He said, "Hey, why are you way back here? Nothing's happening back here. Why don't you move up to the front? You know, you have the megaphone. Why don't you tell the crowd to move way back? Tell the cops to leave the area. They're the ones who are causing all the trouble."

I said, "OK."

MR. WEINGLASS: So what did you do then?

THE WITNESS: So then we spoke a little bit more.

He said, "What's going on up there?"

And I said, "Well, they're throwing tear gas," because I thought it was tear gas, and the cops moved in twice.

MR. WEINGLASS: Now, after your conversation, with Jerry, where did you go?

THE WITNESS: I went up front because I agreed with him that I should go up front to the area where the police and the marchers were close together. I told the marchers to move back, move back. I called for more marshals to come up there to reinforce the line of marshals.

MR. WEINGLASS: What occurred then?

THE WITNESS: Two policemen said, "What's going on here?"

And I said, "Nothing's going on."

And then they said, "Would you move your swine back?"

And I said loudly, "You mean your swine." And they did nothing, they just left.

And shortly after that, the police waded into the crowd, right past the line of marshals, broke up the line of marshals, and proceeded into the bench area and beat people. They beat everything in their path.

After that, there was a great deal of confusion, and finally the police walked out of that area, after beating people, and the medics moved in to pick up people who were injured.

MR. WEINGLASS: Now, did you see where Jerry Rubin went after you left him and moved toward the front?

THE WITNESS: Yes. He went towards the south, toward the extreme rear of the bleacher section right near the bleachers, but he went south away from me, then I went north. We went in opposite directions.

MR. WEINGLASS: And approximately how long after that time that you saw Jerry Rubin did the police charge occur which you have described?

THE WITNESS: Well, I must have been up there ten minutes, eight to ten minutes.

MR. WEINGLASS: Mr. Buff, from the time you first spoke to Lee Weiner about being a marshal the first week in August until the end of the Convention week, did you hear any of the gentlemen who are seated here at this table call for any acts of physical violence or disruption in this city?

THE WITNESS: No.

MR. FORAN: Objection.

THE COURT: I sustain the objection.

MR. WEINGLASS: I have no further questions.

THE COURT: Cross-examination.

• • • • •

MR. FORAN: You know Mr. Frapolly is a policeman now, don't you?

THE WITNESS: Yes.

MR. FORAN: Who told you?

THE WITNESS: I don't remember.

MR. FORAN: You know Mr. Bock is a policeman now, don't you?

THE WITNESS: Yes.

MR. FORAN: Who told you?

THE WITNESS: I read it in the newspaper.

MR. FORAN: You know Mr. Pierson is a policeman now, don't you?

THE WITNESS: Yes.

MR. FORAN: Who told you?

THE WITNESS: Jerry Rubin told me.

MR. FORAN: While you were having that discussion about flares, did you hear Gross say "We're going to have these flares, and we're going to have them lighted," and that "They can be used as a weapon to keep anybody away from us if we're marching"?

Did you hear Gross say that?

THE WITNESS: No.

MR. FORAN: Did you hear Froines say, "They burn at 4,000 degrees Farenheit," and that would keep people away from the marchers?

THE WITNESS: No, definitely not, and you know, that really seems—

MR. FORAN: When the flagpole incident started over at the Bandshell, where were you exactly?

THE WITNESS: When it started I was in the marshals' meeting.

MR. FORAN: The speeches stopped when this started? I mean, there was quite an uproar, wasn't there?

THE WITNESS: They didn't stop because Dellinger took the microphone and made cautionary statements. It is true the program was interrupted, by the police coming in, but the speakers never stopped. There were always directions given to calm the crowd.

MR. FORAN: Now, did you hear people yelling, "Kill the pigs!" and "Kill the cops!" while that was going on at the flagpole?

THE WITNESS: No, I remember people yelling "Pigs!"

MR. FORAN: Did you see fifteen or twenty policemen in uniform attending in front of the trees having rocks thrown at them, dodging and ducking as rocks were thrown at them?

THE WITNESS: Well, I saw policemen lined up in front of the trees. I don't remember if they were dodging or ducking, and I don't remember any rocks being thrown. I didn't hear them land.

MR. FORAN: Isn't it a fact that your heard Mr. Dellinger state from the stand "Those who want to be moving, for example, in the nonviolent march can be gathering over there quietly. Those who want to be leaving in connection with the recommendations of Tom Neumann can begin to be splitting." Didn't you hear Mr. Dellinger say that from the stand?

THE WITNESS: I don't know who Tom Neumann is, so I can't really testify as to whether he spoke. I don't remember his name being mentioned in that.

MR. FORAN: You don't remember Mr. Dellinger introducing him from the Bandstand?

THE WITNESS: I told you I do not know Tom Neumann, so how could I possibly know whether Mr. Dellinger introduced Tom Neumann or not?

MR. FORAN: You feel defensive or something?

THE WITNESS: Of course.

MR. FORAN: Why don't you just answer questions?

THE WITNESS: I am answering questions fully because I was sworn to tell the whole truth and nothing but the truth. Are you trying to make me feel more defensive by that remark?

THE COURT: Mr. Witness—

You have no right to interrogate a lawyer who is examining you. All you must do is answer the questions.

MR. WEINGLASS: I think Mr. Foran's statement is argumentative. I didn't object to it, but I think in light of that the witness should have the opportunity to defend himself.

THE COURT: The witness argued. Mr. Foran did not argue. I overrule the objection.

MR. FORAN: Now, isn't it a fact, Mr. Buff, that when you saw Mr. Rubin, that he came up to you while you were on that microphone telling the crowd to sit down, and he said to you, "Stay off that mike and let the crowd do their thing?" Isn't that a fact?

THE WITNESS: That is false. That is a lie.

MR. FORAN: Mr. Buff, why did you designate that as a lie? Were you told that was said by someone that that was testified to here in this courtroom?

THE WITNESS: I said that it was a lie because it completely contradicts my previous testimony.

MR. FORAN: Were you told that someone had testified in this courtroom that that was said?

THE WITNESS: No. No, sir.

MR. FORAN: And did you talk with Mr. Rubin about the testimony in this case?

THE WITNESS: I never discussed testimony in this case or in this courtroom. I discussed events so as to refresh my memory. That's all I ever discussed.

MR. FORAN: With the defendants?

THE WITNESS: Yes, with the defendants.

MR. FORAN: Thank you. That's all.

THE COURT: Please call your next witness.

MR. FORAN: Your Honor, I note there are a couple of defendants missing.

THE COURT: Are the defendants not here? You lost your gallery, Mr. Kunstler. Your clients aren't here.

MR. KUNSTLER: Well, your Honor, my clients are not my gallery. They are clients.

THE COURT: Well, they have walked out on you.

MR. KUNSTLER: Well, "gallery" doesn't mean interest or lack of interest.

THE COURT: Well, they've gone, so I'll wait until they return. They left without permission. I don't know where they are.

A DEFENDANT: They went to get a witness.

MR. KUNSTLER: They're here.

Testimony of Judy Collins

MR. KUNSTLER: Would you state your name, please?

THE WITNESS: Judy Collins.

MR. KUNSTLER: What is your occupation?

THE WITNESS: I'm a singer. I sing folksongs.

MR. KUNSTLER: Now, Miss Collins, I call your attention to March 17 of 1968 at approximately noontime on that date. Do you know where you were?

THE WITNESS: I was at the Americana Hotel in New York City attending a press conference to announce the formation of what we have now come to know of as the Yippie Movement.

MR. KUNSTLER: Who was present at that press conference?

THE WITNESS: There were a number of people who were singers, entertainers. Jerry Rubin was there, Abbie Hoffman was there. Allen Ginsberg was there, and sang a mantra.

MR. KUNSTLER: Now what did you do at that press conference?

THE WITNESS: Well—[sings] "Where have all the flowers—

THE COURT: Just a minute, young lady.

THE WITNESS: [sings] "—where have all the flowers gone?"

DEPUTY MARSHAL JOHN J. GRACIOUS: I'm sorry. The Judge would like to speak to you.

THE COURT: We don't allow any singing in this court. I'm sorry.

THE WITNESS: May I recite the words?

MR. KUNSTLER: Well, your Honor, we have had films. I think it is as legitimate as a movie. It is the actual thing she did. She sang "Where Have All the Flowers Gone," which is a well-known peace song, and she sang it, and the jury is not getting the flavor—

THE COURT: You asked her what she did, and she proceeded to sing.

MR. KUNSTLER: That is what she did, your Honor.

THE WITNESS: That's what I do.

THE COURT: And that has no place in a United States District Court. We are not here to be entertained, sir. We are trying a very important case.

MR. KUNSTLER: This song is not an entertainment, your Honor. This is a song of peace, and what happens to young men and women during wartime.

THE COURT: I forbid her from singing during the trial. I will not permit singing in this courtroom.

MR. KUNSTLER: Why not, your Honor? What's wrong with singing?

MR. FORAN: May I respond?

This is about the fifth time this has occurred. Each time your Honor has directed Mr. Kunstler that it was improper in the courtroom. It is an old and stale joke in this courtroom, your Honor.

Now, there is no question that Miss Collins is a fine singer. In my family my six kids and I all agree that she is a fine singer, but that doesn't have a thing to do with this lawsuit nor what my profession is, which is the practice of law in the Federal District Court, your Honor, and I protest Mr. Kunstler constantly failing to advise his witnesses of what proper decorum is, and I object to it on behalf of the Government.

THE COURT: I sustain the objection.

MR. KUNSTLER: What did you say at the press conference?

THE WITNESS: I said a great deal. I said I want to see a celebration of life, not of destruction. I said that my soul and my profession and my life has become part of a movement toward hopefully removing the causes for death, the causes for war, the causes for the prevalence of violence in our society, and in order to make my voice heard, I said that I would indeed come to Chicago and that I would sing.

That is what I do, that's my profession. I said that I was there because life was the force that I wished to make my songs and my life known for. I said that I would be in Chicago with thousands of people who want to celebrate life, and I said these words, in the context of a song. I said:

[460]

"Where have all the flowers gone? Long time passing.
Where have all the flowers gone? Long time ago.
Where have all the flowers gone? Young girls have picked them, every one.
           Oh, when will they ever learn?
Where have all the young girls gone? Long time passing.
Where have all the young girls gone? Long time ago.
Where have all the young girls gone? Gone for husbands, every one.
           Oh, when will they ever learn?
Where have all the young men gone? Long time passing.
Where have all the young men gone? Long time ago.
Where have all the young men gone? Gone for soldiers, every one.
           When will they ever learn?
Where have all the soldiers gone? Long time passing.
Where have all the soldiers gone? Long time ago.
Where have all the soldiers gone? Gone to graveyards, every one.
           Oh, when will they ever learn?"

I said that I would give my music and my voice to a situation in which people could express themselves about life with a permit, of course, from the City of Chicago.

MR. KUNSTLER: Now, I call your attention, Miss Collins, to the last or next to last day of April of 1968, did you have an occasion to see Abbie Hoffman on that day?

THE WITNESS: Yes. We met at my house. Abbie Hoffman said that there was a lot of trouble in Chicago getting the permits. I said that I felt if the City of Chicago wanted to provoke violence and wanted to provoke unrest, all they had to do was continue ignoring our requests for grants and also continue the kind of things that had been happening. Daley had just said that he would shoot to kill, and I told Abbie that I was not encouraged by that attitude on the part of the City of Chicago and that I felt that they should further their efforts to get the permits for us to appear.

Abbie Hoffman said that the National Guard was going to be brought in, and I told him at that point that if it was possible, I'd like to arrange to perform and sing also for the National Guard, as they would be there under duress, and they should hear what we all had to say.

MR. KUNSTLER: Now, I call your attention to the third week in June of 1968. Did you have an occasion to have a conversation with Rennie Davis?

THE WITNESS: Yes. Rennie Davis called me, and asked me if I had any desire to join a group of people who were trying to set up coffee houses which would be hosts to GI's all over the country. He invited me to come to Fort Hood.

I told him that I felt that since the USO provides entertainment of a certain kind to GI's, that I would be very willing to go to an installation, a base, and perform at a coffee house to expose the GI's there to my point of view, to the young people's point of view, and to our attempts to create a life force, and to also express to the GI's that we're on their side. We don't want them to die. We don't want them to be exposed to the kind of terror that war will perpetrate.

MR. FORAN: I object, your Honor, as to relevancy. There is no relevancy.

MR. KUNSTLER: Your Honor, the lives and deaths of American soldiers I think is highly relevant. It was the whole purpose or one of the main purposes people came to Chicago.

THE COURT: Life and death are really very wonderful. This is a great place to live in and be alive. I agree with you. But those things are not an issue in this case.

MR. KUNSTLER: Miss Collins, I call your attention to approximately one week before the opening of the convention, the week of August 19, 1968. Did you have an occasion to talk to Abbie Hoffman?

THE WITNESS: Yes. In fact, Abbie did call me to ask me again whether I would participate in the Yippie Celebration of Life.

MR. KUNSTLER: Now, would you relate what he said to you and what you said to him?

THE WITNESS: Well, Abbie told me that what was happening in Chicago was that the police were acting antagonistically towards peace demonstrations. He wanted to warn me that I would be subject to that same kind of provocation as an entertainer performing in a public place without a permit.

I told him that I was frightened, now that I had seen things on television that were disturbing to me and upsetting to me, that I had heard Mayor Daley's declaration of war on me personally.

I said, "Abbie, you must continue to try in every way possible to get those permits, because if we're going to have a celebration, we must do it legally. I don't want to be violent, I'm not going to Chicago to do anything except sing for people in a legal situation."

Abbie asked if I was sure that I wouldn't come if they couldn't get permits because they didn't know if they could or not. And I said that it was doubtful, that I would have to think about it, but as far as my wellbeing went and as far as the wellbeing of all the people, that I feel I represent went, that I could not put myself in a position to jeopardize my physical wellbeing or those of thousands of other young people who would be there to celebrate with us.

MR. KUNSTLER: Did you go to Chicago during Convention week?

THE WITNESS: No, I did not. I stayed away from Chicago because the permits were not granted.

MR. KUNSTLER: And anything that was planned, or generated, or that might cause or be a participating factor in violent activity, you wouldn't want anything to do with it, would you?

THE WITNESS: There was nothing violent about anything that went on in the preparations on our side for this Convention. We were provoked.

MR. KUNSTLER: No further questions.

THE COURT: Cross-examination.

• • • • •

MR. FORAN: Miss Collins, you said in your meeting in April with Mr. Hoffman, didn't you testify that Mr. Hoffman told you that they had been trying to get permits for months in Chicago?

THE WITNESS: Yes, they had been attempting to get permits.

MR. FORAN: This is what he told you.

THE WITNESS: Yes, I knew this was a fact. This wasn't only Abbie Hoffman speaking. This was—

THE COURT: That will be all.

THE WITNESS: That was the consensus that had been going on.

THE COURT: Will you, young lady—

THE WITNESS: There was a refusal to grant it.

THE COURT: Do you hear very well? Do you want to move your hair back?

THE WITNESS: I think so, yes.

THE COURT: I want to ask you, I want to tell you that you have answered the question, you may not go beyond that.

THE WITNESS: Oh, well, I assumed that he wanted to hear more about what statement—

MR. FORAN: Did you know that only one permit had been filed for?

THE WITNESS: I believe that was what I knew then.

MR. FORAN: Did you know that it hadn't been turned down yet?

THE WITNESS: Well it had not been granted. It had been applied for for months.

MR. FORAN: Miss Collins, did Mr. Hoffman tell you that he was planning to tear up Lincoln Park in the city of Chicago?

THE WITNESS: No, I don't believe he ever said that to me. No, I don't think so.

MR. FORAN: I don't think he would tell it to you either.

THE WITNESS: I told him I was going to create an exciting environment with my music, but he didn't say he was going to tear up Grant Park, no.

MR. FORAN: Did Mr. Hoffman tell you that he had come to Chicago prepared to die if necessary to open the city of Chicago up? Did he tell you that?

THE WITNESS: I don't remember that he ever said those exact words.

MR. FORAN: I don't have anything further.

Testimony of Kenneth Paul Potter

THE COURT: Bring the next witness to the stand, please.

MR. KUNSTLER: Would you state your full name, please?

THE WITNESS: Kenneth Paul Potter.

MR. KUNSTLER: Mr. Potter, what is your occupation?

THE WITNESS: I'm a writer.

MR. KUNSTLER: For whom have you worked?

THE WITNESS: I worked for the National Student Association. After graduate school I worked for the Cleveland Community Project, which was an SDS community organizing project.

MR. KUNSTLER: And after that?

THE WITNESS: Well, after that and during that I also worked for Students for a Democratic Society. I was president of that organization in 1964-65.

MR. KUNSTLER: Mr. Potter, when I asked you a question a moment ago, you used the term "the Movement."

Would you explain what you mean by the term "the Movement?"

MR. SCHULTZ: Objection. It is not relevant.

THE COURT: Well, there are so many different movements.

MR. KUNSTLER: Well, he is prepared to explain.

THE COURT: I don't think movements have any place in this case. I'm sorry. I sustain the objection.

MR. KUNSTLER: Now, Mr. Potter, did there come a time when you joined the National Mobilization Committee to End the War in Vietnam?

THE WITNESS: Yes. I attended the March meeting at Lake Villa, which was the first actual contact I had had with the National Mobilization Committee.

MR. KUNSTLER: Did you eventually come to have a position with the project in Chicago?

THE WITNESS: Yes, I did. I was in charge of the movement centers. The movement centers are approximately thirty locations throughout the city where various groups stayed during their presence here at the convention.

MR. KUNSTLER: Now, Mr. Potter, I call your attention to approximately 12:30 A.M. on Tuesday morning, which would be the twenty-seventh of August, a few minutes after midnight. Do you know where you were?

THE WITNESS: I was in the Loop walking down Balbo Street with another member of the Mobilization staff.

MR. KUNSTLER: Now at that time, did you have occasion to see any of the defendants?

THE WITNESS: Yes, we saw Rennie Davis. It was somewhere around 12:15, 12:30.

MR. KUNSTLER: And did you have a conversation with him?

THE WITNESS: Yes, we did. Rennie Davis ran up to us and told us that Tom had just been arrested. His voice was shrill. He was obviously agitated. And he told us that he didn't know what to do.

He was moving around quickly, and he was talking, but he said that he was confused and upset because, apparently, he said, that it had just happened, and he asked us what to do, and I told him to calm down, to try to relax, and we talked for a while. I can't remember all that he said, but then we decided to go back to the Mobilization office.

MR. KUNSTLER: And did you go to the Mobilization office?

THE WITNESS: Yes, we walked back. There was a conversation underway. I don't remember all of it, but I do remember Rennie saying that he feared that the police had simply decided to throw everybody in jail, all of the Mobilization leadership, that he didn't think that Tom had done anything.

MR. KUNSTLER: Now did you eventually arrive at the Mobilization office?

THE WITNESS: Yes.

MR. KUNSTLER: Do you know what time it was, to the best of your recollection, when you arrived there?

THE WITNESS: Well, it was about a ten or fifteen-minute walk. It was somewhere around a quarter to one, twelve-thirty or a quarter to one by the time we got there.

MR. KUNSTLER: What, if anything, happened after you arrived at the Mobilization office?

THE WITNESS: Rennie made some phone calls.

First, he called the legal office to see what was happening with Tom. And second, he sat down and began to call various contacts in the press and begin to try to get the word out that Tom had been arrested again.

MR. KUNSTLER: Did there come a time when you left?

THE WITNESS: Yes, I did. I left sometime after one o'clock, shortly after one o'clock, I think.

MR. KUNSTLER: Was Rennie still there when you left?

THE WITNESS: Yes, he was.

MR. KUNSTLER: Now, Mr. Potter, I call your attention to Wednesday, August 28, approximately 6:00, 6:30 in the early evening. Do you know where you were on that date?

THE WITNESS: I was on the attempted march through Grant Park.

MR. KUNSTLER: Did you have occasion to have a conversation with Dave Dellinger at that time?

THE WITNESS: I went up to Dave and said I was very disturbed about what was happening there, that the march had been stopped for over an hour, perhaps an hour-and-a-half by that time. It was getting close to dusk.

I told Dave that I was afraid that if people just continued to sit there and he continued to try to negotiate with the police for a permit, that when it got dark, there was going to be a massacre. The police simply were going to wade in with clubs, and gas, and everything that was at their disposal.

I urged Dave to tell people for their own safety to leave the park and try to get to the part of Grant Park directly across from the Hilton where on the previous occasions people had been safe.

Dave said that he didn't want to give up the attempt to negotiate this march or this walk, and that he couldn't do that at that time.

MR. KUNSTLER: Now, after that conversation with Dave Dellinger, what did you do?

THE WITNESS: I went and urged people to leave the march and try to make their way to the Hilton for their own safety.

MR. KUNSTLER: No further questions.

THE COURT: Is there cross-examination of this witness?

MR. SCHULTZ: Yes, there is, your Honor.

• • • • •

MR. SCHULTZ: Did Dellinger tell you that he had been negotiating with Deputy Superintendent Rochford right on that corner?

THE WITNESS: I had seen him negotiating with a police officer, I didn't know who.

MR. SCHULTZ: Did he tell you that Deputy Superintendent Rochford said to him, "Please, I'll give you alternatives. Take your people in front of the Hilton Hotel. Have your assembly there." And that he rejected that?

Did he tell you that, sir?

THE WITNESS: He did not tell me that, and I did not hear that. He said that he was committed to march to the Amphitheatre.

MR. SCHULTZ: Did he say to you, sir, that after Deputy Superintendent Rochford gave him these alternatives, Rochford asked him for alternatives, and he said, "I don't listen to you," and turned his head and walked away from Deputy Superintendent Rochford? Did he say that?

THE WITNESS: He didn't say that. I didn't see it. And I don't believe it.

MR. SCHULTZ: How long have you known Rennie Davis?

THE WITNESS: I have known him since 1958. I roomed with him.

MR. SCHULTZ: He is a very close friend of yours, isn't he?

THE WITNESS: He is a close friend, yes.

MR. SCHULTZ: As a matter of fact, sir, you understand, do you not, that there is testimony that Rennie Davis was seen by a number of people in Lincoln Park at the very time that you had him at Michigan and Balbo, isn't that right, sir?

THE WITNESS: I undersood that police informers have testified to that, yes, I do.
MR. SCHULTZ: Who told you, sir?
THE WITNESS: I don't recall.
MR. SCHULTZ: You recall very well, though, don't you, sir, the conversation you had back on August 21, 1968? Would you explain why you have trouble recalling something that you were told recently?
MR. KUNSTLER: Your Honor, I submit that is highly argumentative.
THE COURT: I overrule the objection. I ask the witness to answer.
MR. SCHULTZ: Where were you when you were told?
THE WITNESS: I think my recollection is that I may have seen it in the movement newspaper in Berkeley, *The Tribe,* that carried a lot of coverage of the trial. I may have seen it in one of the regular press.
MR. SCHULTZ: Mr. Potter, you discussed that with Mr. Davis, didn't you?
THE WITNESS: No, I have not.
My only conversation with Mr. Davis concerning what I was going to testify about was on the phone.
I talked to him about a week ago on the phone and said that I was planning to come east, that I wanted to come to Chicago, and I would like to testify at the trial if I could be of any help. He asked me to stop in Chicago and to talk to the defense staff.
MR. SCHULTZ: Did Davis say to you, Mr. Potter, "Paul, please, I want you to come to testify because you have got to tell the jury that I wasn't in Lincoln Park, but I was in the Mobilization Headquarters?"
THE WITNESS: No, he didn't. We did not discuss whether or not I would testify at that time.
MR. SCHULTZ: You mean you hadn't decided at that time what your story was going to be, is that what you are saying, sir?
THE WITNESS: No.
MR. KUNSTLER: Your Honor, that is such an objectionable question.
MR. SCHULTZ: This is absurd.
MR. KUNSTLER: I agree that it is absurd.
Your Honor, they have permitted taps on all the telephones, particularly Rennie Davis. They know what was said.
THE COURT: I will permit him to answer over objection.
MR. SCHULTZ: So yesterday was the first time that you told Davis that you recalled being with him Tuesday morning at the office, is that right?
THE WITNESS: Yes.
MR. SCHULTZ: And approximately how long ago was it that you learned that two people on two separate—two people had seen Davis at Lincoln Park at that time?
THE WITNESS: Over a month ago.
MR. SCHULTZ: When you learned that information, didn't you pick up the phone and call Davis and say, "Rennie, I just learned such-and-such, and I was with you at that time." Didn't you do that, sir?
THE WITNESS: No.
MR. SCHULTZ: After you read this, didn't you grab a phone and call Davis and say, "Rennie, I just learned that they'd got you somewhere where you were doing something allegedly illegal?"
THE WITNESS: No, I did not.
MR. SCHULTZ: Didn't you think that Mr. Davis would welcome such a call from you?
MR. KUNSTLER: Your Honor, I think this is argumentative.
MR. SCHULTZ: He's known Mr. Davis, and they have been roommates, since 1958, and I am asking him whether or not he thought his intimate friend would welcome such a response from this man who is his alibi witness.
THE COURT: I consider it a proper inquiry. I will overrule the objection. I will let you answer.
THE WITNESS: No, I did not call.
MR. SCHULTZ: Isn't it a fact, sir, that the reason why you did not tell Davis when you learned of the testimony that he was in Lincoln Park, when you called him before you came here a week-and-a-half ago, that you did not tell Davis on those occasions that you

were with him at NMC, and you were going to save him on the witness stand here, was because you hadn't made up the story yet? Isn't that a fact?

MR. WEINGLASS: That is an utterly improper question.

MR. KUNSTLER: Your Honor, I object to that.

MR. SCHULTZ: Oh, it is not, your Honor.

MR. KUNSTLER: Improper in any court, and I call for an admonition at this point.

MR. SCHULTZ: Absolutely not.

THE COURT: I will overrule the objection. You may answer, sir.

MR. WEINGLASS: Your Honor, there is something contained in that question which is not accurate.

The Government produced three witnesses on this incident. One placed Rennie Davis at Michigan and Balbo at midnight. One placed Rennie Davis at a barricade in Lincoln Park at approximately 12:20, and one placed him in Old Town at 12:30. Three entirely inconsistent and contradictory stories. Rennie Davis needed no help. That's the fact of the matter.

THE COURT: I don't want to hear anything further. I have overruled the objection.

MR. SCHULTZ: Isn't it a fact, sir, that the reason why you didn't tell Davis on November 15 about you being an alibi witness for him is because you didn't make up the story until you got here yesterday and discussed it with Mr. Davis? Isn't that a fact, sir?

THE WITNESS: No, that is not true.

MR. SCHULTZ: Now, isn't it a fact that you were interviewed by the Federal Bureau of Investigation?

THE WITNESS: No.

MR. SCHULTZ: You were not interviewed?

THE WITNESS: They called me and asked if I wanted to have an interview with them. I said I did not.

MR. WEINGLASS: Your Honor, I object to that.

Mr. Schultz implied that a citizen of this court has an obligation to be interviewed by the FBI. That's not true. May I ask what the purpose of that question is?

MR. SCHULTZ: It's to show that he's taken a side in this case, to show that he would—

MR. WEINGLASS: The side of truth.

MR. FORAN: Bias and prejudice.

THE COURT: May we have order at that table, Mr. Marshal.

THE MARSHAL: Mr. Weiner, will you refrain from talking out loud?

MR. SCHULTZ: What paper did you read about witnesses observing Davis at this time, early Tuesday morning, in Lincoln Park?

THE WITNESS: I'm not sure. I think it might have been one of the Berkeley papers. It could have been the *Times*, either the *L.A. Times* or the *New York Times*, all of which I read.

MR. SCHULTZ: You didn't read it in the paper at all, did you, sir?

THE WITNESS: To the best of my recollection, I did read it in the paper.

MR. SCHULTZ: That's all I have, your Honor.

THE COURT: Redirect examination.

MR. KUNSTLER: Now, Mr. Schultz asked you in one of his questions whether you had been asked to have an interview with the FBI. Will you explain to the jury why you refused to be interviewed by the Federal Bureau of Investigation?

THE WITNESS: I just felt my whole experience with the Federal Bureau of Investigation and government undercover agencies and NSA, where the organization had been corrupted by the CIA, the organization I was intimately involved with—

MR. KUNSTLER: Will you explain what the CIA did to the National Students Association?

MR. SCHULTZ: Objection.

THE COURT: Sustained.

MR. KUNSTLER: That is all I have.

THE COURT: All right, you may go. You are excused.

Mr. Marshal, the Court will be in recess until ten o'clock tomorrow morning.

Testimony of Rennie Davis

January 23, 1970

MR. WEINGLASS: Will you please identify yourself for the record?

THE WITNESS: Rennie Davis.

MR. WEINGLASS: Do you recall the first time you came to the city of Chicago?

THE WITNESS: The first time I came to the city of Chicago was to visit the International Amphitheatre in a poultry judging contest in 1956. It was the international contest and I had just won the Eastern United States Poultry Judging Contest in 4-H and I came to Chicago to participate at the International Amphitheatre in the contest here.

MR. WEINGLASS: How old were you at that time?

THE WITNESS: I was, I guess, sixteen.

MR. WEINGLASS: Your present age?

THE WITNESS: Twenty-nine.

MR. WEINGLASS: What is your occupation?

THE WITNESS: Since 1967 my primary work and concern has been ending the war in Vietnam. Until the time of this trial I was the national coordinator for the National Mobilization to End the War in Vietnam.

MR. WEINGLASS: Now, directing your attention to the early evening of November 20, 1967, do you recall where you were on that night?

THE WITNESS: I was at the University of Chicago in an auditorium called Judd Hall. It was a meeting of a group called The Resistance. I was a speaker with Bob Ross and David Harris who is the husband of Joan Baez.

MR. WEINGLASS: Could you relate now to the Court and jury the words that you spoke, as best you can recall, on that particular night?

THE WITNESS: I began by holding up a small steel ball that was green, about the size of a tennis ball and I said, "This bomb was dropped on a city of 100,000 people, a city called Nam Ding, which is about sixty-five miles south of Hanoi."

I said, "It was dropped by an American fighter jet, an F-105," and that when this bomb exploded over Nam Ding, about 640 of these round steel balls were spewed into the sky. And I said, "When this ball strikes a building or the ground or slows up in any way, these hammers are released, an explosion occurs which sends out about 300 steel pellets."

"Now one of these balls," I explained, "was roughly three times the power of an old-fashioned hand grenade and with 640 of these bombs going off, you can throw steel pellets over an area about a thousand yards long, and about 250 yards wide.

"Every living thing exposed in that 1000-yard area from this single bomb, ninety percent of every living thing in that area will die," I said, "whether it's a water buffalo or a water buffalo boy."

I said that if this bomb were to go off in this room tonight, everyone in the room here would die, but as quickly as we could remove the bodies from the room, we could have another discussion about Vietnam.

I said "This bomb would not destroy this lecture podium, it would not damage the walls, the ceiling, the floor." I said, "If it is dropped on a city, it takes life but leaves the institutions. It is the ideal weapon, you see, for the mentality who reasons that life is less precious than property."

I said that in 1967, the year that we are in, one out of every two bombs dropped on North Vietnam was this weapon. One out of every two. And in 1967 the American Government told the American public that in North Vietnam it was only bombing steel and concrete.

Then I said, "I went to Vietnam not as a representative of the government and not as a member of the military but as an American citizen who was deeply perturbed that we lived in a country where our own government was lying to American people about this war. The American government claimed to be hitting only military targets. Yet what I saw

[467]

was pagodas that had been gutted, schoolhouses that had been razed, population centers that had been leveled."

Then I said that I am going to the Democratic National Convention because I want the world to know that there are thousands of young people in this country who do not want to see a rigged convention rubber stamp another four years of Lyndon Johnson's war.

MR. WEINGLASS: I show you an object marked D-325 for identification and can you identify that object?

THE WITNESS: Yes. This was the bomb that I brought back from Vietnam.

MR. WEINGLASS: If the Court please, the defense would like to offer into evidence D-325, the anti-personnel bomb identified by the witness as the object held by him on the night in question.

MR. FORAN: Your honor, the Government objects to this exhibit for the following reasons.

The Vietnamese war, your honor, has nothing whatsoever to do with the charges in this indictment. The Vietnamese war, which is a major difficulty of this country and a major concern of every citizen in this country, has nothing whatever to do with whether or not people in the United States have a right to travel in interstate commerce to incite a riot.

The methods and techniques of warfare have nothing whatever to do with that charge. The methods and techniques of the seeking of the end of the Vietnam war have nothing to do with the charges of this indictment.

The very purpose of the governmental system of the United States is to handle in a purposeful way within the Constitution of the United States the disposition of such complex and difficult and tragic problems that this nation has lived with for about two hundred years. The charges in this indictment your Honor, have nothing to do with this type of testimony or this kind of concept, and for that reason your Honor, the Government objects.

THE COURT: Objection sustained.

MR. KUNSTLER: Your Honor, at this point I would like to move for a mistrial—

THE COURT: I deny the motion.

MR. RUBIN: You haven't heard it yet.

THE COURT: Oh, there is no ground for a mistrial.

MR. KUNSTLER: But, your Honor—

THE COURT: I direct the marshal to have this man sit down.

MR. KUNSTLER: Every time I make a motion am I going to be thrown in my seat when I argue it?

MR. DELLINGER: Force and violence. The judge is inciting a riot by asking the marshal to have him sit down.

THE COURT: That man's name is Dellinger?

MARSHAL JONESON: Will you be quiet, Mr. Dellinger?

MR. DELLINGER: After such hypocrisy I don't particularly feel like being quiet. I said before the judge was the chief prosecutor, and he's proved the point.

THE COURT: Will you remain quiet? Will you remain quiet, sir?

MR. DELLINGER: You let Foran give a foreign policy speech, but when he tries to answer it, you interrupt him and won't let him speak.

There's no pretense of fairness in this court. All you're doing is employing a riot—employing force and violence to try to keep me quiet. Just like you gagged Bobby Seale because you couldn't afford to listen to the truth that he was saying to you. You're accusing me. I'm a pacifist.

MARSHAL JONESON: Sit down, please, and be quiet.

MR. DELLINGER: I am employing nonviolence, and you're accusing me of violence, and you have a man right here, backed up by guns, jails, and force and violence. That is the difference between us.

MARSHAL JONESON: Will you sit down?

(applause)

THE COURT: Will you continue, please, with the direct examination of this witness?

MR. DELLINGER: There goes the violence right there.

MR. KUNSTLER: That's the Government in operation, your Honor, as it has been throughout this trial.

THE WITNESS: Your Honor, that's my sister they are taking out of the courtroom.

THE COURT: Even your sister—

MR. RUBIN: Bill, they are taking out my wife.

(cries of "Hey, stop it!")

MR. KUNSTLER: Your Honor, must we always have this, the force and power of the Government?

MR. FORAN: Your Honor—

MR. RUBIN: They are dragging out my wife—will you please—

THE COURT: We must have order in the courtroom.

MR. FORAN: Your Honor, traditionally in American law, cases are tried in a courtroom by the participants in the trial, not the audience, not spectators, not by shouting and screaming. This is the American judicial system, and it's worked very well for two hundred years, and it's not going to change now for these people.

MR. DELLINGER: Yes, kept the black people in slavery for two hundred years and wiped out the Indians, and kept the poor people in problems and started the war in Vietnam which is killing off at least a hundred Americans and a thousand Vietnamese every week, and we are trying to stop it.

MARSHAL JONESON: Sit down.

MR. DELLINGER: And you call that ranting and raving and screaming because we speak the truth.

MARSHAL JONESON: Mr. Dellinger, sit down, please.

MR. FORAN: Your Honor, in the American system there is a proper way to raise such issues and to correct them.

MR. DELLINGER: That was the proper way with Fred Hampton, wasn't it?

MR. FORAN: And to correct them, your Honor, by the proper governmental system, and there is a proper way to do that.

MR. KUNSTLER: This is as to Mr. Rubin's wife. She was thrown out of the courtroom, and he is a defendant here. We would like her returned to the courtroom.

THE COURT: No. As long as the marshals are in charge of the behavior of spectators in this courtroom, they will determine who misbehaves.

MR. RUBIN: Am I entitled to a public trial?

THE COURT: No—you have a public trial.

MR. RUBIN: Does a public trial include my wife being in the courtroom? Am I entitled to a public trial?

THE COURT: I don't talk to defendants who have a lawyer.

MR. RUBIN: You didn't listen to my lawyer, so I have to speak. Am I entitled to a public trial?

THE COURT: You may continue with the direct examination of this witness. If you don't, I will just have to ask him to get off the witness stand.

MR. WEINGLASS: Your Honor, the witness has seen from his vantage point his sister forcibly taken from this room. I wonder if we could have a short recess to resolve that?

THE COURT: No recess. No, no. There will be no recess, sir. You will proceed to examine this witness.

MR. WEINGLASS: I direct your attention to February 11, 1968, do you recall where you were?

THE WITNESS: I was in Chicago at what later became the Mobilization office, 407 South Dearborn.

Mr. WEINGLASS: What was occurring in the office?

THE WITNESS: I believe it was a planning meeting to talk about the conference that I had requested of the National Mobilization, a bringing together of all groups interested in Chicago.

MR. WEINGLASS: Did you talk about Chicago?

THE WITNESS: Yes. I said that the key questions before us today was what to do in Chicago, what to do at the Convention itself. Then I listed four positions that I proposed as a kind of agenda.

I said position number one would be we should go to the Democratic Convention to disrupt it.

I said there may be people in this room who do believe that the Democratic Convention, which is responsible for the war, should be physically disrupted, torn apart. I said I don't think that is the MOBE's position—but I think that it is essential that we put it on the agenda. It is an issue that has been created in the press and that we vote it up or down so that we can make ourselves clear on this issue.

So issue poition number one would be disrupt the Convention.

Position number two, I said, that has been talked about, is that the peace movement should support a candidate. Maybe we should support Eugene McCarthy.

Then I said position number three, that had been talked about by some organizations, was what we called stay-home. This was a position that said that Daley is so concerned about the Convention and having demonstrators come into Chicago that he'd bring in the troops, he'd bring in the police, he'd start cracking heads. And in fact this might play right into Johnson's hands. It might show that the Democratic Party is the party of law and order.

So I said position three, that we should talk about here, is whether or not we should have a demonstration at all.

Then I said position number four is a campaign that begins in the spring, it goes into the fall, it goes into the summer, and then finally brings to Chicago literally every possible constituency of the American people.

MR. WEINGLASS: Now, after you outlined these four alternatives, did you say anything further about them then?

THE WITNESS: Well, there was a very long discussion of these four proposals, and I guess at the end of that discussion I said that it was clear that in this meeting of representatives of major national groups across the country there was not a single person who did not favor position number four.

Then Tom interrupted me, and he said he thought that was wrong.

A group of so-called leaders of organizations shouldn't just get together and decide what position to present to everyone. Tom thought that we should now talk about calling a very large conference of organizations to consider all four alternatives, and then he said that each one of these positions should be written up in a paper and presented to—to this conference.

MR. WEINGLASS: Was such a conference called?

THE WITNESS: Yes, it was. It took place at a place called Lake Villa. It was a YMCA camp, just beside a big lake.

MR. WEINGLASS: Now I show you a document which has been marked D-235 for identification, and I ask you if you can identify that document?

THE WITNESS: Yes, I can. Tom Hayden and I wrote this paper. It's called, "Movement Campaign 1968, an Election Year Offensive."

The paper was mimeographed in our office and then presented to every delegate at this Lake Villa meeting outside of Chicago. This was alternative number four that was agreed upon.

MR. WEINGLASS: I offer into evidence D-235 as Defendant's Exhibit Number D-235.

THE COURT: Show it to counsel.

MR. FORAN: Your Honor, this document was offered once before. This document is some twenty-one pages in length. It contains in it a number of broad summary statements that are not supported by factual data.

Each statement in itself has elements in it that are both irrelevant summary statements of a gross character totally unprovable by evidence, and self-serving in nature, and the law, your Honor, is clear that a self-serving declaration of an act or a party is inadmissible in evidence in his favor.*

MR. WEINGLASS: If the Court please, the first time this document was offered, it was through the testimony of the witness Meacham. At that time the Government objected on the ground that the authors of the document were the only persons who could qualify the document for admission. The author is now on the stand, and of course now we are met with the objection that it is self-serving.

If you deny this document then you are proceeding on the assumption, your Honor, that the defendants are guilty and they are contriving documents. That has to be the beginning premise of your thinking if you feel this document is self-serving. If they are innocent, which is what the presumption is supposed to be—then I don't know why the Court would consider that this document would be possibly contrived.

THE COURT: You have here as a witness a very articulate, well-educated, seemingly intelligent witness; why can't he be questioned about his participation in the composition of that document?

MR. WEINGLASS: The defendants are entitled to the benefit of all of the legal evidence they have indicating their innocence, writings as well as spoken words. If this document contained plans to bomb the Amphitheatre or to create a disturbance or riot in the city streets, we clearly would have had this document in evidence in the Government's case, but it contains the contrary and that is why it is being offered. I think they are entitled to the benefit of anything that indicates their innocence as well as their guilt.

THE COURT: I shall not take it in. I sustain the objection of the Government.

MR. WEINGLASS: Your Honor has read the document?

THE COURT: I have looked it over.

THE WITNESS: You never read it. I was watching you. You read two pages.

THE COURT: Mr. Marshal, will you instruct that witness on the witness stand that he is not to address me.

You may continue sir, with your direct examination.

MR. WEINGLASS: Without referring to the document, what did you say about Chicago, if anything?

MR. FORAN: Your Honor, the form of the question is bad.

THE COURT: I sustain the objection.

MR. WEINGLASS: Did you have occasion to speak at the conference?

THE WITNESS: Yes, I spoke at a workshop Saturday evening. Tom and I were both present because we were presenting our paper.

MR. WEINGLASS: Could you relate to the Court and to the jury what you said at the workshop respecting Chicago?

THE WITNESS: Tom spoke about the paper and what was in it and then someone asked Tom why there was an entire page devoted to the issue about disruption and I answered that question.

MR. WEINGLASS: Do you recall your answer?

THE WITNESS: I said that the reason that this document devotes so much attention to the question of violence and disruption at the Convention is because we think that this is not a demonstration where simply the peace movement comes to Chicago. This is, rather, a demonstration where the peace movement is the instrument to bring literally hundreds of thousands of people to Chicago, and I said that is why it is necessary to make crystal-clear our position on disruption.

And I said that is why we feel that we have bent over backwards in this document to make our position on violence and disruption very clear, and we think that we should argue with every organization in the country who is for peace that that must be the strategy in Chicago.

MR. WEINGLASS: Now, directing your attention to the twentieth of July, 1968, do you recall where you were?

THE WITNESS: I was in Cleveland, Ohio, at a meeting in a church in Cleveland.

MR. WEINGLASS: Were any of the other defendants seated here at the table present?

THE WITNESS: Both Dave and Tom were present.

MR. WEINGLASS: Did you speak at that meeting?

THE WITNESS: Yes, I did. I said that I thought what was happening in Chicago was that our original plan to bring a half million American citizens to Chicago was so upsetting to the Mayor of Chicago, who was hosting a Convention of his own party, that there was a real danger that the Mayor had made a decision somewhere along the line to try to scare people away, to try to reduce the numbers of people expected, by stalling on permits and through suggesting that anybody who came to Chicago was going to be clubbed or beaten or Maced.

I said, "On the other hand, I don't want to discourage people into thinking that we are not going to get permits. There are several things in the works that give me a considerable amount of optimism."

I said that the director of the community relations service of the Justice Department, Roger Wilkens, flew into town for the sole purpose of meeting with myself, and that I explained to him in great detail what our plans were, what we hoped to be able to accomplish by this demonstration, and underscored our problems in trying to meet with city officials.

And I reported to the group that the reason I was optimistic was because Mr. Wilkins indicated later to me that he was going to take this matter up with the Attorney General of the United States and with the President of the United States in an effort to try to see if Mayor Daley would meet with me in the negotiations and the discussion of permits.

Then I talked about routes.

I said that the major question to us now was what route the delegates would take because in making our own preparations for how to get to the Amphitheatre, we would be concerned that we choose a route that the delegates would not take. I said at this time we have no idea of knowing what routes the delegates will take. It is one of the reasons we are anxious to meet with the City officials, so we can choose a route that does not conflict with the route the delegates plan to take from the Convention hall to the Loop hotels.

Now, I said that there are several routes that we could consider in going to the Amphitheatre. I said that traditionally when meeting with officials in a city about a parade, the way groups do it, they just pick a route and they pick a place where they want to go and they write it all on a permit and they turn it in and they wait for an answer, yes or no. And I said that my feeling was that we should not do it that way; that really the whole question of routes should be a matter of negotiation and we should never be in a position of making demands on the City that we are only going to go down this route, or we will only settle for this assembly site. I said I think we should be, from the very beginning in discussions with the City, flexible about what routes we are willing to take and what assembly areas we are willing to take in getting to the Amphitheatre.

There was a long discussion in which some decisions were made with respect to routes and assembly areas and I think Dave Dellinger finally summarized those decisions.

Dave said that we've really talked about two demonstrations on August 28. He said the first demonstration would take place in the Loop in the morning, where our hope would be to show millions of Chicagoans that there were many people who were here to express their concern about the war, and Dave said that we should now go ahead with a permit request for a demonstration in the Loop area.

In terms of the evening march Dave said that there may be difficulty through the City negotiating this, and he thought that Halsted Street was an ideal assembly area for our program on the evening of the nomination. So Dave, in summarizing the meeting, said, "We should now proceed to ask for a permit for Halsted Street from 39th on the north to 47th on the south."

MR. WEINGLASS: Now, following this meeting in Cleveland did you take any action with respect to the recommendations that were made there?

THE WITNESS: Within that week, I asked staff people to get permit application forms and I then filled out a permit application for the areas that had been suggested.

MR. WEINGLASS: I show you D-331 for identifcation and D-332, and I ask you if you can identify those two documents?

THE WITNESS: Yes. These are the two permit applications that I filled in on July 25 and submitted to the City a few days after that.

MR. WEINGLASS: Whose signature appears as the applicant?

THE WITNESS: It's my signature.

MR. WEINGLASS: Now, are these two separate applications?

THE WITNESS: Yes, they are. One is for the morning march along State Street and the second is for the evening assembly on August 28.

MR. WEINGLASS: At this time the defendants offer into evidence D-311 and D-322.

MR. FORAN: The Government has no objection to these.

MR. WEINGLASS: Directing your attention to the morning of August 2, 1968, do you recall where you were?

THE WITNESS: I was at the Palmer House, at the coffee shop in the basement. I was meeting with David Stahl, the deputy mayor of the City of Chicago, and with me was Mark Simons.

MR. WEINGLASS: Do you recall, did a conversation occur between yourself and David Stahl?

THE WITNESS: Yes, it did. I said that I felt that given the reports that we had seen in the past, that there was some question about our purposes and intentions in coming to Chicago. I said I did not understand any other explanation for the military sort of saber-rattling that was going on at that time, the constant talks in the past about disruption of the Convention.

I indicated that the character of the demonstration that was planned by our coalition was not like the Pentagon, where civil disobedience was called for, but was more like the character of the April 15 demonstration in New York, where we hoped to be effective in our protest by numbers and not by militant tactics.

I said that I thought the problem areas that we had to work out were, first of all, the matter of a march and an assembly to the Amphitheatre, and that when we had applied for a permit for the use of Halsted, that that was negotiable and that we have at this point not even applied for how to get to Halsted because we wanted to make this an open meeting between you and me.

I then said that the second area of concern for us was the whole matter of parks, that we thought that integral to our program was having park space set aside by City officials so that people could meet and sleep throughout the week of the Convention.

Then Mr. Stahl indicated to me that he thought it might be difficult for the city to grant a permit for the use of a park; that there was a curfew at 11:00 P.M., and that this would be a violation of a city ordinance to give a permit for park space beyond 11:00 P.M.

Mr. Stahl was not sure what the feeling of the City would be with respect to an assembly at the Amphitheatre. I said I thought it was very dangerous for us to even consider an area not adjacent to the Amphitheatre, because people on their own would then go down to the area, they would not have marshals, they would not have organization, and the possibility of disruption and violence would be very great.

Then Mr. Stahl said that he agreed, that it probably would create less problems if people did not march as pedestrians but went in an orderly group.

I then asked him, "Well, how do we begin to talk about these matters?"

And he said, that the mayor's office was not responsible for granting of permits, that these matters were the responsibility of the Park District, the Streets and Sanitation Department and the Police Department and the other agencies directly involved, and then I said, "Mr. Stahl, you're not dealing with an out-of-towner. I live in Chicago, and you can say this to the press, but I really wish you wouldn't say it to me." I said, "Everyone knows in this town who makes decisions like this. You can't tell me that the Streets and Sanitation Department head that's appointed by Mayor Daley is going to make a decision independent of the Mayor," and he sort of smiled at that point and didn't say anything.

Mr. Stahl was very cordial at the end and said, "Thank you very much for what you've said, and I'll relate this back to the appropriate bodies."

MR. WEINGLASS: At approximately six o'clock that night, still on August 21, 1968, do you recall where you were?

THE WITNESS: I was on my way to the Mobilization executive committee meeting, an apartment in Hyde Park.

MR. WEINGLASS: As you were outside, about to enter the apartment, did you have occasion to meet with anyone?

THE WITNESS: Yes. I met with Irv Bock.

MR. WEINGLASS: Now, without going into your conversation with Mr. Bock just now, do you recall what Mr. Bock had in his hand, if anything?

THE WITNESS: He went to his car and he came back and he had—it is hard to describe. It was a very large balloon, and attached to the balloon was a small tube, and stuck in the tube was a cloth fiber, and he took the glass tube and put it into some water, and the air from the balloon would pass through the glass tube in what appeared to be a regular way, so that one bubble would come up and then another and then another and then another, and he explained how this worked.

MR. WEINGLASS: What did he say to you?

THE WITNESS: Well, he said that with this device it's possible to fill the balloon with helium gas and to launch the balloon in the air and allow the helium gas to come out of the balloon in a way that can be computed mathematically so that you know when all of the air will be out of the balloon, and by computing the velocity it's possible to send the balloon up in the air and figure out exactly where it will fall. I said, "Why in the world would anyone be interested in that?"

And he said, "Well, you can attach anything that you want to this balloon, send it up into the air, and then we can drop it on the International Amphitheatre."

And I said, "Well, what would you want to attach to the balloon?"

And he said, "Anything you want."

I thanked Irv for his suggestion and went inside.

MR. WEINGLASS: Now, on August 4, do you recall where you were?

THE WITNESS: Yes. I was at a Mobilization steering committee meeting just outside of Chicago. It was in Highland Park at a sort of old fancy hotel that disgusted me. I mean, it was fancy, so I didn't like it.

MR. WEINGLASS: Now, at noon of that day, do you recall where you were?

THE WITNESS: There was a lunch break around noon or 12:30, and the meeting emptied out down towards the lake. I was on a sandy beach on the edge of Lake Michigan, eating my lunch.

MR. WEINGLASS: Were you alone?

THE WITNESS: No, there were a number of people. Irv Bock was present. Well, Tom Hayden, really, and I were together and we talked and ate lunch together.

MR. WEINGLASS: And did you have a conversation with Tom Hayden on the beach?

THE WITNESS: Yes. I told Tom that I had received a letter from Don Duncan who was a close friend of ours and Don had sent us sort of a list of the various kinds of gases that were being used by the Army in South Vietnam. He described in some detail a gas called CS, which he said caused extreme congestion of the chest, a burning sensation in the face, the eyes filled with tears. Actual burns could occur on the face from this, and in heavy dosage, it could cause death.

Don said that he had information that these kinds of new chemicals being used on the people of Vietnam were now going to be used on the peace movement, and he was especially concerned that this might be the case in Chicago.

MR. WEINGLASS: When you and Tom Hayden had that conversation, did you notice the whereabouts of Irv Bock?

THE WITNESS: He was there. I mean, he was close by.

January 24, 1970

MR. WEINGLASS: Directing your attention to August 13, in the evening at approximately six o'clock, did you have occasion to speak with anyone?

THE WITNESS: I spoke with my attorney, Irving Birnbaum, by phone.

MR. WEINGLASS: Do you recall that conversation you had with him on the phone?

THE WITNESS: Yes. I said, "Irv, things are going very badly with permits. This morning the Park District met. I absolutely cannot understand it. Mr. Barry promised us it was going to be on the agenda and it was not even brought up in the meeting."

I said in addition to that, "Yesterday we had a meeting with David Stahl and Richard Elrod where all of the agency heads were supposed to attend, and none of them did." I said that "I feel, very frankly, that the Mayor is now using the permit issue as a kind of political device to scare people away." And I said, "Very frankly, he's being extremely effective."

I then asked Irv whether or not he thought it made sense to file some kind of lawsuit against the City and take this whole question of permits into the courts.

Irv then said that he thought that would be a practical proposal, that we should draw up a lawsuit against the City, that the City is using its administrative control over permits to deny fundamental First Amendment and Constitutional rights.

I then said to Irv that Mr. Elrod has been quite emphatic with me about the matter of sleeping in the parks beyond 11:00 P.M. "Do we have any legal basis," I said, "for staying in the parks beyond 11:00?"

Irv Birnbaum said that he thought that very definitely that should be included in the lawsuit because he said that parks were made available for the Boy Scouts and for National Guard troops beyond 11:00 P.M., and that under the Civil Rights Act of equal protection under the law, the same kind of facilities should be made available to American citizens, and he indicated that this should be put in the lawsuit.

MR. WEINGLASS: The following Sunday, which was August 18, do you recall where you were in the morning of that day?

THE WITNESS: Yes. In the morning I was at a union hall on Nobel Street. We were having a meeting of the steering committee of the Mobilization.

MR. WEINGLASS: Were there any other defendants present?

THE WITNESS: Yes. John Froines was present.

MR. WEINGLASS: Do you recall what John Froines said at that particular meeting?

THE WITNESS: I recall that John reported on our work with marshals. He said that we were well under way with training sessions in Lincoln Park.

He then went on to talk about some of the problems that we were having, concerns about police violence, the fact that we were going to have to be very mobile through this week if the police came in to break up demonstrations.

I think at one point he said, "We may have to be as mobile as a guerrilla, moving from place to place in order to avoid arrest and avoid police confrontation."

MR. WEINGLASS: Mr. Davis, directing your attention to Wednesday, August 21, at about 10:30 in the morning, do you recall where you were?

THE WITNESS: I was in this building, in Judge Lynch's chambers.

MR. WEINGLASS: Now, who went with you into the Judge's chambers?

THE WITNESS: An attorney, who was assisting the National Mobilization Committee, Stanley Bass. I believe that Richard Elrod was present, Ray Simon, the Corporation Counsel, was present. Judge Lynch, of course, and others.

MR. WEINGLASS: Could you relate to the Court and jury specific conversations in connection with that lawsuit?

THE WITNESS: Well, Mr. Simon proposed to the Mobilization a number of assembly areas for our consideration. He said he made these proposals rather than the one that we suggested because he thought it unreasonable of the Mobilization to insist on a State Street march, that this would disrupt traffic too much.

I then told Mr. Simon that I thought these proposals were quite generous, and I was certain that on this matter we could reach an accommodation.

I said, "The problem with your proposal, Mr. Simon, is that it does not address itself to the fundamental issue for us, which is an assembly in the area of the Amphitheatre at the time of the Democratic nomination."

I went on to say that I would make two concrete proposals at this time. I said that it would be satisfactory to our coalition to consider the area on Halsted Street from 39th on the north to 47th on the south.

I said if that was not acceptable to the City, that there's a large area just west of the parking lot, that would be suitable for our purposes, and I thought would not interfere with the delegates.

Mr. Simons then said that the area on Halsted from 39th on the north to 45th on the south was out of the question for consideration, that it was a security area, he said, and that it was not possible for the City to grant this area to the Mobilization.

He then said that the second area that I had proposed similarly was out of the question because I think he said it was controlled by the Democratic National Convention and the City had no authority to grant that space to the Mobilization.

Then I said, "Assuming both of these areas are just not available, could you, Mr. Simon, suggest an area that would be within eyeshot of the Amphitheatre for an assembly on the evening of the nomination?"

Mr. Simon then said he didn't see why we needed to have an assembly area within eyeshot or close to the Amphitheatre. He said that the City was willing to make other proposals for such an assembly, they would offer us Grant Park, they would offer us Lincoln Park, they would offer us Garfield Park on the west side of Chicago.

MR. WEINGLASS: Incidentally, approximately how far in distance from the Amphitheatre are these parks which the city was offering at that time?

THE WITNESS: Well, Lincoln Park is ten miles and Grant Park is four miles. I said to Mr. Simon, "To go to these areas would be like demonstrating in Detroit."

Then I think that I indicated that we had a right to be at the International Amphitheatre at the time of the nomination, and that we could avoid violence by providing our own marshals to essentially police our own people.

I remember at the end of this conversation Mr. Simon asked me if I intended to have a parade to the International Amphitheatre on the night of the nomination and I indicated that that was our desire, and then Mr. Simon told me that there was a state law forbidding evening and nighttime marches and that under this law this would not be permitted.

Then I believe that session concluded.

MR. WEINGLASS: Now, did another meeting take place in Judge Lynch's chambers?

THE WITNESS: Yes, the following day.

MR. WEINGLASS: Can you relate to the Court and jury the conversation that occurred in your presence?

THE WITNESS: Yes. I said, "Yesterday Mr. Simon told me that Halsted from 39th to 45th was a security zone and for that reason would not be available for an assembly at the Amphitheater.

Then I said that I want to concretely suggest at this time that we consider a large parking lot at the Community Discount Center on the corner of 47th and Halsted. I said that this is not as desirable from our point of view, but in the interest of being reasonable, we offer this at this time as a suggestion.

I then said that Mr. Simon has told me that marching on the Amphitheater is prohibited by state law, so we are prepared to give up this march to the Amphitheater and we will go to the Amphitheater as individuals, as pedestrians.

Mr. Simon then told me that the 11:00 P.M. curfew in parks would be enforced and that we could not stay in parks past 11:00 P.M., and I asked him what we should do, you know, what are people going to do.

He said, well, he thought that it would be reasonable for our committee to rent motel accommodations in Evanston and Park Ridge and Oak Park and far outlying suburban communities.

I said that our coalition has already secured housing for 30,000 people, but that, frankly, we expected more than this number and I just didn't know where people were going to go. I said, "What is going to happen is that they are going to go into the parks, police are going to then come into those parks and clear those parks, and the kids are going to fight back, and the police are going to use Mace and clubs and gas, and it's going to lead to violence, and that's the very kind of situation that more than anything else I want to avoid."

Simon simply said that it would not be possible for us to stay in the parks. Mr. Simon, then, I think, indicated that he would inquire as to the availability of the space at 47th and Halsted. That was the end of the conversation.

MR. WEINGLASS: Now, can you remember where you were in the afternoon of Friday, the twenty-third of August?

THE WITNESS: I think I was in the Mobilization office at that time.

MR. WEINGLASS: Did you receive a phone call at approximately that time in the office?

THE WITNESS: Yes, I did. It was my attorney, Mr. Birnbaum. He said to me that he had just received the opinion of Judge Lynch denying us a permit for an assembly and denying us the right to use parks beyond 11:00 P.M.

I then said, "We should appeal this matter immediately. We are in absolute crisis."

Then Mr. Birnbaum said that, in his professional opinion, no appeal would produce a permit in time for our activities during the week of the Convention, but that he was willing to draw up the papers for appeal for the purpose of preserving the record.

MR. WEINGLASS: I show you D-339 for identification, which is a photograph. Can you identify the persons in that photograph?

THE WITNESS: Myself, Tom Hayden and one of the police tails who followed me through much of the convention week, Ralph Bell.

MR. WEINGLASS: Do you recall when you first saw Mr. Bell, the police tail?

THE WITNESS: Well, on Friday after the phone call from Irv Birnbaum, I then walked out of the building, just to take a long walk alone and to think about what I personally was going to do during this week, and when I came back into the building, there were two men in sort of casual clothes who approached me at the elevator door and flashed badges, said they were policemen, and they were coming up to the office. I went back into the office and they waited outside, and I got Tom, and Tom and I then went back out to talk with them.

MR. WEINGLASS: Could you relate to the Court and jury the conversation that you and Tom Hayden had?

THE WITNESS: Well, one of the gentlemen just flashed his badge for the second time and said, "My name's Officer Bell. This here's Riggio. We're gonna be around you a lot, Davis, so we'll just be around you and going wherever you go from now until the Convention's over," and I said, "Well, what's the purpose of this?"

And Bell said, "Well, the purpose is to give you protection," and I said, "Well, thank you very much, but I'd just as soon not have your protection."

And then Bell said, "Well, just pretend like you're President and got protection everywhere you go, day and night," and I said, "Well, what if I would request not to have this protection."

And then he said, "Motherfucker, you got the protection, and you try to shake me and you're in big trouble. Now, you cooperate, and we'll get along real fine, hear?"

And I said, "Yes, sir," and walked back into the office.

MR. WEINGLASS: I draw your attention to Monday, August 26, at approximately 2:30 in the afternoon of that day.

Do you recall where you were?

THE WITNESS: Well, that afternoon, Monday, I was in Lincoln Park.

MR. WEINGLASS: When Tom Hayden was arrested, were you at the scene of the arrest?

THE WITNESS: No, sir, I was not. I was in the park at the time, yes.

MR. WEINGLASS: Now, when did you first become aware of the fact that he had been arrested?

THE WITNESS: It was around 2:30. A number of people came to me and said that Tom Hayden and Wolfe Lowenthal had been arrested and I could see the people sort of were spontaneously coming together. Many people were talking about marching on to the police station in response to this arrest.

MR. WEINGLASS: And then after receiving that information, what did you do?

THE WITNESS: Well, I talked to a number of marshals about the urgency of getting on with this march and trying to see that it has direction and that our marshals are involved in this march. I was just sort of concerned that people not run out into the streets and down to the police station, so I got on the bullhorn and started to urge people to gather behind the sound for the march to the police station.

MR. WEINGLASS: Approximately how many people joined the march?

THE WITNESS: Well, my recollection is hazy—over a thousand people, I think, joined the march. I was marching about four or five rows from the front with the sound.

MR. WEINGLASS: Were any defendants in your company at that time?

THE WITNESS: Yes. John Froines was with me, really throughout the march that day.

MR. WEINGLASS: And was this march proceeding on the sidewalk, or was it in the roadway?

THE WITNESS: No, it was on the sidewalk, all the way across the sidewalk until a police officer requested that I urge people to stay on one half of the sidewalk.

MR. WEINGLASS: Now, as you were proceeding south on State Street, were you in the company of any officials of the city of Chicago?

THE WITNESS: Yes. I was in the company of two members of the Corporation Counsel, one of whom was Richard Elrod.

MR. WEINGLASS: As you approached the police station, did you have occasion to speak again to Mr. Elrod?

THE WITNESS: Yes. About a block away from the police station, I spoke with Mr. Elrod. I said, "Mr. Elrod, the police station is completely encircled with uniformed police officers. I'm attempting to move the people out of that area and move past the police station, but you've created a situation where we have to move demonstrators down a solid wall of policemen.

"All that has to happen is for one demonstrator to strike a policeman or for one policeman to be too anxious walking past that line, and we've got a full-scale riot on our hands. I'm just not moving this line until those policemen are taken back into that building." And at that point Mr. Elrod said well, he'd see what he could do.

MR. WEINGLASS: Did you observe what Mr. Elrod did after that conversation?

THE WITNESS: I didn't see what he did, but minutes later the policemen in formation marched back into the police headquarters at 11th and State.

MR. WEINGLASS: After the police went back into the police headquarters building what did you do?

THE WITNESS: I urged people to march past the police station staying on the sidewalk, staying together, and I think we began to chant "Free Hayden." We continued then east on 11th Street toward Michigan Avenue, and north on the sidewalk on Michigan.

MR. WEINGLASS: As you were proceeding north, what, if anything, did you observe?

THE WITNESS: To the best of my recollection the march had stopped while we were waiting for the other participants to catch up and it was at that moment that some of the people in the demonstration just sort of broke out of the line of march and ran up a hill, the top of which had the statue of General Jonathan Logan.

MR. WEINGLASS: At that time that the demonstrators broke from the line of march and ran up the hill, were you speaking on the microphone?

THE WITNESS: Not at the time that they broke, no. I had stopped and was waiting for the rest of the people to catch up.

MR. WEINGLASS: Were these people carrying anything in their hands?

THE WITNESS: Yes. They were carrying flags of all kinds, Viet Cong flags, red flags.

MR. WEINGLASS: After you saw them run up the hill to the statue, what, if anything, did you do?

THE WITNESS: A police formation developed at the base of the hill and began to sweep upward toward the statue and at that point I yelled very loudly that people should leave the statue and go to the Conrad Hilton. I said a number of things very rapidly like, "We have liberated the statue, now we should go to the Conrad Hilton. The Conrad Hilton is the headquarters of the people who are responsible for the arrest. Let's leave the statue, let's liberate the Hilton," basically urging people to get away from the statue.

MR. FORAN: I object to the characterization of the words, your Honor.

THE COURT: The use of the word "urging"?

MR. FORAN: "Basically," from the word "basically" on, I move to strike.

THE COURT: Yes. I don't know precisely what it means.

Read the last answer to him. Try to use words that would satisfy the requirements of an answer to the question, Mr. Witness.

THE WITNESS: I can continue. As the police got right up on the demonstrators and began to club the people who were around the base of the statue, I then said as loudly as I could, "If the police want a riot, let them stay in this area. If the police don't want a riot, let them get out of this area."

MR. WEINGLASS: Did there come a time when you left that area?

THE WITNESS: Yes, I left—after I urged people to leave the area, I then left the area myself. I went back to the Mobilization office.

MR. WEINGLASS: Did you have occasion to meet with Tom Hayden that night?

THE WITNESS: Yes, I did. We went to several places and finally we went to the Conrad Hilton. I guess it was a little before midnight. Tom ran into some friends that he knew, a man named Mr. Alder, and some others. I think Jeff Cowan was present, people that I don't know very well.

And they were involved in various capacities in an official way with the Democratic Convention, and they invited Tom to come into the Conrad Hilton to watch the Convention on television. So Tom and myself then accompanied them to the entrance on Balbo Street.

MR. WEINGLASS: Were they successful in getting Tom Hayden into the hotel?

THE WITNESS: No. They returned shortly after that, and Tom said we couldn't get in.

MR. WEINGLASS: Then what did you do?

THE WITNESS: I proceeded to walk across the intersection of Balbo, going north on Michigan. Tom Hayden was directly behind, and I guess I was about halfway across the street on Balbo when I heard someone yell very loudly, "Get him, get him" screaming from a distance, and I turned around and saw the policeman who had been following me through the Convention week, Ralph Bell, running very fast, directly at Tom, and he just charged across Michigan Avenue. Tom and I were sort of frozen in our places, and Bell grabbed Tom around the neck and just drove him to the street.

At that point a second police officer in uniform came from behind and grabbed Tom as well, and I believe he actually held the nightstick against Tom's neck. I then took a few steps towards Bell and Tom and this second police officer, and I yelled at Bell, "What do you think you're doing?"

And then this uniformed policeman took his nightclub and chopped me across the neck and then twice across the chest. Then my second police tail whom I hadn't seen at that point, suddenly had me by my shirt, dragged me across the intersection of Balbo and Michigan, and just threw me up against something. I think it was a lightpole. I remember just being smashed against something, and he said—his name was Riggio—he said, "What do you think you're doing, Davis?"

MR. WEINGLASS: Were you placed under arrest at that time?

THE WITNESS: No, I was not.

MR. WEINGLASS: Did you see what happened to Tom Hayden?

THE WITNESS: Tom was put into a paddywagon, and taken away from the area.

MR. WEINGLASS: What did you do then?

THE WITNESS: Well, I stood still for a moment, just stunned, wandered around alone, then I ran into Paul Potter. Then Paul and I walked back to the office on Dearborn Street.

MR. WEINGLASS: Now, do you recall approximately what time of night you arrived at the office?

THE WITNESS: Well, frankly I don't think that I would recall except that Mr. Riggio when he testified in this trial, indicated the arrest was around midnight, and it's about a five- or ten-minute walk back to the office, so it must have been somewhere between 12:20, 12:30 in that area.

MR. WEINGLASS: When you got back to the office, what, if anything, did you do?

THE WITNESS: Well, I called our legal defense office and explained what had occurred. Then I made a few more phone calls, talked to some people in the office. Paul left the office, and shortly after Paul left, I got in a car and drove towards Lincoln Park.

MR. WEINGLASS: Now, do you recall any of the persons who were in the office at the time you have just indicated?

THE WITNESS: Well, Paul and Carrol Glassman were both in the office, and Jeff Gerth. As a matter of fact, I think it was Jeff Gerth who drove me to Lincoln Park.

MR. WEINGLASS: Now, do you know what time it was that you left the office?

THE WITNESS: Close to one o'clock.

MR. WEINGLASS: Now, when you arrived at Lincoln Park, did you go to the park?

THE WITNESS: No, I did not go into the park. I drove past the park and into the Old Town area, and there I saw Vern Grizzard. I got out of the car and talked to Vernon for a couple of minutes and then Vernon and I got back into the car and we then left the area.

MR. WEINGLASS: Now, approximately twenty-four hours later, very late Tuesday night, do you recall where you were at that time?

THE WITNESS: Well, late Tuesday night I was in Grant Park directly across from the Conrad Hilton Hotel.

MR. WEINGLASS: Now, at 4:00 A.M., were you still in the park?

THE WITNESS: Yes. Yes, I was there certainly up till four o'clock.

MR. WEINGLASS: Did you have occasion at that time to see any of the defendants?

THE WITNESS: Yes. I met with Tom Hayden.

MR. WEINGLASS: Can you describe Tom Hayden's appearance at that time?

THE WITNESS: Well, Tom had a ridiculous hat, and he was sort of dressed in mod clothing. I think he had a fake goatee, as I recall, and for a while he was carrying a handkerchief across his nose and mouth.

I said, "Tom, you look like a fool."

MR. WEINGLASS: Did you and Tom have a conversation after that?

THE WITNESS: Yes. Yes, we did. I said to Tom that I was concerned about the lateness of the hour, I was concerned that television and cameras and photographers and newsmen were now leaving the area; the crowd was thinning out.

I said that this is the kind of situation which could lead to problems, and I told Tom that I thought that someone should make an announcement that this has been a great victory, that we're able to survive under these incredibly difficult conditions, and that people should now be encouraged to leave the park, and return tomorrow morning. Tom then agreed to make that announcement.

MR. WEINGLASS: The following morning, Wednesday, August 28, do you recall where you were?

THE WITNESS: Wednesday morning before Grant Park I was in the Mobilization office. Fifteen people, something like that, were having a meeting.

MR. WEINGLASS: Do you recall who was present at that meeting?

THE WITNESS: I recall that both Tom and Dave Dellinger were present. Linda Morse I think was there.

MR. WEINGLASS: Will you relate to the Court and jury what the defendants said while they were there, including yourself?

THE WITNESS: Dave said that he thought after the rally in Grant Park the most important thing to do was to continue with our plan to march to the Amphitheatre.

Tom said that there is no possibility of going to the Amphitheatre.

Dave said that the City, even though it has not granted permits, has allowed us to have other marches, and that perhaps they will allow us to go to the Amphitheatre.

Tom insisted that we were not going to the Amphitheatre.

Then David said that he felt that even if the police did not allow us to march, that it was absolutely necessary that we assemble, we line up, and we prepare to go to the Amphitheatre. Dave said that if the police indicate that they are going to prevent this march by force, that we have to at that time say to the world that there are Americans who will not submit to a police state by default; that they are prepared to risk arrest and be taken away to jail rather than to submit to the kind of brutality that we had seen all through the week.

Tom said that he agreed that there were people coming who intended to march, but he said as well there are many people who are not prepared to be arrested and he thought that we needed now to suggest another activity for Wednesday afternoon and evening for those people who were not prepared to be arrested.

Dave said he agreed that those people who were unprepared to be arrested should be encouraged to leave the park and return to the hotels as we had the night before.

I then said that I thought that we needed as well to announce that those people who do not want to participate in either activity should simply stay in the park or go home.

Everyone agreed with that and Dave then said that this should be announced from the platform, these three positions, and that I should inform the marshals of these three positions.

MR. WEINGLASS: Now, directing your attention to approximately 2:30 in the afternoon of that same day, do you recall where you were at that time?

THE WITNESS: Yes, I was in Grant Park just south of the refreshment stand. I saw a commotion near the flagpole and shortly after that I heard Dave Dellinger's voice. It was clear that something was happening and Dave indicated that he wanted marshals to move to the flagpole, so I then said to everyone there that we should go toward the flagpole.

MR. WEINGLASS: When you went to the flagpole, did you have anything in your hands?

THE WITNESS: I had a speaker system with a microphone.

MR. WEINGLASS: As you arrived in the vicinity of the flagpole, what was occurring?

THE WITNESS: The flag had been lowered to halfmast and the police were dragging a young man out of the area. The police seemed to be withdrawing from the area as I arrived, and a lot of people who were gathered around the flagpole began to throw anything they could get their hands on at the police who were withdrawing from the crowd. They threw rocks and boards and lunches and anything that was available right on the ground.

MR. WEINGLASS: What were you saying, if anything, at that time on the microphone?

THE WITNESS: I kept directing the marshals to form a line, link arms, and then I constantly urged the people in the crowd to stop throwing things. I said, "You're throwing things at our own people. Move back."

As our marshal line grew, I urged our marshal line to now begin to move back and move the demonstrators away from the police.

MR. WEINGLASS: Where did you go?

THE WITNESS: I continued to stand in front of the marshal line that had been formed.

MR. WEINGLASS: What did you then observe happen?

THE WITNESS: Well, at that time another squadron of policemen in formation began to advance towards my position.

I was standing in front of our marshal line sort of sandwiched in between our marshal line and the advancing police formation.

MR. WEINGLASS: What were you doing as the police were advancing?

THE WITNESS: Well, as the police advanced, I continued to have my back to the police line, basically concerned that the marshal line not break or move. Then the police formation broke and began to run, and at that time I heard several of the men in the line yell, quite distinctly, "Kill Davis! Kill Davis!" and they were screaming that and the police moved on top of me, and I was trapped between my own marshal line and advancing police line.

The first thing that occurred to me was a very powerful blow to the head that drove me face first down into the dirt, and then, as I attempted to crawl on my hands and knees, the policemen continued to yell, "Kill Davis! Kill Davis!" and continued to strike me across the ear and the neck and the back.

I guess I must have been hit thirty or forty times in the back and I crawled for maybe —I don't know how many feet, ten feet maybe, and I came to a chain fence and somehow I managed to crawl either under or through that fence, and a police fell over the fence, trying to get me, and another police hit the fence with his nightstick, but I had about a second or two in which I could stand and I leaped over a bench and over some people and into the park, and then I proceeded to walk toward the center of the park.

MR. WEINGLASS: As you walked toward the center of the park, what, if anything, happened?

THE WITNESS: Well, I guess the first thing that I was conscious of, I looked down, and my tie was just solid blood, and I realized that my shirt was just becoming blood, and someone took my arm and took me to the east side of the Bandshell, and I laid down, and there was a white coat who was bent over me. I remember hearing the voice of Carl Oglesby. Carl said, "In order to survive in this country, we have to fight," and then—then I lost consciousness.

MR. WEINGLASS: I have completed my direct examination.

THE COURT: Is there any cross-examination of this witness?

• • • • •

MR. FORAN: Mr. Davis, could you tell me what you consider conventional forms of protest?

THE WITNESS: Writing, speaking, marching, assembling, acting on your deepest moral and political convictions, especially when the authority that you—

MR. FORAN: I mean methods. You were going along fine.

THE WITNESS: Well, conventional activity would include those forms and others.

MR. FORAN: All right. And do you support those forms of protest or do you like other forms of protest?

THE WITNESS: It depends on what the issue is.

MR. FORAN: Haven't you stated in the past that you opposed the tendency to conventional forms of protest instead of militant action in connection with Chicago?

THE WITNESS: Well, it really depends at what time that was.

MR. FORAN: Well, in March, say.

MR. WEINGLASS: If he is referring to a prior writing, I would like him to identify it so we may follow it.

MR. FORAN: There is no necessity for me to do that, your Honor.

THE COURT: No, no necessity for that. I order the witness to answer the question if he can. If he can't he may say he cannot and I will excuse him.

Now read the question again to the witness.

THE WITNESS: I understand the question. Maybe if Mr. Foran could define for me what he means by the word "militant," because we may have different views about that word.

THE COURT: There is no necessity for defining words.

THE WITNESS: I would like very much to answer your question, Mr. Foran, but I am afraid that your view of militant and mine are very different, so I cannot answer that question as you phrased it.

THE COURT: He said he cannot answer the question, Mr. Foran. Therefore I excuse him from answering the question.

MR. FORAN: Did you tell that meeting at Lake Villa that the summer of '68 should be capped by a week of demonstrations, disruptions, and marches at the Democratic National Convention clogging the streets of Chicago?

THE WITNESS: Well, I certainly might have said "clogging the streets of Chicago."

MR. FORAN: Did you tell them at that meeting what I just said to you?

THE WITNESS: Well, I may have.

MR. FORAN: Did you ever write a document with Tom Hayden called "Discussions on the Democratic Challenge?"

THE WITNESS: Yes, I recall this. This was written very early.

MR. FORAN: When did you write it?

THE WITNESS: I think we wrote that document around January 15.

MR. FORAN: Have you ever said that "Countless creative activities must be employed that will force the President to use troops to secure his nomination?" Have you ever stated that?

THE WITNESS: That's possible.

MR. FORAN: But in January, in your little document that you and Hayden wrote together, that's what you said you were going to do, wasn't it?

THE WITNESS: Well, you've taken it out of context. I would be happy to explain the whole idea.

MR. FORAN: And it was your intention that you wanted to have trouble start so that the National Guard would have to be called out to protect the delegates, wasn't it?

THE WITNESS: No, it was not.

MR. FORAN: You've stated that, haven't you?

THE WITNESS: No. We thought it might be possible the troops would be brought into the city to protect the Convention from its own citizens, it would be another—

MR. FORAN: From the citizens that were outside waiting to pin the delegates in, is that correct?

THE WITNESS: No. It's not correct.

MR. FORAN: On August 2 you met Stahl for breakfast over at the coffee house and you told him that this was an incendiary situation and that you'd rather die right here in Chicago than in Vietnam, didn't you?

THE WITNESS: No, Mr. Foran. I don't want to die in Chicago or Vietnam.

MR. FORAN: Then you saw Stahl again on August 10, that time at the coffee shop on Monroe Street?

THE WITNESS: Yes, that's right.

MR. FORAN: And you told Stahl that you had housing for 30,000 people, didn't you?

THE WITNESS: That's right.

MR. FORAN: And you told Stahl that you expected at least another 70,000 people to come, and they wouldn't have any place to go, so they had to sleep in the park.

THE WITNESS: I think that I did.

MR. FORAN: And Stahl told you about the park ordinance again, didn't he, reminded you of it, that they couldn't sleep overnight in the park? He also told you about the Secret Service security requirements at the Amphitheater, didn't he, at the August 10 meeting?

THE WITNESS: No, no, absolutely not. On the contrary, there was no indication of a security area until August 21.

MR. FORAN: You told the City that you had to be able to march to the Amphitheatre, didn't you?

THE WITNESS: Well, I told the City that we would assemble in any area that was in proximity to the Amphitheatre.

MR. FORAN: That the terminal point of march had to be the Amphitheatre, didn't you say that?

THE WITNESS: No, I never said that. I talked about eyeshot or being near the Amphitheatre.

MR. FORAN: By the way, you people got permits at the Pentagon, didn't you?

THE WITNESS: Yes, permits were granted for the demonstration at the Pentagon.

January 26, 1970

MR. FORAN: And the Mobilization had planned or some people in it had planned civil disobedience at the Pentagon, isn't that right?

THE WITNESS: What do you mean by civil disobedience?

MR. FORAN: In fact, at the Pentagon, you planned both an active confrontation with the warmakers and the engagement of civil disobedience, didn't you?

THE WITNESS: Well, if 150,000 people gathered in assembly is regarded as an active confrontation, as I regard it, the answer, of course, is yes.

MR. FORAN: Isn't it a fact that on the August 12 meeting with Stahl that you told him that during Convention week the demonstrators were going to participate in civil disobedience? Isn't that a fact?

THE WITNESS: No. May I say what I said?

MR. FORAN: Isn't it a fact that you had found that that was a very successful tactic at the Pentagon?

THE WITNESS: No, I believe that Dave Dellinger said that that was a tactic we did not want to use in Chicago. We had one tactic for the Pentagon and another view for Chicago.

MR. FORAN: Isn't it a fact that that tactic, a permit on the one hand and active confrontation combined with civil disobedience on the other hand, gives the movement an opportunity to get both conventional protest groups and active resistance groups to come together in the demonstration? You have heard Dellinger say that, haven't you?

THE WITNESS: No, he never used those words for Chicago, Mr. Foran. What he always said—

MR. FORAN: Did he say it in connection with the Pentagon?

THE WITNESS: Oh, for the Pentagon? There was no doubt there was a conception for civil disobedience which was wholly different from what we wanted to do in Chicago. Can't you understand? It is so simple. The Pentagon was one thing, Chicago was another thing.

MR. FORAN: I know you would like to explain away what happened in Chicago very much, Mr. Davis, but you also have to take into consideration what happened at the Pentagon was the blueprint for Chicago and you know it.

MR. DELLINGER: You are a liar.

MR. KUNSTLER: Your Honor, every time we try to get one of our witnesses to talk about the Pentagon, who was the quickest on his feet to say "That is outside the scope, you can't go into that—

MR. FORAN: Not on cross-examination it isn't outside the scope.

Isn't it a fact that Mr. Dellinger said that the Mobilization at the Pentagon can have its maximum impact when it combines massive action with the cutting edge of resistance? Didn't he say that?

THE WITNESS: What do you mean "cutting edge of resistance?"

MR. FORAN: Did Mr. Dellinger ever say that?

THE WITNESS: Well, I never heard him use those words.

MR. FORAN: In substance did you hear him say it? In substance?

THE WITNESS: Yes, all right.

MR. FORAN: Isn't it a fact that your plan both at the Pentagon and in Chicago was to combine, in Dellinger's words, the peacefulness of Gandhi and the violence of active resistance? Isn't that a fact?

THE WITNESS: No, that is not a fact. In fact, that is not even close.

MR. FORAN: May that be stricken, your Honor?

THE COURT: "In fact, that is not even close," those words may go out and the jury is directed to disregard them.

MR. FORAN: You testified on direct examination that on February 11, 1969, you gave a talk at 407 South Dearborn, didn't you?

THE WITNESS: Yes, sir.

MR. FORAN: Very good.

THE WITNESS: Thank you.

MR. FORAN: In the course of that talk you said on direct examination that "there may be people in this room who do believe that the Democratic Convention which is responsible for the war should be physically disrupted."

THE WITNESS: Yes.

MR. FORAN: Isn't it a fact that among the people in that room at 407 South Dearborn who did believe that the Democratic National Convention should be physically disrupted and torn apart were you and Hayden? Isn't that a fact?

THE WITNESS: No, it is not a fact. If you will read my testimony, you will see that—

MR. FORAN: You and Hayden had written—

THE WITNESS: Yes. Now if you will put that document before the jury—

MR. FORAN: —a "Discussion on the Democratic Convention Challenge," hadn't you?

THE WITNESS: We wrote a paper in January that was substantially revised by that very meeting, sir.

THE WITNESS: So you changed your mind between January 15 and February 11, is that your testimony?

THE WITNESS: We did not change our mind. We dropped some of the language that Dave Dellinger criticized as inappropriate, confusing—I think he said the word "disruption" was irresponsible.

MR. FORAN: In addition to you and Hayden, isn't it a fact that another person in that room who wanted to physically disrupt that National Democratic Convention was Dave Dellinger? Isn't that a fact?

THE WITNESS: Your questions embarrass me, they are so terrible. They really do.

MR. FORAN: Well, answer it.

THE WITNESS: The answer is no.

MR. FORAN: Isn't it a fact that Dellinger ran the show at the Pentagon? Isn't that a fact?

THE WITNESS: Sir, our movement doesn't work that way with one man running the show, as you say. It is a movement of thousands of people who participate each year.

MR. FORAN: You said that the Yippies wanted a gigantic festival in the park in Chicago to show the contrast between your culture and the death-producing culture of the Democratic Convention. Did you so testify?

THE WITNESS: I think I said "the death-producing ritual of the Democratic Convention."

MR. FORAN: Isn't it a fact that all the vile and vulgar propaganda the Yippies were passing out was for the purpose of making the City delay on the permit, and to make the authorities look repressive?

THE WITNESS: Sir, no one had to make the City look repressive. The City was repressive.

MR. FORAN: Isn't it a fact that that vile and vulgar advertising along with all of the talk about a rock festival was for the purpose of attracting the guerrilla active resistance types to your protest?

THE WITNESS: No, sir.

MR. FORAN: And the purpose of the permit negotiations was to attract people who believed in more conventional forms of protest, wasn't it?

THE WITNESS: The purpose of the permits was to allow us to have a legal assembly.

MR. FORAN: That is exactly what you had done at the Pentagon, wasn't it, the synthesis of Gandhi and guerrilla, isn't that what you did at the Pentagon?

THE WITNESS: No.

MR. FORAN: Mr. Davis, you testified that you had young Mark Simons request the use of various park facilities for meeting and for sleeping back around the thirty-first of July, isn't that correct?

THE WITNESS: Yes.

MR. FORAN: Now, isn't it a fact that you were always told by every city official that the 11:00 P.M. curfew in the parks would not be waived, isn't that a fact? Stahl told you that again on August 2, didn't he?

THE WITNESS: Not that emphatically.

MR. FORAN: He told you there was an 11:00 P.M. curfew that did not permit sleeping in the parks, did he say that?

THE WITNESS: But in the context at that time it would be waived, as it was waived all the time for the Boy Scouts and the National Guard troops.

MR. FORAN: Well, you didn't consider the Yippies Boy Scouts, did you?

THE WITNESS: Well, I considered that under the Civil Rights Act that American citizens have equal protection of the law.

MR. FORAN: You think that the Yippies with what they were advertising they were going to do in Lincoln Park are the same as the Boy Scouts? Is that what you are saying?

THE WITNESS: Well, as someone who has been very active in the Boy Scouts during all of his young life, I considered—

MR. FORAN: Did you ever see the Boy Scouts advertise public fornication, for heaven's sake?

THE WITNESS: The Yippies talked about a festival of Life and love and—

MR. FORAN: They also talked about public fornication and about drug use and about nude-ins on the beach? They also talked about that, didn't they?

THE WITNESS: They talked about love, yes, sir.

MR. FORAN: You and I have a little different feeling about love, I guess, Mr. Davis.

Now, isn't it a fact that the continuous demands for sleeping in the park were just for the purpose of again making the authorities appear repressive, isn't that a fact?

THE WITNESS: Oh, no. We wanted Soldiers Field as a substitute, or any facility. I indicated to the superintendent that we would take any facilities that could possibly be made available to get around this ordinance problem.

MR. FORAN: Now, in Judge Lynch's chambers, Raymond Simon proposed four different march routes as alternatives to your proposed march routes, didn't he?

THE WITNESS: Surely.

MR. FORAN: And you told him that while they appeared reasonable for daytime demonstrations, they were completely unacceptable to your coalition because there was no consideration of an assembly at the Amphitheater?

THE WITNESS: Yes, sir, I did.

MR. FORAN: Did you accept any of these proposals of the four routes of march?

THE WITNESS: Yes. Well, we accepted the proposal to assemble in Grant Park at 1:00 to 4:00 P.M.

MR. FORAN: And no other proposals were accepted, is that correct?

THE WITNESS: No other proposals were made.

MR. FORAN: Other proposals that Mr. Simon had made to you, you rejected, did you not? You rejected them saying that you wanted to assemble at the Amphitheatre?

THE WITNESS: They were absurd proposals. People everywhere understood why young people were coming to Chicago: to go to the Convention.

MR. FORAN: After all of these meetings, the cause was argued?

THE WITNESS: On August 22, yes, sir.

MR. FORAN: And it was dismissed on the next day, August 23, is that right?

THE WITNESS: That's right, by the former law partner of Mayor Daley.

MR. FORAN: We can strike that statement.

THE COURT: I strike the remark of the witness from the record, and direct the jury to disregard it.

MR. FORAN: Was a motion to disqualify the judge made by your attorneys in this case?

THE WITNESS: No, it was not.

MR. FORAN: Did you instruct them to do so?

THE WITNESS: We discussed it as to whether or not we could get a fair shake from a former law partner of Mayor Daley, and we decided all of the judges were essentially the same, and that most of them are appointed by Daley.

MR. FORAN: So you thought all eleven judges in this district were appointed by Mayor Daley?

THE WITNESS: Not all eleven judges were sitting at that time. We thought that the court might be a face-saving device for the mayor. A mayor who didn't politically want to give permits might allow the courts to give permits. That is why we went into court.

THE COURT: Did you say all of the judges were appointed by Mayor Daley? Does he have the power to appoint judges?

THE WITNESS: No, I think that I indicated that they were all sort of very influenced and directed by the Mayor of the city of Chicago. There is a lot of feeling about it in the city.

There is a lot of feeling of that in this city, Judge Hoffman. You can't really separate the courts from the Daley machine in this town.

THE COURT: Did you know that I was just about the first judge nominated on this bench by President Eisenhower in early 1953?

THE WITNESS: I do know. I understand that. You are a Republican judge.

THE COURT: I am not a Republican judge; I am a judge of all the people. I happen to be appointed by President Eisenhower in the spring of 1953.

THE WITNESS: Yes, sir, I know that.

THE COURT: So do you want to correct your statement about Mayor Daley? If Mayor Daley had his way, he wouldn't have had me.

I just want to reassure you if you feel that I am here because of Mayor Daley, I am not really.

THE WITNESS: I see.

THE COURT: Mayor Daley, as far as I am concerned, and so I am told, is a good mayor. I don't think I have ever spoken three sentences to him other than—I don't know whether I spoke to him when he was on the stand here or not. Perhaps I did direct him to answer some questions, I don't know.

MR. FORAN: When you were talking to Judge Lynch, you knew that you were going to have your people stay in the park with or without a permit, didn't you, and you didn't tell the judge that, did you?

THE WITNESS: I told the judge that we wanted to avoid violence and that was the most important thing possible.

MR. FORAN: If you wanted to avoid violence so much, did you tell the people out in the ballfield across the Balbo bridge from the Hilton Hotel that you had 30,000 housing units available and if you don't want trouble in the park, why don't you come take advantage of our housing? Did you say that in Grant Park that day?

THE WITNESS: Mr. Foran, we didn't come to Chicago to sleep.

MR. FORAN: Did you say that? Did you tell those people when you were telling them to go back to Lincoln Park that night for the Yippie Festival, did you tell them, "Don't stay in the park tonight, it might cause trouble. We have got plenty of housing available"? Did you tell them that?

THE WITNESS: We made constant references to the availability of housing through our *Ramparts* wall posters, through announcements at the movement centers. We communicated very well—

MR. FORAN: Your Honor, may I have that stricken?

THE WITNESS: —that housing was available.

MR. FORAN: Well, as you were leaving that crowd from Lincoln Park, did you ever announce over that bullhorn, "Now look, we don't want any trouble in the park tonight, so any of you people who don't have housing, just let us know. We have thirty thousand housing units available"?

Did you announce that over the bullhorn while you were conducting that march?

THE WITNESS: On that occasion, no. We had other concerns, namely the arrest of Tom Hayden and Wolfe Lowenthal. But we did make constant announcements about—

MR. FORAN: You heard Oklepek testify, did you not, and it is a fact, isn't it, that at the August 9 meeting if the demonstrators were driven from the park, they ought to move out into the Loop and tie it up and bust it up, and you told the people that at that August 9 meeting, didn't you?

THE WITNESS: That is very close, very close. What I said was that they will drive people out of the parks and people will go into the Loop.

MR. FORAN: Your Honor—

THE COURT: The answer is not responsive. Therefore I must strike it.

THE WITNESS: I heard Mr. Oklepek testify to that but it is not a fact. There was something said that he—

MR. FORAN: You did tell people at that time at that meeting that if the police kept the demonstrators in the park and they couldn't get out, that you had an easy solution for it, just riot. That's what you said, didn't you?

THE WITNESS: I have never in all my life said that to riot was an easy solution to anything, ever.

MR. FORAN: And you sat here in this courtroom and you heard Officer Bock and Dwayne Oklepek and Officer Frapolly testify to all of these things, didn't you?

THE WITNESS: I listened to your spies testify about us, yes, sir, and it was a disgrace to me.

MR. FORAN: And isn't it a fact that you structured your testimony sitting at that table—

THE WITNESS: The answer is no.

MR. FORAN: —on direct examination to appear similar to the testimony of the Government's witnesses but to differ in small essentials because you wanted to lend credibility to your testimony? That is a fact, isn't it?

THE WITNESS: It is not a fact and you know it.

MR. FORAN: May we strike that, your Honor. He whispered to the court reporter "and you know it."

THE COURT: Is that what you told the reporter at the end of your answer to the question?

THE WITNESS: No, I made that man to man to Mr. Foran.

MR. FORAN: Your Honor, a lawyer in court is unable to comment on his personal opinions concerning a witness and because of that reason I ask the jury be instructed to disregard Mr. Davis' comment because I cannot properly respond to it.

THE COURT: "And you know it," to Mr. Foran, words to that effect may go out, and the jury is directed to disregard them.

THE WITNESS: I hope after this trial you can properly respond, Mr. Foran. I really do. I hope we have that chance.

MR. FORAN: I don't know what he is—what are you—

THE WITNESS: That you and I can sit down and talk about what happened in Chicago and why it happened.

THE COURT: Mr. Witness—

THE WITNESS: I would like to do that very much.

THE COURT: Mr. Witness—

MR. FORAN: Your Honor—

THE COURT: Do you hear me, sir?

THE WITNESS: Yes, I do.

THE COURT: You didn't—

THE WITNESS: I am sorry.

THE COURT: You paid no attention to me.

I direct you not to make any volunteered observations. I have made this order several times during your testimony.

THE WITNESS: I apologize.

THE COURT: I do not accept your apology, sir.

January 27, 1970

MR. FORAN: You and your people wanted to have violence in Lincoln Park, didn't you?

THE WITNESS: No, sir. We wanted to avoid violence.

MR. FORAN: You wanted it for one purpose. You wanted it for the purpose of discrediting the Government of the United States, isn't that correct?

THE WITNESS: I wanted to discredit the Government's policies by bringing a half million Americans to Chicago at the time of the Convention.

MR. FORAN: Have you ever said that you came to Chicago to display a growing militant defiance of the authority of the government?

THE WITNESS: I don't recall saying that.

MR. FORAN: Could you have said it?

THE WITNESS: Well, that would be out of context. I would talk about the war. I would talk about racism.

MR. FORAN: Have you ever said it in context or out of context?

THE WITNESS: But the context is all-important, don't you see? It is most important.

MR. FORAN: Not in a statement like that. Have you ever said that?

THE WITNESS: Show me the document.

MR. FORAN: I am asking you a question. I want you to tell me.

THE WITNESS: I don't recall ever saying that.

MR. FORAN: And you wanted violence at the International Amphitheatre also, didn't you?

THE WITNESS: Just the opposite.

MR. FORAN: Isn't it a fact that you wanted violence in order to impose an international humiliation on the people who ruled this country? Isn't that a fact?

THE WITNESS: It is my belief that it was you wanted the violence, Mr. Foran, not me.

MR. FORAN: Your Honor, may that be stricken, and may I have the question answered?

THE COURT: Certainly, the statement may go out. The witness is directed to be careful about his answers. Please read the question for the witness.

(question read)

THE WITNESS: I did not want violence, Mr. Foran.

MR. FORAN: You did want to impose an international humiliation on the people who ruled this country, isn't that correct?

THE WITNESS: I am afraid that our government has already humiliated itself in the world community, sir.

MR. FORAN: Now, you had another alternative to the march to the Amphitheatre, didn't you?

THE WITNESS: Yes, sir.

MR. FORAN: And that was for people who didn't want to march to drift away in small groups from the Bandshell and return to the hotel areas in the Loop.

THE WITNESS: That is right.

MR. FORAN: And it was planned, wasn't it, that they were to come back to the Hilton Hotel in force and cause a violent confrontation with the police, wasn't it?

THE WITNESS: No, of course not.

MR. FORAN: Was the objective of the second alternative to paralyze the "magnificent mile" of Michigan Avenue?

THE WITNESS: No, that is a Government theory, a Government theory to try to figure out and explain away what happened in Chicago.

MR. FORAN: You have actually stated, haven't you, that all of those things I have been asking you about were the things that you accomplished in Chicago, haven't you?

THE WITNESS: You mean violent confrontations and tearing up the city and—

MR. FORAN: That the purpose of your meeting in Chicago was to impose an international humiliation on the people who rule this country, to display a growing militant defiance of the authority of the Government, to paralyze the "magnificent mile" of Michigan Avenue. You have said all of those things, haven't you, that that was your purpose in coming to Chicago and that you achieved it?

THE WITNESS: No, I never indicated that that was our purpose in coming to Chicago.

MR. FORAN: Did you ever write a document, coauthor one with Tom Hayden, called "Politics After Chicago?"

THE WITNESS: I may have.

MR. FORAN: I show you Government's Exhibit No. 104 for identification and ask you if that is a copy of it.

THE WITNESS: Yes. You have butchered the context, just as I suspected.

MR. FORAN: Now, have you and Mr. Hayden stated in this "Politics After Chicago" that since the institutions of this country cannot be changed from within, the people will take to the streets? Have you stated that?

THE WITNESS: Yes. I wish you would read the whole context.

MR. FORAN: You have stated that, have you not?

THE WITNESS: Yes.

MR. FORAN: You have stated "We learned in Chicago what it means to declare that the streets belong to the people."

THE WITNESS: Yes.

MR. FORAN: Did you state that the battle line is no longer drawn in the obscure paddies of Vietnam or the dim ghetto streets, but is coming closer to suburban sanctuaries and corporate board rooms? The gas that fell on us in Chicago also fell on Hubert? The street that was paralyzed was the "magnificent mile" of Michigan Avenue?

THE WITNESS: Yes. That is quite different from what you said before.

MR. FORAN: Did you state this:

"Our strategic purpose is two-fold: To display a growing militant defiance of the authority of the Government."

Did you state that?

THE WITNESS: It is possible. Read the whole document.

MR. FORAN: You stated that, didn't you?

THE WITNESS: Why don't you read the whole document or give it to the jury?

MR. FORAN: You have stated that your program is to discredit the authority of the Government which is deaf to its own system and railroad an election through America as if Vietnam were the caboose?

THE WITNESS: Boy, that's right on.

MR. FORAN: You stated that, did you not, that you wanted to discredit the authority of a Government which is deaf to its own citizens?

THE WITNESS: Well, I embrace those words. I don't know if I said them, but those words are just right.

MR. FORAN: And you believe that you won what you called the Battle of Chicago, don't you?

THE WITNESS: What do you mean by the Battle of Chicago?

MR. FORAN: Have you ever called what occurred in Chicago during the Convention the Battle of Chicago?

THE WITNESS: Yes, and I have defined it and I wonder if you would let me define it here. I will be happy to answer the question.

MR. FORAN: Have you ever stated in the words that I have asked you, "We won the Battle of Chicago"? Have you ever said that in any context?

THE WITNESS: You are not interested in the context, I suppose.

MR. FORAN: In any context, Mr. Davis.

THE WITNESS: Yes, I believe we won the battle in Chicago.

MR. FORAN: That you—it was your—your program would include press conferences, disruptions and pickets dramatizing whatever demands you wanted?

THE WITNESS: May I see the context so we can clarify it?

MR. FORAN: I show you Government's Exhibit No. 99. It starts at the top.

THE WITNESS: Yes. I was right.

MR. FORAN: Now, you feel that the Battle of Chicago continues, don't you?

THE WITNESS: Yes, I believe that contest that will shape the political character in the next decade was really shaped in Chicago in the context between the Daleys and the Nixons, and the Hayakawas, and the Reagans and the young people who expressed their hopes in the streets in Chicago. And I think, frankly, in that context, it is going to be clear it is not the Daleys, or the Humphreys, or the Johnsons who are the future of this country. We are the future of this country.

MR. FORAN: Isn't it a fact that you have said, Mr. Davis, that the Battle of Chicago continues today. The war is on. The reason we are here tonight is to try to figure out how we are going to get the kind of mutiny that Company A started in South Vietnam and spread it to every army base, every high school, every community in this country. That is what you said about the Battle of Chicago continuing today, isn't it?

THE WITNESS: Young people in South Vietnam—

MR. FORAN: Haven't you said just exactly what I read to you, sir?

MR. WEINGLASS: Your Honor, could we have the date of that statement?

THE COURT: Certainly, if you have the date, give it to him.

THE WITNESS: August 28, 1969.

MR. FORAN: On the one year anniversary of what happened on Wednesday, August 28, 1968?

THE WITNESS: A year after the Convention.

MR. FORAN: Isn't it a fact that you have said, "If we go about our own work, and if we make it clear that there can be no peace in the United States until every soldier is brought out of Vietnam and this imperialistic system is destroyed." Have you said that?

THE WITNESS: I don't recall those exact words, but those certainly are my sentiments, that we should not rest until this war is over and until the system—

MR. FORAN: And until this imperialistic system is destroyed?

THE WITNESS: Until the system that made that war is changed, the foreign policy—

MR. FORAN: The way you decided to continue the Battle of Chicago, the way you decided to fight the Battle of Chicago, was by incitement to riot, wasn't it?

THE WITNESS: No, sir, by organizing, by organizing within the army, within high schools, within factories and communities across this country.

MR. FORAN: By inciting to riot within high schools, and within colleges, and within factories, and within the army, isn't that right, sir?

THE WITNESS: No. No, sir. No, I am trying to find a way that this generation can make this country something better than what it has been.

MR. FORAN: Your Honor, he is no longer responding to the question.

THE COURT: I strike the answer of the witness and direct the jury to disregard it.

MR. FORAN: And what you want to urge young people to do is to revolt, isn't that right?

THE WITNESS: Yes, revolt.

MR. FORAN: And you have stated, have you not, "That there can be no question by the time that I am through that I have every intention of urging that you revolt, that you join the Movement, that you become a part of a growing force for insurrection in the United States"? You have said that, haven't you?

THE WITNESS: I was standing right next to Fred Hampton when I said that, who was murdered in this city by policemen.

MR. FORAN: Your Honor, I move to strike that.

THE COURT: Yes, the answer may certainly go out. The question is wholly unrelated to one Fred Hampton.

MR. FORAN: Wouldn't it be wonderful, your Honor, if the United States accused people of murder as these people do without proof, without trial, and without any kind of evidence having been presented in any kind of a decent situation?

MR. KUNSTLER: A man is murdered in his bed, while he is sleeping, by the police.

MR. FORAN: With nineteen guns there.

THE COURT: I am trying this case. I will ask you, Mr. Kunstler, to make no reference to that case because it is not in issue here.

MR. FORAN: In Downers Grove on August 30, you told all of the people out there, "We have won America." Didn't you tell them that? Didn't you tell them that?

THE WITNESS: I believe that I said—

MR. FORAN: Didn't you say that to them out at Downers Grove, sir?

THE WITNESS: Yes, sir, I did.

MR. FORAN: I have no further cross-examination.

THE COURT: Redirect examination.

MR. WEINGLASS: Redirect is unnecessary, your Honor.

(witness excused)

THE COURT: Call your next witness.

Three of the defendants have gone out.

MR. KUNSTLER: They are bringing him in.

THE COURT: Oh, it takes three to bring the next witness in?

MR. KUNSTLER: No, but he likes company.

Testimony of Norman Mailer

MR. KUNSTLER: Would you state your full name, please?

THE WITNESS: Norman Mailer is my full name. I was born Norman Kingsley Mailer, but I don't use the middle name.

MR. KUNSTLER: Would you state, Mr. Mailer, what your occupation is?

THE WITNESS: I am a writer.

MR. KUNSTLER: I show you D-344 for identification and ask you if you can identify this book.

THE WITNESS: This is a book written by me about the march on the Pentagon and its title is *The Armies of the Night*.

MR. KUNSTLER: Can you state whether or not this book won the Pulitzer Prize?

THE WITNESS: It did.

MR. SCHULTZ: Objection.

THE COURT: I sustain the objection. I strike the witness' answer and I direct the jury to disregard it.

MR. KUNSTLER: Can you state what awards this book has won?

THE WITNESS: The book was awarded the National Book Award and the Pulitzer Prize in 1969.

MR. KUNSTLER: I call your attention, Mr. Mailer, to—let me withdraw that.

Did you have a conversation with Jerry Rubin after the Pentagon?

THE WITNESS: Yes, I did in December in my home. I had called Mr. Rubin and asked him to see me because I was writing an account of the march on the Pentagon. I was getting in touch with those principals whom I could locate. Mr. Rubin was, if you will, my best witness. We talked about the details of the march on the Pentagon for hours. We went into great detail about many aspects of it. And in this period I formed a very good opinion of Mr. Rubin because he had extraordinary powers of objectivity which an author is greatly in need of when he is talking to witnesses.

MR. SCHULTZ: Your Honor—Mr. Mailer—

THE COURT: I will have to strike the witness' answer and direct the jury to disregard every word of it.

MR. SCHULTZ: Your Honor, would you instruct Mr. Mailer even though he can't use all of the adjectives which he uses in his work, he should say "he said" and "I said," or if he wants to embellish that, then "I stated" and "he stated." But that's the way it is related before a jury.

THE COURT: We are simple folk here. All you have to do is say "he said", if anything, "I said," if anything, and if your wife said something, you may say what she said.

I strike the witness' answer, as I say, and I direct the jury to disregard it.

MR. KUNSTLER: Now, was anything said in the conversation about what happened at the Pentagon?

THE WITNESS: Mr. Rubin went in to considerable detail about his view of the American military effort in Vietnam and the structure of the military and industrial establishment in America, and it was in Mr. Rubin's view—

MR. SCHULTZ: Your Honor, could he state what Mr. Rubin said relating to what he observed at the Pentagon?

THE WITNESS: This is Mr. Rubin's view. Mr. Rubin said it was his view, Counselor, he said that military-industrial establishment was so full of guilt and so horrified secretly at what they were doing in Vietnam that they were ready to crack at the smallest sort of provocation, and that the main idea in the move on the Pentagon was to exacerbate their sense of authority and control.

MR. KUNSTLER: Mr. Mailer, was anything said about Chicago in this conversation?

THE WITNESS: Yes. Mr. Rubin said that he was at present working fulltime on plans to have a youth festival in Chicago in August of 1968 when the Democratic Convention would take place and it was his idea that the presence of a hundred thousand young people in Chicago at a festival with rock bands would so intimidate and terrify the establishment that Lyndon Johnson would have to be nominated under armed guard.

And I said, "Wow."

I was overtaken with the audacity of the idea and I said, "It's a beautiful and frightening idea."

And Rubin said, "I think that the beauty of it is that the establishment is going to do it all themselves. We won't do a thing. We are just going to be there and they won't be able to take it. They will smash the city themselves. They will provoke all the violence."

And I said, "I think you're right, but I have to admit to you that I'm scared at the thought of it. It is really something."

And he said, "It is. I am going to devote full time to it."

I said, "You're a brave man."

MR. KUNSTLER: Now did you go to Chicago?

THE WITNESS: Yes.

MR. KUNSTLER: I call your attention to approximately 5:00 P.M. on August 27, 1968. Do you know where you were then?

THE WITNESS: Yes. I was in my hotel room with Robert Lowell and David Dellinger and Rennie Davis.

MR. KUNSTLER: Would you state what was said during that conversation?

THE WITNESS: The conversation was about the possibility of violence on a march that was being proposed to the Amphitheatre.

Mr. Lowell and I were a little worried about it because we were McCarthy supporters and we felt that if there was a lot of violence it was going to wash out McCarthy's last remote chance of being nominated.

And Mr. Dellinger said to me, "Look, you know my record, you know I've never had anything to do with violence." He said, "And you know that we have not been the violent ones. For every policeman that has been called a pig, those police have broken five and ten heads. You know that I never move toward anything that will result in violence," he said, "but at the same time I am not going to avoid all activity which could possible result in violence because if we do that, we'll be able to protest nothing at all. We are trying at this very moment to get a permit. We are hoping we get the permit, but if they don't give it to us, we'll probably march anyway because we have to: it's why we're here. We're here to oppose the war in Vietnam and we don't protest it if we stay in our rooms and don't go out to protest it."

He then asked me to speak at Grant Park the next day.

MR. KUNSTLER: Did you accept that invitation?

THE WITNESS: No, I didn't. I said I was there to cover the Convention for *Harper's Magazine,* and I felt that I did not want to get involved because if I did and got arrested, I would not be able to write my piece in time for the deadline, and I was really very concerned about not getting arrested, and losing three, or four, or five days because I had eighteen days in which to write the piece, and I knew it was going to be a long piece.

MR. KUNSTLER: I call your attention to the next day, Wednesday, the twenty-eighth of August, between 3:30 and 4:00 P.M. approximately. Do you know where you were then?

THE WITNESS: Yes, I was in Grant Park. I felt ashamed of myself for not speaking, and I, therefore, went up to the platform and I asked Mr. Dellinger if I could speak, and he then very happily said, "Yes, of course."

MR. KUNSTLER: Can you state what you did say on Wednesday in Grant Park?

THE WITNESS: I merely said to the people who were there that I thought they were possessed of beauty, and that I was not going to march with them because I had to write this piece. And they all said, "Write, Baby." That is what they said from the crowd.

MR. KUNSTLER: Now, Mr. Mailer, I call your attention to Thursday, August 29, did you give another speech that day?

THE WITNESS: Yes, that was in Grant Park on Thursday morning, two or three in the morning.

MR. KUNSTLER: Do you recall what you said?

THE WITNESS: Yes. That was—

MR. SCHULTZ: Objection. What he said is not relevant. What he said at the Bandshell where the Bandshell performance was sponsored by the defendants, that is one thing, but where he makes an independent statement—

THE COURT: There hasn't been a proper foundation for the question.

MR. KUNSTLER: I will ask one question.

THE COURT: I sustain the objection.

MR. KUNSTLER: Mr. Mailer, at the time you spoke, did you see any of the defendants at this table in the vicinity?

THE WITNESS: No, I don't think so.

MR. KUNSTLER: Then I have no further questions.

THE COURT: Is there any cross-examination?

• • • • •

MR. SCHULTZ: A few questions, your Honor.

Mr. Mailer, when you had your conversation with Rubin at your home, did Rubin tell you that the presence of a hundred thousand young people would so intimidate the establishment that Johnson would have to call out the troops and National Guard?

THE WITNESS: He did not use the word intimidate, as I recollect.

MR. SCHULTZ: Did he say that the presence of these people will provoke the establishment and the establishment will smash the city themselves?

THE WITNESS: That was the substance of what he said, yes.

MR. SCHULTZ: All right. Now at your speech in Grant Park, didn't you say that we are at the beginning of a war which would continue for twenty years and the march today would be one battle in that war?

THE WITNESS: Yes, I said that.

MR. SCHULTZ: But you couldn't go on the march because you had a deadline?

THE WITNESS: Yes. I was in a moral quandary. I didn't know if I was being scared or being professional and I was naturally quite upset because a man never likes to know that his motive might be simple fear.

THE COURT: I thought you said you had to do that piece.

THE WITNESS: I did have to do the piece, your Honor, but I just wasn't sure in my own mind whether I was hiding behind the piece or whether I was being professional to avoid temptation.

MR. SCHULTZ: Did you tell the crowd, Mr. Mailer, at the Bandshell, "You have to be beautiful. You are much better than you were at the Pentagon?" Did you tell them that?

THE WITNESS: Yes. I remember saying that.

MR. SCHULTZ: You were talking about their physical appearance rather than their actions?

THE WITNESS: That is right. To my amazement these militant activities seemed to improve their physique and their features.

MR. SCHULTZ: I have no further questions.

THE COURT: Is there any redirect examination?

MR. KUNSTLER: Could you state if Rubin didn't use the word "intimidate" as you have answered Mr. Schultz, what word he did use? What was his language?

THE WITNESS: It would be impossible for me to begin to remember whether Mr. Rubin used the word "intimidate" or not. I suspect that he probably did not use it because it is not his habitual style of speech. He would speak more of diverting, demoralizing the establishment, freaking them out, bending their mind, driving them out of their bird.

I use the word "intimidate" because possibly since I am a bully by nature, I tend to think in terms of intimidation, but I don't think Mr. Rubin does. He thinks in terms of catalysm, of having people reveal their own guilt, their own evil.

His whole notion was that the innocent presence of one hundred thousand people in Chicago would be intolerable for a man as guilt-ridden as Lyndon Johnson. When this conversation took place, Lyndon Johnson was still President and the war in Vietnam gave no sign of ever being diminished in its force and its waste.

MR. KUNSTLER: I have no further questions.

January 28, 1970

MR. SCHULTZ: Your Honor, before the jury comes out, the Government has a matter which it would like to bring to your Honor's attention.

Former Attorney General of the United States, Ramsey Clark, has been subpoenaed by the defense. The former Attorney General was interviewed on Sunday by two defendants and two defense counsel. One of the attorneys who is currently employed with the Department of Justice was present at the interview at Mr. Clark's request.

In the presence of Daniel Murrell, of the Department of Justice, it was discussed what the Attorney General would testify about.

I have spoken with Mr. Murrell, I have read his memorandum of the interview of the meeting, and I would like at this time, before the Attorney General is called in the presence of the jury, first to—well, I'd like your Honor to make a determination of whether or not anything that he has is admissible.*

Normally we wouldn't make such a request, but throughout this trial, Mr. Kunstler and Mr. Weinglass have argued the answers that they are trying to elicit when your Honor has already sustained an objection to the answers. I would like to point out that the Code of Federal Regulations is involved here because it says:

"That no employee or former employee of the Department of Justice shall in response to a demand of a court produce any material contained in the files of the Department of Justice or disclose any information or produce any material acquired as a part of the performance of his official duties without the prior approval of the Attorney General."

That would obviously mean Attorney General Mitchell.

In any event, your Honor, it is our contention that the Attorney General can contribute nothing to this case, everything that he would testify to would be inadmissible because it is not probative, or that it is hearsay.

If you think that there is a reason to believe that none of his testimony would be admissible, I would ask the Court to have him take the stand out of the presence of the jury and let the defendants ask him questions out of the presence of the jury, and the Court can make a determination.

THE COURT: That is one of the ways an offer of proof can be made, by the question and answer method.

MR. SCHULTZ: Yes. Considering that this is the former Attorney General of the United States of America, a very important person, if they try to create impressions with this man before the jury that are erroneous because the questions are improper, they will have seriously prejudiced the Government's case—

I wish Davis, who was such a gentle boy on the stand for the last couple of days, smiling at the jury and pretending he was just the little boy next door, would stop whispering and talking to me while I am talking.

MR. DAVIS: You are a disgrace, sir. I say you are a disgrace. I really say you are a disgrace.

VOICES: Yes, yes.

MR. SCHULTZ: I think he has a split personality, like a schizophrenic.

MR. WEINER: Now he is a psychology student.

THE COURT: Who will reply for the defendants?

MR. KUNSTLER: I will, your Honor.

The argument of Mr. Schultz is the first time that I have ever heard, and I think it is probably the first time in the history of the United States, that an attempt has been made to prevent a witness from taking the stand who himself does not raise any objection.

When a private citizen of the United States, which is what Mr. Clark is, has accepted a subpoena and has stated—

THE COURT: May I interrupt to ask this question?

You remarked that Mr. Clark is a private citizen, and that is true, but does not the regulation referred to by Mr. Schultz refer to former employees of the Government?

MR. KUNSTLER: But that is inapplicable, your Honor, if a former employee of the Government is called to the stand to be asked questions such as "Did you call the Mayor of Chicago, and as a result of that call, did Mr. Wilkins go to Chicago?" Perfectly proper questions, I think, under any interpretation of the rule of evidence. That is not what is covered by the regulation which Mr. Schultz read to you.

If the regulation were interpreted as Mr. Schultz obviously would like it interpreted, this would mean, that nobody in the Federal Government could ever testify after leaving the Federal Government.

I think it would breach every rule and every element of due process of law and fairness if a witness called by the defendant were not permitted to take the stand and be interrogated, subject to any objection which the Government may raise. What they are trying here, is to prevent the jury from ever knowing that a former Attorney General of the United States is here and ready to testify.

THE COURT: Is it not discretionary with the Court as to whether or not a witness may be brought to the witness stand—

MR. KUNSTLER: Absolutely not. In a criminal proceeding, where a defendant's liberty is at stake, he has the absolute right to bring anyone to that stand he wishes, and the only thing that can stop a person from testifying on that stand is if he, himself, moves the Court to quash his subpoena, as J. Edgar Hoover did, and then have the Court grant the motion to quash.

Mr. Clark is a friendly witness. He wants to testify for the defense. The Attorney General's stand and involvement in this is important to us to get to the jury. If they never see him and never know, then we will have been denied fundamental due process of law in that a witness called by the defense will have been prevented from taking the stand. That, to me, is a gross violation of the Constitution of the United States.

MR. SCHULTZ: Your Honor, may I reply?

THE COURT: Yes, you may.

MR. SCHULTZ: They say that he is anxious to testify for them. Mr. Kunstler has misrepresented the Attorney General. The Attorney General didn't say that at all.

He said that he didn't think his testimony was relevant or admissible, but if it was, he said he wanted to testify because he didn't want to withhold valuable evidence for either the prosecution or the defense. That is what he said, but Mr. Kunstler wants to make it appear here that we are trying to hold something back simply because Mr. Kunstler is going to play around with the rules of evidence.

Now Mr. Kunstler didn't mention to you the fact that he wants to ask the Attorney General in the presence of the jury about electronic eavesdropping or about the constitutionality of the statute, or about the conversations in the Oval Room with the President of the United States.

Instead, he limited it to a telephone call so that he could con your Honor into getting the Attorney General out here and then start one of his tirades.

They want to get him here to pull the stunt in front of the jury, and we are objecting to it. They are not going to stand here and ask that man improper questions as they have done with other witnesses—knowing their conduct is contumacious, but not caring—willing to practice the civil disobedience that their clients participated in to prove to their clients that they are in the fold, they are in the Movement.

MR. DAVIS: Outrageous.

MR. SCHULTZ: We are not asking your Honor solely because of the regulation. We are asking your Honor to do this because the testimony is simply not admissible.

THE COURT: It is the Court's view that during the course of this trial the defendants have attempted to inject irrelevant and extraneous evidence despite repeated rulings prohibiting such evidence. The experience with the mayor's testimony was that he was called with much fanfare but was able to give virtually no evidence that was material to this case.

While the defendants have a right to compulsory process to obtain witnesses in their behalf under the Sixth Amendment, the determination of whether or not to allow a witness to take the stand is a matter within the discretion of the trial judge. Thus, the Court is justified in requiring the defense to demonstrate by voir dire questions of the witness, the testimony it expects to elicit from him.

THE COURT: Will you call your witness?

MR. KUNSTLER: Your Honor, we are going to do this under protest. We believe it is a process to screen a witness prior to his testimony, and we think it is grossly unconstitutional.

Testimony of William Ramsey Clark

MR. KUNSTLER: Would you state your full name?

THE WITNESS: William Ramsey Clark.

MR. KUNSTLER: Mr. Clark, what is your occupation?

THE WITNESS: I am a lawyer.

MR. KUNSTLER: What was your occupation in July and August of 1968?

THE WITNESS: I was Attorney General of the United States.

MR. KUNSTLER: Now, Mr. Clark, do you know Wesley Pomeroy?

THE WITNESS: Yes, I do. He was Special Assistant for Law Enforcement Coordination to the Attorney General.

MR. KUNSTLER: Do you know Roger Wilkins?

THE WITNESS: Yes, I do. He was the Director of the Community Relations Service.

MR. KUNSTLER: Do you know where Mr. Wilkins was with relation to the Democratic National Convention?

THE WITNESS: Well, I know that he was in Chicago from time to time in July and August of 1968.

MR. KUNSTLER: Did there come a time when he made a report to you of a trip he had made to Chicago?

THE WITNESS: He made a number of oral reports, and he filed or sent me one memorandum that I am aware of at this time.

MR. KUNSTLER: I will show you D-316 for identification and ask you if that is the written report which he made to you.

THE WITNESS: This appears to be a copy of the written report.

MR. KUNSTLER: Now as a result of receiving the full report, did you have an occasion to call anyone in Chicago?

THE WITNESS: My recollection is that after reading that report and discussing it with Mr. Wilkins, I called Mayor Daley.

MR. KUNSTLER: Without revealing the subject matter of that conversation do you know what Mr. Wilkins did after you had made that call?

THE WITNESS: He came to Chicago and met with Mayor Daley.

MR. KUNSTLER: Now, Mr. Clark, getting back to the conversation with Mayor Daley would you state what that conversation was, what you said and what Mayor Daley said?

THE COURT: I interrupt you, if I may, before the witness replies. I take it the United States Attorneys are omitting to indicate objections for that reason.

MR. SCHULTZ: Your Honor, no, not exactly.

Many of the questions that he has asked, if they were asked in front of the jury, such as this last one, would have been objected to. We are not objecting to many of them now.

We will, however, begin to object if Mr. Kunstler begins to ask former Attorney General about security matters.

THE COURT: Read the question then to the witness, please.

THE WITNESS: Yes, I called Mayor Daley to ask him to meet with Roger Wilkins and Wes Pomeroy. I suggested that he have Superintendent Conlisk of the Chicago police there and described the purpose of their visit as an interchange of information and ideas.

MR. KUNSTLER: All right. Now, after Mr. Wilkins and Mr. Pomeroy met with the Mayor on July 25, 1968, did one or both report back to you as to the results of that meeting?

THE WITNESS: I think that Mr. Wilkins reported back to me shortly after. He said that, you know, roughly, the meeting was not very satisfactory, that he didn't feel that we were likely to get the cooperation that we hoped for and that the attitude from the mayor's office didn't seem conciliatory.

MR. KUNSTLER: Now, did Mr. Wilkins indicate to you what the attitude of Rennie Davis or any other members of the demonstrator groups in Chicago had been?

THE WITNESS: Well, he gave me his opinion of—particularly Rennie Davis, and I guess you'd say he was impressed, he was favorably impressed with him as being a sincere young person.

MR. KUNSTLER: Now, General Clark, I call your attention to 11:50 A.M. on August 20, 1968. Do you recall receiving a telephone call that day?

THE WITNESS: Yes. I received a call from President Johnson at that time.

MR. KUNSTLER: Will you state what President Johnson said to you and what you said to him?

MR. SCHULTZ: Well, your Honor, at this point I do object. I think that a cabinet officer does not have to and should not have to relate a private telephone call that he had with the President of the United States, especially when it is hearsay in this court.

THE COURT: Do you object to the question?

MR. SCHULTZ: Yes.

THE COURT: I sustain the objection.

MR. KUNSTLER: Your Honor, this is voir dire. I thought objections were reserved.

THE COURT: Well, the question is so clearly invalid, it would not in any circumstances be permitted if the witness were to be called before the jury. I sustain the objection.

MR. KUNSTLER: Now, I call your attention, General Clark, to the next day, to August 21, 1968. Did you have occasion to be in the Oval Room of the White House on that day?

THE WITNESS: That day or within a day or two, yes. Probably that day.

MR. KUNSTLER: Who was present in the Oval Room at that time?

THE WITNESS: The President was there. I was there. There were two presidential assistants there, and there were two representatives from the Department of Defense.

MR. KUNSTLER: At that time did you make certain recommendations to the President of the United States?

MR. SCHULTZ: Objection, your Honor. This falls within security matters.

MR. KUNSTLER: Your Honor, we are not asking for subject matter, merely that he did make recommendations.

THE COURT: I sustain the objection.

MR. KUNSTLER: Now as a result of that meeting in the Oval Room of the White House, did the President make a decision?

THE WITNESS: The President made a decision, and I assume that the discussion in the Oval Room contributed to it.

MR. KUNSTLER: Now, General Clark, did the President's decision adopt the position you had taken in the Oval Room—

MR. SCHULTZ: Objection.

MR. KUNSTLER: —on August 21 to 22?

THE COURT: Sustain the objection.

MR. KUNSTLER: I don't even want the conversation. I merely want him to state whether the President agreed with him or not.

THE COURT: I will let my ruling stand.

MR. KUNSTLER: Now, as a result of the President's decision, do you know what, if any, action was taken with reference to Federal troops?

THE WITNESS: Yes. There were Federal troops pre-positioned in the Chicago area before the beginning of the Democratic National Convention. I believe they were flown in from quite some distance, probably Fort Hood or Fort Sill.

MR. KUNSTLER: Do you know yourself whether the Department of Defense approved or disapproved the decision to pre-position federal troops?

MR. SCHULTZ: Objection.

THE COURT: I sustain the objection.

MR. KUNSTLER: Do you know how many, if you do know, troops were involved in this particular pre-positioning?

THE WITNESS: The initial figure in these things—they seem to tend to enlarge—was 5,000. Now whether it went beyond that, I don't recall.

MR. KUNSTLER: Now, in your opinion, General Clark, was this pre-positioning of Federal troops necessary in the Chicago area?

MR. SCHULTZ: Objection.

MR. KUNSTLER: General Clark, in the Code of Federal Regulations, and refer you particularly to Section 16.12, can you state what in your opinion Regulation 16.12 or any of the others in Part B prohibit an Attorney General from testifying to when properly sub-poenaed to appear in a Federal court?

THE WITNESS: The regulations that we have here are revisions that were undertaken while I was in office. The purpose is essentially to keep confidential those things that in the public interest should be confidential.

When an FBI file, as an illustration, is subpoenaed, and someone is asked to bring it with him and testify from it, generally we would wire the court permission.

As far as I remember, it always had to do with documents.

MR. KUNSTLER: And do you feel as a former Attorney General of the United States that your testifying in this court, would violate that Federal regulation?

MR. SCHULTZ: I object to the question.

THE COURT: For him to answer that question, even though he formerly held an office much higher than mine, he would be invading the province in the authority of the Court. It is not for a former Attorney General to interpret the statute.

I sustain the objection.

MR. KUNSTLER: Now, General Clark, I call your attention to August 30, 1968, and ask you if you can recall a telephone call to Thomas Foran, the United States Attorney for the Northern District of Illinois?

THE WITNESS: Yes, my notes show that I talked with Tom Foran on that day. I told him that we wanted to investigate the occurrences during that week concerning the National Convention in the manner that we had developed the investigation of civil rights cases, which is essentially through lawyers as distinguished from a grand jury, and that that was the way that we would proceed in this situation.

MR. KUNSTLER: General Clark, was it your understanding or your intention that the events surrounding the Democratic National Convention were to be investigated without the convening of a grand jury?

MR. SCHULTZ: Objection.

THE COURT: I sustain the objection.

MR. KUNSTLER: I have no further questions, your Honor.

MR. SCHULTZ: I have no questions, your Honor.

I have been making notes of the questions that were asked. The Attorney General's testimony would be cumulative on the things that would be admissible, and, the remaining things are either hearsay, or they are just wholly immaterial for all of the reasons I have stated. Your Honor, we ask that the Court not permit the former Attorney General of the United States to appear before the jury because he cannot present to them any testimony which would assist them in making a determination of guilt or innocence in this case. The only way that the Attorney General could in any way assist the defendants in this case is to have the prestige of having the Attorney General testify as their witness. Now that can't be done. A witness is put on the stand not for his prestige, but for what he can lend evidentiary-wise to the case. The Attorney General cannot lend anything to the case for the reasons that I have stated, and we, therefore, object to his testifying in this case.

THE COURT: You may reply, Mr. Kunstler.

MR. KUNSTLER: There is a remedy available to anyone who wishes to quash a sub-poena. This witness, the former Attorney General, has not utilized that method. He appeared here willing to testify under subpoena. There is relevant testimony here. The doubts are to be resolved in favor of the defendants. What we are concerned with here is a crime of intent. Evaluation by the highest law enforcement officer in the nation of what was happening in Chicago, whether it was overreacting, whether there was a superabundance of military force in this city, and all of those aspects, certainly goes to the relevance of the indictment against these defendants.

If he cannot testify to these things subject to all the regular objections provided by the rules of evidence, they will have been cut off from a source of pertinent testimony.

THE COURT: Let me say this, gentlemen. When this matter was presented to me, I had the strong feeling that this witness could not testify to anything material or relevant. I had that strong feeling. I have given the defendants every opportunity here to demonstrate that this witness could make a relevant or material contribution. They have failed to so demonstrate. I therefore sustain the objection of the Government to having the defense call this witness, Attorney General Clark, before the jury, and I also order both counsel for the Government and the defense not to refer to this hearing or the subject matter thereof before the jury after the jury is brought in.

Thank you, sir.

(witness excused)

MR. KUNSTLER: Your Honor, can we have the jury instructed that we had called the Attorney General of the United States but that for legal reasons decided by the Court he was not permitted to testify?

THE COURT: No, that motion will be denied.

MR. KUNSTLER: Your Honor, can't they even know he was here?

MR. SCHULTZ: Your Honor, if the jury were to know everything we were to start—

THE COURT: I deny the request, Mr. Schultz.

MR. KUNSTLER: Your Honor, we have one more matter out of the presence of the jury.

Your Honor, very briefly, Bobby Seale is now in the building and we were only permitted to have lawyers see him in the lock-up this morning. We are requesting permission because of the fact that there is a conspiracy alleged that we be given permission to meet with him tomorrow early with all defendants present as well as the lawyers. It is utterly impossible to work under the conditions we have now.

THE COURT: I leave that entirely to the Marshal.

But I am not going to have any town meetings with witnesses who are brought here under a writ. You may interview him. You are going to examine him. He is your witness. You say he is here. Put him on, and I request that you put him on soon.

MR. KUNSTLER: The Marshal said that he will leave it to your decision.

THE COURT: I will leave it to him. I assume no responsibility in connection with the custody of defendants, sir.

Testimony of Bobby G. Seale

January 29, 1970

THE COURT: Is the missing witness brought down?
MR. KUNSTLER: Yes.
VOICES: Hey, Bobby! Right on, right on!
THE MARSHAL: Sit down, please.
THE COURT: You are Mr. Bobby Seale?
THE WITNESS: Yes.

(there is laughter in the courtroom)

VOICE: He doesn't know that yet?
THE COURT: Are you about to testify in this matter as a witness?
THE WITNESS: Yes, I am under that assumption.
THE COURT: It is my duty and obligation under the law to inform you that you are under no obligation to testify. You are still under indictment here, and it is your constitutional right here not to testify if you choose not to.
  Do you wish to testify?
THE WITNESS: Yes.
THE COURT: All right.
  Now, Mr. Garry, out of the presence of the jury, I am glad to see you after all of the many months, but I hope your standing at the lectern doesn't mean that you are going to interrogate this witness.
MR. GARRY: That is what it means, your Honor.
MR. SCHULTZ: We object, your Honor.
THE COURT: You are not permitted after all the months. You haven't been here during the more than four months of this trial. Your name was not appended to the petition for a writ of habeas corpus ad testificandum. I must forbid you to examine the witness, Mr. Garry.
MR. GARRY: Then, your Honor, I must respectfully ask the Court that I be permitted to sit next to the witness and advise him of his rights on areas—
THE COURT: I have advised him of his rights. We don't permit lawyers to sit next to a witness. You are too accomplished a trial lawyer not to know that in a trial before a jury, a lawyer may not sit next to a witness.
MR. GARRY: I believe there may be some areas of self-incrimination that may go beyond the area of this trial, and I want to be in a position to protect my client's rights.
THE COURT: I will let you sit at the counsel table there, and if questions are asked that you think are such questions that his answers might incriminate the witness, communicate to Mr. Kunstler or Mr. Weinglass.
MR. GARRY: Very well, your Honor.
THE COURT: Bring in the jury please.
MR. GARRY: May I approach the witness, your Honor?
THE COURT: Yes.

(jury enters)

MR. GARRY: The witness would like to have a glass of water.
THE COURT: Mr. Marshal, will you see that he gets some water. The jury marshal will see that he gets some water.
MR. GARRY: Thank you, your Honor.
THE COURT: Will you swear the witness, Mr. Clerk.

(witness duly sworn)

MR. KUNSTLER: Would you state your full name?
THE WITNESS: Bobby G. Seale.

[501]

MR. KUNSTLER: And, Mr. Seale, what is your occupation?

THE WITNESS: Presently, I am the Chairman of the Black Panther Party.

MR. KUNSTLER: Would you state what is the Black Panther Party for Self-Defense?

THE WITNESS: The Black Panther Party—

MR. SCHULTZ: Objection.

THE COURT: I sustain the objection.

MR. KUNSTLER: Your Honor, every single witness on the stand called by the defense has been entitled to tell what is the organization in which his occupation pertained.

MR. SCHULTZ: We are not litigating the Black Panther Party, your Honor, in this case.

THE COURT: I will let my ruling stand, sir.

MR. KUNSTLER: Mr. Seale, would you state for the Court and jury what your duties are as Chairman of the Black Panther Party?

THE WITNESS: As the Chairman of the Black Panther Party, I am a member of the central committee who have to make speaking engagements, representing the Party's program, the Party's ideology, the social programs that we are setting forth in communities to deal with political, economic, and social evils and injustices that exist in this American society.

I go on a number of speaking engagements. I do quite a bit of coordinating work and direct community organizing in the black community and relate to other organizations whom we have coalitions with. We form alliances and direct these alliances in the same manner that brother Fred Hampton used to do before he was murdered, and we form these alliances with the Young Lords, Puerto Ricans, and also Latino people who are oppressed in America.

MR. KUNSTLER: Mr. Seale, you mentioned the name of Fred Hampton. Who was Fred Hampton?

THE WITNESS: Deputy Chairman—

MR. SCHULTZ: Objection.

THE COURT: I sustain the objection.

MR. SCHULTZ: Your Honor, if you will instruct Mr. Seale that when an objection is pending, he should wait before he answers the question—

THE COURT: Mr. Seale, when an objection is made by the opposing lawyers sitting at that table, wait until the Court decides the objection before you answer, please.

THE WITNESS: Well, should I just give a few seconds to see if there is going to be an objection?

THE COURT: Yes. Wait. It is a good idea.

THE WITNESS: Just to see if there is going to be an objection.

MR. SCHULTZ: I will try to be prompt, your Honor.

MR. KUNSTLER: Mr. Seale, I call your attention to August 27, 1968. Did there come a time when you went to the San Francisco International Airport?

THE WITNESS: Tuesday. That Tuesday in August. It was a Tuesday, I think.

MR. KUNSTLER: Did you then board an airplane?

THE WITNESS: Yes.

MR. KUNSTLER: Do you know the destination of that airplane?

THE WITNESS: Chicago, Illinois.

MR. KUNSTLER: I will ask you now to look at the defense table and I want to ask you this question whether, prior to boarding that airplane, you had ever known Jerry Rubin.

THE WITNESS: No, I had not.

MR. KUNSTLER: David Dellinger?

THE WITNESS: I never seen him before in my life.

MR. KUNSTLER: Abbie Hoffman?

THE WITNESS: I never seen him before in my life before that.

MR. KUNSTLER: Lee Weiner?

THE WITNESS: I never seen him before in my life.

MR. KUNSTLER: Rennie Davis?

THE WITNESS: I never seen him before in my life.

MR. KUNSTLER: Tom Hayden?

THE WITNESS: I had heard of his name but I had never met him or seen him before in my life.

MR. KUNSTLER: John Froines?

THE WITNESS: I never seen him or heard of him before in my life.

MR. KUNSTLER: Can you state to the Court the purpose of your trip to Chicago?

MR. SCHULTZ: Objection, your Honor.

THE COURT: I sustain the objection.

MR. KUNSTLER: Now after you arrived in Chicago on the twenty-seventh of August, did you have occasion at any time later that day to go to Lincoln Park?

THE WITNESS: Yes, it was late in the afternoon.

MR. KUNSTLER: Now when you arrived at Lincoln Park, can you recollect what was going on in the area you went to?

THE WITNESS: The area in the park that I observed was completely occupied by policemen. The park was generally surrounded by policemen, cops everywhere, and many of those who I looked at and observed to be what I would call or define as pigs. This is what I observed, this is the impression, the facts that existed and what I saw. It was just the cops, and I myself defined it as pigs, were piggyback. This is the general way we talk in the ghetto in expressing a lot of these things.

MR. KUNSTLER: Now did there come a time, Mr. Seale, when you spoke in Lincoln Park that afternoon?

THE WITNESS: Yes, there did come a time when I did speak.

MR. KUNSTLER: I show you D-350 for identification, do you think that you could identify for us what it is?

THE WITNESS: This is a transcript from a tape recording of the speech I made there.

MR. KUNSTLER: I will show you 350-B. Is that the tape from which 350 was made?

THE WITNESS: Yes, I can recognize it.

MR. KUNSTLER: Is that tape a fair and accurate reproduction of your speech as you gave it on the afternoon of August 27 in Lincoln Park.

THE WITNESS: Yes, it is, except for the fact that the very first line, about half of the sentence on that tape, the very first line of the first sentence that I pronounced in that speech is not on that tape.

MR. KUNSTLER: With the exception of those first three or four words, it is a fair and accurate representation of the speech?

THE WITNESS: Yes.

MR. KUNSTLER: Then I would offer it into evidence.

MR. SCHULTZ: No objection.

MR. KUNSTLER: Your Honor, before this is played we will furnish to the court reporter, to save her hands, a copy of the speech.

MR. SCHULTZ: No objection.

(tape played)

We've come out to speak to some people who're involved, maybe emotionally and maybe in many respects, in a drastic situation of a developing revolution. The revolution in this country at the time is in fact the people coming forth to demand freedom. The revolution at this time is directly connected with organized guns and force.

We must understand that as we go forth to try and move the scurvy, reprobative pigs: the lynching Lyndon Baines Johnsons, the fat pig Humphreys, the jive double-lip-talkin' Nixons, the slick talkin' McCarthys—these murdering and brutalizing and oppressing people all over the world—when we go forth to deal with them—that they're gonna always send out their racist, scurvy rotten pigs to occupy the people, to occupy the community, just the way they have this park here occupied.

You know the Minister of Information, Eldridge Cleaver, who's been nominated as the Presidential candidate, Black Panther candidate, running on the Peace and Freedom ticket. As you know, the brother always says, "All power to the People."

Now just a second here. You must understand what power is. The Minister of Defense, Huey P. Newton, explains and teaches that power is the ability to defend phenomena and make it act in a desired manner.

What phenomena are we talking about? We're talking about the racist, brutal murders that pigs have committed upon black people. We're talking about lynchings that's been going down for four hundred years on black people's heads. We're talking about the occu-

pation troops, right here in Chicago, occupying the black community and even occupying this park where the people have come forth. The phenomenal situation is this: it's that we have too many hogs in every facet of government that exists in this country. We can define that.

But we said the ability to define this social phenomena and also the ability to make it act in a desired manner. How do you make the social phenomena act in a desired manner? I am saying this here, I'm pretty sure you're quite well aware of how you make it act in a desired manner. If a pig comes up to you and you sit down and start talking about slidin' in, rollin' in, jumpin' in, bugalooin' in, dancin' in, swimmin' in, prayin' in and singing "We Shall Overcome," like a lot of these Toms want us to do—we're jivin'. But if a pig comes up to us and starts swinging a billy club, and you check around and you got your piece—you gotta down that pig in defense of yourself. You gonna take that club, whip him over his head, lay him out on the ground and then this pig is acting in a desired manner. All right.

At the same time, many individuals, many groups will run into situations where the pigs are going to attack. Always. Because the pigs have been sent here by the top hog who gave him orders from the power structure to attack the people.

Now listen here. If you gonna get down to nitty-gritty, brothers and people, and you don't intend to miss no nits and no grits, you got to have some functional organization to not only make one individual pig or a number of pigs act in the desired manner but to make this whole racist, decadent power structure act in a desired manner.

The Black Panther Party went forth when brother Huey P. Newton was busted October the 28. He was charged with making a couple of pigs act in a desired manner. And from there, a coalition between the Peace and Freedom Party, a predominately white group, and the Black Panther Party, a black organization, a revolutionary organization, formed this coalition based on the fact that the white people said they were concerned by the fact that their racist power structure in Oakland in California was going to try to railroad Huey P. Newton to the gas chamber and kill him.

Now this coalition developed into a more functional thing: the Peace and Freedom Party in the white community trying to end the decadent racism, the Black Panthers in the black community trying to convince us we've got to defend ourselves, liberate ourselves from the oppressed conditions that are caused by racism. This coalition has gone forth. We think it's a very functional coalition.

So it's very important that we understand the need for organization, cause that's what we deal with. We're not here to be sitting around a jive table vascillating and jiving ourselves. Too many times in the past, the people sit down around tables. When they sit down around these tables they get to arguing about whether or not this white racist wall that black people are chained against is real or not. They want to come talking about some molecular structure of the wall. And the molecular structure of the wall shows that wall is really ninety percent space. So is the white racist wall that we're talking about real or not? We're saying that it's here. You're damned right it's real. Because we're chained against this wall.

And we say this here: don't be out there jiving, wondering whether the wall is real or not. Make sure if you want to coalesce, work, functionally organize, that you pick up a crowbar. Pick up a piece. Pick up a gun. And pull that spike out from the wall. Because if you pull it on out and if you shoot well, all I'm gonna do is pat you on the back and say "Keep shooting." You dig? We won't be jiving.

Now, there are many kinds of guns. Many, many kinds of guns. But the strongest weapon that we have, the strongest weapon that we all each individually have, is all of us. United in opposition. United with revolutionary principles.

So it's very necessary for us to understand the need for functional organization. It's very necessary for us, especially black brothers—listen close—that we have revolutionary principles to guide ourselves by. Because if we just go out in a jive gang, running around in big groups, with rocks and bottles, we're not going to do nothing against 500 pigs with shotguns and .357 Magnums.

What we got to do is functionally put ourselves in organizations. Get every black man in the black community with a shotgun in his home, and a .357 Magnum, and a .45 if he can get it, and an M-1 if he can get it and anything else if he can get it, brothers. Get it and start doing this.

Then, I want to say this here. On the streets, stop running in large groups. That ain't no right tactic. We should run in groups of fours and fives—all around. We cannot continue using these tactics where we lose 3000 arrested or we lose 1 or 200 dead. We gotta stop. So we want to start running in threes, fours, and fives. Small groups using proper revolutionary tactics. So we can dissemble those pigs who occupy our community, who occupy our community like foreign troops.

Black people, we're saying we're lost. We seem to be lost in a world of white racist, decadent America. I'm saying that we have a right to defend ourselves as human beings. And if some pig comes up to us unjustly treating us injustly, then we have to bring our pieces out and start barbecuing some of that pork.

Brother Huey P. Newton was on the stand yesterday. And they said the brother was so beautiful in cross-examination for a whole day-and-a-half that the jury got mad at the D.A. We hope that brother Huey P. Newton be set free. We go further in our hopes, in our work in our organization to demand that he be set free. And we say that if anything happens to Huey P. Newton, the sky is the limit.

Now here are some buckets around and we are here, Huey needs funds, and we hope that you will donate to the Party and other local organizations.

We hope, we sure that you can begin to set up a few things organizationally to deal with the situation in a very revolutionary manner.

So, Power to the People. Power to All the People. Black Power to Black People. Panther Power. Even some Peace and Freedom Power. Power and Free Huey. Thank you.

(end of tape)

MR. KUNSTLER: Now, Mr. Seale, when you used the term "pig" in that speech, can you define what is meant by the word "pig"?

THE WITNESS: A pig is a person or a policeman who is generally found violating the constitutional rights and the human rights of people, a vile traducer, and he is usually found masquerading as a victim of unprovoked attack.

MR. KUNSTLER: And you also used the term in discussing Huey P. Newton "the sky is the limit." Would you explain what you meant by that?

THE WITNESS: I meant by that that we would exhaust all political and legal means through the courts all the way to the top of the Supreme Court. We would have demonstrations. We will organize the people in together and we will go to the limit to try and get our Minister of Defense free if he is not set free.

MR. KUNSTLER: I have no further question.

THE COURT: Is there any cross-examination?

• • • • •

MR. SCHULTZ: Yes, sir, your Honor, I have some.

Now you said in your speech that was just played before the jury that Huey P. Newton was busted and charged with making a couple of pigs act in a desired manner, did you not, Sir?

THE WITNESS: He was charged with shooting a policeman. He was charged with shooting in defense of himself.

MR. SCHULTZ: So when you said that "individuals should make pigs act in a desired manner," you were referring to shooting policemen in defense if necessary, isn't that right?

THE WITNESS: Organizationally and functionally, if you look at the whole context of the sentence, what I mean is not what you are inferring.

What I mean is this here—

MR. SCHULTZ: I am asking you what you said, sir. I am asking you, did you not state that?

THE WITNESS: But you also asked me what I mean, Mr. Schultz.

MR. KUNSTLER: I thought he asked him what he meant, too, your Honor.

MR. SCHULTZ: Let me rephrase the question if I did.

When you stated to the people in Lincoln Park that "they've got to make one individual pig or a number of individual pigs act in the desired manner," you weren't referring to that same desired manner for which Huey Newton was charged, were you?

THE WITNESS: What was that? Rephrase your question again. I am trying to make sure you don't trip me.

MR. SCHULTZ: It was a little complicated, Mr. Seale. It wasn't very well stated.

THE WITNESS: All right.

MR. SCHULTZ: I will ask it to you again.

You said to the people, "They should make one pig or a number of pigs act in the desired manner." You were not then referring to the same desired manner with which Mr. Newton was charged, that is, shooting a policeman? Were you or were you not?

THE WITNESS: No. I can state it in another way in answering the question.

MR. SCHULTZ: No.

THE WITNESS: If you will let me answer the question.

MR. SCHULTZ: You said you were not.

THE WITNESS: Can I answer the question?

THE COURT: You have answered the question. Ask him another question.

MR. SCHULTZ: Were you referring to shooting policemen in the desired manner when you said this: "But if a pig comes up to us and starts swinging a billy club, you're gonna take that club and whip him over the head, and lay him on the ground, and then the pig is acting in a desired manner."

THE WITNESS: I was referring to defending myself.

MR. SCHULTZ: Now you said to the people, did you not, that they should pull the spike from the wall, because "if you pull it out and if you shoot well, all I am going to do is pat you on the back and say 'Keep on shooting'?" Was that for the purpose of making the pig act in the desired manner?

THE WITNESS: That's for the purpose of telling people they have to defend themselves. In that broad sense of that statement, without taking it out of context, that generally means that, and if any individual is unjustly attacked by any policeman, unjustly, at that point he has a human right—

MR. SCHULTZ: To kill the policeman.

THE WITNESS: To defend himself.

MR. SCHULTZ: And that means if necessary to kill that policeman, does it not?

THE WITNESS: If that policeman is attacking me, if he is violating the law, if he is violating the law unjustly, attacking me,—I am not talking about a policeman down the street stopping somebody—

MR. SCHULTZ: That means killing, if necessary, doesn't it?

THE WITNESS: No.

MR. SCHULTZ: You will not kill a policeman, is that right?

THE WITNESS: It is not the desire to kill, and that's what you are trying to put in the tone of it, and it's not that—

MR. SCHULTZ: Will you answer my question?

THE WITNESS: I won't answer that question with a yes or no, your Honor. I have to answer the question my own way.

MR. SCHULTZ: I can rephrase it.

Were you referring to shooting pigs?

THE WITNESS: I was referring to shooting any racist, bigoted pig who unjustly attacks us or brutalizes us in the process of us doing any kind of organizational and functional work to try to change the power structure and remove the oppression.

MR. SCHULTZ: And you said in that context "unjustly attacking you?"

THE WITNESS: In the context of the whole speech, that's what I am talking about.

MR. SCHULTZ: So when you told the people that what we have to do is get every black man in the black community with a shotgun in his home and a .357 Magnum and a .45, if he can get it, and an M-1, if he can get it—you were referring to getting guns for defense, isn't that right?

THE WITNESS: Getting a gun, put a gun in your home, a shotgun—

MR. SCHULTZ: In defense?

THE WITNESS: —or M-1—you have a right by the Second Amendment of the Constitution to have it.

MR. SCHULTZ: Were you referring to it in self-defense, that is my question, sir?

THE WITNESS: I was referring to it in self-defense against unjust brutal attack by any policeman or pigs or bigots in this society who will attack people.

MR. SCHULTZ: And you said to the people in Lincoln Park "I am referring to unjust brutal attack," didn't you?

THE WITNESS: No. You know what I mean, Mr. Schultz. I am telling you what I am referring to.

MR. SCHULTZ: Now, when you told the people to stop running around in big groups and with rocks and bottles because you can't do anything against 500 pigs with shotguns, and .357 Magnums, was that part of your revolutionary tactics?

THE WITNESS: Definitely. It is a change.

Revolution means change, change away from this old erroneous method of running out in the streets in big numbers and rioting, and throwing rocks and bottles. How are you going to stop a .357 Magnum or shotgun full of some shotgun shells that are being shot at you with rocks and bottles. Stop that. Stop it. Stop the rioting. That is in essence what I am talking about.

Stop those kind of tactics. Use revolutionary tactics. Defend yourself from unjust attacks, et cetera.

MR. SCHULTZ: When you told the people in Lincoln Park, "Pick up a gun, pull the spike from the wall, because if you pull it out and you shoot well, all I'm gonna do is pat you on the back and say, 'Keep on shooting,'" That was part of your revolutionary tactics, too, was it not, sir?

THE WITNESS: Yes, sir, and if you look generally—

MR. SCHULTZ: Please, that is all.

THE COURT: You have answered the question.

THE WITNESS: I strike that answer on the grounds that that particular question is wrong because it ain't clear.

THE COURT: I have some news for you, sir.

(there is applause in the courtroom)

THE COURT: I do the striking here, and will the marshals exclude from the courtroom anyone who applauded. This isn't a theater. Anyone who applauded the witness may go out and is directed to leave.

MR. SCHULTZ: Mr. Seale, are you the Bobby G. Seale who was convicted on April 11, 1968, of being in possession of a shotgun in the vicinity of a jail?

THE WITNESS: Yes, I am the same person who was convicted later of being in possession of a shotgun as they charged me of being adjacent to a jail, but as I know by the law, you could have a shotgun as long as it wasn't concealed and as long as you are in a public place, and I was actually in fact on a public sidewalk. Yes, I was convicted, and the thing was appealed.

MR. SCHULTZ: You had five shotgun shells in that gun, did you not?

THE WITNESS: Yes, in a magazine.

MR. SCHULTZ: Now, Mr. Seale, on Wednesday morning, you gave the second speech, right?

THE WITNESS: I guess that was Wednesday morning, in the middle of the week somewhere.

MR. SCHULTZ: And you said to the people, Mr. Seale, "If the pigs get in the way of our march, then tangle with the blue-helmeted motherfuckers. Kill them and send them to the morgue slab," and you were pointing to policemen at that time, isn't that a fact?

MR. KUNSTLER: This is completely out of the scope of the direct examination, your Honor. It is improper and it is wrong.

THE COURT: No, the witness was brought here to testify about his activities during that period.

I think the Government has the right to inquire. Treating your remarks as objection which you have not made, I overrule the objection.

MR. KUNSTLER: Is your Honor ruling that every witness that takes the stand can be cross-examined on anything?

THE COURT: I said it is my ruling, sir, that that question is a proper one on this record.

MR. SCHULTZ: How many people were you speaking to?

THE WITNESS: Let's see now—

MR. GARRY: Just a minute, Mr. Seale.

I am rising to the part that your Honor has heretofore allowed me to.

Unless we can be given a full transcription of the speech that he gave on that day, I am going to instruct the witness not to answer the question upon the grounds of the Fifth Amendment.

THE COURT: If you so advise him and the witness wants to do it in a proper manner, I will respect his refusal to answer.

MR. GARRY: Mr. Seale, you are entitled and I advise you not to answer this question upon the ground it would tend to incriminate you under the Fifth Amendment of the United States Constitution.

I so advise you to take that advice.

THE COURT: Mr. Seale, you have heard Mr. Garry. If you wish to take advantage of the Fifth Amendment and say to the Court that to answer that question might tend to incriminate you, you may do it, but it must come from you, not from your lawyer.

THE WITNESS: I would like to take the Fifth Amendment on the question, yes, sir.

THE COURT: All right. You needn't answer the question.

MR. SCHULTZ: That is all, your Honor.

THE COURT: Is there any redirect examination?

• • • • •

MR. KUNSTLER: Yes, your Honor.

Mr. Seale, with reference to Mr. Schultz' question regarding the conviction for carrying a shotgun, did you ever go to jail for that?

THE WITNESS: No.

MR. SCHULTZ: Objection, your Honor. That is not proper.

THE COURT: I sustain the objection. The test is the conviction, not the punishment.

MR. KUNSTLER: Mr. Seale, do you recall Mr. Schultz asked you about certain guns?

THE WITNESS: Yes, I do.

MR. KUNSTLER: Now I ask you this question. When you were referring to those guns, did you not use the phrase "in his home"?

THE WITNESS: Yes.

MR. SCHULTZ: Objection to the form of question. Mr. Kunstler is doing the testifying and using the witness as a sounding board.

THE COURT: Yes, the form is bad. I sustain the objection.

MR. KUNSTLER: All right. What did you say in that speech, Mr. Seale, with reference to where those guns were to be?

THE WITNESS: I said "Put the guns in your home, .357 Magnum, M-1, .45s." I referred to these kind of guns or anything else. You have a right to do it, and that's part of our program in the Party, a constitutional right to arm yourself.

THE COURT: All right. You've answered the question.

MR. KUNSTLER: Now, Mr. Seale, as to the speech that you gave in Lincoln Park on August 27, 1968, what type of person was this speech addressed to?

MR. SCHULTZ: Objection. I asked him nothing about the audience.

THE COURT: I sustain the objection to the question.

MR. KUNSTLER: In the light of that ruling, your Honor, I have no further questions.

THE COURT: I have sustained the objection.

MR. SCHULTZ: I have no questions.

THE COURT: You may go. Call your next witness, please.

(witness excused)

VOICES: Power to the people! Power to the people!

Testimony of Staughton Craig Lynd

January 30, 1970

MR. WEINGLASS: Will you please state your full name?

THE WITNESS: Staughton Craig Lynd.

MR. WEINGLASS: Your present address?

THE WITNESS: 7359 South Bennett, Chicago.

MR. WEINGLASS: Will you state for the Court and jury your present occupation?

THE WITNESS: I am a teacher at the Industrial Areas Foundation Training Institute.

MR. WEINGLASS: In what special area do you teach?

THE WITNESS: American history.

MR. WEINGLASS: Directing your attention to the field of American history, and in particular the American Revolution, will you indicate what are the works you have authored?

THE WITNESS: Well, my Masters' essay was published under the title "Anti-Federalism in Duchess County, New York." Then a collection of essays on the period of the American Revolution was published under the title *Class Conflict, Slavery and the United States Constitution*. And a book on the ideas of the American Revolution was published under the title *Intellectual Origins of American Radicalism*.

MR. WEINGLASS: If the Court please, the defense offers Professor Lynd as an expert in the area of American revolution. I feel perhaps my motion in this regard should be had outside the presence of the jury.

MR. FORAN: I would think that is quite likely, your Honor. As to the American revolution, there is no charge in this indictment about that.

THE COURT: I will let you make an offer of proof out of the presence of the jury.

(jury excused)

MR. WEINGLASS: Professor Lynd, based on your research in the area of American history, particularly the American revolution, do you have an expert opinion on the origins of the right of the American people to protest for redress of grievances and when those channels of conventional protest are blocked?

THE WITNESS: I have the opinion that the right which is enumerated in the First Amendment, adopted shortly after the ratification of the United States Constitution, the right to petition for redress of grievances, had a much broader meaning to the men who made the American revolution and who wrote the United States Constitution than we ordinarily assume.

I believe that today we often think of the right to petition as the right to ask a democratically elected legislature to pass a particular law, but I believe that in the light of the experience of the men who made the American revolution and who wrote the First Amendment, we should see that what they meant by the right to petition for redress of grievances was something much broader.

When they used the term "petitioning," in the Declaration of Independence, what they have in mind is the situation in which these men found themselves, in which they had no elected representatives in the British Parliament, in which they were dealing with a governmental machinery over which they had no control through elected representatives, to which they could only appeal through the petitioning process, year after year, in petition after petition, before they finally took up arms.

And what they were doing in this petitionary process prior to the American revolution was not asking for the passage of a particular law, but crying out against what the Declaration of Independence called "a long train of abuses" evincing the design of the attempt to create an absolute despotism.

This is what the petitioning meant to them, and the reason that I think this concept of petitioning is relevant to the situation before this Court is that it seems to me that the First Amendment was involved in what happened in Chicago in 1968 in a far broader sense than in its particular senses of the right to march, the right to use a public park, the right to free speech, and the right of free press.

It seems to me that the jury might wish to consider the entire process of the demonstration as a kind of petitioning process in which people who felt that their elected government was no longer responsive to them, felt themselves to be in the same position as the colonists before the American revolution, came to Chicago to make one last direct appeal to the men of power who were assembled in the Democratic Convention. We can see what was intended in Chicago in August 1968 as a petitioning process equivalent to the great march in London in 1848 when the working men of England approached the Houses of Parliament and asked that all adult males be given the vote, and to the march of working men to the Winter Palace of the Czars in Russia in 1905, asking not for the passage of a particular law or for the redress of any single grievance, but for a change in entire policies of oppression, policy against which the Chicago demonstration was directed.

MR. WEINGLASS: Now, what on the basis of your study of the American history, is the next form of petition for redress of grievances should the normal channels of petitioning become blocked or stagnant through nonuse?

THE WITNESS: Well, I think we have to face very squarely the fact that the American nation began in a revolution and is founded on the assertion of a right to revolution and that this right is asserted not only in the preamble to the Declaration of Independence, but in such revolutionary documents as the Virginia Bill of Rights or the Massachusetts Constitution.

It was reaffirmed as late as 1861 by President Abraham Lincoln in his first inaugural address when he said that this country belongs to the people who live in it, and whenever they grow weary of the existing government, they can exercise their constitutional right of amending it or their revolutionary right to overthrow it.

Assuming then, that the men who made the American revolution intended that the people should continue to have the right to revolution after the particular revolution which they made was over, then it seems to me that what we can assume was in the minds of the founders, in speaking in the First Amendment of a right to Petition, was a spectrum of means of social change, beginning with speech, assembly, petitioning, beseeching, ending, if necessary, as a last resort, with revolution, and including in between those two kinds of social change, a variety of intermediate kinds of resistance which go beyond speech to action but not to the comprehensive armed insurrection of revolution.

This was exactly the kind of intermediate resistance which the makers of the American Revolution themselves carried out from 1765 to 1775. They organized nonviolent boycotts of the importation of English goods. They surrounded men who had been appointed distributors of Stamps under the Stamp Act of 1765, called them names, harassed them, broke into their houses, and forced them to resign.

An incident which I think is particularly suggestive of those intermediate forms of resistance is the sequence of events leading up to the so-called Boston Massacre of March 1770. This is a sequence of events which exhibits a peculiar resemblance, in my opinion, to what happened in Chicago in August 1968.

In 1767 an unheard-of event, four regiments of British soldiers were landed on the town of Boston to keep order there. Previous to that Boston had had a police force of something on the order of ten constables.

The soldiers were irritants to the townspeople because the townspeople were obliged to lodge the soldiers in their homes. The soldiers were irritants to the working people of the city because they moonlighted and competed with American artisans for work on the docks, and of course, the soldiers were an irritant to all the people of Boston because they constituted a standing army in peacetime which that generation of Americans considered a threat to democracy.

What happened on March 5, 1770, was that after a series of minor scuffles and incidents between the soldiers and the townspeople, there came a night when a group of townsfolk of Boston surrounded a particular British sentry, called him names. They called him, for example, lobsterback because of his red coat, a kind of eighteenth century equivalent of "pig." They threw oyster shells and hunks of ice at him, and at a certain point he called out the Guard, which was stationed in an adjacent guardhouse.

The guard came out, the crowd continued to call the soldiers names. Finally the order to fire was given. No one is quite sure by whom. The soldiers opened fire, and five colonists were killed. The British said that the soldiers had been provoked because oyster shells and lumps of ice were thrown at them. But the colonists, Sam Adams and Paul Revere, took the position that the provocation consisted in the presence of the British soldiers having turned the city of Boston into an armed camp. That's why acts of resistance, even though certainly far more than the customary speech and assembly envisioned under the First Amendment, seemed appropriate to people like Sam Adams and Thomas Jefferson, because they were responses to an oppressive situation which had gone far beyond those normal circumstances in which speech and assembly and free press and petition were adequate responses.

It seemed to American colonists in 1770 the Government was not yet sufficiently oppressive to justify revolution and yet the times called for something far more than the mere writing of articles and holding of rallies. And so they felt that these nonviolent direct actions, the boycotts and the harrassing of people who accepted positions under the British colonial administration, were appropriate forms of resistance.

I don't see how we can say that the American people has a right to revolution as a last resort against total oppression, and say that they lack a right of resistance short of revolution to a partially oppressive situation.

And therefore it seems to me that both the experience of the men who made the American revolution and the words that they used, in their revolutionary documents, argues for the kind of resistance under oppressive circumstances as a response to oppressive circumstances such as took place in Boston in 1770 or again in 1773 with the Tea Party and such as I think took place in Chicago in 1968.

MR. WEINGLASS: If the Court please, that completes the offer of proof.

THE COURT: What is the position of the Government in respect to what has been described here by Mr. Weinglass as an offer of proof?

MR. FORAN: The Government objects.

THE COURT: I sustain the objection.

Will you bring in the jury?

(jury enters)

THE COURT: Do you have any additional questions of this witness?

MR. WEINGLASS: No, no further questions.

MR. FORAN: No question, your Honor.

THE COURT: You may go, sir.

Testimony of Renault A. Robinson

MR. WEINGLASS: Mr. Robinson, would you state your name in full?

THE WITNESS: Renault A. Robinson.

MR. WEINGLASS: And your present residence?

THE WITNESS: 7639 South Luella, Chicago.

MR. WEINGLASS: And your present occupation?

THE WITNESS: Patrolman, Chicago Police Department.

MR. WEINGLASS: Could you state for the Court and jury what citations you've received in the course of your service as a patrolman?

THE WITNESS: Citations for service and arrests in excess of about twenty-five for my duties and et cetera.

MR. WEINGLASS: Do you belong to any associations connected with the police force?

THE WITNESS: Yes. I belong to the Afro-American Patrolmen's League.

MR. WEINGLASS: I show you D-357 for identification, and I ask you if you can identify that.

THE WITNESS: Yes, it is. It's the official rule book of the Chicago Police Department.

MR. WEINGLASS: And are the patrolmen advised to read this book and know the contents of the book?

THE WITNESS: Yes, they are.

MR. WEINGLASS: And are they bound by the rules and regulations of the book?

THE WITNESS: Yes, they are.

MR. WEINGLASS: At this time the defense offers into evidence D-357 for identification, that is, the official rules and regulations of the Department. I will not request that the document be given in its entirety to the jury, but if the witness is permitted to testify as to just two rules which appear, they are Rules 30 and 31. These are rules relating to whether policemen are allowed to state publicly criticism of the Department or any member of the Department.

MR. FORAN: Your Honor, I object to those. They don't have a thing to do with the case.

MR. WEINGLASS: The Government has produced approximately fifty-seven witnesses, many of whom were members of the Chicago Police Department. If in fact those witnesses were bound by these rules, which I think they are, those rules would preclude them from giving any testimony that would be detrimental, critical, of any other member of the Department. That's why I think the rule is relevant.

THE COURT: Maybe you misconstrue the meaning of those rules. I'll sustain the objection.

MR. WEINGLASS: Now, directing your attention to the period of time just prior to the Democratic National Convention in August of 1968, were you undergoing any special training as a member of the Police Department at that time?

THE WITNESS: Yes. The entire department is required to go in in-service training for a period of a week in which we learn how to shoot shotguns at lifesize targets and riot formation training, where we march in an armory. We are taught formations with the use of the baton for crowd control and we are instructed by our supervisor that to have maximum effect we should make a chant, make a loud noise, because it has a psychological effect on a crowd that we are trying to control.

MR. WEINGLASS: And what was the chant you were told to use?

THE WITNESS: Well, he just said, "Use a chant." He didn't specify any words. Some of the fellows were, I guess, jokingly chanting "Kill, kill, kill."

MR. WEINGLASS: Now, calling your attention to Sunday, August 25, 1968, could you tell the Court and the jury what assignments were made in your district?

THE WITNESS: The Police Department was put on twelve hour shift and all days off were cancelled. In our district, assignments were being made and volunteers were being asked for Convention duty as opposed to remaining in the district. After a certain amount of men volunteered, the rest were made mandatory assignments, and about half of our men were assigned to riot control and Convention duty, and about the other half remained in stand-by and worked in the district.

MR. WEINGLASS: Now, was any change made in the assignment on Wednesday of that week, August 28?

THE WITNESS: Yes, several of the black officers on Wednesday were reassigned back into the district because of disagreements that had—

MR. FORAN: Objection to giving the causes, your Honor. He is testifying to facts.

THE COURT: Yes. The reason was not asked. Beginning with the word "because," the witness words may go out, and the jury is directed to disregard them.

MR. WEINGLASS: I show you D-358 for identification and ask you to remove the contents from the envelope and examine them in order to identify the contents.

THE WITNESS: This is a standard issue shotgun shell that each man is issued five rounds in a car. This is a Magnum-load .12 gauge shotgun shell that we use in our riot guns and it has nine pellets in, like this.

MR. WEINGLASS: What are those pellets made of?

MR. FORAN: I object to this. We have had no showing at all of any connection with any date, time, place. I think we all know that policemen have guns and shells.

THE COURT: I sustain the objection. Certainly policemen are armed. That evidence is in the record.

MR. WEINGLASS: Well, a shotgun is not standard equipment, if the Court please, and the men were issued shotguns.

THE COURT: I will sustain the objection to the question.

MR. WEINGLASS: Now, directing your attention to the first week of September 1968, did you have occasion to attend a function in the evening at the American Legion Hall on 75th Street run by the captain of your district?

THE WITNESS: Yes, we had a district victory party.

MR. FORAN: Your Honor, I object to that. This is the week after the Convention.

THE COURT: That is right.

MR. WEINGLASS: We have had testimony in this case, your Honor, up to sixteen months after the Convention.

THE COURT: He may ask the question about the date and then if you think the question is objectionable, you may indicate your objection.

MR. WEINGLASS: Do you know what night of the week in the first week of September the victory party for the Police Department occurred?

MR. FORAN: I object to the form of the question.

THE COURT: I sustain the objection.

MR. WEINGLASS: Is the basis of the Court's ruling that we are not permitted to go into the first week of September, or is the basis of the Court's ruling that the form of the question is not proper? I will desist if it is the form—

THE COURT: The question is improper as a matter of form. It is improper with respect to date. There has been no foundation laid for it.

Ask another question.

MR. WEINGLASS: Patrolman Robinson, shortly following the week of the Democratic National Convention, did you have occasion to hear police officers of this city address their superiors as "Seig Heil" at a formal function?

MR. FORAN: Objection, your Honor; I move that be stricken.

THE COURT: I do strike it.

MR. WEINGLASS: Your Honor, I ask that I be permitted to establish the truth of that question through an offer of proof.

THE COURT: I will excuse you for a few minutes while an offer of proof is made out of your presence with my usual orders, ladies and gentlemen.

(jury excused)

MR. FORAN: Your Honor, I would ask that the defendants at counsel table try to look a little less like we are sitting in a living room in front of the fire. We have had a young lady kneeling with her arms in his lap. This is a Federal courthouse, your Honor.

THE MARSHAL: Mr. Weiner, sit up.

THE COURT: Mr. Foran, they are laughing at you back there when you say that. I have tried four and a half months, unsuccessfully, I might add, to maintain a modicum of dignity in this courtroom. They didn't even listen to their own expert witnesses, so-called, but insisted on reading newspapers while the testimony was being given.

We have to have the defendants here when they are tried under the Constitution and it is difficult to control that sort of thing during the trial. I have done my best up to now. I will continue to do my best, Mr. Foran.

Now you may proceed, sir. Make your offer of proof.

MR. WEINGLASS: Mr. Robinson, directing your attention to the first week in September 1968, did you have occasion to attend a party given by the captain of your district at the American Legion Hall on 75th Street?

THE WITNESS: Yes, I did.

MR. WEINGLASS: How many persons were present?

THE WITNESS: Approximately 150 guys, policemen.

MR. WEINGLASS: While you were present at the party, would you relate to the court what you observed and what you heard?

THE WITNESS: Well, they were serving food, guys were eating, they were chanting "Thundering Third District," and in the midst of this a group of police officers stood up and raised their arms and started chanting, "Seig Heil" and one particular officer who had been on duty and had led a contingent of these men stood up at attention and sort of— everybody laughed except the officer.

MR. WEINGLASS: That is the offer of proof, if the Court please.

THE COURT: What is the Government's positions with respect to this so-called offer of proof?

MR. FORAN: I object to it for lack of materiality.

THE COURT: I sustain the objection to the so-called offer.

(jury enters)

MR. WEINGLASS: If your Honor please, that completes the direct examination.

THE COURT: Is there any cross-examination?

MR. FORAN: No cross, your Honor.

THE COURT: You may go, Officer.

THE COURT: Please call your next witness.

Testimony of Jesse Louis Jackson

MR. KUNSTLER: Would you state your full name?

THE WITNESS: Jesse Louis Jackson.

MR. KUNSTLER: Mr. Jackson, what is your position?

THE WITNESS: I am a Christian minister employed by the Southern Christian Leadership Conference.

MR. KUNSTLER: Reverend Jackson, in what capacity are you employed by the Southern Christian Leadership Conference?

THE WITNESS: As director of its economic arm, Operation Breadbasket.

MR. KUNSTLER: Could you state for the jury what Operation Breadbasket is?

THE WITNESS: Operation Breadbasket is an economic movement that is designed to be the antidote to the racist domination of our black community by engaging in boycotts and consumer withdrawals from the companies that have an imperialistic relationship with our community. That is, the companies control the capital and blacks are merely reduced to consumers. So far, we've been able to get about five thousand jobs directly, perhaps ten thousand indirectly, but more importantly we've been able to develop black institutions as a result of this movement.

MR. KUNSTLER: By the way, who is the president of the Southern Christian Leadership movement?

THE WITNESS: Dr. Ralph Abernathy.

MR. KUNSTLER: Now, Reverend Jackson, can you briefly give your background prior to your association with Operation Breadbasket?

THE WITNESS: Well, in 1959 I was a student at the University of Illinois. I was there as an athlete, and because I was black I couldn't play quarterback and couldn't participate in student government affairs. I left and went back south to Greensboro, North Carolina, and became involved in the sit-down movement. I was engaged in the Congress of Racial Equality and became a teacher of nonviolent direct action in schools across the South.

In 1965, when blacks could not vote, we knew that they were locked out of the political process in the North, but it was too subtle here to prove, so we went to Selma and created a movement there that later became Federal law.

From the voting rights field, we came to Chicago. We attempted to give a very social and nonviolent analysis of our situation here. We found here that blacks were hemmed in in a very, very racist box, that is, we were caught as forty-two percent of the population, and yet we only have about forty-five percent of our people registered to vote.

MR. FORAN: Your Honor, could we have Reverend Jackson proceed on a question and answer method a little more? He gave rather substantial background, but—

THE COURT: Yes, I think he is getting away from the question.

MR. KUNSTLER: I had asked him his background, your Honor. I thought Reverend Jackson was trying to comply with that.

MR. FORAN: I think we got off into some of the issues that the Reverend had been involved in, and some of those things, your Honor, should be pursuant to specific questions so that we can focus on the particular—

THE COURT: Yes. I would ask you to put specific questions to the witness, proper questions.

MR. KUNSTLER: All right.

Reverend Jackson, have you completed your background up to Operation Breadbasket, or is there any area you have not covered yet?

THE WITNESS: I guess what I really wanted to say—I hope I have not been out of order, Judge. I don't quite understand court procedure.

THE COURT: Well, I don't think I'd make a perfect minister, either. So we're even.

THE WITNESS: Okay, Judge. We're going to get along.

THE COURT: What did you say? We will or we won't?

THE WITNESS: We will.

THE COURT: We will.

THE WITNESS: What I was trying to explain was that the killing of Dr. King in Memphis simply initiated our more direct involvement in political action, which really comes to Convention time.

MR. KUNSTLER: Reverend Jackson, I call your attention to the third week in August, 1968. Did you have an occasion to see Rennie Davis?

THE WITNESS: Yes. At my house here in Chicago.

MR. KUNSTLER: Did you have a conversation at that time with Mr. Davis?

THE WITNESS: Yes, we had three or four issues to discuss. One was the relationship between the assassination of Dr. King and some things that we wanted to happen during the Convention. Rennie really wanted to know what was on my mind about the Convention and I told him that the reason we had not pursued relentlessly through any legal process who killed Dr. King was, that we thought what killed him was an atmosphere that had been created because the nation was so split over the war question, and somehow if the Democratic Convention really became consistent with democracy, perhaps something could come out in that Convention that would indicate a real sorrow for his assassination as opposed to just a holiday.

Then Rennie told me he would like for me to try to go to Hanoi. He felt if I went to Hanoi that I could talk with the prisoners that were to be released, and that through this process we could make the negotiations in Paris more meaningful.

One of the problems we had developed, I told Rennie, was that those of us who were in the peace movement had developed a kind of image where people thought we were against warriors. We were just against the war, so he told me that perhaps I ought to take that stand, and we were talking about it and we couldn't quite make up our mind.

Then we got deeper involved in the Convention. I told him that we were split as to the technique that we were going to use because an atmosphere had been created in Chicago. Those of us from Chicago had reported to Dr. Abernathy that it would be very dangerous to come here if we didn't make some very special adjustments.

I related to Rennie that the shoot to kill order had come out, and therefore we had heard rumblings that if blacks participated in a big demonstration, that we would be shot down. We had talked with some of the policemen, and we saw some shotgun shells that had overkill pellets in them, so some of us who were afraid that some of the younger blacks might get involved in riots had begun to hold some workshops on the South and West sides.

So Rennie told me that he saw the danger, but what kind of decision was I going to make. I told him we felt if blacks marched downtown, there would be a massacre, and it wasn't that we were afraid to go, but we still were hung up because we had some dissenting delegations among us from Mississippi and Georgia. We wanted to support them.

So Rennie said that perhaps the only thing that could do, rather than my being caught in so much ambiguity, was that he was trying to get a legal permit through the city, and asked me what was my advice in case he didn't get the legal permit. I told him I hoped he got the legal permit, but even if he didn't that it would be consistent with Dr. King's teaching that we then got a moral permit. Rather than getting permission from the city, we'd have to get a commission from our consciences and just have an extralegal demonstration, that probably blacks shouldn't participate, that if blacks got whipped nobody would pay any attention, it would just be history. But if whites got whipped, it would make good news; that is, it would make the newspapers.

Rennie told me he didn't understand what I was saying. I told him that I thought long-haired whites was the new style nigger, and if he didn't think they would get whipped, to try it.

We finally decided that we would explain to our people what the demonstration was about, that we would hope that the permits would come through, that Dr. Abernathy was going to come to the black community with the buggy and the mules. But we were afraid of the tremendous police build-up in our community, so we felt too helpless to just put our heads in a meat grinder, and therefore I would spend my time working in the black community telling blacks not to get involved, and I would hope that those who were involved would appreciate that we were with them, but we just couldn't be there physically because chaos was anticipated as opposed to peace.

This was the substance of that conversation as I recall it.

MR. KUNSTLER: I have no further questions.

THE COURT: Is there any cross-examination of this witness?

MR. FORAN: Reverend Jackson, did you call Mr. Davis or did Mr. Davis call you?

THE WITNESS: He called me, then I called him back.

MR. FORAN: That is all.

THE COURT: You may go. Thank you.

(applause)

The marshals will exclude everyone that they have seen applaud.

MR. KUNSTLER: Your Honor, with the testimony of Reverend Jackson, the defense has concluded its presentation of live witnesses. We do have a film that we hope to qualify. We think we will be able to procure the cameraman. We also have a few documents that we are still working on which we may present to the Court.

THE COURT: I would give consideration to recessing until Monday, provided counsel for the defense will rest or will go forward with the remainder of whatever evidence it has.

MR. SCHULTZ: Your Honor, if that evidence is going to be in addition to what Mr. Kunstler stated—that is, that they not over the weekend decide on another dozen or thirty or forty witnesses to start up again.

THE COURT: Mr. Kunstler represented that was the last live witness, as he put it.

If that is the way you want to leave it, with the condition that you must rest Monday, if you don't have anything further, I am perfectly willing to put this case over to Monday morning.

MR. KUNSTLER: That is agreeable, your Honor.

THE COURT: The jury may now be excused until Monday morning at ten o'clock and I will ask counsel and the parties to remain.

(jury excused)

THE COURT: I wanted to say to counsel for the defendants and the defendants, that it has been brought to my attention that there was a speech given in Milwaukee discussing this case by one of the defendants. I want to say that if such a speech as was given is brought to my attention again, I will give serious consideration to the termination of bail of the person who makes the speech. I think he would be a bad risk to continue on bail. The one who made it knows it. I won't go any further than this.

Monday morning at ten o'clock.

MR. WEINGLASS: If your Honor please, could the Court just identify the defendant who gave the speech?

THE COURT: No. I won't do it. I want them all—

MR. DELLINGER: I made the speech. Was there anything in the speech that suggested I won't show up for trial the next day or simply that I criticized your conduct of the trial?

THE COURT: I didn't ask you to rise, sir, and I am certainly not going to be interrogated.

MR. DELLINGER: Why are you threatening me with revocation of bail for exercising my freedom of speech? What has that got to do with it? I am here, aren't I?

A VOICE: Right on.

MR. HOFFMAN: We all give the same speech.

A VOICE: Right on, Dave.

MR. WEINGLASS: Your Honor, I would like to inquire of the Court if Mr. Dellinger indicated in his speech anything about not being available to the Court—

THE COURT: I am not going to be put on the griddle about it. You are one of the lawyers for the defendants. And I think it is wholly inappropriate for defendants in a criminal case to make the kind of speech that was made and the matter of bail goes beyond mere protection for the Government that the defendant appear. Read the book.

MR. WEINGLASS: But I do not think the matter of bail should be held over their heads in order to reduce the amount of public speaking they are doing.

THE COURT: I will determine what to do if and when speeches of a certain kind and character are brought to my attention. Free speech is not involved here. Mr. Marshal, ten o'clock Monday morning.

February 2, 1970

THE COURT: Mr. Kunstler, I like to rely on the representations of lawyers—have you found the cameraman?

MR. KUNSTLER: No. The cameraman as of ten o'clock this morning, we have been unable to find. I am going to go back on my representation anyway with one more witness, your Honor. We had originally contacted Dr. Ralph Abernathy to be a witness for the defense in this case. Dr. Abernathy was then out of the country and has just returned and is willing to appear as a witness for the defense. He is arriving at this moment at O'Hare Airport.

We think his testimony is crucial inasmuch as the Government has raised the issue of the mule train and I think your Honor may recall the testimony of Superintendent Rochford where the Superintendent tried to give the impression that the mule train was afraid of the demonstrators and therefore the police obligingly led it through the line.

Also Mr. Abernathy made a speech at Grant Park directly related to the events of the night of Wednesday, August 28. I did not know that he would be back in the country when I spoke to your Honor on Friday afternoon. His testimony is not long and it would be the last witness we would offer subject only to those records.

THE COURT: I certainly am not going to wait for him.

Who will speak for the Government?

MR. SCHULTZ: I will, your Honor.

The Government is ready to start its case this morning.

To refresh your Honor's recollection, Deputy Superintendent Rochford testified on cross-examination that a driver of the mule train, not Dr. Abernathy of the mule train, said "Please, get us out of here," and Deputy Superintendent Rochford got them out of there.

Now Dr. Abernathy was not present at that conversation. And his testifying as to his impression of what the people in the mule train thought or didn't think is irrelevant. It doesn't rebut anything and it is hearsay. And a speech that he gave in Grant Park on Thursday, of course, is not admissible. So he can contribute nothing to the case.

We are ready to go and would like to proceed with the trial. We would like to put on our first witness this morning.

THE COURT: There have been several witnesses called here during this trial whose testimony the Court ruled could not even be presented to the jury—singers, performers, and former office holders. I think in the light of the representations made by you unequivocally, sir, with no reference to Dr. Abernathy, I will deny your motion that we hold—

MR. KUNSTLER: Your Honor, I think what you have just said is about the most outrageous statement I have ever heard from a bench, and I am going to say my piece right now, and you can hold me in contempt right now if you wish to.

You violated every principle of fair play when you excluded Ramsey Clark from that witness stand. The *New York Times*, among others, has called it the ultimate outrage in American justice.

VOICES: Right on.

MR. KUNSTLER: I am outraged to be in this court before you. Now because I made a statement on Friday that I had only a cameraman, and I discovered on Saturday that Ralph Abernathy, who is the chairman of the Mobilization, is in town, and he can be here, I am trembling because I am so outraged. I haven't been able to get this out before, and I am saying it now, and then you can put me in jail if you want to. You can do anything you want with me, because I feel disgraced to be here.

To say to us on a technicality of my representation that we can't put Ralph Abernathy on the stand. He is the cochairman of the Mobe. He has relevant testimony. I know that doesn't mean much in this court when the Attorney General of the United States walked out of here with his lips so tight he could hardly breathe, and if you could see the expression on his face, you would know, and his wife informed me he never felt such anger at the United States Government as at not being able to testify on that stand.

I have sat here for four and a half months and watched the objections denied and sustained by your Honor, and I know that this is not a fair trial. I know it in my heart. If I have to lose my license to practice law and if I have to go to jail, I can't think of a better cause to go to jail for and to lose my license for—

A VOICE: Right on.

MR. KUNSTLER: —than to tell your Honor that you are doing a disservice to the law in saying that we can't have Ralph Abernathy on the stand. You are saying truth will not out because of the technicality of a lawyer's representation. If that is what their liberty depends upon, your Honor, saying I represented to you that I had a cameraman that was our only witness, then I think there is nothing really more for me to say.

THE COURT: There is not much more you could say, Mr. Kunstler.

MR. KUNSTLER: I am going to turn back to my seat with the realization that everything I have learned throughout my life has come to naught, that there is no meaning in this court, and there is no law in this court—

VOICES: Right on.

MR. KUNSTLER: —and these men are going to jail by virtue of a legal lynching—

VOICES: Right on.

MR. KUNSTLER: And that your Honor is wholly responsible for that, and if this is what your career is going to end on, if this is what your pride is going to be built on, I can only say to your Honor, "Good luck to you."

VOICES: Right on. Right on.

THE COURT: Out with those applauders.

MR. DAVIS: I applauded too, your Honor. Throw me out.

THE COURT: Unfortunately, you have to remain, Mr. Davis, but we note that you applauded. You say you applauded.

MR. SCHULTZ: Your Honor, may we proceed with this trial?

THE COURT: Yes. But they must—we must have the defendants rest here when they have no more evidence.

MR. KUNSTLER: Your Honor, we are not resting. We are never going to rest, your Honor. Your Honor is going to do the resting for us because we have a witness who is available and ready to testify.

THE COURT: I will do the resting for you.

MR. KUNSTLER: You will have to do it for us, your Honor. We are not resting.

THE COURT: Mr. Clerk, let the record show that the defendants have in effect rested.

MR. SCHULTZ: Your Honor, may the defendants and their counsel then not make any reference in front of this jury that they wanted Dr. Abernathy to testify?

MR. KUNSTLER: No, no.

THE COURT: I order you not to make such a statement.

MR. KUNSTLER: We are not going to abide by any such comment as that. Dr. Ralph Abernathy is going to come into this courtroom, and I am going to repeat my motion before that jury.

THE COURT: I order you not to.

MR. KUNSTLER: Then you will have to send me to jail, I am sorry. We have a right to state our objection to resting before the jury.

THE COURT: Don't do it.

MR. KUNSTLER: Your Honor, what is an honest man to do when your Honor has done what he has done? What am I to do? Am I to stand here and say, "Yes, yes, yes."

THE COURT: I will ask you to sit down. I have heard enough from you along that line this morning, sir. I have never as a lawyer or a judge heard such remarks in a courtroom made by a lawyer.

MR. KUNSTLER: Your Honor, no one has heard of such conduct as is going on in this courtroom from the bench. This is the ultimate outrage. And I didn't say that, the editorial writers of the *New York Times* said that.

MR. SCHULTZ: May we proceed, your Honor?

THE COURT: Yes. I have ordered the jury brought in.

(jury enters)

THE COURT: Good morning, ladies and gentlemen of the jury.

THE JURORS: Good morning, your Honor.

THE COURT: I must inform you that I have called on the defendants to produce whatever witness they had, and they had none ready to proceed, and they did not indicate that they would rest. Hence, I let the record show in your presence that the defendants have rested. The word "rested" in law means they have no further evidence to present.

MR. KUNSTLER: We object to that, your Honor, Dr. Ralph Abernathy is on his way from the airport to this courtroom. We want the jury to understand we do not rest. We are prepared to go ahead. We ask merely a few minutes' recess to bring Dr. Abernathy to the stand.

MR. SCHULTZ: The Government's position is if he were here, we wouldn't object to their putting him on.

MR. KUNSTLER: Now it does, your Honor.

MR. FORAN: Your Honor, may we proceed with the rebuttal case of the Government?

THE COURT: Yes, you may.

Testimony of Robert Lynskey

MR. FORAN: Will you state your name, please?

THE WITNESS: Robert J. Lynskey.

MR. FORAN: What is your occupation?

THE WITNESS: I am a Deputy Chief of Patrol for the City of Chicago.

MR. FORAN: Directing your attention to Saturday, August the twenty-fourth, did you have a conversation with the defendant Hoffman in the Cultural Arts Center in Lincoln Park in which you told him, "Kick me in the shins—"?

MR. KUNSTLER: Your Honor, you talk about leading questions. I have never heard one that started out that way. That is not proper on rebuttal or even under direct, your Honor.

THE COURT: I do not share your view. I overrule your objection.

MR. FORAN: Directing your attention to Saturday, August 24, 1968, did you have a conversation with the defendant Hoffman in the Cultural Arts Center in which you said to him, "Kick me in the shins, and I'll arrest you"?

THE WITNESS: No, I did not.

MR. FORAN: Have you ever had such a conversation with him?

THE WITNESS: No, I did not.

MR. FORAN: Directing your attention to approximately midnight on Sunday, August 25, 1968, where were you, sir?

THE WITNESS: I was on Cannon Drive in Lincoln Park. The police were lining up in two ranks while one police vehicle was being utilized to make an announcement that the park was closed, and that those people still in the park were in violation of the law.

MR. FORAN: How many times was that announcement given?

THE WITNESS: That announcement had been given probably a dozen or more times. I heard it three or four times myself.

MR. KUNSTLER: Your Honor, if I can interrupt, Dr. Ralph Abernathy has just arrived.

THE COURT: Let him sit down.

MR. KUNSTLER: I would like to move to reconsider to put him on the stand for the defense.

THE COURT: Let him sit down. You may continue with your examination, Mr. Foran.

MR. KUNSTLER: Does your Honor deny my motion?

THE COURT: I do, sir. You may continue with your examination.

MR. KUNSTLER: Your Honor, the Government said they would have no objection to have Dr. Abernathy testify. He was flown here from Atlanta to be a witness for the defense.

THE COURT: The Government is not running this courtroom.

MR. KUNSTLER: Would your Honor permit an application for Dr. Abernathy to testify after this witness has testified?

THE COURT: I ask you to sit down.

MR. KUNSTLER: Otherwise we are going to excuse him.

THE COURT: Mr. Marshal, have that lawyer sit down.

MR. KUNSTLER: Can you give me an answer to my question? We want to excuse Dr. Abernathy.

MR. FORAN: Your Honor, the interruption in the midst of the questioning of a witness in the presence of the jury is unheard of, your Honor, I wish he would—

THE COURT: Did you hear what I asked you to do, sir?

MR. KUNSTLER: I am down.

THE COURT: Please continue with your examination.

MR. KUNSTLER: I am going to ask Dr. Abernathy to leave, your Honor. It is obvious he is not going to testify.

THE COURT: You sit down, sir, or we will arrange to have you put down.

MR. HOFFMAN: Are you going to gag the lawyers too?

A VOICE: Chained to the chair—

MR. HOFFMAN: You don't have to gag the jury, because they haven't been able to see our witnesses.

THE COURT: That was Mr. Hoffman that made that remark, Miss Reporter.

MR. HOFFMAN: The past Attorney General of the United States, Ramsay Clark—

THE COURT: Mr. Marshal, if anyone rises to interrupt, I ask you to deal appropriately with it as a marshal should.

You may continue, sir, with the direct examination of this witness.

MR. FORAN: Now, on Monday night, did all of the police officers move out first or did some other—

THE WITNESS: After a final warning had been given, the front line of police officers started moving forward and they were met by a severe hail of missiles and rocks. At this point I ordered twelve police officers to move forward and roll gas and smoke grenades in the area of the barricade and the people behind it.

MR. FORAN: How long have you been specifically familiar with the Lincoln Park area and Lincoln Park itself in this area, Chief?

THE WITNESS: For the last four years, since I have been in charge of this particular area.

MR. FORAN: Are there any indications of the curfew time in the park?

THE WITNESS: There are signs prominently posted in the park.

MR. FORAN: How long have those signs been in the park?

THE WITNESS: They have been there for the four years that I have had knowledge of Lincoln Park.

MR. FORAN: That is all.

THE COURT: Ladies and gentlemen of the jury, we are about to take a recess until two o'clock.

(recess)

Will the Government call its next witness?

MR. FORAN: No, your Honor. They are bringing in the next witness.

THE COURT: Call the next witness.

Testimony of Thomas West

MR. FORAN: Will you state your name, please?

THE WITNESS: Thomas West.

MR. FORAN: What is your occupation?

THE WITNESS: I am a Chicago police officer.

MR. FORAN: Calling your attention to approximately two o'clock on August 20, 1968, where were you?

THE WITNESS: I was in Lincoln Park at that time.

MR. FORAN: And how were you dressed?

THE WITNESS: I was dressed in old clothes, a pair of levis, a sweat shirt, and work boots.

MR. FORAN: And what was the length of your hair?

THE WITNESS: It was longer, much longer that it is now.

MR. FORAN: And what were you doing?

THE WITNESS: I was selling newspapers at the time.

MR. FORAN: What was the name of the newspaper?

THE WITNESS: It was *The Militant*.

MR. FORAN: And at that time—

(laughter in the courtroom)

MR. FORAN: And at that time did you see any one of the defendants?

THE WITNESS: Abbie Hoffman.

MR. HOFFMAN: Now, did you have a conversation with him at that time?

THE WITNESS: Yes, I did, sir. I asked him where the rest of the people were, and he told me, to wait, that the lid would start to come off this town come Sunday.

MR. FORAN: That is all, your Honor.

THE COURT: Cross-examination?

• • • • •

MR. KUNSTLER: Mr. West, when Abbie Hoffman stated this remark, you said you heard about the lid coming off on Sunday—

THE WITNESS: Yes, sir.

MR. KUNSTLER: —did he have a can of fruit cocktail in his hand?

THE WITNESS: No, sir, I don't believe so.

MR. KUNSTLER: Thank you. No further questions.

Testimony of James Murray

February 3, 1970

MR. FORAN: Will you state your name, please?

THE WITNESS: James Murray.

MR. FORAN: What is your occupation, Mr. Murray?

THE WITNESS: A reporter for *Chicago Today*.

MR. FORAN: How long have you been a newspaper reporter?

THE WITNESS: Since 1938.

MR. FORAN: Calling your attention to Tuesday, August 27, 1968, shortly after 9:00 P.M., where were you, sir?

THE WITNESS: I was directly in front of the Conrad Hilton Hotel on Michigan Avenue.

MR. FORAN: At that time, sir, what, if anything, was that crowd doing?

THE WITNESS: The crowd was very noisy, chanting such slogans as "Dump the Hump," "The Hump sucks," "Daley sucks the Hump." They were chanting, "Ho, Ho, Ho Chi Minh." They were waving Viet Cong flags, and many other chantings were going on.

MR. FORAN: At that time, sir, shortly after nine o'clock, was anything being thrown?

THE WITNESS: There were many objects. There were bricks, stones, pieces of wood, and there were several whiffle balls with nails in them.

MR. FORAN: Would you describe those?

THE WITNESS: There was a large ball about the size of a baseball which struck just in front of me and bounced and hit my right leg.

MR. FORAN: Were you injured by that when it struck you?

THE WITNESS: A slight cut on the shinbone of the right leg.

MR. FORAN: Directing your attention to about 7:30 on Wednesday, August 28, where were you?

THE WITNESS: I was again in front of the Conrad Hilton Hotel by the main entrance.

MR. FORAN: Calling your attention to approximately 7:45, what occurred?

THE WITNESS: A Poor People's Caravan started to come down Michigan Avenue from the north, and then it proceeded south through the lines of the police officers.

Within minutes, there was a man with a loudspeaker who hollered, "The street is ours. We don't go. Charge. Let's go."

This crowd started to surge forward. Many of them were waving a Viet Cong flag.

As they charged into the first line of the police, another surging crowd came from the west on Balbo and turned south, and got behind the barriers which the police were in front of, and there was a surging crowd, and fighting and striking at the police officers there.

MR. FORAN: What happened then?

THE WITNESS: I saw a young lady sink her teeth into a police officer's left hand as he was holding the baton up, pushing the crowd back. To her left was a young man swinging with a steel helmet, a World War I vintage steel helmet, swinging at the police officer with the helmet.

MR. FORAN: Go on, describe what happened.

THE WITNESS: Several officers were knocked to the pavement. Other officers kept on pushing. The crowd kept on surging. Windows were broken. There was a lot of crying, shouting. Several officers aided young girls and a couple of young boys and an older lady out from behind the barriers, and let them proceed south down Michigan Avenue.

MR. FORAN: Did you see any injured there at that location?

THE WITNESS: Yes, there was a young lady, a blond-haired young man. She was crying saying that he was hurt, he was injured and he was bleeding. They lifted the one corner of the barricade and let him out. Some officer gave an order to take the young man to a first-aid station.

MR. FORAN: Now, calling your attention to an hour or so later, about 10:30, did you see any missiles thrown at that time?

THE WITNESS: The sidewalk seemed to clear a little bit, and a barrage of missiles and stones were thrown, and looking directly ahead of me, looking east, I saw a police officer fall.

MR. FORAN: Did you go over to that scene?

THE WITNESS: I sure did, sir.

MR. FORAN: What did you see when you arrived at that scene?

THE WITNESS: The police officer's helmet was off. He was laying on his left side. He had blood coming from his cheek bone on the left side. As the officer fell to the street, officers on each side of him leaned down to aid him. I heard a command of "Bring up a squad car." He was put into the back seat of the squad car.

MR. FORAN: That is all, your Honor.

THE COURT: Cross-examination?

• • • • •

MR. KUNSTLER: You have been a reporter how many years?

THE WITNESS: Since 1938.

MR. KUNSTLER: How many of those years have you been a police reporter?

THE WITNESS: Practically all the time.

MR. KUNSTLER: Do you have good friends in the Police Department?

THE WITNESS: I have, sir.

MR. KUNSTLER: Who would you class among your friends in the hierarchy in the Police Department?

THE WITNESS: Conlisk.

MR. KUNSTLER: Did you attend any of the so-called victory parties run by the Chicago Police Department after the incident in Michigan and Balbo?

MR. FORAN: Objection, your Honor.

THE COURT: I sustain the objection.

MR. KUNSTLER: You think, Mr. Murray, that the Chicago Police Department is an important steadying influence in Chicago?

THE WITNESS: I do.

MR. KUNSTLER: Would you lie to protect them?

THE WITNESS: No, sir.

MR. KUNSTLER: Never?

THE WITNESS: No, sir.

MR. KUNSTLER: By the way, can you describe the Viet Cong flag for us?

THE WITNESS: It is a black flag—with a symbol.

MR. KUNSTLER: Are you serious?

MR. FORAN: I object.

MR. KUNSTLER: I am asking a serious question. Are you serious that a black flag is the Viet Cong flag?

THE COURT: I sustain the objection to the question "Are you serious?" It is an improper question.

MR. KUNSTLER: Isn't it true that you don't know what a Viet Cong flag looks like?

THE WITNESS: It is not true, sir.

MR. KUNSTLER: All right. Then describe for me the Viet Cong flag.

THE WITNESS: It is a red flag with a symbol.

MR. KUNSTLER: What is the symbol?

THE WITNESS: I don't recall, sir.

MR. KUNSTLER: It is not a black flag, right?

THE WITNESS: No, not all black, sir.

MR. KUNSTLER: Now when you first said it was black and you heard laughter in the courtroom, is that why you changed from black to red?

THE WITNESS: No, sir.

MR. KUNSTLER: What made you change?

THE WITNESS: Because there were black and red flags there and also white flags.

MR. KUNSTLER: Do you state under oath that you saw a Viet Cong flag—at Michigan and Balbo on the night of August 28?

MR. FORAN: Your Honor, I object to that. He has stated that it is red and other colors with a symbol and that is true.

THE COURT: That is an improper question.

MR. KUNSTLER: Mr. Foran, it is not true.

THE COURT: Mr. Marshal, I wish you would direct the men at that defense table not to shout.

MR. KUNSTLER: No further questions.

Testimony of Robert V. Quigley

MR. SCHULTZ: Please state your name.

THE WITNESS: Robert V. Quigley.

MR. SCHULTZ: Your occupation, please?

THE WITNESS: Special Agent, Federal Bureau of Investigation.

MR. SCHULTZ: Special Agent Quigley, directing your attention to approximately 11:15 in the evening on November 14, 1969, would you tell the Court and jury, please, where you were?

MR. KUNSTLER: Your Honor, we object to this testimony thirteen and fourteen months after the events for which these men stand indicted.

THE COURT: I will let the witness answer the question over objection.

THE WITNESS: I was in Washington, D.C., at George Washington University on the quadrangle behind the school library.

MR. SCHULTZ: Specifically, did a man named Abbott Hoffman speak?

THE WITNESS: Yes, sir.

MR. SCHULTZ: Would you tell the Court and jury, please, what if anything the defendant Hoffman said about a society of love?

THE WITNESS: Abbie Hoffman stated that The society in the United States now had to be changed, and a society of love had to be created, and to accomplish this, there must be violence.

MR. SCHULTZ: That is all, your Honor.

THE COURT: Cross-examination.

· · · · ·

MR. WEINGLASS: Agent Quigley was November 14, 1969, the eve of the National Moratorium to End the War in Vietnam?

MR. SCHULTZ: Objection.

THE COURT: I sustain the objection.

MR. WEINGLASS: Did Abbie Hoffman state during his talk that he was late from the plane?

THE WITNESS: Yes, he did, sir.

MR. WEINGLASS: Did he say he had been arrested for standing up on a seat in an airplane?

THE WITNESS: Yes, he did, sir.

MR. WEINGLASS: Now when Abbie Hoffman spoke did he not state the following: "We believe in a nation dedicated to love but in order to love we must learn how to survive and to survive we must learn how to fight"?

THE WITNESS: Is that a correct quote, sir? I don't—

MR. WEINGLASS: Did you hear those words?

THE WITNESS: In essence, yes.

MR. WEINGLASS: I have no further questions.

· · · · ·

MR. SCHULTZ: I have a couple of redirect, your Honor.

What did Hoffman do at the very end of his talk, please?

THE WITNESS: At the very end of his talk he advised the rally that he had a specially prepared chant to be used on the following day, November 15.

MR. SCHULTZ: What did he say?

THE WITNESS: The chant went as follows:

"One, two, three, four, stop the trial/ Five, six, seven, eight, smash the State."

MR. SCHULTZ: Then what was done, please?

THE WITNESS: Shortly after he told this to the crowd, both he and Jerry Rubin led the crowd in the chant.

MR. SCHULTZ: That is all.

[527]

MR. WEINGLASS: Officer Quigley, did you not also hear Abbie Hoffman say that it was expected that the following day, a hundred thousand people would march on the Justice Department to insist that the trial in Chicago be stopped immediately?
MR. SCHULTZ: It is outside the scope, your Honor. I object.
THE COURT: I will sustain the objection.
MR. WEINGLASS: Nothing further.

Testimony of James D. Riordan

February 4, 1970

MR. SCHULTZ: Please state your name.

THE WITNESS: James D. Riordan.

MR. SCHULTZ: And what is your occupation?

THE WITNESS: Deputy Chief of Police in the Chicago Police Department.

MR. SCHULTZ: Now, calling your attention specifically to approximately 5:45 in the evening on Wednesday, August 28, do you recall where you were?

THE WITNESS: I was about fifty feet south of Balbo on Columbus Drive in Grant Park on the east sidewalk.

There were approximately, about 1500 people on the sidewalk from the location where I was standing back to about 9th Street. This was a group of people that wanted to march.

MR. SCHULTZ: And where were you in relation to this group of people that wanted to march?

THE WITNESS: I was in front of them. I stopped the march.

MR. SCHULTZ: Now, at 5:45 that evening on Columbus Drive, did you have occasion to see David Dellinger?

THE WITNESS: I did. He was confronting me at the head of the march.

MR. SCHULTZ: Now, at approximately 5:45, what if any announcements were made?

THE WITNESS: There was announcement made approximately thirty or forty yards back to the south of the front of the march by an unknown man with a loudspeaker.

MR. SCHULTZ: What if anything did you hear on the bullhorn?

THE WITNESS: I heard this unidentified speaker announce to the group that inasmuch as the march had been stopped, to break up in small groups of fives and tens, and to go over into the Loop, to penetrate into the hotels, the theaters, and stores, and business establishments where the police could not get at them, and disrupt their normal activity, and, if possible, to tie up the traffic in the Loop.

MR. SCHULTZ: After that announcement was made, what if anything did you observe the people in your area do?

THE WITNESS: The march disintegrated, and approximately 500 people crossed Columbus Drive and walked west through the ballfield toward the Illinois Central bridge on Balbo.

MR. SCHULTZ: Did Dellinger say anything when this announcement was made?

THE WITNESS: I did not hear him say anything.

MR. SCHULTZ: Did you see where he went?

THE WITNESS: He left with the head of the group that were carrying the flags.

MR. DELLINGER: Oh, bullshit. That is an absolute lie.

THE COURT: Did you get that, Miss Reporter?

MR. DELLINGER: Let's argue about what you stand for and what I stand for, but let's not make up things like that.

THE COURT: All of those remarks were made in the presence of the Court and jury by Mr. Dellinger.

MR. KUNSTLER: Sometimes the human spirit can stand so much, and I think Mr. Dellinger reached the end of his.

THE COURT: I have never heard in more than a half a century of the bar a man using profanity in this court or in a courtroom.

MR. HOFFMAN: I've never been in an obscene court, either.

THE COURT: I never have as a spectator or as a judge. I never did.

MR. KUNSTLER: You never sat here as a defendant and heard liars on the stand, your Honor.

MR. SCHULTZ: Now, your Honor, I move that that statement—how dare Mr. Kunstler—

MR. KUNSTLER: I say it openly and fully, your Honor.

[529]

MR. SCHULTZ: Your Honor, we had to sit with our lips tight, listening to those defendants, to those two defendants, Mr. Hayden and Mr. Hoffman, perjure themselves. I mean Davis and Hoffman.

MR. KUNSTLER: A little Freudian slip, your Honor.

MR. SCHULTZ: Your Honor, I have no further direct examination.

MR. DELLINGER: You're a snake. We have to try to put you in jail for ten years for telling lies about us, Dick Schultz.

MARSHAL JONESON: Be quiet, Mr. Dellinger.

MR. DELLINGER: When it's all over, the judge will go to Florida, but if he has his way, we'll go to jail. That is what we're fighting for, not just for us, but for all the rest of the people in the country who are being oppressed.

VOICES: Right on.

THE COURT: Take that man into custody, Mr. Marshal. Take that man into custody.

VOICES: Right on, right on.

MR. SCHULTZ: Into custody?

THE COURT: Into custody.

VOICES: Right on.

MR. DAVIS: Go ahead, Dick Schultz, put everybody in jail.

MR. DELLINGER: Dick Schultz is a Nazi if I ever knew one.

MR. SCHULTZ: Your Honor, will you please tell Mr. Davis to walk away from me?

MR. DELLINGER: Put everybody in jail.

THE COURT: Mr. Davis, will you take your chair.

MR. HOFFMAN: Nazi jailer.

THE COURT: You may proceed with your cross-examination.

• • • • •

MR. KUNSTLER: Chief Riordan, what time did the march disintegrate?

THE WITNESS: Oh, I would say about six o'clock.

MR. KUNSTLER: Now, would it surprise you, Chief, to know that some forty minutes later, Superintendent Rochford stated that the march was still present, and that he had a conversation with Dave Dellinger at 6:40 that night on that very spot?

MR. SCHULTZ: Objection, your Honor.

THE COURT: I don't deal in surprises. That is always an improper question.

THE WITNESS: It could have happened.

THE COURT: I sustain the objection.

MR. KUNSTLER: At approximately six o'clock, that time was when you say Dave Dellinger left that scene, isn't that correct?

THE WITNESS: That is true. He left my presence.

MR. KUNSTLER: Have you had any conversation with Superintendent Rochford about this?

THE WITNESS: No, sir.

MR. KUNSTLER: Do you know yourself that Superintendent Rochford was there forty minutes later talking to Dave Dellinger and the march had not disintegrated?

MR. SCHULTZ: Objection, your Honor.

THE COURT: I sustain the objection.

MR. KUNSTLER: Chief Riordan, at any time after you heard this speaker make those remarks, did you get on the radio and alert the police in the city of Chicago that a mob was invading the Loop?

THE WITNESS: No, sir.

MR. KUNSTLER: You heard the words, and did nothing?

THE WITNESS: That's right. I reported in to the Yard, the communications center.

MR. KUNSTLER: When did you do that?

THE WITNESS: When I arrived there.

MR. KUNSTLER: At what time did you arrive there?

THE WITNESS: 6:45.

MR. KUNSTLER: And what you had heard over a loudspeaker forty-five minutes earlier about invading the Loop and penetrating the stores and tying up traffic, you didn't think that was important enough to alert a Chicago policeman, is that correct?

THE WITNESS: That is not correct.
MR. KUNSTLER: I have no further questions.

(jury excused)

THE COURT: I have some observations to make here, gentlemen.

Time and again, as the record reveals, the defendant Dave Dellinger has disrupted sessions of this court with the use of vile and insulting language. Today again he used vile and obscene language which, of course, is revealed by the record.

I propose to try to end the use of such language if possible, and such conduct, by terminating the bail of this defendant.*

I do not, if I can help it, intend to permit such tactics to make a mockery out of this trial.

I hereby, Mr. Clerk, terminate the bail of the defendant David Dellinger and remand him to the custody of the United States Marshal for the Northern District of Illinois for the remainder of this trial.
MR. KUNSTLER: Your Honor, is there not going to be any argument on this?
THE COURT: No argument.
MR. KUNSTLER: I would like to say my piece. He is my client, and I think this is an utterly—

(There is disorder in the courtroom.)

MR. KUNSTLER: You brought this on, your Honor. This is your fault. This is what happened in Chicago. You exerted the power, and I would like to argue the point.
THE COURT: You won't argue the point.
MR. KUNSTLER: I will argue, your Honor, that your Honor's action is completely and utterly vindictive, that there is no authority that says because a defendant blurts out a word in court—
THE COURT: This isn't the first word, and I won't argue this.
MR. DAVIS: This court is bullshit.
THE COURT: There he is saying the same words again.
MR. DAVIS: No, I say it.
MR. KUNSTLER: That was not even David Dellinger who made the last remark.
MR. SCHULTZ: It was Davis, the defendant Davis who just uttered the last—
MR. RUBIN: Everything in this court is bullshit.
MR. DAVIS: I associate myself with Dave Dellinger completely, 100 percent. This is the most obscene court I have ever seen.
MR. RUBIN: You are going to separate us. Take us, too.

Take us all. Show us what a big man you are. Take us all.
MR. DAVIS: Mr. Rubin's wife they are now taking—
MR. RUBIN: Keep your hands off her. You see them taking away my wife?
MR. DAVIS: Why don't you gag the press, too, and the attorneys, gag them?
MR. KUNSTLER: Your Honor, there was no need for your action.
THE COURT: The court will be in recess. Mr. Marshal—
THE MARSHAL: Sit down, Mr.—
MR. KUNSTLER: Your Honor, is there no decency left here? Can't we just argue the point?
THE COURT: You will have to go away from that lectern. You can't stand there and insult the United States District Court.
MR. KUNSTLER: Everything in this case is an insult.
THE COURT: You just insulted me again and you have done if often.
MR. KUNSTLER: Every argument is not an insult.
THE COURT: This case is recessed.
THE MARSHAL: Everyone please rise.
THE COURT: Clear the courtroom.
MR. DAVIS: You can jail a revolutionary, but you can't jail the revolution.
MR. HOFFMAN: You are a disgrace to the Jews. You would have served Hitler better. Dig it.

THE MARSHAL: That was Mr. Hoffman, your Honor.

THE COURT: I saw him and I heard him.

MR. RUBIN: You are a fascist, Hoffman—

THE MARSHAL: Clear the court.

THE COURT: Clear the courtroom, Mr. Marshal.

MR. DAVIS: Get as many people as you can. Just like the Convention all over again.

THE MARSHAL: Clear the court.

THE COURT: Clear the court.

A FEMALE VOICE: You little prick.

MR. RUBIN: You are a fascist.

THE MARSHAL: Get out of the courtroom.

Let's go.

MR. HOFFMAN: Oh, yes, I forgot, it's a public trial.

February 5, 1970

THE CLERK: Your Honor, there is a motion for entry of a draft order.

THE COURT: This order has to do with the termination—I will look at that in chambers.

MR. WEINGLASS: If the Court please, if I may be heard—

THE COURT: Go ahead and make your motion, but I think that the Government should be apprised of it in advance.

I will hear you and give such consideration to your presentation as I think it deserves.

MR. WEINGLASS: If the Court please, yesterday at the conclusion of the session the Court advised the defendant Dellinger that presumably as a result of his conduct in court, particularly the statement which was uttered yesterday in the presence of the jury, the Court felt that it had within its power the authority to revoke Mr. Dellinger's bail.

I say that by way of introduction to my remarks because I wanted the record to be clear that the Court acted yesterday solely and exclusively on the basis of what the Court considered to be improper conduct in the courtroom and for no other reason. There was no recitation of fact or allegation by your Honor that the Court in any way felt that Mr. Dellinger would not make himself available to the Court during the remainder of the proceedings.

I submit to the Court on the basis of our completed research of all of the cases dealing with this issue, that the Court has in law no authority to act to revoke the bail of a defendant except where it is clear to the Court that there is a probability that the defendant will leave the jurisdiction and thereby frustrate the proceeding.

THE COURT: That is a matter that always is left to the discretion of the trial judge, and if there is any court in the land after reading the record in this case who wishes to admit your client to bail, and that court has greater authority than I have, I will have to abide by it.

MR. WEINGLASS: Well, your Honor again is indicating, and I think it is very clear that the Court—

THE COURT: I have beseeched you and Mr. Kunstler throughout this trial, beginning with the Seale episode, to please try to get your clients to behave in this courtroom. At no time did you lift a finger or speak a word either to Mr. Dellinger or any of them. I have been very patient for nearly five and a half months.

MR. RUBIN: You haven't been patient at all. You interrupted my attorney right in the middle of his argument. He was right in the middle of his argument and you interrupted him.

You are not being very patient at all. That is not patience.

THE COURT: Ask that man to sit down.

Note who he is. That is Mr. Rubin.

MR. RUBIN: Jerry Rubin.

Can he finish his argument?

Can he finish his argument?

THE COURT: I will ask you to remain quiet, sir.

MR. RUBIN: I will ask you to remain quiet when our attorney represents us in making his arguments.

MR. WEINGLASS: What the Court has indicated by the elaboration of its comments, I think, is very clearly that the Court intends to punish David Dellinger for what he said. Now I have no quarrel with that, that your Honor has a contempt power, and at the end of this preceeding your Honor can punish—

THE COURT: I have more power than that.

MR. WEINGLASS: No—

THE COURT: I don't like the use of the word "power."

MR. WEINGLASS: You have the—

THE COURT: I have the authority to maintain order in this courtroom.

MR. WEINGLASS: But—

THE COURT: It was very difficult when profanity is being uttered by defendants and the judge is called various kinds of names. A defendant has to be tried and so I must let him be here, but in the circumstances of this case he could have been denied bail right from the beginning without his conduct here.

MR. WEINGLASS: Well, if your Honor please, I would like to just answer the Court's remarks without interruption, if I may. If I may—

THE COURT: I will interrupt you whenever I choose. Any judge has a right to—

MR. RUBIN: That is called justice? That is called justice?

THE COURT: Will you ask your—is he your client? Is Mr. Rubin one of your clients?

MR. WEINGLASS: Your Honor, I am—

THE COURT: Will you ask him to remain silent?

MR. WEINGLASS: I am an officer of this court, but I am not a United States Marshal.

THE COURT: At times you have not acted as one.

MR. WEINGLASS: I represent Mr. Rubin's interests here and Mr. Rubin, I feel, has a right when he feels—

THE COURT: If you feel that way, sir, that I have no right to interrogate a lawyer or say something to a lawyer when he is making an argument before me, I deny your motion.

    That will be all.

MR. WEINGLASS: Your Honor is not going to permit me to continue—

THE COURT: That will be all, sir.

MR. WEINGLASS: —my argument—

THE COURT: I deny the motion. I shall not hear Mr. Kunstler on it. I rely on the record.

MR. KUNSTLER: That is disgraceful.

THE COURT: And note that he said that was disgraceful.

MR. KUNSTLER: You are denying Mr. Dellinger bail because he made a speech at Marquette—

THE COURT: The motion, sir, will be denied, and I will ask you both to sit down.

MR. WEINGLASS: Your Honor cannot cut off legal argument in that manner. We have a right to be heard here.

THE COURT: I will tell you that I considered this very carefully and you know what we went through here yesterday.

MR. KUNSTLER: That isn't the reason, your Honor. He made a speech. You threatened him last week because he made a speech at Marquette University and now you are waiting for the opportunity and that one bit of a profane statement, as you considered it, is what you used—

THE COURT: Mr. Marshal, please have that lawyer sit down—both of them.

MR. DAVIS: May we defend ourselves if our lawyers can't?

MR. KUNSTLER: I think the marshal is going to have to put me in my seat this time. I am not going to sit down unless I am forced to sit down.

THE COURT: I direct you to.

MR. KUNSTLER: I think we ought to argue the motion.

THE COURT: I ask you to sit down and there will be no further argument.

MR. HOFFMAN: Your idea of justice is the only obscenity in the room. You schtunk. *Schande vor de goyim,* huh?

    Obviously it was a provocation. That's why it has gone on here today because you threatened him with cutting off his freedom of speech in the speech he gave in Milwaukee.

THE COURT: Mr. Marshal, will you ask the defendant Hoffman to—
MR. HOFFMAN: This ain't the Standard Club.
THE MARSHAL: Mr. Hoffman—
MR. HOFFMAN: Oh, tell him to stick it up his bowling ball.

How is your war stock doing, Julie? You don't have any power. They didn't have any power in the Third Reich either.
THE COURT: Will you ask him to sit down, Mr. Marshal?
THE MARSHAL: Mr. Hoffman, I am asking you to shut up.
MR. RUBIN: Gestapo.
MR. HOFFMAN: Show him your .45. He ain't never seen a gun.
THE COURT: Bring in the jury, Mr. Marshal.
MR. RUBIN: You are the laughing stock of the world, Julius Hoffman; the laughing stock of the world. Every kid in the world hates you, knows what you represent.
MARSHAL DOBKOWSKI: Be quiet, Mr. Rubin.
MR. RUBIN: You are synonymous with the name Adolf Hitler. Julius Hoffman equals Adolf Hitler today.
THE COURT: You may bring the jury in.

(jury enters)

Ladies and gentlemen of the jury, good morning.
THE JURORS: Good morning, Your Honor.
MR. DELLINGER: Good morning.
THE COURT: Does the Government have another witness?

Testimony of Barbara Lawyer

MR. FORAN: Will you state your name, please?

THE WITNESS: Barbara Lawyer.

MR. FORAN: What is your occupation, Miss Lawyer?

THE WITNESS: I am a cocktail waitress at the Den in the Palmer House.

MR. FORAN: Directing your attention to the month of August 1968, where were you employed at that time?

THE WITNESS: In the Haymarket Lounge in the Conrad Hilton.

MR. FORAN: Now, calling your attention to a period of time shortly after eight o'clock on August 28, 1968, where were you?

THE WITNESS: I had just finished taking a break, and I was crossing the lobby into the Haymarket Lounge to go back to work. I had just come through the doorway into the center of the room.

MR. FORAN: And at that time, what did you see, Miss Lawyer?

THE WITNESS: There were about twenty-five or thirty people running toward me from the window, and they were yelling and shouting and pushing and shoving customers.

I saw them leap over tables where customers were seated, and with their arms they just swept glasses and drinks off the tables onto the floor, knocked over furniture, and one man ran up to the bandstand and pushed the drums off the stand onto the floor, and a lot of yelling.

MR. FORAN: And how were these people dressed? Could you describe these people?

THE WITNESS: Well, they were dressed in the hippie fashion with moccasins and vests, and some were shoeless.

MR. FORAN: And what happened then, after what you have described?

THE WITNESS: Well, I saw a couple of policemen come through from behind these people and try to clear out the room.

MR. FORAN: Now, the people had come through the entrance of the building?

THE WITNESS: They came through a broken window.

MR. FORAN: What occurred then?

THE WITNESS: Well, then the police tried to get them out of the lounge into the lobby and I couldn't see them from there because I was over in the corner of the room.

MR. FORAN: Now, Miss Lawyer, was there anything unusual about the lobby that night?

THE WITNESS: Yes, there was an odor in the lobby.

MR. FORAN: And what type of odor was it?

THE WITNESS: It smelled like vomit. It was very strong.

MR. FORAN: That is all, Miss Lawyer.

(jury excused)

MR. WEINGLASS: Your Honor, I would want at this time, because I sincerely and honestly feel that the Court realizes that its position with respect to the jailing of Dave Dellinger is indefensible in law—

THE COURT: I will not hear you further on that motion.

MR. WEINGLASS: Well, your Honor, you are keeping a man in custody, and you are not permitting a lawyer to make an argument for his freedom. That is unheard of. That is unprecedented in law.

THE COURT: I ask you to sit down, sir

MR. WEINGLASS: Your Honor knows—

THE COURT: Mr. Marshal, will you ask that man to sit down?

MR. WEINGLASS: You have no authority for taking that man's freedom away, and you will not let me make a legal argument in his behalf.

MR. SCHULTZ: That is disgraceful.

MR. WEINGLASS: That is disgraceful.

MR. KUNSTLER: Your Honor, I said yesterday you were vindictive, you are doing this because he spoke. You told us on Thursday, you waited for the opportunity.

THE COURT: Have that man sit down. I will hear no further argument on this motion.

MR. HOFFMAN: You put him in jail because you lost faith in the jury system. I hear you haven't lost a case before a jury in twenty-four tries. Only the Corbiasin people got away. We're going to get away, too. That's why you're throwing us in jail now this way.

Contempt is a tyranny of the court, and you are a tyrant. That's why we don't respect it. It's a tyrant.

THE COURT: Mr. Marshal, will you ask the defendant Hoffman to remain quiet?

MR. HOFFMAN: Schtunk.

MR. RUBIN: You are a tyrant, you know that.

MR. HOFFMAN: The judges in Nazi Germany ordered sterilization. Why don't you do that, Judge Hoffman?

MARSHAL DOBKOWSKI: Just keep quiet.

MR. HOFFMAN: We should have done this long ago when you chained and gagged Bobby Seale. Mafia-controlled pigs. We should have done it. It's a shame this building wasn't ripped down.

THE COURT: Mr. Marshal, order him to remain quiet.

MR. HOFFMAN: Order us? Order us? You got to cut our tongues out to order us, Julie.

You railroaded Seale so he wouldn't get a jury trial either. Four years for contempt without a jury trial.

THE MARSHAL: Mr. Hoffman, will you shut up.

MR. HOFFMAN: No, I won't shut up. I ain't an automaton like you. Best friend the blacks ever had, huh? How many blacks are in the Drake Towers? How many are in the Standard Club? How many own stock in Brunswick Corporation?

THE MARSHAL: Shut up.

THE COURT: Bring in the jury, please.

(jury enters)

THE COURT: You may cross-examine this witness.

• • • • •

MR. KUNSTLER: Miss Lawyer, you stated that there were twenty-five, thirty people that you saw coming through the window, is that correct?

THE WITNESS: They were running from the direction of the window.

MR. KUNSTLER: You were asked how they were dressed. Do you recall that? You said hippie fashion.

THE WITNESS: Yes.

MR. KUNSTLER: Can you state what you mean by hippie fashion?

THE WITNESS: Well, it's the current mode, I guess, of describing dress, moccasins, mod clothes.

MR. KUNSTLER: Yes, what else?

THE WITNESS: And the fact that it includes long hair, beards.

MR. KUNSTLER: Now when you saw the window—did you look at the window?

THE WITNESS: Yes, I did.

MR. KUNSTLER: Did you see glass in the Haymarket Lounge on the floor?

THE WITNESS: Yes, I observed it.

MR. KUNSTLER: Would you describe how much glass you saw on the floor?

THE WITNESS: Well, there was the glass from the broken window pane and there was also glass from all of the glasses that had been knocked off the tables onto the floor.

MR. KUNSTLER: Now, after the people come through the window, did you see any police come through the window?

THE WITNESS: Yes, sir, I saw two.

MR. KUNSTLER: Now, when the police came through, were they carrying stretchers or night sticks?

THE WITNESS: They had nothing in their hands.

MR. KUNSTLER: And how many customers were there in the room at that time?

THE WITNESS: Well, I really don't know because when I got in there, everything was in such confusion that I really couldn't say.

MR. KUNSTLER: Now, lastly, Miss Lawyer, you have told us here today you smelled an odor in the lobby. Do you recall that?

THE WITNESS: Yes.

MR. KUNSTLER: When did you smell that?

THE WITNESS: We smelled that most of the week, but that night also.

MR. KUNSTLER: Did you smell it Monday night?

THE WITNESS: I can't tell you whether we did. I just remember smelling it that week.

MR. KUNSTLER: You are sure about Wednesday night?

THE WITNESS: I am sure.

MR. KUNSTLER: Did you tell the FBI about that?

THE WITNESS: No, I did not.

MR. KUNSTLER: When did it first come to you in a way that you can testify about—when you spoke to the United States Attorney?

THE WITNESS: When I spoke to Mr. Foran, yes, sir.

MR. KUNSTLER: Thank you. No further questions.

THE COURT: Gentlemen, I have been informed by the United States Marshal that the juror Mrs. Shirley Seaholm is not well and does not feel equal to continuing this afternoon. Therefore we shall have to recess until tomorrow morning.

I very much regret her illness.

Tomorrow morning at ten o'clock, ladies and gentlemen.

February 6, 1970

THE COURT: Where are the defendants?

THE COURT: May the record show defendants Hoffman and Rubin came in at 1:28, attired in what might be called collegiate robes.

MR. RUBIN: Judges' robes, sir.

A DEFENDANT: Death robes.

THE COURT: Some might even consider them judicial robes.

MR. RUBIN: Judicial robes.

THE COURT: Your idea, Mr. Kunstler? Another one of your brilliant ideas?

MR. KUNSTLER: Your Honor, I can't take credit for this one.

THE COURT: That amazes me.

MR. KUNSTLER: This is a motion to permit the defendants or some of them to sum to the jury themselves. Just weeks ago the United States District Court for the Southern District of New York in a criminal matter involving Roy M. Cohn, permitted Mr. Cohn to sum to the jury—

THE COURT: Cohn was an able lawyer who understood the limitations of good conduct in a United States District Court.

MR. KUNSTLER: Well, he was a defendant. He was not there as a lawyer.

We are not saying that all are going to sum to the jury. One defendant in particular, David Dellinger, has indicated a strong desire to do so and is in fact now preparing his summation—

THE COURT: Don't have him spend too much time in the library.

MR. KUNSTLER: Well, your Honor, he is preparing his summation, and we say that it is particularly important in a case like this, a political case, motivated by political considerations by the Government of the United States.

There are the most serious and compelling reasons why a defendant should be permitted to sum up to the jury should he desire to do so. The worst that a defendant can do in this case is to hurt himself in summing up. He takes that burden, he waives all the safeguards of the law in that respect. If he helps himself, so much the better.

There is no detriment to the Government in a defendant summing up. There can only be detriment to himself, but that is the risk he assumes.

So we respectfully move the Court that those defendants who desire to do so should be allowed to conduct their own summations under any time limitaions which the Court may see fit to impose.

THE COURT: Does the Government wish to reply?

MR. SCHULTZ: Very briefly, your Honor. The hazards involved of a defendant summing up to a jury are great indeed. A defendant does not know the rules of law. If the defendant goes beyond the evidence which the Government cannot and will not do, then the Government is being prejudiced.

Further, the defendant is facing the jury not subject to cross-examination. Mr. Dellinger wants to be able to present his case without being subject to questioning as to the bases for whatever he is saying. That is why they want to make this presentation in this way.

I submit that in this case the Court should exercise its discretion the same as has been done repeatedly in the past by denying the motion. Mr. Dellinger, whose bond was revoked because of his conduct, because of the epithets screamed at your Honor, obscenities hurled just yesterday. The Court should exercise its discretion against this motion and have the defendants' attorneys representing them in this case present the final arguments to the jury.
THE COURT: Is there anything you want to say in reply to Mr. Schultz?
MR. DELLINGER: I would just like to say I have not screamed, and—
THE COURT: I have asked your lawyer.
MR. DELLINGER: —I have not used repeated vile or obscene language. That's untrue.
THE COURT: Please sit down.
MR. KUNSTLER: I just wanted to refer your Honor to Judge Medina in the trial of the eleven leaders of the Communist Party in the Dennis case, or this part, which is called United States against Foster, where Judge Medina said if he were convinced that the defendant felt that he could better present his case to the jury, that he would, without hesitation, permit him to sum up—which is exactly, of course, what was cited in the Roy Cohn case when Mr. Cohn wanted to sum up.
THE COURT: The defendants have moved for permission to conduct personally their own summation by directly addressing the jury at the close of all the evidence.

A situation remarkably similar to the case at bar arose some twenty years ago, and you have referred to it, Mr. Kunstler, United States vs. Foster.* A defendant sought permission to argue personally to the jury despite the fact that he had been represented by counsel throughout the trial.

Upon concluding that the matter was for the sound discretion of the Court, Judge Medina took note of the defendant's disorderly conduct during the lengthy trial, his participation in various kinds of outbursts, and his attacks in open court upon the Court's rulings. These occurrences were found to establish the defendant's intent to manifest his disrespect for the Court, and Judge Medina thus determined to take appropriate action to see to it that the opportunities for similar misconduct were minimized.

The circumstances that caused the Court in Foster to exercise its discretion in denying the motion are not only present here, they are even more compelling.

From the frequent outbursts of these defendants, and their manifest disrespect for this Court, despite repeated admonitions to discontinue their conduct, I conclude that it is most probable that the defendants would utilize the opportunity they seek to further disrupt this trial.

Mr. Clerk, the defendants' motion for permission to conduct personally their own summation by directly addressing the jury at the close of all the evidence will be denied.

Call your next witness, please.

Testimony of Irwin A. Bock

MR. SCHULTZ: Mr. Bock, will you state your name again for the court reporter?

THE WITNESS: Irwin A. Bock, Chicago—

MR. SCHULTZ: Your occupation, please?

THE WITNESS: Police officer, Chicago, Illinois.

MR. SCHULTZ: Mr. Bock, have you ever on any occasion shown the defendant Rennard Davis a balloon attached to a tube?

THE WITNESS: No, sir, I have not.

MR. SCHULTZ: Have you on any occasion ever discussed with Mr. Davis a balloon attached to a tube of any sort?

THE WITNESS: No, sir, I have not.

MR. SCHULTZ: Have you Mr. Bock, ever demonstrated to Mr. Davis any sound amplifying device of any kind?

THE WITNESS: No, sir, I have not.

MR. SCHULTZ: Mr. Bock, have you ever met and spoken with Davis at the doorstep of an apartment in a building on the South Side of Chicago?

THE WITNESS: No, sir, I have not.

MR. SCHULTZ: Did you ever meet Davis at or near the apartment of Sidney Lenz?

THE WITNESS: No, sir.

MR. SCHULTZ: That is all, your Honor.

THE COURT: Cross-examination.

• • • • •

MR. WEINGLASS: Mr. Bock, you knew Rennie Davis in July and August of 1968?

THE WITNESS: Yes, sir.

MR. WEINGLASS: And on July 27 you were with Rennie Davis?

THE WITNESS: Yes, sir.

MR. WEINGLASS: Do you remember where that was?

MR. SCHULTZ: Objection, your Honor. The conversation which we are rebutting regarding Davis was August 2.

THE COURT: I sustain the objection.

MR. WEINGLASS: Well, if the Court please, if we could establish that this man as a part of his duties was to be with Rennie Davis and he was with him July 27 and 28 and August 1, I think he would have to explain why he wasn't with him on August 2. That is the purpose of my cross-examination.

THE COURT: Regardless of your purpose, the question is bad as a matter of law of evidence, and I sustain the objection.

MR. WEINGLASS: The Court is reading the rule of evidence restrictively against us. Your Honor knows that you have discretion, a wide latitude of discretion.

THE COURT: I will tell you that for you to say I am restricting you to applying rules restrictively against anyone—is an unfair charge against the Court and I resent it. There has been a ruling made, and I ask you, sir, to continue with the cross-examination of this witness without any scurrilous remarks.

MR. WEINGLASS: Mr. Bock, you were with Rennie Davis July 27, 28, and August 1 as part of your duties, were you not?

THE WITNESS: I was, sir.

MR. WEINGLASS: He was attending meetings on each of those days and so were you to keep track of him?

THE WITNESS: Yes.

MR. WEINGLASS: On August 2 did you know Rennie Davis was going to a steering committee meeting with Tom Hayden and Dave Dellinger that night?

THE WITNESS: No, sir, I don't believe I was aware of that.

MR. WEINGLASS: Mr. Bock, if you knew that Rennie Davis would be with Tom Hayden and Dave Dellinger on Friday night, you would make it your business to get there and be with him, wouldn't you?

MR. SCHULTZ: I object to the question.

THE COURT: I sustain the objection.

MR. WEINGLASS: You testified on direct that you never had a conversation on the doorstep of an apartment, of Sid Lenz' apartment, with Rennie Davis, is that correct?

THE WITNESS: That is correct.

MR. WEINGLASS: Did you ever go to Sid Lenz' apartment?

THE WITNESS: I believe I have, yes, sir.

MR. WEINGLASS: Well, as a Peace Council member, as a member of the Chicago Vets for Peace, wouldn't you be invited to a meeting concerning the upcoming demonstration?

THE WITNESS: Not necessarily.

MR. WEINGLASS: So if on August 2, Friday night, Sid Lenz was having Dave Dellinger, Tom Hayden, and Rennie Davis over, it would be something which you would probably know about, wouldn't you?

MR. SCHULTZ: Objection.

THE COURT: Sustain the objection.

MR. WEINGLASS: Now, when Mr. Schultz asked you the question about ever having a conversation, I don't believe you had to think very much about it. You just gave him a very quick answer.

MR. SCHULTZ: Objection to the form of the question.

THE COURT: I sustain the objection.

MR. WEINGLASS: Since you have testified here in court, have you had occasion to talk to Mr. Schultz about where you were on August 2, 1968.

THE WITNESS: Yes, sir, I have.

MR. WEINGLASS: And did he tell you that Rennie Davis had said he saw you on that night, August 2, at Sid Lenz' house?

THE WITNESS: No, sir, I don't believe he did.

MR. WEINGLASS: Mr. Bock, it was part of your job in the Navy to attempt to train people for recovery of downed flyers, isn't that true?

THE WITNESS: To train people for—

MR. WEINGLASS: You were actually training the pilots, I believe, on how to be recovered?

THE WITNESS: Yes, sir. You might say that.

MR. WEINGLASS: And in that training was not a technique used by the Navy, the inflation of a balloon by a downed pilot with a radio attached to give his location so that he could be picked up by search aircraft?

THE WITNESS: I was aware that such a technique existed in the United States Military Service, but we were not teaching that technique, to the best of my knowledge.

MR. WEINGLASS: But you became aware of that technique in the Navy, didn't you?

THE WITNESS: I would say yes, sir, I became aware of it.

MR. WEINGLASS: I have no further questions.

THE COURT: Please call in your next witness.

MR. RUBIN: Tough luck, Irv.

Testimony of Desmond Butler

MR. SCHULTZ: Will you state your full name?
THE WITNESS: Desmond Butler.
MR. SCHULTZ: What is your occupation?
THE WITNESS: Chicago policeman.
MR. SCHULTZ: And on August 28, 1968 at about eight o'clock, where were you stationed, please?
THE WITNESS: Michigan and Balbo.
MR. SCHULTZ: Were you present, Mr. Butler, during any disturbance that occurred on Michigan and Balbo about eight o'clock?
THE WITNESS: Yes, I was.
MR. WEINGLASS: Your Honor, I am going to object to the characterization of something as a disturbance.
MR. SCHULTZ: I will call it a riot. That is what it was. That is what it was.
MR. WEINGLASS: That is what the Walker Report called it, a police riot.
MR. SCHULTZ: They are really desperate, your Honor. They are really desperate. They simply cannot prove a case, so they have got to adopt inaccurately other people's remarks.
THE COURT: I will compromise with you. Let's call it an incident.
MR. SCHULTZ: All right.
   What, if any, objects were being thrown while you were standing there for that period of time, please?
THE WITNESS: There were rocks thrown and sticks.
MR. SCHULTZ: Do you recall any other objects in particular, please, Mr. Butler?
THE WITNESS: There was a piece of a sewer cap which hit an officer behind me.
MR. SCHULTZ: And prior to that piece of a sewer cap hitting the officer behind you, did you see the object in the air?
THE WITNESS: I saw it coming from the park. I ducked, so it wouldn't hit me, and it hit the officer next to me.
MR. SCHULTZ: And where did it hit him, please?
THE WITNESS: It hit him in the stomach.
MR. SCHULTZ: After he was hit what, if anything, occurred?
THE WITNESS: Some other officers behind him took him away.
MR. SCHULTZ: Did you see the object which hit him.
THE WITNESS: Yes, when it fell to the ground, it was a sewer cap, about this wide, this long [*indicating*].
MR. SCHULTZ: We have no further questions.
THE COURT: Cross-examination.

• • • • •

MR. KUNSTLER: Mr. Butler, do you remember being interviewed by the Federal Bureau of Investigations?
THE WITNESS: Yes, sir.
MR. KUNSTLER: It was early in September, do you recall that?
THE WITNESS: Yes.
MR. KUNSTLER: Of '68. Can you remember here whether you told them anything about this incident occurring?
THE WITNESS: No, I can't. I don't know if he might not have asked me that question.
MR. KUNSTLER: I will show you D-371 for identification, and ask you if that refreshes your recollection of whether you told anything to the FBI about this incident.
THE WITNESS: Yes.
MR. KUNSTLER: Is it not a fact that what appears in that statement is a grating from a sewer cap and not a sewer cap?
THE WITNESS: Right, yes, metal grate.

[541]

MR. KUNSTLER: Is it your recollection, after reading the statement, that you told the FBI something different than what you have testified to here today?

THE WITNESS: I really couldn't—don't remember exactly what I told them. I know what it was, though, at the time.

MR. KUNSTLER: Mr. Butler, just one last question. What the FBI has in its statement is different than what you told us today, isn't that correct?

MR. SCHULTZ: Objection, your Honor.

THE COURT: Sustain the objection.

MR. KUNSTLER: I have no further questions, your Honor.

MR. FORAN: The Government rests.

(Thereupon the Government rests its case in rebuttal.)

Closing Argument for the Government—
Mr. Schultz

February 10, 1970

THE COURT: Ladies and gentlemen of the jury:

I might say to you that we have come, as I am sure you all or most of you know, to the point in this trial known as the time when the lawyers make their final arguments to the jury or, as they are sometimes referred to, summations.

Mr. Schultz will open for the Government.

MR. SCHULTZ: Thank you, your Honor.

MR. SCHULTZ: Ladies and gentlemen of the jury:

All seven defendants are charged with conspiring to cross state lines to incite a riot during the Convention. Five of the defendants, Hayden, Dellinger, Davis, Rubin, and Hoffman, are then charged with doing things in Chicago both before and during the Convention where they personally incited a riot.

The final two defendants, Weiner and Froines, are not charged with crossing state lines; they are charged with teaching and demonstrating to others the use of an incendiary device, the one they were going to use to blow up the Grant Park underground garage.

Now the first question that you must ask yourselves is why would anybody want to incite a riot? Why should they want demonstrators to destroy property or police to destroy property pursuant to a riot? Why? Why would they want this?

Well, we can look at the defendants' own statements as to why they would want a riot.

Davis and Hayden wrote after the Convention that they had imposed an international humiliation on the Government and they sought to impose this by creating a riot and then blaming the riot on an illegitimate government fighting for its survival, destroying its people in the streets.

Hayden wanted to create the first step towards the revolution. That is what he said at Downers Grove.

Dellinger said that he wanted to bring the U.S. military machinery to a halt. He referred to the people in Chicago as freedom fighters, and on Thursday, after the violence, that horrible violence, he compared the Americans who were fighting in the streets, compared their actions to the actions of the revolutionaries in Cuba.

In December of 1967 Rubin told Norman Mailer that the presence of one hundred thousand people at the Festival of Life would so terrify the establishment that the Convention would be held under armed guard and the resulting violence by the establishment itself will smash the city, and then he said he was going to devote full time to getting a hundred thousand people here to do just that, to smash the city.

Hoffman stated that he wanted to smash this system by any means at his disposal, in the book that he wrote right after the Convention. He intended to "wreck this fucking society." That's what he said.

The point is that they came here wanting a riot, wanting people to be injured. By creating a situation of violence, where it would appear that the demonstrators were being oppressed, people would be magnetized, would be polarized, would join in with the demonstrators, and a National Liberation Front would be started. This was to be the beginning.

When the riots occurred—and they were riots—Davis said, "We won the Battle of Chicago," and he called for little Chicagos to be created all over. That's what he said as soon as he got his riots.

Hayden called the riots on Wednesday night a tremendous success, and he later termed Chicago the first step toward the revolution.

And Hoffman, what did he do? On Thursday night after the riots, he toasted the victory with champagne in the National Mobilization Committee headquarters. He was happy, and I'm trying to explain to you why, why they were happy.

Now, the defendants could not publicly state and publicly announce that they were bringing people here to incite a riot, to charge into the Convention, to fight the police, because if they did that and then there was violence, the people who might otherwise join their movement would say "you're the ones who are asking for trouble."

People will only join these demonstrators if they think the demonstrators were peaceful and the government was violent, not the other way around, so they had to, for that reason, state publicly, "We are coming for a festival of music and joy and for a counter-convention and for workshops." They could get people here for innocent protest, for proper protest, and then turn it into violence and start their revolution.

Now, a good part of the Government's case, especially the part dealing with the planning activities, was presented by four witnesses, Mr. Bock, Mr. Frapolly, Mr. Oklepek and Mr. Pierson. These witnesses related the defendants' plans for mill-ins, for diverting police, for fighting the police in Lincoln Park, for building barricades, and their other plans for violence.

Now, of course, the defendants deny all of these meetings and these conversations, claiming that Mr. Bock, Mr. Frapolly, Mr. Oklepek, and Mr. Pierson falsified their testimony. The defendants, of course, recognize that if you conclude that these witnesses did not falsify their testimony, that the defendants are guilty as they are charged. It is your duty as jurors here in this case to determine who is telling the truth. Who, if anyone, fabricated testimony?

Well, in determining a witness' credibility, to see if he was telling the truth, you consider, among other things, the witness' demeanor on the stand.

I am sure you noticed a noticeable difference between those four witnesses that I have just mentioned, and many of the defense witnesses, who sort of sat there on that witness stand with a chip on their shoulders. They would argue with the judge. They were there as advocates, many of them. They were there to express a point of view, not to tell the facts impartially so you, the jurors, could, through their eyes, see what occurred and make your determination. They weren't there as independent witnesses.

Now let's look at Mr. Bock. At the time he testified he was on the steering committee of the New Mobilization Committee, away up in the ranks. The defendants suspected him, as you recall. They took his statement to see if he was a policeman. So he gave a statement. He gave a statement which he candidly and immediately acknowledged on the stand. He said, "Yes, I gave that statement. Yes, I said all those things in the statement. I had to say them, and I said them."

He told you, no hesitation, no reluctance, and he told you why. Perfectly reasonable, because if a policeman couldn't make a false statement to a defendant's lawyer, no policeman could work undercover.

Mr. Bock did what he had to do, and he explained it to you.

Mr. Frapolly testified. The defendants' position with him, with Mr. Frapolly, is that he was an agent provocateur. They had a situation which they brought out on cross-examination of Mr. Frapolly where he participated with an SDS group at his campus where they planned to go on the stage while the president of the university was talking and they were going to take the microphone away from him and address the group. What happened was they walked up on the stage, and they pushed the president away from the microphone physcially. Then they ran away, and Mr. Frapolly was thrown out of school. He could have told the school, "I'm an undercover policeman. I was there in my capacity, and please let me stay in school. I am a policeman." He could have said that. He didn't. He didn't to protect his identity; he suffered the humiliation of being suspended for a year from the school, but he is not a provocateur.

Now Mr. Oklepek was spending his summer vacation working for a newspaperman. He was assigned to work at the National Mobilization Committee where he became a member of the staff. He wasn't in very close with the defendants, but he heard some significant conversations and he related to you exactly what he saw and what he heard. He even told you that at one time he believed that they were nonviolent, that they were planning peaceful activities. Would an advocate, someone who had an ulterior motive, say "At one time I thought that they were training to avoid violence"? Would he say that? No.

He realized that he was naive when he thought that. At one time he thought that they were not planning violence. But he learned.

Robert Pierson—he said that on Wednesday in the afternoon in Grant Park when they were rocking that police car he, Mr. Pierson, had his hand on the police car, that everybody was rocking and Rubin didn't. That certainly doesn't help Mr. Pierson nor hurt Mr. Rubin, but that's what happened and that's what he told you.

Now the point is that these witnesses and the other witnesses for the Government testified simply to what they saw, not as advocates. What they saw.

Now what I would like to do is look at the proof relating to each of the defendants referring both to the Government's case and the defense, so that you can analyze the proof, so that you can see it all capsulated.

Rubin. Let's take him first. Rubin was telling Phil Ochs, Arlo Guthrie, Ed Sanders, Jacques Levy, Judy Collins, Allen Ginsberg, Country Joe McDonald, Peter Seeger and other musicians that you heard, he is telling them all, with Hoffman, "We want a peaceful festival. Come to Chicago. It will be a lovely music festival."

What he didn't say was that in December 1967 he had told Mailer in effect that he wanted violence in Chicago. Mailer testified that Rubin said to him in December of '67, before these conversations with the artists, that he wanted a hundred thousand people at the music festival in Chicago, which would so intimidate and so terrify the establishment, that the Convention would be held under armed guard and that violence would result, and the establishment would smash the city. He didn't tell Judy Collins and Phil Ochs and the rest his purpose. He needed them to get the people here, and apparently he wasn't satisfied, once he got here, with just letting the establishment smash the city. He had to sort of help it along by running through Lincoln Park, as he did, giving those "Arm yourself" speeches, "fight the pigs, get the pigs."

Before coming here on July 23 Rubin spoke at a rally in New York sponsored by the anti-imperialistic movement. At that speech on July 23, was a special agent of the FBI named Casper. He testified that Rubin said that people should mass in Chicago and cause disruptions, disruptions to the election system in the United States.

Rubin then came to Chicago. He came here to provoke the riot, to smash the city. He was at the National Mobilization Committee a number of times. He had conversations with the other defendants.

On Sunday, the first day of the Convention week, Rubin was observed by Al Baugher out in the park. He was sitting with Lee Weiner, and as Mr. Baugher walked by and said, "Hi, Jerry," Mr. Rubin called Mr. Baugher a fascist pig. That's the way he talks. All right. Then the action starts.

At 5:30 that night police Officer Barbara Callender—you remember her. She was the redheaded girl assigned to walking around Lincoln Park in somewhat of an undercover capacity—at 5:30 on Sunday she saw Rubin get up on the picnic table and he said to about two hundred people that the park belongs to the people. The park belongs to the people. Rubin's from New York. Hoffman's from New York. They are all from out of town.

The park belongs to the people. Arm themselves, he said. Fight the pigs, break into small groups, wait for instructions from the marshals. Wednesday's the big thing, that they're going to stop the Convention. That's Rubin. That's his music festival.

Between nine and ten o'clock that night, Youth Officer Robert Murray was standing right next to Rubin—right next to him. Rubin started to shout and point to ten policemen by the fieldhouse, and he said, "Look at these motherfucking pigs standing over there," screaming and pointing. That's how you incite people. He used that language, and that's why you heard it, so you can make the determination.

Then he started bringing the people toward these ten policemen, standing up near the fieldhouse, screaming profanities. "They are pig motherfuckers," on and on and on. He called them white honkie mf'ers, "Get out of the park, take off your guns. Look at them standing there with their arms folded. You think you're tough," on and on and on.

Mr. Murray said he saw Rubin flick a cigarette, didn't see him smoke it, saw him flick it. Rubin, according to his witnesses, doesn't smoke cigarettes.

The defendants tried to put in evidence that what happened at the fieldhouse wasn't as Mr. Murray described. They put on Linda Morse. That was the lovely girl with the long blonde hair, the one who shoots the M-1 rifle, practices karate, and is getting ready for the revolution.

She said that she was at the fieldhouse. She didn't see Rubin, and she said that the people were teasing and stuff. That's what Linda Morse said about it.

But then they tried to show you that it wasn't Rubin at the fieldhouse, because on cross-examination of Mr. Murray, whom do they bring into the courtroom but some guy, Levin, with a football helmet and a beard and a jacket, looked pretty tough, and he walked in and stood there, and Mr. Kunstler pointed to him and said, "Mr. Murray, isn't that the man you saw?" Mr. Murray laughed. He said, "No, that's not the man. Absolutely not. He's too large. It's a motorcycle helmet that he is wearing, and Rubin had a football helmet."

You were supposed to look and think, "Could have mistaken him for Rubin." That's what you were supposed to think.

And then we pulled the plug, because he was lying. Levin said on Sunday he had a beard that long—but then we had him two days later with no beard.

The only mistake they made was, they didn't know that we had found some photographs of Levin two days later. It was a fabrication, a fabrication to take Jerry Rubin out of it, the putting on of the helmet, the whole works, and you had to sit through it.

Now, at about ten o'clock Sunday night, either just before or just after the fieldhouse incident, we don't know, Barbara Callender saw Rubin again. He spoke with Hayden, he spoke with Davis.

Then in Davis' and Hayden's presence Rubin gave another one of his speeches filled with four-letter words. Mrs. Callender had heard Rubin say just about eleven. "Don't leave the park. Stay in the park and fight the pigs."

Now Rubin says he wasn't there. Rubin says we got the wrong guy. How does he say it? Well, he puts on Phil Ochs to say that Rubin was home in bed. They went home, went to his house, took him out of bed, brought him to the fringe of the park. Mr. Ochs said that they got to the park just a couple of minutes before the police clearing.

He thought the police clearing was at eleven o'clock.

The fact is the police clearing started that night at about 12:30. So if he had been with Rubin for an hour to an hour-and-a-half before, it means that Rubin could have left the park at 11:00, gone home, met with Mr. Ochs and arrived back in Lincoln Park ten minutes before the clearing at 12:30. It doesn't contradict the evidence at all.

During the early afternoon on Tuesday, Pierson met with Rubin and they walked looking at the posters in the park on the trees.

And then looking at one poster of a fat policeman, that's when Rubin said, "Look at that fat pig. We should isolate one or two and kill them." And Pierson agreed.

That is not a crime, saying, "We ought to kill them." That is not charged. Saying it and trying to get people to do it are two different things. But it tells you what he intended, what he wanted. He said it and Pierson agreed. Then they talked with a number of groups for a few hours.

That night, Pierson was still with Mr. Rubin. Pierson saw the people in their group,

Rubin and Pierson and Albert and five other persons, attack a CTA bus. They stoned the bus on the street, kicked at the doors, even rocking the bus. Judy then gave—you know who Judy is, one of the girls—she gave Rubin and Pierson each a small bottle of paint. They threw it at a squad car. Then someone jumped on the car and kicked the blue light off the roof. Then the girl Judy lit a trash barrel on Armitage and Cleveland. Fire Department trucks came to put out the fire. They sat on the steps of some house and they watched the Fire Department put out the fire. They broke up about two or three in the morning.

Rubin had a busy day on Tuesday.

Now we are on Wednesday.

At the Bandshell we have the flag pole incident and then Pierson observed Rubin screaming wildly when the people were throwing objects, screaming at the people, "Kill the pigs. Kill the cops."

Rubin claims he didn't yell "Kill the pigs."

They produced Mr. Buff. Mr. Buff said Rubin came over to him and said, "Why don't you move up near the flagpole and tell the police to get out of the area instead of back here yelling to the crowd to sit down?" It is simply not true.

Rubin for three days and nights had been inciting people to fight the pigs, saw Steve Buff at that moment trying to cool it for good reasons, because they didn't want the ally to be disrupted, and he told Buff "Get off the microphone." That's what happened.

So we proved with regard to Rubin that he came to this city to incite to violence. On Sunday and Monday, on Tuesday and on Wednesday, he was awfully busy inciting. So we are done with Rubin, and I am losing my voice.

There is Davis next. Let's look at Davis. Davis is much more complicated, much more sophisticated, but with the exact same objects.

The first statement we have by Davis is back at Judd Hall, November 20, 1967. He was talking to the Resistance group.

Mr. Thompson, one of our first witnesses, testified that Davis said to the fifty people from the Resistance that there would be civil disobedience to disrupt the Convention and that he said they would do anything that was possible to disrupt the Convention.

Davis, when he took the stand, changed it. He said, "Yes, I said we were going to disrupt but I said we were going to disrupt the sham of the rigged Convention." Entirely different. What Richard Thompson heard him say was that they were going to do anything possible to disrupt the Convention, and if Davis didn't say that, where were the other fifty people at Judd Hall?

On July 27, at the Universal Church of Christ, of all places, Davis stated—and Mr. Bock heard him state—that there will be war in the streets until there's peace in Vietnam. Davis organized the Chicago demonstrations with the other defendants to humiliate the United States Government. He used those very words in a writing after the Convention. He now thinks that he's gone so far, the Movement has developed so, that he can go to campuses, and call for resurrection—excuse me—insurrection and revolution. "Resurrection" certainly wasn't the right word.

Insurrection and revolution. He couldn't say it back in 1968.

Let's look. Let's look at how Davis organized the violence and planned the violence, and then during the Convention, incited, personally incited, the violence.

On August 9 they have the first marshals' meeting. Davis said they were going to have a mill-in in the Loop to bust it up and shut it down. They were going to, in order to get the march to the Amphitheatre, have disruptions throughout the city to attract the police, to attract the National Guard, so that the march could proceed.

Now, Davis was quick to tell you that everything he planned and discussed was peaceful, and yet practically every time he spoke, except on national television or publicly, he talked about mill-ins, disruptions, disabling jeeps, using Mace, getting the Gaurd out, there would be war in the streets. That is all they had on their minds, looking for the confrontation. And they found it.

Hayden was arrested Monday afternoon in the park. The police saw Hayden in the park at about 2:30 and they arrested him, and they had an issue, a political arrest. Letting the air out of tires is now a political arrest. A political arrest, says Davis, screaming it to the crowd. We are going to march to the police station.

Now Davis very shrewdly—you saw how bright he was, there is no getting around that—Davis said, "Well, I organized the march because I didn't want all the people just running wild to the police station."

It was Davis who was screaming, "It's a political arrest. Let's go free Hayden."

Anyway they march, they marched from Lincoln Park down to State Street, a relatively orderly march. They had a few chants, "What do we want? Revolution. When do we want it? Now. Ho, Ho, Ho Chi Minh. Hell, no." and "Free Hayden." They passed the police station, they walked by the Logan statue. At this time Davis had the PA system and he screamed, "Take the hill. Take the high ground."

At midnight that Monday Hayden and Davis were crossing at Balbo and Michigan. At 12:05, Hayden was arrested and Davis left the area.

Well, within a half-an-hour of that, at 12:30, Davis was seen at the barricade in Lincoln Park, on the megaphone, shouting at the people to fight the pigs. He was seen for a few minutes there, and then he was seen after the clearing of the park, inciting a crowd which was fighting the police.

Davis says he wasn't in Lincoln Park. He is not going to tell you he was. What does he say? He says that he was at the National Mobilization headquarters. Whom does he call to establish that? He calls Paul Potter, a former roommate, a very close friend, who was active during the Mobilization activities during Chicago. Potter said he walked with Davis back to the National Mobilization headquarters.

Potter stated on cross-examination that before taking the witness stand he knew, as he put it, police spies and police informants saw Davis in Lincoln Park at the time that Potter was with Davis at Mobilization.

But Potter, who had this information, presumably since the end of October, didn't tell Davis about it in November, never called Davis, waited until January 15 before he called and said, "Oh, by the way, I'm stopping through," and didn't even discuss it then on the telephone.

Do you believe that?

It didn't happen.

It's clear, ladies and gentlemen of the jury, that Potter was just a last-minute alibi witness, passing through Chicago on the way to Boston, a close friend of Davis, whom they could easily get to change the story, a former national president of SDS, a very close friend of Davis. But he fell apart on cross-examination, because it wasn't properly prepared.

The fact is that Davis left Hayden when Hayden was arrested, and within half-an-hour he arrived at Lincoln Park at the barricade.

All of that evidence proved beyond all doubt that Davis came to Chicago from Cleveland, Ohio, about July 20 with the intent to incite and organize and encourage and promote a riot in this city, and when he got here he did things to plan it and incite it and he did, in fact, plan it and incite it during the Convention.

Now, let's take another defendant. Let's look at Abbott Hoffman.

Like Rubin, Hoffman got people here for his Festival of Life. He said his reason for coming here was to have a music festival. The very day Hoffman arrived in Chicago he told David Stahl that he was prepared to tear up the town and the Convention and he was willing to die in Lincoln Park.

He testified that part of his so-called Yippie myth was that Yippies would be all over the city diverting troops. He testified that it was part of the Yippie myth that there would be so much paranoia, fear, in Chicago that the delegates would need helicopters to fly to and from the Amphitheatre. A Festival of Life?

Let's look at some of Hoffman's pre-Convention plans. On August 9, Hoffman says he was at the meeting for five minutes, he just walked in and walked out. Well, of course, he says that. He takes himself out of every situation where violence is being planned.

At that meeting they discussed diversionary activities to distract the military and the police from the march, to cause riots throughout the city, to draw the police and the Guards away so the march could confront the Amphitheater.

Hoffman said that the Yippies would aid in these diversionary tactics and he discussed building barricades in Lincoln Park to defend the park against the police.

Hoffman denied all these statements, of course.

On the twenty-first of August, Hoffman was in Lincoln Park when they practiced the skirmish lines.

On the twenty-fourth, on Saturday, Hoffman had a conversation. Mr. Bock was present, so was Hayden and Davis and Weiner, and Froines was there, and Hoffman said that if they're not allowed to stay in the park, they ought to think of taking over a hotel for sleeping space. That's not a crime, to say "We are planning to take over a hotel." But it shows you what they were planning, what their intent was.

They didn't take over a hotel. It didn't materialize, but it tells you what they were planning, and you see what they did by their own actions.

When the Convention week then began, Hoffman began to create, as did the other defendants, situations where a physical confrontation would begin.

The first confrontation, Sunday afternoon, was just what he wanted. First it was the truck. The police worked the truck out. The electricity. That was worked out. Everything is fine. A drunk is being arrested—another opportunity. Capitalize on your opportunities, and he did. And when the crowd chased the policemen up the monument, throwing stones at them and hitting one of the policemen with a "Peace Now" sign—Hoffman standing there next to Mr. Baugher saying, "This is beautiful, it's beautiful."

The next day is Monday. Hoffman met Pierson. They had a conversation. Pierson admitted that he brought up the subject and he, Pierson, said that it was quite a confrontation in the park Sunday night with the clearing. And Hoffman said, "Yes, they pushed us out last night, but tonight we're going to hold the park."

And then Hoffman had a map of the park and started showing where everybody should be.

A miniature military operation which was bound on its face to fail, but that didn't make any difference. You see, little kids, little hippies in groups of five or six running back and forth to help to defend the park against the police. They didn't have a chance but they are not supposed to have a chance, they are supposed to get their heads bashed in, they are supposed to fight with the police with their fists and clubs, and there should be blood. And then it will appear that there is military oppression, a fascist state, imperialistic state that has to beat up young people who simply came here for a music festival or to protest the war, because the government can't afford to have free thinkers in the country. That's the way it's got to appear.

Mr. Bock testified that Hoffman said that he had met with the Blackstone Rangers and that the Blackstone Rangers were going to help defend the park and that they had weapons and they weren't afraid to use them. But the Blackstone Rangers weren't bilked by Hoffman. They didn't come.

Tuesday night in Lincoln Park Hoffman is speaking to a group about storming the Hilton Hotel, about using bottles and rocks and golf balls with nails pounded through them and helmets and storming the Hilton the next day.

Hoffman says that wasn't he. He was at the Coliseum. That wasn't he.

All right. Let's look at his alibi. His alibi witness was first Phil Ochs who testified that he first saw Hoffman at the Coliseum at about 8:30 on Tuesday night.

On cross-examination Mr. Ochs admitted that he didn't even have a watch and he didn't know if it was 8:30 or not. All he could specifically recall is that he was at the Coliseum, he was on the microphone, Hoffman upstaged him by grabbing the microphone and led the crowd in a chant of "Fuck you, LBJ."

There is no question that Hoffman was at the Coliseum on Tuesday night. The question is when did he get there. He was seen in Lincoln Park about eight o'clock. He could have spoken to the crowd and he did speak to the crowd and then drive to the Coliseum and address the group.

The following day was Wednesday. There is no evidence of Hoffman during that day because he was in jail most of the day, he was arrested in the morning for having the word "fuck" written on his forehead.

Now we are on Thursday, Thursday the twenty-ninth of August. Richard Thompson, Chicago police officer, is at the Logan statue.

As you recall, Mr. Thompson was black, looked like one of the demonstrators, standing on the curb, with the crowd. Hoffman walked up and said, "Are you with me?" And

Mr. Thompson said, "What do you mean, am I with you?" and Hoffman said, "Well, you see that cat. When we get to the top of the hill, if the cat don't talk right, we're going to hold him there, and the police won't bother us."

Thompson promptly left the area to notify the police, and he did. Hoffman tried. He happened to have gone to a policeman, and nothing happened.

He wrote in his book that he announced publicly the plan to kidnap the head pig and snuff him if they touched us.

When we finally get into it on cross-examination, he says, "Well I wrote that in my book but it was all a myth." A myth. Another word for "myth" or another definition is, whenever it incriminates you, it's a myth. When you don't like it, it's a fairytale.

Well, I think that's enough about Hoffman. We've proved on the substantive count that he came here on August 7 from his home in New York, came here with Rubin from New York, to organize and incite and promote and encourage violence.

Now, let's look at the activities and the planning of Hayden and Dellinger. Their primary role, their primary role, was the Wednesday Bandshell. In early March, before they had planned on not mentioning violence to the public because then there would be discredit, Hayden spoke to a Resistance group in March about disrupting the Convention.

The next time we hear from Hayden is by Mr. Michael Kilian, who was the *Tribune* reporter. He heard Hayden say on the telephone, "Fine. Send them out. We'll start the revolution now. Do they want to fight?"

Hayden tells you that they came here for vigils, for a counter-convention, for the grassroots of America, to show that they're fed up with the Government. "Fine. Send them out. Do they want to start the revolution now—do they want to fight?"

That is what he was saying privately.

All right. Hayden spoke on July 25. Mr. Sweeney, a New York businessman, an advertising executive, testified that he was at the Hayden speech in New York. Now there is nothing illegal about the speech, but it shows what he was coming here for. The United States had broken the rules; they were going to break the rules.

Now, Dellinger on the same day was speaking in the evening in San Diego. Mr. Gilman, the young newsman, heard Dellinger talk about Vietnam and the fighting and the brainwashing of the United States prisoners of war by the American Government after they got them from North Vietnam. At the end of the speech Dellinger said to the group, "I am going to Chicago to the Democratic National Convention where there may be problems." And the crowd went wild.

Then he said, "I will see you in Chicago," with his fist up.

It is not a crime to state that, but it tells you, did he come here for a vigil? Did he come here, as they say, for workshops?

Your Honor, I have pretty much lost my voice. I would ask your Honor if I would be permitted to finish the argument tomorrow.

THE COURT: I won't require you to put a laryngologist on the stand to prove what you say. Ladies and gentlemen of the jury, I have concluded that we will recess tonight now until tomorrow morning at ten o'clock.

February 11, 1970

MR. SCHULTZ: Ladies and gentlemen of the jury, when we recessed last evening, I was discussing Hayden and Dellinger, beginning on Wednesday which culminated at the Bandshell and then Michigan and Balbo.

That morning, that Wednesday morning at about 10:30, there was a meeting, a very large meeting, at the Mobilization headquarters. At this Wednesday morning meeting they discussed what would follow the Bandshell.

Now Mr. Bock and Mr. Frapolly heard that they were going to have a march, but Dellinger said the march would be stopped. He said that the march, though, would be a diversion for the other people who would want to leave the park and go into the Loop, and Mr. Bock heard him say "for militant action."

Well, when Davis took the stand he said that the action in the Loop wasn't for militant action, but it was to have people go into the Loop, to go to the hotels, and to demonstrate at the hotels. That is how he defined it.

That was a very important meeting. It is a key meeting. In addition to the defendants, more than twenty people were present; whom do they call other than the defendants? Nobody.

The reason—it is so simple—the reason is that they did plan that action at that meeting. The did plan it and, in fact, they effectuated it that afternoon, and there was no way around it, so they ignored the meeting. A key meeting. They ignored it.

Then we have the Bandshell. At the Bandshell you have Dellinger saying, "We're not going to have a lot of speeches because this is a meeting for action, not speeches." Then Dellinger gave the alternatives, the alternatives they discussed that morning. How does Dellinger tell the group about the three alternatives? He says, "There are going to be three alternatives. One is a peaceful march and the other—well, I am going to call on someone to tell you about that later."

Dellinger won't say it. He won't say it. He won't say what they planned. He is very careful.

Then Tom Neumann spoke. He presented the second alternative, the one that Dellinger wouldn't say anything about except that it was another action. He said, "We have decided, some of us, to move out of this park in any way we can, to move into their space in any way we can, and defend ourselves in any way we can." He is clearly calling for violence by the demonstrators. When Neumann finished his speech, what does Dellinger say? He has got to say something. He said he didn't hear the speech, but he said, "I'm sure he," referring to Neumann, "made his message clear. Those who are going to do his alternative can begin doing that now."

Dellinger doesn't want anybody to know that he is participating in it, but we know he was participating in it because we heard evidence from the meeting where they planned it for this militant action that Dellinger doesn't want anything to do with. He still hasn't mentioned the action, the violent action. That is Dave Dellinger. Very forthright.

Then Hayden gets on the microphone, and he says, "Make sure if blood is going to flow, let it flow all over the city. If we're going to be disrupted and violated, let the whole stinking city be disrupted. I'll see you in the streets."

Of the 15,000 or so people that were present at the Bandshell, about 1,500 lined up in the march. At about 6:30, Deputy Superintendent Rochford spoke to Dellinger, and there were still people in the march present, and he pleaded with Mr. Dellinger for an alternative to the march to the Amphitheatre. He said, "Stay here at the Bandshell all night. Go to Grant Park across from the Hilton Hotel. Hold an assembly there. Do you have any suggestions?" And then Dellinger said, "We're going to march to the Amphitheatre, and I don't have to listen to you." And Dellinger just turned around and walked away from Rochford.

An assembly, a counter-convention? Is that what it was? They planned a confrontation, and they got it. And the defendants were joyous, joyous over the success of the riot. Well, how do we know that?

The next day in Grant Park Mr. Carcerano heard Hayden say that the demonstrators had created a vanguard of people experienced in fighting for survival, a vanguard, the leaders of the people, experienced in fighting for their survival.

That is what they got out of Chicago, he said. These statements are remarkably similar to Linda Morse's who talked about slowly taking over the cities, war in the cities, a vanguard of people fighting for their survival, Vietnam coming home. Remarkably similar. Think about that.

Dellinger after the riots said, "We want to bring the United States military machinery to a halt." They called it the first step toward their revolution. They compared it to Saigon. They compared it to Cuba and the revolutionaries. That is what they wanted, the beginning. That is why they forced the confrontation.

We have proved beyond all doubt that Hayden and Dellinger came to this city for the purposes of organizing, aiding, inciting, and encouraging a riot, and they did on Wednesday. They did just that at the morning meeting on Wednesday morning alone. They then executed it at the Bandshell, and then after the Bandshell.

All right. Now let's look briefly at Weiner and Froines.

On August 18 at Welsh Hall, Froines spoke about mobile tactics being the same as guerrilla tactics, busting windows, and so on. And Davis said, "That's not what he said. He said that you have to be as mobile as a gorilla."

Well, now, Davis is too smart for that. A gorilla isn't even mobile—maybe a monkey is.

Then you have during Convention week both Weiner and Froines being active.

On Monday afternoon just before the Hayden arrest, Weiner said they should have had flares the night before, that Sunday night, could have thrown them into police cars. On Monday night Froines talked about the ammonia and the soap. You remember that meeting.

The following morning, Tuesday morning at the National Mobilization headquarters, Froines told Hoffman and Mr. Bock about the police car he had busted up the night before.

Now let's get to Thursday morning because that is the principal charge relating to these two men.

On Thursday morning at eleven o'clock in Grant Park, Mr. Bock met with Froines and Weiner and Lowenthal and Shimabukuro and Marilyn Katz. Froines said that they needed more things to use against the police and the Guard. Weiner said they should have some cocktails. Shimabukuro asked Weiner, "Do you mean Molotov cocktails?" And Weiner said, "Yes." He said, "All you need—" he said, "They're easy to make. All you need are gasoline, sand, rags, and bottles." And Weiner said that a good mobile tactic would be to pick a target in the Loop and bomb it.

Weiner then asked Mr. Bock to get some bottles. Bock said he would. Weiner said that he and Shimabukuro would get the other materials that were necessary which would have been the gasoline and the rags and the sand. Bock left. He didn't get the materials. Instead he called his control officer.

Mr. Bock came back for the hour later meeting and didn't find Weiner. He did run into Mr. Froines and Froines said that he, too, was looking for Weiner but hadn't found him.

Mr. Bock never met Weiner or Froines after that. That was the end of it for him. But at 2:30 that afternoon Mr. Frapolly, who didn't know anything about the bombing, saw Froines, Weiner and Shimabukuro and others.

Shimabukuro said to Weiner, "Is Frapolly all right?"

And Weiner, "He's all right," meaning you can talk in front of him.

So then Shimabukuro proceeded to tell Weiner how they had planned for that night at 7:30 to meet at the underground Grant Park garage because they were going to fire bomb it with Molotov cocktails. He said, "Don't tell anybody about it. Just be there at 7:30." That was the plan.

As you know, the Chicago Police Department was notified of this and they had twenty men waiting in the underground Grant Park garage.

The next day, Friday, at Downers Grove, Mr. Bock and Mr. Frapolly were both present when Mr. Weiner discussed the fire bombing of the underground garage. He said that he saw men questioning Shimabukuro and he left the garage. They couldn't arrest Shimabukuro. So that is the plan for blowing up the garage. They failed.

The last thing with regard to Froines is the butyric acid, the stink bombs. They are not charged with stink bombs; they are charged with coming here to disrupt, incite a riot and disruption with stink bombs helps you conclude whether they came here for the purpose of disruption.

The butyric acid was used simply to add to the disruptions. So we have proof of that, of the charges regarding the Molotov cocktail and also the use by Froines of the butyric acid to further disrupt.

Let me briefly discuss the conspiracy charge.

We have shown that these defendants, all seven of them, had a mutual understanding to accomplish the objects of the conspiracy, that they had a common purpose of bringing disruption and inciting a violence in this city, and that all seven of them together participated in working together and siding each other to further these plans. Oh, they never explicitly said, "You do that to blow up that," and "I will do that to incite that crowd," that is not how they did it. It was tacit understanding, a working together in all these meetings and all of these conferences that they had, and that is how they conspired.

The only difference between five of the defendants and the remaining two, Rubin and Hoffman, were the ways of getting the people here. Rubin and Hoffman were going to get their people here by a music festival, and the others were going to get their people here by saying they were going to have a counter-convention of the grassroots of America.

All seven defendants worked together jointly for the common purpose and discussed and planned together for the common purpose of creating violent conflict and disruptions in this city. They were going to incite violence in this city by bringing other people here and by coming here themselves. We have proven the defendants guilty on the substantive counts as well as the conspiracy charge, as we charge.

The last area I want to cover are march permits. Most of Davis' direct examination was to impress you on how genuinely he tried to get march permits and an assembly site at the Amphitheatre. Well, he wanted a march permit and he wanted an assembly permit at the Amphitheatre, but it doesn't follow that because he wanted permits he wanted to avoid violence. Don't be fooled by that. Why did Davis want permits for the Amphitheatre? He wanted permits first to make it look like "We are trying to avoid violence. We want permits."

Number two, he wanted permits because they wanted to be where the TV cameras were, at the Amphitheatre.

And, number three, they wanted permits because they wanted the confrontation right at the Amphitheatre, right at the Amphitheatre.

As Davis and Hayden wrote in January of '68, they were going to cap the Convention week with disruptions and they were going to pin the delegates in the Amphitheatre. That's what he said.

If the defendants really wanted a rally, a rally, as they said, they would have negotiated for a rally site. But they didn't want a rally. They wanted a street confrontation at the Amphitheatre, and anything other than the Amphitheatre was nonnegotiable.

Davis rejected all other march routes and had no alternatives except to the Amphitheatre.

So just because he said he wanted a permit doesn't make his intentions nonviolent. And if he couldn't get a permit, the next alternative was to have the confrontation, try to go without a permit.

A march permit, ladies and gentlemen, wouldn't have made any difference. An assembly at the Amphitheatre wouldn't have made any difference. They have shown you, we have proven to you by their conduct, that they came here for a riot. They insisted on a confrontation and they rejected all alternatives for peaceful assembly, workshops and a counter-convention. They came here to riot. We have proven, ladies and gentlemen, we have proven in this case, we have proven beyond all doubt, all conceivable doubt, that these defendants, all seven of them, every one of them, came to Chicago, came to this city to incite people to riot, bringing them here under peaceful guise, getting them here and manipulating so a riot would result from the confrontation. They wanted the riot to start a Vietnam in the United States. They are guilty of coming here to incite a riot. They came here and they incited a riot.

THE COURT: Mr. Weinglass, you may speak to the jury.

Closing Argument for the Defendants by Mr. Weinglass

Ladies and gentlemen of the jury:

This has been a long and tedious trial for all of us. I think Mr. Schultz has exhausted, utilized every shred and piece of evidence that the Government has been able to accumulate against these seven men since they started their investigation. He used all the evidence he could. He wove the evidence into a very fine, very manicured fabric which fit the Government's theory of this case.

The theory of the Government's case put very briefly at the very end of Mr. Schultz' summation is that seven men long active in the peace movement, men who from all indications worked hard to change and better the future, had suddenly decided to embark upon a totally insane and completely inexplicable course.

What the Government contends that they wanted to do in the spring of 1968 after they knew that the Government had just passed a new law making it a crime to cross state lines to incite or promote violence, was to cross state lines and promote and incite violence, and if there would be any question about who did it, they would sign their names on permit applications, they would insist in meeting with officials of the city, they would go on public television and announce their plan, and they would even meet with the U.S. Attorney, Thomas Foran, just in case there was any question about who was causing the violence.

Now, they have to prove their case beyond a reasonable doubt and you have to believe it beyond a reasonable doubt, and if you can believe the Government's case, that these men plotted to put themselves in jail, that these men conspired to have this trial, then you could find them guilty. But I suggest to you that the whole foundation upon which this case is built, the whole structure of it, put in terms of common sense, is just not acceptable as a rational proposition. Unless they could bring a psychologist before you who could testify as to their lunacy, I don't think you could have the crime that they are suggesting was committed by these men, committed on the basis of everything you have heard in this courtroom.

There is an old maxim in the law—and I am relatively new at practice, but I have heard it—and that is that you can create in a courtroom anything that you have witnesses for. It is actually true.

Doesn't the Government have the obligation to present before you the whole truth? Why only city officials? Why only policemen, undercover agents, youth officers, and paid informers? In all of this time, couldn't they find in this entire series of events that span more than a week one good, human, decent person to come in here to support the theory that Mr. Schultz has given you?

We brought in Ruth Migdal, the woman who lives on the North Side who volunteered to act as a medical aide and was at Michigan and Balbo when she saw the police rush by her chanting "Kill, kill, kill" and go into the crowd.

We brought in delegates. We brought in McCarthy people who came to the city, Sam Brown, Mr. Lynford. We brought in civil rights activists who were here on the streets, Dick Gregory. We brought in the police officer Reggie Robinson, who testified that the black officers were reassigned in the middle of the week after they refused to do what they were told to do.

We brought in a pacifist, Stuart Meacham. We even brought in a revolutionary, Linda Morse, who was referred to so much.

We brought in a number of authors, Mr. Styron, Norman Mailer. We brought in a newsman, Mr. Pew, who saw the boy get clubbed in the revolving door.

We brought in Mark Lane, a noted attorney. We brought in Reverend Dutenhaver who was conducting the service in the park on Tuesday night.

We brought in performers, Arlo Guthrie, Judy Collins, Ed Sanders, Phil Ochs, Country Joe, and we brought in director Jacques Levy.

We brought in Allen Ginsberg, Dr. Leary.

We brought in a nurse, Jean Snodgrass.

We brought into this courtroom people who were there, people who do not belong to the Yippies, people who do not belong to the National Mobilization, people who were there and felt compelled to tell the truth.

Well, look for a minute at who was fooled. We fooled Dick Gregory, we fooled Wesley Pomeroy, a man who has been a police officer for twenty-four years and was a special police consultant to the Attorney General of the United States. We fooled Rev. Dutenhaver and all the rest.

I ask you if you can find decently that these men, men of public affairs, men who have been in life, men who know intimately the workings of the system, could all be fooled, could all be tricked, could all be duped as the Government is suggesting they were.

Now I am not going to rebut point by point every fact which Mr. Schultz relies on. I won't dispute the testimony of Officer Riggio who came before you and said that Tom Hayden, a man who confers with Averell Harriman, a man who has travelled in the company of Robert Kennedy and Julian Bond, came to the city to let air out of a police car tire on Sunday night in the park, and to spit on another officer on a public sidewalk, and this was proof of the fact that he was announcing the beginning of the revolution.

These need not be answered, and I don't think this case will be decided on those kinds of details.

The Government has attempted by bringing in these police officers to recite detail after detail—Mr. Aznavoorian, Jerry Rubin threw a sweater at him. Mr. Pierson said Jerry Rubin threw a small jar of paint at a police car but missed. We don't have to rebut all this. This is a desperate attempt by the Government to piece together many, many details, in order to convince you that their theory of what happened is right.

These men had tails on them twenty-four hours a day, two tails every twelve hours, and rethink, remember, think back, with all of those tails on them, following them twenty-four hours a day, what physical acts have they brought before you that these men have done?

Lee Weiner. Not a thing. Not a thing.

John Froines. Frapolly said he was throwing rocks at police cars.

Jerry Rubin, I indicated to you, was seen throwing a sweater and a small jar of paint.

Tom Hayden—letting air out of a police car and spitting on a police officer on the sidewalk.

Rennie Davis was not seen doing anything except they claim he was on the microphone on two separate occasions urging people to fight the police.

Abbie Hoffman was not seen doing anything of a criminal nature although they, too, say that he was urging people to do things.

David Dellinger, of course, they claim did nothing in the nature of a criminal act while he was here.

I want to go back to the four men on whom Mr. Schultz told you the Government bases its case.

These four men are undercover agents. Their names are Frapolly, Bill Frapolly, Dwayne Oklepek, Bock, and Pierson.

Oklepek, technically, is not an undercover agent. He is a newspaper man. You remember Dwayne talking about it. He was offered $160 a week by Jack Mabley to infiltrate. So he was acting in an undercover capacity not for the police but for a newspaper.

Mr. Schultz says they are very important to the case. As a matter of fact, he spent the first hour of his summation justifying—a little apprehensive as to how they were received. Maybe no one likes an undercover agent. He felt it was necessary to argue that these men are perhaps better than they appeared, and that has to be done for a very simple reason.

There is no honest man or woman who will accept the job of spying and deceiving other people. It is something which an honest man just cannot bring himself to do. Think of it for yourself. From the time you wake up in the morning to the time you go to bed, while you are working on the job, your life is one of deception.

You must lie to the people you are in contact with. You must lie to them, you must convince them, and deceive them. And anybody who undertakes that work for any period of time and does it for a period of time loses the handle of truth and can no longer be honest. This has been true through history.

Neither side trusts an undercover agent, neither the Government nor the other side. And there's reason for it, because the people who work with them know that they can't be trusted.

When I met with Irv Bock, and I did have that meeting with him, we went to lunch. We sat down and talked. We talked about his Navy career and the work he was doing. Irv Bock was as sincere with me as he was with you. I really could believe Irv Bock.

MR. SCHULTZ: Objection, your Honor. If Mr. Weinglass had been a witness, he could say, but he is not. It is not evidence. He shouldn't say what he thought.

THE COURT: Yes, that is inappropriate. I direct the jury to disregard the observation of Mr. Weinglass.

MR. WEINGLASS: I won't go into Bock's testimony.

I would say that of the Government's case, twenty-five to thirty percent depends on the reports of these four men, and I won't go into it step by step.

But about Irv Bock, he testified that when he gave me that statement, in the written statement, he said he knew I was working for the defense, and he knew that he had to maintain his cover because he was still doing work on the inside. He was going to maintain his cover by telling me a series of lies, but the logic of it is just the reverse. The fact of the matter is that Irv Bock had to give me a story that he knew squared with everything else that I was getting from all the other witnesses I was interviewing. He had to. Otherwise, I would have said, probably, "Irv, how can you tell me that? Craig Shimabukuro, or Lee Weiner, or John Froines have said—"

MR. SCHULTZ: Objection to that. We have no way of cross-examining Mr. Weinglass on what Craig Shimabukuro, or Lee Weiner, or John Froines told him. That is improper argument.

THE COURT: I sustain the objection.

MR. WEINGLASS: Your Honor, but if everything the Government said were true, I would know right away that Irv Bock is lying.

MR. SCHULTZ: The point is we can't cross-examine Mr. Weinglass on what was told to him. It is not fair for him to say to the jury what may have been or may not have been told to him.

THE COURT: I sustain your objection, sir. I agree with you.

MR. SCHULTZ: All right.

MR. WEINGLASS: At any rate, it is our position that Irv Bock had to maintain his cover, and he was doing it, and he was doing it by telling the truth because that was the only way that he would not be caught up in a factual inconsistency. He testified about what he said in that statement. He signed it.

In that statement, he said the marshal training was entirely peaceful in nature, that it appeared to him that "it looked like the kids were just having a good time in the park" and he said that there was nothing of a violent nature ever discussed.

And he said that he was with Lee Weiner and John Froines on Thursday morning, but there was no mention or no discussion of any kind of any incendiary device, and during the whole week, he never heard anyone talk about incendiary devices. Never happened anyway, but he said he never heard it. That was his statement. I submit to you Irv Bock told the truth to protect his cover, and he did.

Now the other undercover agent is Bill Frapolly. Bill Frapolly, you will remember, was with a group that had thrown the head of Roosevelt University from behind a lectern, apparently—I don't know if he fell off the stage or not.

He also admitted that he was the one who suggested that they throw some kind of a plant or cable into the front of the barbed wire of a vehicle. You will remember that. He said, "Oh, that was just a joke. That was just a joke."

I don't know what kind of a man would make that suggestion to a group of young people who were coming here to demonstrate, but clearly it was the most violent suggestion made of all. The author is a star witness of the government, Bill Frapolly.

Dwayne Oklepek was a little confused. He wrote that he thought the marshal meetings were peaceful, and that the Mobilization leadership wanted to have a peaceful demonstration. He said he later changed his mind, and apparently he did. You will recall on cross-examination he was interviewed by the FBI, I believe, a total of nine times. I don't know what happened to Dwayne Oklepek, but Dwayne Oklepek had a very different story after he was interviewed by the FBI than he did when he was reporting to Mr. Mabley.

With Dwayne Oklepek, let's take a look at the myth of marshal training. People were coming from all over the country. They were strangers in the park. They were getting together and doing these exercises. They were meeting with Allen Ginsberg and were "om-ing" and they were singing with Phil Ochs. There was a ritual, a sun-up on Tuesday morning at which Abbie Hoffman sat on the beach with Allen Ginsberg, and "om-ing" a sunrise ritual.

They said people were training in karate, people were training in judo. There wasn't one police officer out of 12,500 who were then on the force that has been brought into this courtroom to tell you that any one person ever used karate or judo on them. If they would have had one man, they would have brought him in. This skirmish line which Mr. Schultz has been describing over and over again was never used, not once. You saw the movie when the crowd on Michigan and Balbo faced the police line. They were cheek-and-jowl at one point, the crowd and the police line, a perfect situation for the skirmish line that he is attempting to describe. And it just was not employed. It was never used, never. These were never used and never intended to be used, and they are just being paraded before you in an attempt to show that the young people who were here were violent in nature when there is no other proof to indicate it.

But there has been testimony and substantial testimony about what the marshals actually did do—and what did they actually do?

The most dramatic use of the marshals was at the Bandshell. The crowd did react to the arrest of Angus McKenzie. Ten or fifteen people link arms and take the crowd and walk back twenty or thirty feet away from the police. That is a skirmish line and that was the marshal line being formed and those were the marshals in action. That was the best explanation, the best dramatization of what the marshals did. They pushed that crowd back.

The total marshal picture here is one of brave people, young people working to restore order in conditions that had potential for disorder.

The last class of Government witnesses I will characterize as agents who go about receiving information. These are men, who in some cases were trained, and some cases merely paid, who go to meetings, public meetings that are being held in churches and schools, and they sit there and they go home right away and call the FBI.

Now, starting with Mr. Thompson. Remember Mr. Thompson? November of 1967 he went to hear Rennie Davis speak. He said Rennie Davis said at that time that they would disrupt the Convention.

When Rennie Davis was on the stand, he said, "I said we have to disrupt the sham of the Convention by having a mass assembly."

It is very dangerous to confuse words like that, and if you are going to send a person to prison it has got to be done a little more precisely than that.

MR. SCHULTZ: Objection to that.

THE COURT: I sustain the objection. The jury will not send anybody to prison. The matter of punishment, if any, the responsibility of punishment, if any, is lodged in the Court.

MR. WEINGLASS: Let me give you an example of it, of the danger.

Mr. Schultz in closing his argument said to you that Rennie Davis on Thursday morning, August 29, in Grant Park in this city, said that they should have a National Liberation Front now in the United States which would be just like the Viet Cong in Vietnam. That is Mr. Schultz' quote, "just like the Viet Cong in Vietnam," indicating to you that what Rennie Davis was really saying is that we have got to start a violent uprising like the Viet Cong did in Vietnam.

Rennie Davis was on the stand testifying. He said he called for an American Liberation Front, or a National Liberation Front which was to be a coming together of poor people, students, black people, poor whites, and a number of other unrepresented people into a movement which would try once again to gain representation in this government.

You will recall in reading the Gospel according to St. Matthew, there is a passage in there in which Christ said to his disciples, "I have not come to the earth to bring peace but to bring a sword," and if there had been a Gilman there or Casper there or Salzberg there or a Thompson there, that proof would be paraded before a jury and a court as proof of the fact that this man wanted violence, because any many who says he comes to bring the sword is not a man of peace.

But, if you read the passion into the next paragraph, it explains Christ said, "I have come here to set sons against fathers, daughters against mothers, and daughter-in-law against mother-in-law," and what he meant was that the new idea he was bringing, and this was said a long time before our present generation gap, would set the old generation off from the new generation.

That is in the Passion according to St. Matthew, but you have to understand Christ, you would have to understand what he meant in order not to interpret that as a violent statement.

February 12, 1970

MR. WEINGLASS: I want to discuss with you now the question of what happened in Chicago on the major day of the Convention week, and that is Wednesday, August 28.

Now, Mr. Schultz advanced the Government's theory that there was to be a diversionary march in the city with the intention of allowing a certain number of people to invade the Loop for the purpose of breaking up windows, running through the streets, running through stores, setting off false alarms. And that, according to the Government's theory, was what the whole Bandshell really was about.

MR. SCHULTZ: Your Honor, I object to Mr. Weinglass referring to it as a theory. I was relating what they said in an earlier meeting.

THE COURT: I do not remember the word "theory" being used. I sustain the objection.

MR. WEINGLASS: Now one of the key government witnesses to testify about that was a Bill Frapolly. You recall Bill Frapolly, the undercover agent. He said he was at a meeting of the National Mobilization at approximately eleven o'clock in the morning. And he said on his direct testimony that it was Rennie Davis who proposed going into the Loop and busting it up. On cross-examination, I showed Mr. Frapolly his grand jury testimony and he had to acknowledge that when he was before the grand jury, he only said that Rennie Davis proposed after the rally if they couldn't get to the Amphitheatre, they should go across the street from the Hilton Hotel and have a rally in the park.

All of the testimony indicates that there was a rally at the Bandshell. Then a line of march formed right here on Columbus Drive. It was very peaceful and a very large march. After about two hours of staying on Columbus Drive, the march finally breaks up, and the people are to move north. The National Guard is stationed at Balbo, and there is gassing here, if you remember. They couldn't get over the Balbo Street bridge. The crowd kept moving, and finally at Jackson, they found a bridge was open, and they came across Jackson, without any police interference. When they got to the intersection of Michigan and Jackson, they were right at the doorstep of the Loop, the whole business downtown area of Chicago, and the Loop was laid open to them.

This crowd, this mass of people, could have streamed into the Loop without any interference and busted up the Loop or the business section.

There is not one word of testimony that of all of these people who had free access to the Loop, one got into the Loop to do any damage. Not a window cracked, not a single store broken into. But what happened?

When the crowd got to Michigan and Jackson, they saw the mule train coming, and instead of turning into the Loop, the crowd turned and followed the mule train down Michigan Avenue, heading south toward the Amphitheatre. I would rest our case on the fact that the Government did not produce one shred of evidence, not one, to back up their theory that this crowd, this march, Dave Dellinger's plan, was to get these people into that Loop.

This whole mass of people, several thousand, formed a line behind the mule train and came down the street. When they came down the street, they eventually formed a mass, a large mass of people at the intersection of Michigan and Balbo. The mule train came down and it was stuck in the crowd. The mule train was led out of the crowd and the police had a double line formed and shortly after the mule train was led out, the disturbance erupted. Now the question is, how did the disturbance erupt and why?

Deputy Superintendent Rochford said that people who were quiet before suddenly became noisy and started throwing things and the throwing increased. Sarah Diamant, the woman with the camera, who was standing right there, said, "I didn't see anyone throwing anything at that time. Things seemed to be pretty quiet. There was chanting. There was singing at times." She said it would get very loud at times, very loud, and at other times it would sink down and be absolutely quiet.

Then they saw this line of police coming down Balbo. Some describe them as a single line, some as a double line. The police go right up to the line, a van was driven up, there was a moment's hesitation and then this mass of people who up to that point had been standing in the intersection singing and chanting were set upon by the police. The police waded in and began to strike down the people who were in that intersection by clubbing them on the head.

Ruth Migdal saw it and she told you about it. And everyone was pinned, trapped, people couldn't leave because police were coming from the side and coming from the south and they were caught in the wedge in between, and people were forced through the Haymarket Bar as well, and they went right through that window.

We brought in Ruth Migdal who was by the Sheraton Blackstone. We brought in Jean Snodgrass who was across the street. We brought in Sarah Diamant who was across the street in front of the park. We brought in Mr. Pew—remember he saw the young man getting beaten in the revolving door of the Hilton—who was in the hotel.

They did not look for the violence with the police. They were a crowd that wanted to go to the Amphitheatre, that wanted to march, and they weren't permitted to march. They stayed in the streets, and chanted. But does that mean the police should wade into them and beat them and club them? Is that the way we have come to deal with people in this country who adamantly insist on the right to gather together in the streets and to protest?

If the 60s as a decade meant nothing more, the 60s in this country, historically and socially, meant that Americans literally took to the streets, as Tom Hayden said, to protest their grievances. That is what Martin Luther King had done in Selma, Alabama, and that is what has been done ever since.

MR. SCHULTZ: I object to the reference to Martin Luther King. He didn't protest like this.

MR. WEINGLASS: He served thirty days for it.

MR. SCHULTZ: That is an improper comment. There is no proof in this record that Martin Luther King led crowds like this, and I object to it.

MR. KUNSTLER: Your Honor, I represented him for five years, and that is not true.

MR. SCHULTZ: I object to that.

MR. WEINGLASS: Your Honor, he served a jail term right here in this city.

MR. KUNSTLER: If Mr. Schultz had been with Dr. Martin Luther King, he could say something. He was not.

MR. SCHULTZ: And the jury was not a witness to that.

MR. DELLINGER: We were.

MR. SCHULTZ: Mr. Kunstler did not testify to that.

THE COURT: Mr. Marshal—

(There are noises at the defense table.)

MR. SCHULTZ: I would ask that the defendants not make arguments from counsel table. That is not where statements are made from the defendants.

THE COURT: I sustain the objection because there has been no proof in the record here, in fact, of the activities of the late Dr. Martin Luther King. He is not an issue, and his activities are not an issue in this case. I direct the jury to disregard the reference. That is no reflection on the late Dr. Martin Luther King, certainly, but he is not a part of this case.

MR. KUNSTLER: Your Honor, will you also ask the jury to disregard the reference by Mr. Schultz that Dr. King did not do what he said? Mr. Schultz never saw the march from Selma to Montgomery.

THE COURT: Stand back.

MR. KUNSTLER: Oh, I'm not going to leap over the counter, your Honor.

THE COURT: I am afraid you will. You almost have on a number of occasions. I direct the jury to disregard your remarks.

MR. WEINGLASS: This was the time when Americans in large numbers had a moral permit, and they were exercising their moral permit, but that does not mean a violent permit. Civil disobedience can be nonviolent. It can be people who, because of their feeling of the law, without wanting violence, wanting to exercise their higher right of exercising their moral indignation, but not wanting to attack the police.

Let's talk about the Yippies. These men whom you have been told have no regard for the law, who want to disrupt society, who have no respect for rules, no respect for regulations, flew to Chicago, Abbie Hoffman and Jerry Rubin did, five months before the Convention began on March 26, to submit a legal application for a permit to use the park in the city during the Convention week. What was the City afraid of? Why wouldn't they talk to these men?

We could give a number of reasons, but I think you saw one demonstrated right here in front of you, right before your very eyes. What was employed to keep the Yippies out of Chicago was demonstrated in court when we brought before you Allen Ginsberg, who testified about what happened at the Festival of Life. When Allen Ginsberg testified about his meeting with David Stahl and about everything that happened during convention week, including the om-ing and the sunrise ritual, was he cross-examined on the truth of what he said or the truth of the events? Did Mr. Foran attack his believability or his credibility? No. What was attacked was his poetry, his poetry. "Didn't you write a poem where you had a man in bed with a honeymooning couple? Didn't you write a poem where there was some allusion to homosexuality?"

No attempt on the part of the Government to deal with the truth of what the man said or what he stands for, but just a complete misunderstanding of him as a person and an attack on his poetry.

It is that failure to understand, it is the failure to know and appreciate that there are people working in areas of personal relationships and trying to break new ground in those areas, but because of doing that work in those areas, to condemn them, to think of them in terms of violent people or dangerous people is what motivated the city to close its doors to the Yippies.

There is something amiss and awry in the country with respect to how we approach each other personally, sexually, and intimately. And all of these men are attempting to first get us to confront the reality of what life is about and then attempt to get us to do something about it. It is not like something that is scribbled on the walls of a bathroom like the way Mr. Schultz read it. To take it out of context and to make it sound dirty and bad is just reaching too far to gain a conviction.

Approximately fifty years ago a famous Chicago trial attorney, Clarence Darrow, had occasion to defend three men who were charged with conspiracy to incite violence. These three men were charged—

MR. SCHULTZ: I object to that, your Honor. Mr. Weinglass shouldn't go into another case.

THE COURT: I don't think anything that Clarence Darrow did fifty years ago—and I used to sit and watch him in the Federal courthouse as a young lawyer across the street—

MR. WEINGLASS: Then your Honor will know that in summations, he referred to—

THE COURT: He hasn't any place in this trial.

MR. WEINGLASS: If your Honor listened to his summations, then you know that he referred extensively to literature, to other cases, to history—

THE COURT: Clarence Darrow was like a lot of lawyers. He tried to get into cross-examination, direct examination, or summation matters that were irrelevant and immaterial.

MR. WEINGLASS: In a similar case, Mr. Darrow in summing up to the jury told the jury that:

"There are criminals in this case, gentlemen. There are criminals who in the eye of heaven and in the light of justice have not been guilty of the paltry crime of conspiring to save their fellowmen, but criminals who have conspired against the framework of those institutions that had made these criminals great and strong, and you know their names, and I know their names.

"And whether it is written here or not, if there is a book where the deeds of men are recorded by a judge who can look beneath the hollow pretenses of hollow hearts, upon that record, these other men's names are written down as the men who conspired against the liberty of their fellows and against the country in which they live."

I feel a lot of this testimony in court has an effect of trying to indicate to you that these are men who bear hatred for their country, these are men who are clearly unpatriotic, men not worthy of your consideration.

But I call to your attention the brief biography of a young congressman who was elected to Congress from the State of Illinois about 120 years ago in 1848, and his name was Abraham Lincoln.

When he went to Congress and got into Washington, he began to hear, and learn, and see about a war which the country was then involved with against the Mexican government, and he began to develop feelings about the morality of that war and the legality of that war while we were in the midst of the shooting war, itself. He did what no other congressman has done since or before: he introduced a resolution condemning the war as being immoral and illegal. That act by Abraham Lincoln was met with such public scorn and derision that he had to resign from politics after serving his first term. He returned here to Illinois, to live among his friends and neighbors, a man who was vilified as being a hater of his country, a man who was vilified as being unpatriotic.

Within fifteen years, Abraham Lincoln was President of the United States. And the lesson in all of that is that the true patriots of this country throughout history have been men who loved the principles upon which this country was based more than easy, come-and-go, day-to-day peace and security and sanctity of the country. For when Abe Lincoln became President, when he felt the principle was at stake, he committed this country to a great war, and he did that with the same feeling of patriotism that he did when he opposed openly and brazenly as a freshman congressman our involvement in an unjust war.

It seems to me that if the lesson of the country teaches anything, it is that the true patriots are the people who take a position on principle and hold to it, and if there are people in this country who feel that the people in Vietnam are not our enemies, but another part of the humanity on this planet against whom this country is transgressing, and they take action, peaceful action, to protest their feeling, like Abe Lincoln did 120 years ago, there is nothing terribly unpatriotic about it, and rather than to derive from hatred for their country, it seems to me to derive from love of country, and these people have always had it difficult.

When Dave Dellinger and Tom Hayden and Rennie Davis, all men in the peace movement, stated shortly after the Convention, "We have won, we have won," Mr. Schultz attempts to indicate to you that what they were talking about is that they have won in their plans to have violence.

I submit to you that the more reasonable interpretation of that is that people in the United States have won and the peace movement has won because people stood up for a principle, they stood up for what they thought was right. They were beaten and struck down in the streets. They were gassed in the park. But far from defeat, they stood, and they stood their ground. What happened here in Chicago during the week of the Convention is an unfortunate incident on the record of this country. But like all other wrongs that have happened, they can be righted only by people who are willing to stand up to the wrong and embrace the truth and the justice that they see and to stand by what they believe to be true.

I submit to you this task is now before you, and whether this wrong, which is the prosecution of those who were the victims of official misconduct and are brought to trial in an attempt to justify that conduct, is ever righted, resides solely and exclusively in your province.

Throughout history it has always been easy to go along. They did it at the Salem witch trials. They went along in Jerusalem—

MR. SCHULTZ: Oh, objection, if the Court please.

THE COURT: I see no relationship of the Salem witch trials to this courtroom. I don't think it is comparable. I sustain the objection.

MR. WEINGLASS: I merely want to indicate to you in finishing that this case is more than just the defense of seven men. It involves the more basic issue of whether or not those who stand up to dare can do so without grave personal risk and I think it will be judged in that light, and I think while you deliberate this case, that history will hold its breath until you determine whether or not this wrong that we have been living with will be righted by a verdict of acquittal for the seven men who are on trial here.

Thank you.

Closing Argument for the Defendants by Mr. Kunstler

MR. KUNSTLER: Ladies and Gentlemen of the jury:

This is the last voice that you will hear from the defense. We have no rebuttal. This Government has the last word.

In an introductory fashion I would just like to state that only you will judge this case as far as the facts go. This is your solemn responsibility and it is an awesome one.

After you have heard Mr. Schultz and Mr. Weinglass, there must be lots of questions running in your minds. You have seen the same scenes described by two different people. You have heard different interpretations of those scenes by two different people. But you are the ones that draw the final inference. You will be the ultimate arbiters of the fate of these seven men.

In deciding this case we are relying upon your oath of office and that you will decide it only on the facts, not on whether you like the lawyers or don't like the lawyers. We are really quite unimportant. Whether you like the judge or don't like the judge, that is unimportant, too. Whether you like the defendants or don't like the defendants—

THE COURT: I am glad you didn't say I was unimportant.

MR. KUNSTLER: No. The likes or dislikes are unimportant.

And I can say that it is not whether you like the defendants or don't like the defendants. You may detest all of the defendants, for all I know; you may love all of them, I don't know. It is unimportant. It shouldn't interfere with your decision, it shouldn't come into it. And this is hard to do.

You have seen a long defense here. There have been harsh things said in this court, and harsh things to look at from your jury box. You have seen a man bound and gagged. You have heard lots of things which are probably all not pleasant. Some of them have been humorous. Some have been bitter. Some may have been downright boring, and I imagine many were. Those things really shouldn't influence your decision. You have an oath to decide the facts and to decide them divorced of any personal considerations of your own, and I remind you that if you don't do that, you will be living a lie the rest of your life, and only you will be living with that lie.

Now, I don't think it has been any secret to you that the defendants have some questions as to whether they are receiving a fair trial. That has been raised many times.

MR. FORAN: Your Honor, I object to this.

THE COURT: I sustain the objection.

MR. KUNSTLER: They stand here indicted under a new statute. In fact, the conspiracy, which is Count I, starts the day after the President signed the law.

MR. FORAN: Your Honor, I object to that. The law is for the Court to determine, not for counsel to determine.

THE COURT: I sustain the objection.

MR. KUNSTLER: Your Honor, I am not going into the law. They have a right to know when it was passed.

THE COURT: I don't want my responsibility usurped by you.

MR. KUNSTLER: I want you to know, first that these defendants had a constitutional right to travel. They have a constitutional right to dissent and to agitate for dissent. No one would deny that, not Mr. Foran, and not I, or anyone else.

MR. KUNSTLER: Just some fifty years ago, I think almost exactly, in a criminal court building here in Chicago, Clarence Darrow said this:

"When a new truth comes upon the earth, or a great idea necessary for mankind is born, where does it come from? Not from the police force, or the prosecuting attorneys, or the judges, or the lawyers, or the doctors. Not there. It comes from the despised and the outcasts, and it comes perhaps from jails and prisons. It comes from men who have dared to be rebels and think their thoughts, and their faith has been the faith of rebels.

"What do you suppose would have happened to the working men except for these rebels all the way down through history? Think of the complacent cowardly people who never raise their voices against the powers that be. If there had been only these, you gentlemen of the jury would be hewers of wood and drawers of water. You gentlemen would have been slaves. You gentlemen owe whatever you have and whatever you hope to these brave rebels who dared to think, and dared to speak, and dared to act."

This was Clarence Darrow fifty years ago in another case.

You don't have to look for rebels in other countries. You can just look at the history of this country.

You will recall that there was a great demonstration that took place around the Custom House in Boston in 1770. It was a demonstration of the people of Boston against the people who were enforcing the Sugar Act, the Stamp Act, the Quartering of Troops Act. And they picketed at one place where it was important to be, at the Custom House where the customs were collected.

You remember the testimony in this case. Superintendent Rochford said, "Go up to Lincoln Park, go to the Bandshell, go anywhere you want, but don't go to the Amphitheatre."

That was like telling the Boston patriots, "Go anywhere you want, but don't go to the Custom House," because it was at the Custom House and it was at the Amphitheatre that the protesters wanted to show that something was terribly and totally wrong. They wanted to show it at the place it was important, and so the seeming compliance of the City in saying, "Go anywhere you want throughout the city. Go to Jackson Park. Go to Lincoln Park," has no meaning. That is an excuse for preventing a demonstration at the single place that had meaning, which was the Amphitheatre.

The Custom House in Boston was the scene of evil and so the patriots demonstrated. They ran into a Chicago. You know what happened. The British soldiers shot them down and killed five of them, including one black man, Crispus Attucks, who was the first man to die, by the way, in the American revolution. They were shot down in the street by the British for demonstrating at the Custom House.

You will remember that after the Boston Massacre which was the name the Colonies gave to it, all sorts of things happened in the Colonies. There were all sorts of demonstrations—

MR. FORAN: Your Honor, I have sat here quite a while and I object to this. This is not a history lecture. The purpose of summation is to sum up the facts of the case and I object to this.

THE COURT: I do sustain the objection. Unless you get down to evidence, I will direct you to discontinue this lecture on history. We are not dealing with history.

MR. KUNSTLER: But to understand the overriding issues as well, your Honor—

THE COURT: I will not permit any more of these historical references and I direct you to discontinue them, sir.

MR. KUNSTLER: I do so under protest, your Honor. I will get down, because the judge has prevented me from going into material that I wanted to—
MR. FORAN: Your Honor, I object to that comment.
THE COURT: I have not prevented you. I have ruled properly as a matter of law. The law prevents you from doing it, sir.
MR. KUNSTLER: I will get down to the evidence in this case. I am going to confine my remarks to showing you how the Government stoops to conquer in this case.

The prosecution recognized early that if you were to see thirty-three police officers in uniform take the stand that you would realize how much of the case depends on law enforcement officers. So they strip the uniforms from those witnesses, and you notice you began to see almost an absence of uniforms. Even the Deputy Police Chief came without a uniform.

Mr. Schultz said, "Look at our witnesses. They don't argue with the judge. They are bright and alert. They sit there and they answer clearly."

They answered like automatons—one after the other, robots took the stand. "Did you see any missiles?"

"A barrage."

Everybody saw a barrage of missiles.

"What were the demonstrators doing?"

"Screaming. Indescribably loud."

"What were they screaming?"

"Profanities of all sorts."

I call your attention to James Murray. That is the reporter, and this is the one they got caught with. This is the one that slipped up. James Murray, who is a friend of the police, who thinks the police are the steadying force in Chicago. This man came to the stand, and he wanted you to rise up when you heard "Viet Cong flags," this undeclared war we are fighting against an undeclared enemy. He wanted you to think that the march from Grant Park into the center of Chicago in front of the Conrad Hilton was a march run by the Viet Cong, or have the Viet Cong flags so infuriate you that you would feel against these demonstrators that they were less than human beings. The only problem is that he never saw any Viet Cong flags. First of all, there were none, and I call your attention to the movies, and if you see one Viet Cong flag in those two hours of movies at Michigan and Balbo, you can call me a liar and convict my clients.

Mr. Murray, under whatever instructions were given to him, or under his own desire to help the Police Department, saw them. I asked him a simple question: describe them. Remember what he said? "They are black." Then he heard laughter in the courtroom because there isn't a person in the room that thinks the Viet Cong flag is a black flag. He heard a twitter in the courtroom. He said, "No, they are red."

Then he heard a little more laughter.

Then I said, "Are they all red?"

He said, "No, they have some sort of a symbol on them."

"What is the symbol?"

"I can't remember."

When you look at the pictures, you won't even see any black flags at Michigan and Balbo. You will see some red flags, two of them, I believe, and I might say to you that a red flag was the flag under which General Washington fought at the Battle of Brandywine, a flag made for him by the nuns of Bethlehem.

I think after what Murray said you can disregard his testimony. He was a clear liar on the stand. He did a lot of things they wanted him to do. He wanted people to say things that you could hear, that would make you think these demonstrators were violent people. He had some really rough ones in there. He had, "The Hump Sucks," "Daley Sucks the Hump"—pretty rough expressions. He didn't have "Peace Now." He didn't hear that. He didn't give you any others. Oh, I think he had "Charge. The street is ours. Let's go."

That is what he wanted you to hear. He was as accurate about that as he was about the Viet Cong flag, and remember his testimony about the whiffle balls. One injured his leg. Others he picked up. Where were those whiffle balls in this courtroom?

You know what a whiffle ball is. It is something you can hardly throw. Why didn't the Government let you see the whiffle ball? They didn't let you see it because it can't be thrown. They didn't let you see it because the nails are shiny. I got a glimpse of it. Why didn't you see it? They want you to see a photograph so you can see that the nails don't drop out on the photograph. We never saw any of these weapons. That is enough for Mr. Murray. I have, I think, wasted more time than he is worth on Mr. Murray.

Now, I have one witness to discuss with you who is extremely important and gets us into the alleged attack on the Grant Park underground garage.

This is the most serious plan that you have had. This is more serious than attacking the pigs, as they tried to pin onto the Yippies and the National Mobe. This is to bomb. This is frightening, this concept of bombing an underground garage, probably the most frightening concept that you can imagine.

By the way, Grant Park garage is impossible to bomb with Molotov cocktails. It is pure concrete garage. You won't find a stick of wood in it, if you go there. But, put that aside for the moment. In a mythical tale, it doesn't matter that buildings won't burn.

February 13, 1970

In judging the nonexistence of this so-called plot, you must remember the following things.

Lieutenant Healy in his vigil, supposedly in the garage, never saw anything in anybody's hands, not in Shimabukuro's, whom he says he saw come into the garage, not in Lee Weiner's hands, whom he said he saw come into the garage, or any of the other four or five people whom he said he saw come into the garage. These people that he said he saw come into the garage were looking, he said, in two cars. What were they looking into cars for? You can ask that question. Does that testimony make any sense, that they come in empty-handed into a garage, these people who you are supposed to believe were going to fire bomb the underground garage?

Just keep that in mind when you consider this fairy tale when you are in the jury room.

Secondly, in considering it you have the testimony of Lieutenant Healy, who never saw Lee Weiner before. You remember he said "I never saw him before. I had looked at some pictures they had shown me."

But he never had seen him and he stands in a stairwell behind a closed door looking through a one-foot-by-one-foot opening in that door with chicken wire across it and a double layer of glass for three to four seconds, he said, and he could identify what he said was Lee Weiner in three to four seconds across what he said was thirty to forty yards away.

MR. FORAN: Your Honor, I object to "three or four seconds." It was five minutes.

MR. KUNSTLER: No, sir. The testimony reads, your Honor, that he identified him after three or four seconds and if Mr. Foran will look—

MR. FORAN: Then he looked at him for five minutes.

MR. KUNSTLER: He identified him after three or four seconds.

THE COURT: Do you have the transcript there?

MR. FORAN: Your Honor, I would accept that. He identified him immediately but he was looking at him for five minutes.

MR. KUNSTLER: I just think you ought to consider that in judging Lieutenant Healy's question. This officer was not called before the grand jury investigating that very thing. And I think you can judge the importance of that man's testimony on whether he ever did tell the United States Attorney anything about this in September of 1968.

I submit he didn't because it didn't happen. It never happened. This is a simple fabrication. The simple truth of the matter is that there never was any such plot and you can prove it to yourselves. Nothing was ever found, there is no visible proof of this at all. No bottles. No rags. No sand. No gasoline. It was supposed to be a diversionary tactic, Mr. Schultz told you in his summation. This was a diversionary tactic. Diversionary to what? This was Thursday night.

If you will recall, the two marches to the Amphitheatre that got as far as 16th and 18th streets on Michigan had occurred earlier. The only thing that was left was the Downers

Grove picnic. It was a diversionary operation to divert attention from the picnic at Downers Grove. It was diversionary to nothing. The incident lives only in conversations, the two conversations supposedly overheard by Frapolly and Bock, who are the undercover agents who were characterized, I thought, so aptly by Mr. Weinglass.

Now just a few more remarks. One, I want to tell you that as jurors, as I have already told you, you have a difficult task. But you also have the obligation if you believe that these seven men are not guilty to stand on that and it doesn't matter that other jurors feel the other way. If you honestly and truly believe it, you must stand and you must not compromise on that stand.

MR. FORAN: Your Honor, I object to that. Your Honor will instruct the jury what their obligations are.

THE COURT: I sustain the objection. You are getting into my part of the job.

MR. KUNSTLER: What you do in that jury room, no one can question you on. It is up to you. You don't have to answer as to it to anybody and you must stand firm if you believe either way and not—

MR. FORAN: Your Honor, I object to that.

THE COURT: I sustain the objection. I told you not to talk about that, Mr. Kunstler.

MR. KUNSTLER: I think I have a right to do it.

THE COURT: You haven't a right when the Court tells you not to and it is a matter of law that is peculiarly my function. You may not tell the jury what the law is.

MR. KUNSTLER: Before I come to my final conclusion, I want to thank you both for myself, for Mr. Weinglass, and for our clients for your attention. It has been an ordeal for you, I know. We are sorry that it had to be so. But we are grateful that you have listened. We know you will weigh, free of any prejudice on any level, because if you didn't, then the jury system would be destroyed and would have no meaning whatsoever. We are living in extremely troubled times, as Mr. Weinglass pointed out. An intolerable war abroad has divided and dismayed us all. Racism at home and poverty at home are both causes of despair and discouragement. In a so-called affluent society, we have people starving and people who can't even begin to approximate the decent life.

These are rough problems, terrible problems, and as has been said by everybody in this country, they are so enormous that they staggger the imagination. But they don't go away by destroying their critics. They don't vanish by sending men to jail. They never did and they never will.

To use these problems by attempting to destroy those who protest against them is probably the most indecent thing that we can do. You can crucify a Jesus, you can poison a Socrates, you can hang John Brown or Nathan Hale, you can kill a Ché Guevara, you can jail a Eugene Debs or a Bobby Seale. You can assassinate John Kennedy or a Martin Luther King, but the problems remain. The solutions are essentially made by continuing and perpetuating with every breath you have the right of men to think, the right of men to speak boldly and unafraid, the right to be masters of their souls, the right to live free and to die free. The hangman's rope never solved a single problem except that of one man.

I think if this case does nothing else, perhaps it will bring into focus that again we are in that moment of history when a courtroom becomes the proving ground of whether we do live free and whether we do die free. You are in that position now. Suddenly all importance has shifted to you—shifted to you as I guess in the last analysis it should go, and it is really your responsibility, I think, to see that men remain able to think, to speak boldly and unafraid, to be masters of their souls, and to live and die free. And perhaps if you do what is right, perhaps Allen Ginsberg will never have to write again as he did in "Howl," "I saw the best minds of my generation destroyed by madness," perhaps Judy Collins will never have to stand in any courtroom again and say as she did, "When will they ever learn? When will they ever learn?"

· · · · ·

MR. FORAN: Your Honor, could we have a short recess while I get my notes together?

(brief recess)

Closing Argument on Behalf of the Government by Mr. Foran

MR. FORAN: May it please the Court, counsel, ladies and gentlemen of the jury: The recognition of the truth, which is your job, is a very strange thing. There is a real difference between intellectualism and intelligence. Intellectualism leaves out something that intelligence often had and what it really is is a kind of a part of the human spirit. You know many men will be highly intellectual and yet they will have absolutely terrible judgment.

When you stop and think of it, among the twelve of you there is certainly somewhere in excess of four hundred years of human intelligence and instinct, and that is a lot, and that is important.

Now you are bound by your oath to exercise this obligation that you have fairly, without any fear at all, without any favor, without any sympathy, within the framework of the law as it will be given to you by the Court.

Mr. Schultz summarized in minute detail the evidence that was presented in this case. As for me I have sat silent for the most part and I have heard the overwhelming evidence of the guilt of these defendants that was obvious when you heard a minute, exact, careful and honest presentation of the evidence.

Much of the concept of the assault by the defendants on the Government's case is: Would anybody do some of these wild things? Most people wouldn't. But those defendants would.

Some of the things that the Government's witnesses testified that some of these defendants did were pretty wild things, and it would be hard to believe that most people, most decent people, would ever do anything like it. Is it so hard to believe that these men would do it?

Has any one of you, for instance, noticed how in the last few days as we reach the end of the case and it comes before for decision, the sudden quieting in the courtroom, the sudden respect, the sudden decency that we see in this courtroom? For that, are we to forget the four-and-a-half months of what we saw?

The defendants in this case—first of all, they kind of argued in a very strange way that there was no violence planned by these defendants at the Democratic Convention.

Since they have no evidence that violence wasn't planned, the way they argue it is that they say Bock, Frapolly, and Oklepek and Pierson lied. They state that they lied categorically. They said, "Because Bock, Frapolly, Pierson, and Oklepek were undercover agents for the police or newspapers, and therefore, they cannot be honest men."

Now how dare anybody argue that kind of a gross statement? Some of the bravest and the best men of all the world, certainly in law enforcement, have made their contributions while they were undercover. That statement is a libel and a slander on every FBI agent, every Federal narcotics agent, every single solitary policeman who goes out alone and unprotected into some dangerous area of society to try to find out information that is helpful to his government. It is a slander on every military intelligence man, every Navy intelligence man who does the same thing.

There is something that is very interesting, and I bet you haven't noticed it.

The August 9 meeting, you remember that meeting was at Mobilization headquarters. There was a lot of talk and a lot of planning at that meeting. Frapolly, Bock, and Oklepek were all there. So were Dellinger, Davis, Hayden, Weiner, Froines, and Hoffman.

All three of the Government witnesses testified that the march routes to the Amphitheatre were discussed. All agreed that the dangers of the march routes were discussed. All agreed that mill-ins in the Loop were planned during that week: disruptions, blocking cars driving down the street, smashing windows, shut the Loop down, generally make havoc in the Loop area, setting small fires—and, by the way, it all happened.

All of those things that I just mentioned happened on Wednesday of Convention week, and all of them happened in the downtown area right at Michigan and Balbo.

You know, they were saying, "What did they plan that happened?" Well, everything. That was a pretty good shot on the first big meeting.

In addition to the defendants, who else was there at that meeting? Bosciano, Radford, Baker, Steve Buff, and about eight other people. Where are they? If Bock and Frapolly and Oklepek were lying, why weren't they in here testifying that something else was said at that meeting, or that Davis was telling the truth about what he said was said at that meeting. Where are they?

Buff took the witness stand, and they didn't even ask him about the meeting. They didn't even ask him.

The reason that none of the friends and pals of these defendants that were at those meetings didn't come in here and testify or, if they did, ignored the meetings, was because Bock, Frapolly and Oklepek were telling the truth, and if they talked about those meetings on the witness stand, they would have no choice, they would either have to back Bock and Frapolly and Oklepek or they would have to lie. They were at those meetings planning and organizing for the violence that they were going to instigate and incite in Chicago.

And when all that organizing and planning was completed, the time to start the execution of the plan had arrived.

The first thing they had to do is they had to keep this crowd of people getting excited, getting into trouble, but not so much trouble that they would run into a mass arrest situation before Wednesday because they needed the crowd on Wednesday if they were going to have their big confrontation.

And so what they decided—and stop and think of it, remember at the beginning of this case they were calling them all by diminutive names, Rennie and Abbie and Jerry, trying to pretend they were young kids. These are highly sophisticated, highly educated men, every one of them. They are not kids. Davis, the youngest one, took the witness stand. He is twenty-nine. These are highly sophisticated, educated men and they are evil men.

(laughter)

THE COURT: Mr. Marshal.

MR. FORAN: What they have in mind they need to be sophisticated for and they need to be highly educated for because what they have in mind is what Davis told you he had in mind. It is no judgment of mine. Davis told you from that witness stand after two-and-a-half days of the toughest cross-examination I was ever involved in because he was so smart and so clever and so alert, but at last he told you "Revolution. Insurrection." And he told you—I am not—you heard it right from the witness stand.

And so these sophisticated men decided that the first thing that they had to do was to test the police. They had to find out what they could do, where they would be stepping too far, you know, where they would run into trouble.

So the first march they had on Sunday they sent the whole—most of them went down opposite the Hilton Hotel. They had an orderly legal march, legal picketing, and there was absolutely no trouble.

Remember Davis back at that August 9 meeting, "We'll lure the McCarthy kids and other young people with music and sex and try to hold the park." And all of this was done the first night. The first night they carried out that plan. But to carry out the big plan they had to generate more heat the next day so that by Wednesday the psychological training ground of this crowd and the psychological torture of the police, that combination would have reached the proper mix for what they had in mind for Wednesday night.

Say you are in the park after 11:00 P.M., and the law says you are supposed to go; a policeman says, "Leave." You say, "Hell, no." He has only two choices, doesn't he? He either has to walk away from you and not enforce the law, or he has to use whatever physical force is necessary to make you leave.

So, he reaches down—say he takes you by the arm. Then what do you do? You scream, "Let me alone! Let me alone! Police brutality!" And you start wrestling around. Then he had again only two choices. Either he had to physically subdue you right there on the spot, or he had to get help in order to carry you out.

MR. KUNSTLER: There is no evidence of that at all, your Honor. Mr. Foran is making up a story here. I object, your Honor.

THE COURT: I overrule your objection. You may continue, sir.

MR. FORAN: If the police get tough and wrongfully—and it is wrong for a policeman to say, "This man is not going to go," so he cracks him, that is wrong. He shouldn't do that. But say he does it, which they do, policemen do that, then the crowd takes that as total justification to attack the police with rocks and bottles, and to say, "We are defending ourselves."

The technique is simple, and it can fit any situation, and you have seen it fit situations in this courtroom.

Somebody violates the regulation of this courtroom, and the marshal asks him to leave, and he won't, so he takes him by the arm, "Aaaaccchhh! Dirty rotten marshal!" And that had happened, and that is the way it is done, and it is done. You know, this is done in complicated situations and in simple situations.

Monday night in Lincoln Park as the curfew approached, there was Rubin, "Arm yourselves with anything you can. Now is the time to make our stand." Earlier, he had been doing the same thing. That is the night they built the barricade, just like they planned on August 9.

It was a rough night in the park. There was gas. Davis is there on the bullhorn. He is shouting encouragement to the crowd to "Fight the pigs" and "Hold the park," committing a criminal act, by the way, inciting a crowd. He had just left his cohort, Hayden, downtown who had been arrested near the Hilton.

They seem to think that it is terribly difficult to get from Balbo and Michigan to Lincoln Park in a half-an-hour. It is three miles. In a car, you can be up at Lincoln Park at 12:15 without any trouble at all. At midnight, you can go right up Michigan Avenue and be in Lincoln Park, just like that. It is three miles. Twenty miles an hour, and you are there in ten minutes.

Davis was at that barricade. He whipped that crowd up. He tried to come up with an alibi through Potter. You saw him, Potter. That was false testimony, manufactured testimony, a manufactured alibi. There was another little tricky thing, and it is so typical of Davis.

Rubin, as usual, was in the park on Tuesday. He gives a speech to the crowd telling them to take this country away from the people who run it. "Take to the streets in small groups," just as he told Pierson that the Viet Cong had done, and he finished up his revolution exhortation with, "See you in the streets."

These are criminal acts. They are urging people to violence.

Seale followed on the podium with a wild speech telling the crowd to "Get their pieces and barbecue that pork." And we are supposed to wonder, you know, it doesn't mean what it means. That is what the argument is. "It doesn't mean what it means." Of course, you know what it means. "You get your gun and you kill a policeman." That is what is means. It is as obvious as anything from the context of the speech. You heard the whole speech. To say anything else is ridiculous. It is calling black white.

Up at the park, again, Tuesday night, over and over again, the police were saying,

"Clear the park. Clear the park." Finally, at 12:30 A.M., the police moved forward again, and again they were met with a hail of missiles. This time, Froines was right up in the front line, throwing rocks and stones himself.

The police really let them have it with tear gas that night. They had a dispenser, and there was a lot of gas, and the crowd got out quickly. I don't know, maybe that is a better way, but I don't know. There was a lot of gas. It is a temporary bad feeling, but at least nobody gets hurt. Maybe it is a better way.

The battle plan that had been talked about by Davis on August 9, was almost ready. Young people had been moved into the park. They fought and resisted the police.

And now the time had come to start shifting the scene down to the downtown area, and just as they planned, the Hilton area was going to be the focus of the next action.

The crowd was pretty heated and pretty militant, and it had been whipped up really in Lincoln Park, starting way back on August 13 with all of these things, with that crazy snake dancing, and with the skirmish lines. To be trained in karate is something because karate is a vicious thing. If you are any good at it, you can kill somebody with it. It is a vicious way to fight.

The police had been taunted and insulted and attacked until the weak ones among them, and there are plenty of weak policemen, were losing their professionalism, and they were ripe to be driven into joining some of these participants in rioting.

And then they have that meeting in Mobilization headquarters the next morning where they set it up with a kind of—well, it is a combination of "the massive action with the cutting edge of resistance." They used it successfully at the Pentagon and they were now going to transfer it into the practicalities of Chicago.

Dellinger, Davis, Hayden, Froines, Weiner and Rubin all leave to do their various jobs.

The meeting started at the Bandshell. Dellinger was running the public show up on the stage and Davis was giving instructions to his marshals out behind that refreshment stand, those marshals who, as Froines said, were a lot better street fighters than they ever were what marshals are supposed to be.

He says "Disperse the police. Reduce their effectiveness."

Others of the militant group were seen preparing their vicious, filthy weapons—bags of urine, pointed sticks, sharpening tiles.

The mood of those militants in that crowd was shown real quickly when that flag came down to half-mast. When that flag came down and those six policemen went in to arrest the man, they were grossly attacked by that crowd.

And the honesty of the defense is pointed out most clearly by the argument of counsel that they were throwing their lunches at the police and that these were picnickers throwing lunches at the police. These weren't picnickers unless those picnickers eat rocks and bottles for lunch.

Rubin in his volatile way had been caught up in the excitement and he was in there pitching, "Kill the pigs. Kill the pigs."

But Dellinger and Davis were a lot cooler than that. They let them continue for a while. It went on for about fifteen minutes and then they cooled it down because it was still daylight and things were—you know, it wasn't quite ready yet. And that's when Davis got hit. Look at this picture in the jury room. He's got a cut on his head and he's bleeding some and he's smiling and he looks very alert and he doesn't look like he's going to fall unconscious to me.

The thing that you have got to recognize is that you have to tie the Bandshell back to that meeting Wednesday morning. Exactly what was planned at that meeting Wednesday morning happened at the Bandshell.

A diversionary march was set up by Dellinger. Another action was set up by Dellinger. As I said earlier, I think like a ventriloquist he used Tom Neumann. Neumann's name had been talked about that morning at that meeting at the Mobilization office as one of the speakers. Neumann was one of the men. The plan was made there at that meeting.

You can gather a whole bunch of people, most of them don't want to riot, but maybe want to protest, maybe want to get in on the act, maybe want to have some fun, maybe want to fight policemen. You gather enough people together, and you have some people who are dedicated to causing public disorder for serious purposes. You don't need a big crowd. And that is what these people always try to do. They tried to shift it off on all youth. They are talking about our children.

There are millions of kids who, naturally, if we could only remember how it is—you know, you resent authority, you are impatient for change, you want to fix things up. Maybe you are very sensitive and you feel the horrors of racism which is a real cancer in the American character, there is no question about that. You feel a terrible frustration of a terribly difficult war that maybe as a young kid you are going to have to serve in. Sure, you don't like things like that.

There is another thing about a kid, if we all remember, that you have an attraction to evil. Evil is exciting and evil is interesting, and plenty of kids have a fascination for it. It is knowledge of kids like that that these sophisticated, educated psychology majors know about. They know about kids, and they know how to draw the kids together and maneuver them, and use them to accomplish their purposes. Kids in the 60s, you know, are disillusioned. There is no question about that. They feel that John Kennedy went, Bobby Kennedy went, Martin Luther King went—they were all killed—and the kids do feel that the lights have gone out in Camelot, the banners are furled, and the parade is over.

These guys take advantage of them. They take advantage of it personally, intentionally, evilly, and to corrupt those kids, and they use them, and they use them for their purposes and for their intents. And you know, what are their purposes and intents?

Well, they tell you, these men tell you this, and this is what troubles me, that some of the things you can really taste.

What is their intent? And this is their own words: "To disrupt. To pin delegates in the Convention hall. To clog streets. To force the use of troops. To have actions so militant the Guard will have to be used. To have war in the streets until there is peace in Vietnam. To intimidate the establishment so much it will smash the city. Thousands and thousands of people perform disruptive actions in Chicago. Tear this city apart. Fuck up the Convention. Send them out. We'll start the revolution now. Do they want to fight? The United States is an outlaw nation which had broken all the rules so peace demonstrators can break all the rules. Violate all the laws. Go to jail. Disrupt the United States Government in every way that you can. See you in Chicago."

And these men would have you believe that the issue in this case is whether or not they really wanted permits.

Public authority is supposed to stand handcuffed and mute in the face of people like that and say, "We will let you police yourselves"? How would public authority feel if they let that park be full of young kids through that Convention with no policemen, with no one watching them? What about the rape and the bad trips and worse that public authority would be responsible for if it had?

They tried to give us this bunk that they wanted to talk about racism and the war and they wanted a counter-convention. They didn't do anything but look for a confrontation with the police. What they looked for was a fight, and all that permits had to do with it was where was the fight going to be, and that's all.

And they are sophisticated and they are smart and they are well-educated. And they are as evil as they can be.

Of course, the imperfections of our life cry out for answers. They cry out for legal answers. Just when we need legal answers more than ever before in our history, there descends upon the whole country a new kind of a public attitude toward law. Law is viewed by people like this as just kind of a collection of casual suggestions that they can obey or not obey as they please. And they would have our society as represented by you people become tolerant of that kind of evil, attempt to exercise their deliberate violation of the law because they wish to further what they would have us believe is lofty cause.

The intellectual and practical consequences of that kind of thinking is the legitimation of violence and it would destroy this country.

Effective law is the greatest achievement of mankind yet and I believe that most Americans feel that it is not only necessary but it is highly desirable. We must have law.

Violent disobedience to law differs radically from every decent mode of protest and dissent. The First Amendment is not now and was never intended to protect those who violate the law, whatever the cause they may be espousing. To permit factions to resort to force when they feel that a particular law or policy is wrong, would be to renounce our own experience and the experience of our forefathers whom these men now hold up as if they were their models, after I saw them and you saw them excoriating the founders of the country whose pictures his Honor has on the wall behind him.

MR. KUNSTLER: Your Honor, that is not true. That was Bobby Seale—

THE COURT: One of the defense witnesses.

MR. KUNSTLER: Yes, but Bobby Seale claimed that some of the men on the wall have been slave owners which was absolutely correct. George Washington—

THE COURT: I just had a great art dealer sell me that picture.

MR. FORAN: Your Honor, may I continue, please?

THE COURT: I will let the United States Attorney continue.

THE MARSHAL: Mr. Hoffman, will you keep quiet?

MR. HOFFMAN: No.

MR. FORAN: The First Amendment doesn't intend to leave the limits of freedom to the judgment of coercive dissenters like that. What the First Amendment protects is the advocacy of a cause; it does not protect incitement to riot, participating in a riot. The words themselves in definition let you know what the First Amendment protects. "To advocate" means "to speak or write in favor of." That is why some of those wild speeches that those men gave in other states were not charged as crimes. You can consider them to show their intent, but they are not charged as crimes because they were speaking in favor of a revolutionary cause.

But to incite means to urge to particular action. You know "Kill the pigs. Get 'em. Get 'em. Let's go. Let's go."

The vision and ideals that our forefathers had just can't be corrupted by the haters and the violent anarchists. "The future is with the people who will be truthful and pure and loving."

You know who said that? Gandhi. Dr. King.

"Truthful, pure, loving."

Not liars and obscene haters like those men are.

Can you imagine? You know, the way they name-dropped—Can you imagine—and it is almost blasphemous to say it—they have named St. Matthew and they named Jesus and they named Abraham Lincoln. They named Martin Luther King. Can you imagine those men supporting these men if they—

A SPECTATOR: Yes, I can. I can imagine it because it is true.

THE COURT: Remove those people, Mr. Marshal.

MR. DELLINGER: That's my daughter.

A SPECTATOR: I won't listen to any more of these disgusting lies.

MR. DELLINGER: That's my other daughter. Thank you. Right on. Right on.

Don't hit my daughter that way. I saw you. That man hit her on the head for saying the truth in here.

THE COURT: The marshals will maintain order.

MR. DELLINGER: Yes, but they don't have to hit thirteen-year-old girls who know that I was close to Martin Luther King.

THE COURT: Mr. Marshal, have that man sit down.

MR. FORAN: You see, you see how it works?

Don't hit her.

MR. DELLINGER: He did hit her.

A SPECTATOR: They hit him. He did hit her.

MR. FORAN: Oh, bunk.

MR. DELLINGER: I saw him hit her.

MR. FORAN: Can you imagine? Can you imagine those men supporting anybody—supporting anybody who would try to draw young kids to a park—

A SPECTATOR: Why did Ramsey Clark come here? Why did Ramsey Clark come here?

THE COURT: Remove that woman. Remove her and don't let her return, Mr. Marshal.

MR. KUNSTLER: Your Honor, Mr. Foran wanted to provoke this. That is why he mentioned Dr. King. He knows these people worked with Dr. King and that's why he said it and they couldn't take it.

MR. FORAN: Isn't it interesting that these believers in freedom of speech do not believe that the United States Attorney has the same right?

MR. KUNSTLER: We never use that type of tactics, your Honor, with the United States Attorney.

THE COURT: Please sit down with your tactics and your lecture.

MR. FORAN: "Riots are an intolerable threat to every American and those who lead others to defy the law must feel the full force of the law." You know who said that? Senator Bob Kennedy said that, who they tried to adopt.

"In a government of law and not of men, no man, no mob, however unruly or boisterous, is entitled to defy the law."

Do you know who said that? John Kennedy.

The lights in that Camelot kids believe in needn't go out. The banners can snap in the spring breeze. The parade will never be over if people will remember, and I go back to this quote, what Thomas Jefferson said, "Obedience to the law is the major part of patriotism."

These seven men have been proven guilty beyond any doubt. They didn't attack the planning they were charged with. They didn't say it didn't happen. They are guilty beyond any doubt at all of the charges contained in the indictments against them.

You people are obligated by your oath to fulfill your obligation without fear, favor, or sympathy. Do your duty.

THE COURT: Ladies and gentlemen of the jury, I had hoped to be able to charge the jury this afternoon, but as you can observe, that didn't work out. I shall do so tomorrow morning at 9:30.

Mr. Marshal, court will be in recess.

Judge's Charge to the Jury

February 14, 1970

THE COURT: Ladies and gentlemen of the jury, I should like before I proceed with my instructions, to express my deep and appreciative thanks to each and every one of you for the services you have rendered as jurors in this case for the past four-and-a-half months.

I tell you, members of the jury, that these instructions should be considered together as a connected series and be regarded in their entirety as the law applicable to this case. The jury has no right under the law to disregard or give special attention to any one of the instructions or to question the wisdom of any rule of law.

Members of the jury, the offense charged in Count I is conspiracy to commit certain offenses, and the Government need not prove that the purposes of the conspiracy were in fact accomplished or that the substantive crimes were in fact committed. The evidence to establish a conspiracy is sufficient if it establishes beyond a reasonable doubt that one or more of the means or methods described in the indictment was agreed upon to accomplish the purpose of the conspiracy as charged in the indictment.

Count I of the indictment charges these seven defendants, plus other alleged coconspirators, with one single conspiracy. Thus to convict any of the defendants under Count I you must find beyond a reasonable doubt the existence of a single conspiracy, one single common plan, scheme or design. Proof of two or more separate and distinct conspiracies, even if they involve various of the defendants, would not constitute proof of the one single conspiracy charged in the indictment.

While a conspiracy necessarily includes an agreement to violate the law, it is not necessary that the evidence reveal that the persons charged with being members of that conspiracy met together and entered into any express or formal agreement to accomplish its end. It is sufficient to show that they tacitly came to a mutual understanding to accomplish the unlawful purpose charged. To be a member of the conspiracy, a defendant need not know all the other members, nor all the details of the conspiracy, nor the means by which the objects were accomplished.

It is not necessary that all of the overt acts charged in Count I of the indictment were performed. One overt act is sufficient. It need not be in violation of the law, and the other conspirators need not join in it or even know about it. It is necessary only that such act be in furtherance of the purpose or objects of the conspiracy.

[575]

However, the mere commission of the alleged overt acts set forth in Count I is not sufficient by itself to prove the existence of any agreement.

Members of the jury, whoever aids, abets, counsels, commands, induces or procures the commission of a crime is punishable as a principal. In order to aid or abet the commission of a crime, a person must associate himself with the criminal venture, participate in it and try to make it succeed.

As I am sure all of you remember, ladies and gentlemen of the jury, Count VIII of the indictment involves the defendant Bobby G. Seale.

Evidence in any of acts or statements by the defendant Seale, are not to be considered by you in determining the guilt or innocence of the remaining defendants. However, evidence introduced and admitted when Mr. Seale was on the witness stand, as a witness called to that witness stand by the other defendants on trial, may be given such consideration as you deem appropriate.

In each count of the indictment the defendants are charged with performing certain acts on or about a certain date. The Government is not required to prove or establish with certainty the exact date as set forth in the indictment. However, the Government must have proven that the alleged offense or travel was engaged in on a date reasonably near the date or time alleged in the indictment.

Ladies and gentlemen of the jury, I shall now instruct you as to what kind of conduct is not prohibited by law, and cannot, therefore, constitute grounds for conviction.

Among the most vital and precious liberties which we Americans enjoy by virtue of our Constitution are freedom of speech and freedom of assembly. The freedoms guaranteed by the First Amendment allow criticism of existing institutions, of political leaders, of domestic and foreign policies and our system of government. That right is unaffected by whether or not it may seem to you to be wrong, intemperate or offensive or designed to undermine public confidence in existing government.

The law distinguishes between mere advocacy of violence or lawlessness without more, and advocacy of the use of force or illegality where such advocacy is directed to inciting, promoting, or encouraging lawless actions. The Constitution does not protect speech which is reasonably and knowingly calculated and directed to inciting actions which violate the law. A conviction can rest only on advocacy which constitutes a call to imminent unlawful action.

You must keep in mind this distinction between constitutionally protected and unprotected speech.

In addition it is a constitutional exercise of the rights of free speech and assembly to march or hold a rally without a permit where applications for permits were made in good faith at a reasonable time prior to the date of march or rally and the permits were denied arbitrarily or discriminatorily.

Where the law refers to an act that is committed knowingly and wilfully, it means that the act was done voluntarily and purposely, not because of mistake or accident, with knowledge that it was prohibited by law and with the purpose of violating the law. Thus the defendants cannot be found to have acted wilfully and knowingly unless they or any of them did so with a bad purpose of an evil intent. Such knowledge and intent may be proven by the defendants' conduct and by all of the facts and circumstances of the case as shown by the evidence.

If you are not convinced beyond a reasonable doubt that a defendant acted knowingly and wilfully, then you must find that the Government has failed to prove the intent necessary and you must, in such an event, acquit that defendant.

Ladies and gentlemen of the jury, the final portion of my charge will deal with the matter of your consideration of the evidence in this case. You have seen and heard a great deal in the course of this trial and it is my obligation to explain to you what does and does not constitute evidence upon which you may reach a decision.

I have not intended at any time during this trial, and do not now intend, to express my opinion on any matter of fact. If by chance I have expressed or do express any opinion on any matter of fact, it is your duty to disregard that opinion.

Your verdict or verdicts must be reached from all the evidence in the case, but if any evidence was admitted and later stricken out by the Court, you must wholly disregard that evidence which was stricken out.

If you find that the evidence is insufficient to warrant a conviction of the defendants or any defendant under the instructions that I am now giving to you, then you must find the defendants or that defendant not guilty.

In addition, you must not in any way be influenced by any possible antagonism you may have toward the defendants or any of them, their dress, hair styles, speech, reputation, courtroom demeanor or quality, personal philosophy or life style.

The final area that I will discuss relating to the evidence in this case is the law as it applies to your evaluation of the testimony that has been admitted in evidence. The testimony of an informer or any witness whose self interest is shown to be such as might tend to prompt testimony unfavorable to the defendants or any of them should be considered with caution and weighed with care.

The testimony of a law enforcement officer or any governmental official is not to be given any greater weight than that of any other witness, merely because he is a law enforcement officer or a governmental official.

Furthermore, if you believe from the evidence that any witness in this case took that witness stand and knowingly and wilfully testified falsely during this trial, to any matter material to the case, you may disregard the entire testimony of such witness, except as it may have been corroborated by other credible evidence.

I must direct you, ladies and gentlemen of the jury, to follow the law as I have given it to you in all of these instructions. You should consider these instructions as a connected series and as the entirety of the law applicable to this case. You have no right under the law to disregard or give special attention to anyone of the instructions or to question the wisdom of any rule of law.

Ladies and gentlemen of the jury, I direct you to go to the jury room but not to commence your deliberations until you receive an order from me through the marshal which will come in due course. Until then my usual orders.

You may retire now to the jury room.

(jury excused)

THE COURT: I would call on the Government first to indicate whether it has any objections to the charge of the Court.
MR. SCHULTZ: We have none.
THE COURT: All right. Then I will call on the defense to state any objections it might have.
MR. WEINGLASS: If the Court please, I would state for the record that we object generally and specifically, but I do not want to particularize down to the point where I have to mention the numbers.

Now with respect to the Court's charge generally, your Honor will recall that the Government has consistently maintained in this trial that there was both a lawful and an unlawful combination; that there was an attempt to bring people to the city for lawful and peaceful assembly and protest, and what they contended underlay that was a sinister attempt to bring people here also for the purpose of violence, and the two were intertwined.

Now this calls immediately to mind the case of United States vs. Spock in which the Court announced that where you have such an intertwining of a lawful purpose with an unlawful purpose, you have a bifarious conspiracy.

Where you have a bifarious conspiracy, the Court must instruct the jury that if they find that persons joined that conspiracy, they joined it with specific intent of adopting the unlawful portion of the conspiracy.

I feel that the Court should instruct the jury as to the nature of the conspiracy and the fact that the defendants had to join the illegal portion of it.

Secondly, the Court indicated the conspiracy could exist even though none of the crimes were carried out. But what the Court did not tell the jury, and what I felt should have been properly included immediately after that, was the fact that the jury could take into account the fact that none of these acts were committed in considering whether or not there was an agreement in the first place. And I feel it was an error for the Court not to include that.

So for those reasons I would like to put the defense position on the record with respect to the Court's instructions.

THE COURT: The marshal will inform the jury they may proceed to deliberate and I have another matter to take up here with counsel and the parties.

Contempt Proceedings

THE COURT: The Court now has the responsibility of dealing appropriately with the contemptuous conduct that has pervaded this trial from the very beginning.

Contempt by definition is any act calculated to hinder or disrupt the Court in the administration of justice and to lessen the Court's authority. I have tried right down to the very end without success to stop or put an end to that conduct, but anyone who was in attendance here yesterday afternoon would know what happened—the record will show it.

Our legal system provides adequate and orderly means to challenge and test those rulings. Orderly procedures must be followed because the only alternative is anarchy, and we had during this trial such conduct.

The calculated use of contumacious conduct and the direct encouragement of disruptive outcries from spectators to express dissatisfaction or to intimidate the Court and the jurors are reprehensible and must be punished if our system of justice is to survive.*

Knowingly and deliberately, I find these defendants in this case and the lawyers have committed numerous acts which have evidenced a total disregard for the proper conduct of any trial. Each and every act of misconduct constituted a separate and direct offense against this Court and our judicial system.

Particularly reprehensible was the conduct of counsel, who not only disregarded a duty to advise and direct their clients to observe the rules of this Court but participated with their clients in making a mockery of orderly procedure.

The Court might have halted the trial upon each instance of misbehavior and imposed punishment on the particular transgressor at that time. Other considerations, however, were more compelling. The disruption caused by each improper act or comment would have merely been compounded by an immediate contempt proceeding. No doubt cries of oppression would have greeted the Court if punishment were meted out during the course of the trial.

For these reasons the Court has waited until the close of the trial to deal with this problem.* The Supreme Court in Bloom vs. Illinois recognized that direct contempt committed in the presence of the Court are not suited to jury trials.*

Furthermore, some of the offenders have engaged in such impudent repetition of their misconduct, that the Court finds the imposition of consecutive sentences necessary. Even though the punishment imposed upon several of the offenders is grave, it is, nevertheless, based upon separate and distinct acts.

Once any party to a lawsuit has embarked upon a strategy of disruption such as that displayed in this case, only cumulative sanctions can act as a restraint. Otherwise a first offense would offer immunity for further violations.

I will first consider the conduct of the defendant David Dellinger.†

The Court finds the defendant Dellinger guilty of direct contempt of court committed in the presence of the Court with respect to the following specifications enumerated by the Court in the record. Specification No. 1, the defendant will be committed—by the way, does counsel for Dellinger want to be heard before sentence is imposed?

MR. KUNSTLER: Your Honor, I have a legal argument on the power of the Court after trial and I would present the legal argument.

Your Honor cited United States against Bloom as the authority for your action. Bloom holds that summary contempt is only a method of preventing disturbance during trial, but that after trial a man is entitled to a jury trial.

THE COURT: I will not—

MR. KUNSTLER: And that another judge should sit on it other than your Honor because it does involve what your Honor considers to be insults, et cetera, to you personally. I think it is proper here to indicate that in Bloom the Court says:

"Indeed, in contempt cases an even more compelling argument can be made for providing a right to jury trial as a protection against the arbitrary exercise of official power. We place little credence in the notion that the independence of the judiciary hangs on the power to try contempt summarily. We do not deny that serious punishment must sometimes be imposed for contempt but we reject the contention that such punishment must be imposed without a right to jury trial."

Furthermore, Rule 42(b) of the US criminal code says if the contempt charge involved disrespect to or criticism of a judge, that judge is disqualified from presiding at the trial or hearing except with the defendant's consent.*

A VOICE: Right on.

MR. KUNSTLER: The defendants do not consent to your Honor sitting on their contempts and therefore I think your Honor is totally without jurisdiction to do what you are doing today and to sentence people from summary contempt after the trial is over.

THE COURT: I do not share your view.

Mr. Dellinger, do you care to say anything? Only in respect to punishment. I will hear you.

MR. DELLINGER: Yes. I think it all relates—and I hope you will do me the courtesy not to interrupt me while I am talking.

THE COURT: I won't interrupt you as long as you are respectful.

MR. DELLINGER: Well, I will talk about the facts and the facts don't always encourage false respect.

Now, I want to point first of all that the first two contempts cited against me concerned, one, the moratorium action and, secondly, support of Bobby Seale—the war against Vietnam, and racism in this country, the two issues this country refuses to solve, refuses to take seriously.

THE COURT: I hope you will excuse me, sir. I ask you to say what you want to say in respect to punishment. I don't want you to talk politics.

MR. DELLINGER: You see, that's one of the reasons I have needed to stand up and speak anyway, because you have tried to keep what you call politics, which means the truth, out of this courtroom, just as the prosecution has.

THE COURT: I will ask you to sit down.

MR. DELLINGER: Therefore it is necessary—

THE COURT: I won't let you go on any further.

MR. DELLINGER: You want us to be like good Germans supporting the evils of our decade and then when we refused to be good Germans and came to Chicago and demonstrated, now you want us to be like good Jews, going quietly and politely to the concentration camps while you and this court suppress freedom and the truth. And the fact is that I am not prepared to do that. You want us to stay in our place like black people were supposed to stay in their place—

THE COURT: Mr. Marshal, I will ask you to have Mr. Dellinger sit down.

† See Appendix IV for all contempt proceedings.

MR. DELLINGER: —like poor people were supposed to stay in their place, like people with formal education are supposed to stay in their place, like women are supposed to stay in their place—

THE COURT: I will ask you to sit down.

MR. DELLINGER: Like children are supposed to stay in their place, like lawyers—I thank you—are supposed to stay in their places.

It is a travesty on justice and if you had any sense at all you would know that the record that you read condemns you and not us.

THE COURT: All right.

MR. DELLINGER: And it will be one of thousands and thousands of rallying points for a new generation of Americans who will not put up with tyranny, will not put up with a facade of democracy without the reality.

THE COURT: Mr. Marshal, will you please ask him to keep quiet?

THE MARSHAL: Be quiet, Mr. Dellinger.

MR. DELLINGER: I sat here and heard that man Mr. Foran say evil, terrible, dishonest things that even he could not believe in—I heard him say that and you expect me to be quiet and accept that without speaking up.

People no longer will be quiet. People are going to speak up. I am an old man and I am just speaking feebly and not too well, but I reflect the spirit that will echo—

THE COURT: Take him out—

MR. DELLINGER: —throughout the world—

(applause)

MR. DELLINGER: —comes from my children who came yesterday—

(complete disorder in the courtroom)

MR. DELLINGER: Leave my daughters alone. Leave my daughter alone.

A VOICE: Tyrants. Tyrants.

MR. KUNSTLER: What are you doing to us, your Honor?

A VOICE: That's what you have done, Judge Hoffman. That's what you have done.

MR. RUBIN: Heil Hitler. Heil Hitler. Heil Hitler. Heil Hitler. I hope you're satisfied.

MR. KUNSTLER: My life has come to nothing, I am not anything any more. You destroyed me and everybody else. Put me in jail now, for God's sakes, and get me out of this place. Come to mine now, Judge, please. Please. I beg you. Come to mine. Do me, too. I don't want to be out.

A VOICE: Leave her alone.

THE MARSHAL: Will the press sit down?

A VOICE: Get your fucking storm troopers out of here.

THE CLERK: Be seated, please.

THE MARSHAL: All right, sit down. Have a seat.

MR. DELLINGER: Well, you preserved law and order here, Judge.

The day will come when you'll take every one of us.

MR. RUBIN: Heil Hitler. That's how you should be greeted.

THE COURT: With respect to Specification No. 1 and all of the other Specifications referred to by the Court, the Court finds the defendant Dellinger guilty of direct contempt in the presence of the Court with respect to—

MR. DELLINGER: I don't want to interrupt but there was one thing I wanted to say, namely, that the Court was in contempt of human life and dignity and truth and justice and if that's the way punishment should be decided—

THE COURT: If you don't, then don't.

With respect to Specification No. 1, the Court commits the defendant Dellinger to the custody of the Attorney General of the United States for imprisonment for a period of six months.

Specification No. 2, one month. Specification No. 3, seven days. Specification No. 4, three months. Specification No. 5, seven days. Specification No. 6, one day. Specification No. 7, seven days. Specification No. 8, one month. Specification No. 9, one day. Specification No. 10, one day. Specification No. 11, seven days for imprisonment. Specification No. 12, one day. Specification No. 13, two days for imprisonment. Specification No. 14, four days. Specification No. 15, four days. Specification No. 16, three days. Specification No. 17, six days. Specification No. 18, two days. Specification No. 19, six days. Specification No. 20, four days. Specification No. 21, three days. Specification No. 22, three days. Specification No. 23, five days. Specification No. 24, six months imprisonment. Specification No. 25, seven days. Specification No. 26, four months.

That is 26?

THE CLERK: Twenty-six, yes, your Honor.

THE COURT: Specification No. 27, two days. Specification No. 28, two days. Specification No. 29, seven days. Specification No. 30, five months. Specification No. 31, seven days. Specification No. 32, seven days.

Mr. Marshal, the marshals will please remove Mr. Dellinger into custody. All of these sentences will run cumulatively and consecutively.

MR. DELLINGER: Right on, beautiful people, black people, Vietnamese, poor people, young people, everybody fighting for liberty and justice. Right on.

Not to mention Latin Americans.

MR. KUNSTLER: Your Honor, I would like to make a motion for bail pending appeal for Mr. Dellinger.

THE COURT: I would not bail anybody for contempt, direct contempt in the presence of the Court. It is not bailable. And in view of his conduct here, even if it were bailable, I certainly wouldn't do so.

Besides, I think to admit him to bail on appeal here would be frivolous in the opinion of the Court.

MR. DAVIS: You have just jailed one of the most beautiful and one of the most courageous men in the United States.

THE COURT: All right. Now we will talk about you, Mr. Davis.†

Do you care to be heard?

MR. DAVIS: Yes. This morning you said that the only alternative to what I have done in the courtroom is anarchy, and perhaps you are right. You have said as well that as a matter of law, there is no defense for what we have done, and I believe that there is a defense for what we have done.

I believe what we have done is wholly defensible. You may not believe this, but we came here to have a trial with a law that we regarded as unconstitutional and unfair and a jury that was inadequately selected.

We came here, nevertheless, to present our full case to this jury so that this jury might decide whether or not our Movement was just in coming to Chicago, or whether, as the Government charged, we came here to incite a riot.

THE COURT: You are not speaking to the issue here.

MR. DAVIS: I think it relates very specifically.

THE COURT: I don't think it does and I shall not hear you on anything except what I have outlined.

MR. DAVIS: All right. On October 28, this whole incident about the refusal to rise when you came into the room.

Let me just put that particular incident into context, if I may.

Bobby Seale that day was attempting once again to cross-examine a witness in this case, William Frapolly, because he did not have a lawyer here, a lawyer that has represented him on many previous cases, a lawyer he felt had to represent him here.

THE COURT: I will not hear you in that reference to Bobby Seale.

MR. DAVIS: I am putting the specific incident in context.

THE COURT: I have heard enough about Bobby Seale and the lawyers he said he didn't have and the lawyers he did have. I don't want to hear about that.

MR. DAVIS: How am I going to explain to you that what happened to Bobby Seale directly led to my feeling that I could not stand what you did to Bobby Seale at that moment?

Your refusal to allow him to cross-examine a witness and to have his elementary constitutional rights was the reason I did not stand for you at that time. Bobby Seale did not stand at that time.

THE COURT: In the first place, what you say is not accurate. You know what he called me.

MR. DAVIS: I do.

THE COURT: I wouldn't—

MR. DAVIS: He called you a racist, a fascist, and a pig.

THE COURT: Several times.

MR. DAVIS: Many times, and not enough.

THE COURT: I will ask you to sit down.

MR. DAVIS: I have not completed my response.

THE COURT: I will ask you to sit down. I didn't ask you to get up here to further insult me.

MR. DAVIS: I have a right—

THE COURT: You have no right to make insulting remarks.

MR. DAVIS: Judge, you represent all that is old, ugly, bigoted, and repressive in this country, and I will tell you that the spirit at this defense table is going to devour your sickness in the next generation.

THE COURT: Mr. Clerk, with respect to the Specifications named hereafter, the defendant Davis will be committed to the custody of the Attorney General of the United States or his authorized representative for imprisonment for direct contempt committed in the presence of the court as follows:

Specification No. 1, two days. Specification No. 2, one day. Specification No. 3, one day. Specification No. 4, one day. Specification No. 5, one day. Specification No. 6, two months. Specification No. 7, one day. Specification No. 8, one day. Specification No. 9, fourteen days. Specification No. 10, seven days. Specification No. 11, seven days. Specification No. 12, one day. Specification No. 13, seven days. Specification No. 14, two days—or two months, rather, I beg your pardon.

Specification No. 14, two months. Specification No. 15, two months. Specification No. 16, six months. Specification No. 17, three months. Specification No. 18, fourteen months. Specification No. 19—wait a minute—fourteen days, pardon me.

Specification No. 19, seven days. Specification No. 20, two months. Specification No. 21, five months. Specification No. 22, fourteen days. Specification No. 23, one month.

The United States Attorney is directed to prepare the necessary papers in this connection. I direct the marshal to remove Mr. Davis to the custody of the Attorney General.

The sentences are consecutive.

MR. RUBIN: See you in jail.

MR. HOFFMAN: The whole country is in jail.

MR. WEINER: See you in jail, brother.

THE COURT: We come now to the consideration of the matter of Thomas Hayden.†

Mr. Hayden.

MR. HAYDEN: I wanted to say something about my feelings about punishment. The problem that I think people have who want to punish us is that the punishment does not seem to have effect. Even as the elder Dellinger is taken off for two years, a younger Dellinger fights back.

So, your Honor, before your eyes you see the most vital ingredient of your system collapsing because the system does not hold together.

THE COURT: Oh, don't be so pessimistic. Our system isn't collapsing. Fellows as smart as you could do awfully well under this system. I am not trying to convert you, mind you.

MR. HOFFMAN: We don't want a place in the regiment, Julie.

THE COURT: What did you say? Your turn's coming up.

MR. HOFFMAN: I am being patient, Julie.

THE COURT: Well, I don't—you see? He thinks that annoys me by addressing me by a name—he doesn't know that years ago when I was his age or younger, that's what my friends called me.

MR. HAYDEN: The point I was trying to make is that I was trying to think about what I regretted and about punishment. I can only state one thing that affected my feelings, my own feelings, and that is that I would like to have a child.

THE COURT: There is where the Federal system can do you no good.

MR. HAYDEN: Because the Federal system can do you no good in trying to prevent the birth of a new world.

VOICES: Right on. Right on.

THE COURT: Mr. Clerk, with respect to the defendant Hayden, he will be found guilty of direct contempt committed in the presence of the Court on eleven different occasions.

With respect to Specification No. 1, he will be committed to the custody of the Attorney General of the United States for imprisonment for a period of 2 days.

No. 2, one day. No. 3, one month. No. 4, one day. No. 5, one day. No. 6, one day. No. 7, three months. No. 8, four months. No. 9, one day. No. 10, seven days. No. 11, six months.

Next, Abbott Hoffman.† Will the marshals take care of Mr. Hayden?

MR. FROINES: See you in jail.

THE COURT: I will hear from Mr. Hoffman if he wants to be heard.

MR. HOFFMAN: Well, I think—

THE COURT: If you will be respectful.

MR. HOFFMAN: Respectful?

My six-year-old daughter yesterday sent me a note. She said perhaps when the judge changes his glasses he doesn't have a pair that enables him to see what the defendants are all about.

THE COURT: I will let you speak to the specifications, sir.

MR. HOFFMAN: You said that we did not pay tribute to the highest court in the land, but to us the Federal court is not the highest court in the land.

THE COURT: I didn't hear myself say that. The Supreme Court is.

MR. HOFFMAN: The defendants have no respect for the highest court in the land. It ain't high.

THE COURT: I will have to ask you to sit down.

MR. HOFFMAN: I ain't going to sit down. I am going to fight for my right to speak in the same way that I fought for my right to speak and assemble in Lincoln Park.

THE COURT: You are not going to continue your insults and besides you are making statements—

MR. HOFFMAN: We cannot respect an authority that we regard as illegitimate. We can only offer resistance to such illegitimate authority.

We cannot respect a law that is tyranny and the courts are in a conspiracy of tyranny. And when the law is in tyranny, the only order is insurrection and disrespect, and that's what we showed, and that's what all honorable men of free will will show. That's it.

THE COURT: Mr. Clerk, the Court finds the defendant Hoffman guilty of direct contempt in the presence of the Court and in respect to the Specifications which I shall mention here and designate the punishment in connection with each item:

No. 1, one day in the custody of the Attorney General of the United States or his authorized representative.

No. 2, seven days. No. 3, one day. No. 4, seven days. No. 5, one day. No. 6, one day. No. 7, one day. No. 8, two months. No. 9, one day. No. 10, seven days. No. 11, one month. No. 12, fourteen days. No. 13, fourteen days. No. 14, seven days. No. 15, one day.

No. 17, forty-two days. No. 18, fourteen days. No. 19, seven days. No. 20, two days. No. 21, four days. No. 22, five days. No. 23, six days. No. 24, seven days.

The remaining matters here involving Mr. Rubin, Mr. Weiner, Mr. Froines, Mr. Kunstler, and Mr. Weinglass will be disposed of tomorrow morning.

MR. RUBIN: Could we do it now? I don't want to be separated from my brothers.

MR. FORAN: Oh, no.

THE COURT: Tomorrow morning at ten o'clock.

You don't want to ask a favor of Mr. Hitler, do you, Mr. Rubin?

These matters of contempt will be considered at ten o'clock tomorrow morning.

February 15, 1970

THE COURT: I come now to deal with the conduct of Jerry Rubin during this trial.†

I will hear Mr. Rubin if he desires to be heard.

MR. KUNSTLER: Your Honor, before you hear Mr. Rubin, I want to—

THE COURT: I will not hear counsel.

MR. KUNSTLER: I have to just say for the record we make the same argument that I have made and that Mr. Weinglass has made—

THE COURT: This is conduct—contemptuous conduct, committed in the presence of the Court.

MR. KUNSTLER: Yes, I know, but our claim is you don't have the power—

THE COURT: In such circumstances, I am not obligated here to hear counsel, but if you will want to make a motion on jurisdictional grounds, I will consider that you made it on the same ground that you did yesterday.

THE COURT: I will hear Mr. Rubin, if he desires to be heard, but only if he is respectful to the Court.

MR. RUBIN: I came to this trial, I wanted to be indicted. I issued a statement I was indicted upon the Academy Award protest. I was ready for a trial with lawyers, a full defense. The moment you walked in for the arraignment, we got from you instantly the message we were going to jail. And I think it's interesting that while the jury is out, before it reaches a verdict, the ten of us are going to jail. Who has respect for the law?

THE COURT: Speak to the matters I have referred to or I will have to ask you to sit down.

MR. RUBIN: OK, I am trying.

THE COURT: No, you are not succeeding.

MR. RUBIN: OK.

THE COURT: By "OK", you promise me that you will confine your remarks.

MR. RUBIN: You can punish me for these words, but let me say my opinion.

THE COURT: I won't argue with you.

MR. RUBIN: OK. Can I have a second start?

THE COURT: Go ahead. Take your second start.

MR. RUBIN: Now, I have said, "Julius Hoffman equals Adolf Hitler." I said that because I think what we are experiencing in this courtroom is the tyranny of the state, the tyranny of the law, and you have said to us, "Respect or else," and you haven't given moral arguments, and, as a matter of fact, you have shown more disrespect toward us than we have toward you.

What has been our disrespect toward you?

THE COURT: Now, you are not—my what you call "disrespect" for you isn't an issue.

MR. RUBIN: You have interrupted us every time. You have interrupted us every time we speak.

THE COURT: I will not permit you—

MR. RUBIN: You have accused us of laughing at you.

THE COURT: I have endured just about enough.

MR. RUBIN: You are paranoic sending us off to jail.

THE COURT: I will ask you to sit down.

MR. RUBIN: I am happy to.

THE COURT: I find that the acts, statements and conduct of the defendant Jerry C. Rubin constitute a separate—each constituted a separate contempt of the Court and each constituted a deliberate and wilful attack upon the administration of justice, in an attempt to sabotage the functioning of the Federal judicial system; that this misconduct was of so grave a character as to continually disrupt the orderly administration of justice. Accordingly, I notice that it is difficult, that a reading of this record cannot and does not reflect the true intensity and extent of the disruptions which in some instances were accompanied by physical violence, which occurred in the presence of the Court. Accordingly, I adjudge the defendant Jerry C. Rubin guilty of several criminal contempts which I have described.

On Specification No. 1, the defendant Rubin will be committed to the custody of the Attorney General or his authorized representative for imprisonment for a period of one day;

Specification No. 2, one day. Specification No. 3, one day. Specification No. 4, one day. Specification No. 5, four months. Specification No. 6, one day. Specification No. 7, one day. Specification No. 8, one month. Specification No. 9, six months. Specification No. 10, two months. Specification No. 11, six months. Specification No. 12, six months.

The sentence is to run accumulatively and consecutively.

I direct the United States Attorney to prepare the appropriate documents.

MR. SCHULTZ: You haven't covered the remaining counts. I think there were more counts than 12.

THE COURT: You mean the Specifications—

MR. SCHULTZ: There were fifteen Specifications.

THE COURT: Fifteen.

MR. SCHULTZ: Do you want to leave the remaining Specifications out?

THE COURT: On Specification—what was the last one I read?

THE CLERK: Twelve.

THE COURT: Yes, you are quite right. There is a blank space here.

Specification No. 12, six months. Specification No. 13, seven days. Specification No. 14, seven days. Specificatin No. 15, three days.

Those cover all of the Specifications and I direct the United States Attorney to prepare the necessary documents reflecting the views of the Court and I direct the marshal to take the defendant Rubin into custody.

MR. KUNSTLER: For the record, I would like to move for bail pending appeal for Mr. Rubin.

THE COURT: Bail is not indicated in this case. It would be frivolous in view of what appears on the record itself, Mr. Kunstler.

MR. RUBIN: Sadist.

THE COURT: I deny the motion.

We come now to the consideration of the conduct of defendant Lee Weiner.†

THE COURT: Mr. Weiner, if you will confine your remarks to the thoughts you have in respect to mitigation of punishment, I will hear you, sir.

MR. WEINER: Sure, sure.

THE COURT: I don't think that you can—at least I got the impression that you were a university teacher, and I don't think that you would be insulting to the Court. I will hear you, sir.

MR. WEINER: You caught me not standing four times and take that as a measure of my disrespect for the Court.

I would say that throughout this trial, I have sat in a quiet rage as I have seen over and over again the best men of our country, most of my brother defendants, but this has to do with the witnesses as well, the best men and women belittled and attacked in small ways, and sometimes in very great ways, such as Bobby.

If I didn't stand four times and that constitutes contempt of court, I can only say to you that I feel that contempt of court very deeply, very strongly in my heart.

I think the judicial system is a fairly reasonable one—twelve jurors, the evidence— that is kind of good; that is kind of good.

THE COURT: The judicial system is what?

MR. WEINER: I think the judicial system as an idea, an abstract idea, is a fairly reasonable one, and so I have a great deal of sympathy, and I guess, pity for Lennie and Bill who have worked so hard to gain some expertise in a system which should, if it functioned adequately, provide some opportunity for some kind of an abstract notion of justice. But I think that here, you, not necessarily because you are anything evil, but simply because you are what you are, who you are—you are older than us—

THE COURT: I didn't hear that last. You are talking about me. I want to hear that.

MR. WEINER: I say you are older than us. I say that you are a judge in an institutional form, the courtroom, which supports all your notions of omnipotence. I neither forgive you, nor do I necessarily personally condemn you for being what you are, just as I don't personally condemn Tom or Dicky. They are technicians; they do their job for a fascist state.

THE COURT: I must admonish you, sir—

MR. WEINER: Yes.

THE COURT: —I am supposed to be especially tolerant because years ago when I was a much younger man, I was a member of the faculty of the school that you—I don't know whether you still are—at least it has been suggested here during this trial that you are or were a teacher there.

MR. WEINER: I even understand that there is a plaque naming an auditorium after you at the Law School. At latest report, by the way—

THE COURT: You are nice to tell the assembled spectators here—

MR. WEINER: I tell them actually for an evil reason.

THE COURT: —that there is a Hoffman Hall on Northwestern University's campus.

MR. WEINER: I tell them actually because I am suggesting it is evil.

THE COURT: Perhaps those who think ill of me because of some of the things that have been said might have a little compassion.

MR. WEINER: I am pleased to report to you that the plaque has been ripped off the wall.

THE COURT: The plaque?

MR. WEINER: The plaque has been ripped off the wall in the auditorium. Apparently while the Board of Trustees feel affection for you, the student body does not.

THE COURT: Did they take the sign off the door?

MR. WEINER: They have done their best. They have done their best.

THE COURT: I haven't been there.

MR. WEINER: I wouldn't suggest immediately appearing at the Law School after you get through with this trial. You might get mobbed, not necessarily as a tourist of our law building.

THE COURT: If you have anything to say—

MR. WEINER: About punishment.

THE COURT: —in mitigation of your sentence—

MR. WEINER: Sure, I do. Sure, I do.

THE COURT: I will hear that.

MR. WEINER: I think I agree with you. You see, for now, it is your court. It is your government.

THE COURT: I have done the best I can.

MR. WEINER: I am absolutely positive of that.

THE COURT: My best hasn't accorded with what you perceive and some of your co-defendants perceive to be the best kind of judicial conduct.

MR. WEINER: I think it has been terrific.

THE COURT: One thing I have learned in this work, that a judge can't always please everybody.

MR. WEINER: You have pleased me. I think we ten, and I mean my brothers and sisters here in the audience, and downstairs, and across the country, are only slowly groping toward a revolution. I think that you in your own inimitable style have helped educate people younger than ourselves as to what the real world is.

I used to have some questions or some concern in my heart, my gut, about things and now, now, I feel very much more confident that my three-year-old child will make the revolution that we are only slowly groping for. Thank you for that.

THE COURT: I find that the acts, statements and conduct of the defendant, Lee Weiner, each constitute a separate contempt of this Court, each constituted a deliberate and willful attack upon the administration of justice in an attempt to sabotage the functioning of the Federal judicial system, that finding is supported by the observations of the defendant just made in open court, and that this misconduct was of so great a character as to continually disrupt the orderly administration of justice.

Mr. Clerk, with respect to Specification No. 1, the defendant Weiner will be committed to the custody of the United States Attorney or his authorized representative for imprisonment for a period of one day.

With respect to Specification No. 2, one day. With respect to Specification No. 3, one day. Specification No. 4, one day. Specification No. 5, one month. Specification No. 6, fourteen days. Specification No. 7, one month.

These sentences are to be cumulative and consecutive and the defendant is ordered into the custody of the United States Marshal for the Northern District of Illinois.

We now come to the consideration of the matters involving the defendant John Froines.†

In the same manner as heretofore this morning, I will hear counsel for Mr. Froines.

MR. KUNSTLER: Your Honor, just a nunc pro tunc with reference to Mr. Weiner. We want to move for bail pending appeal for him. We have got to do that.

THE COURT: That will be denied for reasons previously indicated.

Mr. Froines, I give you the same opportunity I accorded all of the others to speak in mitigation of punishment here, but without saying offensive things to the Court.

MR. FROINES: What I feel is that in some respects to speak about the punishment is to dignify it in some way, to dignify this punishment that we are all going to receive. So I feel very tied up in terms of talking about it but I think that some way people should say things. I think things finally have to be said.

THE COURT: I agree, but at an appropriate time. This isn't the time to talk about anything except matters that affect the allegedly contemptuous behavior of yourself and others.

MR. FROINES: Well, I am the last defendant—

THE COURT: That's right.

MR. FROINES: —to be sentenced, although it is quite clear that there are two other defendants at this table besides myself, as there are millions of defendants throughout this country and throughout the world in this particular courtroom who still have to be charged.

I think that as Tom said yesterday, not you nor anybody like you can ever sentence and punish all those people—that you finally and all that is represented will, in fact, finally be vilified by history. When history is written, the men who have sat at this table, men there in the spectators' section who stood all night to come to this courtroom, our people here, that's the heroes. That is what this trial is about.

But what is going to happen in this country and across this world, Vietnam in the living room—

THE COURT: Crowd out of your mind, sir, that I have ever had a desire to be a hero. A judge who sets out to be a hero and all things to all people will end up being a mighty incompetent judge.

MR. FROINES: Well, I am not—

THE COURT: Every man in his own profession can't be perfect, but you and your co-defendants have availed yourself of the benefits of the American, United States judicial system.

MR. FROINES: You have that a little backward because we didn't ask actually to come here.

THE COURT: What do you say?

MR. FROINES: We didn't ask to come here. I would prefer to stay where I was.

THE COURT: If the law enforcement agencies of the Government were to wait for all alleged lawbreakers to invite themselves here, I am afraid that most of the courthouses in the land could be burned down. There would be a lot of people—

MR. FROINES: You have got a thought there.

THE COURT: Sometimes we are held to be right, sometimes wrong, but that is the American way. I know of no better way and I am not being chauvinistic when I say that. Certainly we can't let seven or eight defendants at a defense table try their own cases. Now, maybe it will come to that. If it is—and I am living—I will try to become reconciled to it. I will have to because I will be out of a job.

MR. FROINES: We're working on that one.

THE COURT: What did you say?

MR. FROINES: We're working on that.

THE COURT: I suspect you are, from what I hear.

MR. FROINES: I appreciate the chance to have an interchange about the basic facts of American life, but I would like to go to my friends.

THE COURT: To your friends?

MR. FROINES: Yes, I would.

THE COURT: In conformity with Rule 42(a) of the Federal Rules of Criminal Procedure, I find that the acts, statements and conduct of the defendant Froines, each constitutes a separate contempt of this Court, that each constitutes a deliberate and willful attack upon the administration of justice in an attempt to sabotage the functioning of the Federal judicial system, the result of which was to disrupt the orderly administration of justice.

Mr. Clerk, there will be an order committing—with respect to Specification No. 1, there will be an order committing the defendant Froines to the Attorney General of the United States or his authorized representative for imprisonment for a period of one month.

With respect to Specification No. 2, one day. Specification No. 3, one day. Specification No. 4, one day. Specification No. 5, one month. Specification No. 6, one month. Specification No. 7, fourteen days. Specification No. 8, fourteen days. Specification No. 9, two months. Specification No. 10, fourteen days.

I think that is all there are. The sentence is to run cumulative and consecutive and I commit the defendant Froines to the custody of the United States Marshal for the Northern District of Illinois.

This matter now involves the conduct of Mr. William Kunstler, counsel for some of the defendants here, who has participated in this trial from the very beginning.

I have said here frequently that the Court has never had occasion to hold a lawyer in contempt, and only on one occasion did the Court hold someone who is not a lawyer in contempt. That that sentence in that case was concurrent with the sentence in the main case.

I recognize the obligation of a lawyer to defend a client with vigor, and secure for his client the full benefits under the law. Nevertheless if he crosses the bounds of legal propriety, the Court must deal appropriately with that misconduct. Mr. Kunstler's conduct in this case has created a record replete with many direct violations of the orders of the Court.

I am certifying that I saw and heard the conduct which occurred in the actual presence of the Court, during the trial in the case entitled United States of America vs. David Dellinger and others, and which commenced on September 24, 1969, and continued for about four-and-a-half months.†

Do you wish to be heard, Mr. Kunstler?

MR. KUNSTLER: Yes, your Honor. First of all, I make for myself the same motions that I have made for the other clients whom I have represented, with reference to your Honor's powers or lack of power and jurisdiction to impose summary attempt after the trial is over, and I make that with the same force I made it for my client.

THE COURT: I deny the motion.

MR. KUNSTLER: Then I just have a few words, your Honor.

Your Honor, I have been a lawyer since December of 1948, when I was first admitted to the bar in the state of New York. Since that time, I have practiced before, among other courts, the Supreme Court of the United States, the United States Court of Appeals for the First, Second, Third, Fourth, Fifth, Sixth, Seventh, Tenth District of Columbia Circuits, Federal district courts throughout a great deal of the United States, and the United States Court of Military Appeals.

Until today I have never once been disciplined by any judge, Federal or state, although a large part of my practice, at least for the last decade, has taken place in hostile Southern courts where I was representing black and white clients in highly controversial civil rights cases.

Yesterday, for the first time in my career, I completely lost my composure in a courtroom, as I watched the older daughter of David Dellinger being rushed out of the room because she clapped her hands to acknowledge what amounted to her father's farewell statement to her.

I felt then such a deep sense of utter futility that I could not help crying, something I had not done publicly since childhood.

I am sorry if I disturbed the decorum of the courtroom, but I am not ashamed of my tears. Neither am I ashamed of my conduct in this court, for which I am about to be punished.

I have tried with all of my heart faithfully to represent my clients in the face of what I consider repressive and unjust conduct toward them. If I have to pay with my liberty for such repression, then that is the price of my beliefs and sensibilities.

I can only hope that my fate does not deter other lawyers throughout the country, who, in the difficult days that lie ahead, will be asked to defend clients against a steadily increasing governmental encroachment upon their most fundamental liberties. If they are so deterred, then my punishment will have effects of such terrifying consequences that I dread to contemplate the future domestic and foreign course of this country.

But to those lawyers who may, in learning of what may happen to me, waver, I can only say this, stand firm, remain true to those ideals of the law which even if openly violated here and in other places, are true and glorious goals, and, above all, never desert those principles of equality, justice, and freedom without which life has little if any meaning.

Thank you.

(applause)

THE COURT: The marshals will remove those who have applauded from the courtroom. Remove them from the courtroom. This circus has to end sometime. Please remove everybody who has applauded.

Mr. Kunstler, I have to repeat what I have said in substance, that I have never heard a lawyer say to a judge in substance the things that you have said to me during this trial. I know you are going to say—if I permitted you to reply—you would say that I deserved them.

Now I know you tie in your own personal beliefs with those of your clients, and you live your clients' cases as though they are your own. Nobody disputes that. Anyone under the Constitution of the United States has a right to counsel of his choice. But a man charged with a crime has a right only to a defense properly made, and that does not include what has gone on in this courtroom.

We hear a lot of discussion by men in high political places about crime in this country. I am going to make a rather unorthodox statement. I am one of those who believes that crime, if it is on the increase, and I don't have the statistics before me, it is due in large part to the fact that waiting in the wings are lawyers who are willing to go beyond professional responsibility, professional rights, and professional duty in their defense of a defendant, and the fact that a defendant knows that such a lawyer is waiting in the wings, I think, has rather a stimulating effect on the increase in crime.

All right. I find that the acts, statements and conduct of Mr. William Kunstler specified by me each constituted a separate contempt of this Court, that each constituted a deliberate and willful attack upon the administration of justice in an attempt to sabotage the functioning of the Federal judicial system, that this misconduct, especially in a lawyer, was of so grave a character as to continually disrupt the orderly administration of justice. Warning after warning, and admonition after admonition were given to you, Mr. Kunstler. Instead of heeding them, you characterized them as attempts to intimidate you.

I have dealt with many thousands of lawyers both as a lawyer and judge over the many years. Nobody has ever charged me with trying to intimidate, but nobody.

With respect to punishment, have you finished everything you want to say to me?

MR. KUNSTLER: Yes, your Honor, I have nothing further.

THE COURT: All right. With respect to Specification No. 1, Mr. Kunstler will be committed to the custody of the Attorney General of the United States or his authorized representative for a period of one month.

No. 2, fourteen days. No. 3, three months. No. 4, fourteen months, or fourteen days, I beg your pardon.

No. 5, fourteen days. No. 6, three months. No. 7, three months. No. 8, six months. No. 9, twenty-one days. No. 10, fourteen days. No. 11, seven days. No. 12, fourteen days. No. 13, fourteen days. No. 14, one month. No. 15, twenty-one days. No. 16, two months. No. 17, four months. No. 18, one month. No. 19, one month. No. 20, six months. No. 21, six months. No. 22, four months. No. 23, one month. No. 24, two months.

Mr. Kunstler, because you are counsel of record for the defendants here or some of them, on the Court's own motion, the execution of the judgment of conviction entered on these Specifications will be stayed until Monday, May 4, at nine o'clock in the morning, at which time, I order you to report to the United States Marshal for the Northern District of Illinois.

• • • • •

Now we come to the matter of Leonard Weinglass. I will wait until those who wish to leave the courtroom do so.

With respect to Mr. Leonard Weinglass, in conformity with Rule 42(a) of the Federal Rules of Criminal Procedure, I certify that I saw and heard conduct which took place in the actual presence of the Court during the trial.†

Mr. Weinglass, I will hear from you.

MR. WEINGLASS: This trial is my first trial in the Federal court. I have never tried a case either in or out of New Jersey in the United States District Court.

As I first came to this courtroom and I realized the nature of the charges against the eight defendants, as well as the personalities and the involvement of my clients, I wondered if it would be possible to exclude from this room all that did go before and all that was occurring outside of this courtroom. But even in the midst of all this, I tried and I believe together with Mr. Kunstler, to function as best I could under those circumstances and under what I believe to be the tradition of the law, although we differ greatly with the Court on what the tradition of the law is.

However, we continued to hold our course and do what we felt was our obligation in this courtroom and that is defend eight men as best we could. And it hasn't been easy for anyone. This has been a long, difficult, highly contested proceeding in which all of us at one time or another have lost their sense of professional control and judgment. I only have to cite to the Court Mr. Schultz' reference to the bathroom in front of the jury, for which he later apologized.

But I have no quarrel with either Mr. Foran or Mr. Schultz. They were attorneys involved in a very difficult adversary proceeding and they are entitled to errors of judgment, to loss of control, which they committed in the course of this four-and-a-half months.

For the same understandable defects, Mr. Kunstler and myself will have to serve time in jail. Your Honor has the list of citations, I believe there are thirteen or fourteen—each and every one of those citations, without exception, occurring in the course of legal argument.

What the Court has chosen to label as direct contempt I cite as nothing more than the argument of counsel in the heat of battle, and I think you do a disservice to the profession and you unbalance the adversary proceedings where two parties come before the Court as co-equals.

THE COURT: I am not going to permit a lawyer who has had one case in the Federal court tell me that I do a disservice to the profession.

I am accustomed to having lawyers obey the rules and that you consistently failed to do. The United States of America in this case is the plaintiff—the accuser, Justice Cardozo says, "The accuser has some rights." But there is rapidly growing up a belief in this country that the only person on trial is the defendant—that the only party to the trial is the defendant.

When the United States of America procures an indictment against an individual, the United States of America is the accuser and is entitled as much to the protective rulings of the court as the defendant.

You will get along better—you haven't asked me to advise you but since you tell me this is your first case in the Federal court—you will get along better by being respectful— and I know you and I differ on what being respectful means. It doesn't mean being obsequious; you don't have to bow and scrape to a judge. But you must be respectful in your manner and when you are ordered to do something.

MR. WEINGLASS: If I could just answer that digression for a moment. With respect to our different understandings of respect, I was hopeful when I came here that after twenty weeks the Court would know my name and I didn't receive that which I thought was the minimum—

THE COURT: Well, I am going to tell you about that.

MR. WEINGLASS: You have explained it.

THE COURT: I have got a very close friend named Weinruss and I know nobody by the name of Weinrob—and somehow or other the name of Weinruss stuck in my mind, and it is your first appearance here. I scarcely ever forget a lawyer's name even when he hasn't been in for twenty years.

MR. WEINGLASS: I just want to conclude by saying that we have been able to conduct a vigorous defense because of the people who have assisted us.

I came to this city as a stranger and I didn't know these people, but I say to the Court that there are people sitting in the front row of this courtroom who since September 24 have been sleeping on the floor of my apartment, who have been receiving a sum of $20 a week for their maintenance, who have worked until three and four o'clock in the morning going through transcripts and exhibits, who have given up all of the opportunities that are available to them. Like the defendants, America's best was before them, they merely had to seize it.

THE COURT: I think I would have paid out of my own pocket for a good bed in a respectable place if you had set them a good example by at least trying to get these men to refrain from the personal epithets hurled at the Court.

MR. WEINGLASS: Well, I am off that subject for a moment.

THE COURT: They would have respected you even more than they do now.

ANN FROINES: There is no man in this courtroom I respect more than Leonard Weinglass.

MISS LEANER: And you are a racist and a fascist and a pig and I stand with my brothers Weinglass and Kunstler in this courtroom.

THE COURT: Now see what you have? She is your chief staff member. Probably a very competent person. That is an example of the insults I have had to suffer.

Can you imagine that?

After you just got through praising the staff, saying how wonderful they were.

I shall proceed with the disposition—

MR. WEINGLASS: If I may say one sentence in conclusion—

THE COURT: All right. One thing you may say.

MR. WEINGLASS: I face what I am told will be punishment and I don't mean to undermine whatever punishment means by saying this, but I welcome the opportunity of whatever the Court does which will enable me to once again rejoin the defendants and Bill Kunstler wherever they are and what has been for me the warmest and the richest association of my life.

THE COURT: All right.

As I say, I find that the statements and acts and conduct of Leonard Weinglass each constitute a separate contempt of this court and that this misconduct was of so grave a character as to continue to disrupt the orderly administration of justice.

With respect to Specification No. 1, the court directs that Mr. Weinglass be committed to the custody of the Attorney General of the United States for imprisonment for a period of two days.

With respect to No. 2, for a period of four months. No. 3, fourteen days. No. 4, fourteen days. No. 5, one month. No. 6, one month. No. 7, fourteen days. No. 8, one month. No. 9, one month. No. 10, three months. No. 11, one month. No. 12, five months. No. 13, one month. No. 14, twenty-one days.

All of these periods to run cumulatively and consecutively.

I extend the same courtesy to you as I did to Mr. Kunstler, I stay the execution of the judgment of conviction in this situation to May 4 at ten o'clock.

The court will be in recess.

The Verdict

February 18, 1970

THE COURT: I understand, gentlemen, that the jury has brought in a verdict.

Is the jury here? Have you brought the jury here?

THE MARSHAL: Your Honor, the jury has reached a verdict.

MR. SCHULTZ: Your Honor, before the jury is brought in, may I make a statement? May I address the Court, please?

THE COURT: You certainly may.

MR. SCHULTZ: Your Honor, considering what has gone on in this courtroom before, we would ask your Honor to have the court cleared of all spectators except the press. I have authority for it, if your Honor requires it.

THE COURT: Oh, I have done it often before in the trial of jury cases.

I want to ask you a question, Mr. Schultz, before I call on Mr. Kunstler. I see there a number of ladies. I can identify some one or two as members of the press. You think my rule of exclusion here should apply to the wives of the defendants?

MR. SCHULTZ: Yes, your Honor, in fact, the wives of the defendants have been probably more contumacious than any others.

THE COURT: You may reply, Mr. Kunstler.

MR. KUNSTLER: Your Honor, we would want to voice the strongest possible objection to the application by the Government. To clear the courtroom at what is probably the most significant part of the trial, the rendering of a verdict, of the friends and relatives of the defendants is to deny them a public trial. The verdict of this jury should not be received in secret and I think it is received in secret with or without the press being here. I think this is making a star chamber proceeding out of this procedure.

There have been many claims made by the defendants about this trial, that it has not been a fair trial, that it has been a trial which has been dictated by an almost indecent effort to convict them, and we have made this contention, as your Honor knows, against you and against the prosecution.

This is the last possible motion that the Government can make in this case and the defense is hoping that with this last motion, that your Honor will at long last deny a motion made by the prosecution and not let these men stand here alone in this courtroom that has essentially been their home for five months. I beg and implore you to deny this motion of the Government.

THE COURT: I will decide to enter this order. The following may remain: of course, the defendants and those who have sat at the Government's table throughout this trial. The ladies and gentlemen of the press, all media.

Now all of the parties here other than those I have mentioned are directed to leave the courtroom.

A SPECTATOR (ANITA HOFFMAN): The ten of you will be avenged. They will dance on your grave, Julie, and the grave of the pig empire.

A VOICE: They are demonstrating all over the country for you.

MR. SCHULTZ: I just might point out for the record that we have in the hallway now the same kind of screaming we had in the courtroom.

MR. DELLINGER: That's my thirteen-year-old daughter they're beating on.

MR. HOFFMAN: Why don't you bring your wife in, Dick, to watch it?

MR. DELLINGER: You ought to be a proud man.

MR. HOFFMAN: She would like to hear it.

THE COURT: Mr. Marshal, will you please bring in the jury?

(jury enters)

THE COURT: Good morning, ladies and gentlemen of the jury.

I am informed by the United States Marshal that you have reached a verdict or some verdicts.

Is that true? Is there a forewoman or foreman?

THE FOREMAN: A foreman.

THE COURT: Has the jury reached a verdict or some verdicts?

THE FOREMAN: Yes, your Honor.

THE COURT: Would you hand the verdicts to the marshal, please, and, Mr. Marshal, will you hand them to the clerk?

I direct the clerk to read the verdicts.

THE CLERK: "We, the jury, find the defendant David T. Dellinger guilty as charged in Count II of the indictment and not guilty as charged in Count I."

"We, the jury find the defendant Rennard D. Davis guilty as charged in Count III of the indictment and not guilty as charged in Count I."

"We, the jury, find the defendant Thomas E. Hayden guilty as charged in Count IV of the indictment and not guilty as charged in Count I of the indictment."

"We, the jury, find the defendant Abbott H. Hoffman guilty as charged in Count V of the indictment and not guilty as charged in Count I of the indictment."

"We, the jury, find the defendant Jerry C. Rubin guilty as charged in Count VI of the indictment and not guilty as charged in Count I of the indictment."

"We, the jury, find the defendant Lee Weiner not guilty as charged in the indictment."

"We, the jury, find the defendant John R. Froines not guilty as charged in the indictment."

Signed by Edward F. Kratzke, Foreman, and eleven other jurors.

THE COURT: Thank you, ladies and gentlemen.

I wish I were eloquent enough to express my appreciation to you for your several months of service in this case, one of the most difficult I ever tried, one of the longest, and I know you had a great responsibility also.

I express to you in behalf of everybody concerned our deep and appreciative thanks for your service.

You are excused now.

(whereupon the jury is discharged)

MR. KUNSTLER: I am making an application for bond pending appeal for Messrs. Dellinger, Davis, Hayden, Hoffman and Rubin on their convictions on Counts II, III, IV, V and VI.

THE COURT: I have heard the evidence here. I have watched all of the defendants whom you asked me to release on bail. From the evidence and from their conduct in this trial, I find they are dangerous men to be at large and I deny your motion for bail.

The court, Mr. Marshal, will be in recess until tomorrow morning at ten o'clock.

THE MARSHAL: This honorable court will—

Mr. Hoffman, will you please rise?

This honorable court will be in recess until tomorrow morning at ten o'clock.

Sentencing

February 20, 1970

THE COURT: I now proceed with the imposition of sentence.

MR. KUNSTLER: Your Honor, we were not informed on Wednesday that sentence would occur today.

THE COURT: There is no obligation of a Court to notify you of every step it takes.

MR. KUNSTLER: Well, it is wrong, your Honor, both morally and I think legally.

THE COURT: If you are telling me I am morally wrong in this case, you might add to your difficulty. Be careful of your language, sir. I know you don't frighten very easily.

MR. KUNSTLER: The defendants had no way of knowing they are going to be sentenced today. Their families are not even present, which would seem to me in common decency would be permitted.

THE COURT: The reason they were kept out is my life was threatened by one of the members of the family. I was told they would dance on my grave in one of the hearings here within the last week.

MR. KUNSTLER: Your Honor, are you serious?

THE COURT: Yes, I am, sir.

MR. KUNSTLER: Well, your Honor, I have no answer for that then.

THE COURT: I am not a law enforcement officer.

MR. KUNSTLER: It is your life.

THE COURT: I deny your motion to defer sentencing.

MR. KUNSTLER: I think my other applications, your Honor, can await sentencing. I have several other applications.

THE COURT: All right, I will hear from you first then with respect to the defendant David T. Dellinger.

MR. KUNSTLER: Your Honor, I think for all of the defendants, Mr. Weinglass and I are going to make no statement. The defendants will speak for themselves.

THE COURT: All right. Mr. Dellinger, you have the right to speak in your own behalf.

MR. DELLINGER: I would like to make four brief points.

First, I think that every judge should be required to spend time in prison before sentencing other people there so that he might become aware of the degrading antihuman conditions that persist not only in Cook County Jail but in the prisons generally of this country.

I feel more compassion for you, sir, than I do any hostility. I feel that you are a man who has had too much power over the lives of too many people for too many years. You have sentenced them to those degrading conditions without being aware fully of what you are doing, and undoubtedly feeling correct and righteous, as often happens when people do the most abominable things.

I think that in 1970 perhaps the American people will begin to discover something about the nature of the prison system, the system in which we are now confined and which thousands of other political prisoners are confined.

The Black Panthers have said that all black prisoners are political prisoners, and I think that all people in prison are political prisoners. They are in prison, most of them, because they have violated the property and power concepts of the society. The bank robber I talked to yesterday was only trying to get his in the ways he thought were open to him, just as businessmen and others profiteer and try to advance their own economic cause at the expense of their fellows.

My second point is whatever happens to us, however unjustified, will be slight compared to what has happened already to the Vietnamese people, to the black people in this country, to the criminals with whom we are now spending our days in Cook County jail.

I must have already lived longer than the normal life expectancy of a black person born when I was born, or born now. I must have already lived longer, twenty years longer, than the normal life expectancy in the underdeveloped countries which this country is trying to profiteer from and keep under its domain and control.

Thirdly, I want to say that sending us to prison, any punishment the Government can impose upon us, will not solve the problems that have gotten us into trouble with the Government and the law in the first place, will not solve the problem of this country's rampant racism, will not solve the problem of economic injustice, it will not solve the problem of the foreign policy and the attacks upon the underdeveloped people of the world.

The Government has misread the times in which we live, just like there was a time when it was possible to keep black people in slavery, and then it became impossible. So, this country is growing out of the time when it is possible to keep young people, women, black people, Mexican-American, antiwar people, people who believe in truth and justice and really believe in democracy, when it is going to be possible to keep them quiet or suppress them.

Finally, all the way through this I have been ambivalent in my attitude toward you because there is something spunky about you that one has to admire, however misguided and intolerant I believe you are. All the way through the trial, sort of without consciousness or almost against my own will I keep comparing you to George III of England, perhaps because you are trying to hold back the tide of history although you will not succeed, perhaps because you are trying to stem and forestall a second American revolution.

Our Movement is not very strong today. It is not united, it is not well-organized. But there is the beginning of an awakening in this country which has been going on for at least the last fifteen years, and it is an awakening that will not be denied. Tactics will change, people will err, people will die in the streets and die in prison, but I do not believe that this Movement can be denied because however falsely applied the American ideal was from the beginning when it excluded black people, and Indians and people without property, nonetheless there was a dream of justice and equality and freedom and brotherhood, and I think that that dream is much closer to fulfillment today than it has been at any time in the history of this country.

I only wish that we were all not just more eloquent, I wish we were smarter, more dedicated, more united. I wish we could work together. I wish we could reach out to the Forans and the Schultzes and the Hoffmans, and convince them of the necessity of this revolution.

I think I shall sleep better and happier and with a greater sense of fulfillment in whatever jails I am in for the next however many years than if I had compromised, if I had pretended the problems were any less real than they are, or if I had sat here passively in the courthouse while justice was being throttled and the truth was being denied.

I salute my brothers in Vietnam, in the ghetto, in the women's liberation movement, all the people all over the world who are struggling to make true and real for all people the ideals on which this country was supposed to be founded, but never, never lived up to.

THE COURT: Mr. Davis, would you like to speak in your own behalf? You have that right.

MR. DAVIS: I do not think that it is a time to appeal to you or to appeal the system that is about to put me away. I think that what moves a government that increasingly is controlled by a police mentality is action. It is not a time for words; it is a time that demands action.

And since I did not get a jury of my peers, I look to the jury that is in the streets. My jury will be in the streets tomorrow all across this country and the verdict from my jury will keep coming in over the next long five years that you are about to give me in prison.

When I come out of prison it will be to move next door to Tom Foran. I am going to be the boy next door to Tom Foran and the boy next door, the boy that could have been a judge, could have been a prosecutor, could have been a college professor, is going to move next door to organize his kids into the revolution. We are going to turn the sons and daughters of the ruling class in this country into Viet Cong.

THE COURT: Mr. Hayden, you have a right to speak in your own behalf.

MR. HAYDEN: I have very little that I want to say because I don't have very much respect for this kind of freedom of speech. This is the kind of freedom of speech that I think the Government now wants to restrict us to, freedom to speak in empty rooms, in front of prosecutors, a few feet from your jail cell.

We have known all along what the intent of the Government has been. We knew that before we set foot on the streets of Chicago. We knew that before the famous events of August 28, 1968. If those events didn't happen, the Government would have had to invent them, as I think it did for much of its evidence in this case, because they were bound to put us away.

They have failed. Oh, they are going to get rid of us, but they made us in the first place. We would hardly be notorious characters if they had left us alone in the streets of Chicago last year. But instead we became the architects, the masterminds and the geniuses of a conspiracy to overthrow the government. We were invented. We were chosen by the Government to serve as scape goats for all that they wanted to prevent happening in the 1970s.

I have sat there in the Cook County Jail with people who can't make bond, with people who have bum raps, with people who are nowhere, people who are the nothings of society, people who say to me, "You guys burned your draft cards. I would like to burn my birth certificate so they can never find me again."

I sit there and I watch television, and I hear Mr. Foran say the system works. This trial proves the system works.

Mr. Foran, I would love to see a television cameraman come into Cook County jail and show the people how the system is working. Maybe you could televise us sitting around the table with the roaches running over our wrists while we watch somebody on television, a constitutional expert explaining how the jury verdict demonstrates once again the vitality of the American system of justice.

If you didn't want to make us martyrs, why did you do it? If you wanted to keep it cool, why didn't you give us a permit? You know if you had given us a permit, you know if you had given slightly different instructions, very little would have happened last year in Chicago.

And you know that if this prosecution had never been undertaken, it would have been better for those in power. It would have left them in power a little longer. You know that by doing this to us it speeds up the end for the people who do it to us.

You don't believe it but we have to do this. We have no choice. We had no choice in Chicago. We had no choice in this trial. The people always do what they have to do. Every person who is born now and every person under thirty now feels an imperative to do the kind of things that we are doing. They may not act on them immediately, but they feel the same imperative because they are part of the same generation. They are proclaiming that imperative from the streets. Some day they are going to proclaim that imperative from the bench and from the courthouse. It's only a matter of time. You can give us time. You are going to give us time. But it is only a matter of time.

THE COURT: Mr. Hoffman, the law gives you the right to speak in your own behalf. I will hear from you if you have anything to say.

MR. HOFFMAN: Thank you.

I feel like I have spent fifteen years watching John Daly shows about history. You Are There. It is sort of like taking LSD, which I recommend to you, Judge. I know a good dealer in Florida. I could fix you up.

Mr. Foran says that we are evil men, and I suppose that is sort of a compliment. He says that we are unpatriotic. Unpatriotic? I don't know, that has kind of a jingoistic ring. I suppose I am not patriotic.

But he says we are un-American. I don't feel un-American. I feel very American. I said it is not that the Yippies hate America. It is that they feel the American dream has been betrayed. That has been my attitude.

I know those guys on the wall. I know them better than you, I feel. I know Adams. I mean, I know all the Adams. They grew up twenty miles from my home in Massachusetts. I played with Sam Adams on the Concord Bridge. I was there when Paul Revere rode right up on his motorcycle and said, "The pigs are coming, the pigs are coming. Right into Lexington." I was there. I know the Adams. Sam Adams was an evil man.

Thomas Jefferson. Thomas Jefferson called for a revolution every ten years. Thomas Jefferson had an agrarian reform program that made Mao Tse Tung look like a liberal. I know Thomas Jefferson.

Hamilton: Well, I didn't dig the Federalists. Maybe he deserved to have his brains blown out.

Washington? Washington grew pot. He called it hemp. It was called hemp then. He probably was a pot head.

Abraham Lincoln? There is another one. In 1861 Abraham Lincoln in his inaugural address said, and I quote "When the people shall grow weary of their constitutional right to amend the government, they shall exert their revolutionary right to dismember and overthrow that government."

If Abraham Lincoln had given that speech in Lincoln Park, he would be on trial right here in this courtroom, because that is an inciteful speech. That is a speech intended to create a riot.

I don't even know what a riot is. I thought a riot was fun. Riot means you laugh, ha, ha. That is a riot. They call it a riot.

I didn't want to be that serious. I was supposed to be funny. I tried to be, I mean, but it was sad last night. I am not made to be a martyr. I tried to sign up a few years, but I went down there. They ran out of nails. What was I going to do? So I ended up being funny.

It wasn't funny last night sitting in a prison cell, a 5 x 8 room, with no light in the room. I could have written a whole book last night. Nothing. No light in the room. Bedbugs all over. They bite. I haven't eaten in six days. I'm not on a hunger strike; you can call it that. It's just that the food stinks and I can't take it.

Well, we said it was like Alice in Wonderland coming in, now I feel like Alice in 1984, because I have lived through the winter of injustice in this trial.

And it's fitting that if you went to the South and fought for voter registration and got arrested and beaten eleven or twelve times on those dusty roads for no bread, it's only fitting that you be arrested and tried under a civil rights act. That's the way it works.

Just want to say one more thing.

People—I guess that is what we are charged with—when they decide to go from one state of mind to another state of mind, when they decide to fly that route, I hope they go youth fare no matter what their age.

I will see you in Florida, Julie.

THE COURT: The next defendant, Mr. Rubin, do you desire to speak in your own behalf? You have that privilege.

MR. RUBIN: Well, five months are over. Look at the courtroom, fluorescent lighting. We sat for five months in swivel chairs. The press, the marshals, the judge, now it is over.

This is one of the proudest moments of my life. This is one of the happiest moments of my life, if you can dig what I mean. I am happy because I am in touch with myself, because I know who I am. I am happy because I am associated with Rennie, Tom, Dave, Abbie and myself. That makes me very happy.

This is my life. I used to look like this. I use to look like this, Judge. See? [*displaying picture*]

I was a reporter for a newspaper. Most everybody around this table once looked like this, and we all believed in the American system, believed in the court system, believed in the election system, believed that the country had some things wrong with it, and we tried to change it.

I'm being sentenced to five years not for what I did in Chicago—I did nothing in Chicago. I am going to jail because I am part of a historical movement and because of my life, the things I am trying to do, because, as Abbie said, we don't want to be—we don't want to have a piece of the pie.

We don't just want to be part of the American way of life. We don't want to live in the suburbs. We don't want to have college degrees. We don't want to stand before the judge and say, "Yes, we respect you, Judge, no matter what happens." We don't want that. We are moved by something else. We are moved by a firm belief in ourselves.

And you are sentencing us for being ourselves. That's our crime: being ourselves. Because we don't look like this any more. That's our crime.

Judge, I want to give you a copy of my book. I want you to read it on your vacation in Florida, because this is why I am on trial. I inscribed it. I made two little inscriptions. One says, "Dear Julius, the demonstrations in Chicago in 1968 were the first steps in the revolution. What happened in the courtroom is the second step." Then I decided to add another note, and that was: "Julius, You radicalized more young people than we ever could. You're the country's top Yippie." I hope you will take it and read it.

What you are doing out there is creating millions of revolutionaries. Julius Hoffman, you have done more to destroy the court system in this country than any of us could have done. All we did was go to Chicago and the police system exposed itself as totalitarian. All we did is walk into the courtroom and the court system exposed itself as totalitarian.

And I am glad we exposed the court system because in millions of courthouses across this country blacks are being shuttled from the streets to the jails and nobody knows about it. They are forgotten men. There ain't a whole corps of press people sitting and watching. They don't care. You see what we have done is, we have exposed that. Maybe now people will be interested in what happens in the courthouse down the street because of what happened here. Maybe now people will be interested.

This is the happiest moment of my life.

THE DEFENDANTS: Right on.

THE COURT: I call on the Government to reply to the remarks of the defendants and each of them.

MR. FORAN: The Government has no comment on their remarks, your Honor. I think the evidence in this case speaks for itself.

THE COURT: Mr. Clerk, the defendant David T. Dellinger will be committed to the custody of the Attorney General of the United States or his authorized representative for imprisonment for a term of five years. Further, the defendant Dellinger will be fined the sum of $5,000 and costs of prosecution, the defendant to stand committed until the fine and costs have been paid. That sentence of five years will be concurrent with the sentence the court imposed for contempt of court previously. The two sentences will run concurrently.

Mr. Clerk, the defendant Rennard C. Davis will be committed to the custody of the Attorney General of the United States for a term of five years. Further a fine of—a fine will be imposed against Mr. Davis in the sum of $5,000 and costs of prosecution.

The defendant Thomas C. Hayden will be committed to the custody of the Attorney General of the United States for a term of five years. Further a fine of $5,000 and costs of prosecution will be imposed.

The defendant Abbott H. Hoffman will be committed to the custody of the Attorney General of the United States for imprisonment for a term of five years. Further a fine of $5,000 and costs—

MR. HOFFMAN: Five thousand dollars, Judge? Could you make that three-fifty?

THE COURT: —$5,000 and—

MR. HOFFMAN: How about three and a half?

THE COURT: —and costs will be imposed, costs of prosecution will be imposed.

The defendant Jerry C. Rubin will be committed to the custody of the Attorney General of the United States for a term of five years. Further there will be a fine of $5,000 and cost of prosecution will be imposed.

Not only on the record in this case, covering a period of four months or longer, but from the remarks made by the defendants themselves here today, the Court finds that the defendants are clearly dangerous persons to be at large. Therefore the commitments here will be without bail.

THE COURT: Does the defense have any observations?

MR. KUNSTLER: In conclusion, your Honor, speaking both for Mr. Weinglass and myself, we didn't need to hear our clients speak today to understand how much they meant to us but, after listening to them a few moments ago we know that what they have said here has more meaning and will be longer remembered than any words said by us or by you.

We feel that if you could even begin to understand that simple fact, then their triumph would have been as overwhelming today as is our belief—

THE COURT: I gave you an opportunity to speak.

MR. KUNSTLER: —as inevitable—

THE COURT: I gave you an opportunity to speak at the very beginning. You said counsel did not desire to speak.

MR. KUNSTLER: Your Honor, couldn't I say my last words without you cutting me off?

THE COURT: You said you didn't want to speak.

MR. KUNSTLER: Your Honor, I just said a moment ago we had a concluding remark. Your Honor has succeeded perhaps, in sullying it, and I think that maybe that is the way the case should end, as it began.

ABBIE HOFFMAN: We love our lawyers.

THE COURT: Mr. Marshal, the court will be in recess.

UNITED STATES DISTRICT COURT
NORTHERN DISTRICT OF ILLINOIS
EASTERN DIVISION

UNITED STATES OF AMERICA

—vs—

DAVID T. DELLINGER,
RENNARD C. DAVIS,
THOMAS E. HAYDEN,
ABBOTT H. HOFFMAN,
JERRY C. RUBIN,
LEE WEINER,
JOHN R. FROINES, and
BOBBY G. SEALE

No. 69CR180

Violation: Title 18,
United States Code, Section
371, 231 (a) (1) and 2 101

INDICTMENT

The SEPTEMBER 1968 GRAND JURY charges:

1. Beginning on or about April 12, 1968, and continuing through on or about August 30, 1968, in the Northern District of Illinois, Eastern Division, and elsewhere,

DAVID T. DELLINGER,
RENNARD C. DAVIS,
THOMAS E. HAYDEN,
ABBOTT H. HOFFMAN,
JERRY C. RUBIN,
LEE WEINER,
JOHN R. FROINES and
BOBBY SEALE,

defendants herein, unlawfully, wilfully and knowingly did combine, conspire, confederate and agree together and with

WOLFE B. LOWENTHAL
STEWART E. ALBERT,
SIDNEY M. PECK,
KATHIE BOUDIN,
SARA C. BROWN,
CORINA F. FALES,
BENJAMIN RADFORD,
BRADFORD FOX,
THOMAS W. NEUMANN,

CRAIG SHIMABUKURO,
BO TAYLOR,
DAVID A. BAKER,
RICHARD BOSCIANO,
TERRY GROSS,
DONNA GRIPE,
BENJAMIN ORITZ,
JOSEPH TORNABENE and
RICHARD PALMER

being co-conspirators not named as defendants herein, and with divers other persons, some known and others unknown to the Grand Jury, to commit offenses against the United States, that is:

a. to travel in interstate commerce and use the facilities of interstate commerce with the intent to incite, organize, promote, encourage, participate in, and carry on a riot and to commit acts of violence in furtherance of a riot, and to aid and abet persons in inciting, participating in, and carrying on a riot and committing acts of violence in furtherance of a riot, and during the course of such travel, and use, and thereafter, to perform overt acts for the purpose of inciting, organizing, promoting, encouraging, participating in, and carrying on a riot, and committing acts of violence in furtherance of a riot, and aiding and abetting persons in inciting, participating in, and carrying out a riot, and committing acts of violence in furtherance of a riot, in violation of Section 2101 of Title 18, United States Code; and

b. to teach and demonstrate to other persons the use, application, and making of incendiary devices, knowing, having reason to know, and intending that said incendiary devices would be unlawfully employed for use in and in furtherance of civil disorders which may obstruct, delay and adversely affect commerce and the movement of articles and commodities in commerce and the conduct and performance of federally protected functions, in violation of Section 231 (a) (1) of Title 18, United States Code; and,

c. to commit acts to obstruct, impede, and interfere with firemen and law enforcement officers lawfully enaged in the lawful performance of their official duties incident to and during the commission of civil disorders which obstruct, delay, and adversely affect commerce and the movement of articles and commodities in commerce and the conduct and performance of federally projected functions in violation of Section 231 (a) (3) of Title 18, United States Code.

2. It was a part of said conspiracy that from on or about April 12, 1968, through on or about August 24, 1968, the defendants DAVID T. DELLINGER, RENNARD C. DAVIS, THOMAS E. HAYDEN, ABBOTT H. HOFFMAN and JERRY C. RUBIN, and other co-conspirators not named as defendants herein, would organize and attend various meetings, would publish and cause to be published articles, and would make and cause to be made long distance telephone calls for the purpose of encouraging persons to come to Chicago, Illinois, to participate in massive demonstrations during the period of on or about August 25, 1968, through on or about August 29, 1968.

3. It was a further part of said conspiracy that the defendants DAVID T. DELLINGER, RENNARD C. DAVIS and THOMAS E. HAYDEN, and other co-conspirators not named as defendants herein, would maintain and cause to be maintained an office of the National Mobilization Committee to End the War in Vietnam at 407 South Dearborn Street, Chicago, Illinois, and other "movement centers," to be used for the planning and organizing of activities to take place in Chicago during the period of on or about August 25, 1968, through on or about August 29, 1968.

4. It was a further part of said conspiracy that from on or about August 13, 1968, through on or about August 24, 1968, the defendants DAVID T. DELLINGER, RENNARD C. DAVIS, THOMAS E. HAYDEN, ABBOTT H. HOFFMAN, JERRY C. RUBIN, LEE WEINER and JOHN R. FROINES and other co-conspirators not named as defendants herein, would select and cause to be selected persons designated as "marshals" and would conduct and cause to be conducted training sessions for such "marshals" at which instructions would be given in techniques of resisting and obstructing police action, including karate, Japanese snake dancing, methods of freeing persons being arrested, and counter kicks to knee and groin.

5. It was further part of said conspiracy that from on or about August 1, 1968, through on or about August 29, 1968, the defendants DAVID T. DELLINGER, RENNARD C. DAVIS, THOMAS E. HAYDEN, ABBOTT H. HOFFMAN, JERRY C. RUBIN, LEE WEINER, JOHN R. FROINES and BOBBY G. SEALE, and other co-conspirators not named as defendants herein, would plan, carry into effect, and cause to be carried into effect actions and tactics to be employed by groups of persons in Chicago, Illinois, during the period of on or about August 25, 1968, through on or about August 29, 1968, which actions and tactics would include but would not be limited to the following:

a. large numbers of persons would march to the International Amphitheatre, Chicago, Illinois, even if permits authorizing such marches were denied;

b. large numbers of persons would remain in Lincoln Park, Chicago, Illinois, after 11:00 P.M., even if permits authorizing such persons to remain were denied, and would set up defenses and would attempt to hold the Park against police efforts to clear it, were permits denied;

c. large numbers of persons would break windows, set off false fire alarms, set small fires, disable automobiles, create disturbances at various hotels in the Chicago Loop area, and throughout the city of Chicago, for the purpose of disrupting the city and causing the deployment of military forces;

d. on or about August 28, 1968, large numbers of persons would block, obstruct and impede pedestrian and vehicular traffic in the Chicago Loop area, and would occupy and forcibly hold all or part of the Conrad Hilton Hotel in Chicago.

6. It was a further part of said conspiracy that from on or about August 25, 1968, through on or about August 29, 1968, the defendants DAVID T. DELLINGER, REN-NARD C. DAVIS, THOMAS E. HAYDEN, ABBOTT H. HOFFMAN, JERRY C. RUBIN, LEE WEINER, JOHN R. FROINES and BOBBY G. SEALE, and other co-conspirators not named as defendants herein, would make statements and speeches to assemblages of persons encouraging them to remain in and hold Lincoln Park against police efforts to clear it after permits to remain therein had been denied; to march to the International Amphitheatre after permits authorizing such march had been denied; to make weapons to be used against the police; to shout obscenities at, throw objects, threaten and physically assault policemen and National Guard troops; and to obstruct traffic and damage and seize property in the city of Chicago.

7. It was a further part of said conspiracy that on or about August 27, 1968, BOBBY G. SEALE would travel to Chicago, Illinois, where he would speak to assemblages of persons for the purpose of inciting, organizing, promoting and encouraging a riot.

8. It was a further part of said conspiracy that JOHN R. FROINES and LEE WEINER would teach and demonstrate to other persons the use, application and making of an incendiary device, intending that said incendiary device would be employed to damage the underground garage at Grant Park, Chicago, Illinois, on the evening of August 29, 1968.

9. It was a further part of said conspiracy that the defendants and co-conspirators would misrepresent, conceal, and hide and cause to be misrepresented, concealed and hidden, the purpose of and the acts done in furtherance of said conspiracy.

Overt Acts

At the times hereinafter mentioned the defendants committed, among others, the following overt acts in furtherance of the conspiracy and to effect the objects thereof:

1. The Grand Jury realleges and incorporates by reference the allegations contained in Counts II through VIII of this indictment, each of which count is alleged as a separate and distinct overt act.

2. On or about July 23, 1968, JERRY C. RUBIN spoke to an assemblage of persons at 48th Street and Park Avenue, New York, New York.

3. On or about July 25, 1968, THOMAS E. HAYDEN spoke to an assemblage of persons at the Diplomat Hotel, New York, New York.

4. On or about August 1, 1968, RENNARD C. DAVIS spoke to an assemblage of persons at 30 West Chicago Avenue, Chicago, Illinois.

5. On or about August 15, 1968, RENNARD C. DAVIS, THOMAS E. HAYDEN and JOHN R. FROINES participated in a meeting at Lincoln Park, Chicago, Illinois.

6. On or about August 18, 1968, RENNARD C. DAVIS, LEE WEINER and JOHN R. FROINES participated in a meeting at 1012 North Noble Street, Chicago, Illinois.

7. On or about August 20, 1968, RENNARD C. DAVIS, ABBOT H. HOFFMAN, LEE WEINER and JOHN R. FROINES participated in a meeting at the National Mobilization Committee office at 407 South Dearborn Street, Chicago, Illinois.

8. On or about August 24, 1968, DAVID T. DELLINGER, RENNARD C. DAVIS,

THOMAS E. HAYDEN, ABBOTT H. HOFFMAN, LEE WEINER and JOHN R. FROINES attended a "marshal" training session at Lincoln Park, Chicago, Illinois.

9. On or about August 25, 1968, DAVID T. DELLINGER, RENNARD C. DAVIS, THOMAS E. HAYDEN and ABBOTT H. HOFFMAN met at the National Mobilization Committee office at 407 South Dearborn Street, Chicago, Illinois.

10. On or about August 26, 1968, RENNARD C. DAVIS, JERRY C. RUBIN, LEE WEINER, and JOHN R. FROINES met at Lincoln Park, Chicago, Illinois.

11. On or about August 27, 1968, JERRY C. RUBIN, BOBBY G. SEALE and others spoke to an assemblage of persons at Lincoln Park, Chicago, Illinois.

12. On or about August 28, 1968, DAVID T. DELLINGER, THOMAS E. HAYDEN, JERRY C. RUBIN and others spoke to an assemblage of persons at Grant Park, Chicago, Illinois.

13. On or about August 29, 1968, LEE WEINER and JOHN R. FROINES engaged in a conversation at Grant Park, Chicago, Illinois.

All in violation of Section 371 of Title 18, United States Code.

Count II

The SEPTEMBER 1968 GRAND JURY further charges:
That during the period beginning on or about July 20, 1968, through on or about August 22, 1968,

DAVID T. DELLINGER,

defendant herein, did travel in interstate commerce from outside the State of Illinois to Chicago, Illinois, Northern District of Illinois, Eastern Division, with intent to incite, organize, promote and encourage a riot and, thereafter, on or about August 28, 1968, at Grant Park, Chicago, Illinois, he did speak to an assemblage of persons for the purpose of inciting, organizing, promoting and encouraging a riot, in violation of Title 18, United States Code, Section 2101.

Count III

The SEPTEMBER 1968 GRAND JURY further charges:
That during the period beginning on or about July 20, 1968, through on or about August 1, 1968,

RENNARD C. DAVIS,

defendant herein, did travel in interstate commerce from outside the State of Illinois to Chicago, Illinois, Northern District of Illinois, Eastern Division, with intent to incite, organize, promote and encourage a riot, and thereafter, on or about August 1, 1968, at 30 West Chicago Avenue, Chicago, Illinois, and on or about August 9, 1968, at 407 South Dearborn Street, Chicago, Illinois, and on or about August 18, 1968, at 1012 North Noble Street, Chicago, Illinois, and on or about August 26, 1968, at Grant Park, Chicago, Illinois, he did speak to assemblages of persons for the purpose of inciting, organizing, promoting and encouraging a riot; in violation of Title 18, United States Code, Section 2101.

Count IV

The SEPTEMBER 1968 GRAND JURY further charges:
That during the period beginning on or about July 20, 1968, through on or about August 22, 1968,

THOMAS E. HAYDEN,

defendant herein, did travel in interstate commerce from outside the State of Illinois to Chicago, Illinois, Northern District of Illinois, Eastern Division, with intent to incite, organize, promote and encourage a riot and, thereafter, on or about August 26, 1968, at Grant Park, Chicago, Illinois, he did speak to assemblages of persons for the purposes of inciting, organizing, promoting and encouraging a riot; in violation of Title 18, United States Code, Section 2101.

Count V

The SEPTEMBER 1968 GRAND JURY further charges:
That during the period beginning on or about August 1, 1968, through on or about August 7, 1968,

ABBOTT H. HOFFMAN,

defendant herein, did travel in interstate commerce from outside the State of Illinois to Chicago, Illinois, Northern District of Illinois, Eastern Division, with intent to incite, organize, promote and encourage a riot and, thereafter, on or about August 26, 1968, at Lincoln Park, Chicago, Illinois, and on or about August 27, 1968, at Lincoln Park, Chicago, Illinois, and on or about August 29, 1968, at Grant Park, Chicago, Illinois, he did speak to assemblages of persons for the purpose of inciting, organizing, promoting, and encouraging a riot; in violation of Title 18, United States Code, Section 2101.

Count VI

The SEPTEMBER 1968 GRAND JURY further charges:
That during the period beginning on or about July 23, 1968, through on or about August 21, 1968,

JERRY C. RUBIN,

defendant herein, did travel in interstate commerce from outside the State of Illinois to Chicago, Illinois, Northern District of Illinois, Eastern Division, with intent to incite, organize, promote and encourage a riot and, thereafter, on or about August 25, 1968, at Lincoln Park, Chicago, Illinois, and on or about August 26, 1968, at Lincoln Park, Chicago, Illinois, he did speak to assemblages of persons for the purposes of inciting, organizing, promoting and encouraging a riot; in violation of Title 18, United States Code, Section 2101.

Count VII

The SEPTEMBER 1968 GRAND JURY further charges:
That on or about August 29, 1968, at Chicago, Illinois, in the Northern District of Illinois, Eastern Division,

JOHN R. FROINES and
LEE WEINER,

defendants herein, did teach and demonstrate to other persons the use, application and making of an incendiary device knowing, having reason to know and intending that said incendiary device would be unlawfully employed for use in and in furtherance of a civil disorder which may obstruct, delay and adversely affect commerce and the movement of articles and commodities in commerce; in violation of Title 18, United States Code, Section 231 (a) (1).

Count VIII

The SEPTEMBER 1968 GRAND JURY further charges:
That on or about August 27, 1968,

BOBBY G. SEALE,

defendant herein, did travel in interstate commerce from outside the State of Illinois, to Chicago, Illinois, Northern District, Eastern Division, with intent to incite, organize, promote and encourage a riot and, thereafter, on or about August 27, 1968, at Lincoln Park, Chicago, Illinois, and on or about August 28, 1968, at Grant Park, Chicago, Illinois, he did speak to assemblages of persons for the purposes of inciting, organizing, promoting and encouraging a riot; in violation of Title 18, United States Code, Section 2101.

LEGAL CITATIONS [Appendix II]

Page   5   *General Tire and Rubber Company* v. *Watkins*, 363 F.2d 87 (4th Cir., 1966); certiorari denied, 385 U.S. 899 (1966)

            Popkin v. *Eastern Airlines Incorporated*, 236 F.Supp. 645 (Eastern District of Pennsylvania, 1964).

   26   *Shuttlesworth* v. *The City of Birmingham*, 394 U.S. 147 (1969).

   29   *Dombrowski* v. *Pfister*, 380 U.S. 471 (1965).

   39   *Patriarcha* v. *United States*, 402 F.2d 314 (1st Cir., 1969).

   41   *United States* v. *Zuideveld*, 316 F.2d 873 (7th Cir., 1963).

            United States v. *Wechsler*, 392 F.2d 344 (4th Cir., 1968); certiorari denied, 88 S. Ct. 2283 (1968).

            United States v. *Kubacki*, 237 F.Supp. 638 (Eastern District of Pennsylvania, 1965).

            Leyvas v. *United States*, 371 F.2d 714 (9th Cir. 1967).

   58   *Local 309* v. *Gates*, 75 F.Supp. 620 (Northern District of Indiana, 1948).

            Giancona v. *Johnson*, 335 F.2d 366 (Northern District of Illinois, Eastern Division, 1963); certiorari denied, 85 S. Ct. 718 (1965).

            Anderson v. *Sills*, 106 N.J. Super. 545, 256 A.2d 298 (Superior Court, Chancery Division, 1969).

            Katz v. *United States*, 389 U.S. 347 (1967).

            United States v. *Callahan*, 256 F.Supp. 739 (District of Minnesota, Fourth Division, 1964).

            United States v. *Camp*, 275 F.Supp. 7 (District of South Carolina, 1967).

   71   *United States* v. *Carlissi*, 32 F.Supp. 479 (District of the District of Columbia, 1940).

            Harris v. *United States*, 261 F.2d 792 (9th Cir., 1958).

   72   *United States* v. *Davis*, 103 F.Supp. 457 (Western District of Tennessee, 1951).

            Mathis and Devitt, *Federal Jury Practice* (1964), p. 25.

   96   *Prudowitz* v. *United States*, 336 U.S. 440 (1948).

  107   *Elfbrondt* v. *Russell*, 384 U.S. 11 (1966).

            Edwards v. *South Carolina*, 372 U.S. 229 (1963).

            Dombrowski v. *Pfister*, 380 U.S. 479 (1965).

  111   *Brondenburg* v. *Ohio*, 395 U.S. 444 (1969).

  113   *Adams* v. *United States* ex rel. *McConn*, 317 U.S. 269 (1942).

            United States v. *Platner*, 330 F.2d 271 (2nd Cir., 1964).

            United States v. *Deno*, 348 F.2d 12 (2nd Cir., 1965).

            United States ex rel. *Maldonado* v. *Deno*, 239 F.Supp. 851 (Southern District of New York, 1965).

            Duke v. *United States*, 255 F.2d 721 (9th Cir., 1958); certiorari denied 78 S. Ct. 1361 (1958).

  114   *United States* v. *Berlina*, 319 F.2d 916 (2nd Cir., 1963).

            Butler v. *United States*, 317 F.2d 249 (8th Cir., 1963).

            Jewelich v. *United States*, 342 F.2d 29 (5th Cir., 1965).

            United States v. *Davis*, 260 F.Supp. 1009 (Eastern District of Tennessee, 1966).

  119   *United States* v. *Fiorello*, 276 F. 2d 180 (2nd Cir., 1967).

            People v. *Catalano*, 29 Ill. 2d 197, 193 N.E. 2d 797 (Supreme Court of Illinois, 1963).

            United States v. *Bentuena*, 357 F.2d 58 (2nd Cir., 1966).

            United States ex rel. *Maldonado* v. *Deno*, 239 F.Supp. 851 (Southern District of New York, 1965).

  143   *United States* v. *Spock*, 416 F.2d 165 (1st Cir., 1969).

            1969. Weinglass quotes from Judge Aldrich's opinion on bifarious con-

Page 143
(*cont.*)

spiracy: "Adopting the panoply of rules applicable to a conspiracy having purely illegal purposes, the Government introduced numerous statements of third persons alleged to be co-conspirators. This was improper. The specific intent of one defendant in a case such as this is not ascertained by reference to the conduct or statements of another, even if the conspirator has knowledge thereof."

163   *Moore* v. *Dempsey*, 261 U.S. 86 (1923).

179   *Jones* v. *Mayer*, 392 U.S. 409 (1968).

189   *United States* v. *Scheles*, 352 F.2d 892 (7th Cir., 1965).
Wade v. *Hunter*, 336 U.S. 689 (1948).
United States v. *Aviles*, 274 F.2d 179 (6th Cir., 1960).
Braswell v. *United States*, 200 F.2d 597 (5th Cir., 1952).
United States v. *Difronzo*, 345 F.2d 383 (7th Cir., 1965).
United States v. *Rabinowitz*, 339 U.S. 56 (1950).

192   Chef and Carbo and Sellers
Broom v. *Illinois*, 391 U.S. 194 (1968).
Carbo v. *United States*, 288 F.2d 282 (2nd Cir., 1961).

261   *United States* v. *Smith*, 209 F.Supp. 907 (Eastern District of Illinois, 1962).
United States v. *Brockington*, 21 F.R.D. 102 (District Court of Virginia, 1957).
Palermo v. *United States*, 360 U.S. 343 (1953).

262   *Bowman Dairy Co.* v. *United States*, 341 U.S. 214 (1951).
United States v. *Marchesio*, 344 F.2d 653 (2nd Cir., 1965).
United States v. *Carter*, 15 F.R.D. 367 (District Court of the District of Colombia, 1954).
United States v. *Maloney*, 37 F.R.D. 441 (Western District of Pennsylvania, 1965).

265   *United States* v. *Spock*, 416 F.2d 165 (1st Cir., 1969).
Di Re v. *United States*, 332, U.S. 581 (1948).
Scales v. *United States*, 367 U.S. 203 (1961).

266   *United States* v. *Schneiderman*, 106 S.Supp. 906 (Southern District of California, Central Division, 1952).
Espenhain v. *Barker*, 121 Oregon 621, 256 p. 766 (Supreme Court of Oregon, 1927).
Ex Parte Bernet, 255 F.Supp. 429 (1966).

269   *Emick Motor Corp.* v. *General Motors Corp.*, 181 F.2d 70 (7th Cir., 1950).
Ohio Associated Telephone Co. v. *N.L.R.B.*, 192 F.2d 664 (6th Cir., 1951).
Creaghe v. *Iowa Home Mutual Casualty Co.*, 323 F.2d 978 (10th Circuit, 1963).
Boston and Maine Railroad v. *Aetna Casualty Co.*, 329 F.2d 602 (1st Circuit, 1964).

387   *A.U.S.* v. *Freeman*, 302.
United States v. *Freeman*, 302 F.2d 347 (2d Cir., 1962).
United States v. *Budd*, 144 U.S. 154 (1892).
Civil v. *Waterman Steamship Co.*, 217 F.2d 94 (2d Cir., 1954).
3 Wigmore Evidence, Section 907, 1940.

412   *Biasek* v. *United States*, 253 F.2d 658 (5th Cir., 1958).
American Tobacco Co. v. *United States*, 147 F.2d 93 (6th Cir., 1944).
United States v. *New York Great A&P Tea Co.*, 173 F.2d 79 (7th Cir., 1949).
Pacman v. *United States*, 144 F.2d 562 (9th Cir., 1944).
McDonough v. *United States*, 227 F.2d 402 (10th Cir., 1955).
Beal v. *Missouri Pacific Railroad Corp.*. 312 U.S. 45 (1941).
Douglas v. *City of Jeannette*, 319 U.S. 157 (1943).
Bartkus v. *Illinois*, 359 U.S. 121 (1959).

470   *Truckdriver's Local 421* v. *United States*, 128 F.2d 227 (8th Circuit—certiorari denied, 1941).
United States v. *General Motors Corp.*, 121 F.2d 376, (7th Cir., 1941) certiorari denied, 314 U.S. 618 (1941).

Page 495 *May* v. *United States,* 175 F.2d 994 (D.C. Cir., 1949).
        Overholser v. *DeMarcos,* 149 F.2d 23 (D.C. Cir., 1949).
    531 *Carbo* v. *United States,* 288 F.2d 282 (2nd Cir., 1961).
        Fernandez et al. v. *United States,* 81 Supreme Court 642 (1961).
        United States v. *Rice,* 192 F. 720 (Southern District of New York, 1911).
    537 *NAACP* v. *Button,* 371 U.S. 415 (1963).
        Brotherhood of Railway Trainsmen v. *Virginia* ex rel. *Virginia State Bar,* 377
          U.S. 1 (1964).
    538 *United States* v. *Foster,* 9 F.R.D. 367 (S.D.N.Y. 1949).
        Lee v. *State of Alabama,* 406 F.2d 466 (5th Cir., 1968).
        Duke v. *United States,* 255 F.2d 729 (9th Cir., 1958).
    579 *Cox* v. *Louisiana,* 37 U.S. 559 (1965).
        United States v. *Sehiffler,* 361 F.2d 91 (6th Cir., 1965) certiorari denied, 384
          U.S. 1003 (1966).
        United States v. *Galante,* 298 F.2d 72 (1st Cir., 1962).
        Broom v. *Illinois,* 391 U.S. 194 (1968).
    580 *Broom* v. *Illinois,* 391 U.S. 194 (1968).
        Unger v. *Serglin,* 376 U.S. 575 (1964).

BOBBY SEALE CONTEMPT PROCEEDINGS [Appendix III]

At this point Judge Hoffman read verbatim from the trial transcript the text of sixteen incidents for which Bobby Seale was sentenced for contempt. We have not included Judge Hoffman's reading (which included all dirty words) in this edition, but the incidents referred to are to be found on the following pages:

Specification I:	omitted from text	Specification IX:	page 143
Specification II:	page 89	Specification X:	pages 152-153
Specification III:	page 103	Specification XI:	pages 154-156
Specification IV:	pages 114-115	Specification XII:	pages 159-160
Specification V:	page 119	Specification XIII:	page 162
Specification VI:	page 120	Specification XIV:	pages 165-166
Specification VII:	pages 122-123	Specification XV:	pages 174-175
Specification VIII:	pages 136-137	Specification XVI:	page 187

Bobby Seale's sentence on contempt totaled four years.

CONTEMPT PROCEEDINGS [Appendix IV]

As with the contempt proceedings against Bobby Seale, Judge Hoffman read verbatim from the trial transcript the text of the incidents for which the defendants and their lawyers are sentenced for contempt. Again we have not included Judge Hoffman's readings, but refer the reader to the page in the text at which each incident occurs. Also we have given the length of sentence imposed for each separate "contempt."

David Dellinger

Specification	Reference	Sentence
1	pages 92-3	6 months
2	page 125	1 month
3	page 123	7 days
4	pages 144-45	3 months
5	omitted from text	7 days
6	page 154 (refusal to rise)	1 day
7	page 155	7 days
8	page 159 (interfering)	1 month
9	page 160 (refusal to rise)	1 day
10	page 166	1 day
11	page 169	7 days
12	(refusal to rise)	1 day
13	pages 206, 208	2 days
14	pages 223-24	4 days
15	page 240	4 days
16	omitted from text	3 days
17	omitted from text	6 days
18	omitted from text	2 days
19	omitted from text	6 days
20	page 364	4 days
21	page 402	3 days
22	page 407	3 days
23	page 412	5 days
24	page 424	6 months
25	omitted from text	7 days
26	pages 468-69	4 months
27	omitted from text	2 days
28	omitted from text	2 days
29	omitted from text	7 days
30	pages 529-30	5 months
31	page 538	7 days
32	omitted from text	7 days

Total sentence for contempt: 2 years, 5 months, 16 days

Rennie Davis

Specification	Reference	Sentence
1	page 122	2 days
2	page 154 (refusal to rise)	1 day
3	page 160 (refusal to rise)	1 day
4	page 163 (refusal to rise)	1 day

Rennie Davis (*cont.*)

Specification	Reference	Sentence
5	(refusal to rise)	1 day
6	page 169	2 months
7	(refusal to rise)	1 day
8	(refusal to rise)	1 day
9	page 240	14 days
10	omitted from text	7 days
11	omitted from text	7 days
12	omitted from text	1 day
13	page 418	7 days
14	page 471	2 months
15	omitted from text	2 months
16	"During the time the witness Davis was being cross-examined by the Government Attorney . . . Davis continually volunteered remarks and observations. . . . The Court was required to instruct him no less than 43 times to restrict his answers to the scope of the question posed. This violation of 43 Court orders in the period of three days must be considered contempt-uous."	6 months
17	page 495	3 months
18	page 519	14 days
19	omitted from text	7 days
20	page 530	2 months
21	page 531	5 months
22	page 532	14 days
23	omitted from text	1 month

Total sentence for contempt: 2 years, 1 month, 19 days

Tom Hayden

Specification	Reference	Sentence
1	page 10	1 day
2	page 154 (refusal to rise)	1 day
3	page 155	1 month
4	page 160 (refusal to rise)	1 day
5	page 163 (refusal to rise)	1 day
6	(refusal to rise)	1 day
7	page 168	3 months
8	pages 169-70	4 months
9	omitted from text	1 day
10	omitted from text	7 days
11	omitted from text	6 months

Total sentence for contempt: 1 year, 2 months, 13 days

Abbie Hoffman

Specification	Reference	Sentence
1	page 11	1 day
2	pages 128-29	7 days

Abbie Hoffman (*cont.*)

Specification	Reference	Sentence
3	page 154 (refusal to rise)	1 day
4	omitted from text	7 days
5	page 160 (refusal to rise)	1 day
6	page 163	1 day
7	(refusal to rise)	1 day
8	page 169	2 months
9	(refusal to rise)	1 day
10	omitted from text	7 days
11	omitted from text	1 month
12	omitted from text	14 days
13	page 366	14 days
14	omitted from text	7 days
15	page 424	1 day
16	omitted from text	(judge omits)
17	omitted from text	42 days
18	omitted from text	14 days
19	page 517	7 days
20	page 521	2 days
21	omitted from text	4 days
22	pages 531-32	5 days
23	pages 533-34	6 days
24	"On February 6th, the defendant Hoffman attempted to hold the Court up to ridicule by entering the courtroom in judicial robes. While the transcript does not reflect it, he remained in those robes for a considerable period of time before the jury. Later, he removed the robes, threw them on the floor of the courtroom, and wiped his feet on them."	7 days

Total sentence for contempt: 8 months

Jerry Rubin

Specification	Reference	Sentence
1	page 154 (refusal to rise)	1 day
2	page 160 (refusal to rise)	1 day
3	page 163 (refusal to rise)	1 day
4	(refusal to rise)	1 day
5	page 166	4 months
6	(refusal to rise)	1 day
7	(refusal to rise)	1 day
8	omitted from text	1 month
9	page 469	6 months
10	omitted from text	2 months
11	pages 531-32	6 months
12	pages 532-34	6 months
13	page 537 (robes; see above)	7 days
14	page 540	7 days
15	omitted from text	3 days

Total sentence for contempt: 2 years, 23 days

Lee Weiner

Specification	Reference	Sentence
1	page 154 (refusal to rise)	1 day
2	page 160 (refusal to rise)	1 day
3	page 163 (refusal to rise)	1 day
4	(refusal to rise)	1 day
5	page 248	1 month
6	page 424	14 days
7	page 495	1 month

Total sentence for contempt: 2 months, 18 days

John Froines

Specification	Reference	Sentence
1	page 151	1 month
2	page 154 (refusal to rise)	1 day
3	page 163 (refusal to rise)	1 day
4	(refusal to rise)	1 day
5	omitted from text	1 month
6	page 364	1 month
7	omitted from text	14 days
8	omitted from text	14 days
9	omitted from text	2 months
10	omitted from text	14 days

Total sentence for contempt: 6 months, 15 days

William Kunstler

Specification	Reference	Sentence
1	omitted from text	1 month
2	page 94	14 days
3	page 166	3 months
4	omitted from text	14 days
5	omitted from text	14 days
6	pages 302-3	3 months
7	omitted from text	3 months
8	"In the course of the direct examination of the defense witness Daley. . .Mr. Kunstler asked no less than eighty-three questions which were objectionable, mostly leading and suggestive. . . . His conduct was repeated so many times that it must be considered contemptuous."	6 months
9	page 407	21 days
10	omitted from text	14 days
11	page 424	7 days
12	omitted from text	14 days
13	omitted from text	14 days
14	omitted from text	1 month
15	omitted from text	21 days
16	omitted from text	2 months
17	pages 468-69	4 months
18	omitted from text	1 month

William Kunstler (*cont.*)

Specification	Reference	Sentence
19	omitted from text	1 month
20	page 518	6 months
21	page 519	6 months
22	page 531	4 months
23	page 533	1 month
24	omitted from text	2 months

Total sentence for contempt: 4 years, 13 days

Leonard Weinglass

Specification	Reference	Sentence
1	page 5	2 days
2	omitted from text*	4 months
3	omitted from text	14 days
4	omitted from text	14 days
5	omitted from text	1 month
6	omitted from text	1 month
7	omitted from text	14 days
8	omitted from text	1 month
9	omitted from text	1 month
10	omitted from text	3 months
11	omitted from text	1 month
12	omitted from text	5 months
13	omitted from text	1 month
14	omitted from text	14 days

Total sentence for contempt: 1 year, 7 months, 28 days

*Very few of the incidents for which Mr. Weinglass was cited for contempt appear in the text of this edition because every one of them was during the course of complicated and lengthy legal argument. Weinglass' contesting of Judge Hoffman's rulings was most often the basis of the contempt finding.